Consumer Behavior

7th Edition

Wayne D. Hoyer

University of Texas, Austin

Deborah J. MacInnis

University of Southern California

Rik Pieters

Tilburg University

CENGAGE
Learning·

Australia • Brazil • Mexico • Singapore • United Kingdom • United States

Consumer Behavior, 7e
Wayne D. Hoyer, Deborah J. MacInnis,
Rik Pieters

Senior Vice President, General Manager, Social Sciences, Humanities & Business: Erin Joyner

Product Director: Jason Fremder

Product Manager: Heather Mooney

Content Developer: Bethany Sexton

Marketing Director: Kristen Hurd

Marketing Manager: Charisse Darin

Marketing Coordinator: Casey Binder

Product Assistant: Allie Janneck

Production Management, and Composition: Lumina Datamatics Ltd

Intellectual Property

    Analyst: Diane Garrity

    Project Manager: Sarah Shainwald

Manufacturing Planner: Ron Montgomery

Sr. Art Director: Linda May

Cover Designer: Imbue Design /Kim Torbeck

Internal Designer: Ke Design/ Ted & Trish Knapke

Cover Image: iStockPhoto.com /Baran Ã–zdemir

For product information and technology assistance, contact us at
Cengage Learning Customer & Sales Support, 1-800-354-9706

For permission to use material from this text or product, submit all requests online at **www.cengage.com/permissions**
Further permissions questions can be emailed to
permissionrequest@cengage.com

Library of Congress Control Number: 2016948643

ISBN: 978-1-305-50727-2

Cengage Learning
20 Channel Center Street
Boston, MA 02210
USA

Cengage Learning is a leading provider of customized learning solutions with employees residing in nearly 40 different countries and sales in more than 125 countries around the world. Find your local representative at **www.cengage.com**.

Cengage Learning products are represented in Canada by Nelson Education, Ltd.

To learn more about Cengage Learning Solutions, visit **www.cengage.com**

Purchase any of our products at your local college store or at our preferred online store **www.cengagebrain.com**

Printed in the United States of America
Print Number: 01   Print Year: 2016

*To my wonderful family, Shirley, David, Stephanie, and Lindsey
and to my parents Louis and Doris for their tremendous support
and love. To all of you, I dedicate this book.*

Wayne D. Hoyer

Austin, Texas
September 2016

*To my loving husband, my beautiful children, and my devoted
family. You are my life-spring of energy and my center of gravity.*

Deborah J. MacInnis

Los Angeles, California
September 2016

To Trees who loves me and Thomas who knew everything.

Rik Pieters

Tilburg
September 2016

About the Authors

Wayne D. Hoyer

Wayne D. Hoyer is the James L. Bayless/William S. Farish Fund Chair for Free Enterprise in the McCombs School of Business at the University of Texas at Austin. He received his Ph.D. in Consumer Psychology from Purdue University in 1980. He also holds an honorary doctorate from the University of Bern in Switzerland and was recently given a Humboldt Research Award in Germany. His major area of study is Consumer Psychology and his research interests include consumer information processing and decision-making, customer relationship management, consumer brand sabotage, and advertising information processing (including miscomprehension, humor, and brand personality). Wayne has published over 100 articles in various publications including the *Journal of Consumer Research, Journal of Marketing, Journal of Marketing Research, Journal of Advertising Research*, and *Journal of Retailing*. A 1998 article in the *Journal of Marketing Research* (with Susan Broniarczyk and Leigh McAlister) won the O'Dell Award in 2003 for having the most impact in the marketing field over that five-year period. In addition to Consumer Behavior, he has co-authored two books on the topic of advertising miscomprehension. He is a current area editor for the *Journal of Marketing*, a Senior Editor for the International Journal of Research in Marketing, a former associate editor for the *Journal of Consumer Research* and serves on eight editorial review boards including the *Journal of Marketing Research, Journal of Consumer Research*, and *Journal of Consumer Psychology*. His major areas of teaching include consumer behavior, customer strategy, and marketing communications. He has also taught internationally at the University of Mannheim, the University of Muenster, and the Otto Beisheim School of Management (all in Germany), the University of Bern in Switzerland, the University of Cambridge (UK), and Thammasat University in Thailand. He has also been the Montezemolo Visiting Research Fellow in the Judge School of Business and is a Visiting Fellow of Sidney Sussex College at the University of Cambridge (UK).

Deborah J. MacInnis

Debbie MacInnis (Ph.D., University of Pittsburgh 1986) is the Charles L. and Ramona I. Hilliard Professor of Business Administration and Professor of Marketing at the University of Southern California in Los Angeles, CA. She has previously held positions as Chairperson of the Marketing Department, Vice Dean for Research and Strategy and Dean of the Undergraduate Programs at Marshall. Debbie has published papers in the *Journal of Consumer Research, Journal of Marketing Research, Journal of Marketing, Journal of Personality and Social Psychology, Psychology and Marketing*, and others in the areas of marketing communications, information processing, imagery, emotions, and branding. She has also published two co-edited volumes and a book on branding and consumer-brand relationships. She is former co-editor of the *Journal of Consumer Research*, and served as an Associate Editor for the *Journal of Consumer Research*, the *Journal of Consumer Psychology*, and the *Journal of Marketing* and has won outstanding reviewer awards from these journals. Debbie has served as Conference Co-Chair, Treasurer, and President of the Association for Consumer Research. She has also served as Vice President of Conferences and Research for the Academic Council of the American Marketing Association. She has received major awards for her research, including the Alpha Kappa Psi and Maynard awards, given to the best practice- and theory-based articles, respectively, published in the *Journal of Marketing*. Debbie's research has also been named as a finalist for the Practice Prize Competition for contributions to marketing, and the Converse Award for significant long-term contributions to marketing. She has been named recipient of the Marshall Teaching Innovation Award, the Dean's Award for Community, and the Dean's Award for Research from the Marshall School of Business. She has also received the USC mentoring work for her mentoring of faculty. Her classes have won national awards through the SAA National Advertising Competition. Debbie enjoys travel, reading, and being in nature.

Rik Pieters

Rik Pieters is Professor of Marketing at the Tilburg School of Economics and Management (TISEM) of Tilburg University, the Netherlands. He received his Ph.D. in Social Psychology from the University of Leiden in 1989. Rik believes in interdisciplinary work, and that imagination, persistence, and openness to surprise are a person's biggest assets. He has published over 100 articles in marketing, psychology, economics, and statistics. His work has appeared in *Journal of Consumer Psychology, Journal of Consumer Research, Journal of Marketing, Journal of Marketing Research, Marketing Science, Management Science*, and *International Journal of Research in Marketing*. He has published in the *Journal of Personality and Social Psychology, Organizational Behavior and Human Decision Processes, European Journal of Social Psychology, Emotion, Psychological Science*, and *Journal of Economic Literature*. Currently, Rik is an Associate Editor of the *Journal of Marketing Research*. His research concerns attention and memory processes in marketing communication, and the role of emotions in consumer decision-making. He has served as Co-Chair of the Association for Consumer Research annual conference, and has co-organized special conferences on visual marketing, social communication, and service marketing and management. He has taught internationally at Pennsylvania State University; University of Innsbruck, Austria; Koc University, Turkey; and the University of Auckland, New Zealand. He has won best teaching awards at the school and university levels. He has been Strategy Director for National and International clients at the Publicis/FCB advertising agency, Amsterdam office. He bakes bread, rides bikes, plays the bass, and drinks hoppy, fermented barley beverages, all except the first in moderation. In his spare time, he works.

Brief Contents

Contents

Part 2 The Psychological Core 43

Chapter 2 Motivation, Ability, and Opportunity 44

Chapter 3 From Exposure to Comprehension 72

Chapter 4 Memory and Knowledge 100

Part 3   The Process of Making Decisions   179

Part 4 The Consumer's Culture 291

Chapter 11 Social Influences on Consumer Behavior 292

Chapter 12 Consumer Diversity 321

Chapter 13 Household and Social Class Influences 346

Part 5 Consumer Behavior Outcomes and Issues 403

Chapter 15 Innovations: Adoption, Resistance, and Diffusion 404

Chapter 16 Symbolic Consumer Behavior 429

Preface

At just about every moment of our lives, we engage in some form of consumer behavior. When we look for posts on social media, watch an ad on TV, send a text message to friends about a movie we just saw, brush our teeth, go to a ball game or to a beach party, visit a website, download a new song, or even throw away an old pair of shoes, we are behaving as a consumer. Being a consumer reaches into every part of our lives. Of course, we are much more than just consumers. We are students, teammates, family members, employees, citizens, voters, patrons, patients, clients, neighbors, basketball fans, ice-cream lovers, bloggers, inventors, and more. This book is dedicated to our role as consumers.

Given its omnipresence, the study of consumer behavior has critical implications for areas such as marketing, public policy, and ethics. It also helps us learn about ourselves—why we buy certain things, why we use them in a certain way, and how we remove them from our lives through practices like throwing them away, selling, re-gifting, and donating them.

In this book we explore the fascinating world of consumer behavior, looking at a number of interesting and exciting topics. Some of these are quickly identified with our typical image of consumer behavior. Others may be surprising. We hope you will see why we became stimulated and drawn to this topic from the very moment we had our first consumer behavior course as students. We hope you will also appreciate why we choose to make this field our life's work, and why we are dedicated to this textbook.

Why the New Edition of This Book?

There are a number of consumer behavior books on the market. An important question concerns what this book has to offer and what distinguishes it from other texts. As active researchers in the field of consumer behavior, our overriding goal was to continue providing a treatment of the field that is up to date and cutting edge. There has been an explosion of research on a variety of consumer behavior topics over the last 30 years. Our primary aim was to provide a useful summary of this material for students of marketing. However, in drawing on cutting-edge research, we wanted to be careful not to become too "academic." Instead, our objective is to present cutting-edge topics in a manner that is accessible and easy for students to understand, and provides context for how and why consumer behavior insights are applied in real-world marketing.

Specific changes and improvements to the seventh edition of this book include:

- Accessible explanations of the latest academic research and classic research from consumer behavior studies, and their practical implications for marketing strategy worldwide.

- Global perspective of research and behavioral concepts related to such important contemporary topics as financial management and money decisions, marketing ethics, privacy and transparency, obesity, materialism, self-control and self-regulation, contagion, emotions, mobile marketing, social media, and unconscious consumer behavior.

- Carefully edited narrative and examples make the content easier for students to process and connect with basic marketing principles as well as personal consumer experiences.

- Balanced coverage of marketing controversies and the challenges and opportunities of marketing as a force for social responsibility.

- New and updated examples highlight how all kinds of organizations in many nations use insights into consumer behavior to improve their marketing effectiveness and creativity.

- New database analysis exercises offer students an opportunity to make marketing decisions based on consumer demographics and behavior styles.

- Improved synergistic and digitally accessible supplemental materials allow students the opportunity to participate in self-assessments, polls, and short videos for self-reflection and more; Additional short readings are also available. These materials are both student friendly and extremely helpful for effective learning using the Cengage MindTap platform. A description of the MindTap platform appears later in this preface.

Textbook Features

As award-winning teachers, we have tried to translate our instructional abilities and experience into the writing of this text. The following features have been a natural outgrowth of these experiences.

Conceptual Model

First, we believe that students can learn best when they see the big picture—when they understand what concepts mean, how these concepts are used in business practice, and how these relate to one another. In our opinion, consumer behavior is too often presented as a set of discrete topics with little or no relationship to one another. We have therefore developed an overall conceptual model that helps students grasp the big picture and see how the chapters and topics are themselves interrelated. Each chapter is linked to other chapters by a specific model that fits within the larger model. Further, the overall model guides the organization of the book. This organizing scheme makes the chapters far more *integrative* than most other books. Instructors have told us that this conceptual model is a valuable and beneficial aide to student learning.

Practical Orientation, with an Emphasis on Globalization and Social Media

Second, we believe that insights into consumer behavior are interesting in and of themselves, but also that they should be relevant to managerial practice. The ultimate goal of consumer behavior theory and research is to improve the decision-making ability of managers in profit and nonprofit organizations who aim to cater to consumers' needs, and to help policy makers better protect consumers. Rather than merely translating general psychological or sociological principles and theories to a consumer context, this book is dedicated to understanding consumer behavior in order to improve managerial practice. Given our notion that students enjoy seeing how the concepts in consumer behavior can apply to business practice, a second objective of the book was to provide a very practical orientation. We include a wealth of contemporary real-world examples to illustrate key topics. We also try to broaden students' horizons by providing a number of international examples. Given the importance of online consumer behavior, the new edition also fully treats the advent and implications of the latest digital developments, social media marketing, and mobile marketing applications.

Current and Cutting-Edge Coverage

Third, we provide coverage of the field of consumer behavior that is as current and up to date as possible (including many of the recent research advances). This includes several *novel chapters* that often do not appear in other textbooks: "Attitudes Based on Low Effort," "Judgement and Decision Making Based on Low Effort," and "Marketing Ethics and Social Responsibility in Today's Consumer

Society." These important topics are likely to be of considerable interest to students. Instructors have told us how much they appreciate the cutting-edge nature of our book and its ability to keep abreast of the latest research in consumer behavior. Students appreciate that this material is delivered in an engaging way that's also easy to read.

Balanced Treatment of Micro and Macro Topics

Fourth, our book tries to provide a balanced perspective on the field of consumer behavior. Specifically, we give treatment to both psychological (micro) consumer behavior topics (e.g., attitudes, decision-making) and sociological (macro) consumer behavior topics (e.g., subculture, gender, social class influences). Also, although we typically teach consumer behavior by starting with the more micro topics and then moving up to more macro topics, we realize that some instructors prefer the reverse sequence.

Broad Conceptualization of the Subject

Fifth, we present a broad conceptualization of the topic of consumer behavior. While many books focus on what products or services consumers *buy*, consumer behavior scholars have recognized that the topic of consumer behavior is much broader. Specifically, rather than studying buying per se, we recognize that consumer behavior includes a *set* of decisions (what, whether, when, where, why, how, how often, how much, how long) about *acquisition* (including, but not limited to buying), *usage, sharing,* and *disposition* decisions. Focusing on more than what products or services consumers buy provides a rich set of theoretical and practical implications for both our understanding of consumer behavior and the practice of marketing.

Finally, we consider the relevance of consumer behavior to *many constituents,* not just marketers. Chapter 1 indicates that consumer behavior is important to marketers, public policy makers, ethicists and consumer advocacy groups, and consumers themselves (including students). Some chapters focus exclusively on the implications of consumer behavior for public policy makers, ethicists, and consumer advocacy groups. Other chapters consider these issues as well, though in less detail.

Content and Organization of the Book

One can currently identify two main approaches to the study of consumer behavior: One approach focuses on the individual psychological processes that consumers use to make acquisition, consumption, and disposition decisions. A second approach focuses on group behaviors and the symbolic nature of consumer behavior. This latter orientation draws heavily from such fields as sociology, culture theory, and anthropology. Both orientations are represented in this book. The current book and overall model have been structured around a "micro to macro" organization based on the way we teach this course and the feedback that we have received from reviewers.

Chapter 1 in Part I, "An Introduction to Consumer Behavior," presents an introduction to consumer behavior. It helps students understand the breadth of the field, and its importance to marketers, advocacy groups, public policy makers, and consumers themselves. This chapter introduces some of the newest research and presents the overall model that guides the organization of the text. An Appendix, which follows Chapter 1, introduces methods by which consumer research is conducted.

Part II, "The Psychological Core," focuses on the inner psychological processes that affect consumer behavior. We see that the amount of effort consumers put into their acquisition, usage, and disposition behaviors and decisions has significant effects on the decisions they make. Chapter 2 describes three critical factors that affect effort: the (1) *motivation* or desire, (2) *ability* (knowledge and information), and (3) *opportunity* to engage in behaviors and make decisions. The key role of emotions is also discussed. In Chapter 3, we then examine how consumers process information in their environments (ads, prices, product features, word-of-mouth communications, etc.). We consider how they come in contact with these stimuli (*exposure*), notice them (*attention*), and *perceive* them (perception). Chapter 4 continues by discussing how consumers compare new things they encounter in their environment to their existing knowledge, a process called *categorization,* and how they make sense of or *comprehend* them on a deeper level. Also, because consumers often must remember the information they have previously stored in order to make decisions, this chapter examines the important topic of consumer *memory.* In Chapters 5 and 6, we see how *attitudes* are formed and changed depending on whether the amount of effort consumers devote to forming an attitude is *high* or *low* and whether attitudes are cognitively or affectively based.

Whereas Part II examines some of the internal factors that influence consumers' decisions, a critical domain of consumer behavior involves understanding how consumers make acquisition, consumption, and disposition decisions. Thus, in Part III, "The Process of Making Decisions," we examine the sequential steps of the consumer decision-making process. In Chapter 7, we examine the initial steps of this process—*problem recognition* and *information search.* Similar to the attitude change processes described earlier, we next examine the consumer decision-making process, both when *effort is high* (Chapter 8) and when

it is *low* (Chapter 9). Further, in both chapters we examine these important processes from both a cognitive and an affective perspective. Finally, the process does not end after a decision has been made. In Chapter 10, we see how consumers determine whether they are *satisfied* or *dissatisfied* with their decisions and how they *learn* from choosing and consuming products and services.

Part IV, "The Consumer's Culture," examines how various aspects of *culture* affect consumer behavior. First, Chapter 11 considers how, when, and why the specific *reference groups* (friends, work group, clubs) to which we belong can influence acquisition, usage, and disposition decisions and behaviors. Then, we see how *consumer diversity* (in terms of age, gender, sexual orientation, region, ethnicity, and religion) can affect consumer behavior in Chapter 12. Chapter 13 then examines how *social class* and *household* characteristics influence acquisition, usage, and disposition behaviors. Finally, Chapter 14 examines how external influences affect our *personality, lifestyle,* and *values,* as well as consumer behavior.

Finally, Part V, "Consumer Behavior Outcomes," examines the effects of the numerous influences and decision processes discussed in the previous three sections. Chapter 15 builds on the topics of internal decision-making and group behavior by examining how consumers adopt new offerings, and how their *adoption* decisions affect the spread or *diffusion* of an offering through a market. Because products and services often reflect deep-felt and significant meanings (e.g., our favorite song or restaurant), Chapter 16 focuses on the exciting topic of *symbolic consumer behavior.* Finally, Chapter 17 examines *marketing, ethics,* and *social responsibility,* including a look at marketing controversies and the use of marketing for constructive purposes.

Pedagogical Advantages

Based on our extensive teaching experience, we have incorporated a number of features that should help students learn about consumer behavior.

Chapter Opening Model

Each chapter begins with a conceptual model that shows the organization of the chapter, the topics discussed, and how they relate both to one another and to other chapters. Each model reflects an expanded picture of one or more of the elements presented in the overall conceptual model for the book (described in Chapter 1).

Marketing Implication Sections

Numerous *Marketing Implications sections* are interspersed throughout each chapter. These sections illustrate how various consumer behavior concepts can be applied to the practice of marketing, including such basic marketing functions as market segmentation, target market selection, positioning, market research, promotion, price, product, and place decisions. An abundance of marketing examples (from many countries and many industries) provide concrete applications and implementations of the concepts to marketing practice.

Marginal Glossary

Every chapter contains a set of key terms that are both highlighted in the text and defined in margin notes. These terms and their definitions should help students identify and remember the central concepts described in the chapter.

Rich Use of Full-Color Exhibits

Each chapter contains a number of illustrated examples, including photos, advertisements, charts, and graphs. These illustrations help to make important topics personally relevant and engaging, help students remember the material, and make the book more accessible and aesthetically pleasing, thereby increasing students' motivation to learn. All diagrams and charts employ full color, which serves to both highlight key points and add to the aesthetic appeal of the text. Each model, graph, ad, and photo also has an accompanying caption that provides a simple description and explanation of how the exhibit relates to the topic it is designed to illustrate.

End-of-Chapter Summaries

The end of each chapter provides students with a simple and concise summary of topics. These summaries are a good review tool to use with the conceptual model to help students to get the big picture.

End-of-Chapter Questions

Each chapter includes a set of review and discussion questions designed to help students recall and more deeply understand the concepts in the chapter.

Complete Teaching Package with Online Content

In addition to online content for students including self-assessments, polls, and short videos for self-reflection, a variety of ancillary materials have been designed to help the instructor in the classroom. All of these supplements have been carefully coordinated to support the text and provide an integrated and synergistic set of materials for the instructor. Dr. Angeline Close Scheinbaum of

The University of Texas at Austin authors the digital content and has revised and updated the instructor's teaching manual. She brings a modern approach, and includes experiential aspects of consumer behavior in the supplements. Her objective in this project is twofold:

- Give students digital content so they can have more real-world examples of the theoretical content and opportunities for self-assessment and more critical thinking, while enhancing the student learning experience via more interactive and visually engaging supplements.

- Help instructors, especially newer instructors, by giving modern supplements that are synergistic with each other. That is, the text, the Instructor's Manual, Test Bank, PowerPoint presentations, and quizzes reinforce the same learning objectives and content.

- **MindTap for Marketing: Consumer Behavior**

  As authors, one frustration we've had in the past is providing current examples. Every day, new and interesting video, audio, and print content that relates to consumer behavior is covered in the media. Now technology helps us make such content immediately accessible to students. We have partnered with Cengage Learning to provide students with access to current issues in *Consumer Behavior* through the content of *Business Insights*. We have selected exciting content from *Business Insights* which contains readings and videos from sources like *The New York Times, The Economist* magazine, and *Marketing News* and related it to the concepts in each chapter. We have also created assessments to provide assurances to both students and instructors that learning objectives are being met.

MindTap

The seventh edition of *Consumer Behavior* offers two exciting alternative teaching formats. Instructors can choose between either a hybrid print and digital offering or a version that provides completely integrated online delivery through a platform called MindTap. MindTap is a fully online, highly personalized learning experience built upon authoritative content. By combining readings, multimedia, activities, and assessments into a singular Learning Path, MindTap guides students through their course with ease while promoting engagement. Instructors personalize the Learning Path by customizing Cengage Learning resources and adding their own content via apps that integrate into the MindTap framework seamlessly. Instructors are also able to incorporate the online component of *Consumer Behavior* into a traditional Learning Management System (e.g., Blackboard, Canvas, D2L, etc.) providing a way to manage assignments, quizzes, and tests throughout the semester.

How to Access the Supplements

Consumer Behavior 7e's Instructor's Manual, Test Bank, and PowerPoint supplements, are available on the Instructor's Resource companion site.

Instructor's Manual

The Instructor's Manual is updated to be synergistic with all other supplements. Each chapter includes a summary, learning objectives, chapter outline, review/discussion answers discussion questions, and experiential learning exercises to enhance student learning.

Test Bank

A new test bank is available for CB 7e, also updated to be synergistic with the text and other supplements. Each test bank question has a new system of potential choices. There is one clearly defined correct choice. There are two or three other choices that are clearly incorrect for a precise reason (as indicated by the readings). Then, there is a choice that is not relevant at all. The number of "all of the above" and "none of the above" choices has been reduced. The new CB 7e test bank includes AACSB requirement tags (e.g., ethics).

Test Bank, Cognero Format

The Cognero Testing system is a full-featured, online assessment system that allows you to manage content, create and assign tests, deliver tests through a secure online test center, and have complete reporting and data dissemination at your fingertips. The following are some of the features of the Cognero Testing System:

- *Access from anywhere.* Web-based software that runs in a Web browser. No installs are required to start using Cognero. Works in Windows, Mac, and Linux browsers.

- *Desktop-like interface looks and feels like a desktop application.* Uses the latest Web functionality to imitate desktop usability features like drag-and-drop and wizards.

- *Full-featured test generator.* Author and manage your assessment content as well as build tests using the only online test generator that supports all of the major functionality of its desktop competitors. Cognero is complete with a full-featured word processor, multilanguage support, Math-ML compliant equation editor, algorithmic content support, native support for 15 question types (true/false, modified true/false, yes/no, multiple choice, multiple response, numeric response, completion, matching, objective short answer, subjective short answer, multi-mode, ordering, opinion scale/

Likert, essay, and custom), unlimited metadata, ability to print professional paper tests with multiple styles and versions, and more.

- *Class Management and Assignments.* Manage your students, classes, and assignments with the ease of simple drag-and-drop. You can build or import rosters, have students self-register for a class, and move students easily from class to class. Once your roster is set, simply drag a test to a class to schedule and put your students to work.

- *Secure Online Testing.* Cognero has an integrated secure online testing center for your students. Along with delivering traditional tests, your students can receive immediate feedback on each question and/or receive a detailed end-of-assignment report to help them know exactly how they are doing.

- *Complete Reporting System.* What is the use of assessment without being able to disseminate the data derived from it? Cognero allows you to analyze how your students are performing on a real-time basis and from multiple approaches to allow for immediate intervention. You can also quickly analyze your questions and perform a gap analysis of student testing.

- *Content Management System.* Cognero has a unique set of tools to allow for the creation of products (groups of question sets and tests) for distribution to other users. This system includes workflow management for the shared authoring environment, the ability to authorize specific users to access your content, and the ability to edit content and push changes through to subscribers. There are also a number of design features to make high volume authoring within Cognero very efficient. All content created in this system has built-in digital rights management, meaning that your content is protected against unauthorized use.

PowerPoint Presentation Package

A package of professionally developed PowerPoint slides is available for use by adopters of this textbook. These lecture PowerPoint slides outline the text content, including key figures and tables. CB 7e will have more user friendly, experiential presentations to enhance student learning and break up the monotony of text-based lectures.

Videos

A video package has been provided to supplement and enliven class lectures and discussion. Videos contain real-world scenarios that illustrate certain concepts in a given chapter. The clips are intended to be interesting, to ground the concepts in real life for students, and to provide an impetus for stimulating student input and involvement.

Acknowledgments

Special recognition is extended to Marian Wood, whose assistance was crucial to the completion of this project. Her tireless work on this project is greatly appreciated. We have also been extremely fortunate to work with a wonderful team of dedicated professionals from Cengage Learning. We are very grateful to Jason Fremder, Michael Roche, and Bethany Sexton whose enormous energy and enthusiasm spurred our progress on this seventh edition. We also appreciate the efforts of Angeline Close Scheinbaum of the University of Texas at Austin for her work on the online content and Instructor's Manual. The quality of this book and its ancillary package has been helped immensely by the insightful and rich comments of a set of researchers and instructors who served as reviewers. Their thoughtful and helpful comments had real impact in shaping the final product. In particular, we wish to thank:

Larry Anderson
Long Island University

Mike Ballif
University of Utah

Sharon Beatty
University of Alabama

Sandy Becker
Rutgers Business School

Russell Belk
University of Utah

Joseph Bonnice
Manhattan College

Timothy Brotherton
Ferris State University

Carol Bruneau
University of Montana

Margaret L. Burk
Muskingum College

Carol Calder
Loyola Marymount University

Paul Chao
University of Northern Iowa

Dennis Clayson
University of Northern Iowa

Joel Cohen
University of Florida

Sally Dibb
University of Warwick

Richard W. Easley
Baylor University

Richard Elliott
Lancaster University

Abdi Eshghi
Bentley College

Frank W. Fisher
Stonehill College

Ronald Fullerton
Providence College

Philip Garton
Leicester Business School

Peter L. Gillett
University of Central Florida

Debbora Heflin
Cal Poly, Pomona

Elizabeth Hirschman
Rutgers University

Raj G. Javalgi
Cleveland State University

Harold Kassarjian
UCLA

Patricia Kennedy
University of Nebraska, Lincoln

Robert E. Kleine
Arizona State University

Stephen K. Koernig
DePaul University

Scott Koslow
University of Waikato

Robert Lawson
William Patterson University

Phillip Lewis
Rowan College of New Jersey

Kenneth R. Lord
SUNY, Buffalo

Peggy Sue Loroz
Gonzaga University

Bart Macchiette
Plymouth State College

Michael Mallin
Kent State University

Lawrence Marks
Kent State University

David Marshall
University of Edinburgh

Ingrid M. Martin
California State University, Long Beach

Anil Mathur
Hofstra University

A. Peter McGraw
University of Colorado, Boulder

Matt Meuter
California State University, Chico

Martin Meyers
University of Wisconsin, Stevens Point

Vince Mitchell
UMIST

Lois Mohr
Georgia State University

Risto Moisio
California State University, Long Beach

Rebecca Walker Naylor
University of South Carolina

James R. Ogden
Kutztown University

Thomas O'Guinn
University of Illinois

Marco Protano
New York University

Judith Powell
Virginia Union University

Michael Reilly
Montana State University

Anja K. Reimer
University of Miami

Gregory M. Rose
The University of Mississippi

Mary Mercurio Scheip
Eckerd College

Marilyn Scrizzi
New Hampshire Technical College

John Shaw
Providence College

C. David Shepherd
University of Tennessee, Chattanooga

Robert E. Smith
Indiana University

Eric Richard Spangenberg
Washington State University

Bruce Stern
Portland State University

Barbara Stewart
University of Houston

Jane Boyd Thomas
Winthrop University

Phil Titus
Bowling Green State University

Carolyn Tripp
Western Illinois University

Rajiv Vaidyanathan
University of Minnesota, Duluth

Stuart Van Auken
California State University, Chico

Kathleen D. Vohs
University of Minnesota

Janet Wagner
University of Maryland

John Weiss
Colorado State University

Tommy E. Whittler
University of Kentucky

Carolyn Yoon
University of Michigan

The
Psychological Core
2 Motivation, Ability, and Opportunity
3 From Exposure to Comprehension
4 Memory and Knowledge
5-6 Attitudes Based on Effort

An Introduction
to
Consumer Behavior
1 Understanding Consumer Behavior

The Process of
Making Decisions
7 Problem Recognition and Information Search
8-9 Judgment and Decision-Making Based on Effort
10 Post-Decision Processes

The
Consumer's Culture
11 Social Influences on Consumer Behavior
12 Consumer Diversity
13 Household and Social Class Influences
14 Psychographics: Values, Personality, and Lifestyles

Consumer Behavior Outcomes and Issues
15 Innovations: Adoption, Resistance, and Diffusion
16 Symbolic Consumer Behavior
17 Marketing, Ethics, and Social Responsibility in Today's Consumer Society

iStockphoto.com/Ostill

Part 1

An Introduction to Consumer Behavior

I N PART ONE, you will learn that consumer behavior involves much more than purchasing products. In addition, you will find out that marketers continuously study consumer behavior for clues to who buys, uses, and disposes of what goods and services, as well as clues to when, where, why, and how they make decisions.

Chapter 1 defines consumer behavior and examines its importance to marketers, advocacy groups, public policy makers, and consumers. The chapter also presents the overall model that guides the organization of this book. As this model indicates, consumer behavior covers four basic domains: (1) the psychological core, (2) the process of making decisions, (3) the consumer's culture, and (4) consumer behavior outcomes and issues. In addition, you will read about the implications of consumer behavior for marketing activities.

The Appendix focuses on consumer behavior research and its special implications for marketers. You will learn about various research methods, types of data, and ethical issues related to consumer research. With this background, you will be able to understand how consumer research helps marketers develop more effective strategies and tactics for reaching and satisfying customers.

CHAPTER **1**

Understanding Consumer Behavior

iStockphoto.com/Ostill

LEARNING OBJECTIVES

After studying this chapter, you will be able to:

▶ Define consumer behavior and explain the components that make up the definition.

▶ Identify the four domains of consumer behavior that affect acquisition, usage, and disposition decisions.

▶ Discuss the benefits of studying consumer behavior.

▶ Explain how companies apply consumer behavior concepts when making marketing decisions.

INTRODUCTION

From Starbucks to Samsung and Apple to Amazon, all businesses know that their success depends on understanding consumer behavior and trends so they can create goods and services that consumers will want, like, use, and recommend to others. Charities, schools, government agencies, and other organizations are also interested in how consumers behave and how marketing can influence consumers' thoughts, feelings, and actions.

This chapter provides an overview of (1) what consumer behavior is, (2) what factors affect it, (3) who benefits from studying it, and (4) how marketers apply consumer behavior concepts. Because you are a consumer, you probably have some thoughts about these issues. However, you may be surprised at how broad the domain of consumer behavior is, how many factors help explain it, and how important the field is to marketers, ethicists and consumer advocates, public policy makers and regulators, and consumers like yourself. You will also get a glimpse of the marketing implications of consumer behavior, previewing how we will connect consumer behavior concepts with practical applications throughout this book.

ZUMA Press, Inc./Alamy Stock Photo

1-1 Defining Consumer Behavior

If you were asked to define **consumer behavior**, you might say it refers to the study of how a person buys products. However, consumer behavior really involves quite a bit more, as this more complete definition indicates:

> *Consumer behavior reflects the totality of consumers' decisions with respect to the acquisition, consumption, and disposition of goods, services, activities, experiences, people, and ideas by (human) decision-making units [over time].*[1]

This definition has some very important elements, summarized in Exhibit 1.1. The following sections present a closer look at each element.

> **Consumer behavior** The totality of consumers' decisions with respect to the acquisition, consumption, and disposition of goods, services, time, and ideas by human decision-making units (over time).
>
> **Offering** A product, service, activity, experience, or idea offered by a marketing organization to consumers.

activities, experiences, and ideas such as going to the dentist, attending a concert, taking a trip, and donating to UNICEF.[2] In addition, consumers make decisions about people, such as voting for politicians, reading books by certain authors, streaming movies or TV shows starring certain actors, and attending concerts featuring favorite bands.

Another example of consumer behavior involves choices about the consumption of time, a scarce resource. Will you check to see what's happening on Facebook, search for a YouTube video, watch a sports event live, or record a program and watch it later, for instance?[3] How we use time reflects who we are, what our lifestyles are like, and how we are both the same as and different from others.[4] Because consumer behavior includes the consumption of so many things, we use the simple term **offering** to encompass these entities.

1-1a CONSUMER BEHAVIOR INVOLVES GOODS, SERVICES, ACTIVITIES, EXPERIENCES, PEOPLE, AND IDEAS

Consumer behavior means more than just the way that a person buys tangible products such as bath soap and automobiles. It also includes consumers' use of services,

1-1b CONSUMER BEHAVIOR INVOLVES MORE THAN BUYING

Marketers are intensely interested in consumer behavior related to using and disposing of a product, not just the way that consumers make acquisition decisions. They

---

Exhibit 1.1 ▶ What Is Consumer Behavior?

Consumer behavior reflects more than the way that a product is acquired by a single person at any one point in time. Think of some marketing strategies and tactics that try to influence one or more of the dimensions of consumer behavior shown in this exhibit.

Consumer Behavior Reflects:

The totality of decisions	About the consumption	Of an offering	By decision-making units	Over time
Whether		Products	Information gatherer	Hours
What				
Why	Acquisition	Services		Days
How		Activities	Influencer	
When	Usage		Decider	Weeks
Where		Experiences		
How much/ How often/ How long	Disposition	People	Purchaser	Months
		Ideas	User	Years

Marketing Strategies and Tactics

also study how consumers make decisions about personal finances.

Acquiring an Offering

Buying represents one type of **acquisition** behavior. As shown later in this chapter, acquisition includes other ways of obtaining goods and services, such as renting, leasing, trading, and sharing. It also involves decisions about time as well as money.[5] Consumers sometimes find themselves interrupted during a consumption experience; studies show interruption actually makes a pleasant experience seem more enjoyable when resumed.[6] Deadlines can also affect acquisition behavior: Consumers tend to procrastinate in redeeming coupons and gift cards with far-future deadlines, but move more quickly when deadlines are closer. Why? Because they do not want to regret having missed out and they expect to have more time to enjoy and indulge themselves with the acquisition in the future.[7] Obviously, attitudes toward materialism, status, and self-concept play a role in acquisition behavior, as discussed in later chapters.

Using an Offering

After consumers acquire an offering, they use it, which is why **usage** is at the very core of consumer behavior.[8] Whether and why we use certain products can symbolize something about who we are, what we value, and what we believe. The products we use on Thanksgiving (e.g., making desserts from scratch or buying them in a bakery) may symbolize the event's significance and how we feel about our guests. The music we enjoy (Lady Gaga or Mark Ronson) and the jewelry we wear (nose rings or engagement rings) can also symbolize who we are and how we feel. Moreover, marketers must be sensitive to when consumers are likely to use a product,[9] whether they find it effective,[10] whether they control their consumption of it,[11] and how they react after using it—do they spread positive or negative word-of-mouth reviews about a new movie, for instance?[12]

Disposing of an Offering

Disposition, how consumers get rid of an offering they have previously acquired, can have important implications for marketers.[13] Consumers can give away their used possessions, sell them on eBay or on consignment to vintage stores, rent them via sharing websites, or lend them to others. As discussed in detail in Chapter 17, environmental concerns are growing among consumers and marketers. Eco-minded consumers often seek out biodegradable products made from recycled materials or choose goods that do not pollute when disposed of (see Exhibit 1.2).[14] Municipalities are also interested in how to motivate earth-friendly disposition.[15] Marketers see profit opportunities in addressing disposition concerns. TerraCycle, for example, markets tote bags, pencil cases, and other products made from

Acquisition The process by which a consumer comes to own an offering.

Usage The process by which a consumer uses an offering.

Disposition The process by which a consumer discards an offering.

Exhibit 1.2 ▶ Disposition
Consumers dispose of old products they acquired in a number of ways, oftentimes through recycling or vintage shops.

used packaging and recycled materials. In North and South America, Europe, and the Baltic, the company partners with firms such as PepsiCo to collect mountains of discarded packaging and turn them into usable products for sale.[16]

Managing Money and Making Financial Decisions

How do consumers make financial decisions before, during, and after acquiring an offering? What are their attitudes toward money and prices? These topics are the focus of much study because consumers don't always do a good job of managing money. For example, consumers generally know how to budget and plan for ordinary purchases, but they tend to underestimate spending on out-of-the-ordinary purchases and, in particular, spend more than anticipated on individual purchases.[17] On the other hand, consumers do adjust their budgets in some situations. For example, perhaps because the price of gas is very salient (with prices displayed on store signs and discussed in the news), when gas prices rise, consumers do tend to shop less frequently, switch to one-stop shopping at low-price retail establishments, and reduce overall spending to compensate.[18]

Consumer behavior also affects decisions about managing debt. For instance, consumers are likely to make higher repayments when credit card statements make no mention of a mandatory minimum monthly repayment.[19] Another study found that consumers who close a credit account are more likely to be successful at eliminating their debt, because taking this step motivates them to persist in pursuit of their goal.[20] When consumers feel powerful and in control of their resources, they will put more money in the bank in order to maintain that state of power.[21]

1-1c CONSUMER BEHAVIOR IS A DYNAMIC PROCESS

The sequence of acquisition, consumption, and disposition can occur over time in a dynamic order—hours, days, weeks, months, or years, as shown in Exhibit 1.1. To illustrate, assume that a family has acquired and is using a new car. Usage provides the family with information—whether the car drives well and is reliable—that affects when, whether, how, and why members will dispose of the car by selling, trading, or junking it. Because the family always needs transportation, disposition is likely to affect when, whether, how, and why its members acquire another car in the future.

Entire markets are designed around linking one consumer's disposition decision to other consumers' acquisition decisions. When consumers buy used cars, they are buying cars that others have disposed of. From eBay's online auctions to Goodwill Industries' secondhand clothing stores, from consignment shops to used books sold online, many businesses exist to link one consumer's disposition behavior with another's acquisition behavior. Environmental attitudes and actions are changing, which means marketers must take into account consumers' goals and priorities, perceptions of brands, and internal processes when planning marketing efforts.

Broader changes in consumer behavior occur over time, as well. Fifty years ago, consumers had far fewer brand choices and were exposed to fewer marketing messages. In contrast, today's consumers (particularly millennials) are more connected, easily able to research offerings online, access communications and promotions in multiple media, and check what others think of brands with a quick search or social media post. Later chapters examine these influences in more detail. Consumers can also work with marketers or with each other to collaboratively create new products.[22] For example, thousands of consumers participate when Mountain Dew uses *crowdsourcing* to request ideas for new soft-drink flavors, product logos, and ads.[23]

1-1d CONSUMER BEHAVIOR CAN INVOLVE MANY PEOPLE

Consumer behavior does not necessarily reflect the action of a single individual. A group of friends, a few coworkers, or an entire family may plan a birthday party or decide where to have lunch, exchanging ideas in person, on the phone, via social media, or by e-mail or text message. Moreover, the individuals engaging in consumer behavior can take on one or more roles. In the case of a car purchase, for example, one or more family members might take on the role of information gatherer by researching different models. Others might assume the role of influencer and try to affect the outcome of a decision. One or more members may take on the role of purchaser by actually paying for the car, and some or all may be users. Finally, several family members may be involved in the disposal of the car.

1-1e CONSUMER BEHAVIOR INVOLVES MANY DECISIONS

Consumer behavior also involves understanding whether, why, when, where, how, how much, how often, and for how long consumers will buy, use, or dispose of an offering (look back at Exhibit 1.1).

Whether to Acquire/Use/Dispose of an Offering

Consumers must decide whether to acquire, use, or dispose of an offering. They may need to decide whether to spend or save their money when they earn extra cash. How much they decide to spend may be influenced by their perceptions of how much they recall spending in the past.[24]

They may need to decide whether to order a pizza, clean out a closet, or download a movie. Some consumers collect items, for example, a practice that has created a huge market for buying, selling, transporting, storing, and insuring collectible items.[25] Decisions about whether to acquire, use, or dispose of an offering are often related to personal goals, safety concerns, or a desire to reduce economic, social, or psychological risk. However, such decisions can also be affected by subtle cues in our environment. Did you know that the mere act of hand washing can affect people's decisions to relinquish their own possessions?[26] Also, simply entering a lottery can undermine someone's self-control—making a person more likely, for example, to give in to indulgent purchases.[27] Self-control is an important factor in many consumer behavior situations, as you'll see in later chapters.

What Offering to Acquire/Use/Dispose Of

Consumers make decisions every day about what to buy; in fact, U.S. consumers spend an average of about $90 per day on goods and services in a typical month.[28] In some cases, we make choices among product or service *categories* such as buying food versus downloading new music. In other cases, we choose between *brands* such as whether to buy an Apple iPhone or a Samsung Galaxy phone. Our choices multiply daily as marketers introduce new products, sizes, and packages. Exhibit 1.3 shows how much, on average, U.S. consumers spend for major categories of goods and services every year.

Item	Average annual expenditure by consumers
Housing	$17,148
Transportation	9,004
Food	6,602
Personal insurance, pensions	5,528
Health care	3,631
Entertainment	2,482
Cash contributions	1,834
Clothing and services	1,604
All other expenditures	3,267
TOTAL	$51,100

Source: Adapted from "Consumer Expenditures—2013," *Economic News Release,* September 9, 2014, U.S. Department of Labor, U.S. Bureau of Labor Statistics, Table A, www.bls.gov.

Exhibit 1.3 ▶ Average Annual U.S. Consumer Spending, By Category

On average, U.S. consumers spend more for basics like housing, transportation, and food than for other categories of expenditures.

Why Acquire/Use/Dispose of an Offering

Consumption can occur for a number of reasons. Among the most important reasons, as you will see later, are the ways in which an offering meets someone's needs, values, or goals. Some consumers acquire tattoos as a form of self-expression, to fit into a group, or to express their feelings about someone or something. Taking the self-expression of tattoos into the automotive arena, 3M makes a series of vinyl wrap "tattoos" for car owners to use in personalizing the look of their vehicles.[29] Acquisition may be related to a consumer's attitudes toward money, materialism, status, emotions, and self-control, as discussed in other chapters.

Sometimes our reasons for using an offering are filled with conflict, which leads to some difficult consumption decisions. Teenagers may smoke cigarettes or e-cigarettes, even though they know it is harmful, because they think smoking will help them gain acceptance. Some consumers may be unable to stop acquiring, using, or disposing of products. They may be physically addicted to products such as cigarettes, or they may have a compulsion to eat, gamble, or buy.

Why an Offering Is Not Acquired/Used/Disposed Of

Marketers also try to understand why consumers do *not* acquire, use, or dispose of an offering. For example, consumers may delay buying a particular consumer electronics product because they believe that the product will soon be outdated or that some firms will leave this market, leaving them without after-sale support or service. At times, consumers who want to acquire or consume an offering are unable to do so because what they want is unavailable. Ethics and social responsibility can also play a role. Some consumers may want to avoid products made in factories with questionable labor practices or avoid movies downloaded, copied, and shared without permission.[30] This is why *transparency* is increasingly of concern when consumers want to know what a brand or company stands for.

How to Acquire/Use/Dispose of an Offering

Marketers gain a lot of insight by understanding how consumers acquire, consume, and dispose of an offering.

Ways of Acquiring an Offering

How do consumers decide whether to acquire an offering in a store or mall, online, or at an auction?[31] How do they decide whether to pay with cash, a check, a debit card, a credit card, an electronic system such as PayPal, or a "mobile wallet" smartphone payment app such as

Acquisition Method	Description
Buying	Buying is a common acquisition method used for many offerings.
Trading	Consumers might receive a good or service as part of a trade.
Renting or leasing	Instead of buying, consumers rent or lease cars, furniture, vacation homes, and more.
Bartering	Consumers (and businesses) can exchange goods or services without having money change hands.
Gifting	Each society has many gift-giving occasions as well as informal or formal rules dictating how gifts are to be given, what is an appropriate gift, and how to respond to a gift.
Finding	Consumers sometimes find goods that others have lost (hats left on a bus) or thrown away.
Stealing	Because various offerings can be acquired through theft, marketers have developed products to deter this acquisition method, such as alarms to deter car theft.
Stealing	Another method of acquisition is by sharing or borrowing. Some types of "sharing" are illegal and border on theft, as when consumers copy and share movies.

Exhibit 1.4 ▶ Eight Ways to Acquire an Offering

There are many ways that consumers can acquire an offering.

Apple Pay?[32] These examples relate to consumers' buying decisions, but Exhibit 1.4 shows that consumers can acquire an offering in other ways. As the cost of cars and car insurance rises, some consumers are choosing not to buy cars, but to instead use services like Zipcar or Uber.[33]

Ways of Using an Offering

In addition to understanding how consumers acquire an offering, marketers want to know how consumers use an offering. For obvious reasons, marketers want to ensure that their offering is used correctly. Improper usage of offerings like cough medicine or alcohol can create health and safety problems.[34] Because consumers may ignore label warnings and directions on potentially dangerous products, marketers who want to make warnings more effective have to understand how consumers process label information.

Using an offering can include what we use with the offering (e.g., chips with salsa) as well as how we store and organize the items in our homes. Some interesting research suggests that we like to have things organized in our homes because we feel less anxiety and a greater sense of control over our lives when things are structured.[35] Notably though what seems organized to one person may seem messy to another. Whereas you might think about the items in your room in finely grained categories (e.g., black shirts are different from white shirts, and pants, shoes, and belts are in a different categories altogether), your roommate might have broader categories for thinking of items in their closet (they're all just "my clothes"). You may think her closet is messy; your roommate may think the organization of her closet is perfectly fine.[36]

Ways of Disposing of an Offering

Sometimes nothing but the packaging remains of an offering (such as food) after it has been consumed. This leaves only a decision about whether to recycle or not, and how. Consumers who want to dispose of a tangible product have several options:[37]

- *Find a new use for it.* Using an old toothbrush to clean rust from tools or making shorts out of an old pair of jeans shows how consumers can continue using an item instead of disposing of it.

- *Get rid of it temporarily.* Renting or lending an item is one way of getting rid of it temporarily.

- *Get rid of it permanently.* Throwing away an item, sending it to a recycling center, trading it, giving it away, or selling it are all ways to get rid of it permanently. However, some consumers refuse to throw away things that they regard as special, even if the items no longer serve a functional purpose.

When to Acquire/Use/Dispose of an Offering

The timing of consumer behavior can depend on many factors, including our perceptions of and attitudes toward time itself. Consumers may think in terms of whether it is "time for me" or "time for others" and whether acquiring or using an offering is planned or spontaneous.[38] In cold weather, our tendency to rent movies, call for a tow truck, or shop for clothes is greatly enhanced. At the same time, we are less likely to eat ice cream, shop for a car, or look for a new home during cold weather. Time of day influences many consumption decisions, which is why Panera Bread is adding drive-throughs to accommodate breakfast customers in a hurry and McDonald's now serves breakfast all day, every day.[39]

Our need for variety can affect when we acquire, use, or dispose of an offering. We may decide not to eat a sandwich for lunch today if we have already had it every other day this week. Transitions such as graduation, birth, retirement, and death also affect when we acquire, use, and dispose of offerings. For instance, we buy wedding rings when we get married. When we consume can be affected by traditions influenced by our families, our culture, and the area in which we live.

Decisions about when to acquire or use an offering are also affected by knowing when others might or might not be buying or using it. Thus, we might choose to go to the gym when we know that others will *not* be doing so. In addition, we may wait to buy until we know something will be on sale; even if we have to line up to buy something popular, we are likely to continue waiting if we see many people joining the line behind us.[40] Also, waiting to consume a pleasurable product such as candy increases our enjoyment of its consumption, even though we may be frustrated by having to wait.[41]

Another decision is when to acquire a new, improved version of a product we already own. This can be a difficult decision when the current model still works well or has sentimental value. However, marketers may be able to affect whether and when consumers buy upgrades by providing economic incentives for replacing older products.[42]

Even the first letter of our last name can impact when we acquire products. If your last name begins with a letter that's later in the alphabet (i.e., W, X, Y, or Z) you may be faster in buying the product than consumers whose last name begins with a letter that's in the beginning of the alphabet. Why? One reason is that as a kid you were always last when lines or roll calls were alphabetical. If you've learned to wait, you may develop a desire not to wait, which leads to buying more quickly.[43]

Where to Acquire/Use/Dispose of an Offering

In addition to acquisition decisions, consumers also make decisions about where to consume various products. For example, the need for privacy motivates consumers to stay home when using products that determine whether they are ovulating or pregnant. On the other hand, wireless connections allow consumers in public places to make phone calls, post messages and photos to social media sites, play computer games, and download photos or music from anywhere in the world.

Finally, consumers make decisions regarding where to dispose of goods. Should they toss an old magazine in the trash or the recycling bin? Should they store an old photo album in the attic or give it to a relative? Older consumers, in particular, may worry about what will happen to their special possessions after their death and about how to divide heirlooms without creating family conflict.[44] A growing number of consumers are recycling unwanted goods through recycling agencies or nonprofit groups or giving them directly to other consumers through websites like The Freecycle Network (www.freecycle.org) (see Exhibit 1.5).

How Much, How Often, and How Long to Acquire/Use/Dispose of an Offering

Consumers must make decisions about how much of a good or service they need; how often they need it; and how much time they will spend in acquisition, usage, and disposition.[45] In general, consumers don't like to waste things, and therefore will consider whether they are buying more of a product than what they will use.[46] Interestingly though, we can sometimes mispredict how happy we will be from usage. Although we might want to binge-watch eight episodes of a favorite TV show we've downloaded or streamed, research shows that longer breaks between episodes (e.g., watching one episode a night) will actually make us enjoy the series more.[47] Usage decisions can vary widely from person to person and from culture to culture. For example, consumers in Switzerland eat twice as much chocolate as consumers in Russia—and

Russian consumers eat 10 times as much chocolate as consumers in Mexico.[48] The amount we are willing to spend on items certainly depends on the state of our economy and whether or not we are in a recession.[49] But even if we try to be careful spenders, on the whole we tend to underestimate our spending. And we often don't budget for exceptional purchases.[50]

Sales of a product can be increased when the consumer (1) uses larger amounts of the product, (2) uses the product more frequently, or (3) uses it for longer periods of time. Bonus packages may motivate consumers to buy more of a product, but does this stockpiling lead to higher consumption? In the case of food products, consumers are more likely to increase consumption when the stockpiled item requires no preparation.[51] Usage may also increase when consumers sign up for flat-fee pricing covering unlimited consumption of telephone services or other offerings. However, because many consumers who choose flat-fee programs overestimate their likely consumption, they often pay more than if they had chosen per-usage pricing.[52]

Some consumers experience problems because they engage in more acquisition, usage, or disposition than they should. For example, they may have a compulsion to overbuy, overeat, smoke, or gamble too much. Researchers are also investigating what affects consumers' abilities to control consumption temptations and what happens when self-control falters, an issue for anybody who has tried to diet or make other changes to consumption habits.[53]

Exhibit 1.5 ▶ Where to Dispose
Consumers have a number of options of places to dispose of goods, such as this recycling website.

1-1f   CONSUMER BEHAVIOR INVOLVES EMOTIONS AND COPING

Consumer researchers have studied the powerful role that emotions play in consumer behavior.[54] Positive and negative emotions as well as specific emotions like loneliness,[55] hope,[56] fear,[57] regret,[58] guilt,[59] embarrassment,[60] and general moods[61] can affect how consumers think, the choices they make, how they feel after making a decision, what they remember, and how much they enjoy an experience. Emotions like love sometimes describe how we feel about certain brands, possessions, and experiences.[62] Consumers often use products to regulate their feelings—as when a scoop of ice cream seems like a good antidote to a bad quiz score.[63]

Because issues related to consumer behavior can involve stress, consumers often need to cope in some way.[64] Researchers have studied how consumers cope with difficult choices and an overwhelming array of goods from which to choose;[65] how consumers use goods and services to cope with stressful events[66] like having cancer; and how they cope with losing possessions due to divorce, natural disasters, moving to a residential-care facility, and other significant events.[67] They have even studied the coping behavior of certain market segments, such as low-literacy consumers, who often find it challenging to understand the marketplace without being able to read.[68] In later chapters, you'll learn more about how emotions affect goal pursuit, reactions to marketing stimuli, and other aspects of consumer behavior.

1-2   What Affects Consumer Behavior?

The many factors that affect acquisition, usage, and disposition decisions can be classified into four broad domains, as shown in the model in Exhibit 1.6: (1) The psychological core, (2) the process of making decisions, (3) the consumer's culture, and (4) consumer behavior outcomes. Although the four domains are presented in separate sections of this book, each domain is related to all the others. For example, to make decisions that affect outcomes like buying new products, consumers must first engage in processes described in the psychological core. They need to be motivated, able, and have the opportunity to be exposed to, perceive, and attend to information. They need to think about and comprehend this information, develop attitudes about it, and form memories they can retrieve during the decision process.

The cultural environment also affects what motivates consumers, how they process information, and the kinds of decisions they make. Age, gender, social class, ethnicity, families, friends, and other factors affect consumer values and lifestyles and, in turn, influence the decisions that consumers make and how and why they make them.

In the following overview, we illustrate the interrelationships among the domains with an example of a vacation decision.

1-2a   THE PSYCHOLOGICAL CORE: INTERNAL CONSUMER PROCESSES

Before consumers can make decisions, they must have some source of knowledge or information upon which to base their decisions. This source—the psychological core—covers motivation, ability, and opportunity; exposure, attention, perception, and comprehension; memory and knowledge; and attitudes about an offering.

Motivation, Ability, and Opportunity

Consider the case of a consumer named Jason who is deciding on a ski vacation. In Jason's mind, the vacation decision is risky because it will consume a lot of money and time, and he does not want to make a bad choice. Therefore, Jason is motivated to learn as much as he can about various vacation options, think about them, and imagine what they will be like. He has put other activities aside to give himself the opportunity to learn and think about this vacation. Because Jason already knows how to ski, he has the ability to determine what types of ski vacations he would find enjoyable. Whether he focuses on concrete things (how much the trip will cost) or abstract things (how much fun he will have) depends on how soon he plans to travel and how well the place he plans to visit fits with his self-concept.[69]

Exposure, Attention, Perception, and Comprehension

Because Jason is motivated to decide where to go on vacation and has both the ability and opportunity to do so, he will make sure he is exposed to and attends to any information relevant to his decision. He might look at travel ads and websites, read travel-related articles, check Twitter for special deals, browse photos on Pinterest, and talk with friends and travel agents. Jason will probably not attend to *all* vacation information; in fact, he is likely to be exposed to information he will never consciously perceive or pay attention to. He must identify what he has perceived—is it an ad or something else?—and then determine what country or mountain resort is involved, all as part of the comprehension process. He might infer that Kitzbühel, Austria, is a reasonably priced vacation destination because a website shows information consistent with this interpretation, for example.

Memory and Knowledge

Whether Jason can store what he learns about ski resorts in his memory—and whether he can recall that information later—depends, in part, on his motivation, ability, and opportunity. As he learns something new about ski resorts, he will organize that knowledge according to

Exhibit 1.6 ▶ A Model of Consumer Behavior

Consumer behavior encompasses four domains: (1) The consumer's culture, (2) the psychological core, (3) the process of making decisions, and (4) consumer behavior outcomes and issues. As the exhibit shows, Chapters 2–17 of this book relate to the four parts of this overall model.

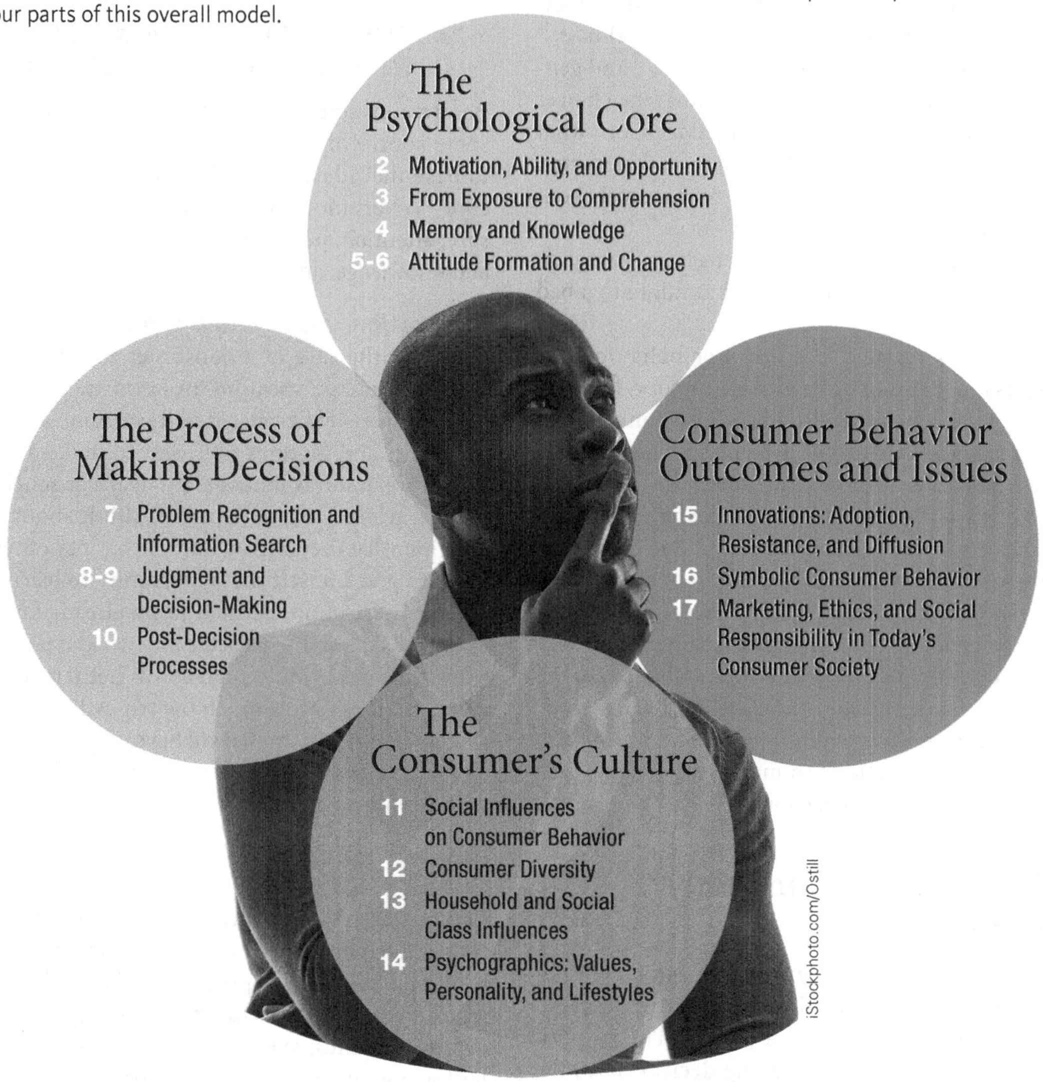

The Psychological Core

2   Motivation, Ability, and Opportunity
3   From Exposure to Comprehension
4   Memory and Knowledge
5-6   Attitude Formation and Change

The Process of Making Decisions

7   Problem Recognition and Information Search
8-9   Judgment and Decision-Making
10   Post-Decision Processes

Consumer Behavior Outcomes and Issues

15   Innovations: Adoption, Resistance, and Diffusion
16   Symbolic Consumer Behavior
17   Marketing, Ethics, and Social Responsibility in Today's Consumer Society

The Consumer's Culture

11   Social Influences on Consumer Behavior
12   Consumer Diversity
13   Household and Social Class Influences
14   Psychographics: Values, Personality, and Lifestyles

iStockphoto.com/Ostill

categories such as "places to stay on a ski vacation." Jason will also associate each new piece of information with other concepts he knows, such as "expensive" or "eco-friendly." Note that Jason may *store* information in memory, but his choices will be based only on the information that can be *retrieved* from memory—a key point for marketers seeking to create strong brand images and develop memorable communications (see Exhibit 1.7).

Forming and Changing Attitudes

Jason is likely to form attitudes toward the vacations he has categorized and comprehended. He may have a favorable attitude toward Kitzbühel because a website describes it as affordable, educational, and fun. However, his attitudes might change as he encounters new information. Attitudes do not always predict behavior. For example, although many of us have a positive attitude toward working out, our attitude and our good intentions do not always culminate in a trip to the gym. For this reason, attitudes and choices are considered as separate topics.

1-2b THE PROCESS OF MAKING DECISIONS

As shown in Exhibit 1.6, the processes that are part of the psychological core are intimately tied to the process of making decisions. This domain involves four stages: Problem recognition, information search, decision-making, and postpurchase evaluation.

Exhibit 1.7 ▶ Forming and Retrieving Memories

Ads that make consumers form and retrieve memories can be effective if the memories are of a positive experience.

Problem Recognition and the Search for Information

Problem recognition occurs when we realize that we have an unfulfilled need. Jason realized that he needed a vacation, for example. His subsequent search for information gave him insight into where he might go, how much the vacation might cost, and when he might travel. He also examined his financial situation. Elements of the psychological core are invoked in problem recognition and search because once Jason realizes that he needs a vacation and begins his information search, he is exposed to information, attends to and perceives it, categorizes and comprehends it, and forms attitudes and memories.

Culture The typical or expected behaviors, norms, and ideas that characterize a group of people.

Reference group A group of people consumers compare themselves with for information regarding behavior, attitudes, or values.

Making Judgments and Decisions

Jason's decision is characterized as a *high-effort decision*, meaning that he is willing to invest a lot of time and to exert mental and emotional energy in making it. He identifies several criteria that will be important in making his choices: The trip should be fun and exciting, safe,

educational, and affordable. Not all decisions involve a lot of effort. Jason also faces low-effort decisions such as what brand of toothpaste to take on the trip.

Again, the psychological core is invoked in making decisions. With a high-effort decision, Jason will be motivated to be exposed to lots of information, think about it deeply, analyze it critically, and form attitudes about it. He may have lasting memories about this information because he has thought about it so much. Consumers are not always aware of what they are thinking and how they are making their choices, so Jason might not be able to explain what affected his choices (background music in a travel agency might even be an influence).[70] Yet the emotions he thinks he will experience from different options (excitement, relaxation) may well influence his ultimate choice.[71] With a low-effort decision, such as what brand of toothpaste to buy, he would probably engage in less information search and process information less deeply, resulting in less enduring attitudes and memories.

Making Postdecision Evaluations

This step allows the consumer to judge, after the fact, whether the decision made was the correct one and whether to purchase that offering again. When he returns from his vacation, Jason will probably evaluate the outcome of his decisions. If his expectations were met and if the vacation was everything he thought it would be, he will feel satisfied. If the vacation exceeded his expectations, he will be delighted. If it fell short of them, he will be dissatisfied. Once again, aspects of the psychological core are invoked in making postdecision evaluations. Jason may seek out information that validates his experiences, he may update his attitudes, and he may selectively remember aspects of his trip that were extremely positive or negative.

1-2c THE CONSUMER'S CULTURE: EXTERNAL PROCESSES

Why did Jason decide to go on a skiing trip in the first place? In large part, our consumption decisions and how we process information are affected by our culture.[72] **Culture** refers to the typical or expected behaviors, norms, and ideas that characterize a group of people. It can be a powerful influence on all aspects of human behavior. Jason had certain feelings, perceptions, and attitudes because of the unique combination of groups to which he belongs and the influence they have on his values, personality, and lifestyle.

Reference Groups and Other Social Influences

When Jason sees groups of others he perceives as similar to himself, he regards them as **reference groups**, people whose values he shares and whose opinions he respects. He might also want to emulate the behavior of people whom he admires and to listen to the advice they offer through *word of mouth* (in person, on Facebook, on Twitter, etc.). Athletes, musicians, or movie stars sometimes serve as reference groups, influencing how we evaluate information and the choices we make (see Exhibit 1.8). Reference groups can also make us feel as if we should behave in a certain way. Jason may feel some pressure to go to Kitzbühel because his friends think that doing so is cool.

Diversity Influences

Jason is a member of many regional, ethnic, and religious groups that directly or indirectly affect the decisions he makes. For example, although his decision to ski at a place far from home is fairly typical for a North American man launched on his career, a consumer from a developing nation or a single woman from a different culture may not have made the same choice. Also, his age, gender, and educational background may all affect his impressions of what constitutes a good vacation, accounting for his interest in a European ski trip. Consider the vacation choices

Symbols External signs that consumers use to express their identity.

shown in Exhibit 1.9, and try to imagine the background factors that predispose consumers to choose these as vacation options.

Household and Social Class Influences

Because Jason is a member of the upper middle class and lives with his parents, these household and social class influences may affect his decision to go to a luxurious European ski resort with friends rather than join his family at a rustic ski area near home.

Values, Personality, and Lifestyle

The choices Jason makes are based, in part, on his beliefs, his personality, and his activities, interests, and opinions. Thus, he may be attracted to a European ski trip because he wants a vacation that he thinks will be exciting and out of the ordinary. He also anticipates that this vacation will test his ability to manage on his own and give himself a sense of accomplishment.

1-2d CONSUMER BEHAVIOR OUTCOMES AND ISSUES

As Exhibit 1.6 shows, the psychological core, decision-making processes, and the consumer's culture affect consumer behavior outcomes through the symbolic use of products and the diffusion of ideas, products, or services through a market. They also influence and are influenced by issues of ethics and social responsibility.

Consumer Behaviors Can Symbolize Who We Are

The groups we belong to and our sense of self can affect the **symbols** or external signs we use, consciously or unconsciously, to express our actual or desired identity. For example, while skiing, Jason may wear a North Face parka and Bollé goggles to communicate his status as an experienced skier. He might use his phone to snap a selfie and take home souvenirs, such as postcards and T-shirts, which symbolize his vacation.

Consumer Behaviors Can Diffuse Through a Market

After Jason makes his vacation decision, he may tell others about his prospective trip, which, in turn, could influence their vacation decisions. In this way, the idea of going to Kitzbühel on vacation may diffuse, or spread, to others. Had Jason resisted going to Kitzbühel (perhaps because he thought it was too expensive or too far away), he might have communicated information that would make others less likely to vacation there. Thus, the diffusion of information can have both negative and positive effects for marketers.

Consumer Behavior, Ethics, and Social Responsibility

Sometimes consumers face potentially conflicting priorities: They try to balance an immediate outcome against a

Source: MilkPEP

Exhibit 1.8 ▶ Influence of Reference Groups
Reference groups are people whose values we share and whose opinions we value, as evidenced in the Got Milk? campaigns.

Exhibit 1.9 ▶ Vacation Choices

The word "vacation" means different things to different people. Can you see how factors like social class, ethnic status, lifestyle, economic conditions, group affiliations, and gender affect the kinds of vacations that appeal to us? These examples show that some marketers are successful because they understand what their customers value.

On vacation, would you like to . . .

Learn how to walk on the moon? Space Camp is the place for you! You'll experience the weightlessness of space flight, launch a rocket, and take a simulated trip to Mars or the Moon. The price for would-be astronauts starts at $499 for a three-day camp experience.

Volunteer to restore parklands? Through the Sierra Club, you can travel to wildlife refuges and parks around the United States when you help preserve wilderness areas and keep up hiking trails. Along with a reasonable price tag—a seven-day stay in the Yosemite Valley to fix hiking trails costs $445, not including transportation—you'll get an insider's view of the local area plus the satisfaction of helping the planet.

See where penguins play? On a National Geographic cruise, you'll start from the tip of South America and sail through Drake Passage. Then you'll travel by kayak along Antarctica's edge, home to penguins, whales, and other marine life. If your itinerary includes the Falkland Islands and South Georgia, you'll pay up to $44,550 (airfare is extra).

Sources: Based on information on www.spacecamp.com; www.sierraclub.org; and www.expeditions.com.

---

long-term outcome, or try to balance their own interests against the interests of others. For instance, a consumer who steals may acquire something right away, but the long-term outcome is personally risky and also problematic to society. Many consumers are interested in whether products have been produced in an ethical manner, with ethically sourced inputs, as discussed in later chapters. Similarly, marketing decisions may involve conflicting priorities and sometimes lead to ethical questions, such as whether marketing efforts promote obesity, whether advertising affects self-image, and whether marketing invades consumers' privacy.

On the other hand, both consumers and marketers can and do use marketing for constructive purposes, balancing short and long-term horizons plus the interests of themselves and others. These efforts by marketers and consumers may be relatively narrow—focusing on satisfying the needs of a particular consumer segment—or much broader, such as protecting the environment or improving the community. In the example of Jason choosing a ski vacation, he might decide to stay at an eco-friendly resort that conserves water and uses energy from clean sources. Or he may decide to buy his gear second-hand on eBay or from a retailer that is transparent about its environmental impact.[73]

1-3 Who Benefits from the Study of Consumer Behavior?

Why do people study consumer behavior? The reasons are as varied as the four different groups who use consumer

research: Marketing managers, ethicists and advocates, public policy makers and regulators, and consumers.

1-3a MARKETING MANAGERS

The study of consumer behavior provides critical information to marketing managers for developing marketing strategies and tactics. The American Marketing Association's definition of **marketing** shows why marketing managers need to learn about consumer behavior:

> *Marketing is the activity, set of institutions, and processes for creating, communicating, delivering, and exchanging offerings that have value for customers, clients, partners, and society at large.*

As this definition makes clear, marketers need consumer behavior insights to understand what consumers and clients value; only then can they develop, communicate, and deliver appropriate goods and services. See the Appendix for more about marketing research.

1-3b ETHICISTS AND ADVOCACY GROUPS

Marketers' actions sometimes raise important ethical questions. Concerned consumers sometimes form advocacy groups to create public awareness of inappropriate practices. They also influence other consumers as well as the targeted companies through strategies such as media statements and boycotts. For example, U.S. advocacy groups such as Consumer Watchdog worry about companies tracking what consumers do online. They and other

> **Marketing** The activity, set of institutions, and processes for creating, communicating, delivering, and exchanging offerings with value for individuals, groups, and society.

groups support an enforceable "do not track" mechanism that would allow consumers to opt out of online tracking systems. The Federal Trade Commission and Federal Communications Commission are weighing input from advertisers and consumers about the privacy issues involved and possible regulatory action.[74] We explore various ethical issues throughout this book and go into more detail in Chapter 17.

1-3c PUBLIC POLICY MAKERS AND REGULATORS

Understanding consumer behavior is crucial for legislators, regulators, and government agencies in developing policies and rules to protect consumers from unfair, unsafe, or inappropriate marketing practices. In turn, marketers' decisions are affected by these public policy actions. Consider the regulatory limits on tobacco marketing that are designed to discourage underage consumers from smoking and to inform consumers of smoking's health hazards. The United States, Canada, and many other nations already ban cigarette advertising on television and radio. Canada also requires large graphic warning labels on each pack.[75] However, electronic cigarettes and vaping are not yet regulated as heavily as traditional tobacco products, despite a steady increase in consumer usage and health concerns about liquid nicotine poisoning.[76]

Understanding how consumers comprehend and categorize information is important for recognizing and guarding against misleading advertising. For instance, researchers want to know what impressions an ad creates and whether these impressions are true. They also want to know how marketing influences consumers' decisions to comply with product usage instructions, such as using medical treatments as prescribed.[77] Consumer behavior research helps government officials understand and try to improve consumer welfare.[78] One example is the increase in childhood obesity over the past few decades, which government officials and regulators are working to address through proposals and actions to shape consumer behavior and influence marketing activities.[79] Even in developing nations where hunger is an ongoing issue, too many children are overweight, a cause for concern around the world.[80] See Chapter 17 for more about this issue.

1-3d ACADEMICS

Understanding consumer behavior is important in the academic world for two reasons. First, academics disseminate knowledge about consumer behavior when they teach courses on the subject. Second, academics generate knowledge about consumer behavior when they conduct research focusing on how consumers act, think, and feel when acquiring, using, and disposing of offerings. In turn, such academic research is useful to marketing managers, advocacy groups, policy makers, regulators, and others who need to understand consumer behavior.

1-3e CONSUMERS AND SOCIETY

Understanding consumer behavior enables marketers and other organizations to provide tools for more informed decision-making. For example, research indicates that we better understand the differences among brands when we can view a chart, matrix, or grid comparing brands and their attributes.[81] Thus, matrices such as those presented in the *Consumer Reports* magazine or on its website are likely to help many consumers make better decisions.

Product, service, and communications developments to protect certain consumer segments have also grown out of understanding how consumers behave. Many people want to protect children against inappropriate advertising or guard themselves against invasion of privacy. Some companies have changed their marketing voluntarily, whereas others have waited until legislators, regulators, or advocacy groups forced them to make changes. Finally, a better understanding of consumer behavior can pave the way for programs that benefit society. As discussed in Chapter 17, research on disposition behavior has the potential to aid recycling programs and other environmental activities, just as research on charitable donations can help nonprofit groups design communications to attract and inform contributors.

1-4 Making Business Decisions Based on the Marketing Implications of Consumer Behavior

As you learn about consumer behavior, you may wonder how businesses use different consumer behavior insights. Starting with Chapter 2, you will find numerous sections titled Marketing Implications that illustrate how marketers apply consumer behavior concepts in the real world. In general, consumer research helps marketers to develop product-specific plans, as well as broader strategies for market segmentation, targeting, and positioning, and to make decisions about the components of the marketing mix.

1-4a DEVELOPING AND IMPLEMENTING CUSTOMER-ORIENTED STRATEGY

Marketing is designed to *provide value to customers*. Thus, marketers must conduct research to understand the various groups of consumers within the marketplace so that they can develop a strategy and specific offerings that will provide such value. Once they develop and implement a suitable strategy, marketers need research to determine how well it is working and whether it is delivering the expected results (such as increasing market share or improving profits).

How Is the Market Segmented?

What one consumer values in a product may not be the same as what another consumer values. Consider the market for orange juice, which can be offered from concentrate, fresh squeezed, with other juices, and in other combinations. For example, Minute Maid, owned by Coca-Cola, has increased sales by adding "Pure Squeezed" orange juices to its product line. A Minute Maid executive explains that "there's a segment of consumers who have an affinity for the not-from concentrate [juice]."[82] Clearly, research helps marketers understand the different groups that make up a market and whether they can make an offering to appeal to one or more of these groups.

How Profitable Is Each Segment?

Consumer research can help marketers identify consumers who have needs that are not being met and can reveal the size and profitability of each segment. For example, Daimler has identified a potentially profitable segment of affluent auto buyers interested in upscale compact vehicles. It is introducing a series of Mercedes-Benz compact cars and SUVs specifically for this segment, fully equipped with accessories for consumers' digital devices, all part of its effort to regain the lead in the premium auto market by 2020.[83]

What Are the Characteristics of Consumers in Each Segment?

After determining how the market is segmented and whether it is potentially profitable, marketers need to learn about the characteristics of consumers in each segment, such as their age, education, and lifestyle. This information helps marketers project whether the segment is likely to grow or to shrink over time, a factor that affects future marketing decisions. For example, sales of fitness goods and services—as well as fitness tracking devices—are increasing as baby boomers, Millennials, and Generation X consumers strive to get and stay in shape.[84]

Are Customers Satisfied with Existing Offerings?

Marketers often do considerable research to learn whether consumers are currently satisfied with the company's offerings and marketing. For example, Harley-Davidson executives regularly ride with members of the Harley Owners Group to see firsthand what satisfies motorcycle buyers and what else they are looking for. They invite customers to submit their own videos online illustrating individual Harley-Davidson experiences, and ask social media users to comment on proposed ad campaigns. This research helps the company come up with new product ideas and new ways to promote bikes to current and potential customers.[85]

1-4b SELECTING THE TARGET MARKET

Understanding consumer behavior helps marketers determine which consumer groups are appropriate targets for marketing tactics and how heavy users of a product differ from light users.[86] Marketers also need to identify who is likely to be involved in acquisition, usage, and disposition

decisions. U.S. home builders like Toll Brothers, for example, are interested in the trend of multigenerational families living in one home. They know that some, if not all, of the family members will want a say in the home purchase, and therefore the homes must have features that will appeal to all the relatives involved in the decision.[87]

1-4c DEVELOPING PRODUCTS

Developing goods and services that satisfy consumers' wants and needs is a critical marketing activity. Marketers apply consumer research when making a number of decisions about products and branding.

What Ideas Do Consumers Have for New Products?

First, marketers need to design an offering that matches what consumers in the target market want. As noted earlier, sometimes customers collaborate with marketers or with each other on the development of innovative new offerings. The jewelry firm Swarovski is one of many companies that have used online competitions to tap the creativity of their customers in designing new products.[88] The entire inventory of Chicago-based online T-shirt company Threadless comes from designs submitted by consumers. After consumers vote (online or via social media), Threadless puts the highest-scoring items into production—with a ready segment of buyers who have a taste for such individualistic designs.[89]

What Attributes Can Be Added to or Changed in an Existing Offering?

Marketers often use research to determine when and how to modify or tailor a product to meet the needs of new or existing groups of consumers. For example, the U.S. Postal Service (USPS) knows that many engaged couples still send printed wedding invitations through the mail instead of communicating electronically. To supplement its regularly updated series of stamps, the USPS designed a stamp specifically for wedding invitations—which generated $375 million in sales within a few years. Now the USPS offers a range of wedding-stamp designs and invites consumers to personalize their own wedding stamps.[90]

How Should the Offering Be Branded?

Consumer research plays a vital role in decisions about choosing a brand and differentiating it from competing brands and from other brands in the company's product portfolio.[91] For example, the Japanese automaker Nissan once marketed cars under the Datsun brand, but eliminated that brand in favor of its corporate name, Nissan, in 1981. Later, the company introduced the Infiniti brand to distinguish its luxury autos from its other cars. Now Nissan is bringing back the Datsun brand for small, low-priced cars to be sold in emerging markets such as Russia, India, and Indonesia. This strategy allows Nissan to maintain a separate brand image and positioning for each of these product lines.[92]

What Should the Package and Logo Look Like?

Many marketers use consumer research when making decisions about packaging and logos. For example, if you were to buy a bag of pretzels, you might infer that a bag with 15 pretzels on the package would contain more pretzels than one that shows only 3 pretzels on the package.[93] ConAgra Foods, which makes products such as Orville Redenbacher popcorn, takes online shopping habits into consideration when designing product packages. By developing smaller packages that cost less to ship, ConAgra increases the opportunities for selling to cost-conscious online shoppers.[94]

1-4d POSITIONING

Another strategic choice is deciding how an offering should be positioned in consumers' minds. The desired image should reflect what the product is and how it differs from the competition. For example, the Window of the World theme park in Shenzhen, China, is positioned as a fun place for Chinese consumers who want to see the world's most famous sights without leaving the country. The park features 130 replicas of well-known landmarks such as the pyramids, the White House, and the Eiffel Tower. This positioning is in contrast to Disneyland Hong Kong and Shanghai Disneyland, which offer rides and other traditional amusement park attractions.[95]

How Are Competitive Offerings Positioned?

Marketers sometimes conduct research to see how consumers view other brands in comparison with their own and then plot the results on a graph called a *perceptual map*. Brands in the same quadrant of the map are perceived as offering similar benefits to consumers. The closer companies are to one another on the map, the more similar they are perceived to be, and hence, the more likely they are to be competitors. Marketers can use perceptual maps to determine how their offerings can be positioned as distinct and different from competing offerings, based on appeals that are sustainable over time.[96]

How Should Our Offerings Be Positioned?

Companies use consumer research to understand what image a new offering should have in the eyes of consumers and what messages will effectively support this image.[97] The positioning should suggest that the product is superior in one or more attributes valued by the target market.[98] For example, Procter & Gamble's research found that many consumers were dissatisfied with traditional dry-cleaning establishments, in part because of inconsistent quality and also due to environmental concerns about cleaning chemicals. Seeing this as an opportunity, P&G positioned its Tide Dry Cleaners chain as clean, green, and friendly—using earth-friendly cleaning products, the power of the Tide brand, and attentive customer service.[99]

Should Our Offerings Be Repositioned?

Consumer research can help marketers reposition existing products (i.e., change their image). Consider how the Versus sports cable channel was repositioned. Originally introduced as Outdoor Life Network in 1995, the U.S. cable channel was repositioned as Versus in 2006 to reflect its broader sports coverage. Even with an audience of 70 million households, Versus fell short of rival ESPN's audience of 100 million households. Knowing that consumers are far more familiar with the NBC brand and coverage, thanks to the network's broadcasting of the Olympics and other high-profile events, Versus was repositioned as NBC Sports Network, broadcasting round-the-clock sporting events and related content.[100]

1-4e MAKING PROMOTION AND MARKETING COMMUNICATIONS DECISIONS

Research can help companies make decisions about promotional/marketing communications tools, including advertising, sales promotions (premiums, contests, sweepstakes, free samples, coupons, and rebates), personal selling, and public relations. One area receiving attention is the use of techniques to measure consumers' physiological and neurological responses to marketing communications and other stimuli.[101] The rise of social media adds another twist to promotion and communications decisions.[102] Word of mouth—which spreads quickly through social media—that is not marketer-controlled, seems more credible to consumers than messages directly controlled by marketers.[103]

What Are Our Communication Objectives?

Consumer research can be very useful in determining advertising objectives. It may reveal, for example, that few people have heard of a new brand, suggesting that the advertising objective should be to enhance brand-name awareness. If research indicates that consumers have heard of the brand but don't know anything about it, the advertising objective should be to enhance brand knowledge. If consumers know the brand name but don't know the characteristics of the brand that make it desirable, the advertising should aim to enhance brand knowledge and encourage positive attitudes about it. And if consumers know neither the brand name nor the product's benefits, the advertising should educate the target market about both.

What Should Our Marketing Communications Look Like?

Research can help marketers determine what words and visuals—and what balance of text and images—would be most effective for ad and brand recognition and recall.[104] A brand name is better remembered when placed in an ad that has interesting, unusual, and relevant visuals. If the visuals are interesting but unrelated to the product, consumers may remember the visuals but forget the product's name.

Online advertising is also being researched. One finding, for instance, is that customizing e-mail messages for targeted customers is an effective way to boost visits to the brand's website.[105] Another study showed that both emotion and physiological arousal are factors in whether an online ad goes viral. Specifically, an ad is more likely to be spread virally when the content evokes a positive emotional response (such as awe) or a negative emotional response (such as anger).[106] As an example, Kleenex's "Unlikely Best Friends" commercial, which featured a man and a dog—both in wheelchairs—attracted tens of millions of online views due to positive emotional response.[107]

Where Should Advertising Be Placed?

When marketers select specific media vehicles in which to advertise, they find demographic, lifestyle, and media usage data very useful. Research shows that more people split their time among many different media and that many people use recording technology to avoid commercials. Knowing this, marketers are choosing media with better targeting or more consumer exposure in mind. For example, Ford has used video ads on Facebook's log-out page to promote its sporty Mustang car, taking advantage of the ability to target by location, gender, and age.[108] A growing number of firms are using sponsorship of cause-related events (such as the Avon Walk for Breast Cancer) that attract the interest of consumers in the targeted segments.[109]

When Should We Advertise?

Research may reveal seasonal variations in purchases due to weather-related needs, variations in the amount of discretionary money consumers have (which changes, for instance, before and after Christmas), holiday buying patterns, and the like. In the weeks leading up to Easter, for instance, the chocolate company Cadbury airs TV commercials, places print ads, sponsors special events, and posts Facebook promotions for its chocolate eggs. In Australia, it has targeted 18- to 30-year-old chocolate lovers with extensive Facebook advertising for new chocolate egg products just before Easter, when this segment is most likely to buy.[110]

Has Our Advertising Been Effective?

Finally, advertisers can research an ad's effectiveness at various points in the advertising development process. Sometimes marketers or ad agencies conduct advertising *copy testing* or *pretesting*, testing an ad's effectiveness before it appears in public. If the objective is creating brand awareness and the tested ad does not enhance awareness, the company may replace it with a new ad. Effectiveness research can also take place after the ads have been placed in the media, such as conducting tracking studies to see whether ads have achieved particular objectives over time.

What About Sales Promotion Objectives and Tactics?

When developing sales promotions, marketers can use research to identify sales promotion objectives and tactics. For example, when Snack Factory wanted to attract new customers to its Pretzel Crisps snacks and increase sales, the firm posted a $1 coupon on Facebook for two weeks. This promotion added 7,000 new Facebook fans and, more importantly, the rate of redemption of the coupons was 87 percent. Without fanfare, Snack Factory switched to a buy one, get one free coupon on Facebook. The new offer went viral, gaining Pretzel Crisps 15,000 fans in two weeks—plus an impressive 95 percent coupon redemption rate. Now the brand has more than 325,000 "likes" and regularly conducts sales promotions on Facebook, Twitter, Pinterest, and other social media sites.[111] Research can also prevent such pitfalls as offering coupons to certain consumers who won't redeem them for fear of looking stingy.[112]

Have Our Sales Promotions Been Effective?

Consumer research can answer this question. Marketers might compare sales before, during, and after a promotion to determine changes in sales. Research can also indicate whether a free sample has been more effective than a price promotion, whether a free gift enhances value perceptions and purchase intentions, and how consumers react after a sales promotion has been discontinued.[113]

How Can Salespeople Best Serve Customers?

Finally, research can help managers make decisions about salespeople. By tracking store patronage at different times of the day or on different days of the week, retailers can determine the appropriate number of store personnel needed to best serve customers at those times. Research also offers insights into selecting salespeople and evaluating how well they serve customers. For example, similarity between the consumer and a salesperson or service provider can influence whether customers comply with these marketing representatives.[114]

1-4f   MAKING PRICING DECISIONS

The price of a product or service can have a critical influence on consumers' acquisition, usage, and disposition decisions. It is therefore very important for marketers to understand how consumers react to price and to use this information in pricing decisions, a topic also covered in later chapters.

What Price Should Be Charged?

Why do prices often end in 99? Consumer research has shown that people perceive $9.99 or $99.99 to be cheaper than $10.00 or $100.00. Perhaps this is one reason why so many prices end in the number 9.[115] Too low a price can make consumers suspect the product's quality.[116] In general, consumers respond better to a discount presented as a percentage off the regular price (e.g., 25 percent subtracted from the price) than to a discount presented as a specific amount of money subtracted from the regular price (originally $25, now only $15).[117]

Also, when making a purchase, consumers consider how much they must pay in relation to the price of other relevant brands or to the price they previously paid for that product, so marketers must be aware of these reference prices.[118] When buying multiple units of a service for one bundled price (such as a multiday ski pass), consumers may not feel a great loss if they use only some of the units because they have difficulty assigning value to each unit. In addition, when consumers buy multiple products for one bundled price (such as a case of wine), they are likely to increase their consumption because unit costs seem low.[119] How much consumers will pay can even be affected by the price of unrelated products they happen to see first. Thus, the price you would be willing to pay for a T-shirt may vary, depending on whether the prices you noticed for shoes in the store next door were high or low.[120]

Also, studies indicate that consumers have differing perceptions of what a product is worth, depending on whether they are buying or selling it. Generally people tend to overestimate how much others will pay for goods, particularly when they are selling a product they own.[121] Sellers should therefore avoid this *endowment effect*; that is, they should not set a higher price than buyers are willing to pay.[122]

How Sensitive Are Consumers to Price and Price Changes?

Research also suggests that consumers have different views of the importance of price. Some consumers are very price sensitive, meaning that a small change in price will have a large effect on consumers' willingness to purchase the product. Other consumers are price insensitive and thus likely to buy an offering regardless of its price. Marketers can use research to determine which consumers are likely to be price sensitive and when. For fashion or prestige goods, a high price symbolizes status. Thus, status-seeking consumers may be less sensitive to a product's price and pay more than $50 for a T-shirt with a prestigious label.

When Should Certain Price Tactics Be Used?

Research also reveals when consumers are likely to be most responsive to various pricing tactics. For example, consumers have traditionally been very responsive to price cuts on bed linens during January. These "white sales" are effective because consumers have come to anticipate them at that time of the year. Similarly, approximately five million U.S. consumers buy new TVs specifically to watch the

Super Bowl every year. Knowing this trend, online and store retailers mount price promotions in the weeks leading up to the Super Bowl, aiming to get their share of these TV purchases.[123]

1-4g MAKING DISTRIBUTION DECISIONS

Another important marketing decision involves how products are distributed and sold to consumers in retail stores. Here, too, marketers can use consumer research.

Where and When Are Target Consumers Likely to Shop?

Marketers who understand the value consumers place on time and convenience have developed distribution channels that allow consumers to acquire or use offerings whenever and wherever it is most convenient for them. For example, 24-hour grocery stores, health clubs, catalog ordering, and online ordering systems give consumers flexibility in the timing of their acquisition, usage, and disposition decisions. Some retailers, including Walmart and Peapod, are testing virtual "stores," actually large posters in transit stations or other busy locations. The posters depict grocery shelves stocked with specific products, each featuring a QR (quick response) code. Consumers use their smartphones to scan the QR codes of items they want to buy, complete the transaction, and schedule delivery for when they know they will be home.[124]

What Do Customers Want to See in Stores?

Retailers want to carry the assortment of merchandise best suited to consumers who shop in their stores. Target, for instance, is experimenting with a new store concept that will help it determine which "smart home" devices, which remotely control lighting and temperature, among other elements of the home environment, are of interest to consumers.[125] Assortment size itself can influence consumer behavior, as you'll see in later chapters.

How Should Stores Be Designed?

Supermarkets are generally designed with similar or complementary items stocked near one another because research shows that consumers think about items in terms of categories based on products' similar characteristics or use. Thus, stores stock peanut butter near jelly because the products are often used together. Consumer research can also help marketers develop other aspects of their retail environments. Music, colors, aromas, the ability to touch product, displays, and store organization can affect consumers' in store behaviors and choices.[126]

Store design also depends on whether consumers are shopping for fun or seeking to quickly accomplish a particular task like buying a certain item.[127] During the back-to-school shopping season, for instance, Target stores display dorm-room products together for consumer convenience.[128] Knowing that some consumers simply like to

AP Images/Imaginechina

Exhibit 1.10 ▶ Targeting Where Consumers Shop

Marketers need to understand how and when consumers best shop. For instance, busy consumers can grocery shop using their smartphones on these boards in subway or bus stations, which is very convenient for them.

shop, retailers are increasingly creating more exciting and aesthetically pleasing store environments.[129] For example, in Shanghai, the distinctive glass exterior, spiral staircase, and gleaming white logo of the Apple store has made such an impression on shoppers that some competitors have opened look-alike stores elsewhere in China.[130]

Given the significant increase in shopping via computer and mobile devices, retailers must design websites for friendly functionality on devices used by targeted consumer groups. Research shows that 38 percent of shoppers only use smartphones when buying from the Amazon retail website, for example; similarly, 44 percent of shoppers only use smartphones when buying from the eBay site.[131] Stores and retail websites must not only function well, they can convey a particular image and shopping atmosphere. To illustrate, the apparel retailer Abercrombie & Fitch added an online playlist so customers who shop via the Internet can click to hear the same songs that play in its stores.[132]

Summary:

Consumer behavior involves understanding the set of decisions (what, whether, why, when, how, where, how much, and how often) that an individual or group of consumers makes over time about the acquisition, use, or disposition of goods, services, ideas, or other offerings. The psychological core exerts considerable influence on consumer behavior. A consumer's motivation, ability, and opportunity affect his or her decisions and influence what a person is exposed to, what he or she pays attention to, and what he or she perceives and comprehends. These factors also affect how consumers categorize and interpret information, how they form and retrieve memories, and how they form and change attitudes. Each aspect of the psychological core has a bearing on the consumer decision-making process, which involves (1) problem recognition, (2) information search, (3) judgments and decision-making, and (4) evaluating satisfaction with the decision.

Consumer behavior is affected by the consumer's culture and by the typical or expected behaviors, norms, and ideas of a particular group. Consumers belong to a number of groups, share their cultural values and beliefs, and use their symbols to communicate group membership. Household and social class influences are involved in consumer behavior, as are each individual's values, personality, and lifestyles. Consumer behavior can be symbolic and express an individual's identity. It is also indicative of how quickly an offering spreads throughout a market. Further, ethics and social responsibility play a role in consumer behavior.

Marketers study consumer behavior to gain insights that will lead to more effective marketing strategies and tactics. Ethicists and advocacy groups are keenly interested in consumer behavior, as are public policy makers and regulators who want to protect consumers from unsafe or inappropriate offerings. Consumers and society can both benefit as marketers learn to make products more user-friendly and to show concern for the environment. Finally, studying consumer behavior helps marketers understand how to segment markets and how to decide which to target, how to position an offering, and which marketing-mix tactics will be most effective.

Questions for Review and Discussion

1. **How is consumer behavior defined?**

2. **What is an offering?**

3. **What are some of the factors in the psychological core that affect consumer decisions and behavior?**

4. **What aspects of the consumer's culture influence decisions and behavior?**

5. **How is *marketing* defined?**

6. **How can public policy decision makers, advocacy groups, and marketing managers use consumer research?**

7. **What kinds of marketing questions can companies use consumer behavior research to answer?**

8. **How can you benefit from studying consumer behavior?**

Endnotes

1   Jacob Jacoby, "Consumer Psychology: An Octennium," in ed. Paul Mussen and Mark Rosenzweig, *Annual Review of Psychology* (Palo Alto, Calif.: Annual Reviews, 1976), pp. 331–358.

2   Karen Page Winterich and Gergana Y. Nenkov, "Save Like the Joneses: How Service Firms Can Utilize Deliberation and Informational Influence to Enhance Consumer Well-Being," *Journal of Service Research* 18, no. 3, 2015, pp. 384–404; and Jennifer Savary, Kelly Goldsmith, and Ravi Dhar, "When Tempting Alternatives Increase Willingness to Donate," *Journal of Marketing Research* 52, no. 1, 2015, pp. 27–38.

3   Subimal Chatterjee and Wilson Lin Chien-Wei, "When Losing Hurts Less: How Spending Time versus Money Affects Outcome Happiness," *Advances in Consumer Research* 40, 2012, pp. 675–677; and Jennifer Aaker, Melanie Rudd, and Cassie Mogilner, "If Money Doesn't Make You Happy, Consider Time," *Journal of Consumer Psychology* 21, April 2011, pp. 126–130.

4   See, for example, Wendy Parkins and Geoffrey Craig, "Slow Living and the Temporalities of Sustainable Consumption," in eds. Tanai Lewis and Emily Potter, *Ethical Consumption: A Critical Introduction* (New York: Routledge, 2011), pp. 189–201; S. P. Mantel and J. J. Kellaris, "Cognitive Determinants of Consumers' Time Perceptions: The Impact of Resources Required and Available," *Journal of Consumer Research*, March 2003, pp. 531–538; and J. Cotte, S. Ratneshwar, and D. G. Mick, "The Times of Their Lives: Phenomenological and Metaphorical Characteristics of Consumer Lifestyles," *Journal of Consumer Research*, September 2004, pp. 333–345.

5 Erica Mina Okada and Stephen J. Hoch, "Spending Time Versus Spending Money," *Journal of Consumer Research* 31, no. 2, 2004, pp. 313–323.

6 Leif D. Nelson and Tom Meyvis, "Interrupted Consumption: Disrupting Adaptation to Hedonic Experiences," *Journal of Marketing Research*, December 2008, pp. 654–664.

7 Suzanne B. Shu and Ayelet Gneezy, "Procrastination of Enjoyable Experiences," *Journal of Marketing Research*, October 2010, pp. 933–944; and Rik Pieters and Marcel Zeelenberg, "A Theory of Regret Regulation 1.0," *Journal of Consumer Psychology* 17, no. 1, 2007, pp. 3–18.

8 Ying-Ching Lin and Chiu-Chi Angela Chang, "Double Standard: The Role of Environmental Consciousness in Green Product Usage," *Journal of Marketing* 76, no. 5, 2012, pp. 125–134; and Rosellina Ferraro, Amna Kirmani, and Ted Matherly, "Look at Me! Look at Me! Conspicuous Brand Usage, Self-Brand Connection, and Dilution," *Journal of Marketing Research* 50, No. 4, August 2013, pp. 477–488.

9 Robyn A. LeBoeuf, "Discount Rates for Time Versus Dates: The Sensitivity of Discounting to Time-Interval Description," *Journal of Marketing Research*, February 2006, pp. 59–72.

10 Baba Shiv, Ziv Carmon, and Dan Ariely, "Placebo Effects of Marketing Actions: Consumers May Get What They Pay For," *Journal of Marketing Research*, November 2005, pp. 383–393.

11 Amar Cheema and Dilip Soman, "The Effect of Partitions on Controlling Consumption," *Journal of Marketing Research*, December 2008, pp. 665–675.

12 Jonah Berger, *Contagious: Why Things Catch On* (New York: Simon & Schuster, 2013).

13 Jacob Jacoby, Carol K. Berning, and Thomas F. Dietworst, "What About Disposition?" *Journal of Marketing*, April 1977, pp. 22–28.

14 Joohyung Park and Sejin Ha, "Understanding Consumer Recycling Behavior: Combining the Theory of Planned Behavior and the Norm Activation Model," *Family and Consumer Sciences Research Journal, Special Issue: The Significance of Community to Individual and Family Well-being* 42, no. 3, 2014, pp. 278–291.

15 Easwar S. Iyer and Rajiv K. Kashyap, "Consumer Recycling: Role of Incentives, Information, and Social Class," *Journal of Consumer Behaviour* 6, no. 1, 2007, pp. 32–47.

16 Tom Szaky, "How Can Identifying Materials Reduce Packaging Waste?" *Packaging Digest*, July 15, 2015, www.packagingdigest.com; Tom Szaky, "The Micro-Multinational," *New York Times*, March 21, 2012, www.nytimes.com; and Penelope Green, "Making Design out of Rubbish," *New York Times*, August 10, 2011, www.nytimes.com.

17 Abigail B. Sussman and Adam L. Alter, "The Exception Is the Rule: Underestimating and Overspending on Exceptional Expenses," *Journal of Consumer Research* 39, no. 4, December 2012, pp. 800–814.

18 Yu Ma, Kusum L. Ailawadi, Dinesh K. Gauri, and Dhruv Grewal, "An Empirical Investigation of the Impact of Gasoline Prices on Grocery Shopping Behavior," *Journal of Marketing* 75, no. 2, March 2011, pp. 18–35.

19 Daniel Navarro-Martinez, Linda Court Salisbury, Katherine N. Lemon, Neil Stewart, William J. Matthews, and Adam J. L. Harris, "Minimum Required Payment and Supplemental Information Disclosure Effects on Consumer Debt Repayment Decisions," *Journal of Marketing Research* 48, supplement 1, October 2011, pp. S60–S77.

20 David Gal and Blakeley B. McShane, "Can Small Victories Help Win the War? Evidence from Consumer Debt Management,"

Journal of Consumer Research 38, no. 4, December 2011, pp. 743–762.

21 Emily N. Garbinsky, Anne-Kathrin Klesse, and Jennifer Aaker, "Money in the Bank: Feeling Powerful Increases Saving," *Journal of Consumer Research* 41, no. 3, October 2014, pp. 610–623.

22 Wayne D. Hoyer, Rajesh Chandy, Matilda Dorotic, Manfred Krafft, and Siddharth S. Singh, "Consumer Cocreation in New Product Development," *Journal of Service Research* 13, no. 3, 2010, pp. 283–296; and Andrea Hemetsberger, "When David Becomes Goliath: Ideological Discourse in New Online Consumer Movements," *Advances in Consumer Research* 33, 2006, pp. 494–500.

23 Bradley Reeves, "Co-Creation Nation," *Media Post*, March 21, 2012, www.mediapost.com.

24 Joydeep Srivastava and Priya Raghubir, "Debiasing Using Decomposition: The Case of Memory-Based Credit Card Expense Estimates," *Journal of Consumer Psychology* 12, no. 3, 2002, pp. 253–264.

25 Russell W. Belk, "Ownership and Collecting," in eds. Randy O. Frost and Gail Steketee, *The Oxford Handbook of Hoarding and Acquiring* (New York: Oxford University Press, 2013), pp. 33–42.

26 Anand Florack, Janet Kleber, Romy Busch, and David Stohr, "Detaching the Ties of Ownership: The Effects of Hand Washing on the Exchange of Endowed Products," *Journal of Consumer Psychology* 24, no. 2, 2014, pp. 284–289.

27 Hyeongmin Kim, "Situational Materialism: How Entering Lotteries May Undermine Self-Control," *Journal of Consumer Research* 40, no. 4, 2013, pp. 759–772.

28 Gallup Poll, June 2015, www.gallup.com/poll.

29 Larry Edsall, "Vehicle Wraps Cover Larger Share of Market," *Detroit News*, December 25, 2014, www.detroitnews.com.

30 Kristine R. Ehrich and Julie R. Irwin, "Willful Ignorance in the Request for Product Attribute Information," *Journal of Marketing Research*, August 2005, pp. 266–277; and Markus Giesler, "Consumer Gift Systems," *Journal of Consumer Research* 33, no. 2, 2006, pp. 283–290.

31 Shibo Li, Kannan Srinivasan, and Baohong Sung, "Internet Auction Features as Quality Signals," *Journal of Marketing*, June 2009, pp. 75–92; Michael Basnjak, Dirk Obermeier, and Tracy L. Tuten, "Predicting and Explaining the Propensity to Bid in Online Auctions: A Comparison of Two Action-Theoretical Methods," *Journal of Consumer Behaviour* 5, no. 2, 2006, pp. 102–116; and Charles M. Brooks, Patrick J. Kaufmann, and Donald R. Lichtenstein, "Travel Configuration on Consumer Trip-Chained Store Choice," *Journal of Consumer Research* 31, no. 2, 2004, pp. 241–248.

32 Nandita Bose, "Exclusive: In 'Year of Apple Pay,' Many Top Retailers Remain Skeptical," *Reuters*, June 5, 2015, www.reuters.com; Bryan Yurcan, "Will Mobile Electronic Wallets Replace Leather Wallets?" *Information Week*, March 20, 2012, www.informationweek.com; and Matthew J. Bernthal, David Crockett, and Randall L. Rose, "Credit Cards as Lifestyle Facilitators," *Journal of Consumer Research* 32, no. 1, 2005, pp. 130–145.

33 Mark Penn, "The Teenage Dream of Owning a Car Is Dying," *Fortune*, July 22, 2015, http://fortune.com; Bardhi Fleura and Giana M. Eckhardt, "Access-Based Consumption: The Case of Car Sharing," *Journal of Consumer Research* 39, no. 4, 2012, pp. 881–898.

34 Jennifer J. Argo and Kelley J. Main, "Meta-Analysis of the Effectiveness of Warning Labels," *Journal of Public Policy & Marketing* 23, no. 2, 2004, pp. 193–208.

35 Keisha M. Cutright, "The Beauty of Boundaries: When and Why We Seek Structure in Consumption," *Journal of Consumer Research* 38, no. 5, 2012, pp. 775–790.

36 Delphine Dion, Ouidade Sabri, and Valerie Guillard, "Home Sweet Messy Home: Managing Symbolic Pollution," *Journal of Consumer Research* 41, no. 3, 2014, pp. 565–589.

37 Jacoby, Berning, and Dietworst, "What About Disposition?"

38 June Cotte, S. Ratneshwar, and David Glen Mick, "The Times of Their Lives: Phenomenological and Metaphorical Characteristics of Consumer Timestyles," *Journal of Consumer Research* 31, no. 2, 2004, pp. 333–345.

39 James F. Peltz, "Offering All-Day Breakfast Is a Made-To-Order Success for McDonald's," *Minneapolis Star-Tribune*, January 2, 2016, www.startribune.com; and John D. Oravecz, "Panera Bread Will Debut Drive-Thru Window in North Hills Store," *Pittsburgh Tribune-Review*, January 3, 2015, http://triblive.com.

40 Rongrong Zhou and Dilip Soman, "Looking Back: Exploring the Psychology of Queuing and the Effect of the Number of People Behind," *Journal of Consumer Research*, March 2003, pp. 517–530.

41 Stephen M. Nowlis, Naomi Mandel, and Deborah Brown McCabe, "The Effect of a Delay between Choice and Consumption on Consumption Enjoyment," *Journal of Consumer Research*, December 2004, pp. 502–210.

42 Erica Mina Okada, "Trade-ins, Mental Accounting, and Product Replacement Decisions," *Journal of Consumer Research* 27, March 2001, pp. 433–446.

43 Kurt A. Carlson and Jacqueline M. Conard, "The Last Name Effect: How Last Name Influences Acquisition Timing," *Journal of Consumer Research* 38, no. 2, 2011, pp. 300–307.

44 Linda L. Price, Eric J. Arnould, and Carolyn Folkman Curasi, "Older Consumers' Disposition of Special Possessions," *Journal of Consumer Research*, September 2000, pp. 179–201.

45 See, for example, Rebecca W. Hamilton, Rebecca K. Ratner, and Debora V. Thompson, "Outpacing Others: When Consumers Value Products Based on Relative Usage Frequency," *Journal of Consumer Research* 37, no. 6, 2011, pp. 1079–1094.

46 Lisa E. Bolton and Joseph Q. Alba, "When Less is More: Consumer Aversion to Unused Utility," *Journal of Consumer Psychology* 22, no. 3, July 2012, pp. 369–383.

47 Jeff Galak, Justin Kruger, and George Loewenstein, "Slow Down! Insensitivity to Rate of Consumption Leads to Avoidable Satiation," *Journal of Consumer Research* 39, no. 5, May 2012, pp. 993–1009.

48 Oliver Nieburg, "The New World of Chocolate," *Confectionery News*, October 9, 2014, www.confectionerynews.com; and "Nestle: Recession Stunts Russian Confectionery Market Growth," *Confectionery News*, August 16, 2011, www.confectionerynews.com.

49 Wagner A. Kamakura and Rex Yuxing Du, "How Economic Contractions and Expansions Affect Expenditure Patterns," *Journal of Consumer Research* 39, no. 2, 2012, pp. 229–247.

50 Abigal B. Sussman and Adam L. Alter, "The Exception is the Rule: Underestimating and Overspending on Exceptional Expenses," *Journal of Consumer Research* 39, no. 4, 2012, pp. 800–814.

51 Pierre Chandon and Brian Wansink, "When Are Stockpiled Products Consumed Faster?" *Journal of Marketing Research*, August 2002, pp. 321–335.

52 Joseph C. Nunes, "A Cognitive Model of People's Usage Estimations," *Journal of Marketing Research* 38, November 2000, pp. 397–409.

53 Kathleen D. Vohs, Roy F. Baumeister, and Dianne M. Tice, "Self-Regulation: Goals, Consumption and Choices, in, eds. Curtis P. Haugtvedt, Paul M. Herr, and Frank R. Kardes, *Handbook of Consumer Psychology* (New York: Psychology Press), pp. 349–367.

54 Allison R. Johnson and David W. Stewart, "A Re-Appraisal of the Role of Emotion in Consumer Behavior: Traditional and Contemporary Approaches," in ed. Naresh Malhotra, *Review of Marketing Research*, vol. 1, 2004, pp. 1–33.

55 Jung Wang, Juliet Zhu, and Baba Shiv, "The Lonely Consumer: Loner or Conformer," *Journal of Consumer Research* 38, no. 6, 2012, pp. 1116–1128.

56 Deborah J. MacInnis and Gustavo deMello, "The Concept of Hope and Its Relevance to Product Evaluation and Choice," *Journal of Marketing*, January 2005, pp. 1–14.

57 Kirsten Passyn and Mita Sujan, "Self-Accountability Emotions and Fear Appeals: Motivating Behavior," *Journal of Consumer Research* 32, March 2006, pp. 583–589; and O. Shehryar and D. Hunt, "A Terror Management Perspective on the Persuasiveness of Fear Appeals," *Journal of Consumer Psychology* 15, no. 4, 2005, pp. 275–287.

58 Eric A. Greenleaf, "Reserves, Regret, and Rejoicing in Open English Auctions," *Journal of Consumer Research* 31, no. 2, 2004, pp. 264–273; Marcel Zeelenberg and Rik Pieters, "A Theory of Regret Regulation 1.0," *Journal of Consumer Psychology* 17, no. 1, 2007, pp. 3–18; Ran Kivetz and Anat Keinan, "Repenting Hyperopia: An Analysis of Self-Control Regrets," *Journal of Consumer Research* 33, no. 2, 2006, pp. 273–282; and Lisa J. Abendroth and Kristin Diehl, "Now or Never: Effects of Limited Purchase Opportunities on Patterns of Regret over Time," *Journal of Consumer Research* 33, no. 3, 2006, pp. 342–351.

59 Darren W. Dahl, Heather Honea, and Rajesh V. Manchanda, "The Three Rs of Interpersonal Consumer Guilt: Relationship, Reciprocity, Reparation," *Journal of Consumer Psychology* 15, no. 4, 2005, pp. 307–315.

60 Darren Dahl, Rajesh V. Manchanda, and Jennifer J. Argo, "Embarrassment in Consumer Purchase: The Roles of Social Presence and Purchase Familiarity," *Journal of Consumer Research*, December 2001, pp. 473–483.

61 Alice M. Isen, "Positive Affect and Decision Processes: Some Recent Theoretical Developments with Practical Implications," in eds. Curtis P. Haugtvedt, Paul M. Herr, and Frank R. Kardes, *Handbook of Consumer Psychology* (New York: Psychology Press, 2008), pp. 273–296.

62 Aaron C. Ahuvia, "Beyond the Extended Self: Loved Objects and Consumers' Identity Narratives," *Journal of Consumer Research* 32, June 2005, pp. 171–184.

63 Joel B. Cohen and Eduardo B. Andrade, "Affective Intuition and Task-Contingent Affect Regulation," *Journal of Consumer Research* 31, no. 2, 2004, pp. 358–367; and Nitika G. Barg, Brian Wansink, and J. Jeffrey Inman, "The Influence of Incidental Affect on Consumers' Food Intake," *Journal of Marketing*, January 2007, pp. 194–206.

64 Adam Duhachek, "Summing Up the State of Coping Research: Prospects and Prescriptions for Consumer Research," in eds. Curtis P. Haugtvedt, Paul M. Herr, and Frank R. Kardes, *Handbook of Consumer Psychology* (New York: Psychology Press, 2008), pp. 1057–1077.

65 Sheena Leek and Suchart Chanasawatkit, "Consumer Confusion in the Thai Mobile Phone Market," *Journal of Consumer Behaviour* 5, no. 6, 2006, pp. 518–532.

66 Teresa M. Pavia and Marlys J. Mason, "The Reflexive Relationship between Consumer Behavior and Adaptive Coping," *Journal of Consumer Research* 31, no. 2, 2004, pp. 441–454.

67 Linda L. Price, Eric Arnould, and Carolyn Folkman Curasi, "Older Consumers' Dispositions of Special Possessions," *Journal of Consumer Research*, September 2000, pp. 179–201.

68 Natalie Ross Adkins and Julie L. Ozanne, "The Low Literate Consumer," *Journal of Consumer Research* 32, no. 1, 2005, pp. 93–105.

69 John G. Lynch and G. Zauberman, "Construing Consumer Decision Making," *Journal of Consumer Psychology* 17, no. 2, 2007, pp. 107–112.

70 John A. Bargh, "Losing Consciousness: Automatic Influences on Consumer Judgment, Behavior, and Motivation," *Journal of Consumer Research*, September 2002, pp. 280–285; Ap Dijksterhuis, Pamela K. Smith, Rick B. Van Baaren, and Daniel H. J. Wigboldus, "The Unconscious Consumer: Effects of Environment on Consumer Behavior," *Journal of Consumer Psychology* 15, no. 3, 2005, pp. 193–202.

71 Deborah J. MacInnis, Vanessa M. Patrick, and C. Whan Park, "Not as Happy as I Thought I'd Be? Affective Misforecasting and Product Evaluations," *Journal of Consumer Research*, March 2007, pp. 479–490; and Deborah J. MacInnis, Vanessa M. Patrick, and C. Whan Park, "Looking Through the Crystal Ball: Affective Forecasting and Misforecasting in Consumer Behavior," *Review of Marketing Research* 2, 2006, pp. 43–80.

72 Donnel Briley, Robert S. Wyer, and En Li, "A Dynamic View of Cultural Influence: A Review," *Journal of Consumer Psychology* 24, no. 4, 2014, pp. 557–571.

73 See, for example, Linn Viktoria Rampl, Tim Eberhardt, Reinhard Schutte, and Peter Kenning, "Consumer Trust in Food Retailers: Conceptual Framework and Empirical Evidence," *International Journal of Retail & Distribution Management* 40, no. 4, 2012, pp. 254–272.

74 Grant Gross, "Group Asks FCC to Make Websites Honor Do-Not-Track Requests," *PC World*, June 15, 2015, www.pcworld.com; and Dina Wisenberg Brin, "The New Technology Advertisers Use to Track Everything You Do," *CNN Money*, June 29, 2015, http://time.com/money.

75 Chantal Mack, "New Tobacco Warnings Become Mandatory," *Post Media News*, March 21, 2012, www.canada.com; and Melissa Healy, "Cigarette Packages in Medical Journals: New Look for a New Age," *Los Angeles Times*, August 4, 2011, www.latimes.com.

76 Samantha Kareen Nair, "FDA Seeks Data on E-Cigarettes after Surge in Poisoning Cases," *Reuters*, June 30, 2015, www.reuters.com.

77 Douglas Bowman, Carrie M. Heilman, and P. B. Seetharaman, "Determinants of Product-Use Compliance Behavior," *Journal of Marketing Research*, August 2004, pp. 324–338.

78 Dipankar Chakravarti, "Voices Unheard: The Psychology of Consumption in Poverty and Development," *Journal of Consumer Psychology* 16, no. 4, 2006, pp. 363–376.

79 Clifton B. Parker, "Targeted Policy Actions Could Help Discourage Obesity, Stanford Expert Says," *Stanford Report (Stanford University)*, October 26, 2015, http://news.stanford.edu.

80 "Child Obesity," Harvard T.H. Chan School of Public Health, www.hsph.harvard.edu.

81 James R. Bettman, *An Information Processing Theory of Consumer Choice* (Reading, Mass.: Addison-Wesley, 1979).

82 Michael Caliah, "Coca-Cola Sales Surprise on Dasani, Minute Maid," *MarketWatch*, April 15, 2014, www.marketwatch.com; and Jeremiah McWilliams, "Coca-Cola to Sell Not-from-concentrate Minute Maid Orange Juice," *Atlanta Journal-Constitution*, August 19, 2011, www.ajc.com/business.

83 Lawrence Ulrich, "German Luxury Car Brands Dominate and Look to Extend Their Lead," *New York Times*, July 2, 2015, www.nytimes.com; and Christiaan Hetzner and Marton Dunai, "Daimler to Launch 4-Door Compact Coupe in 2013," *Reuters*, March 29, 2012, www.reuters.com.

84 Marley Jay, "Fitness Trackers Are Hot, But Do They Really Improve Health?" *Associated Press*, June 30, 2015, www.denverpress.com.

85 Karl Greenberg, "Harley-Davidson Twists the Throttle at Sturgis," *Marketing Daily*, July 16, 2015, www.mediapost.com; and David Booth, "The New Harley-Davidson Wants You," *Edmonton Journal (Canada)*, March 20, 2012, www.edmontonjournal.com.

86 Robert D. Jewell and H. Rao Unnava, "Exploring Differences in Attitudes Between Light and Heavy Brand Users," *Journal of Consumer Psychology* 14, no. 1–2, 2004, pp. 75–80.

87 "Builders Expand Home Size to Capture Multigenerational Trend," *Realtor Mag*, August 18, 2014, http://realtormag.realtor.org; and John Gittelsohn, "Homebuilders Target In-Laws, Dogs as Extended Families Grow," *Businessweek*, November 17, 2011, www.businessweek.com.

88 Johann Füller, Katja Hutter, and Rita Faullant, "Why Co-Creation Experience Matters? Creative Experience and Its Impact on the Quantity and Quality of Creative Contributions," *R&D Management*, June 2011, pp. 259–273.

89 Shambhavi Anand, "VoxPop Ties Up with Threadless Creative Community," *Economic Times (India)*, July 6, 2015, http://articles.economictimes.indiatimes.com; and John Jantsch, "How Threadless Nailed the Crowdsource Model," *Social Media Today*, April 7, 2011, www.socialmediatoday.com.

90 Vincent M. Mallozzi, "The Honor of Your Postage Is Requested," *New York Times*, February 19, 2012, p. ST-17.

91 Judith Lynne Zaichkowsky, "Strategies for Distinctive Brands," *Brand Management* 17, no. 8, 2010, pp. 548–560.

92 Shubham Mukherjee, "'India a Very Complex Market to Understand': Datsun Head," *Times of India*, April 6, 2015, http://timesofindia.indiatimes.com; Jerry Hirsch, "Nissan to Bring Back Datsun Car Brand in Selected Markets," *Los Angeles Times*, March 20, 2012, www.latimes.com.

93 Adriana V. Madzharov and Lauren G. Block, "Effects of Product Unit Image on Consumption of Snack Foods," *Journal of Consumer Psychology* 29, no. 4, 2010, pp. 398–409.

94 Barbara Soderlin, "How Do ConAgra and Other Food Companies Reach Online Consumers?" *Omaha World Herald*, July 21, 2015, www.omaha.com.

95 Will Friedwald, "Celebrating 60 Years of Disneyland," *Wall Street Journal*, July 14, 2015, www.wsj.com; Daniel Roberts, "By the Numbers: Tourism, Wow!" *Fortune*, July 4, 2011, pp. 10–11; and Huang Lan and Huan Cao, "Around the World in a Day," *China Daily*, August 3, 2011, www.chinadaily.com.cn.

96 Cheng-Wen Lee and Chi-Shun Liao, "The Effects of Consumer Preferences and Perceptions of Chinese Tea Beverages on Brand Positioning Strategies," *British Food Journal* 111, no. 1, 2009, pp. 80–96.

97 See Claudiu V. Dimofte and Richard F. Yalch, "Consumer Response to Polysemous Brand Slogans," *Journal of Consumer Research* 33, no. 4, 2007, pp. 515–522.

98 See Alexander Chernev, "Jack of All Trades or Master of One? Product Differentiation and Compensatory Reasoning in Consumer Choice," *Journal of Consumer Research* 33, no. 4, 2007, pp. 430–444.

99 "Tide Dry Cleaners Stores Now Number 30," *American Dry Cleaner*, May 25, 2015, http://americandrycleaner.com; Ray A. Smith, "The New Dirt on Dry Cleaners," *Wall Street Journal*,

July 28, 2011, www.wsj.com; and Andrew Martin, "Smelling an Opportunity," *New York Times*, December 8, 2010, www.nytimes.com.

100 Sofia M. Fernandez, "NBC Sports Network Official Launch Replaces Versus on Monday," *Hollywood Reporter*, January 2, 2012, www.hollywoodreporter.com; and Michael McCarthy, "Versus Set to Become the NBC Sports Network," *USA Today*, August 1, 2011, www.usatoday.com.

101 See, for instance, Thales Teixeira, Michel Wedel, and Rik Pieters, "Emotion-Induced Engagement in Internet Video Advertisements," *Journal of Marketing Research* 49, no. 2, 2012, pp. 144–159; Adam W. Craig, Yuliya Komarova Loureiro, Stacy Wood, and Jennifer M. C. Vendemia, "Suspicious Minds: Exploring Neural Processes During Exposure to Deceptive Advertising," *Journal of Marketing Research* 49, no. 3, 2012, pp. 361–372; and Maarten A. S. Boksem and Ale Smidts, "Brain Responses to Movie Trailers Predict Individual Preferences for Movies and Their Population-Wide Commercial Success," *Journal of Marketing Research* 52, no. 4, August 2015, pp. 482–492.

102 Hyoungkoo Khang, Eyun-Jung Ki, and Lan Ye, "Social Media Research in Advertising, Communication, Marketing, and Public Relations, 1997–2010," *Journalism & Mass Communication Quarterly*, published online March 14, 2012, http://jmq.sagepub.com.

103 W. Glynn Mangold and David J. Faulds, "Social Media: The New Hybrid Element of the Promotion Mix," *Business Horizons* 52, 2009, pp. 357–365.

104 Anocha Aribarg, Rik Pieters, and Michel Wedel, "Raising the Bar: Bias-Adjustment of Advertising Recognition Tests," *Journal of Marketing Research*, June 2010, pp. 387–400.

105 Asim Ansari and Carl Mela, "E-Customization," *Journal of Marketing Research*, May 2003, pp. 131–145.

106 Jonah Berger and Katherine L. Milkman, "What Makes Online Content Viral?" *Journal of Marketing Research* 49, no. 2, April 2012, pp. 192–205.

107 Declan Harty, "Perfect Pair: Dog and Owner Put Kleenex on Top Viral Video Chart," *Advertising Age*, June 30, 2015, www.adage.com.

108 Cotton Delo, "Facebook Sets High Asking Price for Log-Out Ads," *Advertising Age*, March 23, 2012, www.adage.com; and "Facebook Eyes Big Ad Opportunity from Log-Out Ads," *Forbes*, March 28, 2012, www.forbes.com.

109 Carolyn J. Simmons and Karen L. Becker-Olsen, "Achieving Marketing Objectives Through Social Sponsorships," *Journal of Marketing*, October 2006, pp. 154–169.

110 Clare Kermond, "Cadbury Hatches Plan for Three Easter Products," *Canberra Times (Australia)*, March 30, 2012, www.canberratimes.com.au.

111 "Case Study: Snack Brand Doubles Facebook 'Likes' Through Social Coupon," August 16, 2011, www.emarketer.com.

112 Laurence Ashworth, Peter R. Darke, and Mark Schaller, "No One Wants to Look Cheap: Trade-offs between Social Disincentives and the Economic and Psychological Incentives to Redeem Coupons," *Journal of Consumer Psychology* 15, no. 4, 2005, pp. 295–306.

113 Sucharita Chandran and Vicki G. Morwitz, "The Price of 'Free'dom: Consumer Sensitivity to Promotions with Negative Contextual Influences," *Journal of Consumer Research* 33, no. 3, 2006, pp. 384–392; Priya Raghubir, "Free Gift with Purchase: Promoting or Discounting the Brand?" *Journal of Consumer Psychology* 14, no. 1–2, 2004, pp. 181–186; and Luc Wathieu, A. V. Muthukrishnan, and Bart J. Bronnenberg, "The Asymmetric Effect of Discount Retraction on Subsequent Choice," *Journal of Consumer Research* 31, no. 3, 2004, pp. 652–657.

114 Stephanie Dellande, Mary C. Gilly, and John L. Graham, "Gaining Compliance and Losing Weight: The Role of the Service Provider in Health Care Services," *Journal of Marketing* 68, July 2004, pp. 78–91; and Sean Dwyer, Orlando Richard, and C. David Shepherd, "An Exploratory Study of Gender and Age Matching in the Salesperson–Prospective Customer Dyad," *Journal of Personal Selling and Sales Management*, Fall 1998, pp. 55–69.

115 Thomas Manoj and Vicki Morwitz, "Penny Wise and Pound Foolish: The Left-Digit Effect in Price Cognition," *Journal of Consumer Research* 32, no. 1, 2005, pp. 54–64; and Robert M. Schindler and Patrick N. Kirby, "Patterns of Rightmost Digits Used in Advertising Prices: Implications for Nine-Ending Effects," *Journal of Consumer Research*, September 1997, pp. 192–201.

116 Jacob Jacoby, Jerry Olson, and Rafael Haddock, "Price, Brand Name, and Product Composition Characteristics as Determinants of Perceived Quality," *Journal of Applied Psychology*, December 1971, pp. 470–479; and Kent B. Monroe, "The Influence of Price Differences and Brand Familiarity on Brand Preferences," *Journal of Consumer Research*, June 1976, pp. 42–49.

117 Devon DelVecchio, H. Shanker Krishnan, and Daniel C. Smith, "Cents or Percent? The Effects of Promotion Framing on Price Expectations and Choice," *Journal of Marketing*, July 2007, pp. 158–170. For more on pricing effects associated with regular and discount prices, see Keith S. Coulter and Robin A. Coulter, "Distortion of Price Discount Perceptions: The Right Digit Effect," *Journal of Consumer Research*, August 2007, pp. 162–173.

118 Daniel J. Howard and Roger A. Kerin, "Broadening the Scope of Reference Price Advertising Research: A Field Study of Consumer Shopping Involvement," *Journal of Marketing*, October 2006, pp. 185–204; Tridib Mazumdar, S. P. Raj, and Indrajit Sinha, "Reference Price Research: Review and Propositions," *Journal of Marketing*, October 2005, pp. 84–102; Ziv Carmon and Dan Ariely, "Focusing on the Forgone: How Value Can Appear So Different to Buyers and Sellers," *Journal of Consumer Research* 27, December 2000, pp. 360–370; and Tridib Mazumdar and Purushottam Papatla, "An Investigation of Reference Price Segments," *Journal of Marketing Research* 37, May 2000, pp. 246–258.

119 Dilip Soman and John T. Gourville, "Transaction Decoupling: How Price Bundling Affects the Decision to Consume," *Journal of Marketing Research* 38, February 2001, pp. 30–44.

120 Joseph C. Nunes and Peter Boatwright, "Incidental Prices and Their Effect on Willingness to Pay," *Journal of Consumer Research*, November 2004, pp. 457–466.

121 Shane Frederick, "Overestimating Others' Willingness to Pay," *Journal of Consumer Research* 39, no. 1, 2012, pp. 1–21.

122 Dhananjay Nayakankuppam and Himanshu Mishra, "The Endowment Effect: Rose-Tinted and Dark-Tinted Glasses," *Journal of Consumer Research* 32, no. 3, 2005, pp. 390–395.

123 Mike Snider, "Ultra HD TVs, and Egos, Could Revive Super Bowl TV Sales," *USA Today*, January 30, 2015, www.usatoday.com; and Andrea Chang, "TV Prices Plunge Ahead of Super Bowl," *Los Angeles Times*, February 3, 2012, www.latimes.com.

124 Chantal Tode, "QR Code-Enabled Virtual Stores Support Merchants' Mobile Shopping Strategies," *Mobile Commerce Daily*, June 11, 2013, www.mobilecommercedaily.com.

125 Stacey Higginbotham, "Target Opens Up a New Store in San Francisco to Try Out Smart Devices," *Fortune*, July 9, 2015, www.fortune.com.

126 Sevgin A. Eroglu and Karen A. Machleit, "Theory in Consumer-Environment Research: Diagnosis and Prognosis," in eds. Curtis P. Haugtvedt, Paul M. Herr, and Frank R. Kardes, *Handbook of Consumer Psychology* (New York: Psychology Press, 2008), pp. 823–835; James J. Kellaris, "Music and Consumers," in eds. Curtis P. Haugtvedt, Paul M. Herr, and Frank R. Kardes, *Handbook of Consumer Psychology* (New York: Psychology Press, 2008), pp. 837–856.

127 Velitchka D. Kaltcheva and Barton A. Weitz, "When Should a Retailer Create an Exciting Store Environment?" *Journal of Marketing*, January 2006, pp. 107–118.

128 Donna Goodison, "Opening Day Is Right on Target," *Boston Herald*, July 21, 2015, www.bostonherald.com.

129 Risto Moisio and Eric J. Arnould, "Framework in Marketing: Drama Structure, Drama Interaction, and Drama Content in Shopping Experiences," *Journal of Consumer Behaviour* 4, no. 4, 2005, pp. 246–256; and Robert V. Kozinets, John F. Sherry, Diana Storm, Adam Duhachek, Krittinee Nuttavuthisit, and Benét DeBerry-Spence, "Ludic Agency and Retail Spectacle," *Journal of Consumer Research* 31, no. 3, 2004, pp. 658–672.

130 "U.S. Patent for Apple Store in Shanghai," *Shanghai Daily*, March 23, 2012, www.china.org.cn.

131 Bill Siwicki, "Nearly Half of Digital Shoppers at the Top 10 Retailers Are Mobile-Only," *Internet Retailer*, March 9, 2015, www.internetretailer.com.

132 Kevin Woodward, "February Survey: Web Site Design And Usability," *Internet Retailer*, February 1, 2012, www.internetretailer.com; and Zak Stambor, "A Consistent Feel," *Internet Retailer*, November 30, 2011, www.internetretailer.com.

Developing Information About Consumer Behavior

Consumer behavior research helps marketers determine what customers need, how they behave, what they think, and how they feel. Based on research, marketers make decisions about how to profitably satisfy consumer needs. This appendix explains some of the main tools used to collect information about consumers, describes the organizations involved in research, and introduces ethical issues in research.

Consumer Behavior Research Methods

Researchers collect and analyze two types of data for marketing purposes: primary and secondary. Data collected for its own purpose is called **primary data**. When marketers gather data using surveys, focus groups, experiments, and the like to support their own marketing decisions, they are collecting primary data. Data collected by an entity for one purpose and subsequently used by another entity for a different purpose is called **secondary data**. For example, after the government collects census data for tax purposes, marketers can use the results as secondary data to estimate the size of markets in their own industry.

A number of tools are available in the consumer researcher's "tool kit" for gathering primary data, some based on what consumers say and some on what they do (see Exhibit A.1). Researchers may collect data from relatively few people or compile data from huge samples of consumers. Each of these tools can provide unique insights that, when combined, reveal very different perspectives on the complex world of consumer behavior. This is research with a purpose: to guide companies in making more informed decisions and achieving marketing results.

SURVEYS

One of the most familiar research tools is the **survey**, a method of collecting information from a sample of

Primary data Data originating from a researcher and collected to provide information relevant to a specific research project.

Secondary data Data collected for some other purpose that is subsequently used in a research project.

Survey A method of collecting information from a sample of consumers, predominantly by asking questions.

consumers, usually by asking questions, to draw quantitative conclusions about a target population. Some questions may be open-ended, with the consumer filling in the blanks; other questions may ask consumers to use a rating scale or check marks. Surveys can be conducted in person, through the mail, over the phone, or by using the Web.

Although companies often use specialized surveys to better understand a specific customer segment, some organizations carry out broad-based surveys that are made available to marketers. The U.S. Bureau of the Census is a widely used source of demographic information. Its Census of Population and Housing, conducted every 10 years, asks U.S. consumers a series of questions regarding their age, marital status, gender, household size, education, and home ownership. This database, available online (www.census.gov), helps marketers learn about population shifts and other demographic trends that might affect their offerings or their industry.

Survey data can also help marketers understand media usage and product purchasing patterns. For example, the Pew Research Center surveys consumers in different age groups about their Internet usage. One finding is that 96 percent of U.S. adults aged 18–29 are using the Internet today, compared with 70 percent of adults in that age group using the Internet in 2000. In addition, 60 percent of U.S. adults aged 65 or older are using the Internet today, compared with 14 percent of that age group in 2000.[1] Of course, surveys must be properly designed so that respondents can answer accurately and in an unbiased fashion.[2]

Surveys can also be used to collect sensitive information from consumers, by ensuring that their responses to the questions are completely anonymous. In a regular survey, consumers might underreport negative behaviors (e.g., shoplifting, tax evasion, binge drinking, smoking) or over report positive behaviors (e.g., giving to charity, reading books, studying, eating vegetables).[3] Recent developments in market research techniques allow deep insights into the sensitive behaviors of consumers, while still safeguarding their anonymity.[4]

Exhibit A.1 ▶ Tools for Primary Research Investigating Consumer Behavior
There are many different types of tools available to research and get information on consumer behavior.

Tool	Description
Survey	A written instrument that asks consumers to respond to a predetermined set of research questions.
Focus group	A form of interview involving 8 to 12 people who, led by a moderator, discuss a product or other marketing stimulus.
Interview	One-on-one discussion in which an interviewer asks a consumer questions related to consumption behavior and decisions.
Storytelling	Consumers are asked to tell stories about acquisition, usage, or disposition experiences.
Photography and pictures	Showing photographs or pictures to consumers (or asking consumers to take photos or draw pictures) as a way to elicit comments about marketing stimuli.
Diaries	Asking consumers to maintain a written or online diary about product purchasing, media usage, and related behavior.
Experiments	Conducting experiments under laboratory conditions to determine whether and how specific marketing phenomena affect consumer behavior.
Field experiments	Conducting experiments, such as market tests in the real world, to determine actual consumer reaction to marketing stimuli.
Conjoint analysis	A research technique designed to determine the relative importance and appeal of different levels of an offering's attributes.
Observations and ethnographic research	Observing consumers at home or in stores to understand behavior and gain insights that will lead to more effective marketing decisions.
Purchase panels	Tracking what consumers buy on different occasions or in different places.
Database marketing	Combining all research data about consumers and their purchases into a database that can be analyzed to identify behavior patterns as insights for developing marketing programs.
Netnography	Tracking and analyzing online comments and consumer activities to understand consumers' thoughts, feelings, and actions about marketing stimuli.
Psychophysiological reactions and neuroscience	Examining physiological reactions (e.g., eye movements) and applying neuroscience techniques (e.g., measuring brain activity) to understand consumer behavior.

FOCUS GROUPS

Unlike a survey, which may collect input from hundreds of people responding individually to the same questionnaire, a **focus group** brings together small groups of consumers to discuss an issue or an offering. Led by a trained moderator, participants express their opinions about a given product or topic, which can be particularly useful in identifying and testing new product ideas. Focus groups provide qualitative insights into consumer attitudes as opposed to the quantitative (numerical) data resulting from surveys. When Nebraska was readying a new marketing plan to boost state tourism, researchers held focus groups to learn about consumers' perceptions of and attitudes toward the state's varied attractions. Officials put together a tourism plan after determining that some tourists are attracted by Nebraska's "open spaces,"

Focus group A form of interview involving 8 to 12 people; a moderator leads the group and asks participants to discuss a product, concept, or other marketing stimulus.

while others prefer Omaha's faster pace. Additional research prompted the state to brand itself "Nebraska Nice" as a way to emphasize the friendly people that tourists will meet.[5]

A related technique is the computer-based focus group, in which consumers go to a computer lab where their individual comments are displayed anonymously on a large screen for viewing by the group. This method can help researchers gather information on sensitive topics, as can focus groups conducted by telephone or online rather than in person. However, the anonymity prevents researchers from collecting other relevant data, such as nonverbal reactions conveyed by facial expressions and body language that would be available in a traditional focus group. Another alternative is to hold focus groups via Skype or similar technologies, where participants' faces are visible and vocal qualities can be analyzed along with verbal responses.[6]

Some companies convene customer advisory boards, small groups of customers that meet with marketing and service executives once or twice a year (face to face, online, or by phone) to discuss offerings, competitive products, future needs, acquisition and usage problems, strategy, and related issues. Board meetings serve not just as research but also as a tool for strengthening customer relations. Large companies such as Dell and IBM sometimes have multiple customer advisory boards, recruiting key customers to serve on a board for a specific corporate division or a particular product line.[7]

> **Storytelling**
> A research method by which consumers are asked to tell stories about product acquisition, usage, or disposition experiences. These stories help marketers gain insights into consumer needs and identify the product attributes that meet these needs.

INTERVIEWS

Like focus groups, interviews involve direct contact with consumers (see Exhibit A.2). Interviews are often more appropriate than focus groups when the topic is sensitive, embarrassing, confidential, or emotionally charged. They provide more in-depth data than surveys when the researcher wants to "pick consumers' brains."

In some interviews, researchers ask customers about the process they use to make a purchase decision. One research company assigns professional interviewers to tape-record consumers' thoughts while they shop for groceries. This research helps marketers understand how factors in the shopping environment affect purchasing. Interviews can also uncover broader attitudes that affect behavior across product categories. When the Underwriters Laboratories interviewed hundreds of consumers in the United States, Germany, China, and India, it found a belief that high-tech firms were bringing new products to market more quickly than needed. The interviews revealed concerns about the fast pace of new technology and about new products being introduced because companies wanted new products to sell, not necessarily because the products were innovative.[8]

Traditional interviews require a trained interviewer who attempts to establish rapport with consumers. Interviewers also note nonverbal behaviors like fidgeting, voice pitch changes, and folded arms and legs as clues to whether the respondent is open to the discussion or whether certain questions are particularly sensitive. Researchers often record interviews for later transcription so they can examine the results using qualitative or quantitative analysis. Sometimes researchers videotape nonverbal responses that cannot be captured in the transcription process and analyze the interviews later to identify patterns or themes.

STORYTELLING

Another tool for conducting consumer research is **storytelling**, in which consumers tell researchers stories about their experiences with a product. At Patagonia, which markets outdoor clothing and accessories, researchers collect consumer stories about backpacking and other outdoor experiences for use in developing the company's catalogs and online product descriptions. Storytelling not only provides information relevant to the marketing of the product but

CREATISTA/Shutterstock.com

Exhibit A.2 ▶ Interviews

One-on-one interviews with consumers can provide useful feedback to companies or market researchers, especially on sensitive subjects.

also shows that Patagonia is in touch with its customers and values what they say.[9]

Although storytelling involves the real stories of real consumers, sometimes marketers ask consumers to tell or write stories about hypothetical situations that the marketer has depicted in a picture or scenario.[10] The idea is that a consumer's needs, feelings, and perceptions are revealed by the way he or she interprets what is depicted in the picture or scenario. For example, researchers may show a picture of a woman at the entrance to a Zara store with a thought bubble above her head and ask consumers to write what they imagine the woman is thinking. Such stories can reveal what consumers think of a particular store, purchase situation, and so on.

PHOTOGRAPHY AND PICTURES

Some researchers use a technique in which they show pictures of experiences that consumers have had in order to help consumers remember and report experiences more completely. Researchers may also ask consumers to draw or collect pictures that represent their thoughts and feelings about the topic at hand. Still another practice is to ask consumers to photograph their belongings or assemble a collage of pictures that reflects their lifestyles. Researchers then ask about the pictures and the meaning behind them or have the consumer write an essay, which can help integrate the images and thoughts suggested by the pictures.

DIARIES

Asking consumers to keep diaries can provide important insights into their behavior, including product purchasing and media usage. Diaries often reveal how friends and family affect consumers' decisions about money, clothes, music, fast foods, videos, concerts, and so on. For example, several Federal Reserve Banks around the country recruit consumers each year to maintain a diary of financial transactions for several days. The purpose is to understand the use of cash, credit, debit, and electronic payment methods and identify changes in payment preferences over time.[11]

The research firm NPD Group asks more than three million consumers worldwide to maintain online diaries, tracking their purchases in dozens of product categories. Companies buy NPD's diary data to learn whether consumers are brand loyal or brand switching and whether they are heavy or light product users. By linking the data with demographic data, marketers can learn even more about these consumers. Marketers targeting U.S. consumers can also examine yearly data from the government's Consumer Expenditure Diary Survey. As part of this research, selected consumers record all their household purchases of goods and services in certain categories, such as foods, beverages, and nonprescription medical items, during a two-week period. The results provide insights into how purchasing differs by age, home owners versus renters, and other consumer characteristics.

EXPERIMENTS

Consumer researchers can conduct experiments to determine whether certain marketing phenomena affect consumer behavior (see Exhibit A.3). For example, they might design an experiment to learn whether consumers' attitudes toward a brand are affected by the brand name as opposed to factors such as product features, package, color, logo, room temperature, or the consumer's mood. With experiments, researchers randomly assign consumers to receive different "treatments" and then observe the effects of these treatments. To illustrate, consumers might be assigned to groups that are shown different brand names. The researchers collect data about participants' attitudes toward the name and compare attitudes across groups. In a taste-test experiment, they might randomly assign consumers to groups and then ask each group to taste a different product. Comparing evaluations of the

Exhibit A.3 ▶ Experiments
Laboratory testing and field experiments with consumers, such as taste testing, is one way to research new products and marketing trends.

Clandestini/Getty Images

product across the groups will show which product is preferred.

An important aspect of such experiments is that the groups are designed to be identical in all respects except the treatment, called the **independent variable**. Thus, in a taste-test experiment, only the taste of the food or beverage is varied. Everything else is the same across groups—consumers eat or drink the same amount of the product, at the same temperature, from the same kind of container, in the same room, in the presence of the same experimenter, and so on. After consumers taste and rate the product, researchers can compare the groups' responses to see which taste is preferred. Because the groups are identical in all other respects, researchers know that any differences between the two groups are caused by the treatment (the food's taste).

FIELD EXPERIMENTS

Although experiments are often conducted in controlled laboratory situations, marketers can plan and implement experiments in the real world, known as "field experiments." One type of field experiment, a **market test**, reveals whether an offering is likely to sell in a given market and which marketing-mix elements most effectively enhance sales. Suppose marketers want to determine how much advertising support to give to a new product. They could select two test markets of a similar size and demographic composition and spend a different amount of money on advertising in each market. By observing product sales in the two markets over a set period, the marketers would be able to tell whether the added investment in advertising had a significant sales impact.

Before Dr Pepper Snapple introduced its Dr Pepper Ten soft drink throughout the United States—targeting men who drink diet beverages—it tested the product's 10-calorie formula and the supporting marketing mix in six cities. In addition to gauging consumer response to the taste and name, the company wanted to determine how men and women would react to its male-oriented packaging and advertising. As a result of this market test, Dr Pepper Snapple learned that men responded positively—and that women were intrigued enough to try Dr Pepper Ten at least once.[12]

CONJOINT ANALYSIS

Many marketers use the sophisticated research technique of **conjoint analysis** to determine the relative importance and appeal of different levels of an offering's attributes. To start, researchers identify the attributes of the offering, such as package size, specific

Independent variable The "treatment" or the entity that researchers vary in a research project.

Market test A study in which the effectiveness of one or more elements of the marketing mix is examined by evaluating sales of the product in an actual market, for example, a specific city.

Conjoint analysis A research technique to determine the relative importance and appeal of different levels of an offering's attributes.

Ethnographic research In-depth qualitative research using observations and interviews (often over repeated occasions) of consumers in real-world surroundings. Often used to study the meaning that consumers ascribe to a product or consumption phenomenon.

product features, and price points. Next, they determine the levels to be tested for each attribute (e.g., large or small size). Then they ask consumers to react to a series of product concepts that combine these attributes in different ways.

For example, researchers might ask how likely consumers are to buy a large container of liquid Tide laundry detergent that has added stain removal power and costs $10.75; they might also ask how likely consumers are to buy a small container of Tide that lacks added stain removal power and costs $8.50. By analyzing the responses to different combinations, the researchers can see how important each attribute (e.g., size, price) is and the level of a given attribute that customers prefer. Academic researchers have used this methodology to understand, among other things, how much weight consumers give to environmental factors versus price and other attributes when they buy wooden furniture.[13]

OBSERVATIONS AND ETHNOGRAPHIC RESEARCH

At times, researchers observe consumers to gain insight into potentially effective product, promotion, price, and distribution decisions. As an example, VF Corporation, which markets Wrangler and Lee jeans, learned a lot by sending its researchers to observe women shoppers in a department store. The observers noticed that women tried on multiple sizes for each jean style they wanted to buy. Why? Because customers didn't believe they could rely on the labeled sizes. Based on this observation, VF decided to change its size labels and launch an online campaign to help women choose the most flattering jean sizes and styles. VF's revenues soared by millions of dollars as a result of implementing this and other changes based on research insights.[14]

Some companies conduct **ethnographic research**, in which researchers interview and observe (and perhaps videotape) how consumers behave in real-world surroundings. (Ethnographic research can also be applied to Internet activities, as discussed later in this appendix.) Speck, a store located in the high-tech center of California's Silicon Valley, is not in business to make sales of iPhones and other electronic gadgets. Instead, it serves as a retail location for observing and interviewing shoppers as they browse the showcases, handle new products, ask questions, test product functions, and offer comments about the merchandise. "It's a marketing laboratory," explains Speck's CEO. "Sales are nice, but our goal is to be able to talk to people."[15]

PURCHASE PANELS

Sometimes marketers try to understand consumer behavior by tracking what consumers buy on different purchase occasions. This kind of research simply records whether a behavior occurred. Such behavioral data may be collected from special panel members, from a representative sample of the general population, or from the marketer's target market. Every time panel members go shopping, the cash register records their purchases. By merging purchase data with demographic data, marketers can tell who is purchasing a product, whether those consumers are also buying competitors' products, and whether a coupon or other sales promotion was involved. Marketers can also use these data to determine whether, for example, the shelf space allocated to a product, or added advertising in the test area, affected panel members' purchases.

Data mining Searching for patterns in a company database that offer clues to customer needs, preferences, and behaviors.

Netnography Observing and analyzing the online behavior and comments of consumers.

DATABASE MARKETING AND BIG DATA

The increasing availability of large-scale databases filled with consumer information, coupled with technological advances in computing power and advanced analytical models, has led to considerable discussion about the use of "big data" and its potential to transform our understanding of consumer behavior. With big data, marketers combine data from various research sources into a common database. For example, a database might contain information about targeted consumers' demographics and lifestyles combined with data about their purchases in various product categories over time, their media habits, and their usage of coupons and other promotional devices. Data in these databases can be analyzed by techniques that search for patterns in the data, which is called **data mining**. Alternatively, researchers might develop sophisticated analytical models that allow them to test predictions about how consumers will respond to marketing mix activities.

Walmart is at the cutting edge of the big data movement. It follows every piece of merchandise from warehouse to store shelf and when a customer brings an item to the checkout, that purchase is recorded, along with the item's price, the time of sale, and the store location. These data are reported to Walmart hourly and daily by product, by category, by store, by supplier, and so on. The retailer analyzes what else goes into the shopping cart, store by store and region by region, for clues to pricing products in different categories. Walmart also pays attention to what its millions of Facebook fans say and do online. Data mining helps the company identify promising new store locations and stock each store with the right assortment of goods in appropriate quantities. Walmart can even use data mining to be sure that extra quantities of storm-related merchandise gets to individual stores in advance of hurricanes or other extreme weather situations, based on what customers in those stores have bought before and after storms in previous years.[16]

Big data is also used extensively by online companies. Many marketers and digital advertising firms use tracking software or other methods to observe which websites consumers visit, which pages they look at, how long they visit each site, and related data. By analyzing consumer browsing patterns, researchers can determine how to make websites more user-friendly and how to better target online advertising, and how to more effectively move consumers through the "conversion funnel" from product awareness to purchase. Although some marketing researchers proclaim that the advent of big data means the demise of traditional forms of marketing research, most experts agree that insights from large-scale databases are more likely to complement (rather than supplant) traditional marketing research activities.[17]

While marketing researchers may see much potential in big data, privacy advocates are concerned that tracking and recording consumer behavior—especially without the consumer's knowledge or consent—can be intrusive. Even though most companies post privacy policies to explain what details they collect and how they use consumers' data, these policies are not always easy to understand and don't always appear prominently in online or print materials. To protect personal privacy, the European Union now requires companies to obtain consumers' consent before using tracking "cookies" to follow anyone's online activities.[18] Canada requires marketers to disclose how they are tracking consumers online, what information is collected, and how it will be used. "Some people like receiving ads targeted to their specific interests," explains Canada's privacy commissioner. "Others are extremely uncomfortable with the notion of their online activities being tracked. People's choices must be respected."[19]

NETNOGRAPHY

Researchers can use a variety of methods for **netnography**, ethnographic research techniques adapted for the observation and analysis of consumers' online behavior and comments.[20] The content consumers post on social media, brand forums, and websites, as well as data on brand likes and dislikes and consumers' experiences with offerings, all provide rich material for netnography research. However, researchers are still learning to interpret the intentions, attitudes, and emotions inherent in messages and images on Twitter, Facebook, Instagram, Pinterest, and other social media. Tools such as automated content analysis and sophisticated data-mining tools are useful in extracting insights with the goal of fine-tuning marketing elements.[21]

Procter & Gamble, the company behind Tide, Bounty, and many other big brands, looks carefully at the level of social media buzz stimulated by its television commercials and other promotional activities—both the number of consumer messages and the sentiment behind the messages (are the messages positive or negative?). The company coordinates and analyzes its full range of communications, including traditional and digital media, public relations, and in-store promotions, with the goal of engaging customers and encouraging them to be loyal buyers of P&G products.[22]

PSYCHOPHYSIOLOGICAL REACTIONS AND NEUROSCIENCE

Most marketing research involves either collecting verbal responses from consumers (e.g., answers to questions and self-reports about media and purchase behaviors) or observing consumer behavior (e.g., under laboratory conditions, in real life, or online). But verbal reports can be greatly affected by subtle variations in how questions are worded, what sequence they are asked in, and what response scale is used to assess answers (i.e., a 1–7 point agreement scale or a 1–3 point agreement scale).[23] In contrast, the psychophysiological reactions of consumers to marketing actions (e.g., eye and muscle movements) are often automatic and rapid, unable to be verbalized by consumers. The range of potential *psychophysiological reactions* that can be measured is virtually limitless, including pupil dilation, eye movements, skin conductance, facial muscle movements, electrical activity of the brain (using electroencephalogram), and heart rate. Psychophysiological reactions to marketing are an important source of information that cannot easily be collected in any other way.

Neuroscience is the scientific study of the nervous system, which includes the brain, the spinal cord, and the retina. Developments in neuroscience have led to the introduction of new methodologies to collect data on fundamental brain processes involved in consumer behavior. (Note that in marketing, the term *neuro* is often applied in a more general sense to all research techniques that involve some kind of psychophysiological measurement, such as eye tracking.)

Today, consumer researchers are gaining deeper insights by measuring physiological reactions and applying neuroscience to understand how consumers respond to various marketing stimuli.[24] By recording moment-to-moment eye movements and interpreting emotions from facial expressions, for example, researchers can determine which ad messages or websites attract and retain attention, and how competing stimuli affect these processes.[25] Marketers can then apply this learning to increase the "stopping power" of ad messages and websites. In one study, researchers were able to suggest, based on these physiological measurements, how marketers could engage consumers so they will not click away from online video ads.[26] Combining neuroscience with other research techniques can help marketers better understand how consumers process and react to specific marketing stimuli (such as the logos of brand sponsors at a sporting event).[27]

Neuroscientists are seeking to understand consumer behavior by watching which parts of the brain become activated when consumers make a decision, view an ad, or select an investment.[28] For instance, Frito-Lay learned through neuroscience research that consumers like the orange, cheesy residue left on their fingers when they eat Cheetos snacks. Based on this insight, Frito-Lay has played up the messy-fingers angle in its marketing and social media. It also applied this insight when launching Cheetos Sweetos, a sweet snack coated with cinnamon that leaves a brown residue on consumers' fingers.[29] Although neuroscience research raises concerns about manipulation, one advertising executive notes: "Observing brain activity and setting up models for behavior is not the same as forcing a brain into making a consumption decision."[30]

Types of Consumer Researchers

Many entities use market research to study consumer behavior for different reasons, as shown in Exhibit A.4. Organizations such as consumer goods and services companies, ad agencies, and marketing research firms conduct research to make decisions about marketing a specific product or service. Government organizations collect consumer information so as to set laws designed to protect consumers. Academics conduct research to protect consumers or simply to understand why and how consumers behave as they do.

IN-HOUSE MARKETING RESEARCH DEPARTMENTS

The benefits of conducting "in-house" research (conducted by the company for the company) are that the information collected can be kept within the company and that opportunities for information to leak to competitors are minimized. However, internal departments are sometimes viewed as less objective than outside research firms since they may have a vested interest in the research results. For example, employees may be motivated to show that the company is making good decisions,

Exhibit A.4 ▶ Who Conducts Consumer Research?

A number of different organizations conduct research on consumers, although they differ in their objectives. Some do research for application, some for consumer protection, and some for obtaining general knowledge about consumers.

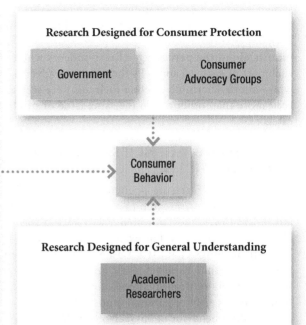

a situation that may unwittingly bias the nature of their research or the outcomes they report. Consequently, some companies use outside research companies to gather their consumer research.

EXTERNAL MARKETING RESEARCH FIRMS

External research firms often help design a specific research project before it begins. They develop measuring instruments to measure consumer responses, collect data from consumers, analyze the data, and develop reports for their clients (see Exhibit A.5). Research firms specializing in neuroscience have helped Procter & Gamble, Campbell Soup, Turner Broadcasting, and others fine-tune their marketing messages and plan new offerings.[31]

Some marketing research firms are "full service" organizations that perform a variety of marketing research services; others specialize in a particular type of research. The GfK Group, for instance, conducts media research, brand awareness

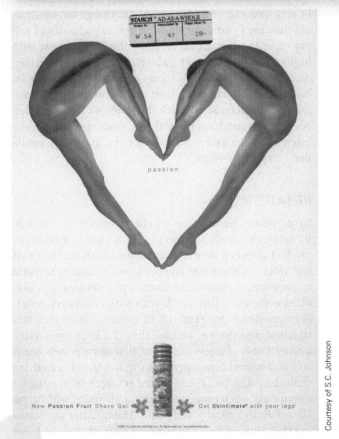

Courtesy of S.C. Johnson

Exhibit A.5 ▶ Working with an External Marketing Research Firm

Companies like Starch collect data on what, if anything, consumers remember from an ad. The numbers noted on the stickers placed at the top of the ad indicate the percentage of respondents sampled who remembered having seen or read various parts of the ad.

research, and other consumer behavior research. In its Starch Advertising Research studies, dozens of readers of a specific magazine go through a recent issue with a trained interviewer. The interviewer asks whether consumers have seen each ad in the issue and whether they saw the picture in each ad, read the headline, read the body copy, and saw the ad slogan. The company compiles reports about the percentage of respondents who saw each part of each ad and sells the results to advertisers who want to determine whether their ads were seen and read more than other ads in the same issue or product category.

ADVERTISING AGENCIES AND MEDIA PLANNING FIRMS

Full-service advertising agencies and media planning firms conduct research to better understand what advertising messages and media will appeal to their clients' target markets. For example, the international home-furnishings chain IKEA asked MEC Global and Ogilvy & Mather to develop a campaign to increase the amount its customers spend during each transaction. When agency researchers studied the buying and consumption behavior of 35-year-old IKEA customers, they found that these shoppers associated the retailer with accessory merchandise, rather than with major furniture pieces and sets. The researchers also discovered that IKEA shoppers were looking for creative ideas they could adapt to personalize their living spaces. Based on this research, the agencies developed a multimedia campaign showing how the store offers choices for furnishing entire rooms with personal flair. The campaign included a brand community where consumers could upload photos of rooms they furnished and decorated with IKEA products, as inspiration for other consumers. The result: IKEA's sales of living room sets rose 9 percent.[32]

Some advertising agencies have departments to test advertising concepts as part of the service they provide to clients. Agencies may also conduct advertising pretesting, using drawings of ads or finished ads, to make sure that an ad is fulfilling its objectives *before* it is placed in the media. In addition, agencies often conduct tracking studies to monitor advertising effectiveness over time. Tracking studies can determine whether the percentage of target market consumers who are aware of a brand has changed as a function of the amount, duration, and timing of its advertising.

SYNDICATED DATA SERVICES

Syndicated data services are companies that collect and then sell the information they collect, usually to firms that market products and services to consumers. For example,

the Yankelovich Monitor study collects data on consumer lifestyles and social trends using 90-minute interviews at the homes of approximately 2,500 adults. Its annual reports describing current and projected lifestyle trends help advertising agencies and company marketers develop content for promotional messages, choose media, identify new product ideas, plan positioning strategy, and make other marketing decisions.

Nielsen is a syndicated data service that tracks the TV viewing habits of thousands of participating U.S. households. Using digital set-top equipment, it records which TV shows each household member is viewing and when. In addition, during "sweeps weeks," it asks two million U.S. consumers to keep a diary indicating the shows they watch. Based on these data, Nielsen assigns a rating that indicates the number and percentage of all households watching a particular TV program, and a specific commercial, along with demographic analyses of the audience. This is how advertisers know how many viewers watch the Super Bowl, for instance.

By combining demographic and TV viewing behavior—including viewing on personal computers, tablet computers, and cell phones, not just on home TV sets—Nielsen can describe the audience for individual shows. Networks, cable stations, and independent channels use this information to determine whether TV shows should be renewed and how much they can charge for advertising time on a particular show. In general, advertisers will pay more to advertise on very popular shows (those with higher Nielsen ratings). Advertisers who buy Nielsen data can assess which TV shows they should advertise in, basing their decisions on how well the audience's demographic characteristics match the sponsor's target market. Nielsen also conducts research into consumers' use of the Internet, video games, mobile devices, and other media that carry ad messages.

RETAILERS

Large retail chains often conduct consumer research. By using electronic scanners to track sales of a brand or product category, they can determine which are their best and worst-selling items and see how consumers respond to coupons, discounts, and other promotions. Because salespeople often interact directly with customers, retailers sometimes use research to measure customer satisfaction and determine how they can improve service quality. Often retailers use research to uncover new needs and understand brand perceptions. Raymond, a clothing chain based in India, conducted research to investigate consumers' preferences and brand attitudes within the United Arab Emirates and Saudi Arabia. After ascertaining that Gulf-region consumers accepted its brand and felt an emotional connection with it, Raymond designed stores specifically for these markets. Now the chain anticipates ongoing expansion in Dubai and other Gulf markets.[33]

RESEARCH FOUNDATIONS AND TRADE GROUPS

Many research foundations and trade groups collect consumer research. A **research foundation** is a nonprofit organization that sponsors research on topics relevant to the foundation's goals. As an example, the nonprofit Advertising Research Foundation seeks to improve the practice of advertising, marketing, and media research. It sponsors conferences and webinars, and publishes reports related to research in these areas. The Marketing Science Institute is another nonprofit organization that sponsors academic research to uncover information useful to marketers.

Specialized trade groups may also collect consumer research to better understand the needs of consumers in their own industries. A **trade group** is an organization formed by people who work in the same industry, such as the Recording Industry Association of America, a group whose members are involved in the music industry through recording, distribution, or retailing activities. This organization has sponsored a host of research projects, including studies to understand how American musical tastes and music consumption patterns have changed over the years.

> **Research foundation** A nonprofit organization that sponsors research on topics relevant to the foundation's goals.
>
> **Trade group** A professional organization made up of marketers in the same industry.

GOVERNMENT

Although government agencies do not use research to help market an offering, businesses frequently use government research for marketing purposes, as when they examine census data to estimate the size of various demographic markets. U.S. government studies by agencies such as the Consumer Products Safety Commission, the Department of Transportation, and the Food and Drug Administration are specifically designed for consumer protection (see Exhibit A.6). As an example, the Federal Trade Commission (FTC) conducts research on potentially deceptive, misleading, or fraudulent advertising. One issue the FTC continues to study, for example, is how consumers perceive goods and services advertised using phrases that suggest environmentally friendly properties. After conducting research, the FTC issued and later clarified guidelines for how marketers are permitted to use specific phrases (e.g., "renewable materials") to avoid misleading consumers about "green" claims.[34] Research can also help resolve court cases involving marketing issues such as whether consumers are confusing a new product's trademark with an established product's trademark, a situation that could hurt the established brand.[35]

CONSUMER ORGANIZATIONS

Independent consumer organizations also conduct research, generally for the purpose of protecting or informing consumers. Consumers Union is an independent, nonprofit testing and information organization designed to serve consumers. The organization publishes the well-known *Consumer Reports* magazine. Many of the products described in *Consumer Reports* are tested in Consumers Union's independent product-testing lab, and the results are posted on the organization's website (www.consumerreports.org).

ACADEMICS AND ACADEMIC RESEARCH CENTERS

Although academic research involving consumers can be used for marketing and may have implications for public policy, studies often are designed simply to enhance our general understanding of consumer behavior. Much of the research reported in this book describes state-of-the-art academic studies. Some academic research centers focus on a specific aspect of consumer behavior. For example, the Restaurant of the Future, on the campus of Wageningen University in the Netherlands, is designed to allow researchers to experiment with lighting, plates, food arrangement, seasonings and ingredients, and other details. The goal is to see their effects on what and how much students and faculty eat.[36]

Exhibit A.6 ▶ Consumer Protection

Government agencies, such as the Consumer Product Safety Commission, are designed for consumer protection, and can issue recall notices such as this one for items unfit for consumer consumption.

Ethical Issues in Consumer Research

Although marketers rely heavily on consumer research in the development of successful goods and services, the conduct of this research raises important ethical issues. As the following sections show, consumer research has both positive and negative aspects. See Chapter 17 for further discussion of ethical issues.

THE POSITIVE ASPECTS OF CONSUMER RESEARCH

Both consumers and marketers can benefit from consumer research. Consumers generally have better acquisition, usage, and disposition experiences. Meanwhile, marketers can learn to build stronger customer relationships by paying attention to consumer research. As a consequence, fewer new products may fail, and more products of interest to consumers will be brought to market, making for a more efficient and effective marketplace.

Better Consumer Experiences

Because consumer research helps marketers become more customer focused, consumers can have better designed products, better customer service, clearer usage instructions, more information that helps them make good decisions, and more satisfying acquisition and postpurchase experiences. Consumer research (by government and consumer organizations) also plays a role in protecting consumers from unscrupulous marketers.

Potential for Building Customer Relationships

Research can help marketers identify ways of establishing and enhancing relationships with customers through a better understanding of their needs, attitudes, and behavior. One example is growing public interest in a marketer's reputation for social responsibility, which in turn affects consumer attitudes and actions. Research shows that consumers will evaluate a product more positively when they know the company is actively engaged in social responsibility programs such as philanthropy. In fact, consumers say they will pay more for offerings from businesses that demonstrate a strong commitment to making a positive social and environmental impact.[37] Being aware of these kinds of broad trends in consumer sentiment is a good foundation from which to approach relationship building.

THE NEGATIVE ASPECTS OF CONSUMER RESEARCH

Consumer research is a very complex process with a number of potentially negative aspects. These include the difficulty of conducting research in foreign countries, the high costs of conducting research, concerns about invasion of privacy, and the use of deceptive practices.

Studying Consumer Behavior in Different Countries

Marketers who want to research consumer behavior in other countries face special challenges. For instance, focus groups are not appropriate in all countries or situations. U.S. marketers often put husbands and wives together in a focus group to explore attitudes toward products like furniture. However, this approach won't work in countries like Saudi Arabia, where women are unlikely to speak freely and are highly unlikely to disagree with their husbands in such settings. Focus groups must also be conducted differently in Japan, where cultural pressures dictate against a person's disagreeing with the views of a group.

Although telephone interviewing is common in the United States, it is far less prevalent in developing nations. Marketers must also consider a country's literacy rate when planning survey research. At a minimum, researchers should word questions carefully and check to ensure that the meaning is being accurately conveyed by first translating questions into the other language and then translating them back into the original language.

Companies may not be able to directly compare secondary data gathered in another country with data gathered in the United States, in part because of different collection procedures or timing. Countries may also use different categorization schemes for describing demographics like social class and education level. Moreover, different or fewer syndicated data sources may be available in other countries, a situation that limits the research available to marketers. Finally, conducting research to examine consumers' online behavior and analyze online comments may be more challenging because of legal, cultural, and language differences from country to country.

Potentially Higher Marketing Costs

Some consumers worry that the process of researching consumer behavior leads to higher marketing costs, which in turn translate into higher product prices. Some marketers, however, argue that they can market to their customers more efficiently if they know more about them. For example, product development, advertising, sales promotion costs, and distribution costs will be lower if marketers know exactly what consumers want and how to reach them.

Invasion of Consumer Privacy

A potentially more serious and widespread concern is that in the process of conducting and using research—especially database marketing—marketers may invade consumers' privacy. Consumers worry that marketers know too much about them and that personal data, financial data, and behavioral data may be sold to other companies or used inappropriately without their knowledge or consent. For example, after two U.S. shopping centers followed shoppers' cellphone signals to track consumers' movements (anonymously) from store to store, legislators objected on privacy grounds. Now malls and retailers planning to use such systems are using incentives such as price promotions to encourage consumers to "opt in" for tracking via their smartphones.[38] The loss of privacy due to improved facial recognition software is another concern as companies and social media sites collect and analyze personal images and videos.[39] Privacy requirements vary from country to country. In some areas, researchers must obtain consumers' permission before collecting and storing personal data.

Deceptive Research Practices

Finally, unscrupulous researchers may engage in deceptive practices. One such practice is lying about the sponsor of the research (e.g., saying it is being conducted by a non-profit organization when it is really being conducted by a for-profit company). Another deceptive practice is promising that respondents' answers will remain anonymous when in fact the company adds identifying information to the data in order to be able to market to these consumers later on. Unscrupulous researchers may also promise to compensate respondents but fail to deliver on this promise.[40] Such deceptive practices are not allowed under the strict codes of conduct developed by professional organizations such as ESOMAR (European Society for Opinion and Market Research) and the Marketing Research Association.

Summary:

Consumer research is a valuable tool that helps marketers design better marketing programs, aids in the development of laws and public policy decisions regarding product safety, and promotes our general understanding of how consumers behave and why. Researchers use a variety of techniques, including collecting data on what consumers say and what they do. These tools may involve data collection from relatively few individuals or from many individuals and may study consumers at a single point in time or track their behavior across time.

Some companies have internal marketing research departments to collect data; others use external research firms to conduct studies. Advertising agencies and syndicated data services are two types of outside agencies that conduct consumer research. Large retail chains often use electronic scanners to track sales of a brand or product category. Research foundations, trade groups, the government, consumer organizations, academics, and academic research centers also collect consumer information. Research supports a consumer-oriented view of marketing and can help companies improve consumption experiences and strengthen customer relationships. However, some critics say research may invade consumers' privacy and lead to higher marketing costs; in addition, unscrupulous marketers can misuse consumer information.

Endnotes

1   Andrew Perrin and Maeve Duggan, "Americans' Internet Access: 2000-2015," *Pew Research Center*, June 26, 2015, www.pewinternet.org.

2   David Gal and Derek D. Rucker, "Answering the Unasked Question: Response Substitution in Consumer Surveys," *Journal of Marketing Research* 48, no. 1, February 2011, pp. 185–195; and Bert Weijters, Maggie Geuens, and Hans Baumgartner, "The Effect of Familiarity with the Response Category Labels on Item Response to Likert Scales," *Journal of Consumer Research* 40, no. 2, 2011, pp. 368–381.

3   Hila Riemer and Sharon Shavitt, "Impression Management in Survey Responding: Easier for Collectivists or Individualists?," *Journal of Consumer Psychology* 21, no. 2, April 2011, pp. 157–168.

4   Martijn G. de Jong, Rik Pieters, and Jean-Paul Fox, "Reducing Social Desirability Bias Through Item Randomized Response," *Journal of Marketing Research*, February 2010, pp. 14–27.

5   Joanne Young, "Tourism Group to Sell State with 'Nebraska Nice,'" *Lincoln Journal Star (Nebraska)*, May 8, 2014, http://journalstar.com; and Scott Koperski, "Tourism Focus Group

Held," *Beatrice Daily Sun (Nebraska)*, December 17, 2011, www
.beatricedailysun.com.

6 Roksana Janghorban, Robab Latifnejad Roudsari, and Ali
Taghipour, "Skype Interviewing: The New Generation of
Online Synchronous Interview in Qualitative Research,"
*International Journal of Qualitative Studies on Health and
Well-Being*, April 2015, www.ncbi.nlm.nih.gov.

7 Anne Fisher, "Should You Join a Customer Advisory Board?
And What Exactly Are They?," *Fortune*, March 13, 2015, www.
fortune.com.

8 Steve Lohr, "Are We Suffering Global Gadget Fatigue?" *New
York Times*, December 12, 2011, www.nytimes.com.

9 "Liberty Partners with Oblo Allowing Consumers to Create
Personalized 'Story-Telling' Lifestyle Photo Products," *Leisure
& Travel Business*, January 14, 2008, p. 27.

10 Sandra Yin, "Marketing Tools: The Power of Images," *American Demographics*, November 2001, pp. 32–33.

11 Shaun O'Brien, "Consumer Preferences and the Use of
Cash: Evidence from the Diary of Consumer Payments
Choice–Working Paper," *Federal Reserve Bank of San Francisco*, July 21, 2014, http://www.frbsf.org/cash/publications/
fed-notes/2014/july/consumer-preferences-cash-use.

12 Elizabeth G. Olson, "Dr. Pepper: A Scrappy Survivor in a Sea of
Struggling Soda Giants," *Fortune*, April 23, 2015, www.fortune.
com; Steven R. Thompson, "Dr Pepper to Test More 10-Cal-
orie Drinks in Columbus," *Dallas Business Journal*, December
20, 2011, www.bizjournals.com; and Mae Anderson, "Dr Pepper Ten 'Not for Women,'" *USA Today*, October 10, 2011, www
.usatoday.com.

13 Roy C. Anderson and Eric N. Hansen, "The Impact of Environmental Certification on Preferences for Wood Furniture: A
Conjoint Analysis Approach," *Forest Products Journal*, March
2004, pp. 42–50.

14 Scott Anthony, "3 Ways to Predict What Consumers Want
Before They Know It," *Fast Company Design*, February 16,
2012, www.fastcodesign.com.

15 Daniel Terdiman, "In Silicon Valley, a Retail Store as Product
Laboratory," *CNet News*, August 18, 2011, http://news.cnet
.com.

16 Matt Weinberger, "How Wal-Mart Hired 2,200 Developers
and Made 'Magic,'" *Business Insider*, July 19, 2015, http://www
.businessinsider.com; Geoff Colvin, "Walmart's Makeover,"
Fortune, December 26, 2011, pp. 50–55; Steve Lohr, "Reaping
Results: Data-Mining Goes Mainstream," *New York Times*,
May 20, 2007, p. BU-3; Constance L. Hays, "What They Know
About You," *New York Times*, November 14, 2004, sec. 3, pp. 1,
9; and Jon Hamilton, "Big-Box Stores' Hurricane Prep Starts
Early," *NPR*, August 26, 2011, www.npr.org.

17 Ben Rossi, "Big Data Doesn't Come of Age: 5 Growing Pains
Facing Businesses Today," *Information Age*, January 5, 2016,
www.information-age.com; and Phil Doriot, "Marketing
Research and Big Data Can Not Only Live Together, They Can
Thrive Together," *Alert! Magazine*, first quarter 2014, www
.marketingresearch.org.

18 Laura Goldsmith, "European Union Cookie Sweep Highlights
Need for Improved Compliance," *National Law Review*, February 27, 2015, www.natlawreview.com.

19 Lisa Abe-Oldenburg, "Using Big Data for Targeted Advertising Could Violate Canadian Privacy Law," *Lexology*, July 16,
2015, www.lexology.com; and Etan Vlessing, "Canada's Privacy
Czar Tells Advertisers to Curb Online Tracking," *Hollywood
Reporter*, December 6, 2011, www.hollywoodreporter.com.

20 Robert V. Kozinets, "The Field Behind the Screen: Using Net-
nography for Marketing Research in Online Communities,"
Journal of Marketing Research, February 2002, pp. 61–72; and
Jonathan Reynolds and Jiyao Xun, "Applying Netnography to
Market Research: The Case of the Online Forum," *Journal of
Targeting, Measurement, and Analysis for Marketing*, March
2010, p. 17.

21 "Can Twitter Predict the Future?" *Economist*, June 4, 2011,
p. 12.

22 Jack Neff, "P&G's Pritchard on Where Marketing, Media and
Metrics Are Going," *Advertising Age*, March 16, 2015, www
.adage.com; and David Talbot, "A Social-Media Decoder,"
Technology Review, November–December 2011, p. 44ff.

23 Kimberlee Weaver and Norbert Schwarz, "Self-Reports in
Consumer Research," in eds. Curtis P. Haugtvedt, Paul M.
Herr, and Frank R. Kardes, *Handbook of Consumer Psychology*
(New York: Psychology Press, 2008), pp. 1081–1102.

24 See Hilke Plassmann, Thomas Zoega Ramsoy, and Milica
Milosavljevic, "Branding the Brain: A Critical Review and
Outlook, *Journal of Consumer Psychology* 22, no. 1, January
2012, pp. 18–36; Rick Scott, "Losses, Gains and Brains: Neu-
roeconomics Can Help to Answer Open Questions about
Loss Aversion," *Journal of Consumer Psychology* 21, no. 4, 2011,
pp. 453–463; and Franz-Rudolf Esch, Thorsten Moll, Bernd
Schmitt, Christian E. Elger, Carolin Neuhaus, and Bernd
Weber, "Brands on the Brain: Do Consumers Use Declarative
Information or Experienced Emotions to Evaluate Brands?"
Journal of Consumer Psychology 22, no. 1, January 2012,
pp. 75–85.

25 Edith Smit, Sophie Boerman, and Lex van Meurs, "The Power
of Direct Context as Revealed by Eye Tracking: A Model
Tracks Relative Attention to Competing Editorial and Promotional Content," *Journal of Advertising Research* 55, no. 22, June
2015, pp. 216–227.

26 Thales Texeira, Michel Wedel, and Rik Pieters, "Emotion-
Induced Engagement in Internet Video Ads," *Journal of Marketing Research*, April 2012, pp. 144–159.

27 See Angeline G. Close, Russell Lacey, and T. Bettina Cornwell, "Can Sporting Event Sponsorships Benefit from the Way
Attendees Process Them?" *Journal of Advertising Research* 55,
no. 2, June 2015, pp. 206–215.

28 Baba Shiv and Carolyn Yoon, "Integrating Neurophysiological
and Psychological Approaches: Toward and Advancement of
Brand Insights," *Journal of Consumer Psychology* 22, January
2012, pp. 2–6.

29 Bruce Horovitz, "Cheetos to Roll Out Sweetos Snacks," *USA
Today*, January 21, 2015, www.usatoday.com; and Adam L.
Penenberg, "NeuroFocus Uses Neuromarketing to Hack Your
Brain," *Fast Company*, August 8, 2011, www.fastcompany.com.

30 Amber Haq, "This Is Your Brain on Advertising," *Business
Week*, October 8, 2007, www.businessweek.com.

31 Anthony Crupi, "Nielsen Buys Neuromarketing Research
Company Innerscope," *Advertising Age*, May 27, 2015, www
.adage.com.

32 Hadley Malcolm, "Ikea Wants to Get a Little More Personal,"
USA Today, June 14, 2015, www.usatoday.com; and Emma
Hutchings, "IKEA Campaign Highlights the Craftsman to
Transform 'Consumer Perceptions,'" *PSFK*, December 15, 2011,
www.psfk.com.

33 Suresh Pattali, "Indian Textile Major Raymond Sizes Up
Fashion Industry," *Khaleej Times*, June 27, 2013, www.khaleej-
times.com; and Manoj Nair, "Raymond Tailors Retail Strategy

to Expand in Gulf Markets," *Gulf News*, December 22, 2011, www.gulfnews.com.

34 Missy Baxter, "FTC Clarifies Green Marketing Guidelines," *Credit Union Times*, May 7, 2014, www.cutimes.com.

35 Chris Pullig, Carolyn J. Simmons, and Richard G. Netemeyer, "Brand Dilution: When Do New Brands Hurt Existing Brands?" *Journal of Marketing*, April 2006, pp. 52–66.

36 Frank Browning, "The Restaurant of the Future: A Living Lab," *NPR*, May 17, 2009, www.npr.org; and Marlise Simons, "In the Netherlands, Eat, Drink, and Be Monitored," *New York Times*, November 26, 2007, p. A4.

37 Alexander Chernev and Sean Blair, "Doing Well by Doing Good: The Benevolent Halo of Corporate Social Responsibility," *Journal of Consumer Research*, April 2015, pp. 1412–1425; and "Global Consumers Are Willing to Put Their Money Where Their Heart Is When It Comes to Goods and Services from Companies Committed to Social Responsibility," *Nielsen News Release*, June 17, 2014, www.nielsen.com.

38 Diane Cardwell, "A Light Bulb Goes On, Over the Mall," *New York Times*, July 19, 2015, www.nytimes.com; and Annalyn Censky, "Malls Stop Tracking Shoppers' Cell Phones," *CNN Money*, November 28, 2011, www.cnn.com.

39 "The Ghost in the Camera," *Consumer Reports*, February 2016, pp. 43–45.

40 Kenneth C. Schneider and Cynthia K. Holm, "Deceptive Practices in Marketing Research: The Consumer's Viewpoint," *California Management Review*, Spring 1982, pp. 89–97.

The
Psychological Core

2 Motivation, Ability, and Opportunity
3 From Exposure to Comprehension
4 Memory and Knowledge
5-6 Attitudes Based on Effort

An Introduction
to
Consumer Behavior

1 Understanding Consumer
Behavior

The Process of
Making Decisions

7 Problem Recognition and
Information Search
8-9 Judgment and Decision-
Making Based on Effort
10 Post-Decision Processes

The
Consumer's Culture

11 Social Influences on
Consumer Behavior
12 Consumer Diversity
13 Household and Social Class
Influences
14 Psychographics: Values,
Personality, and Lifestyles

Consumer Behavior
Outcomes and Issues

15 Innovations: Adoption,
Resistance, and Diffusion
16 Symbolic Consumer Behavior
17 Marketing, Ethics, and Social
Responsibility in Today's
Consumer Society

iStockphoto.com/Ostill

Part 2

The Psychological Core

Consumer behavior is greatly affected by the amount of effort that consumers put into their consumption behaviors and decisions. Chapter 2 describes three critical factors that affect effort: the (1) motivation, (2) ability, and (3) opportunity consumers have to engage in behaviors and make decisions. Chapter 3 discusses how consumers come into contact with marketing stimuli (exposure), notice them (attention), and perceive them.

Chapter 4 continues the topic by discussing how consumers put information into memory, compare information with their existing knowledge, and retrieve it from memory. Chapter 5 describes what happens when consumers exert a great deal of effort in forming and changing attitudes. Finally, Chapter 6 discusses how attitudes can be influenced when consumer effort is low.

© mrcmos / iStock # 85556337

CHAPTER 2

Motivation, Ability, and Opportunity

iStockphoto.com/Ostill

INTRODUCTION

Consumer motivation, ability, and opportunity jointly influence a consumer's acquisition, usage, and disposition decisions, as marketers like Movie Tavern know. Movie Tavern operates movie theaters in 21 locations, also offering restaurant-quality foods and beverages. This combination of film and food is consistent with achieving goals such as saving time and money, and with meeting needs for food and socializing.[1] Making it easy for consumers to find out about the latest movies and menu items (from ads, social media, and other sources) increases the ability and opportunity for purchasing and consumption. Whether motivated consumers actually achieve a goal depends on whether they have the *ability* and the *opportunity* to achieve it. As this chapter explains, ability depends on five categories of resources plus age and education. Opportunity is determined by time, distractions, and the complexity, amount, repetition, and control of information to which consumers are exposed.

Andre Jenny/Alamy Stock Photo

2-1 Consumer Motivation and Its Effects

Motivation comes from the Latin word "movere," which means "to move." Motivation is what moves people. It is defined as "an inner state of activation," with the activated energy directed to achieving a goal.[2] The motivated consumer is energized, ready, and willing to engage in a goal-relevant activity. For example, if you learn that a much-anticipated electronic game will be released next Tuesday, you may be motivated to be ready to buy and download early that morning. Consumers can be motivated to engage in behaviors, make decisions, or process information, and this motivation can be seen in the context of acquiring, using, or disposing of an offering. Let's look first at the effects of motivation, as shown in Exhibit 2.1.

2-1a HIGH-EFFORT BEHAVIOR

One outcome of motivation is behavior that takes considerable effort. For example, if you are motivated to buy a good car, you will research vehicles online, look at ads, visit dealerships, and so on. Likewise, if you are motivated to lose weight, you will buy low-fat foods, eat smaller portions, and exercise. Motivation not only drives the final behaviors that bring a goal closer but also creates a willingness to expend time and energy on preparatory behaviors. Thus, someone motivated to buy a new smartphone may earn extra money for it, drive through a storm to reach the store, and then wait in line to buy it. Note, however, that consumers try to match anticipated and actual effort. If they believe their anticipated effort will be too much—if it is too much trouble to wait on line, for instance—they will simplify the decision (by ordering online or waiting until the next day). Conversely, if consumers think an important decision will be too simple, they will complicate it with extra effort.[3]

2-1b HIGH-EFFORT INFORMATION PROCESSING AND DECISION-MAKING

Motivation also affects how we process information and make decisions.[4] When consumers are highly motivated to achieve a goal, they are more likely to pay careful attention to it, think about it, attempt to understand or comprehend goal-relevant information, evaluate that information critically, and try to remember it for later use. This requires much effort. For example, if you are motivated to buy a new piano keyboard, you might scour websites looking for a sale. If someone mentions an online retailer that has keyboard sales from time to time, you might subscribe to that retailer's promotional e-mails or click to "like" it on Facebook.

Motivation An inner state of activation that provides energy needed to achieve a goal.

Motivated reasoning Processing information in a way that allows consumers to reach the conclusion that they want to reach.

Felt involvement The consumer's experience of being motivated with respect to a product or service, or decisions and actions about these.

However, when consumers have low motivation, they devote little effort to processing information and making decisions. For example, your motivation to purchase the best paper clips on the market is likely to be low. You would devote little attention to learning about the characteristics of paper clips, and you would not stop to think about what it would be like to use various types of paper clips (colored or uncolored, aluminum or steel, small or large). You may use decision-making shortcuts, such as deciding to buy the cheapest brand or the same brand you bought the last time, or the first brand that meets minimum criteria.[5] This is, in fact, how consumers tend to buy common grocery products.

Most research on consumer behavior has focused on consumers' motivation to process information *accurately*, as just described. Recent research has focused on a different type of motivation involved in information processing that is called **motivated reasoning**. When consumers engage in motivated reasoning, they process information in a biased way so that they can obtain the particular conclusion they want to reach.[6] One example of motivated reasoning is a confirmation bias when consumers seek information that supports their conclusion rather than seeking accurate information.

For example, if your goal is to lose weight, and you see an ad for a diet product, you might process the ad in a biased way to convince yourself that the product will work for you. If we want to believe that we are not vulnerable to the ill effects of smoking, we may be more likely to smoke if we are aware of smoking cessation products that are touted as "remedies." Because there are remedies to help us to quit smoking, we can use motivated reasoning to convince ourselves that smoking is not so bad after all or that is less dangerous for us than it is for others, or that eating vegetables and playing sports compensates for the negative consequences of smoking.[7]

As another example, because we want to think about good things that can happen to us rather than bad things, we may underestimate the likelihood of facing problems such as becoming ill—and fail to take preventive steps to avoid doing so.[8] We may be particularly prone to motivated reasoning when our self-esteem is at stake or when we desperately hope to achieve a particular goal (like weight loss) or avoid a negative outcome (like becoming ill).[9] Motivated reasoning returns in later chapters. Here, the focus is on the motivation to process information accurately.

2-1c FELT INVOLVEMENT

A final outcome of motivation is that it evokes a psychological state in consumers called *involvement*. **Felt involvement** is the consumer's experience of being motivated with respect to a product or service, or decisions and actions about these.[10]

Exhibit 2.1 ▶ Chapter Overview: Motivation, Ability, and Opportunity

Motivation, ability, and opportunity (MAO) to engage in various consumer behaviors are affected by many factors. Outcomes of high MAO include (1) goal-relevant behavior, (2) high-effort information processing and decision-making, and (3) felt involvement.

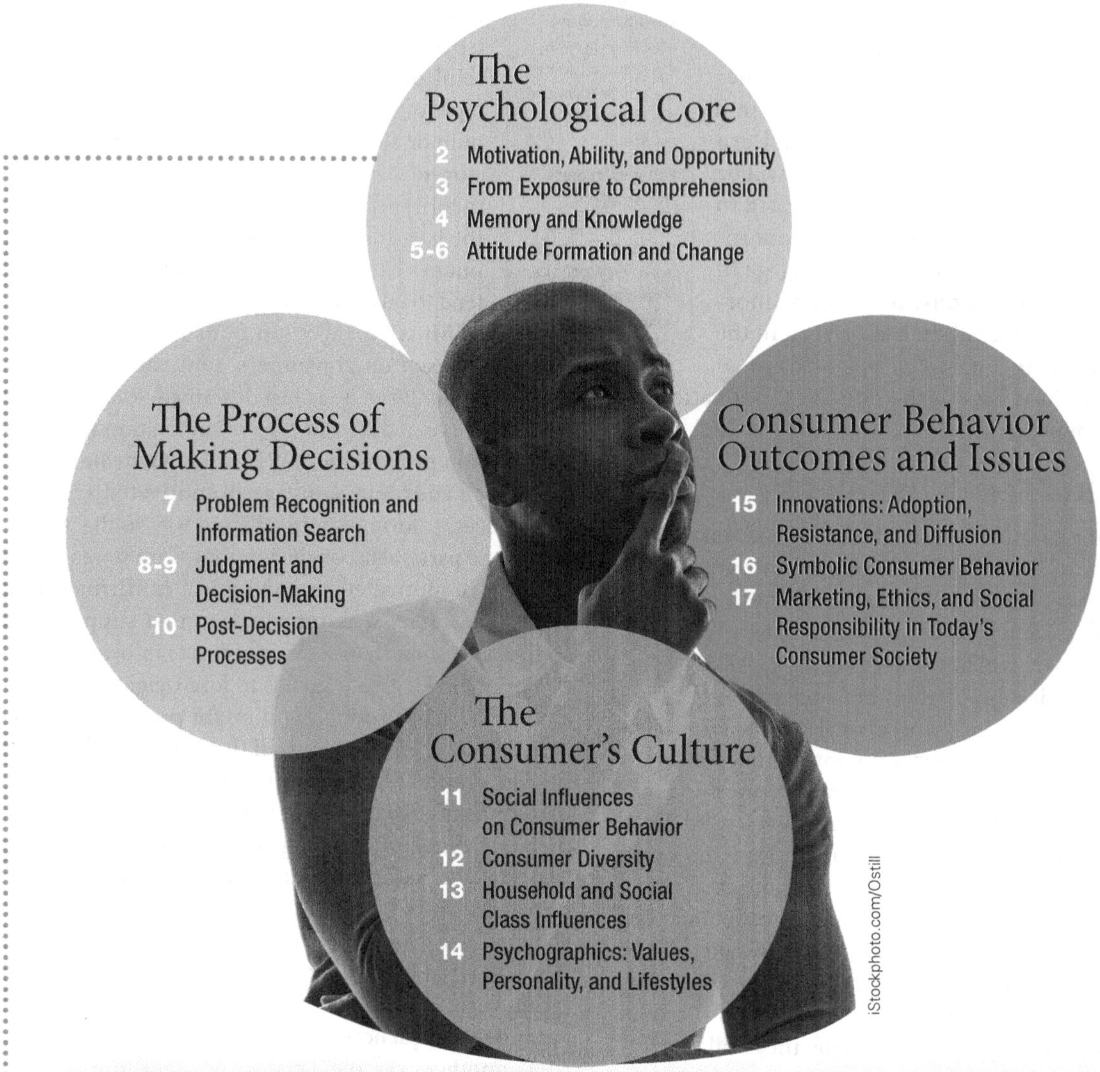

The Psychological Core

2 Motivation, Ability, and Opportunity
3 From Exposure to Comprehension
4 Memory and Knowledge
5-6 Attitude Formation and Change

The Process of Making Decisions

7 Problem Recognition and Information Search
8-9 Judgment and Decision-Making
10 Post-Decision Processes

Consumer Behavior Outcomes and Issues

15 Innovations: Adoption, Resistance, and Diffusion
16 Symbolic Consumer Behavior
17 Marketing, Ethics, and Social Responsibility in Today's Consumer Society

The Consumer's Culture

11 Social Influences on Consumer Behavior
12 Consumer Diversity
13 Household and Social Class Influences
14 Psychographics: Values, Personality, and Lifestyles

iStockphoto.com/Ostill

Motivation

Influenced by:

- Personal relevance (to self-concept, values, needs, goals, and self-control)
- Perceived risk
- Moderate inconsistency with attitudes

Ability

Influenced by:

- Financial, cognitive, emotional, physical, and social and cultural resources
- Education and age

Opportunity

Influenced by:

- Time
- Distractions
- Complexity, amount, repetition, and control of information

- High-effort behavior
- High-effort information processing and decision making
- Felt involvement

Types of Involvement

Felt involvement can be (1) enduring, (2) situational, (3) cognitive, or (4) affective.[11]

Enduring involvement exists when we show interest in an offering or activity over a long period of time.[12] Car enthusiasts are intrinsically interested in cars and exhibit enduring involvement in them. Enthusiasts engage in activities that reveal this interest (e.g., going to car shows, visiting car websites, watching YouTube videos about cars, and going to dealerships). In most instances, consumers experience **situational (temporary) involvement** with an offering or activity. For example, consumers who exhibit no enduring involvement with cars may be involved in the car-buying process when they are in the market for a new car. After they buy the car, their involvement with new cars declines dramatically.

Researchers also distinguish between cognitive and affective involvement.[13] **Cognitive involvement** means that the consumer is interested in thinking about and processing information related to his or her goal. The goal therefore includes learning about the offering. A winter sports fan who is interested in learning all about curling and looks into the Olympic success of the Canadian men's and women's curling teams would be exhibiting cognitive involvement. **Affective involvement** means that the consumer is willing to expend emotional energy in or has heightened feelings about an offering or activity. The consumer who listens to music to experience intense emotions or to relive a particular event in life is exhibiting strong affective involvement.

Objects of Involvement

As many of this chapter's examples indicate, consumers may exhibit cognitive and/or affective involvement in objects. These objects can include *a product or retail category* such as cars or clothing stores or can involve *experiences* such as white-water rafting.[14] You might be involved with clothing because you enjoy shopping for such products and see them as important for your self-expression.[15]

Consumers can also exhibit cognitive and/or affective *involvement with a brand* by being emotionally attached to it, as one might be with a particular musical band or a brand of headphones. When you are emotionally attached to and involved with a brand, you view the brand as an extension of yourself and feel a great deal of passion toward the brand.[16] Intense brand love leads to high customer loyalty and strong motivation to lavish time, money, and energy on that brand.[17] Consumers can also be *involved with ads* that are interesting or relevant to them.[18] In Japan, ads that emphasize interpersonal relationships, social circumstances, and nonverbal expressions generate more involvement than ads with clearly articulated and spoken messages.[19] In addition, consumers may be *involved with a medium* (like TV, newspapers, or the

Enduring involvement Long-term interest in an offering, activity, or decision.

Situational (temporary) involvement Temporary interest in an offering, activity, or decision, often caused by situational circumstances.

Cognitive involvement Interest in thinking about and learning information pertinent to an offering, an activity, or decisions.

Affective involvement Interest in expending emotional energy and evoking deep feelings about an offering, an activity, or a decision.

Response involvement Interest in certain decisions and behaviors.

Internet) or with a particular article or show in which an ad is placed. The huge global audiences of the Super Bowl football game, the FIFA World Cup in soccer, or the Paris Masters and Wimbledon tennis tournaments, demonstrate how involved consumers are with these televised events. A person may get so involved in interacting with a particular company's website or Facebook page that he or she may view it as "play."[20]

Consumers involved in certain decisions and behaviors are experiencing **response involvement**.[21] For example, consumers may be highly involved in the process of deciding between brands. Because consumers can be involved with many different entities, it is important to specify the *object of involvement* when using the term *involvement*. For instance, consumers who are involved with brands because they are attached to them are unlikely to be involved in deciding which brand to buy since they already think their brand is the best. Similarly, consumers can be very involved in an ad because it is funny or interesting, yet they may not be involved in the advertised brand because they are loyal to another brand.

We are motivated to behave, process information, or engage in effortful *decision-making* about things that we feel are personally relevant. And we will experience considerable involvement when buying, using, or disposing of them. Think about all the behaviors that you engaged in when deciding where to go to college—obtaining applications and information packets, searching the Web and social media, visiting campuses, weighing the information about each school, and choosing the school you would attend. You probably found the task of making this decision personally involving and were interested, enthusiastic, and perhaps overwhelmed during the process. Finally, we are also motivated to think deeply about issues pertinent to a given decision when we believe we will have to justify or explain our decisions.[22]

2-2 What Determines Motivation?

Because motivation can affect outcomes of interest to marketers (like goal-relevant behaviors such as purchasing, effortful information processing, and felt involvement), it is important for marketers to understand what affects motivation. If marketers know what the drivers of consumer motivation are, they may be able to predict consumers' motivation to think about, be involved with, and /or process information about their brand or ad and then develop marketing tactics to influence this motivation. As shown in Exhibit 2.1, motivation is affected when consumers regard something as (1) personally relevant; (2) consistent with their self-concept, values, needs, goals, emotions, and self-control processes; (3) risky; and/or (4) moderately inconsistent with their prior attitudes.

2-2a PERSONAL RELEVANCE

Something will be motivating to the extent it has **personal relevance**—that is, the extent to which it has a direct bearing on and significant implications for your life.[23] For example, if you learn that your cellphone's battery is being recalled because it can overheat and cause burns, you will probably find this issue to be personally relevant. Careers, romantic relationships, a car, an apartment or house, clothes, and hobbies are likely to be personally relevant because their consequences are significant for you. This relevance fuels your motivation to process information, make decisions, and take actions.

2-2b CONSISTENCY WITH SELF-CONCEPT

Any kind of offering (a good, a service, a person, a place) may be personally relevant to the extent that it bears on your **self-concept**, or your view of yourself and the way you think others view you. Self-concept helps us define who we are, and it frequently motivates our behavior.[24] Note that different parts of a self-concept can be salient at different times.[25] When we buy clothing, we are often making a statement about some aspect of who we are—such as a professional, a student, or a sports fan. Inconsistency with self-concept can make you feel bad, as might happen when you try on clothing in what you thought was your size only to discover that you need a larger size. When self-concept is threatened in this way, consumers will take action to repair their bruised ego (e.g., buying a product that improves the appearance of their hair).[26]

Identifying with a brand and making an emotional connection with it strengthens brand loyalty and makes those consumers less price sensitive toward that brand.[27] Harley-Davidson customers, for instance, see the brand as relevant to their self-concept and are therefore loyal. Intense affective involvement with a brand may create an almost human-like experience of brand love.[28] In a similar way, reality TV shows can be very relevant when viewers identify with the lives of the people on the show.[29] However, when consumers feel threatened about their social identity, they cope by "motivated forgetting." So if you're a dedicated Pittsburgh Steelers fan and the team is not having a good season, you may very well forget the details of a marketing message linked to that team.[30]

2-2c VALUES

Consumers are more motivated to attend to and process information when they find it relevant to their **values**—abstract beliefs that guide what people regard as important or good. Thus, if you see intellectual development as very important, you are likely to be motivated to engage in behaviors that are consistent with this value, such as pursuing a college degree. Other values may include family security, protecting the environment, and feeling fit (see Exhibit 2.2). (You'll read more about values in Chapter 14.)

2-2d NEEDS

Consumers also find things personally relevant when they have a bearing on activated needs. A **need** is an internal state of tension experienced as a discrepancy between the current state and an ideal or desired state. For example, at certain times of the day, your stomach begins to feel uncomfortable. You realize it is time to get something to eat, and you are

---

Personal relevance Something that has a direct bearing on the self and has potentially significant consequences or implications for our lives.

Self-concept Our mental view of who we are.

Values Abstract, enduring beliefs about what is right/wrong, important, or good/bad.

Need An internal state of tension experienced when there is a discrepancy between the current and an ideal or desired physical or psychological state.

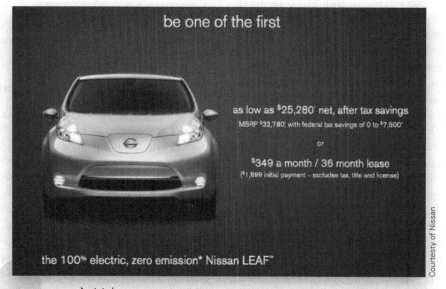

be one of the first

as low as $25,280' net, after tax savings
MSRP $32,780', with federal tax savings of 0 to $7,500'

or

$349 a month / 36 month lease
($1,999 initial payment – excludes tax, title and license)

the 100% electric, zero emission* Nissan LEAF™

Courtesy of Nissan

Exhibit 2.2 ▶ Values

Consumers are more motivated by ads if they appeal to their values, such as organic products that advertise protecting the environment.

motivated to direct your behavior toward certain outcomes (such as opening the refrigerator). Eating satisfies your need and removes the tension—in this case, hunger. Once you are motivated to satisfy a particular need, objects unrelated to that need seem less attractive. Thus, if you are motivated to fix your hair because you're having a bad hair day, a product such as styling gel will seem more attractive and important than, say, popcorn.[31]

Which needs do consumers experience? Psychologist Abraham Maslow's theory groups needs into the five categories shown in Exhibit 2.3: (1) *physiological* (the need for food, water, and sleep); (2) *safety* (the need for shelter, protection, and security); (3) *social* (the need for affection, friendship, and to belong); (4) *egoistic* (the need for prestige, success, accomplishment, and self-esteem); and (5) *self-actualization* (the need for self-fulfillment and enriching experiences).[32] Within this hierarchy, lower-level needs generally must be satisfied before higher-level needs become activated. Before we can worry about prestige, we must meet lower-level needs for food, water, and so on.

The original Maslow's hierarchy is an important starting point but somewhat restrictive and incomplete. First, needs are not always ordered exactly as in this hierarchy. Some consumers might place a higher priority on buying lottery tickets than on buying necessities such as food. Also, consumers may be able to appreciate art and engage in cultural activities even when they feel insecure or socially excluded. People can paint on an empty stomach. Thus, lower-order needs do not always have to be fulfilled before higher-order needs become important to consumers. Second, the ordering of needs may not be consistent across individuals or cultures. In some societies, for instance, social needs and belonging may be higher in the hierarchy than personal needs. Third, the hierarchy ignores the intensity of needs and the resulting effect on motivation. Lower-order needs might be more pressing than higher order-needs in the short-run. Still, the hierarchy is an important idea: Individuals and cultures share certain basic needs, which are hierarchically organized, lower-order needs are generally fulfilled before higher-order needs are addressed, and these needs influence consumer motivation and specific decisions.

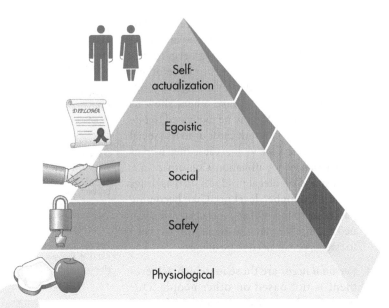

Exhibit 2.3 ▶ Maslow's Hierarchy of Needs

Maslow proposed that needs can be categorized into a basic hierarchy. People generally fulfill lower-order needs (such as physiological needs for food, water, sleep) before they fulfill higher-order needs (such as for self-actualization).

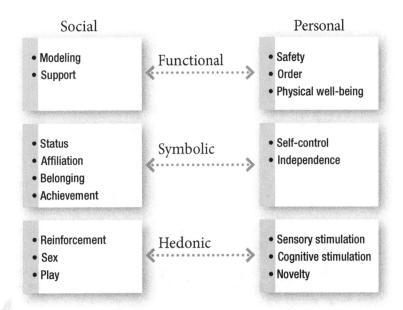

Exhibit 2.4 ▶ Categorizing Needs

Needs can be categorized according to whether they are (1) social or nonsocial and (2) functional, symbolic, or hedonic in nature. This categorization method helps marketers think about consumers' needs.

Types of Needs

Another way to categorize needs is as (1) social and personal needs or as (2) functional, symbolic, and hedonic needs[33] (see Exhibit 2.4).

▪ *Social needs* are externally directed and relate to other individuals. Fulfilling these needs thus requires the presence or actions of other people. For example, the need for status drives our desire to have others hold us in high regard; the need for support drives us to have others relieve us of our burdens; the need for models reflects a wish to have others show us how to behave. We may be motivated to buy products like Hallmark cards or to use social media such as Facebook because they help us achieve a need for affiliation. Consumers may even spend on illegal products such as drugs to satisfy a higher-level need like becoming part of a group.[34] Other products may be valued because they are consistent with our need for status or our need to be unique.

- *Personal needs* are those for which achievement is not based on other people. Our needs for sleep, novelty, control, and understanding, which involve only ourselves, can affect the usage of certain goods and services (see Exhibit 2.5). We might purchase the same brand repeatedly to maintain consistency in our world—or we might buy something different to fulfill a need for variety.

Functional need
Need that motivates the search for offerings that solve consumption-related problems.

Symbolic need
Need that relates to the meaning of our consumption behaviors to ourselves and to others. That is, how we perceive ourselves, how we are perceived by others, how we relate to others, and the esteem in which we are held by others.

Hedonic need Need that relates to sensory pleasure.

- *Functional needs* may be social or nonsocial. **Functional needs** motivate the search for products that solve consumption-related problems. For example, you might consider buying a product like a car equipped with a backup camera because it appeals to your safety needs (a functional, nonsocial need). For mothers with young children, hiring a nanny would solve the need for support (a functional, social need).

- *Symbolic needs* affect how we perceive ourselves and how others perceive us. Achievement, independence, and self-control are **symbolic needs** because they are connected with our sense of self. Similarly, our need for uniqueness is symbolic because it drives consumption decisions about how we express our identity.[35] The need to avoid rejection and the need for achievement, status, affiliation, and belonging are symbolic because they reflect our social position or role. For example, some consumers wear stylish Christian Louboutin shoes—with distinctive red soles—to express their social standing.[36]

- *Hedonic needs* include needs for sensory stimulation, cognitive stimulation, and novelty (nonsocial hedonic needs) and needs for reinforcement, sex, and play (social hedonic needs). These **hedonic needs** reflect our inherent desires for sensory pleasure. In fact, consumers exposed to sexual marketing cues tend to buy sense-rewarding products, like snacks, more quickly than when such cues are not present.[37] If the desire to satisfy hedonic needs is intense enough, it can inspire fantasizing about specific goods, simultaneously pleasurable and discomforting.[38] Consumers in India may go to luxury shopping areas like Mumbai's Palladium Mall for the eye-catching ambiance and the upscale retail experience.[39]

- *Needs for cognition and stimulation* also affect motivation and behavior. Consumers want to understand the world themselves and see some structure in it. Consumers with a high need for cognition[40] (a need for understanding and mental stimulation) enjoy being involved in mentally taxing activities like reading and deeply processing information when making decisions. People with a low need for cognition may prefer activities that require less thought, such as watching TV, and are less likely to actively process information during decision-making. In addition, consumers often need other kinds of stimulation. Those with a high optimum stimulation level enjoy a lot of sensory stimulation and tend to be involved in shopping and seeking brand information.[41] They also show heightened involvement in ads. Consumers with thrill-seeking tendencies enjoy activities like

NOTHING WILL KEEP YOU FROM SOME OF **THE FINEST COCOA BEANS**

NEW **MAGNUM ECUADOR**
For pleasure seekers
Find out more at www.facebook.com/magnum

Image Courtesy of The Advertising Archives

Exhibit 2.5 ▶ Needs
Consumers respond to ads that resonate with their specific needs, such as non-social needs, like this ad for ice cream that targets pleasure and uniqueness.

skydiving or white-water rafting. In contrast, consumers who feel overstimulated want to get away from people, noise, and demands—a desire revealed in the popularity of vacations at nature retreats or monasteries.

Characteristics of Needs

All of the preceding needs share several characteristics:

- *Needs can be internally or externally activated.* Although many needs are internally activated, some needs can be externally cued. Smelling pizza cooking in the apartment next door may, for example, affect your perceived need for food.

- *Need satisfaction is dynamic.* Needs are never permanently satisfied; satisfaction is only temporary. Clearly, eating once will not satisfy our hunger forever. Also, as soon as one need is satisfied, other needs come to the foreground. After we have eaten a meal, we might feel the need to be with others (the need for affiliation) or to work on a personal, creative project (self-actualization). Thus, needs are dynamic : Daily life is a constant process of need fulfillment.

- *Needs exist in a hierarchy.* Although several needs may be activated at any one time, some assume more importance than others. You may experience a need to eat during an exam, but your need for achievement may assume a higher priority—so you stay to finish the test. Despite this hierarchy, many needs may be activated simultaneously and influence your acquisition, usage, and disposition behaviors. Thus, your decision to plan your next holiday with friends over dinner may be driven by a combination of needs for stimulation, companionship, and food.

- *Needs can conflict.* There are various types of need conflicts.

  - An **approach-avoidance conflict** occurs when the consumer wants both to engage in the behavior and to avoid it. Teenagers may experience an approach-avoidance conflict in deciding whether to smoke cigarettes. Although they may believe that others will think they are cool for smoking (consistent with the need to belong and affiliate), they also know that smoking is bad for them (incompatible with the need for safety).

  - An **approach-approach conflict** occurs when the consumer must choose between two or more equally desirable options that fulfill different needs. A consumer who is invited to a career-night function (consistent with achievement needs) might experience an approach-approach

Approach-avoidance conflict An inner struggle about acquiring or consuming an offering that fulfills one need but fails to fulfill another.
Approach-approach conflict An inner struggle about which offering to acquire when each can satisfy an important but different need.
Avoidance-avoidance conflict An inner struggle about which offering to acquire when neither can satisfy an important but different need.

conflict if he is invited to see a basketball game with friends (consistent with affiliation and stimulation needs) on the same evening. This person will experience conflict if he views both options as equally desirable.

  - An **avoidance-avoidance conflict** occurs when the consumer must choose between two equally undesirable options, such as going home alone right after a late meeting (not satisfying a need for safety) or waiting another hour until a friend can drive her home (not satisfying a need for convenience). Conflict occurs when neither option is desirable.

Identifying Needs

Because needs influence motivation and its effects, marketers are keenly interested in identifying and measuring them. However, consumers are often unaware of their needs and cannot readily communicate them to others, even to skilled researchers. Inferring needs from consumers' behaviors is also challenging because a given need might not be linked to a specific behavior. In other words, the same need (e.g., affiliation) can be exhibited in various and diverse behaviors (visiting friends, going to the gym), and the same behavior (going to the gym) can reflect various needs (affiliation, achievement). And even when consumers fulfill a need for affiliation by choosing a brand that represents the group with which they want to affiliate, they can also fulfill the need to express their individuality by selecting specific colors or styles that differentiate them from the group.[42] Moreover, it is sometimes hard to distinguish satisfaction of different needs: Satisfying one need or craving (such as feeling hungry) can lead to the feeling that other needs are being satisfied (such as the need for distinctiveness).[43]

As another example, consider the activity of shopping. The shopping environment itself may activate certain needs. Thus, one study found that when women shop in drugstores, they are mostly seeking information about items that provide peace of mind (satisfying needs for safety and well-being). When they shop in club stores like Costco, they are mostly seeking adventure and entertainment (satisfying the need for stimulation).[44] There are cross-cultural differences in the importance of needs even for the same basic product. For example, some research indicates that U.S. consumers use toothpaste primarily for its cavity-reducing capabilities (a functional need). In contrast, consumers in England and some French-speaking areas of Canada use toothpaste primarily to freshen breath (a hedonic need). French women drink mineral water so they will look better (a symbolic need), whereas German consumers drink it for its health powers (a functional need).[45]

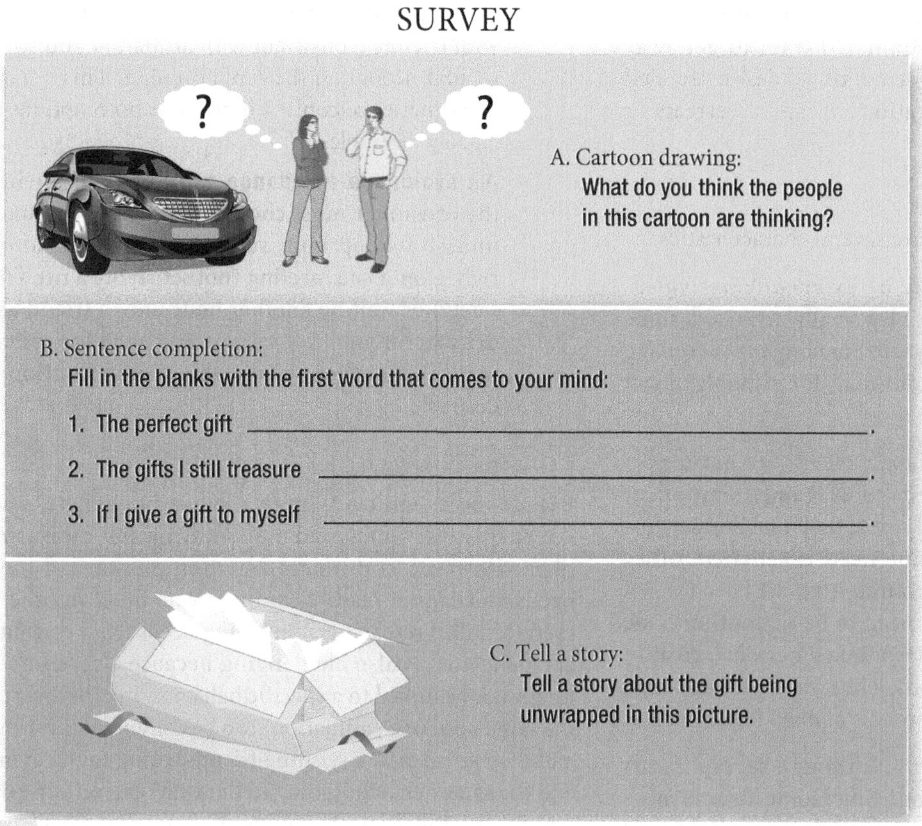

SURVEY

A. Cartoon drawing:
What do you think the people in this cartoon are thinking?

B. Sentence completion:
Fill in the blanks with the first word that comes to your mind:

1. The perfect gift _____.

2. The gifts I still treasure _____.

3. If I give a gift to myself _____.

C. Tell a story:
Tell a story about the gift being unwrapped in this picture.

Exhibit 2.6 ▶ Uncovering Consumers' Needs

Marketers sometimes uncover consumers' needs using indirect techniques, such as asking consumers to describe ambiguous stimuli like cartoon drawings, sentence completion tasks, and tell-a-story tasks. The idea is that consumers will project their needs, wishes, and fantasies onto these ambiguous stimuli, and that this provides more accurate and detailed insight into consumers needs than when asking them directly to report on those.

Given these challenges, marketers sometimes use so-called "indirect" research techniques to uncover consumers' needs.[46] Whereas direct techniques ask people to openly report on their needs, indirect techniques ask for something else and then the researcher tries to infer (indirectly) what the needs of the consumer are. One indirect technique is to ask consumers to interpret a set of relatively ambiguous stimuli such as cartoons, word associations, incomplete sentences, and incomplete stories. Using Exhibit 2.6, one consumer might reveal a need for esteem by interpreting the man in the cartoon as thinking, "My friends will think I'm really cool for riding in this car!" Another might reveal needs for affiliation by filling in the cartoon with "I could take all my friends for rides with me."

2-2e GOALS

Goals are also an important influence on personal relevance and motivation.[47] A **goal** is a particular end state or outcome that a person would like to achieve. Goals

> **Goal** Outcome that we would like to achieve.

are more specific and concrete than needs. For instance, you might have the goals to lose weight before the summer season starts, or to save a particular amount of money to buy a new car, or to study every day for an upcoming exam (see Exhibit 2.7).

Goal Setting and Goal Pursuit

Consumers set goals that they try to pursue over time. Goal setting comprises what to pursue (such as losing weight or saving money) and at what level (such as losing four pounds or saving $500).[48] As shown in Exhibit 2.8, activities during goal pursuit follow a certain sequence. After setting a goal (losing four pounds in one month), consumers are motivated to form a goal intention, plan to take action (seek out low-fat foods, join a gym), implement and control the action (through diet and exercise), and evaluate success or failure in attaining the goal (check weight each week).

Consumers use what they learn from achieving or not achieving the goal as feedback information for future goal

Image Courtesy of The Advertising Archives

Exhibit 2.7 ▶ Consumer Goals

Consumers are more likely to be involved in ads when brands are relevant to consumers' goals (e.g., losing weight).

setting and pursuit. Consumer behavior is a continuous cycle of setting goals, pursuing them, determining success and failure of goal pursuit, and adapting the goals, all with implications for marketing.[49] When consumers fail to achieve everyday subgoals (such as not recycling a newspaper), they may be less committed to long-term end-goals (such as sustaining the environment) and have weaker future intentions to act in ways that enhance quality of life.[50] On the other hand, achieving an intermediate goal, such as losing two pounds of body weight in the first two weeks of a diet, might lead consumers to set higher goals.[51]

Forming the intention to implement a plan for goal achievement can be helpful. In fact, consumers are more likely to actually achieve a goal when they have a fixed rather than a flexible plan for goal pursuit, because it provides a definite set of steps to take in reaching the goal.[52] Both the goal and the plan need to be realistic. Consumers who have a plan may feel demotivated in their pursuit if they believe they are far from their goal, but feel motivated when a recent action toward goal attainment was successful.[53] When consumers form implementation intentions for multiple goals, they anticipate greater difficulty

because completing one step in the process means postponing or ignoring steps toward other goals—which has the effect of lowering goal commitment.[54] Gaining psychological distance from a task (by the simple act of leaning back in your chair, for instance) can reduce the perceived complexity and difficulty, smoothing the way for goal pursuit.[55]

Also, consumers are interested in different things depending on whether they are far from or close to the goal. When they are far from the goal, consumers are concerned about whether they can achieve it. Consumers will be motivated at this stage by assurances that they can achieve their goal. When they are close to the goal, they are concerned about *when* they will achieve it. In fact, the worst time to be interrupted in goal pursuit is right before a goal is being attained.[56] At this stage, consumers are motivated to pursue the goal by being informed that what they are doing is working.[57] Consumers are more likely to continue working toward a goal if they set a target range (such as to lose between two and four pounds this week) rather than a single, very specific goal (such as to lose three pounds this week). This is because consumers perceive the lower number as being more attainable, while the higher number represents a challenge that, if achieved, will lead to a sense of accomplishment.[58]

Moreover, motivation is increased when consumers feel that they are making progress toward a goal by having their attention directed to whichever is better: What they have accomplished so far or what they have remaining to accomplish to attain the goal.[59] When consumers have made little progress toward a goal, they are more motivated when there are a wide variety of ways to achieve it. Conversely, after they have made considerable progress toward a goal, consumers are more motivated when there is less variety in the ways to achieve it.[60] Finally, the ability to set goals can affect consumer satisfaction with the outcome. If poor performers are reminded that they set and then met their own low goals, these consumers are as satisfied as better performers.[61]

Goals and Effort

Consumers vary in how much effort they exert to achieve a goal. You might want to save a large sum of money to spend on a sea cruise in the summer or on a skiing holiday in Colorado in the winter. Furthermore, if you perceive that you have failed in achieving a goal (such as saving a certain amount of money), you will be less motivated and, subsequently, may perform even more poorly in relation to that goal.[62] The more easily consumers can visualize their goals, the more motivated and committed they are to putting in efforts toward those goals.[63] Some research also shows that the amount of effort people exert to achieve a goal depends not only on how important the goal is to them but also on how well they are doing in achieving other, potentially unrelated, goals. For example, if you are making progress toward a goal of getting good grades, you

Exhibit 2.8 ▶ Goal Setting and Pursuit in Consumer Behavior

The process of setting and pursuing goals is circular: How a person feels about achieving or not achieving a goal affects what new goals are being set and why. This process affects the individual's motivation to initiate or continue behaviors relevant to the goal that has been set, and so forth.

Source: Richard P. Bagozzi and Utpal Dholakia, "Goal Setting and Goal Striving in Consumer Behavior," *Journal of Marketing* 63, 1999, p. 20. Reprinted with permission of American Marketing Association.

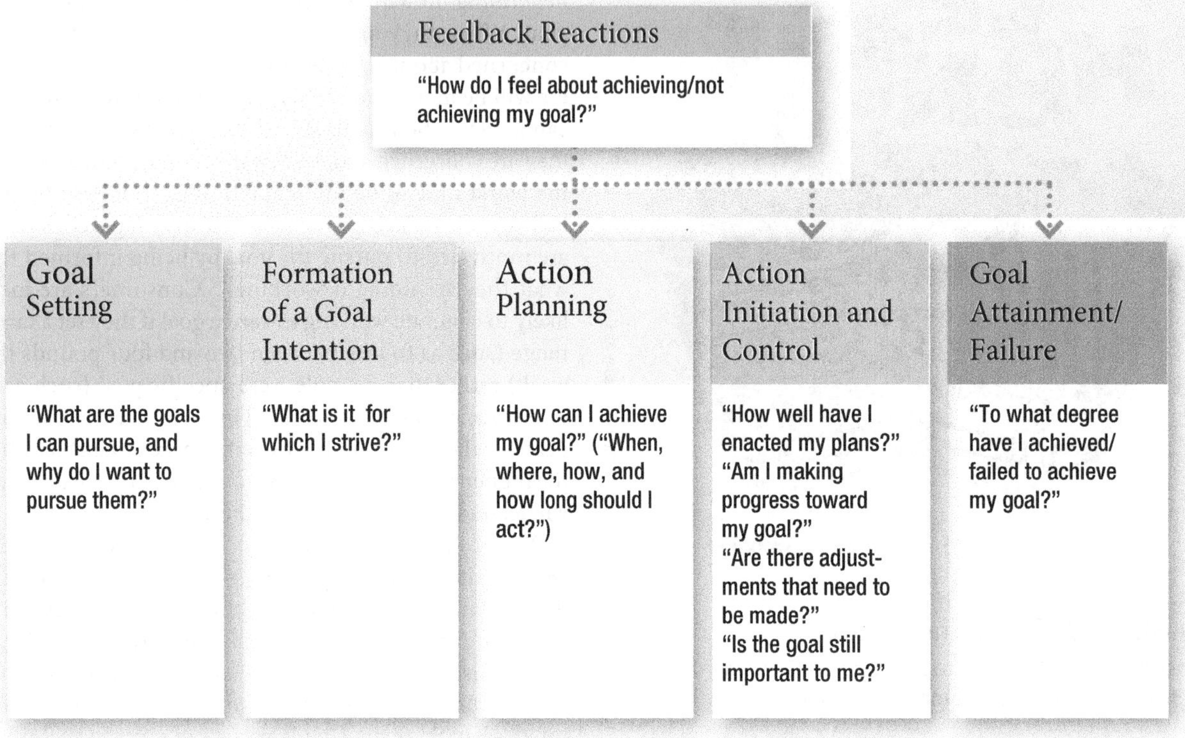

Feedback Reactions

"How do I feel about achieving/not achieving my goal?"

Goal Setting	Formation of a Goal Intention	Action Planning	Action Initiation and Control	Goal Attainment/ Failure
"What are the goals I can pursue, and why do I want to pursue them?"	"What is it for which I strive?"	"How can I achieve my goal?" ("When, where, how, and how long should I act?")	"How well have I enacted my plans?" "Am I making progress toward my goal?" "Are there adjustments that need to be made?" "Is the goal still important to me?"	"To what degree have I achieved/ failed to achieve my goal?"

may also choose to pursue a different goal, such as starting a new exercise routine.[64]

The amount of effort put into achieving a goal also depends on whether consumers have feedback demonstrating their progress toward the goal. You will tend to stick with an exercise routine, for instance, if you notice improvements in your strength and endurance.[65] If you succeed in achieving a recurring goal (such as earning a free travel ticket with frequent-flyer points), you will increase your effort to reach the same goal in the future—if the goal remains challenging.[66] Yet when you are optimistic about your future pursuit of a goal, you will be more motivated to do something when you see your action as a *commitment* to the goal, not as *making progress* toward the goal.[67] Importantly, people often strive to attain multiple goals, such as trying to lose weight, save money, trying to play an instrument, achieve at work, and be a good friend, parent, and spouse. When they are close to attaining one of their goals, people tend to reduce effort on pursuing that goal ("coasting to the finish") and redirect it to other goals. Thus, losing the first three pounds of weight may go faster than losing the last pound, not just because it is harder, but because the consumer's confidence in losing the final pound has increased, and therefore attention already shifted to another goal, such as saving money.

Types of Goals

Although goals (i.e., weight loss) are more concrete than needs (i.e., safety), they can vary in being more *concrete* or *abstract*. Some goals are concrete. They are specific to a given behavior or action and determined by the situation at hand. If you are tired, one of your goals for the evening might be to go to bed before 9:00 PM. If you are often late for a particular class, one of your goals might be to arrive at least five minutes before the start. Other goals are more abstract and endure over a long period, such as being a good student or looking beautiful.[68]

Goals also differ in whether they are *promotion-focused* or *prevention-focused*.[69] With promotion-focused goals, consumers are motivated to act in ways to achieve positive outcomes; that is, they focus on hopes, wants, and accomplishments. With prevention-focused goals, consumers are motivated to act in ways that avoid negative outcomes; they focus on responsibilities, safety, and guarding against risks. However, only consumers who believe that the world is changeable—that their actions make a difference—will be influenced by messages that are framed by a promotion or prevention focus.[70]

To illustrate, if you were going to buy a new car, would you focus on how much fun you would have driving it (promotion-focused goal) or on how much you would have to pay for insurance (prevention-focused goal)? Alternatively, if you were trying to diet, would you focus on how good you would feel if you avoided that slice of cake or how bad you would feel if you ate it?[71] Sometimes consumers engage in behaviors not to express their preferences, goals, and needs, but rather to learn these. Then, they may plan a vacation, for instance, search for information about it, and make a destination choice to explore and express their preferences.[72] There are systematic connections between the consumers' mind and body. When consumers have a highly active goal, such as attaining power, they may actually salivate over material rewards related to that goal—a physical dimension to their "hunger" for what they desire.[73]

2-2f GOALS AND EMOTIONS

The extent to which we are successful or unsuccessful in attaining our goals determines how we feel: We feel good when we make sufficient progress toward goal attainment or have attained our goals (saved enough to buy a new bike) and feel bad when we make insufficient progress toward goal attainment or have failed to attain our goals ("spent too much on clothing again"). According to **appraisal theory**, our emotions are determined by how we think about or "appraise" a situation or outcome. As Exhibit 2.9 shows, appraisal theory proposes that we feel positive emotions like joy and pride when an outcome is consistent with our goals.[74] Appraisal theory also posits other appraisal dimensions that affect how we feel—dimensions like normative/moral compatibility (is the outcome relevant to what is expected of us or what we should do?), certainty (is the outcome certain to occur or not?), and agency (was I the cause of the outcome, did someone else or the environment cause it, or did it happen by chance?).

In some instances, actions and outcomes will result in specific emotions rather than in generally feeling good or bad. If a product doesn't work, consumers might feel guilty, angry, sad, or frustrated, depending on whether the outcome is positive or negative, and who or what is seen as being responsible for the product not working. To illustrate Exhibit 2.9, consumers might

feel proud when a good outcome happens, that they are responsible for, and when the outcome is consistent with a standard of excellence or a desirable goal. In contrast, consumers feel guilty when a bad outcome happens, that they are responsible for, and when the outcome is inconsistent with a standard of excellence or a goal. Conversely, consumers may feel sad when a negative outcome happens that is perceived to be caused by the situation or by bad luck.[75]

Emotions can have wide-ranging long- and short-term consequences for consumer behavior, and these effects are specific to the particular emotion that is being experienced. For example, when consumers feel guilty for having done something bad, they tend to try to compensate for this in other domains, for instance, by buying self-improvement products.[76] On the other hand, when consumers who face a financial decision feel sad, they are more likely to make an impatient choice that yields short-term gain but is less rewarding in the long-term, just for the instant gratification.[77] When consumers feel rejected after an emotional event such as a romantic breakup, they tend to make riskier financial decisions.[78] Also, when consumers feel rejected, they are more likely to choose status-symbol brands to differentiate themselves from the group.[79] Consumers driven by envy will pay more for a product because others who are socially admired have it (benign envy) or pay more for a product because others who are socially admired do not have it (malicious envy).[80]

The positive and negative emotions, pleasure and displeasure, experienced during or after consuming products and services can change over time. When consumers repeat a consumption experience, they tend to like it less over time, a process known as *satiation*. However, when consumers distinguish between the negative and positive emotions they feel during the period of repetition, satiation takes place more slowly due to this cognitive reappraisal.[81] Because emotions play a powerful role in attitudes, choices, and satisfaction, later chapters will return to the role of appraisals in consumers' emotions.[82]

2-2g SELF-CONTROL AND GOAL CONFLICT

Consumers use **self-control** to regulate their feelings, thoughts, and behavior in line with their long-term goals.[83] Self-control conflicts arise when we face decisions about actions related to goals that are in conflict. The various possible conflicts (such as approach-approach: indulge in food today but also be slim tomorrow) are described earlier in this chapter. The mental effort involved in making such a decision between which goal to pursue may result in **ego depletion**, which means the consumer's ability to control his or her behavior

---

Appraisal theory A theory of emotion that proposes that emotions are based on an individual's assessment of a situation or an outcome and its relevance to his or her goals.

Self-control Process consumers use to regulate feelings, thoughts, and behavior in line with long-term goals, rather than to pursue short-term goals.

Ego depletion Outcome of decision-making effort that results in mental resources being exhausted.

Exhibit 2.9 ▶ Appraisal Theory

Emotions are experienced based on how consumers appraise a situation or outcome in the light of their goals, needs, and self-concept.

Source: Based on Allison Johnson and David Stewart, "A Re-Appraisal of the Role of Emotion in Consumer Behavior: Traditional and Contemporary Approaches," *Review of Marketing Research*, vol. 1 (New York: M.E. Sharpe, 2005), pp. 3–34.

CAUSED BY...	Good for Me (consistent with my goals)		Bad for Me (inconsistent with my goals)		
	CERTAIN	UNCERTAIN	CERTAIN	UNCERTAIN	
SELF	Pride	Hope Excitement	Guilt Shame	Fear Anxiety	Relevant to what I should do or should have done
	Happiness	Hope Excitement	Distress	Fear Anxiety	Irrelevant to what I should do or should have done
	Admiration Love	Hope Excitement	Contempt Disgust Envy	Fear Anxiety	Relevant to what I should do or should have done
OTHER	Gratitude Love	Hope Excitement	Anger Enraged Resentful	Fear Anxiety	Irrelevant to what I should do or should have done
ENVIRONMENT	Satisfied Relieved Delighted	Hope Excitement Interest Challenge	Disappointed Threatened Frustrated Regret	Fear Anxiety	Relevant to what I should do or should have done
	Pleased Delighted Relieved	Hope Excitement	Miserable Bored	Fear Anxiety	Irrelevant to what I should do or should have done
NOT SURE	Glad Delighted	Hope Excitement	Pity	Fear Anxiety	Relevant to what I should do or should have done
	Happiness Joy	Hope Excitement	Sadness Miserable	Fear Anxiety	Irrelevant to what I should do or should have done

is impaired. In other words, such challenges deplete a consumer's mental energy, which in turn reduces decision quality.[84]

Suppose one of your goals is to eat healthy and another is to enjoy tasty, not-so-healthy treats. Confronted with the choice of candy or yogurt, you may choose the yogurt in pursuit of your health goal. A little later, when choosing between potato chips and brown rice, your self-control might crumble and the chips would win because of ego depletion. Time plays a role in your self-control: If you repeatedly face the same choice (candy or yogurt), and you first choose yogurt, this initial decision reinforces your self-control and you are more likely to choose yogurt later.[85] Thus, on the one hand, you can train to gain self-control. On the other hand, you may indulge today because you overconfidently believe you will not indulge in the future when faced with similar choices.[86]

The Challenge of Information Processing

Conflicts like these present a challenge to information processing: When evaluating the nutritional value of a meal that combines opposites such as healthy foods and indulgent treats, consumers tend to underestimate the overall calorie content.[87] It turns out that consumers on a diet have better self-control when they have the nutritional information to understand the potential cost of indulging.[88] Faced with an opportunity to indulge, consumers will think back on past behavior to determine whether they have made sufficient progress toward a self-regulatory goal to justify indulgence on this occasion. Impulsive consumers tend to distort their memories of progress toward the goal, thereby giving themselves permission to indulge.[89] Also, when important goals conflict, consumers may change their minds more than once as they face choices that would satisfy competing goals, because the goal that was initially ignored becomes stronger.[90]

Consumers seeking to exert self-control are caught in a psychological conflict between *desire*, which is a short-term, hedonic force (we want that candy NOW, even if we feel regret later) and *willpower*, which is a long-term, more utilitarian force (we think and act to stop ourselves from having that candy now, to have a long-term healthy lifestyle).[91] There is an interesting connection between the mind and the body in self-control. If you anticipate you will require willpower to withstand some immediate desires, you may "firm your muscles." In fact, physically firming one's muscles may even carry through in firming willpower to resist tempting actions (eating candy now), when consumers perceive the long-term benefits of resistance.[92]

Another approach that strengthens self-control is to empower yourself to refuse, saying "I *don't* eat this" instead of "I *can't* eat this," when pursuing an internal goal such as eating healthy.[93] The number of tasks to be completed has an effect on self-control, as well. Even when consumers are highly motivated, they may deplete their resources while completing one task and therefore have lower self-control in a subsequent, unexpected task.[94]

People more readily eat multiple small slices of cake, without experiencing a self-control conflict, than when eating one large slice.[95] Therefore, a further approach that people can use to resist temptations and retain self-control is by "bundling the costs."[96] That is, rather than viewing the eating of an ice-cream cone as a single, isolated indulgent act, which is small and easy to justify ("It is summer, it is my favorite taste, and I deserve it"), it can help to bundle this act together with eating the slice of pie earlier in the day, and drinking the soda later. Likewise, self-control in spending can be helped by keeping large denominations. People tend not to spend when they perceive the purchase as one large amount ($20) rather than as many smaller amounts (10 purchases of $2). In fact, when consciously exerting self-control over their spending, consumers prefer to receive money in large-denomination bills rather than smaller bills.[97]

The Challenge of Emotion Regulation

Consumers not only experience emotions in response to certain behaviors that can turn out right or wrong to them (and others), they also engage in consumer behaviors to experience positive emotions and avoid experiencing negative emotions. They thus actively regulate their moods or emotions.

Consumers frequently have *goals about how they want to feel or do not want to feel*. If you feel depressed, you might have a goal of trying to make yourself feel better,

perhaps by going to the movies or eating an ice cream cone. These goals explain why consumers who are feeling sad may think that "retail therapy" will cheer them up. In fact, this may reduce sadness by allowing them to feel some control over their environment.[98] Feeling sad can lead you to pay more for new items and to eat less healthy food than usual, without conscious awareness of what you are doing.[99] Yet if you're exposed to photos or descriptions of indulgent foods when you feel sad, you will be mindful of the negative consequences of unhealthy eating and not over-indulge to make yourself feel better.[100] Consumers also try to regulate their emotions when planning their consumption activities for maximal pleasure. For example, when on vacation, someone may plan what to do and in what order, to maximize the overall pleasure.[101]

Consumers who actively pursue a self-control goal may lapse when the offering they want (candy, for instance) is far away, in distance or in time. Then, they focus more on the short-term pleasurable experience (good taste) and less on the long-term cost and unpleasurable experience (gaining weight, health concerns). If they cannot access product information from external sources (such as a nutrition label) and instead rely on memory, consumers are also more likely to lose self-control and consume because they focus on the pleasure.[102]

Although self-control can help consumers progress toward long-term goals, and thus stimulate positive emotions such as joy and pride, exerting it can be associated with negative feelings such as anger or regret.[103] Then, firming one's muscles may help willpower, and exerting willpower may firm one's muscles and might carry over into feeling angry. These connections between the mind (feeling angry, exerting willpower) and body (firming one's muscles) are another example of the **embodiment** of the mind, as discussed earlier.[104]

> **Embodiment** Connection between mind and body that influences and expresses consumer self-control and behavior.

Marketing Implications

An understanding of consumers' self-concept, needs, goals, and self-control processes is important in many areas of marketing strategy and tactics. For example, marketers frequently use consumer needs, goals, or values to segment and target specific markets. Targeting the growing segment of vegetarian consumers, Earthbound Farm offers organically grown fruits and vegetables, as well as premade salads mixed with beans and whole grains for convenience and added nutrition.[105] In particular, marketers should keep consumer self-concept, needs, goals, and self-control in mind when planning for communications, product development and positioning, and influencing specific behaviors.

Enhance Motivation to Process Communications

Marketers can enhance consumers' motivation to process and act on promotional material by making the information as personally relevant as possible and appealing to consumers' self-concepts, values, needs, or goals. Similarly, salespeople can explore consumers' underlying reasons for making a purchase and tailor sales pitches to those reasons. In advertising, messages can use a narrative structure to stimulate narrative processing, helping consumers connect the advertised brand with their self-concept.[106] Consumers tend to think more about messages that match their self-concept.[107] Thus, if you see yourself as being extroverted, you are likely to be stimulated to process an ad if it portrays a brand appropriate for extroverted people.

Consumers who value personal growth or achievement will find an ad or marketing message more personally relevant if it appeals to those values. For instance, charity: Water, a nonprofit organization dedicated to bringing safe drinking water to developing nations, appeals to achievement by showing how contributors can make a difference. The charity has more than 300,000 Facebook "likes" and more than 1.5 million Twitter followers. The founder explains: "There are solutions, and we can show people those solutions. It's a story full of hope and redemption."[108]

Product Development and Positioning

Marketers can develop goods or services with features and benefits to help consumers achieve their self-control goals. For instance, Weight Watchers and other weight-loss organizations offer tips and tools for avoiding unhealthy eating (self-control goal) as well as feedback on progress toward reaching the goal. Bundled offerings, in particular, may allow consumers to achieve more than one goal or satisfy more than one need in a single consumption episode.[109] At the restaurant chain Saladworks, a diverse menu of meal-sized salads with fresh, tasty ingredients allows consumers to achieve healthy-eating goals while also satisfying hedonic needs and cravings for variety.[110] Sometimes marketers try to appeal to consumers' unrecognized needs or goals. Franklin Ramsey did this with his idea for a trash can that secures liner bags inside. He took his idea to Edison Nation, which helped get the new product patented and—branded as Pressix—helped market it to consumers who need a convenient way to keep trash bags in place.[111]

In general, a new good or service is likely to be better suited to consumers' needs—and more valued—when consumers are actively involved in its development.[112] This co-creation process is increasingly important for marketing success and customer relationship building. Even then, marketers launching a new product might want to target consumers with promotion-focused goals. Why? Buying a new product may bring new benefits, but often with potential costs (money and uncertainty) in making the change. Prevention-focused consumers tend to preserve the status quo by staying with the option they know, making them less receptive to new products.[113] Companies can also improve offerings to help consumers make decisions involving conflicting goals or needs. The frozen yogurt chain TCBY now offers self-serve counters where customers dish out their own desserts, choose toppings, and pay by the ounce. "If calories are an issue or budget is an issue, [customers are] in control," explains an executive. TCBY has now developed a vending machine that allows consumers to choose their desired size, flavor, and topping, and have the finished dessert in hand within 30 seconds.[114]

Encouraging Specific Behaviors

Marketers can also use the mind-body connection to influence behavior in support of purchase decisions. For example, a real estate agent who wants to emphasize the spacious, open floor-plan of a home could use physical movements such as turning his or her head all the way from left to right and gesturing across the space with his or her arms, encouraging prospective buyers to do the same. Similarly, a furniture salesperson can have consumers sit on a sofa in the store and imagine relaxing on it at home. Such physical actions can help move consumers closer toward purchase decisions.

2-2h PERCEIVED RISK

Exhibit 2.1 shows that another factor of consumers' motivation to process information about a product or brand is **perceived risk**: The extent to which the consumer anticipates negative consequences of buying, using, or disposing of an offering to emerge and positive consequences to not emerge.[115] There are thus two components to perceived risk, namely, the anticipation of outcomes and how certain or uncertain these are (uncertainty component), and the negativity of the outcomes and how severe these are (consequences component). Perceived risk is high when negative outcomes are likely or positive outcomes are unlikely. Consumers are more likely to pay

> **Perceived risk** The extent to which the consumer anticipates negative consequences of an action, for example, buying, using, or disposing of an offering, to emerge and positive consequences to not emerge.

Source: Carbonite

Exhibit 2.10 ▶ Perceived Risk
Consumer products and services are often touted as ways to avoid risky outcomes.

attention to and carefully process marketing communications when perceived risk is high (see Exhibit 2.10). As perceived risk increases, consumers tend to collect more information and evaluate it carefully.

Perceived risk can be associated with any product or service, but it tends to be higher (1) when the offering is new; (2) when the offering has a high price; (3) when the offering is technologically complex; (4) when brands differ fairly substantially in quality and might cause the consumer to make an inferior choice; (5) when the consumer has little confidence or experience in evaluating the offering; (6) when the opinions of others are important, and the consumer is likely to be judged on the basis of the acquisition, usage, or disposition decision, and generally (7) when little information is available about the offering.[116]

Perceptions of risk vary across cultural groups. Also, perceived risk is typically higher when consumers have little expertise in a particular domain and are aware of this, such as

travelers who purchase goods or services in a foreign country.[117] In addition, risk perceptions vary within a culture.[118]

Types of Perceived Risk

It is useful to distinguish six types of risk that consumers can perceive:[119]

- **Performance risk** reflects uncertainty about whether the product or service will perform as expected. Consumer purchases of certified pre-owned vehicles are hitting record levels because buyers know that these cars, SUVs, and pickups have been professionally checked and come with the reassurance of a warranty.[120]

- **Financial risk** is higher if an offering is expensive, such as the cost of buying a home. When consumers perceive high product-category risk due to high price levels, research suggests that their buying decisions can be improved if they research offerings using websites such as epinions.com.[121]

- **Physical (or safety) risk** refers to the potential harm a product or service might pose to one's safety. Many consumer decisions are driven by a motivation to avoid physical risk. For example, consumers often shy away from buying perishable groceries that have passed the stated expiration date because they are afraid of getting sick from eating spoiled food.[122]

- **Social risk** is the potential harm to one's social standing that may arise from buying, using, or disposing of an offering. According to research, antismoking ad messages that conveyed the severe social disapproval risk of smoking cigarettes were more effective in influencing teens' intentions not to smoke than ad messages stressing the health consequences of smoking, such as disease.[123]

- **Psychological risk** reflects consumers' concern about the extent to which a product or service fits with the way they perceive themselves. To illustrate, if you see yourself as an environmentalist, buying disposable diapers may be psychologically risky.

- **Time risk** reflects uncertainties about the length of time that must be invested in buying, using, or disposing of the product or service. Time risk may be high if the offering involves considerable time commitment, if learning to use it is a lengthy process, or if it entails a long commitment period (such as a subscription to cable television services that require a two-year contract).

Performance risk The possibility that the offering will not perform as well as hoped or expected.

Financial risk The extent to which buying, using, or disposing of an offering is perceived to have the potential to create financial harm.

Physical (or safety) risk The extent to which buying, using, or disposing of an offering is perceived to have the potential to create physical harm or harm one's safety.

Social risk The extent to which buying, using, or disposing of an offering is perceived to have the potential to do harm to one's social standing.

Psychological risk The extent to which buying, using, or disposing of an offering is perceived to have the potential to harm one's sense of self and thus create negative emotions.

Time risk The extent to which buying, using, or disposing of the offering is perceived to have the potential to lead to loss of time.

Risk and Involvement

Products and services vary in the extent to which they are personally relevant or involving. Perceived risk is a key determinant of this. Consumers are likely to be more involved in purchasing products such as homes, sports attire, life insurance, and computers than in purchasing picture frames, canned soup, or coffee because the former generate higher levels of performance, financial, safety, social, psychological, or time risk and can therefore have more significant personal consequences.

High risk is generally uncomfortable for consumers. As a result, they are usually motivated to engage in any number of behaviors and information-processing activities to reduce or resolve risk. To reduce the uncertainty component of risk, consumers can collect additional information by consulting social media ("What do my Facebook friends say?"), conducting online research, reading news articles, engaging in comparative shopping, talking to friends or sales specialists, or consulting experts. Consumers also try to reduce the uncertainty component of perceived risk by purchasing famous brands and by remaining brand loyal.

In addition, consumers attempt to reduce the consequence component of perceived risk through various strategies. Some consumers may employ a simple decision rule that results in a safer choice. For example, someone might buy the most expensive offering or choose a heavily advertised brand in the belief that this brand is of higher quality than other brands. When decision risk is high, consumers may be willing to consider less conventional alternatives, particularly when they do not trust traditional products or practices. For example, consumers who believe that conventional medical treatments are too technological or dehumanizing may be open to other healing alternatives.[124]

Marketing Implications

When perceived risk is high, marketers can either reduce uncertainty or reduce the perceived consequences of failure. Darn Tough Vermont, which markets highly durable, premium-quality athletic socks priced at $20 per pair, reduces both financial and performance risk by offering a lifetime guarantee: If a sock ever wears out, the buyer gets a new pair for free.[125] When risk is low, consumers are less motivated to think about the brand or product and its potential consequences. Marketers sometimes need to enhance risk perceptions to make their messages more compelling. For instance, the Scottish government's alcohol moderation campaign, which ran online, in print, and on radio, highlighted negative effects of excessive

drinking with the slogan "Every time you have a drink, it adds up to more than you think."[126]

Interestingly, consumers do not always see a particular action as risky, even when it is. For example, many people fail to realize the risks of unprotected sex, a situation that explains why condom sales are not higher than they are. Despite the health benefits of using sunscreen, some consumers don't fully appreciate the risk they take when suffering a sunburn. This is why New Zealand, which leads the world in melanoma skin cancer mortality rates, has created a Sun Protection Alert graphic for media use in reminding consumers to use sunscreen and avoid the sun during specific hours.[127] Marketers can also enhance consumers' understanding of how behavior can create risky negative outcomes. When consumers think about the role their own behavior plays in acquiring AIDS, they are more likely to follow the advice in ads about reducing that risk.[128]

2-2i INCONSISTENCY WITH ATTITUDES

A final factor affecting motivation, shown in Exhibit 2.1, is the extent to which new information is consistent with previously acquired knowledge or attitudes. We tend to be motivated to process messages that are moderately inconsistent with our knowledge or attitudes because such messages are perceived as moderately threatening or uncomfortable. Therefore, we try to eliminate or at least understand this inconsistency.[129] For example, if a consumer sees a car ad that mentions slightly negative information about the brand she currently owns—such as the brand's getting lower gas mileage than a competitor—she will want to process the information to understand and perhaps resolve the uncomfortable feeling.

On the other hand, consumers are less motivated to process information that is highly inconsistent with their prior attitudes. Thus, for instance, someone who is loyal to the Hertz brand would not be motivated to process information from a comparative ad suggesting that Hertz is bad or that other brands are better. The consumer would simply reject the other brands as nonviable options.

2-3 Consumer Ability: Resources to Act

Ability The extent to which consumers have the required resources to make an outcome happen.

Motivation may not result in action unless a consumer has the ability to process information, make decisions, or engage in behaviors. **Ability** is defined as the extent to which consumers have the necessary resources to make the outcome happen.[130] If our ability to process information is high, we may engage in active decision-making. As shown in Exhibit 2.1, (1) financial resources, (2) cognitive resources, (3) emotional resources, (4) physical resources, and (5) social and cultural resources can affect consumers' abilities to process information about brands and make decisions about and engage in buying, usage, and disposition. In turn, these five resources can be affected by other factors, including education and age.

2-3a FINANCIAL RESOURCES

In some situations, consumers can use money instead of other resources to enhance their ability to make decisions and take actions. For example, many consumers hire financial planners for investment guidance and pay tour guides to show them around a particular area. Obviously, the lack of money constrains consumers who might otherwise have the motivation to engage in a behavior that involves acquisition. Although motivated consumers who lack money can still process information and make buying decisions, they are constrained in their immediate ability to buy in the market. And, as noted in Chapter 1, consumers' management of savings and debts can affect their financial situation. See Chapter 13 for an in-depth discussion of the meaning of money.

2-3b COGNITIVE RESOURCES

Consumers vary greatly in their knowledge about and experience of an offering.[131] They can gain knowledge from product or service experiences such as ad exposures, interactions with salespeople, and information from friends or the media, previous decision-making or product usage, or memory. A number of studies have compared the information-processing activities of consumers who have a lot of product knowledge or expertise with those of consumers who do not.[132] Knowledgeable consumers, or "experts," are better able to think deeply about information than are equally motivated but less knowledgeable consumers, or "novices." These differences in prior knowledge affect how consumers make decisions. For example, consumers trying to lease a car rarely understand the concept of capitalized costs (the figure used to determine lease payments) or the need to negotiate lower costs to lower their payments. The inability to understand these costs may result in a less than optimal decision.

One particular type of expertise concerns knowledge about financial matters, called *financial literacy*. Independent of educational level and income, people low in financial literacy have higher debt rates and lower savings, and are less likely to plan for retirement. One large study among U.S. adults aged 23–28 reported low levels of financial literacy (such as knowledge about the effects of interest rates and inflation), and found that it was associated with lower levels of general cognitive ability.[133] Cognitive ability can also affect buying behavior. Consumers are less likely to use loyalty or reward points when they cannot easily calculate what they will save by using these points.[134]

Novices and experts process information in different ways.[135] Experts can process information about specific attributes (what the product has—such as a three-terabyte hard drive), whereas novices process information better when it's stated in terms of more general benefits (what the product can do—such as store a lot of data). Novices may be able to process information when marketers provide a helpful analogy (e.g., can hold a library's worth of data).[136] In particular, an analogy is persuasive when consumers can transfer their knowledge of one product's attributes to an unfamiliar product and can allocate the resources needed to process this mapping.[137]

Also, consumers may have difficulty evaluating a service provider when they lack product knowledge or experience (or simply because the service outcome is not easy to evaluate, such as whether the doctor provided the best possible advice). In such situations, consumers may judge service providers using *heuristics*, simple cues or rules of thumb such as whether the medical staff was friendly or whether the examination room was clean and in good order.[138] Finally, consumers can differ in *cognitive style*, or their preferences for ways information should be presented. Some consumers are adept at processing information visually (checking a map for directions), whereas others prefer to process information verbally (listening to a GPS unit give verbal directions).

2-3c EMOTIONAL RESOURCES

Consumers' ability to experience empathy and sympathy can affect their processing of information and their decisions about brand choices, consumption, disposition, spending, and so on. Emotional resources also affect the actions consumers take to participate in charitable events or donate to causes. For example, many marketers offer pink-themed products during October, which is Breast Cancer Awareness Month, and donate part of the purchase price to the fight against breast cancer (see Exhibit 2.11). According to research, 84 percent of all U.S. consumers buy pink-themed products during October because they want to help battle the disease.[139]

2-3d PHYSICAL RESOURCES

Physical capabilities—"body power"—can affect how, when, where, and whether consumers make decisions and take actions. As discussed earlier in this chapter, the mind-body connection can play a role in consumers'

Exhibit 2.11 ▶ Emotional Resources

Some ads appeal to a consumer's emotions, such as advertising a product that donates to breast cancer awareness.

Courtesy of Daimler AG

self-control, for example. Physical resources also influence consumers' ability to use certain goods or services. Even when consumers do not accurately assess their physical resources, these resources will affect their decisions. For instance, consumers who feel they are physically capable may decide to take a strenuous hike or buy challenging exercise equipment.

2-3e SOCIAL AND CULTURAL RESOURCES

Social resources derive from the network of social relationships that people have with others and the extent to which they can leverage the resources contained in these relationships. Cultural resources derive from knowledge of and access to the system of (sub)cultural institutions in a society. Knowledge of and access to these resources affect acquisition, consumption, and disposition behavior of consumers. For example, studies show that college freshmen with solid social and cultural resources are more likely to continue into their second year of school, rather than dropping out.[140]

A consumer's social resources also play a role in whether marketing activities conducted on Facebook or in other social media will generate strong word of mouth support and referrals to potential buyers or brand fans. Top YouTube stars like PewDiePie (real name: Felix Kjellberg) have millions of followers viewing and sharing their videos. These social media stars generate income from ads that run alongside their videos, as well as from marketing their own branded products.[141] Being "in the know" socially and (sub)culturally helps consumers to act according to the norms and to be part of the right rituals. Wearing the right clothes, knowing the right music, and speaking the right language increases the likelihood that consumers will have access to particular sports clubs, colleges, companies, and community groups.[142]

2-3f EDUCATION AND AGE

Education and age have also been related to the ability to process information and make decisions. Specifically, better-educated consumers will have more cognitive resources to use in processing complex information and making decisions. Age also accounts for differences in physical resources and processing ability. Older children seem to be more sensitive to the fact that the benefits of searching for information sometimes outweigh the costs, whereas younger children don't seem to have this same ability.[143] Old age has been associated with a decline in certain cognitive skills and thus reduced ability to process information. For instance, older consumers took more time to process nutrition information and made decisions that were less accurate than those of younger consumers.[144]

Marketing Implications

Factors affecting ability suggest several implications for marketers. First, marketers should be sure that targeted consumers have sufficient prior knowledge to process marketing communications. If not, the company may need to develop educational messages as a first step. Marketers also need to be sensitive to the potentially different processing styles, education levels, and ages of each segment. For example, highly motivated but visually oriented parents may be unable to assemble furniture if the written instructions are too complex and thus incompatible with their processing style. IKEA's furniture assembly instructions are appropriate for a broad audience because they have only illustrations and numbers, and they are thoroughly tested to ensure clarity. IKEA even has a website, the Share Space, where customers can post photos after they've assembled their purchases—reassuring others that they can do this, too.[145]

Knowing that a lack of money constrains purchase behaviors, marketers can facilitate first-time and repeat buying by providing monetary aid. Car manufacturers have enhanced consumers' purchasing ability—and boosted sales—by offering low- or no-down-payment programs, low financing rates, and rebates. Marketers can also provide education and information (through advertising, websites, mobile marketing, social media, point-of-purchase displays, and other communications) that help consumers better process information, make more informed decisions, and engage in consumption behaviors.

2-4   Consumer Opportunity

The final factor affecting whether motivation results in action is consumers' opportunity to engage in a behavior. For example, a consumer may be highly motivated to work out and have sufficient money to join a health club (ability); however, when the local health club is being renovated, there is no opportunity to implement the intention to work out. Unavailability of the desired choice option is an important reason why motivated and able consumers cannot do what they set out to do. Independent of this, someone may not take action or make decisions because of three key influences: (1) lack of time, (2) distraction, and (3) the complexity, amount, repetition, and control of information.

2-4a   TIME

Time can affect the consumer's opportunity to process information, make decisions, and perform certain behaviors. Some studies show that time-pressured consumers are more likely to buy things for themselves during the Christmas season because this is one of the few opportunities they have to shop.[146] Knowing that would-be gardeners have little time (or patience) to plant, weed, and water, companies are successfully marketing seed-embedded mats, low-maintenance plants, and fast-maturing trees.[147]

Consumers under time pressure to make a decision will (1) acquire less information, (2) process the information less systematically, and (3) place more emphasis on negative information.[148] For example, a consumer who has to buy 30 items during a 15-minute grocery shopping trip will not have time to process a lot of information about each item. The more time consumers have to think about consumption problems, the more creative they tend to be at coming up with novel solutions.[149]

2-4b   DISTRACTION

Distraction refers to any aspect of a situation that diverts consumers' attention. For example, other people in the subway can divert a consumer's attention from reading a newspaper online. If someone talks while a consumer is viewing an ad or making a decision, that distraction can inhibit the consumer's ability to process the information. Certain background factors in the ad itself, such as music or attractive models, can also distract consumers from an advertised message.[150] Consumers may be distracted from TV commercials if the program during which the commercials appear is very involving.[151] Distraction seems to influence mostly the effect that consumers' (slow) thoughts have on their choices, and less so the effect that their (fast) emotions have on choices.[152]

2-4c   COMPLEXITY, AMOUNT, REPETITION, AND CONTROL OF INFORMATION

The complexity of the information to which consumers are exposed can affect their opportunity to process it. Consumers find technical or quantitative information more difficult to handle than nontechnical and qualitative data, a situation that inhibits processing.[153] Technological and pharmaceutical products typically entail complex information. In addition, messages containing pictures-without-words can be ambiguous and therefore hard to comprehend.[154] Marketers can, however, use visualization tools to communicate complex information and facilitate processing.[155] The consumer's regulatory focus plays a role, as well. When consumers encounter a lot of information about a product, those who are promotion-focused will rely more on positive details and have higher brand evaluations, whereas those who are prevention-focused will rely more on negative details and will have lower brand evaluations.[156]

Information may also be complex if the individual must sift through a huge volume of it. That's why Lowe's, the home improvement retailer, offers consumers the opportunity to educate themselves about repair projects quickly and conveniently by viewing how-to videos or downloading articles in Spanish or English. The retailer also invites customers to design bathrooms and kitchens in-store and visualize the appearance using augmented-reality technology.[157]

Although consumers' ability to process information is limited by time, distraction, and the quality and complexity of the information, one factor—repetition—may actually enhance it.[158] If consumers are repeatedly exposed to information, they have more opportunities to think about, scrutinize, relate to, and remember the information. Advertisers who use television and radio, in particular, must therefore plan to get their messages to the target audience more than once to enhance the opportunity for processing. Of course, frequent exposure to the same ad may lead to irritation, which in turn may hurt the brand. Consumers show more patience for repetition of ads from known, familiar brands.[159]

Consumers remember and learn more when they can control the flow of information by determining what information is presented, for how long, and in what order. With print and many online ads, for example, consumers have much control over which messages they pay attention to, how long they spend processing each message, and the order in which they process the messages. They have more opportunity to select what is appropriate for their own needs and goals, process the information, and apply it to consumption decisions. The same is true for informative company or product review websites. In contrast, consumers exposed to radio or TV commercials do not have such control, so they have less opportunity to process and apply the information.[160] As consumers become proficient in controlling the information flow, they can put more effort into processing the content rather than focusing on the control task.[161]

Marketing Implications

Often marketers can do little to enhance consumers' opportunities to process information, make careful decisions, or engage in purchase, usage, or disposition behaviors. For example, individual advertisers cannot easily make public transportation, cafés, and living rooms less distracting during TV commercials or give consumers more time for shopping. However, companies can play some role in enhancing opportunity.

▶ *Repeating marketing communications* (up to a point) increases the likelihood that consumers will notice and eventually process them. Marketers can also increase the likelihood of processing by presenting messages at a time of day when consumers are least likely to be distracted and pressed for time. Simple messages, with minimal pictures-and-text and a clear connection to the brand, help consumers to understand them. Often companies such as Pepsi will get a message across by restating it in different media (TV commercials, radio ads, billboards, Facebook posts, tweets, etc.). Repetition increases the opportunity to process information in ads, but it can also reduce consumers' motivation to process the information once the ad is worn out.

▶ *Reducing time pressure* can lessen distractions for consumers. For example, stores may extend their hours and offer online buying so consumers can shop when they are least distracted and least time pressured. Amazon.com, among other online retailers, allows consumers to "save" items in their shopping carts for later evaluation and purchase.

▶ *Reducing the time needed to buy, use, and learn about a product or service* allows consumers more opportunities to process information and act on their decisions. In stores, clear signs and directories help consumers locate goods more quickly and increase the likelihood that they will actually buy the goods. For example, Lowe's is testing a robot greeter in some stores to lead customers directly to the products they want to see and buy.[162] Intelligent search engines enable consumers to rapidly find what they seek online.

▶ *Offering information when and where consumers choose to access it* will open more opportunities for processing and acting on information. Increasingly, companies are using mobile marketing to allow consumers to access product information, receive special orders, and place orders via smartphone from anywhere at any time. To illustrate, Simon Property Group has installed beacon technology in its 192 U.S. shopping centers to facilitate mobile communications with shoppers who are interested in specific products, stores, and offers. Nordstrom's shopping app will check inventory in nearby branches, scan barcodes to obtain additional information about particular items, and tote up rewards points for purchases.[163]

Summary:

Motivation reflects an inner state of activation that moves the consumer to engage in goal-relevant behaviors, effortful information processing, and detailed decision-making. Motivated consumers often experience affective or cognitive involvement. In some cases, this involvement may be enduring; in other cases, it may be situational, lasting only until the goal has been achieved. Consumers experience greater motivation when they regard a goal or object as personally relevant, or when it relates to their self-concept, values, needs, emotions, goals, and/or calls for self-control; when it entails perceived risk; or when it is moderately inconsistent with their prior attitudes.

Even when motivation is high, consumers may not achieve their goals if their ability or opportunity to do so is low. Similarly, if consumers lack the financial, cognitive, emotional, physical, or social and cultural resources, they may not have the ability to make a decision. Age and education also affect ability. Highly motivated consumers may also fail to achieve goals if lack of time, distractions, complex or large amounts of information, or lack of control over information flow limit the opportunity to make decisions.

Questions for Review and Discussion

1. What are the three major sources of effort consumers invest in making acquisition, usage, and disposition decisions?

2. How is motivation defined, and how does it affect felt involvement?

3. What are some objects of involvement for consumers?

4. Why are personal relevance, self-concept, and values important for motivation?

5. What determines the ranking of needs in Maslow's hierarchy?

6. What types of goals do consumers have?

7. According to appraisal theory, what do emotions have to do with goals?

8. What is self-control and how does it relate to conflicting goals?

9. Why do conflicting goals pose a challenge to information processing and emotion regulation?

10. What are six types of perceived risk, and how does perceived risk affect personal relevance?

11. What five types of resources affect ability to process information and make decisions?

12. Identify some of the elements that contribute to consumer opportunity for processing information and making decisions, and suggest how marketers can make use of these for marketing purposes.

Endnotes

1 Rebecca Pahle, "Brewing Up a Good Time: Movie Tavern Champions Innovation and Expansion," *Film Journal*, October 28, 2015, www.filmjournal.com.

2 C. Whan Park and Banwari Mittal, "A Theory of Involvement in Consumer Behavior: Problems and Issues," in ed. J. N. Sheth, *Research in Consumer Behavior* (Greenwich, Conn.: JAI Press, 1979), pp. 201–231; and Deborah J. MacInnis, Christine Moorman, and Bernard J. Jaworski, "Enhancing and Measuring Consumers' Motivation, Opportunity, and Ability to Process Brand Information from Ads," *Journal of Marketing*, October 1991, pp. 32–53.

3 Rom Y. Schrift, Oded Netzer, and Ran Kivetz, "Complicating Choice," *Journal of Marketing Research*, April 2011, pp. 308–326.

4 Deborah J. MacInnis and Bernard J. Jaworski, "Information Processing from Advertisements: Toward an Integrative Framework," *Journal of Marketing* 53, October 1989, pp. 1–23; Scott B. MacKenzie and Richard A. Spreng, "How Does Motivation Moderate the Impact of Central and Peripheral Processing on Brand Attitudes and Intentions?" *Journal of Consumer Research*, March 1992, pp. 519–529; Richard E. Petty and John T. Cacioppo, *Communication and Persuasion* (New York: SpringerVerlag, 1986); Anthony Greenwald and Clark Leavitt, "Audience Involvement in Advertising: Four Levels," *Journal of Consumer Research* 11, June 1984, pp. 581–592; Ronald C. Goodstein, "Category-Based Applications and Extensions in Advertising: Motivating More Extensive Ad Processing," *Journal of Consumer Research*, June 1993, pp. 87–99; and Ellen Garbarino and Julie A. Edell, "Cognitive Effort, Affect, and Choice," *Journal of Consumer Research*, September 1997, pp. 147–158.

5 Wayne D. Hoyer, "An Examination of Consumer Decision Making for a Common Repeat Purchase Product," *Journal of Consumer Research*, December 1984, pp. 822–829; James R. Bettman, Mary-Frances Luce, and John W. Payne, "Constructive Consumer Choice Processes," *Journal of Consumer Research* 25, no. 3, 1998, pp. 187–217.

6 Kurt A. Carlson, Margaret G. Meloy, and J. Edward Russo, "Leader-Driven Primacy: Using Attribute Order to Affect Consumer Choice," *Journal of Consumer Research* 32, no. 4, 2006,

pp. 513–518; Nidhi Agrawal and Durairaj Maheswaran, "Motivated Reasoning in Outcome-Bias Effects," *Journal of Consumer Research* 31, no. 4, 2005, pp. 798–805; Getta Menon, Lauren G. Block, and Suresh Ramanathan, "We're at as Much Risk as We're Led to Believe: The Effect of Message Cues on Judgments of Health Risk," *Journal of Consumer Research*, March 2002, pp. 533–549; Shailendra Jain and Durairai Maheswaran, "Motivated Reasoning: A Depth-of-Processing Perspective," *Journal of Consumer Research* 26, no. 4, 2000, pp. 358–371; Ziva Kunda, "The Case for Motivated Reasoning," *Psychological Bulletin*, 1990, pp. 480–498; and Raymond S. Nickerson, "Confirmation Bias: A Ubiquitous Phenomenon in Many Guises," *Review of General Psychology* 2, no. 2, 1998, pp. 175–220.

7 Lisa E. Bolton, Joel B. Cohen, and Paul N. Bloom, "Does Marketing Products as Remedies Create 'Get Out of Jail Free Cards'?" *Journal of Consumer Research* 33, no. 1, 2006, pp. 71–81; and Neil D. Weinstein, S. ED. Marcus, and R. P. Moser, "Smokers' Unrealistic Optimism about Their Risk," *Tobacco Control* 14, 2005, pp. 55–59.

8 Ying-Ching Lin, Chien-Huang Lin, and Priya Raghubir, "Avoiding Anxiety, Being in Denial, or Simply Stroking Self-Esteem: Why Self-Positivity?" *Journal of Consumer Psychology* 13, no. 4, 2003, pp. 464–477.

9 Gustavo de Mello, Deborah J. MacInnis, and David W. Stewart, "Threats to Hope: Effects on Reasoning About Product Information," *Journal of Consumer Research*, August 2007, pp. 153–161; and Deborah J. MacInnis and Gustavo de Mello, "The Concept of Hope and Its Relevance to Product Evaluation and Choice," *Journal of Marketing*, January 2005, pp. 1–14.

10 Richard L. Celsi and Jerry C. Olson, "The Role of Involvement in Attention and Comprehension Processes," *Journal of Consumer Research*, September 1988, pp. 210–224.

11 Marsha L. Richins, Peter H. Bloch, and Edward F. McQuarrie, "How Enduring and Situational Involvement Combine to Create Involvement Responses," *Journal of Consumer Psychology*, September 1992, pp. 143–154; Peter H. Bloch and Marsha L. Richins, "A Theoretical Model for the Study of Product Importance Perceptions," *Journal of Marketing*, Summer 1983, pp. 69–81; Celsi and Olson, "The Role of Involvement in Attention and Comprehension Processes"; Andrew A. Mitchell, "The Dimensions of Advertising Involvement," in ed. Kent Monroe, *Advances in Consumer Research*, vol. 8 (Ann Arbor, Mich.: Association for Consumer Research, 1981), pp. 25–30; and Marsha L. Richins and Peter H. Bloch, "After the New Wears Off: The Temporal Context of Product Involvement," *Journal of Consumer Research*, September 1986, pp. 280–285.

12 Michael J. Houston and Michael L. Rothschild, "Conceptual and Methodological Perspectives on Involvement," in ed. S. Jain, *Research Frontiers in Marketing: Dialogues and Directions* (Chicago: American Marketing Association, 1978), pp. 184–187; Richins and Bloch, "After the New Wears Off: The Temporal Context of Product Involvement"; and Gilles Laurent and Jean-Noel Kapferer, "Measuring Consumer Involvement Profiles," *Journal of Marketing Research*, February 1985, pp. 41–53.

13 C. Whan Park and S. Mark Young, "Consumer Response to Television Commercials: The Impact of Involvement and Background Music on Brand Attitude Formation," *Journal of Marketing Research*, February 1986, pp. 11–24.

14 Judith Lynne Zaichkowsky, "Measuring the Involvement Construct," *Journal of Consumer Research*, December 1985, pp. 341–352; and Laurent and Kapferer, "Measuring Consumer Involvement Profiles," *Journal of Marketing Research*, February 1985, pp. 41–53.

15 Nina Michaelidou and Sally Dibb, "Product Involvement: An Application in Clothing," *Journal of Consumer Behaviour* 5, no. 5, 2006, pp. 442–453.

16 Jennifer Aaker, Susan Fournier, and S. Adam Brasel, "When Good Brands Do Bad," *Journal of Consumer Research*, June 2004, pp. 1–16; and Matthew Thomson, Deborah J. MacInnis, and C. W. Park, "The Ties that Bind: Measuring the Strength of Consumers' Emotional Attachments to Brands," *Journal of Consumer Psychology* 15, no. 1, 2005, pp. 77–91.

17 Rajeev Batra, Aaron Ahuvia, and Richard P. Bagozzi, "Brand Love," *Journal of Marketing* 76, no. 2, March 2012, pp. 1–16.

18 J. Craig Andrews, Syed H. Akhter, Srinivas Durvasula, and Darrel D. Muehling, "The Effect of Advertising Distinctiveness and Message Content Involvement on Cognitive and Affective Responses to Advertising," *Journal of Current Issues and Research in Advertising*, Spring 1992, pp. 45–58; Laura M. Bucholz and Robert E. Smith, "The Role of Consumer Involvement in Determining Cognitive Response to Broadcast Advertising," *Journal of Advertising*, March 1991, pp. 4–17; Darrel D. Muehling, Russell N. Laczniak, and Jeffrey J. Stoltman, "The Moderating Effects of Ad Message Involvement: A Reassessment," *Journal of Advertising*, June 1991, pp. 29–38; and Scott B. MacKenzie and Richard J. Lutz, "An Empirical Examination of the Structural Antecedents of Attitude Toward the Ad in an Advertising Pretesting Context," *Journal of Marketing*, April 1989, pp. 48–65.

19 Barbara Mueller, "Standardization vs. Specialization: An Examination of Westernization in Japanese Advertising," *Journal of Advertising Research*, January–February 1992, pp. 15–24.

20 Ann E. Schlosser, "Computers as Situational Cues: Implications for Consumers Product Cognitions and Attitudes," *Journal of Consumer Psychology* 13, nos. 1 and 2, 2003, pp. 103–112; and Charla Mathwick and Edward Rigdon, "Play, Flow, and the Online Search Experience," *Journal of Consumer Research* 31, no. 2, 2004, pp. 324–332.

21 Houston and Rothschild, "Conceptual and Methodological Perspectives in Involvement"; Peter H. Bloch, Daniel Sherrell, and Nancy Ridgway, "Consumer Search: An Extended Framework," *Journal of Consumer Research*, June 1986, pp. 119–126; Peter H. Bloch, Nancy M. Ridgway, and Scott A. Dawson, "The Shopping Mall as Consumer Habitat," *Journal of Retailing*, Spring 1994, pp. 23–42; Richard L. Celsi, Randall L. Rose, and Thomas W. Leigh, "An Exploration of High-Risk Leisure Consumption Through Skydiving," *Journal of Consumer Research*, June 1993, pp. 1–23; Eric J. Arnould and Linda L. Price, "River Magic: Extraordinary Experience and the Extended Service Encounter," *Journal of Consumer Research*, June 1993, pp. 24–45; Morris B. Holbrook and Elizabeth C. Hirschman, "The Experiential Aspects of Consumption," *Journal of Consumer Research*, September 1982, pp. 132–140; Elizabeth C. Hirschman and Morris B. Holbrook, "Experience Seeking," *Journal of Marketing*, Summer 1982, pp. 92–101; and Morris B. Holbrook, Robert W. Chestnut, Terence A. Oliva, and Eric A. Greenleaf, "Play as a Consumption Experience," *Journal of Consumer Research*, September 1984, pp. 728–739.

22 Yinlong Zhang and Vikas Mittal, "Decision Difficulty: Effects of Procedural and Outcome Accountability," *Journal of Consumer Research* 32, no. 3, 2005, pp. 465–472.

23 Celsi and Olson, "The Role of Involvement in Attention and Comprehension Processes"; Greenwald and Leavitt, "Audience Involvement in Advertising"; Laurent and Kapferer, "Measuring Consumer Involvement Profiles"; Zaichkowsky, "Measuring the Involvement Construct"; Michael L.

Rothschild, "Perspectives on Involvement: Current Problems and Future Directions," in ed. Tom Kinnear, *Advances in Consumer Research*, vol. 11 (Ann Arbor, Mich.: Association for Consumer Research, 1984), pp. 216–217; Andrew A. Mitchell, "Involvement: A Potentially Important Mediator of Consumer Behavior," in ed. William L. Wilkie, *Advances in Consumer Research*, vol. 6 (Ann Arbor, Mich.: Association for Consumer Research, 1979), pp. 191–196; and Petty and Cacioppo, *Communication and Persuasion*.

24 Banwari Mittal, "I, Me, and Mine: How Products Become Consumers' Extended Selves," *Journal of Consumer Behaviour* 5, no. 6, 2006, pp. 550–562. For more background, see M. Joseph Sirgy, "Self-Concept in Consumer Behavior: A Critical Review," *Journal of Consumer Research*, December 1982, pp. 287–300.

25 Americus Reed II, "Activating the Self-Importance of Consumer Selves," *Journal of Consumer Research* 31, no. 2, 2004, pp. 286–295.

26 JoAndrea Hoegg, Maura L. Scott, Andrea C. Morales, and Darren W. Dahl, "The Flip Side of Vanity Sizing: How Consumers Respond to and Compensate for Larger than Expected Clothing Sizes," *Journal of Consumer Psychology* 24, no. 1, January 2014, pp. 70–78.

27 Christian Homburg, Jan Wieseke, and Wayne D. Hoyer, "Social Identity and the Service-Profit Chain," *Journal of Marketing*, March 2009, pp. 38–54; and David Sprott, Sandor Czellar, and Eric Spangenberg, "The Importance of a General Measure of Brand Engagement and Validation of a Scale," *Journal of Marketing Research*, February 2009, pp. 92–104.

28 Rajeev Batra, Aaron Ahuvia, and Richard P. Bagozzi, "Brand Love," *Journal of Marketing* 76, no. 2, March 2012, pp. 1–16.

29 Randall L. Rose and Stacy L. Wood, "Paradox and the Consumption of Authenticity Through Reality Television," *Journal of Consumer Research* 32, no. 2, 2005, pp. 284–296.

30 Amy N. Dalton and Li Huang, "Motivated Forgetting in Response to Social Identity Threat," *Journal of Consumer Research* 40, no. 6, April 2014, pp. 1017–1038.

31 C. Miguel Brendl, Arthur B. Markman, and Claude Messner, "The Devaluation Effect: Activating a Need Devalues Unrelated Objects," *Journal of Consumer Research*, March 2003, pp. 463–473.

32 Abraham H. Maslow, *Motivation and Personality*, 2nd ed. (New York: Harper & Row, 1970).

33 C. Whan Park, Bernard J. Jaworski, and Deborah J. MacInnis, "Strategic Brand Concept–Image Management," *Journal of Marketing*, October 1986, pp. 135–145.

34 Nicole L. Mead, Roy F. Baumeister, Tyler F. Stillman, Catherine D. Rawn, and Kathleen D. Vohs, "Social Exclusion Causes People to Spend and Consume Strategically in the Service of Affiliation," *Journal of Consumer Research*, February 2011, pp. 902–919.

35 Judy Harris and Michael Lynn, "The Manifestations and Measurement of the Desire to Be a Unique Consumer," Proceedings of the 1994 AMA Winter Educators' Conference, Chicago; Kelly Tepper, "Need for Uniqueness: An Individual Difference Factor Affecting Nonconformity in Consumer Responses," Proceedings of the 1994 AMA Winter Educators' Conference, Chicago; and Kelly Tepper Tian, William O. Bearden, and Gary L. Hunter, "Consumers' Need For Uniqueness: Scale Development and Validation," *Journal of Consumer Research* 28, June 2001, pp. 50–66.

36 "7 Easy Ways to Identify a Genuine Christian Louboutin Shoe," *Las Vegas Review-Journal*, August 17, 2015, www.review-journal.com.

37 Bram Van den Bergh, "Bikinis Instigate Generalized Impatience in Intertemporal Choice," *Journal of Consumer Research*, June 2008, pp. 85–97.

38 Russell W. Belk, Güliz Ger, and Soren Askegaard, "The Fire of Desire: A Multisited Inquiry into Consumer Passion," *Journal of Consumer Research*, December 2003, pp. 326–351.

39 Priyanka Ghosh, "High-Occupancy Malls Draw Steep Rental Premiums," *Financial Express (India)*, September 7, 2015, www.financialexpress.com.

40 John T. Cacioppo and Richard E. Petty, "The Need for Cognition," *Journal of Personality and Social Psychology*, February 1982, pp. 116–131; Douglas M. Stayman and Frank R. Kardes, "Spontaneous Inference Processes in Advertising: Effects of Need for Cognition and Self-Monitoring on Inference Generation and Utilization," *Journal of Consumer Psychology* 1, no. 2, 1992, pp. 125–142; and John T. Cacioppo, Richard Petty, and Katherine Morris, "Effects of Need for Cognition on Message Evaluation, Recall, and Persuasion," *Journal of Personality and Social Psychology*, October 1993, pp. 805–818.

41 P. S. Raju, "Optimum Stimulation Level," *Journal of Consumer Research*, December 1980, pp. 272–282; and Jan-Benedict E. M. Steenkamp and Hans Baumgartner, "The Role of Optimum Stimulation Level in Exploratory Consumer Behavior," *Journal of Consumer Research*, December 1992, pp. 434–448.

42 Cindy Chan, Jonah Berger, and Leaf Van Boven, "Identifiable But Not Identical: Combining Social Identity and Uniqueness Motives in Choice," *Journal of Consumer Research* 39, no. 3, October 2012, pp. 561–573.

43 Jonah Berger and Baba Shiv, "Food, Sex, and the Hunger for Distinction," *Journal of Consumer Psychology* 21, no. 4, Special Issue, October 2011, pp. 464–472.

44 Stuart Elliott, "Study Tries to Help Retailers Understand What Drives the Shopping Habits of Women," *New York Times*, January 17, 2001, p. C6.

45 Robert Roth, *International Marketing Communications* (Chicago: Crain Books, 1982), p. 5.

46 H. Murray, *Thematic Apperception Test Manual* (Cambridge, Mass.: Harvard University Press, 1943); Harold Kassarjian, "Projective Methods," in ed. Robert Ferber, *Handbook of Marketing Research* (New York: McGraw-Hill, 1974), pp. 85–100; Ernest Dichter, *Packaging the Sixth Sense: A Guide to Identifying Consumer Motivation* (Boston: Cahners Books, 1975); Dennis Rook, "Researching Consumer Fantasy," in ed. Elizabeth C. Hirschman, *Research in Consumer Behavior*, vol. 3 (Greenwich, Conn.: JAI Press, 1990), pp. 247–270; David Mick, M. De Moss, and Ronald Faber, "A Projective Study of Motivations and Meanings of Self-Gifts," *Journal of Retailing*, Summer 1992, pp. 122–144; and Mary Ann McGrath, John F. Sherry, and Sidney J. Levy, "Giving Voice to the Gift: The Use of Projective Techniques to Recover Lost Meanings," *Journal of Consumer Psychology* 2, no. 2, 1993, pp. 171–191.

47 Rebecca Ratner, "Consumer Goal Pursuit," *Journal of Consumer Research* 40, no. 2, August 2013, pp. vi–viii; Sharon Shavitt, Suzanne Swan, Tina M. Lowrey, and Michaela Wanke, "The Interaction of Endorser Attractiveness and Involvement in Persuasion Depends on the Goal That Guides Message Processing," *Journal of Consumer Psychology* 3, no. 2, 1994, pp. 137–162; Robert Lawson, "Consumer Decision Making Within a Goal-Driven Framework," *Psychology and Marketing*, August 1997, pp. 427–449; and Ingrid W. Martin and David W. Stewart, "The Differential Impact of Goal Congruency on Attitudes, Intentions, and the Transfer of Brand Equity," *Journal of Marketing Research*, November 2001, pp. 471–484.

48 Richard P. Bagozzi and Utpal Dholakia, "Goal Setting and Goal Striving in Consumer Behavior," *Journal of Marketing* 63, 1999, pp. 19–32.

49 Catalina E. Kopetz, Aire W. Kruglanski, Zachary G. Arens, Jordan Etkin, and Heather M. Johnson, "The Dynamics of Consumer Behavior: A Goal Systemic Perspective," *Journal of Consumer Psychology* 22, no. 2, April 2012, pp. 208–223.

50 Berna Devezer, David E. Sprott, Eric R. Spangenberg, and Sandor Czellar, "Consumer Well-Being: Effects of Subgoal Failures and Goal Importance," *Journal of Marketing* 78, no. 2, March 2014, pp. 118–134.

51 Mario Louro, Rik Pieters, and Marcel Zeelenberg, "Dynamics of Multiple Goal Pursuit," *Journal of Personality and Social Psychology* 93, no. 2, 2007, pp. 174–193.

52 Liyin Jin, Szu-Chi Huang, and Ying Zhang, "The Unexpected Positive Impact of Fixed Structures on Goal Completion," *Journal of Consumer Research* 40, no. 4, December 2013, pp. 711–725.

53 Claudia Townsend and Wendy Liu, "Is Planning Good for You? The Differential Impact of Planning on Self-Regulation," *Journal of Consumer Research* 39, no. 4, December 2012, pp. 688–703.

54 Amy N. Dalton and Stephen A. Spiller, "Too Much of a Good Thing: The Benefits of Implementation Intentions Depend on the Number of Goals," *Journal of Consumer Research* 39, no. 3, October 2012, pp. 600–614.

55 Manoj Thomas and Claire I. Tsai, "Psychological Distance and Subjective Experience: How Distancing Reduces the Feeling of Difficulty," *Journal of Consumer Research* 39, no. 2, August 2012, pp. 324–340.

56 Ji Hoon Jhang and John G. Lynch Jr., "Pardon the Interruption: Goal Proximity, Perceived Spare Time, and Impatience," *Journal of Consumer Research* 41, 2015, pp. 1267–1283.

57 Szu-Chi Huang and Ying Zhang, "Motivational Consequences of Perceived Velocity in Consumer Goal Pursuit," *Journal of Marketing Research* 48, no. 6, December 2011, pp. 1045–1056.

58 Maura L. Scott and Stephen M. Nowlis, "The Effect of Goal Specificity on Consumer Goal Reengagement," *Journal of Consumer Research* 40, no. 3, October 2013, pp. 444–459.

59 Minjung Koo and Ayelet Fishbach, "The Small-Area Hypothesis: Effects of Progress Monitoring on Goal Adherence," *Journal of Consumer Research* 39, no. 3, October 2012, pp. 493–509.

60 Jordan Etkin and Rebecca K. Ratner, "The Dynamic Impact of Variety among Means on Motivation," *Journal of Consumer Research* 38, no. 6, April 2012, pp. 1076–1092.

61 Cecile K. Cho and Gita Venkataramani Johar, "Attaining Satisfaction," *Journal of Consumer Research* 38, no. 4, December 2011, pp. 622–631.

62 Dilip Soman and Amar Cheema, "When Goals Are Counterproductive," *Journal of Consumer Research*, June 2004, pp. 52–62.

63 Amar Cheema and Rajesh Bagchi, "The Effect of Goal Visualization on Goal Pursuit," *Journal of Marketing*, March 2011, pp. 109–123.

64 Ayelet Fishbach and Ravi Dhar, "Goals as Excuses or Guides: The Liberating Effect of Perceived Goal Progress on Choice," *Journal of Consumer Research* 32, no. 3, 2005, pp. 370–377.

65 Joseph C. Nunes and Xavier Drèze, "The Endowed Progress Effect: How Artificial Advancement Increases Effort," *Journal of Consumer Research* 32, no. 4, 2006, pp. 504–512.

66 Xavier Drèze and Joseph C. Nunes, "Recurring Goals and Learning," *Journal of Marketing Research*, April 2011, pp. 268–281.

67 Ying Zhang, Ayelet Fishbach, and Ravi Dhar, "When Thinking Beats Doing: The Role of Optimistic Expectations in Goal-Based Choice," *Journal of Consumer Research*, February 2008.

68 Richard P. Bagozzi and Utpal Dholakia, "Goal Setting and Goal Striving in Consumer Behavior," *Journal of Marketing* 63, 1999, pp. 19–32.

69 K. Lee, J. Choi, and Y.J. Li, "Regulatory Focus as a Predictor of Attitudes Toward Partitioned and Combined Pricing," *Journal of Consumer Psychology* 24, no. 3, July 2014, pp. 355–362; and Arnd Florack, Malte Friese, and Martin Scarabis, "Regulatory Focus and Reliance on Implicit Preferences in Consumption Contexts," *Journal of Consumer Psychology* 20, no. 2, April 2010, pp. 193–204.

70 Shailendra Pratap Jain, Pragya Mathur, and Durairaj Maheswaran, "The Influence of Consumers' Lay Theories on Approach/Avoidance Motivation," *Journal of Marketing Research*, February 2009, pp. 56–65.

71 Rui (Juliet) Zhu and Joan Meyers-Levy, "Exploring the Cognitive Mechanism that Underlies Regulator y Focus Effects," *Journal of Consumer Research* 34, no. 1, 2007, pp. 89–98; Jing Wang and Angela Y. Lee, " The Role of Regulator y Focus in Preference Construction," *Journal of Marketing Research*, February 2006, pp. 28–38; Utpal M. Dholakia, Mahesh Gopinath, Richard P. Bagozzi, and Rajan Nataraajan, "The Role of Regulatory Focus in the Experience and Self-Control of Desire for Temptations," *Journal of Consumer Psychology* 16, no. 2, 2006, pp. 163–175; and Jens Förster, E. Tory Higgins, and Lorraine Chen Idson, "Approach and Avoidance Strength During Goal Attainment," *Journal of Personality and Social Psychology*, November 1998, pp. 1115–1131.

72 Jinhee Choi and Ayelet Fishbach, "Choice as an End Versus a Means," *Journal of Marketing Research*, June 2011, pp. 544–554.

73 David Gal, "A Mouth-Watering Prospect: Salivation to Material Reward," *Journal of Consumer Research* 38, no. 6, April 2012, pp. 1022–1029.

74 See, for example, B. McFerran, K. Aquino, and J. L. Tracy, "Evidence for Two Facets of Pride in Consumption: Findings from Luxury Brands," *Journal of Consumer Psychology* 24, no. 4, October 2014, pp. 455–471; and Xun (Irene) Huang, Ping Dong, and Anirban Mukhopadhyay, "Proud to Belong or Proudly Different? Lay Theories Determining Contrasting Effects of Incidental Pride on Uniqueness Seeking," *Journal of Consumer Research* 41, no. 3, October 2014, pp. 697–712.

75 Allison R. Johnson and David W. Stewart, "A Reappraisal of the Role of Emotion in Consumer Behavior," in ed. Naresh K. Malhotra, *Review of Marketing Research*, (London: M.E. Sharpe, 2005), pp. 3–34.

76 Thomas Allard and Katherine White, "Cross-Domain Effects of Guilt on Desire for Self-Improvement Products," *Journal of Consumer Research* 42, October 2015, pp. 401–419.

77 J. S. Lerner, Y. Li, and E. U. Weber, "The Financial Costs of Sadness," *Psychological Science* 24, no. 1, January 2013, pp. 72–79.

78 Rod Duclos, Echo Wen Wan, and Yuwei Jiang, "Show Me the Honey! Effects of Social Exclusion on Financial Risk-Taking," *Journal of Consumer Research* 40, no. 1, June 2013, pp. 122–135.

79 Sara Loughran Dommer, Vanitha Swaminathan, and Rohini Ahluwalia, "Using Differentiated Brands to Deflect Exclusion and Protect Inclusion: The Moderating Role of Self-Esteem on Attachment to Differentiated Brands," *Journal of Consumer Research* 40, no. 4, December 2013, pp. 657–675.

80 Niels van de Ven, Marcel Zeelenberg, and Rik Pieters, "The Envy Premium in Product Evaluation," *Journal of Consumer Research*, April 2011, pp. 984–998.

81 Morgan Poor, Adam Duhachek, and Shanker Krishnan, "The Moderating Role of Emotional Differentiation on Satiation," *Journal of Consumer Psychology* 22, no. 4, October 2012, pp. 507–519.

82 Seunghee Han, Jennifer S. Lerner, and Dacher Keltner, "Feelings and Consumer Decision Making: The Appraisal-Tendency Framework," *Journal of Consumer Psychology* 17, no. 3, 2007, pp. 158–168.

83 Kathleen D. Vohs and Roy F. Baumeister, "Understanding Self-Regulation: An Introduction," in eds. Roy F. Baumeister and Kathleen D. Vohs, *Handbook of Self-Regulation: Research, Theory, and Applications* (New York: Guilford Press, 2004), pp. 1–9.

84 Murat Usta and Gerald Häubl, "Self-Regulatory Strength and Consumers' Relinquishment of Decision Control: When Less Effortful Decisions Are More Resource Depleting," *Journal of Marketing Research* 48, no. 2, April 2011, pp. 403–412.

85 Siegried Dewitte, Sabrina Bruyneel, and Kelly Geyskens, "Self-Regulating Enhances Self-Regulation in Subsequent Consumer Decisions Involving Similar Response Conflicts," *Journal of Consumer Research*, October 2009, pp. 394–405.

86 Uzma Khan and Ravi Dhar, "Where There Is a Way, Is There a Will?" *Journal of Experimental Psychology* 136, 2007, pp. 277–288.

87 Alexander Chernev and David Gal, "Categorization Effects in Value Judgments," *Journal of Marketing Research*, August 2010, pp. 738–747.

88 Remi Trudel and Kyle B. Murray, "Self-Regulatory Strength Amplification through Selective Information Processing," *Journal of Consumer Psychology* 23, no. 1, January 2013, pp. 61–73.

89 Frank May and Caglar Irmak, "Licensing Indulgence in the Present by Distorting Memories of Past Behavior," *Journal of Consumer Research* 41, no. 3, October 2014, pp. 624–641.

90 Kurt A. Carlson, Margaret G. Meloy, and Elizabeth G. Miller, "Goal Reversion in Consumer Choice," *Journal of Consumer Research* 39, no. 5, March 2013, pp. 918–930.

91 For more about strategies for reducing desire and increasing willpower, see Stephen J. Hoch and George F. Loewenstein, "Time-Inconsistent Preferences and Consumer Self-Control," *Journal of Consumer Research*, March 1991, pp. 492–507.

92 Iris W. Hung and Aparna A. Labroo, "From Firm Muscles to Firm Willpower: Understanding the Role of Embodied Cognition in Self-Regulation," *Journal of Consumer Research*, April 2011, pp. 1046–1064.

93 Vanessa M. Patrick and Henrik Hagtvedt, "'I Don't' versus 'I Can't': When Empowered Refusal Motivates Goal-Directed Behavior," *Journal of Consumer Research* 39, no. 2, August 2012, pp. 371–381.

94 Danit Ein-Gar and Yael Steinhart, "The 'Sprinter Effect': When Self-Control and Involvement Stand in the Way of Sequential Performance," *Journal of Consumer Psychology* 21, no. 3, July 2011, pp. 240–255.

95 Rita Coelho do Vale, Rik Pieters, and Marcel Zeelenberg, "Flying under the Radar: Perverse Package Size Effects on Consumption Self-Regulation," *Journal of Consumer Research* 35, no. 3, 2008, pp. 380–390.

96 Hoch and Loewenstein, "Time-Inconsistent Preferences and Consumer Self-Control," *Journal of Consumer Research*, March 1991, pp. 492–507.

97 Priya Raghubir and Joydeep Srivastava, "The Denomination Effect," *Journal of Consumer Research*, December 2009, pp. 701–713.

98 See Eduardo B. Andrade, "Behavioral Consequences of Affect: Combining Evaluative and Regulatory Mechanisms," *Journal of Consumer Research* 32, no. 2, 2005, pp. 355–362; and S. I. Rick, B. Pereira, and K. A. Burson, "The Benefits of Retail Therapy: Making Purchase Decisions Reduces Residual Sadness," *Journal of Consumer Psychology* 24, no. 3, July 2014, pp. 373–380.

99 Nitika Garg and Jennifer S. Lerner, "Sadness and Consumption," *Journal of Consumer Psychology* 23, no. 1, January 2013, pp. 106–113.

100 Anthony Salerno, Juliano Laran, and Chris Janiszewski, "Hedonic Eating Goals and Emotion: When Sadness Decreases the Desire to Indulge," *Journal of Consumer Research* 41, no. 1, June 2014, pp. 135–151.

101 Nathan Novemsky and Ravi Dhar, "Goal Fulfillment and Goal Targets in Sequential Choice," *Journal of Consumer Research* 32, no. 3, 2005, pp. 396–404.

102 Remi Trudel and Kyle B. Murray, "Why Didn't I Think of That?" *Journal of Marketing Research*, August 2011, pp. 701–712.

103 David Gal and Wendy Liu, "Grapes of Wrath: The Angry Effects of Self-Control," *Journal of Consumer Research*, October 2011, p. 445ff.

104 See, for example, Massimiliano Ostinelli, David Luna, and Torsten Ringberg, "When Up Brings You Down: The Effects of Imagined Vertical Movements on Motivation, Performance, and Consumer Behavior," *Journal of Consumer Psychology* 24, no. 2, Special Issue, April 2014, pp. 271–283.

105 Mike Hornick, "Earthbound Farm Brings Kale Caesar to Bowl Line," *The Packer*, July 21, 2015, www.thepacker.com.

106 Jennifer Edson Escalas, "Narrative Processing: Building Consumer Connections to Brands," *Journal of Consumer Psychology* 14, no. 1/2, 2004, pp. 168–180.

107 Nidhi Agrawal and Durairaj Maheswaran, "The Effects of Self-Construal and Commitment on Persuasion," *Journal of Consumer Research* 31, no. 4, 2005, pp. 841–849; and S. Christian Wheeler, Richard E. Petty, and George Y. Bizer, "Self-Schema Matching and Attitude Change: Situational and Dispositional Determinants of Message Elaboration," *Journal of Consumer Research* 31, no. 4, 2005, pp. 787–797.

108 Elise Hu, "How Millennials Are Reshaping Charity and Online Giving," *National Public Radio,* October 13, 2014, www.npr.org; and Gina Pace, "Creating Marketing Campaigns That Matter," *Inc.*, May 16, 2011, www.inc.com.

109 Ravi Dhar and Itamar Simonson, "Making Complementary Choices in Consumption Episodes," *Journal of Marketing Research* 36, February 1999, pp. 29–44.

110 Jason Daley, "Why Fresh Fruits and Veggies Mean Healthy Profits for Fast Food," *Entrepreneur,* October 16, 2015, www.entrepreneur.com.

111 Constance Gustke, "More Older Adults Are Becoming Inventors," *New York Times*, April 17, 2015, www.nytimes.com.

112 Wayne D. Hoyer, Rajesh Chandy, Matilda Dorotic, Manfred Krafft, and Siddharth S. Singh, "Consumer Cocreation in New Product Development," *Journal of Service Research* 13, no. 3, 2010, pp. 283–296.

113 Alexander Chernev, "Goal Orientation and Consumer Preference for the Status Quo," *Journal of Consumer Research* 31, no. 3, 2004, pp. 557–565.

114 Emily Jed, "One-Of-A-Kind TCBY Frozen Yogurt Vending Machine Makes One-Show Debut," *Vending Times*, May 2015, www.vendingtimes.com; and Jaime Levy Pessin, "Yogurt Chains Give Power to the People," *Wall Street Journal*, August 22, 2011, www.wsj.com.

115 Raymond A. Bauer, "Consumer Behavior as Risk Taking," in ed. Robert S. Hancock, *Dynamic Marketing for a Changing*

World (Chicago: American Marketing Association, 1960), pp. 389–398; Grahame R. Dowling, "Perceived Risk: The Concept and Its Measurement," *Psychology and Marketing*, Fall 1986, pp. 193–210; and Lawrence X. Tarpey and J. Paul Peter, "A Comparative Analysis of Three Consumer Decision Strategies," *Journal of Consumer Research*, June 1975, pp. 29–37.

116 James R. Bettman, "Perceived Risk and Its Components," *Journal of Marketing Research*, May 1973, pp. 184–190.

117 Vincent W. Mitchell and Michael Greatorex, "Consumer Purchasing in Foreign Countries," *International Journal of Advertising* 9, no. 4, 1990, pp. 295–307.

118 "Marketing Briefs," *Marketing News*, March 1995, p. 11.

119 Jacob Jacoby and Leon Kaplan, "The Components of Perceived Risk," in ed. M. Venkatesan, *Advances in Consumer Research* vol. 3 (Chicago: Association for Consumer Research, 1972), pp. 382–383; and Tarpey and Peter, "A Comparative Analysis of Three Consumer Decision Strategies," *Journal of Consumer Research*, June 1975, pp. 184–190.

120 Melissa Burden, "AutoTrader: Certified Pre-Owned Car Sales to Grow," *Detroit News*, November 6, 2014, www.detroitnews.com.

121 Vanitha Swaminathan, "The Impact of Recommendation Agents on Consumer Evaluation and Choice," *Journal of Consumer Psychology* 13, no. 1 and 2, 2003, pp. 93–102.

122 Michael Tsiros and Carrie M. Heilman, "The Effect of Expiration Dates and Perceived Risk on Purchasing Behavior in Grocery Store Perishable Categories," *Journal of Marketing*, April 2005, pp. 114–129.

123 Cornelia Pechmann, Guangzhi Zhao, Marvin E. Goldberg, and Ellen Thomas Reibling, "What to Convey in Antismoking Advertisements for Adolescents," *Journal of Marketing*, April 2003, pp. 1–18.

124 Craig J. Thompson, "Consumer Risk Perceptions in a Community of Reflexive Doubt," *Journal of Consumer Research* 32, no. 2, 2005, pp. 235–248.

125 "Darn Tough Is Getting Darn Big," *The Barre Montpelier Times-Argus (VT)*, March 23, 2015, www.timesargus.com.

126 "Scottish Government Reveals Results of Social Marketing Campaigns," *The Drum*, August 18, 2011, www.thedrum.co.uk; and "Scots Gov Launches Alcohol Awareness Social Media Campaign," *The Drum*, January 13, 2011, www.thedrum.co.uk.

127 Kate Mead, "Here Comes the Sun," *Sunday Star Times (New Zealand)*, November 6, 2011, www.stuff.co.nz.

128 Priya Raghubir and Geeta Menon, "AIDS and Me, Never the Twain Shall Meet: The Effects of Information Accessibility on Judgments of Risk and Advertising Effectiveness," *Journal of Consumer Research*, June 1998, pp. 52–63.

129 Shailendra Pratap Jain and Durairaj Maheswaran, "Motivated Reasoning: A Depth-of-Processing Perspective," *Journal of Consumer Research* 26, March 2000, pp. 358–371; and Joan Meyers-Levy and Alice Tybout, "Schema-Congruity as a Basis for Product Evaluation," *Journal of Consumer Research*, June 1989, pp. 39–54.

130 Deborah J. MacInnis and Bernard J. Jaworski, "Information Processing from Advertisements: Toward an Integrative Framework," *Journal of Marketing* 53, October 1989, pp. 1–23.

131 Joseph W. Alba and J. Wesley Hutchinson, "Dimensions of Consumer Expertise," *Journal of Consumer Research*, March 1987, pp. 411–454. For an excellent overview of measures of consumer knowledge or expertise, see Andrew A. Mitchell and Peter A. Dacin, "The Assessment of Alternative Measures of Consumer Expertise," *Journal of Consumer Research*, December 1996, pp. 219–239.

132 Eric J. Johnson and J. Edward Russo, "Product Familiarity and Learning New Information," *Journal of Consumer Research*, June 1984, pp. 542–550; Merrie Brucks, "The Effects of Product Class Knowledge on Information Search Behavior," *Journal of Consumer Research*, June 1985, pp. 1–16; and Alba and Hutchinson, "Dimensions of Consumer Expertise," *Journal of Consumer Research*, March 1987, pp. 411–454.

133 Annamaria Lusardi, Olivia S. Mitchell, and Vilsa Curto, "Financial Literacy Among the Young," *The Journal of Consumer Affairs* 44, no. 2, 2010, pp. 358–380.

134 Jessica Y. Y. Kwong, Dilip Soman, and Candy K. Y. Ho, "The Role of Computational Ease on the Decision to Spend Loyalty Program Points," *Journal of Consumer Psychology* 21, no. 2, April 2011, pp. 146–156.

135 Durairaj Maheswaran and Brian Sternthal, "The Effects of Knowledge, Motivation, and Type of Message on Ad Processing and Product Judgments," *Journal of Consumer Research*, June 1990, pp. 66–73.

136 Jennifer Gregan-Paxton and Deborah Roedder John, "Consumer Learning by Analogy," *Journal of Consumer Research*, December 1997, pp. 266–284.

137 Michelle L. Roehm and Brian Sternthal, "The Moderating Effect of Knowledge and Resources on the Persuasive Impact of Analogies," *Journal of Consumer Research*, September 2001, p. 257.

138 Michael K. Hui, Xiande Zhao, Xiucheng Fan, and Kevin Au, "When Does the Service Process Matter? A Test of Two Competing Theories," *Journal of Consumer Research* 31, no. 2, 2004, pp. 465–475.

139 Liz Szabo, "Pink Ribbon Marketing Brings Mixed Emotions, Poll Finds," *USA Today*, October 7, 2011, www.usatoday.com.

140 Ryan Wells, "Social and Cultural Capital, Race and Ethnicity, and College Student Retention," *Journal of College Student Retention* 10, no. 2, 2008–9, pp. 103–128.

141 Jessica Derschowitz, "PewDiePie tops Forbes' List of Highest-Paid YouTube Stars," *Entertainment Weekly*, October 17, 2015, www.ew.com.

142 Douglas Holt, "Distinction in America? Recovering Bourdieu's Theory of Taste from Its Critics," *Poetics* 25, 1997, pp. 93–120.

143 Jennifer Gregan-Paxton and Deborah Roedder John, "Are Young Children Adaptive Decision Makers? A Study of Age Differences in Information Search Behavior," *Journal of Consumer Research*, March 1995, pp. 567–580.

144 Catherine A. Cole and Gary J. Gaeth, "Cognitive and Age-Related Differences in the Ability to Use Nutrition Information in a Complex Environment," *Journal of Marketing Research*, May 1990, pp. 175–184.

145 John Pavlus, "How Ikea Designs Its (In)famous Instruction Manuals," *Fast Company Design*, October 28, 2015, www.fastcompany.com; and Lisa Boone, "IKEA Launches Share Space for Customers' Project Photos," *Los Angeles Times*, August 18, 2011, www.latimes.com.

146 Cynthia Crossen, "'Merry Christmas to Moi' Shoppers Say," *Wall Street Journal*, December 11, 1997, pp. B1, B14.

147 June Fletcher and Sarah Collins, "The Lazy Gardener," *Wall Street Journal*, June 6, 2001, pp. W1, W16.

148 Rajneesh Suri and Kent B. Monroe, "The Effects of Time Constraints on Consumers' Judgments of Prices and Products," *Journal of Consumer Research*, June 2003, pp. 92–104; and Peter Wright, "The Time Harassed Consumer: Time Pressures, Distraction, and the Use of Evidence," *Journal of Applied Psychology*, October 1974, pp. 555–561.

149 C. Page Moreau and Darren W. Dahl, "Designing the Solution: The Impact of Constraints on Consumers' Creativity," *Journal of Consumer Research* 32, no. 1, 2005, pp. 13–22.

150 Park and Young, "Consumer Response to Television Commercials"; Deborah J. MacInnis and C. Whan Park, "The Differential Role of Characteristics of Music on High and Low-Involvement Consumers' Processing of Ads," *Journal of Consumer Research*, September 1991, pp. 161–173; and Shelly Chaiken and Alice Eagly, "Communication Modality as a Determinant of Persuasion: The Role of Communicator Salience," *Journal of Personality and Social Psychology*, August 1983, pp. 605–614.

151 Kenneth Lord and Robert Burnkrant, "Attention Versus Distraction: The Interactive Effect of Program Involvement and Attentional Devices on Commercial Processing," *Journal of Advertising*, March 1993, pp. 47–61; Kenneth R. Lord and Robert E. Burnkrant, "Television Program Effects on Commercial Processing," in ed. Michael J. Houston, *Advances in Consumer Research*, vol. 15 (Provo, Utah: Association for Consumer Research, 1988), pp. 213–218; and Gary Soldow and Victor Principe, "Response to Commercials as a Function of Program Context," *Journal of Advertising Research*, February–March 1981, pp. 59–65.

152 Baba Shiv and Stephen M. Nowlis, "The Effect of Distractions While Tasting a Food Sample: The Interplay of Informational and Affective Components in Subsequent Choice," *Journal of Consumer Research*, December 2004, pp. 599–608.

153 Richard Yalch and Rebecca Elmore-Yalch, "The Effect of Numbers on the Route to Persuasion," *Journal of Consumer Research*, June 1984, pp. 522–527.

154 Noel Capon and Roger Davis, "Basic Cognitive Ability Measures as Predictors of Consumer Information Processing Strategies, *Journal of Consumer Research*, June 1984, pp. 551–564.

155 Nicole H. Lurie and Charlotte H. Mason, "Visual Representation: Implications for Decision Making," *Journal of Marketing*, January 2007, pp. 160–177.

156 Yeosun Yoon, Gülen Sarial-Abi, and Zeynep Gü Rhan-Canli, "Effect of Regulatory Focus on Selective Information Processing," *Journal of Consumer Research* 39, no. 1, June 2012, pp. 93–110.

157 Hilary Milnes, "Digital DIY: How Home Depot and Lowe's Stack Up Online," *DigiDay*, June 3, 2015, www.digiday.com; and Adam Blair, "Lowe's Mounts Multi-Channel Battle Plan," *Retail Information Systems News*, August 23, 2011, http://ris-news.edgl.com.

158 Rajeev Batra and Michael L. Ray, "Situational Effects of Advertising Repetitions: The Moderating Influence of Motivation, Ability, and Opportunity to Respond," *Journal of Consumer Research*, March 1986, pp. 432–435; Carl Obermiller, "Varieties of Mere Exposure: The Effects of Processing Style and Repetition on Affective Response," *Journal of Consumer Research*, June 1985, pp. 17–30; Arno Rethans, John L. Swazy, and Lawrence J. Marks, "The Effects of Television Commercial Repetition, Receiver Knowledge, and Commercial Length: A Test of the Two-Factor Model," *Journal of Marketing Research*, February 1986, pp. 50–61; Sharmistha Law and Scott A. Hawkins, "Advertising Repetition and Consumer Beliefs: The Role of Source Memory," in ed. William Wells, *Measuring Advertising Effectiveness* (Mahwah, N.J.: Lawrence Erlbaum Associates, 1997), pp. 67–75; and Giles D'Sousa and Ram C. Rao, "Can Repeating an Advertisement More Frequently Than the Competition Affect Brand Preference in a Mature Market?" *Journal of Marketing* 59, no. 2, 1995, pp. 32–43.

159 Margaret C. Campbell and Kevin Lane Keller, "Brand Familiarity and Advertising Repetition Effects," *Journal of Consumer Research*, September 2003, pp. 292–304.

160 Dan Ariely, "Controlling the Information Flow: Effects on Consumers' Decision Making and Preferences," *Journal of Consumer Research* 27, September 2000, pp. 233–248.

161 Ibid.

162 Ken Elkins, "Lowe's Works to Bring Innovation into Space, Closer to Home," *Charlotte Business Journal*, October 29, 2015, www.bizjournals.com.

163 Sabrina Korber, "Retail's 'Beacon' of Hope: Shopping That's Personal," *CNBC*, May 26, 2015, www.cnbc.com; and Hilary Milnes, "In the Race to Digitize, Nordstrom and Macy's Are Neck-and-Neck," *DigiDay*, May 7, 2015, www.digiday.com.

CHAPTER 3

From Exposure to Comprehension

iStockphoto.com/Ostill

Don Arnold/Wireimage/Getty Images

INTRODUCTION

If consumers are to register any message after being exposed to an ad, an Instagram photo of a product, a package on the store shelf, or some other marketing element, they must pay attention to it, use their senses to determine its properties, and make sense of it (see Exhibit 3.1). When the Great Harvest Bake Company in Tempe, Arizona, offers customers a free slice of bread from a warm loaf just out of the oven, it's appealing to four senses: vision, smell, taste, and touch. The bakery plays classic rock music in the background, adding the sensory appeal of sound.[1] A variety of factors affect the four-step process of exposure, attention, perception, and comprehension, which also plays a role in and is influenced by knowledge stored in memory, as described in Chapter 4.

3-1 Exposure and Consumer Behavior

Before an ad, a tweet, a product sample, or a store display can affect consumers, they must be exposed to it. **Exposure** means coming into physical contact with a stimulus. **Marketing stimuli** contain information about products or brands and other offerings communicated by either the marketer (via ads, Facebook messages, Vine videos, salespeople, brand symbols, packages, prices, and so on) or by nonmarketing sources (e.g., news media, word-of-mouth, and consumer reviews of a product).

The best products and services fail to be successful if consumers are not aware of them, and exposure is a precondition to this. Consumers can be exposed to marketing stimuli at any stage of the decision-making process. To some extent, they can select what they will be exposed to and avoid other stimuli, as you know from your own experience. Because exposure is critical to influencing consumers' thoughts and feelings, marketers want consumers to be exposed to stimuli that portray their offerings in a favorable light or at a time when consumers may be interested in such products.

3-1a FACTORS INFLUENCING EXPOSURE

The *position of an ad within a medium* can affect exposure. Consumers' exposure to online ads is more likely when the ads appear high on the search list. Exposure to magazine ads is greatest when they appear on inside cover (next to the table of contents) or on the back cover because the ads are in view whenever the magazine is placed face down. Also, consumers are most likely to be exposed to ads placed next to articles or within TV programs that interest them.[2] Exposure to commercials is higher when they air at the beginning or end of a commercial break within a program, because consumers are still involved in the program or are waiting for the program to resume. Some advertisers sponsor commercial-free TV programs in which the company gets *product placement* within the show or airs a single ad before or after the show. Also, advertisers are placing product images and videos in Facebook news feeds, on Pinterest boards, as pre-roll ads to YouTube videos, and on Twitter, where social-media users will be exposed to them (and, in the case of Pinterest, consumers can click to buy).[3]

Moreover, *product distribution and shelf placement* affect consumers' exposure to brands and packages. The more stores carry the product or brand, the higher the likelihood that consumers will encounter it. Likewise, the product's location (eye-level) or the amount of shelf space allocated to it can increase exposure to a product. Sales of some products increase because of their higher exposure in displays at checkout counters in supermarkets, automotive stores, and restaurants. With growing interest in mobile checkout, which reduces or eliminates the time customers must wait to pay for purchases, traditional distribution and shelf position strategies are being reevaluated with an eye toward targeted exposure.[4]

3-1b SELECTIVE EXPOSURE

While marketers can work hard to affect consumers' exposure to certain products and brands, ultimately consumers control their exposure to marketing stimuli. In other words, consumers can and do actively seek out certain stimuli and avoid or resist others. One reason consumers want to avoid ads is that they are exposed to so many that they cannot possibly process them all. Consumers avoid ads for product categories they do not use (indicating that the ads are irrelevant to them); they also tend to avoid or mentally block out ads they have seen before because they know what these ads will say. When consumers avoid stimuli they find distracting—such as online ads located near content they want to focus on—they are likely to form negative attitudes toward those brands.[5]

Consumers' avoidance of marketing stimuli is a major challenge for marketers. During an ad airing on cable or broadcast TV, consumers can mentally block it out, do something else, leave the room, or avoid it by zipping and zapping (see Exhibit 3.2). With **zipping**, consumers record TV shows with a DVR (digital video recorder) and fast-forward through the commercials when viewing the shows later. Consumers zip through up to 75 percent of the ads in recorded shows—yet they can still identify the brand or product category in many of the ads.[6] Consumers can also skip pre-roll commercials in online channels, such as YouTube. If such skipping or zipping occurs, an ad with extensive brand information in the center of the screen can have a positive influence on brand attitude.[7] Also, despite skipping and zipping, prior exposure to an ad improves consumers' recall of the message but increases consumers' tendency to avoid previously seen ads.[8]

With **zapping**, consumers avoid ads by switching to other channels during commercial breaks. Approximately 20 percent of consumers zap at any one time; more than two-thirds of households with cable TV zap regularly. Men zap more than women do. People are more likely to zap commercials at the half-hour or hour mark than during the program itself.[9]

Beyond skipping, zipping, and zapping, a growing number of consumers are "cutting the cord" by dropping cable or satellite television subscriptions in favor of streaming services such as Netflix, Amazon Prime Video, and Hulu.[10] *Cord-cutting* further challenges how marketers plan for ad exposure, in part because audiences

---

Exposure The process by which the consumer comes in physical contact with a stimulus.

Marketing stimuli Information about commercial offerings communicated either by the marketer (such as ads) or by nonmarketing sources (such as word-of-mouth).

Zipping Fast-forwarding through commercials on a program recorded earlier.

Zapping Use of a remote control to switch channels during commercial breaks.

Exhibit 3.1 ▶ Chapter Overview: From Exposure to Comprehension

Before you can pay attention to a marketing stimulus, you must be exposed to it. By allocating mental resources to a stimulus, you can perceive it and, finally, comprehend what it is, in the context of what you already know.

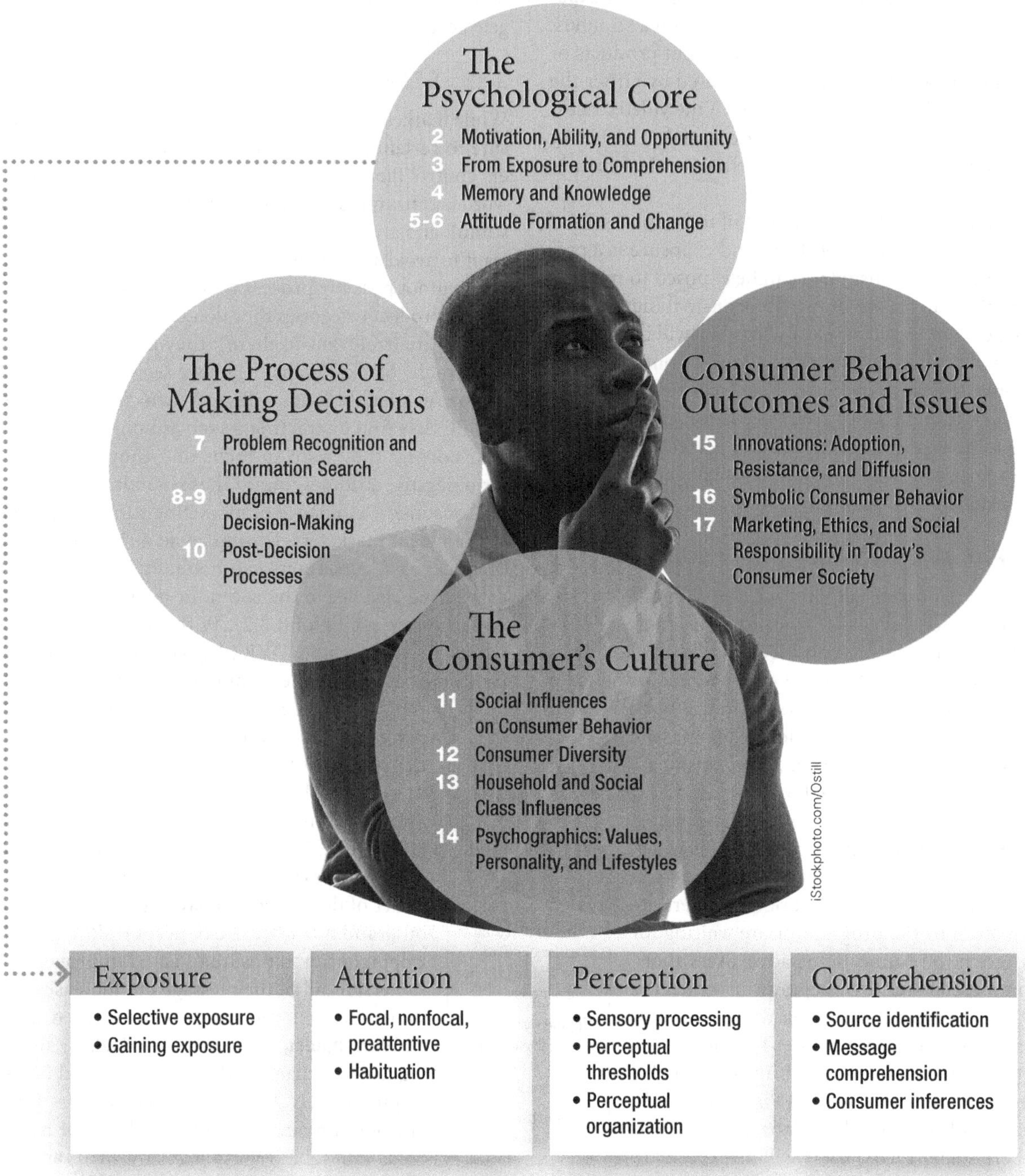

The Psychological Core

2   Motivation, Ability, and Opportunity
3   From Exposure to Comprehension
4   Memory and Knowledge
5-6   Attitude Formation and Change

The Process of Making Decisions

7   Problem Recognition and Information Search
8-9   Judgment and Decision-Making
10   Post-Decision Processes

Consumer Behavior Outcomes and Issues

15   Innovations: Adoption, Resistance, and Diffusion
16   Symbolic Consumer Behavior
17   Marketing, Ethics, and Social Responsibility in Today's Consumer Society

The Consumer's Culture

11   Social Influences on Consumer Behavior
12   Consumer Diversity
13   Household and Social Class Influences
14   Psychographics: Values, Personality, and Lifestyles

iStockphoto.com/Ostill

Exposure	Attention	Perception	Comprehension
• Selective exposure • Gaining exposure	• Focal, nonfocal, preattentive • Habituation	• Sensory processing • Perceptual thresholds • Perceptual organization	• Source identification • Message comprehension • Consumer inferences

are more fragmented among multiple entertainment sources. Moreover, cord-cutters tend to have different media habits, viewing entertainment on computer screens or on mobile devices rather than on TV and viewing on demand, sometimes binge-watching multiple episodes of a series in quick succession.[11]

Cord-cutting shows that consumers are increasingly taking charge of where, when, and for how long they are exposed to certain stimuli, by watching online or on demand, for example, or by downloading programs to view now or later. As viewing shifts to Internet- and mobile-based streaming, and more consumers seek out

Exhibit 3.2 ▶ Selective Exposure
Consumers can selectively control what marketing stimuli they view.

scyther5/Shutterstock.com

events such as celebrity runs that put the brand in the social media spotlight.[14]

Distribution is key to exposure at the retail level, and multiple exposures can be beneficial. According to recent research, consumers found innovative car designs more appealing after multiple exposures, while typical designs lost appeal over time. This effect carried over into actual sales, with atypical car designs outselling typical car designs after about three years. Thus, it is important to keep innovative products on the market long enough for consumers to be exposed multiple times and to develop a positive impression.[15]

online content, the use of ad-blocking software by consumers is increasing. An estimated 200 million people worldwide have downloaded software to avoid being exposed to advertising.[12] In some nations, nearly half of all Internet users have installed such software. This presents a major challenge to online sites that rely on advertising revenue to support content such as news and entertainment—and to marketers seeking to target online audiences.[13]

Marketers are trying other ways of gaining exposure for marketing stimuli, including advertising on racing cars, airport jetways, sports stadium turnstiles, and supermarket floors. Aspen Dental is one of several advertisers with a logo on Danica Patrick's car and jumpsuit during NASCAR races.[16] Mobile marketing is a fast-growing field as marketers experiment with coupons, apps, offers, contests, and other content viewed on consumers' cell phones. Marketers are adapting their websites for smaller screens and enabling consumers to seamlessly access their shopping carts, coupons, rewards points, newsletters, and other elements whether they log in from a laptop, a desktop computer, or a smartphone.[17] Marketers such as Woolworths in Australia have created virtual grocery shelves, projected on the walls of transit stations, to increase exposure and encourage purchasing via cell phone.[18] These are all ways that marketers use to increase the "reach" of messages about their products and brands, and to increase the number of transaction (purchase) possibilities that are open to consumers.

Marketers want to get their messages or products noticed without alienating consumers, a real task when consumers feel bombarded by marketing stimuli. Therefore, some marketers are reaching out through media not yet saturated with messages. As the

Marketing Implications

Marketers start the process of gaining exposure by selecting media, such as Internet and social networking sites, television, radio, and product placements, and developing communications for targeted consumers. For example, to connect with younger consumers—often the most style-conscious and interested in self-expression—Adidas coordinates multiple brand and product messages in multiple media. The firm is expanding its roster of professional hockey, basketball, and football players who endorse its products, to reinforce brand stature among sports fans. Adidas's flagship NEO stores feature eye-catching, colorful displays and head-to-toe outfits geared to the fashion tastes of teenagers in Europe and beyond. Finally, the company plans special image-messaging mobile app SnapChat gained popularity, for instance, Coca-Cola created video ads specifically for the app's Discover section. Knowing the app's users are teens and twenty-something consumers who typically are not attracted to traditional advertising, Coke's videos featured the iconic bottle paired with mouth-watering foods revealed in layers, such as sandwiches with multiple fillings.[19] Targeted e-mail marketing allows firms to communicate regularly with consumers, offering product updates, promotional deals, and other content. Although Internet users resent uninvited messages from companies, many will agree to receive e-mail if they see a benefit and can control the timing.

Television audiences are increasingly fragmented, so advertisers are looking for ways to expand exposure and make the most of their TV budgets. For commercials that will air during high-profile TV programs such as the Super Bowl and the Academy Awards, advertisers are offering online previews and teasers, mobile marketing extras, and social media promotions that build buzz. Another way to encourage ad exposure is by giving consumers some choice about what and how they watch. The TV website Hulu gives consumers the choice of watching one long commercial or a number of separate commercials, and even allows consumers to choose one interactive commercial instead of viewing multiple commercials during a program.[20]

Product placement within a television program or movie is another way to increase exposure among viewers. For example, as many as 17 brands bought product-placement "screen time" in the James Bond movie *Spectre*, including the champagne brand Bollinger, Omega watches, Heineken beer, Tom Ford suits, Sony smartphones, and automotive brands Rolls-Royce, Jaguar, and Aston Martin.[21] Product placement of luxury and regular brands in television programs, when complemented by commercials that air during the programs, can increase the memorability of the ad and the brand as well as increasing positive affect for these.[22]

3-2 Attention and Consumer Behavior

While exposure reflects whether consumers encounter a stimulus, **attention** reflects how much mental activity they devote to it. A certain amount of attention is necessary for information to be perceived—for it to activate people's senses. After consumers perceive information, they may pay more attention to it and continue with the higher-order

> **Attention** The amount of mental activity a consumer devotes to a stimulus.

processing activities discussed in the next few chapters. Thus, attention enables consumers to learn more efficiently from their exposure to marketing stimuli and make more informed decisions.

3-2a CHARACTERISTICS OF ATTENTION

Three key characteristics of attention are shown in Exhibit 3.3. Attention (1) is limited; (2) is selective; and (3) can be divided.

Attention Is Limited

Attention is limited. Consumers cannot possibly attend to all stimuli in the environment, even if they would want to see everything. However, consumers can attend to multiple stimuli (such as products on store shelves) if processing them is relatively automatic, well-practiced, and effortless.[23] When trying to learn a new skill, for instance, like playing an instrument or ordering books online, we need to pay close attention to each specific activity. With practice, we integrate sequences of activities into larger "chunks" and our attention is freed up for other things (The next chapter examines this in more detail).

Attention Is Selective

Because attention is limited, consumers need to select what to pay attention to and simultaneously what not to pay attention to. Being surrounded by a potentially overwhelming number of stimuli, we pay less attention to things we have seen many times before.[24] Attention can also be affected by goals: If we look at a package with the goal of learning how to use the product, we may be more likely to read the directions than to read about its ingredients.[25] If we repeatedly pay selective attention to a particular product and not to certain other products, we are more likely to choose the product that has captured our attention in the past, and reject those products we have previously ignored.[26]

Attention Can Be Divided

We can divide our attentional resources over time, by allocating some attention to one task and some to another, or by very rapidly switching attention between tasks. At the same time, we can become distracted when one stimulus draws attention from another; if we are distracted from an ad, we devote less attention to it.[27]

3-2b FOCAL AND NONFOCAL ATTENTION

These three characteristics of attention raise questions about what happens when we focus on a stimulus (*focal attention*) while simultaneously being exposed to other stimuli (*nonfocal attention*). For example, can we process any information from a roadside billboard in our peripheral vision if we are carefully focusing on the traffic on the road ahead of us? This example is about the information processing that can take place during nonfocal attention.

Characteristic	Example
Attention is limited: Consumers may miss some stimuli, especially when in unfamiliar surroundings.	While watching TV with friends, a consumer may reduce the volume to pay more attention to what friends are saying.
Attention is selective: Consumers decide what to focus on at any one time, choosing not to focus on or mentally process other stimuli.	Shoppers cannot focus on every display or product in a store, so they must decide which they will pay attention to.
Attention can be divided: Consumers can allocate some attention to one task and some to a different task, or rapidly switch between tasks.	While paying attention to their driving, consumers can also notice ads on billboards posted along a highway.

Exhibit 3.3 ▶ Three Characteristics of Attention

To the extent that we can process information from our peripheral vision even if we are not aware of doing so, we are engaged in **preattentive processing**. With preattentive processing, most of our attentional resources are devoted to one thing, which is the focus of attentive processing, leaving limited resources for something else. We devote just enough attention to an object in our peripheral vision to process *something* about it, but we are usually not aware that we are absorbing and processing that information.

Preattentive processing The non-conscious processing of stimuli, such as in peripheral vision.

Do preattentively processed stimuli affect feelings about or choices of brands? Research suggests that consumers will like a brand name more if they have processed it preattentively than if they have not been exposed to it.[28] Preattentive processing makes a brand name familiar, and we generally like familiar things.[29] Preattentive processing of an ad can also affect consumers' consideration of a product, even when they do not remember seeing the ad.[30] In addition, emotions can play a factor in preattentive processing. If TV commercials can engage consumers emotionally, they can build strong brands even at low attention levels.[31] Likewise, emotionally charged headlines in print ads can be processed preattentively, resulting in higher ad and brand awareness.[32]

Marketing Implications

Although consumers can process general information (such as logos and brand names) preattentively, specific information (such as about ingredients and directions for use) will have more impact when consumers devote full attention to it. Unfortunately, a marketing stimulus competes with many other stimuli for attention, and consumers may have limited motivation and

opportunity to attend to marketing stimuli. Consequently, marketers often take steps to attract consumers' attention by making the stimulus (1) personally relevant, (2) pleasant, (3) surprising, and/or (4) easy to process. They can use various research methods to gauge consumers' attention to ads, packages, and products, as shown in Exhibit 3.4.

1. *Make stimuli personally relevant.* Stimuli are personally relevant when they appeal to our needs, values, emotions, or goals.[33] If you are hungry, for example, you are more likely to pay attention to food ads and packages. Products such as candy bars may make use of this by appealing to the need for energy to keep going, or the need for "a break" between tasks. A second way is to show people who are similar to the target audience, such as "typical consumers" in an ad.[34] A third way to increase personal relevance is by using

Exhibit 3.4 ▶ Studying Eye Movements to Gauge and Improve Attention

dramas, mini-stories that depict the experiences of actors or consumers through a narrative in one or more ads. A fourth way to draw consumers into the ad is to ask rhetorical questions, such as "Would you like to win a million dollars?"[35] These questions appeal to the consumer by including the word *you* and by asking the consumer (if only for effect) to consider answering the question.

2. *Make stimuli pleasant.* Because people tend to approach things that are inherently pleasant, marketers can increase consumers' attention to marketing stimuli by:

    ▶ *Using attractive models.* Ads containing attractive models have a higher probability of being noticed because the models arouse positive feelings or basic sexual attraction.[36] Whereas attractiveness can be due to sheer beauty, similarity with the audience and expertise can be deemed attractive as well.

    ▶ *Using music.* Familiar songs and popular entertainers can attract us in pleasant ways.[37] When Fiat Chrysler launched the Jeep Renegade, the head of marketing approached Interscope Records about a song for the introductory campaign. The X Ambassadors were in the process of recording a song titled *Renegades* for an Interscope music label, and it became the Jeep Renegade's advertising theme music. "The genius here is that you tie the name of the car, which is 'Renegade,' to the mindset of the target, which is the millennial target," explains Fiat Chrysler's chief marketing officer.[38]

    ▶ *Using humor.* Humor can be an effective attention getting device.[39] For example, a commercial for Berlitz language schools shows a London double-decker bus landing, flying-saucer style, in Middle Eastern cities as locals flee. The tag line is: "Don't be an alien in a foreign country."[40] Although roughly one in five TV ads contains humor, some are more successful at evoking laughter and in capturing and retaining viewers' attention than others.[41]

3. *Make stimuli surprising.* Consumers are likely to process a stimulus when it is surprising by:

    ▶ *Using novelty.* We are more likely to notice any marketing stimulus (an ad, package, or brand name) that is new or unique, because it stands out relative to other stimuli. For example, Volvo attracted attention when it introduced its XC90 SUV model at the Los Angeles Auto Show using a virtual reality commercial simulating a test-drive. Consumers accessed the commercial through a mobile app paired with the Google Cardboard virtual reality viewer.[42] Although novel stimuli attract attention, people do not like extreme novelty. For example, we may dislike food with a taste or ingredients unlike that of foods we usually eat. Grasshopper Burgers may be new but appealing to only a few.[43] Thus, the factors that make a stimulus novel may not be the same factors that make it likable, and ideally marketing stimuli will attract attention in a positive way.

    ▶ *Using unexpectedness* (see Exhibit 3.5). Unexpected stimuli may not necessarily be new to us, but their placement or content differs from what we are used to, arousing curiosity and causing us to analyze them further to make sense of them.[44] In fact, unexpectedness can affect the extent to which consumers perceive an ad as humorous.[45] For example, slapstick comedy has little to do with buying car tires, so consumers are apt to notice when Bridgestone uses such humor in TV commercials.[46]

    ▶ *Using a puzzle.* Visual rhymes, antitheses, metaphors, and puns are puzzles that attract attention in ads, because they require resolution. To understand puns and metaphors, a shared cultural background is needed, which makes it hard to use them in multinational campaigns—American consumers may not readily understand ads developed in other countries, just as people from other cultures may not readily understand U.S. ads.[47] Although ads that use a puzzle may capture and hold attention, it is important that consumers can solve it to prevent boomerang effects.

Image Courtesy of The Advertising Archives

Exhibit 3.5 ▶ Capturing Attention

Consumers are more likely to pay attention to ads with unexpected elements.

4. *Make stimuli easy to process.* Marketers can enhance attention by boosting consumers' ability to process the stimuli. Four characteristics make a stimulus easy to process:

▶ *Prominent stimuli.* Prominent stimuli stand out relative to the environment because of their intensity. The size or length of the stimulus can affect its **prominence**. For example, consumers are more likely to notice larger or longer ads than smaller or shorter ones.[48] Increasing the amount of space devoted to text within an ad increases the viewers' attention to the entire message; making ads less cluttered focuses attention on the brand, price, and promotion aspects of the message.[49] Movement also increases prominence, which is why attention tends to be enhanced when a commercial uses dynamic, fast-paced action.[50] Movement attracts attention even in the visual periphery, which is why Web ads often make use of it. Also, when choosing among competing products, consumers tend to buy products in packages that appear to be taller than others. Even the ratio of the dimensions of rectangular products or packages can subtly affect consumer preferences.[51]

▶ *Concrete stimuli.* Stimuli are easier to process if they are concrete rather than abstract.[52] **Concreteness** is defined as the extent to which we can imagine a stimulus. Notice how easily you can develop images of the concrete words in Exhibit 3.6 compared with your response to the abstract words. Concreteness applies to brand names as well, which is why a dishwashing liquid such as Sunlight may attract more attention than a competing brand named Joy. Marketers can improve purchase intentions by enhancing mental simulation of product use in a concrete way. Showing a mug of coffee in an ad with the handle on the right makes it easy for right-handed people to mentally visualize picking it up to take a sip.[53]

▶ *Limited number of competing stimuli.* A stimulus is easier to process when few things surround it to compete for your attention.[54] You are more likely to notice a billboard when driving down a deserted rural highway than when in a congested, sign-filled city, just as you are more likely to notice a brand name in a

Concrete Words	Abstract Words
Apple	Aptitude
Bowl	Betrayal
Cat	Chance
Cottage	Criterion
Diamond	Democracy
Engine	Essence
Flower	Fantasy
Garden	Glory
Hammer	Hatred
Infant	Ignorance
Lemon	Loyalty
Meadow	Mercy
Mountain	Necessity
Ocean	Obedience

Source: Allan Paivio et al., *Journal of Experimental Psychology*, Monograph Supplement, January 1968, pp. 1–25. Copyright © 1968 by the American Psychological Association. Adapted with permission.

Exhibit 3.6 ▶ Concreteness and Abstractness
We may pay more attention to things that are concrete and capable of generating images than we do to things that are abstract and difficult to represent visually.

visually simple ad than in one that is visually cluttered. Companies seek moments and locations where competition for attention with their stimuli is limited.

▶ *Contrast with competing stimuli.* Contrast captures attention. Color newspaper ads stand out because they are surrounded by black and white, just as black-and-white TV ads stand out during TV shows broadcast in color. For contrast, some winemakers put images of unusual animals on their labels to help bottles stand out on the shelf.[55] A study on retail advertising found that attention was highest when an ad differed from the other ads, and when these other ads were very similar to each other.[56]

Therefore, attention to a stimulus is high when its signal-to-noise ratio is high. Prominent and concrete stimuli have a high "signal," whereas the "noise" is low when there are few competing stimuli and the stimulus contrasts with those competitors (i.e., because competing ads all look the same).

Prominence The intensity of stimuli that causes them to stand out relative to the environment.

Concreteness The extent to which a stimulus is capable of being imagined.

3-2c CUSTOMER SEGMENTS DEFINED BY ATTENTION

If we do pay attention to things that are relevant, pleasant, surprising, and easy to process, can we identify consumer segments that are more affected by relevance, pleasantness, surprise, and ease of processing? The answer appears to be yes. Researchers have identified a segment of consumers who paid minimal attention to an ad because the elements were not relevant to them. A second segment focused on visually pleasant elements of the ad, such as the picture. The third and last segment spent the longest time looking at the ad and devoted equal time to the picture, package, headline, and body text, perhaps because they viewed the product as personally relevant and its purchase as potentially risky. Hence, the consumers needed sustained attention to properly evaluate the ad's information.[57]

3-2d HABITUATION

When a stimulus becomes familiar, it can lose its attention-getting ability, a result called **habituation** or wear-out. For example, think about the last time you purchased something new for your living room (such as a picture or vase). For the first few days, you probably noticed the object every time you entered the room. Over time, however, you probably noticed the item less and less, as you became habituated to it. It has ceased to be part of the foreground, and became part of the background.

In the same way, consumers become habituated to ads, packages, and other marketing stimuli. To counter this, marketers can alter the stimulus periodically. For example, many companies develop multiple ads that communicate the same basic message but in different ways and different media. Habituation also explains why marketers sometimes change packaging to attract consumers' attention anew. Kellogg is now marketing breakfast cereals in single-serve pouches, an unusual type of packaging for this category, to meet the needs of on-the-go consumers and to capture their attention at the store level.[58]

> **Habituation** The process by which a stimulus loses its attention-getting abilities by virtue of its familiarity.
>
> **Perception** The process of determining the properties of stimuli using vision, hearing, taste, smell, and touch.

3-3 Perception and Consumer Behavior

After we have been exposed to a stimulus and have devoted at least some attention to it, we are in a position to perceive it. **Perception** is the process of determining the properties of stimuli using one or more of our five senses: Vision, hearing, taste, smell, and touch.[59] For instance, consumers judge how much soft drink a can will contain based on its width and height, how much food a plate contains based on the size, which car will drive fastest based on the color (red or green) and the engine's sound (low pitched or high pitched), which fabric softener will make clothes softest based on its smell and color, and so on. Consumers constantly and mostly automatically determine such properties of marketing stimuli using their senses and knowledge of the world. Some of these perceptions are about physical properties such as the size, color, pitch, loudness, smell, and softness of stimuli, while others are meanings associated with these properties, such as whether something feels luxurious.

3-3a PERCEIVING THROUGH VISION

What arouses our visual perception? All of the following factors can combine to impact the beauty or aesthetic qualities of a product or package.[60]

Size and Shape

Consumers perceive that packages in eye-catching shapes contain more of a product.[61] When product or package size is changed, consumers are less sensitive when the change involves only one dimension (height or length or width) than when the change involves all three dimensions. Thus, consumers may "supersize" their order when a product is enlarged along only one dimension, but "downsize" when the product is enlarged along all dimensions, a change more easily perceived.[62] In fact, consumers may not notice downsizing of up to 24 percent if the package shape is elongated at the same time.[63]

Lettering

The size and style of the lettering on a product or in an ad can attract attention and support brand recognition and image.[64] The distinctive, curly Coca-Cola script, for instance, is not only eye-catching but also is instantly identified with the soft-drink brand and expresses its classic meaning.

Image Location on Package

Where product images are located on a package can influence consumers' perceptions and preferences. Images located near the package top, on the left side, or at top-left add to the perception of a product as "lighter." On packages of products where "lighter" is perceived positively—such as healthy snacks—the images should be placed in these "lighter" locations.[65]

Color

Color is a crucial factor in visual perception. A color can be described according to hue, saturation, and lightness. *Hue* is the pigment contained in the color. Colors can be classified into two broad categories of hues: warm colors such as red, orange, and yellow and cool colors such as green, blue, and violet. Saturation (also called *chroma*) refers to the richness of the color, leading to distinctions such as pale pink or deep, rich pink. *Lightness* refers to the depth of tone in the color. A saturated pink could have a lot of lightness (a fluorescent pink) or a lot of darkness (a mauve).

Diagnostic colors are important for attention and perception, such as pink for skincare or blue for the Nivea brand of skincare products. These help consumers to quickly determine the product and brand being advertised, even when the message is shown very fast, in the visual periphery, or with many competing ads.[66]

Color also can influence our physiological responses and moods: Warm colors generally encourage activity and excitement, whereas cool colors are more soothing and relaxing. Thus, cool colors are more appropriate in places such as spas or doctors' offices, where it is desirable for consumers to feel calm or to spend time making decisions. Warm colors are more appropriate in environments such as health clubs and fast-food restaurants, where high levels of activity are desirable. Red appears to arouse an aggressive response and to elicit higher bid increments when used as the background color of an online auction screen.[67]

Finally, colors can have a great effect on consumers' liking of a product. Defying the stainless steel trend in kitchen appliances, General Electric recently introduced two bright new refrigerator colors with retro appeal: Cupcake Blue and Red Pepper.[68] Interestingly, research suggests that consumers of multiple racial groups have an inherent preference for the color white versus the color black in products and advertising messages.[69]

Appearance of Being New or Worn

Research shows that consumers react differently to money—specifically, paper currency—depending on whether the bills look crumpled and well-worn or crisp and new. Consumers spend worn bills more readily than new bills, because they are disgusted at the thought of the used money having passed through so many hands. On the other hand, they will keep fresh, crisp bills because they can feel good about spending this currency when they are in public.[70]

3-3b PERCEIVING THROUGH HEARING

Sound represents another form of sensory input. Perception of sound (auditory stimuli) depends on its intensity.[71] Of course, consumers are more likely to notice loud music or voices and stark noises. When the announcer in a radio or TV ad speaks more quickly, the faster pace disrupts consumers' processing of the information; a low-pitched voice speaking syllables at a faster-than-normal rate induces more positive ad and brand attitudes.[72] When a company uses one person to speak the voice-over lines during many of its ads or plays the same jingle in many commercials, consumers associate those sounds with the product or brand. Apple, Skype, Microsoft, and other firms consciously seek to define a certain *sonic identity*—using specific music or sounds to identify a brand.[73]

Further, consumers infer product attributes and form evaluations using information gleaned from hearing a brand's sounds, syllables, and words—a process known as sound *symbolism*.[74] For instance, the name of Nissan's LEAF electric car reminds consumers of the product's environmental benefits. In addition, because electric cars are very quiet, Nissan created a pleasant, turbine-like hum as a distinctive, non–gasoline-engine noise to signal LEAF's smooth acceleration and deceleration.[75] In addition, consumers will have positive feelings about a brand name with sound repetition in its phonetic structure when spoken aloud, which in turn improves brand evaluations and product choice, such as for Hubba Bubba chewing gum.[76] Background noise can also affect consumer behavior: a moderate level of ambient noise (such as people conversing in a store) stimulates abstract thinking, which in turn can enhance the likelihood that consumers will buy an innovative product.[77]

3-3c PERCEIVING THROUGH TASTE

Food and beverage marketers stress taste perceptions in their marketing stimuli. For example, the major challenge for marketers of low-calorie and low-fat products is to provide healthier foods that still taste good and that, perhaps more importantly, are perceived as such. Yet what tastes good to one person may not taste good to another, and consumers from different cultural backgrounds may have different taste preferences. Interestingly, tasting or sampling a product is the in-store marketing tactic that most influences consumer purchasing, even though stand-alone, in-store displays—perceived through vision—are the marketing tactic that shoppers notice the most.[78] "If you see a four-pack of Oogavé sodas on the grocery shelf alongside all the other soda options, you may not put it in your shopping cart," explains the head of the small Colorado-based company that makes these all-natural drinks sweetened with agave. "But once you've tried it, you'll go looking for it."[79]

Food marketers also understand how the sensory texture of food being chewed affects calorie perceptions. Research shows that when consumers taste foods with a hard or rough texture, they perceive these to be lower in calorie than foods with a soft or smooth texture, perhaps because smooth is associated with fat and this is associated with calories.[80] The next chapter describes such associations with products and brands in more detail.

3-3d PERCEIVING THROUGH SMELL

If you were blindfolded, you (like most consumers) would probably have a hard time identifying many supermarket items based on smell.[81] However, consumers also differ in their ability to label odors. Compared with younger consumers, the elderly have a harder time identifying smells,[82] and women in general are better at the task than men are.[83] Marketers are concerned with the effects of smell on consumer responses, product trial, liking, and buying.

▪ *Effects of smells on physiological responses and moods.* Smell produces both physiological and emotional responses. Some studies show that people can feel tense or relaxed depending on whether or not a scent is present and what it is.[84] This theory has been key to the development of aromatherapy. Some of our most basic emotions are also linked to smell. For example, children hate having their security blankets washed, in part because washing removes comforting smells. In addition, the smell of the ocean, freshly baked cookies, or apple pie can revive emotional or childhood memories.[85]

▪ *Effects of smell on liking.* Retailers, in particular, recognize that smells can attract consumers. For example, The NetCost supermarket in New York City adds grapefruit aroma in its produce department to attract shoppers. Since NetCost began doing this, fruit and vegetable sales have increased 7 percent.[86] Similarly, grocery retailers often locate in-store bakeries up front so that the aroma of fresh bread can be smelled at the main entrance.

▪ *Effects of smell on product trial.* Smell (often in combination with other sensory perceptions) can entice consumers to try or buy a food product. Research suggests that scents in the air can be effective stimuli when related to the product being sold—yet the fit between scent and product is crucial. Thus, a flowery aroma is more appropriate for a lingerie store than for a coffee bar.[87] Some "scratch-and-sniff" ads for perfumes and after-shave lotions are doused with the product to increase sensory processing. However, this technique can backfire if consumers are offended by or have allergic reactions to scents.

▪ *Effects of smell on buying.* Providing a pleasant-smelling environment can have a positive effect on shopping behavior by encouraging more attention to relevant stimuli that consumers encounter, and encouraging consumers to linger longer.[88] Abercrombie & Fitch scents its stores with its branded fragrances, such as the men's fragrance Fierce, for a pleasing shopping experience that appeals to its target market.[89]

3-3e PERCEIVING THROUGH TOUCH

Although individual preferences vary, touch (both what we touch with our fingers and the way things feel as they come in contact with our skin) is an important aspect of many offerings.[90] Consumers like some products because of their feel. Some consumers buy skin creams and baby products for their soothing effect on the skin. In fact, consumers who have a high need for touch tend to like products that provide this opportunity.[91] When considering products with material properties, such as clothing or carpeting, consumers prefer goods they can touch in stores more than products they only see and read about online or in catalogs.[92]

The mere touching of a product (or imagining the action of touching it) can already increase a consumer's perceived ownership of the item.[93] Also, consumers who are briefly touched by a salesperson are more likely to have positive feelings and more likely to evaluate both the store and the salesperson positively. In addition, customers who are touched by the salesperson are more likely to comply with the salesperson's requests.[94] However, reaction to touch in sales situation differs from culture to culture. Consumers in Latin America are more comfortable with touching and embracing than U.S. consumers. In Asia, touching between relative strangers is commonly seen as inappropriate.[95] Another interesting finding is that consumers have higher evaluations of a product that has been touched by an attractive member of the opposite sex, such as a good-looking salesperson or model.[96] This finding shows the symbolic nature of consumer behavior, which Chapter 16 treats in further detail.

Although marketers might attempt to control how consumers perceive marketing stimuli, sensory perceptions are sometimes affected by subtle cues in the environment. For example, exposure to dryness-related images or words can lead consumers to feel thirstier and less energetic, influencing the effort they will invest in decisions.[97] The temperature of an item or a room can also be a factor. Consumers deal more effectively with complex choices in cooler surroundings, because feeling too warm can deplete cognitive resources.[98] Yet warm temperatures typically elicit positive reactions and increase consumers' evaluation of products.[99] Interestingly, consumers perceive the temperature of a restaurant to be lower when they are eating alone, a finding relevant to marketing in-restaurant dining experiences.[100]

 Marketing Implications

Sensory marketing is the process of systematically managing consumers' perception and experiences of marketing stimuli.[101] Many companies seek to enhance consumer perception of marketing stimuli by appealing to the five senses (see Exhibit 3.7).

Vision

Color preferences are in part affected by gender, with men preferring certain colors and women other colors, which marketers must consider when planning marketing stimuli.[102] Because colors can strongly influence attention to and liking of a product, marketers often rely on the advice of "color forecasters" when deciding which colors to use in products and on packages. Why? Because color can make consumers believe they are buying products that are very current or spark nostalgia for earlier times. Color is also important in perceptions of service marketers and their staff. For example, MGM Grand hotel in Las Vegas projects a contemporary image by updating the color and style of employees' uniforms when it redecorates restaurants and other hotel facilities.[103] The National Football League has experimented with a "Color Rush" campaign in which teams wear monochromatic uniforms in bright hues during selected games as a way to break the routine and generate buzz.[104]

Another important point about vision: Consumers' sensory experiences of a product can be influenced by the shape of the packaging and the label, as well as the sound symbolism of the brand name.[105] Products in the center visually attract more attention. Therefore, consumers usually choose a product from the center of the shelf rather than a product from the side of the shelf.[106] Also, recent research shows that seeing more pictures of products being compared can confuse consumers' perceptions and increase choice uncertainty.[107] Finally, the level of light intensity can make a difference: Brighter light increases affective intensity and dimmer light reduces affective intensity.[108]

Hearing

Fast music, like that played at aerobics classes, tends to energize; in contrast, slow music can be soothing. The type of music being played in a retail outlet can affect shopping behavior.[109] A fast tempo creates a more rapid traffic flow, whereas a slow tempo can increase sales as much as 38 percent because it encourages leisurely shopping (although consumers are unaware of this influence).[110] A fast tempo is more desirable in some restaurants because consumers will eat faster, facilitating greater turnover and higher sales.[111] For example, radio ads for the In-N-Out hamburger chain use a slightly retro, fast-paced jingle to reflect both old-fashioned quality and speedy service.[112] Likable and familiar music can induce good moods, whereas discordant sounds can induce bad moods. This effect is important to note because, as you will see in later chapters, bad moods may affect how people feel about products and consumption experiences.[113] Sounds have been increasingly used as trademarks, and some are registered as "sound logos," such as the lion's roar of the MGM entertainment company.

Taste

Marketers often try to monitor consumers' tastes through taste tests. Many food and beverage products are thoroughly taste tested before they are introduced. Ads or food packages sometimes ask consumers to compare the product's taste with that of competing products. However, consumers are not always good at discerning taste, so marketers should consider adding descriptive words or pictures to marketing communications about foods, restaurants, and the like.[114] To engage consumers, some marketers mention taste in an unexpected way. For instance, the slogan of Buckley's Cough Mixture for more than 25 years has been: "It Tastes Awful. And It Works."[115] Marketers such as Frito-Lay use *crowdsourcing* to involve consumers in submitting and voting on new product flavors.[116]

Taste can, at times, interfere with the positive effect of marketing messages, as happened in a study where consumers ate popcorn or chewed gum while viewing commercials for foreign brands.[117] Also, the order in which food products such as chocolates are sampled and the sensory similarities or differences among samples can influence consumer choices. When the products have sensory similarity, consumers tend to prefer the item sampled first. However, when products have sensory dissimilarities, consumers prefer the item

Wear the fragrance of mountain air

Because it's Ariel, even your dirtiest clothes will wash clean as driven snow. And because it's Ariel Alpine, they'll also smell as crisp and fresh as mountain air (even your socks).

ARIEL ALPINE

NEW

Image Courtesy of The Advertising Archives

Exhibit 3.7 ▶ Perception Through Senses
Some products are valued because of the smells they evoke.

sampled last.[118] Whether consumers actively participate in creating something using the product as an input can also affect sensory evaluations. For instance, consumers who used a dinner kit as the basis of meal preparation were more likely to have a positive evaluation of the kit and the meal they created from it.[119]

Smell

Obviously, we like some products—for example, perfumes and scented candles—for the smells they produce. However, we may like other products, such as mouthwashes and deodorants, because they mask aromas. Procter & Gamble's Febreze product, for example, actually started as an odor eliminator. After company research showed how strongly consumers are influenced by scents, marketers introduced aromas into Febreze and added these aromas to many P&G products for the home and laundry. Due to multimedia and social media marketing to reinforce positive perceptions of these Febreze scents, P&G sells more than $1 billion worth of Febreze products annually.[120]

However, smell does not always work to the marketers' advantage: Some consumers may dislike a product scent or find it irritating. In addition, some consumers value particular products because they have no smell, such as unscented deodorants, carpet cleaners, and laundry detergents. Also, consumers' preferences for smells differ across cultures. Although the smell of oranges, vanilla, and cinnamon are liked by many, it seems that only one smell (cola) is universally regarded as pleasant, a finding that is good news for globally operating companies like Coca-Cola and Pepsi.[121] Finally, if a marketing message encourages consumers to imagine they can smell a product (such as a freshly baked cookie), consumers will salivate and desire to eat it only if they can visualize the item.[122]

Touch

The ability to touch a product can influence what consumers buy and how much they are willing to pay.[123] Knowing that consumers prefer to try products before they buy them, many retailers and manufacturers offer trial sizes, samples, and opportunities to handle products. Companies often set up tables or exhibits in transportation hubs and busy shopping districts so consumers can get a feel for products in person. Every November, a weekend-only market featuring made-in-America products opens in Brooklyn, New York, to allow consumers hands-on access to numerous products, such PF Flyers sneakers and Tesla electric cars.[124]

Absolute threshold The minimal level of stimulus intensity needed to detect a stimulus.

Differential threshold/just noticeable difference (jnd) The intensity difference needed between two stimuli before they are perceived to be different.

Weber's law The stronger the initial stimulus, the greater the additional intensity needed for the second stimulus to be perceived as different.

3-3f WHEN DO WE PERCEIVE STIMULI?

Our senses are exposed to numerous inputs at any given time. To perceive each and every one would be overwhelming and extremely difficult. Fortunately, our sensory processing is simplified by the fact that many stimuli do not enter our conscious awareness. For us to perceive something, it must be sufficiently intense. The intensity of a smell can be measured by the concentration of the stimulus in a substance or in the air. Stimulus intensity of sounds can be measured in decibels and frequencies, and stimulus intensity of colors can be measured by properties like lightness, saturation, and hue. In the area of touch, stimulus intensity can be measured in terms of pounds or ounces of pressure. In terms of taste, the bitterness of beers is measured in IBUs (International Bitterness Units).

Absolute Thresholds

The **absolute threshold** is the minimum level of stimulus intensity needed for a stimulus to be perceived. In other words, the absolute threshold is the amount of intensity needed for a person to detect a difference between something and nothing. Suppose you are driving on the highway and a billboard is in the distance. The absolute threshold is that point at which you can first see the billboard. Before that point, the billboard is below the absolute threshold and not sufficiently intense to be seen.

Differential Thresholds

Whereas the absolute threshold deals with whether or not a stimulus can be perceived, the **differential threshold** refers to the intensity difference needed between two stimuli before people can perceive that the stimuli are different. Thus, the differential threshold is a relative concept; it is often called the **just noticeable difference (jnd)**. For example, when you get your eyes checked, the eye doctor may show you a card with rows of letters, with the rows being of an increasingly smaller type size. If you can distinguish two letters on the same line, then the letters have crossed your differential threshold for visual perception. The row with the smallest letters that you can still distinguish reliably indicates your visual acuity.

Weber's law, outlined by psychophysiologist Ernst Weber, states that the stronger the initial stimulus, the greater the additional intensity needed for the second stimulus to be perceived as different. This relationship is shown in the following formula:

$$\frac{\Delta s}{S} = K$$

where S is the initial stimulus value, Δs is the smallest change (Δ) in a stimulus capable of being detected, and K is a constant of proportionality.

Imagine that a marketer finds, through testing, that one ounce would need to be added to a 10-ounce package before consumers notice that the two packages contain different amounts. The marketer has a 50-ounce box and wants to know how much to add before consumers detect a difference. According to Weber's law, $K = 1/10$ or 0.10. To determine how much would need to be added, the marketer uses this formula:

> **Subliminal perception** The activation of sensory receptors by stimuli presented below the perceptual threshold.

$$\frac{\Delta s}{50} = 0.10$$

The answer is 0.10 of the package weight, or five ounces.

 ## Marketing Implications

Thresholds have a number of implications in marketing situations.

Absolute Threshold

Obviously, consumers will only consciously perceive a marketing stimulus when it is sufficiently high in intensity to be above the absolute threshold. Thus, if images or words in a commercial are too small or the sound level is too low, the stimulus will not be consciously perceived.

Differential Threshold

Sometimes marketers *do not* want consumers to notice a difference between two stimuli. In some cases, marketers might not want consumers to notice that they have decreased a product's size or increased its price, or that the taste has changed due to the use of different ingredients. Such situations might be beneficial to the consumers, when a low-sugar, fat-free ice cream tastes as rich and luscious as the regular version. It may raise ethical concerns, as when consumers unknowingly receive less value for their money. For example, when Consumer Reports asked Häagen-Dazs why it reduced the amount of ice cream in its containers by two fluid ounces, the company explained: "Due to the cost of ingredients and facilities costs, it was either change the size of the container or raise the price."[125] This change may have stayed "under-the-radar" for consumers. Note that differential thresholds vary from sense to sense, and that there are large individual differences, as some people are super tasters and others have a "super nose."

Subliminal Perception

"Limen" is the Latin word for threshold, and "sub" means below, as in submarine. Subliminal stimuli are presented below the threshold level of conscious awareness. If such stimuli still have an effect, this is evidence of **subliminal perception**. Subliminal perception is different from preattentive processing. In the case of preattentive processing, we process information which is outside the focus of our attention—for instance, we may preattentively process an ad in the visual periphery of an article that we are reading on a webpage. In principle, we could be made aware of the ad in periphery, namely, by looking there : Stimulus exposure is not subliminal. In the case of subliminal perception, our attention is directed squarely at the stimulus, but the stimulus is being presented subliminally. Subliminal stimuli are presented so quickly or are so degraded that the very act of consciously perceiving is not possible, even if you try hard.

Subliminal perception has been the subject of controversy since a widely known but fraudulent study claimed that consumers at a movie theater bought more popcorn and Coca-Cola after being subliminally exposed to extremely brief on-screen messages that read "Eat popcorn" and "Drink Coke."[126] This study that was never published and perhaps never even conducted still led to much public debate because it appeared to show that advertising could manipulate consumers against their will.[127] What is the evidence? It is important to distinguish between "weak" and "strong" effects of subliminal advertising.

A "strong" effect would be when subliminal advertising could influence people attitudes and behavior *against their will*. There is little evidence for this theory, though. Subliminal perception can influence consumers' attitudes but only when the subliminal stimulus fits with the consumer's current goals or motivations.[128] In other words, consumers who are hungry and ready to eat will be more motivated to act on a subliminal message about popcorn than if they have just had a meal. Here, both a subliminal stimulus and a motivated consumer make the difference for behavioral effects to occur.

A "weak" effect would be when subliminal advertising could influence people in ways that are consistent with their current goals or motivations, or would improve their perception of objects. Unlike the strong effect, there is much evidence for the weak effect.[129] If consumers are subliminally exposed to a word (e.g., razor), they will recognize that word faster than they recognize words to which they have not been exposed subliminally.[130] This research shows that subliminal stimuli can improve perception, and activate various meanings in consumers. In one study, when consumers were exposed subliminally to either the IBM or the Apple brand logo, those exposed to the Apple logo exhibited more creativity when completing a subsequent task. Apple is known for its creativity, and consumers subliminally primed by its logo responded creatively in an automatic way when motivated, without being conscious of any influence.[131] Stimuli that are perceived subliminally may also affect consumers' feelings. Consumers were found to have stronger responses to ads with sexual subliminal implants than to those without them.[132]

Overall, research suggests that the effects of subliminal perception are limited in time, and difficult to obtain outside of controlled laboratory situations.[133] Still, researchers continue to investigate when and how subliminal advertising works to understand fundamental perception processes, also using neuroscience methods.[134] Exposing consumers to a message at or above the threshold level of awareness should generally have just as much, if not more, impact than subliminal stimuli, making the use of subliminal stimuli unnecessary.[135] Moreover, subliminal advertising is banned in the United States, the United Kingdom, Australia, and the Netherlands, among other countries.[136]

3-3g HOW DO CONSUMERS PERCEIVE A STIMULUS?

Consumers tend not to perceive a single stimulus in isolation; rather, they organize and integrate it in the context of the other things around it. Also, many stimuli are really a complex combination of numerous simple stimuli that consumers must organize into a unified whole using **perceptual organization**. This process represents a somewhat higher, more meaningful level of processing than simply having stimuli register on our sensory receptors. Four basic principles related to perceptual organization are figure and ground, closure, grouping, and preference for the whole.

The principle of **figure and ground** suggests that people interpret stimuli in contrast to a background (see Exhibit 3.8). The figure is well defined and in the forefront—the focal point of attention—whereas the ground is indefinite and in the background. Military personnel may use camouflage clothing to blend in with their background, and remain unnoticed. Advertisers should plan for important brand information to be the figure, and not let the background muddle the figure.

> **Perceptual organization** The process by which stimuli are organized into meaningful units.
>
> **Figure and ground** The principle that people interpret stimuli in the context of a background.
>
> **Closure** The principle that individuals have a need to organize perceptions so that they form a meaningful whole.
>
> **Grouping** The tendency to group stimuli to form a unified picture or impression.

Closure refers to the fact that individuals have a need to organize perceptions so that they form a meaningful whole. Even if a stimulus is incomplete, our need for closure will lead us to see it as complete. The key to using the need for closure is to provide consumers with an incomplete stimulus. For example, putting a well-known television ad on the radio can get consumers thinking about the message. The radio version of the ad is an incomplete stimulus, and the need for closure leads consumers to picture the visual parts of the ad. In a television campaign for a coffee brand in Europe, the first stage was a voice-over repeatedly saying ". . . and then there is coffee, brand X coffee, good coffee." In the second stage of the campaign, the voice-over only said: "and then . . . ." so that consumers could complete the sentence themselves. Because of consumers' strong need for closure, such appeals may have positive effects on brand attitude.[138] Recent research shows that consumers perceive companies with incomplete typeface logos as being innovative, because the logos are so interesting.[139]

Grouping refers to the fact that we often group stimuli to form a unified picture or impression, making it easier to process them. We view similar or nearby objects as belonging together. Marketers can influence the image

Maurice Savage/Alamy Stock Photo

Exhibit 3.8 ▶ Figure and Ground

Sometimes marketers play with reversals of figure and ground to attract and retain attention in creative ways, as in this Baskin-Robbins logo. Initially, you may see a large B and R, the "figure," and the rest of the logo is "ground." Then you may discover the number 31 shown in pink, which refers to the original number of ice-cream flavors that Baskin-Robbins is famous for. When you focus on the pink number 31, you cannot see the letters BR. The switching between 31 and BR illustrates figure-ground reversals to convey the brand message. In fact, such playful and multiple-meaning logos may be particularly effective, and withstand repeated exposures.[137]

or perception of an offering by grouping it with other products. In a store, consumers may perceive a table setting as elegant when the napkins, napkin holders, silverware, dishes, and serving bowls are cleverly grouped.

Preference for the whole means that consumers perceive more value in the whole of something than in two or more parts that are equivalent to the whole. Thus, you are more likely to make a $20 purchase if you have two $5 bills and a $10. In contrast, if you have a single $20 bill, your preference for the whole makes you less willing to spend it.[140]

3-4 Comprehension and Consumer Behavior

So far, we have been exposed to a marketing stimulus, focused our attention on it, and used our senses to perceive it. Now, we have to identify what it is and understand the message it conveys. These are the two critical elements in **comprehension**, which is the process of extracting higher-order meaning from what we have perceived in the context of what we already know. Sometimes it is immediately clear that a stimulus to which we are exposed is an ad for a car brand, but the message the car brand wants to convey may be less clear. In that case, the *message comprehension* is challenged. But increasingly, it may be hard to identify whether the stimulus that we are exposed to is an ad or something else, which represents a challenge of *source identification.*

3-4a SOURCE IDENTIFICATION

Source identification is the process of determining what the stimulus that we have detected actually is. Chapter 4 explains in more detail how we use categorization processes to quickly accomplish this identification. Imagine opening a magazine and quickly looking at a page. Source identification is the rapid, perhaps automatic process of determining what a scene, such as a page in a magazine or on a website, contains. When exposed to a page in a magazine, people almost automatically ask themselves the question: "Is it an ad, or something else?" And if it is an ad, they naturally try to determine the brand or product being advertised. Such identification processes are useful because they help consumers to rapidly determine which of the numerous stimuli in their environment are relevant to them (is the ad for ice cream or broccoli?). Research shows that

Preference for the whole The tendency to perceive more value in a whole than in the combined parts that make up a whole, even if the parts have the same objective value as the whole.

Comprehension The process of extracting higher-order meaning from what we have perceived in the context of what we already know.

Source identification The process of determining what the perceived stimulus actually is, that is, what category it belongs to.

Objective comprehension The extent to which consumers accurately understand the message a sender intended to communicate.

Subjective comprehension What the consumer understands from the message, regardless of whether this understanding is accurate.

consumers are remarkably good at identifying the products and brands in ads—when the ads are typical for the category. In fact, after only 100 milliseconds (just a brief, single glance) consumers already know that something is an ad rather than editorial information (such as an article). And if the ad is typical, they know which product category and even which brand is being advertised. Ads that are atypical for the product category require more than a single glance to communicate what they are for, which is why marketers try to retain consumers' attention long enough to allow for source identification.[141]

Because of techniques such as *product placement* (arranging for a product to be shown in a movie, TV show, or digital game), it is not always easy to know whether something is really a marketing message or not. Such blurring of the lines occurs in other media, as well. Is that magazine article actually an *advertorial* (advertising that takes the form of editorial content) or a story unconnected with a sponsor? Is that TV program an *infomercial* (a long-form commercial sponsored by a marketer) or a news story about a product or brand? Is a social-media message consumer-generated or marketer-sponsored? Commercial stimuli try to look noncommercial because that may increase their credibility—although that compromises source identification by consumers. The U.S. Federal Trade Commission (FTC) requires that advertorials, infomercials, and sponsored tweets be clearly labeled as such, but these disclosures generally attract less attention than the rest of the message.

3-4b MESSAGE COMPREHENSION

Once we have identified the source as a marketing message and determined what product or brand is involved, we can start to comprehend which message it brings us—to make sense out of it—on a number of levels. In particular, marketers are concerned with (1) objective and subjective comprehension of messages; (2) the possibility of miscomprehension; (3) the effect of motivation, ability, and opportunity on comprehension; and (4) the effect of culture.

Objective and Subjective Comprehension

Objective comprehension refers to whether the meaning that consumers take from a message is consistent with what the message actually stated. **Subjective comprehension** is the different or additional meaning consumers attach to the message, whether or not these meanings were intended.[142] Whereas *objective comprehension* reflects whether we accurately understand what a sender intended to communicate, *subjective comprehension* reflects what we understand, accurate or not. Marketing mix elements such as price and advertising have a powerful influence on what we think a message is saying. You may infer that a dental gum is as powerful at whitening teeth as whitening toothpastes because the package art has white sparkles, the model in the ad has very white teeth, and the package displays phrases like "whitening agent." Yet the product may not be an effective whitening agent, and the words on the package may not actually say that it is, as you will see later in this chapter.

Miscomprehension

Miscomprehension occurs when consumers inaccurately construe the meaning contained in a message, that is, when their subjective comprehension is incorrect. Several studies have found a surprisingly high level of miscomprehension of TV and magazine ads. The estimated rate of objective comprehension was only about 70 percent for TV ads and 65 percent for magazine ads. Moreover, the rates of miscomprehension for directly asserted information and implied information were fairly equal, as were miscomprehension rates for programming, editorial material, and advertising.[143]

In addition to miscomprehending advertising messages, consumers sometimes miscomprehend product descriptions and usage instructions. The insurance company Aflac (American Family Life Assurance Company) changed its advertising messages after research showed that consumers misunderstood some of its offerings (see Exhibit 3.9). The famous duck that quacks the company's name is still in Aflac ads, but now the ads focus on features and benefits. The "One Day Pay" feature is promoted because "Millennials are a generation of instant gratification, and with this initiative, they are able to get their claims processed and paid within just a day," explains Aflac's chief marketing officer.[144]

Effect of MAO

Consumers may not comprehend a marketing message when they have low motivation and limited opportunity to process it, when the message is complex or shown for only a few seconds, or when the message is viewed only once or twice.[145] Experts are better able to comprehend information about a highly innovative product when prompted by marketing messages that help them make the connections and tap existing knowledge in more than one category.[146] Regarding ability, one study found that

Courtesy of United Healthcare

Exhibit 3.9 ▶ Avoiding Miscomprehension
Here UnitedHealthcare combines their logo and company name (the brand cue), along with a clear description of their services, to avoid miscomprehension.

although consumers want to see nutritional information on packaging (implying high motivation to process it), most do not comprehend it once they have read it.[147] Still, comprehension may improve with expertise and ability, which is the reason that adults often better comprehend the finer points of a message than young children do.[148] Also, marketers should carefully plan written marketing messages to match the reading ability of the target audience.[149]

Effect of the Culture

Consumers in low-context cultures such as those in North America and northern Europe generally separate the words and meanings of a communication from the context in which the message appears. In these cultures, consumers place more emphasis on what is said than on the surrounding visuals. But in high-context cultures (such as many in Asia), much of a message's meaning is implied indirectly and communicated nonverbally rather than stated explicitly through words. The message sender's characteristics, such as social class, values, and age, also play an important role in message interpretation.[150]

Language differences further raise the possibility of miscomprehension, as does the meaning that consumers in different cultures attach to words.[151] For example, in the United Kingdom, a *billion* is "a million million," whereas in the United States, a billion means "a thousand million." Finally, marketing messages can encourage positive product attitudes when they portray the progression of time in the way people from that culture visualize it. Thus, in cultures where people read from left to right, placing product images horizontally to suggest the past at left and the future at right—especially in the context of how the product helps consumers improve over time—will lead to more positive evaluations.[152]

Marketing Implications

Marketers may enhance consumer comprehension and awareness with a variety of tactics.

Marketers can improve objective comprehension in several ways.[153] When consumers accurately identify the advertised product and brand, much is already gained because people can access their prior knowledge. Keeping the message simple helps too. Another way is to repeat the message—stating it multiple times within the same communication and repeating it on multiple occasions. Presenting information in different forms, such as both visually and verbally in a TV commercial or YouTube video, can also help consumers form an accurate mental picture.[154] In fact, consumers who have had more exposure to a brand's marketing messages will be better able to process brand information and have more positive attitudes toward it.[155] Ease in perceiving and processing information is known as **perceptual fluency**. The earlier in life that consumers encounter a brand, and the more regularly they encounter it, the more quickly they will be able to recognize it. As a result, perceptual fluency is high for established brands that have been known for years, compared with new brands just entering the market.[156]

Subjective comprehension involves some interaction between what is in a message and what consumers already know. As a result, a marketer can strongly influence what consumers subjectively perceive by designing a message to be consistent with their prior knowledge. When consumers know little about a new product, marketers may be able to convey information effectively by drawing an analogy between the product and something with similar benefits. For example, a marketer may try to communicate the idea that a particular brand of boots is waterproof, soft, and lightweight by using the analogy of a duck.[157]

As mentioned earlier, product placements are one way marketers seek to increase exposure, counter advertising avoidance, and associate their brands with popular media. Knowing that Chinese audiences responded positively to earlier Transformers movies, Lenovo and other Chinese marketers arranged for product placement in *Transformers 3* and *Transformers 4* to showcase their brands in blockbuster Hollywood movies.[158] Marketers pay some celebrities with large numbers of Twitter followers, such as Snoop Dogg, for tweeting about brands and offerings.[159] (As required by the FTC,

sponsored tweets must be labeled as such, using easily understood hashtags such as #spon or #ad.) Such product placements blur the boundaries between commercial and noncommercial stimuli and may make it harder for consumers to identify the goals and messages of the programs and their contents.

At times, marketers may (knowingly or unknowingly) create inferences that do not accurately characterize an offering, which results in miscomprehension.[160] For instance, Taiwan's Fair Trade Commission fined Colgate for a comparative TV commercial in which the competing toothpaste brand wasn't sufficiently disguised. The ad was intended to convey Colgate's superiority in reducing teeth sensitivity. However, the commission said consumers could be misled into thinking that the competing brand was an inferior toothpaste, even though it also contained ingredients proven to reduce sensitivity.[161] The U.S. Food and Drug Administration has warned some tobacco marketers about making claims that their cigarettes are "natural," thereby suggesting a lower health risk.[162] When consumers associate "natural" cigarettes with lower health risks, this would be an example of a consumer inference.

> **Perceptual fluency**
> The ease with which information is processed.

3-4c CONSUMER INFERENCES

Specific elements of the marketing mix can affect the correct or incorrect inferences consumers make about an offering during comprehension. *Inferences* are the conclusions that consumers draw or interpretations that they form based on the message. Such inferences may lead to conclusions such as (1) if brand A contains attribute 1 then it will also contain attribute 2 (congruent) or (2) if brand A contains attribute 1 then it will not contain attribute 2 (incongruent). Here, we look at the effect of brand names and symbols, product features and packaging, price, message wording, and retail atmospherics and display.

Brand Names and Symbols

Subjective comprehension of a marketing communication can be based on the inferences consumers make from a brand symbol. For example, the Pillsbury Doughboy has slimmed down over the years because the company's marketers were afraid that consumers would infer that he was fat from eating Pillsbury products. Google changed the typeface of its brand not long ago to give it a modern look, enable animation, and make it more readable on smaller screens such as smart watches.[163]

Brand names themselves can create subjective comprehension and inferences. For example, alphanumeric brand names like BMW's X6 tend to be associated with technological sophistication. When presented with brand names such as X-500 and X-700, consumers tend to prefer names with higher numerical values, inferring that the product will have advanced attributes.[164] In addition, consumers tend to make inferences when they evaluate a brand extension by carrying over certain features linked to the parent brand.[165]

Descriptive names can also create inferences. Brand names such as Speedo for bathing suits may create inferences about the particular brand's benefits.[166] Marketers sometimes use old or retired brands to launch new products or enter new markets, banking on recognition and inferences from the past. Nissan, for instance, used to market low-priced vehicles worldwide under the Datsun name before discontinuing the brand in the 1980s. Decades later, Nissan reintroduced the Datsun brand on low-priced cars in India, Russia, and other emerging markets.[167] Exposure to brands can also influence how we behave. One study showed that video-game players drove faster and more recklessly in a racing game when exposed to the Red Bull logo.[168]

Product Features and Packaging

Consumers may subjectively comprehend aspects of an offering based on inferences they make from the product and the way that it is packaged. For example, consumers may infer that a product with a low repair record also has a long warranty.[169] As another example, a consumer who encounters a large, multipack item may use prior knowledge about the correlation between price and package size to infer that the large-sized brand is also a good buy.[170]

Consumers make taste inferences based on nutritional information presented about food products, inferences that affect their buying and consumption decisions. Some research shows that consumers who are given nutritional information about a product are more likely to see it as healthier than when they are not given nutritional information. However, they will also infer that the healthier product will not taste as good as an unhealthier product.[171] Moreover, consumers infer that products with unusual flavors or color names are better than products that use common flavors or color names.[172]

When consumers are searching for information about whether a product will deliver a particular benefit, exposure to irrelevant attributes leads to inferences that the product will not necessarily perform as desired.[173] In highly competitive categories, where differences among products seem minimal, consumers may infer that although the dominant brand is good on observable attributes it has a disadvantage on some unobservable attribute.[174]

Knowledge about a product's country of origin can affect the way consumers think about it.[175] Just as we stereotype people based on where they were born, we stereotype products based on where they were made. Consumers in developing countries, for instance, often infer higher quality for brands perceived as foreign.[176]

Conversely, consumers in some nations believe their country's products are superior to those made elsewhere. Japanese consumers, for example, tend to infer that made-in-Japan products are higher quality than made-in-America products. Therefore, Samsonite markets its pricier luggage in Japan by stressing that the products are designed and made in Japan.[177] Consumers are more likely to make inferences about a brand based on its country of origin when they are unmotivated to process brand information or when their processing goal guides attention toward origin information.[178] If consumers dislike a country's political or social policies, they may respond negatively to its products.[179]

Package characteristics can also stimulate inferences. Although consumers may make inferences about one brand if its packaging looks much like that of the market leader, they do not necessarily react negatively to the copycat brand.[180] As bargain-hunting consumers increasingly seek out cost-effective store brands, more retailers are redesigning their packaging to point out the differences between store and national brands. Walgreens, for example, has renamed and repackaged its store-brand merchandise to stand out and look more distinctive next to national brands.[181]

Price

Consumers sometimes (but not always) make inferences about an offering's quality based on its price.[182] They may know from prior experience that price and quality tend to be correlated in a particular product category, and then infer that a high-priced product is also high in quality.[183] Consumers often make this inference when they believe that brands differ in quality, when they perceive that choosing a low-quality product can be risky, and when they have no information about the brand's quality before they buy it.[184] When consumers use price as a shortcut to infer quality, they may overestimate the relationship between price and quality.[185] Note that some consumers may infer that a low price means poor quality, whereas others may infer that a low price means good value.[186]

Also, consumers judge a product in a smaller package to be of higher quality than the equivalent product in a larger package, because the smaller package carries a higher unit price.[187] Culture can influence perceptions of price and quality as well, because of differences in cognitive styles. Generally, consumers from less individualistic cultures such as Japan and China rely more on price to judge quality than consumers from more individualistic cultures such as France, Canada, and the United States.[188]

Independent of potential quality inference, rounded prices (e.g., $20) are perceived more fluently than non-rounded prices ($19.99 or $20.01) are. This may increase the preference for products with rounded prices, when consumers rely on their feelings (rather than their thoughts) as they shop. When relying on one's feelings, the ease of perceiving rounded prices feels good, and this transfers to the product.[189]

Offering a product with *no* price (meaning *free*, as in a gift with purchase) can increase the consumer's willingness to pay for the product after the promotion expires. The reason is that consumers perceive little or no devaluation of the free product, especially in the purchase context of a high-priced item, because they use the price of the expensive product to estimate the value of the freebie.[190] Method of payment affects inferences about pricing, as well. When consumers have been primed for cash, they focus more on costs in evaluating the product. On the other hand, when they have been primed for credit cards, they tend to focus more on the product's benefits.[191]

Price plays an important role in marketing of medications. According to research, consumers infer that lower-priced medications are more available to people who need them, and this feeling of accessibility increases perceptions of self-risk, resulting in higher consumption. Inferences about higher-priced medications have the opposite effect, decreasing perceptions of self-risk and lowering consumption.[192]

Message Wording

Consumers draw inferences from the way marketing messages are worded. Suppose a product's warranty period is promoted in terms of months (such as 60 months) rather than in terms of years (five years). Here, consumers will focus on the numbers, not the units of measure, which will lead them to perceive greater differences between products that describe warranty periods in terms of larger numbers.[193] Inferences related to the unit of measure come into play in other situations, such as when consumers perceive that a delivery period of "1–2 weeks" seems longer than "7–14 days" because they focus on the magnitude of the measure of time (weeks seem longer than days).[194] If consumers mentally "rehearse" message wording about prices and discounts,

the mere sounds of numbers can influence and distort perception of the numerical magnitude on a nonconscious level.[195]

Retail Atmospherics, Displays, and Distribution

Comprehension can be influenced by retailers' marketing tactics. The inferences you make when walking into a warehouse-type store like Costco are likely to be different from the inferences you make entering a more upscale, service-oriented store like Nordstrom. Atmospherics are a major tool used to develop, elaborate, and change store images. The Duane Reade drug store in New York City's financial district is nothing like the typical drug store, urban or suburban. Housed in a former bank building with marble walls and vaulted ceilings, this store has a two-story lobby and a holographic "greeter" who talks up special features such as the stock ticker, manicure center, and sushi stations.[196] Whether the retail environment is organized or not is another factor, because consumers tend to have lower self-control in a disorganized environment, which affects impulse purchasing.[197] When consumers are in an unstructured setting, they seek out structure by showing a preference for retail environments, products, and brand logos that are tangibly or intangibly bordered.[198]

The context of a product display is also important. In particular, it may lead consumers to rely more on external cues—meaning that a brand's positioning could be undermined by a store's inappropriate retail display decisions.[199]

Moreover, consumers may draw inferences from the way an offering is distributed. For example, food trucks have not traditionally been associated with innovative, top-quality meals or snacks. These days, however, consumers expect novel tastes when they approach one of the many gourmet food trucks crisscrossing streets from Portland, Oregon, to Portland, Maine. Many food trucks announce their routes via Twitter or mobile apps, adding an "insider" association to the experience of being in the right place at the right time.[200]

Summary:

For a marketing stimulus to have an impact, consumers must be exposed to it, allocate some attention to it, and perceive it. Consumers need a basic level of attention to perceive a stimulus before they can use additional mental resources to process the stimulus at higher levels. Exposure occurs when the consumer is presented with a marketing stimulus. Attention occurs when the consumer allocates mental activity to the stimulus. Attention is limited, selective, and can be divided, and may be focal or nonfocal. Consumers perceive a stimulus by using one or more of their five senses.

Perceptual thresholds determine the point at which stimuli are perceived. Consumers can sometimes perceive things outside of their conscious level of awareness, a phenomenon called subliminal perception. Perceptual organization occurs when consumers organize a set of stimuli into a coherent whole, affected by the principles of figure and ground, closure, grouping, and preference for the whole. Comprehension is the process of extracting higher-order meaning from what consumers have perceived in the context of what they know. This starts with source identification ("what is it actually?") and continues with message comprehension ("what about it?"), including objective comprehension (accurately understanding what is stated) and subjective comprehension (what consumers understand from the message). Finally, consumers may make correct or incorrect inferences from various elements of the marketing mix during the comprehension process.

Questions for Review and Discussion

1. **How do skipping, zipping, zapping, and cord-cutting affect consumers' exposure to marketing stimuli such as products and ads?**

2. **What is attention, and what are its three key characteristics?**

3. **In what ways do prominence and habituation affect consumer attention?**

4. **What is perception, and what methods do we use to perceive stimuli?**

5. **Differentiate between the absolute threshold and the differential threshold, and explain how these concepts relate to Weber's law.**

6. **Identify four principles of perceptual organization and describe why marketers need to know about them.**

7. **Discuss how source identification and message comprehension affect consumers' comprehension of a stimulus.**

8. **What are some ways that companies can use marketing-mix elements such as brand names and symbols to affect consumer inferences?**

Endnotes

1   Sue Doerfler, "Marketing Sense: How Retailers Use 5 Senses to Appeal to Customers," *Arizona Republic*, April 24, 2015, www.azcentral.com.

2   Adam Finn, "Print Ad Recognition Readership Scores: An Information Processing Perspective," *Journal of Marketing Research*, May 1988, pp. 168–177.

3   Justin Lafferty, "Adobe Q2 Report: Facebook Beats Google /YouTube at Getting You to Click on Ads," *Adweek*, July 15, 2015, www.adweek.com; and George Slefo, "Pinterest Users Can Now Search With Pictures," *Advertising Age*, November 9, 2015, www.adage.com.

4   Oliver Nieburg, "For Whom the Till Tolls: Could Impulse Candy Buys Flatline as Checkouts Phase Out?" *Confectionery News*, March 7, 2014, www.confectionerynews.com.

5   Brittany R. L. Duff and Ronald J. Faber, "Missing the Mark: Advertising Avoidance and Distractor Devaluation," *Journal of Advertising*, Summer 2011, pp. 51–62.

6   Erik du Plessis, "Digital Video Recorders and Inadvertent Advertising Exposure," *Journal of Advertising Research*, June 2009, p. 236ff; and Steve McClellan, "It's Inescapable: DVRs Here to Stay," *Television Week*, November 29, 2004, p. 17.

7   S. Adam Brasel and James Gips, "Breaking through Fast-Forwarding: Brand Information and Visual Attention," *Journal of Marketing*, November 2008, pp. 31–48.

8   Steven Bellman, Anika Schweda, and Duane Varan, "The Residual Impact of Avoided Television Advertising," *Journal of Advertising*, Spring 2010, pp. 67–81.

9   Dean M. Krugman, Glen T. Cameron, and Candace McKearney White, "Visual Attention to Programming and Commercials," *Journal of Advertising*, Spring 1995, pp. 1–12; and S. Siddarth and Amitava Chattopadhyay, "To Zap or Not to Zap: A Study of the Determinants of Channel Switching During Commercials," *Marketing Science* 17, no. 2, 1998, pp. 124–138.

10 Meg James and Yvonne Villarreal, "Cord Cutters Face a Sea of Streaming Options," *Los Angeles Times*, January 1, 2016, www.latimes.com.

11 Matthew Ingram, "Pay TV Industry: Yes, Cord-Cutting Is Accelerating, But It Could Be Worse!" *Fortune*, November 10, 2015, www.fortune.com; "Adam Flomenbaum, "Why TV Is Going Nowhere, Cord Cutting Is Years Away, and Cable Companies Are Safe," *The Drum*, November 2, 2015, www.thedrum.com.

12 Mark Scott, "Study of Ad-Blocking Software Suggests Wide Use," *New York Times*, August 10, 2015, www.nytimes.com; and Steven M. Edwards, Hairong Li, and Joo-Hyun Lee, "Forced Exposure and Psychological Reactance," *Journal of Advertising*, Fall 2002, pp. 83–95.

13 Trent Gillies, "Advertisers Sweat as Ad Blockers Proliferate," *CNBC*, October 25, 2015, www.cnbc.com.

14 Emma Thomasson, "Adidas Brand to Take Over as NHL Supplier from Reebok in 2017," *Reuters*, September 16, 2015, www.reuters.com; Julie Cruz, "Adidas Targets Teenage Girls for $1.3 Billion in Sales," *Bloomberg News*, February 13, 2012, www.bloomberg.com; Ellen E. Jervell, "Adidas Forecasts Bouncier Sales After Good Quarter," *Wall Street Journal*, November 5, 2015, www.wsj.com; and Katie Richards, "Adidas Taps Influencers for a Unique Run Through the Streets of New York," *Adweek*, October 29, 2015, www.adweek.com.

15 Jan R. Landwehr, Daniel Wentzel, and Andreas Herrmann, "Product Design for the Long Run: Consumer Responses to Typical and Atypical Designs at Different Stages of Exposure," *Journal of Marketing* 76, no. 2, March 2012, pp. 33–46.

16 Brant James, "Danica Patrick Locks Up Sponsorship for All 2016 Sprint Cup Races," *USA Today*, October 30, 2015, www.usatoday.com.

17 George Slefo, "Legacy Retailers Struggle to Ramp Up Mobile Marketing," *Advertising Age*, November 9, 2015, www.adage.com.

18 Chris Griffith, "Woolworths Unveils Virtual Supermarket in Sydney," *The Australian*, February 20, 2012, www.theaustralian.com.

19 Tim Peterson, "How Brands, Publishers Are Tailoring Their Ads for Snapchat Discover," *Advertising Age*, October 20, 2015, www.adage.com.

20 Yvonne Villarreal, "Willing to Interact with an Ad? You Can Watch Some Hulu Shows Commercial-Free If You Do," *Los Angeles Times*, November 3, 2015, www.latimes.com.

21 Sam Creighton, "Making a Killing! 17 Different Brands Linger on Screen in New Bond Film *Spectre* and 007 Himself 'Profits from Each Endorsement," *Daily Mail (UK)*, October 22, 2015, www.dailymail.co.uk.

22 Abe Sauer, "US TV Product Placement Boosts Brands, Even as It's Shrinking," *Brandchannel*, October 19, 2015, www.brandchannel.com.

23 L. Hasher and R. T. Zacks, "Automatic and Effortful Processes in Memory," *Journal of Experimental Psychology: General*, September 1979, pp. 356–388; W. Schneider and R. M. Shiffrin, "Controlled and Automatic Human Information Processing," *Psychological Review*, January 1977, pp. 1–66; and R. M. Shiffrin and W. Schneider, "Controlled and Automatic Human Information Processing," *Psychological Review*, March 1977, pp. 127–190.

24 Rik Pieters, Edward Rosbergen, and Michel Wedel, "Visual Attention to Repeated Print Advertising: A Test of Scanpath Theory," *Journal of Marketing Research* 36, November 1999, pp. 424–438.

25 Rik Pieters and Michel Wedel, "Goal Control of Attention to Advertising: The Yarbus Implication," *Journal of Consumer Research*, August 2007, pp. 224–233.

26 Chris Janiszewski, Andrew Kuo, and Nader T. Tavassoli, "The Influence of Selective Attention and Inattention to Products on Subsequent Choice," *Journal of Consumer Research* 39, no. 6, April 2013, pp. 1258–1274.

27 Scott B. MacKenzie, "The Role of Attention in Mediating the Effect of Advertising on Attribute Importance," *Journal of Consumer Research*, September 1986, pp. 174–195; and Richard E. Petty and Timothy C. Brock, "Thought Disruption and Persuasion," in eds. Richard E. Petty, Thomas Ostrom, and Timothy C. Brock, *Cognitive Responses in Persuasion* (Hillsdale, N.J.: Lawrence Erlbaum, 1981), pp. 55–79.

28 Chris Janiszewski, "Preattentive Mere Exposure Effects," *Journal of Consumer Research*, December 1993, pp. 376–392; Janiszewski, "Preconscious Processing Effects"; and Chris Janiszewski, "The Influence of Print Advertisement Organization on Affect Toward a Brand Name," *Journal of Consumer Research* 17, June 1990, pp. 53–65.

29 Janiszewski, "Preattentive Mere Exposure Effects"; Stewart Shapiro and Deborah J. MacInnis, "Mapping the Relationship Between Preattentive Processing and Attitudes," in eds. John Sherry and Brian Sternthal, *Advances in Consumer Research*, vol. 19 (Provo, Utah: Association for Consumer Research, 1992), pp. 505–513.

30 Stewart Shapiro, "When an Ad's Influence Is Beyond Our Conscious Control," *Journal of Consumer Research* 26, June 1999, pp. 16–36; and Stewart Shapiro, Deborah J. MacInnis, and Susan E. Heckler, "The Effects of Incidental Ad Exposure on the Formation of Consideration Sets," *Journal of Consumer Research*, June 1997, pp. 94–104.

31 Robert Heath, "Emotional Engagement: How Television Builds Big Brands at Low Attention," *Journal of Advertising Research*, March 2009, pp. 62–73.

32 Jesper H. Nielsen, Stewart A. Shapiro, and Charlotte H. Mason, "Emotionality and Semantic Onsets: Exploring Orienting Attention Responses in Advertising," *Journal of Marketing Research*, December 2010, pp. 1138–1150.

33 Richard L. Celsi and Jerry C. Olson, "The Role of Involvement in Attention and Comprehension Processes," *Journal of Consumer Research*, September 1988, pp. 210–224.

34 Arch Woodside and J. William Davenport Jr., "The Effect of Salesman Similarity and Expertise on Consumer Purchasing Behavior," *Journal of Marketing Research*, May 1974, pp. 198–202.

35 Robert E. Burnkrant and Daniel J. Howard, "Effects of the Use of Introductory Rhetorical Questions Versus Statements on Information Processing," *Journal of Personality and Social Psychology*, December 1984, pp. 1218–1230.

36 Grant McCracken, "Who Is the Celebrity Endorser? Cultural Foundations of the Endorsement Process," *Journal of Consumer Research*, December 1989, pp. 310–321; and Jeffrey Burroughs and Richard A. Feinberg, "Using Response Latency to Assess Spokesperson Effectiveness," *Journal of Consumer Research*, September 1987, pp. 295–299.

37 Deborah J. MacInnis and C. Whan Park, "The Differential Role of Characteristics of Music on High and Low-Involvement Consumers' Processing of Ads," *Journal of Consumer Research*, September 1991, pp. 161–173; David W. Stewart and David H. Furse, *Effective Television Advertising: A Study of 1000 Commercials* (Lexington, Mass.: Lexington Books, 1986); James J. Kellaris and Robert J. Kent, "An Exploratory Investigation of Responses Elicited by Music Varying in Tempo, Tonality, and Texture," *Journal of Consumer Psychology*, March 1993, pp. 381–402; and James J. Kellaris, Anthony Cox, and Dena Cox, "The Effects of Background Music on Ad Processing Contingency Explanation," *Journal of Consumer Research*, October 1993, pp. 114–126.

38 Kristina Monllos, "How Jeep Found the Perfect Song to Launch Its Renegade Campaign," *Advertising Age*, April 17, 2015, www.adage.com.

39 Brian Sternthal and Samuel Craig, "Humor in Advertising," *Journal of Marketing*, October 1973, pp. 12–18; and Thomas

Madden and Marc G. Weinberger, "The Effect of Humor on Attention in Magazine Advertising," *Journal of Advertising*, September 1982, pp. 8–14.

40 Iain Akerman, "Berlitz—Don't Be an Alien," *Campaign Middle East*, February 28, 2011, www.campaignme.com.

41 Josephine L. C. M. Woltman Elpers, Ashesh Mukherjee, and Wayne D. Hoyer, "Humor in Television Advertising: A Moment-to-Moment Analysis," *Journal of Consumer Research*, December 2004, pp. 592–598.

42 Lauren Johnson, "Virtual Reality Is Grabbing Brands' Attention but Not Their Ad Dollars," *Adweek*, May 31, 2015, www .adweek.com.

43 Eliza Barklay, "At 'Pestaurant,' Grasshopper Burgers Win Over Eaters Who Say 'Yuck,'" *National Public Radio*, June 10, 2014, www.npr.org.

44 Satya Menon and Dilip Soman, "Managing the Power of Curiosity for Effective Web Strategies," *Journal of Advertising*, Fall 2002, pp. 1–14; Yih Hwai Lee, "Manipulating Ad Message Involvement Through Information Expectancy," *Journal of Advertising* 29, no. 2, Summer 2000, pp. 29–42; and Joan Meyers-Levy and Alice Tybout, "Schema Congruity as a Basis for Product Evaluation," *Journal of Consumer Research*, June 1989, pp. 39–54. Characteristics of music can also cause surprise; see James Kellaris and Ronald Rice, "The Influence of Tempo, Loudness and Gender of Listener on Responses to Music," *Psychology and Marketing* 10, no. 1, 1993, pp. 15–29.

45 Dana L. Alden, Ashesh Mukherjee, and Wayne D. Hoyer, "The Effects of Incongruity, Surprise and Positive Moderators on Perceived Humor in Television Advertising," *Journal of Advertising* 29, no. 2, Summer 2000, pp. 1–15; and Elpers, Mukherjee, and Hoyer, "Humor in Television Advertising : A Moment-to-Moment Analysis."

46 Mae Anderson, "Super Bowl Ads: Slapstick, Cameos Strike a Funny Note," *The Statesman* (Austin, Tex.), February 6, 2011, www.statesman.com.

47 Edward F. McQuarrie and David Glen Mick, "Visual Rhetoric in Advertising," *Journal of Consumer Research* 26, June 1999, pp. 37–54.

48 Rik Pieters and Michel Wedel, "Attention Capture and Transfer in Advertising: Brand, Pictorial, and Text-size Effects," *Journal of Marketing*, April 2004, pp. 36–50.

49 Ibid.

50 S. Shyam Sundar and Sriram Kalyanaraman, "Arousal, Memory, and Impression-Formation Effects of Animation Speed in Web Advertising," *Journal of Advertising*, Spring 2004, pp. 7–17; Werner Krober-Riel, "Activation Research," *Journal of Consumer Research*, March 1979, pp. 240–250; and Morris B. Holbrook and Donald R. Lehmann, "Form vs. Content in Predicting Starch Scores," *Journal of Advertising Research*, August 1980, pp. 53–62.

51 Priya Raghubir and Eric A. Greenleaf, "Ratios in Proportion: What Should the Shape of the Package Be?" *Journal of Marketing*, April 2006, pp. 95–107; Priya Raghubir and Aradhna Krishna, "Vital Dimensions in Volume Perception: Can the Eye Fool the Stomach?" *Journal of Marketing Research* 36, August 1999, pp. 313–326; and Aradhna Krishna, "Interaction of Senses: The Effect of Vision Versus Touch on the Elongation Bias," *Journal of Consumer Research* 32, no. 4, 2006, pp. 557–566.

52 Mackenzie, "The Role of Attention in Mediating the Effect of Advertising on Attribute Importance."

53 Ryan S. Elder and Aradhna Krishna, "The 'Visual Depiction Effect' in Advertising: Facilitating Embodied Mental Simulation through Product Orientation, *Journal of Consumer Research* 38, no. 6, April 2012, pp. 988–1003.

54 Chris Janiszewski, "The Influence of Display Characteristics on Visual Exploratory Search Behavior," *Journal of Consumer Research*, December 1998, pp. 290–301.

55 Walter Nicholls, "The U.S. Is Turned On to Wine," *Washington Post*, January 2, 2008, www.washingtonpost.com.

56 Rik Pieters, Michael Wedel, and Jie Zhang, "Optimal Feature Advertising Design under Competitive Clutter," *Management Science*, November 2007, pp. 1815–1828.

57 Edward Rosbergen, Rik Pieters, and Michel Wedel, "Visual Attention to Advertising: A Segment-Level Analysis," *Journal of Consumer Research*, December 1997, pp. 305–314.

58 Hannah Abdulla, "Kellogg Targets 'Emerging Needs' in US NPD Roll-out," *Just Food*, November 19, 2015, www.just-food.com.

59 See Aradna Krishma, *Customer Sense: How the 5 Senses Influence Buying Behavior* (New York: Palgrave McMillan, 2013).

60 See, for example, Minu Kumar and Nitika Garg, "Aesthetic Principles and Cognitive Emotion Appraisals: How Much of the Beauty Lies in the Eye of the Beholder?" *Journal of Consumer Psychology* 20, no. 4, Special Issue, October 2010, pp. 485–494; and Martin Reimann, Judith Zaichkowsky, Carolin Neuhaus, Thomas Bender, and Bernd Weber, "Aesthetic Package Design: A Behavioral, Neural, and Psychological Investigation," *Journal of Consumer Psychology* 20, no. 4, Special Issue, October 2010, pp. 431–441.

61 Valerie Folkes and Shashi Matta, "The Effect of Package Shape on Consumers' Judgments of Product Volume," *Journal of Consumer Research*, September 2004, pp. 390–401.

62 Pierre Chandon and Nailya Ordabayeva, "Supersize in One Dimension, Downsize in Three Dimensions: Effects of Spatial Dimensionality on Size Perceptions and Preferences," *Journal of Marketing Research*, December 2009, pp. 739–753.

63 Nailya Ordabayeva and Pierre Chandon, "Predicting and Managing Consumers' Package Size Impressions," *Journal of Marketing* 77, no. 5, September 2013, pp. 123–137.

64 John R. Doyle and Paul A. Bottomley, "Dressed for the Occasion: Font-Product Congruity in the Perception of Logotype," *Journal of Consumer Psychology* 16, no. 2, 2006, pp. 112–123.

65 Xiaoyan Deng and Barbara E. Kahn, "Is Your Product on the Right Side? The 'Location Effect' on Perceived Product Heaviness and Package Evaluation," *Journal of Marketing Research*, December 2009, pp. 725–738.

66 Michel Wedel and Rik Pieters, "The Buffer Effect: The Role of Color When Advertising Exposures Are Brief and Blurred," *Marketing Science* 34, no. 1, 2015, pp. 134–143.

67 Rajesh Bagchi and Amar Cheema, "The Effect of Red Background Color on Willingness-to-Pay: The Moderating Role of Selling Mechanism," *Journal of Consumer Research* 39, no. 5, March 2013, pp. 947–960.

68 Brian Bennett, "GE Artistry Fridge Wants to Add a Dollop of Color to Your Kitchen," *Cnet*, January 8, 2015, www.cnet.com.

69 Ioannis Kareklas, Frederic F. Brunel, and Robin A. Coulter, "Judgment Is Not Color Blind: The Impact of Automatic Color Preference on Product and Advertising Preferences," *Journal of Consumer Psychology* 24, no. 1, January 2014, pp. 87–95.

70 Fabrizio Di Muro and Theodore J. Noseworthy, "Money Isn't Everything, But It Helps If It Doesn't Look Used: How the Physical Appearance of Money Influences Spending," *Journal of Consumer Research* 39, no. 6, April 2013, pp. 1330–1342.

71 Peter H. Lindsay and Donald A. Norman, *Human Information Processing: An Introduction to Psychology*, 2nd ed. (New York : Academic Press, 1977).

72 Amitava Chattopadhyay, Darren W. Dahl, Robin J. B. Ritchie, and Kimary N. Shahin, "Hearing Voices: The Impact of Announcer Speech Characteristics on Consumer Response to Broadcast Advertising," *Journal of Consumer Psychology* 13, no. 3, 2003, pp. 198–204.

73 Adi Robertson, "Sound Decision," *The Verge*, October 7, 2015, www.theverge.com.

74 Eric Yorkston and Geeta Menon, "A Sound Idea: Phonetic Effects of Brand Names on Consumer Judgments," *Journal of Consumer Research*, June 2004, pp. 43–51.

75 Chris Dearden, "Electric Vehicles Find Their Voice," *New Zealand Herald*, August 27, 2011, www.nzherald.co.nz.

76 Jennifer J. Argo, Monica Popa, and Malcolm C. Smith, "The Sound of Brands," *Journal of Marketing* 74, no. 4, July 2010, pp. 97–109.

77 Ravi Mehta, Rui (Juliet) Zhu, and Amar Cheema, "Is Noise Always Bad? Exploring the Effects of Ambient Noise on Creative Cognition," *Journal of Consumer Research* 39, no. 4, December 2012, pp. 784–799.

78 Kate Fitzgerald, "In-Store Media Ring Cash Register," *Advertising Age*, February 9, 2004, p. 43.

79 Kathryn Tuggle, "More Businesses Turning to Free Samples to Drum up Business," *Fox Business*, August 15, 2011, http://small-business.foxbusiness.com; and David Phillips, "Natural Sweeteners Help Manufacturers Hit the Beverage Sweet Spot," *Food Processing*, May 14, 2014, www.foodprocessing.com.

80 D. Biswas, C. Szocs, A. Krishna, and D. R. Lehmann, "Something to Chew On: The Effects of Oral Haptics on Mastication, Orosensory Perception, and Calorie Estimation," *Journal of Consumer Research* 41, no. 2, August 2014, pp. 261–273.

81 Trygg Engen, *The Perception of Odors* (New York: Academic Press, 1982); and Trygg Engen, "Remembering Odors and Their Names," *American Scientist*, September–October 1987, pp. 497–503.

82 Hannah Booth, "Sound Minds: Brands These Days Need to Sound Good as Well as Look Good," *Design Week*, April 15, 2004, p. 163.

83 T. Schemper, S. Voss, and W. S. Cain, "Odor Identification in Young and Elderly Persons," *Journal of Gerontology*, December 1981, pp. 446–452; and J. C. Stevens and W. S. Cain, "Smelling via the Mouth: Effect of Aging," *Perception and Psychophysics*, September 1986, pp. 142–146.

84 W. S. Cain, "Odor Identification by Males and Females: Prediction vs. Performance," *Chemical Senses*, February 1982, pp. 129–142.

85 M. S. Kirk-Smith, C. Van Toller, and G. H. Dodd, "Unconscious Odor Conditioning in Human Subjects," *Biological Psychology* 17, 1983, pp. 221–231; Pamela Weentraug, "Sentimental Journeys: Smells Have the Power to Arouse Our Deepest Memories, Our Most Primitive Drives," *Omni*, August 1986, p. 815; Howard Erlichman and Jack N. Halpern, "Affect and Memory," *Journal of Personality and Social Psychology*, May 1988, pp. 769–779; and Frank R. Schab, "Odors and the Remembrance of Things Past," *Journal of Experimental Psychology: Learning, Memory and Cognition*, July 1990, pp. 648–655.

86 James Archer, "Let Them Sniff, Customers Will Buy More," *Inc.*, January 23, 2013, www.inc.com; and Josh Sanburn, "NYC Grocery Store Pipes in Artificial Food Smells," *Time*, July 20, 2011, www.moneyland.time.com.

87 Anick Bosmans, "Scents and Sensibility: When Do (In)Congruent Ambient Scents Influence Product Evaluations?" *Journal of Marketing*, July 2006, pp. 32–43.

88 Maureen Morrin and S. Ratneshwar, "Does It Make Sense to Use Scents to Enhance Brand Memory?" *Journal of Marketing Research*, February 2003, pp. 10–25.

89 Humayun Khan, "How Retailers Manipulate Sight, Smell, and Sound to Trigger Purchase Behavior in Consumers," *Shopify*, May 21, 2014, www.shopify.com.

90 Joann Peck and Terry L. Childers, "Individual Differences in Haptic Information Processing," *Journal of Consumer Research*, December 2003, pp. 430–442.

91 Joann Peck and Jennifer Wiggins, "It Just Feels Good: Customers' Affective Response to Touch and Its Influence on Persuasion," *Journal of Marketing*, October 2006, pp. 57–69.

92 Deborah Brown McCabe and Stephen M. Nowlis, "The Effect of Examining Actual Products or Product Descriptions on Consumer Preference," *Journal of Consumer Psychology* 13, no. 4, 2003, pp. 431–439.

93 Joann Peck, Victor A. Barger, and Andrea Webb, "In Search of a Surrogate for Touch: The Effect of Haptic Imagery on Perceived Ownership," *Journal of Consumer Psychology* 23, no. 2, April 2013, pp. 189–196.

94 Jacob Hornik, "Tactile Stimulation and Consumer Response," *Journal of Consumer Research*, December 1992, pp. 449–458.

95 Sak Onkvisit and John J. Shaw, *International Marketing: Analysis and Strategy* (Columbus, Ohio: Merrill, 1989).

96 Jennifer J. Argo, Darren W. Dahl, and Andrea C. Morales, "Positive Consumer Contagion: Responses to Attractive Others in a Retail Context," *Journal of Marketing Research*, December 2008, pp. 690–701.

97 Idit Shalev, "Implicit Energy Loss: Embodied Dryness Cues Influence Vitality and Depletion," *Journal of Consumer Psychology* 24, no. 2, April 2014, pp. 260–270.

98 Amar Cheema and Vanessa M. Patrick, "Influence of Warm Versus Cool Temperatures on Consumer Choice: A Resource Depletion Account," *Journal of Marketing Research* 49, no. 6, December 2012, pp. 984–995.

99 Yonat Zwebner, Leonard Lee, and Jacob Goldenberg, "The Temperature Premium: Warm Temperatures Increase Product Valuation," *Journal of Consumer Psychology* 24, no. 2, Special Issue, April 2014, pp. 251–259.

100 Seung Hwan (Mark) Lee, Jeff D. Rotman, and Andrew W. Perkins, "Embodied Cognition and Social Consumption: Self-Regulating Temperature through Social Products and Behaviors," *Journal of Consumer Psychology* 24, no. 2, Special Issue, April 2014, pp. 234–240.

101 Aradhna Krishna, Editor, Sensory Marketing: Research on the Sensuality of Products (New York: Routledge, 2010).

102 Gun R. Semin and Tomas A. Palma, "Why the Bride Wears White: Grounding Gender with Brightness," *Journal of Consumer Psychology* 24, no. 2, Special Issue, April 2014, pp. 217–225.

103 Sonya Padgett, "Designer Creates Uniforms MGM Workers Want to Wear," *Las Vegas Review-Journal*, August 28, 2011, www.lvrj. com.

104 Erin Flynn, "NFL Reveals Thanksgiving Color Rush Uniforms for Cowboys vs. Panthers," *Sports Illustrated*, November 20, 2015, www.si.com.

105 Charles Spence, "Managing Sensory Expectations Concerning Products and Brands: Capitalizing on the Potential of Sound and Shape Symbolism," *Journal of Consumer Psychology* 22, no. 1, Special Issue, January 2012, pp. 37–54.

106 A. Selin Atalay, H. Onur Bodur, and Dina Rasolofoarison, "Shining in the Center: Central Gaze Cascade Effect on Product Choice," *Journal of Consumer Research* 39, no. 4, December 2012, pp. 848–866.

107 Jayson Shi Jia, Baba Shiv, and Sanjay Rao, "The Product-Agnosia Effect: How More Visual Impressions Affect Product Distinctiveness in Comparative Choice," *Journal of Consumer Research*, August 2014, pp. 342–360.

108 Alison Jing Xu and Aparna A. Labroo, "Incandescent Affect: Turning on the Hot Emotional System with Bright Light," *Journal of Consumer Psychology* 24, no. 2, Special Issue, April 2014, pp. 207–216.

109 Ronald E. Milliman, "Using Background Music to Affect the Behavior of Supermarket Shoppers," *Journal of Marketing*, Summer 1982, pp. 86–91.

110 Colleen Bazdarich, "In a Buying Mood? Maybe It's the Muzak," *Business 2.0*, March 2002, p. 100.

111 Ronald E. Millman, "The Influence of Background Music on the Behavior of Restaurant Patrons," *Journal of Consumer Research*, September 1986, pp. 286–289; and Richard Yalch and Eric Spannenberg, "Effects of Store Music on Shopping Behavior," *Journal of Services Marketing*, Winter 1990, pp. 31–39.

112 Barry Shlachter, "Fort Worth's Newest Burger Joint Draws In-N-Out Crowd," *Fort Worth Star-Telegram*, August 11, 2011, www.star-telegram.com.

113 Gerald J. Gorn, "The Effects of Music in Advertising on Choice Behavior," *Journal of Marketing*, Winter 1982, pp. 94–101; C. Whan Park and S. Mark Young, "Consumer Response to Television Commercials," *Journal of Marketing Research*, February 1986, pp. 11–24; and MacInnis and Park, "The Differential Role of Characteristics of Music on High and Low-Involvement Consumers' Processing of Ads."

114 JoAndrea Hoegg and Joseph W. Alba, "Taste Perception: More (and Less) than Meets the Tongue," *Journal of Consumer Research*, March 2007, pp. 490–498.

115 Bruce Watson, "Turning Foul Flavors into Sweet Success," *Daily Finance*, September 11, 2010, www.dailyfinance.com; and Jeanne Whalen, "Foul Taste Is Part of the Cure," *Wall Street Journal*, November 5, 2007, p. B4.

116 Lauren Johnson, "How Lay's Is Adding More Social Zest to Its Popular Flavor-Creation Campaign," *Adweek*, February 27, 2015, www.adweek.com.

117 Sascha Topolinski, Sandy Lindner, and Anna Freudenberg, "Popcorn in the Cinema: Oral Interference Sabotages Advertising Effects," *Journal of Consumer Psychology* 24, no. 2, Special Issue, April 2014, pp. 169–176.

118 Dipayan Biswas, Lauren I. Labrecque, Donald R. Lehmann, and Ereni Markos, "Making Choices While Smelling, Tasting, and Listening: The Role of Sensory (Dis)similarity When Sequentially Sampling Products," *Journal of Marketing* 78, no. 1, January 2014, pp. 112–126.

119 Sigurd Villads Troye and Magne Supphellen, "Consumer Participation in Coproduction: 'I Made It Myself' Effects on Consumers' Sensory Perceptions and Evaluations of Outcome and Input Product," *Journal of Marketing* 76, no. 2, March 2012, pp. 33–46.

120 Rachel Feltman, "The Mind-Blowing Science of How Febreze Hides Your Smelliness," *Washington Post*, August 17, 2015, www.washingtonpost.com; and Michal Clements, "How Procter and Gamble Sniffed Out New Markets," *Chicago Now*, September 25, 2013, www.chicagonow.com.

121 Maxine Wilkie, "Scent of a Market," *American Demographics*, August 1995, pp. 40–49.

122 Aradhna Krishna, Maureen Morrin, and Eda Sayin, "Smellizing Cookies and Salivating: A Focus on Olfactory Imagery," *Journal of Consumer Research* 41, no. 1, June 2014, pp. 18–34.

123 A. Festjens, S. Bruyneel, and S. Dewitte, "What a Feeling! Touching Sexually Laden Stimuli Makes Women Seek Rewards," *Journal of Consumer Psychology* 24, no. 3, July 2014, pp. 387–393.

124 Teresa Novellino, "Try a Tesla, Buy U.S.-Made in Brooklyn at American Field Holiday Popup," *New York Business Journal*, November 19, 2015, www.bizjournals.com.

125 "Downsized! More and More Products Lose Weight," *Consumer Reports*, February 2011, pp. 18–19.

126 Stuart Rogers, "How a Publicity Blitz Created the Myth of Subliminal Advertising," *Public Relations Quarterly*, Winter 1992, pp. 12–18.

127 Martha Rogers and Christine A. Seiler, "The Answer Is No," *Journal of Advertising Research*, March–April 1994, pp. 36–46; W. B. Key, *Subliminal Seduction* (Englewood Cliffs, N.J.: Prentice-Hall, 1973); Matthew Fitzgerald, *Media Sex-ploitation* (Englewood Cliffs, N.J.: Prentice-Hall, 1976); W. B. Key, *The Clamplate Orgy* (Englewood Cliffs, N.J.: Prentice-Hall, 1980); Martha Rogers and Kirk H. Smith, "Public Perceptions of Subliminal Advertising," *Journal of Advertising Research*, March–April 1993, pp. 10–19; and Michael Lev, "No Hidden Meaning Here: Survey Sees Subliminal Ads," *New York Times*, June 16, 1991, pp. 22.

128 Erin J. Strahan, Steven J. Spencer, and Mark P. Zanna, "Subliminal Priming and Persuasion: Striking While the Iron Is Hot," *Journal of Experimental Social Psychology*, 2002, pp. 556–568; Johan C. Karremans, Wolfgang Stroebe, and Jasper Claus, "Beyond Vicary's Fantasies: The Impact of Subliminal Priming and Brand Choice," *Journal of Experimental Social Psychology*, 2006, pp. 792–798.

129 See, for example, Thijs Verwijmeren, Johan C. Karremans, Wolfgang Stroebe, and Daniël H.J. Wigboldus, "The Workings and Limits of Subliminal Advertising: The Role of Habits," *Journal of Consumer Psychology* 21, no. 2, April 2011, pp. 206–213; and Martijn Veltkamp, Ruud Custers, and Henk Aarts, "Motivating Consumer Behavior by Subliminal Conditioning in the Absence of Basic Needs: Striking Even While the Iron Is Cold," *Journal of Consumer Psychology* 21, no. 1, Special Issue, January 2011, pp. 49–56.

130 A. J. Marcel, "Conscious and Unconscious Perception," *Cognitive Psychology*, June 1983, pp. 197–237; and A. J. Marcel, "Conscious and Unconscious Perception," *Cognitive Psychology*, September 1983, pp. 238–300.

131 Grainne M. Fitzsimons, Tanya L. Chartrand, and Gavan J. Fitzsimons, "Automatic Effects of Brand Exposure on Motivated Behavior: How Apple Makes You 'Think Different,'" *Journal of Consumer Research*, June 2008, pp. 21–35.

132 Ronald C. Goodstein and Ajay Kalra, "Incidental Exposure and Affective Reactions to Advertising," *Working Paper No. 239*, School of Management, University of California at Los Angeles, January 1994.

133 Sharon Beatty and Del I. Hawkins, "Subliminal Stimulation: Some New Data and Interpretation," *Journal of Advertising*, June 1989, pp. 4–9; Myron Gable, Henry T. Wilkens, Lynn Harris, and Richard Feinberg, "An Evaluation of Subliminally Embedded Sexual Stimuli and Graphics," *Journal of Advertising*, March 1987, pp. 26–32; Dennis L. Rosen and Surendra N. Singh, "An Investigation of Subliminal Embed Effect on Multiple Measures of Advertising Effectiveness," *Psychology and Marketing*, March–April 1992, pp. 157–173; J. Steven Kelly, "Subliminal Embeds in Print Advertising," *Journal of Advertising*, September 1979, pp. 20–24; Anthony R. Pratkanis and Anthony G. Greenwald, "Recent Perspectives

on Unconscious Processing," *Psychology and Marketing*, Winter 1988, pp. 337–353; and Joel Saegert, "Why Marketing Should Quit Giving Subliminal Advertising the Benefit of the Doubt," *Psychology and Marketing*, March–April 1987, pp. 157–173; and "Does Subliminal Advertising Actually Work?" *BBC Magazine*, January 20, 2015, www.bbc.com.

134 David Penn, "Looking for the Emotional Unconscious in Advertising," *International Journal of Market Research* 48, no. 5, 2006, pp. 515–524.

135 Timothy E. Moore, "Subliminal Advertising: What You See Is What You Get," *Journal of Marketing*, Spring 1982, pp. 38–47.

136 Cahal Milmo, "Power of the Hidden Message Revealed," *Independent (UK)*, September 28, 2009, www.independent.co.uk.

137 Chris Janiszewski and Tom Meyvis, "Effects of Brand Logo Complexity, Repetition and Spacing on Processing Fluency and Judgment," *Journal of Consumer Research* 28, June 2001, pp. 18–32.

138 Donna M. Webster and Arie W. Kruglanski, "Cognitive and Social Consequences of the Need for Cognitive Closure," *European Review of Social Psychology* 18, 1997, pp. 133–173.

139 Henrik Hagtvedt, "The Impact of Incomplete Typeface Logos on Perceptions of the Firm," *Journal of Marketing* 75, no. 4, July 2011, pp. 86–93.

140 Himanshu Mishra, Arul Mishra, and Dhananjay Nayakankuppam, "Money: A Bias for the Whole," *Journal of Consumer Research* 32, no. 4, 2006, pp. 541–549.

141 Rik Pieters and Michel Wedel, "Ad Gist: Ad Communication in a Single Eye Fixation," *Marketing Science*, January–February 2012, pp. 59–73.

142 David G. Mick, "Levels of Subjective Comprehension in Advertising Processing and Their Relations to Ad Perceptions, Attitudes, and Memory," *Journal of Consumer Research*, March 1992, pp. 411–424.

143 Jacob Jacoby, Wayne D. Hoyer, and David A. Sheluga, *Miscomprehension of Televised Communication* (New York: American Association of Advertising Agencies, 1980); and Jacob Jacoby and Wayne D. Hoyer, *The Comprehension and Miscomprehension of Print Communications: An Investigation of Mass Media Magazines* (New York: Advertising Education Foundation, 1987); see also Jacob Jacoby and Wayne D. Hoyer, "The Miscomprehension of Mass-Media Advertising Claims: A Re-Analysis of Benchmark Data," *Journal of Advertising Research*, June–July 1990, pp. 9–17; Jacob Jacoby and Wayne D. Hoyer, " The Comprehension–Miscomprehension of Print Communication," *Journal of Consumer Research*, March 1989, pp. 434–444; and Fliece R. Gates, "Further Comments on the Miscomprehension of Televised Advertisements," *Journal of Advertising*, Winter 1986, pp. 4–10.

144 Tanya Gazdik Irwin, "Aflac Introduces One Day Pay Promise in Its Largest Marketing Campaign Ever," *Mediapost*, February 6, 2015, www.mediapost.com; and Suzanne Vranica, "Aflac Partly Muzzles Iconic Duck," *Wall Street Journal*, December 2, 2004, p. B8.

145 Gar y J. Gaeth and Timothy B. Heath, " The Cognitive Processing of Misleading Advertising in Young and Old Adults," *Journal of Consumer Research*, June 1987, pp. 43–54; Deborah Roedder and John and Catherine A. Cole, "Age Differences in Information Processing," *Journal of Consumer Research*, December 1986, pp. 297–315; and Catherine A. Cole and Michael J. Houston, "Encoding and Media Effects on Consumer Learning Deficiencies in the Elderly," *Journal of Marketing Research*, February 1987, pp. 55–63.

146 Richard L. Celsi and Jerry C. Olson, "The Role of Involvement in Attention and Comprehension Processes," *Journal of Consumer Research*, September 1988, pp. 210–224.

147 Jacob Jacoby, Robert W. Chestnut, and William Silberman, "Consumer Use and Comprehension of Nutrition Information," *Journal of Consumer Research*, September 1977, pp. 119–127.

148 C. Page Moreau, Donald R. Lehmann, and Arthur B. Markman, "Entrenched Knowledge Structures and Consumer Response to New Products," *Journal of Marketing Research*, February 2001, pp. 14–29.

149 Haeran Jae, Devon S. DelVecchio, and Terry L. Childers, "Are Low-Literate and High-Literate Consumers Different? Applying Resource-Matching Theory to Ad Processing Across Literacy Levels," *Journal of Consumer Psychology* 21, no. 3, July 2011, pp. 312–323.

150 Edward T. Hall, *Beyond Culture* (Garden City, N.Y.: Anchor Press/Doubleday, 1976); and Onkvisit and Shaw, *International Marketing: Analysis and Strategy*.

151 Onkvisit and Shaw, *International Marketing: Analysis and Strategy*.

152 Boyoun (Grace) Chae and JoAndrea Hoegg, "The Future Looks 'Right': Effects of the Horizontal Location of Advertising Images on Product Attitude," *Journal of Consumer Research* 40, no. 2, August 2013, pp. 223–238.

153 Wayne D. Hoyer, Rajendra K. Srivastava, and Jacob Jacoby, "Examining Sources of Advertising Miscomprehension," *Journal of Advertising*, June 1984, pp. 17–26; Julie A. Edell and Richard Staelin, " The Information Processing of Pictures in Print Advertisements," *Journal of Consumer Research*, June 1983, pp. 45–61; and Ann Beattie and Andrew A. Mitchell, "The Relationship Between Advertising Recall and Persuasion," in eds. Linda F. Alwitt and Andrew A. Mitchell, *Psychological Processes and Advertising Effects* (Hillsdale, N.J.: Lawrence Erlbaum, 1985), pp. 129–156.

154 David Luna, "Integrating Ad Information," *Journal of Consumer Psychology* 15, no. 1, pp. 38–51.

155 Angela Y. Lee and Aparna A. Labroo, "The Effect of Conceptual and Perceptual Fluency on Brand Evaluation," *Journal of Marketing Research*, May 2004, pp. 151–165.

156 Andrew W. Ellis, Selina J. Holmes, and Richard L. Wright, "Age of Acquisition and the Recognition of Brand Names," *Journal of Consumer Psychology* 20, 2010, pp. 43–52.

157 Jennifer Gregan-Paxton and Deborah Roedder John, "Consumer Learning by Analogy: A Model of Internal Knowledge Transfer," *Journal of Consumer Research*, December 1997, pp. 266–284.

158 Abe Sauer, "Hollywood's New China Deal a Goldmine for Product Placement," *Brand Channel*, February 21, 2012, www.brandchannel.com; and Lily Kuo, "Transformers 4 and the Perils of Backfiring Product Placement," *The Atlantic*, July 10, 2014, www.theatlantic.com.

159 Lauren Dugan, "Celebs Are Paid $2,500–$8,000 Per Sponsored Tweet," *Media Bistro*, January 31, 2012, www.mediabistro.com.

160 Richard D. Johnson and Irwin P. Levin, "More Than Meets the Eye: The Effect of Missing Information on Purchase Evaluations," *Journal of Consumer Research*, September 1985, pp. 169–177; Frank Kardes, "Spontaneous Inference Processes in Advertising," *Journal of Consumer Research*, September 1988, pp. 225–233; and Joseph W. Alba and J. Wesley Hutchinson, "Dimensions of Consumer Expertise," *Journal of Consumer Research*, March 1987, pp. 411–454.

161 "Colgate Receives Fine of NT $400,000 in Biased Advertising Case: FTC," *China Post*, August 6, 2011, www.chinapost.com.tw; and "Taiwan Fair Trade Commission Decisions," *Federal Trade Commission*, August 2011, www.ftc.gov.

162 Tripp Mickle, "FDA Warns Cigarette Makers on 'Natural' Labeling," *Wall Street Journal*, August 27, 2015, www.wsj.com.

163 Mark Wilson, "Google's New Logo Is Its Biggest Update in 16 Years," *Fast Company Design*, September 1, 2015, www.fastcodesign.com.

164 Kunter Gunasti and William T. Ross Jr., "How and When Alphanumeric Brand Names Affect Consumers," *Journal of Marketing Research*, December 2010, pp. 1177–1192.

165 Michaela Wänke, Herbert Bless, and Norbert Schwarz, "Context Effects in Product Line Extensions," *Journal of Consumer Psychology* 7, no. 4, 1998, pp. 299–322.

166 Teresa Pavia and Janeen Arnold Costa, "The Winning Number: Consumer Perceptions of Alpha-Numeric Brand Names," *Journal of Marketing*, July 1993, pp. 85–99; France Leclerc, Bernd H. Schmitt, and Laurette Dube, "Foreign Branding and Its Effects on Product Perceptions and Attitudes," *Journal of Marketing Research*, May 1994, pp. 263–270; and Mary Sullivan, "How Brand Names Affect the Demand for Twin Automobiles," *Journal of Marketing Research*, May 1998, pp. 154–165.

167 Lindsay Chappell, "Nissan's Datsun Brand Weighs More Markets," *Auto News*, October 29, 2015, www.autonews.com.

168 S. Adam Brasel and James Gips, "Red Bull 'Gives You Wings' For Better or Worse: A Double-Edged Impact of Brand Exposure on Consumer Performance," *Journal of Consumer Psychology* 21, no. 1, Special Issue, January 2011, pp. 57–64.

169 Susan M. Broniarczyk and Joseph W. Alba, "The Role of Consumers' Intuitions in Inference Making," *Journal of Consumer Research*, December 1994, pp. 393–407.

170 Gary T. Ford and Ruth Ann Smith, "Inferential Beliefs in Consumer Evaluations," *Journal of Consumer Research*, December 1987, pp. 363–371.

171 Rajagopal Raghunathan, Rebecca Walker Naylor, and Wayne D. Hoyer, "The Unhealthy = Tasty Intuition and Its Effects on Taste Interferences, Enjoyment, and Choice of Food Products," *Journal of Marketing*, October 2006, pp. 170–184.

172 Elizabeth G. Miller and Barbara E. Kahn, "Shades of Meaning: The Effect of Color and Flavor Names on Consumer Choice," *Journal of Consumer Research* 32, no. 1, 2005, pp. 86–92.

173 Tom Meyvis and Chris Janiszewski, "Consumers' Beliefs About Product Benefits," *Journal of Consumer Research*, March 2002, pp. 618–635.

174 Alexander Chernev and Gregory S. Carpenter, "The Role of Market Efficiency Intuitions in Consumer Choice," *Journal of Marketing Research*, August 2001, pp. 349–361.

175 Peeter W. J. Verlegh, Jan-Benedict E. M. Steenkamp, and Matthew T. G. Meulenberg, "Country-of-origin Effects in Consumer Processing of Advertising Claims," *International Journal of Research in Marketing*, June 2005, pp. 127–139; Sung-Tai Hong and Robert S. Wyer Jr., "Determinants of Product Evaluation," *Journal of Consumer Research*, December 1990, pp. 277–288; Durairaj Maheswaran, "Country of Origin as a Stereotype," *Journal of Consumer Research*, September 1994, pp. 354–365; Sung-Tai Hong and Robert S. Wyer Jr., "Effects of Country of Origin and Product-Attribute Information on Product Evaluation," *Journal of Consumer Research*, September 1989, pp. 175–187; Johny K. Johansson, Susan P. Douglas, and Ikujiro Nonaka, "Assessing the Impact of Country of Origin on Product Evaluations," *Journal of Marketing Research*, November 1985, pp. 388–396; and WaiKwan Li and Robert S. Wyer Jr., "The Role of Country of Origin in Product Evaluations," *Journal of Consumer Psychology* 2, 1994, pp. 187–212.

176 Rajeev Batra, Venkatram Ramaswamy, Dana L. Alden, Jan-Benedict E. M. Steenkamp, and S. Ramachander, "Effects of Brand Local and Non-local Origin on Consumer Attitudes in Developing Countries," *Journal of Consumer Psychology* 9, no. 2, 2000, pp. 83–95.

177 Enid Tsui, "Samsonite Makes Its Case for Japan," *Financial Times*, August 30, 2011, www.ft.com; and Zeynep Gürhan-Canli and Durairaj Maheswaran, "Cultural Variations in Country of Origin Effects," *Journal of Marketing Research*, August 2000, pp. 309–317.

178 Zeynep Gürhan-Canli and Durairaj Maheswaran, "Determinants of Country-of-Origin Evaluations," *Journal of Consumer Research*, June 2000, pp. 96–108.

179 Sung-Tai Hong and Dong Kyoon Kang, "Country-of-Origin Influences on Product Evaluations," *Journal of Consumer Psychology* 16, no. 3, 2006, pp. 232–239.

180 Luk Warlop and Joseph W. Alba, "Sincere Flattery: Trade-Dress Imitation and Consumer Choice," *Journal of Consumer Psychology*, 2004, pp. 21–27.

181 Sandra M. Jones, "Nice! Touch Comes to Walgreens Shelves as Store Brands Get Makeover," *Chicago Tribune*, August 18, 2011, www.chicagotribune.com.

182 Frank R. Kardes, Maria L. Cronley, James J. Kellaris, and Steven S. Posavac, "The Role of Selective Information Processing in Price–Quality Inference," *Journal of Consumer Research*, September 2004, pp. 368–374.

183 Donald Lichtenstein and Scott Burton, "The Relationship Between Perceived and Objective Price-Quality," *Journal of Marketing Research*, November 1989, pp. 429–443; Etian Gerstner, "Do Higher Prices Signal Higher Quality?" *Journal of Marketing Research*, May 1985, pp. 209–215; Susan M. Petroshius and Kent B. Monroe, "Effect of Product-Line Pricing Characteristics on Product Evaluations," *Journal of Consumer Research*, March 1987, pp. 511–519; Akshay R. Rao and Kent B. Monroe, "The Moderating Effect of Prior Knowledge on Cue Utilization in Product Evaluations," *Journal of Consumer Research*, September 1988, pp. 253–264; and Cornelia Pechmann and S. Ratneshwar, "Consumer Covariation Judgments: Theory or Data Driven?" *Journal of Consumer Research*, December 1992, pp. 373–386.

184 Thomas T. Nagle and Reed K. Holden, *The Strategy and Tactics of Pricing*, 2nd ed. (Englewood Cliffs, N.J.: Prentice-Hall, 1995), pp. 84–85.

185 Maria L. Cronley, Steven S. Posavac, Tracy Meyer, Frank R. Kardes, and James J. Kellaris, "Selective Hypothesis Testing Perspective on Price–Quality Inference and Inference-Based Choice," *Journal of Consumer Psychology* 15, no. 2, 2005, pp. 159–169.

186 Hélène Deval, Susan P. Mantel, Frank R. Kardes, and Steven S. Posavac, "How Naive Theories Drive Opposing Inferences from the Same Information," *Journal of Consumer Research* 39, no. 6, April 2013, pp. 1185–1201.

187 Dengfeng Yan, Jaideep Sengupta, and Robert S. Wyer, Jr., "Package Size and Perceived Quality: The Intervening Role of Unit Price Perceptions," *Journal of Consumer Psychology* 24, no. 1, January 2014, pp. 4–17.

188 Ashok K. Lalwani and Sharon Shavitt, "You Get What You Pay For? Self-Construal Influences Price-Quality Judgments," *Journal of Consumer Research* 40, no. 2, August 2013, pp. 255–267.

189 Monica Wadwha and Kuangjie Zhang, "This Number Just Feels Right: The Impact of Roundedness of Price Numbers on Product Evaluations," *Journal of Consumer Research* 41, February 2015, pp. 1172–1185.

190 Mauricio M. Palmeira and Joydeep Srivastava, "Free Offer Not Equal Cheap Product: A Selective Accessibility Account on the Valuation of Free Offers," *Journal of Consumer Research* 40, no. 4, December 2013, pp. 644–656.

191 Promothesh Chatterjee and Randall L. Rose, "Do Payment Mechanisms Change the Way Consumers Perceive Products?" *Journal of Consumer Research* 38, no. 6, April 2012, pp. 1129–1139.

192 Adriana Samper, Adriana and Janet A. Schwartz, "Price Inferences for Sacred versus Secular Goods: Changing the Price of Medicine Influences Perceived Health Risk," *Journal of Consumer Research* 39, no. 6, April 2013, pp. 1343–1358.

193 Mario Pandelaere, Barbara Briers, and Christophe Lembregts, "How to Make a 29% Increase Look Bigger: The Unit Effect in Option Comparisons," *Journal of Consumer Research* 38, August 2011, pp. 308–322.

194 Ashwani Monga and Rajesh Bagchi, "Years, Months, and Days versus 1, 12, and 365: The Influence of Units versus Numbers," *Journal of Consumer Research* 39, June 2012, pp. 185–198.

195 Keith S. Coulter and Robin Coulter, "Small Sounds, Big Deals: Phonetic Symbolism Effects in Pricing," *Journal of Consumer Research* 37, August 2010, pp. 315–328.

196 Anne Kadet, "Yes, It's Still a Drugstore," *Wall Street Journal*, August 20, 2011, www.wsj.com.

197 Boyoun (Grace) Chae and Rui (Juliet) Zhu, "Environmental Disorder Leads to Self-Regulatory Failure," *Journal of Consumer Research* 40, no. 6, April 2014, pp. 1203–1218.

198 Keisha M. Cutright, "The Beauty of Boundaries: When and Why We Seek Structure in Consumption," *Journal of Consumer Research* 38, no. 5, February 2012, pp. 775–790.

199 Lauranne Buchanan, Carolyn J. Simmons, and Barbara A. Bickart, "Brand Equity Dilution," *Journal of Marketing Research*, August 1999, pp. 345–355.

200 Tiana Kennell, "Food Trucks Rolling Out the Red Carpet with Gourmet Food, Service," *Shreveport Times (Louisiana)*, August 31, 2015, www.shreveporttimes.com.

CHAPTER 4

Memory and Knowledge

LEARNING OBJECTIVES

After studying this chapter, you will be able to:

▶ Distinguish among sensory, working, long-term, implicit, and explicit memory, and explain why marketers must be aware of these different types of memory.

▶ Explain how and why knowledge content and structure, including associative networks, categories, schemas, scripts, and prototypicality, are relevant to marketers.

▶ Discuss what memory retrieval is, how it works, and the ways in which marketers can try to affect it.

INTRODUCTION

As you saw in Chapter 3, once we are exposed to a stimulus (like the Apple brand or logo) and attend to it, we use our senses to perceive and comprehend it (the Apple brand stands for well-designed, playful electronics, not fruit or stuffy machines). Sensory input is the starting point for memory and knowledge. We can store inputs such as a brand name, a logo (like the Apple), or an advertising image in memory for some period of time, ranging from moments to years, to be retrieved for later use. This is why Apple, for example, has used multimedia marketing messages to reinforce its iPhone brand, ending with the slogan: "If it's not an iPhone, it's not an iPhone."[1]

Memory may be explicit or implicit, depending on whether we are aware of trying to retrieve information from it. The content of our knowledge and the way we structure knowledge in memory (i.e., what we know about Apple and iPhones) influence our ability to relate new information to what we already know and our ability to retrieve memory. Finally, memory retrieval can be enhanced in a variety of ways, thus improving our ability to call on knowledge in memory during any part of the decision-making process (see Exhibit 4.1).

Exhibit 4.1 ▶ Chapter Overview: Memory and Knowledge

Marketers need to understand how consumers store and retrieve information about things, experiences, and evaluations. Information may remain in memory temporarily, be moved to working memory for further processing, and finally be stored in our long-term memory. Knowledge content, structure, and flexibility affect our ability to relate new information to what we already know. Marketers can try to enhance retrieval to overcome failures and errors and increase the likelihood that information will be retrieved from memory.

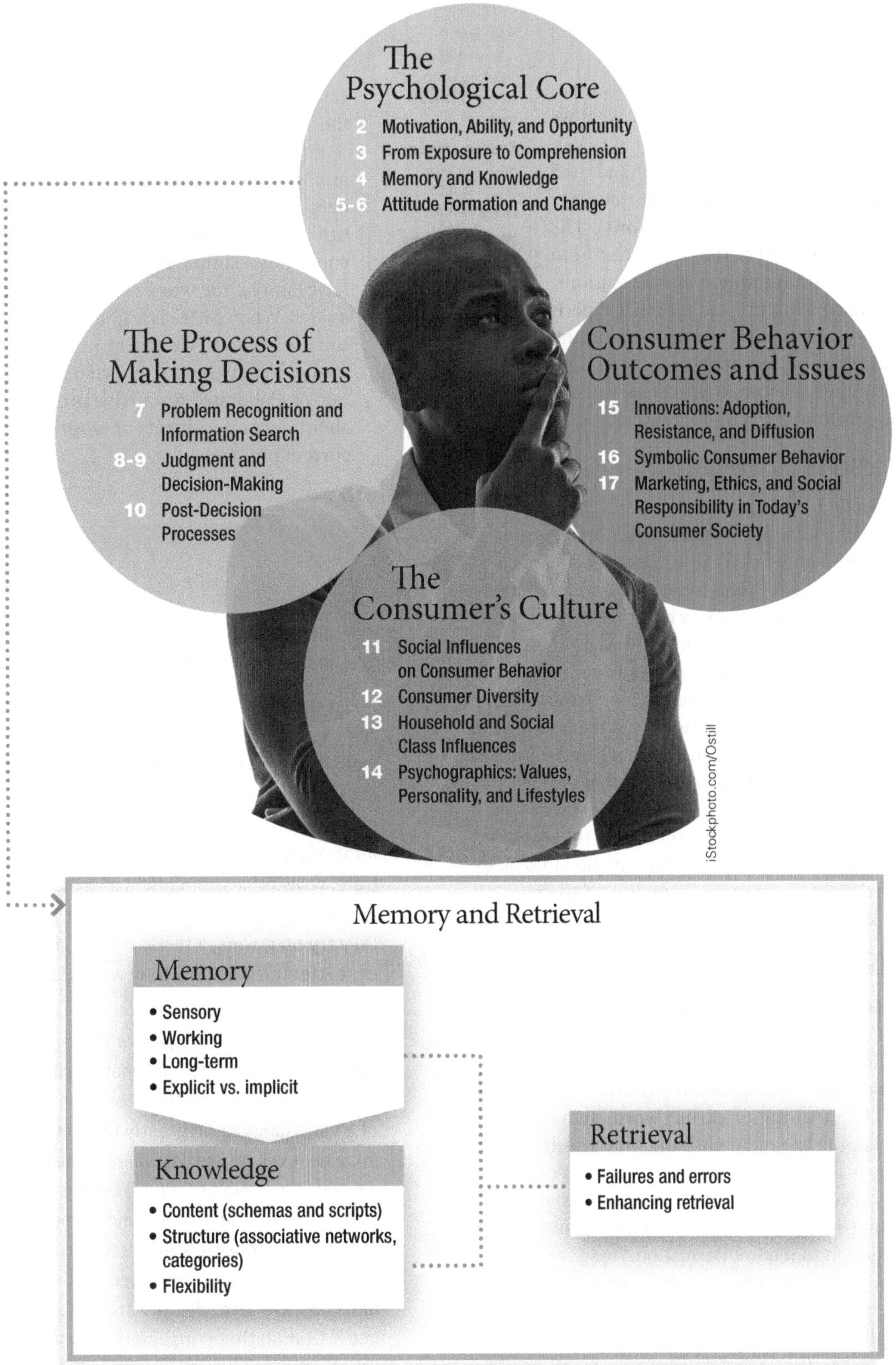

The Psychological Core

2 Motivation, Ability, and Opportunity
3 From Exposure to Comprehension
4 Memory and Knowledge
5-6 Attitude Formation and Change

The Process of Making Decisions

7 Problem Recognition and Information Search
8-9 Judgment and Decision-Making
10 Post-Decision Processes

Consumer Behavior Outcomes and Issues

15 Innovations: Adoption, Resistance, and Diffusion
16 Symbolic Consumer Behavior
17 Marketing, Ethics, and Social Responsibility in Today's Consumer Society

The Consumer's Culture

11 Social Influences on Consumer Behavior
12 Consumer Diversity
13 Household and Social Class Influences
14 Psychographics: Values, Personality, and Lifestyles

iStockphoto.com/Ostill

Memory and Retrieval

Memory

- Sensory
- Working
- Long-term
- Explicit vs. implicit

Knowledge

- Content (schemas and scripts)
- Structure (associative networks, categories)
- Flexibility

Retrieval

- Failures and errors
- Enhancing retrieval

4-1 What Is Memory?

Consumer memory is the persistence of learning over time, via the storage and retrieval of information, which can occur consciously or unconsciously. **Retrieval** is the process of remembering or accessing what was previously stored in memory. We constantly store and remember information that we learn about things, experiences, and evaluations. Specifically, we might remember what brands, products or services, and companies we have used in the past (things); what we paid; the features of these products or services; how, where, when, and why we bought and used them, and on which occasions (experiences)[2]; and whether we liked them (evaluations). The information we store and retrieve is learned from various sources—marketing communications, the media, word-of-mouth, and personal experience. We may retain it in memory for an instant, for a few minutes, or for a long time depending on the type of memory employed: sensory memory, working memory, or long-term memory.

Consumer memory
The persistence of learning over time, via the storage and retrieval of information, either consciously or unconsciously.

Retrieval The process of remembering or accessing what was previously stored in memory.

Sensory memory
Input from the five senses stored temporarily in memory.

Working memory (WM) The portion of memory where incoming information is encoded or interpreted in the context of existing knowledge, and kept available for more processing.

4-1a SENSORY MEMORY

Sensory memory is the ability to temporarily store input from all our five senses. Information is stored automatically and retained only briefly in sensory memory, generally from a quarter of a second to several seconds at most.[3] *Echoic memory* is sensory memory of things we hear, while *iconic memory* is sensory memory of things we see. For instance, you may have found that when someone asks you a question, and you are not really listening, you can say, "What did you say?" and actually "play back" what the person said. Iconic memory is at work when you drive by a sign and see it quickly and then only later realize what the sign was advertising. *Olfactory memory* is at play, for example, when the smell of freshly baked bread still lingers in your mind right after having left a bakery. If the information in sensory memory is relevant, consumers are motivated to process it further and keep it active. This occurs in working memory.

4-1b WORKING MEMORY

Working memory (WM) is the portion of memory where we "encode" or interpret incoming information and keep it available for further processing. As you read this book, you are using your working memory to comprehend what you read. The meaning of earlier words in a sentence need to be kept in memory until the final words. Working memory is where most of our conscious information processing takes place. It is both limited in capacity and short-lived in time, some 20 to 30 seconds at most. Also, it requires attention to retain information.[4]

Information processing in working memory can take one of several forms. When we think about an object—say, an apple—we might use *discursive processing* and represent it with the word apple. Alternatively, we could represent it visually as a picture of an *apple* or in terms of its smell, its feel, what it sounds like when we bite into it, or what it tastes like. Representing the visual, auditory, tactile, and/or olfactory properties of an apple uses *imagery processing*.[5] Unlike discursive processing, an object in imagery processing bears a close resemblance to the thing being represented.[6] Therefore, if you were asked to imagine an apple and a car, imagery processing would ensure that you preserve their relative sizes.

Information represented either as words or images can be elaborated, or thought about more deeply.[7] When motivation, ability, and opportunity (MAO) is low, working memory might consist of a simple reproduction of an object—for example, the word *skier* or a visual image of a skier. When MAO is high, however, consumers can use elaborated imagery processing to engage in daydreams, fantasies, visual problem-solving, or elaborated discursive processing to think about upcoming events or work out solutions to current problems.

Marketing Implications

Working memory, particularly imagery processing, has several key implications for marketers:

1. *Imagery can improve the amount of information that can be processed.* Adding more information to ads, websites, or packages, like lists of attributes, can create information overload and hamper discursive processing. By stimulating visual imagery, more information can be processed and retained. To illustrate, www.brides.com offers a virtual dressing room app, allowing brides to upload their photos and digitally try on gowns, a tactic that might help consumers better imagine how they would look in particular styles.[8]

2. *Imagery can stimulate future choice.* When making choices, we often imagine what consuming the product or service will be like. For example, our choice of a vacation may be greatly influenced by what we imagine it will be like. We value some of the products we buy (e.g., novels or music) because of the imagery they provide.[9] Consumers who immerse themselves in thoughts of using a product or having an experience similar to one simulated in an ad will tend to have positive attitudes toward the ad and the product.[10] Stimulating consumers to imagine how they

would use a product can improve product attitudes even more when the context in which the imagery processing occurs is similar to the situation in which products are normally used.[11]

3. *Realistic imagery can improve consumer satisfaction.* We may create an elaborate image or fantasy of what the product or consumption experience will be like (how great we will look in a new car or how relaxing a vacation will be). If reality does not confirm our imagery, however, we may feel dissatisfied. Realizing this possibility, some marketers help consumers establish realistic imagery. For example, paint brands such as Behr, Valspar, and Benjamin Moore offer apps that let consumers browse colors on their smartphone screens and "paint" virtual rooms to envision the effect before they buy paint.[12]

4-1c LONG-TERM MEMORY

Long-term memory (LTM) is that part of memory where information is permanently stored for later use. The two major types of long-term memory are episodic and semantic memory.

    Episodic (or autobiographical) memory represents knowledge about ourselves and what has happened to us in our past, including emotions and sensations tied to past experiences.[13] These memories tend to be primarily sensory, involving visual images, sounds, smells, tastes, and tactile sensations. For example, we may have episodic memories that relate to product acquisition, such as a specific shopping trip to find a birthday present for a good friend[14] or consumption such as eating at a particular restaurant. Because we each have a unique set of experiences, episodic memory tends to be very personal and idiosyncratic.

    Episodic memory can influence how products and services are evaluated. For example, if you once ate at a particular restaurant and found a hair in your food, the memory of this experience might prevent you from eating there again. This is a form of *operant conditioning*, where one vivid event produces a lasting memory and a changed behavior (see Chapter 10 for more about this concept). Positive experiences would have the opposite effect, as finding a pearl in an oyster at a restaurant might lead to returning to that restaurant. Also, you may remember how much you paid for something the last time you made that purchase,[15] and this memory can affect your future choices. For instance, you may decide not to buy something if you think you overpaid last time or will overpay this time.

> **Long-term memory (LTM)**
> The part of memory where information is permanently stored for later use.
>
> **Episodic (autobiographical) memory** Knowledge we have about ourselves and our personal, past experiences.
>
> **Semantic memory** General knowledge about an entity, detached from specific episodes.

Consumers' expectations about choices do not always match their episodic memories of similar experiences. Consumers who consider indulging in a purchase expect to have more negative than positive feelings when a strong justification for the indulgence is lacking. Yet in one study, consumers reported episodic memories of having enjoyed a recent indulgence, whether they "earned" it.[16]

    Much of what we have stored in memory consists of facts and general knowledge unrelated to specific episodes in our life's history. This is called **semantic memory**. For example, we have memory for the concept called "cola." We know that colas are liquid, come in cans and bottles, are fizzy and brown in color, and are sweet. This knowledge holds for colas in general. It is not tied to any specific consumption experience that we had.

Marketing Implications

Various techniques can leverage the power of episodic memory for marketing.

1. *Promote empathy and identification.* Episodic memories can play a role in creating identification with characters or situations in ads. For example, if an ad for Hefty bags can make consumers think about incidents in which their own garbage bags split open, consumers may be better able to relate to ads showing inferior bags splitting apart while Hefty bags remain strong.

2. *Cue and preserve episodic memories.* Consumers value some brands or products and have a positive attitude toward some ads because they promote episodic memories by creating feelings of nostalgia—a fondness for the past.[17] Many consumers want to preserve personal memories of vacations, graduations, weddings, birthdays, and so on, creating opportunities for marketers of goods and services that help consumers document these occasions. Shutterfly's TripPix app, for instance, enables consumers to make a glossy, printed book from as few as 15 travel photos in only five minutes.[18]

3. *Reinterpret past consumption experiences.* Advertising can affect episodic memories, such as how a consumer remembers past experiences with the advertised product.[19] One study had consumers sample good and bad-tasting orange juices and then watch ads that described the products' good taste. Those exposed to the ads remembered the bad-tasting juice as being better tasting than it actually was.[20] Oreo, the century-old cookie brand, has created a game app

("Twist, Lick, Dunk") to remind consumers of their love for the ritual of eating the black-and-white sandwich cookie with a glass of milk. It has also posted YouTube videos encouraging consumers to try new ways of enjoying Oreos, linking fond memories with anticipation of future consumption.[21]

4-1d EXPLICIT MEMORY, IMPLICIT MEMORY, AND PROCESSING FLUENCY

Memory may be explicit or implicit. **Explicit memory** is when consumers are consciously aware that they remember something. For instance, consumers may remember that they visited a particular website, and what they ordered from the site. **Implicit memory** is when consumers are not consciously aware that they remember something. Implicit memory makes it easier to process information that we have encountered before. This ease-of-processing or *processing fluency* leads to feelings of familiarity. So consumers may not remember that they actually visited a particular website before, but may instead experience a sense of familiarity with it. Much of our memory is implicit, and this is efficient. It would overburden our information-processing ability to constantly and consciously remember everything we encountered and did before. In fact, consciously remembering what we know might prevent many of our automatic behaviors: it may be dangerous to try to remember and speak out loud the exact movements of the hands, feet, body, and head while driving a car or riding a bike.

Suppose you are driving down the highway at high speed and pass a billboard bearing the word *Caterpillar* (a brand of construction machinery). Later you are asked whether you remember seeing a billboard and, if so, what was on it. You have no explicit memory of the billboard and its message. But if you are asked to say the first word you can think of that begins with *cat-*, you might answer "caterpillar." Why? Because when you are asked for a word that begins with *cat-*, your implicit memory brings the brand to mind.

Exposure to brands via advertising and other marketing stimuli enhances perceptual fluency, making it easier for consumers to recognize a brand and process perceptual information about it (text and pictures), and this generally leads to more favorable brand attitudes.[22] Positive attitudes also tend to result from higher conceptual fluency, the ease with which the meaning of an ad or brand comes to mind and can be processed. Such forms of processing fluency are a key element in implicit memory and

Explicit memory When consumers are consciously aware that they remember something.

Implicit memory Memory without a conscious attempt at remembering something. Implicit memory is evidenced when a process that requires memory is executed faster or more accurately.

Recognition The process of identifying whether we have previously encountered a stimulus when reexposed to the stimulus.

Recall The ability to retrieve information about a stimulus from memory without being reexposed to the stimulus again.

in learning new behaviors. (Learning is described in more detail in Chapter 10.)

4-1e HOW MEMORY IS ENHANCED

Because we must attend to something before we can remember it, many of the factors that affect attention (described in Chapter 3) also affect memory and, ultimately, recognition and recall. Explicit memory expresses itself in two forms. **Recognition** occurs when we remember we have seen, heard, smelled, touched, or tasted some stimulus before, after being reexposed to the stimulus again. A brand recognition question could be: "Which of the *following* car brands have you owned before?" after which a list of car brands names and pictures is provided. **Recall** occurs when we remember we have seen, heard, smelled, touched, or tasted a stimulus before *without* being reexposed to the stimulus again. A brand recall question could be: "Which car brands do you remember having owned before?" without providing a list.

Several techniques help to improve working memory and increase the likelihood that information will be transferred to long-term memory, such as chunking, rehearsal, recirculation, and elaboration. A *chunk* is a group of items that are processed as a unit. For example, phone numbers are typically grouped into three chunks: the area code, the exchange, and four numbers. Chunking means that we try to create meaningful combinations (chunks) of information to improve memory. Thus, it may be useful to memorize the word BOATS when going to the supermarket for bananas, oranges, apples, tomatoes, and sardines.

Whereas chunking reduces the likelihood that information will be lost from working memory, rehearsal improves the transfer of information to long-term memory. *Rehearsal* means that we actively and consciously interact with the material that we are trying to remember, perhaps by silently repeating or actively thinking about the information and its meaning (BOATS, BOATS). In marketing contexts, rehearsal is likely to occur mostly when consumers are motivated to process and remember information.

Information can also be transferred to long-term memory by *recirculation*. Just as water is recirculated when it goes through the same pipe again and again, information is recirculated through your working memory when you encounter it repeatedly, such as when passing the harbor with a billboard advertising Malibu boats on your way to the supermarket. Unlike rehearsal, with recirculation we make no active attempt to remember the information. Brand recall is greater when information is repeated at different times rather than when it is presented with a high frequency in a short time period.[23]

Finally, through **elaboration**, we transfer information into long-term memory by processing it at deeper levels of meaning.[24] We can try to remember through rote memorization or rehearsal; however, this type of processing is not always effective over a long period. If you have ever rote-memorized material for an exam, you probably noticed that you forgot most of what you had learned within a few days. More enduring memory is established when we try to relate information to prior knowledge and past experiences. If you see an ad for a new product, for instance, you might elaborate on it by thinking about how you would use the product, how it fits in your lifestyle, which personal benefits it has, and therefore store the brand and the ad with rich associations in your memory.

Elaboration Transferring information into long-term memory by processing it at deeper levels.

Marketing Implications

Marketers can apply chunking, rehearsal, recirculation, and elaboration to help consumers remember their brands, communications, or offerings.

Chunking

Marketers can increase the likelihood that consumers will hold information in short-term memory and transfer it to long-term memory by providing larger bits of information that chunk together smaller bits. For example, acronyms reduce several pieces of information to one chunk. Brand names like KFC and H&M are examples of chunking in a marketing context. Similarly, marketers can facilitate consumers' memory for telephone numbers by using meaningful words rather than individual numbers (e.g., 800-LUNGUSA). Also, ads might draw conclusions that summarize or chunk disparate pieces of information into a single attribute or benefit.

Rehearsal

When motivation is low, marketers may use tactics such as jingles, sounds, and slogans to instigate rehearsal. For example, Kellogg advertises the "snap, crackle, pop" sounds of its Rice Krispies in commercials that include a catchy jingle and the spokescharacters taking selfies with Rice Krispies treats.[25] Sometimes these techniques work too well, as you may know from going through the day singing a commercial's jingle over and over.

Recirculation

Recirculation is an important principle for marketing because it explains why repetition of marketing communications affects memory, particularly in low-involvement situations.[26] Marketers can strengthen the effect of recirculation by creating different ads that repeat the same basic message and repeating the brand name frequently. Studies show that spaced exposures of alternating messages in involving media such as TV commercials and less involving media such as billboards can be highly effective.[27] However, when one brand repeatedly advertises product claims that are similar to claims promoted repeatedly by a close competitor, this may confuse consumers, rather than enhance their memory.[28]

Elaboration

Several strategies mentioned in previous chapters can enhance the likelihood that consumers will elaborate on information. Unexpected or novel stimuli can attract attention and induce elaboration.[29] For example, GEICO's choice of a gecko as a character for its insurance ads is intended to make consumers think about the connection, as is Aflac's choice of a duck. Elaboration may also explain why moderate levels of humor in an ad enhance both encoding and retrieval of the product's claims, whereas strong humor inhibits elaboration of the claims.[30] Further, the ability to elaborate may vary across individuals. Older people may have less ability to elaborate on information from marketing messages, perhaps because of the declining capacity of their working memory. Children may elaborate less because they have less knowledge, which makes it more difficult for them to think extensively about an ad message.[31]

4-2 Knowledge Content, Structure, and Flexibility

Knowledge content reflects the information we have already learned and stored in memory about brands, companies, stores, people, how to shop, how to use public transportation or bake a cake, and so on. *Knowledge structure* describes how we organize knowledge (both episodic and semantic) in memory. When we say we "know" something, it has to do with what we have encountered (knowledge content) and the way in which that knowledge is organized in memory (knowledge structure). Both content and structure are flexible, as discussed later in this chapter.

4-2a KNOWLEDGE CONTENT: SCHEMAS AND SCRIPTS

Knowledge content is not stored in memory as a bunch of random facts. Instead, content takes the form of schemas or scripts. As the next sections explain, schemas are a form of semantic knowledge: knowledge about *what* objects and people are, and what they mean to a consumer. Scripts are a form of procedural knowledge: knowledge about *how to* do things with the objects and people and are related to episodic memory.

Schemas and Associative Networks

A **schema** is the group of associations or *associative network* linked to an object or person (more in general to a "concept").[32] A schema for the concept *banana* has various associations—it has 100 calories, is yellow, and bruises easily, and the peel can be slippery if stepped on. We have schemas for *people* (mothers, Taylor Swift, basketball players), *salespeople* (cosmetics salesperson, car salesperson), *ads* (Taco Bell ads, GEICO ads), *companies* (Apple, Huawei), *places* (LEGOLAND, the Taj Mahal), and so on. The banana example is an illustration of a *product category schema*. We also have schemas for brands, which can be influenced by marketing actions (see Exhibit 4.2). We also have a *self-schema*, and sometimes consider whether a brand's

> **Schema** The set of associations linked to a concept in memory.

schema fits with it.[33] Schemas thus contain subjective knowledge about "what" something is. Of course, our subjective knowledge of products, brands, and ourselves may be inconsistent with objective facts.

Exhibit 4.3 represents one consumer's schema or associative network for the category "vacations," specifically for a St. Moritz ski vacation. The associations are learned based on personal experiences and other information, such as from mass media, word-of-mouth, or advertising. Some associations in the network represent episodic memories and others represent semantic memory.

Notice that in Exhibit 4.3, the links in the associative network vary in strength. Strong links (depicted by the thick lines) are firmly established in memory because they have been rehearsed, recirculated, chunked, and elaborated extensively. Others (depicted by the dashed lines) are weakly established in memory, because they are encountered infrequently, are rarely accessed, or have not been thoroughly processed.

Exhibit 4.2 ▶ Marketers Use Ads, Packages, and Product Attributes to Enhance Consumers' Knowledge About an Offering

Marketers often want consumers to know more about their products (e.g., where the Chinese beer brand Tsingtao is for sale). Ads, packages, and product attributes are useful ways of getting this knowledge across.

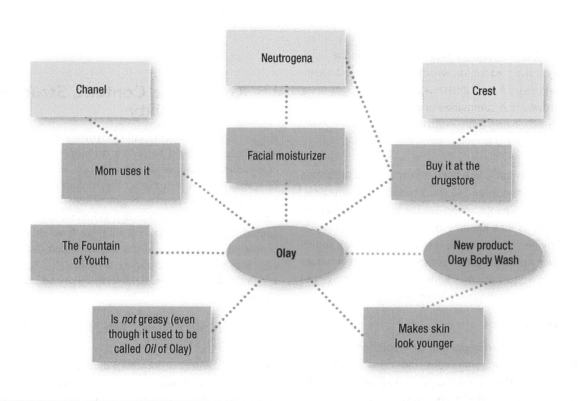

Exhibit 4.3 ▶ An Associative Network for Vacations

An associative network is a set of concepts connected by links. When one concept is activated, others may become activated via the links. Concepts connected by strong links are more likely to activate each other than are those connected by weak links.

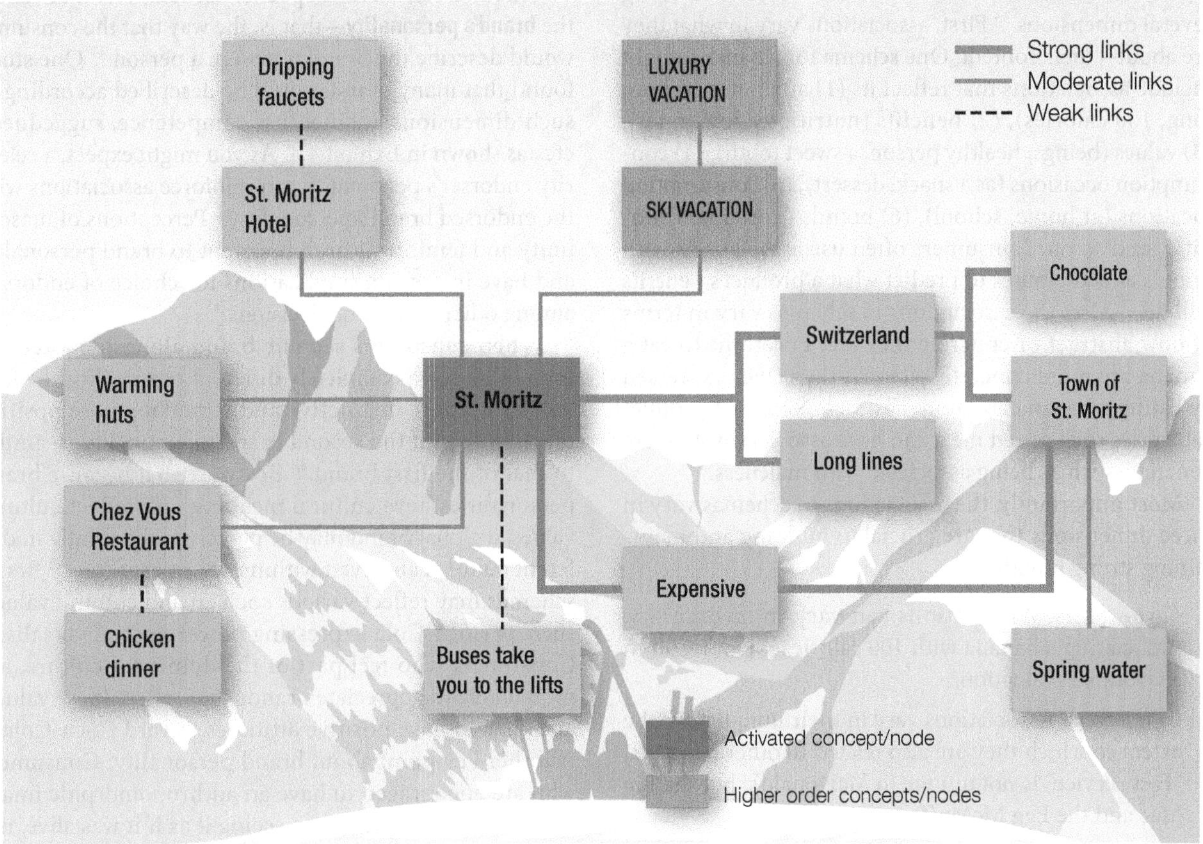

Because associations in the network are connected, activating one part of the associative network leads to a **spreading of activation** to other parts of the network. Using the example in Exhibit 4.3, when the "St. Moritz" concept is activated in the consumer's associative network, the strong link between "St. Moritz" and "expensive" will make the consumer think about "expensive." Because the link connecting "St. Moritz" and "expensive" is very strong, the activation will spread to adjacent concepts in the associative network, particularly along strong links. This spreading of activation will likely lead the consumer to remember the town of St. Moritz and may also activate "Switzerland" and "long lines." Activation from "Switzerland" may, in turn, spread to the concept "chocolate."

Of course, concepts like "Switzerland," "chocolate," and "expensive" are linked to many

Spreading of activation The process by which retrieving a concept or association spreads to the retrieval of a related concept or association.

priming The increased sensitivity to certain concepts and associations due to prior experience based on implicit memory.

associative networks, not just to one. The consumer may think about chocolate when prompted to think about St. Moritz, but chocolate may be strongly linked to other associative networks that can be cued through spreading of activation. Spreading of activation explains why we sometimes have seemingly random thoughts as the activation spreads from one associative network to another. If the consumer's motivation and opportunity to process information are high, the number of activated links can also be quite high.[34]

Spreading of activation may take place consciously. Then, a consumer who sees the purple Milka chocolate bar might think about Alpine cows and the rich milk they give for the Milka chocolate. Spreading of activation may also take place outside of conscious awareness. This concept is called **priming**: the increased sensitivity to certain concepts and associations due to prior experience based on implicit memory.[35] It occurs when a concept is activated by a stimulus (such as when the "Milka" brand activates the concept "Switzerland") and this activation influences consumers' associations, positively or negatively, outside of awareness.

The associations in schemas can be described along several dimensions.[36] First, associations vary in what they are about—their content. One schema for a banana might include associations that reflect its (1) attributes (yellow, long, 100 calories), (2) benefits (nutritious, low in fat), (3) values (being a healthy person, a sweet tooth), (4) consumption occasions (as a snack, dessert), (5) consumption locations (at home, school), (6) brands (Turbana, Chiquita), and so on. Consumers often use associations with brands and attributes to predict what a product's benefits will be.[37] Also, the associations in schemas vary in terms of how abstract or concrete they are. Locations to eat a banana are more concrete, whereas the values expressed by eating a banana are more abstract. Note that product categories such as red meat can have associations that are concrete, such as being associated with maleness.[38]

Most importantly, the associations in schemas vary in three dimensions that are crucial to building and maintaining strong brands:

1. *Favorability.* Associations can vary in favorability. Associating a banana with 100 calories might result in a favorable evaluation.

2. *Uniqueness.* Associations vary in their uniqueness: the extent to which they are also related to other concepts. "Fast service" is not unique to McDonald's, but the Big Mac and the Egg McMuffin are.

3. *Salience.* Associations vary in their salience, or how easily they come to mind. For example, a consumer might always think of the Golden Arches when hearing the McDonald's name. Less salient associations may be remembered only in certain contexts. Thus, the association that McDonald's offers breakfast burritos may be less salient than other associations, and a consumer may think about it only if someone starts talking about fast-food breakfast items.[39] Brands aim to be linked to favorable, unique, salient associations.

Specific Schemas: Brand Image, Personality, and Anthropomorphization

A **brand image** is a specific type of schema that captures what a brand stands for and how favorably consumers view it. For example, our brand image of McDonald's may be favorable, and it may include such associations as a family-friendly place and fast food. An image does not represent *all* the associations linked to a schema—only those that are most salient and

Brand image Specific type of schema that captures what a brand stands for and how favorably it is viewed.

Brand personality The set of associations included in a schema that reflect a brand's personification.

Script A special type of schema that represents knowledge of the sequence of actions involved in performing an activity.

that make the brand different from others in the category. Thus, although we may know that McDonald's also serves low-fat foods, this knowledge need not be used to form our brand image. We also have images for other marketing entities like stores, companies, places, and countries.[40]

Schemas can include specific associations that reflect the **brand's personality**—that is, the way that the consumer would describe the brand if it were a person.[41] One study found that many brands could be described according to such dimensions as sincerity, competence, ruggedness, etc., as shown in Exhibit 4.4. As you might expect, a celebrity endorser's personality can reinforce associations with the endorsed brand's personality.[42] Perceptions of masculinity and femininity are important to brand personality and have important implications for choice of endorser, among other marketing decisions.[43]

When consumers see one brand alongside a second brand that has a completely different personality, the first will seem more distinctive and stimulate more positive reaction than if the second brand's personality is similar to that of the first brand.[44] Be aware that because brand personalities have cultural meaning and reflect cultural values, a global brand may be perceived differently in different cultures and even within the same culture.[45] Brand schemas may reflect various societal and cultural values, such as Coca-Cola expressing power and universalism. Consumers who feel part of the dominant culture, are more likely to appreciate brands that reflect these values, and thus to have positive attitudes toward Coca-Cola.[46] Another key point about brand personality: Consumers who are encouraged to have an anthropomorphic image of a product such as a car—seeing it as if it was alive, not an inanimate object—are more committed to it and less willing to replace it.[47]

Another key element is the fit between the consumer's actual personality and the brand's personality. A consumer will react to a good fit with the feeling that the brand's personality is "like who I really am." Also, research suggests that using a brand with a certain personality can help shape a consumer's personality.[48] Brand personality has an even stronger influence on the consumer's emotional attachment to a brand when involvement, self-esteem, and public self-consciousness are high. The trend toward *cocreation*—consumers collaborating with companies to shape brand personality and develop new products—can go a long way toward enhancing the fit between one's personality and the brand's personality.[49]

Scripts

A **script** represents our knowledge of a sequence of actions involved in performing an activity.[50] For example, you may have a script for how to arrange roses bought from the store: You open

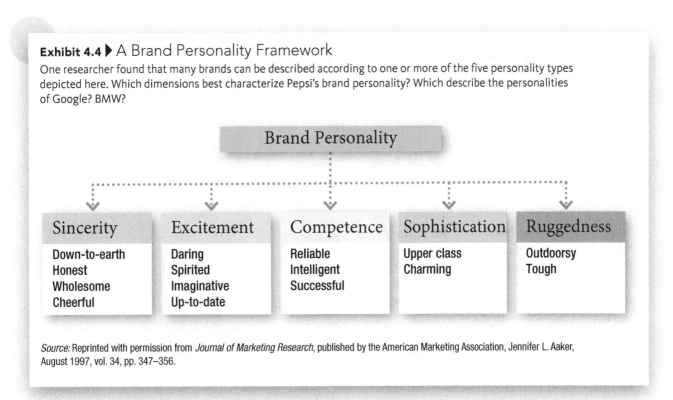

Exhibit 4.4 ▶ A Brand Personality Framework
One researcher found that many brands can be described according to one or more of the five personality types depicted here. Which dimensions best characterize Pepsi's brand personality? Which describe the personalities of Google? BMW?

Brand Personality				
Sincerity	Excitement	Competence	Sophistication	Ruggedness
Down-to-earth Honest Wholesome Cheerful	Daring Spirited Imaginative Up-to-date	Reliable Intelligent Successful	Upper class Charming	Outdoorsy Tough

Source: Reprinted with permission from *Journal of Marketing Research,* published by the American Marketing Association, Jennifer L. Aaker, August 1997, vol. 34, pp. 347–356.

the cellophane wrapping, get scissors, fill a vase with water, run the rose stems under water, cut them, and arrange the flowers in the vase. This script helps you complete the task quickly and easily. But when you do something for the first time, such as renting an apartment from a local host via a company such as Airbnb, not having a script may prolong the task. Some brands and stimuli may activate scripts in consumers' minds, such as when an ad for IKEA makes you think about how to walk through the store and finish the trip with a visit to the restaurant, or how to assemble, step-by-step, the popular BILLY bookcase, if you have done this more often.

 Marketing Implications

Knowledge content is important to marketers. Brands with favorable, unique, and salient associations that are meaningful to consumers have high brand equity and are valuable to the company.[51] Such strong brands can command a higher price and have a more loyal following of consumers. Therefore, marketers need to identify and understand the various favorable, unique, and salient associations that consumers link to a particular brand.[52] Moreover, consumers as young as middle-school age start to associate brand images with their self-images,

seeing brands as "me" or "not me."[53] Understanding the associations that consumers see as part of themselves or want to see as part of themselves helps marketers to create, maintain, change, and protect brand images and personalities.

Creating Brand Images and Personalities

When an offering is new, the marketer has to create a schema, image, and/or personality to help consumers understand what it is, what it can do for them, and how it differs from competing offerings. Creating schemas and images for a company is also important so that consumers understand the types of products it offers. For example, GEICO, the insurance firm with the gecko brand character, wants consumers to know it offers motorcycle insurance as well as car insurance. That association is why it is a major sponsor of the annual Sturgis motorcycle rally in South Dakota.

Also, brands in certain categories (fashion, electronics) often try for a "cool" brand image. Although perceptions of cool differ from individual to individual, brands that break seemingly unnecessary rules may be perceived as cool. As an example, a product might be considered cool if it violates a dress code that consumers view as superfluous, whereas the product will not be viewed as cool if it breaks a more legitimate dress code. Here, the coolness factor stems from qualities of independence and uniqueness compared with the norm.[54]

Creating Brand Extensions

Marketers create a **brand extension** when they use the brand name of a product with a well-developed image (like Dove soap) on a product in a different category (e.g., Dove Deodorant, which belongs to the antiperspirant category, see Exhibit 4.5). Brand extensions have two general effects.

> **Brand extension**
> Using the brand name of a product with a well-developed image on a product in a different category.

First, a transfer of associations takes place from the original brand schema (the "parent": Dove Soap) to the new branded product (the "offspring" : Dove Deodorant).[55] If consumers like the original brand, these feelings will improve their evaluations of the brand extension.[56] Consumers tend to like brand extensions more when (1) the new product fits in some way with the parent brand, and when (2) they really like the parent brand.[57] The fit between brand extension and parent brand or family may be based on similar attributes or benefits, usage goals, or targets.[58] However, consumers' reactions to the brand extension and its fit with the parent brand are also affected by the relative brand familiarity of competitors.[59] Ideally, the brand extension fits the brand's personality, the brand is liked, and the brand extension presents a benefit over products of competitors (see above about "favorability, uniqueness, and salience" of associations).

Second, a transfer of meaning from the new branded product (Dove Deodorant) to the original brand schema (Dove Soap) may take place. One concern is that brand extensions may make the brand schema less coherent and may dilute the brand's image.[60] For example, if the Jeep name appears on too many different products—strollers, clothing—consumers may be confused about what this automotive brand really stands for. On the other hand, sometimes consumers accept a brand extension more readily when the brand is already linked to quite different products because some of the attributes or benefits in one category make the brand extension seem like a good product.[61] Interestingly, visual images can affect consumers' evaluations of brand extensions. Seeing pictures of a brand extension makes it more concrete, so consumers may base their evaluation more on the quality of the brand than the degree to which it fits the parent brand.[62]

There are cross-cultural differences in brand extension effects. One study found that brand dilution would be more pronounced in Eastern cultures, compared with

Image Courtesy of The Advertising Archives

Exhibit 4.5 ▶ Brand Extensions
Certain products can market their success with one product by expanding their brand to other products, like Dove did with their soap and new deodorant.

the effect in Western cultures, if an unsuccessful brand extension is similar to an existing product and consumer motivation is high. This occurs because of differences in processing conflicting information about the brand and the products to which it is linked (i.e., Eastern cultures are more able to deal with conflicting information).[63] Further, the "stretchability" of a brand depends on consumers' ability to process relationships and accept the perceived fit between the parent brand and other products on which it appears, which can vary from culture to culture.[64]

Maintaining Brand Images and Personalities

Once created, marketers must maintain and develop the brand images and personalities. Over time, consistent advertising can help to accomplish this.[65] To develop the brand images and personalities, a company may offer multiple brand extensions (the way Dove did with antiperspirant), link the product to an appropriate sponsorship (the way GEICO did with the motorcycle rally), or highlight additional features and benefits.[66]

Changing Brand Images and Personalities

If a brand or product image becomes stale, outdated, or linked to negative associations, marketers need to add new and positive associations. For example, when Walmart wanted to polish its image as a good corporate citizen, the retail giant publicized its long-term targets for reducing greenhouse gas emissions, using clean energy sources, preserving wildlife habitats, and other sustainability activities. It also increased employee wages above the federally mandated hourly minimum and required meat and poultry suppliers to meet specific standards for animal welfare.[67]

Protecting Brand Images and Personalities

Brand images and personalities may be threatened during a brand crisis that involves potential harm, such as reports of contaminated products or health problems that are linked to specific products. Crises that involve ethical issues can also affect the brand. Volkswagen, for example, faced a crisis after the public revelation that millions of its diesel-engine vehicles used secret software to improve results on government-mandated emissions tests. In the weeks following this revelation, the automaker offered U.S. owners of its diesel vehicles a $500 gift card plus $500 toward repairs. To attract new buyers, Volkswagen promoted zero-downpayment deals and zero-per cent financing.[68]

The way that a company responds to a crisis affects its brand image, but consumers' prior expectations also play a critical role. Companies whose customers held a strong, positive image of the brand prior to the crisis suffered less image damage than did companies whose customers had lower expectations. Strong prior brand images in this way can act as a shock-absorber. Firms with a weaker brand image need to act more aggressively to support their brands after a crisis.[69] Interestingly, firms with a "sincere" brand personality may have difficulty re-establishing strong customer relations after a crisis because fundamental perceptions of the brand have deteriorated. In contrast, firms with an "exciting" brand personality may have an easier time reinvigorating customer relationships after a crisis because consumers are less surprised by nonroutine experiences with such brands.[70]

4-2b KNOWLEDGE STRUCTURE: CATEGORIES

Consumers have various associations with each of the objects and people surrounding them. They also have the natural tendency to group these objects and people together in categories that share certain characteristics, called **taxonomic categories**.[71] A taxonomic category is a specifically defined division within an orderly classification of objects with similar objects in the same category. For example, our schemas for Coke, Pepsi, Diet Coke, and other brands can be clustered in a category called soft drink; we might also use subcategories to cluster specific brands and separate them from others. Thus, we might have one subcategory for diet soft drinks and a different subcategory for nondiet *soft drinks*. In turn, soft drinks may be part of a larger beverage category that also includes coffees, teas, juices, and bottled water, as shown in Exhibit 4.6.

> **Taxonomic category**
> How consumers classify a group of objects in memory in an orderly, often hierarchical way, based on their similarity to one another.

Once we have categorized an object, we know what it is, what it is like, and what it is similar to. Although categories allow us to efficiently process complex information, both the size and the number of categories can affect our perceptions of risk and outcome.[72] Note that consumers do not always categorize offerings correctly. This is why the Timberland brand helps consumers put its Earthkeepers boots in the category of "eco-friendly products" via the product name (Earthkeepers) and the description ("Made with natural and recycled material").[73] When consumers encounter a product or service provider that does not seem to fit the category, they may elaborate more on the information about that provider. And when they categorize the provider as a member of the product category, they may infer that the provider has features or attributes typical of the category.[74] Thus if a financial services firm such as PayPal is categorized as an "online bank," it will be associated with other beliefs that consumers have about banks, such as the availability of savings accounts, even if the firm does not offer these.

On the other hand, marketers may sometimes want consumers to mentally recategorize a product. For example, General Motors faces this situation with its electric-gas hybrid models and forthcoming all-electric models marketed under the Cadillac brand, traditionally known for luxury. Because these cars and SUVs use engine technology similar to that of GM's all-electric Chevrolet Volt model, Cadillac may be able to build on high awareness of the Volt as it encourages consumers to properly categorize the gas-saving Cadillacs.[75]

Graded Structure and Prototypicality

Objects within the same taxonomic category share similar features, which are different from the features of objects in other categories. A category member such as Diet Coke shares many associations with members of its own category of diet colas but shares few associations with members of other categories. In Exhibit 4.6, Diet Coke has associations a–d, and Diet Pepsi has many but not all of the same associations (a–c and e). In this category, you might view Diet Coke as a better example of a soft drink than a lesser-known diet drink. The fact that category

Exhibit 4.6 ▶ Taxonomic Category Structure

Objects can be organized in ordered, hierarchically structured categories, with similar objects in the same category. For example, herbal and nonherbal teas are subordinate to the basic-level category of teas. Teas, coffees, and soft drinks are members of the superordinate category beverages. The letters under each brand signify attributes linked with each brand. Brands with the same letters have the same attributes. For example, three brands share a common attribute "a" (e.g., caffeine) while only Diet Coke and Diet Pepsi share attribute "b" (e.g., low calorie).

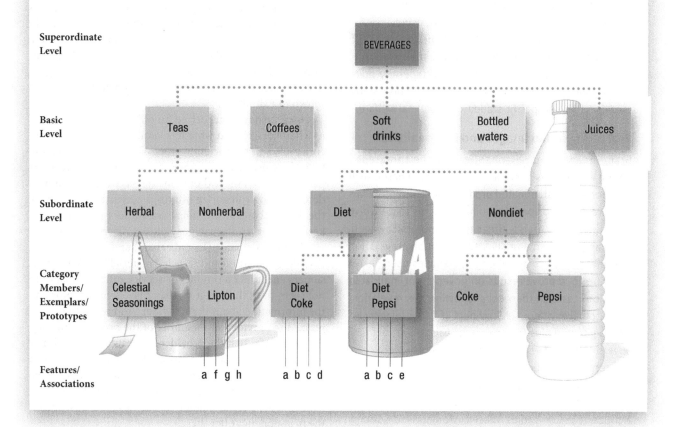

members vary in how well they are perceived to represent a category illustrates the principle of *graded structure*.[76]

Within a category, some category members represent the category better than others. The **prototype** is the category member perceived to be the best example of the category, like Disney being the prototypical theme park, and apple pie being the prototypical pie. **Prototypicality** is the extent to which category members are considered to be representative of the category. To most consumers, a diamond ring may be a more prototypical engagement gift than a tattoo or a nose piercing. To many consumers, the iPad may be the prototypical tablet computer. Exhibit 4.7 identifies brands generally regarded as prototypes in their product categories.

Several factors affect whether a consumer regards something as a category prototype.[77] The first is shared associations: A prototype shares the most associations

> **prototype** The best example of a cognitive (mental) category.
>
> **prototypicality** the extent to which an object is representative of its category.

with other members of its own category and shares the fewest with members from different categories. The second is the frequency with which an object is encountered as a category member. Thus, brands with the highest market share are likely to be considered the prototype. Third, the first or "pioneer" brand in a category—such as Amazon for online books and music—may also become the prototype because it sets a standard against which later brands are compared.[78]

So, what should a new or lesser known brand do to boost its salience in consumers' minds? One approach is to team up with dominant, protypical brands to make use of the latter's prominence, for instance, by engaging in *co-branding activity*. However, this may actually pose an unintended threat to the lesser known brands, when the salient associations of the prototypical brand overshadow the less salient associations of the lesser known one.[79]

Hierarchical Structure

Another way in which taxonomic categories are structured is hierarchically, which affects the number of associations. As Exhibit 4.6 indicates, taxonomic categories can be hierarchically organized into basic, subordinate, and superordinate levels. The broadest level of categorization is the *superordinate level*, where objects share a few associations but also have many different ones. Finer discriminations among these objects are made at the *basic level*. Beverages might be more finely represented by categories such as teas, coffees, and soft drinks. The finest level of differentiation exists at the *subordinate level*. For example, soft drinks might be subdivided into categories of diet and nondiet soft drinks. As you can see, consumers use more associations to describe objects in a progression from the superordinate to the basic to the subordinate levels.

The hierarchical structure of information stored in memory is also influenced by environmental cues. People who ignore environmental cues tend to integrate information and form general brand beliefs, whereas those who pay attention to environmental cues store information in a more context-specific way and do not form general beliefs about product categories.[80]

Correlated Associations

When an associative network contains attributes that are linked in the consumer's mind, these attributes are *correlated*. With automobiles, consumers may expect the size of a car to be negatively correlated with fuel efficiency, or the price to be positively correlated with quality or luxury. Although the attributes may be correlated in consumers' minds, they may or may not actually be correlated. Knowledge about correlated attributes or benefits can significantly affect consumers' inferences about a new brand and the kinds of communications marketers need to create to overcome potentially false inferences. Contrary to the correlations in some consumers' minds, for example, healthy food options can be tasty, and tasty options can be healthy.

When consumers are developing a schema or when they are confronted with ambiguous information, they can mistakenly believe that if a product in a particular category has a type of attribute, other products in that category have similar attributes.[81] To understand these illusory correlations, consider this example: Just as some smokers mistakenly thought that "clean" smokeless cigarettes were safer than regular cigarettes, they may also mistakenly believe that low-toxin and natural cigarettes are safer.[82] Clearly understanding such illusory and real associations between attributes is crucial for marketers and policy makers.

Product Category	Prototypical Brands
Bologna	Oscar Mayer
Car rental service	Hertz
Cold cereal	Kellogg's
Eco-friendly car	Toyota Prius
Greeting cards	Hallmark
Hamburgers	McDonald's
Hook-and-loop fastener	Velcro
Ketchup	Heinz
Laundry detergent	Tide
Motorcycle	Harley-Davidson
Online retailer	Amazon.com
Smartphone	iPhone
Social media	Facebook
Soup	Campbell's
Tablet computer	iPad
Theme park	Disney

Exhibit 4.7 ▶ Prototypical Brands

Brands viewed as the best examples of a product category are called *prototypical brands*. Prototypical brands tend to have many features in common with other brands in the category, are encountered frequently, and may have been the first entrant in the product category.

 Marketing Implications

Prototypes are the main point of comparison used by consumers to categorize a new brand. Therefore, a brand can develop its identity by being positioned as being either similar to or different from the prototype. Because the prototype best defines the category and is well liked, a new brand positioned as being similar to it may appeal to that same (large) segment of consumers. Thus, consumers may well have a positive response to products that look similar to the prototype, including copycat competitors.[83]

Positioning away from the prototype can be an effective way to differentiate a brand. For instance, the small size of the Mercedes-Benz Smart ED electric car (see Exhibit 4.8) clearly differentiates it from the full-size green-car prototype, the Toyota Prius. This tactic can also work with pricing, because consumers judge whether a product's price is high or low by comparing it with the prices of several category members, not just with the price of the prototype.[84]

Helping consumers classify new hybrid products that straddle product categories can be a marketing opportunity and challenge. The smartphone is perhaps an ultimate example of a hybrid product, combining a phone, camera, computer, game device, and even a flashlight. The competitive context of these hybrid products shapes both the inferences consumers draw from the product's classification and their preferences for attributes. As a result, inferences drawn from a single product category (flashlights) don't necessarily determine the consumer's attribute preference when evaluating the hybrid product itself (smartphone).[85]

ROMEO GACAD/AFP/Getty Images

Exhibit 4.8 ▶ Differentiating from the Prototype

Since products are often compared to prototypes, new brands and products can differentiate themselves by positioning themselves away from the prototype, such as the new Mercedes-Benz Smart ED electric car whose small size differentiates it from the green-car prototype, the Toyota Prius.

Applying the concept of correlated associations, when two brands with similar brand concepts become cosponsors of an event such as a soccer championship, a positive image transfer can occur.[86] Understanding consumers' hierarchical category structure also helps marketers identify their competitors and influence perceptions of category attributes and prototypical products.[87] For instance, basic, subordinate, and superordinate category levels have implications for retail store design and merchandising. In grocery stores, objects in taxonomically similar categories are usually shelved together, as are items in the same basic and subordinate-level categories. Thus, most grocery stores have a dairy (superordinate level) section with shelves for milk, yogurt, cheese, and so on (basic level). Thus, soy milks, which are non-dairy, still are typically sold in the supermarket's refrigerated milk section to help consumers find them among category members.

Another key point about retail merchandising: How products are organized on store shelves (by benefit or by feature, for example) can affect consumer perceptions and decisions. When products are organized according to benefit (such as all whitening toothpastes

Goal-derived category Things viewed as belonging in the same category because they serve the same goals.

shelved together and all breath-freshening toothpastes shelved together), consumers will perceive individual products in each category to be less distinctive. As a result, consumers will focus more on price in making the buying decision.[88]

4-2c KNOWLEDGE FLEXIBILITY

The content and structure of a consumer's associative networks and categorizations are flexible and adaptable to the requirements of the tasks that he or she faces. This flexibility depends, in part, on the consumer's specific goals and the time to implement these goals.

Goal-Derived Categories

Taxonomic categories are fairly stable and based on the similarity between objects in terms of attributes ("all drinks that are carbonated"). Consumers may also organize their knowledge in **goal-derived categories**. A goal-derived category contains things that consumers view as similar because they serve the same goal, even though they may belong to very different taxonomic categories.[89] "Lighter, water, beef jerky, and a tent" have very different attributes but they may belong to the goal-directed category "things to take on a camping trip," while "mystery books, T-shirts of hard rock bands, and home-brewed beer" might be part of the category "gifts to take to your grand-dad."

Because consumers have different goals over time, they also have goal-derived categories that change flexibly. Thus, Diet Coke might be part of the taxonomic categories of diet colas, soft drinks, and beverages and also a member of goal-derived categories such as "things to have for lunch" and "things to take on a picnic." And, like taxonomic categories, goal-derived categories exhibit graded structure.

Construal Level

The associations that become activated in consumers' associative networks depend on the time interval between now and the moment of implementing the goals. That is, when consumers are far away from implementing a goal, more abstract knowledge about the desirability of attaining the goal becomes salient (the "why"). This is useful because it helps people to move toward the goal and block out competing goals. However, when people are close to implementing a goal, more concrete knowledge about the feasibility of attaining the goal becomes salient (the "how").[90] This helps people to prepare for the required activity and perform well.

To illustrate, when your wedding day is months away, more abstract associations such as the "union of souls" and "the joy of sharing thoughts and values" are salient in the associative network "my marriage." Yet, as the designated day draws near, more concrete associations about "who to invite" and "which dishes to have on the buffet" become salient. That is, the activated knowledge varies from very abstract to very concrete levels, and the time to act is an important determinant of this.[91]

Construal level theory describes the different levels of abstractness in the associations that a consumer has about concepts (people, products, brands, and activities) and how the consumer's psychological distance from these concepts influences his or her behavior.[92] Attributes of products and brands may have concrete or abstract associations, depending on the time to act, which is an aspect of psychological distance. For instance, the price of a product may be an indicator of quality when the purchase is far in the future; yet price may also be an indicator of the "pain" of paying when a consumer is in the store, and ready to buy (or not).[93] Another important point: When consumers feel confident, they will focus on the abstract aspects of products, whereas when they feel less confident, they will focus on concrete details.[94]

> **Construal level theory** Theory describing the different levels of abstractness in the associations that a consumer has about things (products, brands, people, and activities) and how the consumer's psychological distance influences the abstractness of the associations (far = abstract; close = concrete) and his or her behavior.

Marketing Implications

Positioning an offering as relevant to a goal can be an important marketing objective. To illustrate, in Japan, Nestlé's Kit Kat brand translates into something like "surely win." Thus, Kit Kat candy bars are positioned as "lucky things to eat before school exams."[95]

Supermarkets also apply the idea of goal-derived category structures. Many stores display baby bottles, diapers, and baby food in the same aisle despite these products' taxonomic differences. But these products are part of a goal-derived category—"things you need to take care of a baby." Parents can therefore easily find the items they need in one handy location. Retailers use a hybrid of taxonomic (all frozen products) and goal-derived categories (baby products, impulse products) to manage their assortments across the available store space.

When consumers are made aware of the specific set of brands they will actually have to choose from in the future, they might focus on the concrete associations that they actually will focus on when having to make the final choice. That might help them make accurate decisions.[96] Other factors such as mood may also influence the abstractness of the associations that become salient: Consumers in a positive mood tend to think more abstractly, while those in a negative mood tend to think more concretely.[97]

Brands and products that employ emotion-based appeals should understand that increased distance reduces the intensity of feelings, which works in favor of brands that have unpleasant side effects but works against brands with pleasant associations.[98] So, for example, a nonprofit using an emotion-based marketing message to solicit donations after a natural disaster would want to emphasize the urgency of the need and remind consumers how good they will feel after contributing.

4-2d WHY CONSUMERS DIFFER IN KNOWLEDGE CONTENT AND STRUCTURE

Goals and their timing influence the content and structure of knowledge *within* the minds of consumers. The consumer's culture and level of expertise influence the structure and content of knowledge *between* consumers.

That is, the associations that consumers link to a concept may vary considerably across cultures.[99] In Europe, the Philips brand is associated with consumer electronics while in U.S. markets Philips is closely associated with light bulbs, which it also makes.[100] Cultural groups also vary in how they organize taxonomic and goal-derived categories. In the United States, the category "breakfast products" includes cereal and eggs for many consumers, whereas in Japan it may include fish and rice.

Culture can affect how associations are correlated, as well. For example, price and store size may be negatively correlated in U.S. consumers' knowledge because big stores like Costco and Walmart tend to price products lower than small stores do. In contrast, price and store size may be positively correlated in India and Sri Lanka because large stores in those countries tend to price products higher to cover higher costs.

Prior experience plays a role in the content and structure of consumers' knowledge and the flexibility of using their knowledge. Therefore, consumers vary in their ability to process information based on how much prior experience they have. For instance, experts are consumers with a lot of prior experience and their knowledge and flexibility is well developed. Experts differ from novices in several ways.[101] First, expert consumers have a richer associative network with more associations, and more concrete and abstract associations linked to a concept than novices have. Second, they have more graded and refined taxonomic structure of categories. Third, they exhibit more flexibility in activating suitable associations (concrete or abstract) and categories (superordinate and subordinate) than novices. As a consequence, experts learn better which brands might be appropriate for different usage situations, organize such information by specific product subcategories, and are less motivated than novices to learn about a new product.[102]

Experts can also make finer distinctions among brands. For example, car experts would have many subordinate categories for cars, such as vintage cars and roadsters. In addition, novices tend to seek diverse experiences that will broaden their knowledge of a product category, whereas experts seek more focused experiences that will deepen their knowledge of the category.[103] Although consumers are sometimes overconfident in their knowledge and think they know more than they actually do, novices seek positive feedback and respond to it with increased commitment.[104] When evaluating products, experts have the deeper knowledge and motivation to process knowledge of *nonalignable attributes*—attributes that are not shared by all brands in the category. When novices are motivated or able to enhance their category knowledge, they will do as experts

do, and use a nonalignable attribute as the basis of judgment.[105]

Experts tend to evaluate a brand more favorably when product information is presented in such a way that they feel they are progressing toward their goal of making a decision. They also react favorably when the information presentation involves abstract associations, because these are motivating and expert consumers already have access to the concrete associations themselves.[106]

4-3 Memory and Retrieval

Marketers not only want consumers to store information in memory, properly categorized, and with favorable, unique, salient associations—they want consumers to retrieve this information from memory when making decisions. You have already seen how information becomes salient within the minds of consumers over time when moving toward or away from a decision, and between consumers due to culture and expertise. Marketers also want to understand and influence more specifically how consumers retrieve this information from memory and remember the information.

Marketing communication aims to increase the memorability (recall and recognition) of a brand name and logo, the brand's attributes, benefits, and perhaps personality.[107] Of course, memorable ads are not necessarily the most effective for the brand (see Exhibit 4.9). In one study, consumers who watched the commercials during the Super Bowl incorrectly attributed the advertising slogan of one telecommunications firm to as many as 13 other companies.[108] More importantly, the likelihood that a particular brand is chosen depends on whether it is remembered when consumers make a choice, independent of the attitude that consumers have toward brands.[109] Clearly, marketers want to avoid retrieval failures and retrieval errors for their brand when consumers make a choice.

4-3a RETRIEVAL FAILURES

Three elements in particular contribute to retrieval failures: decay, interference, and serial-position effects.

Decay

Decay occurs when memory strength deteriorates over time, for instance, because it has not been used. Thus, we tend to forget entire events or small details from childhood because they happened so long ago. Decay is reduced by repetition of the information, such as by advertising, and by recirculation, such as when repeatedly retrieving it from memory.

> **Decay** The weakening of memory strength over time.

Courtesy of Geico

Exhibit 4.9 ▶ Memory and Retrieval

Marketers aim to create memorable ads so consumers can easily recall the brand, like this promotion for Geico, featuring their famous gecko.

Interference

Interference occurs when the strength of a memory deteriorates over time because of the presence of other memories that compete with it.[110] Similarity between products, brands, and ads increase the likelihood of memory interference. Suppose you watch an ad that focuses on car brand A's safety, followed by a similar ad that focuses on car brand B's speed. You may then remember that some brand excels in safety but forget which brand it is.[111] Competitive advertising affects interference. When an established brand promotes a new attribute, consumers' knowledge of the brand's old attributes can interfere with retrieval of information about the new one. Yet when competitive advertising is present, consumers are able to suppress older attribute information and effectively retrieve the new attribute information, an accomplishment that works to the brand's advantage.[112]

Interference also affects marketing across cultures. For instance, a study of how interference affects bilingual

Interference When the strength of a memory deteriorates over time because of competing memories.

Primacy and recency effect The tendency to show greater memory for information that comes first or last in a sequence.

consumers concluded that second-language messages are not retrieved as well as first-language messages. To reduce interference, marketers could use visual and textual cues that reinforce each other. This tactic helps consumers to process second-language messages, thereby improving retrieval.[113]

Moreover, interference can result when one concept is activated so frequently that we cannot activate a different one. Suppose you are trying to recall the 10 items that you have on your grocery list. Chances are good that you can recall several items very easily and a few more with some difficulty, but the last ones may be almost impossible to remember. In trying to remember the missing items, you keep remembering the items you have already recalled, and these recollections interfere with your ability to activate the missing ones.[114]

Serial-Position Effects: Primacy and Recency

Decay and interference can be used to explain **primacy and recency effects**—that is, the fact that the things we encountered first or last in a sequence are often those most easily remembered. As an example of primacy effects, consumers are likely to remember the first ad during a commercial break because there is no other ad information to interfere with it. That information may also be less likely to decay if they rehearse it. Sampling two desirable products (such as two new songs), consumers tend to prefer the second sample, because of recency effects.[115] Considering primacy and recency effects, many advertisers believe that the best placement for an ad is either first or last in a commercial sequence or in a paper or digital magazine. Research supports the importance of being first, but the evidence in support of being last is not as strong.[116]

4-3b RETRIEVAL ERRORS

Memory is not always accurate or complete and may be subject to selection, confusion, and distortion. Memory is selective when you only remember the good things that happened on your last vacation but not the bad things that happened. Memory can be confused, as when you remember your friend telling you a great story about a new movie, when it was really your neighbor who told you. This example is a form of *source confusion* because you accurately remember the story about the movie but confuse who the source of the story was.

Finally, memory can be distorted, as when you remember experiences or events that actually did not happen. Perhaps you remember that a waitress who treated you badly at a restaurant clunked your coffee down loudly on the table, and asked for a larger tip. While this "memory" is consistent with the "bad waitress" experience, it might not have actually happened.[117] And virtual interaction with a product leads to more false memories because it generates vivid images that consumers later come to believe were real occurrences.[118]

4-3c   ENHANCING RETRIEVAL

Given the importance of retrieval, marketers need to understand how they can enhance the likelihood that consumers will remember something about specific brands. In addition to memory-enhancing factors mentioned earlier in this chapter, retrieval is affected by: (1) the characteristics of the stimulus itself, (2) what the stimulus is linked to, (3) the way the stimulus is processed, and (4) the consumer's characteristics.

> **Retrieval cue** A stimulus that facilitates the activation of memory.

4-3d   CHARACTERISTICS OF THE STIMULUS

Key characteristics of the stimulus that affect retrieval are salience, prototypicality, redundant cues, and the medium.

- *Salience.* Salient objects tend to attract attention and induce greater elaboration, thereby creating stronger memories.[119] Research has shown that consumers remember longer commercials better than shorter ones and bigger print ads better than smaller ones.[120] Yet 15-second TV commercials are more prevalent than 30-second commercials—and advertisers are testing commercials as brief as six seconds, in part because of the high cost of airing commercials.[121] Rotating ads on websites are often in view for under four seconds before the next one appears.[122]

- *Prototypicality.* We are better able to recognize and recall prototypical or pioneer brands because these have been frequently rehearsed and recirculated and are linked to many other concepts in memory, and pioneers were the first to occupy the links. The fact that we tend to remember these brands may explain why they have been so successful over time and why so many companies fight to establish themselves as category leaders.[123]

- *Redundant cues.* Memory is enhanced when the information items to be learned seem to go together naturally. Marketers can enhance consumers' memory for brands by advertising two complementary products together (such as Jif peanut butter with Smucker's jelly) and explaining why they go together.[124] Event sponsorship enhances memory when the brand is prototypical and the event relates to the brand's core meaning. Even if no clear link exists between the event and the sponsor, sponsor recall can be improved if the company explains why the sponsorship makes sense.[125]

- *The medium in which the stimulus is processed.* Researchers are exploring whether certain media are

more effective than others at enhancing consumer memory. Compared to magazines, television may be more effective because it combines visual and auditory information. Some studies suggest that consumers tend not to look at or remember online ads, whereas other studies suggest online ads can be as or even more effective than traditional media in generating brand memory.[126]

What the Stimulus Is Linked to

Retrieval can also be affected by what the stimulus is linked to in memory. A **retrieval cue** is some stimulus that facilitates the activation of memory.[127] For example, if you want to remember to go to a sale at Macy's, you might leave a note on your desk that says, "Macy's." The note serves as a retrieval cue when you see it some time later and remember the sale.

Retrieval cues can be generated internally or externally. Internally, a thought can cue another thought, as in "Today is November 8. Oh no, it's my sister's birthday!" An external stimulus such as a vending machine, a viral ad video, or an in-store display could also serve as a retrieval cue. Pictures or videos of ourselves engaging in an activity can serve as powerful retrieval cues, too.[128] Effective retrieval cues may differ from culture to culture. One study found sounds to be more effective retrieval cues for English-language ads, whereas visuals were more effective for Chinese-language ads.[129]

The brand name acts as a retrieval cue, when seeing or hearing the name brings the rich association network around the brand to mind.[130] Scents can also serve as retrieval clues.[131] If marketers want consumers to recognize the brand on the store shelf, it is important to have high-frequency words or names to which consumers have been heavily exposed—for example, Axe or Old Spice. If the goal is to have consumers recall the brand and its associations, better brand names (1) evoke rich imagery (Old El Paso), (2) are novel or unexpected (Kindle), or (3) suggest the offering and its benefits (Mr. Clean).

Unfamiliar brands have a retrieval advantage when the name of the brand fits well with the product function, whereas familiar brands have a retrieval advantage when the name features unusual spelling.[132] Images closely related to the brand name also serve as retrieval cues.[133] Revealing the brand name early in an ad message strengthens the memory association between the brand and the consumer's evaluation of the message content, an effect that influences retrieval.[134] Finally, logos, packages, and familiar branding and typefaces can also act as retrieval cues, such as when the Nike swoosh symbol activates associations of intense sports and physical activity.[135] The picture of the girl with the umbrella is likely to cue consumers to remember the Morton seasoning products depicted in Exhibit 4.10.

Morton®, When it Rains it Pours®, and the Morton Umbrella Girl are registered trademarks of Morton.

Exhibit 4.10 ▶ The Package as Retrieval Cue

Packages sometimes contain information that helps consumers remember what they saw in an ad. The girl with the umbrella (who shows that Morton salt still pours even when it rains) is used as a retrieval cue on all Morton seasoning products.

How a Stimulus Is Processed in Working Memory

Another factor affecting retrieval is the way information is processed in working memory. One consistent finding is that messages processed through visual imagery tend to be better remembered than those processed discursively. Importantly, multisensory imagery (text and pictures) can create a greater number of associations in memory, which, in turn, enhance retrieval.[136] This is because mental images are processed as pictures *and* as words. This *dual coding* of information provides extra and stronger associative links in memory, enhancing the likelihood that the item will be retrieved, whereas information encoded verbally is processed just one way and has only one retrieval path. Dual coding is one reason that marketers often use the audio portion of well-known TV ads as radio commercials. When consumers hear the familiar verbal message, they may provide their own imagery of the visual part.

Consumer Characteristics Affecting Retrieval

Consumers' mood and expertise can affect retrieval.[137] First, being in a positive mood can enhance our recall of stimuli in general. Second, we are more likely to recall information that is consistent with our mood. In other words, if we are in a positive mood, we are more likely to recall positive information. Several explanations account for these mood effects. One is that feelings consumers associate with a concept are linked to the concept in memory. Thus, your memory of Disney World may be associated with the feeling of having fun. If you are in a mood for fun, the "fun" concept may be activated, and this activation may spread to the concept of "Disney World."[138] People also appear to process information in more detail when mood is intense than when it is not. More detailed processing leads to greater elaboration and higher levels of recall.[139] Furthermore, mood influences both elaboration and rehearsal. Thus, consumers in a positive mood are more likely to readily learn brand names and engage in brand rehearsal.[140]

Compared with novices, experts have more complex category structures in memory with a greater number of higher and lower-level categories and more detail within each category. Therefore, experts' associative networks are more interconnected than the networks of novices. The complex linkages and the spreading of the activation concept explain why experts can recall more brands, brand attributes, and benefits than novices.[141] Next to the various benefits of being an expert, there is also an unexpected cost. When experts comparing product descriptions infer information that is not actually described, they may base their judgments at least in part on these false memories because of their highly developed category structures and schema.[142] That is, experts more so than novices rely on their intuition and processing fluency, and these may be fallible.

Novices have much less knowledge and therefore they will initially exert considerable effort to recall larger sets of brand and product alternatives, which leads to more negative evaluations when retrieving a lot of information. By comparison, experts already know a lot, and they must exert effort when retrieving smaller sets of information. This leads to more negative evaluations when experts are in situations when they recall small amounts of information.[143] Finally, consumers appear to more quickly access information about brands they encounter when they are young compared to when they are older. As a result, some marketers target children to build brand awareness and recognition at an early age, which in turn facilitates retrieval later in life.[144]

Summary:

Consumer memory is the persistence of learning over time, via the storage and retrieval of information, which can occur consciously or unconsciously. Retrieval is remembering or accessing what is stored in memory. Sensory memory (iconic and echoic) involves a very brief analysis of sensory inputs. Working memory is where we interpret incoming information, involving discursive and imagery processing. Long-term memory represents the permanent memory store, covering both episodic and semantic memory. Explicit memory involves active efforts to remember what's in memory; implicit memory involves remembering without conscious awareness. Chunking, rehearsal, recirculation, and elaboration are useful for influencing working memory.

Knowledge content is represented by a set of associations about an object or an activity linked in schemas and scripts. Knowledge in long-term memory is organized according to associative networks, with concepts connected by associations or links. Objects in memory are stored according to taxonomic categories. Taxonomic categories are structured hierarchically, organized into superordinate, basic, and subordinate levels. A schema is the group of associations linked to something. A script is knowledge of a sequence of actions involved in performing an activity. A prototype is perceived as the best example of its category. Knowledge content and structure are flexible. Objects may become part of the same category because they contribute to the same goal, and more or less abstract associations may become activated depending on the time until consumers make the choice or take the action.

People forget because of retrieval failures (due to decay, interference, and primacy and recency effects), or they may retrieve information that is not accurate. Factors that facilitate retrieval include the characteristics of the stimulus, what it is linked to, the way it is processed, and the characteristics of consumers.

Questions for Review and Discussion

1. How are sensory memory, working memory, and long-term memory linked?

2. What techniques can enhance the storage of information in long-term memory?

3. What is a schema and how can the associations in a schema be described?

4. Why are some links in a semantic or associative network weak, whereas others are strong?

5. What are taxonomic categories and how do consumers use them to structure knowledge in memory?

6. What is a category prototype, and what affects prototypicality?

7. What does it mean to say that consumers organize knowledge according to goal-derived categories?

8. How do high (abstract) and low-level (concrete) associations differ, and what does this mean for knowledge structure?

9. How can priming affect spreading of activation, and why is this important for marketing purposes?

10. Which three elements affect retrieval failures?

11. How can consumers' ability to retrieve information in memory be enhanced?

Endnotes

1 Jonathan Chew, "Apple's Latest Ads Take a Different Approach," *Fortune*, August 10, 2015, www.fortune.com.

2 Loraine Lau-Gesk, "Understanding Consumer Evaluations of Mixed Affective Experiences," *Journal of Consumer Research* 32, no. 1, 2005, pp. 23–28.

3 R. N. Haber, "The Impending Demise of the Icon: A Critique of the Concept of Iconic Storage in Visual Information Processing," *The Behavioral and Brain Sciences*, March 1983, pp. 1–54.

4 Nader T. Tavassoli and Jin K. Han, "Scripted Thought: Processing Korean Hancha and Hangul in a Multimedia Context," *Journal of Consumer Research*, December 2001, pp. 482–493.

5 Deborah J. MacInnis and Linda L. Price, "The Role of Imagery in Information Processing: Review and Extensions," *Journal of Consumer Research*, March 1987, pp. 473–491.

6 Allan Paivio, "Perceptual Comparisons Through the Mind's Eye," *Memory and Cognition*, November 1975, pp. 635–647; Stephen M. Kosslyn, "The Medium and the Message in Mental Imagery," *Psychological Review*, January 1981, pp. 46–66; and MacInnis and Price, "The Role of Imagery in Information Processing."

7 Morris B. Holbrook and Elizabeth C. Hirschman, "The Experiential Aspects of Consumption," *Journal of Consumer Research*, September 1982, pp. 132–140; and Alan Richardson, "Imagery: Definitions and Types," in ed. Aness Sheikh,

Imagery: Current Theory, Research, and Application (New York: Wiley, 1983), pp. 3–42.

8 Genevieve Shaw Brown, "New Wedding Dress App Uses 'Augmented Reality Technology' for Virtual Try-Ons," *ABC News*, September 4, 2014, http://abcnews.go.com.

9 Martin S. Lindauer, "Imagery and the Arts," in ed. Aness Sheikh, *Imagery: Current Theory, Research, and Application* (New York: Wiley, 1983), pp. 468–506.

10 Jennifer Edson Escalas, "Imagine Yourself in the Product," *Journal of Advertising*, Summer 2004, pp. 37–48.

11 Iris W. Hung and Robert S. Wyer Jr., "Shaping Consumer Imaginations: The Role of Self-Focused Attention in Product Evaluations," *Journal of Marketing Research*, April 2011, pp. 381–392.

12 Kimberly Janeway, "5 Ways to Find the Right Paint Hue for You," *Consumer Reports*, April 6, 2015, www.consumerreports.org.

13 Hans Baumgartner, Mita Sujan, and James R. Bettman, "Autobiographical Memories, Affect, and Consumer Information Processing," *Journal of Consumer Psychology* 1, no. 1, 1992, pp. 53–82.

14 See Kathryn A. Braun-LaTour, Michael S. LaTour, and George M. Zinkham, "Using Childhood Memories to Gain Insight into Brand Meaning," *Journal of Marketing*, April 2007, pp. 45–60.

15 Marc Vanhuele, Gilles Laurent, and Xavier Drèze, "Consumers' Immediate Memory for Prices," *Journal of Consumer Research* 33, no. 2, 2006, pp. 163–172.

16 Jing Xu and Norbert Schwarz, "Do We Really Need a Reason to Indulge?" *Journal of Marketing Research*, February 2009, pp. 25–36.

17 Darrel D. Muehling and Vincent J. Pascal, "An Empirical Investigation of the Differential Effects of Personal, Historical, and Non-Nostalgic Advertising on Consumer Responses," *Journal of Advertising*, Summer 2011, pp. 107–122; Darrel D. Muehling and David E. Sprott, "The Power of Reflection: An Empirical Examination of Nostalgia Advertising Effects," *Journal of Advertising*, Fall 2004, pp. 25–36; Morris B. Holbrook, "Nostalgia and Consumer Preferences," *Journal of Consumer Research*, September 1993, pp. 245–256; and Morris B. Holbrook and Robert M. Schindler, "Echoes of the Dear Departed Past," in eds. Rebecca H. Holman and Michael R. Solomon, *Advances in Consumer Research*, vol. 18 (Provo, Utah: Association for Consumer Research, 1991), pp. 330–333.

18 Sarah Perez, "Shutterfly Launches TripPix, A Quick Way to Create Travel Photo Books From Your iPhone," *TechCrunch*, June 10, 2015, www.techcrunch.com.

19 Kathryn A. Braun-LaTour, Michael S. LaTour, Jacqueline E. Pickrell, and Elizabeth F. Loftus, "How and When Advertising Can Influence Memory for Consumer Experience," *Journal of Advertising*, Winter 2004, pp. 7–25.

20 Kathryn A. Braun, "Postexperience Advertising Effects on Consumer Memory," *Journal of Consumer Research*, March 1999, pp. 319–334.

21 Danielle Sacks, "The Story of Oreo: How An Old Cookie Became a Modern Marketing Personality," *Fast Company Create*, October 23, 2014, www.fastcocreate.com.

22 Angela Y. Lee and Aparna A. Labroo, "The Effect of Conceptual and Perceptual Fluency on Brand Evaluation," *Journal of Marketing Research*, May 2004, pp. 151–165.

23 Noel Hayden, "The Spacing Effect: Enhancing Memory for Repeated Marketing Stimuli," *Journal of Consumer Psychology* 16, no. 3, 2006, pp. 306–320.

24 F. I. M. Craik and R. S. Lockhart, "Levels of Processing," *Verbal Learning and Verbal Behavior*, December 1972, pp. 671–684.

25 Jessica Wohl, "Rice Krispies Updates Treat Making with New Jingle," *Advertising Age*, November 20, 2015, www.adage.com.

26 Alan G. Sawyer, "The Effects of Repetition," in eds. G. David Hughes and Michael L. Ray, *Buyer/Consumer Information Processing* (Chapel Hill, N.C.: University of North Carolina Press, 1974), pp. 190–219; George E. Belch, "The Effects of Television Commercial Repetition on Cognitive Response and Message Acceptance," *Journal of Consumer Research*, June 1982, pp. 56–66; H. Rao Unnava and Robert E. Burnkrant, "Effects of Repeating Varied Ad Executions on Brand Name Memory," *Journal of Marketing Research*, November 1991, pp. 406–416; and Murphy S. Sewall and Dan Sarel, "Characteristics of Radio Commercials and Their Recall Effectiveness," *Journal of Marketing*, January 1986, pp. 52–60.

27 Chris Janiszewski, Hayden Noel, and Alan G. Sawyer, "Re-Inquiries: A Meta-Analysis of the Spacing Effect in Verbal Learning," *Journal of Consumer Research*, June 2003, pp. 138–149; see also Sara L. Appleton, Robert A. Bjork, and Thomas D. Wickens, "Examining the Spacing Effect in Advertising," *Journal of Consumer Research* 32, no. 2, 2005, pp. 266–276.

28 Sharmistha Law, "Can Repeating a Brand Claim Lead to Memory Confusion? " *Journal of Marketing Research*, August 2002, pp. 366–378.

29 Susan E. Heckler and Terry L. Childers, "The Role of Expectancy and Relevancy in Memory for Verbal and Visual Information," *Journal of Consumer Research*, March 1992, pp. 475–492.

30 H. Shanker Krishnan, "A Process Analysis of the Effects of Humorous Advertising Executions on Brand Claims Memory," *Journal of Consumer Psychology*, 2003, pp. 230–245.

31 Catherine A. Cole and Michael J. Houston, "Encoding and Media Effects on Consumer Learning Deficiencies in the Elderly," *Journal of Marketing Research*, February 1987, pp. 55–64; and Deborah Roedder John and John C. Whitney Jr., "The Development of Consumer Knowledge in Children," *Journal of Consumer Research*, March 1986, pp. 406–418.

32 Lawrence W. Barsalou, *Cognitive Psychology: An Overview for Cognitive Scientists* (Hillsdale, N.J.: Lawrence Erlbaum, 1992); James R. Bettman, "Memory Factors in Consumer Choice," *Journal of Marketing*, Spring 1979, pp. 37–53; and Merrie Brucks and Andrew A. Mitchell, "Knowledge Structures, Production Systems and Decision Strategies," in ed. Kent B. Monroe, *Advances in Consumer Research*, vol. 8 (Ann Arbor, Mich.: Association for Consumer Research, 1982), pp. 750–757.

33 Vanitha Swaminathan, Karen L. Page, and Zeynep Gurhan-Canli, "'My' Brand or 'Our' Brand: The Effects of Brand Relationship Dimensions and Self-Construal on Brand Evaluations," *Journal of Consumer Research*, August 2007, pp. 248–259.

34 Joseph W. Alba and J. Wesley Hutchinson, "Dimensions of Consumer Expertise," *Journal of Consumer Research*, March 1987, pp. 411–454.

35 Chris Janiszewski and Robert. S. Wyer, Jr., "Content and Process Priming: A Review," *Journal of Consumer Psychology* 24, no. 1, January 2014, pp. 96–118; and Claudiu V. Dimofte and Richard F. Yalch, "The Mere Association Effect and Brand Evaluations," *Journal of Consumer Psychology* 21, no. 1, Special Issue, January 2011, pp. 24–37.

36 Deborah J. MacInnis, Kent Nakamoto, and Gayathri Mani, "Cognitive Associations and Product Category Comparisons," in eds. John F. Sherry and Brian Sternthal, *Advances in*

Consumer Research, vol. 19 (Provo, Utah: Association for Consumer Research, 1992), pp. 260–267; and Kevin L. Keller, "Conceptualizing, Measuring, and Managing Customer-Based Brand Equity," *Journal of Marketing*, January 1993, pp. 1–22.

37 Stijn M. J. Van Osselaer and Chris Janiszewski, "Two Ways of Learning Brand Associations," *Journal of Consumer Research*, September 2001, pp. 202–223.

38 Paul Rozin, Julia M. Hormes, Myles S. Faith, and Brian Wansink, "Is Meat Male? A Quantitative Multimethod Framework to Establish Metaphoric Relationships," *Journal of Consumer Research* 39, no. 3, October 2012, pp. 629–643.

39 Leslie Patton, "McDonald's Sells Chorizo-Style Chicken Burrito," *Bloomberg*, September 25, 2014, www.bloomberg.com.

40 Zeynep Gurhan-Canli and Rajeev Batra, "When Corporate Image Affects Product Evaluations: The Moderating Role of Perceived Risk," *Journal of Marketing Research*, May 2004, pp. 197–205.

41 Ji Kyung Park and Deborah Roedder John, "Capitalizing on Brand Personalities in Advertising: The Influence of Implicit Self-Theories on Ad Appeal Effectiveness," *Journal of Consumer Psychology* 22, no. 3, July 2012, pp. 424–432; Pragya Mathur, Shailendra P. Jain, and Durairaj Maheswaran, "Consumers' Implicit Theories about Personality Influence Their Brand Personality Judgments," *Journal of Consumer Psychology* 22, no. 4, October 2012, pp. 545–557; Gita V. Johar, Jaideep Sengupta, and Jennifer L. Aaker, "Two Roads to Updating Brand Personality Impressions: Trait Versus Evaluative Inferencing," *Journal of Marketing Research*, November 2005, pp. 458–469; T. Plummer, "How Personality Makes a Difference," *Journal of Advertising Research*, December 1984–January 1985, pp. 27–31; William D. Wells, Frank J. Andriuli, Fedele J. Goi, and Stuart Seader, "An Adjective Check List for the Study of 'Product Personality,'" *Journal of Applied Psychology*, October 1957, pp. 317–319; and Jennifer L. Aaker, "Dimensions of Brand Personality," *Journal of Marketing Research*, August 1997, pp. 347–356.

42 Rajeev Batra and Pamela Miles Homer, "The Situational Impact of Brand Image Beliefs," *Journal of Consumer Psychology* 14, no. 3, 2004, pp. 318–330.

43 Bianca Grohmann, "Gender Dimensions of Brand Personality," *Journal of Marketing Research*, February 2009, pp. 105–111.

44 Linyun W. Yang, Keisha M. Cutright, Tanya L. Chartrand, and Gavan J. Fitzsimons, "Distinctively Different: Exposure to Multiple Brands in Low-Elaboration Settings," *Journal of Consumer Research* 40, no. 5, February 2014, pp. 973–992.

45 Yongjun Sung and Spencer F. Tinkham, "Brand Personality Structures in the United States and Korea," *Journal of Consumer Psychology* 15, no. 4, 2005, pp. 334–350.

46 Steven Shepher, Tanya L. Chartrand, and Gavan J. Fitzsimons, "When Brands Reflect Our Ideal Worlds: The Values and Brand Preferences of Consumers who Support versus Reject Society's Dominant Ideology," *Journal of Consumer Research* 42, no. 1, June 2015, pp. 76–92.

47 Jesse Chandler and Norbert Schwarz, "Use Does Not Wear Ragged the Fabric of Friendship: Thinking of Objects As Alive Makes People Less Willing to Replace Them," *Journal of Consumer Psychology* 20, no. 2, April 2010, pp. 138–145.

48 Ji Kyung Park and Deborah Roedder John, "Got to Get You into My Life: Do Brand Personalities Rub Off on Consumers?" *Journal of Consumer Research*, December 2010, pp. 655–669.

49 Lucia Malar, Harley Krohmer, Wayne D. Hoyer, and Bettina Nyffenegger, "Emotional Brand Attachment and Brand Personality: The Relative Importance of the Actual and the Ideal Self," *Journal of Marketing*, July 2011, pp. 35–52.

50 Thomas W. Leigh and Arno J. Rethans, "Experiences in Script Elicitation Within Consumer Decision-Making Contexts," in eds. Richard P. Bagozzi and Alice M. Tybout, *Advances in Consumer Research*, vol. 10 (Ann Arbor, Mich.: Association for Consumer Research, 1983), pp. 667–672; Roger C. Shank and Robert P. Abelson, *Scripts, Plans, Goals, and Understanding* (Hillsdale, N.J.: Lawrence Erlbaum, 1977); Ruth Ann Smith and Michael J. Houston, "A Psychometric Assessment of Measures of Scripts in Consumer Memory," *Journal of Consumer Research*, September 1985, pp. 214–224; R. A. Lakshmi-Ratan and Easwar Iyer, "Similarity Analysis of Cognitive Scripts," *Journal of the Academy of Marketing Science*, Summer 1988, pp. 36–43; and C. Whan Park, Easwar Iyer, and Daniel C. Smith, "The Effects of Situational Factors on In-Store Grocery Shopping Behavior," *Journal of Consumer Research*, March 1989, pp. 422–432.

51 See Girish N. Punj and Clayton L. Hillyer, "A Cognitive Model of Customer-Based Brand Equity for Frequently Purchased Products," *Journal of Consumer Psychology* 14, nos. 1, 2, 2004, pp. 124–131; Kevin Lane Keller, *Building, Measuring, and Managing Brand Equity*, 2nd ed. (Upper Saddle River, N.J.: Prentice-Hall, 2003), p. 60; and Roland T. Rust, Valarie Z. Zeithaml, and Katherine N. Lemon, *Driving Customer Equity* (New York: Free Press, 2000), pp. 80–87.

52 Deborah Roedder John, Barbara Loken, Kyeongheui Kim, and Alokparna Basu Monga, "Brand Concept Maps," *Journal of Marketing Research*, November 2006, pp. 549–563.

53 Lan Nguyen Chaplin and Deborah Roedder John, "The Development of Self-Brand Connections in Children and Adolescents," *Journal of Consumer Research* 32, no. 1, 2005, pp. 119–129.

54 Caleb Warren and Margaret C. Campbell, "What Makes Things Cool? How Autonomy Influences Perceived Coolness," *Journal Of Consumer Research* 41, no. 2, August 2014, pp. 543–563.

55 Tom Meyvis and Chris Janiszewski, "When Are Broader Brands Stronger Brands?" *Journal of Consumer Research* 31, no. 2, 2004, pp. 346–357; Sheri Bridges, Kevin Lane Keller, and Sanjay Sood, "Communication Strategies for Brand Extensions," *Journal of Advertising* 29, no. 4, Winter 2000, pp. 1–11; Elyette Roux and Frederic Lorange, "Brand Extension Research," in eds. Fred von Raiij and Gary Bamoussy, *European Advances in Consumer Research*, vol. 1 (Provo, Utah: Association for Consumer Research, 1993), pp. 492–500; C. Whan Park, Bernard J. Jaworski, and Deborah J. MacInnis, "Strategic Brand Concept–Image Management," *Journal of Marketing*, October 1986, pp. 135–145; David A. Aaker and Kevin L. Keller, "Consumer Evaluations of Brand Extensions," *Journal of Marketing*, January 1990, pp. 27–41; Bernard Simonin and Julie A. Ruth, "Is a Company Known by the Company It Keeps?" *Journal of Marketing Research*, February 1998, pp. 30–42; C. Whan Park, Sung Youl Jun, and Allan D. Shocker, "Composite Branding Alliances," *Journal of Marketing Research*, November 1996, pp. 453–466; MacInnis, Nakamoto, and Mani, "Cognitive Associations and Product Category Comparisons"; David M. Bousch et al., "Affect Generalization to Similar and Dissimilar Brand Extensions," *Psychology and Marketing*, 1987, pp. 225–237; and Susan M. Baroniarczyk and Joseph W. Alba, "The Importance of the Brand in Brand Extension," *Journal of Marketing Research*, May 1994, pp. 214–228.

56 Catherine W. M. Yeung and Robert S. Wyer Jr., "Does Loving a Brand Mean Loving Its Products? The Role of Brand-Elicited Affect in Brand Extension Evaluations," *Journal of Marketing Research*, November 2005, pp. 495–506.

57 Huifang Mao and H. Shanker Krishnan, "Effects of Prototype and Exemplar Fit on Brand Extension Evaluations: A Two-Process Contingency Model," *Journal of Consumer Research* 33, no. 1, 2006, pp. 41–49; Franziska Volkner and Henrik Sattler, "Drivers of Brand Extension Success," *Journal of Marketing*, April 2006, pp. 18–34; David Bousch, Shannon Shipp, Barbara Loken, Esra Genturk, Susan Crocket, Ellen Kennedy, Bettie Minshall, Dennis Misurell, Linda Rochford, and John Strobel, "Affect Generalization to Similar and Dissimilar Brand Extensions," *Psychology and Marketing* 4, no. 3, 1987, pp. 225–237; and Rainer Greifender, Herbert Bless, and Thorston Kurschmann, "Extending the Brand Image on New Products," *Journal of Consumer Behavior* 6, no. 1, 2007, pp. 19–31.

58 Zachary Estes, Michael Gibbert, Duncan Guest, and David Mazursky, "A Dual-Process Model of Brand Extension: Taxonomic Feature-Based and Thematic Relation-Based Similarity Independently Drive Brand Extension Evaluation," *Journal of Consumer Psychology* 22, no. 1, Special Issue, January 2012, pp. 86–101; Ingrid Martin and David Stewart, "The Differential Impact of Goal Congruence on Attitudes, Intentions, and the Transfer of Brand Equity," *Journal of Marketing Research*, November 2001, pp. 471–484; and Alokparna Basu Monga and Deborah Roedder John, "Cultural Differences in Brand Extension Evaluation," *Journal of Consumer Research* 33, no. 4, 2007, pp. 529–536. See also Shailendra Pratap Jain, Kalpesh Kaushik Desai, and Huifang Mao, "The Influence of Chronic and Situational Self-Construal on Categorization," *Journal of Consumer Research* 34, no. 1, 2007, pp. 66–76; and Sandra Milberg, C. W. Park, and Robert Lawson, "Evaluation of Brand Extensions," *Journal of Consumer Research* 18, no. 2, 1991, pp. 185–193.

59 S. J. Milberg, F. Sinn, and R. C. Goodstein, "Consumer Reactions to Brand Extensions in a Competitive Context: Does Fit Still Matter?" *Journal of Consumer Research*, October 2010, pp. 543–553.

60 Deborah Roedder John, Barbara Loken, and Christopher Joiner, "The Negative Impact of Extensions," *Journal of Marketing* 62, January 1998, pp. 19–32.

61 Meyvis and Janiszewski, "When Are Broader Brands Stronger Brands?"

62 Tom Meyvis, Kelly Goldsmith, and Ravi Dhar, "The Importance of the Context in Brand Extension: How Pictures and Comparisons Shift Consumers' Focus from Fit to Quality," *Journal of Marketing Research* 49, no. 2, April 2012, pp. 206–217.

63 Sharon Ng, "Cultural Orientation and Brand Dilution: Impact of Motivation Level and Extension Typicality," *Journal of Marketing Research*, February 2010, pp. 186–198.

64 Rohini Ahluwalia, "How Far Can a Brand Stretch? Understanding the Role of Self-Construal," *Journal of Marketing Research*, June 2008, pp. 337–350.

65 Kathryn A. LaTour and Michael S. LaTour, "Assessing the Long-term Impact of a Consistent Advertising Campaign on Consumer Memory," *Journal of Advertising*, Summer 2004, pp. 49–61.

66 See Kevin P. Gwinner and John Eaton, "Building Brand Image Through Event Sponsorship," *Journal of Advertising* 28, no. 4, Winter 1999, pp. 47–57.

67 Marc Gunther, "Walmart Is Slapping Itself on the Back For Sustainability But It Still Has a Way to Go," *The Guardian*, November 18, 2015, www.theguardian.com; and Kristina Monllos, "Is Walmart Trying to Brand Itself As Socially Conscious?" *Adweek*, May 29, 2015, www.adweek.com.

68 Marco della Cava, "VW Chairman Shifts Focus from Emissions Scandal to Future Car Vision," *USA Today*, January 6, 2016, www.usatoday.com; Christoph Rauwald, "VW's Bad News Drip Continues Two Months After Scandal Started," *Bloomberg*, November 23, 2015, www.bloomberg.com; and David Shepardson, "Volkswagen says 120,000 U.S. Diesel Owners Will Get Gift Cards, Repairs," *Reuters*, November 19, 2015, www.reuters.com.

69 Niraj Dawar and Madan M. Pillutla, "Impact of Product-Harm Crises on Brand Equity," *Journal of Marketing Research*, May 2000, pp. 215–226.

70 Jennifer Aaker, Susan Fournier, and S. Adam Brasel, "When Good Brands Do Bad," *Journal of Consumer Research*, June 2004, pp. 1–16.

71 Eleanor Rosch, "Principles of Categorization," in eds. E. Rosch and B. Lloyd, *Cognition and Categorization* (Hillsdale, N.J.: Lawrence Erlbaum, 1978), pp. 119–160.

72 Mathew S. Isaac and Aaron R. Brough, "Judging a Part by the Size of Its Whole: The Category Size Bias in Probability Judgments," *Journal of Consumer Research* 41, no. 2, August 2014, pp. 310–325.

73 Ian P. Murphy, "Retailers Are Finding That 'Sustainable' Sells," *Retail Dive*, August 19, 2015, www.retaildive.com; and Lauren Johnson, "Timberland Kicks Up Mobile Efforts with Targeted Ad Campaign," *Mobile Commerce Daily*, December 14, 2012, www.mobilecommercedaily.com.

74 Shashi Matta and Valerie S. Folkes, "Inferences About the Brand from Counterstereotypical Service Providers," *Journal of Consumer Research* 32, no. 2, 2005, pp. 196–206.

75 Mike Colias, "Cadillac's Plug-in Play: Hybrids First, Then EV," *Automotive News*, November 23, 2015, www.autonews.com; Greg Migliore, "GM Transplants Chevrolet Volt Technology into the Cadillac ELR Hybrid," *Auto Week*, August 17, 2011, www.autoweek.com.

76 Rosch, "Principles of Categorization"; Barsalou, *Cognitive Psychology*; and Madhubalan Viswanathan and Terry L. Childers, "Understanding How Product Attributes Influence Product Categorization: Development and Validation of Fuzzy Set-Based Measures of Gradedness in Product Categories," *Journal of Marketing Research*, February 1999, pp. 75–94.

77 Lawrence Barsalou, "Ideals, Central Tendency, and Frequency of Instantiation as Determinants of Graded Structure in Categories," *Journal of Experimental Psychology: Learning, Memory and Cognition*, October 1985, pp. 629–649; Barbara Loken and James Ward, "Alternative Approaches to Understanding the Determinants of Typicality," *Journal of Consumer Research*, September 1990, pp. 111–126; James Ward and Barbara Loken, "The Quintessential Snack Food: Measurement of Product Prototypes," in ed. Richard J. Lutz, *Advances in Consumer Research*, vol. 13 (Provo, Utah: Association for Consumer Research, 1986), pp. 126–131; and Gregory S. Carpenter and Kent Nakamoto, "Consumer Preference Formation and Pioneering Advantage," *Journal of Marketing Research*, August 1989, pp. 285–298.

78 Hyeong Min Kim, "Evaluations of Moderately Typical Products: The Role of Within Versus Cross-Manufacturer Comparisons," *Journal of Consumer Psychology* 16, no. 1, 2006, pp. 70–78.

79 Marcus Cunha, Jr., Mark R. Forehand, and Justin W. Angle, "Riding Coattails: When Co-Branding Helps versus Hurts Less-Known Brands," *Journal of Consumer Research* 41, no. 5, February 2015, pp. 1284–1300.

80 Sharon Ng and Michael J. Houston, "Field Dependency and Brand Cognitive Structures," *Journal of Marketing Research*, April 2009, pp. 279–292.

81 See Amos Tversky and Daniel Kahneman, "Extensional versus Intuitive Reasoning: The Conjunction Fallacy," *Psychological Review*, October 1983, pp. 293–315.

82 Tripp Mickle, "FDA Warns Cigarette Makers on 'Natural' Labeling," *Wall Street Journal*, August 27, 2015, www.wsj.com; Bob Garfield, "Softly Lit or Blunt, 'Less Toxic' Cigarette Ads Hint at Health," *Advertising Age*, November 12, 2001, p. 58; and Suein Hwang, "Smokers May Mistake 'Clean' Cigarette for Safe," *Wall Street Journal*, September 30, 1995, pp. B1, B2.

83 Luk Warlop and Joseph W. Alba, "Sincere Flattery: Trade-Dress Imitation and Consumer Choice," *Journal of Consumer Psychology* 14, no. 1/2, 2004, pp. 21–27.

84 Ronald W. Niedrich, Subhash Sharma, and Douglas H. Wedell, "Reference Price and Price Perceptions," *Journal of Consumer Research*, December 2001, pp. 339–354.

85 Theodore J. Noseworthy, Juan Wang, and Towhidul Islam, "How Context Shapes Category Inferences and Attribute Preference For New Ambiguous Products," *Journal of Consumer Psychology* 22, no. 4, October 2012, pp. 529–544.

86 Francois A. Carrillat, Eric G. Harris, and Barbara A. Lafferty, "Fortuitous Brand Image Transfer," *Journal of Advertising*, Summer 2010, pp. 109–123.

87 Barbara Loken, Christopher Joiner, and Joann Peck, "Category Attitude Measures: Exemplars as Inputs," *Journal of Consumer Psychology*, no. 2, 2002, pp. 149–161.

88 Cait Poynor Lamberton and Kristin Diehl, "Retail Choice Architecture: The Effects of Benefit and Attribute-Based Assortment Organization on Consumer Perceptions and Choice," *Journal of Consumer Research* 40, no. 3, October 2013, pp. 393–411.

89 Barsalou, *Cognitive Psychology*.

90 Yaacov Trope, Nira Liberman, and Cheryl Wakslak, "Construal Levels and Psychological Distance: Effects on Representation, Prediction, Evaluation, and Behavior," *Journal of Consumer Psychology* 17, no. 2, 2007, pp. 83–95.

91 Klaus Fiedler, "Construal Level Theory As an Integrative Framework for Behavioral Decision-Making Research and Consumer Psychology," *Journal of Consumer Psychology* 17, no. 2, 2007, pp. 101–106.

92 Yaacov Trope and Nira Liberman, "Temporal Construal," *Psychological Review*, 110, no. 3, 2003, pp. 403–421.

93 Dengfeng Yan and Jaideep Sengupta, "Effects of Construal Level on the Price-Quality Relationship," *Journal of Consumer Research*, August 2011, pp. 376–389.

94 Echo Wen Wan and Derek D. Rucker, "Confidence and Construal Framing: When Confidence Increases Versus Decreases Information Processing," *Journal of Consumer Research* 39, no. 5, March 2013, pp. 977–992.

95 Aimee Thompson, "Kit Kat Chocolates in Japan: Unique Varieties Popular in Regions Across the Country," *Chicago Now*, May 20, 2014, www.chicagonow.com.

96 Frank R. Kardes, Maria L. Cronley, and John Kim, "Construal Level Effects on Preference Stability, Preference-Behavior Correspondence, and the Suppression of Competing Brands," *Journal of Consumer Psychology* 16, no. 2, 2006, pp. 135–144.

97 Aparna A. Labroo and Vanessa M. Patrick, "Psychological Distancing: Why Happiness Helps You See the Big Picture," *Journal of Consumer Research*, February 2009, pp. 800–809.

98 Lawrence E. Williams, Randy Stein, and Laura Galguera, "The Distinct Affective Consequences of Psychological Distance and Construal Level," *Journal of Consumer Research* 40, no. 6, April 2014, pp. 1123–1138.

99 Eleanor Rosch, "Human Categorization," in ed. N. Warren, *Studies in Cross-Cultural Psychology* (New York: Academic Press, 1977), pp. 1–49; A. D. Pick, "Cognition: Psychological Perspectives," in eds. H. C. Triandis and W. Lonner, *Handbook of Cross-Cultural Psychology* (Boston: Allyn & Bacon, 1980), pp. 117–153; and Bernd Schmitt and Shi Zhang, "Language Structure and Categorization: A Study of Classifiers in Consumer Cognition, Judgment and Choice," *Journal of Consumer Research*, September 1998, pp. 108–122.

100 Beth Snyder Bulik, "Philips: We're Not Just Light Bulbs," *Advertising Age*, June 25, 2007, www.adage.com.

101 Alba and Hutchinson, "Dimensions of Consumer Expertise"; Deborah Roedder John and John Whitney Jr., "The Development of Consumer Knowledge in Children," *Journal of Consumer Research*, March 1986, pp. 406–417; Merrie Brucks, "The Effects of Product Class Knowledge on Information Search Behavior," *Journal of Consumer Research*, June 1985, pp. 1–16; Deborah Roedder John and Mita Sujan, "Age Differences in Product Categorization," *Journal of Consumer Research*, March 1990, pp. 452–460; see also Andrew A. Mitchell and Peter A. Dacin, "The Assessment of Alternative Measures of Consumer Expertise," *Journal of Consumer Research*, December 1996, pp. 219–239; and C. Whan Park, David L. Mothersbaugh, and Lawrence Feick, "Consumer Knowledge Assessment," *Journal of Consumer Research*, June 1994, pp. 71–82.

102 Elizabeth Cowley and Andrew A. Mitchell, "The Moderating Effect of Product Knowledge on the Learning and Organization of Product Information," *Journal of Consumer Research*, December 2003, pp. 443–454; and Stacy L. Wood and John G. Lynch Jr., "Prior Knowledge and Complacency in New Product Learning," *Journal of Consumer Research*, December 2002, pp. 416–426.

103 Joshua J. Clarkson, Chris Janiszewski, and Melissa D. Cinelli, "The Desire for Consumption Knowledge," *Journal of Consumer Research* 39, no. 6, April 2013, pp. 1313–1329.

104 Joseph W. Alba and J. Wesley Hutchinson, "Knowledge Calibration," *Journal of Consumer Research*, September 2000, pp. 123–156; and Stacey R. Finkelstein and Ayelet Fishbach, "Tell Me What I Did Wrong: Experts Seek and Respond to Negative Feedback," *Journal of Consumer Research* 39, no. 1, June 2012, pp. 22–38.

105 Myungwoo Nam, Jing Wang, and Angela Y. Lee, "The Difference between Differences: How Expertise Affects Diagnosticity of Attribute Alignability," *Journal of Consumer Research* 39, no. 4, December 2012, pp. 736–750.

106 Jiewen Hong and Brian Sternthal, "The Effects of Consumer Prior Knowledge and Processing Strategies on Judgments," *Journal of Marketing Research*, April 2010, pp. 301–311.

107 Larry Percy and John R. Rossiter, "A Model of Brand Awareness and Brand Attitude in Advertising Strategies," *Psychology and Marketing*, July–August 1992, pp. 263–274.

108 Bonnie Tsui, "Bowl Poll: Ads Don't Mean Sales," *Advertising Age*, February 5, 2001, p. 33.

109 Angela Y. Lee, "Effects of Implicit Memory on Memory-Based versus Stimulus-Based Brand Choice," *Journal of Marketing Research*, November 2002, pp. 440–454.

110 Rik G. M. Pieters and Tammo H. A. Bijmolt, "Consumer Memory for Television Advertising: A Field Study of Duration, Serial Position and Competition Effects," *Journal of Consumer Research*, March 1997, pp. 362–372; Raymond Burke and Thomas K. Srull, "Competitive Interference and Consumer Memory for Advertisements," *Journal of Consumer Research*, June 1988, pp. 55–68; Kevin Keller, "Memory and Evaluation Effects in Competitive Advertising Environments," *Journal of Consumer Research*, March 1991, pp. 463–476; Tom J. Brown and Michael L. Rothschild, "Reassessing the Impact of Television Advertising Clutter," *Journal of Consumer Research*, June 1993, pp. 138–147; Robert J. Kent and Chris T. Allen, "Competitive Interference Effects in Consumer Memory for Advertising," *Journal of Marketing*, July 1994, pp. 97–105; and H. Rao Unnava and Deepak Sirdeshmukh, "Reducing Competitive Ad Interference," *Journal of Marketing Research*, August 1994, pp. 403–411.

111 Anand Kumar and Shanker Krishnan, "Memory Interference in Advertising: A Replication and Extension," *Journal of Consumer Research*, March 2004, pp. 602–661; and Anand Kumar, "Interference Effects of Contextual Cues in Advertisements on Memory for Ad Content," *Journal of Consumer Psychology* 9, no. 3, 2000, pp. 155–166.

112 Robert D. Jewell and H. Rao Unnava, "When Competitive Interference Can Be Beneficial," *Journal of Consumer Research*, September 2003, pp. 283–291.

113 David Luna and Laura A. Peracchio, "Moderators of Language Effects in Advertising to Bilinguals," *Journal of Consumer Research*, September 2001, pp. 28–43.

114 Joseph W. Alba and Amitava Chattopadhyay, "Effects of Context and Part-Category Cues on Recall of Competing Brands," *Journal of Marketing Research*, August 1985, pp. 340–349; Joseph W. Alba and Amitava Chattopadhyay, "Salience Effects in Brand Recall," *Journal of Marketing Research*, November 1986, pp. 363–369; and Manoj Hastak and Anusre Mitra, "Facilitating and Inhibiting Effects of Brand Cues on Recall, Consideration Set, and Choice," *Journal of Business Research*, October 1996, pp. 121–126.

115 Dipayan Biswas, Dhruv Grewal, and Anne Roggeveen, "How the Order of Sampled Experiential Products Affects Choice," *Journal of Marketing Research*, June 2010, pp. 508–519.

116 Rik Pieters and Tammo H. A. Bijmolt, "Consumer Memory for Television Advertising: A Field Study of Duration, Serial Position, and Competition Effects," *Journal of Consumer Research*, March 1997, pp. 362–372; and Burke and Srull, "Competitive Interference and Consumer Memory for Advertising."

117 Elizabeth F. Loftus, "When a Lie Becomes Memory's Truth: Memory and Distortion after Exposure to Misinformation," *Current Directions in Psychological Science*, August 1992, pp. 121–123.

118 Ann E. Schlosser, "Learning Through Virtual Product Experiences," *Journal of Consumer Research* 33, no. 3, 2006, pp. 377–383.

119 Joseph W. Alba, J. Wesley Hutchinson, and John G. Lynch Jr., "Memory and Decision Making," in eds. Thomas S. Robertson and Harold Kassarjian, *Handbook of Consumer Behavior* (Englewood Cliffs, N.J.: Prentice-Hall, 1991), pp. 1–49.

120 Rik G. M. Pieters and Tammo H. A. Bijmolt, "Consumer Memory for Television Advertising: A Field Study of Duration, Serial Position, and Competition Effects," *Journal of Consumer Research*, March 1997, pp. 362–372; David W. Stewart and David H. Furse, *Effective Television Advertising: A Study of 1000 Commercials* (Cambridge, Mass.: Marketing Science Institute,

1986); and Pamela Homer, "Ad Size as an Indicator of Perceived Advertising Costs and Effort: The Effects on Memory and Perceptions," *Journal of Advertising*, Winter 1995, pp. 1–12.

121 Victor Luckerson, "Here's Exactly Why Watching TV Has Gotten So Annoying," *Time*, May 12, 2014, www.time.com.

122 Tim Ash, "Rotating Banners: Why Image Sliders Kill Conversions," *Marketing Land*, July 11, 2014, www.marketingland.com.

123 Frank R. Kardes and Gurumurthy Kalyanaram, "Order of Entry Effects on Consumer Memory and Judgment," *Journal of Marketing Research*, August 1992, pp. 343–357; Frank Kardes, Murali Chandrashekaran, and Ronald Dornoff, "Brand Retrieval, Consideration Set Composition, Consumer Choice, and the Pioneering Advantage," *Journal of Consumer Research*, June 1993, pp. 62–75; and Frank H. Alpert and Michael A. Kamins, "An Empirical Investigation of Consumer Memory, Attitude, and Perceptions Toward Pioneer and Follower Brands," *Journal of Marketing*, October 1995, pp. 34–44.

124 Sridar Samu, H. Shankar Krishnan, and Robert E. Smith, "Using Advertising Alliances for New Product Introduction," *Journal of Marketing*, January 1999, pp. 57–74.

125 T. Bettina Cornwell, Michael S. Humphreys, Angela M. Maguire, Clinton S. Weeks, and Cassandra L. Tellegen, "Sponsorship-Linked Marketing: The Role of Articulation in Memory," *Journal of Consumer Research* 33, no. 3, 2006, pp. 312–321.

126 Rex Briggs and Nigel Hollis, "Advertising on the Web," *Journal of Advertising Research*, March–April 1997, pp. 33–45.

127 Michael Pham and Gita Venkataramani Johar, "Contingent Processes of Source Identification," *Journal of Consumer Research*, December 1997, pp. 249–265.

128 Deborah D. Heisley and Sidney J. Levy, "Autodriving: A Photo-elicitation Technique," *Journal of Consumer Research*, December 1991, pp. 257–272.

129 Nader T. Tavassoli and Yih Hwai Lee, "The Differential Interaction of Auditory and Visual Advertising Elements with Chinese and English," *Journal of Marketing Research*, November 2003, pp. 468–480.

130 Charles D. Lindsey and H. Shanker Krishnan, "Retrieval Disruption in Collaborative Groups due to Brand Cues," *Journal of Consumer Research* 33, no. 4, 2007, pp. 470–478; Joan Meyers-Levy, "The Influence of a Brand Name's Association Set Size and Word Frequency on Brand Memory," *Journal of Consumer Research*, September 1989, pp. 197–207; and Alba and Hutchinson, "Dimensions of Consumer Expertise."

131 Maureen Morrin, Aradhna Krishna, and May O. Lwin, "Is Scent-Enhanced Memory Immune to Retroactive Interference?" *Journal of Consumer Psychology* 21, no. 3, July 2011, pp. 354–361.

132 Tina M. Lowrey, L. J. Shrum, and Tony M. Dubitsky, "The Relation Between Brand-Name Linguistic Characteristics and Brand-Name Memory," *Journal of Advertising*, Fall 2003, pp. 7–17.

133 Jaideep Sengupta and Gerald J. Gorn, "Absence Makes the Mind Grow Sharper: Effects of Element Omission on Subsequent Recall," *Journal of Marketing Research*, May 2002, pp. 186–201.

134 William E. Baker, Heather Honea, and Cristel Antonia Russell, "Do Not Wait to Reveal the Brand Name," *Journal of Advertising*, Fall 2004, pp. 77–85.

135 Judith Lynne Zaichkowsky, "Strategies for Distinctive Brands," *Brand Management* 17, no. 8, 2010, pp. 548–560; and Terry L. Childers and Jeffrey Jass, "All Dressed Up with Something to Say: Effects of Typeface Semantic Associations on

Brand Perceptions and Consumer Memory," *Journal of Consumer Psychology*, 2002, pp. 93–106.

136 David Luna, Marina Carnevale, and Dawn Lerman, "Does Brand Spelling Influence Memory? The Case of Auditorily Presented Brand Names," *Journal of Consumer Psychology* 23, no. 1, January 2013, pp. 36–48; May O. Lwin, Maureen Morrin, and Aradhna Krishna, "Exploring the Superadditive Effects of Scent and Pictures on Verbal Recall: An Extension of Dual Coding Theory," *Journal of Consumer Psychology* 20 no. 3, July 2010, pp. 317–326; Cole and Houston, "Encoding and Media Effects on Consumer Learning Deficiencies in the Elderly"; and Sharmistha Law, Scott A. Hawkins, and Fergus I. M. Craik, "Repetition-Induced Belief in the Elderly: Rehabilitating Age-Related Memory Deficits," *Journal of Consumer Research*, September 1998, pp. 91–107.

137 Alice M. Isen, "Some Ways in Which Affect Influences Cognitive Processes: Implications for Advertising and Consumer Behavior," in eds. Alice M. Tybout and P. Cafferata, *Advertising and Consumer Psychology* (Lexington, Mass.: Lexington Books, 1989), pp. 91–117; see also Patricia A. Knowles, Stephen J. Grove, and W. Jeffrey Burroughs, "An Experimental Examination of Mood Effects on Retrieval and Evaluation of Advertisement and Brand Information," *Journal of the Academy of Marketing Science*, Spring 1993, pp. 135–143; Gordon H. Bower, "Mood and Memory," *American Psychologist*, February 1981, pp. 129–148; Gordon H. Bower, Stephen Gilligan, and Kenneth Montiero, "Selectivity of Learning Caused by Affective States," *Journal of Experimental Psychology: General*, December 1981, pp. 451–473; and Alice M. Isen, Thomas Shalker,

Margaret Clark, and Lynn Karp, "Affect, Accessibility of Material in Memory, and Behavior," *Journal of Personality and Social Psychology*, 1978, pp. 1–12.

138 Alice M. Isen, "Toward Understanding the Role of Affect in Cognition," in eds. Robert S. Wyer and Thomas K. Srull, *Handbook of Social Cognition* (Hillsdale, N.J.: Lawrence Erlbaum, 1984), pp. 179–236.

139 Alice M. Isen, "Some Ways in Which Affect Influences Cognitive Processes: Implications for Advertising and Consumer Behavior," in eds. Patricia Cafferata and Alice M. Tybout, *Cognitive and Affective Responses to Advertising* (Lexington, Mass.: Lexington Books, 1989), pp. 91–118.

140 Angela Y. Lee and Brian Sternthal, "The Effects of Positive Mood on Memory," *Journal of Consumer Research* 26, September 1999, pp. 115–127.

141 Alba and Hutchinson, "Dimensions of Consumer Expertise."

142 Ravi Mehta, Joandrea Hoegg, and Amitav Chakravarti, "Knowing Too Much: Expertise-Induced False Recall Effects in Product Comparison," *Journal of Consumer Research*, October 2011, pp. 535–554.

143 Jayati Sinha and Dhanajay Naykankuppam, "Knowledge Does Not Necessarily Make the Heart Grow Fonder: The Moderating Role of Knowledge on Accessibility Experiences," *Journal of Consumer Psychology* 23, no. 1, January 2013, pp. 49–60.

144 Andrew W. Ellis, Selina J. Holmes, and Richard L. Wright, "Age of Acquisition and the Recognition of Brand Names: On the Importance of Being Early," *Journal of Consumer Psychology* 20, no. 1, January 2010, pp. 43–52.

Attitudes Based on High Effort

LEARNING OBJECTIVES

After studying this chapter, you will be able to:

▶ Discuss how marketers can apply various cognitive models to understand consumers' attitudes based on high-effort thought processes.

▶ Describe some of the methods for using the communication source and the message to favorably influence consumers' attitudes in high-effort situations.

▶ Identify the emotional foundations of attitudes when consumers' processing effort is high.

▶ Explain how and why a company might try to change consumers' attitudes by influencing their feelings.

▶ Outline the three main factors that lead to a positive overall consumer attitude toward an advertisement.

▶ Discuss the various elements that can affect whether a consumer's attitudes will influence his or her behavior.

Source: Patek Philippe & Co.

INTRODUCTION

Luxury, tradition, and achievement are common themes in marketing high-end watches to affluent consumers worldwide. To attract and engage well-to-do buyers, Rolex advertises in luxury lifestyle magazines, arranges endorsements from successful sports figures, sponsors yacht racing, and uses mobile marketing to highlight product details. These marketing activities illustrate several important points that stem from concepts explored in the previous chapter. Consumers probably have certain beliefs about brands such as Rolex that are based on the mental associations they have linked to them (Rolex watches are expensive; Rolex watches are status symbols).[1] These beliefs can affect consumers' attitudes (whether they like a certain brand or a particular style) and their behavior (whether they will travel to a store that carries Rolex watches and buy one). Finally, consumers' attitudes can be based on the offering's functional features (precise time-keeping ability) or the emotional aspects (feeling proud to own a prestige brand). How marketers help consumers form positive brand attitudes based on new beliefs and associations, and to influence buying decisions, are central issues addressed in this chapter.

5-1 What Are Attitudes?

An **attitude** is an overall evaluation that expresses how much we like or dislike an object, issue, person, or action.[2] Attitudes are learned, and they tend to persist over time. Our attitudes also reflect our overall evaluation of something based on the set of associations linked to it. This is the reason why we have attitudes toward brands, product categories, ads, people, stores, websites, activities, and so forth.

5-1a THE IMPORTANCE OF ATTITUDES

Attitudes are important because they (1) guide our thoughts (the **cognitive function**), (2) influence our feelings (the **affective function**), and (3) affect our behavior (the **connative function**). We decide which ads to read, whom to talk to, where to shop, and where to eat, based on our attitudes. Likewise, attitudes influence our behavior in acquiring, consuming, and disposing of an offering. Thus, marketers need to change attitudes in order to influence consumer decision-making and change consumer behavior.

5-1b THE CHARACTERISTICS OF ATTITUDES

Attitudes can be described in terms of five main characteristics: favorability, attitude accessibility, attitude confidence, persistence, and resistance. **Favorability** refers to how much we like or dislike something. **Attitude accessibility** refers to how easily and readily an attitude can be retrieved from memory.[3] If you went to a movie last night, you can probably remember fairly easily what your attitude toward it was, just as you can easily remember your attitude toward an important object, event, or activity (such as your first car).

Attitudes can also be described in terms of their strength, or **attitude confidence**. In some cases we hold our attitudes very strongly and with a great deal of confidence, whereas in other cases we feel much less certain about them.[4] Attitudes may also vary in their **persistence**, or endurance. The attitudes we hold with confidence may last for an extremely long time, whereas others may be very brief. In addition, attitudes can be described in terms of their **resistance** to subsequent change.[5] Consumers may change attitudes easily when they are not loyal to a particular brand or know little about a product. However, attitude change is more difficult when consumers are brand loyal or consider themselves experts in the product category.

Finally, attitudes may be described in terms of **ambivalence**, as when we have strong positive evaluations of one aspect of a brand and strong negative evaluations of other

Attitude A relatively global and enduring evaluation of an object, issue, person, or action.

Cognitive function How attitudes influence our thoughts.

Affective function Katz' notion that our feelings influence our attitudes.

Connative function How attitudes influence our behavior.

Favorability The degree to which we like or dislike something.

Attitude accessibility How easily an attitude can be remembered.

Attitude confidence How strongly we hold an attitude.

Attitude persistence How long our attitude lasts.

Attitude resistance How difficult it is to change an attitude.

Ambivalence When our evaluations regarding a brand are mixed (both positive and negative).

aspects of the brand. Interestingly, someone else's opinion will tend to influence us more when our attitudes are ambivalent, even when we do not see that person as being particularly knowledgeable about the product or category. So if you are shopping, and you can find both good and bad reasons to buy the product, you may be more influenced to buy it if encouraged by a friend.[6]

5-1c FORMING AND CHANGING ATTITUDES

Marketers can better create or influence consumers' attitudes toward new offerings and novel behaviors when they understand how attitudes are formed. This understanding also helps marketers plan strategies for changing consumer attitudes about existing offerings and established behaviors. Exhibit 5.1 summarizes general approaches to attitude formation and change processes that are discussed in this and the next chapter.

The Foundation of Attitudes

As Exhibit 5.1 shows, one approach to attitude formation suggests that attitudes are based on *cognitions* (thoughts) or beliefs.[7] This means that attitudes can be based on thoughts we have about information received from an external source (such as advertising, salespeople, Facebook, or a friend) or on information we recall from memory. One study shows that ad messages with information about product function—what a product's features can do, for example—can provoke thinking about the product and stimulate positive product attitudes.[8]

A second approach suggests that attitudes are based on *emotions*. Sometimes we have a favorable attitude toward an offering simply because it feels good or seems right. Likewise, we can acquire attitudes by observing and vicariously experiencing the emotions of others who use an offering. For example, if you see that people riding skateboards are having fun, you may believe that if you rode one, you would, too. In fact, research suggests that both the hedonic aspect (related to the experience of product use) and the utilitarian aspect (related to the product's function) affect attitudes toward product categories and individual brands.[9]

The Role of Effort in Attitude Formation and Change

How much extensive thinking or *elaboration* consumers put forth affects their attitude formation and change processes as well. As discussed in Chapter 2, consumers sometimes have high motivation, ability, and opportunity (MAO) to process information and make decisions. When MAO is high, consumers are more likely to devote

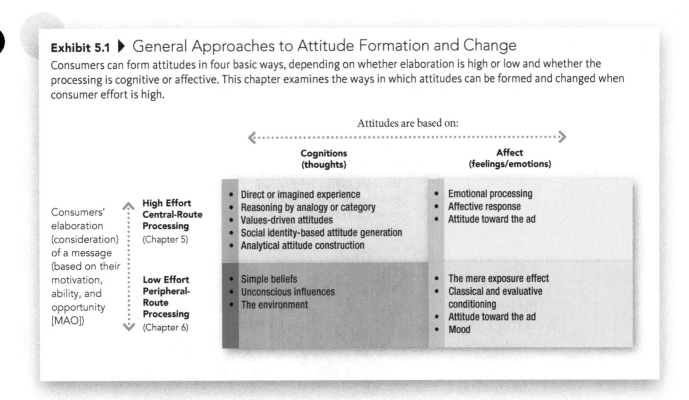

Exhibit 5.1 ▶ General Approaches to Attitude Formation and Change

Consumers can form attitudes in four basic ways, depending on whether elaboration is high or low and whether the processing is cognitive or affective. This chapter examines the ways in which attitudes can be formed and changed when consumer effort is high.

Attitudes are based on:

	Cognitions (thoughts)	Affect (feelings/emotions)
High Effort Central-Route Processing (Chapter 5)	• Direct or imagined experience • Reasoning by analogy or category • Values-driven attitudes • Social identity-based attitude generation • Analytical attitude construction	• Emotional processing • Affective response • Attitude toward the ad
Low Effort Peripheral-Route Processing (Chapter 6)	• Simple beliefs • Unconscious influences • The environment	• The mere exposure effect • Classical and evaluative conditioning • Attitude toward the ad • Mood

Consumers' elaboration (consideration) of a message (based on their motivation, ability, and opportunity [MAO])

---

a lot of effort toward and become quite involved in forming or changing attitudes and making decisions. Some researchers have used the term **central-route processing** to describe the process of attitude formation and change when thinking about a message requires some effort.[10] Processing is central because consumers' attitudes are based on a careful and effortful analysis of the true merits or central issues contained within the message. As a result of this extensive and laborious processing, consumers form strong, accessible, and confidently held attitudes that are persistent and resistant to change.

When MAO is low, however, consumers' attitudes are based on a more tangential or superficial analysis of the message, not on an effortful analysis of its true merits. Because these attitudes tend to be based on peripheral or superficial cues contained within the message, the term **peripheral-route processing** has been used to describe attitude formation and change that involves limited effort (or low elaboration) on the part of the consumer.

This chapter focuses on several ways in which consumers form and change attitudes when effort (i.e., MAO) is high. The next chapter focuses on how consumers form and change attitudes when effort is low. Because attitudes tend to be more accessible, persistent, resistant to change, and held with confidence when consumers' MAO to process information is high, much of the chapter focuses on what affects the favorability of consumers' attitudes.

Central-route processing The attitude formation and change process when effort is high.

peripheral-route processing The attitude formation and change process when effort is low.

As shown in Exhibit 5.2, when consumers are likely to devote a lot of effort to processing information, marketers can influence consumer attitudes either (1) *cognitively*—influencing the thoughts or beliefs they have about the offering or (2) *affectively*—influencing the emotional experiences consumers associate with the offering. Furthermore, marketers can try to influence consumers' attitudes through characteristics of the source used in a persuasive communication, the type of message used, or some combination of both. After attitudes are formed, they may play a powerful role in influencing consumers' intentions and actual behavior.

5-2 The Cognitive Foundations of Attitudes

Researchers have proposed various theories to explain how thoughts are related to attitudes when consumers devote a lot of effort to processing information and making decisions. This section focuses on five cognitive models: (1) direct or imagined experience; (2) reasoning by analogy or category; (3) values-driven attitudes; (4) social identity-based attitude generation; and (5) analytical processes of attitude construction, including expectancy-value models such as the theory of reasoned action (TORA) and the theory of planned behavior.

Exhibit 5.2 ▶ Chapter Overview: Attitude Formation and Change, High Consumer Effort

Following the first two stages (exposure, attention, and comprehension; and knowledge and memory), consumers can either form or change their attitudes. This chapter explains how consumers form high-effort attitudes based on both cognition and affect. It also shows how marketers can influence attitudes through source factors and message factors.

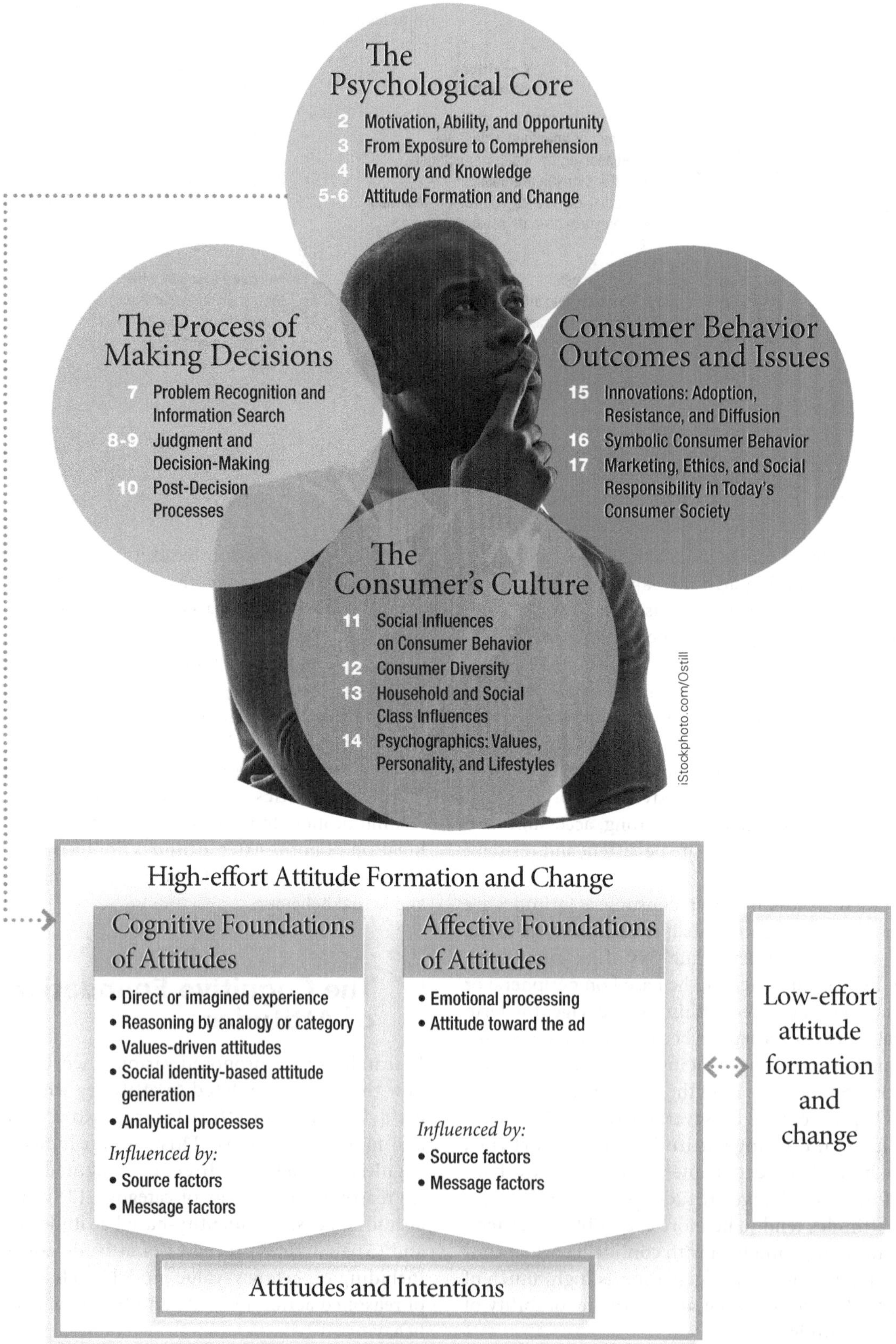

The Psychological Core

- 2 Motivation, Ability, and Opportunity
- 3 From Exposure to Comprehension
- 4 Memory and Knowledge
- 5-6 Attitude Formation and Change

The Process of Making Decisions

- 7 Problem Recognition and Information Search
- 8-9 Judgment and Decision-Making
- 10 Post-Decision Processes

Consumer Behavior Outcomes and Issues

- 15 Innovations: Adoption, Resistance, and Diffusion
- 16 Symbolic Consumer Behavior
- 17 Marketing, Ethics, and Social Responsibility in Today's Consumer Society

The Consumer's Culture

- 11 Social Influences on Consumer Behavior
- 12 Consumer Diversity
- 13 Household and Social Class Influences
- 14 Psychographics: Values, Personality, and Lifestyles

iStockphoto.com/Ostill

High-effort Attitude Formation and Change

Cognitive Foundations of Attitudes

- Direct or imagined experience
- Reasoning by analogy or category
- Values-driven attitudes
- Social identity-based attitude generation
- Analytical processes

Influenced by:
- Source factors
- Message factors

Affective Foundations of Attitudes

- Emotional processing
- Attitude toward the ad

Influenced by:
- Source factors
- Message factors

Low-effort attitude formation and change

Attitudes and Intentions

5-2a DIRECT OR IMAGINED EXPERIENCE

Elaborating on actual experience with a product or service (or even imagining what that experience could be like) can help consumers form positive or negative attitudes. You are likely to form an attitude after test-driving a new car or watching a movie preview, for instance, or even simply by imagining what it would be like to drive that car or watch that movie. JC Penney's "Pennies from Heaven" fundraising campaign to benefit after-school programs asks consumers to "imagine what a penny can do" and reminds them that a lot of small change can make a big difference.[11] Also, you will have a more favorable attitude toward a product like a new car if you use imagery to elaborate on the positive aspects of buying and using it.[12]

On the other hand, if you're looking at a brochure or an ad featuring product photos taken from different perspectives, your attitude will be different depending on your goal. If you're trying to use the photos to construct a mental story about the product experience, the additional processing difficulty will cause you to have a less favorable attitude than if you were simply imagining yourself acquiring information about the experience.[13]

5-2b REASONING BY ANALOGY OR CATEGORY

Consumers also form attitudes by considering how similar a product is to other products or to a particular product category. For instance, if you have never sipped a chilled bottle of Starbucks Frappuccino, but you think it might be similar to the hot Starbucks coffees that you like, your reasoning would lead you to form a positive attitude toward the Frappuccino. As another example, if a tiny key ring-mounted flash drive is advertised as having the portability and convenience of a Swiss Army knife, you might form a positive attitude toward it because the analogy involves a product you like (the knife).[14]

5-2c VALUES-DRIVEN ATTITUDES

Another way that attitudes are generated or shaped is based on individual values.[15] Suppose that environmental protection is one of your most strongly held values. When you think about buying new sneakers, you might have a more positive attitude about a brand that uses recycled materials than you would about a brand that uses nonrecyclable materials. Thus, your values shape your attitude toward those brands (see Exhibit 5.3). This is also true for consumers who value authenticity and therefore form a positive attitude toward a brand or offering they perceive to be genuine, real, and true.[16] For example, now that McDonald's serves breakfast all day, it has decided to buy only eggs produced by cage-free hens. This policy will enhance its image as a fast-food marketer that genuinely cares about animal welfare and wants to make a difference.[17]

Cognitive response
Thought we have in response to a communication.

Exhibit 5.3 ▶ Value-Driven Ads
Consumers are more responsive to ads that reflect their individual values.

5-2d SOCIAL IDENTITY-BASED ATTITUDE GENERATION

The way that consumers view their own social identities can play a role in forming their attitudes toward products or brands. If you consider yourself a very serious sports fan, for instance, that may be a defining aspect of your identity. In turn, you will tend to form positive attitudes toward a brand or product (such as the brand of sports apparel endorsed by your favorite athlete) that enables you to express this social identity.[18] Thus, for example, consumers who see themselves as dedicated snowboarding fans may form positive feelings toward the Northstar Ski Resort in Lake Tahoe, where X Games star Shaun White has designed a two-story half-pipe.[19]

5-2e ANALYTICAL PROCESSES OF ATTITUDE FORMATION

Consumers sometimes use a more analytical process of attitude formation in which, after being exposed to marketing stimuli or other information, they form attitudes based on their cognitive responses. **Cognitive responses** are the thoughts a person has when he or she is exposed to a communication, which may take the form of recognitions, evaluations, associations, images, or ideas.[20] Suppose a man sees an ad for the impotency drug Cialis. In response, he might think, "I really need a product like this," "This product will never work," or "The guy in the ad was paid to praise this product." These spontaneously generated thoughts will, according to cognitive response models, influence his attitude toward Cialis.[21] Positive thoughts can have a favorable impact on attitudes, whereas negative thoughts can have a negative effect.

Cognitive Responses to Communications

According to the cognitive response model, consumers exert a lot of effort in responding to the message—enough effort to generate counterarguments, support arguments, and source derogations.

- **Counterarguments (CAs)** are thoughts that express disagreement with the message. In the example of a man seeing an ad for Cialis, such thoughts might be "This product will never work" or "This product will not cure my problem."

- **Support arguments (SAs)** are thoughts that express agreement with the message. The man may think "This sounds great" or "I really need a product like this."

- **Source derogations (SDs)** are thoughts that discount or attack the message source. Seeing the Cialis ad, the man might think "The guy is lying" or "The guy in the ad was paid to say this."

Counterargument (CA) Thought that disagrees with the message.

Support argument (SA) Thought that agrees with the message.

Source derogation (SD) Thought that discounts or attacks the source of the message.

Belief discrepancy When a message is different from what consumers believe.

Counterarguments and source derogations, in particular, result in a less favorable initial attitude or resistance to attitude change. Thoughts like "It will never work" or "The guy was paid to say this" are likely to lead to a negative attitude toward Cialis. However, consumers do not blindly accept and follow suggestions made in persuasive messages; rather, they may use their knowledge about marketers' goals or tactics to effectively cope with or resist these messages.[22] In fact, consumers do think about how marketers try to influence consumer behavior—and, in turn, these thoughts allow consumers to formulate counterarguments or support arguments in response to marketing activities.[23] Moreover, the presence of support arguments ("This sounds great") results in positive attitudes toward the offering.

Research shows that when consumers resist persuasion and become aware of their own resistance, this awareness reinforces their initial attitudes. In high-elaboration situations, consumers confronted with a persuasive message that conflicts with their own attitudes will generate counterarguments that strengthen their initial attitudes—but only when the message is from an expert source.[24]

Marketing Implications

Although marketers want consumers to be exposed to and to comprehend their marketing messages, they also want consumers' responses to be positive rather than negative. Consumers who generate counterarguments and source derogations will have weak or even negative attitudes toward an offering. To combat this reaction, marketers should test consumers' cognitive responses to communications before running the ads. By asking consumers to think aloud while they view the ad or to record their thoughts right after seeing it, marketers can classify the responses, identify problems, and strengthen the message.

Consumers tend to generate more counterarguments and fewer support arguments when the message content differs from what they already believe. Thus, a message supporting handgun control will generate a lot of counterarguments among National Rifle Association members. This **belief discrepancy** creates more counterarguments because consumers want to maintain their existing belief structures and do so by arguing against the message.[25] Consumers also generate more counterarguments and fewer support arguments when the message is weak. For example, saying that Gillette disposable razors come in many colors is not a strong and compelling reason to buy one. In such a situation, consumers may derogate the source (Gillette) or generate counterarguments ("Who cares about color?").[26]

Consumers come up with more support arguments and fewer counterarguments when they are involved with the TV program in which a commercial appears. The program distracts consumers from counterarguing, enhancing the message's persuasive impact.[27] Another way to decrease counterarguments is through the *disrupt-then-reframe technique*. Disrupting consumers' cognitive processing of the communication in an odd but subtle way ("400 pennies a day vs. $4 a day") clears the way for more effective persuasion when the message is reframed (with a statement such as "this is an incredible bargain").[28] Further, consumers react more favorably to communications when they are in a good mood: They often want to preserve this mood, so they resist counterarguing.[29] Marketers may also want to invite consumers to ask questions in marketing situations, which can positively influence attitudes. Yet in high-involvement situations, this can negatively influence attitudes because consumers must actually come up with questions to ask.[30] Finally, a growing number of brands are inviting consumers to create their ad messages. Although this can lead to skepticism and questions about the ad creator's competence, marketers can increase persuasion by providing information that allows the audience to identify with the ad creator, an especially effective tactic when the consumer is highly brand-loyal and has limited cognitive resources for message processing.[31]

Expectancy-Value Models

Expectancy-value models are analytical processes that explain how consumers form and change attitudes based on (1) the beliefs or knowledge they have about an object or action and (2) their evaluation of these particular beliefs.[32] According to this model, you might like a Volkswagen

Expectancy-value model A widely used model that explains how attitudes form and change.

Theory of reasoned action (TORA) A model that provides an explanation of how, when, and why attitudes predict behavior.

Behavior (B) What we do.

Behavioral intention (BI) What we intend to do.

Attitude toward the act (Aact) How we feel about doing something.

Subjective norm (SN) How others feel about our doing something.

because you believe it is reliable, moderately priced, and environmentally friendly—and you think it is good for a car to have these traits.

The expectancy-value model known as the **theory of reasoned action (TORA)** provides an expanded picture of how, when, and why attitudes predict consumer behavior, particularly in the United States.[33] As shown in Exhibit 5.4, the model proposes that **behavior (B)** is a function of a person's **behavioral intention (BI)**, which in turn is determined by (1) the person's **attitude toward the act (Aact)** and (2) the **subjective norms (SN)** that operate in the situation. Consistent with most expectancy-value models, A_{act} is determined by the consumer's *beliefs* (b_i) about the consequences of engaging in the behavior and the consumer's *evaluation* (e_i) of these consequences. SNs are determined by the consumer's *normative beliefs* (NB_j)—or what the consumer thinks someone else wants him or her to do—and the consumer's *motivation to comply* (MC_j) with such.

Exhibit 5.4 ▶ The Theory of Reasoned Action

TORA is an expectancy-value model that proposes how beliefs influence attitudes and norms, which in turn affect behavior.

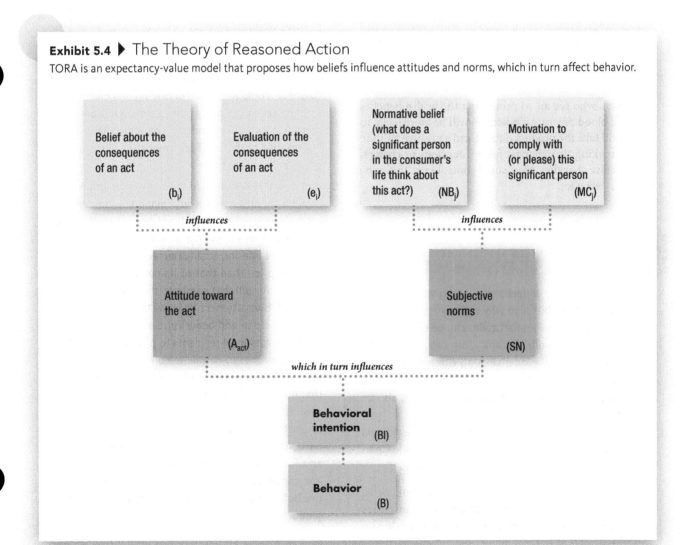

Note that the TORA model takes into account how other people in the social environment influence consumer behavior. In some situations, **normative influences** from others can play a powerful role in how people behave. Hotels use normative influences to encourage eco-friendly behavior when they place signs in guest rooms saying "the majority of guests reuse their towels," in the hope that guests will not request freshly laundered towels every day.[34] Also, the recommendations of other people can have a strong impact on preferences when consumers are making decisions in the distant future rather than the near term.[35] Further, trying to predict BIs from attitudes, as in the TORA model, is much easier than trying to predict actual behaviors because many situational factors could cause a consumer not to engage in an intended behavior.[36] For example, you may *intend* to buy a Volkswagen, but you may not actually make the purchase because you are short of money.

The TORA model assumes that attitudes are accessible since they can only guide behavior if consumers can retrieve them. Attitude confidence and less ambivalence will also increase the relationship between attitudes and behavior.[37] In addition, an extension of TORA, the **theory of planned behavior**, seeks to predict behaviors over which consumers have incomplete control by examining their perceived behavioral control.[38] For instance, older consumers who see an ad promoting the health benefits of taking blood pressure medication will be more likely to obtain and take the product if they form a positive attitude toward making this change, form intentions to change, and perceive that they have some control over this consumption behavior.

Normative influence How other people influence our behavior through social pressure.

Theory of planned behavior An extension of the TORA model that predicts behaviors over which consumers perceive they have control.

Marketing Implications

Marketers need to understand not only what attitudes consumers have but also why consumers have these attitudes and how these attitudes can be changed. The TORA model is useful for analyzing the reasons why consumers may like or dislike an offering, whether they intend to engage in or resist a behavior, and who else might be influential and therefore should also be targeted.

Such models also provide useful guidance on how marketers can change attitudes, intentions, and (marketers hope) behavior through these major strategies:

1. *Change beliefs.* One possible strategy would be to change the strength of the beliefs that consumers associate with the consequences of acquiring an offering. Marketers could try to (1) strengthen beliefs that the offering has positive, important consequences or (2) lessen the belief that it has negative consequences. Although marketers commonly use this strategy when consumers are more likely to consider the message, inducing such change is not easy when consumers have strong prior beliefs. When South Korea's Hyundai first entered global markets such as the United States and South Africa, its cars were perceived as low-price, low-quality products. Hyundai sought to change those beliefs by redesigning its products and consistently advertising the good-quality, high-tech features, and updated styling of its Genesis and Elantra models. Now the automaker's most popular cars are rated high in quality by authorities such as J.D. Power and *Consumer Reports*.[39]

2. *Change evaluations.* Another way to change attitudes is to change consumers' evaluations of the consequences. Consumers' attitudes become more positive when their beliefs are more positive or less negative. For instance, makers of biodiesel-blended heating oil are targeting home-owners with messages that explain the environmental benefits of "bioheat" compared with traditional fuel oil.[40] Interestingly, research shows that a campaign promoting a product category winds up changing the relative importance of the attributes that consumers use to evaluate brands in that category.[41]

3. *Add a new belief.* A third strategy is to add a new belief altogether that would make the consumer's attitude more positive. This strategy is particularly effective when a brand has existing features that are considered inferior, quality perceived to be lower, or a higher price than that of its competitors.[42] After the 2010 oil spill that damaged the Gulf Coast, Florida wanted vacationers to know that most beaches remained clean and beautiful. So the tourism commission asked local residents to post photos of their favorite beaches to floridalive.com, a special site with web-cam feeds as well as photos to reinforce the idea that many beaches were undamaged. The campaign evolved into an ongoing invitation for vacationers to post their Florida photos and attract others—particularly Millennials and families—who love sun and fun.[43] Note that adding novel attributes to a low-complexity product is likely to encourage positive beliefs and a more positive attitude toward that product.[44]

4. *Encourage attitude formation based on imagined experience.* Marketers can communicate information through ads featuring vivid language, detailed pictures, instructions, or virtual reality demonstrations to encourage consumers to imagine the experience. Doing this may produce positive brand attitudes as long as consumers are good at imagining things and as long as they focus on positive aspects rather than potentially negative aspects.[45] For example, Macy's and Neiman Marcus are testing "smart mirror" dressing rooms in some stores. When consumers stand in front of these high-tech mirrors, they can see how different garments will look on them, and wave a hand to change outfits virtually without ever changing in person.[46]

5. *Target normative beliefs.* Another strategy is to develop communications that specifically target strong normative beliefs as a way of influencing behavior. For example, Outagamie County, Wisconsin, is fighting heavy drinking among teens with billboards citing surveys showing that "70 percent of area high school students say it is not okay to binge drink."[47] On the other hand, condom ads have been unsuccessful in increasing sales because they have not stressed normative beliefs (what others will think of you if you do not use them).[48] The importance of normative beliefs does, however, vary across cultures. In countries that stress group values over those of the individual (such as Japan, among other Asian nations), appeals to normative beliefs take on greater significance.[49]

5-3 How Cognitively Based Attitudes are Influenced

As Exhibit 5.2 indicates, both the communication source and the message influence how favorable a consumer's attitude will be. Here we explore how marketing communications can affect consumers' cognitively based attitudes when the processing effort is extensive.

5-3a COMMUNICATION SOURCE

Among consumers who process information extensively, those with attitudes based on cognitions are likely to be influenced by believable information. This means that marketing messages must be credible to generate support arguments, restrict counterarguments and source derogations, and increase belief strength. Several factors, including source credibility and company reputation, enhance the credibility of a message.

Source Credibility

In many marketing messages, information is presented by a spokesperson, usually a celebrity, an actor, a company representative, or a real consumer. In a sales situation, the salesperson is a spokesperson for the company and the offering. Both the **credibility** of these sources and the credibility of the company influence consumers' attitudes.[50] According to research, consumers tend to evaluate product information more thoughtfully when source credibility is low than when source credibility is high.[51]

> **Credibility** Extent to which the source is trustworthy, expert, or has status.

Sources are credible when they have one or more of three characteristics: trustworthiness, expertise, and status. First, someone perceived as trustworthy is more likely to be believed than someone who is not. Stickley Furniture, for instance, has featured customer testimonials in commercials for its wooden and upholstered furniture products.[52] Consumers tend to see other consumers' opinions as less biased than official sources, which is why many check product reviews posted on bizrate.com, yelp.com, Trip Advisor, and other review sites. Research shows that high-quality online reviews (and a high number of reviews) have a positive effect on the purchasing intentions of online shoppers.[53]

Word of mouth is an important and credible source, yet research shows that the type of language used by someone describing a consumption experience can have an effect on that person's intentions to repeat the experience, recommend the experience, and talk about it in the future. Therefore, marketers should consider messages that help word-of-mouth sources understand and explain their experiences in specific ways.[54]

Second, we are more likely to accept a message from someone perceived as knowledgeable or as *an expert* about the topic than from someone who has no experience with it. A salesperson who demonstrates extensive product knowledge will be more credible than an uninformed one. Consumers do, in fact, make buying decisions based on recommendations from expert sources such as *Consumer Reports*—and consumers will quickly change their buying patterns when the magazine retracts its findings.[55] Third, someone with a high position or social status can also be perceived as credible; this is why many firms feature their CEOs or founders in their ads or on their websites. Tom Dickinson is a credible source not only because he founded Blendtec, which makes blenders for home and restaurant use, but also because of his "Will It Blend?" viral videos showing how his products can blend almost anything, from Apple Watches and Avengers weapons to coconuts.[56]

Research shows that credible sources have considerable impact on the acceptance of the message when consumers' prior attitudes are negative, when the message deviates greatly from their prior beliefs, when the message is complex or difficult to understand, and when there is a good "match" between product and endorser.[57] Moreover, source credibility can influence consumer attitudes by influencing the confidence consumers have in their thoughts about the message.[58]

Yet, credible sources will have less impact when consumers hold their existing attitude with confidence (so that even a credible source will not convince them otherwise) and when they have a high degree of ability to generate their own conclusions from the message (they have a lot of product-relevant knowledge, particularly if it is based on direct experience).[59] Also, consumers are less likely to believe that a source is credible when the source (e.g., a celebrity) endorses multiple products.[60] Finally, trust is an important element of credibility for spokescharacters such as the GEICO Gecko. Specifically, trust in a spokescharacter results in favorable brand attitudes if the consumer has had little experience with that brand.[61]

Marketing Implications

David Beckham's soccer achievements make him a credible, trusted endorser for Adidas sports shoes and apparel, even though he's retired from the sport.[62] Expert sources can also be popular, another factor that can contribute to an effective ad. Interestingly, one survey indicated that women endorsers are often seen as more popular and credible than male endorsers.[63] However, the company or product risks losing some credibility if a celebrity endorser gets into trouble or quits. For instance, AT&T, Gatorade, and a few other marketers cancelled their endorsement contracts with golfer Tiger Woods after his personal problems made headlines worldwide.[64]

Ordinary people may also be perceived as credible endorsers. Southwest Airlines and other firms feature employees in their ad campaigns and online marketing because the employees add realism and help make an emotional connection with consumers.[65] Also note that a low-credibility source can be effective in some circumstances. In particular, if a low-credibility source argues against his or her own self-interest, positive attitude change can result.[66] Political ads, for example, may feature a member of the opposing party who endorses a rival candidate. In addition, the impact of a low-credibility source can actually increase over time (assuming the message is powerful). This **sleeper effect** occurs because the consumer's memory of the source can decay more rapidly than his or her memory of the message.[67] Thus, consumers may remember the message but not the source.

> **Sleeper effect**
> Consumers forget the source of a message more quickly than they forget the message.

Company Reputation

When marketing communications do not feature an actual person, consumers judge credibility by the reputation of the company delivering the message.[68] People are more likely to believe—and change their attitudes based on—messages from companies with a reputation for producing quality products, dealing fairly with consumers, or being trustworthy. Online, a company can enhance its reputation and engender positive reactions by sponsoring content on relevant websites; banner ads highly targeted to a site's audience can also elicit positive attitudes toward

Marketing Implications

Knowing that reputation influences consumer perceptions and credibility, companies generally work hard to develop a positive image through corporate advertising. Ford, Toyota, Honda, and other companies have become known for their environmental records and earth-friendly products, which is why they top the list of the world's greenest brands (see Exhibit 5.5).[71] Many firms use advertising, social media, and public relations to communicate their involvement in charitable activities and environmental initiatives. The clothing retailer H&M, based in Sweden, showcases its support of UNICEF in ads, a Facebook page, and Flickr photo-sharing.[72]

These were the world's most environmentally friendly brands in 2014, as ranked by INTERBRAND:
1. Ford (car company based in the United States)
2. Toyota (car company based in Japan)
3. Honda (car company based in Japan)
4. Nissan (car company based in Japan)
5. Panasonic (electronics manufacturer based in Japan)
6. Nokia (telecommunications infrastructure company based in Finland)
7. Sony (electronics manufacturer based in Japan)
8. Adidas (athletic shoe and clothing company based in Germany)
9. Danone (food company based in France)
10. Dell (computer company based in the United States)

Source: Adapted from INTERBRAND, http://interbrand.com/assets/uploads/Interbrand-Best-Global-Green-Brands-2014-Marketing-Toolkit.pdf

Exhibit 5.5 ▶ Top 10 Global Green Brands
A company's reputation for eco-friendly operations can influence perceptions of its credibility and consumer attitudes toward its brands.

the company.[69] More specifically, a brand's perceived trustworthiness exerts more influence on consumers' consideration and behavior than its expertise.[70]

5-3b THE MESSAGE

Just as consumers evaluate whether or not the source is credible when their processing effort is high, they also evaluate whether or not the message is credible. Four factors affect the credibility of a message: the quality of its argument, whether it is a one or two-sided message, and whether it is a comparative message.

Argument Quality

One of the most critical factors affecting whether a message is credible concerns whether it uses strong arguments.[73] **Strong arguments** present the best features or central merits of an offering in a convincing manner. Messages can also present supporting research or endorsements, such as the Good Housekeeping Seal, which is awarded only to products that pass the company's lab testing (see Exhibit 5.6).[74] Strong arguments are likely to be more persuasive if consumers are exposed to such

> **Strong argument**
> A presentation that features the best or central merits of an offering in a convincing manner.
>
> **One-sided message**
> A marketing message that presents only positive information.
>
> **Two-sided message** A marketing message that presents both positive and negative information.
>
> **Comparative message** A message that makes direct comparisons with competitors.

messages after thinking about what they could have done differently to avoid a purchasing experience that led to an undesirable outcome.[75]

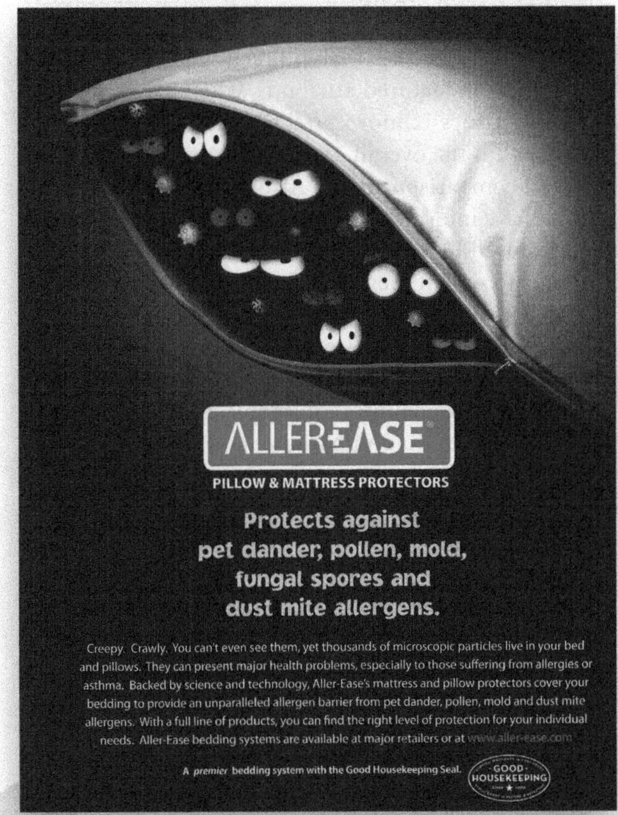

In addition, strong arguments have a greater effect on behavioral intentions when consumers focus on the process of using the product rather than on the outcome of using it, especially for low-to moderate-involvement products.[76] Combining a strong argument with an implicit conclusion in an ad message engenders more favorable brand attitudes and buying intentions among consumers with a high need for cognition.[77] Moreover, consumers are more persuaded by a message containing a strong argument when they devote sufficient cognitive resources to processing the information.[78]

Infomercials—commercial messages that can last 30 to 60 minutes—allow companies enough time to fully explain complicated, technologically advanced, or innovative goods and services. In recent years, some marketers have turned to shorter infomercials—often only two minutes long—to sell products that require more demonstration or explanation than can be squeezed into a 30 or 60-second TV commercial. Infomercials generally include the address of a website or Facebook page where consumers can see more details and place orders.[79]

One- Versus Two-Sided Messages

Most marketing messages present only positive information. These are called **one-sided messages**. In some instances, however, a **two-sided message**, containing both positive and negative information about an offering, can be effective. For example, Buckley's Cough Mixture is marketed using blunt two-sided ad messages such as "It tastes awful. And it works" and "Disgustingly effective."[80] Like strong arguments, two-sided messages may affect consumers' attitudes by making the message more credible (i.e., they increase belief strength) and reducing counterarguments. When consumers see negative information in an ad, they tend to infer that the company is honest, a belief that adds to source credibility.[81] By providing reasons for consumers to be interested in the offering despite these problems, the ad encourages consumers to add a new belief. Note that the persuasive effect of two-sided messages depends, in part, on how much negative information is presented, on the interplay of negative and positive attributes, and—in the case of product reviews—on the consistency between the reviewer's arguments and the reviewer's helpfulness ratings.[82]

Comparative Messages

Comparative messages show how much better the offering is than a competitor's. Two types of comparative messages have been identified.[83] The most common type is the *indirect comparative message*, in which the offering

ALLEREASE
PILLOW & MATTRESS PROTECTORS

Protects against pet dander, pollen, mold, fungal spores and dust mite allergens.

Creepy. Crawly. You can't even see them, yet thousands of microscopic particles live in your bed and pillows. They can present major health problems, especially to those suffering from allergies or asthma. Backed by science and technology, Aller-Ease's mattress and pillow protectors cover your bedding to provide an unparalleled allergen barrier from pet dander, pollen, mold and dust mite allergens. With a full line of products, you can find the right level of protection for your individual needs. Aller-Ease bedding systems are available at major retailers or at www.aller-ease.com

A *premier* bedding system with the Good Housekeeping Seal.   GOOD HOUSEKEEPING

Courtesy of ALLER-EASE

Exhibit 5.6 ▶ Argument Quality
An example of a strong argument message is one based on research and backed by the Good Housekeeping Seal of approval.

is compared with those of unnamed competitors (such as "other leading brands" or "Brand X"). This strategy can improve consumers' perceptions of a moderate-share brand relative to other moderate-share brands (but not to the market leader).[84] Marketers must remember, however, that the effectiveness of comparative advertising differs from culture to culture.[85] In Korea, a culture that values harmony, comparative advertising seems overly confrontational and is rarely used, whereas this technique is frequently used in the United States. In general, most consumers don't like comparative advertising when other brands in the category don't use it, and its use can have a negative effect on ad persuasion.[86]

With *direct comparative advertising*, advertisers explicitly name and attack a competitor or set of competitors on the basis of an attribute or benefit (see Exhibit 5.7). This approach is usually used when the offering has a feature that is purportedly better than that of a competitor's. Salespeople frequently use this technique to convince consumers of the advantages of their offering over the competition. Comparative advertising is also used in political campaigns, where it generates more counterarguments and fewer source derogations than negative political advertising does. This result may be due to the different styles of information processing that the two types of

messages encourage.[87] However, consumers exposed to negative political messages find them less useful for decision-making and have more negative attitudes toward political campaigns than do consumers exposed to positive political advertising.[88]

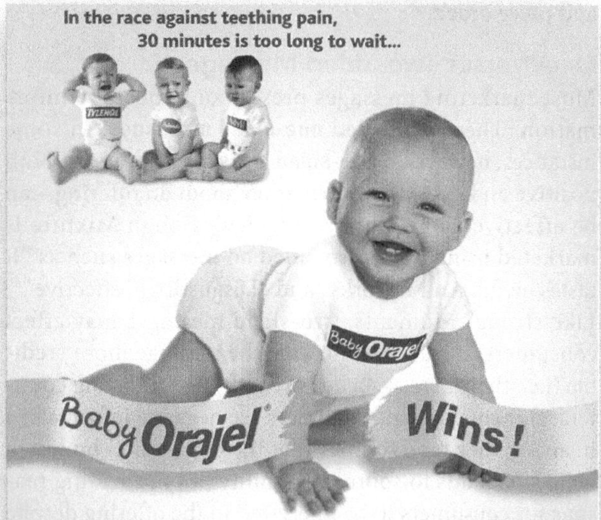

In general, direct comparative messages are effective in generating attention and brand awareness and in positively increasing message processing, attitudes, intentions, and behavior.[89] They do not, however, have high credibility, as noted earlier. These messages are particularly effective for new brands or low-market-share brands attempting to take sales away from more popular brands.[90] Advertising for the new or low-share brand can enhance consumers' attitudes by highlighting how the brand is different from or better than other brands, giving consumers a credible reason for purchasing it. In fact, comparative advertising that stresses differentiation can spur consumers to note the dissimilarities of competing brands.[91] Messages comparing two brands perceived as dissimilar will elicit more elaboration, especially among consumers with a low need for cognition, precisely because the brands are different.[92]

Comparative messages are especially effective when they contain other elements that make them believable—such as a credible source or objective and verifiable claims (a strong argument)[93]— and when the featured attribute or benefit is important within the product category.[94] Still, a message that indirectly indicates a brand's superiority on featured attributes when compared with all competitors is more effective at positioning that brand within the overall market than a noncomparative or direct comparison ad is.[95] Also, consumers who originally receive information in a noncomparative ad and are then exposed to a comparative ad will revise their evaluations more than they will when subsequently exposed to another noncomparative ad.[96] Comparative ads that refer to competitors in a negative way are perceived as less believable and more biased; they cause consumers to develop more counterarguments and fewer support arguments than do comparative ads without negative competitive references.[97]

Marketers should also consider consumers' goals when preparing comparative ads. Promotion-focused consumers, whose goal is to maximize their gains and positive outcomes, will be more responsive to claims that Brand X is superior to Brand Y; prevention-focused consumers, who want to minimize their loss and risk, will be more skeptical of superiority claims and more responsive to claims that Brand X is similar or equivalent to Brand Y.[98] Note that positively framed comparative messages (Brand X performs better than Brand Y) are more effective for promotion-focused consumers (refer to Chapter 2), whereas negatively framed messages (Brand Y has more problems than Brand X) are more effective for prevention-focused consumers.[99] Positively framed comparative messages

In the race against teething pain,
30 minutes is too long to wait...

Baby Orajel Wins!

Baby Orajel works on contact to relieve teething pain instantly, not up to 30 minutes like Children's Tylenol, Children's Advil or Hyland's, which all have to work their way through a baby's system to start to provide relief.

Baby Orajel is fast, safe & effective. No wonder it's the #1 pediatrician recommended brand. In fact, it's trusted by more moms & pediatricians than all other teething brands combined.

Nothing beats Baby Orajel

Courtesy Church & Dwight Co., Inc.

Exhibit 5.7 ▶ Comparative Messages
Ads may compare their products with competitors in direct comparative messaging.

encourage more cognitive processing and prompt consumers to consider other brand information—sparking their buying intentions if the additional information supports the positive argument.[100]

 ## Marketing Implications

If messages are weak, consumers are unlikely to think that they offer credible reasons for buying. Saying that a person should buy a particular brand of mattress because it comes in decorator fabrics is not very convincing. Nevertheless, messages do not always have to focus on substantive features of a product or service. Less important features can actually play a key role in influencing consumers' attitudes when brands are similar and many competitors emphasize the same important attributes.[101] Also, a message should match the amount of effort consumers want to use to process it. A message that is too simple or too complicated is unlikely to be persuasive.[102]

Two-sided messages seem to be particularly effective (1) when consumers are initially opposed to the offering (they already have negative beliefs) or (2) when they will be exposed to strong countermessages from competitors.[103] However, consumers who are exposed to many competing ads during a short period are likely to have difficulty recalling a particular brand's message, which in turn will hurt sales.[104] Two-sided messages are also well received by more intelligent consumers, who prefer neutral, unbiased messages. However, the use of two-sided advertising is not always in the marketer's best interest. In general, the positive effects of two-sided messages on brand attitudes occur only if the negative message is about an attribute that is not extremely important.

When MAO is high, consumers exert more effort in processing direct comparative messages and are less likely to confuse the advertised brand with its competition.[105] Further, when consumers use analytical processing, a comparative ad will be more persuasive than a noncomparative ad; when consumers use imagery processing, a noncomparative ad will be more persuasive.[106] For instance, the SUBWAY sandwich chain has used comparative messages urging consumers to buy their lower-fat, lower-calorie sandwiches, which help consumers make a choice between fast-food categories based on attributes such as nutrition.[107] Bear in mind, however, that comparative messages are not useful in changing a consumer's negative first impression of a brand or company.[108]

All information contained in a comparative message must be factual and verifiable; otherwise, competitors may consider taking legal action. Although comparative ads are widely used in the United States and Latin America, they are illegal in some countries and closely regulated in the European Union.[109] Some consumers dislike comparative advertising. Japanese consumers, for example, respond better to a softer sell than they do to comparative ads.[110] Aggressive use of direct comparative ads can draw complaints from consumers as well as from competitors, and stimulate regulatory scrutiny.[111] Also, messages that compare a company's new, improved product to the same company's original product will be effective only when the improved functions are seen as atypical for that product. Otherwise, consumers are likely to discount the novelty of the new functionality.[112]

5-4 The Affective (Emotional) Foundations of Attitudes

Most of the early consumer research on attitudes when MAO and processing effort are high has focused on the cognitive models of attitude formation. Now, however, researchers are recognizing that consumers might exert a lot of mental energy in processing a message on an emotional basis. Emotional reactions, independent of cognitive structure, may serve as a powerful way of creating attitudes that are favorable, enduring, and resistant to change.[113] This section examines when and how attitudes can be changed through consumers' feelings when MAO and processing effort are high.

When affective involvement with an object or decision is high, consumers can experience fairly strong emotional reactions to or engagement with a stimulus. *Engagement* refers to the extent to which consumers are emotionally connected to a product or ad.[114] A high level of engagement means strong feelings that can, in turn, influence attitudes. In this case, the consumer's *feelings* act as a source of information, and consumers will rely on these feelings to evaluate the stimulus.[115]

Feelings are more likely to influence attitude change when they fit with or are viewed as relevant to the offering.[116] For example, someone who is in love might have a more positive attitude toward an expensive perfume than someone who is not experiencing this emotion would. Consumers tend to like a brand or product when there is a close match between their *emotional receptivity* (predisposition for a certain level of emotion) and the emotional intensity expressed in an ad or by a salesperson.[117] Feelings can also be a factor when consumers see others experiencing strong emotion while using an offering or when situational factors hamper the consumer's effort to develop a cognitive attitude.[118] Thus, consumers under severe time pressure could simply recall a previous emotional experience rather than develop a cognitive attitude.

In marketing situations, certain factors can activate experiences or episodes from memory that may be associated with strong emotions.[119] For example, you might experience positive emotions such as joy and excitement if you suddenly see an ad for the car you just bought. If you are a dog lover, you might experience affective involvement toward a message featuring a cute dog (see Exhibit 5.8). It is no wonder that dogs have, in fact, been included in print advertising for decades.[120]

Attitudes can also be formed through an emotional route to persuasion called *regulatory fit*. Recall that Chapter 2 identified two types of goals consumers might have—promotion and prevention-focused. Consumers with promotion-focused goals are motivated to act in ways to achieve positive outcomes, focusing on hopes, wants, and accomplishments. In contrast, consumers with prevention-focused goals are motivated to avoid negative outcomes, focusing on responsibilities, safety, and guarding against risks.

Affective response
When consumers generate feelings and images in response to a message.

Emotional appeal
A message designed to elicit an emotional response.

Research suggests that a consumer's attitude toward a product depends on the fit between the consumer's goal and the strategies available to achieve that goal. For example, a promotion-focused consumer who sees an ad showing how great it feels to drive a certain car (promotion goal) will be more persuaded than if the ad emphasized safety features. The ad emphasizing safety would, in fact, be more persuasive for consumers with prevention-focused goals. Why? People just feel right when there is a fit between their regulatory goals and the strategies available to help them achieve their goals. This feeling makes them more certain about their attitude evaluation and more likely to regard their attitude or choice as valuable.[121]

When consumers are emotionally involved in a message, they tend to process it on a general level rather than analytically.[122] This process involves the generation of images or feelings, called **affective responses** (or ARs),[123] rather than cognitive responses. In fact, affective responses are generally more influential than cognitive responses in shaping consumers' attitudes toward trying a product.[124] Affective responses are particularly important when the ad builds toward a "peak emotional experience."[125] Consumers can either recall an emotional experience from memory or vicariously place themselves in the situation and experience the emotions associated with it.[126] These feelings will then influence their attitudes, especially if the consumers' emotional receptivity matches the ad's emotional intensity.[127] Consumers focused on goals involving their hopes and aspirations tend to rely on their affective responses to an ad, whereas consumers focused on their responsibilities and obligations tend to rely more on message content.[128]

Cross-cultural differences can also influence the effectiveness of **emotional appeals**. One study found that messages evoking ego-focused responses (such as pride or happiness) led to more favorable attitudes in group-oriented cultures, whereas empathetic messages led to more positive attitudes in individualistic cultures.[129] The reason for this apparent reversal is that the appeal's novelty or uniqueness increases the motivation to process and consider the message.

Negative emotions sometimes have a positive effect on attitude change. In one study, the exposure to a public service announcement about child abuse initially created negative emotions (sadness, anger, fear) but then led to a feeling of empathy, and this response led to a decision to help.[130] In addition, consumers can actively try to avoid making decisions associated with strong negative emotions by making choices to minimize these emotions.[131]

Note that cognition can still influence whether experienced feelings will affect consumer attitudes. For feelings to have a direct impact on their attitudes, consumers must cognitively link them to the offering.[132] To illustrate, if you saw a bank ad showing a tender scene of a

Exhibit 5.8 ▶ Man's Best Friend in Advertising
Pet owners feel strong emotions toward dogs, so an ad featuring a cute dog can be used to stimulate affective involvement.

Courtesy of Mars, Incorporated. CESAR® Canine Cuisine

father holding his baby, you might experience an immediate emotional response (warmth and joy). However, this feeling will affect your attitude toward the bank only if you consciously make a connection between the feeling and the bank ("This bank makes me feel good" or "I like this bank because it cares about people"). Also, an advertising message that relies on emotional appeal will be more effective in helping heavy users of the product access the brand name than in helping light users access the brand name.[133]

Marketing Implications

Marketers can try to influence emotions as a way of affecting consumer attitudes. In particular, marketers can try to ensure that the emotions experienced in a particular situation will be positive. Car salespeople, for example, may try to do everything possible to please customers so they will develop positive attitudes toward the dealer and the car. The importance of creating positive emotions also explains why airlines, financial institutions, and other service providers place a high value on being friendly. For example, L.L. Bean has earned a reputation for customer-oriented service, thanks to its flexible merchandise return policy and its responsive, courteous call-center representatives.[134]

Another way to influence consumers' attitudes and emotions is by focusing attention on the emotional experience of product usage.[135] To illustrate, Subaru ads are known for their emotional overtones. In one of its classic commercials, an anxious father stands next to his Subaru while his five-year-old daughter sits in the driver's seat. The father nervously gives her last-minute safety instructions about driving by herself for the first time. Finally, as he hands over the keys, the audience sees that the driver is now a teenager ready for a solo drive. By portraying an emotional situation that many parents can identify with, Subaru called attention to its vehicles' safety features and specific benefits that buyers will appreciate.[136]

Marketing communications can potentially trigger strong emotions in consumers, although the ability to trigger these emotions is typically quite limited—ads are better at creating low-level moods than they are at creating intense emotions. Think about how commercials that show people enjoying sips of ice-cold Coca-Cola seek to put viewers in a good mood. Nevertheless, in situations in which affective involvement in the product or

Attractiveness A source characteristic that evokes favorable attitudes if a source is physically attractive, likable, familiar, or similar to ourselves.

Match-up hypothesis Idea that the source must be appropriate for the product/service.

service is often high, marketers may be able to generate the images and feelings necessary to change attitudes. This outcome most often occurs in categories in which a strong pleasure-seeking or symbolic motivation is present—when feelings or symbolic meanings are critical. To illustrate, Quaker Oats has run commercials emphasizing the warm feelings shared by families as they eat breakfast together, with the parents thinking about how quickly their young children will grow up.[137] Note that a good mood will not enhance the consumer's evaluation of a brand extension introduced by a core brand seen as undesirable by that consumer.[138]

5-5 How Affectively Based Attitudes Are Influenced

When MAO and effort are high and attitudes are affectively (emotionally) based, several strategies shown in Exhibit 5.1 can be employed to change attitudes. As with cognitively based attitudes, marketers can use characteristics of the source and the message to change consumers' attitudes by affecting their emotions.

5-5a THE SOURCE

Perceived **attractiveness** is an important source characteristic affecting high-effort, emotionally based attitudes. Research on source attractiveness suggests that when consumers' MAO and effort are high, attractive sources tend to evoke favorable attitudes if the sources are appropriate for the offering category (e.g., a luxury automobile, fashion, cosmetics, and beauty treatments).[139] This effect has been called the **match-up hypothesis** (the source should match the offering). The relevant attractive source probably enhances attitudes, either by making the ad informative and likable or by affecting consumers' beliefs that the product must be good. A source that is attractive but not relevant can distract the consumer from the message's ideas.[140]

Research suggests that the match-up hypothesis may be even more powerful for expert sources than for attractive sources, which may explain why tennis star Li Na's endorsement of Nike tennis clothing was particularly effective in China. After the champ retired in 2014, Nike extended the association by naming one of its Shanghai headquarters buildings after her.[141]

The relationship between attractiveness and attitude change applies to selling encounters as well. Consumers perceive physically attractive salespeople as having more favorable selling skills and are more likely to yield to their requests.[142] Customers also tend to be attracted to and to buy from salespeople whom they perceive as similar to themselves.[143]

Exhibit 5.9 ▶ The Importance of Attractiveness
Ads often use attractive models to stimulate positive feelings toward the ad and the product.

Marketing Implications

Although attractiveness is most often thought of in terms of physical features, sources can also be attractive if they are perceived as similar, likable, or familiar (in terms of physical appearance or opinions).[144] One example is Nespresso's long-time deal with actor George Clooney to appear in ads and on in-store posters promoting coffee machines in Europe, Japan, and Russia (see Exhibit 5.9). Clooney was chosen not just because of his likability but also because "he's a worldwide citizen ... and a humanist," says Nespresso's CEO.[145]

> **Emotional contagion** A message designed to induce consumers to vicariously experience a depicted emotion.

5-5b THE MESSAGE

Just as marketers can use characteristics of the source to understand and influence affective processing, they can also use characteristics of the message to influence consumers. In particular, emotional appeals and fear appeals are two important message characteristics.

Emotional Appeals and Emotional Contagion

Marketers sometimes attempt to influence consumers' attitudes by using appeals that elicit emotions such as love, desire, joy, hope, excitement, daring, fear, anger, shame, or rejection. Disgust can be a powerful emotion that, even when stimulated unintentionally through humor or another aspect of a message, can engender negative attitudes and purchase intentions.[146] Moreover, because consumers try to minimize emotions like shame and guilt, an appeal based on these emotions may not be effective.[147] Emotional appeals based on conflicting emotions (such as happiness and sadness) can result in less favorable attitudes among consumers who are less accepting of such contradictions.[148]

In general, positive emotions are intended to attract consumers to the offering, whereas the negatives are intended to create anxiety about what might happen if consumers do not use the offering. Messages or salespeople can also use flattery to elicit positive attitudes.[149] And when consumers identify with and feel a strong emotional connection with a brand or company, they pay more attention to it and are more loyal, as well.[150] Not surprisingly, sales personnel who understand how to interpret and appropriately influence a consumer's emotional state will be more effective in influencing attitudes and buying decisions, as well as reinforcing customer loyalty.[151]

However, emotional appeals may limit the amount of product-related information consumers can process.[152] This can occur because consumers may be thinking more about feeling good than about the product's features, a situation that inhibits cognition about the product and its benefits. Thus, emotional appeals are more likely to be effective when the emotional arousal relates to product consumption or usage, an occurrence that is common when hedonic or symbolic motivations are important. Research suggests that emotional appeals more effectively influence consumer behavior when the type of product being advertised has been on the market for some time. In contrast, ads featuring expert sources and strong arguments are more effective for products in younger markets.[153]

Messages that apply the principle of **emotional contagion** depict people expressing an emotion, with the goal of inducing consumers to vicariously experience that emotion (see Exhibit 5.10). As an example, a U.K. McDonald's commercial shows smiling children enjoying Happy Meals while *Glad All Over*, an upbeat 1960s song, plays in the background. Consumers who "catch" that happy feeling from the children's smiles are likely to transfer it to McDonald's and Happy Meals. McDonald's also used smiling children in Happy Meals commercials to encourage healthier eating during the Free Fruit Fridays campaign.[154] When consumers are drawn into a message through warm, positive feelings, they become more interested and their attitudes become more positive toward the ad, especially if the message is affectively intense.[155]

Exhibit 5.10 ▶ Emotional Contagion

Marketers sometimes attempt to influence consumers' attitudes by using appeals that elicit emotions such as love, desire, joy, hope, and excitement. When consumers feel these emotions in response to an ad, emotional contagion has occurred.

Still, consumers who see sad-faced victims in a charity's ads will also feel sad and will be more inclined to donate to the cause.[156]

Finally, when consumers become immersed in a message's emotionally charged story, they focus less on the costs and more on the positive outcomes of consumption. In the context of an ad featuring lottery winners, for example, consumers who feel lucky would be drawn into the narrative and focus on the good fortune of winning rather than on the low probability of actually hitting the jackpot.[157]

 Marketing Implications

Typically, marketers attempt to arouse emotions by using techniques such as music, emotional scenes or facial expressions, visuals, sex, and attractive sources. To illustrate, an Ad Council campaign focused on the emotions surrounding the adoption of a dog or cat from a local pet shelter, with visuals and voiceovers featuring happy pet owners and contented pets. The multimedia and online campaign, with the tag line "A person is the best thing to happen to a shelter pet. Be that person—Adopt," has significantly increased adoptions since its launch in 2009.[158] However, arousing emotions can be a challenge unless the message has personal relevance for the consumer.

Fear Appeals

> **Fear appeal** A message that stresses negative consequences.

Fear appeals attempt to elicit fear or anxiety by stressing the negative consequences of either engaging or not engaging in a particular behavior. By arousing this fear, marketers hope consumers will be motivated to think about the message and behave in the desired manner.[159] But is fear an effective appeal? Early studies found that fear appeals were ineffective because consumers' perceptual defense helped them block out and ignore the message (due to its threatening nature).[160] This research provides one explanation of why the surgeon general's warning on cigarette packages and ads has been largely ineffective. However, more recent research indicates that fear appeals can work under certain conditions.[161] For example, fear appeals that evoke guilt, regret, or challenge can motivate behavior because they play to feelings of self-accountability that are experienced when the consumer does or does not do something, such as applying sun screen to avoid cancer.[162]

> **Terror management theory (TMT)** A theory which deals with how we cope with the threat of death by defending our world view of values and beliefs.

Terror management theory (TMT) provides additional insight into the use of fear appeals. According to this theory, we develop a worldview of values and beliefs to cope with the terror of knowing that we will die someday, despite our innate impulse toward self-preservation. To avoid being paralyzed by anxiety, we may respond to messages that highlight the threat of death by more strongly defending our worldview. A high-fear appeal using a threat of fatal consequences may be ineffective, therefore, because consumers elaborate so much on the threat that they cannot process the message's suggested change in behavior. So the nature of the fear appeal—specifically, whether it makes mortality more salient—can influence consumers' emotions, their elaboration, and their attitudes.[163]

 Marketing Implications

When can fear appeals be effective? First, the appeal must suggest an immediate action that will reduce the consumer's fear. Consider how Carbonite markets its online backup services. "We found that the only thing that sells our product is fear," says the company's CEO. "The fact that you might wake up tomorrow and your hard drive is dead and all your photos are gone." Carbonite's messages on radio, Facebook, and Twitter stress that consumers can prevent data loss by signing up to try its backup services.[164]

Second, the level of fear must be generally moderate for the appeal to be effective.[165] If the fear induced is too intense, the consumer's perceptual defense will take over and the message will not have an impact. Third, at higher levels of involvement, lower levels of fear can be generated because the consumer has a higher motivation to process the information.[166] Factors such as personality, product usage, and socioeconomic status also have an impact on the effectiveness of fear appeals.[167] Finally, the source providing the information must be credible; otherwise, the consumer can easily discount the message by generating counterarguments and source derogations.

5-6 Attitude Toward the AD

Although most attitude research has focused on consumers' attitude toward the brand, some evidence suggests that the overall **attitude toward the ad (A$_{ad}$)** in which the brand is advertised will influence consumers' brand attitudes and behavior.[168] In other words, if we see an advertisement and like it, our liking for the ad may rub off on the brand and thereby make our brand attitude more positive. Most A$_{ad}$ research has been done in the context of low-effort processing. However, researchers are finding that A$_{ad}$ can also have an impact when consumers devote considerable effort to processing the message.

Three major factors have been found to lead to a positive A$_{ad}$ in the context of high effort.[169] First, more *informative* ads tend to be better liked and to generate positive responses.[170] These reactions to the ad will, in turn, have a positive influence on brand attitudes, a factor called the **utilitarian (or functional) dimension**. For example, consumers often like promotions on the Internet because these are seen as more informative than promotions in other media. On the other hand, consumers may have negative attitudes toward ads that are not informative. A good example is the rising negativity toward political ads that are viewed as "mudslinging" and that provide little useful information about the candidates.[171]

Second, consumers can like an ad if it creates positive feelings or emotions (the **hedonic dimension**).[172] We tend to like ads that either make us feel good or elicit positive experiences from our memory. This positive attitude can transfer to

the brand and make our beliefs about the brand (b$_i$) more positive as well.[173]

Third, consumers can like an ad because it is interesting—that is, it arouses curiosity and attracts attention. When consumers exert a lot of effort and thoughtfully elaborate on a message, it can be viewed as interesting and generate a positive A$_{ad}$.

Marketing Implications

Marketers use a variety of techniques to enhance the hedonic dimension of ad messages, especially online, and to engage consumers to generate a positive A$_{ad}$. For example, Audi has run a series of two-minute advertising episodes called "Untitled Jersey City Project." Along with online extras such as clues and character insights, these ads were created to engage consumers who like the mystery and excitement of a fast-paced dramatic storyline. Throughout the episodes, the AUDI A6 could be seen weaving in and out of traffic through Jersey City streets.[174]

5-7 When Do Attitudes Predict Behavior?

Marketers are interested not only in how attitudes are formed and can be changed but also in knowing whether, when, and why attitudes will predict behavior. The TORA model comes closest to providing this information by predicting which factors affect consumers' BIs. However, as previously noted, what we intend to do does not always predict what we actually will do. Therefore, marketers also need to consider which factors affect the attitude–behavior relationship. These are some of the factors that affect whether a consumer's attitudes will influence his or her behavior:

- *Level of involvement/elaboration.* Attitudes are more likely to predict behavior when cognitive involvement is high and consumers elaborate or think extensively about the information that gives rise to their attitudes.[175] Attitudes also tend to be strong and enduring and therefore more predictive of a consumer's behavior when affective involvement is high. Thus, attitudes toward emotionally charged issues such as owning a handgun or getting an abortion tend to be strongly held and related to behavior. What if consumers are faced with inconsistencies about a brand and learn, for example, that it rates higher against competitors on one

---

Attitude toward the ad (A$_{ad}$) Whether the consumer likes or dislikes an ad.

Utilitarian (or functional) dimension When an ad provides information.

Hedonic dimension When an ad creates positive or negative feelings.

attribute but lower on another attribute? Here, the attitude–behavior relationship is weakened if consumers do not attempt to resolve the inconsistency through elaboration.[176]

- *Knowledge and experience.* Attitudes are more likely to be strongly held and predictive of behavior when the consumer is knowledgeable about or experienced with the object of the attitude.[177] When making a computer-buying decision, for example, an expert is more likely to form an attitude that is based on more detailed and integrated information than is a novice. This attitude would then be more strongly held and more strongly related to behavior.

- *Analysis of reasons.* Research shows that asking consumers to analyze their reasons for brand preference increases the link between attitude and behavior in situations in which behavior is measured soon after attitudes are measured. Marketers should take this finding into account when planning consumer research to support a new product introduction.[178]

- *Accessibility of attitudes.* Attitudes are more strongly related to behavior when they are accessible or "top of mind."[179] Conversely, if an attitude cannot be easily remembered, it will have little effect on behavior. Direct experience (product usage) generally increases attitude accessibility for attributes that must be experienced (e.g., tasted, touched), whereas advertising can produce accessible attitudes for search attributes (e.g., price, ingredients), especially when the level of repetition is high.[180] Also, consumers asked about their purchase intentions toward a product in a particular category are more likely to choose brands toward which they have positive and accessible attitudes; research itself can make attitudes more accessible for brands in that category, thereby changing behavior.[181]

- *Attitude confidence.* As noted earlier, sometimes we are more certain about our evaluations than we are at other times. Therefore, another factor affecting the attitude–behavior relationship is attitude confidence. Confidence tends to be stronger when the attitude is based either on a greater amount of information or on more trustworthy information. And when we are confident, our attitudes are more likely to predict our behaviors.[182] Not surprisingly, strongly held attitudes have more influence on consumers' consideration and choice of brand alternatives than weakly held attitudes.[183] When consumers feel that they have depleted their mental resources (ego depletion) in thoroughly processing the message, they will be more confident of their attitudes, which, in turn, means that their attitudes will exert more influence over buying decisions.[184]

- *Specificity of attitudes.* Attitudes tend to be good predictors of behavior when we are very specific about the behavior that they are trying to predict.[185] Thus, if we wanted to predict whether people will take skydiving lessons, measuring their attitudes toward skydiving in general would be less likely to predict behavior than would measuring their attitudes specifically toward skydiving lessons.

- *Attitude–behavior relationship over time.* When consumers are exposed to an advertising message but do not actually try the product, their attitude confidence declines over time. Marketers should therefore plan their advertising schedules to reactivate consumer attitudes and attitude confidence through message repetition. On the other hand, trial-based brand attitudes are likely to decline over time even though advertising-based attitudes do not. As a result, marketers should use communications to reinforce the effects of the trial experience and thereby reactivate the attitude.[186]

- *Emotional attachment.* Emotional attachment to a brand is a stronger predictor of actual purchase behavior than brand attitudes.[187] The more emotionally attached consumers are to a brand—the more they feel bonded or connected to it—the more likely they will be to purchase it repeatedly over time. In fact, such consumers are more willing to pay a price premium for the brand to which they are committed and remain loyal even if it is involved in a product crisis such as a recall.[188] To increase the emotional attachment, marketers should develop and project a brand personality that fits well with the consumer's actual self-image.[189] Note that consumers who are emotionally attached to a brand will be aroused by negative information about that brand, motivating them to generate more counterarguments against the negative information.[190]

- *Situational factors.* Intervening situational factors can prevent a behavior from being performed and can thus weaken the attitude–behavior relationship.[191] For instance, you might have a very positive attitude toward Porsche, but you might not buy one because you cannot afford to. In another situation, if you had gone to buy the car, your attitude might not have resulted in a purchase if the dealership had none available. In other circumstances, the usage situation may alter the attitude. For example, your attitudes toward different wines might depend on whether you are buying wine for yourself or for a friend. Also, your first impression of a consumption experience such as eating in a restaurant can be affected by whether you are alone or with others. This is because your connection with the other people sharing the experience can influence how you remember and react to it.[192]

Finally, your attitudes are more likely to affect your intentions when you can vividly imagine the outcomes that buying the product will bring you.[193]

- *Normative factors.* According to the TORA model, normative factors are likely to affect the attitude–behavior relationship. For example, you may like going to the ballet, but you may not go because you think your friends will make fun of you for doing so. Although your attitude is positive and should lead to the behavior of attending the ballet, you are more motivated to comply with normative beliefs.

- *Personality variables.* Finally, certain personality types are more likely to exhibit stronger attitude–behavior relationships than are others. Individuals who like to devote a lot of thought to actions will evidence stronger attitude–behavior relationships because their attitudes will be based on high elaboration thinking.[194] Also, people who are guided more by their own internal dispositions (called *low self-monitors*) are more likely to exhibit similar behavior patterns across situations and therefore more consistent attitude–behavior relationships.[195] People who are guided by the views and behaviors of others (called *high self-monitors*), on the other hand, try to change their behavior to adapt to every unique situation. Thus, a high self-monitor's choice of beer might depend on the situation; a low self-monitor would choose the same beer regardless of the circumstances.

Summary:

When consumers' MAO to engage in a behavior or to process a message is high, consumers tend to devote considerable effort to forming their attitudes and to message processing. An attitude is a relatively global and enduring evaluation about an offering, issue, activity, person, or event. Attitudes can be described in terms of their favorability, accessibility, confidence, persistence, and resistance. Consumers' thoughts and feelings in response to this situation can affect their attitudes, through either a cognitive or an affective route to persuasion.

Five types of cognitive models show how thoughts relate to attitudes in high-consumer-effort situations: (1) direct or imagined experience, (2) reasoning by analogy or category, (3) values-driven attitudes, (4) social identity-based attitude generation, and (5) analytical processes of attitude construction, including expectancy-value models such as the TORA and the theory of planned behavior. Under the cognitive response model, consumers exert a lot of effort in responding to the message—enough effort to generate counterarguments, support arguments, and source derogations. Under elaborative processing, messages can be effective if they have a credible source or a strong argument, present positive and negative information (under certain circumstances), or involve direct comparisons (if the brand is not the market leader).

Consumers can experience emotions when they are affectively involved with a communication or when the message involves an emotional appeal. In either case the consumer processes the communication, and the positive or negative feelings that result can determine attitudes. When attitudes are affectively based, sources that are likable or attractive can have a positive impact on affective attitude change. Emotional appeals can affect communication processing if they are relevant to the offering. Fear appeals, a type of emotion-eliciting message, are explained, in part, by terror-management theory. A consumer's attitude toward the ad (A_{ad}) can play a role in the attitude change process if the ad is informative or associated with positive feelings. The A_{ad} can then rub off on brand beliefs and attitudes.

Finally, attitudes will better predict a consumer's behavior when (1) involvement is high, (2) knowledge is high, (3) reasons are analyzed, (4) attitudes are accessible, (5) attitudes are held with confidence, (6) attitudes are specific, (7) the attitude–behavior relationship does not decline over time, (8) emotional attachment is high, (9) no situational factors are present, (10) normative factors are not in operation, and (11) we are dealing with certain personality types.

Questions for Review and Discussion

1. What are attitudes, and what three functions do they serve?

2. How do expectancy-value models seek to explain attitude formation?

3. What role does credibility play in affecting consumer attitudes based on cognitions?

4. What are the advantages and disadvantages of offering a two-sided message about a product?

5. Contrast emotional and fear appeals. Why is each effective? Which do you consider most compelling for products in which you are interested?

6. What three factors may lead to a positive attitude toward the ad (A_{ad}) when consumers devote a lot of effort to processing a message? How can marketers apply these factors when designing advertising messages?

Endnotes

1 See Harry Wallop, "What Are the New Status Symbols for the Ultra Rich?" *The Telegraph (U.K.)*, April 21, 2015, www.telegraph.co.uk.

2 Richard E. Petty, H. Rao Unnava, and Alan J. Strathman, "Theories of Attitude Change," in eds. Thomas S. Robertson and Harold H. Kassarjian, *Handbook of Consumer Behavior* (Englewood Cliffs, N.J.: Prentice-Hall, 1991), pp. 241–280.

3 Ida E. Berger and Andrew A. Mitchell, "The Effect of Advertising on Attitude Accessibility, Attitude Confidence, and the Attitude–Behavior Relationship," *Journal of Consumer Research*, December 1989, pp. 269–279; and Joel B. Cohen and Americus Reed II, "A Multiple Pathway Anchoring and Adjustment (MPAA) Model of Attitude Generation and Recruitment," *Journal of Consumer Research* 33, no. 1, 2006, pp. 1–15.

4 See Derek D. Rucker, Zakary L. Tormala, Richard E. Petty, and Pablo Brinol, "Consumer Conviction and Commitment: An Appraisal-Based Framework for Attitude Certainty," *Journal of Consumer Psychology* 24, no. 1, January 2014, pp. 119–136.

5 Rohini Ahluwalia, "Examination of Psychological Processes Underlying Resistance to Persuasion," *Journal of Consumer Research*, September 2000, pp. 217–232.

6 Joseph R. Priester and Richard E. Petty, "The Gradual Threshold Model of Ambivalence," *Journal of Personality and Social Psychology* 71, 1996, pp. 431–449; Joseph R. Priester, Richard E. Petty, and Kiwan Park, "Whence Univalent Ambivalence?" *Journal of Consumer Research* 34, no. 1, 2007, pp. 11–21; and Martin R. Zemborain and Gita Venkataramani Johar, "Attitudinal Ambivalence and Openness to Persuasion," *Journal of Consumer Research* 33, no. 4, 2007, pp. 506–514.

7 Martin Fishbein and Icek Ajzen, *Belief, Attitude, Intention, and Behavior: An Introduction to Theory and Research* (Reading, Mass.: Addison-Wesley, 1975).

8 Lizbieta Lepkowska-White, Thomas G. Brashear, and Marc G. Weinberger, "A Test of Ad Appeal Effectiveness in Poland and the United States," *Journal of Advertising*, Fall 2003, pp. 57–67.

9 Kevin E. Voss, Eric R. Spangenburg, and Bianca Grohmann, "Measuring the Hedonic and Utilitarian Dimensions of Consumer Attitude," *Journal of Marketing Research*, August 2003, pp. 310–320.

10 Petty, Unnava, and Strathman, "Theories of Attitude Change"; and Richard Petty and John T. Cacioppo, *Communication and Persuasion* (New York: Springer, 1986).

11 Jean Hopfensperger, "Charities Cashing in As Shoppers Round Up at Checkout," *Star-Tribune (Minneapolis)*, December 24, 2014, www.startribune.com; "JC Penney Supports Youth Programs One Penny at a Time," *Retailing Today*, July 22, 2011, www.retailingtoday.com.

12 Cohen and Reed, "A Multiple Pathway Anchoring and Adjustment (MPAA) Model of Attitude Generation and Recruitment;" F. P. Bone and S. P. Ellen, "The Generation and Consequences of Communication-Evoked Imagery," *Journal of Consumer Research*, June 1992, pp. 93–104; Punam Anand Keller and Ann L. McGill, "Differences in the Relative Influence of Product Attributes under Alternative Processing Conditions: Attribute Importance Versus Attribute Ease of Imagability," *Journal of Consumer Psychology* 3, no. 1, 1994, pp. 29–49; and Pham, Michel Tuan, Joel B. Cohen, John W. Pracejus, and G. David Hughes, "Affect Monitoring and the Primacy of Feelings in Judgment," *Journal of Consumer Research* 28, September 2001, pp. 167–188.

13 Yuwei Jiang, Rashmi Adaval, Yael Steinhart, and Robert S. Wyer, "Imagining Yourself in the Scene: The Interactive Effects of Goal-Driven Self-Imagery and Visual Perspectives on Consumer Behavior," *Journal of Consumer Research* 41, no. 3, August 2014, pp. 418–435.

14 Miranda R. Goode, Darren W. Dahl, and C. Page Moreau, "The Effect of Experiential Analogies on Consumer Perceptions and Attitudes," *Journal of Marketing Research* 47, no. 2, April 2010, pp. 274–286; Anton Olsen, "Review: Victorinox Swiss Army Slim Flash Drive," *Wired*, August 18, 2011, www.wired.com; and Jennifer Gregan Paxton and Deborah Roedder John, "Consumer Learning by Analogy: A Model of Internal Knowledge Transfer," *Journal of Consumer Research* 24, December 1997, pp. 266–284.

15 Cohen and Reed, "A Multiple Pathway Anchoring and Adjustment (MPAA) Model of Attitude Generation and Recruitment."

16 Michael B. Beverland and Francis J. Farrelly, "The Quest for Authenticity in Consumption: Consumers' Purposive Choice of Authentic Cues to Shape Experienced Outcomes," *Journal of Consumer Research*, February 2010, pp. 838–856.

17 Stephanie Strom, "McDonald's Plans a Shift to Eggs from Only Cage-Free Hens," *New York Times*, September 9, 2015, www.nytimes.com.

18 Americus Reed II, "Activating the Self-Importance of Consumer Selves," *Journal of Consumer Research* 31, September 2004, pp. 286–295; and Sharon Shavitt and Michelle R. Nelson, "The Social-Identity Function in Person Perception," in eds. Gregory Maio and James M. Olson, *Why We Evaluate: Functions of Attitudes* (Mahwah, N.J.: Lawrence Erlbaum, 2000), pp. 37–57.

19 Finn-Olaf Jones, "36 Hours in Lake Tahoe," *New York Times*, February 25, 2015, www.nytimes.com; and Jason Blevins, "Vail Resorts Lands Endorsement Deal with Shaun White," *Denver Post*, August 17, 2011, www.denverpost.com.

20 Peter L. Wright, "Message-Evoked Thoughts: Persuasion Research Using Thought Verbalizations," *Journal of Consumer Research*, September 1980, pp. 151–175.

21 Jerry C. Olson, Daniel R. Toy, and Philip A. Dover, "Do Cognitive Responses Mediate the Effects of Advertising Content on Cognitive Structure?" *Journal of Consumer Research*, December 1982, pp. 245–262.

22 Marian Friestad and Peter Wright, "The Persuasion Knowledge Model: How People Cope with Persuasion Attempts," *Journal of Consumer Research*, June 1994, pp. 1–31.

23 Peter Wright, "Marketplace Metacognition and Social Intelligence," *Journal of Consumer Research*, March 2002, pp. 677–682.

24 Zakary L. Tormala and Richard E. Petty, "Source Credibility and Attitude Certainty: A Metacognitive Analysis of Resistance to Persuasion," *Journal of Consumer Psychology* 14, no. 4, 2004, pp. 427–442.

25 Daniel R. Toy, "Monitoring Communication Effects," *Journal of Consumer Research*, June 1982, pp. 66–76.

26 Petty, Unnava, and Strathman, "Theories of Attitude Change."

27 Punam Anand and Brian Sternthal, "The Effects of Program Involvement and Ease of Message Counterarguing on Advertising Persuasiveness," *Journal of Consumer Psychology* 1, no. 3, 1992, pp. 225–238; and Kenneth R. Lord and Robert E. Burnkrant, "Attention Versus Distraction: The Interactive Effect of Program Involvement and Attentional Devices on Commercial Processing," *Journal of Advertising*, March 1993, pp. 47–60.

28 Bob M. Fennis, Enny H. H. J. Das, and Ad Th. H. Pruyn, "'If You Can't Dazzle Them with Brilliance, Baffle Them with Nonsense': Extending the Impact of the Disrupt-Then-Reframe Technique of Social Influence," *Journal of Consumer Psychology* 14, no. 3, 2004, pp. 280–290; and B. P. Davis and E. S. Knowles, "A Disrupt-Then-Reframe Technique of Social Influence," *Journal of Personality and Social Psychology* 76, 1999, pp. 192–199.

29 Deborah J. MacInnis and Whan C. Park, "The Differential Role of Characteristics of Music on High and Low-Involvement Consumers' Processing of Ads," *Journal of Consumer Research*, September 1991, pp. 161–173; and Rajeev Batra and Douglas M. Stayman, "The Role of Mood in Advertising Effectiveness," *Journal of Consumer Research*, September 1990, pp. 203–214.

30 Uzma Khan and Zakary L. Tormala, "Inviting Questions," *Journal of Consumer Psychology* 22, no. 3, July 2012, pp. 408–417.

31 Debora V. Thompson and Prashant Malaviya, "Consumer-Generated Ads: Does Awareness of Advertising Co-Creation Help or Hurt Persuasion?" *Journal of Marketing* 77, no. 3, May 2013, pp. 33–47.

32 William L. Wilkie and Edgar A. Pessemier, "Issues in Marketing's Use of Multi-Attribute Models," *Journal of Marketing Research*, November 1973, pp. 428–441.

33 Richard P. Bagozzi, Nancy Wong, Shuzo Abe, and Massimo Bergami, "Cultural and Situational Contingencies and the Theory of Reasoned Action," *Journal of Consumer Psychology* 9, no. 2, 2000, pp. 97–106.

34 Noah J. Goldstein, Robert B. Cialdini, and Vladas Griskevicius, "A Room with a Viewpoint: Using Social Norms to Motivate Environmental Conservation in Hotels," *Journal of Consumer Research*, October 2008, pp. 472–482.

35 Min Zhao and Jinhong Xie, "Effects of Social and Temporal Distance on Consumers' Responses to Peer Recommendations," *Journal of Marketing Research* 48, no. 3, June 2011, pp. 486–496.

36 Icek Ajzen and Martin Fishbein, "Prediction of Goal-Directed Behavior: Attitudes, Intentions, and Perceived Behavioral Control," *Journal of Experimental Social Psychology*, September 1980, pp. 453–474; and Blair H. Sheppard, Jon Hartwick, and Paul R. Warshaw, "The Theory of Reasoned Action," *Journal of Consumer Research*, December 1988, pp. 325–342.

37 Cohen and Reed, "A Multiple Pathway Anchoring and Adjustment (MPAA) Model of Attitude Generation and Recruitment."

38 Arti Sahni Notani, "Moderators of Perceived Behavioral Control's Predictiveness in the Theory of Planned Behavior," *Journal of Consumer Psychology* 7, no. 3, 1998, pp. 247–271.

39 Doron Levin, "How Korean Car Makers Beat Out the Japanese," *Fortune*, June 29, 2015, www.fortune.com.

40 Joanna R. Turpin, "Market Warms to Bioheat," *Air Conditioning-Heating-Refrigeration News*, December 1, 2014, www.achrnews.com; and Erin Voegele, "Building Out for Bioheat," *Biodiesel Magazine*, September 8, 2011, www.biodieselmagazine.com.

41 Amitav Chakravarti and Chris Janiszewski, "The Influence of Generic Advertising on Brand Preferences," *Journal of Consumer Research*, March 2004, pp. 487–502.

42 Stephen M. Nowlis and Itamar Simonson, "The Effect of New Product Features on Brand Choice," *Journal of Marketing Research*, February 1996, pp. 36–46.

43 Yvette C. Hammett, "Local, State Tourism Marketing Efforts Lean on Social Media to Draw Young Adults, Families," *Tampa Tribune*, September 5, 2015, www.tbo.com; and Jennifer Rooney, "How Florida Bounced Back from the Oil Spill," *Advertising Age*, January 3, 2011, www.adage.com.

44 Ashesh Mukherjee and Wayne D. Hoyer, "The Effect of Novel Attributes on Product Evaluation," *Journal of Consumer Research*, December 2001, pp. 462–472.

45 Iris W. Hung and Robert S. Wyer, "Shaping Consumer Imaginations: The Role of Self-Focused Attention in Product Evaluations," *Journal of Marketing Research* 48, no. 2, April 2011, pp. 381–392; Petia K. Petrova and Robert B. Cialdini, "Fluency of Consumption Imagery and the Backfire Effects of Imagery Appeals," *Journal of Consumer Research* 32, no. 3, 2005, pp. 442–452; Punam Anand Keller and Ann L. McGill, "Differences in the Relative Influence of Product Attributes Under Alternative Processing Conditions," *Journal of Consumer Psychology* 3, no. 1, 1994, pp. 29–49; and Michel Tuan Pham, "Representativeness, Relevance, and the Use of Feelings in Decision Making," *Journal of Consumer Research* 25, September 1998, pp. 144–159.

46 Deborah Weinswig, "Are Magic Mirrors the Next Big Thing?" *Retailing Today*, January 22, 2015, www.retailingtoday.com.

47 Lindsay Veremis, "Anti-drinking Billboards Hit Outagamie County," *WLUK-TV*, August 17, 2011, www.fox11online.com.

48 Laura Bird, "Condom Campaign Fails to Increase Sales," *Wall Street Journal*, June 23, 1994, p. B7.

49 Barbara Mueller, "Reflections of Culture: An Analysis of Japanese and American Advertising Appeals," *Journal of Advertising Research*, June–July 1987, pp. 51–59.

50 Yong-Soon Kang and Paul M. Herr, "Beauty and the Beholder: Toward an Integrative Model of Communication Source Effects," *Journal of Consumer Research* 33, no. 1, 2006, pp. 123–130; and Ronald E. Goldsmith, Barbara A. Lafferty, and Stephen J. Newell, "The Impact of Corporate Credibility and Celebrity Credibility on Consumer Reaction to Advertisements and Brands," *Journal of Advertising* 29, no. 3, Fall 2000, pp. 43–54; also see Brian Sternthal, Ruby R. Dholakia, and Clark Leavitt, "The Persuasive Effect of Source Credibility," *Public Opinion Quarterly*, Fall 1978, pp. 285–314.

51 Joseph R. Priester, "The Influence of Spokesperson Trustworthiness on Message Elaboration, Attitude Strength, and Advertising Effectiveness," *Journal of Consumer Psychology* 13, no. 4, 2003, pp. 408–421.

52 Thomas Russell, "Stickley Turns Consumer Testimonials into TV Ads," *Furniture Today*, May 22, 2015, www.furnituretoday.com.

53 Der-Juinn Horng, Sheng-Hsien Lee, and Chin-Lung Lin, "The Effects of Online Reviews on Purchasing Intention," *Social Behavior and Personality: An International Journal*, February 2011, p. 71.

54 Sarah G. Moore, "Some Things Are Better Left Unsaid: How Word of Mouth Influences the Storyteller," *Journal of Consumer Research* 38, no. 6, April 2012, pp. 1140–1154.

55 Uri Simonsohn, "Lessons from an 'Oops' at *Consumer Reports*," *Journal of Marketing Research*, February 2011, pp. 1–12.

56 Kari Kenner, "'Will It Blend?' From the Web: Blendtec Blends Up Some Pina Colada," *Daily Herald (Provo, Utah)*, August 11, 2015, www.heraldextra.com

57 Amna Kirmani and Baba Shiv, "Effects of Source Congruity on Brand Attitudes and Beliefs," *Journal of Consumer Psychology* 7, no. 1, 1998, pp. 25–48.

58 Pablo Briñol, Richard E. Petty, and Zakary L. Tormala, "Self-Validation of Cognitive Responses to Advertisements," *Journal of Consumer Research*, March 2004, pp. 559–573.

59 Chenghuan Wu and David R. Schaffer, "Susceptibility to Persuasive Appeals as a Function of Source Credibility and Prior Experience with the Attitude Object," *Journal of Personality and Social Psychology*, April 1987, pp. 677–688.

60 Carolyn Tripp, Thomas D. Jensen, and Les Carlson, "The Effects of Multiple Endorsements by Celebrities on Consumers' Attitudes and Intentions," *Journal of Consumer Research*, March 1994, pp. 535–547.

61 Judith A. Garretson and Ronald W. Niedrich, "Spokes-Characters: Creating Character Trust and Positive Brand Attitudes," *Journal of Advertising* 33, no. 2, Summer 2004, pp. 25–36.

62 Kurt Badenhausen, "David Beckham Banks His Biggest Year Ever With Earnings Of $75 Million," *Forbes*, March 11, 2015, www.forbes.com.

63 Kevin Goldman, "Women Endorsers More Credible than Men, a Survey Suggests," *Wall Street Journal*, October 22, 1995, p. B1.

64 "Tiger Woods Dropped by Tag Heuer," *Advertising Age*, August 8, 2011, www.adage.com; and Cathy Yingling, "Beware the Lure of Celebrity Endorsers," *Advertising Age*, September 24, 2007, p. 19.

65 Patrick Clarke, "Watch: Southwest Aims for the Funny Bone With New Ads," *Travel Pulse*, March 27, 2015, www.travelpulse.com.

66 Sternthal, Dholakia, and Leavitt, "The Persuasive Effect of Source Credibility."

67 Darlene B. Hannah and Brian Sternthal, "Detecting and Explaining the Sleeper Effect," *Journal of Consumer Research*, September 1984, pp. 632–642.

68 Marvin E. Goldberg and Jon Hartwick, "The Effects of Advertiser Reputation and Extremity of Advertising Claim on Advertising Effectiveness," *Journal of Consumer Research*, September 1990, pp. 172–179.

69 Karen L. Becker-Olsen, "And Now, a Word from Our Sponsor," *Journal of Advertising*, Summer 2003, pp. 17–32.

70 Tülin Erdem and Joffre Swait, "Brand Credibility, Brand Consideration, and Choice," *Journal of Consumer Research*, June 2004, pp. 191–198.

71 Candace Lombardi, "Toyota, 3M, Siemens Top Green Brands in Survey," *CNet News*, July 27, 2011, http://news.cnet.com.

72 Kelly O'Reilly, "H&M to Launch Children's Collection for UNICEF," *NBC New York*, June 15, 2011, www.nbcnewyork .com; and Jeff Beer, "UNICEF and H&M Launch Unicoin, a Charitable Currency to Help Early Childhood Education," *Fast Company Create*, June 11, 2015, www.fastcocreate.com.

73 Petty, Unnava, and Strathman, "Theories of Attitude Change"; and Charles S. Areni and Richard J. Lutz, "The Role of Argument Quality in the Elaboration Likelihood Model," in ed. Michael J. Houston, *Advances in Consumer Research*, vol. 15 (Provo, Utah: Association for Consumer Research, 1987), pp. 197–203.

74 "Marketers, Get Ready: Go o d Housekeeping Makes More Product Tests Public," *Advertising Age*, September 13, 2011, www.adage.com.

75 Parthasarathy Krishnamurthy and Anuradha Sivararman, "Counterfactual Thinking and Advertising Responses," *Journal of Consumer Research*, March 2002, pp. 650–658.

76 Jennifer Edson Escalas and Mary Frances Luce, "Process Versus Outcome Thought Focus and Advertising," *Journal of Consumer Psychology*, 2003, pp. 246–254; and Jennifer Edson Escalas and Mar y Frances Luce, "Understanding the Effects of Process Focused Versus Outcome-Focused Thought in Response to Advertising," *Journal of Consumer Research*, September 2004, pp. 274–285.

77 Brett A. S. Martin, Bodo Lang, and Stephanie Wong, "Conclusion Explicitness in Advertising," *Journal of Advertising*, Winter 2003–2004, pp. 57–65.

78 Keith S. Coulter and Girish N. Punj, "The Effects of Cognitive Resource Requirements, Availability, and Argument Quality on Brand Attitudes," *Journal of Advertising* 33, no. 4, Winter 2004, pp. 53–64.

79 Bridget McCrea, "A Winning Combination," *Response*, March 2011, pp. 36+.

80 Patrick Di Justo, "Minty, Piney, Sticky … I Guess I Feel Better," *Wired*, November 2009, p. 39; and Jeanne Whalen, "Foul Taste Is Part of the Cure," *Wall Street Journal*, November 5, 2007, p. B4.

81 See Gerd Bohner, Sabine Einwiller, Hans-Peter Erb, and Frank Siebler, "When Small Means Comfortable: Relations Between Product Attributes in Two-Sided Advertising," *Journal of Consumer Psychology* 13, no. 4, 2003, pp. 454–463.

82 Martin Eisend, "Two-Sided Advertising: A Meta-Analysis," *International Journal of Research in Marketing* 23, no. 2, June 2006, pp. 187–198; Ann E. Schlosser, "Can Including Pros and Cons Increase the Helpfulness and Persuasiveness of Online Reviews? The Interactive Effects of Ratings and Arguments," *Journal of Consumer Psychology* 21, no. 3, July 2011, pp. 226–239; and Danit Ein-Gar, Baba Shiv, and Zakary L. Tormala, "When Blemishing Leads to Blossoming: The Positive Effect of Negative Information," *Journal of Consumer Research* 38, no. 5, February 2012, pp. 846–859.

83 Cornelia Pechmann and David W. Stewart, "The Effects of Comparative Advertising on Attention, Memory, and Purchase Intentions," *Journal of Consumer Research*, September 1990, pp. 180–191.

84 Pechmann and Stewart, "The Effects of Comparative Advertising on Attention, Memory, and Purchase Intentions"; and Rita Snyder, "Comparative Advertising and Brand Evaluation: Toward Developing a Categorization Approach," *Journal of Consumer Psychology* 1, no. 1, 1992, pp. 15–30.

85 Yung Kyun Choi and Gordon E. Miracle, "The Effectiveness of Comparative Advertising in Korea and the United States," *Journal of Advertising* 33, no. 4, Winter 2004, pp. 75–87.

86 Michael J. Barone and Robert D. Jewell, "How Category Advertising Norms and Consumer Counter-Conformity Influence Comparative Advertising Effectiveness," *Journal of Consumer Psychology* 22, no. 4, October 2012, pp. 496–506.

87 Patrick Meirick, "Cognitive Responses to Negative and Comparative Political Advertising," *Journal of Advertising*, Spring 2002, pp. 49–62.

88 Bruce E. Pinkleton, Nam-Hyun Um, and Erica Weintraub Austin, "An Exploration of the Effects of Negative Political Advertising on Political Decision Making," *Journal of Advertising*, Spring 2002, pp. 13–25.

89 Dhruv Grewal, Sukumar Kavanoor, Edward F. Fern, Carolyn Costley, and James Barnes, "Comparative Versus Noncomparative Advertising," *Journal of Marketing*, October 1997, pp. 1–15.

90 Pechmann and Stewart, "The Effects of Comparative Advertising on Attention, Memory, and Purchase Intentions."

91 Kenneth C. Manning, Paul W. Miniard, Michael J. Barone, and Randall L. Rose, "Understanding the Mental Representations Created by Comparative Advertising," *Journal of Advertising* 3, no. 2, Summer 2001, pp. 27–39.

92 Joseph R. Priester, John Godek, D. J. Nayankuppum, and Kiwan Park, "Brand Congruity and Comparative Advertising," *Journal of Consumer Psychology* 14, nos. 1–2, 2004, pp. 115–123.

93 Jerry B. Gotlieb and Dan Sarel, "Comparative Advertising Effectiveness," *Journal of Advertising* 20, no. 1, 1991, pp. 38–45; and Koprowski, "Theories of Negativity."

94 Cornelia Pechmann and S. Ratneshwar, "The Use of Comparative Advertising for Brand Positioning: Association Versus Differentiation," *Journal of Consumer Research*, September 1991, pp. 145–160.

95 Paul W. Miniard, Michael J. Barone, Randall L. Rose, and Kenneth C. Manning, "A Further Assessment of Indirect Comparative Advertising Claims of Superiority Over All Competitors," *Journal of Advertising* 35, no. 4, Winter 2006, pp. 53–64.

96 A. V. Muthukrishnan and S. Ramaswami, "Contextual Effects on the Revision of Evaluative Judgments: An Extension of the Omission-Detection Framework," *Journal of Consumer Research*, June 1999, pp. 70–84.

97 Shailendra Pratap Jain and Steven S. Posavac, "Valenced Comparisons," *Journal of Marketing Research* 41, no. 1, February 2004, pp. 46–58.

98 Shailendra Pratap Jain, Nidhi Agrawal, and Durairaj Maheswaran, "When More May Be Less: The Effects of Regulatory Focus on Responses to Different Comparative Frames," *Journal of Consumer Research* 33, no. 1, 2006, pp. 91–98.

99 Shailendra Pratap Jain, Charles Lindsey, Nidhi Agrawal, and Durairaj Maheswaran, "For Better or For Worse? Valenced Comparative Frames and Regulatory Focus," *Journal of Consumer Research* 34, no. 1, 2007, pp. 57–65.

100 Anne L. Roggeveen, Dhruv Grewal, and Jerry Gotlieb, "Does the Frame of a Comparative Ad Moderate the Effectiveness

of Extrinsic Information Cues?" *Journal of Consumer Research* 33, no. 1, 2006, pp. 115–122.

101 Timothy B. Heath, Michael S. McCarthy, and David L. Mothersbaugh, "Spokesperson Fame and Vividness Effects in the Context of Issue-Relevant Thinking," *Journal of Consumer Research*, March 1994, pp. 520–534.

102 Laura A. Peracchio, "Evaluating Persuasion-Enhancing Techniques from a Resource Matching Perspective," *Journal of Consumer Research*, September 1997, pp. 178–191.

103 Michael A. Kamins and Henry Assael, "Two-Sided Versus One-Sided Appeals: A Cognitive Perspective on Argumentation, Source Derogation, and the Effect of Disconfirming Trial on Belief Change," *Journal of Marketing Research*, February 1984, pp. 29–39.

104 See Peter J. Danaher, Andre Bonfrer, and Sanjay Dhar, "The Effect of Competitive Advertising Interference on Sales for Packaged Goods," *Journal of Marketing Research*, April 2008, pp. 211–225.

105 Pechmann and Stewart, "The Effects of Comparative Advertising on Attention, Memory, and Purchase Intentions."

106 Debora Viana Thompson and Rebecca W. Hamilton, "The Effects of Information Processing Mode on Consumers' Responses to Comparative Advertising," *Journal of Consumer Research* 32, no. 4, 2006, pp. 530–540.

107 Karlene Lukovitz, "Subway Takes on Grease in Product Launch Spots," *Mediapost*, August 17, 2011, www.mediapost.com; and Kate Macarthur, "Why Big Brands Are Getting into the Ring," *Advertising Age*, May 21, 2007, p. 6.

108 A. V. Muthukrishnan and Amitava Chattopadhyay, "Just Give Me Another Chance: The Strategies for Brand Recovery from a Bad First Impression," *Journal of Marketing Research*, May 2007, pp. 334–345.

109 Dennis Amschewitz, Sarah Bailey, Paola Gelato, and Janna van Olst, "This Article Is Better Than Yours," *Managing Intellectual Property*, April 2011, n.p.; and John Tylee, "New 'Honesty' Laws Could Render Many Campaigns Illegal," *Campaign*, March 17, 2000, p. 16.

110 Barbara Mueller, "Reflections of Culture: An Analysis of Japanese and American Advertising Appeals," *Journal of Advertising Research*, June–July 1987, pp. 51–59.

111 "Number of Complaints Is Soaring, Reports ASA," *Grocer*, May 14, 2011, p. 5.

112 Paschalina (Lilia) Ziamou and S. Ratneshwar, "Innovations in Product Functionality: When and Why Are Explicit Comparisons Effective?" *Journal of Marketing*, April 2003, pp. 49–61.

113 H. Onur Bodur, David Brinberg, and Eloïse Coupey, "Belief, Affect, and Attitude: Alternative Models of the Determinants of Attitude," *Journal of Consumer Psychology* 9, no. 1, 2000, pp. 17–28.

114 Stephen D. Rappaport, "Lessons from Online Practice: New Advertising Models," *Journal of Advertising Research*, June 2007, pp. 135–141.

115 Michel Tuan Pham, "Representativeness, Relevance, and the Use of Feelings in Decision Making," *Journal of Consumer Research*, September 1998, pp. 144–159.

116 MacInnis and Park, "The Differential Role of Characteristics of Music on High and Low-Involvement Consumers' Processing of Ads."

117 Yih Hwai Lee and Elison Ai Ching Lim, "When Good Cheer Goes Unrequited: How Emotional Receptivity Affects Evaluation of Express Emotion," *Journal of Marketing Research*, December 2010, pp. 1151–1161.

118 Deborah J. MacInnis and Douglas M. Stayman, "Focal and Emotional Integration: Constructs, Measures and Preliminary Evidence," *Journal of Advertising*, December 1993, pp. 51–66; and Chris T. Allen, Karen A. Machleit, and Susan Schultz Kleine, "A Comparison of Attitudes and Emotions as Predictors of Behavior at Diverse Levels of Behavioral Experience," *Journal of Consumer Research*, March 1992, pp. 493–504.

119 Deborah J. MacInnis and Bernard J. Jaworski, "Two Routes to Persuasion in Advertising," *Review of Marketing* 10, 1990, pp. 1–25.

120 See Nancy Spears and Richard Germain, "1900–2000 in Review: The Shifting Role and Face of Animals in Print Advertisements in the Twentieth Century," *Journal of Advertising*, Fall 2007, pp. 19–33.

121 Tamar Avnet and E. Tory Higgins, "How Regulatory Fit Affects Value in Consumer Choices and Opinions," *Journal of Marketing Research*, February 2006, pp. 1–10; Tamar Avnet and E. Tory Higgins, "Response to Comments on 'How Regulatory Fit Affects Value in Consumer Choices and Opinions,'" *Journal of Marketing Research*, February 2006, pp. 24–27; Jennifer L. Aaker and Angela Y. Lee, "Understanding Regulatory Fit," *Journal of Marketing Research*, February 2006, pp. 15–19; Aparna A. Labroo and Angela Y. Lee, "Between Two Brands: A Goal Fluency Account of Brand Evaluation," *Journal of Marketing Research*, August 2006, pp. 374–385; and Junsang Yeo and Jongwon Park, "Effects of Parent-Extension Similarity and Self-Regulatory Focus on Evaluations of Brand Extensions," *Journal of Consumer Psychology* 16, no. 3, 2006, pp. 272–282.

122 Whan C. Park and Mark S. Young, "Consumer Response to Television Commercials: The Impact of Involvement and Background Music on Brand Attitude Formation," *Journal of Marketing Research*, February 1986, pp. 11–24.

123 Rajeev Batra and Michael L. Ray, "Affective Responses Mediating Acceptance of Advertising," *Journal of Consumer Research*, September 1986, pp. 234–249.

124 Jooyoung Kim and Jon D. Morris, "The Power of Affective Response and Cognitive Structure in Product-Trial Attitude For mat ion," *Journal of Advertising* 36, no. 1, Spring 2007, pp. 95–106.

125 Hans Baumgartner, Mita Sujan, and Dan Padgett, "Patterns of Affective Reactions to Advertisements: The Integration of Moment-to-Moment Responses into Overall Judgments," *Journal of Marketing Research*, May 1997, pp. 219–232.

126 Deborah J. MacInnis and Bernard J. Jaworski, "Information Processing from Advertisements: Toward an Integrative Framework," *Journal of Marketing*, October 1989, pp. 1–23.

127 Lee and Lim, "When Good Cheer Goes Unrequited."

128 Michel Tuan Pham and Tamar Avnet, "Ideals and Oughts and the Reliance on Affect Versus Substance in Persuasion," *Journal of Consumer Research*, March 2004, pp. 503–518.

129 Jennifer L. Aaker and Patti Williams, "Empathy Versus Pride: The Influence of Emotional Appeals Across Cultures," *Journal of Consumer Research*, December 1998, pp. 241–261.

130 Richard P. Bagozzi and David J. Moore, "Public Service Announcements: Emotions and Empathy Guide Prosocial Behavior," *Journal of Marketing*, January 1994, pp. 56–57.

131 May Frances Luce, "Choosing to Avoid: Coping with Negatively Emotion-Laden Consumer Decisions," *Journal of Consumer Research*, March 1998, pp. 409–433.

132 Joel B. Cohen and Charles S. Areni, "Affect and Consumer Behavior," in eds. Thomas S. Robertson and Harold H. Kassarjian, *Handbook of Consumer Behavior* (Englewood Cliffs, N.J.: Prentice-Hall, 1991), pp. 188–240.

133 Robert D. Jewell and H. Rao Unnava, "Exploring Differences in Attitudes Between Light and Heavy Brand Users," *Journal of Consumer Psychology* 14, no. 1/2, 2004, pp. 75–80.

134 Amanda McGowan, "Make Way For Duck Boots: Explaining the Wild Success of L.L. Bean," *WBGH*, September 8, 2015, http://wgbhnews.org; and Jena McGregor, "Customer Service Champs 2010: L. L. Bean," *Bloomberg Businessweek*, February 18, 2010, www.businessweek. com.

135 See Miranda R. Goode, Darren W. Dahl, and C. Page Moreau, "The Effect of Experiential Analogies on Consumer Perceptions and Attitudes," *Journal of Marketing Research*, April 2010, pp. 274–286.

136 Tim Nudd, "Ad of the Day: Subaru Just Made Another Great Father-Daughter Tearjerker," *Adweek*, June 4, 2015, www .adweek.com; Amy Tokic, "New Subaru Ad Promotes Brand's Safety," *Auto Guide*, August 8, 2010, www.autoguide.com.

137 Susan Krashinsky, "Following WestJet's lead, Quaker Tests Waters of Emotional Advertising," *Globe and Mail (Toronto)*, August 14, 2015, www.theglobeandmail.com.

138 Michael J. Barone and Paul W. Miniard, "Mood and Brand Extension Judgments: Asymmetric Effects for Desirable versus Undesirable Brands," *Journal of Consumer Psychology* 12, no. 4, October 2002, pp. 283–290.

139 Petty, Unnava, and Strathman, "Theories of Attitude Change."

140 Harry C. Triandis, *Attitudes and Attitude Change* (New York: Wiley, 1971).

141 Brian D. Till and Michael Busler, "The Match-Up Hypothesis: Physical Attractiveness, Expertise, and the Role of Fit on Brand Attitude, Purchase Intent, and Brand Beliefs," *Journal of Advertising* 29, no. 3, Fall 2000, pp. 1–13; Angela Doland, "How Nike Reacted to Li Na Announcing Her Retirement Today," *Advertising Age*, September 19, 2014, www.adage.com.

142 Peter H. Reingen and Jerome B. Kernan, "Social Perception and Interpersonal Influence: Some Consequences of the Physical Attractiveness Stereotype in a Personal Selling Situation," *Journal of Consumer Psychology* 2, no. 1, 1993, pp. 25–38.

143 Scott Ward and Frederick E. Webster Jr., "Organizational Buying Behavior," in eds. Thomas S. Robertson and Harold H. Kassarjian, *Handbook of Consumer Behavior* (Englewood Cliffs, N.J.: Prentice-Hall, 1991), pp. 419–458.

144 Herbert Simon, Nancy Berkowitz, and John Moyer, "Similarity, Credibility, and Attitude Change," *Psychological Bulletin*, January 1970, pp. 1–16.

145 Louise Lucas, "Beauty and the Brands," *Financial Times*, August 29, 2011, www.ft.com.

146 Terence A. Shimp and Elnora W. Stuart, "The Role of Disgust as an Emotional Mediator of Advertising Effects," *Journal of Advertising*, Spring 2004, pp. 43–53.

147 Nidhi Agrawal and Adam Duhachek, "Emotional Compatibility and the Effectiveness of Antidrinking Messages," *Journal of Marketing Research*, April 2010, pp. 263–273.

148 Patti Williams and Jennifer L. Aaker, "Can Mixed Emotions Peacefully Coexist?" *Journal of Consumer Research*, March 2002, pp. 636–649.

149 Elaine Chan and Jaideep Sengupta, "Insincere Flattery Actually Works," *Journal of Marketing Research*, February 2010, pp. 122–133.

150 See Christian Homburg, Jan Wieseke, and Wayne D. Hoyer, "Social Identity and the Service-Profit Chain," *Journal of Marketing*, March 2010, pp. 38–54; and David Sprott, Sandor Czellar, and Eric Spangenberg, "The Importance of a General Measure of Brand Engagement on Market Behavior," *Journal of Marketing Research*, February 2009, pp. 92–104.

151 Blair Kidwell, David M. Hardesty, Brian R. Murtha, and Shibin Sheng, "Emotional Intelligence in Marketing Exchanges," *Journal of Marketing*, January 2011, pp. 78–95.

152 Batra and Stayman, "The Role of Mood in Advertising Effectiveness."

153 Rajesh K. Chandy, Gerard J. Tellis, Deborah J. MacInnis, and Pattana Thaivanich, "'What to Say When' Advertising Appeals in Evolving Markets," *Journal of Marketing Research*, November 2001, pp. 399–414.

154 "McDonald's—Happy Box," *Campaign*, July 29, 2011, p. 7; Gillian West, "McDonald's Heralds 'Latest Step in the Evolution of the Happy Meal' with Free Fruit Fridays Launch," *The Drum (U.K.)*, March 7, 2014, www.thedrum.com.

155 Jennifer Edson Escalas, Marian Chapman Moore, and Julie Edell Britton, "Fishing for Feelings? Hooking Viewers Helps!" *Journal of Consumer Psychology* 14, nos. 1, 2, 2004, pp. 105–114.

156 Deborah A. Small and Nicole M. Verrochi, "The Face of Need: Facial Emotion Expression on Charity Advertisements," *Journal of Marketing Research*, December 2009, pp. 777–787.

157 Brent McFerran, Darren W. Dahl, Gerald J. Gorn, and Heather Honea, "Motivational Determinants of Transportation into Marketing Narratives," *Journal of Consumer Psychology* 20, 2010, pp. 306–316.

158 "Shelter Pet Adoption," Ad Council, www.adcouncil.org; and Minda Smiley, "Pupparazzi Pen Makes Its Debut at MTV's Video Music Awards," *The Drum (U.K.)*, August 31, 2015, www .thedrum.com.

159 John F. Tanner, James B. Hunt, and David R. Eppright, "The Protection Motivation Model: A Normative Model of Fear Appeals," *Journal of Marketing*, July 1991, pp. 36–45.

160 Michael L. Ray and William L. Wilkie, "Fear: The Potential of an Appeal Neglected by Marketing," *Journal of Marketing*, January 1970, pp. 54–62.

161 Ibid.

162 Kirsten Passyn and Mita Sujan, "Self-Accountability Emotions and Fear Appeals: Motivating Behavior," *Journal of Consumer Research* 32, no. 4, 2006, pp. 583–589.

163 Omar Shehryar and David M. Hunt, "A Terror Management Perspective on the Persuasiveness of Fear Appeals," *Journal of Consumer Psychology* 15, no. 4, 2005, pp. 275–287.

164 Scott Kirsner, "The Carbonite File," *Boston Globe*, May 12, 2011, www.boston.com; and Scott Kirsner, "Dueling Data Backup Firms Are Rare Bright Spot," *Boston Globe*, January 25, 2009, www.boston.com.

165 Herbert J. Rotfeld, "Fear Appeals and Persuasion: Assumptions and Errors in Advertising Research," in eds. James H. Leigh and Claude R. Martin, *Current Issues and Research in Advertising* (Ann Arbor, Mich.: Graduate School of Business Administration, University of Michigan, 1990), pp. 155–175.

166 John J. Wheatley, "Marketing and the Use of Fear or Anxiety Arousing Appeals," *Journal of Marketing*, April 1971, pp. 62–64; and Peter L. Wright, "Concrete Action Plans in TV Messages to Increase Reading of Drug Warnings," *Journal of Consumer Research*, December 1979, pp. 256–269.

167 John J. Burette and Richard L. Oliver, "Fear Appeal Effects in the Field: A Segmentation Approach," *Journal of Marketing Research*, May 1979, pp. 181–190.

168 Mac Innis and Jaworski, "Two Routes to Persuasion in Advertising."

169 Thomas J. Olney, Morris B. Holbrook, and Rajeev Batra, "Consumer Responses to Advertising: The Effects of Ad Content, Emotions, and Attitude Toward the Ad on Viewing Time," *Journal of Consumer Research*, March 1991, pp. 440–453.

170 Paul W. Miniard, Sunil Bhatla, and Randall L. Rose, "On the Formation and Relationship of Ad and Brand Attitudes," *Journal of Marketing Research*, August 1990, pp. 290–303.

171 Sally Goll Beatty, "Executive Fears Effects of Political Ads," *Wall Street Journal*, April 29, 1996, p. B6.

172 Julie A. Edell and Richard E. Staelin, "The Information Processing of Pictures in Print Advertisements," *Journal of Consumer Research*, June 1983, pp. 45–60.

173 Scott B. MacKenzie, Richard J. Lutz, and George E. Belch, "The Role of Attitude Toward the Ad as a Mediator of Advertising Effectiveness," *Journal of Marketing Research*, May 1986, pp. 130–143; and Pamela M. Homer, "The Mediating Role of Attitude Toward the Ad: Some Additional Evidence," *Journal of Marketing Research*, February 1990, pp. 78–86.

174 Dan Minahan, "Game of Thrones Director Wraps Audi Drama Series," *Shoot Online*, October 21, 2011, www.shootonline.com.

175 Richard E. Petty, John T. Cacioppo, and David W. Schumann, "Central and Peripheral Routes to Advertising Persuasion," *Journal of Consumer Research*, September 1983, pp. 134–148.

176 Jaideep Sengupta and Gita Venkataramani Johar, "Effects of Inconsistent Attribute Information on the Predictive Value of Product Attitudes," *Journal of Consumer Research*, June 2002, pp. 39–56.

177 Robert E. Smith and William R. Swinyard, "Attitude-Behavior Consistency: The Impact of Product Trial Versus Advertising," *Journal of Marketing Research* 20, no. 3, August 1983, pp. 257–267; and Russell H. Fazio and Mark P. Zanna, "Direct Experience and Attitude–Behavior Consistency," in ed. Leonard Berkowitz, *Advances in Experimental Social Psychology* (New York: Academic Press, 1981), pp. 162–202.

178 Jaideep Sengupta and Gavan J. Fitzsimons, "The Effects of Analyzing Reasons for Brand Preferences: Disruption or Reinforcement?" *Journal of Marketing Research* 37, August 2000, pp. 318–330.

179 Russell H. Fazio, Martha C. Powell, and Carol J. Williams, "The Role of Attitude Accessibility in the Attitude-to-Behavior Process," *Journal of Consumer Research*, December 1989, pp. 280–288; and Berger and Mitchell, "The Effect of Advertising on Attitude Accessibility, Attitude Confidence, and the Attitude–Behavior Relationship."

180 Smith and Swinyard, "Attitude–Behavior Consistency"; and Alice A. Wright and John G. Lynch, "Communication Effects of Advertising vs. Direct Experience When Both Search and Experience Attributes Are Present," *Journal of Consumer Research*, March 1995, pp. 708–718.

181 Vicki G. Morwitz and Gavan J. Fitzsimons, "The Mere-Measurement Effect: Why Does Measuring Intention Change Actual Behavior?" *Journal of Consumer Psychology* 14, no. 1/2, 2004, pp. 64–74; and Pierre Chandon, Vicki G. Morwitz, and Werner J. Reinartz, "Do Intentions Really Predict Behavior? Self-Generated Validity Effects in Survey Research," *Journal of Marketing* 69, no. 2, April 2005, pp. 1–14.

182 Berger, "The Nature of Attitude Accessibility and Attitude Confidence."

183 Joseph R. Priester, Dhananjay Nayakankuppam, Monique A. Fleming, and John Godek, "The A2SC2 Model: The Influence of Attitudes and Attitude Strength on Consideration and Choice," *Journal of Consumer Research*, March 2004, pp. 574–587.

184 Echo Wen Wan, Derek D. Rucker, Zakary L. Tormala, and Joshua J. Clarkson, "The Effect of Regulatory Depletion on Attitude Certainty," *Journal of Marketing Research*, June 2010, pp. 531–541.

185 Fishbein and Ajzen, *Belief, Attitude, Intention, and Behavior*.

186 Shanker H. Krishnan and Robert E. Smith, "The Relative Endurance of Attitudes, Confidence, and Attitude–Behavior Consistency," *Journal of Consumer Psychology* 7, no. 3, 1998, pp. 273–298.

187 Whan C. Park, Deborah J. MacInnis, Joseph Priester, Andreas B. Eisingerich, and Dawn Iacobucci, "Brand Attachment and Brand Attitude Strength: Conceptual and Empirical Differentiation of Two Critical Brand Equity Drivers," *Journal of Marketing*, November 2010, pp. 1–17.

188 Matt Thomson, Deborah J. MacInnis, and Whan C. Park, "The Ties that Bind: Measuring the Strength of Consumers' Emotional Attachments to Brands," *Journal of Consumer Psychology* 15, no. 1, 2005, pp. 77–91; Whan C. Park and Deborah J. MacInnis, "What's In and What's Out: Questions on the Boundaries of the Attitude Construct," *Journal of Consumer Research* 33, no. 1, 2006, pp. 16–18; Whan C. Park, Deborah J. MacInnis, and Joseph Priester, "Brand Attachment as a Strategic Brand Exemplar," forthcoming in ed. Bernd H. Schmitt, *Handbook of Brand and Experience Management* (Elgar Publishing, 2009); Rohini Ahluwalia, Robert Burnkrant, and H. Rao Unnava, "Consumer Response to Negative Publicity," *Journal of Marketing Research* 37, no. 2 (May 2000), pp. 203–214; Michael D. Johnson, Andreas Herrmann, and Frank Huber, "The Evolution of Loyalty Intentions," *Journal of Marketing* 70, April 2006, 122–132; and Matthew Thomson, "Human Brands: Invest i gating Ante c e dent s to Consumers' Strong Attachments to Celebrities," *Journal of Marketing* 70, no. 3, July 2006, pp. 104–119.

189 Lucia Malar, Harley Krohmer, Wayne D. Hoyer, and Bettina Nyffenegger, "Emotional Brand Attachment and Brand Personality: The Relative Importance of the Actual and the Ideal Self," *Journal of Marketing*, July 2011, pp. 35–52.

190 Sekar Raju and H. Rao Unnava, "The Role of Arousal in Commitment," *Journal of Consumer Research* 33, no. 2, 2006, pp. 173–178.

191 Krishnan and Smith, "The Relative Endurance of Attitudes, Confidence, and Attitude–Behavior Consistency."

192 Rajesh Bhargave and Nicole Votolato Montgomery, "The Social Context of Temporal Sequences: Why First Impressions Shape Shared Experiences," *Journal of Consumer Research* 40, no. 3, October 2013, pp. 501–517.

193 Bob M. Fennis, Marieke A. Adriaanse, Wolfgang Stroebe, and Bert Pol, "Bridging the Intention-Behavior Gap: Inducing Implementation Intentions Through Persuasive Appeals," *Journal of Consumer Psychology* 21, no. 3, July 2011, pp. 302–311.

194 John T. Cacioppo, Richard E. Petty, Chuan Fang Kao, and Regina Rodriguez, "Central and Peripheral Routes to Persuasion," *Journal of Personality and Social Psychology* 51, 1986, pp. 1032–1043.

195 Mark Snyder and William B. Swan Jr., "When Actions Reflect Attitudes: The Politics of Impression Management," *Journal of Personality and Social Psychology* 34, 1976, pp. 1034–1042.

CHAPTER 6

Attitudes Based on Low Effort

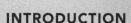

MARCUS BRANDT/Newscom/European Pressphoto Agency, Hamburg/Hamburg/Germany

LEARNING OBJECTIVES

After studying this chapter, you will be able to:

▶ Outline some issues marketers face in trying to change consumers' attitudes when processing effort is low.

▶ Explain the role of unconscious influences on attitudes and behavior in low-effort situations.

▶ Discuss how consumers form beliefs based on low-processing cognitive effort.

▶ Show how marketers can influence cognitive attitudes through communication source, message, context, and repetition.

▶ Describe how consumers form attitudes through affective reactions when cognitive effort is low.

▶ Highlight how marketers can use the communication source, message, and context to influence consumers' feelings and attitudes when processing effort is low.

INTRODUCTION

In Chapter 5, you learned how consumers form attitudes based on high cognitive effort, and how marketing can be used to influence those attitudes. Snack brands such as Frito-Lay face a different challenge: Because consumers tend not to actively process message arguments or become emotionally involved in messages about snacks, these marketers must use other techniques to create positive evaluations of their brands, increase situational involvement, raise awareness of need situations, and stimulate purchasing and consumption. For instance, Frito-Lay connects with consumers and communicates messages through television and other traditional media as well as through social and mobile media like YouTube, Twitter, and texting.[1] This chapter discusses how marketers apply these and other techniques such as sex, humor, attractive sources, and emotion to influence attitudes even when consumers make little effort to process the message.

6-1 High-Effort Versus Low-Effort Routes to Persuasion

When consumers are either unwilling or unable to exert a lot of effort or devote emotional resources to processing the central idea behind a marketing communication, we characterize it as a *low-effort situation*. In such a situation, consumers are unlikely to think about what the product means to them, relate empathetically to the characters in the ad, or generate arguments against or in support of the brand message. When processing effort is low, consumers are passive recipients of the message and usually do not form strong beliefs or accessible, persistent, resistant, or confident attitudes. In fact, attitudes formed under low-effort processing may not even be stored in memory, allowing consumers to form attitudes anew each time they are exposed to a message.[2] Marketers must therefore use a strategy that takes into account these effects of lower-level processing.

One approach is to create communications that use a different route. Instead of focusing on the key message arguments, the message will be more effective if it takes the **peripheral route to persuasion**.[3] Processing is called *peripheral* when consumers' attitudes are based not on a detailed consideration of the message or their ability to relate to the brand empathetically but on other easily processed aspects of the message, such as the source or visuals, called **peripheral cues**. In particular, consumer attitudes can persist over time if peripheral cues such as visuals are related to the offering.[4]

Just as there are both cognitive and affective routes to persuasion when processing effort is high, so too can consumers form low-effort attitudes in both a cognitive and an affective manner. Marketers can try to design their ads to enhance the likelihood that consumers' thoughts (the cognitive base), feelings (the affective base), or both will be favorable. Exhibit 6.1 provides a framework for thinking about the peripheral bases of consumer behavior, including unconscious influences on attitude formation and change.

Marketers need to understand how consumers form attitudes with low effort because, in most cases, consumers will have limited motivation, ability, and/or opportunity (MAO) to process marketing communications. Think about the countless marketing messages you receive every day. How many actually attract your attention and stimulate you to think about the ad and the way that you feel about the offering? When the television is on, do you channel surf during commercials or tune them out because they feature products you do not care about? These behaviors pose challenges for marketers.

Peripheral route to persuasion Aspects other than key message arguments that are used to influence attitudes.

Peripheral cues Easily processed aspects of a message, such as music, an attractive source, picture, or humor.

Thin-slice judgments Evaluations made after very brief observations.

6-2 Unconscious Influences on Attitudes When Consumer Effort Is Low

Recent research indicates that much processing in low-effort situations occurs below conscious awareness. This means that consumers form attitudes on both cognitive and affective bases without being aware of how or why they have done so. For example, a consumer browsing in a store may unconsciously be affected by various aspects of the shopping environment.[5] As another example, when people must stand in line to acquire something (make a purchase, get on a flight), they will perceive the product or experience as more valuable—and have a more positive attitude toward it—as they make progress toward the front of the line.[6] In particular, two unconscious influences being researched are thin-slice judgments based on brief observations and cues from body feedback.

6-2a THIN-SLICE JUDGMENTS

Thin-slice judgments are assessments consumers make after brief observations despite receiving minimal information input. Studies show that consumers can form surprisingly accurate impressions through thin-slice judgments, even though they are not doing so on a conscious level.[7] For example, a consumer may unconsciously form an assessment about a salesperson after a moment of observation or interaction. (This same effect may occur when students judge a professor's class performance after brief observation.) Such an assessment can influence the consumer's decision to buy and satisfaction with the sale. Also, when consumers glance at a product and unconsciously perceive it to have a friendly human face—such as an upturned car grille that seems to be a smile—they are likely to have a positive attitude toward that product.[8] At the same time, an overabundance of information, knowledge, or analysis can impair this kind of intuitive assessment.[9]

6-2b BODY FEEDBACK

Even though consumers may not consciously monitor their own physical reactions, body feedback can influence attitudes and behavior in some circumstances, which is why researchers are studying mind–body connections in more detail. For instance, consumers who were induced to nod had more positive evaluations of favorable brands; when induced to shake their heads, consumers had more negative evaluations. Similarly, pushing up on a table led to more positive evaluations; pushing down led to more negative evaluations. However, consumers must know the meaning of the body feedback they experience in order to explain their behavior. If they do not recognize that

Exhibit 6.1 ▶ Chapter Overview: Attitude Formation and Change: Low Consumer Effort

Attitudes can be formed unconsciously as well as cognitively and affectively in low-effort situations, although not in the same way as they are in high-effort situations. Low-effort cognition involves simple beliefs, and affect involves mere exposure, classical and evaluative conditioning, attitude toward the ad, and mood. Marketers can also influence consumer attitudes cognitively and affectively using source, message, and context factors.

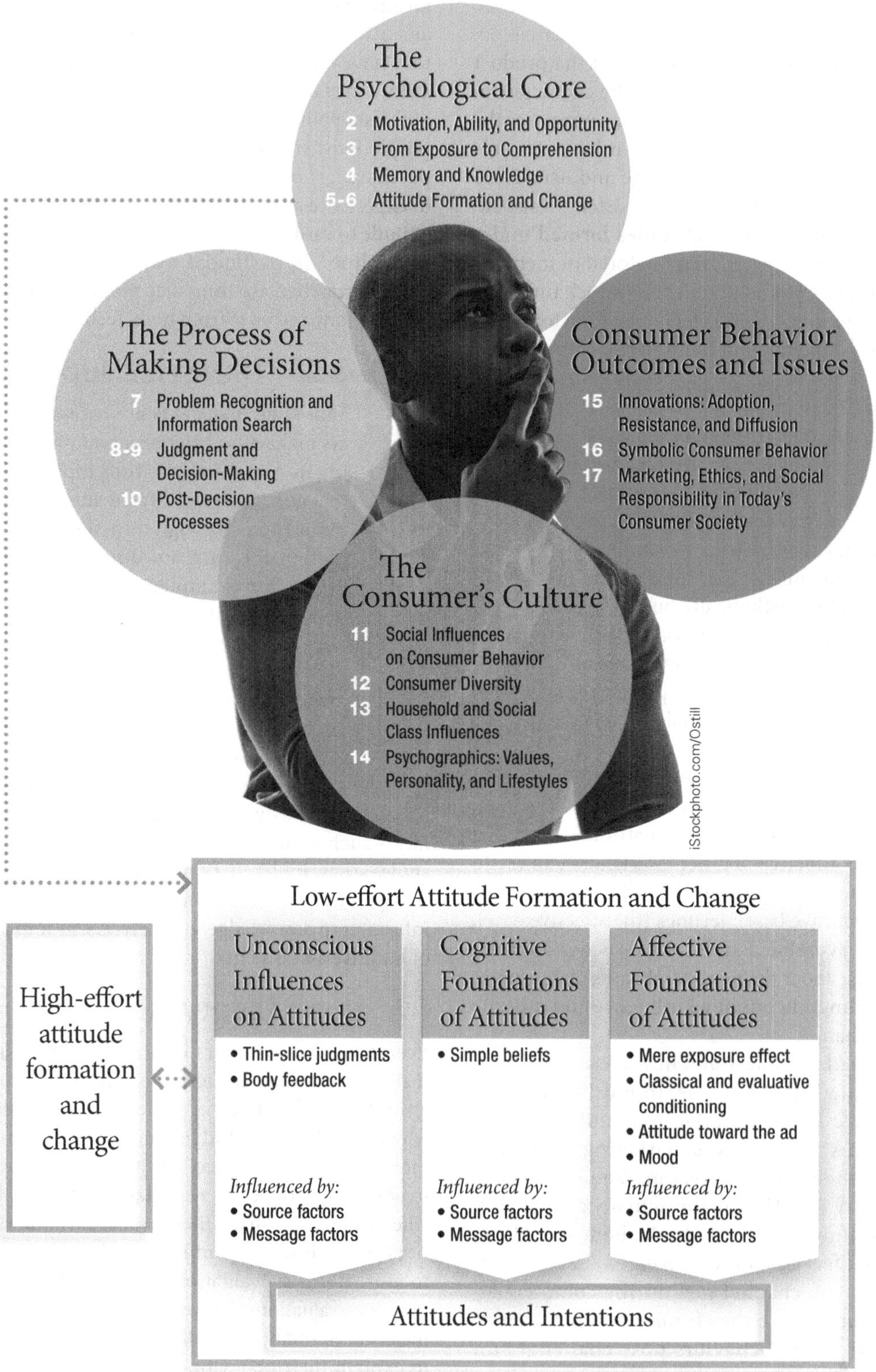

The
Psychological Core

2 Motivation, Ability, and Opportunity
3 From Exposure to Comprehension
4 Memory and Knowledge
5-6 Attitude Formation and Change

The Process of
Making Decisions

7 Problem Recognition and
Information Search
8-9 Judgment and
Decision-Making
10 Post-Decision
Processes

Consumer Behavior
Outcomes and Issues

15 Innovations: Adoption,
Resistance, and Diffusion
16 Symbolic Consumer Behavior
17 Marketing, Ethics, and Social
Responsibility in Today's
Consumer Society

The
Consumer's Culture

11 Social Influences
on Consumer Behavior
12 Consumer Diversity
13 Household and Social
Class Influences
14 Psychographics: Values,
Personality, and Lifestyles

iStockphoto.com/Ostill

Low-effort Attitude Formation and Change		
Unconscious Influences on Attitudes	**Cognitive Foundations of Attitudes**	**Affective Foundations of Attitudes**
• Thin-slice judgments • Body feedback	• Simple beliefs	• Mere exposure effect • Classical and evaluative conditioning • Attitude toward the ad • Mood
Influenced by: • Source factors • Message factors	*Influenced by:* • Source factors • Message factors	*Influenced by:* • Source factors • Message factors

High-effort
attitude
formation
and
change

Attitudes and Intentions

nodding signals agreement, this feedback cue will have no effect on their attitude or behavior.[10] Also, as discussed in Chapter 2, the mind–body connection can affect consumer behavior. As one example, physically firming muscles may help consumers exert self-control in choices such as picking a healthy snack rather than an unhealthy one.[11]

 ## Marketing Implications

Marketers can try to enhance thin-slice judgments and induce positive body feedback, even though consumers will not be consciously aware of these influences. For example, a consumer may unconsciously form an assessment about a salesperson after a moment or two of conversation. Applying body feedback theory, many marketers make product packaging intriguing or attractive enough to cause consumers to pick up a product. In one test, high school students began buying baby carrots after the vegetables were repackaged like popular chip snacks and displayed in bright orange vending machines.[12]

Also, marketers should aim to have consumers read ad copy from top to bottom (and then from bottom to top) to simulate nodding "yes." Such body movements could tip the scale in favor of a purchase if the consumer has a positive perception of the product. Applying unconscious influences in marketing can be tricky, however, because of their complex interactions with conscious influences.[13] For example, after a redesign of the Mazda3 sports car turned the grille into a wide grin, reviewers complained that the car seemed less "aggressive." Mazda does, in fact, use grille design as a differentiator to convey car personality.[14] Finally, when advertising a product and its results, marketers should pay close attention to placement of images within the message. Research suggests that consumers tend to perceive the product as being more effective when its image is shown close to the image of the promised results, especially when consumers are less knowledgeable about the product category.[15]

Simple inferences Beliefs based on peripheral cues.

Heuristics Simple rules of thumb that are used to make judgments.

Frequency heuristic Belief based simply on the number of supporting arguments or amount of repetition.

6-3 Cognitive Bases of Attitudes When Consumer Effort Is Low

Chapter 5 explains how consumers' beliefs form an important cognitive basis for their attitudes. When processing effort is low, attitudes may be based on a few simple and not very strong beliefs because consumers have not processed the message deeply. Interestingly, because these beliefs are not very strong, marketers may actually be *more* successful in changing them than when consumers' processing effort is high.

The attitudes of low-effort consumers may be less resistant to attack than those of high-effort consumers because the low-effort people may "let their guard down" and not resist the message or develop counterarguments. So a company that wants to change consumers' false beliefs about a product will be more successful if it uses a direct refutation to rebut a direct product claim.[16] Also, ads that focus consumers on the process of using the advertised product make consumers more likely to think about a plan to buy the product—and open the way to persuasion by strong message claims.[17]

When processing effort is low, consumers may acquire simple beliefs by forming **simple inferences** based on simple associations. For example, consumers may infer that a brand of champagne is elegant because it is shown with other elegant things, such as a richly decorated room or a woman in an evening dress. If an ad is perceived to be similar to the prototypical ad for a product or service category, consumers may believe that the offering is just like the prototypical brand and may develop similar attitudes toward both.[18] Inferred beliefs may also come from consumers' superficial analysis of the product's brand name, country of origin, price, or color. Inferences may be based upon the product's maker, as well. Research shows that consumers judge ads as more credible when the ad indicates that the manufacturing firm is profitable.[19]

In addition, consumers can form simple beliefs based on attributions or explanations for an endorsement.[20] If consumers attribute an endorsement to a desire to earn a lot of money, they will not find the message believable. The ad is apt to be credible if consumers perceive that the endorser truly cares about the offering. When Maria Sharapova appears in Nike ads for the tennis clothing she's designed, she's believable because she has an insider's understanding of the sport and is known for her sense of style on and off the court.[21] Moreover, childhood exposure to brand advertising can have a positive impact on brand evaluations even after consumers grow up, because of positive feelings toward the ads and because of knowledge structures created at an early age.[22]

Finally, consumers can aid judgments by forming **heuristics**, or simple rules of thumb, that are easy to invoke and require little thought.[23] For example, consumers could use the heuristic "If it is a well-known brand, it must be good" to infer that brands with more frequent ads are also higher in quality.[24] A special type of heuristic is the **frequency heuristic**, with which

Exhibit 6.2 ▶ Endorsement

Ellen DeGeneres is seen here as a brand ambassador.

consumers form a belief based on the number of supporting arguments.[25] They may think, "It must be good because there are ten reasons why I should like it." Research also indicates that consumers are likely to have stronger beliefs about a product when they hear the same message repeatedly, which is known as the **truth effect**.[26] Rather than thinking about and evaluating the information, consumers use familiarity with the message to judge its accuracy ("This 'rings a bell,' so it must be true").

Truth effect When consumers believe a statement simply because it has been repeated a number of times.

6-4 How Cognitive Attitudes Are Influenced

Marketers need to consider multiple factors when trying to influence cognitive attitudes. The strength and importance of consumers' beliefs is one factor. Another factor is the likelihood that consumers will form favorable beliefs based on the inferences, attributions, and heuristics they use in processing the message. In designing communications that overcome these hurdles, marketers must consider three major characteristics of a communication: (1) the communication source, (2) the message, and (3) the context in which the message is delivered and the use of repetition.

6-4a COMMUNICATION SOURCE

Characteristics of the source play an important role in influencing consumers' beliefs when their processing effort is low. Credible sources can serve as peripheral cues for making a simplified judgment, such as "Statements from experts can be trusted" or "Products endorsed by an expert must be good."[27] Note that source expertise is used here as a simple cue in judging the credibility of the message, and unlike the case in high-effort situations, little cognitive effort is required to process the message. Marketers may also increase the chances that consumers will believe the endorsement of a product by using an endorser who does not advertise many other products. Source credibility is also affected by the language used when communicating about the product. Research indicates that consumers who review products are seen as more credible sources when they use polite language and soften the effect of any negative product information they are conveying.[28]

6-4b THE MESSAGE

The message itself can influence attitudes in a number of ways when consumers' processing effort is low.

Category- and Schema-Consistent Information
Many elements of a communication affect the inferences that consumers make about a message. For example, consumers may infer that a brand has certain characteristics based on its name ("Healthy Choice soups must be good for me"). They may make inferences about quality based on price, as discussed in Chapter 4, or about attributes based on color, such as when blue suggests coolness. Thus, in designing ads for low-effort consumers, marketers pay close attention to the immediate associations consumers have about easily processed visual and verbal information. These associations are likely to be consistent with category and schema information stored in the consumer's memory.

Placement in product rankings such as "top 10" listings can affect consumers' inferences. Consumers mentally create subcategories of products according to ranks that end in "0" and "5," and they tend to exaggerate the differences between adjacent subcategories. Thus, when a product improves its ranking from number 11 to number 10, consumers will have a more favorable perception of the shift into the "top 10" subcategory than when a product improves its ranking within the "top 10" from number 10 to number 9.[29]

Many Message Arguments
The frequency heuristic can also affect consumers' beliefs about the message. As a simplifying rule,

consumers do not actually process all the information but form a belief based on the number of supporting arguments. For example, when Kraft introduced MiO concentrated fruit flavors for water, its Facebook promotions and TV commercials featured three arguments to encourage belief formation: MiO flavors make water tastier, MiO-flavored water is more fun to drink, and MiO flavors can be combined for variety.[30] Note that low-effort attitudes can be affected by how easily consumers remember the message arguments. Simply being able to recall some of the arguments can enhance a consumer's preference for the advertised brand.[31] Multiple message supporters can also play a role: Consumers may be persuaded by ads that use consensus claims, like 9 out of 10 dentists prefer a certain toothpaste brand.[32]

Simple Messages

In low-processing situations, a simple message is more likely to be effective because consumers will not have to process a lot of information. Marketers often want to convey basic information about why a particular brand is superior, especially when a point of differentiation distinguishes it from the competition. Thus, rather than overloading low-processing consumers with details, marketers should use a simple message with one or two key points. When Glad advertises its ForceFlex garbage bags, the words and pictures focus on one simple point: The bags stretch when stuffed, but they do not break. When marketing food products on the basis of convenience, marketers should focus attention on one important functional benefit through a literal, direct assertion, such as "ready in just 15 minutes."[33]

Involving Messages

Marketers will sometimes want to *increase* consumers' situational involvement with the message to ensure that the information is received. One common strategy is to increase the extent to which consumers engage in **self-referencing**, or relating the message to their own experience or self-image.[34] A self-referencing strategy can be effective in developing positive attitudes and intentions, especially if it is used at moderate levels and consumers' involvement is not too low. Some marketers use nostalgia in messages to encourage self-referencing and influence positive attitudes.[35]

Even the choice of words can be important elements for involvement. Research shows that when customers expect a close relationship with a brand, they will have more favorable brand evaluations after reading messages that use "we," compared with messages that use wording such as "you and the brand." On the other hand, customers' brand evaluations will be less favorable if the message

Exhibit 6.3 ▶ Simple Message

When effort is low, consumers will not process a lot of information, so advertisers need to provide simple messages, like in this ad.

> **Self-referencing**
> Relating a message to one's own experience or self-image.

uses "we" to imply a closer relationship than the consumers expected.[36]

Remembering and using the consumer's name in a personal selling context also increases purchase behavior.[37] Coca-Cola played on this idea with its "Share a Coke" packaging for 20-ounce bottles of cola. Each bottle featured one of hundreds of common given names in the space where the brand name usually appears. As a result, sales of Coke's 20-ounce bottles increased by 19 percent.[38]

Note that consumers will have more favorable attitudes toward a brand that is highly descriptive on a personality dimension that they consider important or self-descriptive.[39] A mainstream ad with dominant culture cues may stimulate self-referencing among members of a subculture as well as among members of the dominant culture and lead to favorable ad attitudes. If the ad has subcultural cues rather than dominant culture cues, however, it will induce self-referencing and positive ad attitudes only among subculture members.[40]

Marketing Implications

Marketers can increase self-referencing by (1) directly instructing consumers to self-reference ("Think of the last time you had a good meal . . ."), (2) using the word *you* in the ad, (3) asking rhetorical questions ("Wouldn't you like your clothes to look this clean?"),[41] or (4) showing visuals of situations to which consumers can easily relate. As an example, Shutterfly uses the headline

"Bring your adventures to life in minutes" to promote its TripPix app, which allows consumers to turn iPhone photos into printed photo books.[42] However, when a rhetorical question in an ad attracts special attention, consumers wonder why the question is there, shifting their processing effort to the message style instead of the message content.[43]

The **mystery ad** (sometimes called the "wait and bait" ad), which does not identify the brand until the end, if at all, is another way to arouse consumers' curiosity and involvement. Some movies use mystery ads to build audience interest in advance of their release dates. In particular, the mystery ad is effective in generating category-based processing and storing brand associations in memory.[44]

Mystery ad An ad in which the brand is not identified until the end of the message.

Marketers can also employ other techniques to increase situational involvement and processing effort. Online marketers can use avatars to induce more arousal and involve consumers in the website experience.[45] Scratch-and-sniff print ads often increase processing effort because many consumers cannot resist trying something new. Applying this technique, North Carolina and other states have introduced scratch-and-sniff lotto tickets embedded with flavors such as chocolate, barbecue, and bacon.[46] Also, inviting consumers to experience simulated product usage online increases involvement and advertising effectiveness more than an online ad message alone would.[47] The Lego site, for example, features interactive games where players create virtual animals and cities using virtual Lego blocks, demonstrating the product's functionality and fun. In addition, Lego sends Lego experts and displays on tour to major cities so families can experience hands-on fun with the blocks.[48]

Mere exposure effect When familiarity leads to a consumer's liking an object.

6-4c   MESSAGE CONTEXT AND REPETITION

Although source and message factors can influence consumers' attitudes, the context in which the message is delivered can affect the strength of consumers' beliefs and the prominence (or salience) of those beliefs for the consumers. In particular, a company can use message *repetition* to help consumers acquire basic knowledge of important product features or benefits, enhancing the strength and salience of their beliefs. Consumers do not try to process this information actively; rather, the constant repetition increases recall through effortless or **incidental learning**. For example, you may have a prominent belief about

Incidental learning Learning that occurs from repetition rather than from conscious processing.

milk's health benefits because you have been repeatedly exposed to the long-running "Got Milk?" milk mustache ad campaign.

Repetition may enhance brand awareness, make a brand name more familiar,[49] make it easier to recognize in the store, increase the likelihood that consumers will remember it and be better able to process it when making a purchasing decision,[50] and increase consumers' confidence in the brand.[51] Also, as you have seen, repetition can make claims more believable (the truth effect)—an effect that gets even stronger when ads are spaced out over time.[52] TV commercials that air within the context of similar programming (i.e., humorous ads aired during comedy shows) are more likable and better understood by consumers expending low-processing effort.[53] Similarly, ads that fit into the context of the magazines where they appear elicit more positive feelings and are better remembered than ads not in tune with magazine context.[54]

6-5   Affective Bases of Attitudes When Consumer Effort Is Low

The establishment of low-level beliefs based on peripheral cues is not the only way that consumers can form attitudes about brands with little effort. Attitudes can also be based on consumers' affective or emotional reactions to these easily processed peripheral cues. These low-effort affective processes may be due to (1) the mere exposure effect, (2) classical and evaluative conditioning, (3) attitude toward the ad (A_{ad}), and (4) consumer mood.

6-5a   THE MERE EXPOSURE EFFECT

According to the **mere exposure effect**, we tend to prefer familiar objects to unfamiliar ones.[55] Therefore, our attitudes toward an offering such as a new style of clothing should change as we become more and more familiar with it, regardless of whether we perform any deep cognitive analysis of it. The mere exposure effect may explain why many of the top brands in the 1930s are still among the top today. It also explains why the music industry likes to have recordings featured on the radio, TV, and YouTube. Through repeated exposure, consumers become familiar with the music and come to like it.

Because most demonstrations of the mere exposure effect have occurred in tightly controlled laboratory studies, some experts question whether it generalizes to the real world.[56] It is also possible that repeated exposure reduces uncertainty about the stimulus or increases consumers' opportunity to process it[57] and that these factors (rather than mere familiarity) are what affect consumers' attitudes. However, research shows that mere exposure can help an unknown brand compete against other unknown brands if product performance characteristics are equivalent and consumers invest little processing effort at the time of brand choice.[58] Also, when consumers can easily process the information from a stimulus to which they have been exposed in the past, they mistakenly believe that the ease in processing is due to liking, truth, or acceptability.[59]

Marketing Implications

If the mere exposure effect is valid, marketers may be able to enhance consumers' liking of a new product or service by repeatedly exposing consumers to the offering or messages about it. Research suggests that when consumers' MAO is low, marketers need creative tactics for increasing consumers' exposure to products and messages, perhaps by using the right medium, the right placement within the medium, optimal shelf placement, and sampling.

Consistent with the mere exposure effect, some smaller companies are embarking on marketing campaigns to create brand-name familiarity and liking, which are especially important for new brands. For instance, GoldieBlox, which makes construction toys and books for girls, is a fast-growing small business with a small marketing budget. The company has been building its brand and stimulating demand for its products by releasing videos and commercials that go viral and generate lots of buzz on social media.[60]

Some companies pay to have their logos displayed at sporting events, knowing that there will be repeated exposures as race cars go around the track or players move around the field. However, repeated exposures will build familiarity and liking only up to a point.[61] After this, consumers typically experience **wearout,** which means they become bored with the stimulus, and brand attitudes can actually become negative.[62] In fact, once a persuasive ad has effectively reached the targeted consumer segment, wearout causes a loss of persuasiveness.[63] Interestingly, although consumers are irritated by repeated direct mail requests for contributions to charities, their attitude and behavior toward the charities is not negatively affected, perhaps because charities are viewed differently than businesses.[64]

Research shows that when consumers are familiar with a brand, wearout may occur later.[65] Also, the use of rational arguments to promote a well-known brand in a mature

product category tends to be less effective than the use of affectively based tactics because consumers have been exposed to the product information many times before.[66] Still, in low-effort processing situations, brand evaluations do not suffer when consumers are repeatedly exposed to messages about product features.[67]

Marketers can overcome wearout by creating different executions for the same message or variants on the same offering; this is the reason why many advertisers develop a series of ads rather than a single execution.[68] The goal is to get the same message across in many different ways, as Ireland's official tourism agency is doing by creating a three-year multimedia campaign featuring numerous iconic sights such as the Ring of Kerry.[69] The mere exposure effect may not be the only reason that repetition affects brand attitudes. When repetition allows consumers greater opportunity to process information about specific aspects of the brand and the ways that it relates to other brands in the category, brand attitudes improve.[70]

6-5b CLASSICAL AND EVALUATIVE CONDITIONING

One way of influencing attitudes based on low effort is **classical conditioning**, producing a response to a stimulus by repeatedly pairing it with another stimulus that automatically produces this response. Classical conditioning became well known from a study in the 1900s by the Russian scientist Ivan Pavlov. Normally, hungry dogs will salivate automatically just at the sight of food. Pavlov discovered that he could condition hungry dogs to salivate at the sound of a bell. How did he do that?

According to Pavlov, the food was an *unconditioned stimulus (UCS)*, and the salivation response to the food was an *unconditioned response (UCR)* (see the top half of Exhibit 6.4). A stimulus is unconditioned when it automatically elicits an involuntary response. In this situation, the dogs automatically salivated when they saw meat powder. In contrast, a *conditioned stimulus (CS)* is something that does not automatically elicit an involuntary response by itself. Until Pavlov rang the bell at the same time that the food was presented, the bell alone could not make the dogs salivate. By repeatedly pairing the CS (the bell) with the UCS (the meat powder), the involuntary UCR (salivation) was created. The dogs associated the food and the bell so closely that eventually just the ringing bell made them salivate. Because the response could now be evoked in the presence of the CS, the response was said to be a *conditioned response (CR)*. (This is the same phenomenon that makes cats come running when they hear the can opener.)

Wearout Becoming bored with a stimulus.

Classical conditioning Producing a response to a stimulus by repeatedly pairing it with another stimulus that automatically produces this response.

Exhibit 6.4 ▶ Classical and Evaluative Conditioning

In classical conditioning (top), an unconditioned stimulus, or UCS (e.g., food), will automatically produce an unconditioned physiological response, or UCR (e.g., salivation). By repeatedly pairing the UCS with a conditioned stimulus, or CS (e.g., a bell), the CS can be conditioned to produce the same response, a conditioned response, or CR (e.g., salivation). In evaluative conditioning (bottom), a special case of classical conditioning, the UCS may be a pleasant scene and the CS a soft drink. Here, repeatedly pairing the UCS and the CS results in a CR of positive affect, rather than a physiological response. Can you think of any other situations in which this process occurs?

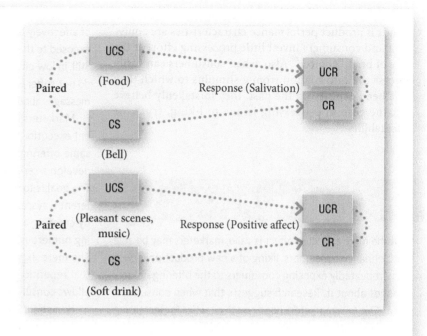

Evaluative conditioning is a special case of classical conditioning that produces an affective response by repeatedly pairing a neutral *CS* (such as a brand) and an emotionally charged *UCS* (such as a well-liked celebrity).[71] This process is shown in the bottom half of Exhibit 6.4. Here, the goal is not to encourage a physiological behavior (salivating, as in Pavlov's classical conditioning) but to encourage a psychological one (positive feeling toward or preference for the CS).

Certain unconditioned stimuli (such as a happy scene or a catchy jingle) automatically elicit an UCR such as joy. By repeatedly pairing one of these unconditioned stimuli with a CS such as a brand name, marketers may be able to evoke the same emotional response (now the CR) to the CS—that is, the brand name itself. Similarly, consumers might be conditioned to have a *negative* emotional response to an offering such as cigarettes if ads or package labels repeatedly show the product with stimuli that elicit a negative emotional response (such as pictures of badly stained teeth or diseased lungs). This is why some countries require graphic warning labels on cigarette packages, and research shows that these warnings have been effective in encouraging smokers to quit in Brazil, Thailand, and several other nations.[72]

> **Evaluative conditioning** A special case of classical conditioning, producing an affective response by repeatedly pairing a neutral conditioned stimulus with an emotionally charged unconditioned stimulus.

of either pleasant or unpleasant music. Subjects who heard pleasant music selected the pen they viewed with that music 79 percent of the time, whereas only 30 percent of those who heard the unpleasant music selected the pen they had viewed.[73] Although these findings could be interpreted in different ways (subjects may have done what they thought the experimenter wanted them to do, or the music may have put the consumers in a better mood),[74] more recent, tightly controlled studies have found support for classical and evaluative conditioning. For example, by using unconditioned stimuli such as *Star Wars* music and pleasing pictures, experimenters have affected consumers' attitudes toward such conditioned stimuli as geometric figures, colas, and toothpaste.[75] Research also shows that attitudes created by classical conditioning can be fairly enduring over time.[76] Brand attitudes influenced by evaluative conditioning are fairly enduring as well, especially when different affective unconditioned stimuli are paired with the CS (the brand).[77] Finally, when consumers have limited or depleted attentional resources, they may not make the connection between the CS and the UCS, which in turn can impair the evaluative conditioning response.[78]

Overall, research suggests that conditioning is most likely to occur under the following circumstances:

▶ The conditioned stimuli–unconditioned stimuli link is relatively novel or unknown. This is the reason why

 Marketing Implications

In one of the first consumer studies to demonstrate classical/evaluative conditioning, subjects viewed a slide of a blue or beige pen matched with a one-minute segment

marketers often use unique visuals, such as pictures of beautiful scenery, exciting situations, or pleasing objects, as unconditioned stimuli to create positive feelings.

▸ The CS precedes the unconditioned stimulus (*forward conditioning*). Conditioning is weaker when the UCS is presented first (*backward conditioning*) or at the same time as the conditioned stimulus (*concurrent conditioning*).

▸ The CS is paired consistently with the UCS.

▸ The consumer is aware of the link between the conditioned and unconditioned stimuli.

▸ A logical fit exists between the conditioned and unconditioned stimuli, such as between NBA star Stephen Curry and the brand he endorses, Under Armour.[79]

Interestingly, the first condition can cause problems for marketers because unconditioned stimuli are often well-known celebrities, music, or visuals for which consumers possess many associations. This finding might suggest that using highly visible celebrities is not as effective a strategy for creating a classical conditioning effect. Other research indicates that the problem can be overcome by using highly familiar stimuli such as popular personalities because they elicit very strong feelings. Some marketers do not shy away from endorsers associated with multiple brands. Bollywood actress Kareena Kapoor endorses more than a dozen brands in India, yet Unilever's Magnum ice-cream brand recently signed her as its spokesperson because of Kapoor's popularity.[80]

Another area of investigation is how choices are affected when consumers are exposed to a stimulus (such as a product message) that activates attitudes without conscious thought. One study found that consumers are likely to rely on their unconscious, conditioned attitudes in situations where they have not explicitly evaluated product attribute information—even when they have both motivation and opportunity to retrieve product information from memory.[81] Even now, researchers are investigating these issues in more detail to understand the mechanisms that trigger response and their short- and long-term effects.

6-5c ATTITUDE TOWARD THE AD

Another concept that has been useful in understanding the affective bases of attitudes in low-effort situations is the consumer's attitude toward the ad (A_{ad}). Sometimes consumers like an ad so much that they transfer their

positive feelings from the ad to the brand.[82] Thus, you may decide that you really like Frito-Lay snacks because the company's ads or YouTube videos are humorous.

One study found that consumers' beliefs or knowledge about the brand did not fully account for brand attitudes and that A_{ad} provided a significant additional explanation—brands with liked ads were evaluated more favorably.[83] Furthermore, research in India, Greece, Denmark, New Zealand, and the United States revealed that the A_{ad} principle was globally applicable.[84] An Advertising Research Foundation project suggests that consumers' attitudes toward ads may be the best indicator of advertising effectiveness.[85]

Dual-mediation hypothesis Explains how attitudes toward the ad influence brand attitudes.

The **dual-mediation hypothesis** is a somewhat more complex explanation of the relationship between consumers' liking of an ad and brand attitude (see Exhibit 6.5).[86] According to this hypothesis, consumers can have a favorable attitude toward an ad either because they find it believable or because they feel good about it. Thus, the dual-mediation hypothesis proposes that A_{ad} can affect attitudes toward the brand (A_b) either through believability or liking. These responses, in turn, may positively affect consumers' intentions to purchase (I_b).

 Marketing Implications

Based on attitude-toward-the-ad theory, marketers may be able to make consumers' A_b more positive by providing ads that please consumers. Thus, by using techniques such as humor, music, pleasant pictures, and sex (all of which will be discussed in more detail shortly), marketers can encourage positive attitudes toward the ad. Kellogg's, for instance, has aired emotion-evoking commercials online and on TV for Frosted Flakes, showing fathers and sons playing sports and then sitting down for a bowl of cereal together, with the tagline: "Share what you love with who you love."[87]

In addition, the effect of ad attitudes on A_b may depend on whether consumers already have a strong attitude toward the brand. When brands are well known and attitudes about them have been formed, consumers may not like the brand more just because they like the ad. However, when brands are new or not well known, consumers' liking of the ad can play a more significant role in their liking of the brand.[88] Studies also suggest that the effect of A_{ad} on attitude toward the brand dissipates over time.[89] As memory of the ad fades, liking of the ad and the brand becomes weaker.

Exhibit 6.5 ▶ The Dual-Mediation Hypothesis

This hypothesis explains how attitudes toward the ad (A_{ad}) can influence attitudes toward the brand (A_b) and intentions (I_b). When you read an ad, you can have responses (C_{ad}) that are both cognitive (this ad has information about a brand) and affective (positive feelings from finding the ad). These responses may cause you to like the ad (A_{ad}), a reaction that can then either (1) make you more accepting of brand beliefs (C_b), leading to a more positive brand attitude (A_b); or (2) give you positive feelings that transfer over to the brand (I like the ad, so I like the brand). Both processes lead to an increase in intention to purchase.

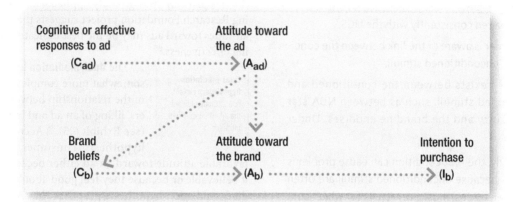

6-5d MOOD

Affective attitudes can also be influenced by the consumer's mood. Here, a stimulus creates a positive or a negative mood; in turn, this mood can affect the consumer's reactions to any other stimulus they happen to evaluate. Thus, we are more likely to say that we like something if we are in a good mood or say that we dislike something if we are in a bad mood. Mood can therefore bias attitudes in a *mood-congruent direction*. Note that mood is different from classical conditioning because mood (1) does not require a repeated association between two stimuli; and (2) can affect consumers' evaluations of any object, not just the stimulus.

According to one study, consumers in a good mood who have a tentative preference for a certain brand tend to ignore negative information about that brand as well as information about a competitor.[90] Another study found that although consumers tend to like a brand extension less when the product is not very similar to the parent product, consumers in a good mood are more likely to like a brand extension that is moderately similar to the parent product than consumers who are not in a good mood.[91] A good mood can act as a resource by increasing elaboration and helping consumers think creatively and see relationships among brands. Specific emotions, not just a general good or bad mood, can also influence attitudes when MAO is low, as long as the emotions are consistent with the consumer's goals.[92]

Moreover, consumers in a good mood tend to give more weight to positive information when evaluating a product, whereas consumers in a bad mood give more weight to negative information.[93] Mood affects compliance with marketing communications, as well. In the case of hedonic products, or utilitarian products being marketed hedonically, assertive advertising language, such as Nike's "Just do it" is more effective in encouraging compliance when consumers are in a good mood.[94] Interestingly, consumers will have more positive attitudes toward a brand if it is present during an experience that provokes fear, because the brand "shared" in that experience.[95]

Consumers may like a brand better when they are put in a good mood by its ads or the programs in which the ads appear. Research has focused on the kinds of emotions or moods that ads invoke and the variety of ways these factors might affect consumers' A_b.[96] One study identified three major categories of affective responses: (1) *SEVA* (surgency, elation, vigor, and activation), which is present when the communication puts the consumer in an upbeat or happy mood; (2) *deactivation feelings*, which include soothing, relaxing, quiet, or pleasant responses; and (3) *social affection*, which are feelings of warmth, tenderness, and caring.[97] Another study found that ad-induced feelings of warmth and humor could have a direct and positive impact on A_b.[98] Thus, when ads for Huggies disposable diapers picture tender moments between babies and parents, they may also generate positive feelings for the brand.

Marketing Implications

On the assumption that mood affects consumer behavior, retailers can use physical surroundings and the behavior of store employees to put consumers in a good mood. Warm colors such as red and orange tend to be more stimulating and exciting, whereas cool colors such as blue, green, and violet tend to be more soothing.[99] Warm colors are more likely to draw customers to an outlet but can also create tension, whereas cool colors are more relaxing but do not attract customers.[100] Therefore, when the goal is to stimulate quick purchases or activity, warm colors are more appropriate, a situation that explains why Target and Costco stores use a red-based color scheme. Warm colors are also appropriate for health clubs, sports stadiums, and fast-food restaurants, where a high level of activity and energy is desirable. Cool colors are more appropriate when the goal is to have consumers feel calm or spend time deliberating. For instance, Apple's modernistic stores are decorated in white, black, tan, and grey, with touches of natural wood and greenery, to provide a clean, uncluttered environment for showcasing high-tech products to shoppers.[101]

Researchers examining how lighting influences mood have found that brighter in-store lighting tends to increase the extent to which shoppers examine and handle merchandise.[102] Brighter lighting does not, however, increase the amount of time consumers spend shopping or the number of purchases they make. A salesperson's mood can influence consumers as well. Consumers in a bad mood are likely to feel worse and downgrade their judgments of the product being sold when they interact with salespeople who seem to be unhappy (unless the decision is so important that they are motivated to shake off their bad mood).[103]

6-6 How Affective Attitudes Are Influenced

When consumers apply little processing effort and form attitudes based on feelings, the same three factors that influence cognitive reasoning also influence affective attitudes: the communication source, the message, and the context. Again, these factors are based on low-effort processes such as mere exposure, classical conditioning, A_{ad}, and mood.

6-6a COMMUNICATION SOURCE

Under conditions of low effort, two factors play a major role in determining whether or not the communication source evokes favorable affective reactions: its physical attractiveness and its likability. These two factors help to explain why marketers like to feature celebrities in ads.

Attractive Sources

Many ads feature attractive models, spokespersons, or celebrities, reflecting the long-held belief that beauty sells—especially in the beauty business. Research studies in a number of nations generally support this notion. One study in Romania found that attractive models in beauty ads stimulated positive ad and product evaluations, but mixed self-judgments. Yet, after a two-week trial of a product advertised by attractive models, these consumers experienced positive self-judgments.[104] When consumers' motivation to process an advertised message is low, attractive sources enhance the favorability of consumers' A_b regardless of whether the message arguments are strong or weak.[105] Consumers also rate ads with attractive models as more appealing, eye-catching, and interesting than ads with unattractive models. These ratings may affect consumers' attitudes toward the products these models sponsor.[106]

Moreover, attractiveness can have beneficial effects on advertiser believability and actual purchase.[107] These effects can occur for both male and female models (consumers are more strongly attracted to models of the opposite sex) and have been found to operate for direct-mail responses, point-of-purchase displays, and personal-selling interactions.[108] Race may be an important factor as well.[109] One study showed that African American consumers who identified strongly with African American culture responded more favorably to ads with African American models. Attractive sources make a difference in personal selling too. In one study, consumers had more positive attitudes and stronger buying intentions when attractive salespeople tried to persuade than when unattractive salespeople were involved.[110]

Note that in the context of high affective involvement, attractive sources directly influence brand-based attitudes because the sources are directly relevant to the product being considered (perfume, fashion, lingerie, etc.) and are thus a central part of the message. In the context of low-effort processing, attractive sources serve as a peripheral cue used to increase situational involvement and to generate a positive A_{ad}.

Likable Sources

The likability of the source can influence affective attitudes.[111] For instance, L'Oreal has found YouTube makeup star Michelle Phan to be a likable and attractive endorser of beauty products because of her personality, enthusiasm,

Un simple viaje puede cambiar el curso de una vida.
Camboya, Mayo de 2011.

Acompañe a Angelina Jolie en lpelouittanourney.com

LOUIS VUITTON

Image Courtesy of The Advertising Archives

Exhibit 6.6 ▶ Influence of Communication Source

Companies use popular movie stars or celebrities like Angelina Jolie to generate positive feelings toward the ad and the product.

and popularity.[112] Consumers also have more favorable attitudes toward brands that use likable celebrity voice-overs.[113] Likable sources may serve as unconditioned stimuli, create a positive mood that affects consumers' evaluations of the ad or brand, and make consumers feel more positive about the endorsed product. Online ads in which consumers assume an avatar to interact virtually with the product can lead to more positive A_b and purchase intentions because consumers feel positive about the endorser (themselves).[114] Sometimes, the source can be physically unattractive but have features or a personality that consumers like. We tend to like people of average looks because they are more similar to ourselves and we can relate to them. In addition, people with disabilities are effective, likable models in catalog photos and online ads for the Nordstrom retail chain because marketers want to represent diversity and because consumers admire courageous individuals.[115]

Celebrity Sources

Physical attractiveness and likability explain why celebrities and well-known cartoon characters are among the

most widely used sources. In this case, the presence of celebrities essentially increases the likelihood that consumers will like the ad (A_{ad}). In particular, celebrity sources can be effective when they are related to the offering (the match-up hypothesis).[116] Teenage consumers find athletes to be especially influential endorsers: The sports stars stimulate discussion about the brand and encourage brand loyalty.[117]

Spokescharacters of long tenure sometimes need makeovers to remain attractive to contemporary eyes. That's why Planters, a Kraft Foods brand, gave its Mr. Peanut character a retro look for nostalgic appeal and, later, hired comedian Bill Hader when it revamped the character's voice.[118] Spokescharacters may engender trust even if they are not directly relevant to the advertised product; trust, in turn, influences A_b.[119] Spokescharacters may be most effective in ads for hedonic services such as restaurants.[120]

Nonprofit organizations also use celebrities to attract attention and influence attitudes. Tennis champion Novak Djokovic and other celebrity endorsers for UNICEF "are of huge value," says the nonprofit's head of celebrity relations. "When a celebrity talks, people listen; there is no better messenger."[121] Using a celebrity endorser entails some risk because the spokesperson might become ill, break the law, or have another problem that could put the brand in a negative light. Yet research shows that a company can actually enhance its reputation by associating with an endorser who is perceived by consumers as having little blame for a problem (such as falling ill).[122] Finally, when MAO is low, consumers like a brand less when it features a celebrity endorser who also endorses lots of other products.[123]

6-6b THE MESSAGE

Just as the source can influence consumers' feelings and moods, so too can characteristics associated with the message. Even the placement of visual images in an ad can have an effect on whether a brand is perceived as friendly or a leader.[124]

Message characteristics that influence feelings in low-effort processing situations include pleasant pictures, music, humor, sex, emotional content, and context.

Pleasant Pictures

Marketers frequently use pleasant pictures to influence consumers' message processing. Visual stimuli can serve as a CS, affect consumers' mood, or make an ad likable by making it interesting. Research has generally supported the view that pleasant pictures can affect ad and A_b when they are processed peripherally, beyond the effect they have on consumers' beliefs about the product.[125] A picture of a sunset, for instance, can influence the choice of a soft drink.[126] As another example, because consumers associate visual art with luxury, the luxury image carries over to ads and packages featuring art.[127] Many advertisers use high-powered special effects rivaling those seen in movies for their TV and online ads. In fact, video ads are now the fastest-growing category of online advertising.[128]

Music

Music is frequently used as a communications tool by many domestic and international companies, including South Korea's Kia Motors, which has used LMFAO's *Rock Party Anthem* to advertise its Soul model in America.[129] Further, the use of music is progressing beyond the traditional use of the "jingle." Sometimes, the music ads become popular and drive album sales, as was the case with U2, whose album *How to Dismantle an Atomic Bomb* became a huge hit after the song "Vertigo" was featured in an iPod TV commercial.[130]

The popularity of music as a marketing device should not be surprising given that music has been shown to stimulate a variety of positive effects.[131] First, music can be an effective CS for a classical conditioning strategy. NBC and other brands use musical "tags" to serve as retrieval cues and add to the brand identity. Second, music can put the consumer in a positive mood and lead to the development of positive attitudes. Third, music can be effective in generating positive feelings such as happiness, serenity, excitement, and sentimentality. Fourth, background music in ads can stimulate emotional memories of experiences or situations.[132] If a song in an ad reminds you of your high school days or of an old romance, the emotions associated with these memories may transfer to an ad, a brand, a store, or other attitude object. Several studies have found that music can have a positive effect on purchase intentions.[133] However, reaction to music can depend on consumers' mood. Consumers who are sad or frustrated prefer music that matches their mood, especially when their negative feelings are due to relationship problems.[134]

Exhibit 6.7 shows several musical characteristics and the emotional responses they may elicit. Whether or not music evokes a positive affective response depends on the music's structure. The style of music used and the product meanings it conveys can vary considerably across different cultures.[135] Marketers must therefore be careful to match their music to the desired affective responses.

Humor

An ad can use humor in many different ways, including puns, understatements, jokes, ludicrous situations, satire, and irony. Humor is common in TV advertising: 24 to 42 percent of all commercials contain some form of humor.[136] Although not as widespread in other traditional media as in TV, the use of humor is nevertheless extensive, particularly in radio.[137] The popularity of humor as a message device is not surprising because it works, increasing consumers' liking of the ad and the brand (see Exhibit 6.8).[138]

Humor appears to be more appropriate for low-involvement offerings in which generating positive feelings about the ad is critical.[139] Unless humor is tied or related

				Emotional Expression						
Musical Element	**Serious**	**Sad**	**Sentimental**	**Serene**	**Humorous**	**Happy**	**Exciting**	**Majestic**	**Frightening**
MODE	Major	Minor	Minor	Major	Major	Major	Major	Major	Minor
TEMPO	Slow	Slow	Slow	Slow	Fast	Fast	Fast	Medium	Slow
PITCH	Low	Low	Medium	Medium	High	High	Medium	Medium	Low
RHYTHM	Firm	Firm	Flowing	Flowing	Flowing	Flowing	Uneven	Firm	Uneven
HARMONY	Consonant	Dissonant	Consonant	Consonant	Consonant	Consonant	Dissonant	Dissonant	Dissonant
VOLUME	Medium	Soft	Soft	Soft	Medium	Medium	Loud	Loud	Varied

Source: Gordon C. Bruner, "Music, Mood, and Marketing," *Journal of Marketing,* October 1990, p. 100. Reprinted by permission.

Exhibit 6.7 ▶ Musical Characteristics for Producing Various Emotional Expressions

Research has pinpointed the specific effect that various aspects of music can have on feelings. As shown here, the mode, tempo, pitch, rhythm, harmony, and volume of music can influence whether individuals feel serious, sad, sentimental, serene, humorous, happy, excited, majestic, or frightened.

Courtesy of Mars Incorporated

Exhibit 6.8 ▶ Humor in Advertising
Humor is a widely used technique in advertising.

to the offering, however, consumers will only pay attention to the humor and ignore the brand.[140] In fact, consumers will have higher recall of an ad when the humor is strong and relates to the message.[141] Consumers who feel the need to seek out amusement and wittiness will develop more favorable attitudes toward humorous ads—and may have less favorable attitudes toward ads with lower levels of humorous content.[142]

How consumers react during a TV ad affects their evaluations of the message as well. Consumers in one study rated TV ads as more humorous when the ad created surprise followed by a humorous response.[143] TV and online ads depicting comedic violence stimulate greater involvement with the message and greater likability. Although these ads do not affect A_b, they do generate buzz and have high pass-along rates, which is why many Super Bowl ads that feature this type of humor go "viral" and gain widespread Internet exposure.[144]

Marketing Implications

Humor tends to work best on TV and radio because these media allow for greater expressiveness than do other traditional media.[145] For example, Progressive Insurance airs funny commercials featuring "Flo" the salesperson, instead of the serious ads that many car insurance firms favor, in order to give the brand a distinctive and likable personality.[146] However, humor is more effective with certain audiences than with others. In particular, younger, more educated males tend to respond most positively—apparently because

aggressive and sexual types of humor appear more frequently than other types of humor, and men enjoy this type of humor more than women do.[147] Also, humor appears to be more effective for consumers who have either a lower need for cognition or a positive attitude toward the advertised brand.[148]

Finally, humor can be used effectively throughout the world. One study examined humorous ads from Germany, South Korea, Thailand, and the United States and found that most humorous ads in all four countries contained the same basic structure—contrasts between expected/possible and unexpected/impossible events.[149] However, ads in Korea and Thailand tended to emphasize humor related to group behavior and unequal status relationships, whereas ads in the other two countries focused the humor on individuals with equal status. In all four countries, humor was more likely to be used for marketing pleasure-oriented products. In addition, not all countries appear to employ humor more often for low-involvement products than for high-involvement ones. German and Thai ads, for example, used humor equally for both types of products, and U.K. firms tend to use humorous ads more than U.S. firms do.[150] Humor is most common in U.S. ads for foods and beverages. In China, however, humor is most prevalent in consumer electronics ads, while in France, humor is most prevalent in ads for services (see Exhibit 6.9).[151] Finally, research finds that the effect of humor varies from culture to culture, depending on the way humor is employed in the ad and the cultural orientation of the consumer.[152]

Sex

Sex as a communication technique appears in two major forms: sexual suggestiveness and nudity. Sexual suggestiveness involves situations that either portray or imply sexual themes or romance. Another use of sex is through nudity or partial nudity, a technique often used by brands in the fragrance industry.[153] Research shows that consumers prefer mildly provocative ads and that such ads can even be effective in promoting social causes that have some connection to sex (match-up hypothesis).[154] Men tend to have a generally positive attitude toward an ad with sexual cues. Women, however, tend to dislike such ads but soften their attitudes when relationship commitment is involved.[155] Further, men who are exposed to sexual cues in ads exhibit more impulsive behavior and are more likely to buy or consume right away rather than waiting.[156]

Country	Product Categories
United States	1. Food and beverages
	2. Automobiles
	3. Services
	4. Medicine
	5. Beauty and personal care
China	1. Consumer electronics
	2. Automobiles
	3. Services
	4. Household appliances
	5. Beauty and personal care
France	1. Services
	2. Food and beverages
	3. Automobiles
	4. Household appliances
	5. Consumer electronics

Source: Adapted from Michel Laroche, Marcelo Vinhal Nepomuceno, Liang Huang, and Marie-Odile Richard, "What's So Funny?" *Journal of Advertising Research* 51, no. 2, 2011: Table 4, p. 409.

Exhibit 6.9 ▶ Humor in U.S., Chinese, and French Advertising: Top Five Product Categories

Although the percentage of ads with sexual overtones has not changed over the years, the type of sex appeal depicted has. From 1964 to 1984, the use of sex in the United States became more overt and blatant.[157] As the country became more conservative in the late 1980s, ads became more playful and subtler—suggestive rather than blunt.[158] In recent years, public response and regulatory scrutiny have prompted some advertisers to tone down their use of sexual references and imagery in traditional advertising. At the same time, some advertisers (like Go Daddy, the Internet hosting service) have used the strategy of airing a slightly risqué TV commercial as a teaser, to attract viewers for a sexier ad posted directly on the brand website. Although the sexy ads significantly boosted brand awareness, Go Daddy stopped using this technique because of the controversy, and because the company wanted to do more marketing to women who own small businesses.[159]

Marketing Implications

Research on sexual themes in messages suggests that they can be effective in several ways. Sexual messages attract the consumer's attention[160] and can evoke emotional responses such as arousal, excitement, or even lust, which in turn can affect consumers' moods and their attitudes toward the ad and the brand.[161] Funny ads featuring sexy women drawn to men wearing Axe brand body spray have been quite effective for Unilever.[162]

For some consumers, however, sexual messages can create negative feelings such as embarrassment, disgust, or uneasiness, any of which would have a negative effect. In particular, women are more likely to react negatively to ads with sexy female models.[163] Men are much more likely than women to buy a product featured in an ad with sexual content. Yet, 61 percent of the respondents in one study said they would be less likely to buy products advertised with sexual imagery. In this research, 53 percent of the respondents preferred love imagery over sex imagery in advertising.[164]

One survey indicated that 84 percent of females and 72 percent of males believe that TV ads place too much emphasis on sex. In another survey, 49 percent said they have been embarrassed in front of friends or family by sexy TV ads, and 47 percent indicated they would not buy a product if they found an ad offensive.[165] The lesson for marketers is that sexual themes should be used carefully and not be demeaning, sexist, or offensive.

Whether consumers will have a positive or negative reaction to a sexual ad often depends on whether the sexual content is appropriate for the product/service. One study found that using a seductive model to sell body oil was very appealing, but having a nude model endorse a ratchet set was not.[166] Thus, sexual themes would be relevant for products such as perfume, cologne, suntan lotion, and lingerie but inappropriate for tools, computers, and household cleaners.

Finally, consumer reaction to sexual messages varies from culture to culture. In some societies, such as in Europe, sexual attitudes are fairly open, and the use of sex in advertising is more widespread than it is in other countries. German and Thai TV commercials typically show more nudity than U.S. and Chinese commercials, for example.[167] In areas where attitudes are more conservative (such as Muslim and some Asian countries), the use of sex is much more restricted. Showing intimacy and kissing, as many U.S. ads do, would be inappropriate and even offensive in these cultures. Consumers in different countries reacted differently to a public service ad for breast cancer awareness in which men admired an attractive woman wearing a sun-dress while an announcer stated, "If only women paid as much attention to their breasts as men do." Japanese consumers appreciated the humor, but French consumers disliked the sexual overtones and light treatment of a serious problem.[168]

Dramas Ads with characters, a plot, and a story.

Emotional Content

Marketers can plan communications to accommodate or enhance consumers' existing MAO and processing effort in the presence of cognitive attitudes. The same holds true for affective attitudes, which is where emotionally involving messages come into play. Note that emotional appeals can be concrete (linked to a specific experience or emotion, such as the joy of winning a race) or abstract (less specific, such as feeling hopeful). Concrete emotional appeals are more effective in stimulating short-term behavioral intentions, whereas abstract emotional appeals are more effective in stimulating long-term intentions.[169]

One special type of emotional message is called **transformational advertising**.[170] The goal of a transformational ad is to associate the experience of using the product with a unique set of psychological characteristics. These ads try to increase emotional involvement by making the use of the product or service a warmer, more exciting, more pleasing, and richer experience as opposed to the approach taken by informational ads, which only present factual information. Coca-Cola, for example, uses transformational advertising to convey that "Coke is a part of the pleasure of everyday life, the pleasure of aliveness, relaxation, and being connected," says the company's chief marketing officer. When Coca-Cola launched its #ShareaCoke campaign on Twitter, consumers who tweeted with

Transformational advertising Ads that try to increase emotional involvement with the product or service.

that hashtag saw a custom emoji of two Coke bottles clinking as a toast, evoking the positive feelings of sharing with a friend.[171]

Dramas can also increase emotional involvement in a message. A drama message has characters, a plot, and a story about the use of the product or service.[172] The aim is to involve consumers emotionally and influence positive attitudes through both sympathy and empathy.[173] For instance, South Korean cosmetics marketer Innisfree recently created two mini-drama commercials starring film actor Lee Min-ho and pop singer Im Yoona to promote its face makeup. One ran for four minutes, the other ran for six minutes, allowing enough time for YouTube viewers to become engaged in the possible on-screen romance between these two well-known celebrities.[174]

Message Context

The program or editorial context in which an ad appears can affect consumers' evaluation of the message. First, ads embedded in a happy TV program may be evaluated more positively than those in sad programs, especially if the ads are emotional.[175] Similarly, how well we like the program can affect our feelings about the ad and the brand.[176] One explanation of this reaction is that the programs influence us to process information in a manner consistent with our mood. Or, according to the excitation transfer hypothesis, we may mistakenly attribute to the ad our feelings about the TV program.[177]

One note of caution: A TV program can become too arousing and can therefore distract viewers from the ads. In an interesting study that compared consumers' reactions to ads broadcast during the Super Bowl, ad responses in the winning city were inhibited in contrast to those in the losing and neutral cities.[178] Another study shows that placing ads in violent programs can inhibit processing and ad recall.[179]

Summary:

Marketers can use a variety of techniques to change consumers' attitudes when motivation, ability, and opportunity (MAO) are low and consumers use little effort to process information, make decisions, or engage in behavior. Often consumers form attitudes unconsciously, without being aware of how or why they have done so. Two unconscious influences in low-effort situations are thin-slice judgments and body feedback. When attitudes of low MAO consumers are based on cognitive processing, the message should affect their beliefs, which may be formed by simple inferences, attributions, or heuristics. Marketers can also affect the salience, strength, or favorability of consumers' beliefs on which attitudes are based. Source credibility, information consistent with the offering category, the number of message arguments, simple arguments, and repetition can all influence beliefs.

According to the mere exposure effect, when effort (MAO) is low, consumers' attitudes toward an offering become more favorable as consumers become more familiar with it. Classical conditioning predicts that consumers' attitudes toward an offering (the conditioned stimulus) are enhanced when it is repeatedly paired with a stimulus (the unconditioned stimulus) that evokes a positive response (the unconditioned response). Evaluative conditioning, a special case of classical conditioning, produces an emotional response (positive or negative) by repeatedly pairing a conditioned stimulus and an emotionally charged unconditioned stimulus. Attitude toward the ad is also a factor: If consumers like an ad, these positive feelings may be transferred to the brand. Consumers' moods and their tendency to evaluate an offering in accordance with their moods can also affect their attitudes.

Finally, marketers can use marketing communications to induce favorable attitudes based on affective processes when consumers' motivation, ability, opportunity, and effort are low. Characteristics of the source (attractiveness, likability), the message (attractive pictures, pleasant music, humor, sex, emotionally involving messages), and the context (repetition, program or editorial context) can all influence affective attitudes.

Questions for Review and Discussion

1. How can unconscious influences affect consumer attitudes and behavior in low-effort situations?

2. What role do source, message, context, and repetition play in influencing consumers' cognitive attitudes in low-effort situations?

3. What is the mere exposure effect, and why is it important to consumers' affective reactions?

4. How do classical conditioning and evaluative conditioning apply to consumers' attitudes when processing effort is low?

5. Explain the dual-mediation hypothesis. What are the implications for affecting consumers' brand attitudes?

6. In low-effort situations, what characteristics of the message influence consumers' affective response?

7. What are the advantages and disadvantages of featuring celebrities in advertising messages?

Endnotes

1 Lauren Johnson, "How Lay's Is Adding More Social Zest to Its Popular Flavor-Creation Campaign," *Adweek*, February 27, 2015, www.adweek.com.

2 Norbert Schwarz, "Attitude Research: Between Ockham's Razor and the Fundamental Attribution Error," *Journal of Consumer Research* 33, no. 1, 2006, pp. 19–21.

3 Richard E. Petty and John T. Cacioppo, *Attitudes and Persuasion: Classic and Contemporary Approaches* (Dubuque, IA: William C. Brown, 1981); and Richard E. Petty, John T. Cacioppo, and David Schumann, "Central and Peripheral Routes to Advertising Effectiveness: The Moderating Role of Involvement," *Journal of Consumer Research*, September 1983, pp. 135–146.

4 Jaideep Sengupta, Ronald C. Goodstein, and David S. Boninger, "All Cues Are Not Created Equal: Obtaining Attitude Persistence under Low Involvement Conditions," *Journal of Consumer Research*, March 1997, pp. 315–361.

5 Ap Dijksterhuis, Pamela K. Smith, Rick B. Van Baaren, and Daniel H. J. Wigboldus, "The Unconscious Consumer: Effects of Environment on Consumer Behavior," *Journal of Consumer Psychology* 15, no. 3, 2005, pp. 193–202.

6 Minjung Koo and Ayelet Fishbach, "A Silver Lining of Standing in Line," *Journal of Marketing Research*, August 2010, pp. 713–724.

7   Nalini Ambady, Mar y Ann Krabbenhoft, and Daniel Hogan, "The 30-Sec Sale: Using Thin-Slice Judgments to Evaluate Sales Effectiveness," *Journal of Consumer Psychology* 16, no. 1, 2006, pp. 4–13.

8   Jan R. Landwehr, Ann L. McGill, and Andreas Herrmann, "It's Got the Look: The Effect of Friendly and Aggressive 'Facial' Expressions on Product Liking and Sales," *Journal of Marketing*, May 2011, pp. 132–146.

9   Frank R. Kardes, "When Should Consumers and Managers Trust Their Intuition?" *Journal of Consumer Psychology* 16, no. 1, 2006, pp. 20–24.

10 Jens Förster, "How Body Feedback Influences Consumers' Evaluation of Products," *Journal of Consumer Psychology* 14, no. 4, 2004, pp. 416–426. See also Ronald S. Friedman and Jens Förster, "The Effects of Approach and Avoidance Motor Actions on the Elements of Creative Insight," *Journal of Personality and Social Psychology* 79, no. 4, 2000, pp. 477–492.

11 Iris W. Hung and Aparna A. Labroo, "From Firm Muscles to Firm Willpower," *Journal of Consumer Research*, April 2011, pp. 1046–1064.

12 Bruce Horovitz, "Baby Carrots Take on Junk Food with Hip Marketing Campaign," *USA Today*, September 3, 2010, www.usatoday.com.

13 Itamar Simonson, "In Defense of Consciousness: The Role of Conscious and Unconscious Inputs in Consumer Choice," *Journal of Consumer Psychology* 15, no. 3, 2005, pp. 211–217.

14 Yoree Koh, "Grilles Come First as Mazda Pushes Personality," *Wall Street Journal*, April 25, 2013, www.wsj.com; "Mazda3 Review: What the Auto Press Says," *U.S. News and World Report*, October 19, 2011, http://usnews.rankingsandreviews.com.

15 Boyoun (Grace) Chae, Li Xiuping, and Rui (Juiliet) Zhu, "Judging Product Effectiveness from Perceived Spatial Proximity," *Journal of Consumer Research* 40, no. 2, August 2013, pp. 317–335.

16 Gita V. Johar and Anne L. Roggeveen, "Changing False Beliefs from Repeated Advertising: The Role of Claim-Refutation Alignment," *Journal of Consumer Psychology* 17, no. 2, 2007, pp. 118–127.

17 Jennifer Edson Escalas and Mary Frances Luce, "Understanding the Effects of Process-Focused versus Outcome-Focused Thought in Response to Advertising," *Journal of Consumer Research* 13, no. 2, 2004, pp. 274–285.

18 Ronald C. Goodstein, "Category-Based Applications and Extensions in Advertising: Motivating More Extensive Ad Processing," *Journal of Consumer Research*, June 1993, pp. 87–99.

19 Steven S. Posavac, Michael Herzenstein, Frank R. Kardes, and Suresh Sundaram, "Profits and Halos: The Role of Firm Profitability Information in Consumer Inference," *Journal of Consumer Psychology* 20, no. 3, July 2010, pp. 327–337.

20 Valerie S. Folkes, "Recent Attribution Research in Consumer Behavior: A Review and New Directions," *Journal of Consumer Research*, March 1988, pp. 548–656.

21 Jennie Bell, "Maria Sharapova's US Open Exit: What It Means For Nike," *Footwear News*, August 31, 2015, www.footwearnews.com.

22 Paul M. Connell, Merrie Brucks, and Jesper H. Nielsen, "How Childhood Advertising Exposure Can Create Biased Product Evaluations That Persist into Adulthood," *Journal of Consumer Research* 41, no. 1, June 2014, pp. 119–134.

23 Shelly Chaiken, "Heuristic versus Systematic Information Processing and the Use of Source versus Message Cues in Persuasion," *Journal of Personality and Social Psychology* 39, 1980, pp. 752–766. See also "The Heuristic Model of Persuasion," in eds. Mark P. Zanna, J. M. Olson, and C. P. Herman, *Social Influence: The Ontario Symposium*, vol. 5 (Hillsdale, N.J.: Lawrence Erlbaum, 1987), pp. 3–49.

24 Amna Kirmani, "Advertising Repetition as a Signal of Quality: If It's Advertised So Much, Something Must Be Wrong," *Journal of Advertising*, Fall 1997, pp. 77–86.

25 Joseph W. Alba and Howard Marmorstein, "The Effects of Frequency Knowledge on Consumer Decision Making," *Journal of Consumer Research*, June 1987, pp. 14–25.

26 Scott A. Hawkins and Stephen J. Hoch, "Low-Involvement Learning: Memory without Evaluation," *Journal of Consumer Research*, September 1992, pp. 212–225; and Lynn Hasher, David Goldstein, and Thomas Toppino, "Frequency and the Conference of Referential Validity," *Journal of Verbal Learning and Verbal Behavior*, February 1977, pp. 107–112.

27 S. Ratneshwar and Shelly Chaiken, "Comprehension's Role in Persuasion: The Case of Its Moderating Effect on the Persuasive Impact of Source Cues," *Journal of Consumer Research*, June 1991, pp. 52–62.

28 Ryan Hamilton, Kathleen D. Vohs, and Ann L. McGill, "We'll Be Honest, This Won't Be the Best Article You'll Ever Read: The Use of Dispreferred Markers in Word-of-Mouth Communication," *Journal of Consumer Research* 41, no. 1, June 2014, pp. 197–212.

29 Mathew S. Isaac and Robert M. Schindler, "The Top-Ten Effect: Consumers' Subjective Categorization of Ranked Lists," *Journal of Consumer Research* 40, no. 6, April 2014, pp. 1181–1202.

30 Ray Latif, "Everyone's Looking for the Big Squeeze," *BevNet*, March 2014, www.bevnet.com; and Barry Silverstein, "Kraft Whets Appetites for Flavored Water with Facebook Freebies, Sassy Gay Friend," *BrandChannel*, February 22, 2011, www.brandchannel.com.

31 Alice M. Tybout, Brian Sternthal, Prashant Malaviya, Georgios A. Bakamitsos, and Se-Bum Park, "Information Accessibility as a Moderator of Judgments: The Role of Content versus Retrieval Ease," *Journal of Consumer Research* 32, no. 1, 2005, pp. 76–85.

32 Traci H. Freling and Peter A. Dacin, "When Consensus Counts: Exploring the Impact of Consensus Claims in Advertising," *Journal of Consumer Psychology* 20, no. 2, April 2010, pp. 163–175.

33 Nancy Spears, "On the Use of Time Expressions in Promoting Product Benefits," *Journal of Advertising*, Summer 2003, pp. 33–44.

34 Jennifer Edson Escalas, "Self-Referencing and Persuasion: Narrative Transportation versus Analytical Elaboration," *Journal of Consumer Research* 33, no. 4, 2007, pp. 421–429; and Claudiu V. Dimofte and Richard F. Yalch, "The Role of Frequency of Experience with a Product Category and Temporal Orientation in Self-Referent Advertising," *Journal of Consumer Psychology* 20, no. 3, July 2010, pp. 343–354.

35 Darrel D. Muehling and Vincent J. Pascal, "An Empirical Investigation of the Differential Effects of Personal, Historical, and Non-Nostalgic Advertising on Consumer Responses," *Journal of Advertising*, Summer 2011, pp. 107–122.

36 Aner Sela, S. Christian Wheeler, and Gülen Sarial-Abi, "We Are Not the Same as You and I: Causal Effects of Minor Language Variations on Consumers' Attitudes toward Brands," *Journal of Consumer Research* 39, no. 3, October 2012, pp. 644–661.

37 Daniel J. Howard, Charles Gengler, and Ambuj Jain, "What's in a Name? A Complimentary Means of Persuasion," *Journal of Consumer Research*, September 1995, pp. 200–211.

38 Tim Nudd, "Coca-Cola Brings Back Personalized Bottles, With Four Times as Many Names," *Adweek*, April 14, 2015, www.adweek.com.

39 Jennifer L. Aaker, "The Malleable Self: The Role of Self-Expression in Persuasion," *Journal of Marketing Research* 36, February 1999, pp. 45–57.

40 Anne M. Brumbaugh, "Source and Nonsource Cues in Advertising and Their Effects on the Activation of Cultural and Subcultural Knowledge on the Route to Persuasion," *Journal of Consumer Research*, September 2002, pp. 258–269.

41 Robert E. Burnkrant and Daniel J. Howard, "Effects of the Use of Introductory Rhetorical Questions versus Statements on Information Processing," *Journal of Personality and Social Psychology*, December 1984, pp. 1218–1230; and James M. Munch, Gregory W. Boller, and John L. Swazy, "The Effects of Argument Structure and Affective Tagging on Product Attitude Formation," *Journal of Consumer Research*, September 1993, pp. 294–302.

42 Sarah Perez, "Shutterfly Launches TripPix, A Quick Way To Create Travel Photo Books From Your iPhone," *TechCrunch*, June 10, 2015, www.techcrunch.com.

43 Rohini Ahluwalia and Robert E. Burnkrant, "Answering Questions about Questions: A Persuasion Knowledge Perspective for Understanding the Effects of Rhetorical Questions," *Journal of Consumer Research*, June 2004, pp. 26–42.

44 Russell H. Fazio, Paul M. Herr, and Martha C. Powell, "On the Development and Strength of Category-Brand Associations in Memory: The Case of Mystery Ads," *Journal of Consumer Psychology* 1, no. 1, 1992, pp. 1–14.

45 Liz C. Wang, Julie Baker, Judy A. Wagner, and Kirk Wakefield, "Can a Retail Website Be Social?" *Journal of Marketing*, July 2007, pp. 143–157.

46 Richard Stradling, "NC Lottery Offers Scratch-and-Sniff 'Smoky BBQ' Tickets," *The State (Columbia, S.C.)*, September 13, 2015, www.thestate.com.

47 David A. Griffin and Qimei Chen, "The Influence of Virtual Direct Experience (VDE) on On-Line Ad Message Effectiveness," *Journal of Advertising*, Spring 2004, pp. 55–68.

48 Courtney Crowder, "The Lego Creativity Tour Hits Des Moines," *Des Moines Register*, September 17, 2015, www.desmoinesregister.com; and Hiawatha Bray, "'Advergames' Spark Concerns of Kids Being Targeted," *Boston Globe*, July 30, 2004, www.bostonglobe.com.

49 Joseph W. Alba, J. Wesley Hutchinson, and John G. Lynch, "Memory and Decision Making," in eds. Thomas S. Robertson and Harold H. Kassarjian, *Handbook of Consumer Behavior* (Englewood Cliffs, N.J.: Prentice-Hall, 1991).

50 Chris Janiszewski and Tom Meyvis, "Effects of Brand Logo Complexity, Repetition, and Spacing on Processing Fluency and Judgment," *Journal of Consumer Research*, June 2001, pp. 18–32; and H. Rao Unnava and Robert E. Burnkrant, "Effects of Repeating Varied Ad Executions on Brand Name Memory," *Journal of Marketing Research*, November 1991, pp. 406–416.

51 Ida E. Berger and Andrew A. Mitchell, "The Effect of Attitude Accessibility, Attitude Confidence, and the Attitude–Behavior Relationship," *Journal of Consumer Research*, December 1989, pp. 269–279.

52 Prashant Malaviya and Brian Sternthal, "The Persuasive Impact of Message Spacing," *Journal of Consumer Psychology* 6, no. 3, 1997, pp. 233–256.

53 Patrick De Pelsmacker, Maggie Geuens, and Pascal Anckaert, "Media Context and Advertising Effectiveness: The Role of Context Appreciation and Context/Ad Similarity," *Journal of Advertising*, September 2002, pp. 49–61.

54 Marjolein Moorman, Peter C. Neijens, and Edith G. Smit, "The Effects of Magazine-Induced Psychological Responses and Thematic Congruence on Memory and Attitude toward the Life in a Real-Life Setting," *Journal of Advertising*, Winter 2002, pp. 27–40.

55 See, for instance, Xiang Fang, Surendra Singh, and Rohini Ahluwalia, "An Examination of Different Explanations for the Mere Exposure Effect," *Journal of Consumer Research* 34, no. 1, 2007, pp. 99–103.

56 Carl Obermiller, "Varieties of Mere Exposure: The Effects of Processing Style and Repetition in Affective Response," *Journal of Consumer Research*, June 1985, pp. 17–30.

57 Arno Rethans, John L. Swazy, and Lawrence J. Marks, "The Effects of Television Commercial Repetition, Receiver Knowledge, and Commercial Length," *Journal of Marketing Research*, February 1986, pp. 50–61.

58 William E. Baker, "When Can Affective Conditioning and Mere Exposure Directly Influence Brand Choice?" *Journal of Advertising* 28, no. 4, Winter 1999, pp. 31–46.

59 Chris Janiszewski and Tom Meyvis, "Effects of Brand Logo Complexity, Repetition, and Spacing on Processing Fluency and Judgment," *Journal of Consumer Research* 28, June 2001, pp. 18–32.

60 Caroline McMillan Portillo, "An In-Depth Look at the Power of Viral Video: How Goldieblox Tapped 'The Holy Grail of Marketing," *Business Journals*, October 21, 2014, www.bizjournals.com.

61 Herbert Krugman, "Why Three Exposures May Be Enough," *Journal of Advertising Research*, December 1972, pp. 11–14.

62 George E. Belch, "The Effects of Television Commercial Repetition on Cognitive Response and Message Acceptance," *Journal of Consumer Research*, June 1982, pp. 56–65.

63 Margaret Henderson Blair, "An Empirical Investigation of Advertising Wearin and Wearout," *Journal of Advertising Research* 40, November 2000, p. 95.

64 Merel van Diepen, Bas Donkers, and Philip Hans Franses, "Does Irritation Induced by Charitable Mailings Reduce Donations?" *International Journal of Research in Marketing* 26, 2009, pp. 180–188.

65 Margaret C. Campbell and Kevin Lane Keller, "Brand Familiarity and Advertising Repetition Effects," *Journal of Consumer Research*, September 2003, pp. 292–304.

66 Deborah J. MacInnis, Ambar G. Rao, and Allen M. Weiss, "Assessing When Increased Media Weight of Real-World Advertisements Helps Sales," *Journal of Marketing Research*, November 2002, pp. 391–407.

67 Christie L. Nordhielm, "The Influence of Level of Processing on Advertising Repetition Effects," *Journal of Consumer Research*, December 2002, pp. 371–373.

68 Marian Burke and Julie A. Edell, "Ad Reactions over Time," *Journal of Consumer Research*, June 1986, pp. 114–118; and Curtis P. Haugtvedt, David W. Schumann, Wendy L. Schneier, and Wendy L. Warren, "Advertising Repetition and Variation Strategies," *Journal of Consumer Research*, June 1994, pp. 176–189.

69 Ishbel Macleod, "Tourism Ireland Begin Filming for Three-Year Global Advertising Campaign," *The Drum (UK)*, October 21, 2011, http://thedrum.co.uk.

70 Prashant Malaviya, "The Moderating Influence of Advertising Context on Ad Repetition Effects: The Role of Amount and Type of Elaboration," *Journal of Consumer Research* 34, no. 1, 2007, pp. 32–40.

71 Steven Sweldens, Stijn M. J. van Osselaer, and Chris Janiszewski, "Evaluative Conditioning Procedures and the Resilience of Conditioned Brand Attitudes," *Journal of Consumer Research*, October 2010, pp. 473–489.

72 "Graphic Warnings on Cigarette Packets Do Help Smokers to Kick the Habit," *Daily Mail Reporter (UK)*, May 27, 2011, www.dailymail.co.uk.

73 Gerald J. Gorn, "The Effects of Music in Advertising on Choice Behavior: A Classical Conditioning Approach," *Journal of Marketing*, Winter 1982, pp. 94–101.

74 Calvin Bierley, Frances K. McSweeny, and Renee Vannieuwkerk, "Classical Conditioning of Preferences for Stimuli," *Journal of Consumer Research*, December 1985, pp. 316–323; James J. Kellaris and Anthony D. Cox, "The Effects of Background Music in Advertising," *Journal of Consumer Research*, June 1989, pp. 113–118; and Chris T. Allen and Thomas J. Madden, "A Closer Look at Classical Conditioning," *Journal of Consumer Research*, December 1985, pp. 301–315.

75 Bierley, McSweeny, and Vannieuwkerk, "Classical Conditioning of Preferences for Stimuli"; Elnora W. Stuart, Terence A. Shimp, and Randall W. Engle, "Classical Conditioning of Consumer Attitudes," *Journal of Consumer Research*, December 1987, pp. 334–349; Terence A. Shimp, Elnora W. Stuart, and Randall W. Engle, "A Program of Classical Conditioning Experiments Testing Variations in the Conditioned Stimulus and Context," *Journal of Consumer Research*, June 1991, pp. 1–12; and Chris T. Allen and Chris A. Janiszewski, "Assessing the Role of Contingency Awareness in Attitudinal Conditioning with Implications for Advertising Research," *Journal of Marketing Research*, February 1989, pp. 30–43.

76 Randi Priluck Grossman and Brian D. Till, "The Persistence of Classically Conditioned Brand Attitudes," *Journal of Advertising*, Spring 1998.

77 Sweldens, van Osselaer, and Janiszewski, "Evaluative Conditioning Procedures and the Resilience of Conditioned Brand Attitudes."

78 Gordy Pleyers, Olivier Corneille, Vincent Yzerbyt, and Olivier Luminet, "Evaluative Conditioning May Incur Attentional Costs," *American Psychological Association* 35, no. 2, 2009, pp. 279–285.

79 Jeff Barker, "Under Armour Doubles Down on Stephen Curry with New Deal," *Baltimore Sun*, September 17, 2015, www.baltimoresun.com; and Terence A. Shimp, "Neo-Pavlovian Conditioning and Its Implications for Consumer Theory and Research," in eds. Thomas S. Robertson and Harold H. Kassarjian, *Handbook of Consumer Behavior* (Englewood Cliffs, N.J.: Prentice-Hall, 1991), pp. 162–187.

80 "For Svelte Kareena Kapoor, Weekend Is a Time for Sweet Indulgence," *India Today*, February 19, 2015, http://indiatoday.intoday.in.

81 Melanie A. Dempsey and Andrew A. Mitchell, "The Influence of Implicit Attitudes on Choice When Consumers Are Confronted with Conflicting Attribute Information," *Journal of Consumer Research*, December 2010, pp. 614–625.

82 Aparna A. Labroo and Suresh Ramanathan, "The Influence of Experience and Sequence of Conflicting Emotions on Ad Attitudes," *Journal of Consumer Research* 33, no. 4, 2007, pp. 523–528; Steven P. Brown and Douglas M. Stayman, "Antecedents and Consequences of Attitude toward the Ad: A Meta-analysis," *Journal of Consumer Research*, June 1993, pp. 34–51; Andrew A. Mitchell and Jerry C. Olson, "Are Product Attribute Beliefs the Only Mediator of Advertising Effects on Brand Attitudes?" *Journal of Marketing Research*, August 1981, pp. 318–322; Terence A. Shimp, "Attitude toward the Ad as a Mediator of Consumer Brand Choice," *Journal of Advertising* 10, no. 2, 1981, pp. 9–15; and Christian M. Derbaix, "The Impact of Affective Reactions on Attitudes toward the Advertisement and the Brand: A Step toward Ecological Validity," *Journal of Marketing Research*, November 1995, pp. 470–479.

83 Mitchell and Olson, "Are Product Attribute Beliefs the Only Mediator of Advertising Effects on Brand Attitudes?"

84 Srinivas Durvasula, J. Craig Andrews, Steven Lysonski, and Richard G. Netemeyer, "Assessing the Cross-National Applicability of Consumer Behavior Models: A Model of Attitude toward Advertising in General," *Journal of Consumer Research*, March 1993, pp. 626–636.

85 Russell I. Haley and Allan L. Baldinger, "The ARF Copy Research Validity Project," *Journal of Advertising Research*, April–May 1991, pp. 11–32.

86 Elizabeth S. Moore and Richard J. Lutz, "Children, Advertising, and Product Experiences: A Multimethod Inquiry," *Journal of Consumer Research* 27, June 2000, pp. 31–48; Scott B. MacKenzie, Richard J. Lutz, and George E. Belch, "The Role of Attitude toward the Ad as a Mediator of Advertising Effectiveness: A Test of Competing Explanations," *Journal of Marketing Research*, May 1986, pp. 130–143; Pamela M. Homer, "The Mediating Role of Attitude toward the Ad: Some Additional Evidence," *Journal of Marketing Research*, February 1990, pp. 78–86; and Brown and Stayman, "Antecedents and Consequences of Attitude toward the Ad."

87 E. J. Schultz, "A Tiger at 60," *Advertising Age*, August 29, 2011, www.adage.com.

88 Brown and Stayman, "Antecedents and Consequences of Attitude toward the Ad."

89 Marian Chapman Burke and Julie A. Edell, "Ad Reactions over Time: Capturing Changes in the Real World," *Journal of Consumer Research*, June 1986, pp. 114–118; and Amitava Chattopadhyay and Prakash Nedungadi, "Does Attitude toward the Ad Endure?" *Journal of Consumer Research*, June 1992, pp. 26–33.

90 Margaret G. Meloy, "Mood Driven Distortion of Product Information," *Journal of Consumer Research* 27, December 2000, pp. 345–359.

91 Michael J. Barone, Paul W. Miniard, and Jean B. Romeo, "The Influence of Positive Mood on Brand Extension Evaluations," *Journal of Consumer Research* 26, March 2000, pp. 386–400.

92 Anick Bosmans and Hans Baumgartner, "Goal-Relevant Emotional Information," *Journal of Consumer Research* 32, no. 3, 2005, pp. 424–434.

93 Rashmi Adaval, "Sometimes It Just Feels Right: The Differential Weighting of Affect-Consistent and Affect-Inconsistent Product Information," *Journal of Consumer Research* 28, June 2001, pp. 1–17.

94 Ann Kronrod, Amir Grinstein, and Luc Wathieu, "Enjoy! Hedonic Consumption and Compliance with Assertive Messages," *Journal of Consumer Research* 39, no. 1, June 2012, pp. 51–61.

95 Lea Dunn and JoAndrea Hoegg, "The Impact of Fear on Emotional Brand Attachment," *Journal of Consumer Research* 41, no. 1, June 2014, pp. 152–168.

96 Julie A. Edell and Marian Chapman Burke, "The Power of Feelings in Understanding Advertising Effects," *Journal of*

Consumer Research, December 1987, pp. 421–433; Douglas M. Stayman and David A. Aaker, "Are All Effects of Ad-Induced Feelings Mediated by Aad?" *Journal of Consumer Research*, December 1988, pp. 368–373; and Morris B. Holbrook and Rajeev Batra, "Assessing the Role of Emotions as Mediators of Consumer Responses to Advertising," *Journal of Consumer Research*, December 1987, pp. 404–420.

97 Rajeev Batra and Michael L. Ray, "Affective Responses Mediating Acceptance of Advertising," *Journal of Consumer Research*, September 1986, pp. 234–249.

98 David A. Aaker, Douglas M. Stayman, and Michael R. Hagerty, "Warmth in Advertising: Measurement, Impact, and Sequence Effects," *Journal of Consumer Research*, March 1986, pp. 365–381.

99 Ayn E. Crowley, "The Two-Dimension Impact of Color on Shopping," *Marketing Letters* 4, no. 1, 1993, pp. 59–69.

100 Joseph A. Bellizzi, Ayn E. Crowley, and Ronald W. Hasty, "The Effects of Color in Store Design," *Journal of Retailing*, Spring 1983, pp. 21–45.

101 Lance Whitney, "Apple Stores May Be Headed for Major Overhaul," *Cnet*, September 1, 2015, www.cnet.com; and Nick Bilton, "Bits Pics: Inside Apple's New Grand Central Store," *New York Times*, August 17, 2011, www.nytimes.com.

102 Charles S. Areni and David Kim, "The Influence of In-Store Lighting on Consumers' Examination of Merchandise in a Wine Store," *International Journal of Research in Marketing*, March 1994, pp. 117–125.

103 Nancy M. Puccinelli, "Putting Your Best Face Forward: The Impact of Customer Mood on Salesperson Evaluation," *Journal of Consumer Psychology* 16, no. 2, 2006, pp. 156–162.

104 Camelia C. Micu, Robin A. Coulter, and Linda L. Price, "How Product Trials Alters the Effects of Model Attractiveness," *Journal of Advertising*, September 2009, pp. 69–81.

105 Curt Haugtvedt, Richard E. Petty, John T. Cacioppo, and T. Steidley, "Personality and Ad Effectiveness: Exploring the Utility of Need for Cognition," in ed. Michael J. Houston, *Advances in Consumer Research*, vol. 15 (Provo, Utah: Association for Consumer Research, 1988), pp. 209–212.

106 Susan M. Petroshius and Kenneth E. Crocker, "An Empirical Analysis of Spokesperson Characteristics on Advertisement and Product Evaluations," *Journal of the Academy of Marketing Science*, Summer 1989, pp. 217–225; and Lynn R. Kahle and Pamela M. Homer, "Physical Attractiveness of the Celebrity Endorser," *Journal of Consumer Research*, March 1985, pp. 954–961.

107 Michael A. Kamins, "An Investigation into the 'Match-Up' Hypothesis in Celebrity Advertising," *Journal of Advertising* 19, no. 1, 1990, pp. 4–13; and Marjorie J. Caballero and Paul J. Solomon, "Effects of Model Attractiveness on Sales Response," *Journal of Advertising* 13, no. 1, 1984, pp. 17–23.

108 Lynn R. Kahle and Pamela M. Homer, "Physical Attractiveness of the Celebrity Endorser," *Journal of Consumer Research*, March 1985, pp. 954–961; Kathleen Debevec and Jerome B. Kernan, "More Evidence on the Effects of a Presenter's Physical Attractiveness," in ed. Thomas C. Kinnear, *Advances in Consumer Research*, vol. 11 (Provo, Utah: Association for Consumer Research, 1984), pp. 127–132; Marjorie J. Caballero and William M. Pride, "Selected Effects of Salesperson Sex and Attractiveness in Direct Mail Advertising," *Journal of Marketing*, January 1984, pp. 94–100; Shelly Chaiken, "Communicator Physical Attractiveness and Persuasion," *Journal of Personality and Social Psychology*, August 1979, pp. 1387–1397; and Peter H. Reingen and Jerome B. Kernan, "Social

Perception and Interpersonal Influence," *Journal of Consumer Psychology* 2, no. 1, 1993, pp. 25–38.

109 Tommy E. Whittler and Joan Scattone Spira, "Model's Race: A Peripheral Cue in Advertising Messages?" *Journal of Consumer Psychology* 12, no. 4, 2002, pp. 291–301.

110 M. Reinhard, M. Messner, and S. Ludwig Sporer, "Explicit Persuasive Intent and Its Impact on Success at Persuasion—the Determining Roles of Attractiveness and Likeableness," *Journal of Consumer Psychology* 16, no. 3, 2006, pp. 249–259.

111 Yong-Soon Kang and Paul M. Herr, "Beauty and the Beholder: Toward an Integrative Model of Communication Source Effects," *Journal of Consumer Research* 33, no. 1, 2006, pp. 123–130; Richard E. Petty, H. Rao Unnava, and Alan J. Strathman, "Theories of Attitude Change," in eds. Thomas S. Robertson and Harold H. Kassarjian, *Handbook of Consumer Behavior* (Englewood Cliffs, N.J.: Prentice-Hall, 1991), pp. 241–280; and Kahle and Homer, "Physical Attractiveness of the Celebrity Endorser."

112 Jack Neff, "Michelle Phan Eclipsed by Newer Beauty Stars on YouTube," *Advertising Age*, June 9, 2015, www.adage.com.

113 Mark R. Forehand and Andrew Perkins, "Implicit Assimilation and Explicit Contrast: A Set/Reset Model of Response to Celebrity Voice-Overs," *Journal of Consumer Research* 32, no. 3, 2005, pp. 435–441.

114 Sun Joo Ahn and Jeremy N. Bailenson, "Self-Endorsing versus Other-Endorsing in Virtual Environments," *Journal of Advertising*, Summer 2011, pp. 93–106.

115 Claire Daniel, "Nordstrom Ads Feature Models with Disabilities, Generate Goodwill," *Adweek*, July 16, 2014, www.adweek.com.

116 Sengupta, Goodstein, and Boninger, "All Cues Are Not Created Equal."

117 Alan J. Bush, Craig A. Martin, and Victoria D. Bush, "Sports Celebrity Influence on the Behavioral Intentions of Generation Y," *Journal of Advertising Research*, March 2004, pp. 108–118.

118 John Patterson, "Bill Hader: 'I'm a Fraud, I Really Shouldn't Be Here,'" *The Guardian (U.K.)*, August 13, 2015, www.theguardian.com; and Stuart Elliott, "Mr. Peanut's New Look? Old School," *New York Times*, November 7, 2010, www.nytimes.com.

119 Judith A. Garretson and Ronald W. Niedrich, "Spokes-Characters," *Journal of Advertising*, Summer 2004, pp. 25–36.

120 Marla Royne Stafford, Thomas F. Stafford, and Ellen Day, "A Contingency Approach: The Effects of Spokesperson Type and Service Type on Service Advertising Perceptions," *Journal of Advertising*, Summer 2002, pp. 17–34.

121 James Waterson, "Novak Djokovic Appointed UNICEF Serbia Ambassador," *Tennis Now*, August 29, 2011, www.tennisnow.com; and Peter Ford and Gloria Goodale, "Why Stars and Charities Need Each Other," *Christian Science Monitor*, January 13, 2005, p. 1.

122 Therese A. Louie and Carl Obermiller, "Consumer Response to a Firm's Endorser (Dis)Association Decisions," *Journal of Advertising*, Winter 2002, pp. 41–52.

123 Dan Hamilton Rice, Katie Kelting, and Richard J. Lutz, "Multiple Endorsers and Multiple Endorsements: The Influence of Message Repetition, Source Congruence and Involvement on Brand Attitudes," *Journal of Consumer Psychology* 22, no. 2, April 2012, pp. 249–259.

124 See Xun (Irene) Huang, Xiuping Li, and Meng Zhang, "'Seeing' the Social Roles of Brands: How Physical Positioning

Influences Brand Evaluation," *Journal of Consumer Psychology* 23, no. 4, October 2013, pp. 509–514.

125 Mitchell and Olson, "Are Product Attributes Beliefs the Only Mediator of Advertising Effects on Brand Attitudes?"; Andrew A. Mitchell, "The Effect of Verbal and Visual Components of Advertisements on Brand Attitudes and Attitude toward the Advertisement," *Journal of Consumer Research*, March 1986, pp. 12–24; and Paul W. Miniard, Sunil Bhatla, Kenneth R. Lord, Peter R. Dickson, and H. Rao Unnava, "Picture-Based Persuasion Processes and the Moderating Role of Involvement," *Journal of Consumer Research*, June 1991, pp. 92–107.

126 Paul W. Miniard, Deepak Sirdeshmukh, and Daniel E. Innis, "Peripheral Persuasion and Brand Choice," *Journal of Consumer Research*, September 1992, pp. 226–239.

127 Henrik Hagtvedt and Vanessa M. Patrick, "Art Infusion: The Influence of Visual Art on the Perception and Evaluation of Consumer Products," *Journal of Marketing Research*, June 2008, pp. 379–389.

128 Robert Hof, "What Double-Dip? Online Ads Keep Clicking—for Now," *Forbes*, September 28, 2011, www.forbes.com.

129 Chris Woodyard, "Kia Brings Back the Hamsters in TV Ad This Sunday," *USA Today*, August 26, 2011, www.usatoday.com.

130 "Mark Sandman, An Instant Classic," *Wall Street Journal*, December 28, 2004, p. D8.

131 Gordon C. Bruner, "Music, Mood, and Marketing," *Journal of Marketing*, October 1990, pp. 94–104; Gerald J. Gorn, "The Effects of Music in Advertising on Choice Behavior," *Journal of Marketing*, Winter 1982, pp. 94–101; Judy I. Alpert and Mark I. Alpert, "Background Music as an Influence in Consumer Mood and Advertising Responses," in ed. Thomas K. Srull, *Advances in Consumer Research*, vol. 16 (Provo, Utah: Association for Consumer Research, 1989), pp. 485–491; Meryl Paula Gardner, "Mood States and Consumer Behavior: A Critical Review," *Journal of Consumer Research*, December 1985, pp. 281–300; and C. Whan Park and S. Mark Young, "Consumer Response to Television Commercials," *Journal of Marketing Research*, February 1986, pp. 11–24.

132 Juliet Rui and Joan Meyers-Levy, "Distinguishing between the Meanings of Music," *Journal of Marketing Research*, August 2005, pp. 333–345.

133 Mark Alpert and Judy Alpert, "Background Music as an Influence in Consumer Mood and Advertising Responses," *Advances in Consumer Research* 16, Fall 1989, pp. 485–491; and Stout and Leckenby, "Let the Music Play."

134 Chan Jean Lee, Eduardo B. Andrade, and Stephen E. Palmer, "Interpersonal Relationships and Preferences for Mood-Congruency in Aesthetic Experiences," *Journal of Consumer Research* 40, no. 2, August 2013, pp. 382–391.

135 Noel M. Murray and Sandra B. Murray, "Music and Lyrics in Commercials: A Cross-Cultural Comparison between Commercials Run in the Dominican Republic and the United States," *Journal of Advertising*, Summer 1996, pp. 51–64.

136 Marc G. Weinberger and Harlan E. Spotts, "Humor in U.S. vs. U.K. T V Advertising," *Journal of Advertising* 18, no. 2, 1989, pp. 39–44; and Paul Surgi Speck, "The Humorous Message Taxonomy," in eds. James H. Leigh and Claude R. Martin, *Current Research and Issues in Advertising* (Ann Arbor, Mich.: University of Michigan, 1991), pp. 1–44.

137 Thomas J. Madden and Marc G. Weinberger, "Humor in Advertising: A Practitioner View," *Journal of Advertising Research*, August–September 1984, pp. 23–29; Stewart and Furse, "Effective Television Advertising," *Marketing News* 20, no. 22, October 24, 1986, p. 1/9; Thomas J. Madden and Marc

C. Weinberger, "The Effects of Humor on Attention in Magazine Advertising," *Journal of Advertising* 1, no. 3, 1982, pp. 8–14; and Marc C. Weinberger and Leland Campbell, "The Use and Impact of Humor in Radio Advertising," *Journal of Advertising Research*, December–January 1991, pp. 44–52.

138 Martin Eisend, "A Meta-analysis of Humor in Advertising," *Journal of the Academy of Marketing Science* 37, 2009, pp. 191–203;

139 Harlan E. Spotts, Marc. G. Weinberger, and Amy L. Parsons, "Assessing the Use and Impact of Humor on Advertising Effectiveness: A Contingency Approach," *Journal of Advertising*, Fall 1997, pp. 17–32.

140 Brian Sternthal and Samuel Craig, "Humor in Advertising," *Journal of Marketing* 37, no. 4, 1973, pp. 12–18; Calvin P. Duncan, "Humor in Advertising: A Behavioral Perspective," *Journal of the Academy of Marketing Science* 7, no. 4, 1979, pp. 285–306; and Weinberger and Campbell, "The Use and Impact of Humor in Radio Advertising."

141 Thomas W. Cline and James J. Kellaris, "The Influence of Humor Strength and Humor–Message Relatedness on Ad Memorability," *Journal of Advertising*, Spring 2007, pp. 55–67.

142 Thomas W. Cline, Moses B. Altsech, and James J. Kellaris, "When Does Humor Enhance or Inhibit Ad Responses?" *Journal of Advertising*, Fall 2003, pp. 31–45.

143 Josephine L. C. M., Woltman Elpers, Ashesh Mukherjee, and Wayne D. Hoyer, "Humor in Television Advertising: A Moment-to-Moment Analysis," *Journal of Consumer Research*, December 2004, pp. 592–598.

144 Mark R. Brown, Roop K. Bhadury, and Nigel K. Li Pope, "The Impact of Comedic Violence on Viral Advertising Effectiveness," *Journal of Advertising*, Spring 2010, pp. 49–65.

145 Madden and Weinberger, "Humor in Advertising"; Weinberger and Campbell, "The Use and Impact of Humor in Radio Advertising"; and Weinberger and Spotts, "Humor in U.S. vs. U.K. TV Advertising."

146 Ashley Rodriguez, "Flo's Progressive Evolution," *Advertising Age*, November 12, 2014, www.adage.com.

147 Madden and Weinberger, "Humor in Advertising"; and Thomas W. Whipple and Alice E. Courtney, "How Men and Women Judge Humor," in eds. James H. Leigh and Claude R. Martin, *Current Research and Issues in Advertising* (Ann Arbor, Mich.: University of Michigan, 1981), pp. 43–56.

148 Yong Zhang, "Responses to Humorous Advertising: The Moderating Effect of Need for Cognition," *Journal of Advertising*, Spring 1996; and Amitava Chattopadhyay and Kunal Basu, "Prior Brand Evaluation as a Moderator of the Effects of Humor in Advertising," *Journal of Marketing Research*, November 1989, pp. 466–476.

149 Dana L. Alden, Wayne D. Hoyer, and Chol Lee, "Identifying Global and Culture-Specific Dimensions of Humor in Advertising: A Multi-National Analysis," *Journal of Marketing*, April 1993, pp. 64–75; and Dana L. Alden, Wayne D. Hoyer, Chol Lee, and Guntalee Wechasara, "The Use of Humor in Asian and Western Advertising: A Four-Country Comparison," *Journal of Asia-Pacific Business* 1, no. 2, 1995, pp. 3–23.

150 Weinberger and Spotts, "Humor in U.S. vs. U.K. TV Advertising."

151 Michel Laroche, Marcelo Vinhal Nepomuceno, Liang Huang, and Marie-Odile Richard, "What's So Funny?" *Journal of Advertising Research* 51, no. 2, 2011, pp. 404–416.

152 Yih Hwai Lee and Elison Ai Ching Lim, "What's Funny and What's Not," *Journal of Advertising*, Summer 2008, pp. 71–84.

153 Sean Poulter, "Beyonce Turns Up the Heat a Little Too Much," *Daily Mail (UK)*, November 17, 2010, www.dailymail.co.uk.

154 Nigel K. Li Pope, Kevin E. Voges, and Mark R. Brown, "The Effect of Provocation in the Form of Mild Erotica on Attitude to the Ad and Corporate Image," *Journal of Advertising*, Spring 2004, pp. 69–82.

155 Darren W. Dahl, Jaideep Sengupta, and Kathleen D. Vohs, "Sex in Advertising: Gender Differences and the Role of Relationship Commitment," *Journal of Consumer Research*, August 2009, pp. 215–231; and Jaideep Sengupta and Darren W. Dahl, "Gender-Related Reactions to Gratuitous Sex Appeals in Advertising," *Journal of Consumer Psychology* 18, 2008, pp. 62–78.

156 Bram Van den Bergh, Siegried Dewitte, and Luk Warlop, "Bikinis Instigate Generalized Impatience in Intertemporal Choice," *Journal of Consumer Research*, June 2008, pp. 85–97.

157 Lawrence Soley and Gary Kurzbard, "Sex in Advertising: A Comparison of 1964 and 1984 Magazine Advertisements," *Journal of Advertising* 15, no. 3, 1986, pp. 46–54.

158 Cyndee Miller, "We've Been 'Cosbyized,'" *Marketing News*, April 16, 1990, pp. 1–2; and Joshua Levine, "Marketing: Fantasy, Not Flesh," *Forbes*, January 22, 1990, pp. 118–120.

159 "It's Not Your Father's GoDaddy, Says New CEO," *Seattle Times*, August 29, 2015, www.seattletimes.com; and Susanna Kim, "Go Daddy Hopes Super Bowl Ads Are Risque Again," *ABC News*, February 4, 2011, www.abcnews.go.com.

160 Robert S. Baron, "Sexual Content and Advertising Effectiveness: Comments on Belch et al. (1981) and Caccavale et al. (1981)," in ed. Andrew A. Mitchell, *Advances in Consumer Research*, vol. 9 (Ann Arbor, Mich.: Association for Consumer Research, 1982), pp. 428–430.

161 Michael S. LaTour, Robert E. Pitts, and David C. Snook-Luther, "Female Nudity, Arousal, and Ad Response: An Experimental Investigation," *Journal of Advertising* 19, no. 4, 1990, pp. 51–62.

162 Evan I. Schwartz, "When Advertising Becomes the Show," *MIT Technology Review*, October 22, 2010, www.technologyreview.com; and Laura Petrecca, "Axe Ads Turn Up the Promise of Sex Appeal," *USA Today*, April 17, 2007, p. 3B.

163 Marilyn Y. Jones, Andrea J. S. Stanaland, and Betsy D. Gelb, "Beefcake and Cheesecake: Insights for Advertisers," *Journal of Advertising*, Summer 1998, pp. 33–52.

164 John Fetto, "Where's the Lovin'?" *American Demographics*, February 28, 2001.

165 Miller, "We've Been 'Cosbyized'"; and "Poll on Ads: Too Sexy," *Wall Street Journal*, March 8, 1993, p. B5.

166 Robert A. Peterson and Roger A. Kerin, "The Female Role in Advertisements," *Journal of Marketing*, October 1977, pp. 59–63.

167 Michelle R. Nelson and Hye-Jin Paek, "Nudity of Female and Male Models in Primetime TV Advertising Across Seven Countries," *International Journal of Advertising* 27, no. 5, 2008, pp. 715–744.

168 Sak Onkvisit and John J. Shaw, "A View of Marketing and Advertising Practices in Asia and Its Meaning for Marketing Managers," *Journal of Consumer Marketing*, Spring 1985, pp. 5–17; and Sarah Ellison, "Sex-Themed Ads Often Don't Travel Well," *Wall Street Journal*, March 31, 2000, p. B7.

169 Cenk Bulbul and Geeta Menon, " The Power of Emotional Appeals in Advertising," *Journal of Advertising Research*, June 2010, pp. 169–180.

170 M. Friestad and Esther Thorson, "Emotion-Eliciting Advertising: Effect on Long-Term Memory and Judgment," in ed. R. J. Lutz, *Advances in Consumer Research*, vol. 13 (Provo, Utah: Association for Consumer Research, 1986), pp. 111–116.

171 Tim Nudd, "Twitter Unveils Its First Paid Brand Emoji, and It's for (Who Else?) Coca-Cola," *Adweek*, September 18, 2015, www.adweek.com; Theresa Howard, "Coke Adds Spark to Ad Campaign," *USA Today*, April 3, 2006, p. 3B; and Christina Cheddar Berk, "Coke to Debut 'Real' Ad on 'Idol,'" *Wall Street Journal*, January 17, 2005, p. B3.

172 Barbara B. Stern, "Classical and Vignette Television Advertising Dramas: Structural Models, Formal Analysis, and Consumer Effects," *Journal of Consumer Research*, March 1994, pp. 601–615; William D. Wells, "Lectures and Dramas," in eds. Pat Cafferata and Alice M. Tybout, *Cognitive and Affective Responses to Advertising* (Lexington, Mass.: D. C. Heath, 1988); and John Deighton, Daniel Romer, and Josh McQueen, "Using Dramas to Persuade," *Journal of Consumer Research*, December 1989, pp. 335–343.

173 Jennifer Edson Escalas and Barbara B. Stern, "Sympathy and Empathy: Emotional Responses to Advertising Dramas," *Journal of Consumer Research*, March 2003, pp. 566–578.

174 Yoon Sarah, "Innisfree Releases Mini-Drama Ads of Lee Min-ho, Yoona," *Asia One*, May 27, 2015, http://news.asiaone.com.

175 Marvin E. Goldberg and Gerald J. Gorn, "Happy and Sad TV Programs: How They Affect Reactions to Commercials," *Journal of Consumer Research*, December 1987, pp. 387–403; and John P. Murray Jr. and Peter A. Dacin, "Cognitive Moderators of Negative-Emotion Effects," *Journal of Consumer Research*, March 1996, pp. 439–447.

176 John P. Murray, John L. Lastovicka, and Surendra Singh, "Feeling and Liking Responses to Television Programs," *Journal of Consumer Research*, March 1992, pp. 441–451.

177 S. N. Singh and Gilbert A. Churchill, "Arousal and Advertising Effectiveness," *Journal of Advertising* 16, no. 1, 1987, pp. 4–10.

178 Mark A. Pavelchak, John H. Antil, and James M. Munch, "The Super Bowl: An Investigation into the Relationship among Program Context, Emotional Experience, and Ad Recall," *Journal of Consumer Research*, December 1988, pp. 360–367.

179 Sally Beatty, "Madison Avenue Should Rethink Television Violence, Study Finds," *Wall Street Journal*, December 1, 1998, p. B8.

The
Psychological Core

2 Motivation, Ability, and Opportunity
3 From Exposure to Comprehension
4 Memory and Knowledge
5-6 Attitudes Based on Effort

An Introduction
to
Consumer Behavior

1 Understanding Consumer
Behavior

The Process of
Making Decisions

7 Problem Recognition and
Information Search
8-9 Judgment and Decision-
Making Based on Effort
10 Post-Decision Processes

The
Consumer's Culture

11 Social Influences on
Consumer Behavior
12 Consumer Diversity
13 Household and Social Class
Influences
14 Psychographics: Values,
Personality, and Lifestyles

Consumer Behavior
Outcomes and Issues

15 Innovations: Adoption,
Resistance, and Diffusion
16 Symbolic Consumer Behavior
17 Marketing, Ethics, and Social
Responsibility in Today's
Consumer Society

iStockphoto.com/Ostill

Part 3

The Process of Making Decisions

PART THREE examines the sequential steps in the consumer decision-making process. Chapter 7 explores the initial steps of this process—problem recognition and information search. Consumers must first realize they have a problem before they can begin the process of making a decision about solving it. They must then collect information to help make this decision.

As with attitude change, decision-making is affected by the amount of effort consumers expend. Chapter 8 examines the decision-making process when consumer effort is high and explores how marketers can influence this extensive decision process. Chapter 9 focuses on decision-making when consumer effort is low and discusses how marketers can influence this kind of decision process. Chapter 10 looks at how consumers determine whether they are satisfied or dissatisfied with their decisions and how they learn from choosing and consuming products and services.

Problem Recognition and Information Search

INTRODUCTION

Making the decision to buy something involves a number of steps, and marketing stimuli can be especially helpful in the early stages of this process. Suppose your car breaks down. Because you need reliable transportation, you realize you have a problem that you need to solve, as shown in Exhibit 7.1. Trying to remember what you know about car brands and features represents internal search. Looking at car ads, browsing at dealerships, and going online to read reviews are all part of external information search. Whether problem recognition, internal information search, and external information search proceed sequentially, simultaneously, or in a different order, these three stages are useful in explaining the basic processes that characterize consumer decision-making.

Exhibit 7.1 ▶ Chapter Overview: Problem Recognition and Information Search

The first step in the consumer decision-making process involves problem recognition (the consumer recognizes a problem that needs to be solved). Next, the consumer searches for information to solve the problem either internally from memory or externally from outside sources (such as experts, magazines, or ads). How much consumers search, what they search for, and the process they go through while searching are all discussed in this chapter.

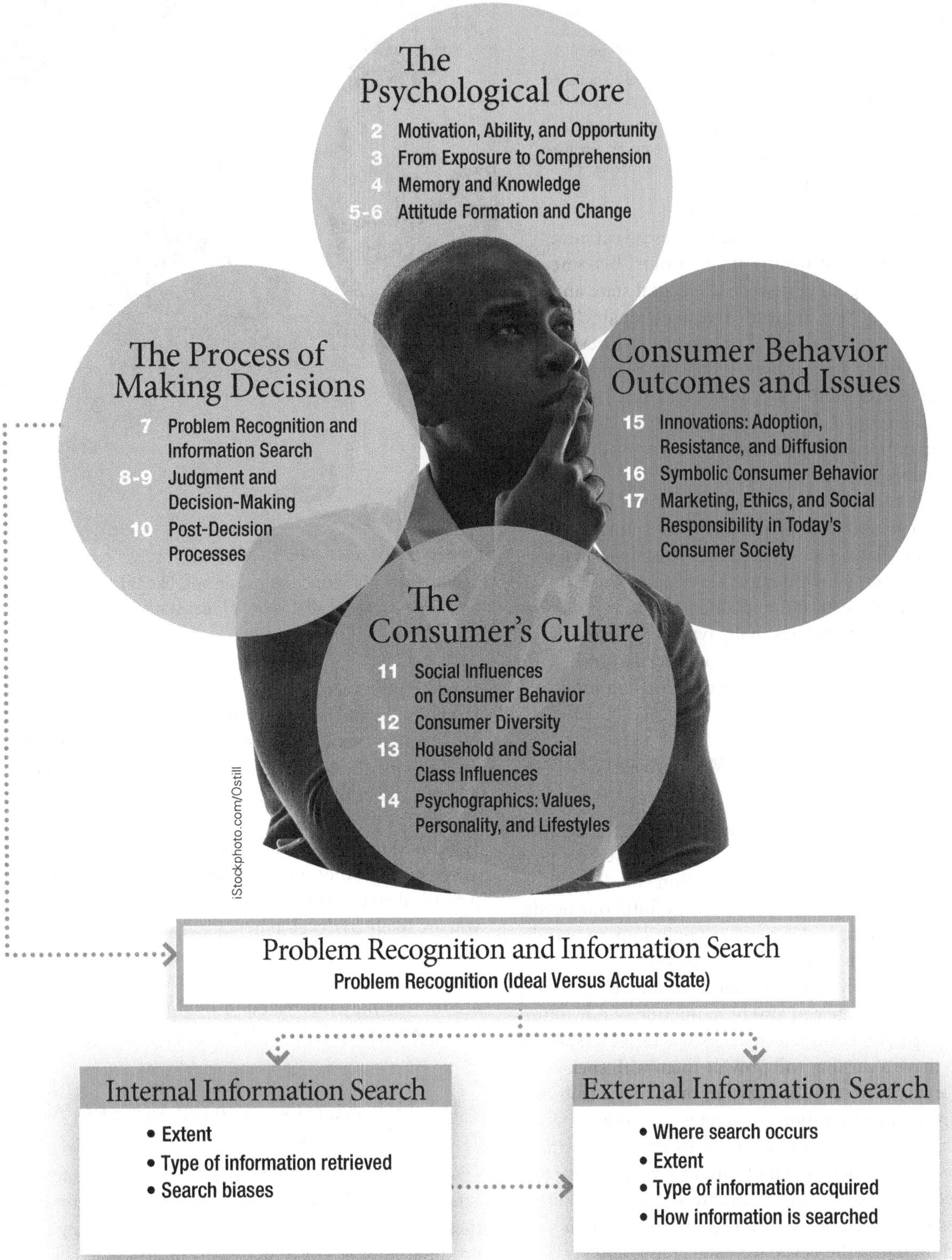

The
Psychological Core

2　Motivation, Ability, and Opportunity
3　From Exposure to Comprehension
4　Memory and Knowledge
5-6　Attitude Formation and Change

The Process of
Making Decisions

7　Problem Recognition and
　　Information Search
8-9　Judgment and
　　Decision-Making
10　Post-Decision
　　Processes

**Consumer Behavior
Outcomes and Issues**

15　Innovations: Adoption,
　　Resistance, and Diffusion
16　Symbolic Consumer Behavior
17　Marketing, Ethics, and Social
　　Responsibility in Today's
　　Consumer Society

The
Consumer's Culture

11　Social Influences
　　on Consumer Behavior
12　Consumer Diversity
13　Household and Social
　　Class Influences
14　Psychographics: Values,
　　Personality, and Lifestyles

iStockphoto.com/Ostill

Problem Recognition and Information Search
Problem Recognition (Ideal Versus Actual State)

Internal Information Search

• Extent
• Type of information retrieved
• Search biases

External Information Search

• Where search occurs
• Extent
• Type of information acquired
• How information is searched

7-1 Problem Recognition

The consumer decision process generally begins when a person identifies a consumption problem that needs to be solved ("I need a new car" or "I would like some new clothes"). **Problem recognition** is the perceived difference between an ideal and an actual state. This is a critical stage in the decision process because it motivates the consumer to action (see Exhibit 7.2).

Problem recognition The perceived difference between an actual and an ideal state.

Ideal state The way we want things to be.

Actual state Current state; the way things actually are.

The **ideal state** is the way that consumers would like a situation to be (having an excellent camera or wearing attractive clothing). The **actual state** is the real situation as consumers perceive it now. Problem recognition occurs if consumers become aware of a discrepancy between the actual state and the ideal state ("My car needs frequent repairs" or "My clothing is out of date"). The greater the discrepancy between the actual and the ideal states, and the higher the level of motivation, ability, and opportunity (MAO), the more likely consumers are to act. If consumers do not perceive a problem, their motivation to act will be low.

Problem recognition relates to consumption and disposition as well as to acquisition. Consumers can recognize problems such as needing to decide what to make for dinner, which item of clothing to wear, or whether to replace an old appliance. Because problem recognition stimulates many types of consumer decision-making, it is important to understand what contributes to differences between the ideal and the actual states.

Exhibit 7.2 ▶ An Ideal State
Consumers may respond to upscale ads, like this one for Jimmy Choo, because that is their ideal state.

Image Courtesy of The Advertising Archives

7-1a THE IDEAL STATE: WHERE WE WANT TO BE

Where do we get our notion of the ideal state? Sometimes we rely on simple expectations, usually based on past experience, about everyday consumption and disposition situations and how products or services fulfill our needs. For example, we consider how we might look in certain clothes, how much fun it would be to vacation in a particular location, which old products we should keep, and so on. The ideal state can also be a function of our future goals or aspirations. For example, many consumers might want to drive a car that will provide them with social status (a Lexus, Mercedes, or Porsche) or to join a club that will bring them admiration or acceptance by others.

Both expectations and aspirations are often stimulated by our own personal motivations—what we want to be based on our self-image—and by aspects of our own culture. Some societies are more materialistic than others, and therefore the desire for many goods and services may be greater in those cultures. Likewise, social class can

exert an influence: Many consumers want to be accepted by members of their class or to raise their social standing, leading them to aspire to a higher ideal state. Reference groups also play a critical role because we strive to be accepted by others and because reference groups serve as a guide to our behavior.

Finally, major changes in personal circumstances, such as getting a promotion or becoming a parent, can instigate new ideal states. When you graduate and start a new job, you are likely to develop new ideal states related to where you live, what you wear, what you drive, and so forth. Newly affluent consumers in South Korea, for example, are increasingly interested in buying world-famous status-symbol brands that signify wealth, such as Bentley cars.[1]

7-1b THE ACTUAL STATE: WHERE WE ARE NOW

Like our perception of the ideal state, our perception of the actual state can be influenced by a variety of factors. Often these are simple physical factors, such as running out of a product, having a product malfunction (the cell phone breaks) or become obsolete (the digital music player has insufficient storage), or unexpectedly needing a service (a cavity requires dental work). Needs also play a critical role. If you are hungry or thirsty or if friends make fun of your clothes, your actual state would not be acceptable. Finally, external stimuli can suddenly change your perceptions of the actual state. If someone tells you that Mother's Day is next Sunday, for example, you might suddenly realize that you have not bought a card or present yet.

Marketing Implications

Marketing can help put consumers in a state of problem recognition and motivate them to start the decision process, leading them to acquire, consume, or dispose of a product or service. In general, marketers use two major techniques to try to stimulate problem recognition. First, they can attempt to create a new ideal state. Forty years ago, few people gave much thought to the performance or style of their athletic shoes. Today we are bombarded with marketing messages featuring athletic shoes that will make us run faster, jump higher, stay healthy, and look more fashionable—a new ideal state.[2]

Second, marketers can try to encourage our dissatisfaction with the actual state, as Saks Fifth Avenue did by fostering shoppers' dissatisfaction with ordinary shopping bags. When Saks created boldly stylish, eco-friendly, reusable bags to hold purchases, it encouraged consumers to view free bags as personal statements about fashion and environmental consciousness. Now many upscale retailers worldwide offer elegant shopping bags. This trend has led some status-conscious South Korean consumers to buy luxury-brand shopping bags from other consumers.[3]

Whether they create a new ideal state or stimulate dissatisfaction with the actual state, marketers are more likely to have their offering chosen if they position it as the solution to the consumer's problem (see Exhibit 7.3). For example, the name of Procter & Gamble's Mr. Clean Magic Eraser sponges and mops suggest that they help consumers quickly and easily "erase" dirt for a cleaner home.

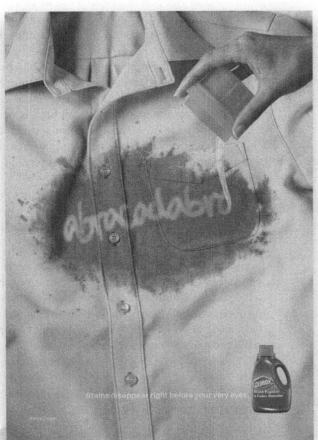

Exhibit 7.3 ▶ Targeting the Ideal State
Marketers can target the ideal state by showing consumers how the product is the solution to their problems.

7-2 Internal Search: Searching for Information from Memory

After problem recognition has been stimulated, the consumer will usually begin the decision process to solve the problem. Typically, the next step is **internal search**. As discussed in Chapter 4, almost all decision-making involves some form of memory processing. Consumers have stored in memory a variety of information, feelings, and past experiences that can be recalled when making a decision.

> **Internal search** The process of recalling stored information from memory.

Because consumers have limited capacity or ability to process information—and because memory traces can decay over time—consumers are likely to recall only a small subset of stored information when they engage in internal search. Researchers are investigating (1) the extent of the search, (2) the nature of the search, and (3) the process by which consumers recall information, feelings, and experiences and enter them into the decision process.

7-2a HOW MUCH DO WE ENGAGE IN INTERNAL SEARCH?

The degree of internal search can vary widely from the simple recall of only a brand name to more extensive searches through memory for relevant information, feelings, and experiences. On a general level, researchers know that the effort consumers devote to internal search depends on their MAO to process information. Thus, consumers will attempt to recall more information when felt involvement, perceived risk, or the need for cognition is high. In addition, consumers can engage in active internal search only if the information is stored in memory. Consumers with a greater degree of knowledge and experience therefore have a greater ability to search internally. Finally, consumers can recall information from memory only if they have the opportunity to do so. Time pressure or distractions will limit internal search.

7-2b WHAT KIND OF INFORMATION IS RETRIEVED FROM INTERNAL SEARCH?

Much of the research on the role of internal search in consumer judgment and decision-making has focused on what is recalled. Specifically, researchers have examined the recall of four major types of information: (1) brands, (2) attributes, (3) evaluations, and (4) experiences.[4]

Recall of Brands

The set of brands that consumers recall from memory whenever problem recognition has been stimulated is an important aspect of internal search that greatly affects decision-making. Rather than remembering all available brands in any given situation, consumers tend to recall a subset of two to eight brands known as a **consideration** or **evoked set**.[5] For example, someone buying toothpaste might consider Colgate and Crest rather than all possible brands. With product proliferation, however, the number of offerings has increased dramatically. Colgate-Palmolive alone offers more than a dozen toothpaste brands worldwide (including Colgate Total, Ultrabrite, and Laser), a situation that increases competition for inclusion in the consideration set.[6]

In general, the consideration set consists of brands that are "top of mind," or easy to remember, when a consumer is making a decision. For instance, some U.S. consumers fly rather than take the train—even when taking the train is faster and cheaper—simply because they do not consider the possibility of train. Conversely, in India, airlines are using marketing to encourage consumers to consider flying rather than taking the train or bus when they travel long distances. The effort has been successful: The number of air travelers is increasing by eight percent or more every year.[7]

A small consideration set is usually necessary because consumers' ability to recall brand information decreases as the size of the set increases. However, even if they do not recall the entire set from memory, stored information aids the recognition process. For example, stored information can help consumers identify brands on the shelf.

> **Consideration (or evoked set)** The subset of top-of-mind brands evaluated when making a choice.

This is one reason why L'Oréal is stepping up social media marketing in dozens of countries, supplementing television and print advertising with content on Facebook, Instagram, and Twitter for new product introductions.[8] By increasing brand recognition and stored information, L'Oréal hopes to strengthen its brand in the consumers' consideration set, despite competition from Unilever and Procter & Gamble.

Studies indicate that consideration sets vary in terms of their size, stability, variety, and *preference dispersion* (the equality of preferences toward brands or products in the set). On more familiar occasions and in more familiar locations, such as when buying snacks at the local movie theater, consumers have consideration sets that are less stable, are larger in size, and have slightly more variety. In such situations, consumers tend to have stronger preferences for one or two items in the consideration set. This phenomenon suggests that a company should enhance its product's linkage with an occasion or situation familiar to consumers—such as eating on the run—to increase the chance that the product will be retrieved from memory as part of the consideration set.[9]

According to research, brands that are recalled are more likely to be chosen.[10] However, a brand's simply being recalled does not guarantee that it will be in a consumer's consideration set because consumers can recall a number of brands and then reject undesirable alternatives. Also, consumers' choices can be altered by the simple manipulation of which brands they recall, even though this manipulation may not change their product preferences. Thus, if consumers cannot recall brands from memory to form a consideration set, the set will tend to be determined by external factors such as the availability of products on the shelf or the suggestions of salespeople.[11]

Researchers have looked at the following factors that increase the possibility of consumers' recalling a particular brand during internal search, and including that brand in their consideration set:

- *Prototypicality.* When consumers engage in internal search, they more easily recall brands that are closest to the prototype or that most resemble other category members, making these more likely to be included in the consideration set than brands that are not typical of the category.[12] For example, Apple's iPad created the category of tablet computer, which it still dominates. This brand is more likely than other brands to be in the consideration set when problem recognition for the product exists (see Exhibit 7.4).

- *Brand familiarity.* Well-known brands are more easily recalled during internal search than unfamiliar brands because the memory links associated with these brands tend to be stronger. As a result,

Exhibit 7.4 ▶ Prototypicality
When you think of a "tablet," Apple's iPad probably comes to mind first, as it is the prototype of the tablet category.

For example, an ad for Kellogg's Frosted Flakes cereal features ESPN anchor Rece Davis, targeting fathers with the tagline "share what you love with who you love." Here, the usage situation is breakfast-time and the goal is to strengthen father–child connections. A Kellogg marketer explains: "Dad loves to share the things that he is passionate about with his kid, and Frosted Flakes and sports are two of those things."[17]

- *Brand preference.* Brands toward which the consumer has positive attitudes tend to be recalled more easily and tend to be included in the consideration set more often than brands that evoke negative attitudes.[18] This tendency highlights the importance of developing positive brand attitudes. In Canada, Molson Coors Brewing encourages positive brand attitudes by appealing to strong patriotic feelings with ads and branded merchandise built on the slogan "I. Am. Canadian."[19]

- *Retrieval cues.* By strongly associating the brand with a retrieval cue, marketers can increase the chance that the brand will be included in the consumer's consideration set. Think of the Target red-and-white bull's-eye. The retailer is emphasizing this cue as it expands into city centers with smaller and mid-sized stores, rather than large-format stores (see Exhibit 7.5).[20] Packaging can also be an important retrieval cue for food products. Therefore, Coca-Cola's iconic glass bottle is still featured in some promotions, even though the bottles are now made with recycled and recyclable plastic.[21]

Recall of Attributes

For a variety of reasons, we access only a small portion of the information stored in memory during internal search. Often we cannot remember specific facts about a product or service because our memory of details decreases over time. Thus, the attribute information we recall tends to be in summary or simplified form rather than in its original detail. For example, we would be more likely to remember that a car gets good gas mileage or that filling the tank is not expensive than to remember the actual miles per gallon the car gets or the exact price of the gas.

Nevertheless, consumers can often recall some details when they engage in internal search, and the recalled attribute information can strongly influence their brand choices.[22] As a result, researchers have been very interested in determining which factors influence the recall of attribute information in the information search and decision-making processes. These are some of the major variables they have identified:

- *Accessibility or availability.* Information that is more accessible or available—having the strongest associative links—is the most likely to be recalled and entered into the decision process.[23] Information

companies need to repeat marketing communications continually to keep brand awareness high and associations strong. In Asian cultures, ads with high-meaning pictures and words (e.g., Superman fences with a picture of Superman) are very effective in increasing brand-name recall.[13] Even in low-MAO situations in which little processing occurs, incidental ad exposure can increase the likelihood of a brand's inclusion in the consideration set.[14] This explains why global brands such as McDonald's have high familiarity worldwide and are likely to be in many consumers' consideration sets. Brand familiarity helps consumers recognize which of the many brands in the store should be attended to and reduces misidentification of brands.[15]

- *Goals and usage situations.* As discussed in Chapter 5, consumers have goal-derived and usage-specific categories in memory, such as drinks to bring to the beach, and the activation of these categories will determine which brands they recall during internal search.[16] Therefore, marketers can attempt to associate products with certain goals and usage situations.

Image Courtesy of The Advertising Archives

Martin Good/Shutterstock.com

Exhibit 7.5 ▶ Retrieval Cues

Brands can create strong retrieval cues, increasing the likelihood of being included in consumers' consideration set. Target stores have done this with their bull's-eye logo, which helps them be known around the world.

that is perceived as being easy to recall is also more likely to be accessible.[24] Simply reminding consumers of the ease of information retrieval can affect their judgments in some situations.[25] Marketers can make information more accessible by repeatedly drawing attention to it in communications or by making the information more relevant.[26]

■ *Diagnosticity.* **Diagnostic information** helps us distinguish objects from one another. If all brands of computers are the same price, then price is not diagnostic, or useful, when consumers are making a decision. On the other hand, if prices vary, consumers can distinguish among them, so the information is diagnostic.[27] If information is both accessible and diagnostic, it has a very strong influence in the decision-making process.[28] However, if accessible information is not diagnostic, it is less likely to be recalled.

Research shows that negative information tends to be more diagnostic than positive or neutral information because the former is more distinctive.[29] Because most brands are associated with positive attributes, negative information makes it easier for consumers to categorize the brand as different from other brands. Unfortunately, consumers tend to give negative information greater weight in decisions, increasing the chances

> **Diagnostic information** That which helps us discriminate among objects.
>
> **Salient attribute** Attribute that is "top of mind" or more important.

that alternatives with negative qualities will be rejected. Therefore, marketers should avoid associating their offerings with negative information, and plan two-sided messages that counter negative information, or divert attention from the negative feature.

In addition, marketers can identify which attributes tend to be most diagnostic for a particular category and seek a competitive advantage on one or more of these attributes. This is what Quirky did with a product named Pivot Power: an adjustable power strip that can accommodate plugs of many sizes and shapes. Invented by a consumer, the product was named to suggest the unique attribute that sets it apart from its competitors, as more consumers seek ways to conveniently plug various types of gadgets into a single power source.[30]

■ *Salience.* Research has clearly shown that consumers can recall very **salient** (prominent) **attributes** even when their opportunity to process is low.[31] The Fitbit's sleek bracelet design and multifunction technology are salient attributes for consumers interested in wearable fitness trackers, for example. In addition, price is a highly salient attribute for many consumers. Note that consumers do not always have a strong belief about the salience of an attribute.[32] Thus, a marketer of stereo systems can improve consumers' recall of its products' sound quality by providing information that makes this attribute more salient, an action that in turn facilitates brand choice.[33] By repeatedly calling attention to an attribute in marketing messages, marketers can increase a product's salience and its impact on the decision.[34] For example, Chobani uses traditional and digital marketing to emphasize both the health benefits and the flavors of its Greek yogurt products, which face intense competition on crowded supermarket shelves.[35]

However, an attribute can be highly salient but not necessarily diagnostic. If you are buying a watch, for example, the attribute "tells time" would be highly salient but not very diagnostic. For information to be recalled and entered into the decision, it must have **attribute determinance**, which means the information is both salient and diagnostic.[36] When Dunkin' Donuts introduced a new breakfast sandwich, the marketing emphasized not only eat-on-the-go convenience but also the use of egg whites, a salient attribute for health-conscious consumers.[37]

> **Attribute determinance** Attribute that is both salient and diagnostic.
>
> **Online processing** When a consumer is actively evaluating a brand as he/she views an ad for it.

- *Vividness.* Vivid information is presented as concrete words, pictures, or instructions to imagine (e.g., imagine yourself on a tropical beach) or through word-of-mouth communication. For example, a photo of an arm wearing an Apple Watch is vivid information. Vivid information is easier to recall than less dramatic information, but it only tends to influence judgment and decision-making when consumers have not formed a strong prior evaluation, especially one that is negative.[38] Also, vividness affects attitudes only when the effort required to process the information matches the amount of effort the consumer is willing to put forth.[39] Otherwise, vivid and nonvivid information affect consumer attitudes in about the same way.

- *Goals.* The consumer's goals will determine which attribute is recalled from memory. If one of your goals in taking a vacation is to economize, you are likely to recall price when considering possible vacation destinations. Marketers can identify important goals that guide the choice process for consumers and can then position their offerings in the context of these goals, such as offering economy vacation packages.

Recall of Evaluations

Because our memory for specific details decays rapidly over time, we find overall evaluations or attitudes (i.e., our likes and dislikes) easier to remember than specific attribute information. In addition, our evaluations tend to form strong associative links with the brand. This tendency is the reason that it is important for a marketer to encourage positive attitudes toward its brand or offering, whether it is a product, service, person, or place. Many businesses do this via social media. In Australia, the founders of Frank Body Scrub use Snapchat, Instagram, Twitter, Facebook, Pinterest, YouTube, and Twitter to show what goes into their personal care products and to offer beauty tips. One of the cofounders notes, "when we get influencers to post for us, there is a large element of trust," which helps to further reinforce positive brand attitudes.[40]

Evaluations are also more likely to be recalled by consumers who are actively evaluating the brand when they are exposed to relevant information. For example, if you are ready to buy a new computer and suddenly see an ad for a particular brand, you will probably determine whether you like the brand when you see the ad. This activity is called **online processing**.[41] Afterward, you will more likely recall this evaluation rather than the specific information that led to it. Many times, however, consumers do not have a brand-processing goal when they see or hear an ad. In such cases they do not form an evaluation and are therefore better able to recall specific attribute information, assuming that their involvement was high and the information was processed.[42] Moreover, consumers are more likely to use online processing in evaluating a family of brands when the brands within that family have low variability and share many attributes.[43]

Recall of Experiences

Internal search can involve the recall of experiences from autobiographical memory in the form of specific images and the effect associated with them.[44] Like information in semantic memory, experiences that are more vivid, salient, or frequent are the most likely to be recalled. For example, if you have an experience with a product or service that is either unusually positive or unusually positive experience with a product or service, it will be easier to recall. To illustrate, minor league baseball is known for wacky promotions that make the in-stadium experience more exciting and memorable. During their season, the popular South Bend Cubs team in Indiana holds crowd-pleasing promotions such as Princess in the Park day, Star Wars night, and Back to the Future night.[45] Research suggests that although advertising may affect how accurately consumers can recall their product experiences, their recall of the product's evaluations is not necessarily affected.[46]

 Marketing Implications

Obviously marketers want consumers to recall positive experiences related to certain products or services. Marketers often deliberately associate their products or services with common positive experiences or images to increase their recall from consumers' memory. For example, the Macy's department store chain generates considerable goodwill through its Thanksgiving Day Parade and its Independence Day fireworks displays in New York City, both of which draw millions of television and Internet viewers every year (see Exhibit 7.6).

Marketers should also monitor reviews posted online and in social media for negative recall experiences. It is important for marketers to respond to comments about negative experiences with speedy, satisfactory responses that are more salient. For instance, after Dell was stung by a lot of negative customer comments a few years ago, the company set up a central "listening post"

Exhibit 7.6 ▶ Recall of Experiences

Marketers can associate their products with positive events, like the Macy's Thanksgiving Day Parade, to promote positive customer recall.

to scour the Web and social media for conversations about its brand and products. The company also created several Twitter accounts specifically for handling customers' complaints. Now, a Dell executive says, "we've seen a significant decline in negative commentary about our products and services, proof that the ability to listen and respond instantly is a smart investment in any company's future and a way to continually improve both business and customer relations."[47]

7-2c   IS INTERNAL SEARCH ALWAYS ACCURATE?

In addition to being influenced by factors that affect what we recall, we all have processing biases that alter the nature of internal search. These search biases can sometimes lead to the recall of information that results in a less-than-optimal judgment or decision. Three biases have important implications for marketing: confirmation bias, inhibition, and mood.

Confirmation Bias

Confirmation bias refers to our tendency to recall information that reinforces or confirms our overall beliefs rather than contradicting them, thereby making our judgment or decision more positive than it should be. This phenomenon is related to the concept of *selective perception*—we see what

Inhibition The recall of one attribute inhibiting the recall of another.

Confirmation bias Tendency to recall information that reinforces or confirms our overall beliefs rather than contradicting them, thereby making our judgment or decision more positive than it should be.

we want to see—and occurs because we strive to maintain consistency in our views. When we engage in internal search, we are more likely to recall information about brands we like or have previously chosen than information about brands we dislike or have rejected. Furthermore, when the confirmation bias is operating, we are more likely to recall positive rather than negative information about favored brands. This response can be a problem because, as mentioned earlier, negative information tends to be more diagnostic.

Nevertheless, we sometimes recall contradictory evidence. In fact, we may recall moderately contradictory information because we had consciously thought about it when we first tried to understand it.[48] In most instances, however, consumers tend to recall information that reinforces their overall beliefs.

Inhibition

Another internal search bias is associated with limitations in consumers' processing capacity.[49] In this case, all the variables that influence the recall of certain attributes—such as accessibility, vividness, and salience—can actually lead to the **inhibition** of recall for other diagnostic attributes.[50] In buying a house, for example, a consumer might recall information such as the selling price, number of bathrooms, and square footage but may not recall other important attributes such as the size of the lot. Inhibition can also lead to a biased judgment or decision because consumers may remember but still ignore important and useful information.

Mood

Recall from Chapter 6 that consumers engaged in internal search are most likely to recall information, feelings, and experiences that match their mood.[51] With this knowledge in mind, advertisers are aware that marketing communications that put consumers in a good mood through the use of humor or attractive visuals can enhance the recall of positive attribute information.

Marketing Implications

From a marketing perspective, confirmation bias presents a real problem when consumers search internally for only positive information about the competition. One way marketers attack this problem is to draw attention to negative aspects of competitive brands through comparative advertising. For example, Samsung promotes the convenient wireless recharging feature of its Galaxy phones, comparing them with the hassles of plugging in competing phones for recharging.[52] By presenting comparative information in a convincing and credible way, marketers may be able to overcome confirmation bias.

Inhibition is an important aspect of internal search for two reasons. First, consumers may not always consider key aspects of a brand when making a decision because they recall other, more accessible attributes instead. If these nonrecalled attributes reflect features that differentiate the brand from others (i.e., if the attributes are diagnostic), the company may want to highlight them in marketing communications. Marketers can sometimes offset the effect of their brand's disadvantages and/or their competitors' advantages by drawing attention to more vivid or accessible attributes.

7-3 External Search: Searching for Information from the Environment

Sometimes a consumer's decision can be based entirely on information recalled from memory. At other times, information may be missing or some uncertainty may surround the recalled information. Then consumers engage in an **external search** of outside sources, such as dealers, trusted friends or relatives, published sources (magazines, pamphlets, or books), advertisements, the Internet, or the product package. Consumers use external search to collect additional information about which brands are available as well as about the attributes and benefits associated with brands in the consideration set.

Two types of external search are prepurchase search and ongoing search. **Prepurchase search** occurs in response to the activation of problem recognition. As an example, consumers seeking to buy a new car or truck can get information by visiting dealers, searching edmunds.com and other websites, checking quality rankings, searching social media sites for tips and opinions,

Ongoing search
A search that occurs regularly, regardless of whether the consumer is making a choice.

External search The process of collecting information from outside sources, for example, magazines, dealers, and ads.

Prepurchase search
A search for information that aids a specific acquisition decision.

talking to friends, and reading *Consumer Reports*. Online prepurchase search is so commonplace that Mercedes coordinates brand-oriented ads on Facebook and Instagram to build traffic to the Mercedes website. Not only has this improved brand awareness, the combination of ads boosted the number of visitors to the car company's website by more than 500 percent.[53]

Ongoing search occurs on a regular and continual basis, even when problem recognition has not been activated.[54] A consumer might consistently read automotive magazines, visit automotive websites, and go to car shows because he or she has a high degree of enduring involvement in cars. Exhibit 7.7 contrasts these two types of searches.

Researchers have examined five key aspects of the external search process: (1) the source of information, (2) the extent of external search, (3) the content of the external search, (4) search typologies, and (5) the process or order of the search.

7-3a WHERE CAN WE SEARCH FOR INFORMATION?

For either prepurchase or ongoing search, consumers can acquire information from a number of external sources:[55]

- *Retailer search.* Visits or calls to stores or dealers, including the examination of package information or pamphlets about brands; in particular, consumers believe they save time by going to stores that are clustered together.[56]

- *Media and social media search.* Information from advertising, online ads, manufacturer-sponsored websites and forums, and other types of marketer-produced communications, as well as from Facebook, Twitter, blogs, and other social media sources. Consumers may use smartphones, tablet computers, laptops, or desktop computers to conduct online and social media searches.

- *Interpersonal search.* Advice from friends, relatives, neighbors, coworkers, and/or other consumers, whether sought in person, by phone, online, text message, or in another way. Sites such as yelp.com and tripadvisor.com offer consumer-generated reviews of restaurants, stores, and other goods and services, for instance. Note that online consumer reviews have no significant effect on sales of brands that enjoy strong brand equity. However, favorable reviews do improve sales of brands with weaker brand equity.[57]

- *Independent search.* Contact with independent sources of information, such as books, nonbrand-sponsored websites like shopping.com, government pamphlets, or magazines.

Exhibit 7.7 ▶ Types of Information Search

Consumers can engage in two major types of external search. Prepurchase search occurs in response to problem recognition; the goal is to make better purchase decisions. Ongoing search results from enduring involvement and occurs on a continual basis (independent of problem recognition). In the latter, consumers search for information because they find searching enjoyable (they like to browse).

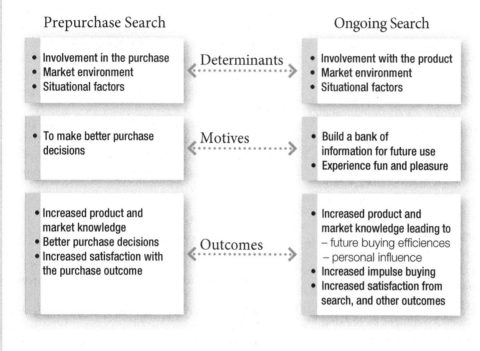

Prepurchase Search — Ongoing Search

Determinants
- Involvement in the purchase
- Market environment
- Situational factors

- Involvement with the product
- Market environment
- Situational factors

Motives
- To make better purchase decisions

- Build a bank of information for future use
- Experience fun and pleasure

Outcomes
- Increased product and market knowledge
- Better purchase decisions
- Increased satisfaction with the purchase outcome

- Increased product and market knowledge leading to
  – future buying efficiencies
  – personal influence
- Increased impulse buying
- Increased satisfaction from search, and other outcomes

Sources: Michael Totty, "So Much Information . . ." *Wall Street Journal*, December 9, 2002, p. R4; and Subodh Bhat, Michael Bevans, and Sanjit Sengupta, "Measuring Users' Web Activity to Evaluate and Enhance Advertising Effectiveness," *Journal of Advertising*, Fall 2002, pp. 97–106.

- *Experiential search.* Using product samples or product/service trials (such as a test-drive) or experiencing the product online.

Traditionally, retailer and media searches, followed by experiential search, have been the most frequently used forms of search. These increase when a consumer's involvement is higher and knowledge is lower.[58] This finding is significant for marketers because such sources are under their most direct control. Other research indicates that consumers browse two or more sources of information (such as the Internet and catalogs) before making a buying decision.[59] Therefore, marketers and retailers should ensure that their brand information is consistent across the various sources.

Consumers increase their use of interpersonal sources as their brand knowledge decreases. Apparently, when consumers' knowledge is limited, they are motivated to seek out the opinions of others. Furthermore, when consumers believe that their purchase and consumption of certain items (usually hedonic or symbolic products and

services such as fashion, music, and furniture) will be judged by others, they tend to seek out interpersonal sources.[60]

Relationships with an expert service provider can influence whether consumers consult other experts for "second opinions." Research indicates that when consumers have a long-term relationship with a trusted professional expert (such as a doctor, financial advisor, or accountant), they are less likely to seek a second opinion. This is because consumers seek to preserve the harmony in their existing expert relationships, even at the expense of their own best interests.[61]

Experiential search is also critical for hedonic products and services. Given the importance of sensory stimulation, consumers want to get a "feel" for the offering, so they often try on clothing or listen to a new song before they buy. When Neutrogena introduced Wipe Clean makeup remover in Brazil, the company arranged for a weekly magazine to create a cover featuring a well-known actress in full makeup, and inserted free product samples with that issue. Consumers were invited to use Wipe Clean to remove the eye makeup and lipstick from the cover. "This interactive piece of press gives consumers the power to star in the campaign," explained Neutrogena's ad agency. "They handle the product, test, prove, and evaluate the outcome."[62]

Cultural characteristics play a role in external search, as well. According to research, consumers who are members of subcultural groups and not culturally assimilated— fully integrated into the surrounding culture—tend to conduct a wider search of external sources. And members of subcultural groups who identify with the surrounding culture are more likely to search for information among media advertisements. Thus, marketers should create informative advertising messages when targeting these consumer segments.[63] Although independent search tends to increase as available time increases, time spent on this type of search is generally quite minimal.

Internet and Social Media Sources

Without leaving their keyboards or smartphones, consumers can use the Internet to search through mountains of data online, locate any details needed to make purchase decisions, and buy. In fact, consumers can use the Internet to get information from all five of the sources just mentioned. Sometimes consumers search for specific information; at other times they simply browse.[64] Consumers tend to use the same Internet search sources over and over, although the emergence of new online sites can disrupt this inertia.[65] One study suggests that women and older consumers visit websites longer than others do.[66] Speed, user control, and two-way communication capability are key elements of website interactivity for conducting online searches.[67]

In general, consumers who have a pleasant experience with a company's website will have more positive attitudes toward the site and its brands.[68] Consumers report higher satisfaction and stronger buying intentions when searching and shopping on sites that use an avatar—an animated "person"— to deliver information.[69] For example, IKEA's Anna is an animated customer service representative that answers online shoppers' questions about the store, its products, and its services. These virtual shopping agents are particularly effective for introducing newcomers to a website's offerings and guiding them through the search and service process.[70] Internet ads can also encourage current customers to search and buy again. Research shows that the number of exposures to Internet ads, the number of websites visited, and the number of pages viewed all have a positive effect on repeat purchasing.[71]

In addition to conducting keyword searches on sites such as Google, consumers can use social media (such as Pinterest, Facebook, Twitter, and blogs) to research brands and products. In-vehicle systems such as General Motors' OnStar information platform now feature product, hotel, and restaurant searches and suggestions.[72] Many consumers download and use mobile phone-based shopping apps to compare prices, including retailer-sponsored apps offered by Walmart and Amazon.[73] Some websites provide assisted search, displaying recommended products based on their prediction of what each consumer will like. In these cases, greater variability causes consumers to search less, which is contrary to what is commonly observed in search without recommendations.[74]

Some consumers use shopping agents such as Shopping.com to organize their search results according to price, retail source, and other attributes. However, consumers do not always accurately assess whether a shopping agent's recommendations are appropriate and effective in a particular buying situation. Thus, consumers may make poor buying decisions by using an inferior shopping agent and by choosing offers they should have avoided.[75] Also, when consumers using a shopping agent receive recommendations about unfamiliar products, they check additional recommendations for familiar products as a context in which to evaluate the unfamiliar products.[76] Over time, analyzing consumers' buying patterns can improve shopping agents' recommendations.[77] Still, consumers who make numerous visits to a website may not buy even when the site offers tools to help them make better decisions.[78]

Information Overload

Consumers today have access to so much information that they can actually become overloaded. Depending on the way in which the information is structured, an overload can lead to a decline in decision quality.[79] Some search sites therefore apply more efficient search techniques that prioritize results by identifying the most popular or frequently accessed sites.[80] An ordered list with the "best" result presented first may actually encourage consumers to keep exploring less-than-optimal options, resulting in less-than-optimal buying decisions. On the other hand, consumers whose searches uncover increasingly better options may have more positive brand evaluations and be motivated to search for superior choices.[81]

Despite the potential for overload, does decision quality suffer when consumers desire more choice options? Some research indicates that choice overload can occur in situations where the problem is complex and the consumer has difficulty dealing with complexity.[82] However, other research suggests that increasing the number of options does not generally reduce choice quality. Nevertheless, marketers should always be sensitive to the amount of information presented in order to ensure that overload does not occur.

Simulations

Advances in technology and graphics have dramatically improved the online experience. Website developers can now simulate the retail experience as well as product trials by creating sites that incorporate special and interactive effects including audio, video, zoom, panoramic views, streaming media, and three-dimensional product representations that can be manipulated. Creating a virtual product experience has a positive effect on consumer product knowledge and brand attitude, thereby reducing perceived risk and increasing purchase intention.[83] Thousands of colleges and universities worldwide are offering virtual campus tours that can be viewed online, on mobile apps, or on social media.[84]

The Online Community

Often people with a common interest or condition related to a product or service go online to share ideas by using websites, discussion forums, text chat, and other tools.[85] Research indicates that the most common interactions focus on product recommendations and how-to-use-it advice.[86] Often this information can be very influential in the consumer's decision process because it is not controlled by marketers and is therefore seen as more credible. The actual words used in a review can influence attitudes. Specifically, consumers will have more favorable attitudes toward hedonic products that were reviewed using figurative language such as metaphors, idioms, hyperbole, and other figurative language.[87]

In fact, one study shows that 80 percent of consumers changed their mind about buying a good or service after reading a negative review online. On the other hand, positive reviews influenced the buying decisions of 87 percent of consumers surveyed.[88] Moreover, consumers place a higher value on the input of reviewers who respond quickly to inquiries and provide a good deal of information.[89] In addition, reviews written by people whose tastes seem to be similar to the consumer's are more persuasive than reviews written by people with dissimilar tastes.[90] And if consumers are evaluating a brand by itself, they are likely to have positive evaluations if they see it has an online fan base similar to themselves—or has at least some brand fans similar to themselves.[91] To improve conversion rates among review readers, marketers should encourage reviewers to describe their product experiences using vivid language that conveys their emotions and using words consistent with the product category.[92]

An increasing number of retailers and manufacturers are tracking consumers' online information search and purchase patterns to provide additional assistance and recommendations. For example, consumers who rent or stream movies from Netflix are encouraged to rate them so that the site can recommend other movies based on what each consumer liked and didn't like. This is Netflix's way of adding movies to the consideration set and providing more information for consumer decision-making.

 Marketing Implications

Consumers are buying online more frequently, making bigger purchases, and choosing a wider variety of products than they did in the early days of the Internet. Still, online marketers tend to be less successful when shoppers cannot judge the quality of a product such as a sofa (as the defunct furniture retailer Living.com found out).[93] Facilitating extended searches for even inexpensive items like books can boost sales significantly, as Amazon.com learned with its "LOOK INSIDE!" feature, which lets consumers read pages from individual books.

When shopping for homes and other major purchases, many consumers use the Internet or mobile apps to search for information and then complete the purchase in person, although a small number will buy without any personal experience of the offering.

Many consumers see product choice as riskier when they lack access to experiential information until after they have completed an online purchase.[94] Sometimes consumers search but then abandon their online shopping carts because of frustration over the time and effort needed to check out; some do not buy because they get no information about shipping fees and taxes until they reach the final screen, or they balk at the fees at the last minute.[95] In some cases, consumers fill their shopping carts for entertainment purposes rather than with a specific purchase in mind; in other cases, they fill their carts as part of the search and return to buy later.[96] Among consumers who abandon carts several times over the course of a month, 48 percent will buy if the marketer makes another approach—and this group will spend more, too, suggesting that filling and leaving an online cart is simply part of the buying decision process for these consumers.[97] Yet in many cases, consumers leave products in the cart because they plan to continue shopping using another device, which is why retailers can encourage return visits simply by e-mailing reminders of products viewed and products in the cart.[98] Among retailers that send e-mail reminders, 60 percent of the reminders stimulate consumers to buy within 24 hours of receipt.[99]

To learn which online tactics are most effective for their site and products, marketers must track consumers' search and purchase behaviors using appropriate measurements. Note that marketers need specific strategies for individual markets because activities that are effective with U.S. consumers will not be effective everywhere. So, for instance, the Web-based book retailer Flipkart offers the usual credit card and debit card options to its customers in India. In addition, it allows buyers to pay cash for their books when delivered or set up a monthly payment plan for their purchases—options not commonly available to U.S. buyers of books online.[100]

7-3b HOW MUCH DO WE ENGAGE IN EXTERNAL SEARCH?

Much of the research on external search has concentrated on examining how much information consumers acquire prior to making a judgment or decision. One of the key findings is that the degree of search activity is usually quite limited, even for purchases that are typically considered important.[101]

With more consumers shopping online, search activity is increasing because online sources are very convenient. Yet consumers' Internet search patterns can differ depending on type of product. Specifically, when researching *experience goods* (products that cannot easily be evaluated until after purchase and use), consumers tend to dig into the details and spend some time on each web page. Consumer-contributed product reviews and multimedia sources such as video demonstrations are particularly helpful during such searches because they enable consumers to better understand these products before the purchase. On the other hand, when researching *search goods* (products that can be evaluated before purchase and use), consumers tend to cast the net wider, searching more sites but spending less time on each web page.[102]

Nevertheless, information search can vary widely from a simple hunt for one or two pieces of information to a very extensive search relying on many sources. In an attempt to explain this variance, researchers have identified a number of causal factors that relate to our motivation, ability, and opportunity to process information.

Motivation to Process Information

As the motivation to process information increases, external search will generally be more extensive. Six factors increase our motivation to conduct an external search: (1) involvement and perceived risk, (2) the perceived costs of and benefits resulting from the search, (3) the nature of the consideration set, (4) relative brand uncertainty, (5) attitudes toward the search, and (6) the level of discrepancy of new information.

■ *Involvement and perceived risk.* To understand how involvement relates to external search, recall the distinction from Chapter 2 between situational involvement—a response to a particular situation—and enduring involvement—an ongoing response. Higher situational involvement will generally lead to a greater prepurchase search,[103] whereas enduring involvement relates to an ongoing search regardless of whether problem recognition exists.[104] Thus, consumers with high enduring involvement with cars are more likely to read automotive magazines, visit car shows and car-related websites, and seek out other information about cars on a regular basis.

Because perceived risk is a major determinant of involvement, it should not be surprising that when consumers face riskier decisions, they engage in more external search activity. One of the key components of perceived risk is uncertainty regarding the consequences of behavior, and consumers use external search as a way to reduce this uncertainty.[105] Consumers are more likely to search when they are uncertain about which brand to choose than when they are uncertain about a brand's specific attribute. Consumers also search more when they are evaluating services rather than products because services are intangible and hence perceived as more uncertain.[106] Finally, consumers will have higher motivation to search if the consequences are more serious, such as those entailing high financial or social risk. This situation explains why consumers often search more extensively for information about higher-priced products or services.

■ *Perceived costs and benefits.* External search activity is also greater when its perceived benefits are high relative to its costs.[107] In these situations, consumers who search will benefit by reducing their uncertainty and increasing the likelihood of their making a better decision, obtaining a better value, and enjoying the shopping process. The costs associated with external search are time, effort, inconvenience, and money (including traveling to stores and dealers). All these factors place psychological or physical strain on the consumer. In general, consumers tend to continue searching until they perceive that the costs outweigh the benefits. The desire to reduce searching costs explains why many supermarkets now offer a variety of nontraditional items like electronics and furniture, becoming places "where people do all their gift shopping."[108] As noted earlier, consumers who uncover increasingly better options will be motivated to keep searching for superior options.[109] Even so, consumers tend to minimize their initial search investment, delay further searches after making a choice, and underestimate the future costs (both search and usage) of switching to another offering.[110]

■ *Consideration set.* If the consideration set contains a number of attractive alternatives, consumers will be motivated to engage in external search to decide which alternative to select. On the other hand, a consideration set that contains only one or two brands reduces the need to search for information.

■ *Relative brand uncertainty.* When consumers are uncertain about which brand is the best, they are more motivated to engage in external search.[111] They also engage in more external search to learn about features when brands vary along unique dimensions, even though continued search may reduce their satisfaction with the eventual decision.[112]

■ *Attitudes toward search.* Some consumers like to search for information and do so extensively.[113] These consumers generally have positive beliefs about the value and benefits of their search. In particular, extensive search activity appears to be strongly related to the belief that "when important purchases are made quickly, they are regretted."[114] Other consumers simply hate searching and do little of it.

Researchers have identified two groups of Internet searchers.[115] Experienced searchers are the most enthusiastic and heaviest users of the Internet, whereas moderate and light users see it as a source of information only, not a source of entertainment or fun. To appeal to the latter group, some companies have created interesting and engaging games to stimulate consumers to search.[116]

■ *Discrepancy of information.* Whenever consumers encounter something new in their environment, they will try to categorize it by using their stored knowledge. If it does not fit into an existing category, consumers will try to resolve this incongruity by engaging in information search, especially when incongruity is at a moderate level and the consumer has limited knowledge about the product category.[117] Consumers are likely to reject highly incongruous information.[118] Marketers can capitalize on this tendency by introducing moderate discrepancies between their brand and other brands.

Exhibit 7.8 ▶ Utilizing Discrepancy

Marketers can use moderate discrepancy between one brand and a competitor such as Diet Pepsi's "skinny can" to encourage consumers to think about their brand in order to resolve the discrepancy.

The same general process applies to the search for information about new products. If a new product is moderately discrepant or incongruent with existing categories of products, the consumer will be motivated to resolve this discrepancy.[119] In particular, consumers explore the most salient attributes in greater depth rather than search for a lot of additional attributes. From a marketing perspective, this behavior suggests that positioning new products as moderately different from existing brands may induce consumers to search for more information that might, in turn, affect their decision-making process.

Ability to Process Information

External search is also strongly influenced by the consumer's ability to process information. Researchers have studied the ways that four variables affect the extent of external information search: (1) consumer knowledge, (2) cognitive abilities, (3) consumer affect, and (4) demographic factors.

■ *Consumer knowledge.* Common sense suggests that expert consumers search less because they already have more complex knowledge stored in memory. However, research results on this subject have been mixed.[120] Part of the problem stems from the way that *knowledge* is defined. Some studies have measured *subjective knowledge*, the consumer's perception about what he or she knows relative to what others know. *Objective knowledge* refers to the actual information stored in memory that can be measured with a formal knowledge test. Researchers have linked objective knowledge to information search, although both types of knowledge are somewhat related. One study found that subjective knowledge influences the locations where consumers search for information as well as the quality of their choices.[121]

Specifically, several studies have found an inverted-U relationship between knowledge and search.[122] Consumers with moderate levels of knowledge search the most. They tend to have a higher level of motivation and at least some basic knowledge, which helps them to interpret new information. Experts, on the other hand, search less because they have more knowledge stored in memory, and they also know how to target their search to the most relevant or diagnostic information, ignoring that which is irrelevant—except when the search involves new products. Because experts have more developed memory structures, they have an advantage when learning novel information and can acquire more information about new products.

■ *Cognitive abilities.* Consumers with higher basic cognitive abilities, such as a high IQ and the ability to integrate complex information, not only are more likely to acquire more information than consumers with little or no knowledge but also are able to process this information in more complex ways.[123]

- *Consumer affect.* Positive affect results in more efficient processing, according to research, whereas negative affect appears to make judgments both less efficient and more effortful.[124]

- *Demographics.* As researchers continue to investigate whether certain types of consumers search more than others, they have discovered a few consistent patterns. For instance, consumers with higher education tend to search more than less educated consumers do. This situation results because consumers with more education have at least moderate levels of knowledge and better access to information sources than the less educated do.[125]

Opportunity to Process Information

Consumers who have the motivation and ability to search for information must still have the opportunity to process that information before an extensive search can take place. Situational factors that might affect the search process include (1) the amount of information, (2) the information format, (3) the time available, and (4) the number of items being chosen.

- *Amount of information available.* In any decision situation, the amount of information available to consumers can vary greatly, depending on the number of brands on the market, the attribute information available about each brand, the number of retail outlets or dealers, and the number of other sources of information, such as magazines or knowledgeable friends. With the use of the Internet and social media, which can generate greater external search, consumers can do more searching as the amount of available information increases, not to mention cell phone access to price comparisons. If information is restricted or not available, however, consumers have a hard time engaging in extensive external search.

- *Information format.* The format in which information is presented can also strongly influence the search process. Sometimes information is available from diverse sources or locations, but consumers must expend considerable effort to collect it (contacting different companies or stores, for instance). In contrast, presenting information in a manner that reduces consumer effort can enhance information search and usage, particularly when the consumer is in the decision mode.[126] As an example, U.S. regulations require foods to carry a concise, easy-to-read nutrition label (see Exhibit 7.9), thereby improving opportunity to process.[127] A related study found that consumers increase their use of nutritional information when the

Nutrition Facts
Serving Size 3/4 Cup (27g)

Amount Per Serving	Cereal	With 1/2 Cup Skim Milk
Calories	90	130
Calories from Fat	10	10
	Daily Value (%)	
Total Fat 1g*	**2**	**2**
Saturated Fat 0 g	**0**	**0**
Trans Fat 0 g	**0**	**0**
Cholesterol 0 mg	**0**	**0**
Sodium 190 mg	**8**	**11**
Potassium 85 mg	**2**	**8**
Total Carbohydrate 23 g	**8**	**10**
Dietary Fiber 5 g	**20**	**20**
Sugars 5 g		
Protein 2 g		
Vitamin A	0	4
Vitamin C	10	15
Calcium	0	15
Iron	2	2

Exhibit 7.9 ▶ Information Format

Public policy makers have tried to make nutrition labels easier for consumers to understand and use by improving the format of this information. How easy do you think it is to understand the nutrition information in this exhibit?

Source: From Peter H. Bloch, Daniel L. Sherrell, and Nancy M. Ridgeway, "Consumer Search: An Extended Framework," *Journal of Consumer Research*, June 1986, p. 120. Reprinted with permission of University of Chicago Press.

rewards of good nutrition are made more explicit.[128] In addition, consumers will engage in more leisurely exploratory searches if the information surrounding an object is visually simple and uncluttered.[129] The order in which options are presented can also influence attitude and preference.[130] If consumers hear a familiar song and then listen to a newer version of that song by another musical group, for example, they tend to prefer the familiar version because they encountered it first.

- *Time availability.* Consumers who face no time restrictions have more opportunity to search. If consumers are under time pressure, however, they will severely restrict their search activity.[131] Further, consumers will spend less time getting information from different sources as time pressure increases.[132] Time pressure is one of the main reasons that consumers search and shop on the Internet. One study found that when consumers revisit a website for search reasons, they spend less total time on the site because they look at fewer pages, not because they spend less time looking at each page.[133]

■ *Number of items being chosen.* When consumers are making a decision about multiple items, research suggests that they will conduct a more extensive search with less variability in search patterns than if the decision involves the purchase or use of only one item.[134]

 ## Marketing Implications

The extent to which consumers search for external information has important implications for marketing strategy. If many consumers tend to search extensively for a particular product or service, marketers can facilitate this process by making information readily available and easily accessible at the lowest cost and with the least consumer effort. To do this, marketers should consider redesigning their product packaging, websites, ads, and other promotional materials to add information that will alter consumers' attitudes and change their buying behavior. Some include QR (quick response) codes in various marketing elements so that consumers can get

more information via cell phone. QR codes, including branded codes and animated codes, are especially popular in China, South Korea, and Japan, which is why marketers such as Alibaba are incorporating them into many marketing activities.[135] Exhibit 7.10 shows how marketers can use QR codes to stimulate information search and processing.

Companies should also provide information about salient and diagnostic attributes, particularly if the brand has a differential advantage. Otherwise, if consumers cannot get the information they need, they may eliminate the brand from their consideration set. Novices, in particular, tend to be influenced by visual cues such as pictures and colors that focus their attention on selected attributes, a factor that affects their external search and, ultimately, their brand choices.[136]

Moreover, marketers can segment the market for a product or service according to search activity. One study identified six clusters of searchers in the purchase of a car.[137] Another found that consumers who search online for cars are younger and better educated and conduct more searches than those who do not use the Internet—and that they would have searched more extensively if they could not have used the Internet.[138]

Do:

- *Have a purpose.* What is the purpose of the QR code? For example, do you want consumers to scan the code so they can watch an instructional video or to download a discount coupon?

- *Explain what will happen.* Let consumers know why they should scan the code. For example, an ad might state: "Scan this code for an exclusive discount."

- *Plan for the small screen.* Whatever content you offer, be sure it looks good shrunk to the size of a phone screen. The words must be readable and graphics must be clear on the small screen.

- *Monitor and evaluate QR code usage.* Beyond monitoring the number of consumers who scan the code daily and weekly, track how much time they spend with the information (do they watch the entire 60-second video?). Also determine how many are repeat visitors and how many click to the brand's Facebook page or website.

Don't:

- *Let design overpower the code.* Consumers should be able to see and scan the QR code wherever it's placed (on a product label or tag, in a magazine ad, etc.)

- *Post once and forget it.* Change the content from time to time to encourage repeat visits and provide additional information if and when consumers search again.

- *Link to content not valued by the audience.* Reward customers for taking the time to scan the code by offering interesting, beneficial content such as exclusive discounts, contests, or interviews with brand spokespeople.

- *Miss the chance to extend the relationship.* Invite consumers who scan the code to subscribe to an e-newsletter or "like" the brand on Facebook for special offers, product specifications, and more details.

Sources: Based on information in Karen M. Kroll, "Decoding ROI in Marketing's QR Codes," *COMPUTERWORLD,* November 14, 2011, www .computerworld.com; Tim Donnelly, "How to Use QR Codes to Market Your Business," *Inc.,* December 16, 2010, www.inc.com; Matthias Galica, "5 Big Mistakes to Avoid in Your QR Code Marketing Campaign," *Mashable,* August 2, 2011, www.mashable.com; and Hamilton Chan, "5 Steps for a Successful QR Code Marketing Campaign," *Mashable,* November 11, 2011, www.mashable.com.

Exhibit 7.10 ▶ Marketing with QR Codes

In high-tech markets, older consumers tend to search information channels that provide fairly uncomplicated information, whereas better educated consumers tend to search all information channels.[139]

Determining which search activities are commonly used for a particular product helps marketers plan to meet the information needs of their targeted consumers. Low-search consumers, for example, will focus on getting a good deal, whereas high searchers will need a lot of attention and information to offset their low levels of confidence and prior satisfaction. Marketers can be very selective in providing low searchers with information, emphasizing only those attributes that are most salient and diagnostic.

Marketers can attempt to stimulate external search by providing information in a highly accessible manner. Retailers and restaurants are offering Wi-Fi to facilitate search and reinforce customer loyalty, as well as the use of apps for ordering, discounts, and payment. When Macy's opened its first Backstage off-price stores, it installed Wi-Fi and encouraged customers to comparison shop, so they could confirm how much they were saving.[140] Such opportunities for additional search may lead low searchers to information that will change their attitudes and affect their buying decisions. Marketers can also provide consumers with incentives to search.

7-3c WHAT KIND OF INFORMATION IS ACQUIRED IN EXTERNAL SEARCH?

Researchers are interested in the types of information that consumers acquire during an external search because this information can potentially play a crucial role in influencing the consumers' judgments and decision-making. When searching external sources, consumers usually acquire information about brand name, price, and other attributes.

Brand Name Information
Brand name is the most frequently accessed type of information because it is a central node around which other information can be organized in memory.[141] Thus, when we know the brand name, we can immediately activate other relevant nodes. For example, we can draw on prior knowledge and associations if we know the brand name is Whirlpool.

Price Information
Price is often the focus of consumer search because it tends to be diagnostic and can be used to make inferences about other attributes such as quality and value.[142] One study found that when price and quality are not directly correlated for a product category, consumers who use quality-screening agents to search for purchase options online are actually more sensitive to price differences.[143] Yet the search for price is less important than we might expect (due to the low overall extent of search), and it does not become more important when price variations increase and costs are higher.[144] In line with construal level theory (see Chapter 4), consumers will rely more on price as a quality cue when the decision is psychologically distant—when it relates to someone else, for instance.[145]

Even when consumers search on the basis of price, prior brand preference plays a role in how other information is processed.[146] Specifically, consumers who switch to a lower-price product during their search still retain some preference for the brand they preferred before search, which tends to bias their information processing in favor of that preferred brand. Consumers who search for price across multiple stores and over a period of time do, in fact, save more than those who search only one way.[147] When searching for a deal, consumers consider not only how much they will save in an absolute sense by buying a particular item (absolute savings), but how much they will save relative to other items they might buy (relative savings).[148] Consumers considering products that are increasing in price may search more extensively to be sure they are getting the most for their money.[149] Also, if marketers announce a product's price before it is launched, consumers who encounter that information in early searches will integrate it as a quality-related element later, when the product is available.[150]

Finally, the importance of price depends on the culture. For example, compared to other countries, consumers in Japan have not traditionally been fond of discounters. However, this has changed as many now search for bargains in low-price stores. Women have traditionally been the target market for 100-yen discount stores, yet a growing number of businessmen are willing to shop there for socks and other basic items.[151]

Information About Other Attributes
After brand and price, attribute information for which consumers will search depends on which attributes are salient and diagnostic in the offering category (see Exhibit 7.11). Consumers are more likely to access information that is relevant to their goals. For example, if a major goal in choosing a snack is to eat healthy, a consumer would probably collect information about each snack's ingredients, how much fat it contains, and how many calories. Note that size labels on food packages affect perceptions because consumers tend to rely on simple heuristics (like number of portions) rather than closely examining the details (such as number of ounces).[152] Also, when consumers switch goals from one purchase occasion to the next, as when looking for an economy car instead of one that is fast, the search they perform for the second task is more efficient because they can transfer the knowledge from the first task.[153]

Image Courtesy of The Advertising Archives

Exhibit 7.11 ▶ Attributes

Consumers respond to ads that show attributes that are both salient and diagnostic.

7-3d IS EXTERNAL SEARCH ALWAYS ACCURATE?

Consumers can be just as biased in their search for external information as they are during internal search. In particular, consumers tend to search for external information that confirms rather than contradicts their overall beliefs. In one study, consumers with a strong price-quality belief tended to search more for higher priced brands.[154] Unfortunately, confirmation bias can lead consumers to avoid important information, resulting in a less-than-optimal decision outcome. Thus, if a lower priced, high-quality brand were available, consumers might never acquire information about it and therefore never select it for purchase.

7-3e HOW DO WE ENGAGE IN EXTERNAL SEARCH?

External search follows a series of sequential steps that can provide further insight into the consumer's decision. These steps include orientation, or getting an overview of the product display; evaluation, or comparing options on key attributes; and verification, or confirming the choice.[155] Researchers have examined the order of information acquisition during evaluation, in particular, because they assume that information acquired earlier in the decision process plays a more significant role than information acquired later.[156] Once a brand emerges as the leader early in the search process, subsequent information acquisition and evaluation are distorted in favor of that brand.[157]

Search Stages

Consumers access different sources and use different decision criteria at different stages of the search process. In the early stages, mass media and marketer-related sources tend to be more influential, whereas interpersonal sources are more critical when the actual decision is made.[158] Early in a search, consumers are more likely to access information that is especially salient, diagnostic, and goal related. However, if they can recall salient, diagnostic information from memory, they will have little need to search for it externally. Therefore, consumers will search first for information on attributes that provoke greater uncertainty or are less favorable.[159]

Early in a search, consumers will use simpler criteria to screen out options and then apply more detailed decision rules later in the search process. How highly a brand ranks early in the search may have little influence on the likelihood that the consumer will select it later in the process.[160] Because consumers tend to search first for brands with a higher perceived attractiveness, it is important for marketers to encourage positive brand attitudes. Consumers who are new to a product or service category will start by searching for information about low-risk, well-known brands; then search lesser known brands; and then consolidate the information leading to a preference for brands that provide the greatest utility.[161]

Searching by Brand or Attribute

Two major types of processes are (1) *searching by brand*, in which consumers acquire all the needed information on one brand before moving on to the next, and (2) *searching by attribute*, in which consumers compare brands in terms of one attribute at a time, such as by price.[162] Consumers generally prefer to process by attribute because doing so is easier.

Consumers are very sensitive to the manner in which information is stored in memory and the format in which it is presented in the store.[163] If information is organized by brand, as is the case in most stores where all the information is on packages, consumers will process information by brand. Experts, in particular, tend to process by brand because they have more brand-based knowledge. The fact that consumers are accustomed to processing by brand may bias processing, however, even when information is organized by attribute.[164] In addition, different search strategies affect consumers' decision processes differently.[165] Consumers who process by brand remain high in uncertainty until the very end of the search process, whereas those who search by attribute gradually reduce their uncertainty.

Nevertheless, consumers with less knowledge will take advantage of opportunities to process by attribute, such as by viewing information in a matrix in *Consumer Reports* or in another format that simplifies searching. One study found that presenting lists of nutritional information in the grocery store is popular with consumers. The *Consumer Reports* rating charts, which provide information about the top brands and best buys in various product categories in a simple format, are popular sources of information. As noted earlier, search engines and shopping agents also make it easier for consumers to process by attribute, especially by price.

Marketing Implications

Marketers have to make the specific information that consumers seek easily and readily available by emphasizing it in communications, whether printed, online, broadcast, accessed through mobile app, or presented through the sales force. It is important to remember that consumers are less likely to choose a brand that performs poorly on attributes that are accessed frequently. Therefore, marketers should be sure that their offerings perform well on attributes that are heavily accessed, including price. In addition, marketers can develop search maps using data about consumers' online search patterns for products at a particular retailer (e.g., Amazon.com). Based on these maps, marketers can see which brands are the strongest competitors and on which attributes they compete.[166]

When marketers promise to match the lowest price that consumers can find, such policies spark more extensive searching when search costs are low (as consumers look for the lowest price) but less extensive searching when search costs are high (and consumers perceive that the policy signals low prices).[167] Many U.S. retailers offer a price-matching guarantee to reassure consumers about their low prices, and some also accept competitors' discount coupons as an added inducement. Finally, companies can pay search sites such as Google to make brand information available in a prominently positioned sponsored link when consumers perform certain keyword searches. In China, Henan Yilong Carpet Factory, which markets handmade silk rugs, credits its use of Google's online and mobile search services as a major factor in boosting annual sales from $700,000 to $5 million within eight years.[168]

Summary:

This chapter examined the initial stages of the consumer decision-making process. Problem recognition, the first stage, is the perceived difference between an ideal state and the actual state. When there is a discrepancy between these two states, the consumer may be motivated to resolve it by engaging in decision-making. Internal search is the recall of information, experiences, and feelings from memory. The extent of internal search generally increases as motivation, ability, and opportunity increase. Aspects of an offer that are more salient, diagnostic, vivid, and related to goals are the most likely to be recalled. Biases that apply to internal search include: confirmation bias (the tendency to remember information that reinforces our overall beliefs), inhibition (the recall of some information inhibits the recall of other attributes), and mood (the tendency to recall mood-congruent information).

When consumers need more information or are uncertain about recalled information, they engage in external search, acquiring information from outside sources such as retailers, media, social media, and product experience through prepurchase search or ongoing search. Consumers will conduct a more extensive search when they have a higher motivation and opportunity to process information. Situational factors affect the consumer's opportunity to process the information. Brand name and price are the most accessed attributes in an external search. Consumers also tend to exhibit a confirmation bias in their external search. More salient and diagnostic information tends to be accessed earlier. Finally, consumers tend to process either by brand or by attribute. Attribute search is easier and preferred, but often the information is not organized to facilitate such processing.

Questions for Review and Discussion

1. **How does a discrepancy between the ideal state and the actual state affect consumer behavior?**

2. **What factors affect the inclusion of brands in the consideration set, and why would a company want its brand in the consideration set?**

3. **How does confirmation bias operate in internal and external searches for information?**

4. **What five broad groups of sources can consumers consult during external search?**

5. **How do involvement and perceived risk, perceived costs and benefits, and the consideration set affect a consumer's motivation to conduct an external search?**

6. **When would a consumer be more likely to conduct an external search by brand rather than by attribute? Which search process would a marketer prefer consumers to use—and why?**

Endnotes

1 "With BMWs Common in Gangnam, Koreans Splurge on Bentleys, Maseratis," *Reuters*, March 9, 2015, www.fortune.com.

2 See Lindsay Crouse, "Forget Barefoot; New Trendsetter in Running Shoes Is Cushioning," *New York Times*, February 16, 2015, www.nytimes.com; and "NY Exhibit Unties History, Culture of Sneakers," *Reuters*, July 8, 2015, www.reuters.com.

3 "One Example of How Much Koreans Love Luxury," *Wall Street Journal*, August 17, 2011, www.wsj.com; and Michael Barbaro, "Never Mind What's in Them, Bags Are the Fashion," *New York Times*, December 16, 2007, www.nytimes.com.

4 Joseph W. Alba, J. Wesley Hutchinson, and John G. Lynch, "Memory and Decision Making," in eds. Thomas C. Roberton and Harold H. Kassarjian, *Handbook of Consumer Behavior* (Englewood Cliffs, N.J.: Prentice-Hall, 1991).

5 John R. Hauser and Birger Wernerfelt, "An Evaluation Cost Model of Consideration Sets," *Journal of Consumer Research*, March 1990, pp. 393–408.

6 P. R. Venkat and Shibani Mahtani, "Colgate Buys Myanmar Toothpaste Brand," *Wall Street Journal*, October 28, 2014, www.wsj.com.

7 "India's Air Passenger Traffic Grows by 8 per cent in 2014," *Business Today India*, February 6, 2015, http://www.business-today.in.

8 Andrew Hutchinson, "Big Brand Theory: L'Oréal Stays Connected with Their Audience via Social," *Social Media Today*, September 9, 2015, www.socialmediatoday.com.

9 Kalpesh Kaushik Desai and Wayne D. Hoyer, "Descriptive Characteristics of Memory-Based Consideration Sets: Influence of Usage Occasion Frequency and Usage Location Familiarity," *Journal of Consumer Research* 27, December 2000, pp. 309–323.

10 Prakash Nedungadi and J. Wesley Hutchinson, "The Prototypicality of Brands: Relationships with Brand Awareness, Preference, and Usage," in eds. Elizabeth C. Hirschman and Morris B. Holbrook, *Advances in Consumer Research*, vol. 12

(Provo, Utah: Association for Consumer Research, 1985), pp. 498–503; and Prakash Nedungadi, "Recall and Consumer Consideration Sets: Influencing Choice Without Altering Brand Evaluations," *Journal of Consumer Research*, December 1990, pp. 263–276.

11 Alba, Hutchinson, and Lynch, "Memory and Decision Making."

12 Nedungadi and Hutchinson, "The Prototypicality of Brands"; and James Ward and Barbara Loken, "The Quintessential Snack Food: Measurement of Product Prototypes," in ed. Richard J. Lutz, *Advances in Consumer Research*, vol. 13 (Provo, Utah: Association for Consumer Research, 1986), pp. 126–131.

13 Siew Meng Leong, Swee Hoon Ang, and Lai Leng Tham, "Increasing Brand Name Recall in Print Advertising Among Asian Consumers," *Journal of Advertising*, Summer 1996, pp. 65–82.

14 Stewart Shapiro, Deborah J. MacInnis, and Susan E. Heckler, "The Effects of Incidental Ad Exposure on the Formation of Consideration Sets," *Journal of Consumer Research*, June 1997, pp. 94–104.

15 Alba, Hutchinson, and Lynch, "Memory and Decision Making."

16 S. Ratneshwar and Allan D. Shocker, "Substitution in Use and the Role of Usage Context in Product Category Structures," *Journal of Marketing Research*, August 1991, pp. 281–295.

17 E.J. Schultz, "A Tiger at 60," *Advertising Age*, August 29, 2011, www.adage.com.

18 Nedungadi and Hutchinson, "The Prototypicality of Brands"; and Ward and Loken, "The Quintessential Snack Food."

19 Susan Krashinsky, "Canadian Pride Gets Louder: Tim Hortons Strikes New Tone with Sidney Crosby Ad," *Globe and Mail (Toronto)*, January 3, 2014, www.globeandmail.com.

20 Phil Wahba, "Target Taking Its Small Express Stores to More Markets," *Fortune*, February 2, 2015, www.fortune.com.

21 Gabriel Beltrone, "Coca-Cola Celebrates Its Iconic Bottle's 100th Birthday With 15 New Ads," *Adweek*, March 2, 2015, www.adweek.com.

22 Gabriel Biehal and Dipankar Chakravarti, "Consumers' Use of Memory and External Information in Choice: Macro and Micro Perspectives," *Journal of Consumer Research*, March 1986, pp. 382–405.

23 Gabriel Biehal and Dipankar Chakravarti, "Information Accessibility as a Moderator of Consumer Choice," *Journal of Consumer Research*, June 1983, pp. 1–14.

24 Michaela Waenke, Gerd Bohner, and Andreas Jurkowitsch, "There Are Many Reasons to Drive a BMW?" *Journal of Consumer Research*, September 1997, pp. 170–177.

25 Shai Danziger, Simone Moran, and Vered Rafaely, "The Influence of Ease of Retrieval on Judgment as a Function of Attention to Subjective Experience," *Journal of Consumer Psychology* 16, no. 2, 2006, pp. 191–195.

26 Meryl Paula Gardner, "Advertising Effects on Attributes Recalled and Criteria Used for Brand Evaluations," *Journal of Consumer Research*, December 1983, pp. 310–318; Scott B. MacKenzie, "The Role of Attention in Mediating the Effect of Advertising on Attribute Importance," *Journal of Consumer Research*, September 1986, pp. 174–195; and Priya Raghubir and Geeta Menon, "AIDS and Me, Never the Twain Shall Meet," *Journal of Consumer Research*, June 1998, pp. 52–63.

27 Fellman and Lynch, "Self-Generated Validity and Other Effects of Measurement"; and John G. Lynch, Howard Marmorstein, and Michael F. Weigold, "Choices from Sets Including Remembered Brands," *Journal of Consumer Research*, September 1988, pp. 169–184.

28 Carolyn L. Costley and Merrie Brucks, "Selective Recall and Information Use in Consumer Preferences," *Journal of Consumer Research*, March 1992, pp. 464–474; and Geeta Menon, Priya Raghubit, and Norbert Schwarz, "Behavioral Frequency Judgments," *Journal of Consumer Research*, September 1995, pp. 212–228.

29 Paul M. Herr, Frank R. Kardes, and John Kim, "Effects of Word-of-Mouth and Product-Attribute Information on Persuasion," *Journal of Consumer Research*, March 1991, pp. 454–462.

30 Steve Lohr, "The Invention Mob, Brought to You by Quirky," *New York Times*, February 14, 2015, www.nytimes.com.

31 Walter Kintsch and Tuen A. Van Dyk, "Toward a Model of Text Comprehension and Production," *Psychological Review*, September 1978, pp. 363–394; and S. Ratneshwar, David G. Mick, and Gail Reitinger, "Selective Attention in Consumer Information Processing," in eds. Marvin E. Goldberg, Gerald Gorn, and Richard W. Pollay, *Advances in Consumer Research*, vol. 17 (Provo, Utah: Association for Consumer Research, 1990), pp. 547–553.

32 Jacob Jacoby, Tracy Troutman, Alfred Kuss, and David Mazursky, "Experience and Expertise in Complex Decision Making," in ed. Richard J. Lutz, *Advances in Consumer Research*, vol. 13 (Provo, Utah: Association for Consumer Research, 1986), pp. 469–475.

33 Stewart Shapiro and Mark T. Spence, "Factors Affecting Encoding, Retrieval, and Alignment of Sensory Attributes in a Memory-Based Brand Choice Task," *Journal of Consumer Research*, March 2002, pp. 603–617.

34 Gardner, "Advertising Effects on Attributes Recalled and Criteria Used for Brand Evaluations"; and Mackenzie, "The Role of Attention in Mediating the Effect of Advertising on Attribute Importance."

35 Craig Giammona, "With Chobani Back on Track, Founder Is Staying Put," *Bloomberg Businessweek*, September 10, 2015, www.bloomberg.com.

36 Mark I. Alpert, "Identification of Determinant Attributes," *Journal of Marketing Research*, May 1971, pp. 184–191.

37 M. R. F. Buckley, "Coffee, Doughnut Giant Has Recipe for Success," *WCVB-TV*, August 14, 2011, www.thebostonchannel.com.

38 Jolita Kiselius and Brian Sternthal, "Examining the Vividness Controversy," *Journal of Consumer Research*, March 1986, pp. 418–431; and Herr, Kardes, and Kim, "Effects of Word-of-Mouth and Product-Attribute Information on Persuasion."

39 Punam Anand Keller and Lauren G. Block, "Vividness Effects," *Journal of Consumer Research*, December 1997, pp. 295–304.

40 Eloise Keating, "Snap To It: Why Snapchat Is the New SME Social Media Secret Weapon," *Smart Company (Australia)*, September 21, 2014, www.smartcompany.com.au.

41 Reid Hastie and Bernadette Park, "The Relationship Between Memory and Judgment Depends on Whether the Judgment Task Is Memory-Based or On-Line," *Psychological Review*, June 1986, pp. 258–268; and Barbara Loken and Ronald Hoverstad, "Relationships Between Information Recall and Subsequent Attitudes," *Journal of Consumer Research*, September 1985, pp. 155–168.

42 Biehal and Chakravarti, "Consumers' Use of Memory and External Information in Choice: Macro and Micro Perspectives"; and Jong-Won Park and Manoj Hastak, "Memory-Based Product Judgments," *Journal of Consumer Research*, December 1994, pp. 534–547.

43 Zeynep Gürhan-Canli, "The Effect of Expected Variability of Product Quality and Attribute Uniqueness on Family Brand Evaluations," *Journal of Consumer Research*, June 2003, pp. 105–114.

44 Hans Baumgartner, Mita Sujan, and James R. Bettman, "Auto-biographical Memories, Affect, and Consumer Information Processing," *Journal of Consumer Psychology* 1, no. 1, 1992, pp. 53–82.

45 Melissa Hudson, "South Bend Cubs Announce Promotions for Upcoming Season," *ABC-57 News (South Bend, IN)*, February 24, 2015, www.abc57.com.

46 Elizabeth Cowley and Eunika Janus, "Not Necessarily Better, but Certainly Different: A Limit to the Advertising Misinformation Effect on Memory," *Journal of Consumer Research*, June 2004, pp. 229–235.

47 Joel Windels, "Social Media Command Centers are Coming of Age," *Brandwatch*, February 12, 2014, www.brandwatch.com; and Jason Duty, "Customer Support in the Virtual Era," *Forbes.com*, September 12, 2011, www.forbes.com.

48 Michael J. Houston, Terry L. Childers, and Susan E. Heckler, "Picture–Word Consistency and the Elaborative Processing of Advertisements," *Journal of Marketing Research*, November 1987, pp. 359–369.

49 Joseph W. Alba and Amitava Chattopadhyay, "Salience Effects in Brand Recall," *Journal of Marketing Research*, November 1986, pp. 363–369; and Kiselius and Sternthal, "Examining the Vividness Controversy."

50 Alba and Chattopadhyay, "Salience Effects in Brand Recall"; and Kiselius and Sternthal, Examining the Vividness Controversy."

51 Gordon H. Bower, "Mood and Memory," *American Psychologist*, February 1981, pp. 129–148; Gordon H. Bower, Stephen Gilligan, and Kenneth Montiero, "Selectivity of Learning Caused by Affective States," *Journal of Experimental Psychology: General*, December 1981, pp. 451–473; and Alice M. Isen, Thomas Shalker, Margaret Clark, and Lynn Karp, "Affect, Accessibility of Material in Memory, and Behavior," *Journal of Personality and Social Psychology*, January 1978, pp. 1–12.

52 Alexandra Burlacu, "Apple iPhone 6 vs. Samsung Galaxy S6: This Ad Convinces You To Change The Way You Charge," *Tech Times*, June 25, 2015, www.techtimes.com.

53 Lauren Johnson, "Mercedes Generated 54% More Traffic by Running Ads on 2 Major Social Sites," *Adweek*, October 1, 2014, www.adweek.com.

54 Peter H. Bloch, Daniel L. Sherrell, and Nancy M. Ridgway, "Consumer Search: An Extended Framework," *Journal of Consumer Research*, June 1986, pp. 119–126.

55 Sharon E. Beatty and Scott M. Smith, "External Search Effort," *Journal of Consumer Research*, June 1987, pp. 83–95.

56 Charles M. Brooks, Patrick J. Kaufmann, and Donald P. Lichtenstein, "Travel Configuration on Consumer Trip-Chained Store Choice," *Journal of Consumer Research* 31, no. 2, 2004, pp. 241–248.

57 Nga N. Ho-Dac, Stephen J. Carson, and William L. Moore, "The Effects of Positive and Negative Online Customer Reviews: Do Brand Strength and Category Maturity Matter?," *Journal of Marketing* 77, no. 6, November 2013, pp. 37–53.

58 Beatty and Smith, "External Search Effort."

59 See Judi Strebel, Tulim Erdem, and Joffre Swait, "Consumer Search in High Technology Markets," *Journal of Consumer Psychology* 14, no. 1–2, 2004, pp. 96–104.

60 David F. Midgley, "Patterns of Interpersonal Information Seeking for the Purchase of a Symbolic Product," *Journal of Marketing Research*, February 1983, pp. 74–83.

61 Janet Schwartz, Mary Frances Luce, and Dan Ariely, "Are Consumers Too Trusting? The Effects of Relationships with Expert Advisers," *Journal of Marketing Research* 48, supplement 1, October 2011, pp. S163–S174.

62 "Brazilian Neutrogena Ad Lets You Wipe the Lipstick Right Off This Actress's Face," *Adweek*, August 7, 2015, www.adweek.com.

63 Denver D'Rozario and Susan P. Douglas, "Effect of Assimilation on Prepurchase External Information-Search Tendencies," *Journal of Consumer Psychology* 8, no. 2, 1999, pp. 187–209.

64 Niranjan J. Raman, "A Qualitative Investigation of Web-Browsing Behavior," in eds. Merrie Brucks and Deborah J. MacInnis, *Advances in Consumer Research*, vol. 24 (Provo, Utah: Association for Consumer Research, 1997), pp. 511–516.

65 Wendy W. Moe and Sha Yang, "Inertia Disruption: The Impact of a New Competitive Entrant on Online Consumer Search," *Journal of Marketing*, January 2009, pp. 109–121.

66 Peter J. Danaher, Guy W. Mullarkey, and Skander Essegaier, "Factors Affecting Web Site Visit Duration: A Cross-Domain Analysis," *Journal of Marketing Research*, May 2006, pp. 182–194.

67 Sally J. McMillan and Jang-Sun Hwang, "Measures of Perceived Interactivity: An Exploration of the Role of Direction of Communication, User Control, and Time in Shaping Perceptions of Interactivity," *Journal of Advertising*, Fall 2002, pp. 29–42; and Yuping Liu and L. J. Shrum, "What Is Interactivity and Is It Always Such a Good Thing," *Journal of Advertising*, Winter 2002, pp. 53–64.

68 Charla Mathwick and Edward Rigdon, "Play, Flow, and the Online Search Experience," *Journal of Consumer Research*, September 2004, pp. 324–332.

69 Martin Holzwarth, Chris Janiszewski, and Marcus M. Neumann, "The Influence of Avatars on Online Consumer Shopping Behavior," *Journal of Marketing*, June 2006, pp. 19–36.

70 Clemens F. Kohler, Andrew J. Rohn, Ko de Ruyter, and Martin Wetzels, "Return on Interactivity: The Impact of Online Agents on Newcomer Adjustment," *Journal of Marketing*, March 2011, pp. 93–108.

71 Puneet Manchanda, Jean-Pierre Dubé, Khim Yong Goh, and Pradeep K. Chintagunta, "The Effect of Banner Advertising on Internet Purchasing," *Journal of Marketing Research*, February 2006, pp. 98–108.

72 John Irwin, "OnStar's Updated Mobile App Offers Shopping Options, Coupons," *Automotive News*, September 15, 2015, www.autonews.com.

73 Shelly Banjo, "Walmart Built the Fastest-Growing Retail App By Focusing on One Key Shopper Habit," *Quartz*, September 16, 2015, www.qz.com.

74 Benedict G. C. Dellaert and Gerald Häubl, "Searching in Choice Mode: Consumer Decision Processes in Product Search with Recommendations," *Journal of Marketing Research* 49, no. 2, April 2012, pp. 277–288.

75 Andrew D. Gershoff, Susan M. Broniarczyk, and Patricia M. West, "Recommendation or Evaluation? Task Sensitivity in Information Source Selection," *Journal of Consumer Research*, December 2001, pp. 418–438.

76 Alan D. J. Cooke, Harish Sujan, Mita Sujan, and Barton A. Weitz, "Marketing the Unfamiliar: The Role of Context and Item-Specific Information in Electronic Agent Recommendations," *Journal of Marketing Research*, November 2002, pp. 488–497.

77 Dan Ariely, John G. Lynch Jr., and Manuel Aparicio IV, "Learning by Collaborative and Individual-Based Recommendation Agents," *Journal of Consumer Psychology* 14, no. 1–2, 2004, pp. 81–95.

78 Caterina Sismeiro and Randolph E. Bucklin, "Modeling Purchase Behavior at an E-Commerce Web Site," *Journal of Marketing Research*, August 2004, pp. 306–323.

79 Nicholas H. Lurie, "Decision Making in Information-Rich Environments: The Role of Information Structure," *Journal of Consumer Research*, March 2004, pp. 473–486.

80 Ross Kerber, "Direct Hit Uses Popularity to Narrow Internet Searches," *Wall Street Journal*, July 2, 1998, p. B4.

81 Kristen Diel, "When Two Rights Make a Wrong: Searching Too Much in Ordered Environments," *Journal of Marketing Research*, August 2005, pp. 313–322; and Kristen Diel and Gal Zauberman, "Searching Ordered Sets," *Journal of Consumer Research* 31, no. 4, 2005, pp. 824–832.

82 Benjamin Scheibehenne, Rainer Greifeneder, and Peter M. Todd, "Can There Ever Be Too Many Options? A Meta-Analytical Review of Choice Overload," *Journal of Consumer Research*, October 2010, pp. 409–425.

83 Hairong Li, Terry Daugherty, and Frank Biocca, "Impact of 3-D Advertising on Product Knowledge, Brand Attitude, and Purchase Intention: The Mediating Role of Presence," *Journal of Advertising*, Fall 2002, pp. 43–57.

84 "Virtual Tours Growing in Popularity," *ICEF Monitor*, August 11, 2015, www.monitor.icef.com.

85 Eileen Fischer, Julia Bristor, and Brenda Gainer, "Creating or Escaping Community? An Exploratory Study of Internet Consumers' Behaviors," in eds. Kim P. Corfman and John G. Lynch, *Advances in Consumer Research*, vol. 23 (Provo, Utah: Association for Consumer Research, 1996), pp. 178–182; and John Buskin, "Tales from the Front," *Wall Street Journal*, December 7, 1998, p. R6.

86 Neil A. Granitz and James C. Ward, "Virtual Community: A Sociocognitive Analysis," in eds. Kim P. Corfman and John G. Lynch, *Advances in Consumer Research*, vol. 23 (Provo, Utah: Association for Consumer Research, 1996), pp. 161–166.

87 Ann Kronrod and Shai Danziger, "'Wii Will Rock You!' The Use and Effect of Figurative Language in Consumer Reviews of Hedonic and Utilitarian Consumption," *Journal of Consumer Research* 40, no. 4, December 2013, pp. 726–739.

88 Sarah Mahoney, "Study: Negative Reviews Grow More Powerful," *MediaPost*, August 31, 2011, www.mediapost.com.

89 Allen M. Weiss, Nicholas H. Lurie, and Deborah J. MacInnis, "Listening to Strangers: Whose Responses Are Valuable, How Valuable Are They, and Why?" *Journal of Marketing Research*, August 2008, pp. 425–436.

90 Rebecca Walker Naylor, Cait Poynor Lamberton, and David A. Norton, "Seeing Ourselves in Others: Reviewer Ambiguity, Egocentric Anchoring, and Persuasion," *Journal of Marketing Research*, June 2011, pp. 617–631.

91 Rebecca Walker Naylor, Cait Poyner Lamberton, and Patricia M. West, "Beyond the 'Like' Button: The Impact of Mere Virtual Presence on Brand Evaluations and Purchase Intentions in Social Media Settings," *Journal of Marketing* 76, no. 6, November 2012, pp. 105–120.

92 Stephan Ludwig, Ko de Ruyter, Mike Friedman, Elisabeth C. Brüggen, Martin Wetzels, and Gerard Pfann, "More Than Words: The Influence of Affective Content and Linguistic Style Matches in Online Reviews on Conversion Rates," *Journal of Marketing* 77, no. 1, January 2013, pp. 87–103.

93 Holly Vanscoy, "Life after Living.com," *Smart Business*, February 2001, p. 68.

94 Stacy L. Wood, "Remote Purchase Environments: The Influence of Return Policy Leniency on Two-Stage Decision Process," *Journal of Marketing Research* 38, May 2001, pp. 157–169.

95 "How to Take Advantage of Shopping Cart Abandonment," *eMarketer*, January 13, 2015, www.emarketer.com.

96 Monika Kukar-Kinney and Angeline G. Close, "The Determinants of Consumers' Online Shopping Cart Abandonment," *Journal of the Academy of Marketing Science* 38, 2010, pp. 240–250.

97 Charles Nicholls, "Can Shopping Cart Abandonment Predict Online Buying Behavior?" *ClickZ*, September 13, 2011, www.clickz.com.

98 Andrew Corselli, "Marketers Shouldn't Abandon Product Page Abandonment," *Direct Marketing News*, June 2, 2015, www.dmnews.com.

99 Matt Lindner, "Personalized Shopping Cart Abandonment e-mails Lead to Sales," *Internet Retailer*, December 2, 2014, www.internetretailer.com.

100 Nivedita Mookerji and Dilasha Seth, "Casting the Net Wider," *Business Standard (India)*, September 12, 2011, www.business-standard.com/india.

101 Jacob Jacoby, Robert W. Chestnut, Karl Weigl, and William A. Fisher, "Prepurchase Information Acquisition," in ed. Beverlee B. Anderson, *Advances in Consumer Research*, vol. 3 (Cincinnati, Ohio: Association for Consumer Research, 1976), pp. 306–314; and Jacob Jacoby, Robert W. Chestnut, and William Silberman, "Consumer Use and Comprehension of Nutrition Information," *Journal of Consumer Research*, September 1977, pp. 119–128.

102 Peng Huang, Nicholas H. Lurie, and Sabyasachi Mitra, "Searching for Experience on the Web: An Empirical Examination of Consumer Behavior for Search and Experience Goods," *Journal of Marketing*, March 2009, pp. 55–69.

103 John O. Claxton, Joseph N. Fry, and Bernard Portis, "A Taxonomy of Prepurchase Information Gathering Patterns," *Journal of Consumer Research*, December 1974, pp. 35–42.

104 Bloch, Sherrell, and Ridgway, "Consumer Search: An Extended Framework."

105 R. A. Bauer, "Consumer Behavior as Risk Taking," in ed. Robert S. Hancock, *Dynamic Marketing for a Changing World* (Chicago: American Marketing Association, 1960), pp. 389–398; and Rohit Deshpande and Wayne D. Hoyer, "Consumer Decision Making: Strategies, Cognitive Effort, and Perceived Risk," in *1983 Educators' Conference Proceedings* (Chicago: American Marketing Association, 1983), pp. 88–91.

106 Keith B. Murray, "A Test of Services Marketing Theory," *Journal of Marketing*, January 1991, pp. 10–25; and Joel E. Urbany, Peter R. Dickson, and William L. Wilkie, "Buyer Uncertainty and Information Search," *Journal of Consumer Research*, September 1989, pp. 208–215.

107 David J. Furse, Girish N. Punj, and David W. Stewart, "A Typology of Individual Search Strategies Among Purchasers of New Automobiles," *Journal of Consumer Research*, March 1984, pp. 417–431; Narasimhan Srinivasan and Brian T. Ratchford, "An Empirical Test of a Model of External Search for Automobiles," *Journal of Consumer Research*, September 1991, pp. 233–242; and Jacob Jacoby, James J. Jaccard, Imran Currim, Alfred Kuss, Asim Ansari, and Tracy Troutman, "Tracing the Impact of Item-by-Item Information Accessing on Uncertainty Reduction," *Journal of Consumer Research*, September 1994, pp. 291–303.

108 Calmetta Y. Coleman, "Selling Jewelry, Dolls, and TVs Next to Corn Flakes," *Wall Street Journal*, November 19, 1997, pp. B1, B8.

109 Diehl and Zauberman, "Searching Ordered Sets."

110 Gal Zauberman, "The Intertemporal Dynamics of Consumer Lock-In," *Journal of Consumer Research*, December 2003, pp. 405–419.

111 Sridhar Moorthy, Brian T. Ratchford, and Debabrata Talukdar, "Consumer Information Search Revisited," *Journal of Consumer Research*, March 1997, pp. 263–277.

112 Jill G. Griffin and Susan M. Broniarczyk, "The Slippery Slope: The Impact of Feature Alignability on Search and Satisfaction," *Journal of Marketing Research*, April 2010, pp. 323–334.

113 Calvin P. Duncan and Richard W. Olshavsky, "External Search: The Role of Consumer Beliefs," *Journal of Marketing Research*, February 1982, pp. 32–43; and Girish N. Punj and Richard Staelin, "A Model of Information Search Behavior for New Automobiles," *Journal of Consumer Research*, September 1983, pp. 181–196.

114 Duncan and Olshavsky, "External Search: The Role of Consumer Beliefs."

115 Kathy Hammond, Gil McWilliam, and Andrea Narholz Diaz, "Fun and Work on the Web: Differences in Attitudes between Novices and Experienced Users," in eds. Joseph W. Alba and J. Wesley Hutchinson, *Advances in Consumer Research*, vol. 25 (Provo, Utah: Association for Consumer Research, 1998), pp. 372–378.

116 Joan E. Rigdon, "Advertisers Give Surfers Games to Play," *Wall Street Journal*, October 28, 1996, pp. B1, B6.

117 Laura A. Peracchio and Alice M. Tybout, "The Moderating Role of Prior Knowledge in Schema-Based Product Evaluation," *Journal of Consumer Research*, December 1996, pp. 177–192.

118 Joan Meyers-Levy and Alice Tybout, "Schema-Congruity as Basis for Product Evaluation," *Journal of Consumer Research*, June 1989, pp. 39–54.

119 Julie L. Ozanne, Merrie Brucks, and Dhruv Grewal, "A Study of Information Search Behavior during Categorization of New Products," *Journal of Consumer Research*, March 1992, pp. 452–463.

120 Punj and Staelin, "A Model of Consumer Information Search Behavior for New Automobiles"; and Kiel and Layton, "Dimensions of Consumer Information Seeking."

121 Christine Moorman, Kristin Diehl, David Brinberg, and Blair Kidwell, "Subjective Knowledge, Search Locations, and Consumer Choice," *Journal of Consumer Research*, December 2004, pp. 673–680.

122 Merrie Brucks, "The Effects of Product Class Knowledge on Information Search Behavior," *Journal of Consumer Research*, June 1985, pp. 1–16; James R. Bettman and C. Whan Park, "Effects of Prior Knowledge and Experience and Phase of the Choice Process on Consumer Decision Processes: A Protocol Analysis," *Journal of Consumer Research*, December 1980, pp. 234–248; Eric J. Johnson and J. Edward Russo, "Product Familiarity and Learning New Information," *Journal of Consumer Research*, June 1984, pp. 542–550; P. S. Raju, Subhas C. Lonial, and W. Glyn Mangold, "Differential Effects of Subjective Knowledge, Objective Knowledge, and Usage Experience on Decision Making," *Journal of Consumer Psychology* 4, no. 2, 1995, pp. 153–180; and Joseph W. Alba and J. Wesley Hutchinson, "Dimensions of Consumer Expertise," *Journal of Consumer Research*, March 1987, pp. 411–454.

123 Noel Capon and Roger Davis, "Basic Cognitive Ability Measures as Predictors of Consumer Information Processing Strategies," *Journal of Consumer Research*, June 1984, pp. 551–563.

124 Paul M. Herr, Christine M. Page, Bruce E. Pfeiffer, and Derick F. Davis, "Affective Influences on Evaluative Processing," *Journal of Consumer Research* 38, no. 5, February 2012, pp. 833–845.

125 For a summary of a number of studies, see Joseph W. Newman, "Consumer External Search: Amount and Determinants," in eds. Arch Woodside, Jagdish Sheth, and Peter Bennett, *Consumer and Industrial Buying Behavior* (New York: North-Holland, 1977), pp. 79–94; and Charles M. Schaninger and Donald Sciglimpaglia, "The Influences of Cognitive Personality Traits and Demographics on Consumer Information Acquisition," *Journal of Consumer Research*, September 1981, pp. 208–216.

126 Scott Painton and James W. Gentry, "Another Look at the Impact of Information Presentation Format," *Journal of Consumer Research*, September 1985, pp. 240–244.

127 J. Edward Russo, Richard Staelin, Catherine A. Nolan, Gary J. Russell, and Barbara L. Metcalf, "Nutrition Information in the Supermarket," *Journal of Consumer Research*, June 1986, pp. 48–70.

128 Christine Moorman, "The Effects of Stimulus and Consumer Utilization of Nutrition Information," *Journal of Consumer Research*, December 1990, pp. 362–374.

129 Chris Janiszewski, "The Influence of Display Characteristics on Visual Exploratory Search Behavior," *Journal of Consumer Research*, December 1998, pp. 290–301.

130 Mario Pandelaere, Kobe Millet, and Bram Van den Bergh, "Madonna or Don McLean? The Effect of Order of Exposure on Relative Liking," *Journal of Consumer Psychology* 20, 2010, pp. 442–451.

131 William L. Moore and Donald L. Lehman, "Validity of Information Display Boards," *Journal of Marketing Research*, November 1980, pp. 296–307; and C. Whan Park, Easwar S. Iyer, and Daniel C. Smith, "The Effects of Situational Factors on In-Store Grocery Shopping Behavior," *Journal of Consumer Research*, March 1989, pp. 422–433.

132 John R. Hauser, Glen L. Urban, and Bruce D. Weinberg, "How Consumers Allocate Their Time When Searching for Information," *Journal of Marketing Research*, November 1993, pp. 452–466.

133 Randolph E. Bucklin and Catarina Sismeiro, "A Model of Web Site Browsing Behavior Estimated on Click-Stream Data," *Journal of Marketing Research*, August 2003, pp. 249–267.

134 Alhassan G. Abdul-Muhmin, "Contingent Decision Behavior," *Journal of Consumer Psychology* 8, no. 1, 1999, pp. 91–111.

135 Davey Alba, "Alibaba Reveals a New Kind of QR Code to Fight Counterfeits," *Wired*, May 18, 2015, www.wired.com.

136 Naomi Mandel and Eric J. Johnson, "When Web Pages Influence Choice: Effects of Visual Primes on Experts and Novices," *Journal of Consumer Research*, September 2002, pp. 235–245.

137 Furse, Punj, and Stewart, "A Typology of Individual Search Strategies among Purchasers of New Automobiles."

138 Brian T. Ratchford, Myung-Soo Lee, and Debabrata Talukdar, "The Impact of the Internet on Information Search for Automobiles," *Journal of Marketing Research*, May 2003, pp. 193–209.

139 Judi Strebel, Tülin Erdem, and Joffre Swait, "Consumer Search in High Technology Markets: Exploring the Use of Traditional Information Channels," *Journal of Consumer Psychology*, 2004, pp. 96–104.

140 Chantal Tode, "How Macy's Backstage Could Innovate Off-Price Retail via Mobile," *Mobile Commerce Daily*, May 7, 2015, www.mobilecommercedaily.com.

141 Jacob Jacoby, Robert W. Chestnut, and William A. Fisher, "A Behavioral Process Approach to Information Acquisition in Nondurable Purchasing," *Journal of Marketing Research*, November 1978, pp. 532–544.

142 Marco Bertini, Luc Wathieu, and Sheena S. Iyengar, "The Discriminating Consumer: Product Proliferation and Willingness to Pay for Quality," *Journal of Marketing Research* 49, no. 1, February 2012, pp. 39–49; and Kent B. Monroe, "The Influence of Price Differences and Brand Familiarity on Brand Preferences," *Journal of Consumer Research*, June 1976, pp. 42–49.

143 Kristin Diehl, Laura J. Kornish, and John G. Lynch Jr., "Smart Agents: When Lower Search Costs for Quality Information Increase Price Sensitivity," *Journal of Consumer Research*, June 2003, pp. 56–71.

144 Dhruv Grewal and Howard Marmorstein, "Market Price Variation, Perceived Price Variation, and Consumers' Price Search Decision for Durable Goods," *Journal of Consumer Research*, December 1994, pp. 453–460.

145 Dengfeng Yan and Jaideep Sengupta, "Effects of Construal Level on the Price-Quality Relationship," *Journal of Consumer Research*, August 2011, pp. 376–389.

146 Kurt A. Carlson, Margaret G. Meloy, and Daniel Lieb, "Benefits Leader Reversion: How a Once-Preferred Product Recaptures Its Standing," *Journal of Marketing Research*, December 2009, pp. 788–797.

147 Dinesh K. Gauri, K. Sudhir, and Debabrata Talukdar, "The Temporal and Spatial Dimensions of Price Search: Insights from Matching Household Survey and Purchase Data," *Journal of Marketing Research*, April 2008, pp. 226–240.

148 Ritesh Saini and Sweta C. Thota, "The Psychological Underpinnings of Relative Thinking in Price Comparisons," *Journal of Marketing Research* 49, no. 2, April 2012, pp. 277–288.

149 Hong Yuan and Song Han, "The Effects of Consumers' Price Expectations on Sellers' Dynamic Pricing Strategies," *Journal of Marketing Research* 48, no. 1, February 2011, pp. 48–61.

150 Torsten Bornemann and Christian Homburg, "Psychological Distance and the Dual Role of Price," *Journal of Consumer Research*, October 2011, pp. 490–504.

151 Leo Lewis, "Japanese Men Embrace Inner Cheapskate in Booming Discount Retailers," *Financial Times*, August 9, 2015, www.ft.com.

152 Nilufer Z. Aydinoglu and Aradhna Krishna, "Guiltless Gluttony: The Asymmetric Effect of Size Labels on Size Perceptions and Consumption," *Journal of Consumer Research*, April 2011, pp. 1095–1112.

153 Cynthia Huffman, "Goal Change, Information Acquisition, and Transfer," *Journal of Consumer Psychology* 5, no. 1, 1996, pp. 1–26.

154 Deborah Roedder John, Carol A. Scott, and James R. Bettman, "Sampling Data for Covariation Assessment," *Journal of Consumer Research*, March 1986, pp. 406–417.

155 J. Edward Russo and France Leclerc, "An Eye-Fixation Analysis of Choice for Consumer Nondurables," *Journal of Consumer Research*, September 1994, pp. 274–290.

156 Jacoby et al., "Prepurchase Information Acquisition."

157 J. Edward Russo, Margaret G. Meloy, and Husted Medvec, "Predecisional Distortion of Product Information," *Journal of Marketing Research*, November 1998, pp. 438–452.

158 Carol A. Berning and Jacob Jacoby, "Patterns of Information Acquisition in New Product Purchases," *Journal of Consumer Research*, September 1974, pp. 18–22.

159 Itamar Simonson, Joel Huber, and John Payne, "The Relationship between Prior Brand Knowledge and Information Acquisition Order," *Journal of Consumer Research*, March 1988, pp. 566–578.

160 Wendy W. Moe, "An Empirical Two-Stage Choice Model with Varying Decision Rules Applied to Internet Clickstream Data," *Journal of Marketing Research*, November 2006, pp. 680–692; and Amitav Chakravarti, Chris Janiszewski, and Gulden Ulkumen, "The Neglect of Prescreening Information," *Journal of Marketing Research*, November 2006, pp. 642–653.

161 Carrie M. Heilman, Douglas Bowman, and Gordon P. Wright, "The Evolution of Brand Preference and Choice Behaviors of Consumers New to a Market," *Journal of Marketing Research* 37, May 2000, pp. 139–155.

162 Jacoby et al., "Prepurchase Information Acquisition"; and James R. Bettman, *An Information Processing Theory of Consumer Choice* (Reading, Mass.: Addison-Wesley, 1979).

163 Eric J. Johnson and J. Edward Russo, "Product Familiarity and Learning New Information," *Journal of Consumer Research*, June 1984, pp. 542–550; and James R. Bettman and P. Kakkar, "Effects of Information Presentation Format on Consumer Information Acquisition Strategies," *Journal of Consumer Research*, March 1977, pp. 233–240.

164 Raj Sethuraman, Catherine Cole, and Dipak Jain, "Analyzing the Effect of Information Format and Task on Cutoff Search Strategies," *Journal of Consumer Psychology* 3, 1994, pp. 103–136.

165 Jacoby et al., "Tracing the Impact of Item-by-Item Information Accessing on Uncertainty Reduction."

166 Jun B. Kim, Paulo Albuquerque, and Bart J. Bronnenberg, "Mapping Online Consumer Search," *Journal of Marketing Research* 48, no. 1, February 2011, pp. 13–27.

167 Joydeep Srivastava and Nicholas Lurie, "A Consumer Perspective on Price-Matching Refund Policies," *Journal of Consumer Research*, September 2001, pp. 296–307.

168 Liu Zheng, "Google Demos Online Marketing Strategies to Support Chinese SMEs," *China Daily*, September 18, 2015, www.chinadaily.com.cn.

CHAPTER 8

Judgment and Decision-Making Based on High Effort

LEARNING OBJECTIVES

After studying this chapter, you will be able to:

▶ Distinguish between judgment and decision-making, and indicate why both processes are important to marketers.

▶ Describe the types of decisions consumers face in situations where motivation, ability, and opportunity to process are high.

▶ Identify two types of cognitive decision-making models and understand how consumers make decisions based on brands, product attributes, and gains and losses.

▶ Explain how affective decision-making models differ from cognitive decision-making models, and discuss the role of appraisals and feelings, affective forecasting, and imagery in high-effort decisions.

▶ Discuss why, in a high-effort situation, consumers may delay a decision, and show how they make decisions when alternatives cannot be compared.

▶ Outline the ways that consumer characteristics, decision characteristics, and other people can influence high-effort decisions.

INTRODUCTION

To be successful in marketing cars, pickups, and SUVs, automakers must understand the types of judgments that vehicle buyers make (such as that electronics can make a car safer) and the criteria that most influence consumers' buying decisions (such as the security of being able to drive and park safely). In addition, all marketers must understand the emotions and feelings that influence consumer decisions (e.g., that a car makes you feel good). This chapter examines high-effort judgments and decisions (see Exhibit 8.1), the kind of judgments and decisions that consumers make when their motivation, ability, and opportunity to process information relevant to the decision are high. By carefully analyzing the factors that enter into judgment and decision-making, marketers can acquire valuable insights that help them develop and market offerings to consumers.[1]

Exhibit 8.1 ▶ Chapter Overview: Judgment and Decision-Making Based on High Consumer Effort

After problem recognition and search, consumers can engage in some form of judgment or decision-making, which can vary in terms of processing effort (from high to low). This chapter looks at high-effort judgment and decision processes. Judgments serve as inputs into decision-making, which can be cognitively or affectively based. Contextual effects also influence this process.

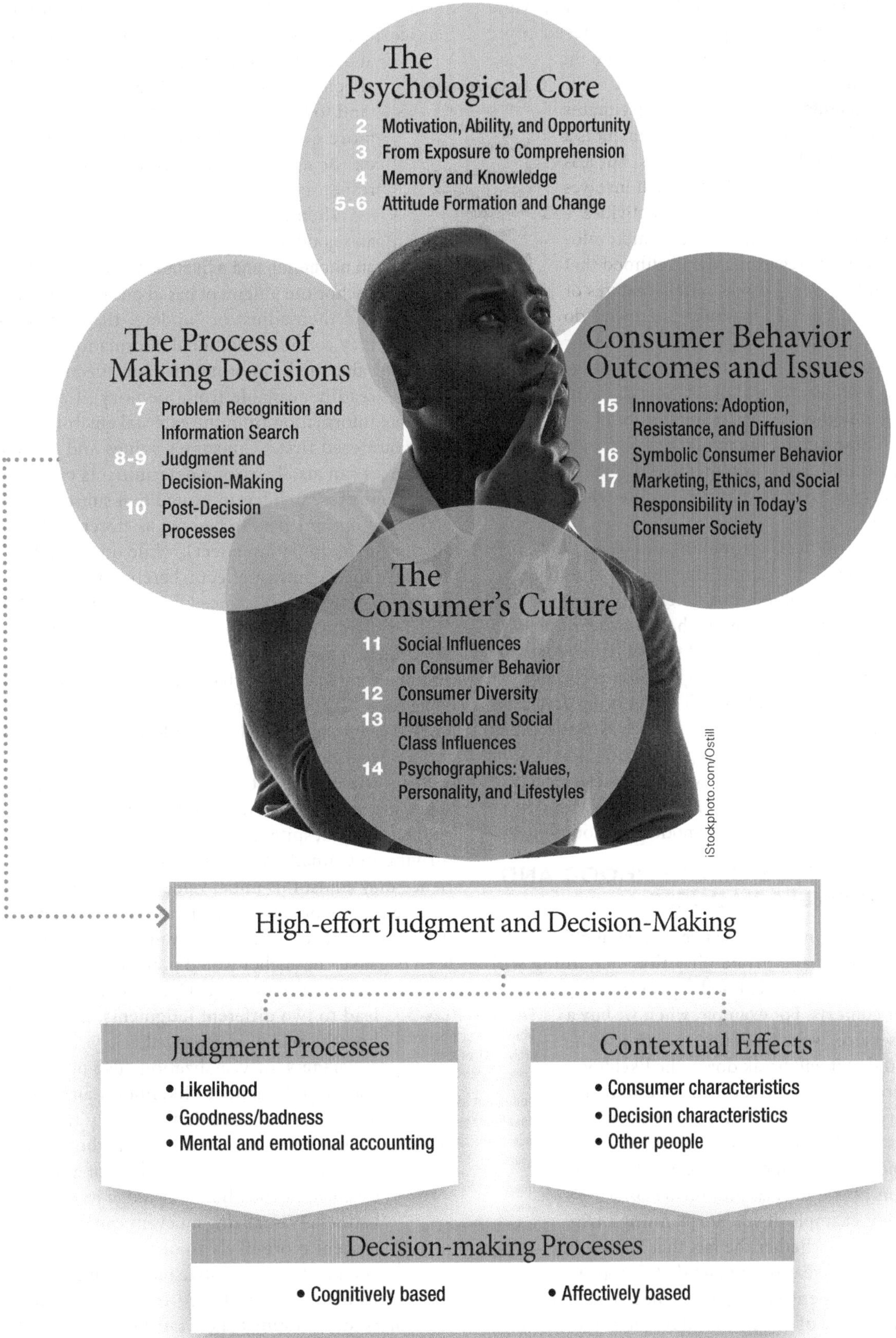

The Psychological Core

2 Motivation, Ability, and Opportunity
3 From Exposure to Comprehension
4 Memory and Knowledge
5-6 Attitude Formation and Change

The Process of Making Decisions

7 Problem Recognition and Information Search
8-9 Judgment and Decision-Making
10 Post-Decision Processes

Consumer Behavior Outcomes and Issues

15 Innovations: Adoption, Resistance, and Diffusion
16 Symbolic Consumer Behavior
17 Marketing, Ethics, and Social Responsibility in Today's Consumer Society

The Consumer's Culture

11 Social Influences on Consumer Behavior
12 Consumer Diversity
13 Household and Social Class Influences
14 Psychographics: Values, Personality, and Lifestyles

iStockphoto.com/Ostill

High-effort Judgment and Decision-Making

Judgment Processes

- Likelihood
- Goodness/badness
- Mental and emotional accounting

Contextual Effects

- Consumer characteristics
- Decision characteristics
- Other people

Decision-making Processes

- Cognitively based
- Affectively based

8-1 High-Effort Judgment Processes

Think about the last time you went to a restaurant. While reviewing the menu, you probably considered some items and thought about how good they would be before making your final choice. You were making **judgments**—evaluations or estimates regarding the likelihood of events. Judgment is a critical input into the decision process, but it is not the same as **decision-making**, which involves making a selection among options or activities.

In a consumer context, *judgments* are evaluations or estimates regarding the likelihood that products and services possess certain features or will perform in a certain manner.[2] Judgments do not require a decision. Thus, if you see an ad for a new Italian restaurant, you can form a judgment as to whether you will like it, how different it will be from other Italian restaurants, or how expensive it will be. These judgments can serve as important inputs into your decision about whether to eat at the restaurant, but they do not require that you decide whether to go there or not.

Judgment and decision-making can also involve different processes.[3] For example, one study found that consumers searched attributes in a different order when they were making judgments than when they were making decisions.[4] Another study found that whether consumers' familiarity with a product helped or hurt the amount of information, they could recall about it depended on whether they were making judgments or making decisions about the brands.[5] Given the importance of judgment in consumers' information processing, marketers need to understand judgments about (1) likelihood, (2) goodness or badness, and (3) mental and emotional accounting.

8-1a JUDGMENTS OF LIKELIHOOD AND GOODNESS/BADNESS

One kind of judgment is an **estimation of likelihood**, the determination of the probability that something will occur. Estimations of likelihood appear in many consumer contexts. For example, when we buy a good or service, we can attempt to estimate the likelihood that it will break down, the likelihood that others will like it, and the likelihood that it will satisfy our needs. When we view an ad, we can assess the likelihood that it is truthful.

Judgments of goodness/badness reflect our evaluation of the desirability of the offering's features. For example, if you are planning a trip, you might judge whether the fact that Europe is cold this time of year or the fact that European travel can be expensive is good or bad. Chapter 5 discussed judgments of goodness and badness in the section

Judgment Evaluation of an object or estimate of likelihood of an outcome or event.

Decision-making Making a selection among options or courses of action.

Anchoring and adjustment process Starting with an initial evaluation and adjusting it with additional information.

Estimation of likelihood Judging how likely it is that something will occur.

Judgment of goodness/badness Evaluating the desirability of something.

Imagery Multisensory mental representation (image) of a stimulus or an event.

on high-effort attitudes. The research presented there suggested that a consumer combines judgments about product attributes or actions associated with a product to form an evaluation of, or attitude toward, the product or service. Judgments of goodness and badness are not only affected by the attributes of a product but also affected by how we feel. Specifically, consumers tend to form judgments of goodness or badness more quickly and consistently based, in part, on the intensity and direction of their affective responses.[6]

When making judgments about likelihood and goodness/badness, consumers often employ an **anchoring and adjustment process**.[7] They first anchor the judgment based on some initial value and then adjust or "update" the evaluation as they consider additional information. The initial value can be information or an affective response readily available from memory; it can also be attribute information from the external environment that is encountered first.[8] Consumer values and normative influences can also be strong determinants of the initial value. Some research has indicated that subsequent evaluations of options tend to be seen as closer to the initial anchor (an assimilation effect), while other studies find evidence for a contrast effect whereby the subsequently estimated options are distanced from the initial anchor.[9]

To illustrate, Walt Disney is strongly associated with the United States and, thanks to its theme parks, movies, and memorable cartoon characters, it has a strong brand image worldwide. So when Disney opened a series of English-language schools for children in China, it used the "Disney" name as a positive initial anchor and encouraged consumers to see the schools—where cartoon characters are incorporated into lessons—as an update to that anchor. And, despite high tuition, Disney's schools are thriving in China.[10] Additional information from experience may adjust this initial value upward or downward, but the judgment is more likely to be positive, based on the Disney image. If the prior evaluation of Disney had been negative, the anchor would probably have resulted in a negative judgment. Thus, the same anchor can lead to two different judgments, depending on how the anchor is perceived.

Imagery, or visualization, also plays a major role in judgments of likelihood and goodness and badness. Consumers can try to construct an image of an event, such as how they will look and feel behind the wheel of a new car, to estimate its likelihood, or judge its goodness or badness. Visualizing an event can actually make it seem more likely to occur because consumers may form a positive bias when they imagine themselves using the product.[11] Imagery may also lead consumers to overestimate how satisfied they will be with a product or service.[12] In addition, imagery may cause consumers to focus on vivid attributes and weigh those attributes more heavily when forming judgments.[13] Particularly valuable to marketers during the planning of new products is the input of consumers who have an "emergent nature" (i.e., they can imagine how product ideas might be developed into actual products).[14]

8-1b MENTAL AND EMOTIONAL ACCOUNTING

As consumers, we use **mental accounting** to categorize spending and saving decisions into "accounts" we mentally designate for specific consumption transactions, goals, or situations. For example, we might have a "vacation" account (to pay for a trip), an "emergency" account (money held in reserve for unexpected expenses), and a "credit card" account (for credit purchases), each associated with a budget range or a dollar amount. The way we mentally account for our money influences judgments about what, when, where, why, how, and how much we should spend or save, borrow, make payments, and behave as a consumer over time. For instance, one study found that consumers were more willing to use a mobile payment service to make everyday purchases if it was linked to a credit card rather than a savings or checking account because of these consumers' mental accounting categories.[15]

> **Mental accounting** Categorizing spending and saving decisions into "accounts" mentally designated for specific consumption transactions, goals, or situations.
>
> **Emotional accounting** The intensity of positive or negative feelings associated with each mental "account" for saving or spending.

The related concept of **emotional accounting** suggests that the intensity of the positive or negative feelings associated with each "account" is another important influence on buying behavior.[16]

Money received under negative circumstances (from a seriously ill relative, for instance) is more likely to be spent on a utilitarian purchase (such as tuition) than on a hedonic purchase (a trip) because the utilitarian purchase helps counter the negative feelings. Clearly, mental and emotional accounting will vary from consumer to consumer, so marketers must research and understand the attitudes and feelings of their target markets.

8-1c BIASES IN JUDGMENT PROCESSES

Judgments are not always objective. Biases and other factors may compromise the quality of the consumer's decision[17] and affect consumer judgment in a variety of ways:

- *Confirmation bias.* If consumers are susceptible to a confirmation bias (see Chapter 7) they will focus more on judgments that confirm what they already believe and will hold those judgments with more confidence. They may ignore information that runs counter to their judgments. Of course, overweighting confirming information and underweighting contrary information in forming judgments can reduce consumers' tendencies to search for more information because they believe they know almost everything about the product.[18] Therefore, the confirmation bias can set consumers up for making less-than-optimal choices.

- *Self-positivity bias.* Consumers can make judgments about the extent to which they or others are vulnerable to having bad things happen to them (e.g., contracting AIDS, getting into an automobile accident). Interestingly, research finds that consumers have a self-positivity bias when making these judgments about the likelihood that bad outcomes will happen. That is, they tend to believe that bad things are more likely to happen to other people than to themselves. As such, they might not process messages that suggest that they themselves might be vulnerable to risks.[19] This is bad news for some marketers (e.g., health-care marketers, insurance marketers) who want to remind consumers that bad things can indeed happen to them.

- *Negativity bias.* With a negativity bias, consumers give negative information more weight than positive information when they are forming judgments. Consumers seem to weigh negative information more heavily in their judgments when they are forming opinions about something that is very important to them and for which they wish to have as accurate a judgment as possible (e.g., which college to attend). But consumers do not engage in a negativity bias when they are already committed to a brand. For example, if you love the school you are now attending, you are unlikely to think much about (or may even discount) any negative information you hear about it.[20]

- *Mood and bias.* Mood can bias consumer judgments in several ways.[21] First, your mood can serve as the initial anchor for a judgment. If you are in a good mood when browsing a menu, you will probably respond positively to new items you might try. Second, moods bias consumers' judgments by reducing their search for and attention to negative information. The reason for this phenomenon is that consumers want to preserve their good mood, and encountering negative information may not serve that goal. Third, mood can bias judgments by making consumers overconfident about the judgments they are reaching.[22]

- *Prior brand evaluations.* When consumers judge a brand to be good based on their past exposure to it, they may subsequently fail to learn (and view as important) information about the brand's attributes that affect its actual quality.[23] In effect, the favorable brand name "blocks" learning about quality-revealing product attributes that should affect consumers' judgments.

■ *Prior experience.* Customers learn from their previous experiences, which can be helpful but may also bias judgments during future decisions. Imagine you are customizing a product (such as a laptop computer) to your own specifications. Based on your experience with decisions made early in the process, you will find subsequent decisions to be easier or more difficult. If later decisions are easier than earlier decisions, you will be more likely to upgrade to expensive features.[24]

■ *Difficulty of mental calculations.* When comparing various prices or discounts, the ease or difficulty of calculating the difference will affect consumers' judgment of the size of these differences. When consumers have little difficulty mentally calculating the difference between two or more prices or discounts, they may think the numerical differences are larger than in reality, which will bias their judgment of the choices.[25]

 Marketing Implications

Marketers can do several things to make sure that their brand serves as a positive anchor in anchoring adjustment decisions. First, they can focus consumers' attention on those attributes that place the brand as the best in its class. For example, by focusing attention on its distinctive design and technology, Fitbit has made its wearable activity tracker the anchor for that product category (and become the market leader).[26] Marketers can also try to affect the set of other products that consumers use in their adjustment.[27] Detroit-based Shinola encourages buyers to think of fashion classics when they think of its vintage-inspired, premium-priced wristwatches, leather goods, and other made-in-America products.[28]

When consumers are exposed to a brand extension, the existing brand name and its positive associations often serve as the anchor for judgments of the new product. A product's country of origin can also serve as an anchor and influence subsequent judgments.[29] For example, although the Kenny Rogers Roasters chain of rotisserie-chicken restaurants no longer has any U.S. outlets, it is quite popular in Asia, where the local franchiser operates 140 restaurants and rings up more than $100 million in annual revenue.[30]

Marketers can also affect judgments of goodness and badness in several ways. First, making consumers feel good (e.g., by manipulating their moods or priming consumers with positive feelings before giving them information) will lead them to evaluate the offering more positively.[31] Second, marketers can affect judgments of goodness and badness by asking consumers to imagine the attributes or benefits of a product or service. A particular kind of pizza will be judged as better than other kinds when consumers imagine how delicious it tastes. It will be judged as worse when consumers imagine the grease it might have on top of it.

Finally, marketers can affect consumers' perceptions of how probable things are (i.e., likelihood estimates). Research shows that consumers primed to consider their family ties are more likely to take a financial risk because they realize that their family can help cushion a monetary loss. However, consumers are less likely to take a social risk when thinking about family ties because of the way that a negative outcome might affect their family.[32] Marketers can also try to reduce consumers' self-positivity judgments. A study on consumers' self-positive bias regarding the likelihood that they could contract AIDS was reduced when consumers were shown that people very similar to them have also gotten AIDS and when they were made to think about actions that they engage in that could result in getting AIDS.[33] Enumerating many (versus few) risk behaviors that can make a person vulnerable to a bad outcome (e.g., contracting AIDS) can also reduce his or her self-positivity bias.[34]

8-2 ## High-Effort Decisions and High-Effort Decision-Making Processes

Acquisition, usage, and disposition all involve some sort of consumer decision—even if the decision is not to select any of the alternatives, which may happen when a great deal of uncertainty exists.[35] In some cases, the consumer first makes a decision about whether or not to buy and then focuses on the selection decision.[36] The selection decision can, in turn, involve other decisions such as decisions about (1) what offerings to consider, (2) what factors are important to the choice, (3) what choice to actually make, (4) whether to make a decision now or to delay a decision, and (5) how to make choices when alternatives cannot be compared. We consider each of these kinds of decisions in this chapter (see Exhibit 8.2). When consumers' motivation, ability, and opportunity (MAO) to process information relevant to a decision are high, consumers put a lot of effort into making these decisions.

Exhibit 8.2 ▶ Types of Decisions That Consumers Face in High-Effort Situations

In high-effort situations, consumers are often confronted with a variety of different types of decisions to make. This exhibit outlines the major ones.

Deciding which brands to consider	Deciding what is important to the choice	Deciding what offerings to choose	Deciding whether to make a decision now	Deciding when alternatives cannot be compared

Consideration set	Goals
	Time
	Framing
		Thought-based
		  decisions
		    Brands
		    Product attributes
		    Gains and losses
		Feeling-based
		  decisions
		    Appraisals and
		    feelings
		    Affective forecasts
			Decision delay	

8-2a DECIDING WHICH BRANDS TO CONSIDER

Consumers today face more options than ever before.[37] In fact, they are reluctant to actually make a decision when they have only one option available to them.[38] When faced with many available options, consumers often first decide which fall into an **inept set** (those that are unacceptable), an **inert set** (those they treat with indifference), and a consideration set (those they want to choose among).[39]

The consideration set is very important to marketers because it affects what brands consumers are choosing among and hence whom the marketer is competing against. Decisions tend to be easier when the consideration set contains brands that can be easily compared.[40] Still, just because a brand is in a consideration set does not mean that it will get much of the consumers' attention.[41] But if it does get a lot of attention, consumers are more likely to select it and to be willing to pay more for it than for the other alternatives.[42] If they focus on one brand at a time, they tend to judge that brand more positively than they would the average of the best brands within that category.[43] When consumers are making a series of decisions, a smaller consideration set develops a maximizing mind-set, which will persist in subsequent decisions even if these decisions involve ever-larger consideration sets.[44]

A consumer's evaluation of a brand in the consideration set depends on the other brands to which it is compared. If one brand is clearly

Inept set Options that are unacceptable when making a decision.

Inert set Options toward which consumers are indifferent.

Attraction effect When the addition of an inferior brand to a consideration set increases the attractiveness of the dominant brand.

more attractive or dominant than the others, making a choice does not require much effort. Changing the alternatives in the consideration set can, however, have a major impact on the consumer's decision, even without a change in preferences.[45] For example, a good brand can look even better when an inferior brand is added to the consideration set. This **attraction effect** occurs because the inferior brands increase the attractiveness of the dominant brand, making the decision easier.[46]

Marketing Implications

The most important implication is that it is critical for a company to get its brand into the consumer's consideration set; otherwise, there is little chance that the brand will be chosen. Repetition of the brand name and messages in marketing communications are needed to ensure that the brand name is "top of mind." Another way to try to gain an advantage is by promoting comparisons of the brand with inferior rather than with equal or superior competitors. Doing this maximizes the attraction effect and results in a more positive evaluation of the brand. Also, marketers can increase sales of a high-margin item simply by offering a higher-priced option.[47] Thus, Amazon.com might increase the sales of its lowest-priced Kindle Fire tablet by offering higher-priced models with much more functionality (see Exhibit 8.3). Even if the higher-priced models aren't best-sellers, they would make the lower-priced model look like a good deal.

Exhibit 8.3 ▶ Attraction Effect

Sometimes a higher-priced option can make a lower-priced option look like a better deal, as is the case with the Kindle products.

JOE KLAMAR/AFP/Getty Images

8-2b DECIDING WHICH CRITERIA ARE IMPORTANT TO THE CHOICE

Before consumers can choose a specific offering from among a set of brands in a consideration set, they need to determine which criteria are relevant to the decision and how important each criterion is to their decision. The relevance and importance of various decision criteria, in turn, depend on consumers' goals, the timing of their decision, and how the decision is framed or represented. Note that in many cases, consumers need to make trade-offs in deciding on various attributes, since they can't find a product that has everything they want. So they may, for example, need to trade off paying a lower price for getting a product with the options they want.[48]

Goals

Goals clearly affect the criteria that will drive a consumer's choice. For example, one goal might be to buy an economical car you can afford; another might be to buy a car that will impress your friends. Consumers whose goal is to influence others will use different criteria when choosing among brands than those used by consumers who do not have this goal.[49]

When the goal is to make a decision, consumers may evaluate products with unique, positive attributes and shared negative attributes as more favorable than products with unique, negative attributes that share positive attributes.[50] If the goal is flexibility in choice, the consumer will seek out a large assortment of choices; if the goal is to simplify the choice, the consumer will seek out a small assortment.[51]

In addition, consumers' goals may change during the decision process. For example, before you go to a store, you may be less certain about what you want to buy—but once you are in the store, your goals may become more certain and concrete.[52] Whether the consumers' goals are prevention- or promotion-focused will also affect their decisions. Promotion-focused consumers, whose goal is to maximize gains and positive outcomes, will put more emphasis on whether they think they have the skills and capacity to use the product to achieve the goal they seek and put less emphasis on the effectiveness of the product itself. Prevention-focused consumers, who are more risk-averse, emphasize the product's efficacy rather than their own skills and capacities to use it.[53]

Time

The timing of a decision also affects which criteria drive our choices. As you learned in Chapter 4, *construal level theory* relates to how we think about (or construe) an offering. Whether we use high (abstract) or low-level (concrete) construals depends on whether we are making a decision about what to buy/do right now or about something we might buy/do in the future.[54]

If the decision is about something we will buy or do immediately (e.g., what restaurant to go to right now), our choices tend to be based on *low-level construals*—specific, concrete elements such as how close it is to home, how much dinner will cost there, and who is coming along. The opposite is true for decisions we anticipate making later: our criteria tend to be more general and abstract (e.g., which restaurant will create the best dining experience). When the decision outcome will be realized far in the future, consumers may consider the hedonic aspects of a decision (how good it will make me feel) to be more important than the more rational aspects of the decision (can I really afford it?).[55] Even when consumers tell researchers that they intend to buy a socially responsible product, they actually make such purchases less often than stated, partly because of the timing of the decision. Yet when consumers come to believe that a marketer is devoting more resources to ethics and social responsibility, they are more likely to follow through on their intentions and purchase that marketer's product.[56]

Framing

Decision framing
The initial reference point or anchor in the decision process.

The way in which the task is defined or represented, **decision framing**, can affect how important a criterion is to our choice. Because the frame serves as the initial anchor in the decision process, all subsequent information is considered in light of that frame.

Early research on framing studied people's willingness to take risks in a gamble. Results showed that people are more willing to take risks when a choice is framed as avoiding a loss rather than as acquiring a gain.[57] Other research has found that messages framed in terms of loss are more persuasive when consumers are in a good mood, whereas messages framed in terms of gain are more persuasive when consumers are in a bad mood.[58] Framing gains and losses also applies to buying and selling: When the outcomes are equally positive, buyers feel better about not losing money while sellers feel better about achieving gains. But when the outcomes are equally negative, buyers feel worse about losses while sellers feel worse about not gaining anything.[59] One study on recycling behavior found that loss-framed messages (we lose so much if we don't recycle) were more effective than gain-framed messages (recycling can make a difference) when consumers were asked to think concretely about recycling, as opposed to thinking abstractly about it. In contrast, gain-framed messages worked better in promoting recycling behavior when consumers were asked to think abstractly, not concretely.[60]

Decisions can also be framed in terms of how the problem is structured in the external environment, such as whether beef is presented as 75 percent lean or as 25 percent fat.[61] Framing the time period can affect decisions as well.

Consumers perceive health hazards as being more immediate and concrete if they are framed as occurring every day but regard them as less immediate and more abstract if they are framed as occurring every year.[62] In another study, industrial buyers who used low price as an initial reference point were less willing to take risks than buyers with a medium or high-price point.[63] Likewise, consumers react more positively when marketers frame the cost of a product as a series of small payments (pennies a day) instead of as a large one-time expense.[64] Moreover, a product framed in the context of higher-priced options will be judged as being less expensive than one framed in the context of lower-priced options.[65] In the case of multi-item package pricing, consumers' evaluations will depend on whether the price (such as $59 for 12 items) or the quantity (12 items for $59) is presented first. Here, the information presented first becomes salient and affects evaluations, particularly when there are more items in the package and it is difficult to calculate unit prices.[66]

Whether a decision is framed positively (How good is this product?) or negatively (How bad is this product?) influences the evaluation differently.[67] Consumers are more likely to choose a brand with negatively framed claims about a competitor when elaboration is low, but higher elaboration may lead them to conclude that the tactics being used are unfair.[68]

Priming certain attributes, such as reliability and creativity, can significantly alter consumers' judgments of both comparable alternatives like different brands of cameras and non-comparable alternatives like computers and cameras.[69] This priming causes consumers to focus their processing on specific attributes rather than on abstract criteria. Priming hedonic or symbolic attributes— such as associations—with political concerns (e.g., reduce toxic waste) rather than with functional ones (e.g., no more hassles) can produce a higher willingness to pay for items or social programs.[70] Consumers primed to respond to a question about liking a product (i.e., one framed positively) answered more quickly than when they were primed to respond to a question about disliking a product (one framed negatively).[71]

 Marketing Implications

Goals, decision timing, and framing have important implications for positioning and market segmentation. First, marketers can position an offering as being consistent with consumers' goal-related or usage categories. That way, marketers can influence the way that consumers frame the decision, and consumers will be more likely to consider the brand and important related information. For example, Tesla markets its premium-priced electric cars as eco-friendly and high-tech, for consumers who want to protect the environment and be on the cutting edge of car technology.[72] Second, marketers can identify and market to large segments of consumers who have similar goal-related or usage-context categories. Thus, for example, the LEGO Group has introduced a video game called *Dimensions*, targeting the segment of fans interested in both LEGO building sets and digital play activities. The game allows players to create customized mashups featuring their favorite LEGO minifigures such as Batman and Doctor Who by moving them around a special game base connected to the video game (see Exhibit 8.4).[73]

Another marketing strategy is to frame or reframe the decision. For example, a marketer might emphasize emotional benefits rather than functional benefits of a product. The Melt, a San Francisco-based chain of grilled-cheese restaurants, focuses on its sandwiches and burgers, tomato soup, and soft-serve ice cream as nostalgic food that "just makes people happy."[74] Sales promotions generally are more successful when framed as gains rather than as a reduced loss—consumers prefer getting something free rather than getting a discount. And consumer decisions can be framed by the location of products in the store, a strategy that influences comparisons. For example, placing wine next to gourmet foods may frame the consumer's decision more broadly as planning to have a nice, romantic meal rather than simply buying a bottle of wine.

Finally, marketers must consider the timing of the consumer's decision when planning and promoting merchandise assortments. Consumers prefer larger assortments when they are making an immediate decision, but prefer smaller assortments when the decision is distant in time or in location. Therefore, stores with smaller assortments would benefit from emphasizing the costs of choosing if the consumer is making a decision on the spot, but downplay the costs if consumers are making the decision later or in a faraway location.[75]

Exhibit 8.4 ▶ Usage-Context
Sometimes ads try to stimulate purchase of new products by targeting consumers who already know the brand (i.e., LEGO® toys).

Ilya S. Savenok/Getty Images

8-3 Deciding What Brand to Choose: Thought-Based Decisions

Researchers have proposed various decision-making models, each of which may accurately describe how consumers make these high-effort decisions. Being opportunistic and adaptive, consumers do not follow a uniform process every time they make a decision.[76] Instead, they choose a model or use bits and pieces of various models, depending on the situation, and they may employ one or more decision rules, sometimes just because they want a change.[77] Furthermore, the choices consumers make may be related to other choices. For example, making one decision (buying a computer) can lead to yet another decision (buying a printer).[78]

Cognitive decision-making models describe how consumers systematically use information about attributes to reach a decision. Researchers also recognize that consumers may make decisions on the basis of feelings or emotions, using **affective decision-making models**.[79] Therefore, marketers need to know how consumers make choices when the decision is either cognitive or more emotional in nature.

Decision-making styles can vary across cultures.[80] Some North Americans, for example, tend to be analytical, rely on factual information, and search for solutions to problems. In contrast, in Asian cultures, and particularly

Cognitive decision-making model The process by which consumers combine items of information about attributes to reach a decision.

Affective decision-making model The process by which consumers base their decision on feelings and emotions.

Exhibit 8.5 ▶ Types of Cognitive Choice Models

Cognitive decision-making models can be classified along two major dimensions: (a) whether processing occurs one brand at a time or one attribute at a time, and (b) whether they are compensatory (bad attributes can be compensated for by good ones) or noncompensatory (a bad attribute eliminates the brand).

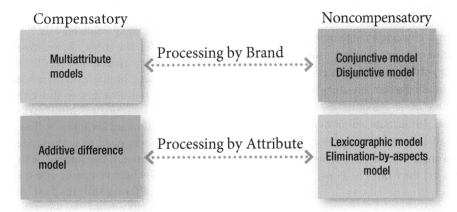

in Japan, logic is sometimes less important than the *kimochi*—the feeling. Similarly, many Saudi Arabians are more intuitive in their decision-making and avoid persuasion based on empirical reasoning. Russians may place more emphasis on values than on facts, and Germans tend to be theoretical and deductive. In North American and European cultures, decisions are usually made by individuals who control their own fate. In Asian cultures, the group is of primary importance, and actions are regarded as arising at random or from other events rather than as being controlled by individuals.

Cognitive models describe the processes by which consumers combine information about attributes to reach a decision in a rational, systematic manner. Two types of cognitive models are (1) compensatory versus noncompensatory and (2) brand versus attribute (see Exhibit 8.5).

With a **compensatory model**, consumers evaluate how good each of the attributes of the brands in their consideration set is (i.e., they make judgments about goodness and badness) and weight them in terms of how important the attributes are to their decisions. The brand that has the best overall score (attribute goodness times importance summed across all of the brand's attributes) is the one consumers choose. This is a kind of mental cost-benefit analysis in which a negative evaluation of one attribute can be compensated for (hence the name *compensatory*) by the positive features on others. To illustrate, for some U.S. consumers, a negative feature of Chinese products is that they are not made in America. However, this evaluation can be overcome if the products rate highly on other criteria deemed important, such as price.

Compensatory model A mental cost-benefit analysis model in which negative features can be compensated for by positive ones.

Noncompensatory model A simple decision model in which negative information leads to rejection of the option.

Cutoff level For each attribute, the point at which a brand is rejected with a noncompensatory model.

With a **noncompensatory model**, consumers use negative information to evaluate brands and immediately eliminate from the consideration set those that are inadequate on any one or more important attributes.[81] These models are called *noncompensatory* because a negative rating on a key attribute eliminates the brand, as is the case when some U.S. consumers reject a product because it is foreign-made. Noncompensatory models require less cognitive effort than compensatory models do because consumers set up **cutoff levels** for each attribute and reject any brand with attribute rankings below the cutoff. Thus, if brands in consumers' consideration set are similar in attractiveness, they must put more effort into making a decision and will probably use a compensatory model.[82]

 Marketing Implications

Given that different models can lead to different choices, marketers may sometimes want to change the process by which consumers make a decision. For example, if most consumers are using a compensatory strategy, switching them to a noncompensatory strategy may be advantageous, particularly if competitors' products have a major weakness. By convincing consumers not to accept a lower level of an important attribute—that is, not to compensate for the attribute—marketers might prompt some consumers to reject competitors' products from consideration. For example, sales of the ITALIKA motorbike have soared in Mexico because the product is not only affordable, it can be conveniently financed and serviced through the hundreds of Elektra stores where it is sold. Those attributes are important to consumers—and competing bikes don't have the same convenient financing and servicing arrangements.[83]

When consumers reject a brand using a noncompensatory strategy, marketers can try to switch them to using a compensatory strategy by arguing that other attributes compensate for a negative. To illustrate, advertising for high-priced, premium brands often stresses the reasons why its offerings are worth the extra money so that consumers do not reject them on price alone.

Brand processing
Evaluating one brand at a time.

Multiattribute expectancy-value model A type of brand-based compensatory model.

Conjunctive model A noncompensatory model that sets minimum cutoffs to reject "bad" options.

brand. This type of **brand processing** occurs frequently because the environment—advertising, dealerships, and so on—is often organized by brands.

Much research has focused on brand-based compensatory models, also called **multiattribute expectancy-value models**.[84] One multiattribute model, the theory of reasoned action (TORA), was discussed in Chapter 5. Note that when considering multiple attributes, consumers tend to give more weight to those that are compatible with their goals.[85] Multiattribute models can be emotionally taxing as well as cognitively taxing when consumers need to make tradeoffs among attributes.[86] For instance, consumers facing emotionally difficult tradeoffs between price and quality may cope by choosing the offering with the best quality.[87] Some consumers may simply avoid making tradeoffs between conflicting attributes.[88]

Using a **conjunctive model**, consumers set up *minimum* cutoffs for *each* attribute that represent the absolute lowest value they are willing to accept.[89] For example, consumers might want to pay less than $10 per hour to rent a car and therefore reject an alternative with a higher hourly cost.

8-3a DECISIONS BASED ON BRANDS

In making a decision, consumers may evaluate *one brand at a time*. Thus, a consumer making a laptop purchase might collect information about an Apple model and make a judgment about it before moving on to the next

---

Exhibit 8.6 ▶ Which Apartment Would You Choose?

Imagine that you visited five apartments (A, B, C, D, and E) and were trying to decide which to rent. You have determined what attributes you get (cost is the most important attribute followed by size and then location). After visiting each apartment, you rate how good each apartment is on each attribute. Which apartment would you rent if you used the following decision rules? Note that different decision rules can lead to different choices.

Evaluations of brands as good or bad based on information retrieved from memory or generated through external search (5 = very good on this attribute; 1 = not at all good on this attribute).

Importance weight of this attribute based on needs, values, goals (higher score means more important: weights add up to 100).

Evaluative Criteria	A	B	C	D	E	Importance
Cost	5	3	4	4	2	35
Size	3	4	5	4	3	25
Location	5	5	5	2	5	20
View	1	3	1	4	1	15
Has a pool	3	3	4	3	5	5

Apartment Chosen Based on the:
1. Compensatory Model (sum of Eval x Imp) _____
2. Conjunctive Model (set minimum cutoff of 2) _____
3. Disjunctive Model (set acceptable cutoff of 3) _____
4. Lexicographic Model (compare on EC in order of Imp) _____
5. Elimination by Aspects Model (set acceptable cutoff of 3) _____

Answers: 1 = C; 2 = B or D; 3 = B; 4 = A; 5 = B

Thus, Enterprise CarShare charges Duke University students $9 per hour to rent a compact car.[90] Because the cutoffs represent the bare minimum belief strength levels, the psychology of a conjunctive model is to rule out unsuitable alternatives (i.e., get rid of the "bad ones") as soon as possible, something that consumers do by weighing negative information.

The **disjunctive model** is similar to the conjunctive model, with two important exceptions. First, the consumer sets up *acceptable* levels for the cutoffs—levels that are more desirable (i.e., find the "good ones"). So even though $10 per hour may be the highest payment a consumer will accept for a car rental, $8 per hour may be more acceptable, especially if the rental will cover several hours. Second, the consumer bases evaluations on several of the *most important* attributes rather than on all of them, putting the weight on positive information. Using the descriptions provided above, see if you can decide which brand you would choose from among the set of brands in Exhibit 8.6, using first the multiattribute decision-making model, then the conjunctive, and finally the disjunctive model. Note that consumers may use several of these decision-making models. When the consideration set is large, they might use the conjunctive or disjunctive model to eliminate undesirable brands and then make their final choice among the brands that remain, using the multiattribute model.[91]

> **Disjunctive model** A noncompensatory model that sets acceptable cutoffs to find options that are "good."

Marketing Implications

Brand-based compensatory models help marketers understand which alternatives consumers may choose or reject and the beliefs that consumers have about the outcomes or attributes associated with a product. If consumers do not strongly believe that positive outcomes or attributes are associated with a decision, marketers should stress these outcomes or attributes through marketing to strengthen consumers' beliefs. For example, Megabus markets its intercity bus services on the basis of low price. It emphasizes its modern vehicles with Wi-Fi and power outlets at every seat, rather than the duration of trips (longer compared with train and air travel) and the inflexibility of trips (compared with private cars). Consumers have the option of paying a small fee to reserve a seat with a view or save a group of seats in advance.[92]

> **Attribute processing** Comparing brands, one attribute at a time.
>
> **Additive difference model** Compensatory model in which brands are compared by attribute, two brands at a time.
>
> **Lexicographic model** A noncompensatory model that compares brands by attributes, one at a time in order of importance.

Marketers can address shortcomings by altering the product and communicating its improvements to consumers. However, when companies make changes to remove competitive disadvantages, they may draw consumers away from competitive offerings, but they may also be reducing differentiation. Therefore, marketers should consider the long-term effects of improvements.[93] Decision models can also help marketers better plan communications. Research shows that consumers with little commitment to a brand will put more weight on negative information because they perceive it as more diagnostic.[94] This is why Radisson, which had aging U.S. hotel properties and struggled with perceptions of undistinguished service, introduced its upscale Radisson Blu from Europe to revitalize its U.S. brand image and expand into the growing Latin American market.[95]

8-3b DECISIONS BASED ON PRODUCT ATTRIBUTES

The previous discussion described how consumers make choices when they first process information one brand at a time. Here, we discuss **attribute processing**, which occurs when consumers compare across brands *one attribute at a time*, such as comparing each brand on price. Although most consumers prefer attribute processing because it is easier than brand processing, they cannot always find information available in a manner that facilitates it. This situation accounts for the increasing popularity of shopping agents. One study found that the inclusion of an attribute in a shopping agent's recommendations list gives that attribute more prominence.[96]

According to the **additive difference model**, brands are compared by attribute, *two brands at a time*.[97] Consumers evaluate differences between the two brands on each attribute and then combine them into an overall preference. This process allows tradeoffs between attributes—that is, a positive difference on one attribute can offset a negative difference on another.

With the **lexicographic model**, consumers order attributes in terms of importance and compare the options one attribute at a time, starting with the most important. If one option dominates, the consumer selects it. In the case of a tie, the consumer proceeds to the second most important attribute and continues in this way until only one option remains. A tie can occur if the difference between two options on any attribute is below the just noticeable difference: one brand priced at $2.77 and one priced at $2.79 would likely be regarded as being tied on price.

The **elimination-by-aspects model** is similar to the lexicographic model but incorporates the notion of an *acceptable cutoff*.[98] This model is not as strict as the lexicographic model, and more attributes are likely to be considered. Consumers first order attributes in terms of importance and then compare options on the most important attribute. Those options below the cutoff are eliminated, and the consumer continues the process until only one option remains. Again using the information shown in Exhibit 8.6, think about which brand you would select if you were to use the various decision models described in this exhibit.

> **Elimination-by-aspects model** Similar to the lexicographic model but adds the notion of acceptable cutoffs.

Marketing Implications

The additive difference model helps marketers determine which attributes or outcomes exhibit the greatest differences among brands and use this knowledge to improve and properly position their brand. On one hand, if a brand performs below a major competitor on a certain attribute, the company needs to enhance consumers' beliefs about that product's superiority. On the other hand, if a brand performs significantly better than competitors on a key attribute, marketers should enhance consumer beliefs by positioning the offering around this advantage. Kyochon Chicken, a Korean restaurant chain specializing in fried chicken, for example, has expanded outside Asia by emphasizing its unique crispy, cooked to-order chicken dishes. Its first U.S. outlet opened in 2007, and the chain continues to open restaurants on both coasts. "Americans have long been accustomed to the flavor of KFC chicken," explains a Kyochon executive. "For them, the soy sauce-coated chicken wing was brand new and attractive."[99]

If many consumers are employing a lexicographic model, and a brand is weak on the most important attribute, the company needs to improve this feature in order to have its brand selected. Also, marketers can try to change the order of importance of attributes so that a major brand advantage is the most critical attribute. Note that when consumers turn to independent expert sources such as *Consumer Reports* for help in assessing attributes and options, they quickly adapt if they learn that the source made a mistake but then corrected its information.[100] In other words, consumers are able to ignore the information and able to update their knowledge based on the new findings.

Identifying consumers' cutoff levels can be very useful for marketers. If an offering is beyond any of the cutoffs that many consumers set, it will be rejected frequently. This result means marketers must change consumers' beliefs about these attributes. For example, consumers concerned that an electric car won't take them far enough on a single charge may be reassured by the growing number of recharging stations being installed across the country. Whole Foods Market has noticed great interest in the recharging stations at its stores in Connecticut, Colorado, and Texas, among other locations.[101]

Marketers can also influence brand choice by affecting how attributes are framed (i.e., whether they are framed negatively or positively). Consumers may not like or choose a brand that is framed as having 25 percent fat and may like a brand framed as being 75 percent lean better. While both brands have the same amount of fat, one is framed in terms of a positive (lean); the other in terms of a negative (fat).[102] Moreover, a marketer can influence whether consumers use an alternative- or attribute-based evaluation strategy by first priming either time or money. Time priming leads consumers to evaluate products on the basis of alternatives, whereas money priming leads consumers to evaluate on the basis of attributes.[103]

Finally, marketers should examine consumers' perceptions of quantity-discount deals. Consumers may view the quantity-discount price of a giant-sized product package as a gain if they think they are saving money relative to what they would have spent on the same amount in regular-sized packages. Conversely, buying smaller-sized versions at the regular price could be perceived as a loss relative to the price of the larger-sized package.[104]

8-3c DECISIONS BASED ON GAINS AND LOSSES

The previous discussion describes the different types of models that consumers can use to make decisions. However, research shows that the decisions consumers make also depend on whether the consumer is motivated to seek gains or to avoid losses. According to *prospect theory*, losses loom larger than gains for consumers even when the two outcomes are of the same magnitude.[105] For example, when asked to set a price for an item to be exchanged, sellers typically ask for a much higher price (because they are experiencing a loss of the item or because they perceive selling as a self-threat[106]) than buyers are willing to pay (gaining the item). This has been called the **endowment effect** because ownership increases the value (and loss) associated with an item. Other research suggests that consumers perceive selling as an implicit self-threat, so sellers, as part of their defense mechanisms, respond to self-threat by enhancing the value of the self-associated object.

> **Endowment effect**
> When ownership increases the value of an item.

Similarly, consumers have a much stronger reaction to price increases than to price decreases and may be more reluctant to upgrade to higher-priced durable items. Thus, consumers may avoid making decisions to a greater degree when a decision involves losses relative to gains. This effect has been demonstrated across a variety of products/services including wine, lottery tickets, basketball tickets, and pizza toppings.

In addition, the consumer's promotion-and-prevention-focused goals will impact this process. For instance, prevention-focused consumers tend to preserve the status quo instead of making a decision that will result in a change because they want to avoid losses. In contrast, promotion-focused consumers are more willing to try new things if they think that changing from the status quo will help them achieve their goals of growth and development.[107]

Marketing Implications

Prospect theory has a number of important marketing implications. First, consumers will be more risk averse and unwilling to buy the product when the decision involves losses. Thus, marketers must make an effort to reduce risks and potential losses. This situation is one of the key reasons that manufacturers and retailers make offers such as the "full money-back guarantee" or "no money down for 12 months with no interest" as well as provide warranty programs. Red Wing Shoes, for example, allows customers 30 days to wear a new pair of shoes and return them if they're unhappy for any reason, with a full refund and "no questions asked."[108]

Second, consumers will react more negatively to price increases or higher-priced items than they will react positively to price decreases. Thus, marketers need to carefully consider the amount of the price increase (i.e., the greater the increase, the stronger the negative reaction). Further, this suggests that if possible, marketers should try to frame these increases as gains rather

than losses (i.e., the increased benefit the consumer might get from the higher-priced item). For example, when Nissan increased the base price of its Leaf electric car models, it also included a more powerful battery and a fast-charge connection as standard equipment, plus additional connectivity and audio technology, enhancements that car buyers value.[109]

8-4 Deciding What Brand to Choose: High-Effort Feeling-Based Decisions

Just as consumers can make high-effort thought-based decisions, so too can they make high-effort feeling-based decisions. With affective decision-making, consumers make a decision because the choice feels right rather than because they have made a detailed, systematic evaluation of offerings. Or they may decide that the chosen option feels like a perfect fit, regardless of their prior cognitive processing.[110] Consumers who make decisions based on feelings tend to be more satisfied afterward than those who make decisions based on product attributes.[111] Moreover, emotions can also help thought-based decision-making since emotions can help consumers gather their thoughts and make judgments more quickly.[112]

As explained in Chapter 6, brands can be associated with positive emotions such as love, joy, pride, and elation as well as with negative emotions such as guilt, hate, fear, anxiety, anger, sadness, shame, and greed. These emotions can be recalled to play a central role in the decision process, particularly when consumers perceive them as relevant to the offering.[113] This affective processing is frequently experience-based.[114] In other words, consumers select an option based on their recall of past experiences and the associated feelings. When consumers choose among brands in memory, they must work harder to process information, so their feelings carry considerable weight. In contrast, when they choose among brands based on information in ads or other external stimuli, they can focus more on the offering's attributes and less on their feelings.[115]

Consumer feelings are particularly critical for offerings with hedonic, symbolic, or aesthetic aspects.[116] Feelings also influence decisions about what we will consume and for how long.[117] We tend to buy offerings that make us feel good more often and for longer periods than we buy offerings that do not have these effects. Note that consumers sometimes buy a product, such as jewelry, simply to make themselves feel better (see Exhibit 8.7). In other situations, they may make a choice because of a negative feeling, buying a product out of guilt or shame.

WEAR IT AND BLOOM

A rose is not just a rose. Stack our floral inspired RING UPON RING series with the beautifully hand-carved rose in black onyx, set in sterling silver.

be inspired at pandora.net

PANDORA
UNFORGETTABLE MOMENTS

Image Courtesy of The Advertising Archives

Exhibit 8.7 ▶ Affective Decision-Making

Consumers sometimes make purchase decisions based on how they feel, as opposed to product attributes. Ads for Pandora jewelry, seen here, feature good feelings and memories.

8-4a APPRAISALS AND FEELINGS

As discussed in Chapter 2, *appraisal theory* examines how our emotions are determined by the way that we think about or "appraise" the situation, a field being explored by many researchers.[118] This theory also explains how and why certain emotions (including those carried over from previous decisions) can affect future judgments and choices. People who are fearful tend to see more risk in new situations than do people who are angry, for example.

In situations involving disposition of objects, people who are disgusted tend to view this activity as an opportunity to get rid of their current possessions while people who are sad tend to view

it as an opportunity to change their circumstances.[119] Even the emotional reaction to a desired product being out of stock can affect a consumer's feelings about and appraisals of subsequent purchases in the same environment.[120]

Consumers also consider how they will feel if a hedonic experience is interrupted. Although consumers prefer that a positive experience (such as watching a movie) be uninterrupted, they actually enjoy it more with an interruption, because the pleasure is intensified after the break. Similarly, their appraisal of a negative experience may cause them to want an interruption, yet research shows that interrupting such experiences actually increases irritation.[121] Finally, consumers appraise their feelings of envy when considering a purchase. If their appraisal is benign envy, they will put a premium on purchases to keep up with higher-status consumers; if their appraisal is malicious envy, they will put a premium on purchases that set them apart from higher-status consumers.[122]

8-4b AFFECTIVE FORECASTS AND CHOICES

Consumers' predictions of what they will feel in the future—**affective forecasting**—can influence the choices they make today. For instance, someone may buy a dishwasher after forecasting the relief she will feel at having an appliance to handle this time-consuming chore. You may decide to go to Mexico instead of Colorado over spring break because you think the Mexico trip will make you feel more relaxed. As shown in Exhibit 8.8, we can forecast (1) how we think we will feel as a result of a decision, (2) how intensely we will have this feeling, and (3) how long this feeling will last. Any one of these

> **Affective forecasting** A prediction of how you will feel in the future.

Exhibit 8.8 ▶ Affective Forecasting

Affective forecasting occurs when consumers try to predict how they will feel in a future consumption situation. Specifically, they try to predict what feelings they will have, how strongly these feelings will be, and how long the feelings will last.

What Will I Feel?	How Much Will I Feel It?	How Long Will I Feel This Way?
Valence (good or bad) Nature of feeling (specific emotion such as happiness, regret, guilt, shame)	Intensity	Duration

forecasts can affect our decision about whether to go to Mexico. Affective forecasting is not always accurate, however, and we can be wrong about any or all of the above-noted forecasts.[123] Consequently, after our vacation, instead of feeling relaxed, we may feel stressed; instead of feeling extremely relaxed, we may feel only mildly relaxed; or instead of feeling relaxed for a week, our post-vacation feelings of relaxation may only last until we reach home (and see the pile of work we now have to do).

While anticipating postdecision levels of happiness (or relaxation, as illustrated in the example above) can impact the choices consumers make, so too can anticipated regret about making a wrong decision impact the choices consumers make. For instance, if they are participating in an auction and anticipate feeling deep regret should another bidder win, consumers will place a higher bid on an item than they would otherwise have placed.[124] Similarly, consumers who anticipate regret at later finding out that today's sale price was better than a future sale price are more likely to buy the item on sale now.[125]

Waking to the music of tropical birds greeting the sunrise
An afternoon stroll on the golden beaches
Dinner at one of the best restaurants in the world

It doesn't get better than Barbados

$\mathcal{B}$ARBADOS
www.visitbarbados.co.uk

Image Courtesy of The Advertising Archives

Exhibit 8.9 ▶ Stimulating Imagery Through Advertising

Ads sometimes try to induce consumers to imagine themselves in certain situations. When they do, consumers may experience the feelings and emotions that are associated with this situation.

8-4c IMAGERY

Imagery plays a key role in emotional decision-making.[126] Consumers can attempt to imagine themselves consuming the product or service and can use any emotions they experience as input for the decision. In choosing a vacation, you can imagine the excitement you might experience by being in each destination (see Exhibit 8.9). If these images are pleasant (or negative), they will exert a positive (or negative) influence on your decision process. Imagery can also ignite consumer desire for and fantasizing about certain products.[127] Inviting consumers to interact with a product through an online demonstration can evoke vivid mental images of product use and increase purchase intentions.[128]

Adding information actually makes imagery processing easier because more information makes it easier for consumers to form an accurate image (whereas it may lead to *information overload* under cognitive processing). For instance, consumers who see an ad asking them to imagine how good they would feel using the advertised product are likely to react positively and like the product more.[129] Moreover, imagery encourages brand-based processing because images are organized by brand rather than by attribute. Also, companies that design new products by encouraging customers to imagine or create a new image rather than recall one from memory can produce more original product designs.[130]

Marketing Implications

Marketers can employ a variety of advertising, sales, and promotional techniques to add to the emotional experience and imagery surrounding an offering. Good service or pleasant ambiance in a hotel, restaurant, or store, for example, can produce consumers' positive feelings and experiences that may influence their future choices. This is why the Ritz-Carlton hotel chain spends so much time and money training its 35,000 employees to deliver exemplary service and make every guest feel pampered. The hotel's advertising focuses on the emotional experience, "measuring a stay in the number of memories, so you get your memory's worth, not just your money's worth," explains the ad agency. Thanks to Ritz-Carlton's reputation for quality service, it can also market service training programs to other businesses and facilities, like the Erlanger Health System in Chattanooga, Tennessee.[131]

8-5 Additional High-Effort Decisions

In addition to deciding which brands to include in a consideration set, deciding what is important to the choice, and deciding what offerings to choose, consumers in high-effort situations face two more key decisions. First, should they delay the decision or make it right now? And second, how can they make a decision when the alternatives cannot be compared?

8-5a DECISION DELAY

If consumers perceive the decision to be too risky or if it entails an unpleasant task, they may delay making a decision.[132] They may also delay if they have too many attractive choices that are difficult to compare.[133] Another reason for delaying a decision is if consumers feel uncertain about how to get product information. Delaying a decision can affect a consumer's evaluation of brands that have features in common, regardless of whether those features are positive or negative. Specifically, the delay seems to make the shared features easier to recall and therefore has a greater impact on consumers' evaluations of the brands being considered.[134]

> **Noncomparable decision** The process of making a decision about products or services from different categories.
>
> **Alternative-based strategy** Making a noncomparable choice based on an overall evaluation.
>
> **Attribute-based strategy** Making a noncomparable choice by making abstract representations of comparable attributes.

 Marketing Implications

Should marketers encourage consumers to decide on a purchase right away? Many sales promotion techniques, including coupons and discounts, are available only to consumers who act quickly. On the other hand, if consumers delay making their decisions, marketers may have more time to offer additional information to bolster the chances that their brand will be chosen. Tesla used this strategy to good advantage when it began to hype its much-anticipated Model 3 electric car nearly two years before the U.S. launch, using traditional media and social media to reveal information little by little. Tesla's founder, Elon Musk, first publicized the $35,000 base price and other details on his Twitter account, where he has three million followers—building anticipation and interest in advance of the car's preorder date.[135]

8-5b DECISION-MAKING WHEN ALTERNATIVES CANNOT BE COMPARED

Consumers sometimes need to choose from a set of options that cannot be directly compared on the same attributes. For instance, you might be trying to select entertainment for next weekend and may have the choice of going to the movies, eating at a nice restaurant, renting a video, or attending a party. Each alternative has different attributes, making comparisons among them difficult.

In making these **noncomparable decisions**, consumers adopt either an alternative-based strategy or an attribute-based strategy.[136] Using the **alternative-based strategy** (also called *top-down processing*), they develop an overall evaluation of each option—perhaps using a compensatory or affective strategy—and base their decision on it. For example, if you were deciding on weekend entertainment, you could evaluate each option's pros and cons independently and then choose the one you liked the best.

Using the **attribute-based strategy**, consumers make comparisons easier for themselves by forming abstract representations that will allow them to compare the options. In this strategy (also called *bottom-up processing*), the choice is constructed or built up. To make a more direct comparison of options for an entertainment decision, for example, you could construct abstract attributes for them such as "fun" or "likelihood of impressing a date." Because using abstractions simplifies the decision-making process, consumers tend to use them even when the options are easy to compare.[137]

Note that both strategies can be employed in different circumstances. When the alternatives are less comparable, consumers tend to use an alternative-based strategy because it is harder for them to create attribute abstractions.[138] Alternative-based strategies also suit consumers who have well-defined goals because they can easily recall the various options and their results. For example, if your goal is to find enjoyable things to do with a date, you could immediately recall a set of options like going to a movie or eating out, along with your overall evaluation of each option. You would then pick the option with the strongest evaluation. On the other hand, when consumers lack well-defined goals, they tend to use attribute-based processing.

Remember that price is often the one attribute on which alternatives can be compared directly. Consumers typically use price to screen alternatives for the consideration set rather than as the main basis of comparison among noncomparable alternatives. Thus, when selecting from among entertainment alternatives, you might use cost to generate a set of options that are reasonably affordable, and then use an alternative or attribute-based strategy to make the final decision.

Marketing Implications

Because of the way that consumers approach noncomparable decisions, marketers should look at each product's or brand's competition in broad terms as well as understand how the product or brand stacks up to specific competitors. For example, when consumers are deciding where to go on vacation, their alternatives may reflect competition between different types of destinations (such as cities or beaches), activities (such as going to museums or going surfing), and so on. Therefore, marketers might identify the abstract attributes that consumers use to make these noncomparable evaluations. To illustrate, stressing an attribute like "historic" could make it easier for consumers to compare products. Then communications about travel destinations like Scotland could feature multiple attributes (historic landmarks, old-fashioned steam trains, majestic castles) and suggest how visiting the destination will fit the "historic" attribute.[139] Pricing is also an important marketing tactic for getting a brand into the consideration set when consumers cannot directly compare the attributes of various alternatives. Thus, tourism marketers often use pricing promotions to attract consumers' attention and encourage them to make further comparisons based on their goals or on individual attributes.

8-6 What Affects High-Effort Decisions?

As you have seen, consumers can use many different strategies when making decisions. However, the best strategy to use for making a specific decision depends on the consumer and the nature of the decision.[140] This final section looks at how characteristics of (a) consumers, (b) the decision, and (c) the group that they are a part of can affect their decisions.

8-6a CONSUMER CHARACTERISTICS

Characteristics associated with consumers—such as their expertise, mood, extremeness aversion, time pressure, and metacognitive experiences—can affect the decisions they make.

Expertise

Consumers are more likely to understand their preferences and decisions when they have detailed consumption vocabularies—meaning that they can articulate exactly why they like or dislike the brands that they do.

For example, a consumer who is an expert in wine may know that he or she likes wines that are buttery, dry, and smooth, whereas a novice might not know how to articulate these preferences.[141] Consumers who have this "consumption vocabulary" can use more attributes and information when making a decision. Expert consumers have more brand-based prior experience and knowledge and, as a result, tend to use brand-based decision strategies.[142] These consumers know how to identify relevant information and ignore irrelevant attributes in their decision-making. When consumers consider complex information, they may simplify the processing task by focusing more on brand effects and less on attributes, especially if they face more than one complex choice task.[143]

Mood

Consumers who are in a reasonably good mood are more willing to process information and take more time in making a decision than those who are not in a good mood.[144] When in a good mood, consumers pay closer attention to the set of brands being considered and think about a higher number of attributes connected with each brand, a process that can result in more extreme (positive or negative) evaluations.[145] Another study showed that consumers in a high-arousal mood—feeling excited or very sad, for instance—tend to process information less thoroughly. Recall is also affected: Consumers in a bad mood are more likely to accurately recall what a marketing message said, a factor that may affect what attributes they consider when making their choices.[146] Being in a good mood can also make people think more about the future and more about the big picture, rather than thinking about the details associated with the future.[147]

Mood can also influence how positively consumers judge products and their attributes.[148] One study found that when consumers' moods were subconsciously influenced by music, consumers in a good mood rated a set of audio speakers more positively than did consumers in a bad mood.[149] Interestingly, consumers may deliberately manipulate their moods to help themselves improve their decision performance.[150] Finally, consumers in a good mood are more willing to try new products because they perceive lower probabilities of incurring losses.[151]

Time Pressure

As time pressure increases, consumers initially try to process information relevant to their choices faster.[152] If doing this does not work, they base their decision on fewer attributes and place heavier weight on negative information, eliminating bad alternatives by using a noncompensatory decision strategy. Time pressure, one of the major reasons that consumers fail to make intended purchases, can reduce shopping time and the number of impulsive purchases.[153] Time pressure also affects consumers' decisions to delay their choices.[154] Moreover, whether a consumer is present or future-oriented can lead to different motivations and choices for different products.[155] *Present-oriented consumers* want to improve their current well-being and prefer products that help them to do so, such as relaxing vacations and entertaining books. *Future-oriented consumers* want to develop themselves and select life-enriching vacations and books.

Extremeness Aversion

Consumers tend to exhibit **extremeness aversion**, meaning that options for a particular attribute that are perceived as extreme will seem less attractive than those perceived as intermediate. This tendency is the reason that people often find moderately priced options more attractive than options that are either very expensive or very inexpensive.

When consumers see the attributes of one alternative as being equally dispersed (rather than very close together or very far apart), they will view this alternative as the compromise option even when it is not at the overall midpoint among options.[156] According to the **compromise effect**, a brand will gain share when it is seen as the intermediate or compromise choice rather than as an extreme choice.[157]

Also, consumers prefer a brand with attributes that score equally well on certain criteria more than a brand that has unequal scores across attributes, a phenomenon known as **attribute balancing**.[158]

Metacognitive Experiences

One final set of consumer characteristics that affects the decision-making process is that of **metacognitive experiences**. These are factors based on our decision-processing experience, such as how easy it is to recall information in memory and to form thoughts as well as how easy it is to process new information.[159] Metacognitive experiences affect decisions beyond formal knowledge by influencing retrieval ease, inferences, and biases. Thus, it is not just the content of the information that influences the decision; rather, *how* this information is processed is also critical.

According to one study, the pleasant experience of being able to process a brand name easily can lead to a consumer's favorable attitudes toward that brand. Yet in some cases in which consumers can process information about the brand more easily—such as seeing the mention of product benefits in an ad message—they may develop less favorable attitudes toward the brand because they may attribute that ease of processing to the persuasiveness of the information rather than to the attractiveness of the brand itself. Other studies have found that individuals are more likely to regard a statement as true when it is printed in an easy-to-read color or if the words rhyme.[160] In short, metacognitive experiences affect choices in concert with stimuli and consumer characteristics such as mood.[161]

Extremeness aversion Options that are extreme on some attributes are less attractive than those with a moderate level of those attributes

Compromise effect When a brand gains share because it is an intermediate rather than an extreme option.

Attribute balancing Picking a brand because it scores equally well on certain attributes rather than faring unequally on these attributes.

Metacognitive experiences How the information is processed beyond the content of the decision.

8-6b CHARACTERISTICS OF THE DECISION

In addition to consumer characteristics, decision characteristics can affect how consumers make their choices. Two decision characteristics of particular note are the availability of information on which to base a decision and the presence of trivial attributes.

Information Availability

The amount, quality, and format of the information can affect the decision-making strategy that consumers use. When a consumer has more information, the decision becomes more complex, and the consumer must use a more detailed decision-making strategy, such as the multiattribute choice strategy. Having more information will lead to making a better choice only up to a point, however; after that, the consumer will experience information overload.[162] For example, pharmaceutical firms are legally

Exhibit 8.10 ▶ Information Availability

Providing relevant information is important in consumer purchasing, but the marketer must be aware not to provide too much information or the consumer will experience information overload and most likely will not process all this information.

required to provide detailed prescription information and to disclose side effects of medications in their ads, yet the amount of such information can be overwhelming.

If the information provided is useful and relevant to our decision criteria, decision-making is less taxing, and we can make better decisions.[163] Essentially, we can narrow the consideration set relatively quickly because we can focus on those attributes that are most important to our decision. Hence, it is better for marketers to focus on providing relevant information, not just more information (see Exhibit 8.10). If the information provided is not useful or if some information is missing, we will need to infer how the product might rate on that attribute, perhaps by using other attributes of the brand in question to make that inference.[164] Interestingly, the mere suggestion that consumers might reject all items in the choice set can affect how consumers make decisions. Specifically, consumers tend to engage in more alternative- than attribute-based processing and focus on attributes that are meaningful to them when the choice set includes a "none of these products" option.[165]

If the available information is ambiguous, consumers are more likely to stay with their current brand than to risk purchasing a new competitive brand—even a superior one.[166] Consumers can also compare numerical attribute information faster and more easily than they can compare verbal information.[167] For example, to help parents select video games, a group of manufacturers developed a rating system to indicate the amount of sex and violence in their games. Also, decisions are sometimes affected by information about attributes to which consumers have been exposed in a previous choice.[168]

Information Format

The format of the information—the way that it is organized or presented in the external environment—can also influence the decision strategy that consumers use. If information is organized by brand, consumers will likely employ a brand-based decision-making strategy such as a compensatory, conjunctive, or disjunctive model. If information is organized by attribute or in a matrix, consumers can use an attribute-processing strategy. For example, one study found that organizing yogurt by flavor instead of by brand encouraged more comparison shopping on the basis of attribute processing.[169]

Sometimes consumers will even restructure information into a more useful format, especially in a matrix. Consumers are less likely to choose the cheapest brand of consumer electronics product when the offerings are organized by model (similar offerings by different companies grouped together) rather than by brand.[170] Thus, companies with high-priced brands would want the display to be organized by model, whereas companies offering low-priced brands would prefer a brand-based display. When the option to see pricing information is presented with the higher price first, consumers are more likely to choose the higher priced option. On the other hand, they are more likely to choose the lowest price if the options are presented from lowest to highest price.[171]

The presence of a narrative format for presenting information about brands can also impact consumers' choices. When researchers presented consumers with a narrative message about vacations, the consumers used holistic processing to sequence and evaluate the information. The narrative structure is similar to the way in which consumers acquire information in daily life, so processing was easier. In processing the narrative, consumers did not consider individual features, a situation that meant negative information had less impact.[172] Also note that consumers who tend to elaborate on the potential benefits and potential risks of the outcome before making a decision are less susceptible to information format biases.[173]

Trivial Attributes

Consumers sometimes finalize decisions by looking at trivial attributes. For example, if three brands in the consideration set are perceived as equivalent with the exception that one contains a trivial attribute, the consumer is likely to choose the brand with the trivial attribute (arguing that its presence may be useful). If, however, two of the three brands in the consideration set have a particular trivial attribute, the consumer is likely to choose the one without that attribute (arguing that the attribute is unnecessary). In both cases, the trivial attribute was used to complete and justify the decision.[174]

8-6c GROUP CONTEXT

Consumers' decisions can be affected by the presence of other people, or even a relationship with someone else.[175] For example, men are more likely to spend more money when shopping with a friend. However, women are more likely to spend more when shopping alone.[176]

Many decisions are made in a group context, such as when a group of people is dining out and each member is deciding what to order. As each group member makes a decision in turn, he or she attempts to balance two sets of goals: (1) goals that are attained by the individual's action alone (*individual alone*) and (2) goals that are achieved depending on the actions of both the individual and the group (*individual group*).[177] Because consumers may have to choose a different alternative to achieve each set of goals, they cannot always achieve both sets of goals simultaneously in group settings.

In a group, consumers face three types of individual-group goals, as shown in Exhibit 8.11:

■ *Self-presentation.* Consumers seek to convey a certain image through the decisions they make in a group context. When consumers want to use unique choices as positive self-presentation cues or to express their

Exhibit 8.11 ▶ Goal Classes That Affect Consumer Decision-Making

Consumers are not always able to achieve both individual-alone and individual-group goals when making decisions in the context of a group. Trying to achieve individual-group goals can result in either group variety or group uniformity, while trying to achieve individual-alone goals allows the consumer to satisfy his or her own taste through the decision.

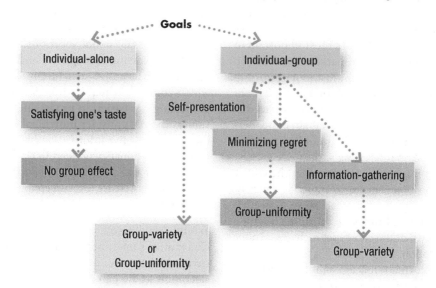

Note: In cases where informational social influence is present during the decision process, an outcome of group uniformity or variety seeking can result.

Source: From Dan Ariely and Jonathan Levav, "Sequential Choice in Group Settings: Taking the Road Less Traveled and Less Enjoyed," *Journal of Consumer Research*, December 2000, p. 281. Reprinted with permission of The University of Chicago Press.

individuality, the result will be variety seeking at the group level. Yet consumers are often more concerned about social norms and therefore make similar choices to blend in, resulting in uniformity at the group level. Interestingly, consumers may actually feel less confidence in their publically stated decision if they see others make the same decision but offer a different explanation for their choice.[178]

■ *Minimizing regret.* Consumers who are risk averse and want to minimize regret will tend to make choices that are similar to those made by the rest of the group, leading to uniformity at the group level. Making this choice allows group members to avoid any disappointment they might feel if someone else's choice seemed better than their own.

■ *Information gathering.* Consumers can learn more about the different choices each has made through interaction with other group members. Whether members actually share choices or simply share their reactions, the result is variety in the totality of choices within the group when consumers see information gathering as a priority. However, when group members are more concerned with self-presentation or loss aversion than with information gathering,

they will make similar choices, resulting in group uniformity.

When making a decision in a group context, we try to balance these three individual-group goals with our individual-alone goals. In most group situations, the result is group uniformity, even though individual members may ultimately feel less satisfied by the outcome.

 Marketing Implications

Marketers can develop some interesting strategies by understanding how consumer characteristics affect high-effort decisions. One technique is to sell a new, improved model alongside the old model at the same price, a tactic that makes the new one look better. In addition, marketers need to think about the information in their ads and on their packaging because irrelevant information can sometimes influence consumers' decisions—even in the presence of more relevant information.[179]

Providing the right amount of information at the right time is a challenge marketers face all over the world. One study found that consumers in Romania and Turkey have experienced great confusion in judging quality and making choices because "there are so many alternatives now."[180] Marketers should therefore present a few key points, not a flood of information. However, providing too little information can also hamper decision-making, resulting in poorer quality decisions and a lower level of satisfaction. A lack of both products and information has been a major problem in some former communist countries.[181]

When consumers face difficult decisions, have difficulty comparing alternatives, or have difficulty organizing the consideration set, marketers may want to consider providing decision aids such as product filtering tools, product comparison tools, or product recommendations. However, such decision aids should be planned carefully to avoid increasing the complexity of the decision process or leading consumers to extended search and less-optimal choices.[182]

Marketers can use communications to make individual-group goals a higher priority in group situations, leading to more uniformity of choice in favor of the advertised brand. Beer marketers, for instance, often show group members enjoying only the advertised brand, an image that reinforces strong social norms and encourages consumers to order that brand when they drink in a social setting.

Summary:

Judgments involve forming evaluations or estimates—not always objective—of the likelihood of the occurrence of events, whereas decisions entail choosing from among options or courses of action. Consumers make judgments about likelihood, about goodness or badness, and using mental accounting.

Once they recognize a problem, consumers may address it by using cognitive decision-making models (deciding in a rational, systematic manner) or affective decision-making models (deciding on the basis of their feelings or emotions). Consumers face a number of other decisions in high-effort situations: which brands to consider (developing the consideration set), what is important to the choice (how it is affected by goals, decision timing, and decision framing), what offerings to choose, whether to make a decision now or delay the decision, and what to do when alternatives cannot be compared (when they can use an alternative-based or attribute-based strategy).

In thought-based decisions about offerings, consumers may use compensatory or noncompensatory models, process by brand or by attribute, and consider gains versus losses. Feeling-based decisions about offerings may rely on appraisals and feelings, affective forecasts and choices, and imagery. Finally, three types of contextual factors that can influence the decision process are (1) consumer characteristics (expertise, mood, time pressure, extremeness aversion, metacognitive experiences), (2) decision characteristics (information availability, information format, trivial attributes), and (3) the presence of other people.

Questions for Review and Discussion

1. How does consumer judgment differ from consumer decision-making?

2. What is the anchoring and adjustment process, and how does it affect consumer judgment?

3. How do consumers use compensatory and noncompensatory decision-making models?

4. Explain how consumers use their goals, decision timing, and framing to decide which criteria are important for a particular choice.

5. Why do marketers need to know that attribute processing is easier for consumers than brand processing?

6. How do appraisals and feelings as well as affective forecasting influence consumer decision-making?

7. Under what circumstances do consumers use an alternative-based strategy or an attribute-based strategy for decision-making?

8. In what ways do the characteristics of consumers, the decision, and the group context influence consumer decision-making?

Endnotes

1   See, for example, Jack Ewing, "Apple and Google Create a Buzz at Frankfurt Motor Show," *New York Times*, September 17, 2015, www.nytimes.com.

2   Michael D. Johnson and Christopher P. Puto, "A Review of Consumer Judgment and Choice," in ed. Michael J. Houston, *Review of Marketing* (Chicago: American Marketing Association, 1987), pp. 236–292.

3   Eloise Coupey, Julie R. Irwin, and John W. Payne, "Product Category Familiarity and Preference Construction," *Journal of Consumer Research*, March 1998, pp. 459–468.

4   Itamar Simonson, Joel Huber, and John Payne, "The Relationship between Prior Brand Knowledge and Information Acquisition Order," *Journal of Consumer Research*, March 1988, pp. 566–578.

5   Eric J. Johnson and J. Edward Russo, "Product Familiarity and Learning New Information," *Journal of Consumer Research*, June 1984, pp. 528–541.

6   Michel Tuan Pham, Joel B. Cohen, John W. Pracejus, and G. David Hughes, "Affect Monitoring and the Primacy of Feelings in Judgment," *Journal of Consumer Research*, September 2001, pp. 167–188.

7   Gita Venkataramani Johar, Kamel Jedidi, and Jacob Jacoby, "A Varying-Parameter Averaging Model of Online Brand Evaluations," *Journal of Consumer Research*, September 1997, pp. 232–247; and Daniel Kahneman and Amos Tversky, "On the Psychology of Prediction," *Psychology Review*, July 1973, pp. 251–275; and Wegener, T. Duane, Richard E. Petty, Kevin L. Blankenship, and Brian Detweiler-Bedell, "Elaboration and Numerical Anchoring: Implications of Attitude Theories for Consumer Judgment and Decision Making," *Journal of Consumer Psychology* 20, no. 1, January 2010, pp. 5–16.

8   Joan Meyers-Levy and Alice M. Tybout, "Context Effects at Encoding and Judgment in Consumption Settings: The Role of Cognitive Resources," *Journal of Consumer Research*, June 1997, pp. 1–14.

9   Alexander Chernev, "Semantic Anchoring in Sequential Evaluations of Vices and Virtues," *Journal of Consumer Research* 37, no. 5, February 2011, pp. 761–774.

10 Howard Yu and Stefan Michel, "Disney Rethinks Its China Strategy," *Financial Times*, December 2, 2013, www.ft.com; and "Middle Kingdom Meets Magic Kingdom," *Economist*, August 28, 2010, p. 52.

11 John Carroll, "The Effect of Imagining an Event on Expectations for the Event," *Journal of Experimental Social Psychology*, January 1978, pp. 88–96.

12 Deborah J. MacInnis and Linda L. Price, "The Role of Imagery in Information Processing: Review and Extensions," *Journal of Consumer Research*, March 1987, pp. 473–491.

13 Baba Shiv and Joel Huber, "The Impact of Anticipating Satisfaction on Consumer Choice," *Journal of Consumer Research* 27, September 2000, pp. 202–216.

14 Donna L. Hoffman, Praveen K. Kopalle, and Thomas P. Novak, "The 'Right' Consumers for Better Concepts: Identifying Consumers High in Emergent Nature to Develop New Product Concepts," *Journal of Marketing Research* 47, no. 5, October 2010, pp. 854–865.

15 Irene C. L. Ng and Nick K.T. Yip, "Theoretical Foundations in the Pricing of Intermediating Services: The Case of Payments Via Mobile Phones," *Journal of Revenue and Pricing Management* 9, no. 3, 2010, pp. 217–227.

16 Jonathan Levav and A. Peter McGraw, "Emotional Accounting: How Feelings about Money Influence Consumer Choice," *Journal of Marketing Research*, February 2009, pp. 66–80.

17 Arul Mishra and Dhananjay Nayakankuppam, "Consistency and Validity Issues in Consumer Judgments," *Journal of Consumer Research* 33, no. 3, 2006, pp. 291–303.

18 Calvin P. Duncan and Richard W. Olshavsky, "External Search: The Role of Consumer Beliefs," *Journal of Marketing Research*, February 1982, pp. 32–43.

19 Geeta Menon, Lauren G. Block, and Suresh Ramanathan, "We're at as Much Risk as We Are Led to Believe," *Journal of Consumer Research*, March 2002, pp. 533–549.

20 Rohini Ahluwalia, "Re-Inquiries: How Prevalent Is the Negativity Effect in Consumer Environments?" *Journal of Consumer Research*, September 2002, pp. 270–279; and Rohini Ahluwalia, H. Rao Unnava, and Robert E. Burnkrant, "The Moderating Effect of Commitment on the Spillover Effect of Marketing Communications," *Journal of Marketing Research*, November 2001, pp. 458–470.

21 Meryl Paula Gardner, "Mood States and Consumer Behavior: A Critical Review," *Journal of Consumer Research*, December 1985, pp. 281–300.

22 Margaret G. Meloy, J. Edward Russo, and Elizabeth Gelfand, "Monetary Incentives and Mood," *Journal of Marketing Research*, May 2006, pp. 267–275.

23 Stijn M. J. Van Osselaer and Joseph W. Alba, "Consumer Learning and Brand Equity," *Journal of Consumer Research* 27, June 2000, pp. 1–16.

24 Keith Wilcox and Sangyoung Song, "Discrepant Fluency in Self Customization," *Journal of Marketing Research*, August 2011, pp. 729–740.

25 Manoj Thomas and Vicki G. Morwitz, "The Ease-of-Computation Effect," *Journal of Marketing Research*, February 2009, pp. 81–91.

26 Sarah Perez, "Apple Watch Not A Flop–Now #2 Wearable, Just Behind Fitbit," *TechCrunch*, August 27, 2015, www.techcrunch.com.

27 Paul M. Herr, "Priming Price: Prior Knowledge and Context Effects," *Journal of Consumer Research*, June 1989, pp. 67–75.

28 Robert Klara, "How Shinola Went From Shoe Polish to the Coolest Brand in America," *Adweek*, June 22, 2015. www.adweek.com.

29 Sung-Tai Hong and Robert S. Wyer Jr., "Effects of Country-of-Origin and Product-Attribute Information," *Journal of Consumer Research*, September 1989, pp. 175–187.

30 Daniel Khoo, "Bfood Eyes 20% Growth," *The Star (Malaysia)*, January 24, 2015, www.thestar.com/my; and Maureen Morrison, "Now-Rare U.S. Brands Thriving Overseas," *Advertising Age*, September 5, 2011, www.adage.com.

31 James R. Bettman and Mita Sujan, "Effects of Framing on Evaluation of Comparable and Noncomparable Alternatives by Expert and Novice Consumers," *Journal of Consumer Research*, September 1987, pp. 141–151.

32 Naomi Mandel, "Shifting Selves and Decision Making: The Effects of Self-Construal Priming on Consumer Risk-Taking," *Journal of Consumer Research*, June 2003, pp. 30–40.

33 Priya Raghubir and Geeta Menon, "AIDS and Me, Never the Twain Shall Meet," *Journal of Consumer Research*, June 1998, pp. 52–63.

34 Menon, Block, and Ramanathan, "We're as at Much Risk as We Are Led to Believe."

35 Ravi Dhar and Itamar Simonson, "The Effect of Forced Choice on Choice," *Journal of Marketing Research*, May 2004, pp. 146–160; and Ravi Dhar, "Consumer Preference for a No-Choice Option," *Journal of Consumer Research*, September 1997, pp. 215–231.

36 Ravi Dhar and Stephen M. Nowlis, "To Buy or Not to Buy," *Journal of Marketing Research*, November 2004, pp. 423–432.

37 "The Rise of the Superbrands," *Economist*, February 5, 2005, pp. 63–65.

38 Daniel Mochon, "Single-Option Aversion," *Journal of Consumer Research* 40, no. 3, October 2013, pp. 555–566.

39 F. May and R. Homans, "Evoked Set Size and the Level of Information Processing in Product Comprehension and Choice Criteria," in ed. William D. Perrault, *Advances in Consumer Research*, vol. 4 (Chicago: Association for Consumer Research, 1977), pp. 172–175.

40 Amitav Chakravarti and Chris Janiszewski, "The Influence of Macro-Level Motives on Consideration Set Composition in Novel Purchase Situations," *Journal of Consumer Research*, September 2003, pp. 244–258.

41 Frank R. Kardes, David M. Sanbonmatsu, Maria L. Cronley, and David C. Houghton, "Consideration Set Overvaluation," *Journal of Consumer Psychology*, 2002, pp. 353–361.

42 Steven S. Posavac, David M. Sanbonmatsu, and Edward A. Ho, "The Effects of Selective Consideration of Alternatives on Consumer Choice and Attitude–Decision Consistency," *Journal of Consumer Psychology*, 2002, pp. 203–213.

43 Steven S. Posavac, David M. Sanbonmatsu, Frank R. Kardes, and Gavan J. Fitzsimons, "The Brand Positivity Effect: When Evaluation Confers Preference," *Journal of Consumer Research*, December 2004, pp. 643–651.

44 Jonathan Levav, Nicholas Reinholtz, and Claire Lin, "The Effect of Ordering Decisions by Choice-Set Size on Consumer Search," *Journal of Consumer Research* 39, no. 3, October 2012, pp. 585–599.

45 Ryan Hamilton, Jiewen Hong, and Alexander Chernev, "Perceptual Focus Effects in Choice," *Journal of Consumer Research*, August 2007, pp. 187–199; and Itamar Simonson and Amos Tversky, "Choice in Context: Tradeoff Contrast and Extremeness Aversion," *Journal of Marketing Research*, August 1992, pp. 281–295.

46 Jongwon Park and JungKeun Kim, "The Effects of Decoys on Preference Shifts," *Journal of Consumer Psychology* 15, no. 2, 2005, pp. 94–107; Sanjay Mishra, U. N. Umesh, and Donald E. Stem, "Antecedents of the Attraction Effect," *Journal of Marketing Research*, August 1993, pp. 331–349; Yigang Pan, Sue O'Curry, and Robert Pitts, "The Attraction Effect and Political Choice in Two Elections," *Journal of Consumer Psychology* 4, no. 1, 1995, pp. 85–101; Sankar Sen, "Knowledge, Information Mode, and the Attraction Effect," *Journal of Consumer Research*, June 1998, pp. 64–77; Timothy B. Heath and Subimal Chatterjee, "Asymmetric Decoy Effects on Lower-Quality Versus Higher-Quality Brands," *Journal of Consumer Research*, December 1995, pp. 268–284; and Elizabeth Cowley and John R. Rossiter, "Range Model of Judgments," *Journal of Consumer Psychology* 15, no. 3, 2005, pp. 250–262; and Selin A. Malkoc, William Hedgcock, and Steve Hoeffler, "Between a Rock and a Hard Place: The Failure of the Attraction Effect Among Unattractive Alternatives," *Journal of Consumer Psychology* 23, no. 3, July 2013, pp. 317–329.

47 Simonson, "Get Closer to Your Consumers by Understanding How They Make Choices."

48 Gabriele Paolacci, Katherine A. Burson, and Scott I. Rick, "The Intermediate Alternative Effect: Considering a Small Tradeoff Increases Subsequent Willingness to Make Large Tradeoffs," *Journal of Consumer Psychology* 21, no. 4, October 2011 Special Issue, pp. 384–392.

49 Rebecca W. Hamilton, "Why Do People Suggest What They Do Not Want? Using Context Effects to Influence Others' Choices," *Journal of Consumer Research*, March 2003, pp. 492–506.

50 Jim Wang and Robert S. Wyer Jr., "Comparative Judgment Processes: The Effects of Task Objectives and Time Delay on Product Evaluations," *Journal of Consumer Psychology*, 2002, pp. 327–340.

51 Alexander Chernev, "Decision Focus and Consumer Choice among Assortments," *Journal of Consumer Research* 33, no. 1, 2006, pp. 50–59.

52 Leonard Lee and Dan Ariely, "Shopping Goals, Goal Concreteness, and Conditional Promotions," *Journal of Consumer Research* 33, no. 1, 2006, pp. 60–70.

53 Punam A. Keller, "Regulatory Focus and Efficacy of Health Messages," *Journal of Consumer Research* 33, no. 1, 2006, pp. 109–114.

54 John G. Lynch and G. Zauberman, "Construing Consumer Decision Making," *Journal of Consumer Psychology* 17, no. 2, 2007, pp. 107–112.

55 Ran Kivetz and Itamar Simonson, "Self-Control for the Righteous: Toward a Theory of Precommitment to Indulgence," *Journal of Consumer Research*, September 2002, pp. 199–217.

56 Reetika Gupta and Sankar Sen, "The Effect of Evolving Resource Synergy Beliefs on the Intentions-Behavior Discrepancy in Ethical Consumption," *Journal of Consumer Psychology* 23, no. 1, January 2013, pp. 114–121.

57 Daniel Kahneman and Amos Tversky, "Prospect Theory," *Econometrica*, March 1979, pp. 263–291.

58 Punan Anand Keller, Isaac M. Lipkus, and Barbara K. Rimer, "Affect, Framing, and Persuasion," *Journal of Marketing Research*, February 2003, pp. 54–64.

59 Ashwani Monga and Rui Zhu, "Buyers versus Sellers: How They Differ in Their Responses to Framed Outcomes," *Journal of Consumer Psychology* 15, no. 4, 2005, pp. 325–333.

60 Katherine White, Rhiannon MacDonnell, and Darren W. Dahl, "It's the Mind-Set That Matters: The Role of Construal Level and Message Framing in Influencing Consumer Efficacy and Conservation Behaviors," *Journal of Marketing Research* 48, no. 3, June 2011, pp. 472–485.

61 I. P. Levin, "Associative Effects of Information Framing on Human Judgments," Paper presented at the annual meeting of the Midwestern Psychological Association, May 1987, in Chicago, Ill.

62 Sucharita Chandran and Geeta Menon, "When a Day Means More Than a Year: Effects of Temporal Framing on Judgments of Health Risk," *Journal of Consumer Research*, September 2004, pp. 375–389.

63 Christopher P. Puto, W. E. Patton, and Ronald H. King, "Risk Handling Strategies in Industrial Vendor Selection Decisions," *Journal of Marketing*, January 1987, pp. 89–98.

64 John T. Gourville, "Pennies-a-Day: The Effect of Temporal Reframing on Transaction Evaluation," *Journal of Consumer Research*, March 1998, pp. 395–408.

65 Rashmi Adaval and Kent B. Monroe, "Automatic Construct and Use of Contextual Information for Product and Price

Evaluations," *Journal of Consumer Research*, March 2002, pp. 572–588.

66 Rajesh Bagchi and Derick F. Davis, "$29 for 70 Items or 70 Items for $29? How Presentation Order Affects Package Perceptions," *Journal of Consumer Research* 39, no. 1, June 2012, pp. 62–73.

67 Yaacov Schul and Yoav Ganzach, "The Effects of Accessibility of Standards and Decision Framing on Product Evaluations," *Journal of Consumer Psychology* 4, no. 1, 1995, pp. 61–83.

68 Baba Shiv, Julie A. Edell, and John W. Payne, "Factors Affecting the Impact of Negatively and Positively Framed Ad Messages," *Journal of Consumer Research*, December 1997, pp. 285–294.

69 James R. Bettman and Mita Sujan, "Effects of Framing on Evaluation of Comparable and Noncomparable Alternatives by Expert and Novice Consumers," *Journal of Consumer Research* 14, no. 2, 1987, pp. 141–154.

70 Donald P. Green and Irene V. Blair, "Framing and Price Elasticity of Private and Public Goods," *Journal of Consumer Psychology* 4, no. 1, 1995, pp. 1–32.

71 Paul M. Herr and Christine M. Page, "Asymmetric Association of Liking and Disliking Judgments: So What's Not to Like?" *Journal of Consumer Research*, March 2004, pp. 588–601.

72 Brian Halla, "Piecing Together the Tesla Strategy Puzzle," *Harvard Business Review*, September 16, 2015, https://hbr .org.

73 Richard Milne, "Sales Jump Secures Lego's Crown as World's Biggest Toymaker," *Financial Times*, September 2, 2015, www .ft.com.

74 Melia Robinson, "This California Grilled-Cheese Chain Hired NASA Engineers to Design Its Delivery Vehicles," *Business Insider*, February 13, 2015, www.businessinsider.com; and Josh Ozersky, "Cheesed Off: A Childhood Staple Becomes a Fad," *Time*, September 5, 2011, www.time.com.

75 Joseph K. Goodman and Selin A. Malkoc, "Choosing Here and Now versus There and Later: The Moderating Role of Psychological Distance on Assortment Size Preferences," *Journal of Consumer Research* 39, no. 4, December 2012, pp. 751–768.

76 Itamar Simonson, "Get Closer to Your Consumers by Understanding How They Make Choices," *California Management Review*, Summer 1993, pp. 68–84; and John W. Payne, James R. Bettman, and Eric J. Johnson, "The Adaptive Decision-Maker," in ed. Robin M. Hogarth, *Insights in Decision Making: A Tribute to Hillel Einhorn* (Chicago: University of Chicago Press, 1990).

77 Aimee Drolet, "Inherent Rule Variability in Consumer Choice: Changing Rules for Change's Sake," *Journal of Consumer Research*, December 2002, pp. 293–305; James R. Bettman, Mary Frances Luce, and John W. Payne, "Constructive Consumer Choice Processes," *Journal of Consumer Research*, December 1998, pp. 187–217; James R. Bettman, Mary Frances Luce, and John W. Payne, "Constructive Consumer Choice Processes," *Journal of Consumer Research*, December 1998, pp. 187–217; Denis A. Lussier and Richard W. Olshavsky, "Task Complexity and Contingent Processing in Brand Choice," *Journal of Consumer Research*, September 1979, pp. 154–165; and Eric J. Johnson and Robert J. Meyer, "Compensatory Choice Models of Noncompensatory Processes," *Journal of Consumer Research*, June 1984, pp. 542–551.

78 Sanjay Sood, Yuval Rottenstreich, and Lyle Brenner, "On Decisions That Lead to Decisions: Direct and Derived Evaluations of Preference," *Journal of Consumer Research*, June 2004, pp. 17–18.

79 Seymour Epstein, "Integration of the Cognitive and the Psychodynamic Unconscious," *American Psychologist*, August 1994, pp. 709–724.

80 Mariele K. De Mooij and Warren Keegan, *Worldwide Advertising* (London: Prentice-Hall International, 1991).

81 Peter Wright, "Consumer Choice Strategies: Simplifying vs. Optimizing," *Journal of Marketing Research*, February 1975, pp. 60–67; and Noreen Klein and Stewart W. Bither, "An Investigation of Utility-Directed Cutoff Selection," *Journal of Consumer Research*, September 1987, pp. 240–256.

82 Simonson, "Get Closer to Your Consumers by Understanding How They Make Choices."

83 "Buzzing into Brazil," *Economist*, August 20, 2011, p. 61.

84 For a review of multiattribute models, see William L. Wilkie and Edgar A. Pessemier, "Issues in Marketing's Use of Multiattribute Models," *Journal of Marketing Research*, November 1983, pp. 428–441; and Blair H. Sheppard, Jon Hartwick, and Paul R. Warshaw, "The Theory of Reasoned Action," *Journal of Consumer Research*, December 1988, pp. 325–342.

85 Alexander Chernev, "Goal-Attribute Compatibility in Consumer Choice," *Journal of Consumer Psychology*, 2004, pp. 141–150.

86 Mary Frances Luce, "Choosing to Avoid: Coping with Negatively Emotion-Laden Consumer Decisions," *Journal of Consumer Research*, March 1998, pp. 409–433; and Ellen C. Garbarino and Julie A. Edell, "Cognitive Effort, Affect, and Choice," *Journal of Consumer Research*, September 1997, pp. 147–158.

87 Mary Frances Luce, John W. Payne, and James R. Bettman, "Emotional Trade-off Difficulty and Choice," *Journal of Marketing Research* 36, May 1999, pp. 143–159.

88 Aimee Drolet and Mary Frances Luce, "The Rationalizing Effects of Cognitive Load on Emotion-Based Tradeoff Avoidance," *Journal of Consumer Research*, June 2004, pp. 63–77; see also Tiffany Barnett White, "Consumer Trust and Advice Acceptance: The Moderating Roles of Benevolence, Expertise, and Negative Emotions," *Journal of Consumer Psychology* 15, no. 2, 2005, pp. 141–148.

89 David Grether and Louis Wilde, "An Analysis of Conjunctive Choice," *Journal of Consumer Research*, March 1984, pp. 373–385.

90 Lisa Brown, "Enterprise CarShare Membership Nearly Doubled in a Year," *St. Louis Post-Dispatch*, October 22, 2014, www.stltoday.com; and Bryan Roth, "Volts Give Car-Sharing a New Charge," *Duke Today*, August 31, 2011, http://today.duke .edu.

91 Lussier and Olshavsky, "Task Complexity and Contingent Processing in Brand Choice"; and Johnson and Meyer, "Compensatory Choice Models of Noncompensatory Processes."

92 Nancy Trejos, "Megabus Adds Reserved Seating, for a Fee," *USA Today*, April 1, 2015, www.usatoday.com; and Ben Austen, "The Mega Bus," *Bloomberg Businessweek*, April 11, 2011, pp. 63–67.

93 Timothy B. Heath, Gangseog Ryu, Subimal Chatterjee, Michael S. McCarthy, David L. Mothersbaugh, Sandra Milberg, and Gary J. Gaeth, "Asymmetric Competition in Choice and the Leveraging of Competitive Disadvantages," *Journal of Consumer Research* 27, December 2000, pp. 291–308.

94 Rohini Ahluwalia, Robert E. Burnkrant, and H. Rao Unnava, "Consumer Response to Negative Publicity: The Moderating Role of Commitment," *Journal of Marketing Research* 37, May 2000, pp. 203–214.

95 David Phelps, "Radisson Blu Taps into Growing Latin American Market," *Minneapolis Star-Tribune*, July 27, 2015, www.startribune.com; Josh Noel, "Radisson Betting on Blu," *Chicago Tribune*, August 26, 2011, www.chicagotribune.com; and Paris Wolfe, "Radisson's Brand Transformation Progresses," *Lodging Hospitality*, August 25, 2011, http://lhonline.com.

96 Gerald Häubl and Kyle B. Murray, "Preference Construction and Persistence in Digital Marketplaces: The Role of Electronic Recommendation Agents," *Journal of Consumer Psychology*, 2003, pp. 75–91.

97 Amos Tversky, "Intransitivity of Preferences," *Psychological Review*, January 1969, pp. 31–48.

98 Amos Tversky, "Elimination by Aspects: A Theory of Choice," *Psychological Review*, July 1972, pp. 281–299.

99 Violet Kim, "Watch Your Wing, KFC! Korean Fried Chicken (and Beer) Is Here," *CNN*, June 21, 2015, www.cnn.com; and "Korean Restaurant Chains Seek Success Abroad," *Korea Herald*, September 9, 2011, www.koreaherald.com.

100 Uri Simonsohn, "Lessons from an 'Oops' at Consumer Reports: Consumers Follow Experts and Ignore Invalid Information," *Journal of Marketing Research* 48, no. 1, February 2011, pp. 1–12.

101 David R. Baker, "Startup's Big Idea: Free EV Charging at Whole Foods, Other Stores," *San Francisco Chronicle*, June 11, 2015, www.sfgate.com; and Jeff DeLong, "Retail Outlets Adding Electric Car Charging Stations," *USA Today*, January 18, 2011, www.usatoday.com.

102 Irwin Levin, "Associative Effects of Information Framing," *Bulletin of the Psychonomic Society*, March 1987, pp. 85–86.

103 L. Su and L. L. Gao, "Strategy Compatibility: The Time versus Money Effect on Product Evaluation Strategies," *Journal of Consumer Psychology* 24, no. 4, October 2014, pp. 549–556.

104 Zheyin (Jane) Gu and Sha Yang, "Quantity-Discount-Dependent Consumer Preferences and Competitive Nonlinear Pricing," *Journal of Marketing Research* 47, no. 6, December 2010, pp. 1100–1113.

105 Nathan Novemsky and Daniel Kahneman, "The Boundaries of Loss Aversion," *Journal of Marketing Research*, May 2005, pp. 119–128; Colin Camerer, "Three Cheers—Psychological, Theoretical, Empirical—for Loss Aversion," *Journal of Marketing Research*, May 2005, pp. 129–133; and Dan Ariely, Joel Huber, and Klaus Wertenbroch, "When Do Losses Loom Larger Than Gains?" *Journal of Marketing Research*, May 2005, pp. 134–138.

106 Promothesh Chatterjee, Caglar Irmak, and Randall L. Rose, "The Endowment Effect as Self-Enhancement in Response to Threat," *Journal of Consumer Research* 40, no. 3, October 2013, pp. 460–476.

107 Alexander Chernev, "Goal Orientation and Consumer Preference for the Status Quo," *Journal of Consumer Research* 31, no. 3, 2004, pp. 557–565.

108 "17 American Companies That Offer Great Guarantees," *Consumer Reports*, September 23, 2014, www.consumerreports.org.

109 G. Chambers Williams III, "Nissan's Updated Leaf Electric Car Gets a Bigger Battery, Longer Range for 2016," *San Antonio Express News*, September 21, 2015, http://blog.mysanantonio.com.

110 Douglas E. Allen, "Toward a Theory of Consumer Choice as Sociohistorically Shaped Practical Experience," *Journal of Consumer Research*, March 2002, pp. 515–532.

111 Peter R. Darke, Amitava Chattopadhyay, and Laurence Ashworth, "The Importance and Functional Significance of Affective Cues in Consumer Choice," *Journal of Consumer Research* 33, no. 3, 2006, pp. 322–328; and Stephen J. Hoch and George F. Lowenstein, "Time-Inconsistent Preferences and Consumer Self-Control," *Journal of Consumer Research*, March 1991, pp. 492–507.

112 Michel Tuan Pham, "The Logic of Feeling," *Journal of Consumer Psychology* 14, no. 4, 2004, pp. 360–369.

113 Michel Tuan Pham, "Representativeness, Relevance, and the Use of Feelings in Decision Making," *Journal of Consumer Research*, September 1998, pp. 144–159.

114 Epstein, "Integration of the Cognitive and the Psychodynamic Unconscious."

115 Yuval Rottenstreich, Sanjay Sood, and Lyle Brenner, "Feeling and Thinking in Memory-Based Versus Stimulus-Based Choices," *Journal of Consumer Research* 33, no. 4, 2007, pp. 461–469.

116 Pham, "Representativeness, Relevance, and the Use of Feelings in Decision Making"; Morris B. Holbrook and Elizabeth C. Hirschman, "The Experiential Aspects of Consumption," *Journal of Consumer Research*, September 1982, pp. 132–140; and Erica Mina Okada, "Justification Effects on Consumer Choice of Hedonic and Utilitarian Goods," *Journal of Marketing Research*, February 2005, pp. 43–53.

117 Stacy L. Wood and James R. Bettman, "Predicting Happiness: How Normative Feeling Rules Influence (and Even Reverse) Durability Bias," *Journal of Consumer Psychology* 17, no. 3, 2007, pp. 188–201; and Morris B. Holbrook and Meryl P. Gardner, "An Approach to Investigating the Emotional Determinants of Consumption Durations: Why Do People Consume What They Consume for as Long as They Consume It?" *Journal of Consumer Psychology* 2, no. 2, 1993, pp. 123–142.

118 See Jennifer S. Lerner, Seunghee Han, and Dacher Keltner, "Feelings and Consumer Decision Making: Extending the Appraisal Tendency Framework," *Journal of Consumer Psychology* 17, no. 3, 2007, pp. 184–187; J. Frank Yates, "Emotional Appraisal Tendencies and Carryover: How, Why, and ... Therefore?" *Journal of Consumer Psychology* 17, no. 3, 2007, pp. 179–183; and Baba Shiv, "Emotions, Decisions, and the Brain," *Journal of Consumer Psychology* 17, no. 3, pp. 174–178.

119 Seunghee Han, Jennifer S. Lerner, and Dacher Keltner, "Feelings and Consumer Decision Making: The Appraisal-Tendency Framework," *Journal of Consumer Psychology* 17, no. 3, 2007, pp. 158–168.

120 Ibid.

121 Leif D. Nelson and Tom Meyvis, "Interrupted Consumption: Disrupting Adaptation to Hedonic Experiences," *Journal of Marketing Research*, December 2008, pp. 654–664.

122 Niels van de Ven, Marcel Zeelenberg, and Rik Pieters, "The Envy Premium in Product Evaluation," *Journal of Consumer Research*, April 2011, pp. 984–998.

123 Deborah J. MacInnis, Vanessa M. Patrick, and C. Whan Park, "Not as Happy as I Thought I'd Be? Affective Misforecasting and Product Evaluations," *Journal of Consumer Research*, March 2007, pp. 479–490; and Deborah J. MacInnis, Vanessa M. Patrick, and C. Whan Park, "Looking Through the Crystal Ball: Affective Forecasting and Misforecasting in Consumer Behavior," *Review of Marketing Research* 2,

2006, pp. 43–80; and Stephen X. He and Samuel D. Bond, "Word-of-mouth and the Forecasting of Consumption Enjoyment," *Journal of Consumer Psychology* 23, no. 4, October 2013, pp. 464–482.

124 Eric A. Greenleaf, "Reserves, Regret, and Rejoicing in Open English Auctions," *Journal of Consumer Research* 31, no. 2, 2004, pp. 264–273.

125 I. Simonson, "The Influence of Anticipating Regret and Responsibility on Purchase Decisions," *Journal of Consumer Research* 19, 1992, pp. 105–118.

126 Ann L. McGill and Punam Anand Keller, "Differences in the Relative Influence of Product Attributes under Alternative Processing Conditions," *Journal of Consumer Psychology* 3, no. 1, 1994, pp. 29–50; and MacInnis and Price, "The Role of Imagery in Information Processing: Review and Extensions."

127 Russell W. Belk, Güliz Ger, and Søren Askegaard, "The Fire of Desire: A Multisited Inquiry into Consumer Passion," *Journal of Consumer Research*, December 2003, pp. 326–351.

128 Ann E. Schlosser, "Experiencing Products in the Virtual World: The Role of Goal and Imagery in Influencing Attitudes versus Purchase Intentions," *Journal of Consumer Research*, September 2003, pp. 184–198.

129 Jennifer Edson Escalas, "Imagine Yourself in the Product," *Journal of Advertising*, Summer 2004, pp. 37–48.

130 Darren W. Dahl, Amitava Chattopadhyay, and Gerald J. Gorn, "The Use of Visual Mental Imagery in New Product Design," *Journal of Marketing Research* 36, February 1999, pp. 18–28.

131 Micah Solomon, "Ritz-Carlton President Herve Humler's Leadership, Culture and Customer Service Secrets," *Forbes*, April 21, 2015, www.forbes.com; Stuart Elliott, "Luxury Hotels Market the Memories They Can Make," *New York Times*, September 13, 2011, www.nytimes.com; Carmine Gallo, "Employee Motivation the Ritz-Carlton Way," *BusinessWeek*, February 29, 2008, www.businessweek.com; and Molly Gamble, "Luxury Hotel Chain Ritz-Carlton to Help Tennessee Hospital Achieve Service Excellence," *Becker's Hospital Review*, August 26, 2011, www.beckershospitalreview.com.

132 Eric A. Greenleaf and Donald R. Lehmann, "Reasons for Substantial Delay in Consumer Decision Making," *Journal of Consumer Research*, September 1995, pp. 186–199.

133 See Benjamin Scheibehenne, Rainer Greifeneder, and Peter M. Todd, "Can There Ever Be Too Many Options? A Meta-Analytic Review of Choice Overload," *Journal of Consumer Research*, October 2010, pp. 409–425.

134 Thomas A. Brunner and Michaela Wänke, "The Reduced and Enhanced Impact of Shared Features on Individual Brand Evaluations," *Journal of Consumer Psychology* 16, no. 2, 2006, pp. 101–111.

135 Kirsten Korosec, "Tesla's Elon Musk Reveals When Customers Can Pre-Order the Cheaper Model 3," *Fortune*, September 2, 2015, www.fortune.com.

136 Michael D. Johnson, "Consume r Choice Strategies for Comparing Noncomparable Alternatives," *Journal of Consumer Research*, December 1984, pp. 741–753; and Michael D. Johnson, "Comparability and Hierarchical Processing in Multialternative Choice," *Journal of Consumer Research*, December 1988, pp. 303–314.

137 Kim P. Corfman, "Comparability and Comparison Levels Used in Choices Among Consumer Products," *Journal of Marketing Research*, August 1991, pp. 368–374.

138 C. Whan Park and Daniel Smith, "Product-Level Choice: A Top-Down or Bottom-Up Process?" *Journal of Consumer Research*, December 1989, pp. 289–299.

139 "Global 'Buzz' Goal Set for Borders to Edinburgh Railway," *BBC News*, September 14, 2015, www.bbc.com/news.

140 Girish N. Punj and David W. Stewart, "An Interaction Framework of Consumer Decision Making," *Journal of Consumer Research*, September 1983, pp. 181–196.

141 Patricia M. West, Christina L. Brown, and Stephen J. Hoch, "Consumption Vocabulary and Preference Formation," *Journal of Consumer Research*, September 1996, pp. 120–135.

142 Johnson and Russo, "Product Familiarity and Learning New Information"; and James R. Bettman and C. Whan Park, "Effects of Prior Knowledge and Experience and Phase of the Choice Process on Consumer Decision Processes, A Protocol Analysis," *Journal of Consumer Research*, December 1980, pp. 234–248.

143 Joffre Swait and Wiktor Adamowicz, "The Influence of Task Complexity on Consumer Choice," *Journal of Consumer Research*, June 2001, pp. 135–148.

144 Elaine Sherman and Ruth Belk Smith, "Mood States of Shoppers and Store Image: Promising Interactions and Possible Behavioral Effects," in eds. Paul Anderson and Melanie Wallendorf, *Advances in Consumer Research*, vol. 14 (Provo, Utah: Association for Consumer Research, 1987), pp. 251–254.

145 Rashmi Adaval, "How Good Gets Better and Bad Gets Worse: Understanding the Impact of Affect on Evaluations of Known Brands," *Journal of Consumer Research*, December 2003, pp. 352–367.

146 Stewart Shapiro, Deborah J. MacInnis, and C. Whan Park, "Understanding Program-Induced Mood Effects: Decoupling Arousal from Valence," *Journal of Advertising*, Winter 2002, pp. 15–26.

147 Jin Seok Pyone and Alice M. Isen, "Positive Affect, Intertemporal Choice, and Levels of Thinking: Increasing Consumers' Willingness to Wait," *Journal of Marketing Research* 48, no. 3, June 2011, pp. 532–543.

148 Catherine W. M. Yeung and Robert S. Wyer Jr., "Affect, Appraisal, and Consumer Judgment," *Journal of Consumer Research*, September 2004, pp. 412–424.

149 Gerald J. Gorn, Marvin E. Goldberg, and Kunal Basu, "Mood, Awareness, and Product Evaluation," *Journal of Consumer Psychology* 2, no. 3, 1993, pp. 237–256.

150 Joel B. Cohen and Eduardo B. Andrade, "Affective Intuition and Task-Contingent Affect Regulation," *Journal of Consumer Research*, September 2004, pp. 358–367.

151 Alexander Fedorikhin and Catherine A. Cole, "Mood Effects on Attitudes, Perceived Risk, and Choice: Moderators and Mediators," *Journal of Consumer Psychology* 14, no. 1/2, 2004, pp. 2–12.

152 Payne, Bettman, and Johnson, "The Adaptive Decision-Maker."

153 C. Whan Park, Easwar S. Iyer, and Daniel C. Smith, "The Effects of Situational Factors on In-Store Grocery Shopping Behavior: The Role of Store Environment and Time Available for Shopping," *Journal of Consumer Research*, March 1989, pp. 422–433.

154 Ravi Dhar and Stephen M. Nowlis, "The Effect of Time Pressure on Consumer Choice Deferral," *Journal of Consumer Research* 25, March 1999, pp. 369–384.

155 Michelle M. Bergadaa, "The Role of Time in the Action of the Consumer," *Journal of Consumer Research*, December 1990, pp. 289–302.

156 Alexander Chernev, "Extremeness Aversion and Attribute-Balance Effects in Choice," *Journal of Consumer Research*, September 2004, pp. 249–263.

157 Ran Kivetz, Oded Netzer, and V. Srinivasan, "Alternative Models for Capturing the Compromise Effect," *Journal of Marketing Research*, August 2004, pp. 237–257; and Ravi Dhar, Anil Menon, and Bryan Maach, "Toward Extending the Compromise Effect to Complex Buying Contexts," *Journal of Marketing Research*, August 2004, pp. 258–261.

158 Alexander Chernev, "Context Effects without a Context: Attribute Balance as a Reason for Choice," *Journal of Consumer Research* 32, no. 2, 2005, pp. 213–223.

159 Norbert Schwarz, "Metacognitive Experiences in Consumer Judgment and Decision Making," *Journal of Consumer Psychology* 14, no. 4, 2004, pp. 332–348; and S. B. Park and S.J. Bae, "Different Routes to Metacognitive Judgments: The Role of Accuracy Motivation," *Journal of Consumer Psychology* 24, no. 3, July 2014, pp. 307–319.

160 Rolf Reber and Norbert Schwarz, "Effects on Perceptual Fluency on Judgments of Truth," *Consciousness and Cognition* 8, 1999, pp. 338–342; and Matthew S. McGlone and Jessica Tofighbakhsh, "Birds of a Feather Flock Conjointly(?): Rhyme as Reason in Aphorisms," *Psychological Science* 11, no. 1, 2000, pp. 424–428.

161 See Joel Huber, "A Comment on Metacognitive Experiences and Consumer Choices," *Journal of Consumer Psychology* 14, no. 4, 2004, pp. 356–359; and Norbert Schwarz, "Metacognitive Experiences: Response to Commentaries," *Journal of Consumer Psychology* 14, no. 4, 2004, pp. 370–373.

162 Jacob Jacoby, "Perspectives on Information Overload," *Journal of Consumer Research*, March 1984, pp. 569–573; and Kevin Lane Keller and Richard Staelin, "Effects of Quality and Quantity of Information on Decision Effectiveness," *Journal of Consumer Research*, September 1987, pp. 200–213.

163 Keller and Staelin, "Effects of Quality and Quantity of Information on Decision Effectiveness."

164 Ran Kivetz and Itamar Simonson, "The Effects of Incomplete Information on Consumer Choice," *Journal of Marketing Research* 37, November 2000, pp. 427–448.

165 Jeffrey R. Parker and Rom Y. Schrift, "Rejectable Choice Sets: How Seemingly Irrelevant No-Choice Options Affect Consumer Decision Processes," *Journal of Marketing Research* 48, no. 5, October 2011, pp. 840–854.

166 A. V. Muthukrishnan, "Decision Ambiguity and Incumbent Brand Advantage," *Journal of Consumer Research*, June 1995, pp. 98–109.

167 Madhubalan Viswanathan and Sunder Narayanan, "Comparative Judgments of Numerical and Verbal Attribute Labels," *Journal of Consumer Psychology* 3, no. 1, 1994, pp. 79–100.

168 Joseph R. Priester, Utpal M. Dholakia, and Monique A. Fleming, "When and Why the Background Contrast Effect Emerges," *Journal of Consumer Research* 31, no. 3, 2004, pp. 491–501; Joel Huber, John W. Payne, and Christopher Puto, "Adding Asymmetrically Dominated Alternatives: Violations of Regularity and the Similarity Hypothesis," *Journal of Consumer Research*, June 1982, pp. 90–98; and Ravi Dhar and Itamar Simonson, "Making Complementary Choices in Consumption Episodes," *Journal of Marketing Research*, February 1999, pp. 29–44.

169 Itamar Simonson and Russell S. Winer, "The Influence of Purchase Quantity and Display Format on Consumer Preference for Variety," *Journal of Consumer Research*, June 1992, pp. 133–138.

170 Itamar Simonson, Stephen Nowlis, and Katherine Lemon, "The Effect of Local Consideration Sets on Global Choice between Lower Price and Higher Quality," *Marketing Science*, Fall 1993.

171 Kwanho Suk, Jiheon Lee, and Donald R. Lichtenstein, "The Influence of Price Presentation Order on Consumer Choice," *Journal of Marketing Research* 49, no. 5, October 2012, pp. 708–717.

172 Rashmi Adaval and Robert S. Wyer Jr., "The Role of Narratives in Consumer Information Processing," *Journal of Consumer Psychology* 7, no. 3, 1998, pp. 207–245.

173 Gergana Y. Nenkov, J. Jeffrey Inman, John Hulland, and Maureen Morrin, "The Impact of Outcome Elaboration on Susceptibility to Contextual and Presentation Biases," *Journal of Marketing Research*, December 2009, pp. 764–776.

174 Christina L. Brown and Gregory S. Carpenter, "Why Is the Trivial Important? A Reasons-Based Account for the Effects of Trivial Attributes on Choice," *Journal of Consumer Research*, March 2000, pp. 372–385.

175 Jeffry A. Simpson, Vladas Griskevicius, and Alexander J. Rothman, "Consumer Decisions in Relationships," *Journal of Consumer Psychology* 22, no. 3, July 2012, pp. 304–314.

176 Didem Kurt, J. Jeffrey Inman, and Jennifer J. Argo, "The Influence of Friends on Consumer Spending: The Role of Agency-Communion Orientation and Self-Monitoring," *Journal of Marketing Research* 48, no. 4, August 2011, pp. 741–754.

177 Dan Ariely and Jonathan Levav, "Sequential Choice in Group Settings," *Journal of Consumer Research* 27, December 2000, pp. 279–290.

178 Cait Poynor Lamberton, Rebecca Walker Naylor, and Kelly L. Haws, "Same Destination, Different Paths: When and How Does Observing Others' Choices and Reasoning Alter Confidence in Our Own Choices?" *Journal of Consumer Psychology* 23, no. 1, January 2013, pp. 74–89.

179 Stijn M. J. van Osselaer, Joseph W. Alba, and Puneet Manchanda, "Irrelevant Information and Mediated Intertemporal Choice," *Journal of Consumer Psychology* 14, no. 3, 2004, pp. 257–270.

180 Guliz Ger, "Problems of Marketization in Romania and Turkey," in eds. Clifford Schultz, Russell Belk, and Guliz Ger, *Consumption in Marketizing Economies* (Greenwich, Conn.: JAI Press, 1995).

181 Sabrina Tavernise, "In Russia, Capitalism of a Certain Size," *New York Times*, July 29, 2001, sec. 3, p. 6; and Guliz Ger, Russell Belk, and Dana-Nicoleta Lascu, "The Development of Consumer Desire in Marketing and Developing Economies," in eds. Leigh McAlister and Michael L. Rothschild, *Advances in Consumer Research*, vol. 20 (Provo, Utah: Association for Consumer Research, 1993), pp. 102–107.

182 See Susan Broniarczyk and Jill G. Griffin, "Decision Difficulty in the Age of Consumer Empowerment," *Journal of Consumer Psychology* 24, no. 4, October 2014, pp. 608–625; and Joseph K. Goodman, Susan Broniarczyk, Jill G. Griffin, and Leigh McAlister, "Help or Hinder? When Recommendation Signage Expands Consideration Sets and Heightens Decision Difficulty," *Journal of Consumer Psychology* 23, no. 2, April 2013, pp. 165–174.

CHAPTER 9

Judgment and Decision-Making Based on Low Effort

LEARNING OBJECTIVES

After studying this chapter, you will be able to:

▶ Identify the types of heuristics that consumers can use to make simple judgments.

▶ Explain why marketers need to understand both unconscious and conscious decision-making processes in low-effort situations.

▶ Highlight how consumers learn to apply choice tactics through operant conditioning.

▶ Discuss how consumers make thought-based low-effort decisions using performance-related tactics, habit, brand loyalty, price-related tactics, and normative influences.

▶ Describe how consumers make affect-based low-effort decisions using feelings as a simplifying strategy, brand familiarity, variety seeking, and impulse purchasing.

INTRODUCTION

When consumers have low motivation, ability, and opportunity (MAO) to process information (as when purchasing everyday products like shampoo), their judgment and decision processes are different and involve less effort than when MAO is high (as when buying luxury goods). Consumers may simplify their decisions by repeatedly buying a brand they like or from a store they like. Or they may be guided by their feelings toward a familiar brand or store. Also, the marketer can try to increase the excitement (or situational involvement) by offering free merchandise and coupons on its website, through social media, via smartphones, by mail, or in the store. Bed Bath & Beyond, for example, frequently sends 20 percent off coupons to customers by mail and via smartphone, as well as offering them for download from Facebook.[1] This chapter examines the nature of low-effort judgment and decision-making, as shown in Exhibit 9.1. The focus here is on the cognitive and affective shortcuts or heuristics that consumers use to make judgments and decisions, as well as on how consumers make unconscious and conscious decisions in low-effort situations.

Exhibit 9.1 ▶ Chapter Overview: Judgment and Decision-Making: Low Consumer Effort
In low-effort processing situations, consumers tend to use heuristics or ways of simplifying the judgment or decision. Both cognitively based heuristics (performance-based tactics, habit, price-related tactics, brand loyalty, and normative influences) and affectively based heuristics (affect-related tactics, variety seeking, and impulse) are used to make decisions.

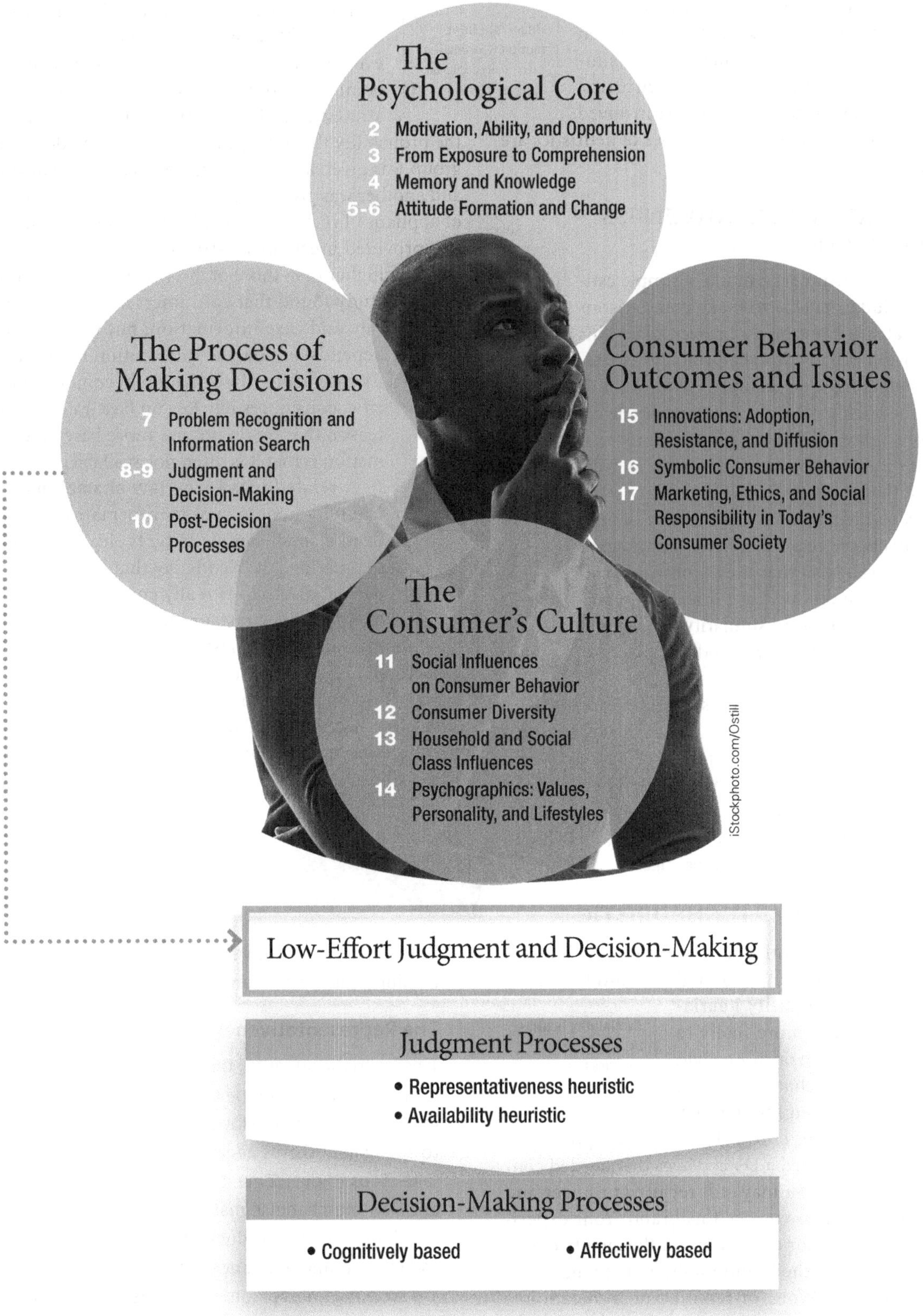

The
Psychological Core

2   Motivation, Ability, and Opportunity
3   From Exposure to Comprehension
4   Memory and Knowledge
5-6 Attitude Formation and Change

The Process of
Making Decisions

7   Problem Recognition and
    Information Search
8-9 Judgment and
    Decision-Making
10 Post-Decision
    Processes

Consumer Behavior
Outcomes and Issues

15 Innovations: Adoption,
    Resistance, and Diffusion
16 Symbolic Consumer Behavior
17 Marketing, Ethics, and Social
    Responsibility in Today's
    Consumer Society

The
Consumer's Culture

11 Social Influences
    on Consumer Behavior
12 Consumer Diversity
13 Household and Social
    Class Influences
14 Psychographics: Values,
    Personality, and Lifestyles

iStockphoto.com/Ostill

Low-Effort Judgment and Decision-Making

Judgment Processes

• Representativeness heuristic
• Availability heuristic

Decision-Making Processes

• Cognitively based   • Affectively based

9-1 # Low-Effort Judgment Processes

Chapter 8 explained that when effort is high, consumers' judgments—such as estimations of likelihood, judgments of goodness/badness, and mental accounting—can be cognitively complex. In contrast, when MAO is low, individuals are motivated to simplify the cognitive process by using heuristics, or rules of thumb, to reduce the effort involved in making judgments.[2] Two major types of heuristics are representativeness and availability.

9-1a THE REPRESENTATIVENESS HEURISTIC

One way that consumers can make simple estimations or judgments is to make comparisons with the category prototype or exemplar. This categorization process is called the **representativeness heuristic**.[3] For example, if you want to estimate the likelihood that a new laundry detergent is of high quality, you might compare it with your prototype for detergents, such as Tide. If you see that the new brand is similar to the prototype, you will assume that it is also of high quality. This is the reasoning behind packaging many store brands so that they look similar to leading brands in product categories. The retailers hope that the outward similarity will suggest to consumers that the store products possess the same good qualities.

Like any shortcut, the representativeness heuristic can also lead to biased judgments. For instance, consumers who see Hallmark as the prototype of a greeting card may assume that it offers only paper-based products. To overcome these biased judgments, Hallmark has added a variety of tech-enhanced products, including e-cards and a mobile app for sending digital greetings.[4]

9-1b THE AVAILABILITY HEURISTIC

Judgments can also be influenced by the ease with which instances of an event can be brought to mind, a shortcut called the **availability heuristic**.[5] Consumers are more likely to recall more accessible or more vivid events, a tendency that influences their judgments—even though they may be unaware of this effect.[6] To illustrate, suppose that years ago you purchased a DVD player that needed constant repair. Today you may still recall your anger and disappointment when you see this brand. Your experiences greatly color your estimations of the quality of this brand, even though the brand might actually have few breakdowns today. Word-of-mouth communication is another example of accessible information that leads to

> **Base-rate information** How often an event really occurs on average.

> **Representativeness heuristic** Making a judgment by simply comparing a stimulus with the category prototype or exemplar.

> **Law of small numbers** The expectation that information obtained from a small number of people represents the larger population.

> **Availability heuristic** Basing judgments on events that are easier to recall.

use of the availability heuristic. If a friend says she had problems with a certain brand of DVD player, this information is likely to affect your estimates of the brand's quality, even though her experience might have been an isolated event.

These judgments are biased because we tend to ignore **base-rate information**—how often the event really occurs—in favor of information that is more vivid or accessible. One study demonstrated this effect in the context of estimating the probability that refrigerators would break down.[7] One group was given a set of case histories told by consumers, and another was given actual statistics about the incidence of appliance breakdown. People who read the case histories provided breakdown estimates that were 30 percent higher than those of the statistics group. Another study found that consumers can use both base-rate and case information, but their judgment depends on how the information is structured.[8] As case history information becomes more specific, consumers rely less on base rates. Another reason that we do not use more base-rate information is that it is often not available.

A related bias is the **law of small numbers**, whereby people expect information obtained from a small sample to be typical of the larger population.[9] If friends say that a new song by a particular group is really good or that the food at a particular restaurant is terrible, we believe that information, even if most people do not feel that way. In fact, reliance on small numbers is another reason that word-of-mouth communication can be so powerful. We tend to have confidence that the opinions of friends or relatives are more reflective of the majority than they may actually be.

 ## Marketing Implications

Both the representativeness and availability heuristics are important to marketers.

The Representativeness Heuristic

This heuristic suggests that companies position offerings close to a prototype that has positive associations in consumers' minds. However, when the shortcut leads to a judgment that is negatively biased, marketers must take steps to overcome it. For example, some consumers view merchandise made in China as the prototype for cheaply made products. Chinese companies such as Haier (home appliances) and Lenovo (computers) are working to overcome this bias by designing cutting-edge products and opening local manufacturing facilities in the United States and other countries where they market.[10]

The Availability Heuristic

Marketers can attempt either to capitalize on or to overcome the availability bias. To capitalize, they can provide consumers with positive and vivid product-related experiences through the use of marketing communications, or they can ask consumers to imagine such situations. Both strategies will increase consumers' estimates that these events will occur. Or marketers can attempt to stimulate positive word-of-mouth communication. For instance, *Entertainment Weekly* magazine invites consumers to participate in live online chats with its editors and post to Twitter or Facebook while watching popular TV shows. The idea is to get consumers talking about *Entertainment Weekly* and the TV shows.[11]

Marketers can attempt to overcome the availability bias by providing consumers with base-rate information about the general population. If this information is vivid and specific (such as "chosen 2 to 1 over its competitors"), it can help consumers make a less biased judgment. The Internet is an excellent vehicle for providing base-rate information. To illustrate, consumers interested in buying books at Amazon.com can see a summary rating, read consumer-submitted reviews, and click to preview the book. The availability bias is also a common problem in the context of sweepstakes and lotteries. Although the likelihood of their winning is exceedingly small, consumers often overestimate the odds because they are exposed to highly vivid and available images of winners in the media. Regulators have attempted to overcome this bias by requiring marketers to clearly post the odds of winning.

9-2 Low-Effort Decision-Making Processes

Most low-effort judgment and decision situations are not very important in consumers' lives relative to other decisions in their lives. Clearly, career and family decisions are far more important than deciding which toothpaste or peanut butter to buy. Thus, the consumer usually does not want to devote a lot of time and effort to these relatively mundane decisions.[12] So how do consumers make decisions in these low-elaboration situations? Researchers suggest that such decisions are sometimes made unconsciously and sometimes consciously, but with little effort.

9-2a UNCONSCIOUS LOW-EFFORT DECISION-MAKING

In some low-effort situations, consumers may make a decision without being consciously aware of how or why they are doing so. As much as 50 percent of all shopping decisions are made spontaneously and unconsciously while consumers are in the store.[13] Such unconscious choices may be strongly affected by environmental stimuli such as the fragrance of a perfume in a department store.[14] With "all of the other senses, you think before you respond, but with scent, your brain responds before you think," observes one expert.[15] Other environmental stimuli that might trigger choices and behavior without the consumer's being consciously aware of the effect are novel shapes, color, brand logos, certain places or social situations, and the presence of other people.[16] When making choices quickly, consumers' decisions are often affected more by visual aspects of the package than by their prior preferences.[17]

Several influences mentioned in Chapter 6 play a role in unconscious, low-effort decision-making. For example, evaluative conditioning can influence attitudes and unconscious brand choices.[18] In addition, consumers may form accurate yet unconscious impressions through thin-slice judgments.[19] Consumers may have a positive attitude toward a product they unconsciously perceive as having a friendly human face—such as a car that seems to smile.[20] Body feedback can also play a role. In one study, consumers who were induced to nod had more positive evaluations of positively valenced brands (and more negative evaluations when induced to shake their heads).[21] Another factor affecting unconscious evaluations of products is how the floor feels to a shopper. The comfortable feeling of standing on carpeting prompts shoppers to evaluate nearby products as more comforting than products that are not close at hand.[22] Even the way products are stocked on store shelves can influence purchase decisions. Interestingly, consumers are less likely to buy food and beverage products when the product display seems disorganized and quantities are limited—but more likely to buy non-food products like fabric softeners when few products are on display and the shelves are not organized.[23]

Some researchers argue that certain choices represent goal-related behavior (e.g., buying fast food), even though consumers are pursuing the goal almost automatically, without conscious thought.[24] Others point out that although many consumer behaviors operate on a conscious level, unconscious choices and behaviors are also important, even if poorly understood and unpredictable.[25] More research is needed to explain how and why consumers use unconscious decision-making.

Marketing Implications

Because environmental stimuli strongly influence unconscious choices, many hotels, stores, and restaurants scent the air with aromas that serve as unconscious reminders of certain products, brands, or situations. Upscale hotels often create signature scents for their lobbies. As an example, each Ritz-Carlton hotel uses a scent appropriate for its particular location. The scent chosen for the Ritz-Carlton in Kyoto, Japan features jasmine, while the scent chosen for the Ritz-Carlton in Washington, D.C. features the fragrance of cherry blossoms.[26] Marketers can also use music, color, displays, and other sensory cues.

9-2b CONSCIOUS LOW-EFFORT DECISION-MAKING

In the previous chapter, you learned that consumers have certain beliefs about each alternative that are combined to form an attitude that leads to a conscious behavior or a choice. The consumer engages in *thinking*, which leads to *feelings*, which result in behaving, a progression known as the hierarchy of effects. However, studies show that this **traditional hierarchy of effects** does not apply to all decision-making situations.[27]

Instead, researchers have proposed a **hierarchy of effects for low-effort situations** that follows a *thinking-behaving-feeling* sequence.[28] The consumer enters the decision process with a set of low-level beliefs based on brand familiarity and knowledge obtained from repeated exposures to advertising, in-store exposure, or prior usage. In the absence of any attitude, these beliefs serve as the foundation for the decision or behavior. After making the decision and while using the product, the consumer evaluates the brand and may or may not form an attitude, depending on how strongly the brand is liked or satisfies needs. In fact, when users have an "aha" moment and gain conceptual insights into usage after trying a product for the first time, the experience can increase positive feelings and usage intentions toward that product.[29]

Some researchers have challenged the belief-behavior link in the low-involvement hierarchy, saying that consumers sometimes base a decision solely on how they feel rather than on what they think.[30] For example, you might select a new candy or download a TV program based on positive feelings rather than on beliefs or knowledge. Here, the sequence would be feeling,

Traditional hierarchy of effects Sequential steps used in decision-making involving thinking, then feeling, then behavior.

Low-effort hierarchy of effects Sequence of thinking-behaving-feeling.

Satisfice Finding a brand that satisfies a need even though the brand may not be the best brand.

behaving, and thinking. This type of decision-making, which clearly does occur, suggests that consumers can process in both a cognitive and an affective manner—a factor in many low-elaboration situations.

9-2c USING SIMPLIFYING STRATEGIES WHEN CONSUMER EFFORT IS LOW

Low-effort purchases represent the most frequent type of decisions that consumers make in everyday life. One in-store study of laundry detergent purchases found that the median amount of time taken to make a choice was only 8.5 seconds.[31] A study of coffee and tissues found very low levels of decision activity, particularly among consumers who purchased the product frequently and had a strong brand preference.[32] Some research has examined consumer decision processes across a number of product categories and has even questioned whether there is any decision process at all.[33] Other research suggests that if you have low motivation and ability, you may simply delegate a buying decision by asking someone else to make the decision. Of course, the outcome will depend on how well the other person knows you.[34]

Under low motivation and low processing opportunity, how a marketing message is framed will influence how consumers react. A negatively framed marketing message is more effective than a positively framed message for low MAO, for instance.[35] Research also shows that consumers with a low need for cognition are more susceptible to the influence of a negatively framed message.[36] And when a decision is framed in terms of subtracting unwanted options from a fully loaded product, consumers will choose more options with a higher total option price than they will if the decision is framed in terms of adding wanted items to a base model.[37]

A decision process probably does occur in low-effort situations, but it is simpler, involves less effort, and is qualitatively different from processes that occur when MAO is high. Two other factors influence the low-MAO decision process. First, the goal is not necessarily to find the best possible brand, called *optimizing*, as is the case with high-elaboration decisions. To optimize here would require more effort than consumers are typically willing to expend. Instead, consumers are more willing to **satisfice**, to find a brand that is good enough to simply satisfy their needs. The effort required to find the best brand may simply not be worth it.[38] Also, low-effort decisions can be easily influenced by the situation. For example, simply thinking about the concept of "balance" may cause consumers to choose a compromise option, one that may be just acceptable on all features even if other options are actually better on one or two features.[39] As another example of how the situation can influence low effort choice, research shows that when people are shopping in crowded environments, thoughts about safety come to mind, which makes them more risk averse and more prevention focused.[40]

Second, most low-elaboration decisions are made frequently and repeatedly. In these decisions, consumers may rely on previous information and judgments of satisfaction or dissatisfaction from past consumption. Think of all the times that you have purchased toothpaste, breakfast cereal, and shampoo. You have acquired information by using these products and by seeing ads, checking websites, talking to friends, and so forth. Instead of searching for information every time you are in the store, you can simply remember previous decisions and use that information to make your next choice.

In these common, repeat-purchase situations, consumers can develop decision heuristics called **choice tactics** for quick, effortless decision-making.[41] Rather than comparing various brands in detail, consumers apply these rules to simplify the decision process. The study of laundry detergents mentioned earlier supports this view.[42] When consumers were asked how they made their choices, several major categories of tactics emerged, including *price tactics* (it's the cheapest or it's on sale), *affect tactics* (I like it), *performance tactics* (it cleans clothes better), and *normative tactics* (my mother bought it). Other studies have identified *habit tactics* (I buy the same brand I bought last time), *brand-loyalty tactics* (I buy the same brand for which I have a strong preference), and *variety-seeking tactics* (I need to try something different). Research has found similar patterns in Singapore, Germany, Thailand, and the United States.[43]

Consumers can develop a choice tactic for each repeat-purchase, low-elaboration decision in the product or service category. If the consumer's decision is observed only once, it will appear very limited. Because all prior purchases serve as input to the current decision, it is important to look at a whole series of choices and consumption situations to fully understand consumer decision-making. Thus, low-effort decision making is very dynamic in nature.

> **Choice tactics** Simple rules of thumb used to make low-effort decisions.

9-3 Learning Choice Tactics

To understand low-elaboration decision-making, marketers need to know how consumers learn to apply choice tactics. Certain concepts from the behaviorist tradition in psychology are relevant to understanding the way that consumers learn. **Operant conditioning** views behavior as a function of previous actions and of the reinforcements or punishments obtained from these actions.[44] For example, while you were growing up, your parents may have given you a reward for making good grades

> **Operant conditioning** A process of learning drive by the use of rewards to reinforce desired behavior and punishment to discourage objectionable behavior.

or an allowance for mowing the lawn. You learned that these were good behaviors, and you were more likely to do these things again because you had been rewarded for them.

9-3a REINFORCEMENT

Reinforcement usually comes from a feeling of satisfaction that occurs when we as consumers perceive that our needs have been adequately met. This reinforcement increases the probability that we will purchase the same brand again. For example, if you buy Crest toothpaste and are impressed by the results after using it, your purchase will be reinforced, and you will be more likely to buy this brand again. In one study, past experience with a brand was by far the most critical factor in brand choice—more important than quality, price, and familiarity.[45] Other research has shown that the information that consumers receive from product trials tends to be more powerful and influential than that received from advertising.[46] The thoughts and emotions experienced during a trial can have a particularly powerful influence on evaluations.[47] Reinforcement in the form of frequent-buyer rewards can also be effective. One study found that consumers actually accelerated their purchasing as they got closer to earning a reward.[48]

Note that consumers often perceive few differences among brands of many products and services.[49] Thus, they are unlikely to develop a strong positive brand attitude when no brand is seen as clearly better than another. As long as the consumer is not dissatisfied, the choice tactic he or she used will be reinforced. Suppose you buy the cheapest brand of paper towels. If this brand at least minimally satisfies your needs, you are likely to buy the cheapest brand again—and it may be a different brand next time. Thus, reinforcement can occur for either the brand or the choice tactic.

9-3b PUNISHMENT

Alternatively, consumers can have a bad experience with a product or service, form a negative evaluation of it, and never purchase it again. In operant conditioning terms, this experience is called *punishment*. If you did something bad when you were growing up, your parents may have punished you to make sure that you would not behave that way again. In a consumer context, punishment occurs when a brand does not meet our needs and we are dissatisfied, so we learn not to buy that brand again. Punishment may also lead consumers to reevaluate the choice tactic and use a different tactic for the next purchase. If you buy the cheapest brand of trash bags, and the bags burst when you take out the trash, you could either employ a new tactic (buy the most expensive or the most familiar brand) or upgrade your tactic (buy the cheapest *national* brand).

9-3c REPEAT PURCHASE

Consumers learn when the same act is repeatedly reinforced or punished over time, a process summarized in Exhibit 9.2. This process occurs whenever we buy a common, repeat-purchase product. Thus, we learn and gradually acquire a set of choice tactics that will result in making a satisfactory choice in each decision situation. Decision-making models have traditionally ignored the key role of consumption in the decision process, focusing more attention on the processing that occurs immediately prior to the decision. But clearly what takes place while the product is being consumed has important implications for future acquisition, usage, and disposition decisions. In other words, whether the consumer forms a positive or negative evaluation of the brand or tactic can be an important input into future decisions.

9-3d CHOICE TACTICS DEPEND ON THE PRODUCT

The choice tactics we use often depend on the product category that we are considering.[50] For example, we might be brand loyal to Heinz ketchup but always buy the cheapest trash bags. The tactic we learn for a product

category depends on which brands are available and our experiences with them. The amount of advertising, price variations, and the number and similarity of brands also influence the type of tactic that we employ.[51] Interestingly, the study from Singapore mentioned earlier found a greater similarity in the tactics that consumers use for the same product in different cultures (the United States and Singapore) than in tactics that they use for different products in the same culture.[52] In general, our experiences help us learn what works for each product, and we use these tactics to minimize our decision-making effort for future purchases.

9-4 Low-Effort Thought-Based Decision-Making

Each tactic consumers learn for making low-elaboration decisions can have important implications for marketers. As in high-elaboration decisions, these strategies can be divided into two broad categories: thought-based and feeling-based decision-making. This section examines cognitive-based decision-making, which includes performance-related tactics, habit, brand loyalty, price-related tactics, and normative influences.

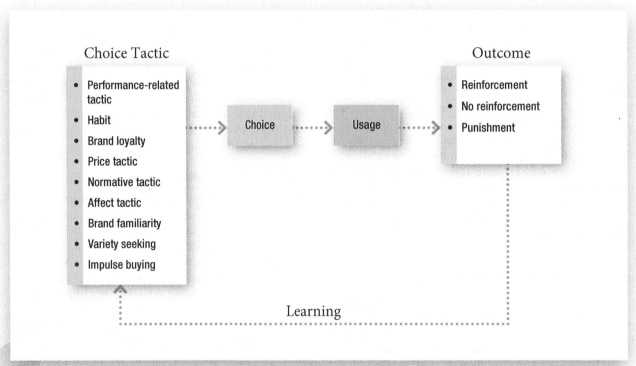

Exhibit 9.2 ▶ The Learning Process

This diagram shows how the outcome of a decision can help consumers learn which choice tactic to apply in a given situation. After consumers apply one of the seven basic types of tactics to make a choice, they take the brand home and use it. During consumption, they can evaluate the brand, an action that results in one of three basic outcomes: reinforcement (satisfaction leading to positive attitude and repurchase), no reinforcement (leading to tactic reinforcement, but no attitude toward the brand), or punishment (leading to a negative attitude, no repurchase, and tactic reevaluation).

9-4a PERFORMANCE AS A SIMPLIFYING STRATEGY

When the outcome of the consumption process is positive reinforcement, consumers are likely to use **performance-related tactics** to make their choices. These tactics can represent an overall evaluation (works the best) or focus on a specific attribute or benefit (gets teeth whiter, tastes better, or has quicker service). Satisfaction is the key: Satisfied consumers are likely to develop a positive evaluation of the brand or service and repurchase it based on its features.

> **Performance-related tactics** Tactics based on benefits, features, or evaluations of the brand.

as a signal of lower quality when they are not category experts, when the promotion is not typical of the industry, and when the brand's past behavior is inconsistent. Domino's, for instance, has been working to change quality perceptions after years of emphasizing price via coupons and other promotions. These days, when Domino's launches new products, its marketing focuses on great taste and fresh ingredients—especially in Italy, where it is trying to establish itself by emphasizing local ingredients and local taste favorites.[56]

Marketing Implications

A principal objective of marketing strategy should be to increase the likelihood of satisfaction through offering quality. Only then can a brand consistently achieve repeat purchases and loyal users. Kohl's, for example, offers basic clothing products and national brands as well as higher-quality private-label fashion lines by Jennifer Lopez and Marc Anthony. Customers return to Kohl's because they appreciate the product quality and store policies such as no-hassle merchandise returns.[53]

Advertising can play a central role in influencing performance evaluations by increasing the consumer's expectation of positive reinforcement and satisfaction and lessening the negative effects of an unfavorable consumption experience.[54] Because we see what we want to see and form our expectations accordingly, marketers should select product features or benefits that are important to consumers, help to differentiate the brand from competitors, and convince consumers that they will be satisfied if they buy the product. Earthbound Organic, which markets organically grown vegetables and fruits, makes a good impression by stacking romaine lettuce leaves in one direction within the bag, which research shows consumers prefer. Within salad kits, it packages grain and bean add-ins separately from greens to preserve quality and texture.[55]

Sales promotions such as free samples, price deals, or coupons are often used to induce consumers to try an offering. Marketers hope that if consumers find the product satisfactory, they will continue to buy it after the promotions end. However, these strategies only work if product performance satisfies and reinforces the consumer. They will not overcome dissatisfaction due to poor product quality or other factors. Another caution is that consumers may perceive a price promotion

9-4b HABIT AS A SIMPLIFYING STRATEGY

> **Habit** A learned behavior that involves regular performance of the same act repeatedly over time. Behaviors are often performed unconsciously and may be difficult to discontinue.

Humans are creatures of **habit**. Once we find a convenient way of doing things, we tend to repeat it without really thinking: following the same routine every morning, driving the same route to work or school, shopping at the same stores. We do these things because they make life simpler and more manageable.

Sometimes consumers' acquisition, usage, and disposition decisions are based on habit, too. Habit is one of the simplest, most effortless types of consumer decision-making, characterized by (1) little or no information seeking and (2) little or no evaluation of alternatives. However, habit does not require a strong preference for an offering; rather, it simply involves repetitive behavior and regular purchase.[57] Decision-making based on habit also reduces risk.[58] Consumers know the brand will satisfy their needs because they have bought it a number of times in the past. Research supports the effect of habit on low-priced, frequently purchased products. Yet the longer consumers wait to make their next purchase in a product category, the less likely they are to buy the brand that they habitually purchase.[59]

Marketing Implications

Habit-based decision-making has several important implications for marketers who want to develop repeat-purchase behavior and to sell their offerings to habitual purchasers of both that brand and competing products.

Developing Repeat-Purchase Behavior

Getting consumers to acquire or use an offering repeatedly is important because repeat purchases lead to profitability. Marketers can use an operant conditioning technique called **shaping** that leads consumers through a series of steps to a desired response: purchase.[60] Companies often use sales promotions to shape repeat purchasing. First, they might offer a free sample to generate brand trial, along with a high-value coupon to induce purchasing. The next step might be to provide a series of lower-value coupons to promote subsequent repurchase, hoping that when the incentives end, consumers will continue to buy the product by habit. Finally, many marketers reinforce repeat purchasing through loyalty programs that encourage and reward habitual buying of their brands.[61] Kellogg's, for instance, has a rewards program that reinforces habitual purchasing of the company's brands, including Kellogg's cereals, Eggo waffles, and Nutri-Grain bars. By buying Kellogg's brands, program participants earn points that can be redeemed for electronic products, retail discount cards, and other rewards.[62]

> **Shaping** Leading consumers through a series of steps to create a desired response.

Marketing to Habitual Purchasers of Other Brands

Another major marketing goal is to break consumers' habits and induce them to switch to the company's brand. Because the habitual consumer does not have a strong brand preference, this goal is easier to achieve than it is for brand-loyal consumers. To induce brand switching, marketers use sales promotion techniques, such as demonstrations (online or in person), pricing deals, coupons, free samples, and premiums intended to capture consumers' attention and get them to try the new brand (see Exhibit 9.3). For example, after Jade Yoga mailed out 500 small samples of its specially designed non-slip yoga mat, it received 300 responses. This and other promotions have helped the company build its customer base year after year.[63] Once the old habit is broken, consumers may continue to purchase the new brand either because they like it or because they have developed a new habit.

Marketers can also break habits by introducing a new and unique benefit that satisfies consumers' needs better than existing brands. This differential advantage then needs to be heavily promoted to get the word out to consumers. For example, Amazon originally set up its Prime program to provide two-day delivery for a flat annual membership fee. But the online pioneer then expanded Prime to offer additional benefits valued by customers, including free streaming of movies and

Source: World's Best Cat Litter

Exhibit 9.3 ▶ Sales Promotions

Companies often try to get consumers to switch brands by touting their products as superior and utilizing sales promotions for free trials or discounted prices.

TV shows, free Kindle book downloads, and free music streaming. With 40 million members, Amazon Prime has helped the company attract and retain loyal customers and compete with rivals such as Walmart, eBay, and Netflix.[64]

Finally, distribution policies are very important for habitual purchasing. In general, the greater the amount of shelf space a brand has in the store, the more likely the brand is to get consumers' attention. A product's location may be enough to capture the habitual consumer's attention and plant the idea in his or her mind to buy something else. An end-of-aisle display may increase a brand's sales by 100 to 400 percent.[65] In one study, eye-catching displays increased sales of frozen dinners by 245 percent, laundry detergent by 207 percent, and salty snacks by 172 percent.[66]

Marketing to Habitual Purchasers of One's Own Brand

Marketers do not want repeat-purchase customers to break their buying habits. Because habitual consumers are susceptible to competitors' deals, marketers need to offer comparable deals to build resistance to switching. This situation explains why a fare cut by any one airline is usually matched immediately by all of its major competitors. At the same time, it's important for marketers to understand what drives its customers to be repeat purchasers, because not all brand-loyal customers react the same way to marketing stimuli. Attitudinal loyalty is a key factor in customers' positive reactions to promotions for cross-selling products from the same brand, for example, whereas consumers who buy out of habit resist changing their behavior inside the store.[67]

Distribution and inventory control are also used to prevent habitual consumers from switching to another brand. Without a strong preference, consumers are more likely to break the habit and buy another brand if their usual brand is out of stock rather than to go to another store. In one study, 63 percent of consumers said they would be willing to buy another brand of groceries if their preferred brand were not available.[68] Widespread distribution can ensure that the consumer is not forced to buy something else. When Hostess Brands took over the Hostess cupcake brand, along with Ding-Dongs, Twinkies, and other established brands, it built on customer loyalty by expanding distribution to movie theaters, fast-food restaurants, and drug stores.[69]

Finally, advertising and other marketing communications can induce resistance to switching. By occasionally reminding the consumer of a reason for buying the brand and keeping the brand name "top of mind," marketers may be able to keep consumers from switching.

9-4c BRAND LOYALTY AS A SIMPLIFYING STRATEGY

Brand loyalty occurs when consumers make a conscious evaluation that a brand or service satisfies their needs to a greater extent than others do and decide to buy the same brand repeatedly for that reason.[70] Essentially, brand loyalty results from *very* positive reinforcement of a performance-related choice tactic. Brand loyalty can also develop when a consumer becomes skillful in using a particular offering, such as a specific brand of money-management software. Faced with the learning curve needed to switch to a different brand of software, the consumer tends to remain brand loyal because of *cognitive lock-in*.[71]

Note that the level of commitment to the brand distinguishes brand loyalty from habit. The higher the degree of

> **Brand loyalty** Buying the same brand repeatedly because of a strong preference for it.

brand loyalty, the stronger this evaluation becomes over time. For instance, if you buy Heinz ketchup and decide that it is thicker and tastes better than other brands, you will purchase it again. If this evaluation is reinforced repeatedly, you will develop strong brand loyalty. Consumers can also be **multibrand loyal**, committed to two or more brands that they purchase repeatedly.[72] For example, if you prefer and purchase only Coke and Sprite, you exhibit multibrand loyalty for soft drinks.

> **Multibrand loyalty** Buying two or more brands repeatedly because of a strong preference for them.

Brand loyalty results in low-effort decision-making because the consumer does not need to process information when making a decision and simply buys the same brand each time. However, because of their strong commitment to the brand or service, brand-loyal consumers have a relatively high level of involvement with the *brand* regardless of whether their involvement with the product or service category is high or low. Thus, even though ketchup might typically be thought of as a low-involvement product, the brand-loyal consumer can exhibit a high level of involvement toward the brand, for example, Heinz. Brand loyalty also affects choice of retail outlet: Loyalty to a bricks-and-mortar retail brand can lead to higher intentions to shop at that brand's online outlet.[73]

 Marketing Implications

Brand-loyal consumers form a solid base on which companies can build brand profitability. By identifying the characteristics of these consumers, marketers might discover ways to strengthen brand loyalty. Unfortunately, doing this is difficult because marketers cannot obtain a general profile of the brand-loyal consumer that applies to all product categories.[74] In fact, brand loyalty depends on the product category; the consumer who is loyal for ketchup may not be loyal for peanut butter. This situation means that marketers must assess brand loyalty for each specific category.

Identifying Brand-Loyal Customers

One way that marketers can identify brand-loyal consumers is to focus on consumer purchase patterns. Consumers who exhibit a particular sequence of purchases (three to four consecutive purchases of the same brand) or proportion of purchases (seven or eight out of 10 purchases for the same brand) are considered brand loyal.[75] The problem is that because brand loyalty involves both repeat purchases and a commitment to the brand, purchase-only measures do not accurately distinguish between habitual and brand-loyal consumers. To truly identify the brand-loyal consumer, marketers must assess both repeat-purchase behavior and brand preference. In one study, a measure that looked only at repeat-purchase behavior identified more than 70 percent of the consumer sample as brand loyal. Adding brand preference as a qualifier reduced the percentage to less than 50 percent.[76]

With the availability of scanner data and online buying information, marketers now have a wealth of information about consumer purchase patterns that they can analyze to understand how coupons or pricing changes affect buying. Nevertheless, firms that want to study brand loyalty should be measuring both purchase patterns and preference.

Developing Brand Loyalty

Companies seek to develop brand loyalty because they know these customers have a strong brand commitment and are more resistant to competitive efforts and switching than other consumers are. However, the widespread use of pricing deals in the United States has gradually eroded consumer loyalty toward many brands, leading more consumers to buy on the basis of price. Therefore, marketers are now striving to develop consumer loyalty through nonprice promotions or through less drastic price promotions. To illustrate, before being acquired by Men's Wearhouse, the men's clothing retailer Jos. A. Bank was well known for its frequent and deep discounts. After the acquisition, Jos. A. Bank polished its brand and encouraged loyalty by cutting back on price promotions, adding a frequent-buyer rewards program, and emphasizing trendier fashions and accessories.[77]

Developing Brand Loyalty Through Product Quality

One obvious and critical way to develop brand loyalty is to satisfy the consumer with a high-quality product (see Exhibit 9.4). Consumers may also become brand loyal to high-quality brands that are perceived to be priced fairly, a result that explains why some companies have lowered prices on major brands.[78]

Developing Brand Loyalty Through Sales Promotions

Many companies cultivate brand loyalty through sales promotions such as discount coupons and giveaways to brand loyalists. For example, in the United Kingdom, Wilkinson Sword differentiates its razor-blade brand

Image Courtesy of The Advertising Archives

Exhibit 9.4 ▶ Using Quality to Encourage Brand Loyalty

Having high-quality products is a key way to develop brand loyalty.

through social media campaigns that offer consumers the opportunity to win product goodie bags for participation in branded online events.[79]

Frequent-buyer programs build loyalty by encouraging consumers to buy a product or service repeatedly so that they can earn points toward free trips or other rewards. Marketers must take care, however, in planning loyalty rewards and program requirements. The reward should have some brand connection if it is to increase accessibility of favorable brand associations. However, if the reward is too valuable, it will draw more attention than the brand itself.[80] Also, consumers perceive more value in a loyalty program when they think that they have an advantage in earning points.[81] Moreover, consumers who must do more to earn loyalty points will tend to choose luxury rewards (especially when they feel guilty about luxury consumption).[82] Another important point to note is that customers who do not spend enough to maintain their frequent-buyer status will become less loyal if the program "demotes" them to a lower level.[83]

Marketing to Brand-Loyal Consumers of Other Brands

Marketers want to induce brand-loyal users of competitive brands to switch to their brands. However, because these consumers are strongly committed to other brands, getting them to switch is extremely difficult. As a result, it is usually better to avoid these consumers and to try to market toward nonloyal or habitual consumers, except when a brand has a strong point of superiority or differentiation when compared with the competition. In this case, the superior attribute might be enough to persuade brand-loyal consumers to switch. For example, Coca-Cola's high-tech Freestyle vending machine allows consumers to custom-mix their own soft drinks in moments, with nearly 200 different flavor combinations. There's even a Freestyle app so consumers can configure their favorites using a smartphone. Given the novelty and customization, the Freestyle has become a point of differentiation for Coca-Cola in its rivalry with PepsiCo.[84]

9-4d PRICE AS A SIMPLIFYING STRATEGY

Consumers are most likely to use **price-related tactics** such as buying the cheapest brand, buying the brand on sale, or using a coupon when they perceive few differences among brands and when they have low involvement with the brands in the consideration set. Although price is a critical factor in many decisions, consumers generally do not remember price information, even for a brand they have just selected.[85] This reaction occurs because price information is always available in the store, so consumers have little motivation to remember it. Note that consumers who worry about losing money are more concerned about

> **Price-related tactics** Simplifying decision heuristics that are based on price.

Sometimes marketers mistakenly assume that consumers always look for the lowest possible price. Although this assumption is true in some instances, a more accurate statement is that consumers have a **zone of acceptance** regarding what constitutes an appropriate range of prices for a particular category.[86] As long as the brand falls within this price range, consumers will consider it but reject brands falling either above or below the range. For example, all the major fast-food chains have created value menus to appeal to price-conscious consumers, with a variety of items priced at about $1 each (see Exhibit 9.5). At the same time, McDonald's has tested pricier, limited-time menu items such as the Sirloin Burger, part of the chain's strategy to compete with Five Guys and other increasingly popular burger restaurants.[87]

> **Zone of acceptance** The acceptable range of prices for any purchase decision.

price, whereas those who are sensitive to gains look at brand features as well as price.[88] Also, when marketers use price promotions, consumers perceive lower risk in the purchase and tend to use less effort and extensive processing in making the decision, allowing affect to play a larger role.[89]

Importantly, the consumer's processing goal affects perceptions of prices within a range of products. When the goal is discrimination, consumers will be more aware of the contrast with higher-priced prices in the range if the marketer slashes the lowest price—which makes the other prices seem more expensive. Yet when the goal is generalization, consumers will see higher-priced products as less expensive if the marketer slashes the lowest price in the range.[90]

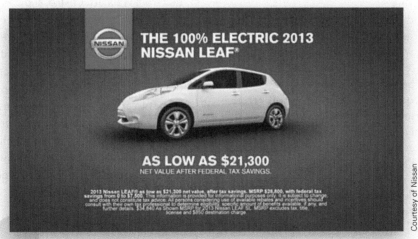

Exhibit 9.5 ▶ Price as a Simplifying Strategy
Sometimes companies stress low price and good value in their ads.

Consumers may reject low-priced products because they infer that something is wrong with the products. Buyers would be suspicious of a pair of expensive designer jeans on sale for $9.99. As noted earlier, consumers sometimes use price as a heuristic to judge quality (higher price means higher quality). Retailers must also consider that consumers view store design (layout and ambiance) as a pricing cue and expect higher prices at stores that look upscale.[91] Finally, when stores that have high selling costs advertise low prices, the revenue generated may not justify the increased cost of servicing the customers who respond.[92]

Price Perceptions

Consumer perceptions play an important role in the use of price-related tactics. Remember that for consumers to perceive two prices as different, the variation must be at or above the just noticeable difference. Thus, consumers might not care if one brand of toothpaste is priced at $1.95 and another at $1.99. Consumers also compare a product's price with an internal reference price for such products that is based on past prices paid, competing product prices, and other factors, including incidental products in some cases.[93] Typically, consumers use a range of prices rather than a single price point when they think of products.[94]

In addition, perceptual processes play a role in the consumer's reaction to different price points. Research has consistently indicated that consumers perceive odd prices (those ending with an odd number) as significantly lower than even prices (those ending with an even number); a movie priced at $14.99 will be perceived as less expensive than one priced at $15.00.[95] Consumers who see a much higher-priced item in a catalog that also has moderately priced products will form a higher reference point for the moderately priced items.[96]

Consumers tend to be more responsive to price decreases than they are to price increases.[97] Lowering the price of an offering will increase sales to a greater degree than increasing price by the same amount will decrease sales. Moreover, when a company heavily discounts a product on an infrequent basis, consumers will perceive the average price as lower than if the product goes on sale often but with less of a price reduction.[98] One study found that when companies establish a purchase or time limit, consumers perceive the deal as more valuable, but only when motivation to process is low.[99]

How companies describe the deal can also make a difference. One study found that comparing the sale price to the "regular price" worked better in the store, whereas comparison to competitors' prices was more effective at home.[100] Also, paying for products in a foreign currency (as when traveling) affects price perceptions and spending behavior: When the foreign currency is valued as a multiple of the home-country currency (such as 8 Swedish krona = $1), consumers tend to spend more than when the foreign currency is valued as a fraction (such as 0.9 euros = $1).[101] Consumers tend to perceive a price increase as less fair if they learn about it from a personal source (such as a sales rep) rather than from nonpersonal sources such as a store sign.[102]

The Deal-Prone Consumer

Deal-prone consumer A consumer who is more likely to be influenced by price.

Marketers are interested in identifying **deal-prone consumers** because this segment is suitable for more directly targeted price-related strategies, but research findings on this issue have been mixed. One study found that deal-prone consumers are more likely to be lower-income, older, and less educated than non-deal-prone consumers; other studies have found that higher-income consumers have better access to price information and are therefore more able to act on it.[103] Part of the problem is that consumers react differently to different types of deals: Some will be more responsive to coupons, whereas others will be more responsive to price cuts and to rebates.[104]

 ## Marketing Implications

Marketers can use a variety of pricing techniques, including coupons, price-offs, rebates, and two-for-ones, as long as the savings are at or above the just noticeable difference and within the zone of acceptance.

Deals and Deal Sites

The importance of deals is evidenced by the deep price cuts supermarkets have made, spurred by stiff competition from Walmart, Costco, and other discounters. Many brands have lowered their prices in response to competition from store brands, which are promoted as being equal in quality to national brands but priced lower. Although many shoppers like shopping online because they can search for price deals, some companies prefer not to attract consumers who use price-comparison sites or apps. Now some retailers are offering their own apps to encourage shoppers to check prices and buy while in the store or from the company's website.[105] Also, many consumers check daily deal sites such as LivingSocial for special price offers.[106]

The Importance of Value

Many consumers are looking for good value—that is, a high-quality brand at a good price. SUBWAY's $5 foot-long sandwich menu has helped the chain compete with other fast-food companies even during a bad economy, for example.[107] Value does not always mean lower price: Consumers will pay more if they believe the offering provides an important benefit that consumers are convinced is worth the extra cost. Apple products (including the iPhone and Apple Watch) command a price premium, for instance, because of their sleek designs and user-friendly technology. Even the distinctive packaging is considered part of an Apple product's value.

Special Pricing

If marketers use pricing deals too often, consumers will perceive the special price as the regular price and will not buy unless the brand is on sale—resulting in lost profits. This result has happened in the past to several food chains. Too many deals can also damage brand loyalty as consumers become too deal oriented and switch brands more often. Thus, deals tend to work best when used intermittently and selectively. Lower brand loyalty has become a major concern in numerous product categories in the United States and is the reason that many firms want to move toward brand-building strategies such as advertising and sampling.[108]

The use of pricing deals also varies with the country. Coupons are common in the United States: More than 300 billion are offered by manufacturers and retailers every year, although only a small fraction are actually redeemed. Digital coupons—obtained by visiting coupon websites, branded websites, social media sites, daily-deal coupon sites, or via mobile marketing—account for about 10 percent of all coupons redeemed in the United States.[109] Digital coupons are expanding in other countries, as well; for instance, in India, more than 10 percent of consumers with Internet access have used digital coupon sites.[110]

Price Consciousness Is Not Static

Consumers tend to be more price conscious in difficult economic times than in times of prosperity. In many countries, stores that sell merchandise at one low, fixed price—one dollar, one pound sterling, or 100 yen—generally did well during the recent recession, fueled by higher consumer demand for low-priced everyday items. Daiso Japan, which operates thousands of 100-yen stores, has been expanding into other countries, including the United States and Australia, targeting bargain hunters interested in deep-discount goods.[111] But it's not just low-income consumers who seek deals: The discount grocery chain Aldi, based in Germany, expanded

throughout California to serve middle-income customers who appreciated the retailer's low prices and private-label brand quality even after the recession ended.[112] Price consciousness can affect whether consumers are willing to pay for store or private-label brands as opposed to national brands. Many factors, including the economic situation and the extent to which private-label brands are new to a market, determine whether consumers are willing to pay for a more expensive national brand rather than a less expensive private-label brand.[113] Some price-conscious consumers continue their new frugality once the economy improves, while others return to their former buying patterns.

9-4e NORMATIVE INFLUENCES AS A SIMPLIFYING STRATEGY

Normative choice tactics Low-elaboration decision-making that is based on others' opinions.

Sometimes other individuals can influence consumers' low-elaboration decision-making. For instance, a college freshman may buy the brand of laundry detergent that his mother uses at home; a sophomore might buy clothing that her friends like. Our use of such **normative choice tactics** can result from (1) *direct influence*, in which others try to manipulate us; (2) *vicarious observation*, in which we observe others to guide our behavior; and (3) *indirect influence*, in which we are concerned about the opinions of others. Normative tactics are particularly common among inexperienced consumers who have little knowledge. Online communication can increase the importance of normative influence in decision-making because consumers can contact each other so easily. If normative tactics are particularly evident in a product or service category, companies can emphasize these motivations in advertising. Marketers can also attempt to stimulate word-of-mouth communication, as described in Chapter 11.

9-5 Low-Effort Feeling-Based Decision-Making

The final category of low-effort strategies covers decisions that are based more on feelings than on cognitive processing. These types of strategies include affective tactics, brand familiarity, variety seeking, and impulse purchasing.

9-5a FEELINGS AS A SIMPLIFYING STRATEGY

At times, consumers will select a brand or service because they like it, even though they may not know why. This behavior relies on very basic, low-level feelings, or **affect**. Affect differs from cognitive strategies such as performance-related attitudes in that it does not necessarily result from a conscious recognition of need satisfaction and is usually weaker than an attitude. Simply being in the presence of someone you like who is smiling happily can make you smile and feel happy—and, in turn, can have a positive influence on your evaluation of a product.[114]

Affect is most likely to be part of the decision process when the offering is hedonic (rather than functional) and when other factors, such as performance evaluations, price, habit, and normative influences, are not in operation. If you buy Hellmann's mayonnaise because it best satisfies your needs or if you usually buy only the cheapest brand of paper towels, affect is less likely to influence your decision. However, when these factors do not operate in low-effort situations, affect can play a central role. Interestingly, research shows that trying to suppress feelings ties up cognitive resources and undermines consumers' ability to judge product performance—leading them to rely more on feelings when making the choice.[115] Another important point is that when consumers trust their feelings, they may make a choice because it "feels right" even when their feelings aren't relevant to the decision at hand.[116]

Affect-related tactics use a form of category-based processing.[117] In other words, we associate brands with global affective evaluations we recall from memory when making a choice, a process called **affect referral** or the "How do I feel about it?" heuristic.[118] For instance, when we hear the name *Starbucks*, we might associate it with general feelings of happiness, and we might decide to get coffee there based on these feelings rather than on a detailed evaluation of Starbucks.

In one study, consumers choosing between a healthy dessert and a less healthy chocolate cake chose the dessert associated with the most positive affect (the cake) when they had little opportunity to think about the choice. When they had more time to think, they chose the healthier dessert, a reaction that suggests that affect referral is more of a factor under low processing effort.[119] Another study found that positive feelings toward promotions can also transfer not only to the promoted product but to unrelated products as well.[120] Moreover, when consumers feel happy and are focused on the future, they tend to choose more exciting options in decision situations; on the other hand, when consumers feel happy and are focused on the present, they tend to choose more calming options.[121] Interestingly, consumers rely more on feelings when making decisions to achieve near-term goals than when making decisions to achieve longer-term goals.[122]

> **Affect** Low-level feelings.

> **Brand familiarity** Easy recognition of a well-known brand.

> **Affect-related tactics** Tactics based on feelings.

> **Affect referral** A simple type of affective tactic whereby we simply remember our feelings for the product or service.

> **Co-branding** An arrangement by which the two brands form a partnership to benefit from the power of both.

Whenever a consumer encounters a new brand, he or she can also compare it with other brands in the same category. To the extent that the new brand is similar to previously encountered brands, the affect associated with that category can be transferred to the new instance and influence choice.[123] On the other hand, if the new brand is perceived as being dissimilar, the consumer is more likely to switch to piecemeal processing, evaluating attributes in the manner described in the previous chapter.[124] For example, when Unilever introduced new damaged-hair shampoos under its Dove brand, the director of Unilever Hair Brands explained, "Intrinsic to Dove is to be about 'real beauty,' and each category has a different take on what that means. In the hair category, 'real beauty' is about having not damaged, not overly dry hair, having healthy hair." As a result of extending this brand to shampoos, consumers may be able to evaluate the new Dove products on their own merits.[125]

9-5b BRAND FAMILIARITY

Affect can also be generated from **brand familiarity** (through the mere exposure effect). In one study, beer drinkers with well-established brand preferences could not distinguish their preferred brand from others in a blind taste test.[126] However, when the beers were identified, consumers rated the taste of their preferred brand significantly higher than that of the others. Another study found that "buying the most familiar brand" was a dominant choice tactic for inexperienced purchasers of peanut butter. Even when the quality of the most familiar brand was manipulated to be lower than that of unfamiliar brands, consumers still greatly preferred the familiar brand.[127] Another study found that brand name was a more important heuristic cue in low-elaboration situations than in high-elaboration ones.[128]

These findings were replicated in a study in Singapore, suggesting that the impact of brand familiarity may be a cross-cultural phenomenon.[129] Coca-Cola is a household name due, in part, to its consistent, highly visible marketing. Yet aggressively promoted local brands can match or outsell Coca-Cola and other global brands in certain areas. Local brand IRN-BRU, for instance, sells at least as well as Coca-Cola in Scotland.[130]

Many companies now engage in **co-branding**, an arrangement by which two brands form a partnership to benefit from the combined power and familiarity of the two.[131] To illustrate, Kellogg's teamed with J.J. Smucker to launch a cobranded breakfast cereal called Jif Peanut Butter cereal.[132] The most successful product launch in the history of the Taco Bell restaurant chain came when the company partnered with Dorito's, owned by Frito-Lay, to introduce the co-branded menu item Doritos Locos Tacos.[133] See another example in Exhibit 9.6.

SOME COMBINATIONS
WERE JUST MEANT TO BE.

Campbell's Goldfish

Tomato soup with Goldfish® crackers. Made for each other, to make your kids smile.
It's amazing what soup can do.

Tomato SOUP

Courtesy of Campbell Soup Company

Exhibit 9.6 ▶ Co-Branding

Sometimes companies engage in co-branding by advertising two different brands together.

Marketing Implications

Given that feelings can play an important role in the decision process, marketers can attempt to create and maintain brand familiarity, build category-based associations, and generate affect through advertising that creates positive attitudes toward the ad. By creating positive affect toward their brand, marketers can increase the probability that, all other things being equal, their brand will be selected.

Affect plays a key role in determining aesthetic responses to marketing stimuli, especially when visual properties are the only basis for judgment. An earlier study found, for example, that in Yellow Pages advertising (now on yp.com), consumers are more likely to consider firms with color ads and more likely to call those with product-enhancing color.[134] One study showed that two key aspects of a product's design generate more positive affective responses to the product.[135] These are **unity**, which means that the visual parts of the design connect in a meaningful

Unity When all the visual parts of a design fit together.

way, and *prototypicality*, which means that the object is representative of its category.

Brands that have positive cross-cultural affect can be marketed internationally. The U.S. image has benefited many firms that market in China. For instance, Starbucks has been successful in positioning itself as a prestigious American brand offering premium-priced coffees and teas adapted for local tastes.[136] In particular, hedonic offerings—those that involve style or taste—rely heavily on affective associations.

9-5c DECISION-MAKING BASED ON VARIETY-SEEKING NEEDS

Another common consumer-choice tactic in low-effort situations is to try something different, a phenomenon called **variety seeking**. A consumer might regularly buy Starbucks coffee but one day have an urge to try Dunkin' Donuts coffee—then return to Starbucks for later coffee purchases. Consumers seek variety for two major reasons: *satiation* and *boredom*.[137] If you had the same food for dinner every night or watched only one movie over and over, satiation would occur, driving you to do something different. Consumer decisions that occur repeatedly can become monotonous. This result explains why some consumers switch for the sake of change, even though they would have derived more immediate enjoyment from repeating their usual choice.[138] Another reason consumers seek variety in public situations is because they anticipate that others will evaluate their decision more positively.[139] Consumers may engage in variety seeking because they perceive the costs of switching to a new product to be lower than do consumers who are not variety seekers.[140]

Variety seeking Trying something different.

However, variety seeking is not expressed in every product category. It is most likely to occur when involvement is low, there are few differences among brands, and the product is more hedonic than functional.[141] It also tends to occur when consumers become satiated with a particular sensory attribute of a product, such as its smell, taste, touch, and visual appearance.[142] Marketers can therefore reduce consumers' boredom simply by providing more variety in a product category (see Exhibit 9.7).[143] In fact, demonstrating to consumers that they have a variety of categories from which to choose—*the mere categorization effect*—can increase feelings of satisfaction with conscious decisions in low-effort situations.[144] Also note that when consumers have more variety from which to choose, they tend to select choices they can easily justify.[145]

Exhibit 9.7 ▶ Courting Variety Seekers

Sometimes consumers need variety in their choices, so advertisers can promote multiple choices in their ads.

Consumers are motivated to relieve their boredom because their level of arousal falls below the **optimal stimulation level (OSL)**—an internal ideal level of stimulation.[146] Repetitive purchasing causes the internal level of stimulation to fall below the OSL, and buying something different is a way of restoring it. In addition, certain consumers need more stimulation and are less tolerant of boredom than others are. These **sensation seekers** are more likely to engage in variety seeking and to be among the first to try new and trendy products; therefore, these consumers are a good market for new offerings.[147]

Note that purchasing something different is only one way to seek stimulation. Consumers can also express their variety drive by engaging in vicarious exploration.[148] **Vicarious exploration** occurs when consumers collect information about a product, either by reading or talking with others or by putting themselves in stimulating shopping environments. For example, many people like to go to stores simply to look around or browse—not to buy, just to increase their stimulation.

Optimal stimulation level (OSL) The level of arousal that is most comfortable for an individual.

Sensation seeker A consumer who actively looks for variety.

Vicarious exploration Seeking information simply for stimulation.

Impulse purchase An unexpected purchase based on a strong feeling.

Marketers should recognize consumers' need for variety and accommodate these needs appropriately, as Frito-Lay does by introducing new flavors and PepsiCo does by introducing new cans on a regular basis. Marketers can attempt to induce brand switching among variety seekers by encouraging consumers to "put a little spice into life" and try something different. Many breweries, for example, produce limited-time seasonal beers to attract variety seekers. Wolf's Ridge Brewing Company and North High Brewing Company, both in Columbus, Ohio, brew pumpkin spice beers every autumn, part of a major trend toward offering pumpkin foods and beverages during the fall season.[149] However, consumers may not like too much variety. Note that simply altering the way that the product assortment is presented (e.g., how items are arranged on the store shelves) can increase consumers' perceptions of variety and trigger higher consumption, a finding that is particularly relevant for food retailers.[150]

9-5d BUYING ON IMPULSE

Another common decision process that has a strong affective component is the **impulse purchase**, which occurs when consumers suddenly decide to purchase something they had not planned on buying. Impulse purchases are characterized by (1) an intense or overwhelming feeling of having to buy the product immediately, (2) a disregard for potentially negative purchase consequences, (3) feelings of euphoria and excitement, and (4) a conflict between control and indulgence.[151] In Asian countries, where interdependence and emotional control are emphasized and power distance belief is high (meaning people accept disparities in power or prestige), consumers engage in less impulse purchasing than do consumers in Western countries, where personal independence and hedonistic pleasures are emphasized.[152] Impulse purchasing and consumption, especially when related to unfulfilled pleasure-seeking needs, are often triggered by the consumer's exposure to an external stimulus, such as an in-store display, a Web ad, or a TV ad with a phone number.[153]

Some research suggests that impulse purchases are prompted by a failure of consumers' self-control.[154] Applying self-control is taxing, a factor that explains why consumers who exert self-control in one area—such as not eating sweets while dieting—may be less able to maintain self-control in another area and will therefore buy something on impulse.[155] Making a series of decisions can deplete consumers' self-control even further.[156] Yet consumers may be unable to control impulse purchasing even when they engage in a great deal of conscious processing.[157] Among the methods that consumers can use to effectively limit impulse buys are making shopping lists, visiting fewer aisles or departments, making shorter and more frequent shopping trips, and paying with cash.[158]

Recent research indicates that consumers may, through the use of mental accounting, plan to buy "on impulse" based on an amount they mentally allocate for unspecified in-store purchasing.[159] Researchers estimate that anywhere from 27 to 62 percent of consumer purchases can be considered impulse buys.[160] However, it is important to distinguish between impulse buying and partially planned purchases, or those for which the consumer has an intention to buy the product category but uses the store display to decide which brand to select. When this distinction is made, the proportion of impulse purchases is usually lower.[161] Also, consumers tend to make more impulse purchases when they choose the store based on favorable pricing; conversely, they make fewer impulse purchases when they choose the store as part of several they visit during one shopping trip.[162]

The tendency to engage in impulse purchasing varies; some consumers can be considered highly impulsive buyers, whereas others are not.[163] The tendency to buy on impulse is probably related to other traits such as general acquisitiveness and materialism, sensation seeking, and a liking for recreational shopping.[164] If the costs of impulsiveness are made salient or if normative pressure such as the presence of others with negative opinions is high, consumers will engage in less impulse purchasing.[165] The presence of peers increases the urge to make impulse purchases, while the presence of family members has the opposite effect.[166] Interestingly, some research suggests that physiological factors, such as eating foods that enhance levels of neurotransmitters, can contribute to impulse buying.[167]

 ## Marketing Implications

Marketers can influence impulse purchases in a number of ways. Many stores organize their merchandise to maximize impulse purchases. As discussed earlier in this chapter, eye-level and eye-catching displays, including end-of-aisle displays and blinking lights, can increase sales dramatically—mostly of impulse items.[168] Package design can also increase impulse purchases—the reason that Kleenex tissues introduced boxes designed like ice-cream cones for summer displays and boxes designed like cake slices for winter displays.[169] Consumers' preshopping goals ("stocking up on basics" or "taking advantage of a special deal") have been shown to affect unplanned buying. Also, although outside-the-store marketing alone does not directly influence impulse buying, the combination of outside-the-store and in-store marketing can encourage consumers to make unplanned purchases.[170] One study of mobile marketing found that when consumers have to walk further into a store to find a product for which they have received a digital coupon, they are more likely to make unplanned purchases than if they stuck to their usual path through the store.[171]

Impulse purchasing tends to decline in difficult economic times. In China, for example, where constant inflation is causing steady price increases, research shows consumers are doing more planning for purchases and cutting back on impulse buys.[172] On the other hand, regardless of economic circumstances, many U.S. consumers are indulging themselves with affordable luxuries such as visiting BLO, Drybar, or other salons that only wash, dry, and style hair.[173]

Summary:

This chapter examines the nature of consumer judgment and decision-making when motivation, ability, and opportunity—and consequently elaboration—are low. In these situations, consumers often make judgments using simplified heuristics or decision rules. When using the representativeness heuristic, consumers base their judgments on comparisons to a category prototype. When using the availability heuristic, they base their judgments on accessibility of information.

Sometimes low-effort decisions are made unconsciously, sometimes consciously. Unconscious decisions may be strongly affected by environmental cues. Conscious low-effort decision-making can follow a hierarchy of effects in which thinking leads to behaving and results in feeling; in contrast, the hierarchy of effects for high-effort decision-making is typically thinking-feeling-behaving. For simplicity, consumers making low-effort decisions may satisfice rather than optimize. They may also devise choice tactics over repeat purchase occasions through a process similar to operant conditioning. Cognitively based choice tactics include performance, habit, brand loyalty, price, and normative influences; affective-based choice tactics include affect referral, brand familiarity, variety seeking, and impulse buying.

Questions for Review and Discussion

1. How do base-rate information and the law of small numbers bias judgments made on the basis of the availability heuristic?

2. How is the high-effort hierarchy of effects similar to and different from the low-effort hierarchy?

3. How do unconscious factors influence consumer behavior?

4. What operant conditioning concepts apply to consumer learning?

5. Why is quality an important ingredient in cognitive-based decision-making?

6. What is brand loyalty, and what role does it play in low-effort decision-making?

7. How do price and value perceptions affect low-effort decision-making?

8. When is affect likely to be more of a factor in low-effort decision-making?

9. If habit is a simplifying strategy, why do consumers sometimes seek variety?

Endnotes

1. Rafi Mohammed, "Bed Bath & Beyond's Persistent Coupons and the Return of Thrifty Consumers," *Harvard Business Review*, October 6, 2015, http://hbr.org.

2. Rohit Deshpande, Wayne D. Hoyer, and Scott Jeffries, "Low Involvement Decision Processes: The Importance of Choice Tactics," in eds. R. F. Bush and S. D. Hunt, *Marketing Theory: Philosophy of Science Perspectives* (Chicago: American Marketing Association, 1982), pp. 155–158; Alan Newell and Herbert A. Simon, *Human Problem Solving* (Englewood Cliffs, N.J.: Prentice-Hall, 1972); and Daniel Kahneman and Amos Tversky, "On the Psychology of Prediction," *Psychological Review*, July 1973, pp. 237–251.

3. Daniel Kahneman and Amos Tversky, "Subjective Probability: A Judgment of Representativeness," *Cognitive Psychology*, July 1972, pp. 430–454.

4. Matt Hamblen, "Hallmark's New E-Card Mobile App Hopes to Target 'Soulless' Interactions," *Computerworld*, May 8, 2015, www.computerworld.com; and "Digital Tells New Tale in Greeting Card Aisle," *MMR*, May 16, 2011, p. 34.

5. Valerie S. Folkes, "The Availability Heuristic and Perceived Risk," *Journal of Consumer Research*, June 1988, pp. 13–23; and Johnson and Puto, "A Review of Consumer Judgment and Choice," in ed. Michael J. Houston, *Review of Marketing* (Chicago: American Marketing Association, 1987), pp. 236–292.

6. Geeta Menon and Priya Raghubir, "Ease-of-Retrieval as an Automatic Input in Judgments: A Mere-Accessibility Framework?" *Journal of Consumer Research*, September 2003, pp. 230–243.

7. Peter R. Dickson, "The Impact of Enriching Case and Statistical Information on Consumer Judgments," *Journal of Consumer Research*, March 1982, pp. 398–408.

8. Chezy Ofir and John G. Lynch Jr., "Context Effects on Judgment under Uncertainty," *Journal of Consumer Research*, September 1984, pp. 668–679.

9. Amos Tversky and Daniel Kahneman, "Belief in the Law of Small Numbers," *Psychological Bulletin*, August 1971, pp. 105–110; and Amos Tversky and Daniel Kahneman, "Judgment Under Uncertainty: Heuristics and Biases," *Science*, September 1974, pp. 1124–1131.

10. James R. Hagerty, "Haier Looks to Expand Toehold in U.S. Appliances," *Wall Street Journal*, August 20, 2015, www.wsj.com; and Marc Worth, "Chinese Brands: When Will They Succeed?" *Forbes*, September 22, 2011, www.forbes.com.

11   Nat Ives, "Entertainment Weekly Adds Co-Viewing Platform for TV Shows from 'Glee' to Football," *Advertising Age*, September 16, 2011, www.adage.com.

12   Wayne D. Hoyer, "An Examination of Consumer Decision Making for a Common Repeat Purchase Product," *Journal of Consumer Research*, December 1984, pp. 822–829.

13   Martin Lindstrom, *Buyology: Truth and Lies About Why We Buy* (New York: Doubleday, 2008).

14   Ap Dijksterhuis, Pamela K. Smith, Rick B. van Baaren, and Daniel H. J. Wigboldus, "The Unconscious Consumer: Effects of Environment on Consumer Behavior," *Journal of Consumer Psychology* 15, no. 3, 2005, pp. 193–202.

15   James Vlahos, "Scent and Sensibility," *Key (New York Times Real Estate Magazine)*, Fall 2007, pp. 68–73.

16   Michal Maimaran and S. Christian Wheeler, "Circles, Squares, and Choice: The Effect of Shape Arrays on Uniqueness and Variety Seeking," *Journal of Marketing Research*, December 2008, pp. 731–740; and Tanya L. Chartrand, "The Role of Conscious Awareness in Consumer Behavior," *Journal of Consumer Psychology* 15, no. 3, 2005, pp. 203–210.

17   Milica Milosavljevic, Vidhya Navalpakkam, Christof Koch, and Antonio Rangel, "Relative Visual Saliency Differences Induce Sizable Bias in Consumer Choice," *Journal of Consumer Psychology* 22, no. 1, January 2012 Special Issue, pp. 67–74.

18   Melanie A. Dempsey and Andrew A. Mitchell, "The Influence of Implicit Attitudes on Choice When Consumers Are Confronted with Conflicting Attribute Information," *Journal of Consumer Research*, December 2010, pp. 614–625.

19   Nalini Ambady, Mary Ann Krabbenhoft, and Daniel Hogan, "The 30-Sec Sale: Using Thin-Slice Judgments to Evaluate Sales Effectiveness," *Journal of Consumer Psychology* 16, no. 1, 2006, pp. 4–13.

20   Jan R. Landwehr, Ann L. McGill, and Andreas Herrmann, "It's Got the Look: The Effect of Friendly and Aggressive 'Facial' Expressions on Product Liking and Sales," *Journal of Marketing*, May 2011, pp. 132–146.

21   Jens Förster, "How Body Feedback Influences Consumers' Evaluation of Products," *Journal of Consumer Psychology* 14, no. 4, 2004, pp. 416–426. See also Ronald S. Friedman and Jens Förster, "The Effects of Approach and Avoidance Motor Actions on the Elements of Creative Insight," *Journal of Personality and Social Psychology* 79, no. 4, 2000, pp. 477–492.

22   Joan Meyers-Levy, Rui Zhu, and Lan Jiang, "Context Effects from Bodily Sensations: Examining Bodily Sensations Induced by Flooring and the Moderating Role of Product Viewing Distance," *Journal of Consumer Research*, June 2010.

23   Iana A. Castro, Andrea C. Morales, and Stephen M. Nowlis, "The Influence of Disorganized Shelf Displays and Limited Product Quantity on Consumer Purchase," *Journal of Marketing* 77, no. 4, July 2013, pp. 118–133.

24   Chris Janiszewski and Stijn M. J. van Osselaer, "Behavior Activation Is Not Enough," *Journal of Consumer Psychology* 15, no. 3, 2005, pp. 218–224.

25   Ap Dijksterhuis and Pamela K. Smith, "What Do We Do Unconsciously? And How?" *Journal of Consumer Psychology* 15, no. 3, 2005, pp. 225–229.

26   Colleen Clark, "Why Do Fancy Hotels Pipe in Such Powerful Fragrances?" *Bloomberg Businessweek*, September 18, 2015, www.businessweek.com.

27   Herbert E. Krugman, "The Impact of Television Advertising: Learning Without Involvement," *Public Opinion Quarterly*, Fall 1965, pp. 349–356.

28   Michael L. Ray, *Marketing Communications and the Hierarchy of Effects* (Cambridge, Mass.: Marketing Science Institute, 1973).

29   Arun Lakshmanan and H. Shanker Krishnan, "The Aha! Experience: Insight and Discontinuous Learning in Product Usage," *Journal of Marketing* 75, no. 6, November 2011, pp. 105–123.

30   Robert B. Zajonc, "Feeling and Thinking: Preferences Need No Inferences," *American Psychologist*, February 1980, pp. 151–175; and Robert B. Zajonc and Hazel B. Markus, "Affective and Cognitive Factors in Preferences," *Journal of Consumer Research*, September 1982, pp. 122–131.

31   Hoyer, "An Examination of Consumer Decision Making for a Common Repeat Purchase Product."

32   Cathy J. Cobb and Wayne D. Hoyer, "Direct Observation of Search Behavior in the Purchase of Two Nondurable Products," *Psychology and Marketing*, Fall 1983, pp. 161–179.

33   Richard W. Olshavsky and Donald H. Granbois, "Consumer Decision Making: Fact or Fiction?" *Journal of Consumer Research*, September 1979, pp. 93–100.

34   Andrew D. Gershoff and Gita Venkataramani Johar, "Do You Know Me? Consumer Calibration of Friends' Knowledge," *Journal of Consumer Research* 32, no. 4, 2006, pp. 496–503.

35   Baba Shiv, Julie A. Edell Britton, and John W. Payne, "Re-Inquiries: Does Elaboration Increase or Decrease the Effectiveness of Negatively Versus Positively Framed Messages?" *Journal of Consumer Research*, June 2004, pp. 199–208.

36   Yong Zhang and Richard Buda, "Moderating Effects of Need for Cognition on Responses to Positively versus Negatively Framed Advertising Messages," *Journal of Advertising*, Summer 1999, pp. 1–15.

37   C. Whan Park, Sung Youl Jun, and Deborah J. MacInnis, "Choosing What I Want Versus Rejecting What I Do Not Want: An Application of Decision Framing to Product Option Choice Decisions," *Journal of Marketing Research*, May 2000, pp. 187–202.

38   William E. Baker and Richard J. Lutz, "An Empirical Test of an Updated Relevance–Accessibility Model of Advertising Effectiveness," *Journal of Advertising* 29, no. 1, Spring 2000, pp. 1–13.

39   Jeffrey S. Larson and Darron M. Billetera, "Consumer Behavior in 'Equilibrium': How Experiencing Physical Balance Increases Compromise Choice," *Journal of Marketing Research* 50, no. 4, August 2013, pp. 535–547.

40   Ahreum Maeng, Robin J. Tanner, and Dilip Soman, "Conservative When Crowded: Social Crowding and Consumer Choice," *Journal of Marketing Research* 50, no. 6, December 2013, pp. 739–752.

41   Deshpande, Hoyer, and Jeffries, "Low Involvement Decision Processes: The Importance of Choice Tactics."

42   Hoyer, "An Examination of Consumer Decision Making for a Common Repeat Purchase Product."

43   Siew Meng Leong, "Consumer Decision Making for Common, Repeat-Purchase Products: A Dual Replication," *Journal of Consumer Psychology* 2, no. 2, 1993, pp. 193–208; and Dana L. Alden, Wayne D. Hoyer, and Guntalee Wechasara, "Choice Strategies and Involvement, A Cross-Cultural Analysis," in ed. Thomas K. Srull, *Advances in Consumer Research*, vol. 16 (Provo, Utah: Association for Consumer Research, 1989), pp. 119–126.

44   Walter A. Nord and J. Paul Peter, "A Behavior Modification Perspective on Marketing," *Journal of Marketing*, Spring 1980, pp. 36–47; and Michael Rothschild and William C. Gaidis,

"Behavioral Learning Theory: Its Relevance to Marketing and Promotions," *Journal of Marketing*, Spring 1981, pp. 70–78.

45 Holly Heline, "Brand Loyalty Isn't Dead—But You're Not Off the Hook," *Brandweek*, June 7, 1994, p. 14.

46 Robert E. Smith and William R. Swinyard, "Information Response Models: An Integrated Approach," *Journal of Marketing*, Winter 1982, pp. 81–93; and Robert E. Smith and William R. Swinyard, "Attitude–Behavior Consistency: The Impact of Product Trial vs. Advertising," *Journal of Marketing Research*, August 1983, pp. 257–267.

47 Deanna S. Kempf and Robert E. Smith, "Consumer Processing of Product Trial and the Influence of Prior Advertising: A Structural Modeling Approach," *Journal of Marketing Research*, August 1998, pp. 325–338.

48 Ran Kivetz, Oleg Urminsky, and Yuhuang Zheng, "The Goal-Gradient Hypothesis Resurrected: Purchase Acceleration, Illusionary Goal Progress, and Customer Retention," *Journal of Marketing Research*, February 2006, pp. 39–58.

49 Michael L. Rothschild and Michael J. Houston, "The Consumer Involvement Matrix: Some Preliminary Findings," in eds. Barnett A. Greenberg and Danny N. Bellenger, *Proceedings of the American Marketing Association Educators' Conference*, Series no. 41, 1977, pp. 95–98.

50 Wayne D. Hoyer, "Variations in Choice Strategies Across Decision Contexts: An Examination of Contingent Factors," in ed. Richard J. Lutz, *Advances in Consumer Research*, vol. 13 (Provo, Utah: Association for Consumer Research, 1986), pp. 32–36.

51 Wayne D. Hoyer and Cathy J. Cobb-Walgren, "Consumer Decision Making Across Product Categories: The Influence of Task Environment," *Psychology and Marketing*, Spring 1988, pp. 45–69.

52 Leong, "Consumer Decision Making for Common, Repeat-Purchase Products: A Dual Replication."

53 Rick Romell, "Kohl's Steps Up Emphasis on National Brands to Revive Slumping Sales," *Milwaukee Journal Sentinel*, May 15, 2014, www.jsonline.com.

54 Robert E. Smith, "Integrating Information from Advertising and Trial: Processes and Effects on Consumer Response to Product Information," *Journal of Marketing Research*, May 1993, pp. 204–219.

55 Sarah Nassauer, "Marketers Hope Guest Veggies Will Get Americans to Eat More Greens," *Wall Street Journal*, July 27, 2011, www.wsj.com.

56 Mari Jo Valero, "Is Selling Domino's Pizza in Italy a Bad Idea?," *Atlanta Journal Constitution*, October 11, 2015, www.ajc.com; Ashley Lutz, "Domino's Made 3 Changes to Become the World's Top Pizza Chain," *Business Insider*, April 13, 2015, www.businessinsider.com; Rae Ann Fera, "Should 'Domino's' and 'Artisan' Be Used in the Same Pizza Ad?" *Fast Company*, September 26, 2011, www.fastcompany.com; and Priya Raghubir and Kim Corfman, "When Do Price Promotions Affect Pretrial Brand Evaluations?" *Journal of Marketing Research* 36, May 1999, pp. 211–222.

57 Adwait Khare and J. Jeffrey Inman, "Habitual Behavior in American Eating Patterns: The Role of Meal Occasions," *Journal of Consumer Research* 32, no. 4, 2006, pp. 567–575; and Jacob Jacoby and David B. Kyner, "Brand Loyalty vs. Repeat Purchasing Behavior," *Journal of Marketing Research*, February 1973, pp. 1–9.

58 Ted Roselius, "Consumer Rankings of Risk Reduction Methods,"*Journal of Marketing*, January 1971, pp. 56–61.

59 P. B. Seetharaman, Andrew Ainslie, and Pradeep K. Chintagunta, "Investigating Household State Dependence Effects Across Categories," *Journal of Marketing Research* 36, November 1999, pp. 488–500.

60 Rothschild and Gaidis, "Behavioral Learning Theory."

61 Conor M. Henderson, Joshua T. Beck, and Robert W. Palmatier, "Review of the Theoretical Underpinnings of Loyalty Programs," *Journal of Consumer Psychology* 21, no. 3, July 2011, pp. 256–276.

62 Elyse Dupre, "Kellogg's Rewards Program Doesn't Flake Out on Digital," *Direct Marketing News*, July 1, 2015, www.dmnews.com.

63 Ilan Mochari, "Give it Away Now: Why Free Product Samples Always Pay Off," *Inc.*, October 3, 2014, www.inc.com.

64 Neal Ungerleider, "It Has 40 Million Subscribers. Now Amazon Prime Is Eyeing The Competition," *Fast Company*, July 9, 2015, www.fastcompany.com.

65 Gary F. McKinnon, J. Patrick Kelly, and E. Doyle Robinson, "Sales Effects of Point-of-Purchase In-Store Signing," *Journal of Retailing*, Summer 1981, pp. 49–63.

66 Kathleen Deveny, "Displays Pay Off for Grocery Marketers," *Wall Street Journal*, October 15, 1992, pp. B1, B5.

67 Yuping Liu-Thompkins and Leona Tam, "Not All Repeat Customers Are the Same: Designing Effective Cross-Selling Promotion on the Basis of Attitudinal Loyalty and Habit," *Journal of Marketing* 77, no. 5, September 2013, pp. 21–36.

68 "Brand Loyalty in the Food Industry," *The Food Institute Report*, November 5, 2001, p. 3.

69 Julie Jargon, "No Wonder: Twinkies Owner Adds Bread," *Wall Street Journal*, September 17, 2015, www.wsj.com.

70 George S. Day, "Two-Dimensional Concept of Brand Loyalty," *Journal of Advertising Research*, August–September 1969, pp. 29–36; Jacoby and Kyner, "Brand Loyalty vs. Repeat Purchasing Behavior"; and Jacob Jacoby and Robert W. Chestnut, *Brand Loyalty: Measurement and Management* (New York: Wiley, 1978).

71 Kyle B. Murray and Gerald Häubl, "Explaining Cognitive Lock-In: The Role of Skill-Based Habits of Use in Consumer Choice," *Journal of Consumer Research* 34, no. 1, 2007, pp. 77–88.

72 Jacob Jacoby, "A Model of Multi-Brand Loyalty," *Journal of Advertising Research*, June–July 1971, p. 26.

73 Her-Sen Doong, Gordon R. Foxall, and Hui-Chih Wang, "An Investigation of Consumers' Webstore Shopping," *International Journal of Information Management*, June 2011, pp. 210–216.

74 Ronald E. Frank, William F. Massy, and Thomas L. Lodahl, "Purchasing Behavior and Personal Attributes," *Journal of Advertising Research*, December 1969–January 1970, pp. 15–24.

75 R. M. Cunningham, "Brand Loyalty—What, Where, How Much," *Harvard Business Review*, January–February 1956, pp. 116–128; and "Customer Loyalty to Store and Brand," *Harvard Business Review*, November–December 1961, pp. 127–137.

76 Day, "A Two-Dimensional Concept of Brand Loyalty."

77 Daphne Howland, "Jos. A. Bank to End Aggressive Promotions, Revamp Clothes," *Retail Dive*, September 22, 2015, www.retaildive.com.

78 Heline, "Brand Loyalty Isn't Dead—But You're Not Off the Hook."

79 David Moth, "Eight of the Best Social Campaigns from June 2014," *E-Consultancy*, June 30, 2014, www.econsultancy.com.

80 Michelle L. Roehm, Ellen Bolman Pullins, and Harper A. Roehm Jr., "Designing Loyalty-Building Programs for

Packaged Goods Brands," *Journal of Marketing Research*, May 2002, pp. 202–213.

81 Ran Kivetz and Itamar Simonson, "The Idiosyncratic Fit Heuristic: Effort Advantage as a Determinant of Consumer Response to Loyalty Programs," *Journal of Marketing Research*, November 2003, pp. 454–467.

82 Ran Kivetz and Itamar Simonson, "Earning the Right to Indulge: Effort as a Determinant of Customer Preferences toward Frequency Program Rewards," *Journal of Marketing Research*, May 2002, pp. 155–170.

83 Tillmann Wagner, Thorsten Hennig-Thurau, and Thomas Rudolph, "Does Customer Demotion Jeopardize Loyalty?" *Journal of Marketing*, May 2009, pp. 69–85.

84 Katie Little, "Design Your Own Soda? There's an App For That," *CNBC*, May 5, 2014, www.cnbc.com; and Don Worthington, "Moe's Drinks Go High-Tech at Manchester Restaurant," *The Herald (Rock Hill, S.C.)*, September 26, 2011, www .heraldonline.com.

85 Peter D. Dickson and Alan G. Sawyer, "Methods to Research Shoppers' Knowledge of Supermarket Prices," in ed. Richard J. Lutz, *Advances in Consumer Research*, vol. 12 (Provo, Utah: Association for Consumer Research, 1986), pp. 584–587.

86 Chris Janiszewski and Donald R. Lichtenstein, "A Range Theory Account of Price Perception," *Journal of Consumer Research* 25, March 1999, pp. 353–368; and Kent B. Monroe and Susan M. Petroshius, "Buyers' Perception of Price: An Update of the Evidence," in eds. Harold H. Kassarjian and Thomas S. Robertson, *Perspectives in Consumer Behavior*, 3rd ed. (Dallas, Tex.: Scott-Foresman, 1981), pp. 43–55.

87 Marilyn Geewax, "The Latest Item on McDonald's Shifting Menu: A $5 Burger," *National Public Radio*, April 8, 2015, www .npr.org.

88 Tulin Erdem, Glenn Mayhew, and Baohung Sun, "Understanding Reference-Price Shoppers: A Withinand Cross-Category Analysis," *Journal of Marketing Research*, Novemb er 2001, pp. 445–457.

89 Aylin Aydinli, Marco Bertini, and Anja Lambrecht, "Price Promotion for Emotional Impact," *Journal of Marketing* 78, July 2014, pp. 80–96.

90 Marcus Cunha Jr. and Jeffrey D. Shulman, "Assimilation and Contrast in Price Evaluations," *Journal of Consumer Research* 37, no. 5, February 2011, pp. 822–835.

91 Julie Baker, A. Parasuraman, Dhruv Grewal, and Glenn B. Voss, "The Influence of Multiple Store Environment Cues on Perceived Merchandise Value and Patronage Intentions," *Journal of Marketing*, April 2002, pp. 120–141.

92 Jiwoong Shin, "The Role of Selling Costs in Signaling Price Image," *Journal of Marketing Research*, August 2005, pp. 302–312.

93 Lisa E. Bolton, Luk Warlop, and Joseph W. Alba, "Consumer Perceptions of Price (Un)Fairness," *Journal of Consumer Research*, March 2003, pp. 474–491; and Joseph C. Nunes and Peter Boatwright, "Incidental Prices and Their Effect on Willingness to Pay," *Journal of Marketing Research*, November 2004, pp. 457–466.

94 Tuo Wang, R. Venkatesh, and Rabikar Chatterjee, "Reservation Price as a Range: An Incentive-Compatible Measurement Approach," *Journal of Marketing Research*, May 2007, pp. 200–213.

95 Mark Stiving and Russell S. Winer, "An Empirical Analysis of Price Endings with Scanner Data," *Journal of Consumer Research*, June 1997, pp. 57–76; and Zarrel V. Lambert,

"Perceived Prices as Related to Odd and Even Price Endings," *Journal of Retailing*, Fall 1975, pp. 13–22.

96 Aradhna Krishna, Mary Wagner, Carolyn Yoon, and Rashmi Adaval, "Effects of Extreme-Priced Products on Consumer Reservation Prices," *Journal of Consumer Psychology* 16, no. 2, 2006, pp. 176–190.

97 Kent B. Monroe, "The Influence of Price Differences and Brand Familiarity on Brand Preferences," *Journal of Consumer Research*, June 1976, pp. 42–49.

98 Joseph W. Alba, Carl F. Mela, Terence A. Shimp, and Joel E. Urbany, "The Effect of Discount Frequency and Depth on Consumer Price Judgments," *Journal of Consumer Research*, September 1999, pp. 99–114.

99 J. Jeffrey Inman, Anil C. Peter, and Priya Raghubir, "Framing the Deal: The Role of Restrictions in Accentuating Deal Value," *Journal of Consumer Research*, June 1997, pp. 68–79.

100 Dhruv Grewal, Howard Marmorstein, and Arun Sharma, "Communicating Price Information Through Semantic Cues," *Journal of Consumer Research*, September 1996, pp. 148–155.

101 Priya Raghubir and Joydeep Srivastava, "Effect of Face Value on Product Valuation in Foreign Currencies," *Journal of Consumer Research*, December 2002, pp. 335–347.

102 Margaret C. Campbell, "'Says Who?!' How the Source of Price Information and Affect Influence Perceived Price (Un)Fairness," *Journal of Marketing Research*, May 2007, pp. 261–271.

103 *Supermarket Shoppers in a Period of Economic Uncertainty* (New York: Yankelovich, Skelly, & White, 1982), p. 53; and Robert Blattberg, Thomas Buesing, Peter Peacock, and Subrata K. Sen, "Who Is the Deal-Prone Consumer?" in ed. H. Keith Hunt, *Advances in Consumer Research*, vol. 5 (Ann Arbor, Mich.: Association for Consumer Research, 1978), pp. 57–62.

104 Donald R. Lichtenstein, Richard G. Netemeyer, and Scot Burton, "Assessing the Domain Specificity of Deal Proneness: A Field Study," *Journal of Consumer Research*, December 1995, pp. 314–326.

105 Mark Hachman, "Retailers Discover Useful In-Store Apps Keep Shoppers from Escaping," *PC Magazine*, September 27, 2011, www.pcmag.com.

106 John Pietz, "Daily Deal Duel," *Crain's Chicago Business*, November 9, 2011, www.chicagobusiness.com.

107 "Fast-Food Chains Bringing Back Cheap Eats with Special Deals," *Chicago Sun-Times*, September 27, 2011, www .suntimes.com.

108 Kathleen Deveny, "How Country's Biggest Brands Are Faring at the Supermarket," *Wall Street Journal*, March 24, 1994, p. B1.

109 Geoffrey Wilson, "Clipping Coupons Cuts Down Grocery Bills," *Poughkeepsie Journal*, September 21, 2015, www .poughkeepsiejournal.com; and David Pitt, "Now That Have Gone Digital, It's Hip to Be Frugal, Executive Says," *Boston Globe*, September 8, 2011, www.boston.com.

110 "Trend for Coupon Sites Growing in India," *The Independent (U.K.)*, July 31, 2011, www.indendent.co.uk.

111 Maria Halkias, "Daiso Japan Dollar Store Expands into Texas," *Dallas Morning News*, July 31, 2015, www.dallasnews.com; "100 Yen Stores—That's $2.80—Come to Australia," *CNN Go*, September 15, 2011, www.cnngo.com.

112 Jon Springer, "Discount Redefined: Aldi in the USA," *Supermarket News*, September 3, 2015, www.supermarketnews .com.

113 Jan-Benedict E. M. Steenkamp, Harald J. Van Heerde, and Inge Geyskens, "What Makes Consumers Willing to Pay a Price

Premium for National Brands over Private Labels?" *Journal of Marketing Research* 47, no. 6, December 2010, pp. 1011–1024.

114 Daniel J. Howard and Charles Gengler, "Emotional Contagion Effects on Product Attitudes," *Journal of Consumer Research*, September 2001, pp. 189–201.

115 Cheng Qui, Yih Hwai Lee, and Catherine W. M. Yeung, "Suppressing Feelings: A Double-edged Sword to Consumer Judgment and Choice," *Journal of Consumer Psychology* 19, 2009, pp. 427–439.

116 Tamar Avnet, Michel Tuan Pham, and Andrew T. Stephen, "Consumers' Trust in Feelings as Information," *Journal of Consumer Research* 39, no. 4, December 2012, pp. 720–735.

117 Susan T. Fiske, "Schema Triggered Affect: Applications to Social Perception," in eds. Margaret S. Clark and Susan T. Fiske, *Affect and Cognition: The 17th Annual Carnegie Symposium on Cognition* (Hillsdale, N.J.: Lawrence Erlbaum, 1982), pp. 55–77; and Mita Sujan, James R. Bettman, and Harish Sujan, "Effects of Consumer Expectations on Information Processing and Selling Encounters," *Journal of Marketing Research*, November 1986, pp. 346–353.

118 Peter L. Wright, "An Adaptive Consumer's View of Attitudes and Choice Mechanisms as Viewed by an Equally Adaptive Advertiser," in ed. William D. Wells, *Attitude Research at Bay* (Chicago: American Marketing Association, 1976), pp. 113–131.

119 Baba Shiv and Alexander Fedorikhin, "Heart and Mind in Conflict: The Interplay of Affect and Cognition in Consumer Decision Making," *Journal of Consumer Research* 26, December 1999, pp. 278–292.

120 Rebecca Walker Naylor, Rajagopal Raghunathan, and Suresh Ramanathan, "Promotions Spontaneously Induce a Positive Evaluative Response," *Journal of Consumer Psychology* 16, no. 3, 2006, pp. 295–305.

121 Cassie Mogilner, Jennifer Aaker, and Sepandar D. Kamvar, "How Happiness Affects Choice," *Journal of Consumer Research* 39, no. 2, August 2012, pp. 429–443.

122 Hannah H. Chang and Michel Tuan Pham, "Affect as a Decision-Making System of the Present," *Journal of Consumer Research* 40, no. 1, June 2013, pp. 42–63.

123 Susan T. Fiske and Mark A. Pavelchak, "Category-Based Versus Piecemeal-Based Affective Responses: Developments in Schema-Triggered Affect," in eds. R. M. Sorrentino and E. T. Higgins, *The Handbook of Motivation and Cognition: Foundations of Social Behavior* (New York: Guilford, 1986), pp. 167–203; and David M. Boush and Barbara Loken, "A Process-Tracing Study of Brand Extension Evaluation," *Journal of Marketing Research*, February 1991, pp. 16–28.

124 Fiske, "Schema Triggered Affect: Applications to Social Perception"; and Mita Sujan, "Consumer Knowledge: Effects on Evaluation Strategies Mediating Consumer Judgments," *Journal of Consumer Research*, June 1985, pp. 31–46.

125 "Dove Campaign Stars Rashida Jones, Focuses on Common Complaints: Bad Hair Days," *Washington Post*, September 19, 2011, www.washingtonpost.com.

126 Ralph I. Allison and Kenneth P. Uhl, "Influence of Beer Brand Identification on Taste Perception," *Journal of Marketing Research*, August 1964, pp. 36–39.

127 Wayne D. Hoyer and Stephen P. Brown, "Effects of Brand Awareness on Choice for a Common, Repeat-Purchase Product," *Journal of Consumer Research*, September 1990, pp. 141–148.

128 Leong, "Consumer Decision Making for Common, Repeat Purchase Products: A Dual Replication."

129 M. Carole Macklin, "Preschoolers' Learning of Brand Names from Visual Cues," *Journal of Consumer Research*, December 1996, pp. 251–261.

130 "Scottish fact of the day: Irn-Bru," *The Scotsman*, November 13, 2014, www.scotsman.com.

131 Eric Yang, "Co-brand or Be Damned," *Brandweek*, November 21, 1994, pp. 21–24.

132 E. J. Schultz, "Yogurt Body Wash, Anyone? Uptick in Co-branding Brings Some Unusual Combos," *Advertising Age*, June 23, 2014, www.adage.com.

133 "Making Co-Branding a Success," *Nation's Restaurant News*, May 4, 2015, www.nrn.com.

134 Karen V. Fernandez and Dennis L. Rosen, "The Effectiveness of Information and Color in Yellow Pages Advertising," *Journal of Advertising* 29, no. 2, Summer 2000, pp. 61–73.

135 Robert W. Veryzer and J. Wesley Hutchinson, "The Influence of Unity and Prototypicality on Aesthetic Responses to New Product Designs," *Journal of Consumer Research*, March 1998, pp. 374–394.

136 Angela Doland, "Defying Tough Times, These Four Foreign Brands Are Successful in China," *Advertising Age*, June 29, 2015, www.adage.com.

137 See Ayelet Fishbach, Rebecca K. Ratner, and Ying Zhang, "Inherently Loyal or Easily Bored?: Nonconscious Activation of Consistency versus Variety-Seeking Behavior," *Journal of Consumer Psychology* 21, no. 1, January 2011 Special Issue, pp. 38–48.

138 Rebecca K. Ratner, Barbara E. Kahn, and Daniel Kahneman, "Choosing Less-Preferred Experiences for the Sake of Variety," *Journal of Consumer Research* 26, June 1999, pp. 1–15.

139 Rebecca K. Ratner and Barbara E. Kahn, "The Impact of Private versus Public Consumption on Variety-Seeking Behavior," *Journal of Consumer Research*, September 2002, pp. 246–257.

140 Rosario Vázquez-Carrasco and Gordon R. Foxall, "Positive versus Negative Switching Barriers: The Influence of Service Consumers' Need for Variety," *Journal of Consumer Behavior* 5, no. 4, 2006, pp. 367–379.

141 Hans C. M. Van Trijp, Wayne D. Hoyer, and J. Jeffrey Inman, "Why Switch? Product Category-Level Explanations for True Variety Seeking," *Journal of Marketing Research*, August 1996, pp. 281–292; and Wayne D. Hoyer and Nancy M. Ridgway, "Variety Seeking as an Explanation for Exploratory Purchase Behavior: A Theoretical Model," in ed. Thomas C. Kinnear, *Advances in Consumer Research*, vol. 11 (Ann Arbor, Mich.: Association for Consumer Research, 1984), pp. 114–119.

142 J. Jeffrey Inman, "The Role of Sensory-Specific Satiety in Attribute-Level Variety Seeking," *Journal of Consumer Research* 28, June 2001, pp. 105–120.

143 Saatya Menon and Barbara E. Kahn, "The Impact of Context on Variety Seeking in Product Choices," *Journal of Consumer Research*, December 1995, pp. 285–295.

144 Cassie Mogilner, Tamar Rudnick, and Sheena S. Iyengar, "The Mere Categorization Effect," *Journal of Consumer Research*, August 2008, pp. 201–215.

145 Aner Sela, Jonah Berger, and Wendy Liu, "Variety, Vice, and Virtue: How Assortment Size Influences Option Choice," *Journal of Consumer Research*, April 2009, pp. 941–951.

146 Erich A. Joachimsthaler and John L. Lastovicka, "Optimal Stimulation Level–Exploratory Behavior Models," *Journal of Consumer Research*, December 1984, pp. 830–835.

147 Albert Mehrabian and James Russell, *An Approach to Environmental Psychology* (Cambridge, Mass.: MIT Press, 1974).

148 Linda L. Price and Nancy M. Ridgway, "Use Innovativeness, Vicarious Exploration and Purchase Exploration: Three Facets of Consumer Varied Behavior," in ed. Bruce Walker, *American Marketing Association Educators' Conference Proceedings* (Chicago: American Marketing Association, 1982), pp. 56–60.

149 J. D. Malone, "Pumpkin Beer Proves Popular," *Columbus Dispatch (Ohio)*, October 14, 2015, www.dispatch.com.

150 Barbara E. Kahn and Brian Wansink, "The Influence of Assortment Structure on Perceived Variety and Consumption Quantities," *Journal of Consumer Research*, March 2004, pp. 519–533.

151 Fritz Strack, Lioba Werth, and Roland Deutsch, "Reflective and Impulsive Determinants of Consumer Behavior," *Journal of Consumer Psychology* 16, no. 2, 2006, pp. 205–216; Dennis W. Rook, "The Buying Impulse," *Journal of Consumer Research*, September 1987, pp. 189–199; and Craig J. Thompson, William B. Locander, and Howard R. Pollio, "The Lived Meaning of Free Choice: Existential–Phenomenological Description of Everyday Consumer Experiences of Contemporary Married Women," *Journal of Consumer Research*, December 1990, pp. 346–361.

152 Yinlong Zhang, Karen Page Winterich, and Vikas Mittal, "Power Distance Belief and Impulsive Buying," *Journal of Marketing Research*, October 2010, pp. 945–954; and Jacqueline J. Kacen and Julie Anne Lee, "The Influence of Culture on Consumer Impulsive Buying Behavior," *Journal of Consumer Psychology* 12, no. 2, 2002, pp. 163–176.

153 See Suresh Ramanathan and Geeta Menon, "Time-Varying Effects of Chronic Hedonic Goals on Impulsive Behavior," *Journal of Marketing Research*, November 2006, pp. 628–641.

154 Roy F. Baumeister, "Yielding to Temptation: Self-Control Failure, Impulsive Behavior, and Consumer Behavior," *Journal of Consumer Research*, March 2002, pp. 670–676.

155 Kathleen D. Vons and Ronald J. Faber, "Spent Resources: Self-Regulatory Resource Availability Affects Impulse Buying," *Journal of Consumer Research* 33, no. 4, 2007, pp. 537–548.

156 Kathleen D. Vohs, "Self-Regulatory Resources Power the Reflective System: Evidence from Five Domains," *Journal of Consumer Psychology* 16, no. 3, 2006, pp. 217–223.

157 Deborah J. MacInnis and Vanessa M. Patrick, "Spotlight on Affect: Affect and Affective Forecasting in Impulse Control," *Journal of Consumer Psychology* 16, no. 3, 2006, pp. 224–231.

158 J. Jeffrey Inman, Russell S. Winer, and Rosellina Ferraro, "The Interplay Among Category Characteristics, Customer Characteristics, and Customer Activities on In-Store Decision Making," *Journal of Marketing*, September 2009, pp. 19–29.

159 Karen M. Stilley, J. Jeffrey Inman, and Kirk L. Wakefield, "Planning to Make Unplanned Purchases?" *Journal of Consumer Research*, August 2010, pp. 264–278.

160 J. Jeffrey Inman and Russell S. Winer, "Where the Rubber Meets the Road: A Model of In-store Consumer Decision Making," *Marketing Science Institute Report Summary*, December 1998, pp. 98–122; "How We Shop ... From Mass to Market," *Brandweek*, January 9, 1995, p. 17; and Danny Bellenger, D. H. Robertson, and Elizabeth C. Hirschman, "Impulse Buying Varies by Product," *Journal of Advertising Research*, December 1978–January 1979, pp. 15–18.

161 Cathy J. Cobb and Wayne D. Hoyer, "Planned vs. Impulse Purchase Behavior," *Journal of Retailing*, Winter 1986, pp. 384–409.

162 David R. Bell, Daniel Corsten, and George Knox, "From Point of Purchase to Path to Purchase: How Preshopping Factors Drive Unplanned Buying," *Journal of Marketing* 75, no. 1, January 2011, pp. 31–45.

163 Rook, "The Buying Impulse."

164 Russell W. B elk, "Materialism: Trait Aspects of Living in a Material World," *Journal of Consumer Research*, December 1985, pp. 265–280; P. S. Raju, "Optimum Stimulation Level: Its Relationship to Personality, Demographics, and Exploratory Behavior," *Journal of Consumer Research*, December 1980, pp. 272–282; and Danny Bellenger and P. K. Korgaonkar, "Profiling the Recreational Shopper," *Journal of Retailing*, Fall 1980, pp. 77–92.

165 Dennis W. Rook and Robert J. Fisher, "Normative Influences on Impulsive Buying Behavior," *Journal of Consumer Research*, December 1995, pp. 305–313; and Radhika Puri, "Measuring and Modifying Consumer Impulsiveness: A Cost–Benefit Accessibility Framework," *Journal of Consumer Psychology* 5, no. 2, 1996, pp. 87–114.

166 Xueming Luo, "How Does Shopping with Others Influence Impulsive Purchasing?" *Journal of Consumer Psychology* 15, no. 4, 2005, pp. 288–294.

167 Arul Mishra and Himanshu Mishra, "We Are What We Consume: The Influence of Food Consumption on Impulsive Choice," *Journal of Marketing Research*, December 2010, pp. 1129–1137.

168 Inman and Winer, "Where the Rubber Meets the Road: A Model of In-store Consumer Decision Making."

169 Sarah Nassauer, "A Season (or 13) for Shopping," *Wall Street Journal*, August 17, 2011, www.wsj.com.

170 David R. Bell, Daniel Corsten, and George Knox, "From Point of Purchase to Path to Purchase," *Journal of Marketing*, January 2011, pp. 31–45.

171 Sam K. Hui, J. Jeffrey Inman, Yanliu Huang, and Jacob Suher, "The Effect of In-Store Travel Distance on Unplanned Spending: Applications to Mobile Promotion Strategies," *Journal of Marketing* 77, no. 2, March 2013, pp. 1–16.

172 Shaun Rein, "Rein: Chinese Women Keep Shopping Despite the Gloom," *CNBC*, September 26, 2011, www.cnbc.com.

173 Laura Mazurak, "This Salon Trend Is Growing in the Triad," *Triad Business Journal (Greensboro/Winston-Salem)*, July 22, 2015, www.bizjournals.com.

CHAPTER ⑩

Post-Decision Processes

LEARNING OBJECTIVES

After studying this chapter, you will be able to:

▶ Distinguish between the dissonance and the regret that consumers may experience after acquisition, consumption, or disposition.

▶ Explain how consumers can learn from experience and why marketers need to understand this post-decision process.

▶ Discuss what happens when consumers experience satisfaction or dissatisfaction with their decisions about acquisition, consumption, or disposition.

▶ Outline the ways in which consumers may respond to dissatisfaction, and highlight the importance to marketers.

▶ Discuss whether customer satisfaction alone is enough to maintain customer loyalty.

▶ Describe how consumers may dispose of something, why this process is more complex for meaningful objects, and what influences consumer recycling behavior.

INTRODUCTION

When Delta Air Lines passengers are grounded by weather delays, or luggage goes missing, they can tweet @DeltaAssist for help—and get a response within the hour.[1] Delta, like other airlines, knows that customer satisfaction is the foundation of a successful business. In turn, customer satisfaction depends on good performance, creating positive feelings, and perceptions of equity (a fair exchange). Further, consumers learn about offerings by experiencing them directly, as customers do when flying on Delta Air Lines or tweeting for customer service. Finally, Delta's promise to respond quickly demonstrates a commitment to handling complaints. All of these phenomena occur after the consumer has made a decision. This chapter examines the four post-decision processes shown in Exhibit 10.1, which have important implications for marketers: dissonance and regret, consumer learning, satisfaction/dissatisfaction, and disposition.

Exhibit 10.1 ▶ Chapter Overview: Post-Decision Processes

The process does not end after consumers have made the decision to acquire a product or service, and have made their choice for a specific brand or version of the product or service. Consumers can experience dissonance (discomfort over whether they made the correct decision) or regret after a purchase, learn about the offering by using it, experience satisfaction or dissatisfaction with it, and eventually dispose of it.

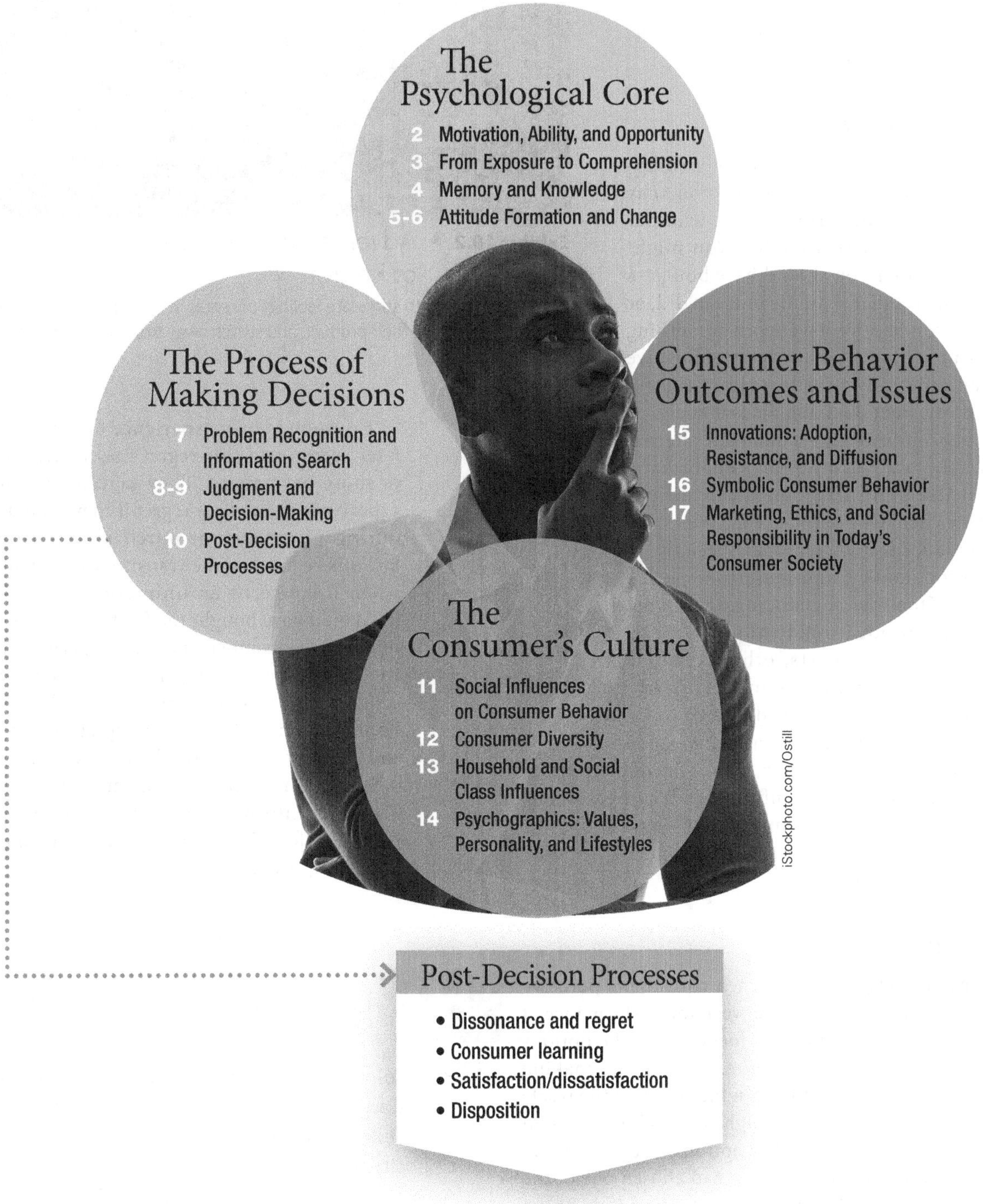

The Psychological Core

2 Motivation, Ability, and Opportunity
3 From Exposure to Comprehension
4 Memory and Knowledge
5-6 Attitude Formation and Change

The Process of Making Decisions

7 Problem Recognition and Information Search
8-9 Judgment and Decision-Making
10 Post-Decision Processes

Consumer Behavior Outcomes and Issues

15 Innovations: Adoption, Resistance, and Diffusion
16 Symbolic Consumer Behavior
17 Marketing, Ethics, and Social Responsibility in Today's Consumer Society

The Consumer's Culture

11 Social Influences on Consumer Behavior
12 Consumer Diversity
13 Household and Social Class Influences
14 Psychographics: Values, Personality, and Lifestyles

iStockphoto.com/Ostill

Post-Decision Processes

- Dissonance and regret
- Consumer learning
- Satisfaction/dissatisfaction
- Disposition

10-1 Post-Decision Dissonance and Regret

Consumers are not always confident about their acquisition, consumption, or disposition decisions. They may feel uncertain about whether they made the correct choice or may even regret the decision that they made, as the following sections show.

10-1a DISSONANCE

After you make an acquisition, consumption, or disposition decision, you may sometimes feel uncertain about whether you made the correct choice. You might wonder whether you should have bought a shirt or dress other than the one you did, or whether you should have worn something else to a party, or whether you should have kept an old teddy bear instead of throwing it away. **Post-decision dissonance** is most likely to occur when more than one alternative is attractive and the decision is important.[2]

Post-decision dissonance can influence consumer behavior because consumers would like to reduce the discomfort, especially when motivation, ability, and opportunity (MAO) are high. One way of reducing dissonance is to search for additional information from sources such as experts, other consumers, web resources, and magazines. This search is typically selective and is designed to make the chosen alternative more attractive and the rejected ones less attractive, thereby reducing dissonance. This is a form of confirmation bias, because the additional information is intended to confirm that the right choice was indeed made. See Chapter 7 for more about confirmation bias.

10-1b REGRET

Post-decision regret occurs when consumers perceive an unfavorable comparison between the performance of the chosen option and the performance of the options not chosen.[3] If you consider three cars before making your purchase decision and then find out that the resale value of the car that you bought is much lower than that of either of the two other options, you may regret your purchase and wish that you had chosen one of the other cars. In fact, you may feel regret even if you have no information about the nonchosen alternatives—especially if you cannot reverse your decision, have a negative outcome from your chosen alternative, or have made a change from the norm or status quo (see Exhibit 10.2).

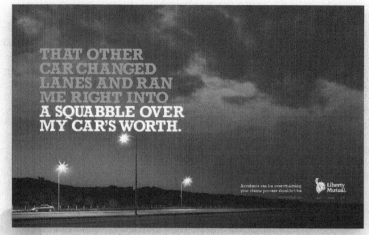

Source: Liberty Mutual Insurance

Exhibit 10.2 ▶ Advertising Based on Feelings of Regret

Sometimes ads try to stimulate feelings of regret in consumers in order to have them purchase their product, and switch away from the product they currently have.

Post-decision dissonance A feeling of discomfort about whether or not the correct decision was made.

Post-decision regret The negative feeling that one should have made another purchase, consumption, or disposition decision than one actually did.

Consumers may experience immediate and later regret, and this regret may be transitory or more permanent. They may, for instance, experience immediate regret if they do not buy during a limited-time purchase opportunity, but this regret may be transitory (short-lived) when it concerns an unimportant purchase ("I should have bought the fruit tea when it was on sale").[4] Consumers may also experience later (postponed) regret. For instance, when exercising repeated self-control and working long hours early in life, they may regret this later in life and feel they have missed out by not living enough in the moment.[5] Consumers can regulate postpurchase regret by seeking information, switching to another option, and also by focusing on what they can learn from this decision to improve future decisions.[6]

 Marketing Implications

By helping consumers reduce post-decision dissonance and regret, marketers can diminish negative feelings related to the offering and contribute to positive brand attitudes. For example, Subaru of America's website lists a number of non-vehicle-related ownership benefits, including a discount on pet health insurance (showcasing the brand's pet-friendly side) and a discount on National Smithsonian Zoo membership (highlighting the brand's family- and nature-friendly associations). It also reinforces positive feelings by offering owners a free, personalized "Badge of Ownership" and inviting them to submit photos of themselves with their cars for the Subaru website and social media such as Instagram and Facebook. To stay connected with buyers, Subaru also publishes a free monthly e-mail newsletter. These activities help to reduce dissonance and regret, and encourage positive attitudes toward the brand.

10-2 Learning from Consumer Experience*

Earlier chapters explained how consumers acquire knowledge through processes such as information search, exposure to marketing communications, and observation of others. From a practical perspective, we most often think about this type of consumer learning because much of it is under the direct control of the company, which provides information through marketing communications. However, the influence of such marketer-controlled information is often limited because of its low credibility.[7] Consumers assume that these messages are intended to persuade them to like and buy the offering, and are therefore generally skeptical about the marketing claims.

Consumers also acquire knowledge by direct experience, which is often less marketer-controlled. Direct experience is an important source of consumer knowledge for several reasons. First, because it is less under marketing control, information from direct experience is often more credible. Second, experiencing an event is more involving and interesting than being informed about it in mass media. Third, information acquired from experience is more vivid, and therefore easier to remember than other types of information.[8] Information about attributes that must be experienced through taste, touch, or smell exerts a stronger influence on consumers' future behavior when it comes from experience or product trial than when it is acquired from ads or word of mouth.[9] An ad can state that a product will taste good, but actually eating it is more likely to generate a strong attitude. For these reasons, marketers often stimulate consumers to experience their offerings

Hypothesis testing Comparing prior belief or expectations with new information, such as evidence from experience.

Hypothesis generation Forming expectations about the brand, product, or service.

Exposure to evidence Actually experiencing the brand, product, or service.

Encoding of evidence Processing the information that one experiences.

Integration of evidence Combining new information with stored knowledge.

before making a choice, by means of free product trials, test drives, initial subscriptions at lower rates, and so forth.

This may have unintended boomerang effects. When consumers can directly experience the choice options before actually making the choice ("test driving the various cars"), they may become so attached to them that any choice may be regretted because it means giving up the alternatives.[10] Moreover, the information gained from experiential learning is not always accurate and may, in fact, be biased and erroneous.[11] Fortunately, repeated exposure to ads can often approximate the effect of direct experience, in particular for search attributes such as price or ingredients.[12]

10-2a A MODEL OF LEARNING FROM CONSUMER EXPERIENCE

Consumers can learn from experience by engaging in a process of **hypothesis testing**, much the way scientists test hypotheses. On the basis of past experience or other sources such as word of mouth or advertising, consumers form hypotheses about the attributes of a brand, product or service for purchase, about a consumption experience, or a disposition option and then set out to test it. A hypothesis is a belief or expectation about some future event or state. Such hypotheses are important because they enable consumers to learn from experience. Consumers go through four stages in testing hypotheses for learning: (1) hypothesis generation, (2) exposure to evidence, (3) encoding of evidence, and (4) integration of evidence and prior beliefs (see Exhibit 10.3). The following example illustrates these four stages.

Suppose a consumer sees an ad for a new movie with the actor Steve Carell. He also remembers some of Carell's previous movies, such as *Date Night* and *The Big Short*. Based on all this information, he forms a prediction (**hypothesis generation**) about the likely quality of the new movie ("It must be great"). Next, he seeks out **exposure to evidence** to test this hypothesis by going to see the new movie. While watching it, he can assess whether or not it is in fact great, a step called **encoding the evidence**. After watching the movie, the consumer can **integrate the evidence** with his existing knowledge or beliefs. If he really likes it, confirming the hypothesis, he may have learned that "you can always count on a Steve Carell movie to be great." However, if he does not like it, he may form the new belief that "not all Carell films are great, and I must be careful in the future."

Consumers can form hypotheses in relation to any aspect of consumer behavior: acquisition ("using an app to buy groceries will be useful"), consumption ("listening

---

*Some of this section draws heavily from an article by Stephen J. Hoch and John Deighton, "Managing What Consumers Learn from Experience," *Journal of Marketing*, April 1989, pp. 1–20.

Exhibit 10.3 ▶ A Model of Learning from Experience

Consumers can acquire much information about products and services by actually experiencing them. This entire process is influenced by consumer familiarity, motivation to process, and the ambiguity of the information. It is also influenced by processing biases, specifically the confirmation bias and overconfidence on the part of the consumer.

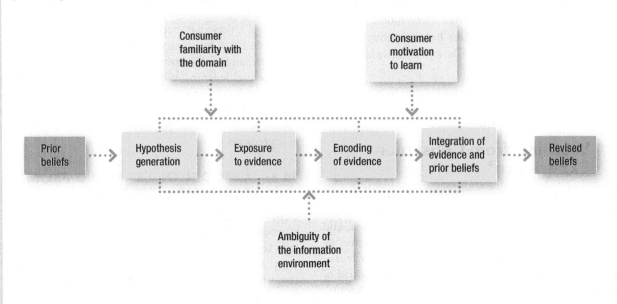

Source: Stephen J. Hoch and John Deighton, "Managing What Consumers Learn from Experience," *Journal of Marketing*, April 1989, pp. 1–20. Reprinted by permission.

to the concert will be fun"), or disposition ("trading in my old car will be easy"). Learning from experience is also important when consumers use an electronic shopping agent or app, or when they react to recommendations from retail sites such as Amazon.com. Using feedback from repeated hypothesis tests, the agent or site learns what the consumer likes and can present more appropriate options.[13]

Consumers' hypothesis testing also influences learning about brands and their personality. Thus, when firms with a "sincere" brand personality suffer a product crisis, they may have much difficulty reconnecting with customers because the fundamental beliefs about the brand may have deteriorated. In contrast, firms with an "exciting" brand personality may re-establish customer relationships more easily after a similar product crisis because consumers are less surprised by nonroutine experiences with such brands (excitement involves variation, positive and negative).[14]

10-2b WHAT AFFECTS LEARNING?

Four factors affect consumers' learning from experience: (1) motivation, (2) prior knowledge or ability, (3) ambiguity of the information environment or lack of opportunity, and (4) processing biases.

Motivation

When consumers are motivated to process information, they will generate a number of hypotheses and seek out information to test them, actively engaging in the process of learning from experience. To help consumers learn more about their offerings, many marketers post video snippets of product and service demonstrations. New York Yoga, for instance, invites consumers to watch a video of a typical yoga class, so they can envision themselves in the experience. Online retailer Net-A-Porter posts videos of models walking in clothing being offered for sale, to show how a garment looks in actual use. Such videos motivate consumers, help them to imagine how the consumption experience will be, and thereby increase the likelihood of purchase.[15] When motivation is low, consumers will rely less on hypothesis testing, which is an effortful cognitive process, and more on classical and operant conditioning to learn (see Chapters 6 and 9). Marketers can facilitate learning both when motivation is high and when it is low, as shown later in this chapter.

Prior Knowledge or Ability

Consumers' prior knowledge or ability affects the extent to which they learn from experience. When knowledge is high, consumers are likely to have well-defined beliefs and expectations and are therefore less likely to generate new hypotheses. In contrast, low-knowledge consumers lack skills to develop hypotheses to guide the learning process.[16] Without guiding hypotheses, consumers have difficulty collecting evidence and learning from it. Thus, moderately knowledgeable consumers are the most likely to generate hypotheses and learn from experience. Of course, experts have an advantage in learning information about new products and services due to their more extensive knowledge base.[17] The amount of prior experience and the breadth (variety) of prior experience also affect consumer learning and individual preferences for novel products.[18]

Ambiguity of the Information Environment or Lack of Opportunity

Some situations do not readily provide the opportunity to learn from experience, even when consumers have well-formed hypotheses. This is particularly true when the consumption experience is ambiguous.[19] There is **ambiguity of information** when it is hard to establish how good the product or service experience actually is, such as in the case of fashion clothing, or when several offerings are very similar in performance. Making the initial choice in a context of ambiguity affects consumers' certainty about the decision and, if the actual experience is uninformative, can lead to persistent preferences for the chosen option's attributes.[20]

> **Ambiguity of information** When there is not enough information from the consumption experience to confirm or disprove one's hypotheses.

Ambiguous consumption information reduces consumers' ability to learn from experience. On the one hand, when consumers have difficulty determining product quality (for such products as fashion clothing or beer), they tend to confirm rather than test their hypotheses with information from advertising or word of mouth. Because consumers cannot easily disprove the information by experiencing the product, they see the product as being consistent with their prior expectations.[21] Thus, for many years consumers believed that Listerine mouthwash prevented colds because the brand's advertising claim could not be disproved by usage. Later, the U.S. Federal Trade Commission required Listerine to run corrective advertising stating that the mouthwash "will not help prevent colds or sore throats or lessen their severity."[22] The marketer in such a situation has an unfair advantage, a situation that explains why deception in advertising is an important topic.

On the other hand, when evidence is unambiguous and the product is clearly good or bad, consumers base their

Exhibit 10.4 ▶ Encouraging Learning to Facilitate Switching

Marketers can encourage consumers to learn about their own brand in order to get them to switch from their current brand.

perceptions on actual experience and learn a great deal. Unambiguous information tends to be better remembered and to have more impact on future decisions.[23] When evidence is ambiguous, evaluations by both experts and novices are strongly influenced by country-of-origin expectations (e.g., knowing that leather handbag was made in France), but when evidence is unambiguous, experts ignore this information and make evaluations based on actual quality.[24]

Processing Biases

Confirmation bias and overconfidence can pose major hurdles to the learning process, particularly when evidence is ambiguous.[25] Specifically, these biases inhibit learning by making consumers avoid both negative and highly diagnostic information. For example, a consumer who believes that all Chinese electronics products are of high quality may ignore contrary evidence and this prevents accurate knowledge of the situation. Experience which unambiguously disconfirms prior beliefs can have a strong and rapid impact on consumer learning.[26]

Marketing Implications

Ambiguous information and processing biases often inhibit consumer learning about products and services. These biases have strategic implications, depending on the offering's market position.[27]

Top-Dog Strategies

A product, service, or brand that is the market leader or has a large market share is called a **top dog**. Limitations on learning are advantageous to top dogs because consumers will simply confirm existing beliefs and expectations and be overconfident, particularly when the motivation to learn is low. When motivation to learn is high, the consumer will try to acquire information that could be disproving and lead to a switch. To avoid this, the top dog can make specific claims that justify consumers' evaluation of the brand. Or the top dog can encourage consumers not to acquire new information, which is called *blocking exposure to evidence*. If top-dog evidence is unambiguous, the consumer simply needs reinforcement of messages telling why this brand is satisfying—called *explaining the experience*—and encouragement to try it. Coca-Cola's slogans over the years, including "Live positively" and "Open happiness," are good examples.

Underdog Strategies

Underdogs (lower-share brands) want to encourage consumer learning because new information may lead consumers to switch to them. First, when consumers are not motivated, underdogs can instigate learning through comparisons of their brand with the market leader, side-by-side displays, or information provided online (see Exhibit 10.4). The underdog needs a strong and distinct advantage if it is to overcome overconfidence and confirmation biases.

Second, underdogs can create expectations and use promotions to provide the actual experience for consumers. If the evidence is ambiguous, consumers' expectations are not likely to be disconfirmed. For example, the Czech beer brand Budweiser Budvar, which competes with Anheuser-Busch InBev's U.S. Budweiser beer in many global markets, promotes its quality ingredients and traditional brewing methods. For its

Top dog A market leader or brand with a large or the largest market share.

Satisfaction The feeling that a purchase decision, consumption experience, or disposition decision meets or exceeds one's expectations.

Dissatisfaction The feeling that a purchase decision, consumption experience, or disposition decision falls short of one's expectations.

Underdog A lower-share brand that is perceived to be doing well in spite of the odds against it.

120th anniversary, Budvar gave away free samples of its beer in Europe and hosted a contest with the grand prize of a VIP trip to its brewery in Ceské Budejovice.[28]

Finally, when consumers' motivation to learn is low and the evidence is unambiguous, facilitating product trial is critical because the evidence from experience will lead to positive learning and possibly to attitude change.

10-3 How Do Consumers Make Satisfaction or Dissatisfaction Judgments?

After consumers have made acquisition, consumption, or disposition decisions, they can evaluate the outcomes of their decisions. If their expectations are confirmed (needs are met) or even exceeded, consumers experience **satisfaction**. Thus, they can feel satisfied with the purchase of a new smartphone, a haircut, a buying experience, a salesperson, or a retail outlet.[29] If their expectations are disconfirmed (needs are not met), consumers experience **dissatisfaction**. Thus, they can feel dissatisfied with a movie, a salesperson, a store, or with having thrown something away. Dissatisfaction is a general negative evaluation, but it can be more specific and intense, as when consumers experience distress, sadness, regret, disgust, or anger.[30]

Feelings of satisfaction and dissatisfaction can concern offerings that consumers are able to evaluate on *utilitarian dimensions*, that is, how well the product or service functions (such as a vacuum cleaner: does it do what it is supposed to do?), as well as on *hedonic dimensions*, that is, how the product makes someone feel (such as a soft drink: does it make the person feel calm or invigorated?).[31] In fact, all aspects of the product or brand experience—its sensory, affective, behavioral, and cognitive appeals—can influence satisfaction or dissatisfaction.[32] When forming satisfaction and dissatisfaction judgments, consumers compare their predictions (beliefs, hypotheses) with the actual performance.[33] Satisfaction varies with consumer involvement, consumer characteristics, and time.[34] High-involvement consumers tend to express higher satisfaction immediately after a purchase, probably due to their more extensive evaluation, but their satisfaction declines over time. Lower-involvement consumers exhibit lower satisfaction at first, but their satisfaction increases with greater usage over time. When consumers make their own choices of hedonic products (such as buying a ticket for next week's concert), they are more satisfied when they delay consumption only a short time after making the decision. If choices are made for them by others, however, consumers' satisfaction will decrease the longer that consumption is delayed.[35]

Exhibit 10.5 ▶ The American Consumer Satisfaction Index (ACSI)

The ACSI measures customer satisfaction performance across a variety of different industries. Here are a few examples.

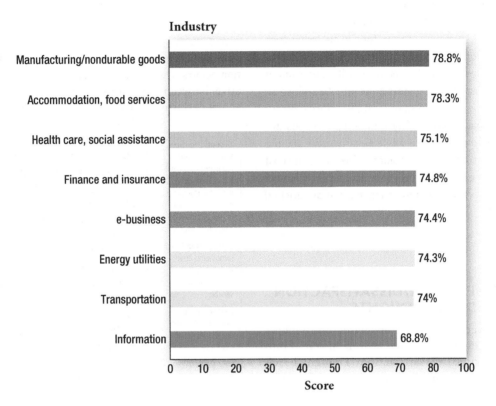

Industry

Manufacturing/nondurable goods	78.8%
Accommodation, food services	78.3%
Health care, social assistance	75.1%
Finance and insurance	74.8%
e-business	74.4%
Energy utilities	74.3%
Transportation	74%
Information	68.8%

0   10   20   30   40   50   60   70   80   100

Score

Source: Data from ACSI, 2015.
Note: Higher scores indicate higher satisfaction.

Marketing Implications

Customer satisfaction is critical to business success because satisfied customers are willing to pay higher prices, particularly if they buy the product repeatedly.[36] They are also more likely to remain customers, be brand loyal, and be committed to the product.[37] Moreover, they will tell others about their experiences, increasing the likelihood that those consumers will then buy the product.[38] Attracting new customers is more expensive than marketing to existing customers, a situation that means that retaining satisfied customers is cost-efficient and generally profitable.[39] When the product category is important to consumers, satisfaction can also lead to more frequent purchasing, especially when it is convenient for the consumer to buy.[40]

When they make purchases, consumers tend to spend more on the brand or with the company that gives them satisfaction in that product category.[41] For example, the founder of Zane's Cycles in Branford, Connecticut, estimates that over a lifetime of purchasing bicycles, parts, and service, his average customer will spend $12,500. Not surprisingly, this store aims to provide superior customer service and encourage repeat purchasing through policies such as free lifetime bicycle tune-ups.[42] In fact, there is strong evidence that customer satisfaction is associated with company profitability. And even though the causality of this relationship may be reversed, because profitable firms may have the financial and other resources to invest in customer satisfaction, it is still the case that improvements in customer satisfaction can pay off in more positive stock recommendations to investors, as well.[43]

For these reasons, many companies actively monitor customer satisfaction. The American Customer Satisfaction Index (ACSI) monitors levels of satisfaction across various product categories. The National Customer

Satisfaction Index (NCSI) does the same for product categories in the United Kingdom. Global marketers should be aware of the cultural, socioeconomic, and political factors that can influence satisfaction.[44]

Marketers also try to understand the roots of dissatisfaction because of the potential for bad outcomes such as negative word-of-mouth communication, complaints, and lower sales and profits. Note that if a department store loses just 167 customers a month, it can lose an estimated $2.4 million in sales (and $280,000 in profit) in just one year.[45] Importantly, it takes up to 12 positive experiences to overcome a single negative one, and the cost of attracting a new customer is five times the cost of keeping an existing one.[46] This emphasizes the power of negative consumption experiences, and dissatisfied customers.

10-3a SATISFACTION/DISSATISFACTION BASED ON THOUGHTS

Just as consumers make decisions based on thoughts and feelings, these thoughts and feelings also feed into their satisfaction or dissatisfaction. Thought-based judgments of satisfaction/dissatisfaction can relate to

Disconfirmation When expectations do not match the actual brand, product or service performance, because performance is either better or worse than expected.

Expectation Belief (hypothesis) about the performance of a brand, product, or service.

Performance The extent to which the product/service does what it is supposed to do and fulfills consumers' needs.

(1) whether consumers' beliefs and expectations about the offering are confirmed or disconfirmed by its actual performance, (2) thoughts about causality and blame, and (3) thoughts about fairness and equity.

Expectations and Performance: The Disconfirmation Paradigm

As diagrammed in Exhibit 10.6, expectation **disconfirmation** occurs when there is a discrepancy, positive or negative, between our prior expectations and the product's actual performance (see the red arrows in the exhibit).[47]

In this case, **expectations** are desired or anticipated product/service outcomes and include "pre-consumption beliefs about overall performance, or . . . the levels or attributes possessed by a product (service)."[48] For example, you might expect a Japanese car to be reliable and fuel efficient, expectations based on advertising, inspection of the product, prior experience with similar offerings, and the experiences of other consumers that are relevant to you.[49]

Performance indicates whether the expected outcomes have been achieved. Performance can either be *objective*—based on the actual

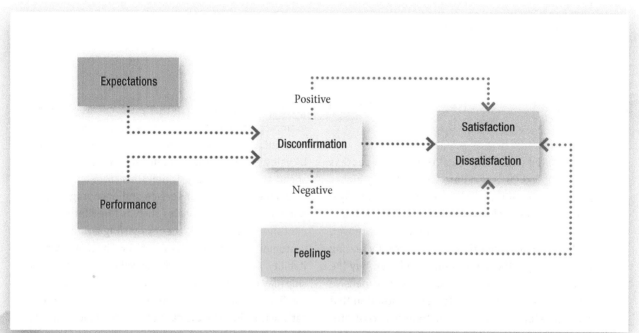

Exhibit 10.6 ▶ The Disconfirmation Paradigm

The disconfirmation paradigm shows how satisfaction or dissatisfaction can occur. Using an example of a new Steve Carell movie, the consumer enters the situation with expectations ("Steve Carell movies are entertaining"). Once the consumer sees the movie, she can evaluate its performance. Positive disconfirmation occurs when the movie is as entertaining or more entertaining than expected, and this leads to satisfaction. Negative disconfirmation occurs when the movie is less entertaining than expected, and this leads to dissatisfaction.

performance, which is fairly constant across consumers—or *subjective*—based on individual feelings, which can vary across consumers. The objective performance of a car describes what its maximum speed and fuel efficiency are, and subjective performance includes how stylish it is and how well it reflects one's personality.

Customers' evaluation of services is susceptible to disconfirmation as well.[50] Customers have expectations related to various elements of service performance and to intangible characteristics of the facilities and the personnel.[51] It is not surprising that consumers who focus on the service provider's obligations (e.g., to respond to their needs) will be more dissatisfied with service failures if they are on friendly terms with the provider. Then, they have higher expectations about what the service provider should deliver, and these are more likely to be negatively disconfirmed. Yet in the same situation, consumers will be less dissatisfied if they focus on their *own* obligations within the relationship.[52] One way that online retailers such as Amazon can manage expectations and avoid dissatisfaction is by providing plenty of information, such as stating the cutoff date for ordering merchandise to be delivered by Christmas, and to provide track-and-trace information so that consumers have knowledge about the exact delivery date, time, and location of their orders.

Satisfaction need not be transaction-specific but can be relation-specific, for instance, when consumers are satisfied with a specific purchase from an online retailer but are dissatisfied about the performance of the retailer in general. These evaluations may change over time, such as when you are dissatisfied today about a statistics course in college but may begin to appreciate it once you are working for an investment banker.[53]

Consumers who have many choices will feel more satisfied when they decide on an option that turns out well, and when they can give themselves credit for making a good decision (but they will be dissatisfied if they choose an option that turns out to be bad because they will blame themselves for making a bad decision).[54] Consumers may experience greater negative disconfirmation and therefore more dissatisfaction when they choose an option from a large assortment.[55] One reason is that then they forgo many alternatives, each of which might have been as good as or better than the one chosen. When consumers choose from a large set of options, performing an act of closure (such as putting unchosen alternatives out of sight) helps discourage unfavorable comparisons between chosen and unchosen options and therefore improves satisfaction.[56] Interestingly, such actual effects of choosing from a large assortment might be reversed before

making the actual choice. Imagining the opportunity to choose from a large assortment can actually lead to the highest satisfaction.[57]

When consumers expect to evaluate an offering, they pay closer attention to negative aspects during consumption and therefore provide less favorable quality and satisfaction evaluations—unless they have low expectations at the outset.[58] Distrust, another consequence of negative disconfirmation, can carry over even to unrelated products or firms.[59] Also, customers who buy at a discount may perceive that they benefit less from the product's consumption than if they had paid full price.[60] Even when price has no bearing on a product's quality, consumers' beliefs about the price–quality relationship will affect their experience of the product's performance.[61] And sometimes, superstition-driven expectations (such as preference for a "lucky" number of items in a package) can play a role in product or service evaluation and disconfirmation.[62]

Exhibit 10.6 shows how performance, expectations, and feelings can affect satisfaction, *independent* of disconfirmation (as reflected by the blue arrows).[63] To fully understand why satisfaction or dissatisfaction occurs, we must account for these dimensions together and separately. How feelings affect satisfaction and dissatisfaction will be explored later in this chapter.

Marketing Implications

Based on the disconfirmation paradigm, better performance is more likely to fulfill expectations and thus to build satisfaction. Expectations created by marketers about product performance can influence satisfaction or dissatisfaction, but in unexpected ways. Raising consumers' expectations of how well the product or service will perform can increase ratings of product performance.[64] Whole Foods Market, the natural foods grocery chain, has cooking coaches on staff to advise shoppers about questions such as how to select dried chili peppers and how to prepare faro. In-store technology provides instant access to additional recipes and cooking tips, helping consumers understand what to expect from the fresh foods they buy at Whole Foods Market. Further, how-to videos on the retailer's YouTube channel and website teach healthy cooking techniques.[65] On the other hand, marketers are setting themselves up for a potential negative disconfirmation and dissatisfaction if customer expectations are too high, and companies make promises they cannot keep.

Providing consumers with a good warranty or guarantee can create positive expectations that will lead to satisfaction (see Exhibit 10.7).[66] Zane's Cycles provides a lifetime service guarantee for every bicycle—covering parts and service—as well as a 30-day test ride period, enabling buyers to determine whether they selected the bike that best fits their needs. The guarantee and test-ride period are both promoted on Zane's Facebook page, its website, and in the store. Even product recalls can open the way to confirmations of customer satisfaction. Zane's educated its employees and had staff ready to answer questions when a well-known bicycle manufacturer announced a recall not long ago. "If you look at it as an opportunity to engage and spend time with your customers that you might not have had, then at least the effort and energy doesn't go to waste," the founder explains.[67]

Causality and Blame: Attribution Theory

Attribution theory describes how individuals think about explanations for or causes of effects or behavior.[68] In a marketing context, when a product or service does not fulfill consumers'

> **Attribution theory** A theory of how individuals find explanations for events.

needs, they will attempt to find an explanation based on three factors:

- *Locus.* Is the problem consumer or marketer related?

- *Controllability.* Is the event under the customer's or marketer's control?

- *Stability.* Is the cause of the event temporary or permanent?

Customers are more likely to be dissatisfied if the cause is perceived to be marketer-related, controllable, and stable. Suppose you find a crack in the windshield of your new car. If you perceive that this is your fault, and an accident (a rock hit the window while driving), you will probably not be dissatisfied with the car manufacturer. On the other hand, suppose you discover that many other consumers have had similar problems over a long period of time, even without rocks hitting their windshields. Here, the cause seems more permanent, company related, and under the company's control. Then you are more likely to be dissatisfied with the car manufacturer.

Attribution theory also applies to services. For instance, consumers were dissatisfied with a travel agent if the problem they had experienced was due to the firm, under the firm's control, and permanent.[69] In a study of passengers delayed at an airport, attributions determined the desire either to complain or to fly the same airline again. If consumers saw the delay as permanent and under the airline's control, they were more likely to complain and less likely to fly the airline again.[70] Consumers who can choose whether to participate in a service are likely to attribute at least part of any negative outcome to their own involvement, whereas they will attribute a good part of any positive outcome to their own participation.[71] Satisfaction with services also depends on whether the consumer holds the company responsible for the outcome and believes the outcome stems from a stable or unstable cause.[72] Finally, consumers are more satisfied when companies exert extra effort to serve them, even when the offerings are not that great.[73]

Exhibit 10.7 ▶ Warranty

Companies can create positive expectations that lead to satisfaction by offering excellent warranties on their products and services, so customers have little to lose if the product or service underperforms.

Source: L.L.Bean Inc.

Marketing Implications

Attribution theory can provide marketers with guidance in how to deal with potential or existing perceptions of consumer dissatisfaction. If the cause of the dissatisfaction actually is marketer-related, under the marketer's control, and permanent, something must be done to correct the problem or provide the consumer with restitution.

Interestingly, when consumers themselves are actually to blame for a post-purchase product failure, they will seek to shift blame and restore self-worth by complaining to the marketer about the product—and despite complaining, these consumers will have negative product evaluations. To counter such negative impact, it helps when marketers first affirm consumers before giving them the opportunity to complain. This diffuses the self-threat and prompts consumers to suggest constructive feedback for product improvements.[74] No wonder L.L. Bean (among other retailers) has a "no questions asked" guarantee, reassuring consumers that no matter who is at fault, a problematic product will be replaced for free, even years after the purchase.[75]

Fairness and Equity: Equity Theory

Equity theory concerns the nature of exchanges between individuals and their perceptions of these exchanges. In marketing, it has been applied to examining the exchange between a buyer and a seller or a more general institution.[76] According to equity theory, consumers form perceptions of their own inputs and outputs into a particular exchange and compare these perceptions with their perceptions of the inputs and outputs of the salesperson, dealer, or company. For example, when buying a car, a consumer's inputs might include information search, decision-making effort, psychological anxiety, and money. The output would be a satisfactory car. Seller inputs might include a quality product, selling effort, and a financing plan; seller output might be a fair profit.

Equity theory also applies to the way consumers perceive exchanges in which they *didn't* participate. For instance, if consumers miss out on a deal involving products that are easily counted (i.e., buy one, get one free), they are more upset than if the deal involves products not easily counted (i.e., a larger size product at a discount).[77]

> **Equity theory** A theory about the fairness of exchanges between individuals, which helps in understanding consumer satisfaction and dissatisfaction.

> **Fairness in the exchange** The perception that the inputs and outputs of people involved in an exchange are equal.

For equity to occur, the buyer must perceive **fairness in the exchange**. Thus, the car buyer might perceive a fair exchange if he or she purchased a desirable car at a fair price. Satisfaction is even higher if consumers perceive that they have gotten a bargain.[78] Consumers will be dissatisfied if they perceive inequity in an exchange—for example, if the salesperson did not pay enough attention to the buyer, given the high cost of the purchase. For equity to occur, the consumer must perceive that the seller is also being dealt with fairly. Nevertheless, fairness perceptions by consumers tend to be self-centered, biased more toward the buyer outcomes and seller inputs, than to the buyer inputs and seller outcomes.[79]

Moreover, consumers judge the equity of the payment exchanged for service usage by asking themselves, "Am I using this service enough, given what I pay for it?" They will perceive the exchange as more equitable when they have high expectations of service usage levels at first or when the service performance exceeds their normative expectations. When they perceive the price/usage exchange to be more equitable, they will be more satisfied.[80] Also, perceptions of equity can shift over time. For instance, as the end of a car's warranty period approaches, owners become increasingly dissatisfied with attributes they believe can be remedied; in turn, these attributes become more highly related to product quality satisfaction.[81]

Equity theory complements the disconfirmation paradigm in that equity theory specifies another way dissatisfaction can occur. The disconfirmation focuses on the consumer's predictions and experiences, and equity theory focuses on the consumer's inputs and outputs versus those of others. Both types of processes can operate at the same time.

 Marketing Implications

As long as consumers perceive that their inputs and outputs are equitable in relation to those of the seller, they will be satisfied. This reaction holds for the offering itself as well as for the interactions with employees when resolving a complaint. In other words, consumers who perceive that they have been treated fairly in the complaint process will be more satisfied, more likely to buy again, and more likely to spread positive word of mouth.[82] If an inequity is perceived ("Others received their money back, but I didn't"), consumers will be dissatisfied. Moreover, when a problem occurs, a company that reacts respectfully will be perceived more favorably by consumers who chose the brand based on value (i.e., price) compared with consumers who feel an emotional connection with the brand. Why? Because consumers who chose the brand based on value tend to view the respectful treatment as above and beyond the expectations of the fairness exchange.[83]

Marketers must work toward providing fair exchanges, even though consumers' perceptions of fairness tend to be biased toward themselves. One area in which marketers can directly affect equity perceptions is the salesperson-customer interaction. Salespeople must make every effort to ensure that their inputs match customer inputs by listening to consumer needs, answering questions, and trying to offer a good deal. At Chow Tai Fook, a Hong Kong-based jewelry chain with 2,100 stores across China and Hong Kong, salespeople serve tea to browsing customers. When asked to bargain on price, they offer discounts in a respectful but responsive way.[84]

Promotions can also increase perceptions of fairness in an exchange. Offering a lower price or a free gift with purchase can make consumers feel that they are getting more out of the exchange. Further, store policies regarding the return of purchased products can play a role in satisfaction, because of the cognitive and physical effort involved in making returns.[85] Finally, some retailers try to reduce post-purchase dissatisfaction and regret by offering low-price guarantees and refunding money upon request to customers who find an even lower price after buying. Communicating that the store does not claim to have the very lowest prices reduces post-purchase regret among information-focused buyers who later find a lower price elsewhere and apply for the store's refund.[86]

10-3b SATISFACTION/DISSATISFACTION BASED ON FEELINGS

Consumers can also experience satisfaction and dissatisfaction on the basis of feelings, specifically (1) experienced emotions (and coping with these emotions) and (2) mispredictions about emotions.

Experienced Emotions and Coping

The positive and negative **post-decision emotions** we experience help to explain satisfaction or dissatisfaction judgments (independent of disconfirmation, as you saw in Exhibit 10.6).[87] If we feel good (or bad) while using a product or service, we are more likely to be satisfied (or dissatisfied), independent of our expectations and evaluations of its performance. Consumers who are happy or

Post-decision emotions Positive or negative emotions experienced while using or disposing of the acquired brands, products, or services.

content are most likely to be satisfied, followed by those who experience pleasant surprise. Most consumers around the world find enjoyment and satisfaction in their buying experiences. One study found that more than 90 percent of durable goods purchases were associated with positive feelings.[88] Positive post-decision emotions are important: actively building strong, positive emotional bonds with customers can enhance both satisfaction and loyalty.[89]

Satisfaction is also a factor when rewarding consumers for loyalty. Consumers who receive preferential treatment (such as unexpected service upgrades at the airport) which they feel they haven't earned will be less satisfied if the upgrade takes place in the presence of others who do not receive the preferential treatment. Then, the feeling of being treated positively, but unfairly in comparison to fellow consumers, harms customer satisfaction. Therefore, marketers who reward consumers in public should take care to communicate how and why rewards are earned to ensure customer satisfaction.[90]

Dissatisfaction is most likely to strike consumers who feel angry or upset, followed by those who experience unpleasant surprise.[91] Feelings expressed by service employees also affect customer satisfaction. When employees appear to be expressing genuinely positive emotions, consumers are more satisfied with the service encounter.[92]

Consumers who are dissatisfied with a purchase, consumption, or disposition decision may need to cope with the feelings of stress that dissatisfaction involves.[93] How they cope depends on whether they feel threatened or challenged by the stress and whether they think that they have the motivation, ability, and opportunity to deal with it. For example, a consumer might cope with a technological product failure by reading the instruction manual (active coping), by calling a friend who knows that technology (instrumental support seeking), or by denying that the failure has occurred (see Exhibit 10.8).

Consumers' satisfaction tends to be tied to specific consumption experiences—we may be satisfied (or not) with the automotive oil change that the garage took care of yesterday. Our satisfaction may be different the next time we use this service, in particular if we expect the service to change.[94] Thus, satisfaction is often transitory and dependent on a specific situation. Sequences of satisfying or dissatisfying experiences eventually boil down to an attitude about a brand, product, or service, which is more lasting an overall evaluation.[95] In addition, consumers' satisfaction tends to be influenced strongly by post-decision emotions during and immediately after the experience, but this influence decreases over time. Conversely, thoughts and beliefs have more influence on satisfaction judgments as time goes by.[96] Of course, a post-decision evaluation can differ from a pre-decision evaluation in that after using the product, a consumer may judge

Active Coping	Expressive Support Seeking	Avoidance
ACTION COPING • I concentrate on ways the problem could be solved • I try to make a plan of action **RATIONAL THINKING** • I analyze the problem before reacting • I try to control my emotions **POSITIVE THINKING** • I try to look on the bright side of things	**EMOTIONAL VENTING** • I take time to express my emotions • I delve into my feelings to understand them **INSTRUMENTAL SUPPORT** • I ask friends with similar experience what they did • I try to get advice from someone about what to do **EMOTIONAL SUPPORT** • I seek out others for comfort • I rely on others to make me feel better	**AVOIDANCE** • I avoid thinking about it • I try to take my mind off of it by doing other things **DENIAL** • I deny that the event has happened • I refuse to believe that the problem has occurred

Source: Adapted from Adam Duhachek, "Coping: A Multidimensional, Hierarchical Framework of Responses to Stressful Consumption Episodes," *Journal of Consumer Research* 32, June 2005, pp. 41–53.

Exhibit 10.8 ▶ Coping with Dissatisfaction Due to Consumption Problems
Consumers may cope with dissatisfaction through active coping, expressive support seeking, or avoidance.

different attributes and cutoff levels than he or she did before.[97] For example, before choosing a new cell phone plan, the monthly rate might be crucial, whereas after choosing it, the data limit and bandwidth may be more important.

Mispredictions About Emotions

While post-decision feelings themselves can affect satisfaction judgments, so too can the difference between these post-decision feelings and the feelings that we predicted we would experience. This relates to a phenomenon known as *affective forecasting* (see Chapter 8). That is, prior to consumption, we form expectations about how we will feel when owning or consuming a brand, product, or service, and we compare this with our actual feelings once this happens. In other words, we tend to be more dissatisfied not only when a product fails to perform as we thought it would (negative performance disconfirmation) but also when a product makes us feel worse than we forecasted that it would (negative affective disconfirmation). This phenomenon may be a fairly common occurrence because people tend to be poor predictors of how decisions, experiences, and outcomes will make them feel.[98] Thus, even when we eagerly anticipate enjoying a new product before the purchase, our satisfaction with its performance can fade as we grow accustomed to the performance over time.[99] Affective forecasting applies to services as well as tangible products. When we predict the outcome of uncertain events (such as who will be voted off a reality TV program), we enjoy those events less than people who make no predictions. Why? Because we are wary of anticipated regret.[100]

 Marketing Implications

Marketers should make sure that customers' feelings after trying, buying, and using their offerings are as positive as possible. For this reason, many banks are marketing value-added services such as financial advice, electronic bill payment, and mobile banking apps that meet the needs of target groups such as Millennials. Bank of America, for example, appeals to Millennials by partnering with Kahn Academy to offer money-management videos that help this target audience plan for repaying student debt and saving for a home.[101]

Some marketers use promotions and special deals to increase consumers' positive post-decision feelings. In fact, research shows that when consumption occurs immediately after payment, discounts make consumption more enjoyable.[102] To increase satisfaction, marketers can run product promotions during specific times when consumers are likely to have more money in their budgets to make purchases. To reduce the potential for negative reactions when money is scarce, marketers can offer special pricing or coupons during specific times when consumers typically have little left in their budgets.[103]

Businesses and nonprofits can build relationships with consumers and contributors by encouraging their involvement and identification with the organization through communications and other activities.[104] Harley-Davidson, for example, works hard to get and keep its customers emotionally involved with the brand. Customers receive invitations to owners-only special events and acquire a sense of community through extensive marketing contacts, both online and offline. Combined with expanded distribution and new products, these marketing activities have helped Harley-Davidson win high customer satisfaction and long-term loyalty.[105]

Finally, knowing that dissatisfied consumers may feel stress, companies can help them to cope by providing easily accessible feedback opportunities and expert advice. For example, the well-trained Genius Bar experts in Apple stores stand ready to listen to customer complaints or inquiries and to offer knowledgeable ideas and solutions (see Exhibit 10.9).[106]

Exhibit 10.9 ▶ Decreasing Customer Dissatisfaction

Some companies help elevate consumer's dissatisfaction after purchase by providing easily accessible mechanisms for feedback or technical support, like the Apple Genius bar.

10-4 Responses to Dissatisfaction

Marketers must understand the nature of consumers' responses to dissatisfaction because a variety of mostly negative consequences for the firm can result. Specifically, dissatisfied consumers can take no action (but remain dissatisfied), discontinue purchasing the brand, product, or service (switch to another option), complain to the company or to a third party and perhaps return the item, respond to any service recovery efforts, or engage in negative word-of-mouth communication.[107] The last three behaviors are of special interest here.

10-4a COMPLAINTS

Surprisingly, the majority of dissatisfied consumers do not complain to the company.[108] Because of this, even a few consumer complaints can already indicate marketing-related problems that need attention, because these few may be the tip of the iceberg. Complaining is more likely when motivation, ability, and opportunity are high. It is also more likely as the level of dissatisfaction or the severity of the problem increases.[109] In equity theory terms, the unfairness of the exchange is higher, and the consumer is more motivated to act.[110] However, the severity of the dissatisfaction alone does not explain complaining behavior. In particular, consumers are less likely to act if they perceive that complaining will take a lot of time and effort, that their chances of benefiting from doing so are low, or that the offering is insignificant.[111]

When consumers do complain, they can voice their dissatisfaction to the manufacturer or service provider, the retailer, regulatory agencies, the media, or to peers through websites such as yelp.com, tripadvisor.com, and social media sites. Customers can also use apps such as GripeO to get their complaints submitted to businesses for response.[112] Such apps and review websites reduce the costs of filing complaints and this increases the numbers of dissatisfied customers who voice their dissatisfaction.[113] Sometimes consumers seek formal redress from governmental agencies or through legal means, such as a class action lawsuit. Thus, marketers increasingly focus on when complaints are likely to occur, which consumers complain, and why.[114]

Attribution theory, which was introduced earlier in this chapter, helps to explain when dissatisfied consumers are more likely to complain. Dissatisfied consumers are more likely to complain when the perceived cause of their dissatisfaction is (1) marketer-related ("they are to blame"), (2) controllable ("they could have prevented it"), and (3) stable ("they always do this").[115] If dissatisfaction is so strong that complainers want "revenge" against the company, they will even resort to a suboptimal alternative, such as switching to a more costly competing product.[116]

You might expect that consumers who are aggressive and self-confident would be more likely to complain than those who are not[117] or that consumers with more experience or knowledge about how to complain might be more likely to do so than their less savvy counterparts. Neither idea has been strongly supported by evidence, although findings suggest experience may influence the likelihood of consumer complaints. Consumers are more likely to complain when they have the time and easy access to formal channels of communication to do so.

Research suggests that there are four types of complainers.[118] *Passives* are the least likely to complain. *Voicers* are likely to complain directly to the retailer or service provider. *Irates* are angry consumers who are most likely to engage in negative word of mouth, stop buying patronage, and complain to the provider but not to a third party such as the media or government. *Activists* engage heavily in all types of complaining, including to a third party. Activists can now reach thousands of people by posting negative comments on blogs, on websites, or on social media such as Twitter.

Although there is no one best way to handle complaints, customer characteristics can provide insights to guide marketers in developing the most appropriate response.[119] In particular, companies should pay close attention to four customer characteristics when preparing complaint-resolution policies and practices:

- *Customer's perceptions of the problem.* How severe does the problem seem to be? Is the company seen as being responsible for the problem? How important is the product to the customer? It is easy for a company to make mistakes here because what may seem to be a minor issue to a company may be a major issue to the consumer.

- *Customer–company relationship.* How often does the customer buy from the company? How long has the customer been buying from the company?

- *Customer psychographics.* Does the customer have a propensity to complain? Consumers are more likely to complain when they are experts or are self-confident and aggressive. How much appreciation of quality does the customer exhibit?

- *Personal characteristics.* What is the age of the customer? What is the gender of the customer?

In general, consumers are more concerned with the fairness of a company's resolution to a complaint—the redress—than with the fairness of the procedure for handling complaints or the fairness of the interactions with the company's representatives.[120] Companies that respond quickly and offer solutions that complainers view as fair (such as a refund) are more likely to earn positive word of mouth and win repeat business.

Marketing Implications

Although a large percentage of consumers do not complain, it is still in the marketer's best interests to be responsive when any consumers do. Speedy response is important: 57 percent of the consumers in one survey said that how quickly a website responds to e-mail influences their decision to buy from that site in the future.[121] In another survey, 42 percent of consumers complaining in social media said they expect a 60-minute response time.[122] Clearly, consumers will be more satisfied and are more likely to buy again if they get a speedy response, especially if it involves getting money back or a fair exchange or refund policy. Bharti Airtel, India's largest cell phone firm, recognizes the importance of responding quickly and heading off negative word of mouth—especially among users of social media or websites. "Online, these situations are fraught with risk," says an Airtel manager. "Unlike call centers, conversation online is one-to-many and a bad response to one can spread like wildfire."[123]

At the same time, dissatisfied consumers who have been treated fairly can become even more loyal in the future, leading to positive word of mouth. Nissan, for instance, moves very quickly to answer complaints that appear on Facebook and other places online. In the interest of transparency, the automaker never takes down negative comments from its Facebook page, which has 14 million fans. Nor does it request that customers post compliments after Nissan has fixed the problem. "But when they decide on their own to do that, that's a great message for those . . . [Facebook] fans to see," a Nissan marketer observes.[124]

However, if consumers experience more than one problem with a company, their satisfaction and repurchase intent will drop, even if the problems are quickly resolved. This reflects the importance of the stability dimension of causal attributions: one resolved problem is excusable, but two are more difficult to ignore. In fact, consumers tend to rate the second problem as even more severe than the first and are more likely to see a pattern in which the company is to blame.[125] Thus, not only do companies need an efficient and responsive mechanism for handling problems, but also must make changes to avoid similar lapses in the future. For instance, when the Massachusetts-based supermarket chain Big Y studied the slow progress of customers through its self-checkout lanes, it learned that delays were caused by issues such as customer confusion over what to do with coupons. Finding that its customers were more satisfied with full-service checkouts, Big Y removed its self-checkouts. CVS has also removed self-checkouts from some of its drug stores as it continues to streamline the checkout process.[126]

Positive disconfirmation of warranty and service expectations—a better-than-expected response—can result in satisfaction with the complaint resolution.[127] Sometimes a company may want to encourage complaints because information about these can help to improve product and service quality and also because dissatisfied consumers who do not complain are more likely to stop buying and switch to a competitor.[128] But when companies are too responsive to complaints—that is, too eager to please—some customers may be more likely to complain, even when a complaint is not justified, because they perceive a greater likelihood of compensation.[129] Still, by encouraging justified complaints and by actively managing customer problems, the company can attract new customers and retain current, valued consumers.

10-4b RESPONDING TO SERVICE RECOVERY

If customers are dissatisfied, marketers need to find ways of making up for this dissatisfaction to win back the customers' business. How consumers will respond to service recovery efforts will depend on their expectations.[130] When consumers expect to maintain a good relationship despite a mishap, the business should sincerely apologize and promise to prevent such mishaps in the future, and deliver on the promise. When consumers expect to respond aggressively and to control the situation, the business should take their complaints seriously, give them choices, and help them feel in control. When consumers expect a rational response based on costs and benefits, the business should offer a discount or some other benefit to restore some level of satisfaction. In general, the frequency, timing, proximity, and sequence of service failures, recoveries, and positive experiences affect customers' perceptions of service quality.[131]

Marketing Implications

Research indicates that consumers prefer service recovery efforts that correspond to the type of failure experienced.[132] In the case of inattentive service, for instance, restoring good service and quickly apologizing can reduce dissatisfaction and help restore satisfaction. When dissatisfied consumers perceive that the cause of the service problem is marketer related, under the firm's control and permanent when in fact it is not, marketers need to correct these misperceptions. Providing consumers with logical explanations for service failure, especially if it was not the company's fault, or providing some form of compensation such as a gift or refund can often reduce consumers' feelings of dissatisfaction.[133]

10-4c RESPONDING BY NEGATIVE WORD OF MOUTH

When consumers are dissatisfied with a product or service, they are often motivated to tell others in order to relieve their frustration and to convince others not to purchase the product or to do business with the company. **Negative word-of-mouth communication** is more likely to occur when consumers perceive that the company is at fault, the problem is severe, and when they are unhappy with the company's responsiveness.[134] Word of mouth between consumers tends to have a large impact on subsequent purchase decisions because it is very vivid (and therefore easily remembered) and it is credible.[135] Word-of-mouth communication that focuses on reasons why the consumers likes or dislikes owning or using an offering rather than why the consumer bought it is particularly persuasive for hedonic products (such as novels or movies).[136]

> **Negative word-of-mouth communication**
> The act of consumers sharing negative information about a brand, product, or service with other consumers.

Negative word of mouth can go global very quickly as consumers air gripes on blogs, social media sites, and specialized websites such as yelp.com—even in cases where the information may be unfair, nasty, or inappropriate. In one study, 59 percent of the consumers surveyed said they regularly use social media to air complaints about negative experiences with products or businesses. The same study found that 74 percent of participants were influenced in their buying decisions by the comments they found about companies on social media and other online sources.[137] Understanding the power of negative comments on social media, computer maker Dell actively monitors social media, analyzes the comments it finds, and responds quickly when issues arise.[138] Such monitoring and responding to social media is an increasingly common, core marketing activity of firms.[139]

Marketing Implications

Marketers need to be responsive to negative word of mouth, make an effort to identify the reason for or source of the difficulty, and take steps to rectify or eliminate the problem with restitution or communications. Consider what happened when the department store JCPenney began promoting a girls' T-shirt bearing the slogan "I'm too pretty to do my homework so my brother has to do it for me." Controversy quickly spread across social media as consumers complained that the shirt was sexist. Within 24 hours, JCPenney withdrew the shirt and issued this public apology: "We agree that the 'Too Pretty' T-shirt does not deliver an appropriate message, and we have immediately discontinued its sale. We would like to apologize to our customers." Because the retailer moved quickly to rectify the situation and made a sincere apology, it showed that its customers' concerns are taken seriously.[140]

When consumers post negative reviews or comments on review sites or social media, some companies post their own comments to show how responsive they are to customer complaints. The owner of a lawn care company in Garland, Texas, explains that consumers appreciate seeing both sides of the conversation: "It's not unusual for me to get a call from somebody saying 'Hey, I read all of your reviews, including the bad ones, and I was impressed by the way you responded to them. You were respectful and gave your side of the story.'"[141]

10-5 Is Customer Satisfaction Enough?

When consumers are not strongly satisfied, they are more prone to defect by switching to a competitor.[142] But even strong customer satisfaction may often not be enough to keep customers loyal. Earlier, 65 to 85 percent of customers who defected to competitors' brands said that they had been either satisfied or very satisfied with the product or service they left.[143] Put differently, the correlation between satisfaction and repurchase is not always very high.[144] Thus, customers may need to be "extremely satisfied" to stay with a brand or company.[145] And it helps when the

brand, product, or service is part of a social network that the company is able to maintain.[146] As mentioned earlier, Harley-Davidson actively cultivates a community feeling among its customers, which enhances customer satisfaction and long-term loyalty.

A related issue is the relationship between customer satisfaction and market share (often an important element in marketing strategy). Customer satisfaction generally does not seem to predict a company's future market share very well. In fact, market share turns out to be a strong *negative* predictor of a company's future customer satisfaction, possibly because consumers prefer many choices in the marketplace or because the offerings of high-market-share firms need to appeal to broad segments and thus cannot excel.[147] One implication is that customer satisfaction and market share may be different objectives for companies to strive for, because attaining one of the objectives does not necessarily imply attaining the other.

10-5a CUSTOMER RETENTION

Customer retention The practice of retaining customers by building long-term relationships with them.

Marketers should strive for **customer retention**, the practice of working to satisfy customers with the intention of developing long-term relationships with them. A customer-retention strategy attempts to build customer commitment and loyalty by continually paying close attention to all aspects of customer interaction, especially after-sales service. Customer loyalty programs can, over the long term, strengthen relationships with customers and increase purchasing.[148] Specifically, profits can be increased through repeat sales, reduced costs, and referrals.[149] Customer relationship management systems can help companies learn more about their customers, information that, in turn, helps marketers better serve, satisfy, and retain customers.[150]

10-5b PRODUCT-HARM CRISES

Businesses have to work especially hard to reassure and retain customers after a crisis in which a product or service has harmed people. Honda, for example, faced such a crisis when safety air bags made by a supplier, Takata, were implicated in fatalities that occurred when air-bag inflators ruptured during a crash. In response, Honda and other automakers that have installed Takata's air bags recalled millions of vehicles to replace the inflators. Honda also switched air-bag suppliers for new Honda and Acura models under development.[151]

When a product-harm crisis occurs, consumers will be understandably uncertain about the product's quality, which will affect their buying and consumption behavior. They will look for cues to product quality in usage experience and also in communications (such as media coverage) about the crisis itself.[152] When consumers have positive beliefs about a brand, they are more likely to consider contextual information (such as the industry frequency of crises) in attributing the cause of the current crisis. Consumers won't let a particular brand off the hook unless there are clear and compelling alternative explanations for what caused the situation. However, consumers may have a less negative reaction when marketers emphasize the rarity of such a crisis.[153] This is once more consistent with the "stability" dimension of causal attributions.

Marketing Implications

Given the cost of acquiring new customers and the potential profit in repeat purchasing, companies should take steps such as the following to retain their customers:[154]

▶ *Care about customers.* Two-thirds of consumers defect because they believe that the company does not care about them. Thus, demonstrating a little caring can go a long way. For instance, Cole Hardware, a family-owned retail chain in San Francisco, offers a lot of service extras. Seniors who need a lift to the store can call for a ride. The store will lend customers a digital camera to photograph a project for which they need help in selecting tools or materials. Cole offers discounts to students, seniors, and other special groups. It also hosts evening events with wine and coupons, and provides space for recycling. "We try really hard to be a community center," explains one of the owners. "It's not just a place to buy nuts and bolts."[155]

▶ *Remember customers between sales.* Companies can contact consumers to make sure that they are not having any problems with the offering or to acknowledge special occasions such as birthdays. Marketers who do most or all of their business online often communicate between transactions through e-mail newsletters and requests for feedback about purchased products and services. Crutchfield, for example, a major catalog and Web retailer of electronics products, does all this and more for its customers. It also alerts customers to its ever-expanding list of online videos that show how to choose, install, and use many of the items sold by the company. And customers are invited to e-mail their comments to owner Bill Crutchfield directly from the home page.[156]

▶ *Build trusting relationships.* Provide consumers with expertise and high-quality offerings that meet their needs, now and into the future. For example, USAA Federal Savings Bank trains its employees to discuss customers' needs more broadly and suggest meaningful long-term alternatives. Even if a particular product is under consideration, employees may recommend that a customer "not buy that product, if that is the right thing to do for the member in that situation," notes a senior USAA manager. This is one reason for USAA's 98 percent customer retention rate.[157]

▶ *Monitor the service-delivery process.* Companies should monitor customer service and make every effort to respond quickly and with care when an offering requires service or repairs. Many service organizations use *mystery shoppers*, consumers or researchers who pose as customers to test the quality of service at each location. For instance, the Montreal taxi bureau recently asked 150 mystery shoppers to report back on the quality of customer service they experienced riding in some of the city's 11,000 taxis.[158] Online stores commonly send e-mail links to satisfaction surveys soon after delivery of the ordered products.

▶ *Provide extra effort.* Companies that put special effort into satisfying customers are more likely to build lasting relationships than companies that do the minimum. Ocado, for example, an online grocery shopping service operating in the United Kingdom, adds extra convenience by allowing customers to choose a one-hour window for their purchases to be delivered. "It would be cheaper for us to offer a two-hour slot, but it's better for the customer that we can offer them one," an Ocado executive explains. Ocado empowers its drivers to resolve customer complaints on the spot, another plus that helps keep its time-strapped customers loyal despite increasing competition.[159]

10-6 Disposition

At the most basic level, *disposition* or disposal is the getting rid of meaningless or used-up items or what is left of them (e.g., packaging). Yet disposition is of course a much richer and more detailed process.[160] We tend to think of possessions as physical things, but they can be defined much more broadly as anything that reflects an extension of the self, including even one's body and body parts, other persons, pets, places, services, time periods, and events. For example, you could end a relationship, give a friend an idea, donate an organ or money, abandon an unhealthy lifestyle, use up all your leisure time, or discontinue your cable TV service. Thus, the study of disposition relates to all of these types of possessions.

Many options are available when a consumer decides that a possession is no longer of immediate use or that others have a better use for it, as outlined in Exhibit 10.10.[161] Note that disposition can be *temporary* (loaning or renting the item) or *involuntary* (losing or destroying

the item).[162] Here we will focus on permanent, voluntary disposition.

Consumers can have logical and reasonable motives behind their disposition actions.[163] For example, people sell things to earn an economic return and come out ahead. In contrast, they may choose to donate something without getting a tax deduction, or they may pass an item along out of a desire to help someone as well as a desire

	VOLUNTARY DISPOSITION OF POSSESSIONS		
FORM	**FOCUS**		
	Personal: The giver is the primary beneficiary	**Interpersonal:** The recipient is the primary beneficiary	**Societal:** A group, collective or society at large is the primary beneficiary
Give away a possession	Give away or give up used or new possessions to feel good about giving (up) or to expect a later return favor.	Give away used clothes, bikes, furniture, equipment or donate a body organ to a specific person who needs it (more than you do)	Give surplus food, clothes and so forth to church, a charitable organization or donate it for a fund raiser with a good cause. Donate a vintage Madonna T-shirt to the local museum
Trade possession for something else.	Trade an unused guitar for desired electronic equipment.	Exchange vegetable and flower seeds with friends who are thrilled with yours	Exchange used possessions for a raffle ticket in a charity lottery
Sell possessions for money	Sell one's artwork, woodwork, the jam and juices from one's garden for money	Sell one's possessions to buy a gift for a friend	Sell one's possessions to donate the money to a good cause
Recycle possessions for another use	Make a quilt of scraps of cloth for personal use; Make compost from vegetable waste for your own garden Make a swing with a piece of rope and a used car tire.	Recycle newspapers, glass bottles, aluminum cans, batteries to support a specific person. Recycle clothing for a friend who makes new dolls out of them.	Recycle newspapers, glass bottles, aluminum cans, batteries to help society
Discard possessions in a socially acceptable manner.	Use garbage bins at your home.	Use garbage bins at a friend's place. Help a friend bring large possessions to the local garbage dump	Use litter bins on the streets, in parks and in campgrounds. Bring large items to the local garbage dump.
Discard possessions in a socially unacceptable manner.	Litter garbage in public places because it is easy; Abandon an old car on the roadside just to get rid of it.	Abandon a pet on someone's doorstep, throw garbage in another person's garden. Leave old clothes behind in someone's apartment.	Litter garbage in public places because "everybody does it"

Note – Obviously when discarding possessions in a socially unacceptable way (category 6), and the focus is interpersonal or societal there are costs rather than benefits to others and/or to society.

Exhibit 10.10 ▶ Disposition Options
Disposition often means throwing things away; however, there are other ways of disposing of possessions (e.g., give away, trade, recycle). In addition, disposition can have a personal focus (you are the primary beneficiary), an interpersonal focus (specific others are the primary beneficiaries), or a societal focus (certain groups, collectives, or society at large gains).

not to let the product go to waste. Situational and product-related factors can also affect disposition options.[164] For example, when consumers have limited time or storage space, they may be more likely to dispose of a possession by throwing it away, giving it away, or abandoning it. Consumers disposing of a possession of high value are likely to sell it or to give it to someone special rather than to throw it away. In general, the frequency of different disposition behaviors varies by product category.

There are also various ways that consumers can dispose of unwanted gifts.[165] They can be laterally recycled (swapped, sold, or passed on to someone else), destroyed, or returned. Destruction is a way of getting revenge against the giver but is usually more of a fantasy than a real action. Retailers need to be aware that returning a gift to a store can be a negative emotional experience for consumers. Disposition can involve more than one individual, as when consumers give old clothes to someone, sell a car, or participate in a neighborhood cleanup, or it can consist of activities of a collective or societal nature, such as recycling waste water.[166]

10-6a DISPOSING OF MEANINGFUL OBJECTS

Although disposal often means simply getting rid of unwanted, meaningless, or used-up possessions, the process is more involved for certain significant items. Possessions can sometimes be important reflections of the self that are infused with significant symbolic meaning.[167] They define who we are, and they catalog our personal history.[168] In these situations, disposition involves two processes: physical detachment and emotional detachment.

We most often think of disposition in terms of **physical detachment**, for example, when an item is physically transferred to another person or location. However, **emotional detachment** is a more detailed, lengthy, and sometimes painful process. Often, consumers remain emotionally attached to possessions long after they have become physically detached. For example, it may take a person years to come to grips with selling a valued house or car. Giving up a baby or pet for adoption is an example of difficult emotional detachment that sometimes results in grief and mourning. In fact, some pack rats and hoarders have a difficult time disposing of even minimally valued possessions—as evidenced by overflowing shelves, basements, closets, and garages. Even when an item can be traded in for a discount on a new replacement, emotional attachment enhances the value consumers perceive in the old item, complicating the disposition and purchase decision.[169] Research based on mental accounting shows that consumers who trade a product in place more weight on receiving a favorable trade-in value than on paying the lowest price for the new item.[170]

> **Physical detachment** Physically disposing of an item.
>
> **Emotional detachment** Emotionally disposing of a possession.

The disposition process can be particularly important during periods of role transition, such as puberty, graduation, and marriage.[171] In these instances, consumers acquire possessions that are symbols of new roles and dispose of possessions that are symbols of old roles. Upon getting married, for example, many people dispose of items that signify old relationships, such as pictures, jewelry, and gifts. The disposition of shared possessions is a critical process during divorce. Two types of such disposition have been identified: *disposition to break free*, in which the goal is to free oneself from the former relationship, and *disposition to hold on*, in which the intent is to cling to possessions with the hope that the relationship can be repaired.[172] Consumers also specify how their possessions will be distributed upon their death. This can include giving away valued items to important family members, other individuals, and organizations such as charities and schools as well as distributing monetary wealth through a will.

 Marketing Implications

Marketers need to understand disposition for several reasons. First, disposition decisions often influence later acquisition decisions. Thus, someone who must buy a new refrigerator because the old one stopped working may decide that the old one did not last long enough and may eliminate this brand from future consideration. By understanding why consumers dispose of older brands, particularly when a problem has occurred, marketers may be able to improve their offerings for the future.

Second, marketers have become interested in the way that consumers trade, sell, or give away items for secondhand purchases through used-merchandise retail outlets and websites, flea markets, garage sales, and classified ads in newspapers and online (see Exhibit 10.11). Flea markets are popular, not only because they are a different way of disposing of and acquiring products but also because of the hedonistic experience they provide.[173] Consumers enjoy searching and bargaining for items, the festive atmosphere— almost like a medieval fair—and the social opportunities. This enjoyment is also true of consumers who use sites such as eBay, Facebook, craigslist, and Alibaba to search for and buy goods. Online trading, selling, and auctioning present important new business opportunities across the globe, both in setting up and managing such sites and markets as well as in making use of them. There are 2,000 reported eBay millionaires in the UK alone.[174]

Third, product disposition behaviors can sometimes have a major impact on society in general. For example, if product life can be extended by getting consumers to trade or resell items, waste and resource depletion could be reduced. Fourth, by examining broad disposition patterns, marketers can gain important insights. For example, one study examined household garbage to identify group differences in food consumption.[175] It turns out that the region of the country accounted most strongly for differences in consumption patterns, followed by cultural status. For instance, lobster is especially popular in New England—so much so that some McDonald's outlets in Maine, New Hampshire, Massachusetts, Rhode Island, and Connecticut sell lobster rolls in season.[176]

Fourth, the disposition of products and services, as well as other parts of the extended self (money, time, and even body parts), leads to what has been called "hybrid economies." In such hybrid economies, market-based exchange where sales and profit motives are more important and non-market based exchange without such motives are intertwined. Hybrid economies emerge when consumers collaborate with producers and among themselves to create value, such as in Internet-based collaborative networks like Couchsurfing (www.couchsurfing.com) or Etsy (www.etsy.com).[177] In this way, new market and non-market hybrids of disposition and acquisition provide new opportunities and challenges for marketers to explore.

Exhibit 10.11 ▶ The Disposition Process

Consumers can dispose of unwanted items in a variety of ways, such as through online auctions, yard sales, or flea markets.

Blue Tulip/Alamy Stock Photo

10-6b RECYCLING

Because of concerns about conserving natural resources, studying disposition behaviors can provide valuable insights for the development of recycling programs (see Exhibit 10.12). In light of this fact, a number of researchers have been interested in examining factors that relate to recycling.[178] For instance, studies show that attitudes toward recycling influence waste recycling and recycling shopping behaviors.[179] More consumers are participating in recycling than ever before, in part because they are more informed about the issues and in part because behaving in an eco-friendly way gives them a good feeling.[180] The most useful variables in understanding consumer recycling are motivation, ability, and opportunity to recycle.

Motivation to Recycle

Consumers are more likely to recycle when they perceive that the benefits outweigh the costs, including money, time, and effort.[181] Immediate benefits or goals include avoiding filling up landfills, reducing waste, reusing materials, and saving the environment. Higher-order goals are to promote health and avoid sickness, achieve life-sustaining ends, and provide for future generations.[182] These benefits are likely to vary across segments. For example, focusing on environmental effects may have little meaning in neighborhoods where violence is a major problem.[183] Also, consumers who perceive that their efforts will have an impact are more motivated to recycle than consumers who do not.[184] Having a clean, convenient place to bring recyclable materials improves consumer motivation as well. Note that when products change size or form during consumption, consumers perceive them to be less useful and are more likely to dispose of them rather than recycling.[185]

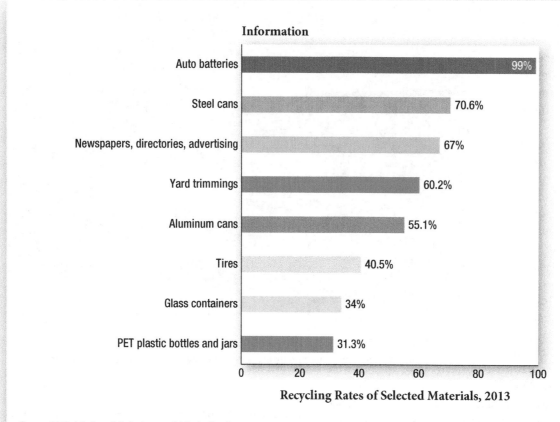

Information

Recycling Rates of Selected Materials, 2013

- Auto batteries: 99%
- Steel cans: 70.6%
- Newspapers, directories, advertising: 67%
- Yard trimmings: 60.2%
- Aluminum cans: 55.1%
- Tires: 40.5%
- Glass containers: 34%
- PET plastic bottles and jars: 31.3%

Source: 2013 data from U.S. Environmental Protection Agency, www.epa.gov

Exhibit 10.12 ▶ What Do U.S. Consumers Recycle?
Car batteries are by far the most recycled products in the United States.

Ability to Recycle

Consumers who know how to recycle are more likely to do so than those who do not.[186] One study of Dutch consumers found that a lack of knowledge led to incorrect disposal and therefore less recycling.[187] Consumers must also possess general knowledge about the positive environmental effects of recycling and must remember to recycle as part of their daily routine, such that it becomes a habit.

Opportunity to Recycle

If separating, storing, and removing recyclable materials is difficult or inconvenient, consumers will usually avoid doing so. In addition, consumers must break old waste disposal habits and develop new recycling behaviors. Providing easy-to-use containers also helps consumers in this regard (see Exhibit 10.13). Also, consumers who buy products such as soft drinks for consumption on the go have fewer opportunities to recycle the empty bottles and cans.[188] Ironically, the opportunity to recycle might actually cause consumers to use more of a given product. One study found that consumers' use of hand towels in restrooms increased when the recycling bin carried a "recycle" label, compared with towel usage when the bin had no "recycle" label.[189]

 Marketing Implications

Marketers can facilitate recycling by increasing consumers' MAO to recycle. Special incentives such as contests can increase motivation. Not long ago, the American Chemistry Council publicized a sweepstakes to increase awareness about the wide range of plastics that can be recycled and to encourage consumer participation, offering a tablet computer as the grand prize.[190] Communications that focus on the negative consequences of not recycling and that are conveyed in person are especially effective in increasing motivation.[191] The only drawback is that these techniques must be reintroduced periodically because their effects are usually temporary.

Marketers can increase consumers' ability to recycle by teaching them how to recycle through personally relevant and easy-to-remember communications from

Exhibit 10.13 ▶ Recycling
Providing color-coded recycling containers makes consumers more willing to recycle since it is easy and convenient.

community leaders, flyers, or public service announcements in traditional and social media. Also, offering tags to place on the refrigerator door can remind consumers to recycle.[192] Offering easily recycled products is another way to increase the opportunity to recycle.

Providing separate containers so that recyclable items can easily be put out and collected along with the trash can increase the opportunity to recycle. Portland, Oregon, for example, is one of a growing number of U.S. cities putting bottle, can, and paper recycling containers in public areas. Retailers often set up recycling centers for bottles and cans purchased at their stores, as well as for unwanted plastic bags. For instance, the U.K. grocery chain Tesco offers frequent-buyer points, cash, and charitable donations to encourage recycling of printer ink cartridges, batteries, and other materials at its recycling centers. Colleges and universities are also helping to motivate recycling behavior by providing convenient bins for used batteries and other recyclable items.

Finally, making products and packaging as environmentally friendly as possible— and promoting the benefits of doing so—can help marketers attract consumers who like the convenience of *not* having to recycle. Heinz, PepsiCo, and other companies are using bottles that decompose more quickly than traditional plastic containers, another step toward using packaging that need not be recycled.[193] Trash can also be the raw material of new products. TerraCycle, for example, specializes in creating and marketing products from used juice pouches, cigarette butts, and other products that have been discarded. The company's annual revenues have grown beyond $20 million as it has diverted more than two billion discarded wrappers and butts from landfills by turning them into products for sale.[194]

Summary:

Consumers sometimes develop post-decision disso-nance—a feeling of discomfort regarding a purchasing decision after it has been made. On occasion, they may feel regret when they perceive an unfavorable comparison between the performance of the chosen option and the performance of the unchosen options. These feelings of regret can directly influence the consumer's intention to buy the same product in the future. Consumers can learn from experience through hypothesis testing, in which they try to confirm or disprove expectations by actually engaging in acquisition, consumption, or disposition of a product. This process is influenced by motivation, prior knowledge or ability, ambiguity of information or lack of opportunity, and two types of biases: the confirmation bias and overconfidence.

Satisfaction is both a subjective feeling and an objec-tive evaluation that a decision has fulfilled a need or goal. Dissatisfaction occurs when consumers have neg-ative feelings and believe that their goals or needs have not been fulfilled. Thought-based judgments of satisfac-tion/dissatisfaction can relate to (1) whether consumers' thoughts and expectations are confirmed or disconfirmed by product performance (the disconfirmation paradigm), (2) thoughts about causality and blame (attribution the-ory), and (3) thoughts about fairness and equity (equity theory). Consumers also judge satisfaction and dissatis-faction on the basis of feelings and emotions.

Consumers can respond to dissatisfaction by doing nothing, not buying the product again, complaining, reacting to service recovery, and engaging in negative word of mouth. Marketers also need to consider whether customer satisfaction is enough, given the importance of customer retention and the potential threat of prod-uct-harm crises. Finally, consumers can dispose of products in various ways, actions that have important implications for marketing strategy and for an under-standing of consumer behavior. Recycling, one form of disposition, depends on consumers' motivation, ability, and opportunity to act.

Questions for Review and Discussion

1. **How does post-decision dissonance differ from post-decision regret, and what effect do these have on consumers?**

2. **Describe how consumers acquire information by learn-ing from their experiences with brands, products, and services.**

3. **How do expectations and performance contribute to disconfirmation?**

4. **Describe** *attribution theory* **and** *equity theory***, and explain how they relate to dissatisfaction.**

5. **What is the role of post-decision emotions in influenc-ing satisfaction and dissatisfaction?**

6. **Why is complaining important to marketers, and how should complaints be handled?**

7. **What influence can experienced emotions and mispre-dictions about emotions have on consumer satisfac-tion or dissatisfaction?**

8. **What is customer retention and what are its marketing implications?**

9. **In what eight ways can consumers dispose of something?**

10. **Why is it important for marketers to consider both physical and emotional detachment aspects of con-sumer disposition?**

Endnotes

1   Laura Laurenzetti, "Delta Will Respond to Your Thanksgiv-ing Travel Mishaps Via Twitter," *Fortune*, November 25, 2015, www.fortune.com.

2   For a review, see William H. Cummings and M. Venkatesan, "Cognitive Dissonance and Consumer Behavior: A Review of the Evidence," *Journal of Marketing Research*, August 1976, pp. 303–308; also see Dieter Frey and Marita Rosch, "Infor-mation Seeking After Decisions: The Roles of Novelty of Information and Decision Reversibility," *Personality and Social Psychology Bulletin*, March 1984, pp. 91–98.

3   Michael Tsiors and Vikas Mittal, "Regret: A Model of Its Antecedents and Consequences in Consumer Decision Making," *Journal of Consumer Research* 26, March 2000, pp. 401–417.

4   Lisa J. Abendroth and Kristin Diehl, "Now or Never: Effects of Limited Purchase Opportunities on Patterns of Regret over Time," *Journal of Consumer Research* 33, no. 3, 2006, pp. 342–351.

5   Ran Kivetz and Anat Keinan, "Repenting Hyperopia: An Anal-ysis of Self-Control Regrets," *Journal of Consumer Research* 33,

no. 2, 2006, pp. 273–282; and Rik Pieters and Marcel Zeelenberg, "A Theory of Regret Regulation 1.0," *Journal of Consumer Psychology* 17, no. 1, 2007, pp. 3–18.

6   Pieters and Zeelenberg, "A Theory of Regret Regulation 1.0"; J. Jeffrey Inman, "Regret Regulation: Disentangling Self-Reproach from Learning," *Journal of Consumer Psychology* 17, no. 1, 2007, pp. 19–24.

7   Stephen J. Hoch and John Deighton, "Managing What Consumers Learn from Experience," *Journal of Marketing*, April 1989, pp. 1–20.

8   Allan Pavio, *Imagery and Verbal Processes* (New York: Holt, Rinehart, & Winston, 1981).

9   Robert E. Smith and William R. Swinyard, "Information Response Models," *Journal of Marketing*, Winter 1982, pp. 81–93; and Deanna S. Kempf and Robert E. Smith, "Consumer Processing of Product Trial and the Influence of Prior Advertising," *Journal of Marketing Research*, August 1998, pp. 325–338.

10 Ziv Carmon, Klaus Wertenbroch, and Marcel Zeelenberg, "Option Attachment: When Deliberating Makes Choosing Feel Like Losing," *Journal of Consumer Research*, June 2003, pp. 15–29.

11 Eric M. Eisenstein and J. Wesley Hutchinson, "Action-Based Learning: Goals and Attention in the Acquisition of Market Knowledge," *Journal of Marketing Research*, May 2006, pp. 244–258.

12 Ida E. Berger and Andrew A. Mitchell, "The Effect of Advertising on Attitude Accessibility, Attitude Confidence, and the Attitude-Behavior Relationship," *Journal of Consumer Research*, December 1989, pp. 269–279; and Alice A. Wright and John G. Lynch Jr., "Communication Effects of Advertising vs. Direct Experience When Both Search and Experience Attributes Are Present," *Journal of Consumer Research*, March 1995, pp. 708–718.

13 Patricia M. West, "Predicting Preferences: An Examination of Agent Learning," *Journal of Consumer Research*, June 1996, pp. 68–80.

14 Jennifer Aaker, Susan Fournier, and S. Adam Brasel, "When Good Brands Do Bad," *Journal of Consumer Research*, June 2004, pp. 1–16.

15 Brad Jefferson, "Why Video Marketing Is One of the Most Effective Ways To Reach Millennials," *Mashable*, October 8, 2015, www.mashable.com; and Bob Tedeschi, "To Raise Shopper Satisfaction, Web Merchants Turn to Videos," *New York Times*, July 2, 2007, p. C4.

16 Joseph W. Alba and J. Wesley Hutchinson, "Dimensions of Consumer Expertise," *Journal of Consumer Research*, March 1987, pp. 411–454.

17 Eric J. Johnson and J. Edward Russo, "Product Familiarity and Learning New Information," *Journal of Consumer Research*, June 1984, pp. 542–551.

18 Steve Hoeffler, Dan Ariely, Pat West, and Rod Duclos, "Preference Exploration and Learning: The Role of Intensiveness and Extensiveness of Experience," *Journal of Consumer Psychology* 23, no. 3, July 2013, pp. 330–340.

19 Stephen J. Hoch and Young-Won Ha, "Consumer Learning: Advertising and the Ambiguity of Product Experience," *Journal of Consumer Research*, October 1986, pp. 221–233.

20 A. V. Muthukrishnan and Frank R. Kardes, "Persistent Preferences for Product Attributes," *Journal of Consumer Research*, June 2001, pp. 89–104.

21 Paul Herr, Steven J. Sherman, and Russell H. Fazio, "On the Consequences of Priming," *Journal of Experimental Social Psychology*, July 1983, pp. 323–340; and Hoch and Ha, "Consumer Learning: Advertising and the Ambiguity of Product Experience."

22 "The Too-Good-to-Be-True Product Hall of Fame," *Time*, October 6, 2011, www.time.com; and Timothy S. Robinson, "Listerine Ordered to Correct Claims," *New York Times*, August 3, 1977, www.nytimes.com.

23 Reid Hastie, "Causes and Effects of Causal Attributions," *Journal of Personality and Social Psychology*, July 1984, pp. 44–56; and Thomas K. Srull, Meryl Lichtenstein, and Myron Rothbart, "Associative Storage and Retrieval Processes in Person Memory," *Journal of Experimental Psychology: General* 11, no. 6, 1985, pp. 316–435.

24 Durairaj Maheswaran, "Country of Origin as a Stereotype: Effects of Consumer Expertise and Attribute Strength on Product Evaluations," *Journal of Consumer Research*, September 1994, pp. 354–365.

25 John Deighton, "The Interaction of Advertising and Evidence," *Journal of Consumer Research*, December 1984, pp. 763–770; and Hoch and Ha, "Consumer Learning: Advertising and the Ambiguity of Product Experience."

26 Bernard Weiner, "Spontaneous Causal Thinking," *Psychological Bulletin*, January 1985, pp. 74–84.

27 Hoch and Deighton, "Managing What Consumers Learn from Experience."

28 Brea Carter, "Budweiser Budvar to Host Brewery Experience," *Event*, October 9, 2015, www.eventmagazine.co.uk.

29 Youjae Yi, "A Critical Review of Consumer Satisfaction," *Review of Marketing* (Chicago: American Marketing Association, 1992), pp. 68–123.

30 Richard L. Oliver, "Processing of the Satisfaction Response in Consumption," *Journal of Consumer Satisfaction, Dissatisfaction, and Complaining Behavior* 2, 1989, pp. 1–16; and Haim Mano and Richard L. Oliver, "Assessing the Dimensionality and Structure of the Consumption Experience," *Journal of Consumer Research*, December 1993, pp. 451–466.

31 Mano and Oliver, "Assessing the Dimensionality and Structure of the Consumption Experience."

32 J. Josko Brakus, Bernd H. Schmitt, and Lia Zarantonello, "Brand Experience: What Is It? How Is It Measured? Does It Affect Loyalty?" *Journal of Marketing*, May 2009, pp. 52–68.

33 Michael D. Johnson, Eugene W. Anderson, and Claes Fornell, "Rational and Adaptive Performance Expectations in a Customer Satisfaction Framework," *Journal of Consumer Research*, March 1995, pp. 695–707.

34 Marsha L. Richins and Peter H. Bloch, "Post-purchase Satisfaction: Incorporating the Effects of Involvement and Time," *Journal of Business Research*, September 1991, pp. 145–158; and Vikas Mittal and Wagner A. Kamakura, "Satisfaction, Repurchase Intent, and Repurchase Behavior," *Journal of Marketing Research*, February 2001, pp. 131–142.

35 Elaine Chan and Anirban Mukhopadhyay, "When Choosing Makes a Good Thing Better: Temporal Variations in the Valuation of Hedonic Consumption," *Journal of Marketing Research*, June 2010, pp. 497–507.

36 Christian Homburg, Nicole Koschate, and Wayne D. Hoyer, "Do Satisfied Customers Really Pay More? A Study of the Relationship Between Customer Satisfaction and Willingness to Pay," *Journal of Marketing*, April 2005, pp. 84–96.

37 David M. Szymanski and David H. Henard, "Customer Satisfaction: A Meta-Analysis of the Empirical Evidence," *Journal of the Academy of Marketing Science* 29, no. 1, 2001, pp. 16–35; and Anders Gustafsson, Michael D. Johnson, and Inger Roos,

"The Effects of Customer Satisfaction, Relationship Commitment Dimensions, and Triggers on Customer Retention," *Journal of Marketing*, October 2005, pp. 210–218.

38 Todd A. Mooradian and James M. Oliver, "'I Can't Get No Satisfaction': The Impact of Personality and Emotion on Postpurchase Processes," *Psychology and Marketing* 14, no. 4, 1997, pp. 379–393; and Xueming Luo and Christian Homburg, "Neglected Outcomes of Customer Satisfaction," *Journal of Marketing*, April 2007, pp. 133–149.

39 Gustafsson et al., "The Effects of Customer Satisfaction, Relationship Commitment Dimensions, and Triggers on Customer Retention;" Christopher Ratcliff, "What Is Customer Lifetime Value (CLV) and Why Do You Need To Measure It?" *Econsultancy*, September 11, 2014, www.econsultancy.com.

40 Kathleen Seiders, Glenn B. Voss, and Dhruv Grewal, "Do Satisfied Customers Buy More? Examining Moderating Influences in a Retailing Context," *Journal of Marketing*, October 2005, pp. 26–43.

41 Bruce Cooil, Timothy L. Keiningham, and Lerzan Aksoy, "A Longitudinal Analysis of Customer Satisfaction and Share of Wallet: Investigating the Moderating Effect of Customer Characteristics," *Journal of Marketing*, January 2007, pp. 67–83.

42 Lisa Reisman, "Best Bicycle Store, Zane's Cycles, Branford," *Shoreline Times (CT)*, December 3, 2015, www.shorelinetimes.com; and "The True Value of Customer Service," *Costco Connection*, August 2011, p. 11.

43 Xueming Luo, Christian Homburg, and Jan Wieseke, "Customer Satisfaction, Analyst Stock Recommendations, and Firm Value," *Journal of Marketing Research*, December 2010, pp. 1041–1058.

44 Forrest V. Morgeson III, Sunil Mithas, Timothy L. Keiningham, and Lerzan Aksoy, "An Investigation of the Cross-National Determinants of Customer Satisfaction," *Journal of the Academy of Marketing Science*, April 2011, pp. 198–215.

45 Terry Vavra, "Learning from Your Losses," *Brandweek*, December 7, 1992.

46 Charlotte Klopp and John Sterlickhi, "Customer Satisfaction Just Catching on in Europe," *Marketing News*, May 28, 1990.

47 Richard L. Oliver, "A Cognitive Model of the Antecedents and Consequences of Satisfaction Decisions," *Journal of Marketing Research*, November 1980, pp. 460–469; and Yi, "A Critical Review of Consumer Satisfaction," p. 92; see also Douglas M. Stayman, Dana L. Alden, and Karen H. Smith, "Some Effects of Schematic Processing on Consumer Expectations and Disconfirmation Judgments," *Journal of Consumer Research*, September 1992, pp. 240–255.

48 Yi, "A Critical Review of Consumer Satisfaction;" and Stayman, Alden, and Smith, "Some Effects of Schematic Processing on Consumer Expectations and Disconfirmation Judgments."

49 Praveen K. Kopalle and Donald R. Lehman, "The Effects of Advertised and Observed Quality on Expectations About New Product Quality," *Journal of Marketing Research*, August 1995, pp. 280–291; Stephen A. LaTour and Nancy C. Peat, "The Role of Situationally-Produced Expectations, Others' Experiences, and Prior Experiences in Determining Satisfaction," in ed. Jerry C. Olson, *Advances in Consumer Research* (Ann Arbor, Mich.: Association for Consumer Research, 1980), pp. 588–592; and Ernest R. Cadotte, Robert B. Woodruff, and Roger L. Jenkins, "Expectations and Norms in Models of Consumer Satisfaction," *Journal of Marketing Research*, August 1987, pp. 305–314.

50 Ruth N. Bolton and James H. Drew, "A Multistage Model of Customers' Assessments of Service Quality and Value," *Journal of Consumer Research*, March 1991, pp. 375–384; and Michael D. Johnson, Eugene W. Anderson, and Claes Fornell, "Rational and Adaptive Performance Expectations in a Customer Satisfaction Framework," *Journal of Consumer Research*, March 1995, pp. 695–707.

51 Glenn B. Voss, A. Parasuraman, and Dhruv Grewal, "The Roles of Price, Performance, and Expectations in Determining Satisfaction in Service Exchanges," *Journal of Marketing*, October 1998, pp. 46–61; and A. Parasuraman, Valarie A. Zeithaml, and Leonard L. Berry, "SERVQUAL: A Multiple-Item Scale for Measuring Consumer Perceptions of Service Quality," *Journal of Retailing*, Spring 1988, pp. 12–36.

52 Lisa C. Wan, Michael K. Hui, and Robert S. Wyer Jr., "The Role of Relationship Norms in Responses to Service Failures," *Journal of Consumer Research*, August 2011, pp. 260–277.

53 Susan Fournier and David Glen Mick, "Rediscovering Satisfaction," *Journal of Marketing* 63, October 1999, pp. 5–23.

54 Simona Botti and Ann L. McGill, "When Choosing Is Not Deciding: The Effect of Perceived Responsibility on Satisfaction," *Journal of Consumer Research* 33, no. 2, 2006, pp. 211–219.

55 Kristin Diel and Cait Poynor, "Great Expectations?! Assortment Size, Expectations, and Satisfaction," *Journal of Marketing Research*, April 2010, pp. 312–322.

56 Yangjie Gu, Simona Botti, and David Faro, "Turning the Page: The Impact of Choice Closure on Satisfaction," *Journal of Consumer Research* 40, no. 2, August 2013, pp. 268–283.

57 Claude Messner and Michaela Wänke, "Unconscious Information Processing Reduces Information Overload and Increases Product Satisfaction," *Journal of Consumer Psychology* 21, no. 1, Special Issue, January 2011, pp. 9–13.

58 Chezy Ofir and Itamar Simonson, "In Search of Negative Customer Feedback," *Journal of Marketing Research* 38, May 2001, pp. 170–182.

59 Peter Darke, Laurence Ashworth, and Kelley Main, "Great Expectations and Broken Promises," *Journal of the Academy of Marketing Science*, Summer 2010, pp. 347–362.

60 Baba Shiv, Ziv Carmon, and Dan Ariely, "Placebo Effects of Marketing Actions," *Journal of Marketing Research*, November 2005, pp. 383–393.

61 Caglar Irmak, Lauren G. Block, and Gavan J. Fitzsimons, "The Placebo Effect in Marketing," *Journal of Marketing Research*, November 2005, pp. 406–409.

62 Lauren Block and Thomas Kramer, "The Effect of Superstitious Beliefs on Performance Expectations," *Journal of the Academy of Marketing Science* 37, 2009, pp. 161–169.

63 David K. Tse and Peter C. Wilson, "Models of Consumer Satisfaction Formation," *Journal of Marketing Research*, May 1988, pp. 204–212; Richard L. Oliver, "Cognitive, Affective, and Attribute Bases of the Satisfaction Response," *Journal of Consumer Research*, December 1993, pp. 418–430; and Richard L. Oliver and Wayne S. DeSarbo, "Response Determinants in Satisfaction Judgments," *Journal of Consumer Research*, March 1988, pp. 495–507.

64 Richard W. Olshavsky and John A. Miller, "Consumer Expectations, Product Performance, and Perceived Product Quality," *Journal of Marketing Research*, February 1972, pp. 469–499.

65 Bonnie S. Benwick, "Shop Till You Learn Something New at the Market," *Washington Post*, June 7, 2011, www.washingtonpost.com.

66 Diane Halstead, Cornelia Droge, and M. Bixby Cooper, "Product Warranties and Post-purchase Service," *Journal of Services*

Marketing 7, no. 1, 1993, pp. 33–40; and Joshua Lyle Wiener, "Are Warranties Accurate Signals of Product Reliability?" *Journal of Consumer Research*, September 1985, pp. 245–250.

67 Graham Winfrey, "Trek Bike Recall Is a Case Study in Crisis Response," *Inc.*, April 24, 2015, www.inc.com; and Gina Pace, "Making Life Easier for His Customers," *Inc.*, May 9, 2011, www.inc.com.

68 Bernard Weiner, "Reflections and Reviews: Attributional Thoughts About Consumer Behavior," *Journal of Consumer Research* 27, December 2000, pp. 382–287; Valerie S. Folkes, "Consumer Reactions to Product Failure," *Journal of Consumer Research*, March 1984, pp. 398–409; Valerie S. Folkes, "Recent Attribution Research in Consumer Behavior," *Journal of Consumer Research*, March 1988, pp. 548–565; and Richard W. Mizerski, Linda L. Golden, and Jerome B. Kernan, "The Attribution Process in Consumer Decision Making," *Journal of Consumer Research*, September 1979, pp. 123–140.

69 Mary Jo Bitner, "Evaluating Service Encounters," *Journal of Marketing*, April 1990, pp. 69–82.

70 Valerie S. Folkes, Susan Koletsky, and John L. Graham, "A Field Study of Causal Inferences and Consumer Reaction," *Journal of Consumer Research*, March 1987, pp. 534–539.

71 Neeli Bendapudi and Robert P. Leone, "Psychological Implications of Customer Participation in Co-Production," *Journal of Marketing*, January 2003, pp. 14–28.

72 Michael Tsiros, Vikas Mittal, and William T. Ross Jr., "The Role of Attributions in Customer Satisfaction," *Journal of Consumer Research*, September 2004, pp. 476–483.

73 Andrea C. Morales, "Giving Firms an E for Effort: Consumer Responses to High-Effort Firms," *Journal of Consumer Research* 31, no. 4, 2005, pp. 806–812.

74 Lea Dunn and Darren W. Dahl, "Self-Threat and Product Failure: How Internal Attributions of Blame Affect Consumer Complaining Behavior," *Journal of Marketing Research* 49, no. 5, October 2012, pp. 670–681.

75 "Consumer Reports: For Returns, Some Stores Are Naughty and Some Are Nice," *Richmond Times-Dispatch (VA)*, January 2, 2016, www.richmond.com.

76 Richard L. Oliver and John E. Swan, "Equity and Disconfirmation Paradigms as Influences on Merchant and Product Satisfaction," *Journal of Consumer Research*, December 1989, pp. 372–383; and Elaine G. Walster, G. William Walster, and Ellen Berscheid, *Equity: Theory and Research* (Boston: Allyn & Bacon, 1978).

77 Jingjing Ma and Neal J. Roese, "The Countability Effect: Comparative versus Experiential Reactions to Reward Distributions," *Journal of Consumer Research* 39, no. 6, April 2013, pp. 1219–1233.

78 Peter R. Darke and Darren W. Dahl, "Fairness and Discounts: The Subjective Value of a Bargain," *Journal of Consumer Psychology* 13, no. 3, 2003, pp. 328–338.

79 Richard L. Oliver and John L. Swan, "Consumer Perceptions of Interpersonal Equity and Satisfaction in Transactions," *Journal of Marketing*, April 1989, pp. 21–35.

80 Ruth N. Bolton and Katherine N. Lemon, "A Dynamic Model of Customers' Usage of Services," *Journal of Marketing Research* 36, May 1999, pp. 171–186.

81 Rebecca J. Slotegraaf and J. Jeffrey Inman, "Longitudinal Shifts in the Drivers of Satisfaction with Product Quality," *Journal of Marketing Research*, August 2004, pp. 269–280.

82 James G. Maxhamm III and Richard G. Netemeyer, "Firms Reap What They Sow: The Effects of Shared Values and Perceived Organizational Justice on Customers' Evaluations of Complaint Handling," *Journal of Marketing*, January 2003, pp. 46–62.

83 Pankaj Aggarwal and Richard P. Larrick, "When Consumers Care About Being Treated Fairly: The Interaction of Relationship Norms and Fairness Norms," *Journal of Consumer Psychology* 22, no. 1, Special Issue, January 2012, pp. 114–127.

84 Anjie Zheng, "Chow Tai Fook Takes a Shine to Hong Kong as China Demand Dims," *Wall Street Journal*, August 20, 2015, www.wsj.com; and Jason Chow and Prudence Ho, "Huge for Its Bling, Unknown in West," *Wall Street Journal*, November 12, 2011, www.wsj.com.

85 Narayan Janakiraman and Lisa Ordonez, "Effect of Effort and Deadlines on Consumer Product Returns," *Journal of Consumer Psychology* 22, no. 2, April 2012, pp. 260–271.

86 Sujay Dutta, Abhijit Biswas, and Dhruv Grewal, "Regret from Postpurchase Discovery of Lower Market Prices: Do Price Refunds Help?" *Journal of Marketing* 75, no. 6, November 2011, pp. 124–138.

87 Diane M. Phillips and Hans Baumgartner, "The Role of Consumption Emotions in the Satisfaction Response," *Journal of Consumer Psychology* 12, no. 3, 2002, pp. 243–252; Robert A. Westbrook and Richard L. Oliver, "The Dimensionality of Consumption Emotion Patterns and Consumer Satisfaction," *Journal of Consumer Research*, June 1991, pp. 84–91; and Mano and Oliver, "Assessing the Dimensionality and Structure of the Consumption Experience."

88 Robert A. Westbrook, "Product/Consumption-Based Affective Responses and Postpurchase Processes," *Journal of Marketing Research* 24, August 1987, pp. 258–270.

89 Chi Kin (Bennett) Yim, David K. Tse, and Kimmy Wa Chan, "Strengthening Customer Loyalty Through Intimacy and Passion," *Journal of Marketing Research*, December 2008, pp. 741–56.

90 Lan Jiang, JoAndrea Hoegg, and Darren W. Dahl, "Consumer Reaction to Unearned Preferential Treatment," *Journal of Consumer Research* 40, no. 3, October 2013, pp. 412–427.

91 Westbrook and Oliver, "The Dimensionality of Consumption Emotion Patterns and Consumer Satisfaction."

92 Thorsten Hennig-Thurau, Markus Groth, and Michael Paul, "Are All Smiles Created Equal?" *Journal of Marketing*, July 2006, pp. 58–73.

93 Adam Duhachek and Dawn Iacobucci, "Consumer Personality and Coping," *Journal of Consumer Psychology* 15, no. 1, 2005, pp. 52–63; and Adam Duhachek, "Coping: A Multidimensional, Hierarchical Framework of Responses to Stressful Consumption Episodes," *Journal of Consumer Research* 32, June 2005, pp. 41–53.

94 Jing Wang, Nathan Novemsky, and Ravi Dhar, "Anticipating Adaptation to Products," *Journal of Consumer Research*, August 2009, pp. 149–159.

95 Richard L. Oliver, "Measurement and Evaluation of Satisfaction Processes in Retail Settings," *Journal of Retailing*, Fall 1981, pp. 25–48; and Richard L. Oliver, *Satisfaction: A Behavioral Perspective on the Consumer*, 2nd ed. (New York: Taylor and Francis, 2010).

96 Christian Homburg, Nicole Koschate, and Wayne D. Hoyer, "The Role of Cognition and Affect in the Formation of Customer Satisfaction: A Dynamic Perspective," *Journal of Marketing*, July 2006, pp. 21–31; and Stacy L. Wood and C. Page Moreau, "Loathing? How Emotion Influences the Evaluation and Early Use of Innovations," *Journal of Marketing*, July 2006, pp. 44–57.

97 Sarah Fisher Gardial, D. Scott Clemons, Robert B. Woodruff, David W. Schumann, and Mary Jane Burns, "Comparing Consumers' Recall of Prepurchase and Postpurchase Evaluation Experiences," *Journal of Consumer Research*, March 1994, pp. 548–560.

98 Vanessa M. Patrick, Deborah J. MacInnis, and C. Whan Park, "Not As Happy As I Thought I'd Be? Affective Misforecasting and Product Evaluations," *Journal of Consumer Research* 33, no. 4, 2007, pp. 479–489; Daniel T. Gilbert, Elizabeth C. Pinel, Timothy D. Wilson, Stephen J. Blumberg, and Thalia P. Wheatley, "Immune Neglect: A Source of Durability Bias in Affective Forecasting," *Journal of Personality and Social Psychology* 75, no. 3, 1998, pp. 617–638; and George Loewenstein and David A. Schkade, "Wouldn't It Be Nice? Predicting Future Feelings," in eds. N. Schwartz, D. Kahneman, and E. Diener, *Well-Being: The Foundations of Hedonic Psychology* (New York: Russell Sage Foundation, 1999), pp. 85–105.

99 Wang, Novemsky, and Dhar, "Anticipating Adaptation to Products."

100 Naomi Mandel and Stephen M. Nowlis, "The Effect of Making a Prediction about the Outcome of a Consumption Experience on the Enjoyment of That Experience," *Journal of Consumer Research*, June 2008, pp. 9–20.

101 Lauren Lyons Cole, "Mobile Banking On The Rise, Thanks To Tech-Savvy Millennials," *International Business Times*, December 5, 2015, www.ibtimes.com; and Meredith Verdone, "How to Be Hip: Big Banks Can Market to Millennials," *Advertising Age*, June 24, 2015, www.adage.com.

102 Leonard Lee and Claire I. Tsai, "How Price Promotions Influence Postpurchase Consumption Experience over Time," *Journal Of Consumer Research* 40, no. 5, 2014, pp. 943–959.

103 Robin L. Soster, Andrew D. Gershoff, and William O. Bearden, "The Bottom Dollar Effects: The Influence of Spending to Zero on Pain of Payment and Satisfaction," *Journal of Consumer Research* 41, no. 3, October 2014, pp. 656–677.

104 C. B. Bhattacharya and Sankar Sen, "Consumer-Company Identification: A Framework for Understanding Consumers' Relationships with Companies," *Journal of Marketing*, April 2003, pp. 76–88; and Dennis B. Arnett, Steve D. German, and Shelby D. Hunt, "The Identify Salience Model of Relationship Marketing Success: The Case of Nonprofit Marketing," *Journal of Marketing*, April 2003, pp. 89–105.

105 James R. Hagerty, "Harley-Davidson to Ramp Up Marketing, as Sales Skid," *Wall Street Journal*, October 20, 2015, www.wsj.com.

106 John Patrick Pullen, "7 Secrets of the Apple Genius Bar Everybody Should Know," *Time*, August 4, 2015, www.time.com.

107 Ralph L. Day, "Modeling Choices Among Alternative Responses to Dissatisfaction," in ed. Thomas C. Kinnear, *Advances in Consumer Research*, vol. 11 (Provo, Utah: Association for Consumer Research, 1984), pp. 496–499; and Marsha L. Richins, "Word-of-Mouth Communication as Negative Information," *Journal of Marketing*, Winter 1983, pp. 68–78.

108 Day, "Modeling Choices Among Alternative Responses to Dissatisfaction"; and Arthur Best and Alan R. Andreasen, "Consumer Response to Unsatisfactory Purchases," *Law and Society*, Spring 1977, pp. 701–742.

109 William O. Bearden and Jesse E. Teel, "Selected Determinants of Consumer Satisfaction and Complaint Reports," *Journal of Marketing Research*, February 1983, pp. 21–28.

110 William O. Bearden and Jesse E. Teel, "Selected Determinants of Consumer Satisfaction and Complaint Reports," *Journal of Marketing Research*, February 1983, pp. 21–28.

111 Day, "Modeling Choices Among Alternative Responses to Dissatisfaction"; and Jagdip Singh and Roy D. Howell, "Consumer Complaining Behavior: A Review," in eds. H. Keith Hunt and Ralph L. Day, *Consumer Satisfaction, Dissatisfaction, and Complaining Behavior* (Bloomington, Ind.: Indiana University Press, 1985).

112 Nathan Benson, "Innovate WNY: GripeO," *WGRZ TV* (Buffalo, NY), November 16, 2015, www.wgrz.com.

113 Jo Causon, "Customer Complaints Made Via Social Media on the Rise," *The Guardian*, May 21, 2015, www.theguardian.com.

114 Micah Solomon, "5 Social Media Customer Service Best Practices To Handle (Or Prevent) Customer Complaints," *Forbes*, January 28, 2015, www.forbes.com.

115 Folkes, "Consumer Reactions to Product Failure."

116 Nada Nasr Bechwati and Maureen Morrin, "Outraged Customers: Getting Even at the Expense of Getting a Good Deal," *Journal of Consumer Psychology* 13, no. 4, 2003, pp. 440–453.

117 Kjell Gronhaug and Gerald R. Zaltman, "Complainers and Noncomplainers Revisited: Another Look at the Data," in ed. Kent B. Monroe, *Advances in Consumer Research* (Ann Arbor, MI: Association for Consumer Research, 1981), pp. 159–165.

118 Jagdip Singh, "A Typology of Consumer Dissatisfaction Response Styles," *Journal of Retailing*, Spring 1990, pp. 57–99.

119 Christian Homburg, Andreas Furst, and Nicole Koschate, "On the Importance of Complaint Handling Design: A Multi-level Analysis of the Impact in Specific Complaint Situations," *Journal of the Academy of Marketing Science* 38, 2010, pp. 265–287.

120 Chiara Orsingher, Sara Valentini, and Matteo de Angels, "A Meta-analysis of Satisfaction with Complaint Handling in Services," *Journal of the Academy of Marketing Science* 38, 2010, pp. 169–186.

121 Tiffany Kary, "Online Retailers Fumble on Customer Care," *CNET News.com*, January 3, 2002, http://cnet.com.

122 Blair Nicole, "Use Social Media to Turn a Complaining Customer Into a Raving Fan," *Social Media Today*, August 27, 2015, www.socialmediatoday.com.

123 Sean Mclain, "Bharti Airtel to Spend $9 Billion to Improve Mobile Network in India," *Wall Street Journal*, November 30, 2015, www.wsj.com; and Ishan Srivastava, "Mobile Complaint? Your Tweet May Help," *Times of India*, September 22, 2011, www.timesofindia.com.

124 Al Urbanski, "Nissan Leads the Pack on Facebook," *Direct Marketing News*, March 9, 2015, www.dmnews.com; and Lindsay Chappell, "Nissan: Facebook May Replace Phone Banks," *Automotive News*, July 25, 2011, p. 6.

125 James G. Maxham III and Richard G. Netemeyer, "A Longitudinal Study of Complaining Customers' Evaluations of Multiple Service Failures and Recovery Efforts," *Journal of Marketing*, October 2002, pp. 57–71.

126 Barb Darrow, "Yay! Human Cashiers Prevail Over Automation At Some CVS Stores," *Fortune*, October 20, 2015, www.fortune.com; and Stephanie Reitz, "Some Supermarkets Bag Self-Serve Checkouts," *Seattle Times*, September 26, 2011, www.seattletimes.com.

127 Halstead, Droge, and Cooper, "Product Warranties and Postpurchase Service."

128 Claes Fornell and Nicholas M. Didow, "Economic Constraints on Consumer Complaining Behavior," in ed. Jerry C. Olson, *Advances in Consumer Research*, vol. 7 (Ann Arbor, Mich.: Association for Consumer Research, 1980), pp. 318–323; and Claes Fornell and Birger Wernerfelt, "Defensive Marketing Strategy by Customer Complaint Management," *Journal of Marketing Research*, November 1987, pp. 337–346.

129 Claes Fornell and Robert A. Westbrook, "The Vicious Cycle of Consumer Complaints," *Journal of Marketing*, Summer 1984, pp. 68–78.

130 Torsten Ringberg, Gaby Odekerken-Schröder, and Glenn L. Christensen, "A Cultural Models Approach to Service Recovery," *Journal of Marketing*, July 2007, pp. 194–214.

131 K. Sivakumar, Mei Li, and Beibei Dong, "Service Quality: The Impact of Frequency, Timing, Proximity, and Sequence of Failures and Delights," *Journal of Marketing* 78, no. 1, January 2014, pp. 41–58.

132 Amy K. Smith, Ruth N. Bolton, and Janet Wagner, "A Model of Customer Satisfaction with Service Encounters Involving Failure and Recovery," *Journal of Marketing Research* 36, August 1999, pp. 356–372.

133 Bitner, "Evaluating Service Encounters."

134 Richins, "Word-of-Mouth Communication as Negative Information."

135 Yi, "A Critical Review of Consumer Satisfaction."

136 Sarah G. Moore, "Attitude Predictability and Helpfulness in Online Reviews: The Role of Explained Actions and Reactions," *Journal of Consumer Research* 42, no. 12, 2015, pp. 30–44.

137 Linda Dobel, "Contact Center Managers Should Already Be Rolling with the Flow of Social Media," *TMC*, October 20, 2011, www.tmcnet.com.

138 Jim Tierney, "Listening Is Social Media Cornerstone at Dell," *Multichannel Merchant*, November 3, 2011, www.multichannelmerchant.com.

139 "The Ignored Side of Social Media: Customer Service," *Knowledge@Wharton*, January 2, 2014, http://knowledge.wharton.upenn.edu.

140 Tim Donnelly, "How to Issue a Great Apology," *Inc.*, September 14, 2011, www.inc.com.

141 Kate Spirgen, "Word of Mouth," *Lawn & Landscape*, December 1, 2015, www.lawnandlandscape.com.

142 Murali Chandrashekaran, Kristin Rotte, Stephen S. Tax, and Rajdeep Grewal, "Satisfaction Strength and Customer Loyalty," *Journal of Marketing Research*, February 2007, pp. 153–163.

143 Frederick F. Reichheld, *The Loyalty Effect* (Boston: Harvard Business School Press, 1996).

144 Priscilla La Barbera and David W. Mazursky, "A Longitudinal Assessment of Consumer Satisfaction/Dissatisfaction," *Journal of Marketing Research*, November 1983, pp. 393–404; and Ruth Bolton, "A Dynamic Model of the Duration of the Customer's Relationship with a Continuous Service Provider," *Marketing Science* 17, no. 1, 1998, pp. 45–65.

145 Thomas O. Jones and W. Earl Sasser, "Why Customers Defect," *Harvard Business Review*, November–December 1995, pp. 88–99.

146 Richard L. Oliver, "Whence Consumer Loyalty?" *Journal of Marketing* 63, 1999, pp. 33–44; and René Algesheimer, Utpal M. Dholakia, and Andreas Herrmann, "The Social Influence of Brand Community: Evidence from European Car Clubs," *Journal of Marketing* 69, July 2005, pp. 19–34.

147 Lopo L. Rego, Neil A. Morgan, and Claes Fornell, "Reexamining the Market Share–Customer Satisfaction Relationship," *Journal of Marketing* 77, no. 5, September 2013, pp. 1–20.

148 Michael Lewis, "The Influence of Loyalty Programs and Short-Term Promotions on Customer Retention," *Journal of Marketing Research*, August 2004, pp. 281–292.

149 Frederick F. Reichheld and W. Earl Sasser, "Zero Defections," *Harvard Business Review*, September 1990, pp. 105–111; Eugene Anderson, Claes Fornell, and Donald H. Lehman, "Customer Satisfaction, Market Share, and Profitability," *Journal of Marketing*, July 1994, pp. 53–66; and Rajendra K. Srivastava, Tassadduq A. Shervani, and Liam Fahey, "Market-Based Assets and Shareholder Value," *Journal of Marketing* 62, no. 1, 1998, pp. 2–18.

150 Werner Reinartz, Manfred Krafft, and Wayne D. Hoyer, "The Customer Relationship Management Process: Its Measurement and Impact on Performance," *Journal of Marketing Research*, August 2004, pp. 293–305; and Suni Mithas, M. S. Krishnan, and Claes Fornell, "Why Do Customer Relationship Management Applications Affect Customer Satisfaction?" *Journal of Marketing*, October 2005, pp. 201–209.

151 Craig Trudell, "Takata Looks Way Past Its Air Bag Woes," *Bloomberg*, January 7, 2016, www.bloomberg.com; Kana Inagaki, "Takata Crisis Deepens with Honda Boycott of Component," *Financial Times*, November 4, 2015, www.ft.com; "Everything You Need to Know about the Takata Airbag Recall," *Consumer Reports*, November 3, 2015, www.consumerreports.org; and David Shepardson, "Honda, Takata Settle Airbag Suits, Lose Round in Class Action Case," *Reuters*, December 3, 2015, www.reuters.com.

152 Yi Zhao, Ying Zhao, and Kristiaan Helsen, "Consumer Learning in a Turbulent Market Environment: Modeling Consumer Choice Dynamics After a Product-Harm Crisis," *Journal of Marketing Research* 48, no. 2, April 2011, pp. 255–267.

153 Jing Lei, Niraj Dawar, and Zeynep Gürhan-Canli, "Base-Rate Information in Consumer Attributions of Product-Harm Crises," *Journal of Marketing Research* 49, no. 3, June 2012, pp. 336–348.

154 Becky Ebenkamp, "The Complaint Department," *Brandweek*, June 18, 2001, p. 21; and Reichheld, *The Loyalty Effect*.

155 Maya Mirsky, "Cole Hardware Opening First Store Outside of S.F. in Rockridge," *Contra Costa Times* (Calif.), December 31, 2014, www.contracostatimes.com; and "Cole Hardware—Leading the Way in Eco-friendly Retailing," *Hardware Retailing*, July 2011, p. 60.

156 Kasey Wehrum, "Learning and Relearning to Listen," *Inc.*, March 2011, pp. 64–69.

157 Stephen Shapiro, "Do You Know What Makes Your Company Distinctive?," *Harvard Business Review*, January 17, 2014, www.hbr.org; and Jeremy Quittner, "USAA Tech Overhaul Makes Remote Banking Less Remote," *American Banker*, July 12, 2011, p. 1.

158 James Foster, "Mystery Shoppers Checking in on Montreal Cabbies," *CJAD News*, December 2, 2015, www.cjad.com.

159 Sam Chambers, "The Freshest Thing About the World's Biggest Online Grocer Isn't Food," *Bloomberg Business*, August 28, 2015, www.bloomberg.com; and Lawrence Hene, "Star Order," *Grocer*, July 16, 2011, p. 20.

160 Melissa Martin Young and Melanie Wallendorf, "Ashes to Ashes, Dust to Dust: Conceptualizing Consumer Disposition of Possessions," in *Proceedings, Marketing Educators' Conference* (Chicago: American Marketing Association, 1989), pp. 33–39.

161 Young and Wallendorf, "Ashes to Ashes, Dust to Dust: Conceptualizing Consumer Disposition of Possessions;" see also Erica Mina Okada, "Trade-Ins, Mental Accounting, and Product Replacement Decisions," *Journal of Consumer Research*, March 2001, pp. 433–446; Jacob Jacoby, Carol K. Berning, and Thomas F. Dietvorst, "What About Disposition?" *Journal of Marketing*, April 1977, pp. 22–28; and Gilbert D. Harrell and Diane M. McConocha, "Personal Factors Related

to Consumer Product Disposal," *Journal of Consumer Affairs*, Winter 1992, pp. 397–417.

162 Jacoby, Berning, and Dietvorst, "What About Disposition?"; and Young and Wallendorf, "Ashes to Ashes, Dust to Dust: Conceptualizing Consumer Disposition of Possessions."

163 Harrell and McConocha, "Personal Factors Related to Consumer Product Disposal Tendencies."

164 Jacoby, Berning, and Dietvorst, "What About Disposition?"

165 John B. Sherry, Mary Ann McGrath, and Sidney J. Levy, "The Disposition of the Gift and Many Unhappy Returns," *Journal of Retailing*, Spring 1992, pp. 40–65.

166 Young and Wallendorf, "Ashes to Ashes, Dust to Dust."

167 Russell W. Belk, "Possessions and the Extended Self," *Journal of Consumer Research*, September 1988, pp. 139–168.

168 Young and Wallendorf, "Ashes to Ashes, Dust to Dust."

169 Okada, "Trade-Ins, Mental Accounting, and Product Replacement Decisions."

170 Rui (Juliet) Zhu, Zinlei (Jack) Chen, and Srabana Dasgupta, "Can Trade-ins Hurt You? Exploring the Effect of a Trade-in on Consumers' Willingness to Pay for a New Product," *Journal of Marketing Research*, April 2008, pp. 159–170.

171 Melissa Martin Young, "Disposition of Possessions During Role Transitions," in eds. Rebecca H. Holman and Michael R. Solomon, *Advances in Consumer Research*, vol. 18 (Provo, Utah: Association for Consumer Research, 1991), pp. 33–39.

172 James H. Alexander, "Divorce, the Disposition of the Relationship, and Everything," in eds. Rebecca H. Holman and Michael R. Solomon, *Advances in Consumer Research*, vol. 18 (Provo, Utah: Association for Consumer Research, 1991), pp. 43–48.

173 Ibid; Russell W. Belk, John F. Sherry, and Melanie Wallendorf, "A Naturalistic Inquiry into Buyer and Seller Behavior at a Swap Meet," *Journal of Consumer Research*, March 1988, pp. 449–470.

174 Jennifer Smith, "The eBay Millionaires," *Daily Mail Online* (UK), August 20, 2014, www.dailymail.co.uk.

175 Michael D. Reilly and Melanie Wallendorf, "A Comparison of Group Differences in Food Consumption Using Household Refuse," *Journal of Consumer Research*, September 1987, pp. 289–294.

176 Mary Bowerman, "McDonald's Offers Lobster Roll in New England," *USA Today*, June 30, 2015, www.usatoday.com.

177 Daiane Scaraboto, "Selling, Sharing, and Everything in Between: The Hybrid Economies of Collaborative Networks," *Journal of Consumer Research* 42, no. 1, 2015, pp. 152–176.

178 For a review, see L. J. Shrum, Tina M. Lowrey, and John A. McCarty, "Recycling as a Marketing Problem," *Psychology and Marketing*, July–August 1994, pp. 393–416.

179 Abhijit Biswas, Jane W. Licata, Daryl McKee, Chris Pullig, and Christopher Daughtridge, "The Recycling Cycle," *Journal of Public Policy and Marketing* 19, Spring 2000, pp. 93–105.

180 Aaron Baar, "Survey: Americans Much More Likely to Recycle," *Media Post*, October 5, 2011, www.mediapost.com.

181 Rik G. M. Pieters, "Changing Garbage Disposal Patterns of Consumers," *Journal of Public Policy and Marketing*, Fall 1991, pp. 59–76.

182 Richard P. Bagozzi and Pratibha Dabholkar, "Consumer Recycling Goals and Their Effect on Decisions to Recycle," *Psychology and Marketing*, July–August 1994, pp. 313–340.

183 E. Howenstein, "Marketing Segmentation for Recycling," *Environment and Behavior*, March 1993, pp. 86–102.

184 Shrum, Lowrey, and McCarty, "Recycling as a Marketing Problem."

185 Remi Trudel and Jennifer J. Argo, "The Effect of Product Size and Form Distortion on Consumer Recycling Behavior," *Journal of Consumer Research* 40, no. 4, December 2013, pp. 632–643.

186 Susan E. Heckler, "The Role of Memory in Understanding and Encouraging Recycling Behavior," *Psychology and Marketing*, July–August 1994, pp. 375–392.

187 Pieters, "Changing Garbage Disposal Patterns of Consumers."

188 Susan Warren, "Recycler's Nightmare: Beer in Plastic," *Wall Street Journal*, November 16, 1999, pp. B1, B4.

189 Jesse R. Catlin and Yitong Wang, "Recycling Gone Bad: When the Option to Recycle Increases Resource Consumption," *Journal of Consumer Psychology* 23, no. 1, January 2013, pp. 122–127.

190 "Plastics Makers Urge Expanded Recycling in Honor of America Recycles Day," *Recycling Today*, November 10, 2015, www.recyclingtoday.com.

191 Kenneth R. Lord, "Motivating Recycling Behavior," *Psychology and Marketing*, July–August 1994, pp. 341–358.

192 Heckler, "The Role of Memory in Understanding and Encouraging Recycling Behavior."

193 Simone Sebastian, "Soft Drink Giants Put New Life into Their Containers," *Houston Chronicle*, September 25, 2011, www.chron.com.

194 Emily Young, "Waste Not, Want Not: Making Money From Rubbish," *BBC News*, February 2, 2015, www.bbc.com.

The
Psychological Core

2 Motivation, Ability, and Opportunity
3 From Exposure to Comprehension
4 Memory and Knowledge
5-6 Attitudes Based on Effort

An Introduction
to
Consumer Behavior

1 Understanding Consumer Behavior

The Process of
Making Decisions

7 Problem Recognition and Information Search
8-9 Judgment and Decision-Making Based on Effort
10 Post-Decision Processes

The
Consumer's Culture

11 Social Influences on Consumer Behavior
12 Consumer Diversity
13 Household and Social Class Influences
14 Psychographics: Values, Personality, and Lifestyles

Consumer Behavior
Outcomes and Issues

15 Innovations: Adoption, Resistance, and Diffusion
16 Symbolic Consumer Behavior
17 Marketing, Ethics, and Social Responsibility in Today's Consumer Society

iStockphoto.com/Ostill

Part 4

The Consumer's Culture

PART FOUR REFLECTS a "macro" view of consumer behavior, examining how various aspects of the consumer's culture affect each other and, individually and in combination, how they affect the consumer's behavior. As Chapter 11 explains, our behaviors and decisions are influenced by certain individuals, specific groups (such as friends and co-workers), and both traditional and social media. Chapter 12 focuses on diversity, specifically on the roles that age; gender; sexual orientation; and regional, ethnic, and religious influences play in consumer behavior.

Chapter 13 looks at various types of households and families and explores how household members influence acquisition and consumption decisions. It also examines how social class affects consumer decisions and behaviors. The combination of diversity, social class, and household influences can affect our values, personality, and lifestyle—the topics covered in Chapter 14. All of these factors influence consumer behavior and therefore have many implications for marketers.

CHAPTER 11

Social Influences on Consumer Behavior

iStockphoto.com/Ostill

INTRODUCTION

The information that individuals or groups provide, as **social influences**, can have a big impact on consumers. When you hear about a game from your friends, that information can be very credible. Social influence is also powerful when individuals within groups are in frequent contact and can communicate information in a way that builds buzz. Certain people (such as famous athletes, politicians, and movie stars) have influence because their power or expertise makes others want to follow what they believe, do, or say. Groups can influence not only what consumers know but also what they do (such as downloading a game). Therefore, marketers need to understand what kinds of social entities create influence, what kinds of influence they create, and how their influence can affect other consumers. Exhibit 11.1 summarizes the social influences that can affect consumers.

> **Social influence**
> Information by and implicit or explicit pressures from individuals, groups, and the mass media that affects how a person behaves.

Zhao Changchun/Xinhua News Agency/HELSINKI/Newscom

Exhibit 11.1 ▶ Chapter Overview: Social Influences

This chapter describes three sources of influence (general, special, and groups) and the characteristics of influence (normative and informational). Information may be positive or negative, and may be provided verbally or nonverbally.

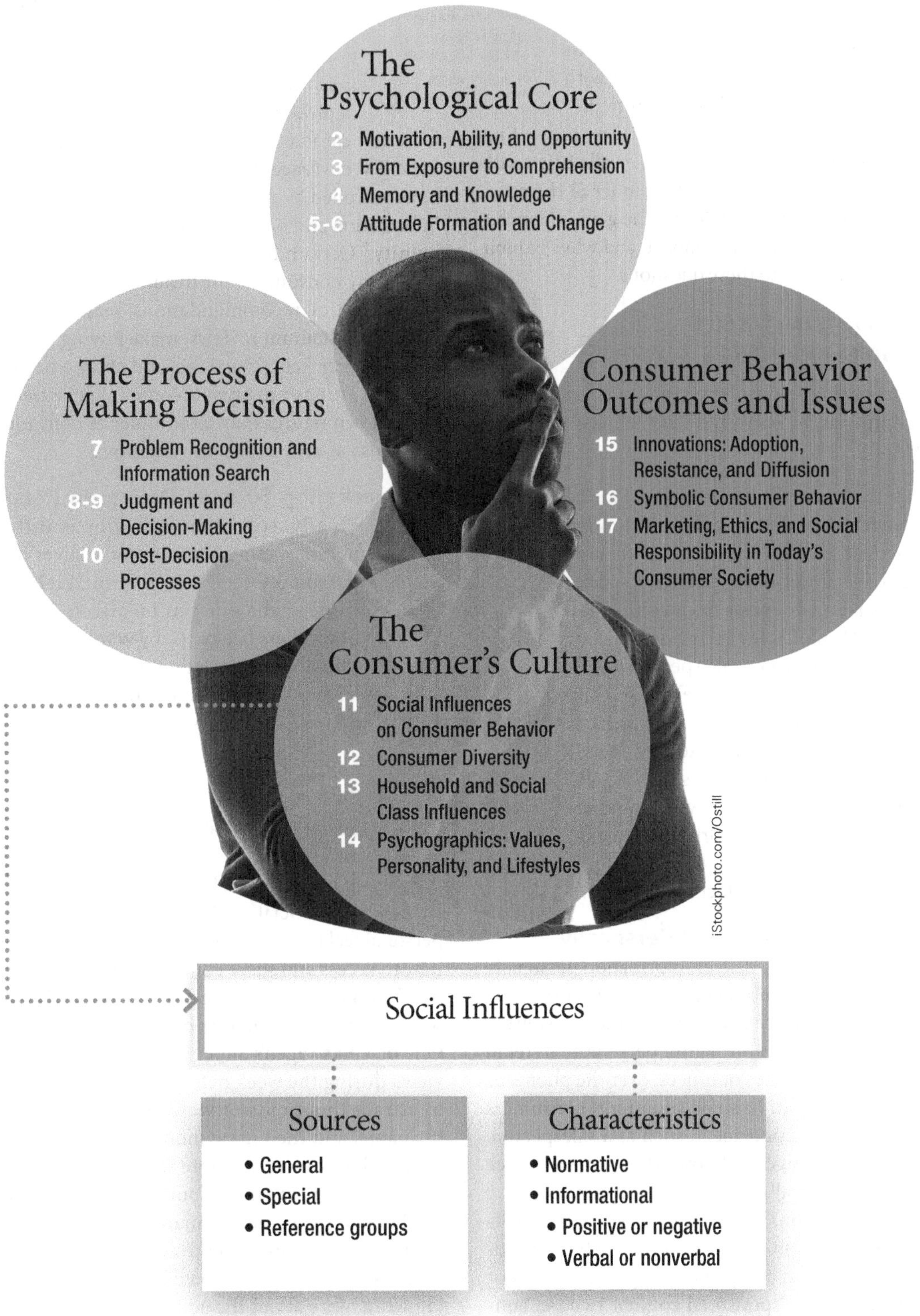

The
Psychological Core

2 Motivation, Ability, and Opportunity
3 From Exposure to Comprehension
4 Memory and Knowledge
5-6 Attitude Formation and Change

The Process of
Making Decisions

7 Problem Recognition and
Information Search
8-9 Judgment and
Decision-Making
10 Post-Decision
Processes

Consumer Behavior
Outcomes and Issues

15 Innovations: Adoption,
Resistance, and Diffusion
16 Symbolic Consumer Behavior
17 Marketing, Ethics, and Social
Responsibility in Today's
Consumer Society

The
Consumer's Culture

11 Social Influences
on Consumer Behavior
12 Consumer Diversity
13 Household and Social
Class Influences
14 Psychographics: Values,
Personality, and Lifestyles

iStockphoto.com/Ostill

Social Influences

Sources	Characteristics

• General
• Special
• Reference groups
	• Normative
	• Informational
	  • Positive or negative
	  • Verbal or nonverbal

11-1 Sources of Influence

Many people learn about products through advertising, Facebook, Pinterest, Instagram, e-mail, publicity, samples and coupons, personal experience, other people, and other sources.[1] Building buzz can be effective because it uses the influence of third parties to amplify initial marketing efforts.[2] For example, Rovio Entertainment teamed up with Britain's Prince William to call attention to illegal animal poaching of endangered species by promoting a special downloadable Angry Birds game called *Roll with the Pangolin*. Involving a prominent member of the royal family boosted the level of buzz during the game's launch.[3] But which sources have the most impact, and why? Exhibit 11.2 offers some answers to these questions.

> **Nonmarketing source** Influence delivered from an entity outside a marketing organization, for example, friends, family, and the media.

11-1a MARKETING AND NONMARKETING SOURCES

Influence can come from marketing and nonmarketing sources and can be delivered via the mass media or personally.

Marketing Sources Delivered via Mass Media

Marketing sources that deliver influence through the mass media (cell 1 in Exhibit 11.2) include advertising, sales promotions, publicity, special events, and social media posts from companies. Macy's and McDonald's try to influence your purchase behavior by promoting special sales or new products in newspapers, on television, and on Facebook. Marketing messages delivered via cell phones also fall under this category. Macy's includes QR (quick response) codes in some ads, in-store displays, and store windows. Consumers simply scan the code with a smartphone to view brief interviews with fashion designers, see promotional materials, or obtain more product information.[4]

> **Marketing source** Influence delivered from a marketing agent, for example, advertising, personal selling.

> **Word of mouth** Influence delivered verbally from one person to another person or group of people.

Marketing Sources Delivered Personally

Marketing sources can also deliver information personally (cell 3 in Exhibit 11.2). Salespeople, service representatives, and customer service agents are marketing sources of influence who deliver information personally in retail outlets, at consumers' homes or offices, over the phone, or via e-mail or online chat. In some situations, consumers will respond to a marketing agent, such as a salesperson, by making use of the agent's knowledge and assistance to further their personal goals. When consumers worry about undue persuasion, however, they will adopt techniques to fend off unwanted attention.[5] Some buzz-building tactics, such as when companies pay people to blog or tweet about a brand or "sponsored content" where "content" in a magazine or website is actually designed to serve as a promotional opportunity for the brand, blur the line between marketing and nonmarketing sources.

Nonmarketing Sources Delivered via Mass Media

As cell 2 in Exhibit 11.2 shows, sources that are not working for marketing companies (**nonmarketing sources**) can also wield influence via mass media–delivered messages. Consumer behavior may be affected by news items about new products, movies, and restaurants; product contamination; accidents involving products; and incidences of product abuse or misuse. Consumers shopping for a new car may learn about recalls and quality problems from TV coverage, Internet sites, blogs, and other media not controlled by marketers.[6] Some may be influenced by information and opinions obtained through a virtual community.[7] Certain media sources are particularly influential. Many consumers, for instance, choose movies based on film critics' recommendations, make dining decisions based on restaurant reviews, make buying decisions based on *Consumer Reports* articles, and choose books based on readers' ratings on Amazon.com. Celebrities and other well-known figures may also influence consumers' acquisition, usage, and disposition decisions.

Nonmarketing Sources Delivered Personally

Finally, consumer behavior is influenced by nonmarketing sources who deliver information personally (cell 4 in Exhibit 11.2).[8] Our consumer behavior can be affected by observing how others behave or by **word of mouth**, information about offerings communicated verbally by friends, family, neighbors, casual acquaintances, and even strangers.

Marketing and Nonmarketing Sources Delivered via Social Media

Social media platforms, such as Facebook, Vine, and YouTube, are increasingly used by both marketing and nonmarketing sources (cells 1 and 2 in Exhibit 11.2). Social media have a mass reach but a more personal feel because consumers choose when, where, and how to access and share content. For example, some Super Bowl ads go viral after being posted on YouTube, multiplying the number of viewers before and after the big game. One of Volkswagen's Super Bowl ads attracted 10 million views during the week before the Super Bowl, continued to attract thousands of viewers during the weeks after the game, and then drew more than one million viewers during the two weeks before the next year's Super Bowl.[9] Consumer-generated ads (nonmarketing sources encouraged or even rewarded by many marketers) can stimulate a range of social media conversations, from positive and negative comments, to debate over content and interest in knowing more about the ad and the brand.[10] Reaction to marketing sources delivered via social media is likely to be positive when the content is entertaining, informative, or is valued in some other way by the consumer audience.[11]

Exhibit 11.2 ▶ Sources of Influence

Social influence can come from marketing or nonmarketing sources and can be delivered via the mass media or in person. Nonmarketing sources tend to be more credible. Information delivered via the mass media can reach many people but may not allow for a two-way flow of communication.

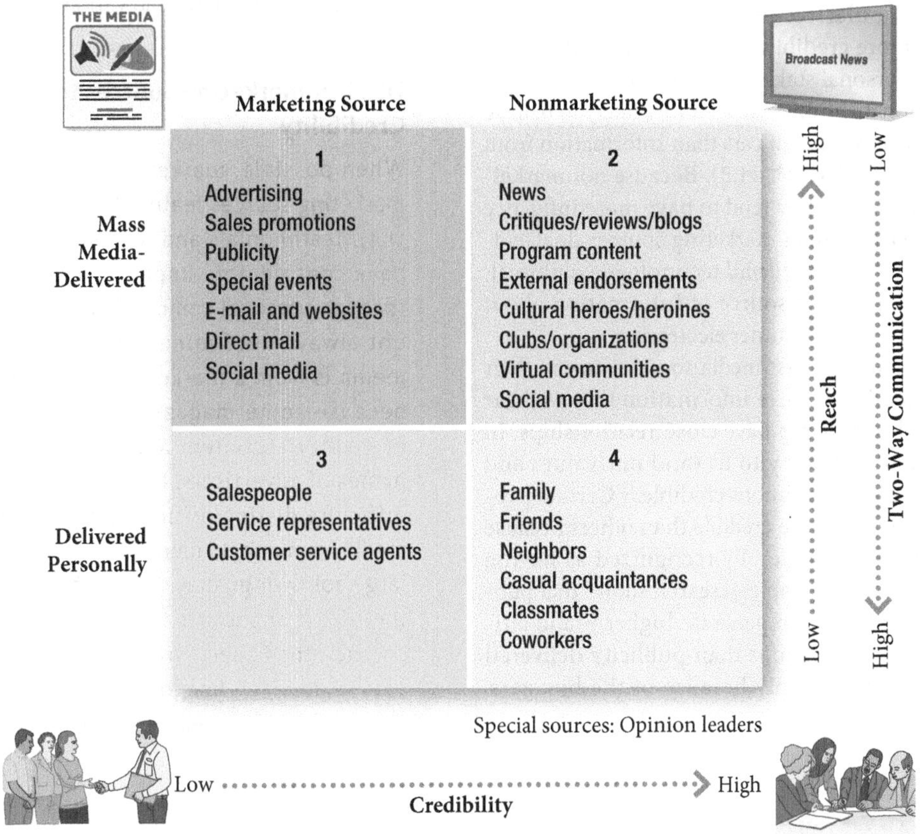

	Marketing Source	Nonmarketing Source	
Mass Media-Delivered	**1** Advertising Sales promotions Publicity Special events E-mail and websites Direct mail Social media	**2** News Critiques/reviews/blogs Program content External endorsements Cultural heroes/heroines Clubs/organizations Virtual communities Social media	High → Low Reach → Two-Way Communication
Delivered Personally	**3** Salespeople Service representatives Customer service agents	**4** Family Friends Neighbors Casual acquaintances Classmates Coworkers	Low → High

Special sources: Opinion leaders

Low ·················· → High
Credibility

11-1b HOW DO THESE GENERAL SOURCES DIFFER?

The influence sources shown in Exhibit 11.2 differ in terms of their reach, capacity for two-way communication, and credibility. In turn, these characteristics affect how much influence each source can have with consumers.

Reach

Mass media sources are important to marketers because they reach large consumer audiences. A 30-second TV commercial during the FIFA World Cup can reach tens of millions of viewers in the United States, Europe, and around the world. The Internet, cell phones, and other technologies are spreading marketing messages, product news, information about the behavior of public figures, and TV programs to an increasingly large audience, thus expanding marketers' reach dramatically.

Capacity for Two-Way Communication

Personally delivered sources of influence are valuable because they allow for a two-way flow of information. For example, a car salesperson may have more influence than a car ad because the salesperson can tailor sales information to fit the buyer's information needs, rebut counterarguments, reiterate important and/or complex information, and answer the buyer's questions. Personal conversations are often more casual and less purposeful than mass media–delivered information. During a conversation, people are less likely to anticipate what will be said and hence are less likely to take steps to avoid information inconsistent with their own frames of reference. Information from a personal source may also seem more vivid than information from the mass media because the person speaking somehow makes it more real, a factor that may make it more persuasive.[12]

Credibility

While personal and mass media sources differ in their reach and capacity for two-way communication, marketing and nonmarketing sources differ in their credibility. Consumers tend to perceive information delivered through marketing sources as being less credible, more biased, and manipulative. In contrast, nonmarketing sources appear more credible because we do not believe that they have a personal stake in our purchase, consumption, or disposition decisions. We are more likely to believe a *Consumer Reports* article on cars than information from a car salesperson (see Exhibit 11.3). Because nonmarketing sources are credible, they tend to have more influence on consumer decisions than marketing sources do. Geoffrey Fowler, a *Wall Street Journal* technology columnist, is a credible, independent source of information about smartphones and other consumer electronics.

Specific personal and mass media sources vary in their credibility. We tend to believe information that we hear from people with whom we have close relationships, in part because their similarity to us (and our values and preferences) makes their opinions credible.[13] Certain people are also regarded as more credible than others because they are experts or are generally recognized as having unbiased opinions. For example, research shows that publicity delivered via blogs can generate higher brand attitudes and purchase intensions than publicity delivered via online magazines, simply because of the bloggers' credibility.[14]

 Marketing Implications

Marketers can build on these differences in credibility, reach, and two-way communication capability to influence consumer behavior in various ways.

Use Nonmarketing Sources to Enhance Credibility

When possible, marketers should try to have nonmarketing sources feature their offerings (see Exhibit 11.4). Testimonials and word-of-mouth referrals may have considerable impact, particularly if delivered through personal communications.[15] Consumers cannot always determine whether information in the media is from a marketing or nonmarketing source because some magazine and newspaper ads look like editorial content and some articles mention the names of advertisers. Likewise, consumers may have difficulty distinguishing paid testimonials in social media from unpaid mentions. Some Twitter users with large followings may tweet about a brand because they like it or because they're paid to do so. For transparency, the Federal Trade Commission suggests that paid tweets and images carry a tag such as "#spon," "#sponsored," or "#promotion."[16] Online, marketers

Exhibit 11.3 ▶ Nonmarketing Sources Enhance Credibility

Nonmarketing sources of influence like Consumer Reports can have a powerful impact on consumer' purchase decisions because they are regarded as highly credible.

I CARRY TWO BADGES. THIS ONE'S FOR HOPE.

Lee/Splash News/Newscom/Splash News/New York/PRINT AD/United States

Exhibit 11.4 ▶ Celebrities as Opinion Leaders

Nonmarketing sources can yield powerful influence because they are often seen as more objective and less biased.

can also reach targeted groups by connecting with a virtual community structured around consumers' common interests (such as cooking or sports).[17]

Use Personal Sources to Enhance Two-Way Communication

Marketing efforts may be more effective when personal information sources are used. Hosts of home shopping parties are credible as sales representatives because "people want to buy from people they like and know," says the head of Tastefully Simple, which sells gourmet foods through such parties.[18] Many companies encourage managers and employees to post comments to social-media sites such as Twitter and Facebook, using appropriate hashtag identifiers, as a way of generating or continuing a dialogue with customers.[19] Best Buy, the electronics retailer, maintains a variety of blogs and Twitter accounts, through which executives and employees engage consumers in social media conversations about new products, tips about technical issues, and answers to customers' questions.[20]

Use a Mix of Sources to Enhance Impact

Because marketing and nonmarketing sources differ in their impact, the effect on consumers may be greatest when marketers use complementary sources of influence. Best Buy benefits from the combination of marketing sources (such as advertising and sales promotions) and nonmarketing sources (such as customer reviews on its website). Some companies stimulate referrals by rewarding customers with discounts or prizes when they refer other people, adding the credibility of a nonmarketing source (current customers) with the inducement of a marketing source (sales promotion).[21] One study of bank customers in Germany found that those who were referred by existing customers were significantly more likely to remain loyal and more profitable than average.[22]

11-1c OPINION LEADERS

Opinion Leader An individual who acts as an information broker between the mass media and the opinions and behaviors of an individual or group.

A special source of social influence is the **opinion leader**, someone who acts as an information broker between the mass media and the opinions and behaviors of an individual or group. Opinion leaders have some position, expertise, or firsthand knowledge that makes them particularly important sources of relevant and credible information, usually in a specific domain or product category. Thus, for example, National Basketball Association star Stephen Curry is an opinion leader for sports shoes (which is why Under Armour pays him for endorsing its products).[23]

Opinion leaders are regarded as nonmarketing sources of influence, a perception that adds to their credibility. They are not necessarily well-known people; they may be friends and acquaintances or professionals like doctors, dentists, or lawyers who advise patients and clients. Opinion leaders are part of a general category of **gatekeepers**, people who have special influence or power in deciding whether a product or information will be disseminated to a market.

Gatekeeper A source that controls the flow of information.

Researchers studying opinion leaders have observed several characteristics.[24] Opinion leaders tend to learn a lot about products, are heavy users of mass media, and tend to buy new products when they are first introduced. Opinion leaders are also self-confident, gregarious, and willing to share product information. They may become opinion leaders because of an intrinsic interest in and enjoyment of certain products—in other words, they have enduring involvement with a product category.[25] Opinion leaders might also like the power of having information and sharing it with others, or they may communicate information because they believe that their actions will help others.[26]

Opinion leaders have influence because they generally have no personal stake in whether their opinions are heeded, so their opinions are perceived as unbiased and credible. They are also regarded as knowledgeable about acquisition, usage, and disposition options because of their product knowledge and experience. These characteristics explain why consumers who enjoy cooking value the comments of celebrity chefs. In fact, after celebrity chefs Jamie Oliver and Delia Smith began promoting the use of shallots in recipes, U.K. sales of shallots rose by 46 percent in one year.[27] However, simply because opinion leaders serve as information brokers does not mean that information only flows from opinion leaders to consumers. Indeed, opinion leaders often get information by seeking it from consumers, manufacturers, and retailers.[28]

Whereas opinion leaders are important sources of influence about a particular product or service category, researchers have also identified another special source of influence—a **market maven**, someone who seems to have a lot of information about the marketplace in general.[29] A market maven seems to know all about the best products, the good sales, and the best stores or retail websites.

> **Market maven** A consumer on whom others rely for information about the marketplace in general.

The goal is to encourage positive, personal reviews, and thereby influence the attitudes and buying behavior of consumers who follow these bloggers. When Spin Master reformulated its Moon Dough molding dough, the company sent samples to hundreds of mommy bloggers. Their positive comments stimulated high interest and resulted in double-digit sales increases within weeks.[33]

Use Opinion Leaders in Marketing Communications

Although opinion leaders' influence may be less effective when delivered through a marketing source, their expertise and association can still support an offering. For example, the NBA's Stephen Curry doesn't just appear in ads for Under Armour sports shoes—he's also in ads funded by the Produce Marketing Association, urging teenagers to eat more fresh fruits and vegetables.[34] As an alternative, marketers may use simulated opinion leaders, such as a dentist's wife endorsing a toothpaste brand, because her affiliation with a dental professional presumably adds credibility.

Refer Consumers to Opinion Leaders

In many cases, marketers ask consumers to contact a knowledgeable opinion leader. Pharmaceutical manufacturers do this by suggesting that consumers consult their doctors (opinion leaders) about how a particular advertised product can help them. Research shows that these opinion leaders can influence the attitudes and behavior of other physicians as well as of consumers.[35]

Marketing Implications

Marketers use several tactics to influence opinion leaders.

Target Opinion Leaders

Given their potential impact and the fact that they are both seekers and providers of marketplace information, an obvious strategy is to identify and target opinion leaders directly.[30] For example, LEGO, a Danish toymaker, targets adult leaders of LEGO fan groups worldwide, seeking their input and, through them, influencing tens of thousands of fans who meet regularly to swap ideas and show off new LEGO creations.[31]

In Brazil, clothing brands target popular fashion bloggers before placing advertising because bloggers are particularly influential opinion leaders.[32] In another example, toy manufacturers often send free samples to "mommy bloggers," mothers whose blogs attract sizable audiences.

> **Associative reference group** A group to which we currently belong.

11-2 Reference Groups as Sources of Influence

Social influence is exerted by individuals such as opinion leaders as well as by specific groups of people. A reference group is a set of people with whom individuals compare themselves for guidance in developing their own attitudes, knowledge, and/or behaviors.

11-2a TYPES OF REFERENCE GROUPS

Consumers may relate to three types of reference groups: aspirational, associative, and dissociative. **Aspirational reference groups** are groups we admire and wish to be like but are not currently a member of. For example, a younger brother may want to be like his older brother and other older children. Given the high respect accorded to education in

South Korea, teachers often serve as an aspirational reference group for students there. Celebrities and athletes are also admired in Asia, which is why tennis champ Li Na has been signed to endorse Nike, Rolex, Mercedes-Benz, and other global brands marketed in her home country of China.[36]

Associative reference groups are groups to which we actually belong, such as a clique of friends, an extended family, a particular work group, a club, or a school group. The gender, ethnic, geographic, and age groups to which you belong are also associative reference groups with whom you may identify. Even consumers who think of themselves as individual-minded react well to products linked to appropriate associative reference groups.[37] However, when consumers misunderstand their relative position in a reference group, they tend to make poor acquisition or consumption decisions.[38] For example, if you believe you are one of the most skillful cyclists or skiers in your class—when in reality, you are just beyond beginner status—you may buy equipment or services unsuited to your capabilities.

> **Aspirational reference group** A group that we admire and desire to be like.

Associative reference groups can form around a brand, as is the case with clubs like the HOG (Harley Owners Group), which is made up of Harley-Davidson fans. A **brand community** is a specialized group of consumers with a structured set of relationships involving a particular brand, fellow customers of that brand, and the product in use.[39] A consumer who is a member of a brand community thinks about brand names (e.g., Harley-Davidson), the product category (e.g., motorcycles), other customers who use the brand (e.g., HOG members), and the marketer that makes and promotes the brand.[40] Members of a brand community not only buy the product repeatedly, but they are extremely committed to it, share their information and enthusiasm with other consumers, and influence other members to remain loyal.[41] Interestingly, such communities may survive even after the brand is discontinued.[42]

> **Brand community** A specialized group of consumers with a structured set of relationships involving a particular brand, fellow customers of that brand, and the product in use.

Dissociative reference groups are groups whose attitudes, values, and behaviors we disapprove of and do not wish to emulate. U.S. citizens, for instance, serve as dissociative reference groups to religious groups in some Arab countries, and neo-Nazis serve as dissociative reference groups for many people in Germany and the United States. Note that the influence of dissociative reference groups can depend, in part, on whether a product is consumed in public or in private.[43]

> **Dissociative reference group** A group we do not want to emulate.

 ## Marketing Implications

The influence of various reference groups has some important implications for marketers.

Associate Products with Aspirational Reference Groups

Knowing their target consumers' aspirational reference group enables marketers to associate their product with that group and to use spokespeople who represent it. Because celebrities are an aspirational reference group for some, many organizations use celebrities to endorse products or communicate with targeted audiences.[44] For example, do-it-yourself home improvement expert Carter Oosterhouse, whose TV shows have included Million Dollar Rooms and Trading Spaces, actively participates in Habitat for Humanity construction projects, using his celebrity status to encourage consumers to donate money or time.[45]

Accurately Represent Associative Reference Groups

Marketers can also identify and appropriately represent target consumers in ads by accurately reflecting the clothing, hairstyles, accessories, and general demeanor of their associative reference groups.[46] To sell products like skateboards and mountain climbing equipment, for example, many sports marketers develop promotions featuring actual skateboarders and mountain climbers.

Help to Develop Brand communities

Many brands now create the framework for communities on Facebook or on dedicated websites. These brand communities bring together like-minded consumers, reinforce brand loyalty, encourage positive attitudes toward the brand and its products, and disseminate information about the brand. For example, the Boston Red Sox baseball team maintains a Facebook page with more than five million "likes," plus a website that is home to the Kid Nation and Red Sox Nation brand communities. Before, during, and after baseball season, thousands of Red Sox fans worldwide enjoy interacting within these brand communities.

Avoid Using Dissociative Reference Groups

When appropriate, companies should not use dissociative reference groups in their marketing. Some marketers drop celebrity spokespeople who commit crimes or exhibit other behavior that is offensive to the target market. For example, after the disclosure that Lance Armstrong had taken performance-enhancing drugs during his celebrated bicycle-racing career, he lost lucrative sponsorship deals with Nike and Trek Bicycle, among other brands.[47]

Homophily The overall similarity among members in the social system.

11-2b CHARACTERISTICS OF REFERENCE GROUPS

Reference groups can be described according to the degree of contact, formality, similarity among members, group attractiveness, density, degree of identification, and strength of the ties connecting members.

Degree of contact

Reference groups vary in their degree of contact. We may have direct and extensive contact with some reference groups like our immediate circle of friends or family but may have less contact with others like politicians. Reference groups with which we have considerable contact tend to exert the greatest influence.[48] A group with which we have face-to-face interaction, such as family, peers, and professors, is a **primary reference group**. In contrast, a **secondary reference group** is one that may influence us even though we have no personal contact with most of its members. We may be members of groups like an Internet chat group or a musical fan club. Although we may interact with some members of the group only through such impersonal communication channels as newsletters, its behavior and values can still influence our behavior.

Primary reference group Group with whom we have physical face-to-face interaction.

Secondary reference group Group with whom we do not have direct contact.

Formality

Reference groups also vary in formality. Groups like fraternities, athletic teams, clubs, and classes are formally structured, with rules outlining the criteria for group membership and the expected behavior of members. For example, you must satisfy certain requirements—gaining admission, fulfilling class prerequisites—before you can enroll in particular college courses. Once enrolled, you must follow rules for conduct by submitting assignments on time. Other groups are more ad hoc, less organized, and less structured. For example, your immediate group of friends is not formally structured and probably has no official rules. People who attend the same party

or vacation on the same cruise also may constitute an informal group.

Homophily: The Similarity Among Group Members

Groups vary in their **homophily**, the similarity among the members. When groups are homophilous, reference-group influence is likely to be strong because similar people tend to see things in the same way, interact frequently, and develop strong social ties.[49] Group members may have more opportunity to exchange information and are more likely to accept information from one another. Because senders and receivers are similar, the information that they share is also likely to be perceived as credible.

Group Attractiveness

The attractiveness of a particular peer group can affect how much consumers conform to the group.[50] When members perceive a group as being very attractive, they have stronger intentions to conform to what the group does—even its illicit consumption behavior. This situation implies that making substance abusers seem less attractive may help U.S. children and teens resist illicit activities.

Density

Dense groups are those in which group members all know one another. For example, an extended family that gets together every Sunday operates as a dense social network. In contrast, the network of faculty at a large university is less dense because its members have fewer opportunities to interact, share information, or influence one another. In many countries, network density varies by geographic area. A rural village may have high density because its families have known each other for generations whereas many of the 10 million residents of Seoul may not know one another, so network density there is low.

Degree of Identification

Some characteristics of an individual within a group contribute to the ways in which groups vary. One is the degree of identification that a consumer has with a group. Just because people are members of a group does not mean that they use it as a reference group. The influence that a group has on an individual's behavior is affected by the extent to which he or she identifies with it.[51] One study found that consumers who attend sporting events were more likely to buy a sponsor's products when they strongly identified with the team and viewed such purchases as a group norm.[52] Moreover, a marketing stimulus that focuses attention on consumers' identification with a certain group (such as ethnic or religious identity) and is relevant to that identification will more likely elicit a positive response.[53]

Tie-Strength

Another characteristic describing individuals within a group is **tie-strength**.[54] A strong tie means that two people are connected by a close, intimate relationship often characterized by frequent interpersonal contact. A weak tie means that the people have a more distant relationship with limited interpersonal contact. Exhibit 11.5 illustrates these concepts.

Tie-strength The extent to which a close, intimate relationship connects people.

consumers are in frequent contact and are connected by strong ties, information about acquiring, using, and disposing of an offering—or related offerings—is likely to be transmitted quickly. The best way to disseminate information rapidly within a market is to target individuals in dense networks characterized by strong ties and frequent contact.

For example, social media users read posted messages and replies of their friends and the brand or products they follow or like—and they spread the word by retweeting, reposting, and adding comments of their own, both positive and negative. Knowing this, McDonald's and other marketers announce new products and promotions on Facebook and other social media to take advantage of the rapidfire spread of information.[55]

Formal Reference Groups as Potential Targets

Formal reference groups can provide marketers with clear targets for marketing efforts. For example, the U.K.-based charity Comic Relief targets formal groups like companies, schools, and rugby clubs to encourage fundraising activities in connection with its two major events, Red Nose Day and Sport Relief. Partnering with supporters such as the grocery chain Sainsbury's, the BBC television network, and neighborhood schools, Comic Relief has raised more than $1.5 billion to help children in need.

Marketing Implications

Marketers pay close attention to the characteristics of reference groups because of their influence on targeting and communication.

Understanding Information Transmission

Homophily, degree of contact, tie-strength, and network density can significantly influence whether, how much, and how quickly information is transmitted within a group. Within dense networks, in which

Exhibit 11.5 ▶ Tie-Strength and Social Influence
The thick red line shows that Anne has strong ties to three school friends: Maria, Kyeung, and Keshia. The blue line indicates that Anne is less closely tied to Jeff, someone she knows from her health club. Another blue line indicates that Maria does not have a close relationship with her distant cousin Tyrone. If you were a marketer, whom would you target in this network? Why?

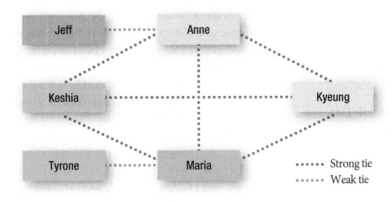

The charity has now established Red Nose Day in the United States, with Walgreens as its retail partner and a bevy of celebrity supporters.[56]

Homophilous Consumers as Targets

Marketers may use the concept of homophily to market their products. For example, if you log on to amazon.com and find a book you like, the recommendation system points you to more books you might like based on the purchases of consumers who bought the first book. The principle is that you might share the reading tastes of people that the site considers to be similar to you. The same goes for Netflix's movie recommendation system.

Targeting the Network

Sometimes it makes sense for marketers to target the network itself. Verizon Wireless, for example, offers one large pool of monthly cell phone minutes and data to be shared among family members. Marketers may also encourage referrals by asking consumers to "tell a friend about us." Ticketmaster, for example, has an app that targets users' Facebook networks. Integrated with the Spotify digital music service, the app recommends upcoming entertainment events based on each user's listening history. Users can click on individual concerts to post Facebook messages like "I want to go" or "I just bought tickets," which encourages discussion among friends and purchases of tickets to attend concerts together. "People who are friends on Facebook generally have very similar interests, and Spotify connected with Facebook is a great way to learn what other people are listening to," explains a Ticketmaster executive.[57]

Research shows that within social networks, one-fifth of a user's friends actually influence that user's activity level on the site. As a result, marketers need to study the interactions among social media users when planning to target the network.[58]

Understanding the Strength of Weak Ties

Although weak ties may seem to have little potential for marketers, the opposite is true. Because weak ties often serve as "bridges" connecting groups, they can play a powerful role in propagating information across networks.[59] In Exhibit 11.5, for instance, Maria is a bridge between her close friends (Keshia, Kyeung, and

Embedded market
Market in which the social relationships among buyers and sellers change the way the market operates.

Jeff Greenberg/PHOTOEDIT

Exhibit 11.6 ▶ Embedded Markets
The Girl Scouts is an example of an embedded market, as they often sell to people within their social network.

Anne) and her distant cousin (Tyrone). Once she gives information to Tyrone, he can communicate it to others with whom he has ties.

In fact, researchers have found that word of mouth spreads more broadly among people with weak ties. Moreover, marketers can use weak ties to identify new networks for marketing efforts. For example, direct-selling organizations like Avon and charitable groups like the American Cancer Society target individual consumers as selling (or fundraising) agents and rely on their interpersonal networks to reach others.

Individuals can tap not only consumers with whom they have strong ties but also those with whom they have weak ties. Girl Scouts, for example, sell cookies to friends and relatives as well as to neighbors, parents' co-workers, and people shopping at grocery stores (see Exhibit 11.6). These are called **embedded markets** because

the social relationships among buyers and sellers change the way that the market operates.[60] Thus, your social relationship with a seller may influence the way that you react to his or her selling efforts. You are more likely to buy Girl Scout cookies from a neighbor's daughter than from a girl you have never met, because you want to remain on good terms with your neighbor. Or you can use the Girl Scouts' app to locate the nearest source of Girl Scout cookies in your area. Girl Scout cookies even have a dedicated Facebook page with more than 700,000 likes.[61]

11-2c REFERENCE GROUPS AFFECT CONSUMER SOCIALIZATION

One way that reference groups influence consumer behavior is through socialization, the process by which individuals acquire the skills, knowledge, values, and attitudes that are relevant for functioning in a given domain. **Consumer socialization** is the process by which we learn to become consumers and come to know the value of money; the appropriateness of saving versus spending; and how, when, and where products should be bought and used.[62] Through socialization, consumers learn consumption values as well as gain the knowledge and skills for consumption.[63]

Consumer socialization can occur in many ways, as the following sections show.

People as Socializing Agents

Reference groups like family and friends play an important role as socializing agents. Parents may, for example, instill values of thriftiness by directly teaching their children the importance of saving money, letting the children observe them being thrifty, or rewarding children for being thrifty. One study found that direct teaching was most effective for instilling consumer skills in younger children and observational learning was most effective for older children.

Intergenerational influence—information, beliefs, and resources being transmitted from one generation (parents) to the next (children)—affects consumers' acquisition and use of certain product categories and preferred brands.[64] Research shows that children are using brand names as cues for consumer decisions by the time they are 12 years old.[65] Note that parenting styles and socialization patterns vary from culture to culture.[66] In individualistic cultures like Australia and the United States, where many parents are relatively permissive, children develop consumer skills at an earlier age. In contrast, children in a collectivist culture such as India, where parents tend to be stricter, understand advertising practices at a later age.

Moreover, parents affect socialization by influencing what types of products, TV programs, and ads their children are exposed to and how much control they have over buying products that they want.[67] Some observers worry that exposure to these socializing agents encourages children to see the acquisition of material goods as a path to happiness, success, and achievement.[68] Some parents are very concerned about their children's exposure to violent and sexually explicit programming and products and actively regulate what their children watch and what games they play.[69]

The effect of reference groups as socializing agents can change over time. Parents have substantial influence on young children, but their influence wanes as children grow older and interact more with their peers.[70] Similarly, your high school friends probably had a more powerful effect on your values, attitudes, and behaviors when you were younger than they do now. Because we associate with many groups throughout our lives, socialization is a life-long process.

The Media and the Marketplace as Socializing Agents

TV programs, movies and videos, music, video games, the Internet, and ads can also serve as socializing agents. For example, in ads, boys are sometimes depicted as more knowledgeable, aggressive, active, and instrumental to actions than girls are; these sex role stereotypes can affect children's conceptions of what it is like to be a boy rather than a girl.[71]

Comic Relief, the previously discussed nonprofit organization active in the United Kingdom and the United States, is a great example of harnessing the socializing power of media for a good cause. By partnering with the BBC television network (in the United Kingdom) and the NBC television network (in the United States) and inviting involvement through multiple traditional and digital media, Comic Relief raises a sizeable sum for charitable causes. Millions of people see promotional messages on television leading up to each charity day, and then watch during prime time as entertainers perform and talk about the progress toward the fundraising goal. For the inaugural U.S. Red Nose Day, NBC created an app that enabled users to paste a virtual red nose on their social-media profile photos. Other fundraising partners offered to donate money when consumers used designated hashtags on social media sites. Sharing and resharing sent these promotions viral and helped Comic Relief raise more than $21 million by the end of its first U.S. event.[72]

11-3 Normative Influence

Thus far you have learned about various sources of influence—general, special, and group. These sources can exert two types of influence, normative and informational (see Exhibit 11.7). Assume that you are at a dinner interview

Consumer socialization The process by which we learn to become consumers.

Exhibit 11.7 ▶ Sources of Influence and Types of Influence

Marketing and nonmarketing sources, special influence sources, and certain groups can affect consumer behavior by exerting normative and/or informational influences.

Sources of Influence

SOURCES OF INFLUENCE
- Marketing or nonmarketing source
- Delivered personally or by social or mass media
- Differ in reach, capacity for two-way communication, credibility

SPECIAL INFLUENCE SOURCES
- Opinion leaders
- Market mavens

GROUPS AS INFLUENCE SOURCES
- Aspirational
- Associative
- Dissociative
- Groups vary in contact, formality, homophily, density, identification, tie-strength

Exert Influence

NORMATIVE INFLUENCE
- Can affect brand choice congruence, conformity, compliance, or reactance

INFORMATIONAL INFLUENCE
- Affected by characteristics of the product, the consumer, and the group

with a prospective employer who tells you that she is a vegetarian. You may be reluctant to order beef, which you love, because you want to make a good impression.

Normative influence is social pressure designed to encourage conformity to the expectations of others.[73] Chapter 5 discusses normative influences in the context of how they affect intentions and consumption behaviors. The term normative influence derives from **norms**, society's collective decisions about what behavior should be. For example, we have norms for which brands, stores, and styles are "in" as well as norms that discourage stealing and impulse buying.[74] Morals also exert normative influence about what is right and wrong, and they can strongly influence attitudes—as they do in people's views of cigarette smoking, for example.[75]

Normative influence implies that consumers will be sanctioned, punished, or ridiculed if they do not follow the norms,[76] just as it also implies that they will be rewarded for performing the expected behaviors. To illustrate, a prospective boss may reward you with a job offer or deny you a job, depending on your behavior in the interview. Middle-school girls impose sanctions by treating classmates differently when they do not conform to the dress norm.[77]

Norm Collective decision about what constitutes appropriate behavior.

Brand-choice congruence The purchase of the same brand as members of a group.

Conformity The tendency to behave in an expected way.

11-3a HOW NORMATIVE INFLUENCE CAN AFFECT CONSUMER BEHAVIOR

Normative influence can have several important effects on consumption behaviors.

Brand-Choice Congruence and Conformity

Normative influence affects **brand-choice congruence**—the likelihood that consumers will buy what others in their group buy. If you compare the types of clothes, music, hairstyles, and cars that you buy with the selections of your friends, you will probably find that you and your friends make similar choices.[78] The presence of others can influence the enjoyment of shared stimuli (such as going to a movie together) and affect congruence as well.[79] Friends, relatives, and others in your social network may also influence the types of goods and services that you buy as gifts.[80] Simply rehearsing what to say in anticipation of discussing a particular brand purchase with others can change the way that consumers think and feel about the product and its features.[81]

Normative influence can also affect **conformity**, the tendency for an individual to behave as the group behaves. Conformity and brand-choice congruence may be related. For instance, you might conform by buying the same brands as others in your group do,[82] although brand-choice congruence is not the only way for you to conform. You may also conform by performing activities that the group wants you to perform, such as participating in initiation rites or acting in the way that the group acts. For example, your actions at a party might depend on whether you are there with your parents or your friends. In each case, you are conforming to a certain set of expectations regarding appropriate behavior. One study found that the norms established by social and brand relationships can influence consumer behavior as well.[83]

Pressures to conform can be substantial.[84] Research examining group pressure toward underage drinking and drug consumption found that students worried about how others would perceive them if they refused to conform to the group's expected behavior. Other studies have shown that conformity increases as more people in the group conform. However, identity-based thinking ("I am an environmentalist") is very strong and resistant to conformity pressures.[85] Note that conformity varies by culture. Compared with U.S. consumers, for example, Japanese consumers tend to be more group oriented and conform more to group desires.

Compliance Versus Reactance

Compliance, a somewhat different effect of normative influence, means doing what someone explicitly asks you to do. You are complying if, when asked, you fill out a marketing research questionnaire or purchase the products sold at a home party. Parents comply with children by purchasing foods or toys or allowing activities (such as parties) that kids request. In a virtual community, members may *not* comply as readily with the group's desires because the members are anonymous and can withdraw at will.[86]

> **Compliance** Doing what the group or social influencer asks.

When we believe our freedom to choose is being threatened, a boomerang effect occurs and we engage in **reactance**—doing the opposite of what a person or group wants us to do.[87] For example, if a salesperson pressures you too much, you may engage in reactance by refusing to buy whatever he or she is trying to sell, even if you wanted to buy it in the first place. Reactance can occur in brand communities too. When a member feels too much pressure to perform certain rituals or assume certain roles, desire to participate in the community or buy the brand in the future may be lowered.[88]

> **Reactance** Doing the opposite of what the individual or group wants us to do.

Social-Relational Theory

According to social-relational theory, consumers conduct their social interactions according to (1) the rights and responsibilities of their relationship with group members, (2) a balance of reciprocal actions with group members, (3) their relative status and authority, and (4) the value placed on different objects and activities. In turn, these relationships and their unspoken rules wield normative influence on consumer behavior.[89] For instance, consumers may regard as taboo transactions in which they are asked to pay for something held to have morally significant value, such as love, friends, family, or even votes in an election. Taboos based on cultural or historical elements may also apply to buying and selling transactions.[90]

11-3b WHAT AFFECTS NORMATIVE INFLUENCE STRENGTH

The strength of normative influence depends on the characteristics of the product, the consumer, and the group to which the consumer belongs.

Product Characteristics

Reference groups can influence two types of decisions: (1) whether we buy a product within a given category and (2) what brand we buy. However, whether reference groups affect product and brand decisions also depends on whether the product is typically consumed in private or in public and whether it is a necessity or a luxury.[91] As Exhibit 11.8 shows, mattresses and hot-water heaters are considered privately consumed necessities, whereas jewelry and inline skates are considered publicly consumed luxuries. This exhibit reflects predictions about when reference groups will affect these decisions.

One prediction is that because we must buy necessity items, reference groups are likely to have little influence on whether we buy such products. However, reference groups might exert some influence on whether we buy a luxury item. For example, your friends will probably not influence whether you buy tissues, a necessity you would buy in any case. But friends might influence whether you get an Apple Watch, in part because luxury products communicate status—something that may be valued by group members. Also, luxury items may communicate your special interests and values and thus convey who you are and with whom you associate.

A second prediction is that products consumed in public—such as the cars we drive—give others the opportunity to observe which brand we have purchased (whether it is a Ford F-150 or a Prius). In contrast, few people see which brand of mattress we buy because we consume this product in private. Different brand images communicate different things to people, so reference groups are likely to have considerable influence on the brand we buy when the product is publicly consumed but not when it is privately consumed. Moreover, a publicly consumed product provides opportunities for sanctions, whereas it would be difficult for groups to develop norms and sanctions for violations when the product is consumed privately. Therefore, reference groups influence product category choice for

Exhibit 11.8 ▶ Reference Group Influences on Publicly and Privately Consumed Products

Reference groups tend to influence consumption of a *product category* only when the product is a luxury (not a necessity). Reference groups tend to influence consumption of a particular *brand* only when the product is consumed in public (not when it is consumed in private). Give some examples of your own to illustrate the matrix.

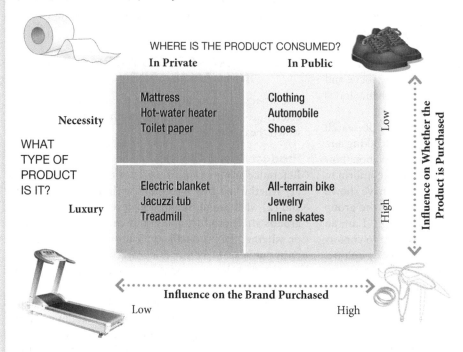

WHERE IS THE PRODUCT CONSUMED?

	In Private	**In Public**	
Necessity	Mattress Hot-water heater Toilet paper	Clothing Automobile Shoes	Low
Luxury	Electric blanket Jacuzzi tub Treadmill	All-terrain bike Jewelry Inline skates	High

WHAT TYPE OF PRODUCT IS IT?

Influence on Whether the Product is Purchased

Influence on the Brand Purchased

Low .... High

luxuries but not for necessities and they influence brand choice for products consumed in public but not for those consumed in private.[92]

The significance of the product to the group also affects normative influence.[93] Some products designate membership in a certain group. A varsity sports jacket may signify team membership and play a significant role in designating in and out-group status. The more central a product is to the group, the greater the normative influence the group exerts over its purchase. Finally, whether a product is perceived as embarrassing may also influence acquisition and consumption behavior that occurs in a more public setting.[94]

Consumer Characteristics

The personalities of some consumers make them readily susceptible to influence by others.[95] The trait of competitiveness, for instance, can influence conspicuous consumption behavior.[96] Several researchers have developed the scale of "susceptibility to interpersonal influence," which includes some of the items in Exhibit 11.8. Consumers who are susceptible to interpersonal influence try to enhance their self-image by acquiring products that they think others will approve of. These consumers are also willing to

Coercive power The extent to which the group has the capacity to deliver rewards and sanctions.

conform to others' expectations about which products and brands to buy.

In addition, a personality characteristic called "attention to social comparison information" (ATSCI) is related to normative influence. Exhibit 11.9 shows several items from an ATSCI scale. People who are high on this personality trait pay close attention to what others do and use this information to guide their own behavior. For example, research shows that people feel lower self-esteem when they are exposed to idealized ad images of financial success or physical attractiveness.[97] When consumers are susceptible to normative influence, they tend to react more positively to communications highlighting product benefits that help them avoid social disapproval.[98]

Tie-strength also affects the degree of normative influence. When ties are strong, individuals presumably want to maintain their relationships with others, so they are therefore motivated to conform to the group's norms and wishes.[99] Normative influence is also affected by a consumer's identification with the group.[100] When a member of a group such as a family or subculture does not identify with that group's attitudes, behaviors, and values, normative reference-group influence will be weak.

Group Characteristics

Finally, the characteristics of the group can impact the degree of normative influence. One characteristic is the extent to which the group can deliver rewards and sanctions, known as the degree of reward power or **coercive power**.[101] To illustrate, your friends probably have more influence over your clothing choices than your neighbors do because friends have greater coercive power. That is, they are better able to deliver sanctions if they consider your clothing inappropriate or out of style. In fact, men tend to spend more when they shop with a friend than they would alone, although this does not occur when women shop with a friend. The influence is also different for high self-monitoring, agentic consumers, who tend to spend more when they shop with a friend than when they shop alone.[102]

Items Indicating Susceptibility to Interpersonal Influence	1. I rarely purchase the latest fashion styles until I am sure my friends approve of them. 2. If other people can see me using a product, I often purchase the brand they expect me to buy. 3. I often identify with other people by purchasing the same products and brands that they purchase. 4. To make sure that I buy the right product or brand, I often observe what others are buying and using. 5. If I have little experience with a product, I often ask my friends about the product. 6. I frequently gather information from friends or family about a product before I buy it.
Items Indicating Attention to Social Comparison Information	1. It is my feeling that if everyone else in a group is behaving in a certain manner, this must be the proper way to behave. 2. I actively avoid wearing clothes that are not in style. 3. At parties, I usually try to behave in a manner that allows me to fit in. 4. When I am uncertain about how to act in a social situation, I look to the behavior of others for cues. 5. I tend to pay attention to what others are wearing. 6. The slightest look of disapproval in the eyes of a person with whom I am interacting is enough to make me change my approach.

Source: Susceptibility to Interpersonal Influence Scale from William O. Bearden, Richard G. Netemeyer, and Jesse E. Teel, "Measurement of Consumer Susceptibility to Interpersonal Influence," *Journal of Consumer Research*, March 1989, pp. 472–481. Reprinted with permission of The University of Chicago Press.

Exhibit 11.9 ▶ Measuring Susceptibility to Interpersonal Influence and Attention to Social Comparison Information

Individuals differ in whether they are susceptible to influence from others and whether they pay attention to what others do. What conclusions can you draw about yourself based on your answers to these questions? What implications do these questions have for marketers?

Group cohesiveness and group similarity also affect the degree of normative influence.[103] Cohesive groups and groups with similar members may communicate and interact on a regular basis. Thus, they have greater opportunity to convey normative influences and deliver rewards and sanctions. Research shows that if a company calls consumers' attention to their cultural identity, their increased awareness of their membership in a particular group can influence their decisions based on group norms.[104] Normative influence tends to be greater when groups are large and when group members are experts.[105] For example, you might be more inclined to buy a bottle of wine recommended by a group of wine experts than one recommended by a casual acquaintance.

Finally, consumers from cultures where collectivism is strong—such as China—are more sensitive to how differences in pricing affect those in their group, compared with consumers from cultures where individualism is strong, such as the United States.[106] This accounts, in part,

for why the practice of *tuangou*, the self-organized banding together of consumers to get discounts by shopping as a group, is especially popular in China. Online group buying grows year after year in China, where digital retailers like Alibaba and Tencent account for more than 80 percent of the $12.6 billion market.[107]

 Marketing Implications

Marketers can take a variety of actions based on normative influences and the factors that affect their strength.

Demonstrate Rewards and Sanctions for Product Use/Nonuse

Marketers may be able to create normative influence by using advertising to demonstrate rewards or sanctions that can follow from product use or nonuse. For example, beer or liquor ads often show friends approving of the purchase or consumption of the advertised brand.

Create Norms for Group Behavior

Marketing organizations may create groups with norms to guide consumers' behavior. Because influence is greater when consumption is public, another strategy is to make a private behavior public, either in person or online via apps, communities, or websites. Under Armour, for example, offers apps that allow consumers to track their fitness activities and compare performance with that of other users in the group. App users can challenge each other to improve and they can also see when they meet or exceed group norms (by being more active or performing better in a particular sport or fitness technique). And by using datamining to analyze app users' data, Under Armour will gain a better understanding of what active consumers do and want.[108]

> **Foot-in-the-door technique** A technique designed to induce compliance by getting an individual to agree first to a small favor, then to a larger one, and then to an even larger one.

Stimulate Referrals Through Normative Influence

Companies can use normative influence to encourage referrals from current customers. "Bring a friend" promotions are one example. The Swedish retailer IKEA uses Facebook among other media to promote its "Bring Your Own Friend Day," offering two-for-one specials in its in-store cafeterias plus discounts, gift-card giveaways, decorating seminars, free shopping bags, and more. Its Facebook page suggested sending invitations to friends designated as "my personal shoppers." For each Facebook friend invited by an IKEA fan, the company donated $1 to a children's charity, another inducement to spread the word and participate.[109] Although referral programs can pay off in the form of higher sales and profits, marketers need to target and test carefully, because not all customers are equally profitable or loyal.[110]

> **Door-in-the-face technique** A technique designed to induce compliance by first asking an individual to comply with a very large and possibly outrageous request, followed by a smaller and more reasonable request.

> **Even-a-penny-will-help technique** A technique designed to induce compliance by asking individuals to do a very small favor—one that is so small that it almost does not qualify as a favor.

Create Conformity Pressures

Marketers may also attempt to create conformity. For example, they may actively associate a product with a certain group so that their product becomes a badge of group membership. They may simulate conformity by showing actors in an ad behaving similarly with respect to a product, as some antismoking campaigns do by portraying teens who do not smoke.[111] Conformity may also be enhanced by publicizing others' conformity, a situation that happens at Mary Kay cosmetics parties and at charity fundraisers like telethons.

Use Compliance Techniques

With the **foot-in-the-door technique**, marketers try to enhance compliance by getting a consumer to agree first to a small favor, then to a larger one, and then to an even larger one. For example, a salesperson may first ask a consumer his or her name and then ask what the person thinks of a given product. After complying with these requests, the consumer may be more inclined to comply with the salesperson's ultimate request to purchase the product.[112]

With the **door-in-the-face technique**, the marketer first asks the consumer to comply with a very large and possibly outrageous request, and then presents a smaller and more reasonable request. For example, a salesperson might ask a consumer whether she wants to buy a $500 piece of jewelry. When the consumer says no, the salesperson might then ask if she wants to buy a set of earrings on sale for only $25.[113] Because the consumer perceives that the requester has given something up by moving from a large to a small request, he or she may feel obligated to reciprocate by responding to the smaller request. Moreover, compared to the large initial request, the second seems much more modest.

A third approach is the **even-a-penny-will-help technique**.[114] Here, marketers ask the consumer for a very small favor—so small that it almost does not qualify as a favor. Marketers collecting money for a charity may indicate that even a penny will help those in need. For example, Pennies, a U.K. charity, uses this technique by asking consumers to donate small change electronically when paying by credit card at Domino's Pizza and other participating merchants. If they agree, the purchase is rounded up to the next whole number and the charity receives the few cents' difference. In the first five years, Domino's customers donated more than $2 million to Pennies.[115] Salespeople making cold calls may even tell prospective clients that even one minute of their time will be valuable. Because people would look foolish denying these tiny requests, they often comply and give an amount appropriate for the situation.

Ask Consumers to Predict Their Behavior

Simply asking consumers to predict their own behavior in taking a certain action often increases the likelihood that they will actually behave in that way.[116] For example, a marketer of products containing recycled parts might ask consumers to predict their behavior in supporting the environment by buying or using products made with reclaimed materials.[117] This request may remind consumers that they have not been doing enough to live up to their own standards in supporting the environment—in turn, leading to purchases that will fulfill the consumers' self-prophecy.

Provide Freedom of Choice

Because reactance usually occurs when people feel that their freedom is being threatened, marketers need to ensure that consumers believe that they have freedom of choice. For example, a salesperson might show a consumer a variety of smartphones, discussing the advantages of each. In this situation, the consumer will feel a greater sense of control over whether to buy at all, and if so, which item to buy. Marketers often offer multiple products within a product line to allow for more choices of features, benefits, and price points, as consumers consider their personal needs and priorities.

Use Expert Service Providers Who Are Similar to Target Customers

Some research shows that consumers are more likely to comply with what a service provider asks (and be more satisfied with the outcome) when the provider and customer have similar attitudes and when the expert clarifies the customer's role.[118]

11-4 Informational Influence

In addition to normative influence, reference groups and other influence sources can exert **informational influence** by offering information to help consumers make decisions.[119] For example, chat groups on Internet travel sites exert informational influence by providing travel tips to prospective travelers. Friends exert informational influence by telling you which movie is playing at the local theater, and the media exert informational influence by reporting that certain foods may be health hazards.

Informational influence can affect how much time and effort consumers devote to information search and decision-making. If you can get information easily from a friend, you may be reluctant to conduct an extensive, time-consuming information search when making a decision. Therefore, if you want a new tablet computer, and a trusted friend says that the one he just bought is

> **Informational influence** The extent to which sources influence consumers simply by providing information.

the best he has ever had, you might simply buy the same one.

11-4a FACTORS AFFECTING INFORMATIONAL INFLUENCE STRENGTH

The extent to which informational influence is strong or weak depends on the characteristics of the product, of the consumer and the influencer, and of the group.

Product Characteristics

Consumers tend to be susceptible to informational influence when considering complex products such as electronic appliances that consumers cannot easily understand how to use.[120] They are also more susceptible to informational influence when they perceive product purchase or usage to be risky.[121] Thus, consumers may be affected by information that they receive about cosmetic surgery, given its formidable financial and safety risks or investment decisions, given its economic risks. Consumers may also be more open to informational influence when they themselves cannot tell the difference between brands.[122]

Consumer and Influencer Characteristics

Characteristics of both the consumer and the influencer affect the extent of informational influence. Such influence is likely to be greater when the source or group communicating the information is an expert,[123] especially if the consumer either lacks expertise or has had ambiguous experiences with the product. For example, given their lack of knowledge and confidence about the home-buying process, first-time home buyers may carefully consider the information conveyed by experts such as real estate agents. Personality traits, such as consumers' susceptibility to reference group influence or open-mindedness, also influence the extent to which consumers look to others for cues on product characteristics.[124]

Like normative influence, informational influence is affected by tie-strength. Individuals with strong ties tend to interact frequently, a situation that provides greater opportunities for consumers to learn about products and others' reactions to them. Note that informational influence may actually affect the ties between individuals. When people establish social relationships that involve sharing information, for example, they may become friends in the process.[125] Informational influence can also be affected by interactions with strangers online. Specifically, consumers seeking information online will assess how quickly and frequently an information provider—such as an anonymous reviewer—responds to questions and comments.[126]

Finally, culture may affect informational influence. One study found that U.S. consumers were more likely than Korean consumers to be persuaded by information-packed ads. Because the Korean culture often focuses on the group and group compliance, Korean consumers may be more susceptible to normative influence than U.S. consumers are.[127]

Group Characteristics

Group cohesiveness also affects informational influence. Specifically, members of cohesive groups have both greater opportunity and perhaps greater motivation to share information.

Marketing Implications

Marketers can apply informational influence in several ways.

Create Informational Influence by Using Experts

Because source expertise and credibility affect informational influence, marketers can use sources regarded as expert or credible for the product category, as Under Armor does when it uses sports stars such as skier Lindsey Vonn and football player Brandon Jennings in its ads.[128]

Create a Context for Informational Influence

Marketers should try to create a context for informational influence to occur. One way to do this is by hosting or sponsoring special product-related events where people can talk to one another about the company's products. Another way is to host online chats or social media accounts to spark company or brand conversations. The home-goods retailer West Elm maintains a series of popular blogs and invites customer comments about its posts and images concerning home fashions, entertaining friends at home, and similar interests.[129] In addition, inviting consumers to rate products on the marketers' website provides a forum for online discussion and stimulates word of mouth—especially where ratings vary—which in turn contributes to higher product sales.[130]

Create Informational and Normative Influence

Marketing efforts may be most successful when both normative and informational influences are involved. One study found that only 2 percent of consumers donated blood in the absence of any type of influence, but between 4 and 8 percent did so when either informational or normative influence was present. However, when both forms of influence were used, 22 percent of

the consumers donated blood.[131] Also, because source similarity enhances both normative and informational influence, advertisers might enhance influence by using sources that are similar to their target audience. Using web-based recommendation systems is another approach to using both normative and informational influence.[132] Finally, marketers can provide clues to product scarcity—such as notifying customers that "due to high demand, only five are left in stock." This strategy acts as an informational normative influence and encourages consumers to "join the crowd" and purchase the item, to avoid being left out.[133]

11-4b DESCRIPTIVE DIMENSIONS OF INFORMATION

In the context of consumer behavior, information can be described by the dimensions of valence and modality.

Valence: Is Information Positive or Negative?

> **Valence** Whether information about something is good (positive valence) or bad (negative valence).

Valence describes whether the information is positive or negative. This distinction is very important because researchers have found that negative and positive information affect consumer behavior in different ways.[134] More than half of the dissatisfied consumers engage in negative word of mouth. Moreover, dissatisfied consumers talk to three times more people about their bad experiences than satisfied consumers do about their good experiences.[135] People who like to post online comments about products react more to negative information than do people who read without posting—perhaps because the posters want to make it look like they have high standards.[136]

Researchers hypothesize that people pay more attention to and give more weight to negative information than they do to positive information.[137] Negative information may be diagnostic—that is, it has more significance because it seems to tell us how offerings differ from one another. Most of the information we hear about offerings is positive, so negative information may receive more attention because it is surprising, unusual, and different.[138] Negative information may also prompt consumers to attribute problems to the offering itself, not to the consumer who uses it.[139] Thus, if you learn that a friend got sick after eating at a new restaurant, you may attribute the outcome to bad food rather than to your friend's eating too much. Although some brands may be reluctant to use negative advertising, brands such as Campbell's Soup have been successful in using negative information to attract consumer attention to competitive comparisons of specific product attributes and benefits.[140]

Modality: Does Information Come from Verbal or Nonverbal Channels?

Another dimension describing influence is the modality through which it is delivered—is it communicated verbally or nonverbally? Although norms about group behavior might be explicitly communicated by verbal description, consumers can also infer norms through observation. For instance, a consumer may learn that a particular brand of can openers is bad either by observing someone struggling with it or by hearing people discuss their experiences with the product.

11-4c THE PERVASIVE AND PERSUASIVE INFLUENCE OF WORD OF MOUTH

Marketers are especially interested in word of mouth, both online and offline, which can affect many consumer behaviors. Your neighbor may recommend a hair stylist; you may overhear a stranger say that Nordstrom's semiannual sale is next week. Or you may go to a new movie because your friend posted a positive comment on Facebook. In fact, word of mouth before a movie is released and during its first week in theaters has been shown to strongly influence other consumers' movie-going intentions.[141] When Paramount released *Mission: Impossible—Rogue Nation*, it relied on last-minute word of mouth from bloggers and the buzz from reaction to the exciting in-theater trailer to draw movie-goers on the first weekend. The strategy worked: The movie opened to strong initial demand, and positive comments from viewers increased demand in the crucial early days of release.[142]

A variety of factors can influence whether people seek word-of-mouth advice from others. For example, whereas 60 percent of affluent households use a financial advisor, only 2 percent of middle class households do so. This is unfortunate because financial advisors can have considerable impact on the retirement savings of middle class households.[143]

What motivates individuals to provide word of mouth? Although one might assume that people engage in word-of-mouth behavior to be altruistic and helpful to others, research suggests that motivations are more often driven by self (vs. other) desires.[144] In particular, people engage in word of mouth to make themselves look good (smart, in the know), which should also make them feel better about themselves. They also do so as a way of feeling connected to others, and perhaps by encouraging others to share what they know. Of course, sometimes people just love a product so much that they want to persuade others to buy it too. In addition to personal motives, product characteristics also affect word of mouth. People are also more likely to provide word of mouth for products that are publically visible and cued by the environment (i.e., accessible in memory). Marketers can play a significant role in cueing a product by virtue of its advertising and promotional activities.[145]

Not only is word of mouth *pervasive* but also more *persuasive* than written information is.[146] It is also extremely influential in purchases of printed and electronic books. "Even in this digital age, the best sales tool remains word of mouth," says a spokesman for Random House, the largest U.S. book publisher. "Nothing trumps that."[147]

Online Word of Mouth

Online forums, review sites, websites, and e-mail magnify the effect of word of mouth because consumers can notify many people about their good or bad experiences with a few clicks of the mouse. For instance, in any given month, 61 million consumers worldwide read reviews of local businesses that consumers post on yelp.com; tripadvisor.com has 50 million consumer-contributed reviews of hotels and other travel businesses. People can provide online word of mouth in several different ways. They can *explain* what a new product is or how it works, *evaluate* it (provide pros and cons), *endorse* (recommend) it, or personally *embrace* it.[148] Research shows that the most persuasive consumer-generated reviews of a good or service offer evidence to support an overall recommendation ("Buy the Divine chocolate, because it tastes good and is fair trade") and include information about key features ("70% cocoa content").[149]

Customers' purchasing decisions are also influenced by observing what others do online after being exposed to the same online word of mouth. For example, consumers who use Amazon.com can read product reviews and then look at the items displayed under the banner "What Other Items Do Customers Buy After Viewing This Item?" This combination is especially influential in the case of products with high word-of-mouth volume.[150]

Social Media Word of Mouth

Social media such as Twitter, YouTube, Pinterest, Instagram, and Facebook are truly *social*, disseminating word of mouth through public messages and through messages visible only to friends (see Exhibit 11.10). In turn, other consumers may keep the conversation going by reposting the original message, echoing it in their own words, rebutting it, recording a video response, or in other ways. These social exchanges can themselves spark word of mouth and get more consumers involved in the conversation and the brand or product. When a product or brand "trends" on Twitter, for example, many users will click to see what others are tweeting about. Similarly, when a YouTube video attracts so many views that it lands on the YouTube home page, that additional exposure is responsible for more views.

Marketers who provide consumers with opportunities to comment via social media during product acquisition or consumption are, in effect, facilitating real-time word of mouth. Simply facilitating sharing of TV program content via social media can increase viewership, according to a recent study. Consumers who click on the content shared via social media are more than twice as likely to become new viewers of the program itself.[151]

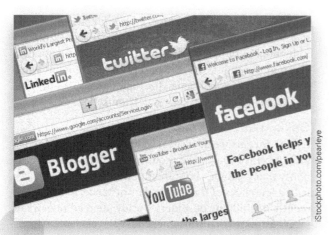

iStockphoto.com/pearleye

Exhibit 11.10 ▶ Social Media Word of Mouth

Word of mouth is now often real-time due to social media and all its many outlets.

 Marketing Implications

Word of mouth can have a dramatic effect on consumers' product perceptions and an offering's marketplace performance. **Viral marketing** refers to the rapid spread of brand/product information among a population of people stimulated by brands. Viral marketing has contributed in large part to the global success of products such as Angry Birds video games. Marketers want brand or product information to "go viral" because of the opportunity to influence many people in a short period. But virality is most likely to occur when the information is emotionally evocative—it induces awe, anger, interest, surprise—and when the information is useful. [152]

Often, small businesses such as hairstylists and preschools cannot afford to advertise in traditional media and rely almost exclusively on word-of-mouth referrals, consumer reviews online, and mentions in social media. Doctors, dentists, and lawyers often rely heavily on word of mouth because they fear that extensive advertising will cheapen their professional image. Moreover, success in some industries (such as entertainment) is ultimately tied to favorable word of mouth. For this reason, companies routinely watch for mentions of their brands online and in social media. Just as important, marketers can actively stimulate discussion by posting information and responding to comments and questions online, often with special emphasis on social media.

Yet word of mouth can have unexpected implications. One study found that consumers with a high need

Viral marketing
Rapid spread of brand /product information among a population of people stimulated by brands.

for uniqueness prefer not to provide positive word of mouth for publicly consumed products that they own, although they will provide word of mouth for privately consumed products. Why? Because positive word of mouth often results in higher sales of a product, which would dilute the uniqueness of publicly consumed products, at least in the eyes of these consumers. [153]

Engineering Favorable Word of Mouth

Marketers can try to engineer favorable word of mouth by targeting opinion leaders and using networking opportunities at trade shows, conferences, and public events. Many have social media strategies that include YouTube, Facebook, Twitter, and other popular sites. Many marketers post product advertisements on YouTube. [154] Film companies routinely post previews on YouTube and on branded sites devoted to each movie, with the goal of building anticipation and prelaunch positive buzz. When consumers are familiar with a brand, positive word of mouth is especially influential, more so than negative word of mouth. On the other hand, consumers resist positive word of mouth about brands they are highly unlikely to purchase (and resist negative word of mouth about brands they are highly likely to purchase). [155] Original products—those that are highly innovative—generate more word of mouth than nonoriginal products. If the product is both original and useful, meaning it meets consumer needs, it is more likely to promote positive word of mouth. [156]

Engineering favorable word of mouth should be an ongoing effort across marketing activities. For instance, an employee group at Gatorade monitors social media mentions, responds to comments, and coordinates social media activities with other marketing efforts. The company integrates its traditional advertising with its social media strategy by, for example, "using the hashtag very purposefully when we're trying to get the conversation going," says a top Gatorade official. [157]

Preventing and Responding to Negative Word of Mouth

Marketers must act to prevent negative word of mouth, whether offline or online, and work to rectify it once it occurs. In the event of a major crisis, a firm must take immediate steps to address the issues, restore confidence, and begin rebuilding its reputation (see Exhibit 11.11). [158]

Rather than ignoring complaints or derogatory comments, firms that empathize with consumers' complaints, address the issues, and respond in a meaningful

DO:	DON'T:
• Listen carefully to understand public perceptions.	• Ignore the crisis.
• Address the issues quickly, consistently, and appropriately.	• Delay your response.
• Be as transparent as possible.	• Evade the issues.
• Make customers your priority.	• Respond with indifference anger or impatience.
• Have a contingency plan to win back customers' trust.	• Ignore regular business operations during the crisis.

Exhibit 11.11 ▶ Restoring a Company's Reputation
Crisis management experts suggest that companies under siege take certain steps (and avoid others) to rebuild their reputation.

way will be more successful at reducing negative word of mouth. For example, L.L. Bean closely monitors product reviews posted by customers and responds to negative comments by reexamining the product's improvement potential and, in some cases, withdrawing the product. "There's value in these conversations," explains the chief marketing officer, "but if you're not acting upon them, you're missing it."[159] In fact, one study of negative online comments found that when a firm responds, 33 percent of customers will follow up with a positive comment and 34 percent of customers will take down the original negative comment.[160]

All kinds of customer comments about a product or brand can go viral. Not long ago, a parent's tweet went viral after she complained about Target separating children's toys by gender and reinforcing gender stereotypes. Within weeks of this viral conversation, the retailer announced it would change its displays so children's toys are not grouped by "boy" or "girl." It also changed its toy signage to avoid using pink or blue to denote gender.[161]

Handling Rumors and Scandals

Rumors are a special case of negative word of mouth.[162] Scandals can also touch off negative word of mouth, even affecting a company's competitors.[163] Companies should be aware of what consumers are saying about their brands and products, offline, online, and in social media—and be ready to deal with rumors and scandals.

▶ *Do nothing.* Often companies prefer to do nothing because more consumers may actually learn about a rumor from marketers' attempts to correct it. However, this strategy can also backfire. For example,

after Nike was accused of condoning low wages and abusive conditions in its Asian factories, its image suffered when it did not respond vigorously to the attacks. The company has since responded in various ways, including putting links to labor standards on its website and severing ties with suppliers that violate those standards. Apple, which produces iPhones and iPads in China, faced similar criticism and now publicizes its annual factory audits, as well as investigating complaints that arise.[164]

▶ *Do something locally.* Some companies react locally, putting the rumor to rest on a case-by-case basis. For example, the firm might send a detailed explanation to people who write or call about a particular rumor. In such cases, companies should brief staff members about the rumor and how to respond to consumers.

▶ *Do something discreetly.* Companies may want to respond discreetly to a rumor. For example, when rumors circulated that oil companies were contriving oil shortages out of greed, the firms ran a public relations campaign highlighting their socially desirable activities. They did not mention the rumor, but the gist of the campaign clearly ran contrary to the rumor's content.

▶ *Do something big.* At times, companies may respond with all the media resources at their disposal. They may use advertising to directly confront and refute the rumor or explain the scandal, create news, and conduct media interviews to communicate their perspective, and hire credible outside opinion leaders to help present factual information. For example, when reports surfaced about the all-electric Chevrolet Volt's battery catching fire following government safety tests, parent company General Motors quickly, publicly, and repeatedly pointed to the car's real-world safety record. It offered Volt owners a free GM loaner car to drive while the safety issue was under investigation. Within weeks, GM had redesigned the battery case to reduce the risk of fire and installed it without charge in Volts already on the road.[165]

Tracking Word of Mouth

Whether word of mouth is positive (like referrals) or negative (like rumors), companies may want to try to identify the source. Marketers can find out where consumers heard the information and then ask all of those sources where, in turn, they heard the story.[166] Companies such as Dell have special departments devoted to analyzing online and social media comments to see where and when they originated and how they're spreading. With this information, the firms can be prepared to

respond accordingly. Marketers can also ask consumers about the specific details that they heard from particular sources, to identify who is distorting information and who is perpetuating the distortions. Then the company can follow up by, for example, thanking or rewarding individuals who communicate positive word of mouth and provide referrals.

Summary:

Consumers are influenced by many sources—marketing and nonmarketing; those that are delivered through the mass media and those that are delivered personally. Consumers regard nonmarketing sources as more credible than marketing sources. Information delivered personally has less reach but more capacity for two-way communication compared with information from mass media sources. Marketers may want to target opinion leaders, online and offline, who are sources of influence because they are experts in a product category.

Reference groups, people with whom individuals compare themselves, may be associative, aspirational, or dissociative; they can be described according to their degree of contact, formality, homophily, group attractiveness, density, identification, and tie-strength. These influence sources exert normative and informational influence. Normative influence tends to be greater for products that are publicly consumed, considered luxuries, or regarded as a significant aspect of group membership. Normative influence is also strong for individuals who tend to pay attention to social information and when groups are cohesive, members are similar, and the group can deliver rewards and sanctions.

Informational influence operates when individuals affect others by providing information. Consumers are most likely to seek and follow informational influence when products are complex, purchase or use is risky, and

brands are distinctive. Social influence varies in valence and modality. Negative information is communicated to more people and given greater weight in decision-making than positive information is. Marketers are particularly interested in word of mouth, both positive and negative, online and offline, and in social media.

Questions for Review and Discussion

1. **How do sources of influence differ in terms of marketer domination and delivery?**

2. **How are social media affecting social influence?**

3. **Why do companies sometimes target opinion leaders for marketing attention?**

4. **What are the three types of reference groups, and how can these groups be described?**

5. **How might consumers respond to normative influence?**

6. **What three techniques can marketers use to encourage consumer compliance?**

7. **Differentiate between information valence and modality.**

8. **Why is word of mouth so important for marketers?**

Endnotes

1   See http://www.socialmediatoday.com/social-networks /2015-04-13/worlds-21-most-important-social-media-sites-and-apps-2015

2   Greg Metz Thomas, "Building the Buzz with the Hive in Mind," *Journal of Consumer Behaviour* 4, no. 1, 2004, pp. 64–72.

3   Ella Alexander, "Prince William Launches Angry Birds Video Game to Protest Against Animal Poaching," *The Independent*, November 17, 2014, www.independent.co.uk.

4   Alex Samuely, "Macy's Leverages In-Store QR Codes for Black Friday Giveway," *Mobile Commerce Daily*, November 25, 2014, www.mobilecommercedaily.com; and Giselle Tsirulnik, "Macy's Is 2011 Mobile Marketer of the Year," *Mobile Marketer*, December 9, 2011, www.mobilemarketer.com.

5   Amna Kirmani and Margaret C. Campbell, "Goal Seeker and Persuasion Sentry: How Consumer Targets Respond to Interpersonal Marketing Persuasion," *Journal of Consumer Research* 31, December 2004, pp. 573–582.

6   Tracy Rickman Cosenza, Michael R. Solomon, and Wi-suk Kwon, "Credibility in the Blogosphere: A Study of Measurement and Influence of Wine Blogs as an Information Source," *Journal of Consumer Behaviour* 14, no. 2, 2015, pp. 71–91.

7   Huynh Thi Xuan Mai and Svein Otta Olsen, "Consumer Participation in Virtual Communities: The Role of Personal Values and Personality," *Journal of Marketing Communications* 21, no. 2, 2015, pp. 144–164.

8   See Mehdi Mourali, Michel Larouche, and Frank Pons, "Antecedents of Consumer Relative Preference for Interpersonal Information Sources in Pre-Purchase Search," *Journal of Consumer Behaviour* 4, no. 5, 2005, pp. 307–318.

9   Cotton Delo, "Doritos' Latest Super Bowl Ad Contest Storms Viral Video Chart," *Advertising Age*, January 12, 2012, www.adage.com.

10 Colin Campbell, Leyland F. Pitt, Michael Parent, and Pierre R. Berthon, "Understanding Consumer Conversations Around Ads in a Web 2.0 World," *Journal of Advertising* 40, Spring 2011, pp. 87–102.

11 David G. Taylor, Jeffrey E. Lewin, and David Strutton, "Friends, Fans, and Followers: Do Ads Work on Social Networks?" *Journal of Advertising Research* 51, March 2011, pp. 258–275.

12 Frederick Koenig, *Rumor in the Marketplace* (Dover, Mass.: Auburn House, 1985); and Paul M. Herr, Frank R. Kardes, and John Kim, "Effects of Word-of-Mouth and Product-Attribute Information on Persuasion: An Accessibility-Diagnosticity Perspective," *Journal of Consumer Research* 17, March 1991, pp. 454–462.

13 Ali Faraji-Rad, Bendik M. Samuelsen, and Luk Warlop, "On the Persuasiveness of Similar Others: The Role of Mentalizing and the Feeling of Certainty," *Journal of Consumer Research*, 2015, forthcoming 42, no. 3 pp. 458–471.

14 Jonas Colliander and Micael Dahlen, "Following the Fashionable Friend: The Power of Social Media," *Journal of Advertising Research* 51, March 2011, pp. 313–320.

15 Andreas B. Eisingerich, Hae Eun Helen Chun, Yeyi Liu, He Michael Jia, and Simon J. Bell, "Why Recommend a Brand Face-to-face But Not on Facebook? How Word-of-Mouth on Online Social Sites Differs from Traditional Word-of-Mouth," *Journal of Consumer Psychology* 25, no. 1, 2015, pp. 120–128.

16 Buchalter Nemer, "New FTC Guidelines for Promoting Products on Social Media," *Lexology*, July 28, 2015, www.lexology.com.

17 Karine Raïes, Hans Mühlbacher, and Marie-Laure Gavard-Perret, "Consumption Community Commitment: Newbies' and Longstanding Members' Brand Engagement and Loyalty," *Journal of Business Research* 68 no. 12 (2015): 2634–2644.

18 Susan B. Garland, "So Glad You Could Come. Can I Sell You Anything?" *New York Times*, December 19, 2004, sec. 3, p. 7; and Rachel Sammon and Kyoung-Nan Kwon, "Host's Interpersonal Influence on Guests in a Home Sales Party," *Journal of Retailing and Consumer Services* 23, no. 1, 2015, pp. 32–38.

19 Garett Sloane, "Essential Tips for Turning Employees into Social Media Ambassadors," *Adweek*, February 18, 2015, www.adweek.com.

20 Richard S. Levick, "4 Strategic Requirements for Corporate Tweeting," *Fast Company*, January 20, 2012, www.fastcompany.com.

21 Gangseog Ryu and Lawrence Feick, "A Penny for Your Thoughts: Referral Reward Programs and Referral Likelihood," *Journal of Marketing* 71, January 2007, pp. 84–94.

22 Philipp Schmitt, Bernd Skiera, and Christophe Van den Bulte, "Why Customer Referrals Can Drive Stunning Profits," *Harvard Business Review*, June 2011, www.hbr.org.

23 John Consoli, "MBPT Spotlight: Under Armour's Athlete Endorsers Starting to Resonate with Consumers," *Broadcasting & Cable*, August 4, 2015, www.broadcastingcable.com.

24 Hans Risselada, Peter C. Verhoef, and Tammo HA Bijmolt, "Indicators of Opinion Leadership in Customer Networks: Self-Reports and Degree Centrality," *Marketing Letters* 26, no. 1, 2015, pp. 1–12. Regarding innovativeness, see Terry L. Childers, "Assessment of the Psychometric Properties of an Opinion Leadership Scale," *Journal of Marketing Research* 23, May 1986, pp. 184–187.

25 Marsha L. Richins and Teri Root-Shafer, "The Role of Involvement and Opinion Leadership in Consumer Word of Mouth," in ed. Michael J. Houston, *Advances in Consumer Research*, vol. 15 (Provo, Utah: Association for Consumer Research, 1988), pp. 32–36.

26 Piotr S. Bobkowski, "Sharing the News Effects of Informational Utility and Opinion Leadership on Online News Sharing," *Journalism & Mass Communication Quarterly* 92, no. 2, pp. 320–345, 2015.

27 "Why We Love Shallots: Sales Double in a Year Thanks to Jamie and Delia," *Daily Mail (UK)*, January 21, 2011, www.dailymail.co.uk.

28 Lawrence F. Feick, Linda L. Price, and Robin Higie, "People Who Use People," in ed. Richard J. Lutz, *Advances in Consumer Research*, vol. 13 (Provo, Utah: Association for Consumer Research, 1986), pp. 301–305; see also Jagdish N. Sheth, "Word-of-Mouth in Low-Risk Innovations," *Journal of Advertising Research* 11, June–July 1971, pp. 15–18.

29 Ronald E. Goldsmith, Ronald A. Clark, and Elizabeth Goldsmith, "Extending the Psychological Profile of Market Mavenism," *Journal of Consumer Behavior* 5, no. 5, 2006, pp. 411–419; and Lawrence F. Feick and Linda L. Price, "The Market Maven: A Diffuser of Marketplace Information," *Journal of Marketing* 51, January 1987, pp. 83–97.

30 See, for example, Dorothy Leonard-Barton, "Experts as Negative Opinion Leaders in the Diffusion of a Technological Innovation," *Journal of Consumer Research* 11, March 1985, pp. 914–926.

31 Thane Grauel, "Lego Builds Adult Fan Base," *Journal News (Westchester, NY)*, November 28, 2014, www.usatoday.com; and Daniel Michaels, "For Some Grown-Ups, Playing with Legos Is a Serious Business," *Wall Street Journal*, November 17, 2011, www.wsj.com.

32 "Eye on Brazil," *WWD*, September 22, 2011, www.com.

33 Mae Anderson, "Mom my Bloggers Can Make or Break Toys," *San Francisco Chronicle*, December 26, 2011, www.sfgate.com.

34 Tom Karst, "Celebrities Endorse Fresh Produce in New Marketing Campaign," *The Packer*, February 26, 2015, www.the-packer.com.

35 Lee Al, "Who Are the Opinion Leaders?" *Journal of Health Communication* 15, September 2010, pp. 629–655.

36 Bill Wilson, "Wimbledon 2014: Li Na Courts Fans and Sponsors," *BBC News*, June 22, 2014, www.bbc.com; and Malcolm Moore, "Li Poised to Become Richest Woman in Sports," *Telegraph (UK)*, August 2, 2011, www.telegraph.co.uk.

37 Jennifer Edson Escalas and James R. Bettman, "Self-Construal, Reference Groups, and Brand Meaning," *Journal of Consumer Research* 32, no. 3, 2005, pp. 378–389.

38 Andrew D. Gershoff and Katherine A. Burson, "Knowing Where They Stand: The Role of Inferred Distributions of Others in Misestimates of Relative Standing," *Journal of Consumer Research* 38, October 2011, pp. 407–419.

39 Albert M. Muniz Jr. and Thomas C. O'Guinn, "Brand Community," *Journal of Consumer Research* 27, March 2001, pp. 412–432; and James H. McAlexander, John W. Schouten, and Harold F. Koenig, "Building Brand Community," *Journal of Marketing* 66, January 2002, pp. 38–54.

40 James H. McAlexander, John W. Schouten, and Harold Koenig, "Building Brand Community," *Journal of Marketing* 66, no. 1, 2002, pp. 38–54.

41 Richard P. Bagozzi and Utpal M. Dholakia, "Antecedents and Purchase Consequences of Customer Participation in Small Group Brand Communities," *International Journal of Research in Marketing* 23, no. 1, 2006, pp. 45–61.

42 Albert M. Muniz Jr. and Hope Jensen Schau, "Religiosity in the Abandoned Apple Newton Brand Community," *Journal of Consumer Research* 31, no. 4, 2005, pp. 737–747.

43 Katherine White and Darren W. Dahl, "To Be or Not Be? The Influence of Dissociative Reference Groups on Consumer Preferences," *Journal of Consumer Psychology* 16, no. 4, 2006, pp. 404–414; and Katherine White and Darren W. Dahl, "Are All Out-Groups Created Equal? Consumer Identity and Dissociative Influence," *Journal of Consumer Research* 34, no. 4, 2007, pp. 525–536.

44 Jennifer Edson Escalas and James R. Bettman, "Managing Brand Meaning Through Celebrity Endorsement," *Brand Meaning Management* 12, 2015, pp. 29–52; Aoi Tanaka, Cathy Nguyen, and Jenni Romaniuk, "The Strengths and Weaknesses of Celebrities as Branding and Creative Design Elements in Advertising," *Journal of Design, Business & Society* 1, no. 1, 2015, pp. 57–75.

45 Jesse Strauch, "Oosterhouse Helps Build Houses for the Needy," *MSNBC*, January 18, 2012, www.msnbc.msn.com.

46 Basil G. Englis and Michael R. Solomon, "To Be and Not to Be: Lifestyle Imagery, Reference Groups, and the Clustering of America," *Journal of Advertising* 24, March 1995, pp. 13–28.

47 Daniel Roberts and Benjamin Snyder, "Ray Rice and 11 Other Athletes Who Lost Their Endorsements," *Fortune*, September 20, 2014, www.fortune.com.

48 A. Benton Cocanougher and Grady D. Bruce, "Socially Distant Referent Groups and Consumer Aspiration," *Journal of Marketing Research* 8, August 1971, pp. 379–383.

49 Linda L. Price, Lawrence Feick, and Robin Higie, "Preference Heterogeneity and Coorientation as Determinants of Perceived Informational Influence," *Journal of Business Research* 19, November 1989, pp. 227–242; Jacqueline J. Brown and Peter Reingen, "Social Ties and Word-of-Mouth Referral Behavior," *Journal of Consumer Research* 14, December 1987, pp. 350–362; Mary C. Gilly, John L. Graham, Mary Wolfinbarger, and Laura Yale, "A Dyadic Study of Interpersonal Information Search," *Journal of the Academy of Marketing Science* 26, no. 2, pp. 83–100; an d George Moschis "Social Comparison and Informal Group Influence," *Journal of Marketing Research* 13, August 1976, pp. 237–244.

50 Randall L. Rose, William O. Bearden, and Kenneth C. Manning, "Attributions and Conformity in Illicit Consumption: The Mediating Role of Group Attractiveness," *Journal of Public Policy & Marketing* 20, no. 1, Spring 2001, pp. 84–92.

51 Sharon E. Beatty, Alexa M. Givan, George R. Franke, and Kristy E. Reynolds, "Social Store Identity and Adolescent Females' Store Attitudes and Behaviors," *Journal of Marketing Theory and Practice* 23, no. 1, 2015, pp. 38–56.

52 Robert Madrigal, "The Influence of Social Alliances with Sports Teams on Intentions to Purchase Corporate Sponsors' Products," *Journal of Advertising* 29, no. 4, Winter 2000, pp. 13–24.

53 Americus Reed II, "Activating the Self-Importance of Consumer Selves: Exploring Identity Salience Effects on Judgments," *Journal of Consumer Research* 31, September 2004, pp. 286–295.

54 Jonathan K. Frenzen and Harry L. Davis, "Purchasing Behavior in Embedded Markets," *Journal of Consumer Research* 17, June 1990, pp. 1–12; Brown and Reingen, "Social Ties and Word-of-Mouth Referral Behavior"; Jonathan K. Frenzen and Kent Nakamoto, "Structure, Cooperation, and the Flow of Market Information," *Journal of Consumer Research* 20, December 1993, pp. 360–375; and Bryan Johnson and Matthew T. Seevers, "Developing Interpersonal Influence in Retail Purchasing Networks: An Exploratory Analysis of Tie Quantity, Tie Strength, and Tie Type," *International Journal of Marketing Studies* 7, no. 1, 2015, pp. 39–54.

55 Azadeh Williams, "Salesforce: McDonald's Has Captured the Future of Marketing," *CMO Magazine (Australia)*, July 17, 2015, www.cmo.com.

56 Adam Forrest, "Red Nose Day: Why Comic Relief Relies on Celebrities," *Forbes*, May 20, 2015, www.forbes.com; and Mark Chillingworth, "A Source of Much Relief for Charity CIO Marcus East," *CIO UK*, December 30, 2011, www.cio.co.uk.

57 Ray Waddell, "Ticketmaster Launches New Facebook App," *Billboard*, January 18, 2012, www.billboard.com.

58 Michael Trusov, Anand V. Bodapati, and Randolph E. Bucklin, "Determining Influential Users in Internet Social Networks," *Journal of Marketing Research* 47, August 2010, pp. 643–658.

59 Reingen and Kernan, "Analysis of Referral Networks in Marketing"; and Brown and Reingen, "Social Ties and Word-of-Mouth Referral Behavior"; see also Frenzen and Nakamoto, "Structure, Cooperation, and the Flow of Market Information."

60 Frenzen and Davis, "Purchasing Behavior in Embedded Markets."

61 Dan Myers, "Things You Didn't Know About Girl Scout Cookies," *Fox News*, July 16, 2015, www.foxnews.com.

62 Chankon Kim, Zhiyong Yang, and Hanjoon Lee, "Parental Style, Parental Practices, and Socialization Outcomes: An Investigation of Their Linkages in the Consumer Socialization Context," *Journal of Economic Psychology* 49, no. 1, 2015, pp. 15–33.

63 Deborah Roedder John, "Consumer Socialization of Children: A Retrospective Look at Twenty-Five Years of Research," *Journal of Consumer Research* 26, December 1999, pp. 183–213.

64 Elizabeth S. Moore, William L. Wilkie, and Richard J. Lutz, "Passing the Torch: Intergenerational Influences as a Source of Brand Equity," *Journal of Marketing*, April 2002, pp. 17–37; Yuanyuan Cai, Guangzhi Zhao, and Jiaxun He, "Influences of Two Modes of Intergenerational Communication on Brand Equity," *Journal of Business Research* 68, no. 3, 2015, pp. 553–560.

65 Gwen Bachmann Achenreiner and Deborah Roedder John, "The Meaning of Brand Names to Children," *Journal of Consumer Psychology*, 13, no. 3, 2003, pp. 205–219.

66 Gregory M. Rose, Vassilis Dalakas, and Fredric Kropp, "Consumer Socialization and Parental Style Across Cultures," *Journal of Consumer Psychology* 13, no. 4, 2003, pp. 366–376.

67 Anirban Mukhopadhyay and Catherine W. M. Yeung, "Building Character: Effects of Lay Theories of Self-Control on the Selection of Products for Children," *Journal of Marketing Research* 47, April 2010, pp. 240–250.

68 John, "Consumer Socialization of Children: A Retrospective Look at Twenty-Five Years of Research."

69 Ann Walsh, Russell Laczniak, and Les Carlson, "Mothers' Preferences for Regulating Children's Television," *Journal of Advertising* 27, Fall 1998, pp. 23–36; and Vince Mitchell, Dan Petrovici, Bodo B. Schlegelmilch, and Ilona Szőcs, "The Influence of Parents versus Peers on Generation Y Internet Ethical Attitudes," *Electronic Commerce Research and Applications* 14, no. 2, 2015, pp. 95–103.

70 Moschis, "The Role of Family Communication in Consumer Socialization of Children and Adolescents"; Conway Lackman and John M. Lanasa, "Family Decision Making Theory," *Psychology and Marketing* 10, March–April 1993, pp. 81–93; and George P. Moschis, *Acquisition of the Consumer Role by Adolescents* (Atlanta, Ga.: Georgia State University, 1978).

71 Alexandra C. Kirsch and Sarah K. Murnen, "'Hot' Girls and 'Cool Dudes': Examining the Prevalence of the Heterosexual Script in American Children's Television Media," *Psychology of Popular Media Culture* 4, no. 1, 2015, p. 18.

72 Liza Ramrayka, "Doing the Funny Business: Why Red Nose Day USA Paid Off," *The Guardian (UK)*, May 28, 2015, www.theguardian.com.

73 Robert E. Burnkrant and Alain Cousineau, "Informational and Normative Social Influence in Buyer Behavior," *Journal of Consumer Research* 2, December 1975, pp. 206–215; and Morton Deutsch and Harold B. Gerard, "A Study of Normative and Informational Influence upon Individual Judgment," *Journal of Abnormal and Social Psychology*, November 1955, pp. 629–636.

74 Dennis Rook and Robert Fisher, "Normative Influences on Impulsive Buying Behavior," *Journal of Consumer Research* 22, December 1995, pp. 305–313.

75 Paul Rozin and Leher Singh, "The Moralization of Cigarette Smoking in the United States," *Journal of Consumer Psychology* 8, no. 3, 1999, pp. 321–337.

76 David B. Wooten, "From Labeling Possessions to Possessing Labels: Ridicule and Socialization Among Adolescents," *Journal of Consumer Research* 33, no. 2, 2006, pp. 188–198.

77 Margaret Talbot, "Girls Just Want to Be Mean," *New York Times Magazine*, February 24, 2002, p. 24.

78 Peter Reingen, Brian Foster, Jacqueline Brown, and Stephen B. Seidman, "Brand Congruence in Interpersonal Relations," *Journal of Consumer Research* 11, December 1984, pp. 771–783.

79 Rajagopal Raghunathan and Kim Corfman, "Is Happiness Shared Doubled and Sadness Shared Halved? Social Influence on Enjoyment of Hedonic Experiences," *Journal of Marketing Research* 43, August 2006, pp. 386–394.

80 Tina M. Lowrey, Cele C. Otnes, and Julie A. Ruth, "Social Influences on Dyadic Giving over Time," *Journal of Consumer Research* 30, March 2004, pp 547–558.

81 Ann E. Schlosser and Sharon Shavitt, "Anticipating Discussion About a Product: Rehearsing What to Say Can Affect Your Judgments," *Journal of Consumer Research* 29, June 2002, pp. 101–115.

82 James E. Stafford, "Effects of Group Influence on Consumer Brand Preferences," *Journal of Marketing Research* 3, February 1966, pp. 68–75.

83 Pankaj Aggarwal, "The Effects of Brand Relationship Norms on Consumer Attitudes and Behavior," *Journal of Consumer Research* 31, June 2004, pp. 87–101.

84 Randall L. Rose, William O. Bearden, and Jesse E. Teel, "An Attributional Analysis of Resistance to Group Pressure Regarding Illicit Drug and Alcohol Consumption," *Journal of Consumer Research* 19, June 1992, pp. 1–13; Bobby J. Calder and Robert E. Burnkrant, "Interpersonal Influences on Consumer Behavior: An Attribution Theory Approach," *Journal of Consumer Research* 3, June 1977, pp. 29–38, 71; Solomon E. Asch, "Effects of Group Pressure upon the Modification and Distortion of Judgment," in ed. H. Guetzkow, *Groups, Leadership and Men* (Pittsburgh, Pa.: Carnegie Press, 1951); and Sak Onkvisit and John J. Shaw, *International Marketing: Analysis and Strategy* (Columbus, Ohio: Merrill, 1989); see also Chin Tiong Tan and John U. Farley, "The Impact of Cultural Patterns on Cognition and Intention in Singapore," *Journal of Consumer Research* 13, March 1987, pp. 540–544.

85 Lisa E. Bolton and Americus Reed II, "Sticky Priors: The Perseverance of Identity Effects on Judgment," *Journal of Marketing Research* 41, November 2004, pp. 397–410.

86 Utpal M. Dholakia, Richard P. Bagozzi, and Lisa Klein Pearo, "A Social Influence Model of Consumer Participation in Networkand Small-Group-Based Virtual Communities," *International Journal of Research in Marketing* 21, no. 3, 2004, pp. 241–263.

87 Beverly Wright, Alphonso O. Ogbuehi, Leon C. Prieto, and Naveen Donthu, "The Power of Can't: Reactance & Product Preference among Young Consumers," *Academy of Marketing Studies Journal* 19, no. 1, 2015, p. 149.

88 Rene Algesheimer, Utpal M. Dholakia, and Andreas Hermann, "The Social Influence of Brand Community," *Journal of Marketing* 69, July 2005, pp. 19–34.

89 A. Peter McGraw and Philip E. Tetlock, "Taboo Trade-Offs, Relational Framing, and the Acceptability of Exchanges," *Journal of Consumer Psychology* 15, no. 1, 2005, pp. 2–15. See also Gita Venkataramani Johar, "The Price of Friendship: When, Why, and How Relational Norms Guide Social Exchange Behavior," *Journal of Consumer Psychology* 15, no. 1, 2005, pp. 22–27; Barbara E. Kahn, "The Power and Limitations of Social Relational Framing for Understanding Consumer Decision Processes," *Journal of Consumer Psychology* 15, no. 1, 2005,

pp. 28–34; and Philip E. Tetlock and A. Peter McGraw, "Theoretically Framing Relational Framing," *Journal of Consumer Psychology* 15, no. 1, 2005, pp. 35–37.

90 Russell W. Belk, "Exchange Taboos from an Interpretive Perspective," *Journal of Consumer Psychology* 15, no. 1, 2005, pp. 16–21.

91 White and Dahl, "To Be or Not Be? The Influence of Dissociative Reference Groups on Consumer Preferences."

92 William O. Bearden and Michael J. Etzel, "Reference Group Influence on Product and Brand Purchase Decisions," *Journal of Consumer Research* 9, no. 2, 1982, pp. 183–194.

93 Raffaele Filieri, "What Makes Online Reviews Helpful? A Diagnosticity-Adoption Framework to Explain Informational and Normative Influences in e-WOM," *Journal of Business Research* 68, no. 6, 2015, pp. 1261–1270; and Robert E. Witt and Grady D. Bruce, "Group Influence and Brand Choice Congruence," *Journal of Marketing Research* 9, November 1972, pp. 440–443.

94 Jennifer J. Argo, Darren W. Dahl, and Rajesh V. Manchanda, "The Influence of a Mere Social Pressure in a Retail Context," *Journal of Consumer Research* 32, no. 2, 2005, pp. 207–212; and Darren W. Dahl, Rajesh V. Manchanda, and Jennifer J. Argo, "Embarrassment in Consumer Purchase," *Journal of Consumer Research* 28, December 2001, pp. 473–481.

95 Bobby J. Calder and Robert E. Burnkrant, "Interpersonal Influences on Consumer Behavior," *Journal of Consumer Research* 3, June 1977, pp. 29–38; William O. Bearden, Richard G. Netemeyer, and Jesse E. Teel, "Measurement of Consumer Susceptibility to Interpersonal Influence," *Journal of Consumer Research* 15, March 1989, pp. 473–481; and William O. Bearden and Randall L. Rose, "Attention to Social Comparison Information," *Journal of Consumer Research* 16, March 1990, pp. 461–471.

96 John C. Mowen, "Exploring the Trait of Competitiveness and Its Consumer Behavior Consequences," *Journal of Consumer Psychology* 14, no. 1, 2004, pp. 52–63.

97 Charles S. Gulas and Kim McKeage, "Extending Social Comparison," *Journal of Advertising* 29, no. 2, Summer 2000, pp. 17–28.

98 David B. Wooten and Americus Reed II, "Playing It Safe: Susceptibility to Normative Influence and Protective Self-Presentation," *Journal of Consumer Research* 31, December 2004, pp. 551–556.

99 C. Whan Park and Parker Lessig, "Students and Housewives: Differences in Susceptibility to Reference Group Influence," *Journal of Consumer Research* 3, September 1977, pp. 102–110.

100 Robert Fisher and Kirk Wakefield, "Factors Leading to Group Identification: A Field Study of Winners and Losers," *Psychology and Marketing* 15, January 1998, pp. 23–40.

101 John R. French and Bertram Raven, "The Bases of Social Power," in ed. D. Cartwright, *Studies in Social Power* (Ann Arbor, Mich.: Institute for Social Research, 1969), pp. 150–167.

102 Didem Kurt, J. Jeffrey Inman, and Jennifer J. Argo, "The Influence of Friends on Consumer Spending: The Role of Agency-Communion Orientation and Self-Monitoring," *Journal of Marketing Research* 48, August 2011, pp. 741–754.

103 Reingen et al., "Brand Congruence in Interpersonal Relations"; and Park and Lessig, "Students and Housewives: Differences in Susceptibility to Reference Group Influence."

104 Donnel A. Briley and Robert S. Wyer Jr., "The Effect of Group Membership Salience on the Avoidance of Negative Outcomes," *Journal of Consumer Research* 29, December 2002, pp. 400–415.

105 Dana-Nicoleta Lascu, William O. Bearden, and Randall L. Rose, "Norm Extremity and Interpersonal Influences on Consumer Conformity," *Journal of Business Research* 32, March 1995, pp. 200–212.

106 Lisa E. Bolton, Hean Tat Keh, and Joseph W. Alba, "How Do Price Fairness Perceptions Differ Across Culture?" *Journal of Marketing Research* 47, June 2010, pp. 564–576.

107 "China's H1 Group-Buying Turnover Exceeds 12-Bln-USD," *Shanghai Daily*, July 28, 2015, www.shanghaidaily.com; and Tae-Hyung Kim, Kevin Lam, and Christopher Tsai, "The Groupon Effect in China," *Knowledge@Wharton*, January 3, 2012, http://knowledge.wharton.upenn.edu.

108 Zach Miners, "Under Armour Snaps Up MyFitnessPal to Become Largest Health Tracker," *PC World*, February 5, 2015, www.pcworld.com.

109 Korky Vann, "Bring a Friend Day at IKEA," *Hartford Courant (CT)*, March 5, 2015, www.courant.com; and Christopher Heine, "IKEA Wants Facebook Fans to Bring Friends to Stores," *ClickZ*, December 20, 2011, www.clickz.com.

110 Philipp Schmitt, Bernd Skiera, and Christophe Van den Bulte, "Referral Programs and Customer Value," *Journal of Marketing* 75, January 2011, pp. 46–59.

111 Social influence, attitudes toward the ads, and prior trial behavior all affect antismoking beliefs, as discussed in J. Craig Andrews, Richard G. Netemeyer, Scot Burton, D. Paul Moberg, and Ann Christiansen, "Understanding Adolescent Intentions to Smoke," *Journal of Marketing* 68, July 2004, pp. 110–123.

112 J. L. Freeman and S. Fraser, "Compliance Without Pressure: The Foot-in-the-Door Technique," *Journal of Personality and Social Psychology* 4, August 1966, pp. 195–202.

113 John C. Mowen and Robert Cialdini, "On Implementing the Door-in-the-Face Compliance Strategy in a Marketing Context," *Journal of Marketing Research* 17, May 1980, pp. 253–258; see also Edward Fern, Kent Monroe, and Ramon Avila, "Effectiveness of Multiple Request Strategies," *Journal of Marketing Research* 23, May 1986, pp. 144–152; and Nicolas Guéguen, "Door-in-the-Face Technique and Delay to Fulfill the Final Request: An Evaluation With a Request to Give Blood," *The Journal of Psychology* 148, no. 5, 2014, pp. 569–576.

114 Alice Tybout, Brian Sternthal, and Bobby J. Calder, "Information Availability as a Determinant of Multiple Request Effectiveness," *Journal of Marketing Research* 20, August 1983, pp. 279–290; and John T. Gourville, "Pennies-a-Day: The Effect of Temporal Reframing on Transaction Evaluation," *Journal of Consumer Research* 24, March 1998, pp. 395–408.

115 Seb Joseph, "Domino's 'Doubling Down' on Mobile Site to Tackle 'Embarrassing Conversions'," *The Drum*, April 21, 2015, www.thedrum.com; and Hadley Jones, "Pennies: Electronic Microdonations for Charity at the Point of Sale," *Point of Sale News*, December 29, 2011, http://pointofsale.com.

116 Eric R. Spangenberg and David E. Sprott, "Self-Monitoring and Susceptibility to the Influence of Self-Prophecy," *Journal of Consumer Research* 32, no. 4, 2006, pp. 550–556; and Eric R. Spangenberg and Anthony G. Greenwald, "Social Influence by Requesting Self-Prophecy," *Journal of Consumer Psychology* 8, no. 1, 1999, pp. 61–89.

117 For more about self-prophecy, see Eric R. Spangenberg, David E. Sprott, Bianca Grohmann, and Ronn J. Smith, "MassCommunicated Prediction Requests," *Journal of Marketing* 67, July 2003, pp. 47–62.

118 Stephanie Dellande, Mary C. Gilly, and John L. Graham, "Gaining Compliance and Losing Weight," *Journal of Marketing* 68, July 2004, pp. 78–91.

119 Deutsch and Gerard, "A Study of Normative and Informational Influence upon Individual Judgment"; Park and Lessig, "Students and Housewives: Differences in Susceptibility to Reference Group Influences"; and Dennis L. Rosen and Richard W. Olshavsky, "The Dual Role of Informational Social Influence," *Journal of Business Research* 15, April 1987, pp. 123–144.

120 Jeffrey D. Ford and Elwood A. Ellis, "A Re-examination of Group Influence on Member Brand Preference," *Journal of Marketing Research* 17, no. 1, 1980, pp. 125–133; and Linda L. Price and Lawrence F. Feick, "The Role of Interpersonal Sources in External Search," in ed. Thomas Kinnear, *Advances in Consumer Research*, vol. 11 (Ann Arbor, Mich.: Association for Consumer Research, 1984), pp. 250–255.

121 Arch G. Woodside and M. Wayne DeLosier, "Effects of Word-of-Mouth Advertising on Consumer Risk Taking," *Journal of Advertising* 5, September 1976, pp. 17–26.

122 Henry Assael, *Consumer Behavior and Marketing Action*, 4th ed. (Boston: PWS-Kent, 1992).

123 John R. French and Bertram Raven, "The Bases of Social Power," in ed. D. Cartwright, *Studies in Social Power* (Ann Arbor, Mich.: Institute for Social Research, 1959), pp. 150–167; Dana-Nicoleta Lascu, William Bearden, and Randall Rose, "Norm Extremity and Interpersonal Influences on Consumer Conformity," *Journal of Business Research* 32, March 1995, pp. 200–212; and David B. Wooten and Americus Reed II, "Informational Influence and the Ambiguity of Product Experience," *Journal of Consumer Psychology* 7, no. 1, 1998, pp. 79–99.

124 Bearden, Netemeyer, and Teel, "Measurement of Consumer Susceptibility to Interpersonal Influence"; Bearden and Rose, "Attention to Social Comparison Information"; and Karen Page Winterich and Gergana Y. Nenkov, "Save Like the Joneses: How Service Firms Can Utilize Deliberation and Informational Influence to Enhance Consumer Well-Being," *Journal of Service Research* 18, no. 3, 2015, pp. 384–404.

125 Gerald Zaltman and Melanie Wallendorf, *Consumer Behavior: Basic Findings and Management Implications*, 2nd ed. (New York: Wiley, 1983); and Reingen et al., "Brand Congruence in Interpersonal Relations."

126 Allen M. Weiss, Nicholas H. Lurie, and Deborah J. MacInnis, "Listening to Strangers: Whose Responses Are Valuable, How Valuable Are They, and Why?" *Journal of Marketing Research* 45, August 2008, pp. 425–436.

127 Charles R. Taylor, Gordon E. Miracle, and R. Dale Wilson, "The Impact of Information Level on the Effectiveness of U.S. and Korean Television Commercials," *Journal of Advertising* 26, Spring 1997, pp. 1–18.

128 Andrea K. Walker, "Under Armour's Rookie Strategy for Endorsement Deals," *Baltimore Sun*, July 25, 2011, www.baltimoresun.com.

129 Jordan Kretchmer, "Gone In 15 Seconds: The Top 3 Reasons People Leave Your Website," *MarketingLand*, July 31, 2015, http://marketingland.com. For more about Web-based chatting, see George M. Zinkhan, Hyokjin Kwak, Michelle Morrison, and Cara Okleshen Peters, "Web-Based Chatting," *Journal of Consumer Psychology* 13, nos. 1 and 2, 2003, pp. 17–27.

130 Wendy M. Moe and Michael Trusov, "The Value of Social Dynamics in Online Product Ratings Forums," *Journal of Marketing Research* 48, June 2011, pp. 444–456.

131 Stephen A. LaTour and Ajay Manrai, "Interactive Impact of Informational and Normative Influence on Donations," *Journal of Marketing Research* 26, August 1989, pp. 327–335.

132 Asim Ansari, Skander Essegaier, and Rajeev Kohli, "Internet Recommendation Systems," *Journal of Marketing Research* 37, August 2000, pp. 363–375.

133 Erica Van Herpen, Rik Pieters, and Marcel Zeelenberg, "When Demand Accelerates Demand: Trailing the Bandwagon," *Journal of Consumer Psychology* 19, no. 3, 2009, pp. 301–312.

134 Johan Arndt, "Role of Product-Related Conversations in the Diffusion of a New Product," *Journal of Marketing Research* 4, August 1967, pp. 291–295. For more information, see Nathalia Purnawirawan, Martin Eisend, Patrick De Pelsmacker, and Nathalie Dens, "A Meta-analytic Investigation of the Role of Valence in Online Reviews," *Journal of Interactive Marketing* 31, 2015, pp.17–27.

135 Marsha L. Richins, "Negative Word of Mouth by Dissatisfied Consumers," *Journal of Marketing* 47, January 1983, pp. 68–78.

136 Ann E. Schlosser, "Posting Versus Lurking: Communication in a Multiple Audience Context," *Journal of Consumer Research* 32, no. 2, 2005, pp. 260–265.

137 Herr, Kardes, and Kim, "Effects of Word-of-Mouth and Product Attribute Information on Persuasion: An Accessibility-Diagnosticity Perspective"; and Richard W. Mizerski, "An Attribution Explanation of the Disproportionate Influence of Unfavorable Information," *Journal of Consumer Research* 9, December 1982, pp. 301–310.

138 See Suman Basuroy, Subimal Chatterjee, and S. Abraham Ravid, "How Critical Are Critical Reviews?" *Journal of Marketing* 67, October 2003, pp. 103–117.

139 Daniel Laufer, Kate Gillespie, Brad McBride, and Silvia Gonzalez, "The Role of Severity in Consumer Attributions of Blame," *Journal of International Consumer Marketing* 17, no. 2/3, 2005, pp. 33–50.

140 Tom Denari, "Negative Ads Might Just Be Positive for Your Brand," *Advertising Age*, November 4, 2014, www.adage.com.

141 Yong Liu, "Word of Mouth for Movies: Its Dynamics and Impact on Box Office Revenue," *Journal of Marketing* 70, no. 3, July 2006, pp. 74–89.

142 Scott Mendelson, "Box Office: How Tom Cruise, 'Mission: Impossible Rogue Nation' Beat The Tracking," *Forbes*, August 3, 2015, www.forbes.com.

143 Danielle D. Winchester and Sandra J. Huston, "All Financial Advice for the Middle Class is Not Equal," *Journal of Consumer Policy* 38, no. 3, 2015, pp. 1–18.

144 Jonah Berger, "Word of Mouth and Interpersonal Communication: A Review and Directions for Future Research," *Journal of Consumer Psychology*, 24, no. 4, 2014, pp. 586–607; and Alixandra Barasch and Jonah Berger, "Broadcasting and Narrowcasting: How Audience Size Affects What People Share," *Journal of Marketing Research*, 51, no. 3, June 2014, pp. 286–299.

145 Jonah Berger and Eric M. Schwartz, "What Drives Immediate and Ongoing Word of Mouth?" *Journal of Marketing Research*, 48, no. 5, October 2011, pp. 869–880.

146 Herr, Kardes, and Kim, "Effects of Word-of-Mouth and Product Attribute Information on Persuasion: An Accessibility-Diagnosticity Perspective"; see also Judith A. Chevalier and Dina Mayzlin, "The Effect of Word of Mouth on Sales: Online Book Reviews," *Journal of Marketing Research* 43, no. 3, 2006, pp. 345–354.

147 Allen Pierleoni, "Best-Sellers Lists," *Sacramento Bee*, January 22, 2012, www.sacbee.com.

148 Robert Kozinets, Andrea C. Wojnicki, Sarah J. S. Wilner, and Kristine De Valck, "Networked Narratives: Understanding Word-of-Mouth Marketing in Online Communities," *Journal of Marketing* 74, March 2010, pp. 71–89.

149 Jin Li and Lingjing Zhan, "Online Persuasion: How the Written Word Drives WOM," *Journal of Advertising Research* 51, March 2011, pp. 239–257.

150 Yubo Chen, Qi Wang, and Jinhong Xie, "Online Social Interactions: A Natural Experiment on Word of Mouth Versus Observational Learning," *Journal of Marketing Research* 48, April 2011, pp. 238–254.

151 Adam Flomenbaum, "Share This Report Highlights Role of Social Media in TV Viewing," *AdWeek*, May 6, 2015, www.adweek.com.

152 Jonah Berger, *Contagious: Why Things Catch On* (New York: Simon and Schuster, 2013); and Jonah Berger and Katherine L. Milkman, "What Makes Online Content Viral?" *Journal of Marketing Research* 49, no. 2, 2012, pp. 192–205.

153 Amar Cheema and Andrew M. Kaikati, "The Effect of Need for Uniqueness on Word of Mouth," *Journal of Marketing Research* 47, June 2010, pp. 553–563.

154 "We Asked, You Voted: Your Favorite YouTube Ad of the Past Decade," *Google agency Blog*, June 2, 2015, http://adwordsagency.blogspot.com/2015/06/we-asked-you-voted-your-favorite.html.

155 Robert East, Kathy Hammond, and Wendy Lomax, "Measuring the Impact of Positive and Negative Word of Mouth on Brand Purchase Probability," *International Journal of Research in Marketing* 25, no. 3, 2008, pp. 215–224.

156 Sarit Moldovan, Jacob Goldenberg, and Amitava Chattopadhyay, "The Different Roles of Product Originality and Usefulness in Generating Word-of-Mouth," *International Journal of Research in Marketing* 28, no. 2, 2011, pp. 109–119.

157 Giselle Abramowitz, "5 Companies That Took Command of Listening to Social Conversations," *CMO Magazine*, February 25, 2014, www.cmo.com; and Natalie Zmuda, "Gatorade's New Selling Point: We're Necessary Performance Gear," *Advertising Age*, January 2, 2012, www.adage.com.

158 Sabine A. Einwiller and Sarah Steilen, "Handling Complaints on Social Network Sites–An Analysis of Complaints and Complaint Responses on Facebook and Twitter pages of Large US Companies," *Public Relations Review* 41, no. 2, 2015, pp. 195–204; and Dallas Lawrence, "6 Tips for Handling Breaking Crises on Twitter," *Mashable*, January 17, 2012, http://mashable.com.

159 Why Terrible Online Reviews Are Actually Good for You," *Advertising Age*, September 15, 2011, www.adage.com.

160 Ekaterina Walter, "How to Respond to Facebook Attacks," *Fast Company*, May 3, 2011, www.fastcompany.com.

161 Jessica Contrera, "Target Will Stop Separating Toys, Bedding by Gender," *Chicago Tribune*, August 10, 2015, www.chicagotribune.com.

162 Michael Kamins, Valerie Folkes, and Lars Perner, "Consumer Responses to Rumors," *Journal of Consumer Psychology* 6, no. 2, 1997, pp. 165–187.

163 Michelle L. Roehm and Alice M. Tybout, "When Will a Brand Scandal Spill Over, and How Should Competitors Respond?" *Journal of Marketing Research* 43, August 2006, pp. 366–373.

164 Tim Higgins, "Apple Reviewing Claims of New Labor Violations in China," *Bloomberg*, September 5, 2014, www.bloomberg.com; Erica Gies, "Is This Apple's Nike Moment?" *Forbes*, January 20, 2012, www.forbes.com; and Lars Paronen, "Apple Reveals Child Labor at Some Suppliers," *Reuters*, January 13, 2012, www.reuters.com.

165 "GM CEO Says Chevy Volt Fire Problem Handled Properly," *Fox News*, January 25, 2012, www.foxnews.com; and Jake Holmes, "GM Considering Volt Buybacks, Offers Loaner Cars During Fire Investigation," *Motor Trend*, December 2, 2011, www.motortrend.com.

166 Reingen and Kernan, "Analysis of Referral Networks in Marketing."

CHAPTER 12

Consumer Diversity

LEARNING OBJECTIVES

After studying this chapter, you will be able to:

▶ Explain how the consumer's age affects acquisition, consumption, and disposition behavior, and why marketers need to consider age influences when planning marketing activities.

▶ Describe how gender and sexual orientation each affects consumer behavior and how companies can create more effective marketing by understanding these influences.

▶ Discuss how regional influences, both within the United States and across the world, can affect consumer behavior and why marketers must consider these influences for targeting purposes.

▶ Highlight the effect of ethnic and religious influences on consumer behavior and the marketing implications for marketers.

iStockphoto.com/Ostill

Pacific Mall, Fatehabad Road

Stuart Kelly/Alamy Stock Photo

INTRODUCTION

When Yum! Brands opens a Pizza Hut, Taco Bell, or KFC restaurant outside the United States, it carefully tailors its offerings to regional and religious preferences. In India, for instance, its branded outlets offer numerous vegetarian dishes, because Hindu consumers do not eat beef.[1] Yum! Brands, like many successful marketers, pays close attention to diversity influences that affect consumer behavior (see Exhibit 12.1). First, the region in which its customers reside can influence consumer behavior, including the foods and flavors they favor. Second, consumer behavior can vary among subgroups of individuals with unique patterns of religion because of different traditions, customs, and preferences. To develop and implement effective marketing strategies and tactics, companies must understand how these and other diversity influences (such as age, gender, and sexual orientation) affect consumers.

Exhibit 12.1 ▶ Chapter Overview: Consumer Diversity

This chapter examines how diversity influences such as age, gender, sexual orientation, the region in which one lives, ethnic groups, and religion can affect consumer behavior.

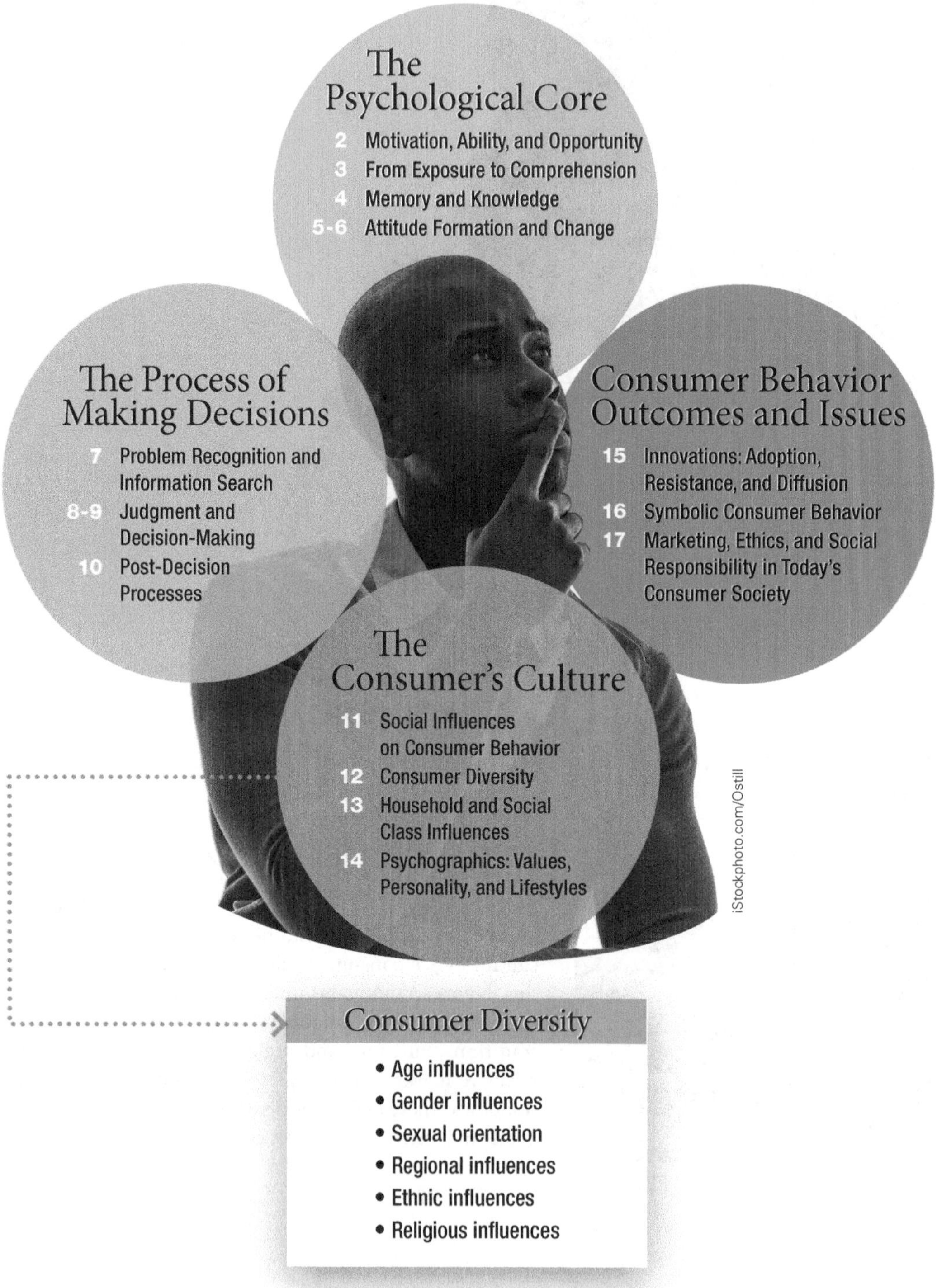

The Psychological Core

2   Motivation, Ability, and Opportunity
3   From Exposure to Comprehension
4   Memory and Knowledge
5-6 Attitude Formation and Change

The Process of Making Decisions

7   Problem Recognition and Information Search
8-9 Judgment and Decision-Making
10 Post-Decision Processes

Consumer Behavior Outcomes and Issues

15 Innovations: Adoption, Resistance, and Diffusion
16 Symbolic Consumer Behavior
17 Marketing, Ethics, and Social Responsibility in Today's Consumer Society

The Consumer's Culture

11 Social Influences on Consumer Behavior
12 Consumer Diversity
13 Household and Social Class Influences
14 Psychographics: Values, Personality, and Lifestyles

iStockphoto.com/Ostill

Consumer Diversity

- Age influences
- Gender influences
- Sexual orientation
- Regional influences
- Ethnic influences
- Religious influences

12-1 How Age Affects Consumer Behavior

Marketers often segment consumers by age. The basic logic is that people of the same age are going through similar life experiences and therefore share many common needs, experiences, symbols, and memories, which, in turn, may lead to similar consumption patterns.[2] Regardless of country, age groups are constantly shifting as babies are born, children grow up, adults mature, and people die. This section opens with an overview of U.S. age trends and continues with an examination of four major age cohorts being targeted by marketers: (1) teens and millennials, also known as Generation Y; (2) Generation X; (3) baby boomers; and (4) seniors.

12-1a AGE TRENDS IN THE UNITED STATES

The median age of U.S. consumers in 1980 was 30 years. Today, the median age is 37 years, reflecting a huge bulge in the over-40 population. Adults aged 18 and over now make up more than 76 percent of the overall U.S. population (see Exhibit 12.2). Thanks in part to better medical care and healthier lifestyles, people are living longer, which is why the senior market is an attractive target market. Marketers also target age segments of consumers who are entering the workplace and those who are setting up their own households, seeking to build and sustain brand loyalty during these critical periods.

> **Millennial** Individuals born between 1980 and about 1994; also known as *Generation Y.*

12-1b TEENS AND MILLENNIALS

Your own experience may confirm that this segment has considerable influence in household purchases and enjoys a good deal of financial independence. Teens shop more frequently than consumers in other segments, check prices online and via cell phone as well as in stores before they buy, and put a high value on price and convenience.[3] Just as important, U.S. consumers under 18 years of age have hundreds of friends (referring primarily to social media contacts) whose buying power and brand preferences they may influence.[4] Friends are a major source of information about products, and socializing is one of the major reasons that teens like to shop. Many teens discuss brands in text messages, instant messages, blogs, social networking, and online reviews.[5] Having grown up with recycling, many in this segment consider a product's environmental impact before buying.

A common teen "culture" is spreading around the world, although marketers must take care not to overlook localized culture and its effects on teen consumer behavior.[6] A study of teens in 44 countries revealed common behaviors, values, and preferences that cross national boundaries in six distinct segments.[7] The "thrills and chills" segment, including teens in the United States,

Germany, and other countries, consists of fun-seeking, free-spending consumers from middle or upper-class backgrounds. Teens in the "resigned" segment, covering Denmark, South Korea, and elsewhere are alienated from society and have low expectations of the future and of material success. High-aspiration teen "world savers" in Hungary, Venezuela, and other countries are characterized by their altruism. Ambitious teen "quiet achievers" in Thailand, China, and other nations conform to societal norms. "Bootstrappers" in Nigeria, Mexico, the United States, and other countries are family-oriented achievement seekers with hopes for the future. Finally, dutiful and conforming "upholders" in Vietnam, Indonesia, and other nations seek a rewarding family life and uphold traditional values. Other research has revealed additional segments in the global teenage market, including "materialists" who practice conspicuous consumption, "ecologists" who are interested in protecting the environment, and "netizens" who are heavy users of Internet-connected devices.[8]

Age cohorts are groups of consumers who are born in the same time period. Age cohorts share similar early life experiences that shape their values, preferences, and behaviors throughout their lives. Consumers born during the years 1980 through about 1994 are part of the **millennial** generation, also known as Generation Y. More than any other age cohort, millennials describe their generation as "idealistic."[9] Millennials are also media and tech savvy; they seek four benefits from tech devices: immediacy, entertainment, social interaction, and self-expression.[10] In fact, 92 percent of teens say they go online every day—and nearly one in four report going online "almost constantly."[11]

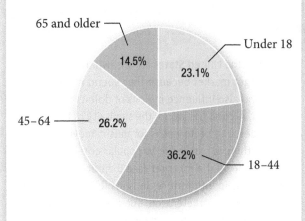

Exhibit 12.2 ▶ The U.S. Population by Age

Consumers up to the age of 18 comprise 23 percent of the U.S. population; by comparison, consumers aged 65 and older comprise 14.5 percent of the population.

65 and older — 14.5%
Under 18 — 23.1%
45–64 — 26.2%
36.2%
18–44

Source: Data from U.S. Census Bureau, "Projections of the Size and Composition of the U.S. Population: 2014 to 2060, Table 1," March 2015.

It is important to distinguish age groups from birth cohorts. An age group could be "consumers between 21 and 35 years old," and this same age group could be targeted now or 20 years from now. Of course, 10 years from now the age group of then 21 to 35 year olds would comprise different people. A birth cohort can be millennials, which includes people who were between about 21 and 36 years old in 2015. After 20 years, the birth cohort would comprise the same people who have grown older and are then in their 40s and 50s. All members of an age cohort experience the same major environmental events during their formative years, such as the millennials, in their teens and 20s at the start of the 21st century, who experienced the rise of social media, the economic rise of China, the global economic downturn of recent years, and so forth.[12]

For economic reasons, including high levels of student debt and the high cost of housing, many consumers in their 20s and 30s have been delaying their economic independence. A significant number are boomerangers, moving back with their parents after college or after being on their own (see Chapter 13 for more about household structure). One study found that in 1999 roughly 30 percent of 25-year-olds in the United States lived with their parents. Fourteen years later, the number who were living with their parents had increased to nearly 50 percent.[13] This trend toward "doubled-up households" isn't confined to the United States: In Australia, for instance, a growing number of adult children aren't leaving home until their mid-20s or later.[14] In Italy, nearly 79 percent of young adults are living with their parents, according to a study from the E.U. agency Eurofound.[15] Boomerangers marry and settle down later and, if they have paid jobs, have more discretionary income to spend on entertainment because their parents pay for essentials. Compared with peers who live independently, such boomerangers are more likely to buy items like a new car or the latest electronics.

 Marketing Implications

Teens in the United States and elsewhere are an important target market because they spend money on their own and also influence billions of dollars in family purchases. Around the world, the similarity of teens' tastes, attitudes, and preferences for music, movies, and fashion clothing is partly due to popular entertainment and partly due to the Internet (see Exhibit 12.3). Nonetheless, teens in different regions exhibit differences too, which is why marketers must do their homework before addressing local tastes and behaviors.

Consumers in their late teens and early 20s are also a prime target for many marketers because they need to acquire many goods and services during their college years and beyond, as they start their adult lives. In particular, they are often early adopters of new technology, intensely interested in brand interactions that take place digitally, and eager to share their brand experiences with others.[16] They are actively searching and shaping the fashion clothing landscape by buying and adapting new and vintage clothing, and contributing to fashion blogs, social media, and web forums.[17] However, having seen parents and peers struggle during the recent recession, and sometimes carrying student debt of their own, many millennials are debt-averse—and have low financial literacy—which affects their purchasing behavior.[18]

Brand Loyalty

Research shows that consumers are able to access internal information about brand names learned early in life more quickly and easily than brand names acquired later.[19] Therefore, marketers seek to build early brand awareness and preference among teens and young millennial consumers, working toward having that brand loyalty carry over into adulthood. For example, 50 percent of female teens have developed cosmetic brand loyalties by the age of 15.[20] Millennials seek out brands they perceive as authentic, and they tend to be highly loyal to their favorites.[21] They also will participate in loyalty programs that reward them for engaging with the brands they like.[22]

Positioning

Some marketers position their products as helpful for dealing with the adolescent pressures of establishing an identity, rebelling, and being accepted by peers. Because teens can be trendsetters, particularly in fashion and music, companies such as Coca-Cola and Pepsi are constantly researching what these consumer like and want. *Teen Vogue*, for example, positions itself as the source for style news and advice with ever-changing printed and online magazine content, plus smartphone apps and social media content to attract and engage teens.[23] Of course, teen tastes can change very quickly, and popular brands or stores may become overexposed and can quickly lose their cachet.[24]

Advertising Messages

Marketers are reaching out to teens and millennials through multiple media that these consumers favor. For instance, Mercedes-Benz is targeting millennials with Instagram and Facebook campaigns for lower-priced

Exhibit 12.3 ▶ Targeting to Teens

Advertising to teens, such as the one seen here, is important since teens shop more frequently than other consumers.

Source: Candies Brand

car models loaded with digital gadgets. "We've realized that visual storytelling through Instagram and Facebook is a really powerful tool for the younger consumer," explains a Mercedes marketing manager.[25] For teens, effective advertising often incorporates symbols, issues, and language to which this younger audience can relate. Popular music and sports figures are frequently featured in ads for soft drinks, snacks, and other products. However, messages need to talk to teens, not at them. Furthermore, because they have grown up with videos, computers, and texting, today's teens seem to process information faster than older consumers—and they prefer short, snappy phrases to long-winded explanations. Yet using contemporary slang can sometimes be dangerous, because if a phrase is out-of-date when the ad appears, the offering will look "uncool."

Traditional and Social Media

Marketers can target teens and millennials through certain TV networks, TV programs, magazines, radio stations, the Internet, and social media. For example, when the media firm Time Warner launched an antibullying campaign, it began with advertising on the Cartoon Network and then partnered with Facebook to promote an app and a Facebook page for promoting the antibullying message.[26] Online news sites like Mic tailor their content to millennials, which is why advertisers are partnering with Mic to post or sponsor branded content for this audience.[27]

Other Marketing Activities

Some marketers reach teens through recreation or special events that showcase the brand or product in a lifestyle or sports setting. For example, Red Bull, the energy drink, sponsors musical events and extreme sporting activities such as skateboard demonstrations, to reach its audience of millennials.[28] In addition, marketers of all types are rethinking their distribution strategies to reach teen consumers. The Cleveland Public Library made headlines when it began inviting teens (and others) who hold library cards to legally download some music for free, as part of a partnership with the Rock and Roll Hall of Fame. Ohio's Cuyahoga County Public Library offers cardholders access to streaming video and music, as well.[29]

12-1c GENERATION X

Individuals born between about 1965 and 1979 are often called **Generation X**. In the United States, within this diverse group of 49 million, some are underachievers while some are career-oriented. Nonetheless, Gen Xers who believe that they may not be able to match or surpass their parents' level of success may feel a bit disillusioned and less materialistic than other age groups. In fact, compared with consumers a decade ago who were 30 to 40 years old, far fewer Gen Xers own their own homes today.[30] In Canada and the United States, many women of this generation are delaying motherhood because of time-consuming work schedules, financial difficulties due to the recession, and shifting societal norms.[31] Yet many Gen Xers are doing well by being at the cutting edge of technology and finding ways to balance their work and personal lives.

> **Generation X** Individuals born between about 1965 and 1979.

Marketing Implications

The Generation X market has considerable buying power, despite the student debt that many are still paying off.[32] In a single year, this age group's $32 billion in furniture purchases account for one-third of the value of all furniture expenditures.[33] Gen X consumers take the time to research a purchase and like to customize offerings to their personal needs and tastes.[34] Understanding Gen Xers' attitudes and behavior is vital for marketers who seek to reach this group. Campbell's Soup, for instance, recognized that Gen Xers prefer the speed of microwave cooking and the convenience of opening a shelf-stable pouch for quick-serve meals. That's why Campbell's has introduced a steady stream of new, easy-to-use products, including Soup at Hand, Skillet Sauces, and Slow Kettle soups.[35] Moreover, this age cohort is accustomed to shopping in stores and online, which means that retailers use multiple distribution channels to accommodate buying patterns.[36]

> **Baby boomers** Individuals born between 1946 and 1964.

Advertising Messages

Born and bred on TV and electronics, Gen Xers tend to be cynical about obvious marketing techniques. They sometimes find objectionable ads that contain exaggerated claims, stereotypes, unpopular products like cigarettes and alcohol, and sexually explicit, political, religious, or social messages. However, Gen Xers do react positively to messages they see as clever or in tune with their values, attitudes, and interests. They notice messages that appeal to nostalgia for their younger days, as evidenced by their active participation in social media themes like "Throwback Thursday."

Traditional and Social Media

Marketers can reach Gen Xers through media vehicles such as popular or alternative music radio stations and network or cable TV. These consumers tend to watch TV at home, compared with lower at-home viewership among millennials.[37] Ads in music-related publications and messages displayed at concerts, sporting events, and popular vacation spots can also be effective. Thus, for example, Nissan, among many other companies, sponsors various college sporting events to attract and retain Gen Xers through such special interests.[38] Marketers are increasingly using the Internet, mobile marketing, and social media to reach these tech-savvy consumers. AXA, which markets life insurance, educates Gen Xers about the product's value through an online game called "Pass It On!," which invites players to walk through a virtual New York City streetscape in search of gold. If players buy life insurance for their characters, they gain a shield that protects them as they advance through higher game levels.[39]

12-1d BOOMERS

The 76 million **baby boomers** born between 1946 and 1964 remain a large and influential U.S. demographic group, although their numbers are declining year by year due to mortality.[40] The oldest boomers are retiring, but many are still working, which means this group has a lot of buying power (see Exhibit 12.4). Younger boomers make saving for retirement a high priority, which is why they spend less than older boomers spend on travel, electronics, home maintenance, and other goods and services.[41] Boomers are a diverse group, yet they share many common experiences of the 1960s and 1970s, when they grew up (an economy on the rise, the first man on the moon, the Vietnam war, the assassinations of President Kennedy and Martin Luther King, the rise of popular youth culture). Boomers strongly value individualism and want the freedom to do what they want, when and where they want.[42] Most boomers grew up with TV and as they get older, tend to watch it more. They also spend time browsing the Internet and are increasingly active in social media, although less so than younger segments.

Some researchers have identified subgroups of boomers based on five-year divisions or other definitions, meaning that the oldest and youngest would tend to be the most different—especially since the oldest are now seniors. Research suggests that boomers around the world, like teens around the world, share certain attitudes and values. Despite many differences, boomer parents

Verizon Wireless

Exhibit 12.4 ▶ Targeting to Boomers

Marketers often try to target and appeal to the lifestyles of baby boomers since they comprise a large segment that has great economic power.

and their adult children share some common characteristics, such as mothers and daughters often choosing to shop in the same stores.[43] In the past, boomers were called the "sandwich generation" because so many were simultaneously involved with their children's upbringing and caring for aging parents. This affected boomers' lifestyles and activities, and their spending patterns, as they looked ahead to their own retirement and saved for their children's education.[44] Now children of the oldest boomers—Gen Xers—are becoming a sandwich generation as their parents age.

Marketing Implications

Baby boomers have so much buying power that they are the target for many products and services, including cars, housing, travel, entertainment, recreational equipment, and motor homes.[45] For example, many have the time and money to pursue once-in-a-lifetime experiences such as visiting polar regions or playing

onstage alongside music icons in the Rock and Roll Fantasy Camp.[46] Boomers are heavy consumers of financial services as they look toward retirement and juggle expenses such as paying for their children's college educations, helping aging parents, and supporting boomerangers who live at home.

Some firms are developing offerings specifically for the needs of baby boomers. For example, apparel marketers have created jeans in larger sizes and different styles to accommodate the middle-aged physique. The Chico's chain has grown to more than 1,500 stores by specializing in loose-fitting yet stylish casual clothing for baby-boom women.[47] Personal care products, fitness goods and services, cosmetic surgery, and similar offerings are especially attractive to boomers who are sensitive to the idea of aging.[48] Coca-Cola and Pepsi, among other marketers, use nostalgia to appeal to this segment. Coca-Cola recently brought back its caffeinated Surge citrus soda, originally introduced in the 1990s and fondly remembered by many boomers. Pepsi introduced a limited-edition Pepsi Perfect soda not long ago, appealing to devoted baby-boom fans of the 1989 movie *Back to the Future II*.[49] BMW introduced its Mini Cooper car in the U.S. market in 2002, which is re-engineered but still reminiscent of the 1960's Mini and the era of optimism that it stands for.[50]

However, brands that have traditionally prospered by marketing to boomers must be prepared to adjust their targeting and tactics as this group ages and their behavior changes. Motorcycle manufacturer Harley-Davidson, for example, has long focused marketing attention on boomers, and enjoys enviably high brand loyalty among these customers. Yet to support future revenue and profit growth, the company is increasingly aiming to attract younger buyers who are familiar with the brand's image and who are interested in lower-priced bikes designed for urban areas.[51]

12-1e SENIORS

Gray market
Individuals over 65 years old.

In the **gray market** of consumers over 65, women outnumber men because women tend to live longer. Due to advances in medical care and healthier lifestyles, seniors are living longer and healthier than ever, which is why the U.S. population of seniors 85 and older will triple in size by 2040.[52] Because information-processing skills tend to deteriorate with age, seniors are less likely to search for information and more likely to have difficulty remembering information and making more complex decisions.[53] Thus, they tend to engage in

**WHEN ONE HEART GOES HEART HEALTHY,
TWO HEARTS CELEBRATE.**

Campbell's

**Healthy
Request**

Heart Healthy Soups • Low Cholesterol • 0 Grams Trans Fat • Healthy Level of Sodium

It's amazing what soup can do.™

Courtesy of Campbell Soup Company

Exhibit 12.5 ▶ Targeting to Seniors
Today's seniors think, feel, and act younger than those of previous generations; and today's advertisements appeal to those values and lifestyles.

simpler, more schematic processing.[54] Furthermore, poor recognition memory makes some seniors susceptible to the "truth effect" (believing that often-repeated statements are true—see Chapter 6).[55] As a result, some may need help or education when making decisions.[56] Some seniors resent being assisted in everyday experiences such as shopping or going to the doctor, because it signals that others perceive them as "old." These seniors may react by acting independently or by participating with care-givers in joint consumption experiences.[57]

Nonetheless, younger seniors in particular tend to be healthier and more active than those of previous generations (see Exhibit 12.5). Given recent economic conditions, many are working later in life out of need, to add to their retirement accounts, or to fund special purchases. At the same time, many seniors rekindle their interest in self-expression and affiliation, which they achieve through identity-inspired consumption such as joining hobby groups and paying for lessons.[58]

Marketing Implications

In the United States, 46.2 million consumers are aged 65 and older, making the senior market important to many businesses.[59] Seniors represent a critical and growing market for health-related products and services and for retirement communities (particularly in warmer states), as well as for recreational goods and services. In general, seniors tend to be brand-loyal, tend to know more about brands from long-standing experience, may not search extensively when planning high-ticket purchases, and have less motivation and cognitive capacity to deal with new, unfamiliar brands.[60]

While some seniors want the latest technology, others care more about basic functionality. For example, Telstra, a global telecommunications firm, runs a "Connected Seniors" program to teach Australian seniors how to choose digital gadgets and use the Internet.[61] Many seniors, less physically mobile than in the past, are heavy Internet and social media users to stay in touch with family members and friends.[62] As with other groups, marketers must carefully research seniors' needs and preferences. In Japan, for instance, Ueshima coffee shops cater to older consumers by having wider aisles, lower tables, and menus with large letter font.[63]

Advertising and Media

Marketers can target boomers through the use of media geared to this group's interests, including oldies rock 'n' roll programs and websites, activity-specific publications and TV shows, and lifestyle-related events such as home shows. Seniors perceive ads with positive older role models as more credible than those with younger models.[64] However, because of America's youth focus, seniors are less likely to appear in ads—or to be depicted positively—although this situation has been changing over time.[65] In recent years, luxury brands like L'Oréal, Kate Spade, and Louis Vuitton have all reached out to tap the "silver economy" with splashy campaigns featuring actress Helen Mirren, the former fashion model Twiggy, and other women celebrities over 65.[66] In general, ads should show seniors as active, contributing members of society, and messages should focus on only a few key attributes. Also, older consumers like and can better recall messages that focus on avoiding negative emotions, possibly because they want to avoid the negative outcomes that are associated with age.[67]

Distribution, Sales, and Promotions

Retailers can design their outlets to provide a more age-friendly shopping environment for baby boomers and seniors, with features such as wider aisles and well-lit aisles and parking lots.[68] Seniors value service, and many develop brand loyalty by taking advantage of discounts offered by retailers such as Kohl's, restaurant chains such as Denny's, and hotels such as Hyatt.[69] However, because older consumers who seek social interaction from telemarketing calls may not recognize fraudulent offers, education and protection are needed to help this segment avoid being victimized by scams.[70]

12-2 How Gender and Sexual Orientation Affect Consumer Behavior

Clearly the two genders, male and female, can differ in traits, attitudes, and activities that affect consumer behavior. The following sections discuss a few key issues that have been the focus of consumer research (complete coverage of the contrasts between the male and female genders is beyond the scope of this book). Remember that these sections describe only general tendencies, which are subject to considerable individual variation.

Also bear in mind that an individual's gender identity may or may not be the same as that person's biological sex designated at birth. In the case of someone who is *transgender*, the gender identity may differ from cultural expectations and social norms based on that person's biological sex designated at birth.[71]

12-2a SEX ROLES

In most cultures, men and women are expected to behave according to sex-role norms learned early in childhood. Until recently, males in Western society were expected to be strong, assertive, and emotionless. They were the primary breadwinners and were guided by **agentic goals** that stress mastery, self-assertiveness, and self-efficacy.[72] Women, on the other hand, have been guided more by **communal goals** of forming affiliations and fostering harmonious relations with others and have been expected to be relatively submissive, emotional, and home-oriented.

On a very general level, men tend to be more competitive, independent, externally motivated, and willing to take risks.[73] Expressing "man-of-action" masculinity may take the form of hypercompetitive breadwinner behavior or a rebel approach (including entrepreneurial breadwinner behavior).[74] In contrast, women tend to be cooperative, interdependent, intrinsically motivated, and risk averse.

Agentic goal Goal that stresses mastery, self-assertiveness, self-efficacy, strength, and no emotion.

Communal goal Goal that stresses affiliation and fostering harmonious relations with others, submissiveness, emotionality, and home orientation.

Women's hormonal cycles can also affect product choice, influencing women to prefer appearance-enhancing clothing during fertile days of their monthly cycle.[75]

Over time, however, female and male roles have been evolving. In particular, more U.S. women are delaying marriage and childbearing in favor of building a career, as noted earlier. This trend has led to higher standards of living for women and to changes in women's attitudes, particularly an emphasis on independence. More men are staying home to care for their children, and many of them exhibit a "rebel" mentality about challenging traditional notions of masculinity, which affects their consumption attitudes and behavior.[76]

Traditional sex roles are changing in many countries, even those that are conservative and male dominated. For example, in India, where arranged marriages are still the norm, women's attitudes toward careers, marriage, and the family are undergoing radical changes as more women pursue higher education, build careers, make financial decisions, and plan for purchases.[77] In fact, the earnings of educated women in India, Brazil, Russia, and China (referred to as the BRIC countries) are growing faster than those of their male counterparts—and women control two-thirds of the household spending in these nations.[78]

Sex roles and appropriate behavior may vary from one culture to another. Sex roles can, in fact, be influenced by various sources. In a recent Canadian study, 66 percent of teenagers reported experiencing peer pressure to conform to traditional sex roles, and nearly half felt pressure from media sources to conform.[79] In the United States, some men feel uncomfortable hugging each other, whereas this behavior is widely accepted in European and Latin societies, often as a greeting.

In general, contemporary ad messages portray stereotyped sex roles less often than in the past. However, stereotyping is still prevalent, mainly in ads that show a man or woman in a particular occupation.[80] And sex roles in ads can provoke differing responses among consumers. For example, women in the Czech Republic have been shown to react less favorably to ads in which female models are depicted in roles that seem superior to those of male models.[81] Moreover, how sex roles are portrayed in advertising for children can influence consumer attitudes toward the message and the brand. Specifically, children who are open-minded about sex roles and stereotyping will have a more positive attitude toward ads with gender content.[82]

12-2b DIFFERENCES IN ACQUISITION AND CONSUMPTION BEHAVIORS

Despite sex-role changes, men and women still exhibit a number of differences in their consumption behaviors. Women appear more likely to engage in a detailed, thorough examination of a message and to make extended decisions based on product attributes (similar to high motivation, ability, and opportunity, MAO, decision-making), whereas men seem more selective information processors, driven more by overall themes and simplifying heuristics (similar to low-MAO decision-making).[83] Men tend to be more sensitive to personally relevant information (consistent with agentic goals), and women pay attention to both personally relevant information and information relevant to others (consistent with communal goals).[84]

Men appear to be more sensitive to trends in positive emotions experienced during consumption, such as feeling enthusiastic and strong, whereas women display a tendency for negative emotions, such as feeling scared and nervous.[85] In addition, men and women differ in the symbolic meaning that they attach to products and services.[86] Women are more likely to have shared brand stereotypes for fashion goods, whereas men are more consistent in their images of automobiles.

In general, American women see shopping as a pleasurable, stimulating activity and a way of obtaining social interaction, whereas men see shopping merely as a way of acquiring goods and as a chore, especially if they hold traditional sex-role stereotypes. These patterns also hold true in other countries such as Turkey and the Netherlands. Finally, men and women tend to exhibit different eating patterns. In particular, women are more likely to engage in compensatory eating—responding to depression or making up for deficiencies such as a lack of social contact by eating.[87]

Marketing Implications

Obviously, many products (such as clothing for men and feminine hygiene products for women) are geared toward gender-specific needs. In addition, certain offerings may be perceived as being more appropriate for one gender than for the other. A tie may be seen as more masculine, whereas a food processor may be seen as more feminine. However, some products are becoming less sex-typed as sex roles evolve. For example, more than 12 percent of Harley-Davidson's motorcycle sales are to women. The company is attracting more women customers with bikes such as the Switchback, ergonomically suited to women riders, and with "garage parties" where women are invited to look at bikes without having to go to a dealership.[88] Meanwhile, products that were traditionally perceived as female-oriented are now being positioned as appropriate for men's needs. As an example, Hindustan Unilever advertises Vaseline moisturizers and face cleaners to men in India.[89]

Another important point is that women tend to be more loyal than men to individuals (such as a particular hair stylist), whereas men tend to be more loyal than women to groups (such as a particular company).[90] Moreover, it appears that men respond more positively than women to loyalty programs that emphasize status, but only when their higher status is highly visible to others. In contrast, women respond more positively than men to loyalty programs that emphasize personalization, but only for personalization in private settings.[91] Gender differences apply to the influence of online product reviews, as well. Women's purchase intentions tend to be more strongly influenced by online reviews than men's purchase intentions.[92]

Targeting a Specific Gender

Marketers often target a particular gender. For example, Home Depot and Lowe's know that women initiate 80 percent of home improvement projects, making them a key target market. Home Depot is targeting women with coordinated lines of house paints and home décor accessories for easy room makeovers. Lowe's has renovated its U.S. stores with brighter lighting and more informative displays, as well as introducing virtual decorating tools and online wish lists, to attract women do-it-yourselfers.[93] "Girls' Night Out" promotions in many areas attract women of all ages to local businesses, with discounts, demonstrations, tastings, and other activities geared to this targeted segment.[94]

In addition, women are often targeted because of their role in household purchases. Procter & Gamble, for instance, targets mothers worldwide with ads and social media promotions for Pampers, among other products for children. It has also targeted mothers in China with marketing for beauty products. One award-winning campaign called "Pretty Mom" featured multiple P&G beauty products for new mothers to use as they returned to work after maternity leave.[95] With traditional gender roles changing, fathers are increasingly doing more housework, grocery shopping, and childcare, and are targeted in advertising for this.[96]

Studies show that men and women respond differently to emotional advertising.[97] In line with changing sex roles, men in ads are increasingly shown in emotional and caring roles, whereas women are appearing more frequently in important situations and professional positions. A study of magazine ads found a similar trend in Japan as well.[98] Yet traditional roles have not disappeared: In China, where women are increasingly assertive and independent, men are now drawn to marketing that "suggest[s] or reinforce[s] a feeling of control," says an advertising agency manager.[99] Ads targeting men for a gender-specific product such as perfume (purchased as a gift) have been shown to be more effective when a male spokesperson is used. In contrast, ads targeting women who buy perfume for themselves are more effective with a female spokesperson.[100]

Traditional and Social Media

Some sex differences still exist in media patterns. Marketers can reach men through certain TV and radio programs, especially those focused on sports, and through automotive and sports magazines such as *Sports Illustrated* as well as sports- and car-oriented websites. One way that Domino's Pizza reaches men in the 18 to 34 age group is through digital "billboards" inserted into video and online games.[101]

Online and social media patterns are important, as well. For example, women tend to use social media more than men and to check social media sites more frequently.[102] This is why some of Nike's social media and online marketing are geared to targeting men and women separately. Nike has a popular Twitter account, @Nikewomen, for gender-specific promotions, and a mobile app, Nike Training Club, for helping women achieve the goal of feeling fit. Nike rings up $5 billion in women's products worldwide, compared with $14 billion in men's products worldwide, and is planning new marketing programs to significantly increase its sales to women in the future.[103]

12-2c GENDER AND SEXUAL ORIENTATION

Gender refers to a biological state (male or female), whereas **sexual orientation** reflects a person's preference toward certain behaviors. Masculine individuals (whether male or female) tend to display male-oriented traits, and feminine individuals tend toward female characteristics. In addition, some individuals can be androgynous, having both male and female traits. Sexual orientations are important because they can influence consumer preferences and behavior. For example, women who are more masculine tend to prefer ads that depict nontraditional women.[104]

Gay, lesbian, bisexual, and transgender consumers may have different needs and preferences compared with consumers who identify as traditionally masculine or feminine in sexual orientation. This is why marketing research is essential for understanding the various segments within an overall market.

Gender Biological state of being male or female.

Sexual orientation A person's preference toward certain behaviors.

Marketing Implications

An increasing number of marketers are using sexual orientation to target gay and lesbian consumers for a wide range of offerings (see Exhibit 12.6). In part, this strategy is due to a dramatic rise in the number of same-sex U.S. households. Although gay and lesbian consumers tend to dislike and distrust ad messages more than heterosexual consumers do, they are likely to respond favorably to sexual orientation symbols in advertising and to ads that "reflect their lives and culture."[105] They respond to marketing that they perceive as gay friendly (and condemn seemingly antigay marketing activities).[106] For instance, the Las Vegas Convention and Visitors Authority promotes a variety of gay-themed events to appeal to gay vacationers, and New York City promotes itself as a destination for same-sex weddings.[107]

The Greater Fort Lauderdale Convention and Visitors Bureau has targeted lesbian and gay consumers for two decades. Not long ago, it conducted research to understand the specific needs and behavior of transgender travelers, learning that 62 percent of transgender consumers travel alone. Another key finding: Transgender consumers tend to be more cost-conscious than gay and lesbian consumers when it comes to travel expenditures. The bureau's multimedia marketing to these market segments has won awards and has attracted thousands of visitors annually who spend millions of dollars on hotels, restaurants, and other travel-related goods and services in Fort Lauderdale.[108]

Marketers in many areas of the world are seeking to reach gay, lesbian, bisexual, and/or transgender consumers. Businesses in China, for example, have learned that consumers in this segment have more disposable income and are more brand-loyal than the general population. These Chinese consumers also travel more frequently than the general population, especially to international destinations. Ads targeting Chinese consumers in this segment frequently use rainbow flags or other subtle cues, to avoid controversy.[109]

12-3 How Regional Influences Affect Consumer Behavior

Because people tend to work and live in the same area, residents in one part of the country can develop patterns of behavior that differ from those in another area. For

Rachel Epstein/PhotoEdit

Exhibit 12.6 ▶ Targeting to Gay and Lesbian Consumers

Companies are increasingly targeting gay and lesbian consumers, shown in this bank ad.

example, a consumer from New England might enjoy lobster and skiing, whereas someone from Texas may prefer barbecues and rodeos. This section explores how the region in which people live can affect their consumer behavior, both within the United States and in various regions across the world.

12-3a REGIONS WITHIN THE UNITED STATES

The United States is a vast country in which various regions have developed distinctive identities, apart from the overall American culture, based on differing environment, ethnic, and cultural histories. For example, California and the Southwest were originally part of Mexico and therefore reflect a Mexican character; the Southwest also has Native American and frontier roots. The eastern seaboard from New England to Georgia reflects the region's roots as the original 13 British colonies. The great expanses of the West and Northwest are reflected in the free-spirited personalities of these regions, and the Deep South from Louisiana to Florida owes some of its character to agriculture as

Clustering The grouping of consumers according to common characteristics, such as demographics and consumption lifestyles, using statistical techniques.

well as to the Confederacy's rebellion during the Civil War. Finally, the Midwest is noted for its farms and agriculture.

Such descriptions represent very broad generalizations. Although each region also has many unique influences and variations that are too numerous to mention, regional differences can affect consumption patterns. Immigration patterns, such as a large number of Mexican-born consumers moving into California and Texas, can add ethnic influences to certain regions as well.[110] For instance, due to a strong Mexican influence, consumers in the Southwest prefer spicy food and dishes such as tortillas and salsa. Interestingly, some Tex-Mex foods were first developed in the United States and then became popular in Mexico.[111]

Because considerable variation exists in values and lifestyles among consumers within a region, researchers have looked for ways to describe consumers on the basis of more specific characteristics, a statistical technique called cluster analysis or *clustering*. **Clustering** is based on the principle that "birds of a feather flock together."[112] This notion suggests that consumers in the same neighborhood tend to buy the same types of cars, homes, appliances, and other products or services.[113] Then the clustering is based on geographic areas only. Systems such as Mosaic (from Experian) and PRIZM (from Nielsen) group areas and neighborhoods into more precise clusters based on consumers' similarities in demographic characteristics and consumption lifestyles. These systems can define a cluster according to similarity of income, education, age, household type, degree of urbanity, attitudes, and product/service preferences, including the type of car owned and preferred radio format.

For example, PRIZM has identified 66 U.S. consumer segments and grouped them geographically (urban, suburban, second city, and town/rural) as well as by lifestage (according to age and the presence or absence of children at home). Here is a sampling of the individual consumer segments:[114]

- *Young Digerati* are affluent, well-educated, tech-savvy 25- to 44-year-olds living in urban areas.

- *Kids & Cul-de-sac* consumers are upper-middle-income, white-collar 25- to 44-year-olds, mostly college grads and home-owners, who live in suburbia with their children.

- *Boomtown Singles* are college-educated consumers under the age of 35, working in entry-level jobs and living in smaller cities where the singles scene thrives.

- *Mobility Blues* are single, lower-income consumers who live in smaller cities, are under the age of 55, and have a high school education.

Marketing Implications

Marketers can develop an offering or communication to appeal to different regions of the United States. For example, Frito-Lay markets "Cajun Herb & Spice" potato chips only in southeastern states, "Chipotle Ranch" chips only in southwestern states, and "Balsamic Sweet Onion" chips only on the west coast. Also, some products are identified with certain regions: Florida orange juice, Hawaiian macadamia nuts, and Texas beef are a few examples. Smaller firms catering to local tastes can develop a loyal following in certain regions. Even though Frito-Lay sells more potato chips across America than all of its smaller competitors combined, Utz chips are popular in Pennsylvania, and Better Made chips are popular in Michigan.[115]

On the other hand, companies sometimes consolidate regional brands because of the expense and complications of marketing multiple products. After years of regional marketing, Dean Foods changed the marketing of its 31 milk brands to focus on a single "DairyPure" national umbrella brand. Dean's key competitive differentiation remains the use of fresh, locally produced milk in each region.[116]

Also, marketers can use clustering systems to help find new customers, learn what their customers like, develop new products, buy advertising, locate store sites, and target consumers through media.[117] Retailers use clustering to identify neighborhoods of consumers most likely to purchase certain merchandise. For example, Petco, which sells pet products, uses clustering to pinpoint neighborhoods where home ownership is high because "usually renters don't own animals," a manager says.[118]

Clustering systems are also available for other countries and across national borders. Experian's Mosaic Global system clusters consumers into a few common lifestyle categories so that global marketers can target consumers with similar characteristics in different parts of the world. For example, "sophisticated singles" are city-dwelling, unmarried consumers with high incomes; at the other end of the affluence scale are "low-income elders," older consumers, mainly living in urban areas, with low incomes.

Marketers should be cognizant of the large regional differences in preferences and consumption behaviors that exist in countries other than their own. To illustrate, the foods and wines in Italy differ markedly across regions, from rice and corn-based polenta dishes in the North to pizza in the South, with many wines and cheeses having their own Denominazione di Origine Controllata (official controlled origin). The same holds for other countries in Europe, for regions in China and elsewhere, and for non-food-product consumption.[119]

12-3b REGIONS ACROSS THE WORLD

Clearly, the area of the world in which a consumer resides can influence consumption patterns. As we have learned, cross-cultural variations exist in just about every aspect of consumer behavior. Some nations are strongly associated with certain products (such as beer in Germany, sports cars in Italy, and sushi in Japan) while the consumption of specific types of products is forbidden in other regions. Drinking alcohol and smoking are not allowed in Muslim countries, and religious restrictions forbid the consumption of pork in Israel and beef in India.

Cultural influences also affect behaviors such as patience. Consumers in Western cultures tend to be less patient and value immediate consumption more than consumers in Eastern cultures do, for instance.[120] Also, cultural influences can affect cognitive approaches to consumption situations. For instance, consumers from Eastern cultures characterized by holistic thinking tend to have more positive evaluations of brand extensions than do consumers from Western cultures characterized by analytic thinking.[121]

In a broader sense, the ways in which cultures differ can affect how consumers think and behave. These differences can be viewed along three main dimensions:

- *Individualism versus collectivism.* Consumers from cultures high in individualism (many Western cultures) put more emphasis on themselves as individuals than as part of the group; consumers from cultures high in collectivism (many Eastern cultures) emphasize connections to others rather than their own individuality.[122] Marketers might apply this distinction to the way in which they depict consumers in ads for each culture—as ruggedly individual or as part of a group, for instance.

- *Horizontal versus vertical orientation.* Consumers from cultures with a horizontal orientation value equality, whereas consumers from cultures with a vertical orientation put more emphasis on hierarchy.[123] This distinction is especially important to marketers of status-symbol products that will appeal to consumers influenced by vertical orientation.

- *Masculine versus feminine.* Consumers from masculine cultures (such as the United States) tend to be more aggressive and focused on individual advancement; in contrast, consumers from feminine cultures (such as Denmark) tend to be more concerned with social relationships.[124] Therefore, advertising with aggressive themes is more likely to strike a chord in masculine cultures than in feminine cultures.

All the consumers in a particular culture may not be affected by cultural influences in the same way, however. The extent of the influence depends on how each consumer processes information and the personal knowledge that he or she relies on when making a judgment.[125]

Marketing Implications

Marketers need to understand global differences in consumer behavior so that they can alter marketing strategy, where necessary, to appeal to specific regions and countries. For example, money-back guarantees give U.S. consumers confidence, but Latin Americans do not believe them because they never expect to get their money back. Also, the strategies of using famous endorsers or being the official product of a sporting event are much more effective in Venezuela and Mexico than in the United States.

Many companies adjust their marketing activities to accommodate global consumer differences.[126] For example, Procter & Gamble developed different versions of a TV ad for Pampers disposable diapers to account for variations in slang and accent in different regions of the German-speaking world. Not heeding important cross-cultural differences can embarrass a company and cause its products to fail. In Germany, Vicks had to change its brand name to Wicks because the former term is slang for sexual intercourse. Also, because many countries require products to be labeled with the country of origin, marketers should be aware of how a foreign-sounding brand will be perceived in the country of consumption.[127]

Marketers should also remember that, as in the United States, consumers in different parts of one country may exhibit different consumer behavior. In Canada, for example, consumers in Quebec have distinctly different food preferences than consumers in British Columbia. Finally, for products available in more than one region, marketers must look at all targeted segments' preferences. General Motors, for example, knows that its Buick vehicles are extremely popular in some parts of China. As a result, the company caters to both U.S. and Chinese consumers' tastes when designing new Buick models. In fact, GM is about to import Buick-branded Envision compact luxury SUVs made in China for sale to U.S. consumers.[128]

Ethnic group Subculture with a similar heritage and values.

Acculturation Learning how to adapt to a new culture.

12-4 How Ethnic and Religious Influences Affect Consumer Behavior

In addition to age, gender and sexual orientation, and regional influences, both ethnic groups and religion are major factors affecting consumer behavior. It is important to emphasize that the generalizations discussed in this chapter are only broad tendencies and may or may not apply to individual consumers. Marketing to any consumer group requires careful research to get beyond stereotypes and to identify specific characteristics and behavioral patterns that can be addressed using appropriate strategies and tactics. Moreover, ethnic influences and religious beliefs are only two of the many cultural elements that, in combination, affect how consumers think, feel, and act.

Immigration creates not only a unique national culture in each country, but also a number of subcultures or **ethnic groups** within the larger society. Members of these ethnic groups share a common heritage, set of beliefs, religion, and experiences that set them apart from others in society. This is the situation in the United States and around the world.

Ethnic groups are bound together by cultural ties that can strongly influence consumer behavior. Moreover, through the process of **acculturation**, members of another culture or an immigrant group learn to adapt to the host culture. During acculturation, consumers acquire knowledge, skills, and behavior through social interaction, by modeling the behavior of others, and through reinforcement or receipt of rewards for certain behaviors.[129]

Acculturation is strongly influenced by family, friends, and institutions such as the media, place of worship, and school and combines with traditional customs to form a unique consumer culture. Meanwhile, members of a larger culture who like to learn about new cultures and think that cultural diversity is important will, at times, adopt a subculture's ethnic-oriented products.[130] Note that even acculturated consumers may find their second-language processing disrupted by visual cues in the environment, such as symbolic icons, that prime cultural associations with their first language.[131]

Racism and ethnocentrism can have the opposite effect, prompting such consumers to avoid products associated with particular ethnic groups.[132] When members of ethnic groups experience rejection and discrimination, their choices are more limited, which increases the possibility of negative consequences in business and in personal life.[133]

12-4a ETHNIC GROUPS WITHIN THE UNITED STATES

Individuals from many different cultures and countries have come to America over the years. Larger groups include consumers from the Hispanic, African American, Asian, Italian, Irish, Jewish, Muslim, Scandinavian, and Polish countries and cultures. More than 90 percent of the U.S. population growth from 2000 to 2014 was due to growth in Hispanic American, African American and,

Asian American, among other subcultural groups, a trend that is projected to continue for some time.[134]

Not surprisingly, **multicultural marketing**, the use of strategies that simultaneously appeal to a variety of cultures, is important. This approach requires both long-term commitment and consideration of all targeted groups from the outset, not as an afterthought. McDonald's, for example, has a separate marketing director and multimillion-dollar budget for communicating with Hispanic American consumers, with African American consumers, and with Asian American consumers. "We make it our job to know our consumers, and the cultural things that are important to them, and recognize this country is changing dramatically," explains a senior marketing executive at McDonald's.[135] The next sections focus on these three large ethnic groups within the United States.

> **Multicultural marketing** Strategies used to appeal to a variety of cultures at the same time.

Hispanic American Consumers

Hispanic Americans represent one of the largest ethnic groups in the United States today, covering people from countries of origin such as Mexico, Puerto Rico, Cuba, Salvador, and Guatemala, among other areas.[136] The median income of Hispanic American households is more than $42,000, and nearly 39 percent of Hispanic Americans have an income of $50,000 or more, making the segment an attractive one for marketers.[137] Hispanics can also be divided into several groups based on their level of acculturation to the host culture: (1) the *acculturated*, who speak mostly English and have a high level of assimilation; (2) the *bicultural*, who can function in either English or Spanish; and (3) the *traditional*, who speak mostly Spanish.[138] The rate of acculturation can be slow, usually taking four generations, although some Hispanic Americans resist assimilation out of a desire to maintain their ethnic identity.[139]

The consumer's level of acculturation affects consumption patterns, as does the **intensity of ethnic identification**.[140] Consumers who strongly identify with their ethnic group and are less acculturated into the mainstream culture are more likely to exhibit the consumption patterns of the ethnic group. Strong Hispanic identification leads to a higher level of husband-dominant decisions (discussed in greater detail in Chapter 13).[141] Furthermore, strong identifiers are more likely to be influenced by radio ads, billboards, family members, and coworkers and are less likely than weak identifiers to use coupons.[142]

> **Intensity of ethnic identification** How strongly people identify with their ethnic group.

Marketing Implications

Hispanic Americans make up 17 percent of the overall U.S. population, and have a combined annual buying power exceeding $1.5 trillion.[143] Marketers of many goods and services have devised a variety of approaches to reach this growing segment, as the following examples show.

Product Development and Distribution

Marketers are building customer loyalty by developing offerings specifically for Hispanic Americans. Univision, a major Spanish language network, recently created a subscription-based live streaming option for its two channels, Univision and Unimas, targeting Hispanic American millennials with Apple and Android digital devices.[144] Procter & Gamble has added specially scented household products, such as Brazilian Carnaval Febreze air freshener, to appeal to this segment, and increased the number of products with Spanish-language labeling.[145]

More marketers are tailoring distribution to Hispanic American consumers. The regional supermarket chain Publix, for example, operates eight Sabor stores designed specifically to cater to Hispanic Americans, with merchandise tailored to the specific preferences and buying habits of local shoppers.[146] Walmart has significantly increased the shelf space devoted to food products favored by Hispanic American consumers in Florida, Texas, and other target areas.[147] As another example, Nissan enjoys a 26 percent share of the car market in Mexico. Noting that purchases by Hispanic Americans account for much of the growth in its U.S. car sales, Nissan helped three of its dealers from Mexico to open dealerships in Los Angeles, San Francisco, and Houston, strengthening its distribution outreach to this key segment.[148]

Media and Communications

Because Hispanic Americans tend to be concentrated in certain areas and share a common language, many can be targeted in Spanish-language media, including TV, radio, print, billboards, and websites. From Univision and Telemundo to *People en Espanol* to Spanish Broadcasting System radio and beyond, marketers have choices to engage this audience. For example, State Farm Insurance runs Spanish-language commercials on TV as well as on ESPN Deportes, the Spanish language sports station, aiming particularly at consumers under 30 making first-time decisions about auto and home insurance.[149] Hispanic Americans prefer web content that reflects their culture and language. Having Spanish language customer support available for Internet users is especially important for less acculturated Hispanic Americans.[150]

Advertising is particularly important in this segment because many Hispanic Americans prefer prestigious or nationally advertised brands (see Exhibit 12.7). This is why P&G, like many other firms, is spending more to reach the segment and creating English and Spanish language messages that appeal to Hispanic Americans in multiple media. P&G uses celebrities such as actress Eva Mendes who is originally form Cuba in its ads for Pantene shampoo to appeal more broadly but also specially to the Hispanic American segment, and it has Spanish language brand websites for Pampers and other big P&G brands. The company also sponsors a special website, Orgullosa, targeting Latina women, with recipes, interviews, product promotions, and user-generated content and conversations.[151]

Hispanic Americans tend to react positively to ads using ethnic spokespeople, who are perceived as more trustworthy, leading to consumers' having more positive attitudes toward the brand being advertised. This strategy is most effective in environments in which ethnicity is more salient (i.e., the group is in the minority).[152] Ads that draw attention to ethnicity can trigger "ethnic self-awareness" and generate more favorable responses from the targeted group.[153] Marketers who develop ads specifically for Hispanic Americans or other groups should realize that although members of the overall culture also may be exposed to the ads, they are unlikely to react in the same way as the targeted group does because they are less familiar with the cues in the ads.[154] Also, some advertisers try to make ethnic representation in ads proportional to the group's size relative to the general population.[155]

Accommodation theory can also apply when marketers develop advertising for Hispanics. This theory specifies that the more effort a source puts into communicating with a group—for example, by using role models and the native language—the greater the response by members of this group and the more positive their feelings. It is another version of the "fit = good" principle, which means that matching marketing stimuli to consumer characteristics is usually effective (the key idea behind targeting). Therefore, advertising in Spanish increases perceptions of the company's sensitivity toward and solidarity with the Hispanic community, creating consumers' positive feelings toward the brand and the firm.[156] Verizon, for example, has developed Spanish language ads and tweets, Facebook pages, and promotions that focus on Hispanic traditions such as the Quinceañera party for 15-year-old girls, that target teens, their parents,

Accommodation theory The more effort one puts forth in trying to communicate with an ethnic group, the more positive the reaction.

¿por qué dejarlo manejar tan pequeño?

Porque con Bounty sí puedes.

Como una esponja de papel.   Úsala   Enjuágala   Reúsala   ¡Listo!

Exhibit 12.7 ▶ Hispanic American Consumers
Some marketers target to subcultures, such as this one in Spanish.

and their grandparents.[157] Volkswagen shoots some TV commercials twice—once in English, once in Spanish—to reach Hispanic bilinguals and those who have a preference for either Spanish or English.[158]

However, using Spanish messages *exclusively* can lead to negative ad perceptions. Many ads directed toward Hispanic Americans are delivered in English because these consumers are often bilingual or highly acculturated. An even more effective strategy may involve using both English and Spanish, for example, the method employed by P&G with its bilingual website orgullosa.com and Facebook page featuring beauty and household tips for women.[159] When an ad targeting Hispanic Americans mixes English and Spanish, it is likely to be more persuasive if the text is mainly in Spanish with one word switched to English instead of mainly in English with one Spanish word. Note that consumers may like a code-switching message less if it mixes words incorrectly.[160]

African American Consumers

African Americans represent a large and diverse group—13 percent of the U.S. population—consisting of many subsegments across different levels of income and education, occupations, and regions, from urban to rural areas. One-third of the households have an income of $50,000 or higher, and 20 percent have a college degree or achieved a higher educational level.[161] This segment represents more than $1 trillion in annual buying power.[162]

As with any subculture, African American consumers have some similarities to the general population and also differ in certain ways. For example, African Americans are more likely to believe that people should feel free to live, dress, and look the way that they want to.[163] They also do not necessarily aspire to assimilate with the majority culture.[164] As incomes rise, a strong desire to preserve a cultural identity also develops. According to a study by Nielsen, African Americans are, compared to the general population, 30 percent more likely to believe that diversity in advertising is important, and 38 percent are more likely to make a purchase when the advertisements include African American people.[165]

Exhibit 12.8 ▶ Targeting to African-American Consumers

Some ads specifically target African-American consumers with specific products or brands.

Marketing Implications

African American consumers, like other segments, respond positively to offerings and communications targeted toward them (see Exhibit 12.8). Generally, they are less likely to trust or buy brands that are not advertised.[166] Marketers are addressing this group's specific needs and interests in a number of ways.

Product Development and Distribution

Many marketers focus primarily on products for the unique needs of the African American market. One World Dolls, based in Houston, targets this market with high-quality African-American and African dolls under the Prettie Girls brand, featuring a variety of skin tones and head types. Annual sales have increased beyond $1 million as One World expands distribution to Walmart and other national chains.[167] As another example, Hallmark and American Greetings both offer a line of greeting cards created specifically for this segment.[168] Marketers can also adjust distribution strategies for this segment.

Media and Communications

African Americans have more positive attitudes toward ads than do Anglo consumers, according to studies.[169] Research also shows that strong ethnic identifiers among African American consumers act more positively than weak identifiers to ads placed in racially targeted media.[170] Marketers can use multiple media that target this segment specifically, including TV networks such as Black Entertainment Television, targeted websites such as BET.com, magazines such as *Ebony*, and more. Compared with other groups, more African Americans are cable TV subscribers.[171] Moreover, Google's research suggests that African American consumers are more open to Web and mobile ads than the overall U.S. population, indicating that digital media are effective for reaching this segment.[172]

Some of the largest U.S. advertisers, including General Motors, Procter & Gamble, and Johnson & Johnson, are investing in ad campaigns specifically for this segment. As noted earlier, subcultures such as African Americans will identify more strongly and have more positive evaluations when the advertising source is of the same ethnic group as the target.[173] Therefore, marketers must take the unique values and expectations of African Americans into account when planning communications, also because they pay attention to whether they are represented accurately and fairly in ads.[174]

Marketers must also be aware of the effect that African American models and actors in ads may have on consumers outside the targeted segment. According to Coors's director of ethnic marketing, the company's targeted advertising has boosted the beer's overall sales, not just its sales to African American consumers, "because African American consumers in urban markets have a lot of influence on what's cool with the general market."[175]

Asian American Consumers

Asian Americans are the third largest and fastest growing subculture in the United States, making up 5 percent of the population. The Asian American community consists of people from more than 29 countries, from the Indian subcontinent to the Pacific Ocean, each with its own values and customs. The six largest groups include immigrants from China, the Philippines, India, South Korea, Vietnam, and Japan. In light of this tremendous diversity, marketers should research the specific subsegment they wish to target.

Despite individual differences, one common denominator of most Asian cultures is the strong emphasis on the family, tradition, and cooperation.[176] These consumers shop frequently and enjoy shopping with friends. They prefer brand names and are willing to pay for top quality, even though they react positively to bargains. Asian Americans are more than twice as likely as the average consumer to check prices and products on the Internet before they buy.[177] Consumers in this group also tend to save money, be highly educated, have higher computer literacy, and hold a higher percentage of professional and managerial jobs than the general population does.[178] More tend to be highly assimilated by the second and third generations.

 Marketing Implications

Asian Americans are a rapidly growing group with a median income of $74,000, significantly higher than the overall U.S. median income of $53,700.[179] Many marketers target this segment, as the following examples show.

Product Development and Distribution

Marketers are increasingly developing more offerings for Asian Americans and tailoring distribution

accordingly. To illustrate, East West Bank, based in California, has introduced special banking services for this segment and invites its customers to bank in Cantonese, Mandarin, or Vietnamese (Spanish is also an option). The company also maintains several bank branches in China.[180] Yet caution is needed to avoid missteps: One company mistakenly offered golf balls in a four-pack instead of the usual three-pack, not knowing that the word four is considered unlucky because it sounds similar to the word for death in both Japanese and Chinese.

Media and Communications

To reach this diverse group, marketers often use native-language newspapers, magazines, broadcast and cable TV, radio, and, of course, the Internet. Messages delivered to Asian Americans in their native language are often more effective than those delivered in English. Despite the diversity of languages within this subculture, marketers may find the effort worthwhile when many consumers from a single subgroup are concentrated in an area. Subaru, for example, has used a "keeping children safe" theme in U.S. TV commercials produced in Cantonese and Mandarin as well as English.[181] Asian Americans tend to respond well to subtle messages that focus on tradition, the family, and cooperation as well as to ads featuring Asian models.[182]

12-4b ETHNIC GROUPS AROUND THE WORLD

Ethnic subcultures exist in many nations. Although it is beyond the scope of this book to discuss each of the numerous ethnic groups around the world, a few examples illustrate their importance and the challenges and opportunities of reaching specific groups within a particular country.

In Canada, the French-speaking subculture has unique motivations and buying habits.[183] Compared with the rest of the Canadian population, French Canadians use more staples for original or "scratch" cooking; drink more soft drinks, beer, wine, and instant beverages; and consume fewer frozen vegetables, diet drinks, and hard liquor. Canada is home to many other groups, as well, meaning multicultural marketing is important. For instance, to reach the entire country during the nationwide launch of its electric Volt car, Chevrolet Canada relied on marketing messages in English, French, Cantonese, Hindi, Mandarin, Punjabi, and Tamil, delivered on TV and in print, on YouTube, in search-engine ads, and on social media sites. The next generation Chevy Volt was marketed on GM's Canadian websites in English and French, and on the brand's English-language and French-language social media sites.[184]

In Thailand, more than 80 percent of the population is of Thai origin, but several sizable ethnic subcultures still flourish. The largest, 10 percent of the population, has Chinese roots, and this segment has influenced the Thai culture to a significant degree.[185] Chinese consumers in Thailand exert a powerful economic force because they own many businesses; their influence is also felt in art, religion, and food. Other, smaller, ethnic groups in Thailand include people of Laotian, Indian, and Burmese origin.

India has a diverse ethnic population, with more than 80 languages and 120 dialects spoken in the country. Some villagers need travel only 30 miles from home to reach a destination where they are not able to speak the language. Within India, consumers have differing preferences and buying patterns. As mentioned early in the chapter, Yum! Brands recognizes how diversity affects consumer behavior in India and other markets, and it fine-tunes its offerings for each targeted group. As another example, the instant noodle brand Wai Wai markets its products with different flavors for consumers in particular regions of India. In the southeast region, Wai Wai is flavored with locally favored Kerala spices, Tamil spices, and Andhra Pradesh spices.[186]

12-4c THE INFLUENCE OF RELIGION

A final cultural influence is based on religious beliefs. Religion provides people with a structured set of beliefs and values that serve as a code of conduct or guide to behavior. It also provides ties that bind people together and make one group different from another. According to research, the majority of Americans are either Protestant or Catholic. In comparison, only a small fraction of Americans identify themselves as being Jewish, Mormon, Buddhist, Muslim, Hindu, or a follower of another religion. Nearly 23 percent of the U.S. population has no religious affiliation.[187]

Although individual differences certainly come into play, some religious influences or traditions can affect consumer behavior. For example, religion can prevent consumption of certain products or services. Mormons are prohibited from using liquor, tobacco, and caffeine, including cola. Orthodox Jews do not eat pork or shellfish, and all meat and poultry to be consumed must be certified as kosher. Muslims cannot drink liquor or eat pork, and all other meat and poultry to be consumed must be certified as halal. Catholic consumers may choose to abstain from eating meat on Fridays, in particular during the season of Lent. On the other hand, after Lent (Catholics) and Ramadan (Muslims) consumption of sweets and treats may be higher. Religious beliefs can also affect attitudes and actions regarding issues such as environmental protection.[188]

Religious subcultures are clearly present in many parts of the world. In India, for example, most of the population is Hindu, but large groups of Muslims, Christians, and Sikhs exhibit different patterns of consumption. Because Hindus are predominantly vegetarian, Indian manufacturers of food and cosmetics must use vegetable-based rather than animal-based oils and shortening in their products. The Sikh religion forbids the consumption of beef and tobacco, and the sales of such products are low in areas where many Sikhs live. Finally, the color green has significance for Muslims as it is mentioned in the Quran to describe the state of the inhabitants of paradise, a factor that has led to its frequent use on product packages for this group.

 ## Marketing Implications

In general, global marketers must understand how religion affects attitudes and behavior in each market where they are active, to encourage positive reactions and minimize negative reactions.[189] Marketers can segment the market by focusing on religious affiliation, delivering targeted messages and promotions or using certain media to deliver them. They can target Christian consumers through religious radio and TV stations and programs, which reach millions of U.S. consumers. In addition, marketers can advertise in one of the many publications geared to specific religious affiliations or reach a particular group via specialized websites or social media interaction. Some deep-discount websites target religious groups with carefully tailored offerings. For example, Jdeal offers deals on Jewish holiday foods, magazine subscriptions, and other products.[190]

Marketing tactics should demonstrate understanding and respect for the targeted group's beliefs and customs, a strategy that will also generate positive word of mouth. The ITC hotel group now offers Eva floors at its hotels in India exclusively for female travelers. Only women employees serve guests on those floors, providing everything from concierge services to room service. "Many women traveling from Muslim countries may not feel comfortable with male attendants delivering food to their rooms," says an ITC marketing official.[191]

Marketers can also distribute religious products through specialized stores and websites that retail items such as religious artwork, books, and jewelry. Some marketers use religious symbols and themes in their advertising, which is an effective way to generate a positive reaction from consumers who are religious.[192] However, some marketers avoid products or messages with overt religious meaning, to avoid controversy. Even that approach can cause controversy, as Starbucks found out in 2015 when it began serving coffee in holiday-red disposable cups without any seasonal symbols related to Christmas.[193]

Summary:

Six major aspects of consumer diversity have important effects on consumer behavior: age, gender, sexual orientation, regional differences, ethnic differences, and religious differences. Age is a key factor because people of the same age have similar life experiences, needs, symbols, and memories that may lead to similar consumption patterns. Four important age groups are teens and millennials (also known as Generation Y), Generation X, baby boomers, and seniors over 65 years old (the gray market). Gender differences, including the influence of changing sex roles, also affect consumer behavior. Men and women differ in terms of their consumer traits, information-processing styles, decision-making styles, and consumption patterns. In addition, more marketers are using sexual orientation to target gay, lesbian, bisexual, and transgender consumers for various goods and services.

Consumption patterns may differ in various regions of the United States and the world, leading some marketers to tailor their strategies specifically to these regions. Clustering helps marketers describe consumers in different regions based on similar demographic and consumption characteristics rather than on geographic location only. The three largest U.S. ethnic groups are African Americans, Hispanic Americans, and Asian Americans. Many marketers are taking a multicultural approach, appealing to several subcultures instead of just one. Finally, religious values and customs can influence consumer behavior and form the basis of some marketing strategies.

Questions for Review and Discussion

1. What type of U.S. consumers are in the Generation X, millennial generation, and baby boomer segments?

2. What is the difference between gender and sexual orientation, and why is this distinction important for marketers?

3. What is clustering, and why do marketers use it?

4. What are the three main subcultures within the U.S. population?

5. How do acculturation and intensity of ethnic identification affect consumer behavior?

6. Define the accommodation theory, and explain its importance for marketers who target Hispanic Americans.

7. Why would a company adopt multicultural marketing rather than target a single subculture?

8. Why do marketers have to consider regional influences when targeting consumers within the United States or in another country?

9. Identify some of the ways in which religion can influence consumer behavior.

Endnotes

1   Leslie Patton and Christie Boyden, "Can the World Learn to Love Taco Bell? Yum Is Under Pressure to Find Out," *Bloomberg*, October 7, 2015, www.bloomberg.com.

2   Charles D. Schewe and Geoffrey Meredith, "Segmenting Global Markets by Generational Cohorts: Determining Motivations by Age," *Journal of Consumer Behavior* 4, no. 1, 2004, pp. 51–63.

3   Bryant Ott, "Marketing to Tweeters and Their Facebook Friends," *Gallup Management Journal*, April 11, 2011, n.p.

4   Beth Snyder, "The iGeneration: There's a Market for That," *Advertising Age*, October 17, 2011, www.adage.com.

5   Rick Garlick and Kyle Langley, "Reaching Gen Y on Both Sides of the Cash Register," *Retailing Issues Letter*, Center for Retailing Studies at Texas A&M University 18, no. 2, 2007, pp. 1–2.

6   Dannie Kjeldgaard and Søren Askegaard, "The Globalization of Youth Culture," *Journal of Consumer Research* 33, no. 2, 2006, pp. 231–247.

7   The Six Value Segments of Global Youth," *Brandweek*, May 22, 2000, pp. 38–44.

8   Agnieszka Kacprzak and Katarzyna Dziewanowska, "Does a Global Young Consumer Exist? A Comparative Study of South Korea and Poland," *Journal of Marketing and Consumer Behaviour in Emerging Markets* 1, no. 1, 2015, pp. 47–61.

9   "Most Millennials Resist the 'Millennial' Label," *Pew Research Center*, September 3, 2015, www.people-press.org.

10 Cole J. Engel, Reginald L. Bell, Robert J. Meier, Michael J. Martin, and Joan H. Rumpel, "Young Consumers in the New Marketing Ecosystem: An Analysis of Their Usage of Interactive Technologies," *Academy of Marketing Studies Journal* 15, no. 2, 2011, pp. 23–44.

11 Amanda Lenhart, "Teens, Social Media, and Technology Overview 2015," *Pew Research Center*, April 9, 2015, www.pewinternet.org.

12 Beth Ann Bovino, "Why Millennials and the Depression-era Generation Are More Similar Than You Think," *Fortune*, April 29, 2015, www.fortune.com.

13 Mark Thoma, "What's Fueling the Boomerang Generation?" *CBS Moneywatch*, February 10, 2015, www.cbsnews.com.

14 John Masanauskas, "Kids Who Won't Leave Home Put Squeeze on Families," *Herald Sun* (Victoria, Australia), August 9, 2011, www.heraldsun.com.au.

15 Shiv Malik, "The Dependent Generation: Half Young European Adults Live with Their Parents," *The Guardian (U.K.)*, March 24, 2014, www.theguardian.com.

16 Lisa Jennings, "Generation App, Study: Millennials Eager to Interact with Brands in Digital Domain," *Nation's Restaurant News*, September 12, 2011, p. 44.

17 Pierre-Yan Dolbec and Eileen Fischer, "Refashioning a Field? Connected Consumers and Institutional Dynamics in Markets," *Journal of Consumer Research* 41, April 2015, pp. 1447–1468.

18 Annamaria Lusardi, "The Alarming Facts About Millennials and Debt," *Wall Street Journal*, October 5, 2015, www.wsj.com.

19 Andrew W. Ellis, Selina J. Holmes, and Richard L. Wright, "Age of Acquisition and the Recognition of Brand Names: On the Importance of Being Early," *Journal of Consumer Psychology* 20, 2010, pp. 43–52.

20 Paula Dwyer, "The Euroteens (and How to Sell to Them)," *BusinessWeek*, April 11, 1994, p. 84.

21 Geoff Smith, "Study: Millennials Are the Most Brand-Loyal Generation," *Inc.*, September 30, 2015, www.inc.com.

22 Laurie Sullivan, "Millennials Want Loyalty Points for Engagement with Brands," *MediaPost*, July 21, 2015, www.mediapost.com.

23 Emma Bazilian, "Teen Vogue Debuts Condé Nast's First Sponsored Cover Ad," *Adweek*, April 21, 2015, www.adweek.com.

24 Kerri Anne Renzulli, "Why Teens Hate Shopping at 'Teen' Clothing Stores," *Time*, January 9, 2015, www.time.com.

25 John McDermott, "Mercedes-Benz Uses Instagram to Sell Cars to Millennials," *DigiDay*, July 10, 2014, www.digiday.com.

26 "Facebook, Time Warner Launch Anti-Bullying App," *KBTX-TV* (Texas), July 17, 2014, www.kbtx.com.

27 Julia Greenberg, "Stop With the Millennial Niche News Sites Already," *Wired*, June 8, 2015, www.wired.com.

28 Marshall Heyman, "A Stage for Skaters," *Wall Street Journal*, September 8, 2011, www.wsj.com.

29 John Caniglia, "Libraries Turn the Page to Keep Up with Changing Times," *Plain Dealer* (Cleveland, OH), September 26, 2011, www.cleveland.com; and Robert Rua, "Cuyahoga County Public Library Expands Its Free Streaming Video Collection," *Plain Dealer* (Cleveland, OH), November 10, 2015, www.cleveland.com.

30 Kathryn Vasel, "Gen-Xers Don't Want to Be Homeowners," *CNN Money*, June 25, 2015, http://money.cnn.com.

31 Tralee Pearce, "For Generation X, It's All Work and No Kids, Study Finds," *Globe and Mail* (Canada), September 21, 2011, www.theglobeandmail.com.

32 See Carol Hymowitz, "Generation X Has It Worse Than Baby Boomers, Millennials," *Bloomberg News*, June 10, 2015, www.bostonglobe.com; and Jackie Crosby, "Viewpoint: How Generation X can avoid a fate as 'Generation Debt,'" *Star-Tribune (Minneapolis)*, January 2, 2016, www.startribune.com.

33 Dana French, "Gen X Comprises 33% of All Furniture Dollars," *Furniture Today*, July 15, 2015, www.furnituretoday.com.

34 Angrisani, "X Marks the Spot."

35 Stephanie Strom, "Campbell Rethinks Its Soup Recipe as Consumer Tastes Change," *New York Times*, November 9,

2015, www.nytimes.com; and Abram Brown, "Doug Conant Pulled the Brand Out from a Circle of Doom," *Business Insider*, September 15, 2011, www.businessinsider.com.

36 Arthur Zaczkiewicz, "Study: Retailers Need a Multigenerational Marketing Approach," *WWD*, August 6, 2015, www.wwd.com.

37 "Age of Technology: Generational Video Viewing Preferences Vary by Device and Activity," *Nielsen*, April 22, 2015, www.nielsen.com.

38 Dale Buss, "Nissan Launches 'Widest-Reaching' College-Sports Sponsorship in Marketing History," *Forbes*, November 6, 2015, www.forbes.com.

39 Matthew Sturdevant, "Marketing Life Insurance Is a Game for AXA Equitable, Online," *Hartford Courant*, November 13, 2011, www.courant.com.

40 "Table 1: Projections and Distribution of the Population in the Baby Boom Ages and Total Population by Race and Hispanic Origin for the United States: 2012, 2030, and 2060," *The Baby Boom Cohort in the United States: 2012 to 2060*, U.S. Census Bureau, May 2014, www.census.gov.

41 John H. Fleming, "Baby Boomers Are Opening Their Wallets," *Gallup*, January 30, 2015, www.gallup.com.

42 Cheryl Russell, "The Power of One," *Brandweek*, October 4, 1993, pp. 27–28, 30, 32.

43 Stephen Reily, "How Marketing to Moms Is Like Marketing to Boomers," *MediaPost*, September 29, 2011, www.mediapost.com.

44 Rodney Brooks, "Retirement Reset: Sandwiched Boomers Put Plans on Hold," *USA Today*, August 21, 2014, www.usatoday.com.

45 Sandra Yin, "More at Home on the Road," *American Demographics*, June 2003, pp. 26–27.

46 Kathy Witt, "Dreams Come True with Bucket-List Adventures," *Modesto Bee* (California), September 23, 2011, www.modbee.com.

47 Casey Logan, "For Chico's, a 'Perfect Storm' in September," *News-Press* (Fort Myers, FL), November 24, 2015, www.news-press.com.

48 Casey Dowd, "Graying Baby Boomers' Quest to Look Younger," *Fox Business*, September 8, 2011, www.foxbusiness.com.

49 Hal Conick, "Nostalgic Flavors: Coca-Cola and Pepsi Create Buzz with Throwback Drinks," *Beverage Daily*, December 3, 2015, www.beveragedaily.com.

50 Diana T. Kurylko, "Goofy Ads, Variants Help Mini Rule Its Own Little World," *Automotive News*, May 20, 2013, www.autonews.com.

51 James R. Hagerty, "Harley-Davidson's Hurdle: Attracting Young Motorcycle Riders," *Wall Street Journal*, June 19, 2015, www.wsj.com.

52 "Aging Statistics, Administration on Aging," U.S. Department of Health and Human Services, no date, http://www.aoa.acl.gov.

53 Catherine A. Cole and Gary J. Gaeth, "Cognitive and Age-Related Differences in the Ability to Use Nutritional Information in a Complex Environment," *Journal of Marketing Research*, May 1990, pp. 175–184; Catherine A. Cole and Siva K. Balasubramanian, "Age Differences in Consumers' Search for Information," *Journal of Consumer Research*, June 1993, pp. 157–169; and Deborah Roedder John and Catherine A. Cole, "Age Differences in Information Processing," *Journal of Consumer Research*, December 1986, pp. 297–315.

54 Carolyn Yoon, "Age Differences in Consumers' Processing Strategies," *Journal of Consumer Research*, December 1997, pp. 329–342.

55 Sharmistha Law, Scott A. Hawkins, and Fergus I. M. Craik, "Repetition-Induced Belief in the Elderly," *Journal of Consumer Research*, September 1998, pp. 91–107.

56 Catherine A. Cole and Gar y J. Gaeth, "Cognitive and Age-Related Differences in the Ability to Use Nutritional Information in a Complex Environment," *Journal of Marketing Research*, May 1990, pp. 175–184; Cole and Balasubramanian, "Age Differences in Consumers' Search for Information"; and John and Cole, "Age Differences in Information Processing."

57 Michelle Barnhart and Lisa Peñaloza, "Who Are You Calling Old? Negotiating Old Age Identity in the Elderly Consumption Ensemble," *Journal of Consumer Research* 39, no. 6, April 2013, pp. 1133–1153.

58 Hope Jensen Schau, Mary C. Gilly, and Mary Wolfinbarger, "Consumer Identity Renaissance: The Resurgence of Identity-Inspired Consumption in Retirement," *Journal of Consumer Research*, August 2009, pp. 255–276.

59 "Millennials Outnumber Baby Boomers and Are Far More Diverse, Census Bureau Reports," *U.S. Census Bureau News Release*, June 25, 2015.

60 Raphaëlle Lambert-Pandraud, Gilles Laurent, and Eric Lapersonne, "Repeat Purchasing of New Automobiles by Older Consumers," *Journal of Marketing*, April 2005, pp. 97–113; and Lambert-Pandraud and Gilles Laurent, "Why Do Older Consumers Buy Older Brands? The Role of Attachment and Declining Innovativeness," *Journal of Marketing* 74, no. 5, September 2010, pp. 104–121.

61 "Telstra: 'Connection Is a Basic Human Right'," *Bandt*, January 24, 2014, www.bandt.com.au.

62 Mary Madden, "Older Adults and Social Media," *Pew Internet and American Life Project*, August 27, 2010, http://pewinternet.org.

63 "Turning Silver into Gold," *Economist*, July 30, 2011, p. 60.

64 Ronald E. Milliman and Robert C. Erffmeyer, "Improving Advertising Aimed at Seniors," *Journal of Advertising Research*, December 1989–January 1990, pp. 31–36.

65 Robin T. Peterson, "The Depiction of Senior Citizens in Magazine Advertisements," *Journal of Business Ethics*, September 1992, pp. 701–706; Anthony C. Ursic, Michael L. Ursic, and Virginia L. Ursic, "A Longitudinal Study of the Use of the Elderly in Magazine Advertising," *Journal of Consumer Research*, June 1986, pp. 131–133; and John J. Burnett, "Examining the Media Habits of the Affluent Elderly," *Journal of Advertising Research*, October– November 1991, pp. 33–41.

66 Emma Bazilian, "Why Older Women Are the New It-Girls of Fashion," *Adweek*, April 6, 2015, www.adweek.com.

67 Patti Williams and Aimee Drolet, "Age-Related Differences in Responses to Emotional Advertisements," *Journal of Consumer Research* 32, no. 3, 2005, pp. 343–354.

68 America's Aging Consumers," *Discount Merchandiser*, September 1993, pp. 16–28; and John and Cole, "Age Differences in Information Processing."

69 Emma Sapong, "Super Saver Seniors," *Buffalo News*, October 3, 2011, www.buffalonews.com.

70 Teresa Mears, "How to Guard Against Common Scams That Target Seniors," *U.S. News & World Report*, October 27, 2015, www.usnews.com.

71 See Lin Fraser, "Gender Dysphoria: Definition and Evolution through the Years," in eds. C. Trombetta et al., *Management of Gender Dysphoria: A Multidisciplinary Approach* (Milan: Springer-Verlag Italia, 2015), pp. 19–31.

72 Joan Meyers-Levy, "The Influence of Sex Roles on Judgment," *Journal of Consumer Research*, March 1988, pp. 522–530.

73 Charles S. Areni and Pamela Kiecker, "Gender Differences in Motivation: Some Implications for Manipulating Task-Related Involvement," in ed. Janeen Arnold Costa, *Gender and Consumer Behavior* (Salt Lake City, Utah: University of Utah Printing Service, 1993), pp. 30–43; and Brenda Giner and Eileen Fischer, "Women and Arts, Men and Sports: Two Phenomena or One?" in ed. Janeen Arnold Costa, *Gender and Consumer Behavior* (Salt Lake City, Utah: University of Utah Printing Service, 1993), p. 149.

74 Douglas B. Holt and Craig J. Thompson, "Man-of-Action Heroes: The Pursuit of Heroic Masculinity in Everyday Consumption," *Journal of Consumer Research*, September 2004, pp. 425–440.

75 Kristina M. Durante, Vladas Griskevicius, Sarah E. Hill, Carin Perilloux, and Norman P. Li, "Ovulation, Female Competition, and Product Choice: Hormonal Influences on Consumer Behavior," *Journal of Consumer Research*, April 2011, pp. 921–934.

76 Gokcen Coskuner-Balli and Craig J. Thompson, "The Status Costs of Subordinate Cultural Capital: At-Home Fathers' Collective Pursuit of Cultural Legitimacy through Capitalizing Consumption Practices," *Journal of Consumer Research* 40, no. 1, June 2013, pp. 19–41.

77 Rahul Sachitanand, "Why Women Consumers Matter and What Companies Are Doing About It," *Economic Times (India)*, March 27, 2012, http://articles.economictimes.indiatimes.com; and Alladi Venkatesh, "Gender Identity in the Indian Context, a Socio-Cultural Construction of the Female Consumer," in ed. Costa, *Gender and Consumer Behavior*, pp. 119–129.

78 Matt Wade, "Business Tigresses Are Burning Bright," *Sydney Morning Herald* (Australia), September 20, 2011, www.smh.com.au.

79 Tamara Baluja, "Canadian Teens Ambivalent about Gender Equality," *Globe and Mail* (Canada), September 22, 2011, www.theglobeandmail.com.

80 Martin Eisend, "A Meta-Analysis of Gender Roles in Advertising," *Journal of the Academy of Marketing Science*, Fall 2010, pp. 418–440.

81 Timothy M. Smith, Srinath Gopalakrishna, and Paul M. Smith, "Men's and Women's Responses to Sex Role Portrayals in Advertisements," *Journal of Marketing* Research, March 2004, pp. 61–77.

82 Aysen Bakir and Kay M. Palan, "How Are Children's Attitudes Toward Ads and Brands Affected by Gender-Related Content in Advertising?" *Journal of Advertising*, Spring 2010, pp. 35–48.

83 Joan Meyers-Levy and Durairaj Maheswaran, "Exploring Differences in Males' and Females' Processing Strategies," *Journal of Consumer Research*, June 1991, pp. 63–70; William K. Darley and Robert E. Smith, "Gender Differences in Information Processing Strategies," *Journal of Advertising*, Spring 1995, pp. 41–56; and Barbara B. Stern, "Feminist Literary Criticism and the Deconstruction of Ads," *Journal of Consumer Research*, March 1993, pp. 556–566.

84 Meyers-Levy, "The Influence of Sex Roles on Judgment"; and Joan Meyers-Levy, "Priming Effects on Product Judgments," *Journal of Consumer Research*, June 1989, pp. 76–86.

85 Laurette Dube and Michael S. Morgan, "Trend Effects and Gender Differences in Retrospective Judgments of Consumption Emotions," *Journal of Consumer Research*, September 1996, pp. 156–162.

86 Richard Elliot, "Gender and the Psychological Meaning of Fashion Brands," in ed. Janeen Arnold Costa, *Gender and*

Consumer Behavior (Salt Lake City, Utah: University of Utah Printing Service, 1993), pp. 99–105.

87 Suzanne C. Grunert, "On Gender Differences in Eating Behavior as Compensatory Consumption," in ed. Janeen Arnold Costa, *Gender and Consumer Behavior*, pp. 74–86.

88 Micah Maidenberg, "What's Next for Harley-Davidson," *Crain's Chicago Business*, September 23, 2015, www.chicagobusiness.com; Wevonneda Minis, "Women on a Roll," *Post and Courier* (Charleston, S.C.), September 25, 2011, www.postandcourier.com; and Clifford Krauss, "Women, Hear Them Roar," *New York Times*, July 25, 2007, pp. C1, C9.

89 Kala Vijayraghavan and Sagar Malviya, "Hindustan Unilever's Shift to Personal Products After Soaps and Detergents," *Economic Times* (India), September 21, 2011, www.economictimes.com.

90 Valentyna Melnyk, Stijn M. J. van Osselaer, and Tammo H. A. Bijmolt, "Are Women More Loyal Customers Than Men? Gender Differences in Loyalty to Firms and Individual Service Providers," *Journal of Marketing*, July 2009, pp. 82–96.

91 Valentyna Melnyk and Stijn M. J. van Osselaer, "Make Me Special: Gender Differences in Consumers' Responses to Loyalty Programs," *Marketing Letters* 23, no. 3, September 2012, pp. 545–559.

92 Soonyong Bae and Taesik Lee, "Gender Differences in Consumers' Perception of Online Consumer Reviews," *Electronic Commerce Research* 11, no. 2, 2010, pp. 201–214.

93 Gina Hall, "The DIY Movement Is Filling Home Improvement Aisles, with Women," *Biz Women Business Journals*, April 24, 2014, www.bizjournals.com; Stephanie Clifford, "Revamping, Home Depot Woos Women," *New York Times*, January 28, 2011, www.nytimes.com; "Lowe's to Debut New Campaign, Tagline," *Advertising Age*, September 15, 2011, www.adage.com; and Amy Tsao, "Retooling Home Improvement," *BusinessWeek*, February 14, 2005, www.businessweek.com.

94 Philip Weyhe, "Upcoming Girl's Night Out Gives St. Peter Businesses Marketing Opportunity," *St. Peter Herald (St. Peter, MN)*, September 18, 2015, www.southernminn.com.

95 Normandy Madden, "P&G's Take on Targeting China's Fast-Changing Consumers," *Advertising Age*, August 20, 2014, www.adage.com.

96 Ana Swanson, "What Super Bowl Manvertising Says About Men's New Role in America," *Washington Post*, January 2, 2015, www.washingtonpost.com.

97 Robert J. Fisher and Laurette Dubé, "Gender Differences in Responses to Emotional Advertising," *Journal of Consumer Research* 31, no. 4, 2005, pp. 850–858.

98 John B. Ford, Patricia Kramer, Earl D. Honeycutt Jr., and Susan L. Casey, "Gender Role Portrayals in Japanese Advertising," *Journal of Advertising*, Spring 1998, pp. 113–124.

99 Geoffrey A. Fowler, "Marketers Take Heed: The Macho Chinese Man Is Back," *Wall Street Journal*, December 18, 2002, p. B1.

100 Thomas W. Whipple and Mary K. McManamon, "Implications of Using Male and Female Voices in Commercials: An Exploratory Study," *Journal of Advertising*, Summer 2002, pp. 79–91.

101 Alex Sood, "The Lost Boys Found: Marketing to Men Through Games," *Fast Company*, March 10, 2011, www.fastcompany.com.

102 "Social Networking Site Use by Gender, 2005–2011," *Pew Research Center's Internet & American Life Project Studies*, May 2011, www.pewinternet.org.

103 Ira Boudway, "Nike Is Finally Selling U.S. Women's Soccer Team Jerseys to Men," *Bloomberg*, April 22, 2015, www.bloomberg.com; and Gillian Shaw, "Getting Off the Couch and Counting Crunches," *Vancouver Sun*, September 27, 2011, www.vancouversun.com.

104 Lynn J. Jaffe and Paul D. Berger, "Impact on Purchase Intent of Sex-Role Identity and Product Positioning," *Psychology and Marketing*, Fall 1988, pp. 259–271.

105 John Fetto, "In Broad Daylight," *American Demographics*, February 2001, pp. 16–20; and Ronald Alsop, "Cracking the Gay Market Code," *Wall Street Journal*, June 29, 1999, p. B1.

106 Steven M. Kates, "The Dynamics of Brand Legitimacy: An Interpretive Study in the Gay Men's Community," *Journal of Consumer Research*, September 2004, pp. 455–464; Whithney Ginder and Sang-Eun Byun, "Past, Present, and Future of Gay and Lesbian Consumer Research: Critical Review of the Quest for the Queer Dollar," *Psychology & Marketing* 32, no. 8, 2015, pp. 821–841.

107 Dave Berns, "Late to the Party, Las Vegas Businesses Targeting Gay Community," *Vegas Inc.*, July 18, 2011, www.vegasinc.com; and Lisa Fickenscher, "Tourism Industry to Capitalize on Same-Sex Marriage," *Crain's New York Business*, June 27, 2011, www.crainsnewyork.com.

108 Diane Daniel, "Courting Transgender Tourists," *New York Times*, September 16, 2015, www.nytimes.com; and Arlene Satchell, "Tourism Bureau's 'Love is Love' Wedding Campaign Nabs Several Awards," *Sun-Sentinel (Florida)*, September 4, 2015, www.sun-sentinel.com.

109 Mark Magnier, "Gay Consumers' Spending Power Draws Attention in China, But Stigma Remains," *Wall Street Journal*, November 25, 2015, www.wsj.com.

110 Sandra Yin, "Home and Away," *American Demographics*, March 2004, p. 15.

111 Antonio Arellano, "Tex-Mex vs Mexican food: Which Side of the Border Does Your Food Come From?" *San Antonio Express-News*, September 30, 2015, www.mysanantonio.com.

112 Susan Mitchell, "Birds of a Feather," *American Demographics*, February 1995, pp. 40–48.

113 Michael Weiss, "Parallel Universe," *American Demographics*, October 1999, pp. 58–63.

114 Adapted from PRIZM Segment Lookup, Nielsen My Best Segments, www.claritas.com.

115 Marti Benedetti, "Detroit's Better Made Has Chipped Away at Customer Tastes for 85 Years," *Crain's Detroit Business*, November 27, 2015, www.crainsdetroit.com.

116 Ilan Brat, "Dean Foods Bets on One National Milk Brand," *Wall Street Journal*, May 4, 2015, www.wsj.com.

117 Mitchell, "Birds of a Feather."

118 Mike Freeman, "Clusters of Customers," *San Diego Union-Tribune*, December 19, 2004, www.signosandiego.com.

119 Bjoern Frank, Gulimire Abulaite, and Takao Enkawa, "Regional Differences in Consumer Preference Structures within China," *Journal of Retailing and Consumer Services* 21, 2014, pp. 203–210; and Don Strachan, "Italy's 20 Regions, Dish by Delicious Dish," *CNN*, January 27, 2014, www.cnn.com.

120 Haipeng (Allan) Chen, Sharon Ng, and Akshay R. Rao, "Cultural Differences in Consumer Impatience," *Journal of Marketing Research*, August 2005, pp. 291–301.

121 Alokparna Basu Monga and Deborah Roedder John, "Cultural Differences in Brand Extension Evaluation: The Influence of Analytic versus Holistic Thinking," *Journal of Consumer Research* 33, no. 4, March 2007, pp. 529–536.

122 See Daphna Oyserman, "High Power, Low Power, and Equality," *Journal of Consumer Psychology* 16, no. 4, 2006, pp. 352–356.

123 Sharon Shavitt, Ashok K. Lalwani, Jing Zhang, and Carlos J. Torelli, "The Horizontal/Vertical Dimension in Cross-Cultural Consumer Research," *Journal of Consumer Psychology* 16, no. 4, 2006, pp. 325–342; Joan Meyers-Levy, "Using the Horizontal/Vertical Distinction to Advance Insights into Consumer Psychology," *Journal of Consumer Psychology* 16, no. 4, 2006, pp. 347–351; Jennifer L. Aaker, "Delineating Culture," *Journal of Consumer Psychology* 16, no. 4, 2006, pp. 343–347; and Sharon Shavitt, Ashok K. Lalwani, Jing Zhang, and Carlos J. Torelli, "Reflections on the Meaning and Structure of the Horizontal/ Vertical Dimension," *Journal of Consumer Psychology* 16, no. 4, 2006, pp. 357–362.

124 Michelle R. Nelson, Frédéric F. Brunel, Magne Supphellen, and Rajesh V. Manchanda, "Effects of Culture, Gender, and Moral Obligations on Responses to Charity Advertising Across Masculine and Feminine Cultures," *Journal of Consumer Psychology* 16, no. 1, 2006, pp. 45–56.

125 Donnel A. Briley and Jennifer L. Aaker, "When Does Culture Matter? Effects of Personal Knowledge on the Correction of Culture-Based Judgments," *Journal of Marketing Research*, August 2006, pp. 395–408.

126 Steven M. Kates and Charlene Goh, "Brand Morphing," *Journal of Advertising*, Spring 2003, pp. 59–68.

127 Valentyna Melnyk, Kristina Klein, and Franziska Volckner, "The Double-Edged Sword of Foreign Brand Names for Companies from Emerging Countries," *Journal of Marketing* 76, no. 6, November 2012, pp. 21–37.

128 Mark Phelan, "Why Buick Is Right to Import the Envision from China," *Detroit Free Press*, December 13, 2015, www.freep.com; and "Chinese May Sway Porsche Designs," *Automotive News*, August 22, 2011, p. 26.

129 George P. Moschis, *Consumer Socialization* (Lexington, Mass.: D. C. Heath, 1987); and Lisa Penaloza, "Atravesando Fronteras/Border Crossings," *Journal of Consumer Research*, June 1994, pp. 32–54.

130 Sonya A. Grier, Anne M. Brumbaugh, and Corliss G. Thornton, "Crossover Dreams: Consumer Responses to Ethnic-Oriented Products," *Journal of Marketing*, April 2006, pp. 35–51.

131 Aurelia Mok and Michael W. Morris, "Bicultural Self-Defense in Consumer Contexts: Self-Protection Motives Are the Basis for Contrast versus Assimilation to Cultural Cues," *Journal of Consumer Psychology* 23, no. 2, April 2013, pp. 175–188.

132 Jean-Francois Ouellet, "Consumer Racism and Its Effects on Domestic Cross-Ethnic Product Purchase: An Empirical Test in the United States, Canada, and France," *Journal of Marketing*, January 2007, pp. 113–128.

133 Sterling A. Bone, Glenn L. Christensen, and Jerome D. Williams, "Rejected, Shackled, and Alone: The Impact of Systemic Restricted Choice on Minority Consumers' Construction of Self," *Journal Of Consumer Research* 41, no. 2, August 2014, pp. 451–474.

134 "The Making of a Multicultural Super Consumer," *Nielsen Newswire*, March 18, 2015, www.nielsen.com.

135 Laurel Wentz, "McDonald's Is Marketer of the Year at AHAA's Hispanic Conference," *Advertising Age*, May 1, 2014, www .adage.com.

136 "Facts For Features: Hispanic Heritage Month 2015," *U.S. Census Bureau*, September 14, 2015, www.census.gov.

137 "Table 1: Income and Earnings Summary Measures by Selected Characteristics, 2013 and 2014," in *Income and Poverty in the United States, 2014*, U.S. Census Bureau, September 2015, www .census.gov; and "Table 690: Money Income of Households,"

Statistical Abstract of the United States 2012, U.S. Census Bureau, p. 452.

138 Carrie Goerne, "Go the Extra Mile to Catch Up with Hispanics," *Marketing News*, December 24, 1990, p. 13; and Marlene Rossman, *Multicultural Marketing* (New York: American Management Association, 1994).

139 Penaloza, "Atravesando Fronteras/Border Crossings."

140 Humberto Valencia, "Developing an Index to Measure Hispanicness," in eds. Elizabeth C. Hirschman and Morris B. Holbrook, *Advances in Consumer Research*, vol. 12 (Provo, Utah: Association for Consumer Research, 1981), pp. 18–21; and Rohit Deshpande, Wayne D. Hoyer, and Naveen Donthu, "The Intensity of Ethnic Affiliation," *Journal of Consumer Research*, September 1986, pp. 214–220.

141 Cynthia Webster, "Effects of Hispanic Ethnic Identification on Marital Roles in the Purchase Decision Process," *Journal of Consumer Research*, September 1994, pp. 319–331.

142 Cynthia Webster, "The Effects of Hispanic Subcultural Identification on Information Search Behavior," *Journal of Advertising Research*, September–October 1992, pp. 54–62; and Naveen Donthu and Joseph Cherian, "Hispanic Coupon Usage," *Psychology and Marketing*, November–December 1992, pp. 501–510.

143 Sarah Berger, "Hispanic Buying Power 2015," *International Business Times*, July 2, 2015, www.ibtimes.com.

144 "Univision's Big Bet on Streaming," *Media Life Magazine*, November 19, 2015, www.medialifemagazine.com.

145 Ellen Byron, "Hola: P&G Seeks Latino Shoppers," *Wall Street Journal*, September 15, 2011, www.wsj.com.

146 Walter Michot, "The Power of Publix: Market Battles for Dominance as It Expands," *Miami Herald*, May 10, 2015, www .miamiherald.com.

147 Mark Harper, "Wal-Mart Adds Grocery Store in Deltona," *Daytona Beach News-Journal*, September 28, 2015, www .news-journalonline.com.

148 Lindsay Chappell, "Sales to Hispanics Outpacing the Market," *Automotive News*, May 18, 2015, www.autonews.com.

149 Mike Reynolds, "Hispanic TV Summit," *Multichannel News*, September 20, 2011, www.multichannel.com.

150 Nitish Singh, Daniel W. Baack, Arun Pereira, and Donald Baack, "Culturally Customizing Websites for U.S. Hispanic Online Consumers," *Journal of Advertising Research*, June 2008, pp. 224–234.

151 Katie Dupere, "'Proud to Be Me': New Ad Campaign Aims to Inspire Modern Latinas," *Mashable*, September 19, 2015, www.mashable.com; and Byron, "Hola: P&G Seeks Latino Shoppers."

152 Rohit Deshpande and Douglas M. Stayman, "A Tale of Two Cities: Distinctiveness Theory and Advertising Effectiveness," *Journal of Marketing Research*, February 1994, pp. 57–64.

153 See Claudia V. Dimofte, Mark R. Forehand, and Rohit Deshpandé, "Ad Schema Incongruity as Elicitor of Ethnic Self Awareness and Differential Advertising Response," *Journal of Advertising*, Winter 2003–2004, pp. 7–17; and Mark R. Forehand and Rohit Deshpandé, "What We See Makes Us Who We Are: Priming Ethnic Self-Awareness and Advertising Response," *Journal of Marketing Research*, August 2001, pp. 336–348.

154 Anne M. Brumbaugh, "Source and Nonsource Cues in Advertising and Their Effects on the Activation of Cultural and Subcultural Knowledge on the Route to Persuasion," *Journal of Consumer Research*, September 2002, pp. 258–269.

155 Robert E. Wilkes and Humberto Valencia, "Hispanics and Blacks in Television Commercials," *Journal of Advertising*, March 1989, pp. 19–25.

156 Scott Koslow, Prem N. Shamdasani, and Ellen E. Touchstone, "Exploring Language Effects in Ethnic Advertising," *Journal of Consumer Research*, March 1994, pp. 575–585.

157 Chris Daniels, "Consumer Tech Brands Answer Call to Tap Hispanic Audience," *PR Week (US)*, May 2011, p. 18.

158 Laurel Wentz, "With an Ever-Growing Population of 'Fusionistas,' Consistency Is Key," *Advertising Age*, October 17, 2011, p. 28.

159 Laurel Wentz, "Few Marketers Target U.S. Hispanics with Spanish-Language Facebook Fan Pages," *Advertising Age*, September 27, 2011, www.adage.com.

160 David Luna and Laura A. Peracchio, "Advertising to Bilingual Consumers," *Journal of Consumer Research* 31, no. 4, 2005, pp. 760–765; and David Luna, Dawn Lerman, and Laura A. Peracchio, "Structural Constraints in Code-Switched Advertising," *Journal of Consumer Research* 32, no. 3, 2005, pp. 416–423.

161 "Table 229: Educational Attainment by Race and Hispanic Origin, 1970 to 2010," *Statistical Abstract of the United States 2012*, U.S. Census Bureau, p. 151; and "Table 690: Money Income of Households."

162 "The Power of the Multicultural Dollar," *Black Enterprise*, September 1, 2015, www.blackenterprise.com.

163 "Where Blacks, Whites Diverge," *Brandweek*, May 3, 1993, p. 22.

164 Howard Schlossberg, "Many Marketers Still Consider Blacks 'Dark-Skinned Whites,'" *Marketing News*, January 18, 1993, pp. 1, 13.

165 "Connecting Through Culture: African-Americans Favor Diverse Advertising," *Nielsen*, October 20, 2014, www.nielsen.com.

166 Corliss L. Green, "Ethnic Evaluations of Advertising," *Journal of Advertising* 28, no. 1, Spring 1999, pp. 49–64; and Pepper Miller and Ronald Miller, "Trends Are Opportunities for Targeting African-Americans," *Marketing News*, January 20, 1992, p. 9.

167 Shern-Min Chow, "Houston Man Turns Wife's Unhappiness into Million Dollar Toy Idea," *KHOU News (Houston)*, November 27, 2015, www.khou.com.

168 "A Mirror for American Diversity," *MMR*, February 7, 2011, p. 24; and "African-Americans Go Natural," *MMR*, December 17, 2001, p. 43.

169 Alan J. Bush, Rachel Smith, and Craig Martin, "The Influence of Consumer Socialization Variables on Attitude Toward Advertising," *Journal of Advertising* 28, no. 3, Fall 1999, pp. 13–24.

170 Green, "Ethnic Evaluations of Advertising."

171 Albert and Jacobs, "Television Attitudes and TV Types."

172 Ki Mae Heussner, "Google Study Sees African-Americans More Responsive to Digital Marketing," *Adweek*, September 18, 2011, www.adweek.com.

173 Jennifer L. Aaker, Anne M. Brumbaugh, and Sonya A. Grier, "Nontarget Markets and Viewer Distinctiveness," *Journal of Consumer Psychology* 9, no. 3, 2000, pp. 127–140.

174 Donnel A. Briley, L. J. Shrum, and Robert S. Wyer Jr., "Subjective Impressions of Minority Group Representation in the Media," *Journal of Consumer Psychology* 17, no. 1, 2007, pp. 36–48; and William J. Qualls and David J. Moore, "Stereotyping Effects on Consumers' Evaluation of Advertising," *Psychology and Marketing*, Summer 1990, pp. 135–151.

175 Sonia Alleyne, "The Magic Touch," *Black Enterprise*, June 1, 2004, n.p.

176 Jonathan Burton, "Advertising Targeting Asians," *Far Eastern Economic Review*, January 21, 1993, pp. 40–41.

177 Rebecca Gardyn and John Fetto, "The Way We Shop," *American Demographics*, February 2003, pp. 30–33.

178 "Table 229, Educational Attainment by Race and Hispanic Origin: 1970 to 2010," *Statistical Abstract of the United States 2012*, U.S. Census Bureau, p. 151; and "Asian Americans Lead the Way Online," *Min's New Media Report*, December 31, 2001.

179 "Table 1: Income and Earnings Summary Measures by Selected Characteristics, 2013 and 2014."

180 Russell Flannery, "East West Bank Becomes First L.A. Bank with Branch in Shenzhen," November 18, 2014, *Forbes*, www.forbes.com; and E. Scott Reckard, "East West Surges into Banking Mainstream," *Los Angeles Times*, February 9, 2011, www.latimes.com.

181 Peter Van Allen, "Subaru Advertising Targets Chinese-Americans, Parents," *Philadelphia Business Journal*, May 20, 2011, www.bizjournals.com/philadelphia.

182 Jonathan Burton, "Advertising Targeting Asians," *Far Eastern Economic Review*, January 21, 1993, pp. 40–41; and Brett A. S. Martin, Christina Kwai-Choi Lee, and Yang Feng, "The Influence of Ad Model Ethnicity and Self-Referencing on Attitudes," *Journal of Advertising*, Winter 2004, pp. 27–37.

183 Onkvisit and Shaw, *International Marketing*; and Charles M. Schaninger, Jacques C. Bourgeois, and W. Christian Buss, "French-English Canadian Subcultural Consumption Differences," *Journal of Marketing*, Spring 1985, pp. 82–92.

184 Simon Houpt and Greg Keenan, "The Biggest Launch in Chevrolet's History," *The Globe and Mail* (Canada), October 3, 2011, www.theglobeandmail.com.

185 Hans Hoefer, *Thailand* (Boston: Houghton Mifflin, 1993).

186 Rosemary Marandi, "Nepali CG Corp's Wai Wai on the Boil," *Nikkei Asian Review*, December 10, 2015, http://asia.nikkei.com.

187 "America's Changing Religious Landscape, Chapter 1: The Changing Religious Composition of the U.S.," *Pew Research Center*, May 12, 2015, www.pewforum.org.

188 Matthew Feinberg and Robb Willer, "The Moral Roots of Environmental Attitudes," *Psychological Science* 24, no. 1, January 2013, pp. 56–62.

189 See, for example, Elif Izberk-Bilgin, "Infidel Brands: Unveiling Alternative Meanings of Global Brands at the Nexus of Globalization, Consumer Culture, and Islamism," *Journal of Consumer Research* 39, no. 4, December 2012, pp. 663–687.

190 Mitchell Hartmann, "Niche Daily Dealer Focuses on Jewish Buyers," *Marketplace*, December 13, 2012, www.marketplace.org.

191 Divya Sathyanarayanan, "OYO WE: Budget Hotels Marketplace—OYO Rooms Launches Exclusive Brand for Women," *The Economic Times (India)*, September 15, 2015, http://articles.economictimes.indiatimes.com; and Rachel Lee Harris, "Hotels in India Offer Women-Only Floors," *New York Times*, October 16, 2011, p. TR-2.

192 Valerie A. Taylor, Diane Halstead, and Paula J. Hayes, "Consumer Responses to Christian Religious Symbols in Advertising," *Journal of Advertising*, Summer 2010, pp. 79–92.

193 "Beyond the Red Cup: How Holiday Consumers Are Changing," *Knowledge@Wharton*, November 25, 2015, http://knowledge.wharton.upenn.edu.

Household and Social Class Influences

LEARNING OBJECTIVES

After studying this chapter, you will be able to:

▶ Describe the various types of households and families, and explain how the family life cycle and other forces affect household structure.

▶ Discuss the roles that household members play in acquisition and consumption decisions, and how companies can build on these roles to market more effectively.

▶ Outline the social class hierarchy and the major determinants of social class standing, and show how social class changes over time.

▶ Explain how social class influences consumer behavior and why these influences are considerations when marketers plan strategy and tactics.

▶ Describe the consumption patterns of specific social classes and the implications for marketers.

INTRODUCTION

Marketers around the world, including Procter & Gamble, recognize that household influences and social class definitely affect consumer behavior (see Exhibit 13.1). For example, mothers in the emerging markets targeted by P&G often have more of a say than other family members in decisions about choosing and using household products. As a result, P&G reaches out to mothers using a variety of communications and promotions for each of its brands, from Pantene to Puffs and Pampers. Social class also affects what and how consumers buy. When lower-status consumers aspire to become middle class, they may buy products to improve their opportunities for advancement or choose a brand preferred by the middle class. As you read this chapter, remember that the generalizations about household and social class are broad group tendencies and may or may not apply to individual consumers.

Exhibit 13.1 ▶ Chapter Overview: Household and Social Class Influences

The first section of this chapter examines household influences on consumer behavior, including the various types of households, trends in household structure, and the decision roles that household members play in acquiring and using an offering. Next is a discussion of the determinants of social class (e.g., occupation, education, income), changes in social class over time, and how social class affects consumption.

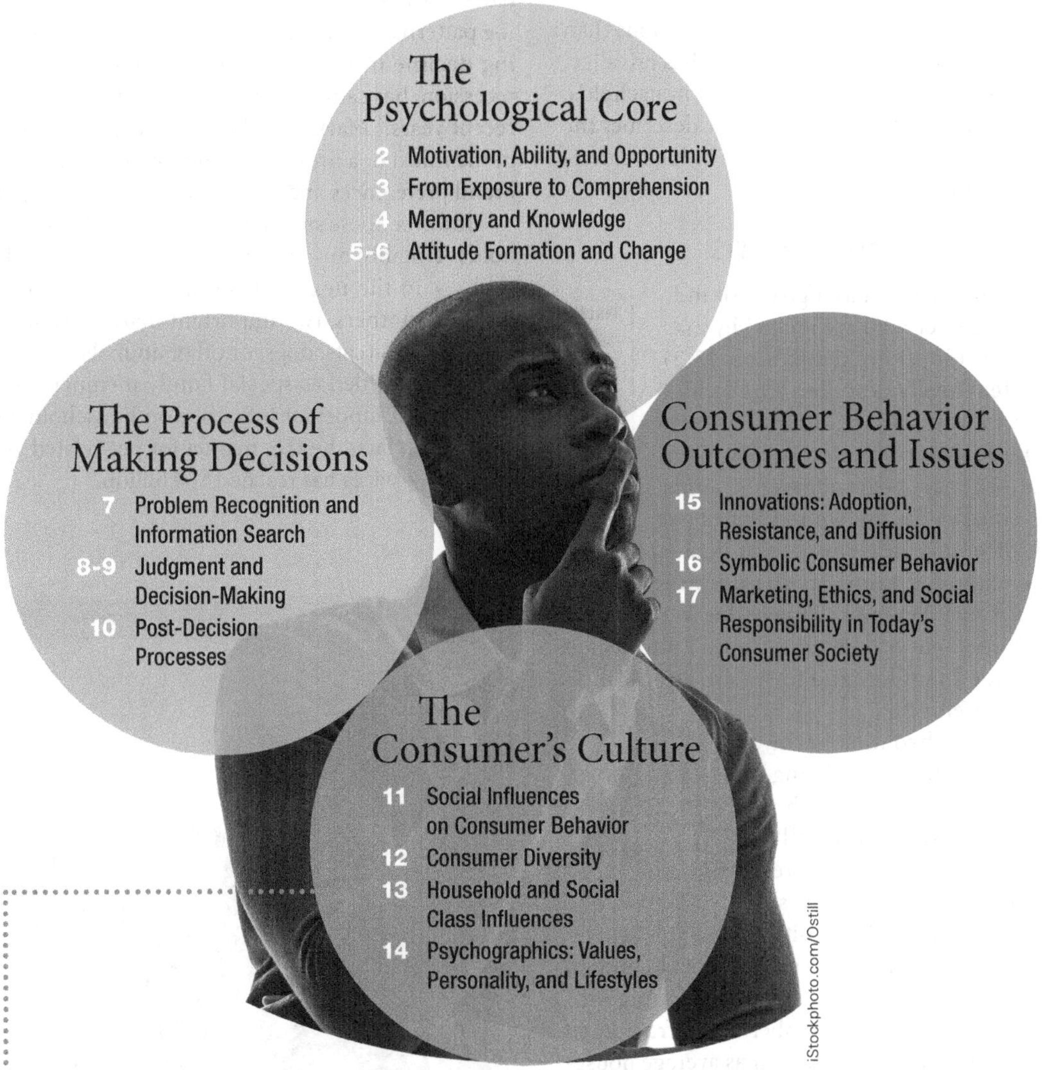

The Psychological Core

2   Motivation, Ability, and Opportunity
3   From Exposure to Comprehension
4   Memory and Knowledge
5-6   Attitude Formation and Change

The Process of Making Decisions

7   Problem Recognition and Information Search
8-9   Judgment and Decision-Making
10   Post-Decision Processes

Consumer Behavior Outcomes and Issues

15   Innovations: Adoption, Resistance, and Diffusion
16   Symbolic Consumer Behavior
17   Marketing, Ethics, and Social Responsibility in Today's Consumer Society

The Consumer's Culture

11   Social Influences on Consumer Behavior
12   Consumer Diversity
13   Household and Social Class Influences
14   Psychographics: Values, Personality, and Lifestyles

iStockphoto.com/Ostill

Household Influences

- Types of households
- Structure of households
- Household decision roles

Social Class Influences

- Social class influences
- Determinants of social class
- Changes in social class over time
- Social class and consumption
- Specific social classes

13-1 How the Household Influences Consumer Behavior

13-1

You know from your own experience how many decisions the members of a household face every day, every week, and every month. In fact, some researchers see the household as the most important unit of analysis for consumer behavior because households make many more acquisition, consumption, and disposition decisions than individuals do. Not all households and families are alike, however. This section defines families and households, examines the different types of households, describes the family life cycle, and looks at how families influence decisions and consumption.

13-1a TYPES OF HOUSEHOLDS

A *family* is usually defined as a group of individuals living together who are related by marriage, blood, or adoption (see Exhibit 13.2). The term **nuclear family** describes a household with a father, mother, and children. The term **extended family** describes the nuclear family plus relatives such as grandparents, aunts, uncles, and cousins. In the United States, we often think of *family* in terms of the nuclear family, whereas the extended family is the defining unit in many other nations. Yet today, largely due to economic conditions, 26 percent of U.S. adults aged 18 to 34 are living in extended families and fewer are establishing independent households.[1]

Nuclear family
Father, mother, and children.

Extended family
The nuclear family plus relatives such as grandparents, aunts, uncles, and cousins.

Household is a broader term that includes a single person living alone or a group of individuals who live together in a common dwelling, regardless of whether they are related. Because of later marriages, cohabitation (two people of opposite sex or same sex living together), divorce, dual careers, boomerang children returning to live with their parents, people living longer, and a lower birth rate, the number of nontraditional households has greatly increased, even as average household size is getting smaller. Exhibit 13.3 shows how U.S. households are changing.

Household A single person living alone or a group of individuals who live together in a common dwelling, regardless of whether they are related.

13-1b HOUSEHOLDS AND FAMILY LIFE CYCLE

Households can differ in terms of stage in the **family life cycle**. As shown in Exhibit 13.4, families can be characterized in terms of the age of the parents, the number of parents or grandparents present, the age and number of children living at home, and so on.[2] Changes such as death or divorce can alter household structure

Family life cycle
Different stages of family life, depending on the age of the parents and how many children are living at home.

by, for instance, creating single-parent households, as the arrows in Exhibit 13.4 indicate.

Marketers must consider the great variation in needs over the family life cycle and the effect on consumer behavior within households. In general, spending increases as households shift from young singles to young married and then remains high until falling sharply at the older married or older single stages.[3] Still, household buying patterns can change over time: For example, the ongoing decline in U.S. birth rates, coupled with economic recession, has caused sales of disposable diapers to drop in recent years.[4] Marketers should be aware that households in the midst of a life cycle change are more likely to switch brand preferences and be receptive to marketing efforts.[5]

However, these stages do not capture all types of households. Notably missing are same-sex couples (discussed in the next section) and never-married single mothers, two important market segments. Also, pets (cats, dogs, or other animals) are sometimes regarded as special family members and can be an important influence on household spending. In fact, the U.S. market for pet-related goods and services has reached $60 billion.[6]

uniqlo undercover   NEW COLLECTION AVAILABLE MARCH 16   www.undercover.uniqlo.com   MADE FOR ALL

Store information Regent Street / 311 Oxford Street / uniqlo.com

Image Courtesy of The Advertising Archives

Exhibit 13.2 ▶ Family Life
Families come in all shapes and sizes.

Exhibit 13.3 ▶ Changes in Household Types

The composition of U.S. households is changing. In particular, there are more men and women alone, and more nonrelated people living together, even as the percentage of married couples living with children continues to decrease.

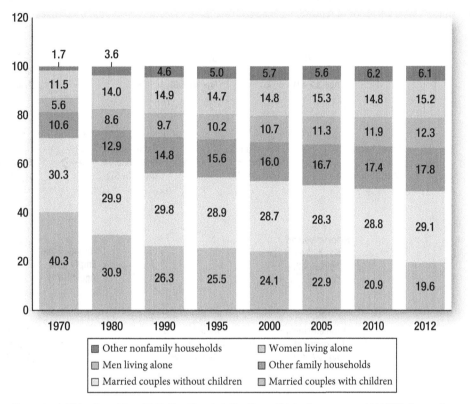

Source: Jonathan Vespa, Jamie M. Lewis, and Rose M. Kreider, "America's Families and Living Arrangements: 2012," U.S. Census Bureau, August 2013, http://www.census.gov/prod/2013pubs/p20-570.pdf, Figure 1.

13-1c CHANGING TRENDS IN HOUSEHOLD STRUCTURE

Five main factors are altering the basic structure and characteristics of households. These include (1) delayed marriage and cohabitation, (2) dual careers, (3) divorce, (4) smaller families, and (5) same-sex couples.

Delayed Marriage and Cohabitation

In many Western societies, an increasing number of individuals are either delaying or avoiding getting married. Today the median age at which U.S. men first marry is 28; for U.S. women, the median age is 26.[7] This delayed marriage may occur because career is a higher priority, because of cohabitation, or because consumers want to reduce their debt. Marketers look at this trend because single-person households exhibit unique consumption patterns. For example, single women pay a greater percentage of their income on housing, health care, and personal care products than do single men.[8]

As a result of changing social norms, more consumers are living with members of the opposite sex outside of marriage.[9] Nonetheless, many unmarried partners share expenses, and because both are likely to work, they often have higher discretionary income than married couples of a similar age in which one spouse works.

Dual-Career Families

Dual-career families have several important implications for consumer behavior, starting with higher discretionary spending. These families tend to spend more than other families do on childcare, eating out, and services in general. Also, juggling work and family roles, or *role overload*, leaves less time for cooking, housekeeping, and other activities. This is why dual-career families particularly value offerings that save time. No wonder more than half of all fast-food restaurant sales take place in the drive-through lane; at McDonald's, more than 60 percent of sales come from drive-through customers.[10] In these families, many husbands take on household responsibilities,

Exhibit 13.4 ▶ Household Life Cycles in the United States

This chart depicts how households change as the family life cycle changes. Each box represents a stage in the family life cycle; each line and arrow represents a type of change (marriage, divorce, death, children entering or leaving, aging). Note that this diagram accounts for numerous possibilities (divorce, becoming a single parent, being a childless couple, never marrying). What stage is your family in right now?

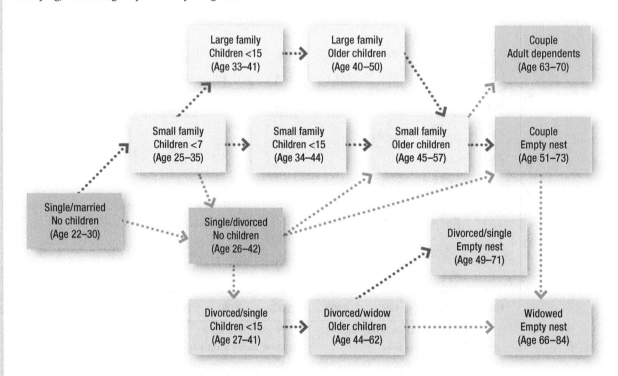

Source: Rex Y. Du and Wagner A. Kamakura, "Household Life Cycles and Lifestyles in the United States," *Journal of Marketing Research*, February 2006, Figure 1, p. 126.

and a small but growing number of men (as many as two million fathers) stay home to care for children.[11] As a result, more ads are geared toward men who, for example, share responsibility for cooking. In Asia, however, such ads may prompt a negative response from both men and women because sex roles are viewed more traditionally, even though more men are handling more housework.

Divorce

More than 4 of every 10 U.S. marriages are likely to end in divorce. Although the trend has leveled off over the past 30 years, many divorces still occur each year, with important implications for consumer behavior.[12] During this transition, consumers perform critical tasks such as disposing of old possessions, forming a new household, and creating new patterns of consumption.[13] Acquiring goods and services can help consumers form a new identity and relieve stress during and after the divorce. For example, a newly divorced consumer might buy a new car, furniture, or clothing; get a new hairstyle; or begin going to singles events.

Divorce also influences household structure. If the couple was childless, the newly divorced often adopt the kinds of singles' acquisition and consumption patterns discussed earlier. However, these new singles are typically older and, if they work, have greater discretionary income for housing, transportation, and clothing. Also, divorce creates single-parent families when children are involved, which means that convenience offerings—such as packaged foods—may become a necessity. Compared with married parents, single parents tend to have lower incomes, spend less on most things, and tend to be renters rather than home owners. Finally, divorced individuals with children form stepfamilies and have unique consumption needs, such as duplicate supplies of clothing and other items that children need when spending time in two households.

Smaller Families

In many countries, the average household size is getting smaller. The average U.S. household size has dropped below three people, even as the number of one-person households has risen.[14] A smaller family means more discretionary income to spend on recreation, vacations, education, and entertainment. Smaller families can also spend more on each child. Childless married couples have more discretionary income than other households and spend more on food, restaurant meals, entertainment, liquor, clothing, and pets.[15]

Same-Sex and Transgender Households

According to the U.S. Census, there are more than 645,000 same-sex households in the United States.[16] The U.S. Supreme Court has ruled that states cannot deny marriage licenses to gay and lesbian couples, and the number of same-sex couples who choose to marry continues to increase.[17] This trend is prompting some marketers to reach out to same-sex couples with targeted marketing communications and products. For instance, Tiffany, Target, and Subaru have featured same-sex couples in their ads, and the Las Vegas Convention and Visitors Authority uses newspaper advertising to encourage same-sex couples to get married in Las Vegas.[18] As societal views continue to change internationally, a growing number of countries now allow same-sex marriage. In 2015, the same year when same-sex marriage became legal in the United States, it also became legal in Finland, Greenland, and Ireland.[19] In addition, more marketers are creating products for transgender consumers. For example, Brooklyn-based retailer Bindle and Keep now markets suits for men, women, and transgender consumers.[20]

Household decision roles Roles that different members play in a household decision.

with offerings that help reduce the stress of these transitions.[24]

Marketers are targeting same-sex couples through sponsorships of gay pride events, ads in targeted magazines such as *Out*, *Winq*, and *The Advocate*, specialized websites, billboards in selected neighborhoods, and TV ads depicting same-sex couples. Some marketers that openly target this segment, however, have become targets of conservative groups opposed to homosexuality.[25] Marketers who target same-sex couples also must understand how these consumers make decisions; for instance, purchasing decisions by lesbian couples tend to be made in a more egalitarian manner than decisions in husband- or wife-dominated traditional households are.[26]

13-2 Roles that Household Members Play

A key aspect of households is that more than one individual can become involved in acquisition and consumption. This section discusses various elements of household consumer behavior, with particular emphasis on **household decision roles** and how household members influence decision processes. Household members may perform a variety of tasks or roles in acquiring and consuming a product or service:

- *Gatekeeper.* Household members who collect and control information important to the decision.

- *Influencer.* Household members who try to express their opinions and influence the decision.

- *Decider.* The person or persons who actually determine which product or service will be chosen.

- *Buyer.* The household member who purchases or acquires the product or service.

- *User.* The household members who consume the product.

Each role can be performed by different household members, by a single individual, a subset of individuals, or the entire household. For example, parents might make the final decision about which movie to download, but the children may play a role, either directly (by stating their preferences) or indirectly (when parents keep their children's preferences in mind). One parent may actually obtain the movie, but the entire family might watch it. Exhibit 13.5 divides household purchases into nine categories, depending on the decision maker and the user.

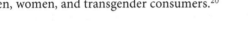

Marketing Implications

Products and services that offer convenience can be marketed specifically to dual-career and divorced households. In two-income families, working wives gain influence over household acquisition and consumption decisions for vacations, cars, and other offerings.[21] Therefore, marketers of costly offerings must appeal to both husband and wife. Nontraditional families are also being targeted: For example, Hallmark offers greeting cards aimed at blended family relationships, without mentioning the word "step."[22] Single men and women are also an attractive target for many marketers. The Canadian grocery chain Metro recently held a "singles night" in Toronto. Shoppers tied a red ribbon to their carts to signal their participation, while a DJ played romantic songs to put shoppers in the mood.[23] And marketers can target consumers who are experiencing family life cycle changes such as divorce

Exhibit 13.5 ▶ Buyers and Users

Household purchase decisions can be made by one, some, or all members of the family. Acquired products and services may be consumed by one, some, or all members. Here is an example of three cells that result from crossing these two factors. Can you think of examples that would fit into the other six cells?

A Purchase Decision Maker

A Consumer		One member	Some members	All members
	One member	1	2 Tennis racket	3
	Some members	4 Sugar Pops	5	6
	All members	7	8	9 Refrigerator

For Example:

1. Mom and Dad go to buy a new tennis racket for Mom. Dad advises Mom on her purchase. Some members are decision makers and one member is a consumer: cell 2.

2. Mom goes to the grocery store to buy Sugar Pops cereal for her children. She'll never eat the stuff. One member is a decision maker and some members are consumers: cell 4.

3. Mom, Dad, and the kids go to the department store to buy a refrigerator. All members are decision makers and all are consumers: cell 9.

Source: Robert Boutilier, "Pulling the Family's Strings," *American Demographics,* August 1993, pp. 44–48. American Demographics © 1993. Reprinted with permission.

Household decision roles can be **instrumental**, meaning that they relate to tasks affecting the buying decision, such as when and how much to purchase. Roles can also be **expressive**, which means they indicate family norms, such as choice of color or style.[27] Traditionally, the husband fulfilled the instrumental role and the wife the expressive role, but sex-role changes are altering this pattern.

Conflict can often occur in fulfilling different household roles based on (1) the reasons for buying, (2) who should make the decision, (3) which option to choose, and (4) who gets to use the product or service.[28] Conflict may occur in decisions about "green" consumption, such as using organic food and conserving water or energy.[29] In general, households resolve conflicts through problem solving, persuasion, bargaining, and politics, with persuasion and problem solving being the most frequently used methods.[30] Note that resolution is often not systematic and rational, but rather a "muddling-through" process in which

> **Instrumental roles**
> Roles that relate to tasks affecting the buying decision.
>
> **Expressive roles**
> Roles that involve an indication of family norms.

the household makes a series of small decisions to arrive at a solution.[31] Moreover, many households avoid rather than confront conflict.

Joint household decisions are more likely when the perceived risk associated with the decision is high, the decision is very important, there is ample time to make a decision, and the household is young. In addition, household members can influence each other in terms of brand preferences and loyalties, information search patterns, media reliance, and price sensitivities.[32]

13-2a THE ROLES OF SPOUSES

Husbands and wives play different roles in making decisions, and the nature of their influence depends on the offering and the couple's relationship. In examining husband–wife influence, a landmark study conducted in Belgium (and replicated in the United States) identified four major decision categories:[33]

- A **husband-dominant decision** is made primarily by the male head-of-household (e.g., the purchase of lawn mowers and hardware).

- A **wife-dominant decision** is made primarily by the female head-of-household (e.g., children's clothing, women's clothing, groceries, and toiletries).

- An **autonomic decision** is equally likely to be made by the husband or the wife, but not by both (e.g., men's clothing, luggage, toys and games, sporting equipment, and cameras).

- A **syncratic decision** is made jointly by the husband and wife (e.g., vacations, refrigerators, TVs, living room furniture, financial planning services, and the family car).

Husband-dominant decision Decision made primarily by the male head-of-household.

Wife-dominant decision Decision made primarily by the female head-of-household.

Autonomic decision Decision equally likely to be made by the husband or wife, but not by both.

Syncratic decision Decision made jointly by the husband and wife.

As spouses come closer to a final decision, the process tends to move toward syncratic decision-making, particularly for more important decisions. These role structures are only generalities, however; the actual influence exerted depends on many factors. First, a spouse who brings more financial resources to the family and has a high involvement level may have more influence on the decision. Second, demographic factors, such as total family income and education, are related to the degree of husband–wife influence. Combined, these factors provide a spouse with a perception of power in the decision-making situation. The higher the degree of perceived power, the more likely the spouse will exert influence.[34]

When the family has a strong traditional sex-role orientation, certain tasks are stereotypically considered either masculine or feminine, and more decisions tend to be husband-dominated than they are in less traditional families.[35] For example, Mexican American families tend toward a traditional orientation and husband-dominant decisions. Still, sex-role changes are influencing husband–wife decisions. In Thailand, nearly half of the husbands surveyed said that they decided what foods their households would eat and that they did the family food shopping, traditionally to be considered the wife's role.[36] While men do much of the grocery shopping in many U.S. households, few advertisers target them directly in connection with these decisions.[37] Also in the United States, joint decision-making is most common among Anglo families and wife dominance is more prevalent in African American families. Other aspects of spousal decision-making have also been studied. For example, through the processes of *bargaining* (which involves a fair exchange) or *concession* (in which a spouse gives in on some points to get what he or she wants in other areas), couples tend to make equitable decisions that result from compromises.[38]

Couples typically follow an informal process for decision-making in which they have limited awareness of each other's knowledge and decision strategy.[39] Husbands and wives are generally not good at estimating their spouse's influence and preferences—and in fact, they have less success predicting preferences as relationships progress—but they do learn from previous decisions and make adjustments over time.[40] Further, when the spouses have opposite spending tendencies—one is a spender, one is not—decision-making can be marked by conflict, which in turn may have a negative effect on the marriage.[41]

13-2b THE ROLE OF CHILDREN

Children play an important role in household decisions by attempting to influence their parents' acquisition, usage, and disposition behavior. The most common stereotype is that children nag until their parents finally give in. Research finds that the success of such attempts depends on the type of offering, characteristics of the parents, age of the child, and stage of the decision process.[42] Children are more likely to use their influence for child-related products such as cereals, snacks, cars, vacations, and new computer technologies.

Children tend to have less influence when parents are more involved in the decision process or are more traditional and conservative. Working and single parents, on the other hand, are more likely to give in because they face more time pressures.[43] Another important finding is that the older the child, the more influence he or she will exert.[44] However, even when the family includes two or more children, parents still exert the most influence over decisions about buying and consuming new offerings.[45] Also, parents who believe self-control can be increased over time tend to make buying decisions that will help the child improve self-control,[46] while materialism in parents may foster materialism in their children.[47] Note that even as parents act as a socializing influence on children's consumption decisions and actions, children in turn can be a resocializing influence on parents by sharing knowledge and attitudes.[48] The influence that children have on their parents does vary by whether the economy is emerging or developed and, within emerging economies, by country.[49]

One study examined the strategies adolescents use in trying to influence parental and family decision-making, which include bargaining (making deals), persuasion (trying to influence the decision in their favor), emotional appeals (using emotion to get what they want), and requests (directly asking).[50] Parents, in turn, can use not only the same strategies on their children but also expert (knowledge), legitimate (power), and directive (parental authority) strategies.

The type of household determines the nature of children's influence. Authoritarian households stress obedience, while neglectful households exert little control. Democratic households encourage self-expression, and

Exhibit 13.6 ▶ Targeting to Children Consumers
Children's game sites combine toys and safe online play areas for kids.

permissive households remove constraints. Children are more likely to have direct decision control in permissive and neglectful families and are more likely to influence decisions in democratic and permissive ones.[51] Also, children's influence varies at different stages of the decision process. It is greatest early in the decision-making process (problem recognition and information search) and declines significantly in the evaluation and choice phases.[52]

Marketing Implications

Marketers need to recognize that appealing only to deciders or purchasers may be too narrow a strategy, because different household members may play different decision roles. For instance, marketers who exclusively target children for toys ignore the fact that parents are usually influencers, deciders, and purchasers of these products. Therefore, marketers should determine which family members are involved in each acquisition decision and appeal to all important parties.

Companies such as General Mills and Sara Lee that target mothers who make decisions about products like breakfast cereal and breads are adapting their products and using ads as well as product reviews by "mommy bloggers" with a sizable social media audience.[53] For other decisions, such as family outings, both spouses may play a key role. KidZania play centers—designed for children from 4 to 14 years old— target parents in Mexico, Japan, Europe, and the Middle East who want to give their children a taste of different careers. The entrance fee allows children to "play" at various occupations using branded props from sponsors such as Procter & Gamble and H&M.[54]

More U.S. children are using the Internet for e-mail, visiting websites, and playing in virtual worlds created especially for youngsters, opening opportunities for established brands and newcomers alike.[55] Children's game sites such as Club Penguin have attracted millions of paid subscribers worldwide because parents see them as a safe place for children to play online. Note that parenting style plays an important role in socializing children as consumers and influences how children learn to respond to advertising.[56] Yet marketing to children raises ethical and legal issues; for that reason, websites for children under 13 must comply with the federal Children's Online Privacy Protection Act and obtain parental permission before collecting information from children. Some states also have special rules protecting the personal details of children who access online sites.[57]

Social class hierarchy The grouping of members of society according to status, high to low.

13-3 Social Class

Most societies have a **social class hierarchy** that confers higher status to some classes of people than to others. These social classes consist of identifiable groups of individuals whose behaviors and lifestyles differ from those of members of the other classes. Members of a particular social class tend to share similar values and behavior patterns. Note that social classes are loose collections of individuals with similar life experiences, not formal groups with a strong identity.[58]

Exhibit 13.7 ▶ U.S. Social Classes

Researchers have classified the U.S. social classes in a variety of ways. This exhibit shows a typical classification scheme, with two classes at the top, two in the middle, and two at the lower end of the social classes.

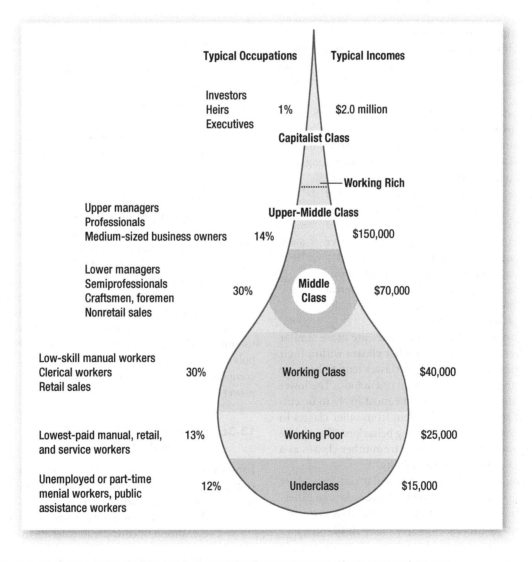

Source: Dennis L. Gilbert, *The American Class Structure in an Age of Growing Inequality,* 9th ed., Sage Publications, 2014, p. 14.

Many societies view these distinctions as important because they recognize that everyone has a role to play in order for society to function smoothly. However, some roles, such as medical doctor or executive, are more prestigious and more aspirational than others, such as toll taker or janitor. Nonetheless, the concept of social class is not inherently negative. Even with the inequalities, social class distinctions can help individuals determine what their role in society is or what they would like it to be (their aspirations). Furthermore, all levels of the social class hierarchy make an important contribution to society.

13-3a TYPES OF SOCIAL CLASS SYSTEMS

Most societies have three major classes: high, middle, and lower. Often, however, finer distinctions are made. The United States, for example, is typically divided into the seven levels presented in Exhibit 13.7, with up to 70 percent of the population concentrated in the middle classes.[59] Although most societies have some kind of hierarchical structure, the size and composition of the classes depend on the relative prosperity of a particular country.[60]

Compared with the United States, Japan and Scandinavia have an even larger and more predominant middle class with much smaller groups above and below. This distribution means that there is greater equality among people in those two countries than in other societies. The Japanese structure represents a concerted government effort to abolish the social class system and mix together people from all levels of society.[61] Yet the very competitive and selective Japanese educational system still restricts entry to higher-status corporate and government positions. In developing areas such as Latin America and India, the largest concentrations are in the lower classes (see Exhibit 13.8).

In most societies, the upper classes are more similar to each other than they are to other classes within their own countries because the upper classes tend to be more cosmopolitan and international in orientation. The lower classes, on the other hand, are the most likely to be culture bound and the most different from other classes in terms of lifestyles, dress, and eating behaviors. The middle classes are most likely to borrow from other classes as a way to achieve upward social mobility.

Even though members of a particular class may share similar values, they may maintain these values in different ways. In addition, a particular social class may contain different economic substrata. Specifically, families whose income level is 20 to 30 percent more than the median of their class are considered **overprivileged** because they have funds to buy more than basic necessities.[62]

Class average Families with an average income in a particular class.

Underprivileged Families below the average income in their class.

Status float Trends that start in the lower and middle classes and move upward.

Trickle-down effect Trends that start in the upper classes and then are copied by lower classes.

Overprivileged Families with an income higher than the average in their social class.

Class average families have an income level that is average for their social class and can therefore afford the type of symbols expected for their status, such as a house or appropriate clothing. The **underprivileged**, whose incomes are below the median, have trouble meeting class expectations.

13-3b SOCIAL CLASS INFLUENCES

Social class structures are important because they strongly affect norms and values and, therefore, behavior. Given that members of a social class interact regularly with each other (both formally and informally), people are more likely to be influenced by individuals in their own social class than by those in other classes. Note that social class influence merely reflects the fact that people with similar life experiences tend to exhibit similar lifestyles and behaviors.[63] In addition, social class structure can change. This is most likely to happen when there are dramatic economic or social changes that destabilize the prevailing social structure.[64]

The norms and behaviors of consumers in one class can also influence consumers in other classes, who, seeking to raise their social standing, copy trends that begin in the upper classes. They also accept upper-class influence if they lack the cultural knowledge to make their own judgments of what is and is not acceptable.[65] For example, the middle class often looks to the upper class for guidance on cultural matters of music, art, and literature. However, the universal validity of the **trickle-down** theory has been questioned. In some instances, a **status float** can occur, whereby trends (in clothing, music, etc.) start in the lower and middle classes and then spread upward. Moreover, there are complex ways in which various social classes can interact in terms of consumption. Researchers have found instances in which lower social classes do not seek to emulate the upper social classes, but reject the symbols of the upper classes or use consumption displays to compete with the dominant social class for visibility and power.[66]

13-3c HOW SOCIAL CLASS IS DETERMINED

Examining how social class affects consumer behavior requires a way of classifying consumers into different social classes. Unfortunately, this is a complex task, and the exact determinants of social class have been the subject of considerable debate over the years.

Income Versus Social Class

Income is only weakly related to social class, for several reasons.[67] First, income levels

Exhibit 13.8 ▶ Class Structure by Culture

The relative sizes and structures of social classes vary by culture. Japan and Scandinavia, for example, are characterized by a large middle class with few people above or below it. India and Latin America, on the other hand, have a greater proportion of individuals in the lower classes. The United States has a large middle class but also has significant proportions in the upper and lower classes.

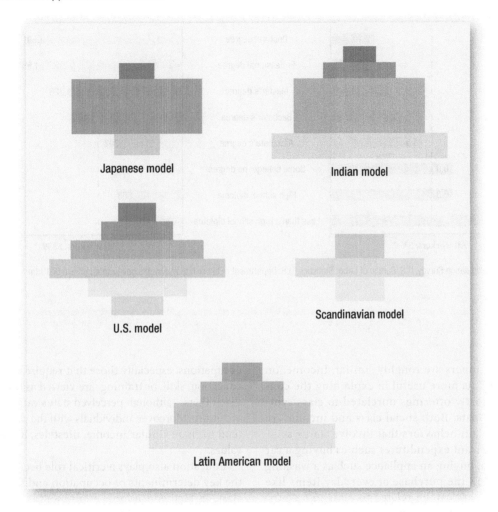

Japanese model

Indian model

U.S. model

Scandinavian model

Latin American model

Source: Adapted from Edward W. Cundiff and Marye T. Hilger, *Marketing in the International Environment* (Englewood Cliffs, N.J.: Prentice-Hall, 1988); and Marieke K. de Mooij and Warren Keegan, *Advertising Worldwide* (Englewood Cliffs, N.J.: Prentice-Hall, 1991), p. 96.

often overlap social classes, particularly at the middle and lower levels. For example, many U.S. blue-collar workers have higher incomes than some white-collar workers, yet they do not have higher social standing. Second, although income increases greatly with age, older workers do not automatically achieve higher social status. Finally, dual-career families may generate a higher than average income but do not necessarily attain higher status. Thus, although income is one factor related to social class, other factors play key roles as well.

Although some researchers argue that income can be a better predictor of consumer behavior than social class, a more common view is that both factors are important in explaining behavior in different situations.[68] Social class is a better predictor of consumption when it reflects lifestyles and values and does not involve high monetary expenditures, such as purchasing clothes or furniture. For example, middle and lower-class consumers favor different styles of furniture, but middle-class consumers tend to spend more money on home furnishings even when the incomes of both

Exhibit 13.9 ▶ Earnings and Unemployment Rates by Educational Attainment

For U.S. consumers aged 25 and older, higher educational achievement translates into higher median weekly earnings and lower unemployment rates. In 2015, consumers without a high school diploma earned only $493 per week, significantly less than consumers who completed high school and then went on to higher education.

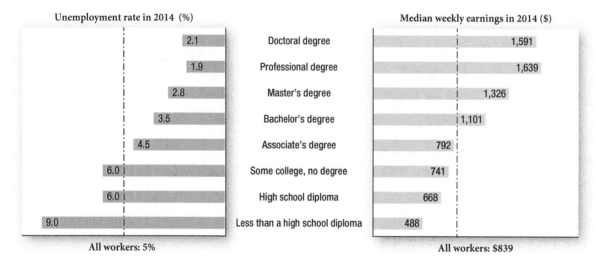

Unemployment rate in 2014 (%)

Median weekly earnings in 2014 ($)

	Unemployment rate	Degree	Median weekly earnings
	2.1	Doctoral degree	1,591
	1.9	Professional degree	1,639
	2.8	Master's degree	1,326
	3.5	Bachelor's degree	1,101
	4.5	Associate's degree	792
	6.0	Some college, no degree	741
	6.0	High school diploma	668
	9.0	Less than a high school diploma	488

All workers: 5%

All workers: $839

Source: Current Population Survey, U.S. Bureau of Labor Statistics, U.S. Department of Labor http://www.bls.gov/emp/ep_chart_001.htm

classes of consumers are roughly similar. Income, on the other hand, is more useful in explaining the consumption of costly offerings unrelated to class symbols, such as boats. Both social class and income are needed to explain behaviors that involve status symbols and significant expenditures such as buying a car or, as in Africa, buying an appliance such as a washing machine.[69] Even the purchase of everyday items like disposable diapers can be related to class in a country like China. Procter & Gamble found this out when middle-class consumers bypassed its "made in China" affordably priced Pampers diapers and instead splurged on higher-priced premium diaper brands made by competitors in Japan.[70]

Although income cannot always explain social class, social class can often explain how income is used. As one illustration, upper-class consumers are more likely to invest money, whereas the lower classes are more likely to rely on savings accounts in banks. The key point is that social class aids in the understanding of consumer behavior and that social standing is determined by a variety of factors in addition to income.

Occupation and Education

The greatest determinant of class standing is occupation, particularly in Western cultures. Specifically, some occupations, especially those that require higher levels of education, skill, or training, are viewed as higher in status than others—although perceived status varies from culture to culture. Moreover, individuals with the same occupation tend to share similar income, lifestyles, knowledge, and values.

Education also plays a critical role because it is one of the key determinants of occupation and therefore social class. In fact, educational attainment is considered the most reliable determinant of consumers' income potential and spending patterns.[71] Consider that in 2014, the median weekly income of a U.S. consumer with a high school diploma was $668, whereas the median weekly income of a college graduate was nearly twice as high, at $1,101 (see Exhibit 13.9).[72] Well-educated consumers not only earn more but also read and travel more, are healthier, and are often more receptive to new offerings than the rest of the population.[73] Higher education is particularly important for gaining entry into higher-status occupations.

Other Indicators of Social Class

Factors such as area of residence, possessions, family background, and social interactions can also indicate class level. The neighborhood in which we live and the number and types of possessions we have are visible signs that often communicate class standing. In terms of family background, researchers distinguish between **inherited status**, which is adopted from parents at birth, and **earned status**, which is acquired later in life from personal achievements.[74] Inherited status is the initial anchor point from which values are learned and from which upward or downward mobility can occur. As mentioned earlier, members of a social class often interact with each other, so the company we keep also helps us to identify our social standing. Note, however, that the relative importance of these determinants of social class varies from country to country.

> **Inherited status** Status that derives from parents at birth.
>
> **Earned status** Status acquired later in life through achievements.

Social Class Indexes

All of the preceding factors must be taken into account to determine social class standing, and sociologists have developed a number of indexes to accomplish this task. For this purpose, researchers use indexes that assess consumers' education, occupation, area of residence, and financial situation. When consumers are consistent across the various dimensions, social class is easy to determine and **status crystallization** occurs. Sometimes, however, individuals are low on some factors but high on others. Thus, a new doctor from an inner-city neighborhood might be inconsistent on factors such as occupation and income. It is also difficult for marketers to neatly categorize such consumers into one social class or another.

> **Status crystallization** When consumers are consistent across indicators of social class income, education, occupation, etc.
>
> **Downward mobility** Losing one's social standing.

13-3d HOW SOCIAL CLASS CHANGES OVER TIME

Social class structures are not necessarily static, unchanging systems. Three of the key forces producing an evolution in social class structures in many countries are (1) upward mobility, (2) downward mobility, and (3) social class fragmentation.

Upward Mobility

In many cultures, consumers can raise their status level through **upward mobility**, usually by educational or occupational achievement. In other words, lower or middle-class individuals can take advantage of educational opportunities, particularly a college education, to gain entry into higher-status occupations. However, the percentage of U.S. college graduates from poverty-level households has remained low for decades, reflecting the challenge of paying for college—especially during tough financial times—and the difficulty of bridging the gap between the lower and middle classes while in college.[75]

> **Upward mobility** Raising one's status level.

Clearly, upward mobility is not guaranteed. The lower classes, particularly some minorities, still face limited economic and cultural resources as well as limited educational opportunities and are statistically less likely than are the upper classes to have access to higher-status occupations.[76] Individuals from higher-status families are twice as likely to maintain their status as members of lower classes are to achieve a higher status. Even after achieving upward mobility, an individual's behavior can still be heavily influenced by his or her former class level because the behaviors associated with the social class in which people grow up are strongly learned.[77] Another important point about upward mobility is that consumers often inaccurately estimate their comparisons with others, which affects their buying decisions.[78]

Note that the degree of upward mobility may vary across cultures and even from region to region within individual nations.[79] Typically, Western nations offer the most opportunities, although opportunities for upward mobility have actually decreased in the United States, Canada, and Great Britain during some periods.[80] The size of the middle class has been exploding in many developing countries because international trade is making affordable goods more available, dual-career families are earning greater income, and more professionals are needed to support growing economies.

Downward Mobility

Downward mobility, or moving to a lower class, is an increasing trend in some industrialized societies. In the past 30 years, millions of U.S. families have slid downward in status as jobs were sent overseas or eliminated by technology and companies lowered wages or laid off workers. Although many parents dreamed of providing their children with a better life and higher status, some children may have difficulty reaching their parents' status level, a situation labeled *status panic*.[81] In fact, a recent U.K. study found that a growing number of people born in the second half of the 20th century will not match the social status of their parents because of reduced employment opportunities in key professions.[82] Meanwhile, because of increasing material desires and economic uncertainties, more upper-middle and middle-class families are having difficulty maintaining their lifestyles—or even saving money to cover college, retirement, and emergencies.[83]

Downward mobility creates disappointment and disillusionment. Sometimes acquisition and consumption can help protect personal self-worth. For example, a consumer might buy a new truck or other item to feel good about himself or herself. Alternatively, downward mobility can lead to a loss of possessions, such as a car or home, or to a decrease in consumption if people choose to spend less on items that are less important.

Social Class Fragmentation

Interestingly, the old social class distinctions are beginning to disintegrate—a phenomenon called **social class fragmentation**—due to several factors.[84] First, both upward and downward mobility have blurred class divisions. Second, the increased availability of mass media, especially TV and the Internet is exposing consumers worldwide to the values and norms of diverse classes and cultures, leading some people to adopt elements of other groups' behavior. A third reason

> **Social class fragmentation** The disappearance of class distinctions.

is that advances in communication technology have increased interaction across social class lines. These factors have led to the emergence of many social class subsegments with distinct patterns of values and behavior. The United States now has dozens of classes ranging from the suburban elite (super-rich families) to the hardscrabble (poor, single-parent families).[85] Similar trends are occurring in other countries as well. Exhibit 13.10 shows some traditional and emerging classes in the United Kingdom.

Social Class	Characteristics	Occupations Represented
Elite	Highly educated, extremely wealthy, involved in elite cultural institutions and events.	CEOs, financial executives, judges and lawyers, and information technology executives, among others
Established middle class	Second-wealthiest social class, highly social and gregarious, culturally engaged.	White-collar managers, professionals, electrical engineers, and occupational therapists, among others
Technical middle class	Prosperous but less socially connected than higher classes and less involved in elite cultural activities.	Pharmacists, pilots, higher education professionals, and scientists, among others
New affluent workers	Younger people with moderate income and savings, active both socially and culturally, but not as well educated as higher classes.	Electricians, postal workers, retail cashiers, and catering assistants, among others
Traditional working class	Modest savings yet high number of home owners, less educated and less involved socially and culturally than higher classes.	Secretaries, truck drivers, daycare workers, and electronic technicians, among others
Emergent service workers	Relatively young people in urban settings, with modest household income and savings, and a high proportion of minority backgrounds.	Nursing assistants, bar staff, and customer service workers, among others
Precariat	Lowest household income of any of the classes, limited social and cultural activity, and low in educational achievement.	Cleaners, caretakers, and carpenters, among others

Source: Adapted from Mike Savage, Fiona Devine, Niall Cunningham, Mark Taylor, Yaojun Li, Johs. Hjellbrekke, Brigitte Le Roux, Sam Friedman, and Andrew Miles, "A New Model of Social Class? Findings from the BBC's Great British Class Survey Experiment," *Sociology* 47, no. 2, 2013, pp. 219–250; and "Huge Survey Reveals Seven Social Classes in UK," *BBC News*, April 3, 2013, www.bbc.com.

Exhibit 13.10 ▶ British Social Classes

This exhibit describes seven distinct social classes within the United Kingdom, as defined by economic capital (wealth), as well as by social and cultural involvement. The largest social class is the established middle class. Two newly emerging classes identified by recent research are the technical middle class and the emergent service workers.

13-4 How Does Social Class Affect Consumption?

Social class is often viewed as a cause of or motivation for consumer acquisition, consumption, and disposition behaviors. This section examines four major topics: (1) conspicuous consumption and voluntary simplicity, (2) status symbols, (3) compensatory consumption, and (4) the meaning of money.

13-4a CONSPICUOUS CONSUMPTION AND VOLUNTARY SIMPLICITY

Conspicuous consumption, also related to social class, is an attempt to offset deficiencies or a lack of esteem by devoting attention to consumption.[86] Conspicuously consumed items are important to their owner because of what they tell others.[87] Only if these items are visible will the message be communicated. According to research, both uniqueness and conformity play a role in conspicuous consumption.[88] Even in societies with fewer distinctions between status levels, conspicuous consumption can prompt lower-status consumers to feel socially competitive and increase their consumption to "get ahead of the Joneses."[89] Another explanation, from *terror management theory*, suggests that such materialism helps relieve consumers' anxiety over the inevitability of death.[90]

In addition, consumers can engage in **conspicuous waste**. For example, wealthy individuals may buy houses they never use and pianos that no one plays.[91] On the other hand, some consumers are moving away from conspicuous consumption toward **voluntary simplicity**, consciously limiting their acquisition and consumption for a less material, eco-friendly lifestyle.[92]

13-4b STATUS SYMBOLS AND JUDGING OTHERS

Highly related to conspicuous consumption is the notion that people often judge others on the basis of what they own. In other words, goods or services become **status symbols** to indicate their owners' place in the social hierarchy. Someone who owns an expensive watch or car will likely be viewed as upper class. While some luxury brands send subtle status signals that only members of the upper class will recognize, other brands use highly distinctive logos or other prominent elements to publicly announce status.[93] Consumers sometimes use the spatial density of stores to make inferences about the social class of the store's patrons. The less crowded the store, the more likely consumers are to infer that store patrons are of higher (vs. lower) social classes.[94]

Consumers' quest to acquire items that reflect not only their current social class but also their class aspirations can explain some acquisition and consumption behaviors (see Exhibit 13.11). By acquiring items that members of their own social class cannot typically afford, consumers can increase their perception of self-worth. In the United States, as well as in Brazil, Indonesia, and other nations, braces for teeth have become a visible symbol of status for teens and adults.[95] Depictions of the material success of peers can spur the desire for luxurious status symbols as well.[96] Even relatively affordable luxuries—like a posh $20 nail polish or the lowest-priced Mercedes car—"enable less affluent consumers to trade up to higher levels of quality, taste, and aspiration," says a Boston Consulting Group expert. "These are the luxuries that continue to sell even when the economy is shaky, because they often meet very powerful emotional needs."[97]

Interestingly, status symbols can sometimes move in a reverse direction, which is called a **parody display**.[98] For example, middle and upper-class Brazilians feel hip if they practice capoeira, a blend of dance and martial arts traditionally popular among members of the lower class.[99] In addition, if certain status symbols become widely possessed, they can lose their status connotations and become **fraudulent symbols**. For example, recognizing that luxury brands are often copied to produce low-price knock-offs for the mass market, Coach and others have redesigned their products with subtler logos. The new products are unmistakably upscale but don't "scream 'Coach, Coach, Coach,'" observes a Coach designer. At the same time, Coach is introducing new, higher-priced products to reinforce its brand's status-symbol image.[100]

13-4c COMPENSATORY CONSUMPTION

Compensatory consumption behavior, also related to social class, is an attempt to offset deficiencies or a lack of esteem by devoting attention to consumption.[101] A consumer who is experiencing frustration or difficulties, particularly in terms of career advancement or status level, may compensate by purchasing status symbols, such as a car or nice clothes, to help restore lost self-esteem. Traditionally, some working-class consumers would exhibit compensatory consumption by mortgaging their future to buy a house and other status symbols. More recently, however, many

Conspicuous consumption The acquisition and display of goods and services to show off one's status.

Parody display Status symbols that start in the lower-social classes and move upward.

Fraudulent symbol Symbol that becomes so widely adopted that it loses its status.

Conspicuous waste Visibly buying products and services that one never uses.

Voluntary simplicity Limiting acquisition and consumption to live a less material life.

Status symbol Product or service that tells others about someone's social class standing.

Compensatory consumption The consumer behavior of buying products or services to offset frustrations or difficulties in life.

Exhibit 13.11 ▶ Conspicuous Consumption and Status Symbols

Sometimes consumers buy items because they signal a message of status or eliteness to others, like expensive eyeglasses or cars.

middle and upper-middleclass U.S. consumers, disappointed at stalled careers and lower prosperity levels than their parents, have exhibited compensatory consumption behavior. Knowing this tendency, companies such as Kate Spade and Gucci have created offerings that are somewhat more affordable than their existing luxury brands.[102]

13-4d THE MEANING OF MONEY

An important concept related to social class is money. At the most basic level, economists define *money* as a medium of exchange or standard of payment. Under this view, money fulfills a very functional or utilitarian purpose, enabling people to acquire items needed for everyday living. Research shows that in poor nations where basic human needs can be met, consumers with a high degree of relatedness and autonomy can feel a sense of life satisfaction. However, in poor nations where consumers who live in extreme poverty cannot meet basic daily needs, there is a pervasive feeling of hopelessness.[103]

Often in Western nations, money comes to symbolize security, power, love, and freedom. Consumers learn the meaning of money early in childhood. Parents easily discover that they can control their children by dispensing rewards and punishments based on money and by buying or not buying things.[104] Children learn that if they behave, get good grades, or do their chores, their parents will buy things for them. This early learning later translates into adult life when money is viewed as a means of acquiring things that will bring not only happiness and fulfillment but also a sense of status and prestige. In some societies, this belief can lead to an almost insatiable desire and quest for making money, which is enhanced by media coverage of those who have "made it" and by the belief that "it could happen to anyone, including me." This belief is one reason that state lotteries are popular among certain classes.

Marketers must understand money and what it stands for in order to understand consumption patterns. Money allows consumers to acquire status objects as indicators of social class standing or as a way to rise to a higher level through acquisition. However, the increase in credit and debit card usage shows that money need not involve physical cash. Even in nations like Kenya, where cash is the dominant payment method, more consumers are qualifying for credit cards so that they can buy now and pay later. And now that many consumers in Kenya and other African nations have access to cell phones, mobile payments are commonplace for everyday transactions even in rural areas.[105]

Money as Both Good and Evil

Money can be perceived as the just reward for hard work and can lead to the acquisition of needed items, a higher quality of life, and the ability to help others and society in general. On the downside, the quest for money can lead to obsession, greed, dishonesty, and potentially harmful practices such as gambling, prostitution, and drug dealing (see Chapter 17). The quest for money can also lead to negative emotions such as anxiety, depression, anger, and helplessness.[106] Moreover, individuals who do not share their wealth with others may be seen as selfish and greedy. Interestingly, consumers with yearly household incomes under $25,000 donate about 4 percent of their income to charities, whereas consumers with household incomes of $100,000 or more contribute less than 3 percent of their income to charities. Yet during the recent recession, high-income households reduced the percentage of income they donated, whereas low- and middle-income households increased the percentage of income donated.[107]

Money and Happiness

The popular belief (especially in Western countries) that money can buy happiness is rarely true. After some people acquire tremendous wealth, money can become meaningless and no longer highly desired. Furthermore, wealthy people can often afford to hire others to handle many of the activities that they formerly enjoyed, such as gardening and do-it-yourself projects. And, of course, money simply cannot buy love, health, true friendship, and children, among other things. In fact, as time becomes scarcer than money, consumers are consciously spending time in ways that will make them happy, such as being with friends and family—experiences that cannot be purchased.[108] Still, research suggests that consumers can get more happiness for their money in a number of ways, including buying experiences rather than material possessions, buying multiple small pleasures rather than a few large pleasures, using money to benefit other people, and delaying consumption to prolong the pleasure of anticipation.[109]

One study on money, acquisition, and happiness indicates that acquiring money is distinct from acquiring an offering, because consumers tend to focus on external information—the face value— when acquiring money, rather than the consumption experience it can buy.[110] Another study shows that the positive emotions that consumers feel when they buy an experience (such as a day at a theme park) tend to last longer than the good feelings they have from acquiring and owning a material possession. However, any negative feeling from a bad purchase is forgotten more quickly than a negative feeling from a bad experience.[111]

Also, some consumers will spend money to acquire what they want now, whereas others will engage in self-denial to save. Interestingly, parents' relative spending on girls versus boys depends to a certain extent on whether the economy is in recession or in an upswing. Parents tend to spend more on girls (than boys) during a recession.[112] Recent research suggests that spending less can benefit consumers by lowering debt and increasing the appreciation of positive acquisition experiences.[113]

Marketing Implications

Tapping into the desire for visible signs of upward mobility can be effective in marketing certain offerings. For example, targeting upper-class consumers who want to wear signs of wealth, Bulgari offers a $59,000 pair of designer sunglasses studded with diamonds and sapphires.[114] In China, where status-symbol brands are coveted as a sign of wealth, Burberry appeals to sophisticated high-income consumers with limited-edition fashions that convey status in a more subtle way.[115] Downward mobility is also prompting marketers of everyday products, such as Heinz and Coca-Cola, to market products in smaller-size packages that can be sold at lower, more affordable prices.[116] Hallmark now offers "sorry you lost your job" cards, indicating a niche segment large enough for such products.[117]

The use of credit and debit cards is rising in many nations, presenting both opportunities and challenges. However, excess use of credit also contributes to higher consumer bankruptcy rates, a situation that raises ethical and public policy issues. Increasingly, consumers in the United States, China, and elsewhere are using their cell phones to pay for purchases, instead of cash or credit cards, despite concerns about security.[118]

13-5 The Consumption Patterns of Specific Social Classes

Earlier sections examined how social class influences acquisition and consumption in general. This section extends the discussion by examining, in broad generalities, the consumption patterns of specific social classes. Although class distinctions are becoming blurred, for the sake of simplicity, this discussion will focus on (1) the upper class, (2) the middle class, (3) the working class, and (4) the homeless. Remember that these are broad tendencies and individual behavior may differ; marketers must delve deeper to identify subsegments of consumers with specific and unique consumption patterns.

Exhibit 13.12 ▶ Targeting to Upper-Class Consumers

Some ads target upper-class consumers with luxury or limited access items.

13-5a THE UPPER CLASS

The *upper class* of most societies is a varied group of individuals who include the aristocracy, the "old money" of inherited wealth, the new social elite (or nouveaux riches), and the upper-middle class (professionals). In the United States, upper class "old money" consumers tend to save and invest money more than members of other classes. Although many of these consumers are price-conscious, they are more likely than other consumers to carefully research their purchases using product characteristics, not price, as an indicator of quality.[119]

The upper class is small but diverse, and its members share a number of common values and lifestyles that relate to consumption behavior. These consumers tend to view themselves as intellectual, political, and socially conscious, leading to an increase in behaviors such as attending the theater, investing in art and antiques, traveling, and giving time and money to charities and civic issues.[120] Self-expression is also important, resulting in the purchase of high-quality, prestige brands in good taste (see

Exhibit 13.12). Even during the recent recession, luxury brands continued to sell well in the United States, China, India, Brazil, and other countries because of upper-class spending.[121]

More than 10 million U.S. households are now among the millionaire ranks, and 1.3 million households have $5 million or more in assets.[122] From a global perspective, the United States is home to more millionaires than any other nation, although China is catching up quickly: During one recent year, a million Chinese households joined the millionaire ranks.[123]

13-5b THE MIDDLE CLASS

The U.S. *middle class* consists primarily of white-collar workers, many of whom have attended college (although some have not earned a degree). The values and consumption patterns of middle-class consumers vary, yet many look to the upper class for guidance on certain behaviors such as proper dining etiquette, clothing (especially important for those with aspirations of upward mobility), and leisure activities such as golf and tennis. This tendency extends to theater attendance, vacations, and adult education classes for self-improvement. Yet during the past decade, financial difficulties have caused many middle-class families to lose purchasing power and experience lower living standards in a downward mobility trend that may not be reversed until the economy is much stronger.[124]

In Latin America, the fast-growing middle-class population will soon be larger than the lower-class population. However, even as millions of consumers in Brazil and Chile have joined the middle class, lower-class consumers in other countries within the region continue to struggle economically.[125] In Mexico, the middle class has many similarities with the traditional spending patterns of the U.S. middle class: spending much of its disposable income on cars, clothing, vacations, and household goods.[126] In Africa, the middle class is growing rapidly enough to attract the attention of multinational corporations such as Ford, Yum! Brands, and Walmart, looking to tap this segment's increased disposable income.[127]

13-5c THE WORKING CLASS

The *working class* is mainly represented by blue-collar workers. The stereotype of a hard-hatted, middle-aged man is changing as the working class becomes younger, more ethnically diverse, more female, somewhat more educated, and more alienated from employers. Working-class consumers depend heavily on family members for economic and social support in many areas, including job opportunities and advice—particularly for key purchases and help during difficult times.[128] As a result, they tend to have more of a local orientation socially, psychologically, and geographically than other classes. For example, working-class men exhibit strong preferences for local athletic teams, news segments, and vacations.

Consumers in the working class are more likely to spend than to save, but when they do save, many choose savings accounts over investments and seek financial stability.[129] Working-class consumers who are "unbanked"—without accounts in traditional financial institutions—wind up paying fees to stores or specialized services for each function, such as cashing a check.[130] In addition, working-class consumers are more likely to judge product quality on the basis of price (higher price means higher quality), to shop in discount stores, and to have less product information when purchasing.[131] And they may exhibit distinctly different product preferences than those of consumers in other social classes. For instance, only 15 percent of U.S. adults with an income below $25,000 say they drink wine, compared with 52 percent of adults in the top-income bracket and 28 percent in middle-income brackets.[132]

13-5d THE HOMELESS

At the low end of the status hierarchy are *homeless* consumers who lack shelter and live on the streets or in makeshift structures, cars, or vacant houses.[133] The homeless represent a sizable segment of society in some countries. Official U.S. estimates indicate that about 610,000 people are homeless on any given night, although other estimates of this population range above seven million, with the numbers growing during the recent recession.[134] This group includes unemployed or underemployed consumers, drug and alcohol abusers, mentally ill people, members of female-headed households, and people who have experienced financial setbacks such as losing their homes. Children are also part of this group: According to a recent study, as many as 2.5 million U.S. children—1 in 30—are homeless.[135]

An overriding characteristic of the homeless is the struggle for survival. With little or no income, homeless consumers have difficulty acquiring daily necessities such as food, housing, and medical care. They are not helpless but rather are a "resourceful, determined, and capable group that proactively deals with its lack of resources in the consumer environment."[136] A particularly important survival activity for homeless consumers is *scavenging*, finding used or partially used goods that others have discarded. Many vary their scavenging patterns to avoid detection as they move between areas to find the needed items, making this a mobile or nomadic society. Despite their poverty, most homeless consumers have some valued possessions, and they get the maximum use out of items, discarding something only if they have absolutely no further use for it.

Marketing Implications

Social class can serve as an effective way of segmenting the market, thereby influencing product or service development, messages, media selection, and channel selection.

Product or Service Development

Social class motives and values can determine which offerings consumers desire. For example, to satisfy their need for prestige and luxury, many upper-class consumers prefer high-end automobiles, imported wines, fancy restaurants, exotic or deluxe vacations, and couture clothing. Working class consumers want good quality at a fair price, and many offerings—family-rate motels, buffet restaurants, basic versions of branded items—are designed to fulfill this desire. Buying power can be an issue, which is why in Mexico, the Elektra retail chain caters to working-class customers by making credit available for purchases of appliances and cars.[137]

Sometimes marketers develop different product lines for different classes. For example, Procter & Gamble targets higher-class customers with $50 antiaging Olay face creams and lower-class customers with basic $6 Olay skin moisturizers.[138] Many marketers target a particular class, get to know the needs of those consumers in depth, and create offerings specifically for them. For example, Italy-based fashion house Loro Piana targets upper-class customers worldwide by creating fine cashmere and wool clothing that does not flaunt the brand and is not mass marketed, enhancing its aura of exclusivity.[139] Also, marketers can create products that appeal to consumers' aspirations for upward mobility. For example, top designers such as Jason Wu and Lilly Pulitzer have reached beyond couture customers into the middle class with lines of moderately priced clothing sold only in Target stores.[140]

Messages

Advertisers targeting a particular social class within the larger population can be effective by tapping into the group's distinctiveness; when targeting the upper classes, for instance, the advertiser might suggest the group's status as a small, elite group.[141] Other messages for the upper classes might focus on themes of "a just reward for hard work," "you've made it," or "pamper yourself because you deserve it." Certain offerings can be advertised as coveted status symbols. Marketers of cars priced above $100,000 advertise stylish design, ultra-high performance, and—increasingly

Exhibit 13.13 ▶ Working-Class Appeal
Stores such as Walmart or the Dollar Tree appeal to working-class consumers with everyday low prices.

AP Images/Jae C. Hong

important—environmentally friendly engines.[142] Messages for the working class might take on a more localized orientation, focusing on home and friends as well as favored activities such as hunting and watching sports events. In addition, messages can use typical members of a social class as role models.

Media Exposure

The classes differ in their exposure to certain media. Advertisers try to reach the upper classes through targeted magazines such as the *Robb Report*, special events such as collectible cars shows, sponsorships on public TV and radio, and cultural events. Many marketers think "three screens" when they want to reach middle and upper-class consumers: television, personal computer, and cell phone or tablet computer. Fashion marketers such as Yoox are also using mobile apps to connect with affluent, style-conscious consumers in China and elsewhere.[143] Lower-class consumers tend to be heavy watchers of TV and less likely than other classes to read magazines and newspapers. Middle-class consumers, particularly those with only some college education, are unique because they tend to be heavy TV watchers as well as magazine readers. However, online streaming of

TV and other entertainment content is altering media consumption habits among all classes, which means marketers must understand the trends and plan carefully to reach target audiences.[144]

Marketers targeting upper-class consumers can make goods available through channels that sell exclusive merchandise with personalized service.[145] For example, Vertu sells its luxury cell phones (priced at $6,000 and up) through upscale boutiques on prestigious shopping streets such as Rodeo Drive in Beverly Hills.[146] Conspicuous consumption can play a role when consumers want to acquire items in the "correct" store, especially if they can be seen doing so.[147] Dollar stores such as Dollar Tree attract working-class consumers and—especially during tough economic times—some middle-class consumers with value pricing of everyday goods. Walmart attracts consumers from the lower and middle classes, although the retailer lost some of its most price-conscious shoppers to dollar stores during the recent recession (see Exhibit 13.13).[148]

Note of Caution

Marketers have had difficulty in using social class as a segmentation variable for several reasons. As noted earlier, social class is difficult to assess because a variety of factors such as occupation and income can have opposite effects on class. Also, variations within a class make social class a better predictor of broad behavior patterns, such as conspicuous product-level choice, than of specific behaviors such as brand choice. Finally, because of social class fragmentation, traditional class distinctions may be becoming too broad to be truly useful. Therefore, marketers are using technology to segment markets and to target consumers more precisely through database marketing, the Internet, direct mail, and other tools. It's also important that we not think of social class as constant, because social class structures can change. For example, in certain Indian villages, status hierarchies that were originally based on caste are being reformed based on marketization and privatization, creating a new social order that changes the long-lived hierarchical caste system.[149]

Summary:

Households, which include families and unrelated people living together as well as singles, exert considerable influence on acquisition and consumption patterns. The proportion of nontraditional households has increased because of factors such as (1) later marriages and cohabitation, (2) dual-career families, (3) divorce, (4) smaller families, and (5) same-sex and transgender households. Members can play different roles in the decision process (gatekeeper, influencer, decider, buyer, and user). Also, husbands and wives vary in their influence on the decision process, depending on whether the situation is husband dominant, wife dominant, autonomic, or syncratic. The nature of children's influence on acquisition, usage, and disposition decisions partly depends on whether the household is authoritarian, neglectful, democratic, or permissive.

Individuals in a society can be grouped into status levels (upper, middle, and lower), making up a social class hierarchy. Class distinctions are significant because members of a particular class tend to share common life experiences and therefore also share values and consumer behavior patterns (despite variations within groups). Individuals are most likely to be influenced by members of their own class because they regularly interact with them. Still, influence can cross class lines through the *trickle-down effect* (when lower classes copy upper-class values and behavior) or *status float* (when trends start in the lower classes and spread upward).

A variety of factors determine social class, the most critical of which are occupation and education. Three major trends producing an evolution in social class structure are upward mobility, downward mobility, and social class fragmentation. Social class influences consumer behavior in four major ways: through (1) conspicuous consumption (acquiring and displaying offerings to show class standing) or voluntary simplicity (consciously choosing a less material lifestyle); (2) status symbols (offerings that demonstrate social standing); (3) compensatory consumption (buying as a way to offset some deficiency); and (4) the meaning of money. Despite the blurring of social class lines, four classes make up sizable segments within the overall market: the upper, middle, and working classes, and the homeless.

Questions for Review and Discussion

1. Define the terms nuclear family, extended family, and household.

2. What five key factors have altered the basic structure and characteristics of households?

3. What five roles might a household member perform in acquiring and consuming something?

4. What is the social class hierarchy?

5. What are the determinants of social class?

6. Why is social class fragmentation taking place?

7. Why would a consumer engage in conspicuous consumption, conspicuous waste, or voluntary simplicity?

8. How does parody display differ from status symbols?

9. Under what circumstances does compensatory consumption occur?

10. Why might a company develop different offerings for consumers in different social classes?

Endnotes

1   Richard Fry, "More Millennials Living with Family Despite Improved Job Market," *Pew Research Center*, July 29, 2015, www.pewsocialtrends.org.

2   Rex Y. Du and Wagner A. Kamakura, "Household Life Cycles and Lifestyles in the United States," *Journal of Marketing Research* 43, February 2006, pp. 121–132; Mary C. Gilly and Ben M. Enis, "Recycling the Family Life Cycle," in ed. Andrew A. Mitchell, *Advances in Consumer Research*, vol. 9 (Ann Arbor, Mich.: Association for Consumer Research, 1982), pp. 271–276; and William D. Danko and Charles M. Schaninger, "An Empirical Evaluation of the Gilly-Enis Updated Household Life Cycle Model," *Journal of Business Research* 21, August 1990, pp. 39–57.

3   Joy Wilkie, "Having Children Major Driver of Spending Patterns in U.S.," *Gallup Economy*, March 4, 2014, www.gallup .com/poll/167705/having-children-major-driver-spending-patterns.aspx.

4   Hannah Karp, "How Tough Are Times? Parents Cut Back Diapers," *Wall Street Journal*, October 4, 2011, www.wsj.com.

5   Anil Mathur, George p. Moschis, and Euehun Lee, "A Study of Changes in Brand Preferences," *Asia Pacific Advances in Consumer Research* 4, 2001, pp. 133–139.

6   Ben Crair, "Animal Haus," *Bloomberg Businessweek*, August 19, 2015, pp. 60–65.

7   "U.S. Census Bureau Reports Men and Women Wait Longer to Marry," *U.S. Census Bureau*, November 10, 2010, www.census.gov.

8   Bella DePaulo, "What Do Singles Spend Their Money On?" *Psychology Today*, April 7, 2011, www.psychologytoday.com.

9   Jonel Aleccia, "'The New Normal': Cohabitation is on the Rise, Study Finds," *NBC Health News*, April 4, 2013, http://www .nbcnews.com/health.

10 Katie Little, "McDonald's Ditches More Sales for Accuracy," *CNBC*, May 22, 2015, www.cnbc.com; and Karl Taro Greenfeld, "Fast and Furious," *Businessweek*, May 9, 2011, pp. 64–69.

11 See Kim Parker, "5 Facts About Today's Fathers," *Pew Research Center*, June 18, 2015, www.pewresearch.org.

12 Claire Cain Miller, "The Divorce Surge Is Over, but the Myth Lives On," *New York Times*, December 2, 2014, www.nytimes .com; and Joan Raymond, "The Ex-Files," *American Demographics*, February 2001, pp. 60–64.

13 James H. Alexander, John W. Shouten, and Scott D. Roberts, "Consumer Behavior and Divorce," in eds. Janeen Costa and Russell W. Belk, *Research in Consumer Behavior*, vol. 6 (Greenwich, Conn.: JAI Press, 1993), pp. 153–184.

14 "U.S. Census Bureau Reports Men and Women Wait Longer to Marry," *U.S. Census Bureau*, November 10, 2010, www.census.gov.

15 Pamela Paul, "Childless by Choice," *American Demographics*, November 2001, pp. 45–50.

16 "Census Bureau Releases Estimates of Same-Sex Married Couples," U.S. Census Bureau, September 27, 2011, www .census.gov. See also, Gillian W. Oakenfull, "What Matters: Factors Influencing Gay Consumers' Evaluations of 'Gay-Friendly' Corporate Activities," *Journal of Public Policy & Marketing* 32, Special Issue, 2013, pp. 79–89.

17 "Same-Sex Marriage Laws," *National Conference of State Legislation*, June 26, 2015, www.ncsl.org.

18 Michelle Castillo, "How the Business of Same-Sex Weddings May Change," *CNBC*, June 26, 2015, www.cnbc.com.

19 "Gay Marriage Around the World," *Pew Research Center*, June 26, 2015, www.pewforum.org.

20 Matt McCue, "These Retailers Are Betting on Transgender Customers," *Fortune*, May 21, 2015, www.fortune.com.

21 Suraj Commuri and James W. Gentry, "Resource Allocation in Households with Women as Chief Wage Earner," *Journal of Consumer Research* 32, no. 2, 2005, pp. 185–195.

22 Carol Morello, "Blended Families More Common," *Washington Post*, January 23, 2011, www.washingtonpost.com.

23 Jennifer Smith Cross, "Price Check on Love: Liberty Village Grocery Store Is Having a Singles Night," *Metro News*, May 20, 2015, www.metronews.ca.

24 Anil Mathur, George p. Moschis, and Euehun Lee, "A Longitudinal Study of the Effects of Life Status Changes on Changes in Consumer Preferences," *Journal of the Academy of Marketing Science* 36, 2008, pp. 234–246.

25 Jane C. Timm, "Evangelical Pastor Franklin Graham: Boycott Gay-Friendly Businesses," *MSNBC*, June 9, 2015, www.msnbc .com; Andy Bagnall, "Does This Ad Make Me Look Gay?" *Advertising Age*, June 8, 2011, www.adage.com; and Ronald Alsop, "As Same Sex Households Grow More Mainstream, Businesses Take Note," *Wall Street Journal*, August 8, 2001, pp. B1, B4.

26 Robert E. Wilkes and Debra A. Laverie, "Purchasing Decisions in Non-Traditional Households: The Case of Lesbian Couples," *Journal of Consumer Behavior* 6, no. 1, 2007, pp. 60–73.

27 Harry L. Davis, "Dimensions of Marital Roles in Consumer Decision Making," *Journal of Marketing Research* 7, May 1970, pp. 168–177; Conway Lackman and John M. Lanasa, "Family Decision Making Theory: An Overview and Assessment," *Psychology and Marketing* 10, March–April 1993, pp. 81–93; and Stephan Muehlbacher, Eva Hofmann, Erich Kirchler, and Christine Roland-Levy, "Household Decision-Making: Changes of Female and Male Partners' Role?" *Psychology and Economics* 2, January 2009, https://www.researchgate .net.

28 Rina Makgosa and Jikyeong Kang, "Conflict Resolution Strategies in Joint Purchase Decisions for Major Household Consumer Durables: A Cross-Cultural Investigation," *International Journal of Consumer Studies* 33, no. 3, 2009, pp. 338–348.

29 Alice Gronhoj, "Communication About Consumption: A Family Process Perspective on 'Green' Consumer Practices," *Journal of Consumer Behavior* 5, no. 6, 2006, pp. 491–503.

30 Sheth, "A Theory of Family Buying Decisions"; and Michael A. Belch, George E. Belch, and Donald Sciglimpaglia, "Conflict in Family Decision Making: An Exploratory Investigation," in ed. Jerry C. Olson, *Advances in Consumer Research*, vol. 7 (Chicago: Association for Consumer Research, 1980), pp. 475–479.

31 W. Christian Buss and Charles M. Schaninger, "The Influence of Family Decision Processes and Outcomes," in eds. Richard p. Bagozzi and Alice M. Tybout, *Advances in Consumer Research*, vol. 10 (Ann Arbor, Mich.: Association for Consumer Research, 1983), pp. 439–444.

32 Terry L. Childers and Akshay R. Rao, "The Influence of Familial and Peer-Based Reference Groups on Consumer Decisions," *Journal of Consumer Research* 19, September 1992, pp. 198–211. See also "The Status of Women in The Middle East and North Africa," *International Foundation for Electoral Systems*, http:// swmena.net/en/report/126.

33 Harry L. Davis and Benny p. Rigaux, "Perception of Marital Roles in Decision Processes," *Journal of Consumer Research* 1, June 1974, pp. 5–14; and Mandy Putnam and William R. Davidson, *Family Purchasing Behavior: 11 Family Roles by Product Category* (Columbus, Ohio: Management Horizons, Inc., A Division of Price Waterhouse, 1987).

34 Tara L. Queen, Cynthia A. Berg, and William Lowrance, "A Framework for Decision Making in Couples across Adulthood," *Aging and Decision Making: Empirical and Applied Perspectives*, 2015, pp. 371–392.

35 William J. Qualls, "Household Decision Behavior: The Impact of Husbands' and Wives' Sex Role Orientation," *Journal of Consumer Research* 14, September 1987, pp. 264–279; and Larry Neale, Renee Robbie, and Brett Martin, "Gender Identity and Brand Incongruence: When in Doubt, Pursue Masculinity," *Journal of Strategic Marketing* 23, May 2015, pp. 1–13.

36 Michael Flagg, "Asian Marketing," *Asian Wall Street Journal*, March 19, 2001, p. A12.

37 Jack Neff, "The Consumer Is Not a Moron, He Is Your Child's Father," *Advertising Age*, October 17, 2011, www.adage.com.

38 Michael B. Menasco and David J. Curry, "Utility and Choice: An Empirical Study of Wife/Husband Decision Making," *Journal of Consumer Research* 16, June 1989, pp. 87–97; and Qualls, "Household Decision Behavior: The Impact of Husbands' and Wives' Sex Role Orientation."

39 C. Whan Park, "Joint Decisions in Home Purchasing: A Muddling Through Process," *Journal of Consumer Research* 9, September 1982, pp. 151–162; Harry L. Davis, Stephen J. Hoch, and E. K. Easton Ragsdale, "An Anchoring and Adjustment Model of Spousal Predictions," *Journal of Consumer Research* 13, June 1986, pp. 25–37; and Robert F. Krampf, David J. Burns, and Dale M. Rayman, "Consumer Decision Making and the Nature of the Product: A Comparison of Husband and Wife Adoption Process Location," *Psychology and Marketing* 10, March–April 1993, pp. 95–109.

40 Benjamin Scheibehenne, Jutta Mata, and Peter M. Todd, "Older but Not Wiser," *Journal of Consumer Psychology* 21, 2011, pp. 184–191; Davy Lerouge and Luk Warlop, "Why It Is So Hard to Predict Our Partner's Product Preferences," *Journal of Consumer Research* 33, no. 3, 2006, pp. 393–402; and Chenting Su, Edward F. Fern, and Keying Ye, "A Temporal Dynamic Model of Spousal Family Purchase-Decision Behavior," *Journal of Marketing Research* 41, August 2003, pp. 268–281.

41 Scott I. Rick, Deborah A. Small, and Eli J. Finkel, "Fatal (Fiscal) Attraction," *Journal of Marketing Research* 48, April 2011, pp. 228–237.

42 Laura A. Williams, Kathleen A. Krentler, and Albert Caruana, "Is Pulling Mom & Dad's Strings a Global Phenomenon? (A Study of Children's Purchase Influence in the United States and Malta)," *Global Perspectives in Marketing for the 21st Century* (Springer International Publishing, 2015), pp. 304–307.

43 Sharon E. Beatty and Salil Talpade, "Adolescent Influence in Family Decision Making: A Replication with Extension," *Journal of Consumer Research* 21, September 1994, pp. 332–341.

44 William K. Darley and Jeen-Su Lim, "Family Decision Making in Leisure Time Activities: An Exploratory Analysis of the Impact of Locus of Control, Child Age Influence Factor and Parental Type on Perceived Child Influence," in ed. Richard J. Lutz, *Advances in Consumer Research*, vol. 13 (Ann Arbor, Mich.: Association for Consumer Research, 1986), pp. 370–374; George p. Moschis and Linda G. Mitchell, "Television Advertising and Interpersonal Influences on Teenagers' Participation in Family Consumer Decisions," in ed. Lutz, *Advances in*

Consumer Research, vol. 13, pp. 181–186; and Beatty and Talpade, "Adolescent Influence in Family Decision Making: A Replication with Extension."

45 June Cotte and Stacy L. Wood, "Families and Innovative Consumer Behavior: A Triadic Analysis of Sibling and Parental Influence," *Journal of Consumer Research* 31, June 2004, pp. 78–86.

46 Anirban Mukhopadhyay and Catherine W. M. Yeung, "Building Character: Effects of Lay Theories of Self-Control on the Selection of Products for Children," *Journal of Marketing Research* 47, April 2010, pp. 240–250.

47 Marsha L. Richins and Lan Nguyen Chaplin, "Material Parenting: How the Use of Goods in Parenting Fosters Materialism in the Next Generation," *Journal of Consumer Research* 41, no. 6, 2015, pp. 1333–1357.

48 Adya Sharma and Vandana Sonwaney, "Theoretical Modeling of Influence of Children on Family Purchase Decision Making," *Procedia—Social and Behavioral Sciences* 133, 2014, pp. 38–46.

49 Monica Chaudhary, "Family Decision–Making in Emerging Economies," *International Journal of Business and Globalisation* 14, no. 3, 2015, pp. 310–320.

50 Kay M. Palan and Robert E. Wilkes, "Adolescent–Parent Interaction in Family Decision Making," *Journal of Consumer Research* 24, September 1997, pp. 159–169.

51 Les Carlson and Sanford Grossbart, "Parental Style and Consumer Socialization of Children," *Journal of Consumer Research* 15, June 1988, pp. 77–94.

52 Belch, Belch, and Ceresino, "Parental and Teenage Influences in Family Decision Making."

53 Michael Hughlett, "General Mills Scrambling to Win Millennials," *The Columbus Dispatch (OH)*, January 2, 2016, www.dispatch.com; Joel Wee, "For PR Firms, Focus Shifts from Newspapers to Social Media," *Philadelphia Inquirer*, August 12, 2015, www.philly.com; and Andrea Gordon, "Big Brands Are Lining up to Harness the Clout of Online Moms," *The Star (Toronto)*, October 13, 2011, www.thestar.com.

54 Harry Wallop, "KidZania: The Educational Theme Park Where Kids Play at Being Adults," *The Telegraph (U.K.)*, June 25, 2015, www.telegraph.co.uk; and John Paul Rathbone, "The Last Word: Advertiser-Funded Theme Parks That Make the World of Work Child's Play," *Financial Times*, June 24, 2011, p. 12.

55 Amanda C. Kooser, "Virtual Playground," *U.S. News & World Report*, April 1, 2008, www.usnews.com.

56 Les Carlson, Russell N. Laczniak, and Chad Wertley, "Parental Style," *Journal of Advertising Research* 51, June 2011, pp. 427–435.

57 "Delaware's Online Privacy and Protection Act Now in Effect," *Lexology*, January 4, 2016, www.lexology.com.

58 Pierre Bourdieu, *Language and Symbolic Power* (Cambridge, Mass.: Harvard University Press, 1991).

59 Richard p. Coleman, "The Continuing Significance of Social Class to Marketing," *Journal of Consumer Research* 10, December 1983, pp. 265–280; and Wendell Blanchard, *Thailand, Its People, Its Society, Its Culture* (New Haven, Conn.: HRAF Press, 1990), cited in Sak Onkvisit and John J. Shaw, *International Marketing: Analysis and Strategy* (Columbus, Ohio: Merrill, 1989), p. 293.

60 Edward W. Cundiff and Marye T. Hilger, *Marketing in the International Environment* (Englewood Cliffs, N.J.: Prentice-Hall, 1988), as cited in Mariele K. DeMooij and Warren Keegan, *Advertising Worldwide* (Englewood Cliffs, N.J.: Prentice-Hall, 1991), p. 96.

61 Onkvisit and Shaw, International Marketing: Analysis and Strategy.

62 Richard p. Coleman, "The Significance of Social Stratification in Selling," in ed. Martin L. Bell, *Marketing: A Maturing Discipline* (Chicago: American Marketing Association, 1960), pp. 171–184.

63 Douglas E. Allen and Paul F. Anderson, "Consumption and Social Stratification: Bourdieu's Distinction," in eds. Chris T. Allan and Deborah Roedder John, *Advances in Consumer Research*, vol. 21 (Provo, Utah: Association for Consumer Research, 1994), pp. 70–73.

64 Ram Manohar Vikas, Rohit Varman, and Russell W. Belk, "Status, Caste and Market in a Changing Indian Village," *Journal of Consumer Research* 42, no. 3, October 2015, pp. 472–498.

65 Pierre Bourdieu, *Distinction: A Social Critique of the Judgment of Taste* (Cambridge, Mass.: Harvard University Press, 1984).

66 Tuba Ustuner and Douglas B. Holt, "Toward a Theory of Status Consumption in Less Industrialized Countries," *Journal of Consumer Research* 37, June 2010, pp. 37–56; Tuba Ustuner and Craig J. Thompson, "How Marketplace Performances Product Interdependent Status Games and Contested Forms of Symbolic Capital," *Journal of Consumer Research* 38, February 2012, pp. 796–814.

67 Coleman, "The Continuing Significance of Social Class to Marketing."

68 See Joan M. Ostrove and Elizabeth R. Cole, "Privileging Class: Toward a Critical Psychology of Social Class in the Context of Education," *Journal of Social Issues* 59, Winter 2003, pp. 677–692; and Charles M. Schaninger, "Social Class Versus Income Revisited: An Empirical Investigation," *Journal of Marketing Research* 18, May 1981, pp. 192–208.

69 "Pleased to Be Bourgeois," *Economist*, May 14, 2011, p. 58.

70 Serena Ng and Laurie Burkitt, "P&G Tripped Up by Its Assumptions About Diapers in China," *Wall Street Journal*, August 13, 2015, www.wsj.com.

71 Diane Crispell, "The Real Middle Americans," *American Demographics*, October 1994, pp. 28–35; and Michael Hout, "More Universalism, Less Structural Mobility: The American Occupational Structure in the 1980s," *American Journal of Sociology*, May 1988, pp. 1358–1400.

72 Tiffany Julian and Robert Kominski, "Education and Synthetic Work-Life Earnings Estimates," *U.S. Census Bureau American Community Survey Reports*, September 2011, p. 2.

73 Peter Francese, "The College–Cash Connection," *American Demographics*, March 2002, http://adage.com/article/americandemographics; and Patricia Cohen, "Forget Lonely. Life Is Healthy at the Top," *New York Times*, May 15, 2004, p. B9.

74 William L. Wilkie, *Consumer Behavior*, 2nd ed. (New York: Wiley, 1990).

75 Tami Luhby, "The Rich Are 8 Times Likelier to Graduate College Than the Poor," *CNN Money*, February 4, 2015, http://money.cnn.com.

76 Allen and Anderson, "Consumption and Social Stratification: Bourdieu's Distinction."

77 Jake Ryan and Charles Sackrey, *Strangers in Paradise: Academics from the Working Class* (Boston: South End Press, 1984).

78 Andrew D. Gershoff and Katherine A. Burson, "Knowing Where They Stand," *Journal of Consumer Research* 38, October 2011, pp. 407–419.

79 Jim Zarroli, "Study: Upward Mobility No Tougher in U.S. Than Two Decades Ago," *National Public Radio*, January 23, 2014, www.npr.org.

80 Ariel Zirulnick, "US Losing Its Competitive Edge Due to Higher Costs of Higher Education: OECD," *Christian Science Monitor*, September 13, 2011, www.csmonitor.com; Amelia Hill, "Upward Mobility Less Likely for Women and Low Earners, Says Study," *Guardian (UK)*, September 23, 2011, www.guardian.co.uk; Mary Janigan, Ruth Atherley, Michelle Harries, Brenda Branswell, and John Demont, "The Wealth Gap," *Maclean's*, August 28, 2000, pp. 42; and Bernstein, "Waking Up from the American Dream."

81 Katherine S. Newman, *Falling from Grace: The Experience of Downward Mobility in the American Middle Class* (New York: Free Press, 1988); and Donna Haraway and Patricia Hill Collins, "Variations on the Theory of Power and Knowledge: The Fractured Matrix of Power," in eds. Anthony Elliott and Charles Lemert, *Introduction to Contemporary Social Theory* (New York: Routledge, 2014), p. 232ff.

82 Chris Green, "Downward Mobility on the Rise for the First Time in Generations," *The Independent (U.K.)*, November 6, 2014, www.independent.co.uk.

83 Allison Schrager, "Even the Upper Middle Class Struggles to Save Money," *Bloomberg Businessweek*, August 12, 2014, www.bloomberg.com.

84 Kenneth Labich, "Class in America," *Fortune*, February 7, 1994, pp. 114–126.

85 Ibid.

86 Joseph C. Nunes, Xavier Dreze, and Yong Jee Han, "Conspicuous Consumption in a Recession: Toning it Down or Turning it Up?," *Journal of Consumer Psychology* 21, no. 2, 2011, pp. 199–205; Philip J. Mazzocco, Derek D. Rucker, Adal D. Galinsky and Eric T. Anderson, "Direct and Vicarious Conspicuous Consumption: Identification with Low Status Groups Increases the Desire for High Status Goods," *Journal of Consumer Psychology* 22, no. 4, October 2012, pp. 520–528; and John Brooks, *Showing Off in America: From Conspicuous Consumption to Parody Display* (Boston: Little, Brown, 1981).

87 Aron O'Cass and Hmily McEwen, "Exploring Consumer Status and Conspicuous Consumption," *Journal of Consumer Behavior* 4, no. 1, 2004, pp. 25–39.

88 Wilfred Amaldoss and Sanjay Jain, "Pricing of Conspicuous Goods: A Competitive Analysis of Social Effects," *Journal of Marketing Research* 42, February 2005, pp. 30–42.

89 Nailya Ordabayeva and Pierre Chandon, "Getting Ahead of the Joneses," *Journal of Consumer Research* 38, June 2011, pp. 27–41.

90 Jamie Arndt, Sheldon Solomon, Tim Kasser, and Kennon M. Sheldon, "The Urge to Splurge: A Terror Management Account of Materialism and Consumer Behavior," *Journal of Consumer Psychology* 14, no. 3, 2004, pp. 198–212.

91 Janeen Arnold Costa and Russell W. Belk, "Nouveaux Riches as Quintessential Americans: Case Studies of Consumption in the Extended Family," in ed. Russell W. Belk, *Advances in Nonprofit Marketing*, vol. 3 (Greenwich, Conn.: JAI Press, 1990), pp. 83–140.

92 "You Choose," *Economist*, December 18, 2010, pp. 123–125; and Mustapha Harzallah Ibtissem, "Application of Value Beliefs Norms Theory to the Energy Conservation Behaviour," *Journal of Sustainable Development*, June 2010, p. 129ff.

93 Jonah Berger and Morgan Ward, "Subtle Signals of Inconspicuous Consumption," *Journal of Consumer Research* 37, December 2010, pp. 555–569; and Ben Steverman, "Conspicuous Consumption Is Back," *Businessweek*, January 27, 2011, www.businessweek.com.

94 Thomas Clayton O'Guinn, Robin J. Tanner, and Ahreum Maeng, "Turning to Space: Social Density, Social Class and

the Value of Things in Stores," *Journal of Consumer Research* 42, no. 2, 2015, pp. 196–213.

95 Dave McGinn, "Once the Height of Teen Embarrassment, Braces Have Somehow Become Cool," *Globe and Mail (Toronto)*, August 13, 2015, www.theglobeandmail.com.

96 Naomi Mandel, Petia K. Petrova, and Robert B. Cialdini, "Images of Success and the Preference for Luxury Brands," *Journal of Consumer Psychology* 16, no. 1, 2006, pp. 57–69.

97 Tamara Abraham, "As Sales Soar 54 Percent in a Year, How Nail Polish Replaced Lipstick as Women's Favourite Recession-Proof Luxury," *Daily Mail (UK)*, September 30, 2011, www.dailymail.co.uk; and Rebecca Gardyn, "Oh, the Good Life," *American Demographics*, November 2002, pp. 30–35.

98 Brooks, Showing Off in America: From Conspicuous Consumption to Parody Display.

99 Stephen Buckley, "Brazil Rediscovers Its Culture; Poor Man's Cocktail, Martial Art Hip Among Middle Class," *Washington Post*, April 15, 2001, p. A16.

100 Sarah Halzack, "Coach Is Buying Stuart Weitzman. Is That a Smart Move for the Troubled Brand?" *Washington Post*, January 6, 2015, www.washingtonpost.com; and Teri Agins, "Now, Subliminal Logos," *Wall Street Journal*, July 20, 2001, p. B1.

101 Derek D. Rucker and Adam D. Galinsky, "Desire to Acquire: Powerlessness and Compensator y Consumption," *Journal of Consumer Research* 35, August 2008, pp. 257–267.

102 Alexander Fury, "Accessible luxury: Brands May Be Devaluing 'Luxury'–But They're Making a Mint," *The Independent (UK)*, August 16, 2015, www.independent.co.uk.

103 Kelly D. Martin and Ronald Paul Martin, "Life Satisfaction, Self-Determination, and Consumption Adequacy at the Bottom of the Pyramid," *Journal of Consumer Research* 38, no. 6, April 2012, pp. 1155–1168.

104 Russell W. Belk and Melanie Wallendorf, "The Sacred Meanings of Money," *Journal of Economic Psychology* 11, March 1990, pp. 35–67.

105 Heidi Vogt, "Making Change: Mobile Pay in Africa," *Wall Street Journal*, January 2, 2015, www.wsj.com; and Abraham McLaughlin, "Africans' New Motto: 'Charge It,'" *Christian Science Monitor*, February 14, 2005, p. 6.

106 Adrian Furnham and Alan Lewis, *The Economic Mind: The Social Psychology of Economic Behavior* (Brighton, Sussex: Harvester Press, 1986); and Belk and Wallendorf, "The Sacred Meanings of Money."

107 Alex Daniels, "As Wealthy Give Smaller Share of Income to Charity, Middle Class Digs Deeper," *Chronicle of Philanthropy*, October 5, 2014, https://philanthropy.com; and Rebecca Gardyn, "Generosity and Income," *American Demographics*, December 2002–January 2003, pp. 46–47.

108 Jennifer L. Aaker, Melanie Rudd, and Cassie Mogilner, "If Money Does Not Make You Happy, Consider Time," *Journal of Consumer Psychology* 21, no. 2, 2011, pp. 126–130.

109 Elizabeth W. Dunn, Daniel T. Gilbert, and Timothy D. Wilson, "If Money Doesn't Make You Happy, Then You Probably Aren't Spending It Right," *Journal of Consumer Psychology* 12, no. 2, 2011, pp. 115–125; Michel Tuan Pham, "On Consumption Happiness: A Research Dialogue," *Journal of Consumer Psychology* 25, no. 1, January 2015, pp. 150–151; and Thomas Gilovich, Amit Kumar, and Lily Jampol, "A Wonderful Life: Experiential Consumption and the Pursuit of Happiness," *Journal of Consumer Psychology* 25, no. 1, 2015, pp. 152–165.

110 Christopher K. Hsee, Yang Yang, Naihe Li, and Luxi Shen, "Wealth, Warmth, and Well-Being: Whether Happiness Is Relative or Absolute Depends on Whether It Is About Money, Acquisition, or Consumption," *Journal of Marketing Research* 46, June 2009, pp. 396–409.

111 Leonardo Nicolao, Julie R. Irwin, and Joseph K. Goodman, "Happiness for Sale: Do Experiential Purchases make Consumer Happier than Material Purchases?" *Journal of Consumer Research* 36, August 2009, pp. 188–198.

112 Kristina M. Durante, Vladas Groslevocois, Joseph p. Redden, and Andrew Edward White, "Spending on Daughters versus Sons in Economic Recessions," *Journal of Consumer Research* 42, October 2015, pp. 435–457.

113 See Joseph Chancellor and Sonja Lyubomirsky, "Happiness and Thrift: When (Spending) Less Is (Hedonically) More," *Journal of Consumer Psychology* 21, no. 2, 2011, pp. 131–138.

114 Marshall Heyman, "At New York Parties, Visions of Grandeur," *Wall Street Journal*, October 6, 2011, www.wsj.com.

115 Clarissa Sebag-Montefiore, "Foreign Brands Go Native in China," *Campaign*, October 21, 2014, www.campaignlive.com.

116 E. J. Schultz, "Packages Shrink to Fit Spending-Power Decline," *Advertising Age*, October 17, 2011, www.adage.com.

117 "How Marketers Sell to the Long-Term Jobless," *Advertising Age*, October 16, 2011, www.adage.com.

118 Will Hernandez, "No Surprise: Gallup Finds Mobile Wallets Low Priority for Consumers," *Mobile Payments Today*, July 21, 2015, www.mobilepaymentstoday.com; and Shen Jingting, "HTC, Unionpay Target Mobile Wallets," *China Daily*, August 10, 2011, www.chinadaily.com.cn.

119 Mercedes M. Cardona, "Affluent Shoppers Like Their Luxe Goods Cheap," *Advertising Age*, December 1, 2003, p. 6.

120 See "Old Money," *American Demographics*, June 2003, pp. 34–37.

121 "India's Luxury Market," *India Knowledge@Wharton*, September 1, 2011, http://knowledge.wharton.upenn.edu; and Shobhana Chandra and Anthony Feld, "Rich Americans Raise Consumer Spending with Little Help from Middle Class," *Bloomberg News*, January 18, 2011, www.bloomberg.com.

122 Robert Frank, "More Millionaires Than Ever Are Living in the US," *CNBC*, March 10, 2015, www.cnbc.com.

123 Chris Matthews, "Millionaires Now Control an Even Bigger Share of the World's Wealth," *Fortune*, June 15, 2015, www.fortune.com.

124 Brad Tuttle, "The Sad, Sorry State of the Middle Class," *Time*, September 8, 2011, http://moneyland.time.com.

125 Christopher Sabatini, "Latin America's Middle-Class Growing Pains," *U.S. News & World Report*, April 18, 2014, www.usnews.com.

126 "What Will an Emerging First World Mexico Mean for California?" *San Francisco Chronicle*, June 5, 2015, www.sfgate.com.

127 Patrick McGroarty, "Africa's Middle Class to Boom," *Wall Street Journal*, October 13, 2011, www.wsj.com.

128 Coleman, "The Continuing Significance of Social Class to Marketing."

129 Paul C. Henry, "Social Class, Market Situation, and Consumers' Metaphors of (Dis)Empowerment," *Journal of Consumer Research* 31, no. 4, 2005, pp. 766–778.

130 Bridgit Bowman, "More and More People in Kansas City Are 'Unbanked,'" *Kansas City Star*, August 15, 2015, www.kansascity.com.

131 Prasad, "Socioeconomic Product Risk and Patronage Preferences of Retail Shoppers"; and Stuart Rich and Subhish Jain, "Social Class and Life Cycle as Predictors of Shopping Behavior," *Journal of Marketing Research* 24, June–July 1987, pp. 51–59.

132 John Fetto, "Watering Holes," *American Demographics*, June 2003, p. 8.

133 Ronald Paul Hill and Mark Stamey, "The Homeless in America: An Examination of Possessions and Consumption Behaviors," *Journal of Consumer Research* 17, December 1990, pp. 303–321.

134 "The State of Homelessness in America 2014," *National Alliance to End Homelessness*, May 27, 2014, http://www.endhomelessness.org/library/entry/the-state-of-homelessness-2014.

135 Stav Ziv, "Child Homelessness in U.S. Reaches Historic High, Report Says," *Newsweek*, November 17, 2014, www.newsweek.com.

136 Ronald Paul Hill, "Homeless Women, Special Possessions, and the Meaning of 'Home': An Ethnographic Case Study," *Journal of Consumer Research* 18, December 1991, pp. 298–310.

137 Anthony Harrup, "Mexico's Grupo Elektra Hires Former Banorte Chief to Head Bank," *Wall Street Journal*, January 16, 2015, www.wsj.com; and Peter Katel, "Petro Padillo Longoria: A Retailer Focused on Working-Class Needs," *Time International*, October 15, 2001, p. 49.

138 Prior and Nagel, "P&G's McDonald Out to Cover Globe."

139 Alessandro Di Fiore, "A Different Premium Brand Strategy," *Harvard Business Review*, October 10, 2011, www.hbr.org.

140 "Target Overwhelmed By Demand for Lilly Pulitzer Collection," *ABC 11 News*, April 11, 2015, http://abc11.com; and Sally Shin, "Target Partners with Designer Jason Wu," *CNBC*, October 7, 2011, www.cnbc.com.

141 Sonya A. Grier and Rohit Deshpandé, "Social Dimensions of Consumer Distinctiveness: The Influence of Social Status on Group Identity and Advertising Persuasion," *Journal of Marketing Research* 38, May 2001, pp. 216–224.

142 Jeremy Cato, "Why the $100,000-and-Up Car Market Is Booming," *Globe and Mail (Toronto)*, March 2, 2015, www.theglobeandmail.com.

143 Yanie Durocher, "Yoox's Luca Martines: Mobile Sales and Niche Labels are Key for E-Commerce in China," *Jing Daily*, April 23, 2015, https://jingdaily.com.

144 See, for example, Yvonne Villarreal, "From Binge-Viewing to Cord-Cutting: Four Takeaways from the 2015 TCA Press Tour," *Los Angeles Times*, August 14, 2015, www.latimes.com.

145 Rich and Jain, "Social Class and Life Cycle as Predictors of Shopping Behavior."

146 Alistair Charlton, "Vertu Signature Touch Review: This Isn't a Phone, It's an £8,500 Experience with Its Own Concierge," *International Business Times*, April 30, 2015, www.ibtimes.co.uk; and Diana Ben-Aaron and Matthew Campbell, "Diamond-Crusted Vertu Phone Defies Slump," *Bloomberg News*, September 29, 2011, www.bloomberg.com.

147 Christine Page, "A History of Conspicuous Consumption," in eds. Floyd Rudmin and Marsha Richins, *Meaning, Measure, and Morality of Materialism* (Provo, Utah: Association for Consumer Research, 1993), pp. 82–87.

148 "Grocery Shoppers Leave Walmart for Dollar Stores," *NPR*, August 19, 2011, www.npr.org.

149 Vikas, Varman, and Belk, "Status, Caste, and Market in a Changing Indian Village."

Psychographics: Values, Personality, and Lifestyles

LEARNING OBJECTIVES

After studying this chapter, you will be able to:

▶ Define and describe values and the value system, identify some of the values that characterize Western cultures, and list the main factors that influence values.

▶ Discuss the personality characteristics most closely related to consumer behavior, and show why these are important from a marketing perspective.

▶ Explain how lifestyles are represented by activities, interests, and opinions.

▶ Describe how psychographic applications in marketing combine values, personality, and lifestyle variables.

INTRODUCTION

The ongoing trend toward product customization illustrates the influence of values, personality, and lifestyles on consumer behavior, all topics discussed in this chapter. Values determine whether consumers care more about individualism or put more emphasis on social groups, for instance. A consumer who values individualism and whose personality leans toward creativity will be more likely than someone disinterested in creativity, to try a website like Zazzle, which sells products customized to individual taste and also markets products such as aprons and travel mugs that can be customized to fit the consumer's lifestyle.[1]

Together, values, personality, and lifestyles constitute the basic components of **psychographics,** the description of consumers based on their psychological and behavioral characteristics (see Exhibit 14.1). Traditionally, psychographics measured consumer lifestyles, but more modern applications also include the consumers' psychological makeup, values, personality, and behavior with respect to specific products (usage patterns, attitudes, and emotions). Marketers use psychographics to gain a more detailed understanding of consumer behavior than they can get from demographic variables like ethnicity, social class, age, gender, and religion.

Exhibit 14.1 ▶ Chapter Overview: Psychographics: Values, Personality, and Lifestyles

Previous chapters demonstrated how membership in certain cultural groups (regional, ethnic, social class, and so on) can affect group behaviors. This chapter examines the effect of these cultural influences on an individual level—namely, on values (deeply held beliefs), personality (consumer traits), and lifestyles (behavioral patterns that are manifestations of values and personality). Each of these factors is useful in understanding consumer behavior; in addition, marketers often combine them to obtain an overall psychographic profile of consumers.

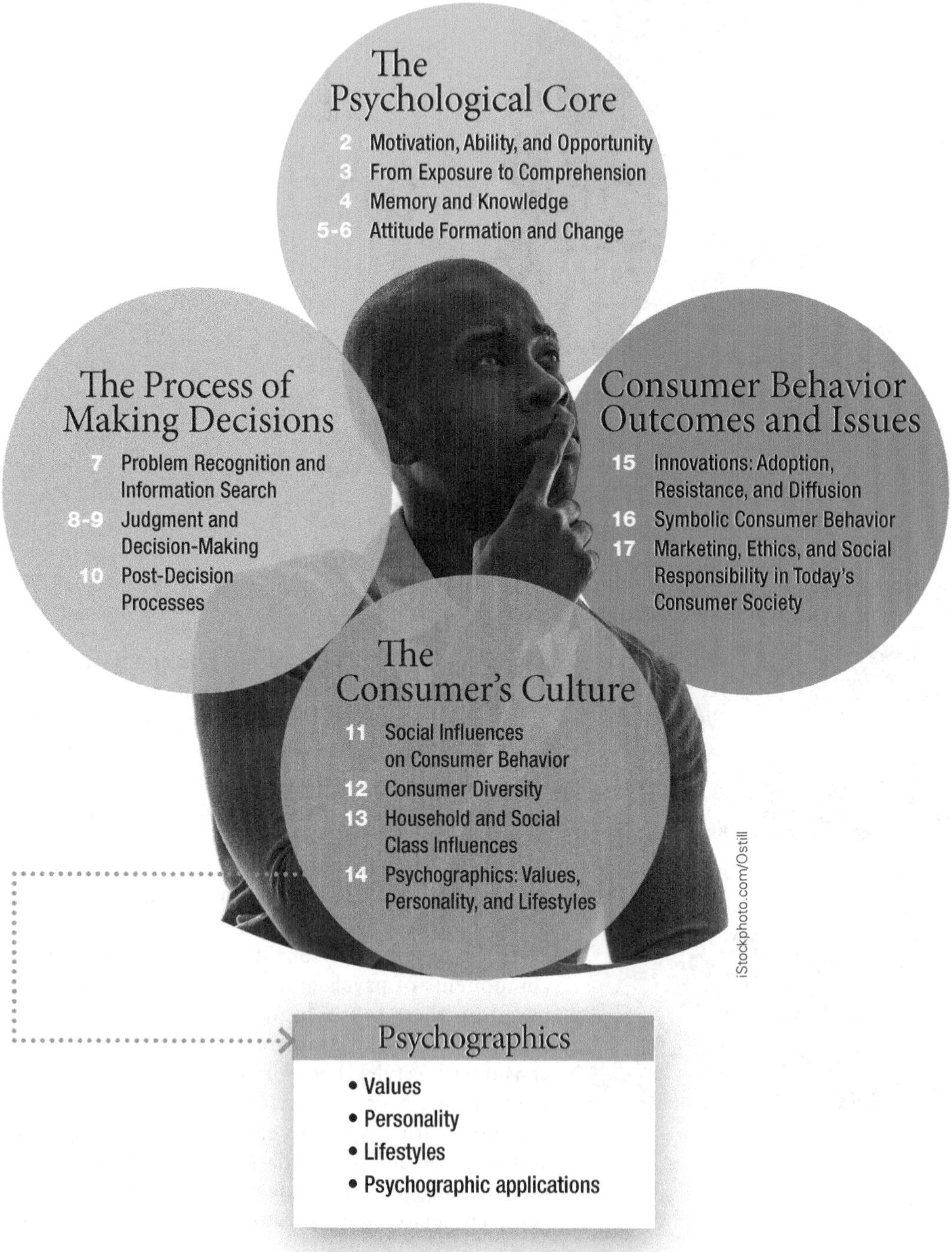

The
Psychological Core
2   Motivation, Ability, and Opportunity
3   From Exposure to Comprehension
4   Memory and Knowledge
5-6   Attitude Formation and Change

The Process of
Making Decisions
7   Problem Recognition and
    Information Search
8-9   Judgment and
    Decision-Making
10   Post-Decision
    Processes

Consumer Behavior Outcomes and Issues
15   Innovations: Adoption,
    Resistance, and Diffusion
16   Symbolic Consumer Behavior
17   Marketing, Ethics, and Social
    Responsibility in Today's
    Consumer Society

The
Consumer's Culture
11   Social Influences
    on Consumer Behavior
12   Consumer Diversity
13   Household and Social
    Class Influences
14   Psychographics: Values,
    Personality, and Lifestyles

iStockphoto.com/Ostill

Psychographics
• Values
• Personality
• Lifestyles
• Psychographic applications

14-1 **Values**

Values are enduring beliefs about abstract outcomes and behaviors that are good or bad.[2] For example, you may believe that it is good to be healthy, keep your family safe, have self-respect, and be free. As enduring beliefs, your values serve as standards that guide your behavior across situations and over time. Thus, how much you value the environment generally determines the extent to which you litter, recycle, buy products made from recycled materials, or drive an electric or hybrid car. Values are so ingrained that people are often not conscious of them and have difficulty describing them.

Our total set of values and their relative importance to us constitute our **value system**. The way that we behave in a given situation is often influenced by how important one value is to us relative to others.[3] For instance, deciding whether to spend Saturday afternoon relaxing with your family or exercising will be determined by the relative importance that you place (this Saturday) on family versus health. You experience a *value conflict* when you do something that is consistent with one value but inconsistent with another equally important value. This dynamic can be illustrated with the example of parents who place equal value on convenience and concern for the environment. They may experience a value conflict when they buy disposable diapers for their babies. Consumers facing such decisions consider not only the product's immediate consumption outcomes but also the product's general effect on society, including how the manufacturer behaves (e.g., toward the environment).[4]

Because values are among the first things that children learn, value systems are often in place by age 10. As discussed in Chapter 11, people learn values through the process of socialization, which results from exposure to reference groups and other sources of influence.[5] You may therefore place a high value on education because your parents went to college and because they and your teachers encouraged this value. Because individuals learn values through exposure to others in institutions and cultures, people within the same group often hold similar values and value systems.

Acculturation is the process by which individuals learn the values and behaviors of a new culture (see Chapter 12). For example, immigrants arriving in the United States learn new values to acculturate to American life, and transmit some of their own values back.[6] Consumers are more likely to adopt the values of a new culture if they view that culture as attractive and as having values similar to their own. Acculturation also happens faster when people in the new culture are cohesive, give a lot of verbal and nonverbal signals about what their values are, and express pride in the values that they hold.[7]

Psychographics
A description of consumers based on their psychological and behavioral characteristics.

Values Enduring beliefs about abstract outcomes and behaviors that are good or bad, such as health, independence, family life, and peace.

Value system Our total set of values and their relative importance.

Global values A person's most enduring, strongly held, and abstract values that hold in many situations.

Terminal values Highly desired end states such as social recognition and pleasure.

Instrumental values The values needed to achieve the desired end states such as ambition and cheerfulness.

Domain-specific values Values that may only apply to a particular area of activities.

14-1a **HOW VALUES CAN BE DESCRIBED**

Values can vary in terms of their specificity. At the broadest, most abstract level are **global values**, which represent the core of an individual's value system. These highly enduring, strongly held, and abstract values apply in many situations. For example, because much of U.S. political philosophy is based on the idea of freedom, that value permeates many domains of our lives. This leads to a belief in the freedom to speak, to go where we want, to dress as we please, and to live where we want.

One of the many ways of characterizing global values is depicted in Exhibit 14.2. This scheme divides global values into seven categories: maturity, security, prosocial behavior (doing good things for others), restrictive conformity, enjoyment, achievement, and self-direction. Note that similar categories are placed close together. Thus, achievement and self-direction reflect a similar orientation toward the individual as a person, whereas prosocial behavior and restrictive conformity reflect values that relate to how an individual should deal with others.

Within the seven domains there are two types of global values: terminal and instrumental. **Terminal values** (shown with an asterisk) are highly desired *end* states, and **instrumental values** (shown with a plus sign) are intermediate values that are needed to achieve these desired end states. For example, the two terminal values in the prosocial category are equality and salvation. The instrumental values of loving, forgiving, helpfulness, honesty, and belief in God help one to achieve these terminal values.[8] Also notice in Exhibit 14.2 that values tend to be polarized: Consumers who place a high value on one set of terminal values place less value on the set on the opposite side of the figure. This situation means that individuals who value security, maturity, and a prosocial orientation might place less value on enjoyment (on the opposite side). Those who emphasize self-direction and achievement would value prosocial behaviors and restrictive conformity less. That is, people cannot value everything to the same extent but have natural orderings from values that are the most to the least important to them.

Global values are different from **domain-specific values**, which are relevant only to particular areas of activity, such as religion, family, or consumption. Materialism is a domain-specific value because it relates to the way that we view the acquisition of material goods. Although they differ, global and domain-specific values can be related in that achievement of domain-specific values (such as health) can be instrumental to the achievement of one or more global values (such as inner harmony or self-respect).

Exhibit 14.2 ▶ Global Values and Value Categories

One scheme for classifying global values identifies seven major categories. Some values are individual oriented (e.g., self-direction, achievement); others are more collective or group oriented (e.g., prosocial, restrictive conformity). Note that categories close to each other are similar; those farther apart are less so. Terminal values (or highly desired end states) are marked with an asterisk (*); instrumental values have a plus sign (+).

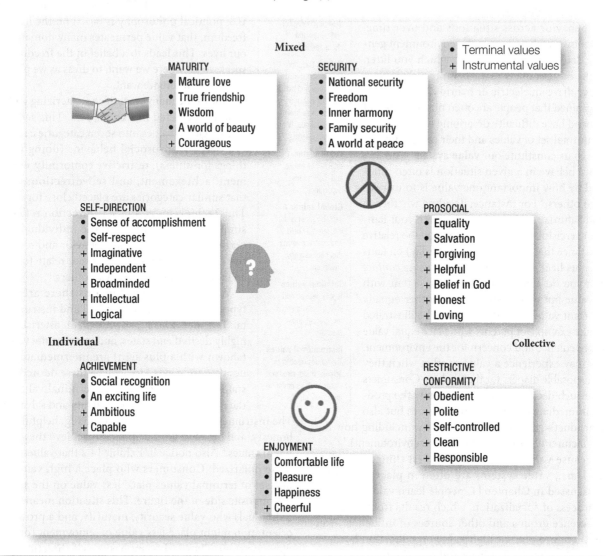

14-1b THE VALUES THAT CHARACTERIZE WESTERN CULTURES

Given that values are an important influence on behavior, marketers need to understand some of the values that characterize consumption in Western societies. These include materialism, the home, work and play, individualism, family and children, health, hedonism, youth, authenticity, the environment, and technology.

Materialism

One value that has become increasingly prevalent in Western cultures is **materialism**.[9] People are materialistic when they place a high importance on acquiring and owning material possessions,

Materialism Placing a high importance on acquiring and owning material goods and money.

and money. Then they seek pleasure in the act of shopping itself, believe that they would be happier than they currently are if only they would have more material possessions, and measure their success in life based upon the amount and type of material possessions they have accumulated. Materialistic individuals tend to value items like cars, jewelry, and boats (see Exhibit 14.3). In contrast, symbolic items such as a mother's wedding gown, family mementos, and photos are more important to those low in materialism.[10]

There is some evidence that materialists are more likely to spend more than they can afford, possibly because they anticipate that buying will do more to increase their happiness than it actually does. That is, the anticipation of a purchase

Exhibit 14.3 ▶ Materialism

Ads for expensive items, like Coach, Prada, and Gucci, target consumers who focus on materialism as a gauge of satisfaction.

boosts positive emotions in the short term, more intensely than the positive feelings consumers have after the purchase.[11] Because materialistic consumers believe that they would be happier if they had a bigger house, a nicer car, or more expensive clothes—and because this boost is often only temporary—they may experience more stress and reduced subjective well-being.[12] In fact, placing too much importance on material possessions and money might detract attention from social endeavors and spending time with others, and this might contribute to feelings of loneliness.[13] Consumers who are materialistic and who also value social endeavors may experience a value conflict ("You cannot have your cake and eat it too"), which further reduces well-being.[14] Materialism need not be universally negative for well-being. Materialistic consumers may work harder to achieve and earn more, which may build self-confidence, and there is evidence that enjoying the act of searching and shopping can improve overall well-being.[15]

Still, during the recent global economic recession, some financially constrained consumers who previously placed a high value on materialism began shifting away from this value. They have been seeking to gain hedonic value from positive experiences, smaller purchases, and other alternatives to materialism.[16] Refocusing on experiences makes sense because the happiness associated with acquired possessions fades quickly, while the positive feelings associated with experiences lingers longer.[17] In addition, financially constrained consumers might shift from spending on experiences such as baseball game tickets, dinner cruises, or Broadway show tickets to more tangible and lasting purchases such as a winter coat, videogame console, or tablet computer. Thus, financial constraints might lead consumers to make less expensive purchases and shift to more tangible, durable purchases.[18]

Brands can benefit by refocusing consumers on the positive experiences that they have with brands themselves. This avoids the regret and dissatisfaction that consumers may feel when they believe they chose the best product but later learn another option could have been better.[19]

Materialism may relate to several of the terminal values noted in Exhibit 14.2. For example, possessions may be instrumental in achieving the higher-order value of social recognition. Or materialism may reflect a high value on accomplishment if people judge self-worth by what they have acquired or by their achievement of a comfortable life. Such values are transmitted between consumers and across generations by the media, the commercial environment of stores, promotions, and so on, and from parents to their children by specific socialization practices.[20] However, materialism may also have more fundamental roots. According to *terror management theory* (see Chapter 13), materialism is rooted, in part, in consumers' drive to relieve anxiety over the inevitability of death by deriving self-esteem and status from acquiring and possessing things.[21] On the other hand, members of communes and certain religious orders have chosen a lifestyle that rejects material possessions, and some people more generally try to live a life of material simplicity.[22]

Regardless, U.S. consumers generally have materialistic tendencies, as do consumers in China, India, and many other nations.[23] In a materialistic society, consumers will be receptive to marketing tactics that facilitate the acquisition of goods, such as phone-in or online orders, special pricing, convenient distribution, and communications that associate acquisition with achievement and status, like ads for a Rolex watch. Consumers also want to protect their possessions, creating opportunities for services such as insurance and security companies that protect consumers against loss, theft, or damage. Still, for consumers who remained materialistic during the recent recession, luxury marketers noticed a shift toward products that conveyed status and wealth more subtly, and away from products emblazoned with high-end brand names or symbols.[24]

Home

Many consumers place a high value on the home and believe in making it as attractive and as comfortable as possible (see Exhibit 14.4). Currently, 64 percent of U.S. residents own their own home.[25] Because the outside world is becoming more complex, exhausting, and dangerous, consumers often consider their home a haven, but they also look for opportunities to connect with others.[26] The home is "command central"—a place to coordinate activities and pool resources before family members enter the outside world. Two-thirds of all U.S. residences have a speedy broadband Internet connection to facilitate the use of technology at home, including TVs, game devices, computers, and smartphones.[27]

Work and Play

Not everyone in every culture shares the same values of work and play. In the United States, consumers are working harder and longer than ever before, partly due to corporate downsizing, an emphasis on productivity, and a drop in real income. In fact, 60 percent of U.S. employees say they work at least part of the time when on vacation—and 35 percent of millennials work every day during vacation.[28]

Image Courtesy of The Advertising Archives

Exhibit 14.4 ▶ Placing a High Value on the Home

As consumers are placing a greater value on the home and are spending more time there, companies are advertising more to appeal to that value.

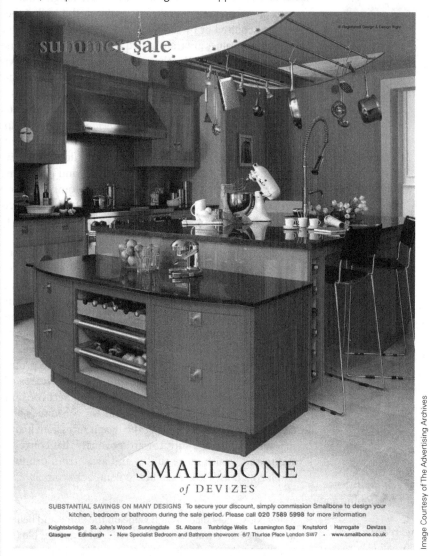

However, consumers increasingly value work for its instrumental function in achieving other values such as a comfortable lifestyle, family security, and accomplishing their life goals. Thus, the idea of valuing work itself and delaying gratification to the exclusion of leisure and pleasure is less characteristic of U.S. consumers than it was a century ago.

When people work longer hours, they value leisure time as much as they value money, and they will pay for services so that they can spend more nonwork time on leisure activities. The online grocery retailer Peapod, owned by the Dutch supermarket company Royal Ahold, has built a multimillion-dollar business catering to U.S. consumers who have better things to do than go to the supermarket to pick out tomatoes and tissues. Already, U.S. consumers spend $24 billion buying groceries online every year. Samsung now markets a refrigerator with an Internet-connected touchscreen door for convenience in ordering groceries from online stores.[29] Many consumers make leisure-time choices with the express purpose of getting completely away from work, a goal that has made exotic resorts and remote destinations more popular for vacations, along with hobbies that can be pursued during a few hours of free time.[30] Themed cruises for lovers of chocolate, needlework, music, tattoo art, and other interests are increasingly popular because they offer the opportunity to get away from home for a few nights or even longer.[31]

Individualism

Western cultures generally place a high value on individualism. The traditional "rugged individualist" consumer values independence and self-reliance, tending to see the individual's needs and rights as a higher priority than the group's needs and rights.[32] Marketers who target men for products such as hunting gear often use advertising imagery and words to make explicit the connection between owning and using these products and expressing rugged individualism. Despite the frontier roots of individualism in America, some consumers worry about violence and other possible negative consequences of unbridled individualism. Also note that marketing appeals that are consistent with the consumer's underlying political beliefs (based on either individualizing or binding moral foundations) can be effective in encouraging sustainability intentions and behavior.[33] Placing a high value on individualism and being independent can also be expressed less ruggedly than by hunting boots, such as when people place a high value on owning their own car rather than using public transportation, value individual sports (golf, biking, running) more than team sports (basketball), or rely on self-medication rather than consulting a physician.

Even in a generally individualistic society, there are *allocentric* consumers who prefer interdependence and social relationships. In contrast, *idiocentric* consumers tend to put more emphasis on individual freedom and assertiveness.

Exhibit 14.5 ▶ Valuing Family and Children

Advertisers target children and family, by focusing on the value of spending quality time together with games or hobbies.

Image Courtesy of The Advertising Archives

Companies are increasing the number of weeks of paid maternity and paternity leave available to employees, and well-known leaders such as Facebook founder Mark Zuckerberg are publicly advocating the advantages of using parental leave to spend time with their new babies.[35]

U.S. parents are generally quite receptive to child-related products, as are families in many cultures (see Exhibit 14.5). LEGO, based in Denmark, is now the world's largest toy company because so many families are buying its plastic interlocking blocks for children who want to build structures straight out of the Harry Potter books and Star Wars movies.[36] Marketers are targeting children with an endless range of cereals, juices, desserts, soft drinks, and other snack products, not to mention games and other playthings. When targeting children, brands in certain product categories face limitations and strict guidelines for marketing. For instance, due to concerns over children's wellness, Taiwan now bans offering free toys with children's fast-food meals.[37]

Health

Many U.S. consumers place a high value on health due to reasons of self-esteem (the way the body looks) and concerns about longevity and survival. The value of health is reflected in the popularity of foods low in fat, calories, carbohydrates, salt, sugar, or cholesterol, as well as foods with special nutritional benefits. Grocery chains such as Dave's Supermarkets in Cleveland now use green "Go! Food" stickers to show shoppers which fruits, vegetables, side dishes, and entrees are low in fat and sodium.[38] Responding to trends in health consciousness, the Wendy's fast-food chain has introduced a gluten-free menu and notifies consumers of all potential allergens in its foods.[39]

Growing concern about pesticides, additives, food-related illnesses, and contaminants has enhanced U.S. demand for organic foods year after year. As Exhibit 14.6 shows, sales of organic nonfood products have also

The behavior of these two types of consumers reflects such differences. Idiocentric consumers in the United States exhibit more interest in sports and adventure, financial satisfaction, gambling, and brand consciousness. Allocentric consumers exhibit more interest in health consciousness, group socializing, reading, and food preparation.[34]

Family and Children

Cultures also differ in the values that they place on their families and children. Parents in Europe and Asia, for example, tend to value education more than U.S. parents do. Among Asian middle-class families, educating children is second in priority only to providing food. American consumers do still place a high value on children.

Exhibit 14.6 ▶ U.S. Sales of Organic Food and Nonfood Products

From 2006 to 2014, annual sales of organic foods and organic nonfood products in the United States rose year after year.

Type of Organic Product	U.S. Sales (in billions of dollars)		
	2006	2010	2014
Organic foods	$17.2	$26.7	$35.9
Organic nonfoods	$0.9	$2.0	$3.2

Source: Organic Trade Association, State of the Organic Industry 2015 and 2011 Organic Industry Survey, www.ota.com.

increased as U.S. consumers seek out natural products in all categories. Moreover, consumers who value health tend to be less price sensitive than consumers who do not hold that value—an important consideration because organic foods sometimes cost more than nonorganic foods.[40]

The emphasis on health has also paved the way for walk-in medical clinics located inside popular stores. CVS has located Minute Clinics in hundreds of its U.S. stores and inside dozens of Target stores, since its acquisition of Target's pharmacy departments.[41] Antismoking campaigns, bans on smoking in public places, and tobacco and alcohol warning labels in many Western nations are consistent with health values. Wellness vacations are increasingly popular, not just for weight loss but also for fitness and other health-related reasons. Health concerns also figure in new home construction, as consumers choose building and decorating materials that are safe and avoid materials that give off fumes or that contain harmful chemicals.[42] Health and fitness apps and gadgets are in high and ever-increasing demand.[43]

Values and behavior can differ, however. Although many Americans talk about a healthy diet, more than 30 percent of U.S. adults are obese, and obesity is also on the increase in Europe and other regions.[44] Some marketers have been criticized for offering excessively large food portions or packages, whereas others have come under fire for the ingredients they put into (or do not take out of) food products (see Chapter 17 for more on this issue). These concerns have resulted in fast-food restaurants posting nutritional information on their websites and on their menus, as well as prompting them to add healthier menu items. McDonald's has downsized the packet of fries that comes with Happy Meals and includes apple slices with each order to encourage children to eat healthier, along with choices like clementines and yogurt.[45]

Hedonism The principle of pleasure seeking.

Hedonism

Consumers are increasingly operating on the principle of **hedonism**, or pleasure seeking, searching for goods, services, and experiences that simply make them feel good, such as luxury cars, good-tasting foods and beverages, digital innovations, and exciting vacations. Boldly flavored foods are selling well, including barbecued meals, gourmet pickles, and spicy sauces such as sriracha, popularized by Huy Fong Foods and now available from Tabasco and other U.S. companies.[46] Furthermore, despite their concerns about health, consumers will not switch to low-fat, low-calorie varieties unless they taste good. In fact, one study found that consumers possess an implicit intuition that healthy foods taste bad.[47]

Youth

Compared with other cultures, the United States has long placed a high value on youth, as evidenced by the wide range of offerings for combating or reducing signs of aging (think of wrinkle creams, hair dye, and hair transplants). Cosmetic surgery is one of the fastest-growing medical specialties for both men and women. Beauty products are riding the wave of this emphasis on youth: For instance, L'Oréal, a global cosmetic brand based in France, is seeing profitable results targeting women in the United States, China, and India who buy hair coloring, makeup, and nail polish. It is increasing its digital marketing to reach these consumers, knowing that they often research beauty products online before purchasing.[48] Marketing communications also indicate the value placed on youth and products that help consumers feel youthful.

Authenticity

People generally value authentic things, either the original article (such as the actual furniture that George Washington owned, which is displayed in his Mount Vernon home) or a faithful reproduction (such as furniture made to look like that of George Washington and shown in a museum or available for purchase).[49] Cheap knockoffs or counterfeits tend to be valued much less. Consumers may feel a close attachment to brands they perceive to be "authentic"—and may drop or even disparage brands that cease to seem authentic.[50] For example, U.S. craft beer brands, brewed locally or in small batches, are often viewed as more authentic than mass-produced beer brands.[51] A service or experience may also be valued for its authenticity. For example, some consumers may perceive the experience of sipping espresso in a small, locally owned coffee shop as a more authentic experience than going to Starbucks, which has a global presence and a consistent in-store brand

Exhibit 14.7 ▶ Valuing the Environment

Environmental concerns are an increasingly important value trend, for consumers and businesses alike.

identity. Sales of major league sports-branded merchandise such as team caps and jerseys are increasing as fans seek out authentic products that mirror what star athletes actually wear during sporting events.[52]

The Environment

Environmental protection has become an important value among U.S. and European consumers, who are interested in conserving natural resources, preventing pollution, and supporting environmentally friendly goods, services, and activities. Businesses can profit from many aspects of environmental values. Procter & Gamble, for example, is demonstrating its green side by replacing petroleum-based packaging and products with sustainable materials, which appeals to consumers who want to buy and use eco-friendly goods.[53] The Nissan LEAF and the Toyota Prius are two car models attracting buyers because they run more cleanly and deliver more fuel efficiency (see Exhibit 14.7). Interest in the environment is fueling the popularity of ecotourism, both domestically and internationally, and increasing demand for hands-on vacations where volunteers help endangered places and species.

Technology

Consumers in many cultures are fascinated by technological advances. More than ever before, consumers in the United States, Japan, and other nations believe that computers, smartphones, digital cameras, and the Internet improve the quality of their lives. As one example, more than 70 percent of Americans with a bank account use a computer or a smartphone for convenience in managing their finances.[54] Nevertheless, technological changes can be so rapid that we have trouble keeping up, resulting in a renewed emphasis on simplicity or at least on managing complexity. Still, products with features that work automatically are popular because they make it easier to use the products properly. Thus, consumers appear to value technology for how it makes their lives easier rather than for its own sake, making technology an instrumental rather than a terminal value. Intel, which makes computer chips for computers and smartphones, is fine-tuning its marketing strategy in line with that insight. "A brand that helps people achieve and offers opportunity has a phenomenal brand attribute," says Intel's director of marketing research.[55]

14-1c WHY VALUES CHANGE

Because societies and their institutions are constantly evolving, value systems are also changing. In addition to the key trends already discussed, U.S. values are moving toward casualness in living, greater sophistication in behavior, a change in sex roles, and the desire to be modern.[56] Although the United States was different from Western Europe 100 years ago, both cultures (and to a certain extent Japan as well) are now becoming more similar in values, even though differences still exist. This increase in value consistency is driven in part by the increase in global communication. Still, value systems are not completely homogenous around the world, which means marketers must dig deep to understand consumer values in each market they are targeting.

14-1d INFLUENCES ON VALUES

How do values differ across groups of consumers? This section explores the ways that culture, ethnicity, social class, and age can influence our values.

Culture and Values

People in different countries are exposed to different cultural experiences, a situation that leads to cross-cultural differences in values. One study found that the three most important values among Brazilians are true friendship, mature love, and happiness, whereas U.S. consumers named family security, world peace, and freedom.[57] Consumers in China place the most importance on values such as preserving the best that one has attained, being sympathetic to others, having self-control, and integrating enjoyment, action, and contemplation.

A study of women in Germany, France, and the United Kingdom found that the value of "having a familiar routine" is most important for German women, but only 10th in importance for the British and 23rd for the French.[58] On the other hand, some values cross national boundaries. Research spanning 28 countries found that an emphasis on materialism is associated with positive attitudes toward global and local products, for example.[59]

In a classic study, Geert Hofstede found that cultures can vary along four main value dimensions:[60]

▪ *Individualism versus collectivism.* The degree to which a culture focuses on the individuals rather than the group.

▪ *Uncertainty avoidance.* The extent to which a culture prefers structured to unstructured situations.

▪ *Masculinity versus femininity.* The extent to which a culture stresses masculine values (as defined by Hofstede) such as assertiveness, success, and competition over feminine values such as quality of life, warm personal relationships, and caring.

▪ *Power distance.* The degree to which a society's members are equal in terms of status.

All cultures can be classified according to these four dimensions. Understanding where a given culture falls may provide insight into cross-cultural differences. For example, research showed that tipping in restaurants is less likely to occur in countries where power distance and uncertainty avoidance are low, feminine values are strong, and individualism is high.[61] Another study found that humorous ad themes are more likely to focus on groups in collectivist societies like Thailand and South Korea and more likely to focus on unequal status relationships in countries with high power distance like the United States and Germany.[62] Finally, studies suggest that U.S. men use everyday consumption to support their view of themselves as men of action, a value in a culture high on masculinity.[63]

Ethnic Identification and Values

Ethnic groups within a larger culture can have some values that differ from those of other ethnic subcultures. As noted in Chapter 12, Hispanic Americans strongly value the family and home; similarly, African American and Asian American consumers place a high value on the extended family.[64] Consumers in different countries may have different ethnic values. For example, consumers in China seek out premium brands for status reasons, and are especially insistent on premium brands for gift-giving situations. Knowing this, Ferrero has profited in China by positioning itself as a premium chocolate brand and marketing boxed assortments appropriate for every gift occasion.[65]

Social Class and Values

Different social classes hold specific values, as discussed in Chapter 13, which in turn affect their acquisition and consumption patterns. As countries in Eastern Europe and Latin American are now embracing market economies, the size of the global middle class is increasing dramatically, along with middle-class values of materialism and a desire for less government control over their lives and greater access to information. Upper–upper-class consumers have the resources and value giving back to society, a characteristic that explains why they become active in social, cultural, and civic causes. These consumers also prize self-expression as reflected in their homes, clothing, cars, and other forms of consumption.[66]

Age and Values

Members of a generation often share similar values that differ from those of other generations. For example, people who grew up during the Great Depression and suffered economic hardship as children may value security over hedonism. Many of that generation therefore view hedonic activities as frivolous and unacceptable. Baby boomers who grew up in the 1960s—a time of political upheaval, self-indulgence, and rebellion—often value hedonism, morality, self-direction, and achievement.[67] Note that it is sometimes very difficult to distinguish values we acquire with age from those we learn from our era. Nevertheless, differences by virtue of age or cohort do exist, and they influence the way that we behave as consumers.

Marketing Implications

Marketers need to understand how consumer values affect consumption patterns, market segmentation, new product development, ad development strategy, and ethics.

Consumption patterns

Consumers usually buy, use, and dispose of products in a manner consistent with their values.[68] Thus, marketers can know more about what consumers like if they understand their values. For example, those who value warm relationships with others are more likely to buy gifts and send cards than those who place less value on relationships.[69] A growing number of consumers place a high value on sustainability, which is why retailers such as Marks & Spencer have created aggressive targets for reducing waste, minimizing energy use, and conserving natural resources. In a six-year period, the U.K. retailer reduced the amount of packaging used in home deliveries by 60 percent and improved the energy efficiency of its U.K. and Irish stores by 36 percent.[70] However, marketers sometimes adopt an ethnocentric perspective, assuming that consumers in other cultures hold values similar to their own, which may not be true.

Market Segmentation

Marketers can identify groups of consumers who have a common set of values that differ from those of other groups, a process called **value segmentation**. Even the market for something as basic as pencils can be segmented in this way. Faber-Castell, for example, which sells two billion pencils every year, offers products for different value segments, including consumers who value quality, creativity, durability, status, and style.[71] Marketers can also use values to understand the attributes that consumers in a particular segment may find important in a product and that may motivate them to choose one brand over another. When buying clothes, individuals who value status might look for attributes like price and luxury, those who value fitting in with the crowd might look for clothing that is trendy, and those who value uniqueness might look for new or nonmainstream styles. For example, uniqueness is a key segmentation variable for Of a Kind, an online retailer owned by Bed, Bath, and Beyond that offers limited-edition fashion clothing by up-and-coming designers.[72] The Body Shop, a beauty retailer owned by L'Oréal, appeals to the segment of millennials who prefer natural ingredients, who seek out ethical businesses, who are environmentally conscious, and who expect value for their money.[73]

> **Value segmentation** The grouping of consumers by common values.

New Product Ideas

Values can also influence consumers' reactions to new and different products. The more a new product is consistent with important consumer values, the greater the likelihood of its success. For example, good-tasting, microwaveable, low-fat, and low-calorie frozen entrees have succeeded in part because these items are consistent with multiple values like hedonism, time, convenience, health, and technology. Yet sometimes balancing conflicting values can be a challenge for marketers with new product ideas. This was the case for the Campbell Soup Company, which tried to balance hedonism and health values. When the firm noticed that sales of its all-natural Select Harvest soups had plateaued, the company increased the amount of salt because consumers "didn't come back," according

to a spokesperson. "The reality is, if it doesn't taste good, people are not going to buy it." Tapping into the trend toward bolder flavors influenced by regional and local tastes, Campbell's is now marketing Select Harvest soups featuring the flavors of New Orleans, New England, and the Southwest.[74]

Ad Development Strategy

Examining the target segment's value profile can help marketers design more appealing ads.[75] Value-laden ads can instigate value-consistent behavior (such as buying a product related to that value), especially when consumers have a positive attitude toward the advertising.[76] The more compatible the ad copy is with consumers' values, the more likely consumers are to become involved in the message and find it relevant. Clearly, marketers must connect product attributes and benefits to consumer values because these represent the end state consumers desire to achieve—the driving force behind their consumption of the product. To stay in tune with its customers, Harley-Davidson, for example, is using crowdsourcing via Facebook to generate advertising ideas and, in the process, learn more about the target audience. A Harley-Davidson official says: "The added benefit is we get insights into what people are thinking about the brand." The company has also crowdsourced new product ideas.[77] Marketers must also avoid communications that conflict with cultural values within one nation or when reaching audiences in multiple nations.

Ethical Considerations

Consumers use values to gauge the appropriateness of others' behaviors—including the behavior of marketers. For example, those who value morality might disapprove of products such as cigarettes and X-rated videos, consumption practices like prostitution and gambling, and sexually explicit ads. In Valencia, Spain, a bus company removed transport ads promoting escort bars and erotic phone services after receiving many complaints about the nature of the ads.[78] Consumers also evaluate marketers' behavior for fairness, ethics, and appropriateness.[79] As Chapter 17 explains, marketers should be aware that consumers may boycott, protest, or complain about practices that seem inconsistent with their values of fairness. As one example, some U.S. liquor stores stopped carrying Russian vodkas to protest Russia's actions in the Crimea.[80]

14-1e HOW VALUES CAN BE MEASURED

To segment the market by values, marketers need some means of identifying consumers' values, gauging their importance, and analyzing changes or trends in values. Unfortunately, values are often hard to measure. One reason is that people do not often think about their values and may therefore have a hard time articulating what is really important to them. Another reason is that people may sometimes feel social pressure to respond to a values questionnaire in a certain way to make themselves look better in the eyes of the researcher. Therefore, marketers usually use less obtrusive or more indirect ways of assessing values.

Inferring Values from the Cultural Milieu

The least obtrusive way to measure values is to make inferences based on a culture's milieu. Advertising has often been used as an indicator of values.[81] Research examining the values portrayed in U.S. print ads between 1900 and 1980 revealed that practicality, the family, modernity, frugality, wisdom, and uniqueness were among the values that appeared most frequently. Researchers can also use ads to uncover cross-cultural differences and track trends in values. One study found that because the People's Republic of China, Taiwan, and Hong Kong are at different levels of economic development and have different political ideologies, different values were reflected in each country's ads.[82] At the time, ads from China focused on utilitarian themes and promised a better life, Hong Kong ads stressed hedonism and an easier life, and Taiwan ads fell between the other two. Now, with the economic changes occurring in China, the trend in local advertising is away from utilitarian themes and toward variety in products and product assurances.

Marketers can infer values just by looking at product names. Product names reflecting values of materialism (Grand Hyatt hotels), hedonism (Obsession perfume), time (Ronzoni Quick Cook Pasta), technology (Microsoft), and convenience (Reddi-wip topping) are common in the United States. Values are also reflected in magazine titles (such as *Money*), book and movie titles, TV programs, the types of people regarded as heroes or heroines, and popular songs. In China, foreign brands are more valued than local brands, so companies like Cadillac and Hilton simply translate their brand names phonetically to emphasize their U.S. origins.[83]

One criticism of cultural milieu as an indicator of values is that researchers never know whether culture reflects values or creates them. In light of this problem, researchers have introduced other methods to measure values.

Means-End Chain Analysis

Marketers can use the **means-end chain analysis** to gain insight into consumers' values by better understanding which attributes they find

Means-end chain analysis A technique that can help to explain how values link to attributes in products and services.

important in products. Armed with this information, researchers can work backward to uncover the values that drive consumer decisions.[84] One way to do this is through *value laddering*, determining the root values related to product attributes that are important to consumers.[85] Suppose a consumer likes light beer because it has fewer calories than regular beer. If a researcher asks why it is important to have a beer with fewer calories, the respondent might say, "Because I don't want to gain weight." If the researcher asks why not, the consumer might respond by saying, "I want to be healthy." If asked why again, the consumer might say, "Because I want to feel good about myself." This example is illustrated in the top line of Exhibit 14.8.

Note that this means-end chain has several potential levels. First, the consumer mentioned an important attribute followed by a concrete benefit that the attribute provides. Then the consumer indicated that this benefit was important because it served some instrumental value. This entire process is called a *means-end chain* because the attribute provides the means to a desired end state or terminal value (in this case, self-esteem).

Looking at Exhibit 14.8, you can also see that a particular attribute can be associated with very different values. For example, first, rather than valuing light beer for its health benefits, some consumers may like light beer because they drink it in a social context that leads to a greater sense of belonging. Second, the same value may be associated with very different products and attributes. Thus, attributes associated with both light beer and rice may appeal equally to the value of belonging. Third, a given attribute may be linked with multiple benefits and /or values, meaning that a consumer might like light beer because it makes her feel healthier and because it facilitates belonging.

Marketers can use means-end chain analysis to identify product attributes that will be consistent with certain values.[86] At one time, consumers generally considered sports cars to be expensive and uncomfortable, and ownership of them took on an aspect of "arrogance and irresponsibility." Then, to be more in line with current values, manufacturers began offering comfortable cars positioned for "people who have friends."[87] The means-end chain model is also useful for developing advertising strategy. By knowing which attributes consumers find important and which values they associate with those attributes, advertisers can design ads that appeal to these values and emphasize related attributes. Note that the ad need not explicitly link a given attribute with a motive, but it can allow consumers to implicitly make the linkage.

Finally, marketers can use the means-end chain to segment global markets and appeal to consumers on the basis of specific benefits and related values.[88] To market yogurt, for instance, a company could identify one segment

Exhibit 14.8 ▶ An Example of Means-End Chains

According to the means-end chain analysis, product and service attributes (e.g., fewer calories) lead to benefits (e.g., I won't gain weight) that reflect instrumental values (e.g., helps make me healthy) and terminal values (e.g., I feel good about myself). This analysis helps marketers identify important values and the attributes associated with them. Can you develop a means-end chain for toothpaste or deodorant?

Product	Attribute	Benefit	Instrumental Value (driving force)	Terminal Value
Light beer (I)	Fewer calories	I won't gain weight.	Helps make me healthy	I feel good about myself (self-esteem).
Light beer (II)	Fewer calories Great taste Light taste	Less filling Enjoyable/relaxing Refreshing	Good times/fun Friendship	Belonging
Rice	Comes in boiling bag	Convenient No messy pan to clean up	Saves time	I can enjoy more time with my family (belonging).

Source: Adapted from Jonathan Gutman, "A Means-End Chain Model Based on Consumer Categorization Processes," *Journal of Marketing*, Spring 1982, pp. 60–72; and Thomas J. Reynolds and John P. Rochan, "Means-End Based Advertising Research: Copy Testing Is Not Strategy Assessment," *Journal of Business Research*, March 1991, pp. 131–142.

that values health and reach this segment by focusing on product attributes such as low fat and could identify a second segment that values enjoyment and reach this segment through attributes such as fruit ingredients (see Exhibit 14.9).

Value Questionnaires

Marketers can directly assess values by using questionnaires. Some types of questionnaires, such as the material values scale, focus only on specific aspects of consumer behavior.[89] Others cover a range of values. One of the best known of these is the **Rokeach Value Survey (RVS)**. This questionnaire asks consumers about the importance that they attach to the 19 instrumental values and 18 terminal values identified in Exhibit 14.2. This questionnaire is standardized, and everyone responds to the same set of items, a procedure that helps researchers identify the specific values that are most important to a given group of consumers, determine whether values are changing over time, and learn whether values differ for various groups of consumers. One drawback is that some values measured by the RVS are less relevant to consumer behavior (such as salvation, forgiving, and being obedient). Some researchers have therefore recommended using a shortened form of the RVS containing only the values most relevant to a consumer context.[90]

Others have advocated the use of the **List of Values (LOV)**. Consumers are presented with nine primary values

Rokeach Value Survey (RVS) A survey that measures instrumental and terminal values.

List of Values (LOV) A survey instrument that efficiently measures nine principal values driving consumer behavior.

New Sveltesse yogurt. Deliciously creamy tasting and rich in fruit

Exhibit 14.9 ▶ Products' Benefits and Values

Marketers are finding new ways to appeal to both a products' benefits (such as 0% fat) and its valuable attributes (100% pleasure).

and asked either to identify the two most important or to rank all nine values by importance. The nine values are (1) self-respect, (2) warm relationships with others, (3) sense of accomplishment, (4) self-fulfillment, (5) fun and enjoyment in life, (6) excitement, (7) sense of belonging, (8) being well respected, and (9) security.[91] The first six are internal values because they derive from the individual; the others are external values. The values can also be described in terms of whether they are fulfilled through interpersonal relationships (warm relationships with others, sense of belonging), personal factors (self-respect, being well respected, self-fulfillment), or nonpersonal things (sense of accomplishment, fun, security, and excitement).

In one study, the LOV predicted consumers' responses to statements that describe their self-reported consumption characteristics (e.g., "I am a spender, not a saver"), their actual consumption behaviors (the frequency with which they watch movies or the news, read certain magazines, and engage in activities like playing tennis), and their marketplace beliefs ("I believe the consumer movement has caused prices to increase"). Compared with the RVS, the LOV is a better predictor of consumer behavior, is shorter, and is easier to administer. Finally, the LOV is useful for identifying segments of consumers with similar value systems.[92]

14-2 Personality

Although individuals with comparable backgrounds tend to hold similar values, it is important to remember that people do not always act the same way even when they hold the same values. In listening to a sales pitch, one consumer may state demurely that she finds the product interesting but is not ready to make up her mind right now. Another might act more assertively, interrupting the salesperson midway through his pitch to indicate that she has no interest whatsoever in the product. Therefore, consumers vary in terms of their personality or the way in which they respond to a particular situation.

Personality consists of the distinctive patterns of behaviors, tendencies, qualities, or personal dispositions that make one individual different from another and lead to a consistent response to environmental stimuli. These patterns are internal characteristics that we are born with or that result from the way we have been raised. The concept of personality helps us understand why people behave differently in different situations.

> **Personality** General, enduring differences between people in terms of behavior patterns, feeling, and thinking.

14-2a RESEARCH APPROACHES TO PERSONALITY

The social sciences provide various approaches to studying personality. This section reviews five approaches that consumer researchers apply: psychoanalytic approaches,

trait theories, phenomenological approaches, social-psychological theories, and behavioral approaches.

Psychoanalytic Approaches

According to psychoanalytic theories, personality arises from a set of dynamic, unconscious internal struggles within the mind.[93] The psychoanalyst Sigmund Freud proposed that we pass through several developmental stages in forming our personalities. In the first stage, the oral stage, the infant is entirely dependent on others for need satisfaction and receives oral gratification from sucking, eating, and biting. At the anal stage, the child is confronted with the problem of toilet training. Then in the phallic stage, the youth becomes aware of his or her genitals and must deal with desires for the opposite-sex parent.

Freud believed that the failure to resolve the conflicts from each stage could influence one's personality. For example, the individual who received insufficient oral stimulation as an infant may reveal this crisis in adulthood through oral-stimulation activities like gum chewing, smoking, and overeating or by distrusting others' motives (including those of marketers). At the anal stage, an individual whose toilet training was too restrictive may become obsessed with control and be overly orderly, stubborn, or stingy, resulting in neatly organized closets and records, list making, and excessive saving or collecting. These individuals may also engage in extensive information search and deliberation when making decisions. On the other hand, those whose training was overly lenient may become messy, disorganized adults.

Although some of Freud's theories have been questioned, one key point is that the subconscious can influence behavior. Another key point is that natural and sometimes unconscious impulses to act (which he termed the "id"), are under the influence of more conscious, rational ("ego") and normative considerations ("superego"), and that people and situations differ in the strength of these latter forces. Some businesses, advertising agencies, and consulting firms conduct research to delve deep into consumers' psyches and uncover subconscious reasons why they buy a particular product.[94] Ford Motor Company produces an annual report about the top 10 trends that will affect consumer behavior in the near future, with an eye toward understanding how consumers are consuming media and making vehicle purchases.[95]

Trait Theories

Trait theorists propose that personality is composed of a set of characteristics that describe and differentiate individuals.[96] For example, people might be described as aggressive, easygoing, quiet, moody, shy, or rigid. Psychologist Carl Jung developed one of the most basic trait theory schemes, suggesting that individuals could be categorized according to their levels of introversion and extroversion.[97] Introverts are shy, prefer to be alone, and are anxious in the presence of others. They tend to avoid social channels and may not find out about new products from others. They are also less motivated by social pressure and more likely to do things that please themselves. In contrast, extroverts are outgoing, sociable, and typically conventional.

There is much evidence that five major personality traits tend to account for the most variance in personality (the "Big 5"): agreeableness, conscientiousness, emotional stability, openness, and extraversion.[98] Recent work has also found that the trait of stability, or consistency in behavior, when combined with the introversion/extroversion dimension, can be used as a basis to represent various personality types (see Exhibit 14.10). For example, a person who is reliable tends to be high on both introversion and stability. In contrast, a passive person is introverted but neither highly stable nor highly

Locus of control
People's tendency to attribute the cause of events to the self (internal) or not the self (external, such as others, the situation, or luck).

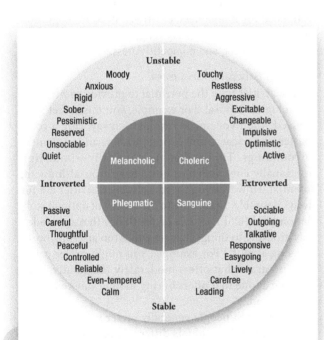

Exhibit 14.10 ▶ A Trait Conception of Personality Types

Consumers can be classified according to whether they have introverted or extroverted personality traits. These traits can lead to the identification of various personality types (e.g., moody, peaceful, lively, and aggressive). Interestingly, these traits can be collected into four major groups that correspond to the basic temperaments identified by the ancient Greek physician Hippocrates centuries ago. How would you classify your personality according to this scheme?

Source: Adapted from Hans Eysenck and S. Rachman, The Causes and Cures of Neurosis: An Introduction to Modern Behavior Therapy Based on Learning Theory and Principles of Conditioning (San Diego, Calif.: Knapp, 1965, p. 16). Reprinted by permission from EdITS.

unstable. One interesting feature about this scheme is that the personality types identified by these two dimensions match the four temperaments identified by the Greek physician Hippocrates centuries ago—for example, a phlegmatic person is introverted and stable; a melancholic person is introverted and unstable.

Phenomenological Approaches

Phenomenological approaches propose that personality is largely shaped by an individual's interpretations of life events.[99] For example, according to this approach, depression is caused by the way that someone interprets key events and the nature of that interpretation rather than by internal conflicts or traits.

A key concept of the phenomenological approaches is **locus of control**, or people's interpretations of why specific things happen, attributing the cause of events to the self or to others.[100] Individuals with an internal locus of control attribute more responsibility to themselves for good or bad outcomes, so they might blame themselves or see themselves as having been careless when a product fails. This fits in with attribution theory, which was introduced in Chapter 10. Externally controlled individuals place responsibility on other people, events, or places rather than on themselves. Thus, they might attribute product failure to faulty manufacturing or poor packaging.

Also, when consumers have a strong desire for control yet a lower perceived ability to exert it, they will show more preference for "lucky" products they associate with positive outcomes, such as a team winning a sporting event when fans are wearing the team's colors (or drinking a certain soft drink).[101] Consuming the lucky product evokes an illusion of control in this situation. Locus of control extends to how people feel about their fate. If consumers think they can change their fate, even in a small way, they become more indulgent when they think an unfavorable day is ahead of them.[102]

Locus of control can heavily influence consumers' perceptions of satisfaction in a consumption experience and determine how the consumer feels. To illustrate, consumers who blame themselves for product failure might feel shame, whereas those who blame product failure on an external source might feel anger and irritation. In addition, someone's life theme or goals (concerns that we address in our everyday lives) can greatly influence the meanings that he or she derives from ads.[103] As a result, a person who is more concerned with family might interpret an ad differently than someone who is more concerned with his or her private self. Finally, some consumers have a tendency to see time in terms of human characteristics (think of the character of "Father Time" and the idea of "killing time"). These consumers will have difficulty summoning the will to wait for an acquisition or a consumption experience, especially if they feel powerless.[104]

Social-Psychological Theories

Another group of theories focuses on social rather than on more biological explanations of personality, proposing that individuals act in social situations to meet their needs. The researcher Karen Horney, for instance, believed that behavior can be characterized by three major orientations.[105] *Compliant* individuals are dependent on others and are humble, trusting, and tied to a group. *Aggressive* individuals need power, move against others, and are outgoing, assertive, self-confident, and tough-minded. *Detached* individuals are independent and self-sufficient but suspicious and introverted. These three orientations are measured by the CAD scale.[106] One study found that assertiveness and aggressiveness were significantly related to styles of interaction with marketing institutions.[107] In particular, highly assertive and aggressive people were likely to perceive complaining as acceptable and to enjoy doing it.

In social-psychological theory, researchers distinguish between state-oriented consumers ("thinkers"), who are more likely to rely on subjective norms to guide their behavior, and action-oriented consumers ("doers"), whose behavior is based more on their own attitudes.[108] Consumers also vary in terms of their attention to information that helps them compare themselves with others (social comparison information). Individuals high on this factor are more sensitive to normative pressure than are those low on this factor.

Behavioral Approaches

In contrast to other explanations of personality, behavioral approaches propose that differences in personality are more a function of how individuals have been rewarded or punished in the past. According to behavioral approaches, individuals are more likely to have traits or engage in behaviors for which they have been rewarded: positive reinforcement. They are less likely to maintain characteristics and behaviors for which they have been punished: negative reinforcement.[109] Thus, an individual might be extroverted because parents, caretakers, and other individuals rewarded outgoing behaviors and punished introverted behaviors. Likewise, a consumer might prefer colorful clothing if he or she previously received positive reinforcement for wearing it. Note that these behavioral approaches to personality involve the principles of operant conditioning discussed in Chapter 9.

14-2b DETERMINING WHETHER PERSONALITY CHARACTERISTICS AFFECT CONSUMER BEHAVIOR

Much of the consumer-related personality research has followed the trait approach, trying to identify specific personality traits that explain differences in consumers' purchase, use, and disposition behavior. Personality traits are not always a strong predictor of specific consumer behaviors.[110] This is not surprising, because traits cover broad domains of consumer behavior, and are not specific to a single behavior. Therefore, general personality traits tend to influence many behaviors a little bit rather than a few specific behaviors a lot. Still, traits may sometimes have a stronger influence on specific consumer behaviors.

First, the association between personality and consumer behavior may be stronger for some types of consumer behavior than for others. For example, personality traits may help marketers to understand why some people are more susceptible to persuasion, particularly like a certain ad, or engage in more information processing. Likewise, our choice of offerings that involve subjective or hedonic features such as looks, style, and aesthetics may be more strongly related to personality. A good example is the selection of a greeting card, which represents a personal message and therefore is an extension of the sender's personality.

Second, certain types of personality traits may be more related to consumer behavior than others.[111] As described below, these include optimal stimulation level, dogmatism, need for uniqueness, creativity, need for cognition, susceptibility to influence, frugality, self-monitoring, national character, and competitiveness.

Optimal Stimulation Level

Some activities have the potential to provide some sort of physiological arousal. For example, you might feel more aroused when you speed on the highway, ride a roller coaster, see a scary movie, or go to new and unfamiliar surroundings. Things that are physically stimulating, emotionally energizing, or novel have arousal-inducing potential. However, highly stimulating activities are not always desirable. According to the theory of optimal stimulation level (OSL), people prefer things that are moderately arousing to things that are either too arousing or not arousing at all.[112] For example, you might prefer eating at a restaurant that offers moderately imaginative food to eating at one that offers boring food or one that offers unusual food.

Even though people generally prefer moderate levels of stimulation, individuals differ in the level of arousal they regard as moderate and optimal. Individuals with a low optimal stimulation level tend to prefer less arousing activities because they want to avoid going over the edge. In contrast, individuals with a high optimal stimulation level are more likely to seek activities that are very exciting, novel, complex, and different. Consumers with a high need for stimulation might enjoy activities like skydiving, gambling, and river rafting.[113] They are also more likely to be innovative and creative.

Individuals with high and low needs for stimulation also differ in the way in which they approach the marketplace. Those with high stimulation needs tend to be the first to buy new products, to seek information about them, and to engage in variety seeking (buying something different).[114] They are more curious about the ads they see but may also be easily bored by them. These consumers are more likely to buy products associated with greater risk, enjoy shopping in malls with many stores and products, and prefer offerings that deviate from established consumption practices.

Dogmatism

Consumers can vary in terms of being open- or closed-minded. **Dogmatism** refers to an individual's tendency to be resistant to change and new ideas. Dogmatic, or closed-minded, consumers are relatively resistant to new products, new promotions, and new ads. For example, one study found that Nigerian consumers' acceptance of new products depended on how dogmatic the consumers were.

Need for Uniqueness

Consumers who pursue a unique position and experiences through the purchase, use, and disposition of goods and services display a **need for uniqueness (NFU)**.[115] Need for uniqueness covers three behavioral dimensions: creative choice counter-conformity (the consumer's choice reflects social distinctiveness yet is one that others will approve of), unpopular choice counter-conformity (choosing products and brands that do not conform to establish distinctiveness despite possible social disapproval), and avoidance of similarity (losing interest in possessions that become commonplace to avoid the norm and hence reestablish distinctiveness). In one study, consumers with a high need for uniqueness who were asked to explain their decisions made unconventional choices, showing that they were aware that their choices and reasoning were outside the norm.[116] Thus, consumers with a high need for uniqueness may avoid well-known global brands in favor of small, local brands.[117] They may also dispose of clothing that has become too popular in favor of emerging fashion trends, seek out handcrafted or personalized items, and customize products to their own specifications, as described in this chapter's opening example.

Creativity

In terms of consumer behavior, *creativity* means "a departure from conventional consumption practice in a novel and functional way."[118] For instance, if confronted with an everyday problem such as lacking the right ingredients to make dinner, a consumer high in creativity would locate substitutes. This solution would enable the consumer to complete the activity in a novel yet practical way. Such creativity enhances the consumer's mood as well. To illustrate, the Pillsbury website and Facebook pages encourage creativity with videos demonstrating cooking techniques, recipes organized by ingredient and occasion, and forums for consumers to exchange ideas about menus,

> **Dogmatism** A tendency to be resistant to change or new ideas.
>
> **Need for uniqueness (NFU)** The desire for a unique position and experiences through the purchase, use, and disposition of products and services.
>
> **Need for cognition (NFC)** A trait that describes how much people like to think.

entertaining, and more.[119] Various environmental factors can also affect how creative we are. For example, we tend to be more creative when exposed to images that suggest creativity (like lightbulbs going on).[120]

Need for Cognition

Consumers who enjoy thinking extensively about things like products, attributes, and benefits are high in the **need for cognition (NFC)**.[121] Those with a low need for cognition do not like to think and prefer to take shortcuts or to rely on their feelings. Interestingly, need for cognition is associated with education, but not strongly. Thus, one can have a low education, e.g., due to economic circumstance, but be high in need for cognition. Consumers with different needs for cognition differ in terms of their product interests, information search, and reaction to different ad campaigns. Specifically, those with a high need for cognition enjoy products and experiences that carry a serious learning and mastery component such as chess, educational games, and TV shows like *Jeopardy*. They derive satisfaction from searching for and discovering new product features and react positively to long, technically sophisticated ads with details about products or services. They might also scrutinize messages more carefully than other consumers do, considering the credibility or merits of the message.[122] Consumers with a low need for cognition, on the other hand, react more positively to short messages using attractive models, humor, or other cues. These individuals tend to make decisions that involve little thinking.

Susceptibility to Influence

Consumers also vary in their susceptibility to persuasion attempts, especially those who are interpersonal or face to face. Some consumers have a greater desire to enhance their image as observed by others and are therefore willing to be influenced or guided by them.[123] Consumers with lower social and information processing confidence tend to be more influenced by ads than are those with higher self-confidence.

Frugality

Frugality is the degree to which consumers take a disciplined approach to short-term acquisitions and are resourceful in using products and services to achieve longer-term goals. Consumers who are high on frugality will, for example, pack leftovers for lunch at work (rather than buy takeout food or eat in a restaurant). Such consumers are less materialistic, less susceptible to the influence of others, and more conscious of price and value.[124] Sometimes governments or firms will actively encourage frugality to conserve scarce resources such as electric power.[125] During the recent global economic recession, with high unemployment and economic uncertainty an ongoing concern, many consumers embraced a deeper

Exhibit 14.11 ▶ Appealing to Frugality

Some consumers possess the value of frugality, especially in tough economic times, so some ads stress these saving money values.

CUT YOUR HEATING AND COOLING COSTS UP TO 80%.

Cut your energy bills. ClimateMaster geothermal systems tap the constant temperature of the earth to provide heating, cooling, and hot water. Your home stays comfortable year-round while trimming your energy use by up to 80%. And now with new federal tax credits, you will save an additional 30% on the total installation. Best of all, ClimateMaster systems are not only a good investment, they are a cleaner choice for the environment. To learn more about how the geothermal technology leader can help you cut your energy bills, visit climatemaster.com or call 877-436-6263 today.

CLIMATEMASTER®
Geothermal Heat Pump Systems
An LSB Industries, Inc. Company (NYSE: LXU)

sense of frugality, dramatically changing their saving and spending habits.[126] These consumers switched to lower-priced, private-label brands; postponed nonessential purchases; limited their use of credit; and actively comparison shopped to stretch their budgets (see Exhibit 14.11). However, it is unclear yet whether this embrace of frugality will endure as a long-term trait once the economy has recovered.

> **National character**
> The personality of a country.

Self-Monitoring

Individuals differ in the degree to which they look to others for cues on how to behave. High self-monitors are typically sensitive to the desires and influences of others as guides to behavior, and low self-monitors are guided more by their own preferences and desires and are less influenced by normative expectations.[127] High and low self-monitors also differ in their responsiveness to advertising appeals. High self-monitors are more responsive to image-oriented ads and more willing to try and pay more for products advertised with an image consistent with high self-monitoring. In contrast, low self-monitors are generally more responsive to ads that make a quality claim and are more willing to try these products and pay extra for them. Marketers can prime awareness of self-monitoring through techniques such as calling the consumer by name. In turn, this higher awareness can encourage the consumer to make decisions that better fit their personal preferences and therefore improve satisfaction.[128] These consumers are also less likely to accept compromise options (see Chapter 8) and variety in their choice set. Yet studies also show that consumers do not always accept information they learn about themselves—which means they may not apply their knowledge of themselves to make more informed decisions.[129]

National Character

Personality traits can sometimes be used to stereotype people of a particular country as having a **national character**. These characterizations represent only very broad generalizations about a particular country; obviously, individuals vary a great deal. To illustrate, French and Italian people are often characterized as emotional and romantic; the British as more reserved; and German, French, and Americans have been characterized as more assertive than their British, Russian, or Italian counterparts.

U.S. consumers are considered more impulsive, risk-oriented, and self-confident than Canadians, who are stereotyped as more cautious, restrained, and reserved. Researchers have characterized how countries differ in their needs for achievement, levels of introversion and extroversion, perceptions of human nature, and flexibility.[130] Marketers must consider how differences in national character may influence reactions to advertising and other communications. For example, when German retailer Media Markt ran ads in Turkey depicting human bodies with animal heads—intended to suggest that only animals would be foolish enough to overpay for certain products—outraged consumers forced the removal of the ads.[131]

Competitiveness

The personality trait of competitiveness has been associated with the desire to outdo others through conspicuous consumption of material items such as the newest electronic gadgets. It also plays a role in consumers' wanting to do better than others in a direct way (e.g., through a sport or by gambling) or an indirect way (such as when watching a sporting event).[132] Marketers who want to appeal to competitive consumers often use messages emphasizing the opportunity to be among the first to try or buy a new product or service. Some marketers appeal to competitiveness by downplaying explicit branding on products in favor of subtle status cues that can be recognized by consumers who are "in the know."[133] Note that when lower-status consumers focus on conspicuous consumption and are aware of their potential for gains relative to higher-status consumers, this creates a competitive mindset and stimulates them to increase consumption.[134]

Marketing Implications

Because some personality traits may be related to consumption behavior, marketers can develop offerings and communications that appeal to various personality types. International marketing efforts can make use of known differences between countries in national culture and personality. For example, ads targeting compliant or extremely self-monitoring consumers can focus on the approval of others, whereas ads and promotions appealing to high optimal stimulation-level consumers or those with a strong need for uniqueness might focus on trying something new and different.

Targeting consumers who enjoy stimulation, Ben & Jerry's ice cream launched a Facebook app in Europe that combines a "personality test" based on ice cream preferences with an invitation to vote for new ice cream flavors.[135] Appealing to consumers who are competitive, the Los Angeles Kings hockey team added a game to its website so that visitors get points for activities such as posting messages about the Kings to social media sites. As they earn points, winners unlock exclusive rewards such as personalized messages from team members. The team also targets consumers who appreciate edgy communications with snarky tweets that sometimes anger fans of opposing teams. "If you are not taking risks, you are really going to fall behind," explains the team's manager of social media.[136]

14-3 Lifestyles

> **Lifestyles** People's patterns of behavior.
>
> **Activities, interests, and opinions (AIOs)** The three components of lifestyles.

Lifestyles relate closely to consumers' values and personality. Whereas values and personality represent internal states or characteristics, **lifestyles** are manifestations or actual patterns of behavior. In particular, they are represented by a consumer's **activities, interests, and opinions (AIOs)**, as illustrated in Exhibit 14.12.

14-3a LIFESTYLE AND BEHAVIOR PATTERNS

What people do in their spare time is often a good indicator of their lifestyle. One consumer might like outdoor activities such as skiing, whereas another might prefer to surf the Web. Political opinions, ideology, and involvement can also affect acquisition, consumption, and disposition decisions.[137] Consumers who engage in different activities and have differing opinions and interests may in fact represent distinct lifestyle segments for marketers. For instance, one lifestyle segment consists of people with an affinity for *nostalgia*, involving a desire for things of the past.[138] This segment clearly represents a key market for old movies, books, and antiques, but also for products that were popular in a consumer's childhood. As another example, consumers who participate in extreme sports such as snowmobiling are a key market for companies that sell related equipment. A common behavior pattern revolves around following a favorite TV series and forming an informal brand community based on discussions of the series, its characters, and various plot developments. The end of that series can bring about the end of the consumption sociality built around that particular brand.[139]

Lifestyle research can help marketers understand how a product fits into consumers' general behavior patterns. For example, the Slow Food movement, which began in Italy, has spread around the world and now influences the lifestyle of many consumers, including how they buy foods and beverages and their attitudes toward cooking and eating with others. Slow Food enthusiasts favor locally grown ingredients, enjoy the process of cooking, and welcome the social experience of sharing a meal with friends and family.[140]

Importantly, consumers in different countries may have characteristic lifestyles. For instance, compared with U.S. women, Japanese women are more home focused, less price sensitive, and less likely to drive.[141] Given these preferences, Japanese women would probably spend more time than U.S. women would preparing meals at home and would therefore pay more for products that enhance meal quality. Popular lifestyle activities among Russian consumers include going to the movies and theater and participating in sports like soccer, ice hockey, and figure skating.[142]

Exhibit 14.12 ▶ Activities, Interests, and Opinions

Lifestyles are represented by consumers' activities, interests, and opinions. Here are some major examples of each category. Note that these lifestyles provide a more detailed profile of consumers than their demographics do (the last column).

Activities	Interests	Opinions	Demographics
Work	Family	Themselves	Age
Hobbies	Home	Social issues	Education
Social events	Job	Politics	Income
Vacations	Community	Business	Occupation
Entertainment	Recreation	Education	Family size
Club membership	Fashion	Economics	Dwelling
Community	Food	Products	Geography
Shopping	Media	Culture	City size
Sports	Achievements	Future	Life cycle stage

Source: Joseph T. Plummer, "The Concept and Application of Life Style Segmentation," *Journal of Marketing*, January 1974, pp. 33–37. Reprinted with permission.

14-3b VOLUNTARY SIMPLICITY

As defined in the previous chapter, *voluntary simplicity* means consciously limiting acquisition and consumption for a less materialistic, more eco-friendly lifestyle. Voluntary simplicity is not the same as frugality. Whereas frugality is a personality trait reflecting disciplined spending and consumption of goods and services, voluntary simplicity is a lifestyle choice for consumers who do not want the accumulation of possessions to be the focus of their lives. Instead, those who follow this lifestyle will borrow items when needed, buy used or share products with family and friends, pay in cash to avoid debt, and reuse items (such as coffee mugs) rather than buying disposable products.[143] This shows how more general traits such as frugality may be associated with a lifestyle of voluntary simplicity, and to the specific activities, interests, and opinions that are part of the lifestyle.

Marketing Implications

Consumer lifestyles can have important implications for market segmentation, communication, and new product ideas.

Segmentation and Targeting

Marketers can make use of information about lifestyles to identify consumer segments for specific offerings. Services such as day-care centers and housecleaning services save time and provide convenience, two benefits that particularly appeal to dual-career couples, working women, and other consumers with busy lifestyles.[144] For example, a group of Dutch firms that export flowering bulbs to U.S. garden centers is targeting busy gardening hobbyists with a campaign that explains how easy it is to plant and grow blooms from bulbs.[145]

As another example, Ford is using lifestyles to target busy, eco-minded college students who are the new car buyers of tomorrow (see Exhibit 14.13). Ford is supplying Zipcar—the by-the-hour rental firm—with Ford Focus and Escape vehicles for rent on college campuses, and subsidizing students' rental fees. "This program enables today's new drivers to experience our latest fuel-efficient vehicles, while helping them reduce their cost of living and help relieve [traffic] congestion on campus," explains the company's executive chairman. In London, Ford is showcasing its brand by renting vehicles by the hour via the company's GoDrive app, a way to appeal to consumers who don't currently own a car.[146]

Exhibit 14.13 ▶ Segmenting and Targeting

Zipcar segments and targets eco-minded and frugal college students, who can rent their fuel-efficient vehicles, thereby saving money and protecting the environment.

Kelvin Ma/Bloomberg/Getty Images

Marketers also monitor lifestyle changes to identify new opportunities.[147] For instance, time-pressured consumers all over the world are now seeking services at all hours. Metro Bank, based in London, offers extended banking hours every day of the week, so that consumers can complete transactions at their convenience. A new bank in London, Atom Bank, plans access via smartphone or tablet computer only, with facial recognition or voice recognition log-on rather than conventional password entry to access accounts. The idea is to strengthen security and reduce the time and energy consumers exert trying to remember and use passwords, a benefit for busy consumers who like mobile devices.[148]

Communications

Marketers can design ad messages and promotions to appeal to certain lifestyles, featuring products in the context of desired lifestyles.[149] Using the Internet, social media, and mobile marketing can be very targeted ways to communicate with a variety of lifestyle segments. This is why sites like mycoke.com and others regularly post new features such as music and games on the Web, on Facebook pages, on YouTube, and via Twitter links to keep brand fans returning again and again. The maker of Flip-Pal, a small, portable scanning device, advertises extensively on genealogy blogs to reach consumers who are interested in researching their family trees and need an easy way to digitize photos and documents.

New Product Ideas

Often marketers can develop new product and service ideas by uncovering unfulfilled needs of certain lifestyle segments. For example, Japan's NTT DOCOMO recognized that many of its customers are avid travelers who like to try different foods when out of the country. In response to this need, the company developed a smartphone app that can instantly translate any restaurant menu written in Chinese or English to Japanese. The telecom company also offers an iPhone app that will translate spoken words or sentences from English, Chinese, Korean, Thai, or Indonesian into Japanese instantly, another way to help its customers who travel.[150]

14-4 Psychographics: Combining Values, Personality, And Lifestyles

This chapter opened by observing that psychographic research today combines values, personality, and lifestyle variables. To illustrate this key point, this last section provides a brief description of several psychographic applications in marketing.

14-4a VALS™

One of the most widely known psychographic tools is *VALS*, formerly known as *Values and Lifestyles*, and is owned by Strategic Business Insights. VALS analyzes the behavior of U.S. consumers to create segments based on two factors. The first factor is resources, including self-confidence, innovativeness, intellectualism, novelty seeking, impulsiveness, leadership, energy level, and vanity. The second factor is primary motivation. Consumers motivated by ideals are guided by intellectual aspects rather than by feelings or other people's opinions. Those who are motivated by achievement tend to buy goods and services that reflect their success for others to see. And those who are motivated by self-expression desire social or physical action, variety, activity, and personal challenge.[151]

Combining the resource and motivation variables plus key demographics such as income, age, and education, VALS has identified eight consumer segments (see Exhibit 14.14). At the low end of the resource hierarchy are the survivors, who have the lowest incomes. Their focus is on meeting basic day-to-day needs; they are careful with their money, not concerned with wearing trendy clothing, and are brand-loyal. Believers have low resources and are motivated by ideals, seeking inspiration from faith and spirituality. Because they do not change easily, believers tend to prefer familiar, established products and brands. The other group motivated by ideals is the thinkers, who are mature and well educated and who actively conduct information searches when planning purchases. Thinkers have more resources than believers and are value oriented in their consumption practices, valuing durability over style.

The two achievement-oriented segments are the strivers (who have limited discretionary income yet strive to emulate more successful people) and achievers (who have higher resources, are focused on work and families, and value technology that improves productivity). In the self-expression segment, makers value self-sufficiency, have a high desire to own land, and are interested in the outdoors and in automotive products and accessories. Experiencers like being the first to participate in a trend (and the first to leave it behind), seek out stimulation, and are highly sociable. Innovators have the greatest resource base, with plenty of self-confidence, high incomes, and education, so they can indulge in all three primary motivations to some extent. These consumers will accept new products and technologies, but they have a high level of skepticism toward advertising.

14-4b OTHER APPLIED PSYCHOGRAPHIC RESEARCH

Although VALS is well-known and widely used, there are various other ongoing psychographic surveys. One is the Futures Company's MONITOR MindBase, a psychographic segmentation system with nine broad segments.[152] Based on attitudes, life-stage data, gender, age, and other inputs, MindBase determines how consumers in each segment behave and why, and then interprets this information for marketing purposes. Consumers in MindBase's "I am at capacity" segment, for instance, have as their motto "Time is of the essence" because they are extremely busy; therefore, this segment values convenience, control, and simplification. Those in the "I am expressive" segment live by the motto "YOLO" (you only live once). They see themselves as trendsetters and express their personality freely, meaning they value creative and hedonic offerings.

Some researchers question whether psychographic techniques fully capture all the variation in consumers' lifestyles. Rather than relying on the traits measured in the preceding research, one researcher identifies some consumption patterns that do not fit into the VALS framework. These include canonical aesthetics (which relates to traditional Western thought and artistic tastes), nurturing mother (in which consumption centers on the home and child-care), and Jeffersonian America (related to the styles and traditions of a pastoral United States).[153] Another researcher warns that segments can shift with societal changes, economic changes, technological changes, and competitive changes.[154]

 Marketing Implications

Marketers use tools such as VALS and other psychographic applications for market segmentation, new product and promotion ideas, and ad development. One area being pursued is methodology for analyzing social media interactions for more precise targeting, message development, and media selection according to individuals' interests and lifestyle activities.[155]

Often, marketers will use psychographic applications in combination with demographic analyses to understand and reach their target markets. This is what Hilton Garden Inn does when it plans its communications and promotional targeting. One online contest called "Life's Ultimate To-Do List" targeted experienced, knowledgeable, active travelers in the 30- to 54-year-old age group with a $75,000 household income and a drive to succeed in life. Such promotions support Hilton Garden Inn's advertising slogan, "We Speak Success."[156]

Exhibit 14.14 ▶ VALS American Segments

VALS classifies consumers into eight major segments based on two dimensions: resources (education, income, intelligence, and so on) and primary motivation (ideals, achievement, self-expression), as described in this exhibit.

Into which group would you fall? Go to www.strategicbusinessinsights.com/vals/presurvey.shtml and take the VALS survey to find out.

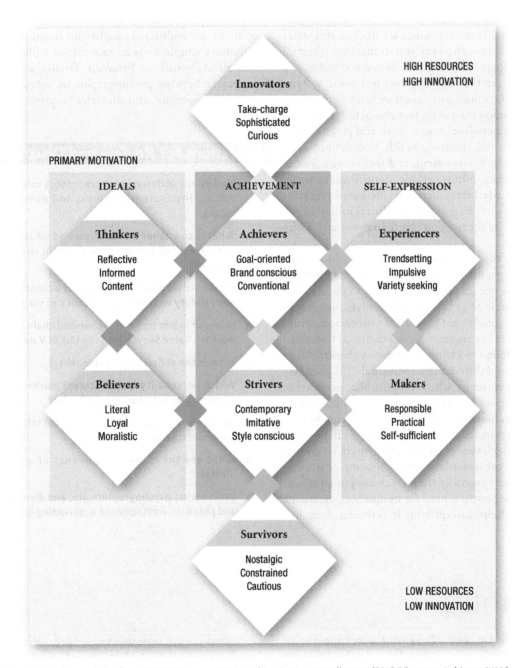

Source: Reprinted with permission from VALS™ Program. SRI Consulting Business Intelligence (SRIC-BI), www.sric-bi.com/VALS.

Summary:

Consumers learn values—enduring beliefs about things that are important—through the processes of socialization and acculturation. Our values exist in an organized value system, in which some are viewed as more important than others. Terminal values are desired end states that guide behavior in many situations, instrumental values help people achieve those desired end states, and global values are the core of someone's value system. Domain-specific values are relevant within a given sphere of activity. Among the values that characterize Western cultures are materialism, home, work and play, individualism, family and children, health, hedonism, youth, authenticity, the environment, and technology. Values are influenced by culture, ethnic identification, social class, and age. Marketers identify value-based segments by inferring values based on the cultural milieu of the group, using the means-end chain analysis, and using questionnaires.

Personality consists of the patterns of behaviors, tendencies, and personal dispositions that make people different from one another. Approaches to the study of personality include (1) the psychoanalytic approach, which sees personality as the result of unconscious struggles to complete key stages of development; (2) trait theories, which attempt to identify personality characteristics that describe and differentiate individuals; (3) phenomenological approaches, which propose that personality is shaped by an individual's interpretation of life events; (4) social-psychological theories, which focus on how individuals act in social situations; and (5) behavioral approaches, which view personality in terms of behavioral responses to past rewards and punishments. Marketers may find some personality traits (such as optimal stimulation level, dogmatism, need for uniqueness, creativity, need for cognition, susceptibility to influence, frugality, self-monitoring, national character, and competitiveness) relate to consumer behavior.

Marketers are also interested in examining lifestyles, which are patterns of behavior or activities, interests, and opinions, for additional insight into consumer behavior. Voluntary simplicity is an example of a lifestyle choice that affects consumer behavior. Finally, some marketing researchers use psychographic techniques involving values, personality, and lifestyles to predict consumer behavior.

Questions for Review and Discussion

1. Explain the differences among global values, terminal values, instrumental values, and domain-specific values.

2. What is consumer materialism and what are some of the ways it influences consumer behavior in Western cultures?

3. What four main value dimensions according to Hofstede's theory explain how cultures can vary?

4. How can marketers use means-end chain analysis, the Rokeach Value Survey, and the List of Values?

5. What is the definition of personality?

6. Which personality traits interest marketers because these may affect consumer behavior?

7. How does a person's locus of control influence his or her beliefs and evaluations?

8. What are the three components of a consumer's lifestyle?

9. Define what psychographics are, and discuss their use and potential limitations in a marketing context.

Endnotes

1 Allison Enright, "E-retailer Zazzle Will Acquire Custom Goods Firm Coveroo," *Internet Retailer*, November 24, 2015, www .internetretailer.com.

2 Milton Rokeach, *The Nature of Human Values* (New York: Free Press, 1973), p. 5.

3 Wagner A. Kamakura and Jose Alfonso Mazzon, "Value Segmentation," *Journal of Consumer Research*, September 1991, pp. 208–218; see also Milton Rokeach and Sandra J. Ball-Rokeach, "Stability and Change in American Value Priorities, 1968–1981," *American Psychologist*, May 1989, pp. 775–784;

Milton Rokeach, *Understanding Human Values* (New York: Free Press, 1979); and Shalom H. Schwartz and Wolfgang Bilsky, "Toward a Universal Psychological Structure of Human Values," *Journal of Personality and Social Psychology*, September 1987, pp. 550–562.

4 Kim A. Nelson, "Consumer Decision Making and Image Theory," *Journal of Consumer Psychology* 14, no. 1/2, 2004, pp. 28–40.

5 Francesco M. Nicosia and Robert N. Mayer, "Toward a Sociology of Consumption," *Journal of Consumer Research*,

September 1976, pp. 65–75; and Hugh E. Kramer, "The Value of Higher Education and Its Impact on Value Formation," in eds. Robert E. Pitts and Arch G. Woodside, *Personal Values and Consumer Psychology* (Lexington, Mass.: Lexington Books, 1984), pp. 239–251.

6   Marius K. Luedicke, "Indigenes' Responses to Immigrants' Consumer Acculturation: A Relational Configuration Analysis," *Journal of Consumer Research*, June 2015, pp. 109–129.

7   Mar y Gilly and Lisa Penaloza, "Barriers and Incentives in Consumer Acculturation," in eds. W. Fred van Raaij and Gary J. Bamossy, *European Advances in Consumer Research*, vol. 1 (Provo, Utah: Association for Consumer Research, 1993), pp. 278–286.

8   Rokeach, *The Nature of Human Values*; and Schwartz and Bilsky, "Toward a Universal Psychological Structure of Human Values."

9   Russell W. Belk, "Materialism: Trait Aspects of Living in the Material World," *Journal of Consumer Research*, December 1985, pp. 265–280; and Russell W. Belk, "Three Scales to Measure Constructs Related to Materialism," in ed. Thomas p. Kinnear, *Advances in Consumer Research*, vol. 11 (Provo, Utah: Association for Consumer Research, 1984), pp. 291–297.

10 Marsha L. Richins, "Special Possessions and the Expression of Material Values," *Journal of Consumer Research*, December 1994, pp. 522–533.

11 Marsha L. Richins, "When Wanting Is Better Than Having: Materialism, Transformation Expectations, and Product-Evoked Emotions in the Purchase Process," *Journal of Consumer Research* 40, no. 1, June 2013, pp. 1–18.

12 James A. Roberts, John F. Tanner Jr., and Chris Manolis, "Materialism and the Family Structure–Stress Relation," *Journal of Consumer Psychology* 15, no. 2, 2005, pp. 183–190; and Helga Dittmar, Richard Bond, M. Hurst, and Tim Kasser, "The Relationship between Materialism and Personal Well-Being: A Meta-Analysis," *Journal of Personality and Social Psychology* 107, no. 5, 2014, pp. 879–924.

13 Rik Pieters, "Bidirectional Dynamics of Materialism and Loneliness: Not Just a Vicious Cycle," *Journal of Consumer Research* 40, no. 4, December 2013, pp. 615–631.

14 James E. Burroughs and Aric Rindfleisch, "Materialism and Well-Being," *Journal of Consumer Research*, December 2002, pp. 348–370.

15 Pieters, "Bidirectional Dynamics of Materialism and Loneliness: Not Just a Vicious Cycle."

16 Elizabeth W. Dunn, Daniel T. Gilbert, and Timothy D. Wilson, "If Money Doesn't Make You Happy, Then You Probably Aren't Spending It Right," *Journal of Consumer Psychology* 21, 2011, pp. 115–125; Jennifer L. Aaker, Melanie Rudd, and Cassie Mogilner, "If Money Does Not Make You Happy, Consider Time," *Journal of Consumer Psychology* 21, 2011, pp. 126–130; and Joseph Chancellor and Sonja Lyubomirsky, "Happiness and Thrift: When (Spending) Less Is (Hedonically) More," *Journal of Consumer Psychology* 21, 2011, pp. 131–138.

17 Leonardo Nicolao, Julie R. Irwin, and Joseph K. Goodman, "Happiness for Sale: Do Experiential Purchases Make Consumers Happier than Material Purchases?" *Journal of Consumer Research*, August 2009, pp. 188–198.

18 Stephanie M. Tully, Hal E. Hershfield, and Tom Meyvis, "Seeking Lasting Enjoyment with Limited Money: Financial Constraints Increase Preference for Material Goods over Experiences," *Journal of Consumer Research* 42, June 2015, pp. 59–75.

19 Jingjing Ma and Neal J. Roese, "The Maximizing Mind-Set," *Journal of Consumer Research* 41, no. 1, June 2014, pp. 71–92.

20 Marsha L. Richins and Lan Nguyen Chaplin, "Material Parenting: How the Use of Goods in Parenting Fosters Materialism in the Next Generation," *Journal of Consumer Research* 41, April 2015, pp. 1333–1357.

21 Jamie Arndt, Sheldon Solomon, Tim Kasser, and Kennon M. Sheldon, "The Urge to Splurge: A Terror Management Account of Materialism and Consumer Behavior," *Journal of Consumer Psychology* 14, no. 3, 2004, pp. 198–212; Jamie Arndt, Sheldon Solomon, Tim Kasser, and Kennon M. Sheldon, "The Urge to Splurge Revisited," *Journal of Consumer Psychology* 14, no. 3, 2004, pp. 225–229; Durairaj Maheswaran and Nidhi Agrawal, "Motivational and Cultural Variations in Mortality Salience Effects," *Journal of Consumer Psychology* 14, no. 3, 2004, pp. 213–218; and Aric Rindfleisch and James E. Burroughs, "Terrifying Thoughts, Terrible Materialism? Contemplations on a Terror Management Account of Materialism and Consumer Behavior," *Journal of Consumer Psychology* 14, no. 3, 2004, pp. 219–224.

22 Marsha L. Richins and Scott Dawson, "A Consumer Values Orientation for Materialism and Its Measurement," *Journal of Consumer Research*, December 1992, pp. 303–316.

23 Bree Feng, "Chinese Respondents Top Materialism Poll," *New York Times Sinosphere*, December 20, 2013, www.nytimes.com.

24 Sarah Halzack, "Why Louis Vuitton, Gucci, and Prada Are in Trouble," *Washington Post*, June 15, 2015, www.washingtonpost.com.

25 U.S. Census Bureau, "Residential Vacancies and Homeownership in the Third Quarter 2015," *U.S. Department of Commerce*, October 27, 2015, www.census.gov.

26 Meg Dupont, "Cocooning Morphs into Hiving," *Hartford Courant*, October 29, 2004, p. H2.

27 John B. Horrigan and Maeve Duggan, "Home Broadband 2015," *Pew Research Center*, December 21, 2015, www.pewinternet.org.

28 Brad Tuttle, "A Huge Number of Millennials Can't Escape Work While on Vacation," *Time*, July 6, 2014, www.time.com; and Josh Eidelson, "For Every Education Level, Real Wages Have Gone Down So Far This Year," *Bloomberg*, August 27, 2014, www.bloomberg.com.

29 Mark Sullivan, "Samsung's New Refrigerator Wants to Do Away With Your Trips to the Grocery Store," *Fast Company*, January 5, 2016, www.fastcompany.com; Allison Enright, "The E-grocery Explosion," *Internet Retailer*, August 3, 2015, www.internetretailer.com; and Robin van Daalen, "Ahold Cuts Costs, Ups Dividend with New Strategy," *Wall Street Journal*, November 21, 2011, www.wsj.com.

30 Emma Seppälä, "If You Can't Take a Vacation, Get the Most Out of Minibreaks," *Harvard Business Review*, July 14, 2015, www.hbr.org.

31 Fran Golden, "The World's Oddest Theme Cruises," *USA Today*, January 5, 2015, www.usatoday.com.

32 Elizabeth C. Hirschman, "Men, Dogs, Guns, and Cars," *Journal of Advertising*, Spring 2003, pp. 9–22.

33 Blair Kidwell, Adam Farmer, and David M. Hardesty, "Getting Liberals and Conservatives to Go Green: Political Ideology and Congruent Appeals," *Journal of Consumer Research* 40, no. 2, August 2013, pp. 350–367.

34 Mohan J. Dutta-Bergman and William D. Wells, "The Values and Lifestyles of Idiocentrics and Allocentrics in an Individualist Culture," *Journal of Consumer Psychology* 12, no. 3, 2002, pp. 232–242.

35 Jena McGregor, "How Mark Zuckerberg's Paternity Leave Affects the Rest of Us," *Los Angeles Times*, December 6, 2015, www.latimes.com.

36 Richard Milne, "Sales Jump Secures Lego's Crown as World's Biggest Toymaker," *Financial Times*, September 2, 2015, www.ft.com.

37 Stephanie Chao, "Ban on Junk Food Marketing to Nation's Kids Takes Effect Jan. 1," *The China Post*, December 25, 2015, www.chinapost.com/tw.

38 Evelyn Theiss, "Dave's Supermarkets Joins Cleveland Clinic's Healthy Food Program," *Cleveland Plain Dealer*, November 18, 2011, www.cleveland.com.

39 Dan Eaton, "Egg-Topped Burgers? Ghost Pepper Fries? Wendy's Willing to Consider It," *Columbus Business Insider (OH)*, February 4, 2015, www.bizjournals.com.

40 Ashutosh Prasad, Andrei Strijnev, and Qin Zhang, "What Can Grocery Basket Data Tell Us About Health Consciousness?" *International Journal of Research in Marketing* 25, 2008, pp. 301–309.

41 John Ewoldt, "CVS Completes Acquisition of Target Pharmacy and Clinic Business," *Star-Tribune (Minneapolis, MN)*, December 16, 2015, www.startribune.com.

42 Laura Kusisto, "Here's What Architects See in Homes of the Future," *Wall Street Journal*, December 29, 2015, www.wsj.com.

43 Jennifer Elias, "In 2016, Users Will Trust Health Apps More Than Their Doctors," *Forbes*, December 31, 2015, www.forbes.com.

44 Tanya Albert Henry, "U.S. Obesity Rate Projected to Reach 50% by 2030," *American Medical News*, September 12, 2011, www.ama-assn.org.amednews.

45 Julie Jargon, "Less Soda Being Chosen With McDonald's Happy Meals," *Wall Street Journal*, June 25, 2015, www.wsj.com; and Donna Goodison, "How 'Bout Them Apples?" *Boston Herald*, October 26, 2011, www.bostonherald.com.

46 Margaret Littman, "How Sriracha Got So Hot," *Time*, June 25, 2015, www.time.com.

47 Raj Raghunathan, Rebecca Walker Naylor, and Wayne D. Hoyer, "The 'Unhealthy = Tasty Intuition' and Its Effects on Taste Inferences, Enjoyment, and Choice of Food Products," *Journal of Marketing* 70, no. 4, 2006, pp. 170–184.

48 Lucy Whitehouse, "L'Oreal on Digital Marketing," *Cosmetics Design Europe*, November 6, 2014, www.cosmeticsdesign-europe.com; and Jack Neff, "Zigging Where Others Zagged, L'Oréal Focuses on U.S., to Beautiful Effect," *Advertising Age*, November 7, 2011, www.adage.com.

49 Kent Grayson and Radan Martinec, "Consumer Perceptions of Iconicity and Indexicality and Their Influence on Assessments of Authentic Market Offerings," *Journal of Consumer Research* 31, no. 2, 2004, pp. 296–312.

50 Craig J. Thompson, Aric Rindfleisch, and Zrsel Zeynep, "Emotional Branding and the Strategic Value of the Doppelganger Brand Image," *Journal of Marketing*, January 2006, pp. 50–64.

51 Gerry Khermouch, "Secret Origins of Authentic Brands," *BEVNET*, November 14, 2011, www.bevnet.com.

52 Daniel Roberts, "The NBA's New Store Is a Tech-ified Basketball Temple," *Fortune*, December 18, 2015, www.fortune.com.

53 Mara Lemos Stein, "Talking About Waste with P&G," *Wall Street Journal*, September 12, 2011, www.wsj.com.

54 "Consumers and Mobile Financial Services, 2015," Board of Governors, U.S. Federal Reserve System, March 2015.

55 Adam L. Penenberg, "NeuroFocus Uses Neuromarketing to Hack Your Brain," *Fast Company*, August 8, 2011, www.fastcompany.com.

56 Sak Onkvisit and John J. Shaw, *International Marketing: Analysis and Strategy* (Columbus, Ohio: Merrill, 1989), p. 243.

57 K. S. Yang, "Expressed Values of Chinese College Students," in eds. K. S. Yang and Y. Y. Li, *Symposium on the Character of the Chinese* (Taipei, Taiwan: Institute of Ethnology Academic Sinica, 1972), pp. 257–312; see also Oliver H. M. Yau, *Consumer Behavior in China: Customer Satisfaction and Cultural Values* (New York: Rutledge, 1994).

58 Alfred S. Boote, cited in Rebecca Piirto, *Beyond Mind Games* (Ithaca, N.Y.: American Demographic Books, 1991).

59 Jan-Benedict E. M. Steenkamp and Martijn G. de Jong, "A Global Investigation into the Constellation of Consumer Attitudes Toward Global and Local Products," *Journal of Marketing*, November 2010, pp. 18–40.

60 Geert Hofstede, "National Cultures in Four Dimensions," *International Studies of Management and Organization*, Spring–Summer 1983, pp. 46–74.

61 Michael Lynn, George M. Zinkhan, and Judy Harris, "Consumer Tipping: A Cross-Country Study," *Journal of Consumer Research*, December 1993, pp. 478–488.

62 Dana L. Alden, Wayne D. Hoyer, and Chol Lee, "Identifying Global and Culture-Specific Dimensions of Humor in Advertising," *Journal of Marketing*, April 1993, pp. 64–75.

63 Douglas B. Holt and Craig J. Thompson, "Man-of-Action Heroes: The Pursuit of Heroic Masculinity in Everyday Consumption," *Journal of Consumer Research* 31, no. 2, 2004, pp. 425–440.

64 Van R. Wood and Roy Howell, "A Note on Hispanic Values and Subcultural Research: An Alternative View," *Journal of the Academy of Marketing Science*, Winter 1991, pp. 61–67; see also Humberto Valencia, "Hispanic Values and Subcultural Research," *Journal of the Academy of Marketing Science*, Winter 1989, pp. 23–28; and Thomas E. Ness and Melvin T. Smith, "Middle-Class Values in Blacks and Whites," in eds. Pitts and Woodside, *Personal Values and Consumer Psychology*, pp. 231–237.

65 Lianne van den Box, "Nestlé Results Confirm Its Need to Rethink China/US Strategy," *Food Magazine (Australia)*, February 23, 2015, www.foodmag.com.au.

66 Richard P. Coleman, "The Continuing Significance of Social Class to Marketing," *Journal of Consumer Research*, December 1983, pp. 265–280.

67 William Strauss and Neil Howe, "The Cycle of Generations," *American Demographics*, April 1991, pp. 25–33, 52; see also William Strauss and Neil Howe, *Generations: The History of America's Future, 1584 to 2069* (New York: William Morrow, 1992).

68 Sharon Beatty, Lynn R. Kahle, Pamela Homer, and Shekhar Misra, "Alternative Measurement Approaches to Consumer Values: The List of Values and the Rokeach Value Survey," *Psychology and Marketing*, Fall 1985, pp. 181–200.

69 Lynn R. Kahle, *Social Values and Social Change: Adaptation to Life in America* (New York: Praeger, 1983).

70 Ben Bold, "M&S Plan A in Numbers," *Marketing Magazine*, June 4, 2015, www.marketingmagazine.co.uk.

71 Jack Ewing, "Hands-On Bavarian Count Presides Over a Pencil-Making Empire," *New York Times*, December 3, 2013, www.nytimes.com.

72 Ryan Cormier, "Wilmington Native Sells Fashion Company to Bed, Bath & Beyond," *Delaware Online*, August 21, 2015, www.delawareonline.com.

73 Pete Born, "Visionary of The Year: Jean-Paul Agon of L'Oréal," *WWD*, December 10, 2015, www.wwd.com.

74 Lauren R. Hartman, "Flavor Trends: Soups Ladle Up the Flavor," *Food Processing*, November 2, 2015, www.foodprocessing.com; and Katie Moisse, "Campbell's Panned for Adding Salt to Soups," *ABC News*, July 14, 2011, http://abcnews.go.com.

75 Patricia F. Kennedy, Roger J. Best, and Lynn R. Kahle, "An Alternative Method for Measuring Value-Based Segmentation and Advertisement Positioning," in eds. James H. Leigh and Claude R. Martin Jr., *Current Issues and Research in Advertising*, vol. 11 (Ann Arbor, Mich.: Division of Research, School of Business Administration, University of Michigan, 1988), pp. 139–156; and Daniel L. Sherrell, Joseph F. Hair Jr., and Robert p. Bush, "The Influence of Personal Values on Measures of Advertising Effectiveness," in eds. Pitts and Woodside, *Personal Values and Consumer Psychology*, pp. 169–185.

76 Christine Defever, Mario Pandelaere, and Keith Roe, "Inducing Value-Congruent Behavior Through Advertising and the Moderating Role of Attitudes Toward Advertising," *Journal of Advertising*, Summer 2011, pp. 25–37.

77 Michael McCarthy, "Latest Items on Harley-Davidson's Crowd-Sourcing List: The Actual Bikes," *Advertising Age*, September 13, 2013, www.adage.com; and Rick Barrett, "Harley Draws on Fan Base for Ad Ideas," *Journal Sentinel (Milwaukee)*, November 9, 2011, www.jsonline.com.

78 Jennifer Leighfield, "Valencia Bus Company Removes 'Explicit' Ads," *Euro Weekly News*, November 2, 2011, www.euroeeweeklynews.com.

79 Robert E. Pitts, John K. Wong, and D. Joel Whalen, "Consumers' Evaluative Structures in Two Ethical Situations," *Journal of Business Research*, March 1991, pp. 119–130.

80 Suzanne McGee, "Top Tips for Making Your Consumer Boycott Effective," *The Guardian (U.K.)*, July 20, 2014, www.theguardian.com.

81 Russell W. Belk and Richard W. Pollay, "Materialism and Status Appeals in Japanese and U.S. Print Advertising," *International Marketing Review*, Winter 1985, pp. 38–47; see also Russell W. Belk, Wendy J. Bryce, and Richard W. Pollay, "Advertising Themes and Cultural Values: A Comparison of U.S. and Japanese Advertising," in eds. K. C. Mun and T. S. Chan, *Proceedings of the Inaugural Meeting of the Southeast Asia Region Academy of International Business* (Hong Kong, China: The Chinese University of Hong Kong, 1985), pp. 11–20.

82 Tse, Belk, and Zhou, "Becoming a Consumer Society."

83 Michael Wines, "Picking Brand Names in China Is a Business Itself," *New York Times*, November 12, 2011, www.nytimes.com.

84 For more on means-end chain analysis, see Beth A. Walker and Jerry C. Olson, "Means-End Chains: Connecting Products with Self," *Journal of Business Research*, March 1991, pp. 111–118; Thomas J. Reynolds and John p. Richon, "Means-End Based Advertising Research," *Journal of Business Research*, March 1991, pp. 131–142; Jonathan Gutman, "Exploring the Nature of Linkages Between Consequences and Values," *Journal of Business Research*, March 1991, pp. 143–148; Thomas J. Reynolds and Jonathan Gutman, "Laddering Theory, Method, Analysis and Interpretation," *Journal of Advertising Research*, February/March 1988, pp. 11–31; and Thomas J. Reynolds and Jonathan Gutman, "Laddering: Extending the Repertory Grid Methodology to Construct Attribute– Consequence–Value Hierarchies," in eds. Pitts and Woodside, *Personal Values and Consumer Psychology*, pp. 155–167.

85 Dawn R. Deeter-Schmelz and Jane L. Sojka, "Wrestling with American Values," *Journal of Consumer Behavior* 4, no. 2, 2004, pp. 132–143.

86 Thomas J. Reynolds and J. p. Jolly, "Measuring Personal Values," *Journal of Marketing Research*, November 1980, pp. 531–536; Reynolds and Gutman, "Laddering"; and Jonathan Gutman, "A Means-End Model Based on Consumer Categorization Processes," *Journal of Marketing*, Spring 1982, pp. 60–72.

87 T. L. Stanley, "Death of the Sports Car?" *Brandweek*, January 2, 1995, p. 38.

88 Frenkel Ter Hofstede, Jan-Benedict E. M. Steenkamp, and Michel Wedel, "International Market Segmentation Based on Consumer–Product Relations," *Journal of Marketing Research* 36, February 1999, pp. 1–17.

89 Marsha L. Richins, "The Material Values Scale," *Journal of Consumer Research*, June 2004, pp. 209–219.

90 J. Michael Munson and Edward F. McQuarrie, "Shortening the Rokeach Value Survey for Use in Consumer Research," in ed. Michael J. Houston, *Advances in Consumer Research*, vol. 15 (Provo, Utah: Association for Consumer Research, 1988), pp. 381–386.

91 Lynn R. Kahle, Sharon Beatty, and Pamela Homer, "Alternative Measurement Approaches to Consumer Values: The List of Values (LOV) and Values and Life Style (VALS)," *Journal of Consumer Research*, December 1986, pp. 405–409; and Kahle, *Social Values and Social Change: Adaptation to Life in America*.

92 Wagner Kamakura and Thomas p. Novak, "Value-System Segmentation," *Journal of Consumer Research*, June 1992, pp. 119–132.

93 Sigmund Freud, *Collected Papers*, vols. I–V (New York: Basic Books, 1959); Erik Erickson, *Childhood and Society* (New York: Norton, 1963); and Erik Erickson, *Identity: Youth and Crisis* (New York: Norton, 1968).

94 Yumiko Ono, "Marketers Seek the 'Naked' Truth," *Wall Street Journal*, May 30, 1997, pp. B1, B13.

95 Laurie Sullivan, "10 Behavioral Trends Guiding Advertising In 2016," *MediaPost*, December 29, 2015, www.mediapost.com.

96 Gordon Allport, *Personality: A Psychological Interpretation* (New York: Holt, Rinehart, & Winston, 1937); and Raymond B. Cattell, *The Scientific Analysis of Personality* (Baltimore: Penguin, 1965).

97 Carl G. Jung, *Man and His Symbols* (Garden City, N.Y.: Doubleday, 1964); see also Hans J. Eysenck, "Personality, Stress and Disease," *Psychological Inquiry* 2, 1991, pp. 221–232.

98 For example, see Lara K. Kammrath, Daniel R. Ames, and Abigail R. Scholer, "Keeping Up with Impressions: Inferential Rules for Impression Change Across the Big Five," *Journal of Experimental Social Psychology* 43, 2007, pp. 450–457; and William Fleeson, "Situation-Based Contingencies Underlying Trait-Content Manifestation in Behavior," *Journal of Personality* 75, no. 4, 2007, pp. 825–862.

99 Carl R. Rogers, "Some Observations on the Organization of Personality," *American Psychologist*, September 1947, pp. 358–368; and George A. Kelly, *The Psychology of Personal Constructs*, vols. 1 and 2 (New York: Norton, 1955).

100 Bernard Weiner, "Attribution in Personality Psychology," in ed. Lawrence A. Pervin, *Handbook of Personality: Theory and Research* (New York: Guilford, 1990), pp. 465–484; and Harold H. Kelly, "The Processes of Causal Attribution," *American Psychologist*, February 1973, pp. 107–128.

101 Eric J. Hamerman and Gita V. Johar, "Conditioned Superstition: Desire for Control and Consumer Brand Preferences,"

Journal of Consumer Research 40, no. 3, October 2013, pp. 428–443.

102 Hyeongmin (Christian) Kim, Katina Kulow, and Thomas Kramer, "The Interactive Effect of Beliefs in Malleable Fate and Fateful Predictions on Choice," *Journal of Consumer Research* 40, no. 6, April 2014, pp. 1139–1148.

103 David Glen Mick and Claus Buhl, "A Meaning-Based Model of Advertising Experiences," *Journal of Consumer Research*, December 1992, pp. 317–338.

104 Frank May and Ashwani Monga, "When Time Has a Will of Its Own, the Powerless Don't Have the Will to Wait: Anthropomorphism of Time Can Decrease Patience," *Journal of Consumer Research* 40, no. 5, February 2014, pp. 924–942.

105 Karen B. Horney, *Our Inner Conflicts* (New York: Norton, 1945).

106 Joel B. Cohen, "An Interpersonal Orientation to the Study of Consumer Behavior," *Journal of Marketing Research*, August 1967, pp. 270–277; and Jon p. Noerager, "An Assessment of CAD," *Journal of Marketing Research*, February 1979, pp. 53–59.

107 Marsha L. Richins, "An Analysis of Consumer Interaction Styles in the Marketplace," *Journal of Consumer Research*, June 1983, pp. 73–82.

108 Richard p. Bagozzi, Hans Baumgartner, and Youjae Yi, "State Versus Action Orientation and the Theory of Reasoned Action," *Journal of Consumer Research*, March 1992, pp. 505–518; William O. Bearden and Randall L. Rose, "Attention to Social Comparison Information," *Journal of Consumer Research*, March 1990, pp. 461–471; and Bobby J. Calder and Robert E. Burnkrant, "Interpersonal Influence on Consumer Behavior," *Journal of Consumer Research*, December 1979, pp. 29–38.

109 B. F. Skinner, *About Behaviorism* (New York: Knopf, 1974); and B. F. Skinner, *Beyond Freedom and Dignity* (New York: Knopf, 1971).

110 Jacob Jacoby, "Multiple Indicant Approaches for Studying New Product Adopters," *Journal of Applied Psychology*, August 1971, pp. 384–388; and Harold H. Kassarjian, "Personality and Consumer Behavior: A Review," *Journal of Marketing Research*, November 1971, pp. 409–418; see also Harold H. Kassarjian, "Personality: The Longest Fad," in ed. William L. Wilkie, *Advances in Consumer Research*, vol. 6 (Ann Arbor, Mich.: Association for Consumer Research, 1979), pp. 122–124.

111 William O. Bearden, David M. Hardesty, and Randall L. Rose, "Consumer Self-Confidence," *Journal of Consumer Research* 28, June 2001, pp. 121–134.

112 D. E. Berlyne, *Conflict, Arousal and Curiosity* (New York: McGraw-Hill, 1960); and D. E. Berlyne, "Novelty, Complexity, and Hedonic Value," *Perception and Psychophysics*, November 1970, pp. 279–286.

113 Marvin Zuckerman, *Sensation Seeking: Beyond the Optimal Level of Arousal* (Hillsdale, N.J.: Lawrence Erlbaum, 1979); and Elizabeth C. Hirschman, "Innovativeness, Novelty Seeking, and Consumer Creativity," *Journal of Consumer Research*, December 1980, pp. 283–295.

114 R. A. Mittelstadt, S. L. Grossbart, W. W. Curtis, and S. p. DeVere, "Optimal Stimulation Level and the Adoption Decision Process," *Journal of Consumer Research*, September 1976, pp. 84–94; p. S. Raju, "Optimum Stimulation Level," *Journal of Consumer Research*, December 1980, pp. 272–282; Jan-Benedict E. M. Steenkamp and Hans Baumgartner, "The Role of Optimum Stimulation Level in Exploratory Consumer Behavior," *Journal of Consumer Research*, December 1992, pp. 434–448; and Erich A. Joachimsthaler and John

Lastovicka, "Optimal Stimulation Level—Exploratory Behavior Models," *Journal of Consumer Research*, December 1984, pp. 830–835.

115 Kelly Tepper Tian, William O. Bearden, and Gary L. Hunter, "Consumers' Need for Uniqueness," *Journal of Consumer Research* 28, June 2001, pp. 50–66.

116 Itamar Simonson and Stephen M. Nowlis, "The Role of Explanations and Need for Uniqueness in Consumer Decision Making," *Journal of Consumer Research* 27, June 2000, pp. 49–68.

117 Craig J. Thompson and Zeynep Arsel, "The Starbucks Brandscape and Consumers' (Anticorporate) Experiences of Globalization," *Journal of Consumer Research* 31, no. 3, 2004, pp. 631–642.

118 James E. Burroughs and David Glen Mick, "Exploring Antecedents and Consequences of Consumer Creativity in a Problem-Solving Context," *Journal of Consumer Research*, September 2004, pp. 402–411.

119 Stuart Elliott, "A Push to Promote Familiar Brands Online," *New York Times*, November 17, 2011, www.nytimes.com.

120 Alex Marin, Martin Reimann, and Raquel Castano, "Metaphors and Creativity: Direct, Moderating, and Mediating Effects," *Journal of Consumer Psychology* 24, no. 2, Special Issue, April 2014, pp. 290–297.

121 John T. Cacioppo, Richard E. Petty, and Chuan F. Kao, "The Efficient Assessment of Need for Cognition," *Journal of Personality Assessment*, June 1984, pp. 306–307; Curtis R. Haugtvedt, Richard E. Petty, and John T. Cacioppo, "Need for Cognition and Advertising: Understanding the Role of Personality Variables in Consumer Behavior," *Journal of Consumer Psychology* 1, no. 3, 1992, pp. 239–260; Rajeev Batra and Douglas M. Stayman, "The Role of Mood in Advertising Effectiveness," *Journal of Consumer Research*, September 1990, pp. 203–214; and John T. Cacioppo, Richard E. Petty, and K. Morris, "Effects of Need for Cognition on Message Evaluation, Recall and Persuasion," *Journal of Personality and Social Psychology*, October 1983, pp. 805–818.

122 Susan Powell Mantel and Frank R. Kardes, "The Role of Direction of Comparison, Attribute-Based Processing, and Attitude-Based Processing in Consumer Preference," *Journal of Consumer Research* 25, March 1999, pp. 335–352.

123 William O. Bearden, Richard G. Netemeyer, and Jesse H. Teel, "Measurement of Consumer Susceptibility to Interpersonal Influence," *Journal of Consumer Research*, March 1989, pp. 472–480; and Peter Wright, "Factors Affecting Cognitive Resistance to Ads," *Journal of Marketing Research*, June 1975, pp. 1–9.

124 John L. Lastovicka, Lance A. Bettencourt, Renée Shaw Hughner, and Ronald J. Kuntze, "Lifestyle of the Tight and Frugal," *Journal of Consumer Research* 26, June 1999, pp. 85–98.

125 Terrence H. Witkowski, "World War II Poster Campaigns," *Journal of Advertising*, Spring 2003, pp. 69–82.

126 Matthew Egol, Andrew Clyde, and Kasturi Rangan, "The New Consumer Frugality," *Strategy + Business*, March 15, 2010, www.strategy-business.com.

127 Richard C. Becherer and Lawrence C. Richard, "Self-Monitoring as a Moderating Variable in Consumer Behavior," *Journal of Consumer Research*, December 1978, pp. 159–162; and Mark Snyder and Kenneth G. DeBono, "Appeals to Image and Claims about Quality," *Journal of Personality and Social Psychology*, September 1985, pp. 586–597.

128 Caroline Goukens, Siegried Dewitte, and Luk Warlop, "Me, Myself, and My Choices: The Influence of Private Self-Awareness on Choice," *Journal of Marketing Research*, October 2009, pp. 682–692.

129 Eugenia C. Wu, Keisha M. Cutright, and Gavan J. Fitzsimons, "How Asking 'Who Am I?' Affects What Consumers Buy: The Influence of Self-Discovery on Consumption," *Journal of Marketing Research*, April 2011, pp. 296–307.

130 Terry Clark, "International Marketing and National Character: A Review and Proposal for an Integrative Theory," *Journal of Marketing*, October 1990, pp. 66–79.

131 Adam Wooten, "Marketers Beware of Using Animals in International Campaigns," *Deseret News (Salt Lake City)*, September 23, 2011, www.deseretnews.com.

132 John C. Mowen, "Exploring the Trait of Competitiveness and its Consumer Behavior Consequences," *Journal of Consumer Psychology* 14, no. 1/2, 2004, pp. 52–63.

133 Jonah Berger and Morgan Ward, "Subtle Signals of Inconspicuous Consumption, *Journal of Consumer Research*, December 2010, pp. 555–569.

134 Nailya Ordabayeva and Pierre Chandon, "Getting Ahead of the Joneses: When Equality Increases Conspicuous Consumption Among Bottom-Tier Consumers," *Journal of Consumer Research*, June 2011, pp. 27–41.

135 "Social Media: PepsiCo and Unilever Aim to Connect with Consumers," *Just-Food*, June 30, 2011, www.just-food.com.

136 Martin Beck, "Social Media Lessons From the Stanley Cup Champion Of Twitter," *MarketingLand*, June 20, 2014, www.marketingland.com; and Zachary Sniderman, "L.A. Kings Are First Pro Sports Team to Get Gamified," *Mashable*, October 20, 2011, www.mashable.com.

137 David Crockett, "The Role of Normative Political Ideology in Consumer Behavior," *Journal of Consumer Research* 31, no. 3, 2004, pp. 511–528.

138 Morris B. Holbrook, "Nostalgia and Consumption Preferences," *Journal of Consumer Research*, September 1993, pp. 245–256.

139 Cristel Antonia Russell and Hope Jensen Schau, "When Narrative Brands End: The Impact of Narrative Closure and Consumption Sociality on Loss Accommodation," *Journal of Consumer Research* 40, no. 6, April 2014, pp. 1039–1062.

140 Christine Rodenbaugh, "Eat Slow. Shop Local," *St. Augustine Record (FL)*, December 3, 2015, www.staugustine.com.

141 Onkvisit and Shaw, *International Marketing: Analysis and Strategy*, p. 283.

142 Leonidas C. Leonidou, "Understanding the Russian Consumer," *Marketing and Research Today*, March 1992, pp. 75–83.

143 Wendy Koch, "Why Are We Obsessed with Stuff and More Stuff ?" *USA Today*, March 24, 2010, www.usatoday.com; and Wendy Koch, "Getting to the Heart of 'Simple Living,'" *USA Today*, June 2, 2010, www.usatoday.com.

144 See Leonard L. Berry, Kathleen Seiders, and Dhruv Grewal, "Understanding Service Convenience," *Journal of Marketing Research*, July 2002, pp. 1–17.

145 Sara Tambascio, "Refreshing the Bulb Market with Dig, Drop, Done," *Today's Garden Center*, July 2011, www.todaysgardencenter.com.

146 Laura Lorenzetti, "Ford's Zipcar-Killer Is Launching in This City," *Time*, May 27, 2015, www.time.com; and Joann Muller, "Ford's Zipcar Deal Is a Clever Marketing Move," *Forbes*, August 31, 2011, www.forbes.com.

147 Jerri Stroud, "'Bankers' Hours' Now Include Evenings and Sundays," *St. Louis Post-Dispatch*, September 4, 2007, n.p.

148 Tom Groenfeldt, "Atom Is First UK Mobile-Only Bank To Receive License," *Forbes*, December 23, 2015, www.forbes.com.

149 Basil G. Englis and Michael R. Solomon, "To Be and Not to Be: Life Style Imagery, Reference Groups, and the Clustering of America," *Journal of Advertising*, Spring 1995, pp. 13–28.

150 "NTT Docomo Makes Voice Translator App Available for iPhone," *Japan Times*, January 19, 2015, www.japantimes.co.jp; and "'Smart' Apps Becoming Lifestyle Game-Changer," *Japan Times*, November 25, 2011, www.japantimes.co.jp.

151 Strategic Business Insights, www.strategicbusinessinsights.com/vals.

152 "Mindbase," The Futures Company, http://thefuturescompany.com/mindbase.

153 Douglas B. Holt, "Poststructuralist Lifestyle Analysis," *Journal of Consumer Research*, March 1997, pp. 326–350.

154 Marvin Shoenwald, "Psychographic Segmentation: Used or Abused?" *Brandweek*, January 22, 2001, p. 34.

155 See, for example, Michael Learmonth, "Penry Price: Why Social Is the Next Frontier of Ad Targeting," *Advertising Age*, June 23, 2011, www.adage.com.

156 Tanya Irwin, "Hilton Garden Inn Launches 'To-Do List' Contest," *Mediapost*, August 9, 2011, www.mediapost.com.

The Psychological Core

2 Motivation, Ability, and Opportunity
3 From Exposure to Comprehension
4 Memory and Knowledge
5-6 Attitudes Based on Effort

An Introduction to Consumer Behavior

1 Understanding Consumer Behavior

The Process of Making Decisions

7 Problem Recognition and Information Search
8-9 Judgment and Decision-Making Based on Effort
10 Post-Decision Processes

The Consumer's Culture

11 Social Influences on Consumer Behavior
12 Consumer Diversity
13 Household and Social Class Influences
14 Psychographics: Values, Personality, and Lifestyles

Consumer Behavior Outcomes and Issues

15 Innovations: Adoption, Resistance, and Diffusion
16 Symbolic Consumer Behavior
17 Marketing, Ethics, and Social Responsibility in Today's Consumer Society

iStockphoto.com/Ostill

Part 5

Consumer Behavior Outcomes and Issues

Part five examines key issues related to the influences, processes, and outcomes that were examined in Parts Two, Three, and Four. Chapter 15 builds on the topics of decision-making and group processes by exploring how consumers adopt innovative offerings and how their adoption decisions affect the spread (diffusion) of a new offering through a market. This chapter also looks at factors that make a difference in consumers' resistance to an innovation, an adoption of an innovation, and the diffusion of an offering through a marketplace.

Chapter 16 discusses the fascinating topic of symbolic consumer behavior. Both goods and services can have deeply felt and significant meanings for consumers. These meanings may be affected by rituals related to acquisition, ownership, use, and disposal. Moreover, the meaning of an offering can be transferred through gift-giving.

Chapter 17 examines the role of ethics and social responsibility in marketing. It also looks at positive and negative aspects of consumer behavior and marketing, including problematic behaviors such as compulsive buying and productive behaviors such as consumer-led marketing efforts to benefit charities.

CHAPTER 15

Innovations: Adoption, Resistance, and Diffusion

iStockphoto.com/Ostill

INTRODUCTION

Many factors influence consumers' decisions about innovative offerings such as mobile payment services and smart-home appliances and apps (see Exhibit 15.1). This chapter opens with an explanation of the types of innovations, which can vary in both novelty and benefits. Next, we explore what affects whether consumers will resist a new product or adopt it. The final section examines the factors affecting how quickly a new product spreads, or diffuses, through a market.

15-1 Innovations

The ability to develop successful new products is critical to a company's sales, future growth, and long-term survival potential. Innovation is so important to the future of the Swiss food company Nestlé that the top management team receives monthly reports on the 10 most promising products in development. The firm has even established a Silicon Valley Innovation Outpost to extend partnerships with high-tech firms for further marketing innovation.[1] Given the role that new products play in a company's sales and profitability, it is vital for marketers to understand new products and what drives their success in the market.

Dai Sugano/MCT/Newscom

Exhibit 15.1 ▶ Chapter Overview: Innovations: Adoption, Resistance, and Diffusion
Consumers may decide to adopt (e.g., purchase) or resist adopting a new offering (an innovation). Diffusion reflects how fast an innovation spreads through a market. The type of innovation, its breadth, its characteristics, and the social system into which it is introduced can influence adoption, resistance, and diffusion.

The
Psychological Core

2   Motivation, Ability, and Opportunity
3   From Exposure to Comprehension
4   Memory and Knowledge
5-6   Attitude Formation and Change

The Process of
Making Decisions

7   Problem Recognition and
    Information Search
8-9   Judgment and
    Decision-Making
10   Post-Decision
    Processes

Consumer Behavior
Outcomes and Issues

15   Innovations: Adoption,
    Resistance, and Diffusion
16   Symbolic Consumer Behavior
17   Marketing, Ethics, and Social
    Responsibility in Today's
    Consumer Society

The
Consumer's Culture

11   Social Influences
    on Consumer Behavior
12   Consumer Diversity
13   Household and Social
    Class Influences
14   Psychographics: Values,
    Personality, and Lifestyles

iStockphoto.com/Ostill

| Innovations | ⋯⋯ | Adoption or Resistance | ⋯⋯ | Diffusion |

Factors Affecting Adoption, Resistance, and Diffusion

- Perceived value
- Uncertainty
- Consumer learning requirements
- Social relevance
- Legitimacy and adaptability
- Social factors

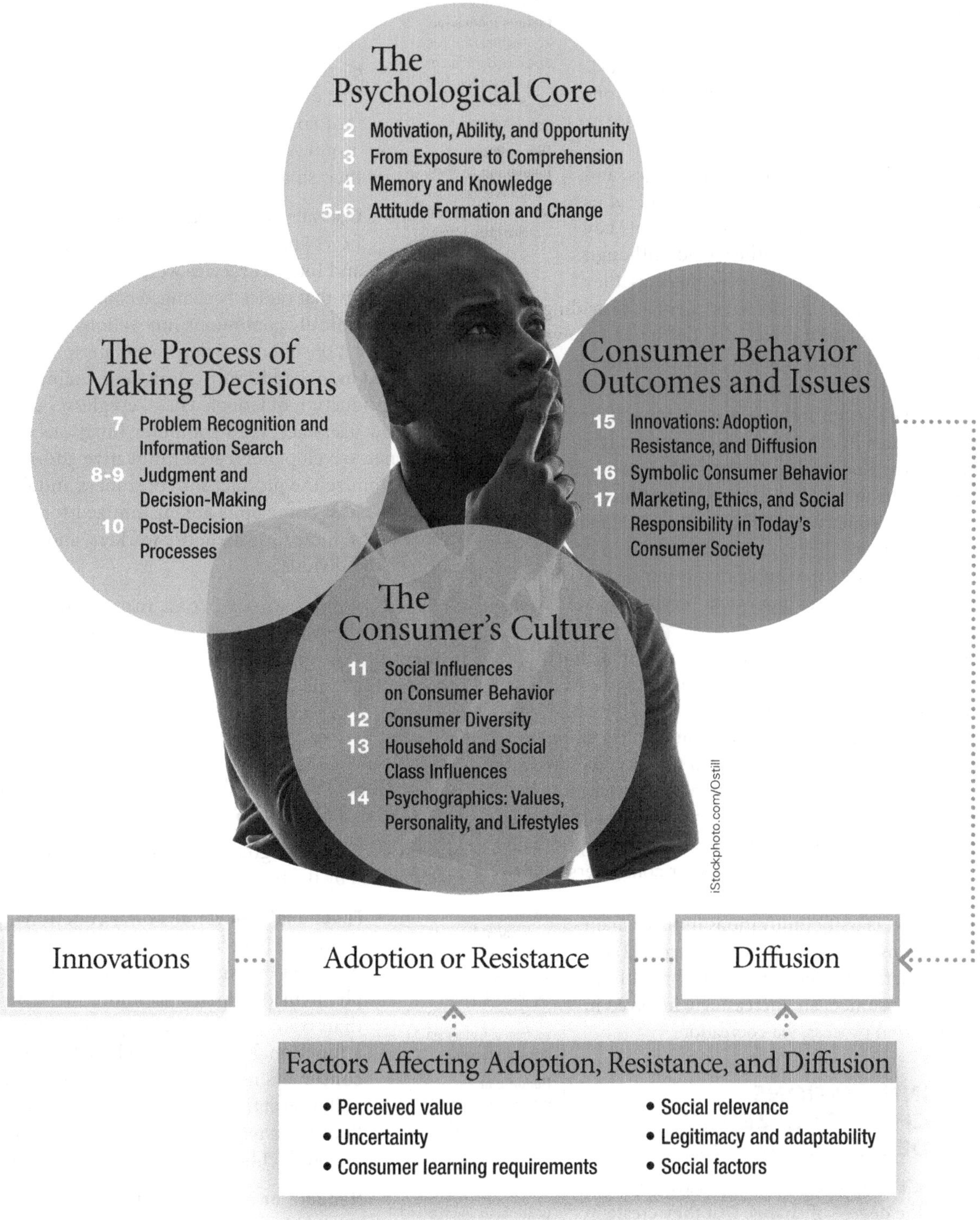

15-1a DEFINING AN INNOVATION

A new product, or an **innovation**, is an offering that is new to the marketplace. More formally, an innovation is any product, service, attribute, or idea that consumers within a market segment perceive as new and that has an effect on existing consumption patterns.[2] Services such as movie downloads and identity fraud insurance can be innovations, as can ideas. For example, social marketers have been active in persuading consumers to adopt such ideas as practicing safe sex and preventing bullying.

Products, services, attributes, packages, and ideas are innovations if they are *perceived* as being new by consumers, whether or not they actually are new. On the other hand, although products can be marketed as new offerings, they can fail if consumers do not view them as providing any unique benefits.[3] Marketers also define an innovation with respect to a market segment. Consumers in developing countries may regard certain appliances and electronic gadgets as entirely new, even though Americans and consumers in other Western countries regard these items as near necessities. On the other hand, U.S. and European consumers may consider something to be new that has been available to consumers in developing countries for some time. For example, consumers in Africa and India had the ability to complete cash transactions via cell phones years before such payment services became commonplace in U.S. markets.[4]

Innovations can bring about changes in acquisition, consumption, and disposition patterns. Microwave ovens have changed the way we cook; e-mail and text messaging have changed the way we communicate; cell phones with built-in cameras have changed the way we take and share photographs. Increased attention to recycling has brought about innovations such as recyclable and reusable packaging. Finally, online sites such as eBay, craigslist, and Freecycle provide innovative ways for consumers to dispose of unwanted items.

Marketers classify innovations in three main ways: in terms of (1) the innovation's type, (2) the type of benefits it offers, and (3) its breadth. In addition, consumers are increasingly involved in the innovation process, via cocreation.

15-1b INNOVATIONS CHARACTERIZED BY DEGREE OF NOVELTY

One way to characterize innovations is to describe the degree of change that they create in our consumption patterns.[5]

- **Continuous innovations** have a limited effect on existing consumption patterns; the

Innovation An offering that is perceived as new by consumers within a market segment and that has an effect on existing consumption patterns.

Dynamically continuous innovation An innovation that has a pronounced effect on consumption practices and often involves a new technology.

Discontinuous innovation An offering that is so new that we have never known anything like it before.

innovation is used in much the same way as the products that came before it. Not surprisingly, most new products are continuous innovations.

- **Dynamically continuous innovations** have a pronounced effect on consumption practices. Often these innovations incorporate a new technology. Smart watches such as the Samsung Galaxy Gear and the Apple Watch were dynamically continuous innovations when first introduced because they changed the way that consumers tracked physical activities, monitored messages, and accessed apps on their smartphones.[6]

- **Discontinuous innovations** are so new that we have never known anything like it before.[7] Airplanes and Internet service were once discontinuous innovations that radically changed consumer behavior. Like dynamically continuous innovations, discontinuous innovationsoften spawn a host of peripheral products and associated innovations. For example, after the introduction of Google Glass, eyeglasses designed to allow users access to computer functions and the Internet, developers created innovative add-on apps to customize the product for consumers and for corporate users. Some apps are customized for medical specialties, some for warehouse workers, and some for disabled individuals.[8]

Based on these three broad innovation types—continuous, dynamically continuous, and discontinuous—innovations can be characterized more specifically according to their degree of novelty on a continuum of newness (see Exhibit 15.2).

15-1c INNOVATIONS CHARACTERIZED BY BENEFITS OFFERED

In addition to their degree of novelty, innovations can be characterized by the type of benefits that they offer.

Functional innovation A new product, service, attribute, or idea that has utilitarian benefits that are different from or better than those of alternatives.

Hedonic or aesthetic innovation An innovation that appeals to our aesthetic, pleasure-seeking, and/or sensory needs.

Continuous innovation An innovation that has a limited effect on existing consumption patterns.

- **Functional innovations** offer functional performance benefits that are better than those provided by existing alternatives. For example, hybrid vehicles are more fuel-efficient than traditional gasoline-powered vehicles, a functional performance benefit that saves consumers money on fuel costs and reduces pollution at the same time. Functional innovations often rely on new technology that makes the product better than existing alternatives.

- **Hedonic or aesthetic innovations** appeal to our aesthetic, pleasure-seeking, and/or sensory needs.[9] New forms of dance or exercise, new types of music, new clothing styles, and new types of food all qualify as hedonic or

Exhibit 15.2 ▶ The Innovation Continuum

Innovations vary in how much behavioral change they require on the part of consumers. Discontinuous innovations (products that are radically new when they are first introduced) require considerable change in consumption patterns, whereas continuous innovations (often extensions of existing products) require very little change.

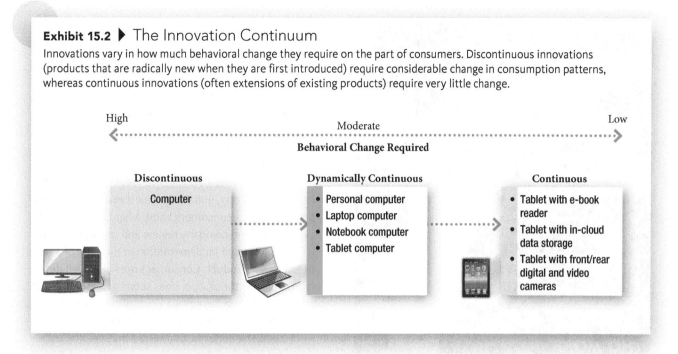

aesthetic innovations. Technology is fueling a variety of hedonic innovations, such as 3D printers that can make chocolates customized with personal portraits.[10] Hedonic innovations are a point of differentiation and also affect consumers' processing of feature performance. Interestingly, consumers may sometimes exhibit a bias in favor of aesthetically less appealing products because they are stimulated to elaborate on the contrast between the look of the product and information about its performance.[11]

▪ **Symbolic innovations** have new social meanings carried by their use and ownership. In some cases, a symbolic innovation is a new offering that is used exclusively by a particular group of consumers. Using the innovation, therefore, conveys meaning about a consumer's group membership. New styles of clothing that convey membership in a particular ethnic, age, or gender group may be regarded as symbolic innovations. In some cases, it is the meaning of the product and not the product itself that is new. For example, although condoms have been around for a long time, their meaning is now couched in terms of preventing the spread of AIDS or STDs as opposed to controlling conception. Earrings, once worn by women, are now fashionable for men as well. Finally, tattoos, once a symbol of machismo, have gained wide appeal and have different meanings among various consumer groups.

> **Symbolic innovation** A product, service, attribute, or idea that has new social meaning.

> **Cocreation** Actively involving consumers in creating value through participation in new product development, among other marketing activities.

Many new products represent blends of innovation types. Nutrition bars are designed to offer the functional benefits of protein and vitamins, with the hedonic benefit of good taste, and the social meanings of being health-conscious.

15-1d INNOVATIONS CHARACTERIZED BY BREADTH

Innovations can also be characterized in terms of their *breadth*, or the range of new and different uses for a particular product (see Exhibit 15.3). Baking soda, for example, has enjoyed a long life in part because it has innovation breadth; it has been used as a baking ingredient, a tooth polisher, a carpet deodorizer, and a refrigerator deodorizer. Teflon, originally developed to keep food from sticking to cookware, is now used in oven mitts, men's clothing (to help repel stains caused by spills), snow shovels (so snow will slide off the shovel), and many other products. The cell phone became the personal organizer, camera, global positioning system, and central device for socializing.

15-1e INNOVATIONS AND COCREATION

Traditionally, companies have controlled the innovation process, developing new offerings based on detailed knowledge of their customers' needs and purchasing patterns, specific customer requests, new technology, and similar market inputs.[12]

Today, however, many companies are pursuing innovations via **cocreation**, actively involving consumers in creating value through participation in new product development, among other marketing activities. Consumers who get involved enjoy the cocreation experience and get satisfaction from seeing some of these ideas

Exhibit 15.3 ▶ Innovations and cocreation
Nivea used cocreation to create a successful new product in its line of personal care products—deodorant.

Cocreation is increasingly popular and is now used in a wide variety of industries. Nivea, for example, used cocreation to develop a new deodorant product that became the most successful deodorant in the company's history. Now it is involving consumers in other innovation projects, as well.[17] Dell, best known for its computers, has refined the site ideastorm.com since its launch in 2007, enhancing the transparency of the process so that consumers know what is happening to every idea, from company review and posting for votes to acceptance and implementation in the form of a new or improved product. Consumer votes help Dell determine which of the 23,000 ideas submitted are the most popular, although the company's business criteria must be met before any ideas are implemented.[18]

Despite the benefits, marketers that employ cocreation must deal with concerns such as the secrecy of new product ideas and the challenges of developing an idea into a commercially feasible innovation. They must also attract, retain, and motivate a community of consumers to participate in cocreation.[19]

transformed into innovative products.[13] From the company's perspective, it is particularly useful to involve consumers who are capable of imagining how a product concept might be developed for the mainstream marketplace.[14]

The Internet and social media have accelerated the cocreation trend by providing convenient, accessible forums for interaction between marketers and consumers. One way consumers may become involved is by submitting new product ideas and voting on other consumers' ideas. Dell set up the site ideastorm.com just for this purpose; its most active consumer participants have suggested more than 200 ideas each and voted on thousands of other ideas.

Potential benefits of cocreation include:[15]

- Innovations that spring from cocreation are likely to fit better with consumer needs.

- Gathering ideas from consumers via social media or a website is relatively fast and inexpensive.

- Involving consumers in cocreation strengthens the relationship with the company.

- Consumers who are involved in selecting the products to be marketed exhibit higher demand for them, because they feel a sense of psychological ownership.[16]

15-1f THE CONSEQUENCES OF INNOVATIONS

Although innovations often offer relative benefits and advantages that may not have previously existed, they need not always be good for society at large. One study examined the diffusion of the steel ax among a tribe of aborigines who lived in the Australian bush.[20] Before the innovation was introduced, the stone ax had served as the tribe's principal tool. It was used only by men and was awarded to them as a gift and as payment for work performed. It was generally regarded as a symbol of masculinity and respect. However, missionaries came into the social system with the steel ax and distributed it to men, women, and children. This distribution scheme disrupted the sex and age roles among tribal members and thus affected the social system.

Innovations may also have negative socioeconomic consequences. For example, a study examining the diffusion of the CAT scanner through the medical community identified two important sociological consequences. First, the innovation tended to diffuse to markets that were generally wealthy, leaving the technology unavailable to families who lived in poorer rural areas. Second, the innovation was expensive and was viewed as driving up health-care costs.[21] As another example, the diffusion of electronic payment systems may lead to increased borrowing and debts, without the proper socialization of consumers. Marketers, policy makers, and we as consumers should be aware of the potential unanticipated social and economic consequences of the adoption and diffusion of innovations, and try to prevent or minimize the negatives.

> **Resistance** A desire not to buy the innovation, even in the face of pressure to do so.

15-2 Resistance Versus Adoption

Because the success of their new offerings is so important to companies, marketers need to understand how a consumer or household chooses to buy or adopt an innovation. Initially, marketers are interested in learning whether consumers would even consider the **adoption** of an innovation or whether they would choose to resist buying it. Marketers also want to know how consumers adopt products and how they decide whether to buy an innovation. Finally, marketers are interested in learning when a consumer would buy an innovation in relation to when other consumers would purchase it.

> **Adoption** A purchase of an innovation by an individual consumer or household.

15-2a WHETHER CONSUMERS ADOPT AN INNOVATION

Adoption will take place only if consumers do not resist the innovation. Consumers who resist an innovation

choose not to buy it, even in the face of pressure to do so.[22] Consumers sometimes resist adopting an innovation because it is simpler or seems preferable for them to continue using a more familiar product or service. **Resistance** may also be high if consumers think that using the new product would involve some risk. Lengthy battles between incompatible technology standards, for instance, affected adoption of products such as DVD players and are one reason for slow adoption of home appliances that connect wirelessly as part of the "Internet of things."[23]

Exhibit 15.4 shows that consumers often resist new technologies until they perceive that the negative effects from having to deal with something new are outweighed by the positive effects the new product might bring.[24] Research also indicates that consumers with low needs for change and cognition are most likely to resist innovations, whereas consumers with high needs for change and cognition are least likely to resist them.[25] Moreover, when consumers identify with a brand, they will resist switching to a new innovation marketed under a different brand.[26]

Note that resistance and adoption are separate concepts. An individual can resist purchasing an innovation without ever progressing to the point of adoption. If an individual does adopt a product, he or she has

Paradox	Description
Control/chaos	Technology can facilitate regulation or order, and technology can lead to upheaval or disorder.
Freedom/enslavement	Technology can facilitate independence or fewer restrictions, and technology can lead to dependence or more restrictions.
New/obsolete	New technologies provide the user with the most recently developed benefits of scientific knowledge, and new technologies are already or soon to be outmoded as they reach the marketplace.
Competence/incompetence	Technology can facilitate feelings of intelligence or efficacy, and technology can lead to feelings of ignorance or ineptitude.
Efficiency/inefficiency	Technology can facilitate less effort or time spent in certain activities, and technology can lead to more effort or time spent in certain activities.
Fulfills/creates needs	Technology can facilitate the fulfillment of needs or desires, and technology can lead to the development or awareness of needs or desires previously unrealized.
Assimilation/isolation	Technology can facilitate human togetherness, and technology can lead to human separation.
Engaging/disengaging	Technology can facilitate involvement, flow, or activity, and technology can lead to disconnection, disruption, or passivity.

Source: From David Glen Mick and Susan Fournier, "Paradoxes of Technology: Consumer Cognizance, Emotions, and Coping Strategies," *Journal of Consumer Research* 25, September 1998, p. 126. Reprinted with permission of The University of Chicago Press.

Exhibit 15.4 ▶ Eight Central Paradoxes of Technological Products
Consumers sometimes have mixed reactions to technologies because they create some of the paradoxes noted here. When the negative sides of these paradoxes are salient, consumers will likely resist an innovation.

presumably overcome any resistance to purchasing that might have existed initially. Marketers have to understand whether, why, and when consumers resist innovations—because the product will fail if resistance is too high. Typically, marketers can use a number of tactics to reduce consumers' resistance to an innovation. As discussed later in this chapter, the characteristics of the innovation, the social system in which the consumers operate, and marketing tactics all influence consumers' resistance to innovations.

15-2b HOW CONSUMERS ADOPT AN INNOVATION

Whether consumers choose to adopt or resist an innovation depends, in part, on whether they are prevention or promotion-focused. Prevention-focused consumers, whose priority is safety and protection, are more likely to resist new offerings because of the perceived risk and uncertainty that new offerings entail.[27] Promotion-focused consumers, whose priority is advancement and growth, are more likely to adopt new offerings, at least when the risks are not salient.[28]

The way in which consumers adopt innovations can vary, depending on whether the adoption decision is a high or low-effort one. The **high-effort hierarchy of effects**, illustrated in the top half of Exhibit 15.5, corresponds to the high-effort information search, attitude formation, judgment, and choice processes described in earlier chapters. Here, the consumer becomes aware of an innovation, thinks about it, gathers information about it, and forms an attitude based on this information. If his or her attitude is favorable, the consumer may try the product. If the trial experience is favorable, the consumer may decide to adopt the new product.

High-effort hierarchy of effects A purchase of an innovation based on considerable decision-making effort.

Consumers' motivation, ability, and opportunity (MAO) determine whether a high-effort adoption process occurs. A high-effort adoption process often takes place when consumers see that the innovation not only has benefits but also incurs psychological, social, economic, financial, or safety risks. For example, the consumer may think that wearing a new style of clothing is socially risky and will wait for others to buy it first. At one time, consumers carefully considered the benefits of buying a DVD player because of the high cost of replacing an entire collection of videotapes with DVDs. These days, DVD sales are plummeting as consumers adopt Internet-capable gadgets that stream movies and TV shows from online sources such as Netflix and Amazon Prime.[29]

Consumers are more likely to follow a high-effort decision-making process when the innovation is discontinuous (as opposed to continuous) because they know less about the innovation and must learn about it. Novice consumers need more information before they can understand and appreciate the benefits of a discontinuous innovation.[30] Also, a high-effort adoption process may be used when many people are involved in the decision, as in a family or an organization.[31]

When the new product involves less risk (as might be the case with a continuous innovation) and when fewer people are involved in the buying process, decision-making may follow the low-effort hierarchy of effects illustrated in the bottom half of Exhibit 15.5. Here, consumers devote less decision-making effort to considering and researching the product before they try it, and then they form attitudes based on the trial. If their attitudes are positive, they may adopt the innovation. With a low-effort hierarchy of effects, the time between awareness of the innovation and its trial or adoption may be brief.

Exhibit 15.5 ▶ Adoption Decision Process

The amount of effort we engage in before we decide to adopt an innovation varies. In some cases, we engage in considerable effort (e.g., extensive information search and evaluation of an offering). In other cases, the adoption process involves limited effort. In such cases, we first adopt the innovation and then decide whether we like it.

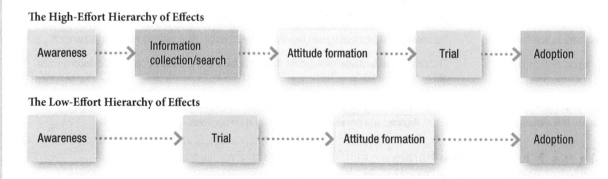

The High-Effort Hierarchy of Effects

Awareness ····▷ Information collection/search ····▷ Attitude formation ····▷ Trial ····▷ Adoption

The Low-Effort Hierarchy of Effects

Awareness ····▷ Trial ····▷ Attitude formation ····▷ Adoption

Marketing Implications

Understanding whether consumers' adoption decisions are based on a high or low-effort adoption process has important implications for marketers. For example, if the adoption involves low effort, marketers need to do all they can to encourage trial. Because the time between trial and purchase is low, trial may be very effective at encouraging consumers to adopt and buy the product. This is true for free offerings, as well. To illustrate, Google's Wave service, which combined the communication capabilities of e-mail with the immediacy of instant messaging, was launched with much fanfare in 2009. Although Google tried various methods to induce trial, Wave never attracted the many thousands of consumers it was created to serve. The company dropped Wave after two years, saying it "has not seen the user adoption we would have liked."[32]

If the adoption process is a high-effort one, marketers need to do all they can to reduce the perceived risk of adopting the innovation. For example, consumers have largely resisted adopting the Segway, a self-balancing scooter with a top speed of about 13 miles per hour and maneuverability well suited to paved streets and park paths. Some of this resistance may be due to the high price and some due to concerns about learning to ride safely. Despite high awareness after intense media coverage of its introduction in 2001, relatively few consumers have actually tried riding a Segway. Now, years after its launch, the Segway is most often purchased by travel businesses for use by tour groups and by municipalities for use by police officers on patrol.[33] An initial trial experience of the Segway as part of a tour group may convince consumers to buy one for their own use.

15-2c WHEN CONSUMERS ADOPT INNOVATIONS

Consumers differ in when they adopt an innovation. One framework identifies five adopter groups based on the timing of their adoption decisions, as shown in Exhibit 15.6.[34] The first 2.5 percent of the market to adopt the innovation are described as *innovators*. The next 13.5 percent are called *early adopters*. The next 34 percent are called the *early majority*. The *late majority* represents the next 34 percent of adopters, and the last 16 percent to purchase the product are called *laggards*.

Characteristics of Adopter Groups

The adopter groups tend to exhibit different characteristics, as shown in the exhibit. Research indicates, for example, that innovators who are enthusiastic about technology want to be the first to get a new high-tech product, even if there are a few bugs or inefficiencies.[35] For example, devotees of Apple iPhones have been known to endure hours of waiting in front of local Apple stores just to be among the first buyers of each new version. Some electronic games inspire similar enthusiasm.

Early adopters are visionaries in the product category. They admire a technologically new product not so much for its features as for its abilities to create a revolutionary breakthrough in how things are done.

The early majority are pragmatists, seeking innovations that offer incremental, predictable improvements on an existing technology. Because they do not like risk, they care deeply about who is making the innovation and the reputation of the company. They are interested in how well the innovation will fit with their current lifestyle and the products they own now, and they are concerned about the innovation's reliability. They are price sensitive, and they are happy when competitors enter the market because they can then compare features and be more assured about the product's ultimate feasibility.

Late-majority consumers are more conservative, wary of progress, and rely on tradition. They often fear high-tech products, and their goal in buying them is to not get stung. They like to buy preassembled products that include everything in a single, easy-to-use package. Laggards, the slowest group to adopt, are skeptics. Although laggards may resist innovations, marketers can gain insights from understanding why this group is skeptical of an innovation. Why, for example, do some people shun smartwatches in favor of other methods of handling tasks such as tracking physical activity and checking messages? Do they fear they will never learn to use all the product's features? Are they worried about rapid obsolescence or about changes in fashion? The answers can help companies like Samsung and Apple market more effectively to this group.[36]

Application of Adopter Group Categories

An important implication of adopter groups is that if an innovation is to spread through the market, it must appeal to every group. Unfortunately, many potentially useful innovations have never gained mass-market appeal because the marketing efforts for them did not acknowledge the characteristics of the adopter groups. This result was the case with short-lived products such as the Apple Newton Message Pad, the Flip pocket camcorder, and the Flooz system of online buying credits.[37]

The five-category scheme of adopter groups is a useful but somewhat idealized way of looking at who adopts innovations when. That is, there may be more or fewer adopter groups, depending on the innovation.[38] For example, when Vespa scooters became a fashion item

Exhibit 15.6 ▶ Profile of Adopter Groups

Researchers have identified five groups of consumers that differ in when they adopt an innovation relative to when others do. Innovators are the first in a market to adopt an innovation, and laggards are the last. Certain characteristics are associated with each adopter group.

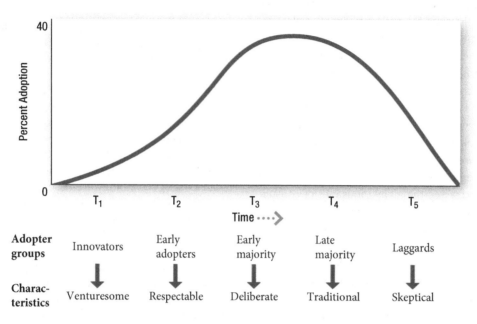

Source: Based on *Diffusion of Innovations*, 3rd edition by Everett M. Rogers.

in Europe, some early adopters in America imported their own before the product was introduced to the U.S. market. Such consumers could be called "preinnovators," because they adopt the innovation before it is even officially introduced.

Also, the shape of adoption curves may differ from the regular bell-shape, such as the positively skewed shape of fashion adoption curves (steep growth, sometimes with steep declines) or the negatively skewed shape of certain health-related innovations (slow growth, slow decline). Thus, instead of attracting the percentages of adopters that form the bell-shaped curve in Exhibit 15.6, certain products may attract the first 1 percent of adopters as innovators, the next 60 percent as early adopters, the next 30 percent as the early majority, the following 5 percent as the late majority, and the last 4 percent as laggards. It is important that marketers use the idea of adoption groups and adoption curves flexibly, and examine how many groups, of which size, and at what times consumers adopt new products in the specific markets where the company operates. We return to this issue later in the chapter when describing the diffusion of innovations.

Exhibit 15.7 ▶ Use-Diffusion Patterns for Home Technology Innovations

Studying the difference in diffusion and usage patterns of consumers can help marketers to understand the diffusion of innovations.

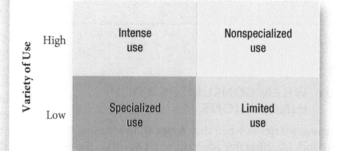

Source: From R. James H. McAlexander, John W. Schouten, and Harold F. Koenig, "Building Brand Community," *Journal of Marketing 66*, no. 1, January 2004, pp. 38–54. Reprinted with permission of American Marketing Association.

Marketing research suggests that it can be useful to examine the rate of use and variety of use to understand how an innovation diffuses through the market.[39] As an example, the use-diffusion model in Exhibit 15.7 identifies specific types of users of home technology such as PCs: intense users (who have many uses for an innovation and show a high rate of use), specialized users (high rate of use but low variety of uses), nonspecialized users (high variety of uses but low rate of use), and limited users (low variety of uses and low rate of use).

Marketing Implications

Whether or not marketers accept the five-category adopter scheme, they recognize that consumers who are the first to buy a new product are important for several reasons. First, because innovators adopt new products independently of the opinions of other people, they are more likely to be receptive to information about new products, including information provided by marketers. Second, by virtue of their experience with the innovation, they may also communicate information to others and thus exact normative and informational influence through the adoption decisions of others (see Chapter 11). Given these issues, many researchers want to better understand who innovators are and how they can be reached through marketing communications and appropriate media.

Demographics

Several of the demographic variables described in Chapters 12 and 13 have been linked with innovators.[40] For example, innovators tend to be younger, more affluent, and better educated than other consumers; laggards are typically older, have less income and education, and have lower occupational status. Yet, even here, marketers need to be aware that unexpected opportunities may emerge. For example, when the cholesterol-free Becel margarine targeted to younger consumers was introduced in Europe, older consumers in particular were ready to adopt it early on. Focusing on taste as much as on health benefits is helping Unilever fuel wider adoption of Becel Gold margarine in global markets.[41] Religion is sometimes linked with innovation adoption. Amish consumers, for example, avoid many innovations, including cars, electricity, and telephones.

The general links between these demographic variables and innovativeness make sense. First, highly educated people tend to be heavier users of media and therefore tend to learn about new products earlier than less educated people do. Second, high-income consumers can afford to buy innovations, and they may perceive less financial risk in adopting something new. Demographic variables such as family influence[42] and culture of origin have also been linked with innovativeness. Consumers in Japan, for example, are regarded as innovators for new technology. This market was among the first to adopt high-tech offerings such as paying for purchases via smartphone, even as the "mobile wallet" has been slow to catch on elsewhere.[43]

Social Influence

Innovators have been linked with the social influence factors discussed in Chapter 11.[44] They tend to have a great deal of social influence beyond their immediate groups, and they tend to be opinion leaders. Although this finding has not been observed in all research, it makes sense that innovators have influence because their opinions are shared with and respected by nonadopters. Importantly, consumers who participate in a brand community are more likely to adopt a new product marketed by that brand—and to resist adoption of new products from competing brands.[45]

Personality

Several personality characteristics have also been linked with the adoption of innovations.[46] For example, innovators are high in their need for stimulation, are inner directed, and are less dogmatic than other consumers. Innovators also do less planning and deliberate less than other consumers do when making buying decisions.[47]

Therefore, it is better to use a mixed approach to understanding innovativeness. That is, in addition to measuring "innate innovativeness" (as a personality trait that some consumers are high on, across all consumption domains) it is useful to examine consumers' willingness to be innovative in a specific consumption domain. For example, an innovator of alternative music might respond positively to statements like "In general, I am among the first in my circle of friends to download a new alternative-rock song" or "I know the names of new alternative-rock acts before other people do." Innovators in the area of fashion, however, might not respond similarly to these statements.[48] Consumers may be innovators or early adopters in one domain but laggards in another, and some consumers may more generally be ready to adopt innovations.

Cultural Values

Adoption of innovations has been linked with culture of origin and the values tied to the culture. One study of 11 European countries found that innovativeness was associated with cultures that value individualism over collectivism, those that value assertiveness over nurturing, and those that value openness to change over conservatism.[49]

Media Involvement

Innovators have been shown to be heavy media users and to rely extensively on external information.[50] They tend to think of themselves as active seekers and disseminators of information.[51] This finding makes sense because to affect others' adoption decisions, innovators must not only get their information somewhere but also be willing to transmit it. Brands are increasingly reaching out via social media to innovators who seek external information and enjoy sharing what they know online.

Usage

Finally, innovators may be heavy users within the product category.[52] Consumers who frequently drink soft drinks may be innovators of new beverages because they are in the market often and hence are likely to notice these new products. In addition, innovators are usually experts in the product category, perhaps because of their heavy media involvement and product usage.

15-3 Diffusion

As increasing numbers of consumers in a market adopt an innovation, the innovation spreads or diffuses through the market. While adoption reflects the behavior of an individual, **diffusion** reflects the behavior of the marketplace of consumers as a group. More specifically, diffusion reflects the percentage of the population that has adopted an innovation at a specific point in time. To illustrate, cell phones are owned by nearly 90 percent of the population in the United States, South Africa, and several other countries.[53]

> **Diffusion** The percentage of the population that has adopted an innovation at a specific point in time.

Because marketers are interested in successfully spreading their offering through a market, they want to understand two important diffusion issues: how an offering diffuses through the market and how quickly it does so.

15-3a HOW OFFERINGS DIFFUSE THROUGH A MARKET

One way to examine how offerings spread through a market is to look at the pattern of adoption over time. From the marketers' perspective, life would be easy if everyone adopted the new offering just as soon as it was introduced into the market (assuming sufficient production capacity to meet the demand). However, this occurrence is rarely the case; in fact, several diffusion patterns have been identified.

> **S-shaped diffusion curve** A diffusion curve characterized by slow initial growth followed by a rapid increase in diffusion.

The S-Shaped Diffusion Curve

Some innovations exhibit an **S-shaped diffusion curve**, as shown in Exhibit 15.8(a).[54] Following this pattern, adoption of the products begins relatively slowly; as the exhibit shows, a relatively small percentage of the total market has adopted the product between times 1 and 2 in the exhibit. After a certain period, however, the rate of adoption increases dramatically, with many consumers adopting the product within a relatively short period of time. Between times 2 and 3, a dramatic increase occurs in the number of consumers adopting the product. Then adoptions grow at a decreasing rate, and the curve flattens out.

As an example, the diffusion of electronic books and e-book-readers was initially very slow. Then it began to increase as more consumers became aware of and knowledgeable about the technology and additional firms entered the market. As a wider variety of downloadable content (books, magazines, newspapers) became available, and more affordably priced devices were introduced by Amazon, Barnes & Noble, and others, millions of consumers purchased e-book readers. Then tablet computers and large-screen smartphones with e-book-reading apps became popular. The pace of e-book-reader adoption slowed as consumers began to read books on these multifunction digital devices rather than buying single-function e-readers. Now e-book reader sales are down, but Amazon is selling more e-books than printed books. Another sign of adoption: 95 percent of U.S. public libraries have added e-books to their collection of circulating materials.[55]

> **Exponential diffusion curve** A diffusion curve characterized by rapid initial growth.

The Exponential Diffusion Curve

Another type of adoption curve is the **exponential diffusion curve**, illustrated in Exhibit 15.8(b).[56] In contrast to the S-shaped curve, the exponential diffusion curve starts out much more quickly, with a large percentage of the market adopting the product as soon as it is available. However, with each additional time period, the adoption rate increases at a slower pace.

15-3b FACTORS AFFECTING THE SHAPE OF THE DIFFUSION CURVE

Many factors influence the ultimate shape of the diffusion curve. In general, marketers might expect an S-shaped diffusion curve when the innovation is associated with some

Exhibit 15.8 ▶ Diffusion and Product Life Cycle Curves

Several diffusion patterns have been identified: (a) with an S-shaped diffusion curve, diffusion starts out slowly, increases rapidly, and then flattens out again; (b) with an exponential diffusion curve, many people adopt the innovation quickly; and (c) the product life cycle curve depicts sales (not cumulative diffusion) of an offering over time.

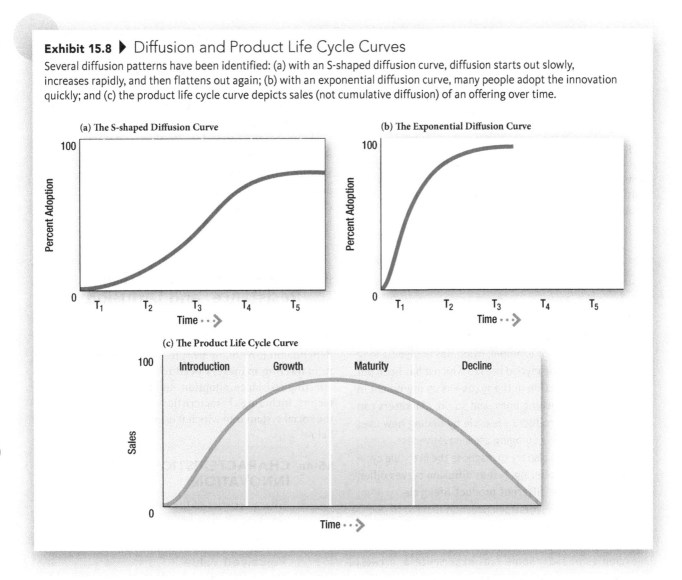

(a) The S-shaped Diffusion Curve

(b) The Exponential Diffusion Curve

(c) The Product Life Cycle Curve

social, psychological, economic, performance, or physical risk. In such situations, consumers might wait to see how other people use and react to the innovation before adopting it. Diffusion may also be slow initially if consumers are not sure whether the product will be on the market for long or whether its use carries high switching costs. The diffusion of computers and CD players followed this S-shaped curve. An S-shaped diffusion pattern might also occur when consumers are physically far apart, do not discuss the innovation with others, or do not share the same beliefs.

In contrast, when the innovation involves little risk, when switching costs are low, when consumers are similar in their beliefs and values, and/or when people talk often about the product and quickly disseminate knowledge throughout the social system, the product may have a rapid takeoff period that follows the exponential curve for diffusion. Note that these curves reflect only the rate at which consumers in the market adopt a product, not the

> **Product life cycle**
> A concept that suggests that products go through an initial introductory period followed by periods of sales growth, maturity, and decline.

time period under analysis. In other words, an S-shaped or an exponential curve could reflect diffusion that has occurred over a 1-year or a 30-year period. Furthermore, the curves could reflect the diffusion of either a functional, symbolic, or hedonic innovation.

15-3c HOW DIFFUSION RELATES TO THE PRODUCT LIFE CYCLE

The **product life cycle** concept, illustrated in Exhibit 15.8(c), proposes that products initially go through a period of introduction, followed by relatively rapid growth as more competitors enter the market and more consumers adopt the product. With greater competition, weaker competitors drop out, and product sales plateau. At some point, however, consumer acceptance wanes, and product sales decline.

Product diffusion and the product life cycle are related but different concepts. Diffusion focuses on the *percentage of the market* that has adopted the product; diffusion is complete when 100 percent of the market has purchased the product. The product life cycle, on the other hand, deals with *sales of the product* over time. Moreover, diffusion curves are generally cumulative—that is, they continue to increase or at least level off over time. However, the product life cycle curve may decline as consumers decide not to purchase the product in the future. For instance, after an innovation such as the cell phone diffused through an entire market, it was replaced by another innovation, the multifunction smartphone, and sales of the old product eventually declined as the new innovation took hold.

> **Classic** A successful innovation that has a lengthy product life cycle.

colors for consumers who want to update their existing kitchen appliances.[59] In contrast, a classic is a successful innovation that has a lengthy product life cycle. For example, Jeans are an American **classic**, as are rock 'n' roll music and hamburgers.

Although the terms fad, fashion, and classic have most often been applied to aesthetic or hedonic innovations, they can also describe functional and symbolic innovations because the life cycle of these innovations similarly can be variable.

 Marketing Implications

Marketers who understand a product's life cycle can try to prevent that product's decline— perhaps by finding new uses for it. For example, nylon has enjoyed a long life cycle given the myriad uses to which it has been put since its introduction in the 1940s—as an ingredient in clothing, rope, fishing lines, and so on. Marketers can lengthen their product's life cycle by finding new uses for a product or encouraging use innovativeness.

Marketers can also try to diagnose the likely life cycle pattern of their offering. Just as diffusion curves differ, so too are there different product life cycle curves. A **fad** is a successful innovation that has a very short product life cycle. Teenage Mutant Ninja Turtles, scooters, and certain diets are examples of fads. Some fads experience a revival years after their first appearance. Hula hoops, for example, came back, more than 40 years after the original fad, as a product to use to stay fit.[57] As another example, yo-yos have been through multiple fashions and fads in usage since the 1930s. Marketers are sometimes interested in the phenomenon of **contagion**, which refers to the degree to which people influence one another in the diffusion of a new product. Marketing researchers have developed models that managers can use to estimate the degree of contagion in a market.[58]

A **fashion** or trend is a successful innovation with a lengthier and potentially cyclical life. For example, certain aesthetic styles like art deco run in fashion cycles, as do styles of clothing and shoes. Colors of laptops, coffeemakers, washing machines, and other electrical items run in fashion cycles, as well. That's why General Electric's FirstBuild Studio is offering 3D-printed replacement knobs in fashion

> **Fad** A successful innovation that has a very short product life cycle.
>
> **Contagion** The degree to which consumers influence each other in the diffusion of a new product.

> **Fashion** A successful innovation that has a moderately long and potentially cyclical product life cycle.
>
> **Relative advantage** Benefits in an innovation superior to those found in existing products.

15-4 Influences on Adoption, Resistance, and Diffusion

Knowing that innovations may diffuse quickly or slowly through a market and that the success of a new product depends on how many people within the market adopt it, marketing managers need to understand the factors affecting resistance, adoption, and diffusion. A number of factors, including characteristics of the innovation and of the social system into which it is introduced, are described below.

15-4a CHARACTERISTICS OF THE INNOVATION

Characteristics of the innovation that can affect resistance, adoption, and diffusion include perceived value, benefits, and costs.

Perceived Value

Consumers perceive that an innovation has value if it offers greater perceived benefits or lower perceived costs than existing alternatives do. Products with high perceived value may be more readily adopted than those with low perceived value. Smartphones, for instance, were adopted quickly because consumers perceived the value in a handheld device that could be used for communication and—with easily downloaded apps—other functions like streaming entertainment, playing games, and reading e-books. This was a big improvement over carrying multiple single-function devices such as early cell phones, electronic book readers, portable videogame devices, and portable DVD players.

Perceived Benefits

An innovation's value to consumers is affected by its perceived **relative advantage**, the extent to which it offers benefits superior to those of existing products. Something new offers a relative advantage if it can help consumers avoid risks, fulfill their needs, solve problems, or achieve

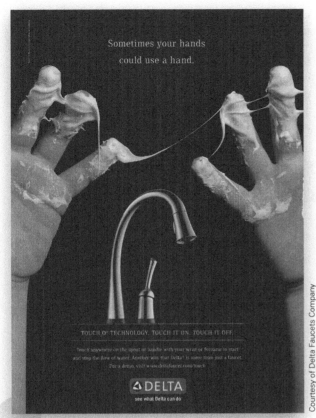

Courtesy of Delta Faucets Company

Exhibit 15.9 ▶ Relative Advantage

Innovations that have a clear relative advantage tend to be adopted more quickly.

their goals—criteria that affect consumers' adoption decisions. In fact, research indicates that product advantage is one of the most important predictors of new-product success (see Exhibit 15.9).[60] Note that a relative advantage is something the product does for the consumer—not something that exists in the product. Thus, the relative advantage of hybrid cars such as the Toyota Prius lies not in their features but rather in the owners' ability to save money on gasoline and help save the environment.

However, if consumers do not perceive a new product's advantage over the benefits of existing alternatives or think the advantage is unimportant, the innovation will face resistance. In addition, consumers often have difficulty concretely imagining the circumstances of buying and using a radically new product.[61] Yet consumers who are able to visualize the value of the novel new benefits will have higher evaluations of a dramatically different innovation.[62] Consumers are likely to perceive a product's benefits as being more valuable when they can adapt it for use in different contexts. **Use innovativeness** means using products in a new or creative way, as in the way that a consumer might use baking soda to solve problems like deodorizing a kitty litter box.[63]

> **Use innovativeness**
> Finding use for a product that differs from the product's original intended usage.

Perceived Costs

Another aspect of the value of a product is its perceived costs, meaning all types of costs, including the money, time, and effort required to adopt the product. The higher the purchase cost, the greater the resistance, and hence the slower the diffusion. Consider hybrid gas-electric cars like the Prius, which tend to have a higher initial cost than comparable conventional cars. Although the higher perceived cost slowed its adoption at first, the car's relative advantage became apparent after the pump price of gasoline skyrocketed, resulting in higher demand for fuel-efficient cars. In contrast, digital music players have experienced much more rapid diffusion as competition and manufacturing efficiencies have brought prices down. *Switching costs*—the costs of changing from the current product to a new one—are part of the total costs. For example, consumers who upgrade computer operating systems may have to replace a peripheral device such as a printer because of incompatibility with the new system.

 ## Marketing Implications

If consumers do not perceive that an innovation has a relative advantage, marketers may need to add one by physically redesigning or reengineering the innovation.

Communicate and Demonstrate the Relative Advantage

The company must educate consumers who do not understand a product or its relative advantages. For instance, the mobile wallet had been available in different forms for several years, with offerings by Google and other providers, before Apple Pay was introduced for the iPhone. Apple and its financial-services partners, including American Express, used advertising, social-media posts, and media coverage to demonstrate the convenience and security of mobile-wallet payments. Very quickly, Walgreens and other retailers reported a significant increase in mobile-wallet usage.[64] Another way to communicate an innovation's advantage is through highly credible and visible opinion leaders. To promote their Wi-Fi-connected stereo speakers, brands such as Bose, Denon, and LG have all provided samples to the influential *Wall Street Journal* columnist Geoffrey Fowler, who writes about tech products.[65]

Use Price Promotions to Reduce Perceived Costs

If consumers perceive that a product is too costly, the company can use special price-oriented sales promotions such as price-offs, rebates, or refunds to reduce the perceived cost. Marketers can also provide guarantees or warranties that make the product seem less expensive. Alternatively, the marketer may find a cheaper way to manufacture the product and pass on the savings in the form of lower prices for consumers, a strategy that marketers of digital watches used.

Provide Incentives for Switching

If innovations are not adopted because consumers think switching costs are high, marketers might provide incentives for switching. This situation explains why razor companies often give away free razor handles to get consumers to switch to new-generation blades. Companies might also use advertising to inform consumers about the costs associated with not switching. Finally, marketers might be able to force their innovation to become the industry standard, for instance, by having such high quality, ease of use, or low price that they become the dominant alternative.

15-4b UNCERTAINTY

In addition to the characteristics of the innovation, uncertainty surrounding the innovation can affect its adoption, resistance, and diffusion. Several aspects of uncertainty are particularly important. One is doubt about what will become the industry standard. To illustrate, as Panasonic, Samsung, General Electric, and other manufacturers wrangle over the details of industry standards, consumers have been slow to adopt innovations such as home appliances that connect for convenient management via smartphone apps.[66]

Another aspect is uncertainty about the relative advantage of a product that requires the consumer to make significant behavioral changes.[67] Consumers are often more uncertain about the usefulness of a discontinuous (vs. a continuous) innovation.[68] Surprisingly, giving consumers more information about a high-tech product that combines a new interface with new functionality actually makes consumers more uncertain about the product's advantages. This phenomenon may happen because consumers pay more attention to the new interface and, in processing the information, reason through the possible negative outcomes of product adoption.[69]

A third aspect of uncertainty is the length of the product life cycle. Consumers are more likely to resist buying a fad than a fashion or a classic. For example, you may forgo spending $100 on spike-heeled shoes if you think they will soon be out of style, or you may wait to buy a tablet computer because you think the next generation will have longer battery life. This type of uncertainty is a legitimate concern in clothing and high-tech markets, where products are frequently changed or improved.

Finally, consumers' specific uncertainty concerns differ according to the length of time before adoption. For example, people are more concerned about the downside of uncertainties such as switching costs when they plan to adopt an innovation in the near future, compared to when adoption is in the distant future.[70]

Marketing Implications

When consumers resist innovations because they are worried about an offering's short life cycle, marketers might show how adaptable the product is and hence how likely it is to have a long life cycle. For example, marketers of digital book readers can address consumers' fears of the product's rapid obsolescence by demonstrating how their products may be upgraded, connected to advanced systems, or used in other ways that extend the life cycle by continuing to deliver perceived value. Amazon's Kindle—one of the original e-book readers—has been upgraded numerous times to improve the reading experience, enhance functionality for multiple uses, and add value even as the price is reduced.[71]

15-4c CONSUMER LEARNING REQUIREMENTS

A third characteristic affecting resistance, adoption, and diffusion is consumer learning requirements—or what consumers need to do to use the innovation effectively. These learning requirements involve compatibility, trialability, and complexity.

Compatibility

Compatibility The extent to which an innovation is consistent with one's needs, values, norms, or behaviors.

Consumers often resist innovations because they see them as incompatible with their needs, values, norms, or behaviors.[72] The more **compatible** the innovation is with consumers' values, norms, and behaviors, the less their resistance and the greater the product diffusion. For example, when Patagonia introduced the first jacket made of Polartec polyester fleece, it was an immediate hit because it was warm yet lightweight, durable, and washable. Today, Polartec is made from recycled material, adding to the eco-friendly appeal.[73] On the other hand, Bernard Matthews Farms, a large U.K. turkey grower, withdrew a line of gourmet-branded turkey steaks in crust and turkey roasts with stuffing after only six months on the market. Why? Turkey is not as mature a product category in the United Kingdom as it is in the United States, and U.K.

consumers are accustomed to cooking whole turkeys rather than buying ready-to-cook specialty turkey entrees positioned on the basis of convenience.[74]

Some potentially serious consequences can arise when an innovation is incompatible with consumers' values, goals, and behaviors. One case in particular is marketers' attempts to encourage bottle-feeding by mothers in Latin American, African, and Asian markets. Manufacturers' ads showed pictures of mothers with beautiful, fat, healthy babies. The ad copy read, "Give your baby love and Lactogen" (Lactogen is an infant formula). The modern look of the ad attracted upper-income, well-educated consumers as well as peasant families who aspired to be like the well-educated. Unfortunately, most peasant families could not afford the expensive formula, so they diluted it with water, leaving their babies malnourished. Furthermore, they were unfamiliar with practices like sterilizing nipples and bottles; as a result, bacteria in these items made the babies sick. The lack of compatibility between the innovation and the consumers' behavior therefore caused unanticipated problems.[75]

Trialability

A second aspect of consumer learning requirements is the **trialability** of the innovation, the extent to which the product can be tried on a limited basis before it is adopted. Products like microwaveable meals can be tested and tasted

> **Complexity** The extent to which an innovation is complicated and difficult to understand or use.

> **Trialability** The extent to which an innovation can be tried on a limited basis before it is adopted.

in just a few minutes (see Exhibit 15.10). Similarly, many software firms offer limited-use trials so consumers can experience the features and benefits before they buy. However, trialability is virtually impossible with innovations like laser eye surgery. Because a trial allows a consumer to assess the product's relative advantages and potential risks, products that are easy to try tend to diffuse through the market more quickly than those that do not.

Trialability is often important to innovators and early adopters because they have little else on which to base the value of the innovation. Trialability can be less important for later adopters, who are likely to know people who have already adopted the innovation and who can therefore speak to its efficacy.[76]

Complexity

Complexity is a final learning requirement related to adoption and diffusion. Diffusion is likely to be slow when consumers perceive they will have difficulty understanding or using a new product. Then, the mental or thinking costs are high. Products that are loaded with many features may appear useful, yet the fact that they have so many features leads them to be perceived as being overly complex.[77] In fact, consumers may form a lower evaluation of a complex product with novel attributes because they worry about the time needed to understand the new features.[78] This perception is a challenge for marketers because consumers tend to

Exhibit 15.10 ▶ Trialability
Consumers' learning experience benefits from a products' trialability, such as trying samples of food, before they purchase.

underestimate how well they can manage complexity.[79] Digital photography initially diffused at a relatively slow rate because consumers perceived that it would be complex to transfer digital images from the camera to the computer, figuring out the software for enhancing images, and printing high-quality photos.[80]

Marketing Implications

Marketers can use several tactics to reduce consumers' resistance to innovations.

Enhance Compatibility or Reduce Complexity

Marketers may be able to reposition an innovation so that it is viewed as more consistent with consumers' needs and values. For example, after experiencing lower sales, Campbell Soup Company recently implemented a marketing campaign to reposition its soups and other packaged food products as healthy, wholesome, and convenient—benefits highly valued by consumers, as research shows.[81] Sometimes, however, companies must redesign an offering to overcome incompatibility and reduce complexity. When Apple introduced the voice-activated personal assistant Siri app on its iPhone, consumers responded to the convenience and simplicity of asking questions in plain English to accomplish tasks and receive information via smartphone. Now Google and Microsoft both offer voice-activated personal assistant apps for smartphones.[82]

Educate About Compatibility

Companies can use promotions to show how their innovations actually are compatible with consumers' needs, values, norms, or behaviors. For example, connecting with friends via texting and using touch-screen electronics are common behaviors for many millennial generation consumers, the target market for PepsiCo's recently introduced touch-screen soft-drink vending machines. To promote this innovation, PepsiCo initially created a how-to video for YouTube. Later tests of its touch-screen vending machines instructed users to log into Facebook and "like" to receive free samples of Pepsi beverages.[83] Advertising can also show how a new offering is easier to use or has more benefits than current alternatives do, even if it requires adopting new behaviors.

Use Change Agents

Another way to enhance perceived compatibility is to use change agents such as opinion leaders. Marketers in diverse industries have aimed new products at influential and highly respected people who can be convinced of a new product's merits and who will then spread positive word of mouth to others. For example, companies are eager to have their products included in the gift bags distributed to movie stars at the annual Academy Awards event because product adoption by these celebrities (or a few words of praise) will encourage trial among fans. Silvercar Rentals, eager to be associated with the glamour of the Oscars, recently put into the bag a certificate good for $20,000 worth of rentals from its all-Audi fleet of vehicles.[84]

Fit with a System of Products

Some marketers address incompatibility by designing the innovation to fit with a system of existing products. This can also work with a packaging innovation or an innovative form of a product that is established. For example, Campbell Soup introduced single-serve "fresh brewed" chicken soup in a K-cup, and Nature Valley introduced single-serve oatmeal in a K-cup. Both product innovations were designed to fit with the many coffeemakers that use K-cup refills, adding convenience to a wider range of foods without requiring consumers to buy new food-preparation accessories.[85]

Force the Innovation to Be the Industry Standard

Marketers can sometimes work with regulators to require adoption of the innovation. For example, smoke detectors, seat belts, and lead-free gasoline are all innovations that have been forced into usage by government mandate. Manufacturers are introducing more hybrid and electric cars because states' clean-air requirements are mandating zero-emission vehicles.[86]

Use Promotions to Enhance Trialability

Companies can stimulate trial through various promotions. Free samples, for example, encourage trial by people who might otherwise resist using the product. Many supermarkets encourage trial by distributing samples of new food products, and Costco is known for the number and variety of sampling opportunities that shoppers encounter as they browse its cavernous stores.

Demonstrate Compatibility and Simplicity

Live demonstrations (at trade shows or conducted by salespeople) and demonstrations in ads and online videos can show a product's ease of use and its compatibility with consumers' needs, values, and

Exhibit 15.11 ▶ Compatibility and Simplicity
Consumers respond to innovations that are shown to be simple and compatible with their values, like the live demonstrations of the Blendtec's blenders.

behaviors. Sales of Blendtec's blenders increased dramatically after the firm posted videos on YouTube to demonstrate how rugged the blenders are and how quickly and easily they work (see Exhibit 15.11). The company continues to film and post at new "Will It Blend?" videos, showing products such as the Apple Watch being pulverized in moments. Now Blendtec's YouTube channel has more than 800,000 subscribers and some of its videos have been viewed more than 12 million times.[87]

Simulate Trial

At times, a company may need to simulate trial rather than have consumers actually try the product. IKEA, for example, offers a free "augmented reality" app that shows, on a smartphone screen, how a particular sofa or bed pictured in the catalog will look in the consumer's own living room or bedroom.[88] On Benjamin Moore's website, consumers can use a "personal color viewer" to preview how different paint colors would look on the walls of different rooms.

15-4d SOCIAL RELEVANCE

> **Social relevance**
> The extent to which an innovation can be observed or the extent to which having others observe it has social cachet.

A fourth major factor that affects resistance, adoption, and diffusion is the innovation's **social relevance**, particularly its observability and social value. *Observability* is the extent to which consumers can see others using the innovation. In general, the more consumers can observe others using the innovation, the more likely they are to adopt it.[89] For example, a new shoulder strap designed to distribute the weight of a golf bag gained acceptance among caddies after they saw others using the product.[90] On the other hand, a new scale that announces your body weight is unlikely to be very observable because few people want to weigh themselves in public (or want others to hear their weight!).[91] Thus, diffusion is also affected by the public or private nature of the product's consumption, as described in Chapter 11.

Social value reflects the extent to which the product has social cachet, which means that it is seen as socially desirable and/or appropriate and therefore generates imitation, speeding diffusion. One study found that farmers adopted certain farming innovations because the innovations were expensive and thus had social prestige value. These studies also found that the earlier someone adopted the innovation, the more prestige was associated with it.[92] Consumers sometimes adopt aesthetic innovations like new fashions, hairstyles, and cars based on the social prestige they confer on the user.

Although social value may enhance diffusion, the diffusion of a product based on a prestige image may actually shorten its life cycle because once a product is adopted by the masses, it is no longer prestigious. For example, designer jeans, once associated with prestige and exclusivity, lost prestige when everyone in the market started to wear them.[93]

 Marketing Implications

Observability can be enhanced by the use of distinctive packaging, styling, and color or unique promotions,[94] using the attention and perception enhancement techniques described in Chapter 3. Also, associating the product with a well-known person or creating ads to suggest that the consumer will be socially rewarded for using the product may enhance observability. An innovation's social relevance can be heightened through advertising— particularly advertising that ties product use with potential social approval. Finally, marketers can enhance social value by associating the product with some social entity, cause, or value. For example, China-based Yingli Green Energy, which makes solar panels, is a sponsor of the Fifa World Cup because it wants a high-profile way to associate its brand with the world's most popular sport—especially now that the company is targeting individual consumers, not just business customers.[95]

15-4e LEGITIMACY AND ADAPTABILITY

Legitimacy and adaptability also influence resistance, adoption, and diffusion, particularly for symbolic and aesthetic innovations.[96] **Legitimacy** refers to the extent to which the innovation follows established guidelines for what seems appropriate in the category. An innovation that is too radical or that does not derive from a legitimate precursor lacks legitimacy.

When Starbucks, for example, introduced the coffee culture to U.S. consumers, it also had to educate consumers to the benefits of waiting a few extra minutes for made-to-order espressos or lattes. Once Starbucks paved the way, other coffee chains that brewed to order were not perceived as too radical. Blue Bottle Coffee, a small but fast-growing chain of cafes, is now expanding the boundaries of that legitimacy. Customers have to wait about five minutes while an employee grinds fresh-roasted beans and brews each cup individually, using a special filtering system. "There's a chance that people are going to be enraged by us and hate us," admits Blue Bottle's founder. With 19 locations in the United States and Japan, however, the company has found that once customers taste its top-quality coffee, most are willing to wait (see Exhibit 15.12).[97]

Adaptability, the innovation's potential to fit with existing products or styles, is another factor affecting adoption and diffusion.[98] For example, certain fashion or furniture is highly adaptable because it can fit with a variety of other fashion or furniture trends. Some functional products, such as cell phones, have high adaptability because they can perform a variety of functions.

> **Legitimacy** The extent to which the innovation follows established guidelines for what seems appropriate in the category.

> **Adaptability** The extent to which the innovation can foster new styles.

Marketing Implications

Marketers may enhance legitimacy by demonstrating how the innovation came into being or marketing it in a way that is consistent with consumers' perceptions

dbimages/Alamy Stock Photo

Exhibit 15.12 ▶ Legitimacy

Innovations must be based on a legitimate precursor, or push the boundaries to prove their legitimacy, like Blue Bottle Coffee.

of what is appropriate for the category. Frito-Lay did this when it tried marketing Latin-flavored Doritos and Lay's chips to Hispanic Americans. Adoption was slow because the targeted consumers "were looking for authentic flavors but didn't expect to see them on those brands," says Frito-Lay's chief marketing officer. Instead, the firm started importing its Sabritones Chile & Lime wheat snacks from Mexico, initially stocking them only in stores serving Mexican American communities. Adoption was so enthusiastic that the product was soon made available in other outlets.[99]

Conversely, if consumers believe the product lacks adaptability, marketers can show that it has uses beyond its original function. For example, the makers of cranberry sauce ask consumers to consider other uses for their product besides serving it as a condiment at Thanksgiving dinner.[100]

15-4f CHARACTERISTICS OF THE SOCIAL SYSTEM

Innovations diffuse rapidly or slowly in part because of product characteristics and in part because of the characteristics of the social system into which they are introduced. Both the kinds of people in the target market and the nature of the relationships among the people in the social system will affect the innovation's acceptance.

- *Modernity.* Resistance, adoption, and diffusion are affected by the social system's **modernity**, the extent to which the system's consumers have a positive attitude toward change. Consumers in modern systems value science, technology, and education and are technologically oriented in terms of the goods produced and the skill of the labor force.[101] The more modern the social system, the more receptive its consumers are to novel products.

> **Modernity** The extent to which consumers in the social system have positive attitudes toward change

- *Physical distance.* Diffusion tends to be faster when members of the social system are physically close. Some marketers in Japan have found that high school girls excel at setting trends. No doubt this ability is due to the physical and emotional proximity of girls and their tendency to talk about new products they have seen and used.[102] Likewise, an innovation may experience slower diffusion when consumers are physically separated.[103]

- *Homophily.* Diffusion tends to be faster when consumers in the market are similar in education, values, needs, income, and other dimensions.[104] This

type of similarity, called homophily, is another type of closeness. Why does similarity increase diffusion rate? First, the more similar people's backgrounds are, the more likely they are to have similar needs, values, and preferences. Second, similar people are more likely to interact with one another and transmit information. Third, similar people tend to model each other. Also, normative influence is likely to be higher as homophily grows, increasing the pressure for adopting the innovation and speeding adoption and diffusion.

- *Opinion leadership.* As noted in Chapter 11, people with credibility, such as experts or opinion leaders, can have considerable influence on product adoption and diffusion because they may spread positive or negative product information to others.[105] Interestingly, opinion leaders both influence others and are influenced by information from others when they are central to their social network—meaning they have many ties within the network and serve to connect individuals within the network.[106]

- *Cultural self-perspectives.* Individualism versus collectivism, a cultural distinction we noted in Chapter 14, also affects the degree to which consumers have a positive attitude toward change. Research finds that consumers in individualistic cultures are more likely to buy really new innovations, whereas those in collectivist cultures are more likely to buy incremental innovations.[107]

 ## Marketing Implications

Marketing efforts can influence resistance, adoption, and diffusion by affecting the social system. For example, if members of the target market are very different from one another, companies may need to use targeted communications that show the product's relevance to consumers' unique needs, values, or norms and may need to place the messages in specialized (target market–specific) media to reach these consumers.

Companies might also identify consumers who have not adopted the innovation yet. There are three types of nonadopters: (1) passive consumers who have tried the product but are unlikely to provide much information to others about it; (2) active rejectors who have tried the product and are likely to provide unfavorable word of mouth to others; and (3) potential adopters who have not yet tried the product but who may be influenced by active rejectors, active acceptors, or marketers. Different marketing strategies may be appropriate for different adopter and nonadopter groups.[108] If potential adopters are unaware of the innovation, for instance, advertising can help build awareness and encourage adoption. Product improvements may, however, be necessary to attract active rejectors.

Because marketing activities can influence diffusion by affecting both the innovation and the social system, it is not surprising that the more intensive the marketing effort, the faster the innovation spreads through a market.[109] Media coverage of an innovation generally has more credibility than the company's communications do. Targeting opinion leaders and targeting the network, rather than the consumer, can also stimulate positive word of mouth, as can new product demonstrations at trade shows and in videos posted online and on social-media sites. And marketers can take a number of steps to track word of mouth, generate positive word of mouth, and counteract negative word of mouth.

Summary:

Innovations are products, services, ideas, or attributes that consumers in a market segment perceive to be new. Innovations can be characterized as functional, symbolic, or hedonic and may vary in the degree of behavioral change their adoption requires. Companies are increasingly using cocreation to develop innovative new products. Product innovativeness ranges along a continuum from continuous to discontinuous. Innovations may represent fads, fashions, or classics and hence may exhibit a short, moderate, or long life cycle. Marketers can extend a product's life cycle by enhancing the breadth of the innovation and encouraging consumers to find innovative uses for familiar products.

Strategies for marketers of innovations include reducing consumers' resistance to innovations, facilitating consumers' adoption of the innovation, and affecting the diffusion of the innovation through the marketplace. A high-effort as opposed to low-effort hierarchy-of-effects adoption process occurs when the innovation is seen as risky. Some individuals, called innovators, are among the first to adopt new products independently of the decisions of other people. Companies may target innovators because their adoption of products influences other consumers' adoption decisions through word of mouth or social modeling.

Resistance, adoption, and diffusion are affected by the characteristics of the innovation and the social system into which it is introduced. Overcoming resistance is easiest when the innovation is perceived to provide value to consumers such as a relative advantage, low price, or low switching costs. Resistance will be lower when the innovation requires minimal learning and is highly compatible with consumers' existing needs, values, and behaviors; easy to try; easy to use; and low risk. Innovations viewed as high in social relevance, legitimacy, and adaptability encounter less resistance than those regarded as low in such factors. The characteristics of the social system in which the innovation operates also affect resistance, adoption, and diffusion. However, it is possible that the diffusion of an innovation may entail some negative social and economic consequences.

Questions for Review and Discussion

1. How can innovations be described in terms of degree of novelty and types of benefits? How does the degree of novelty affect consumers' behavioral change?

2. What is cocreation and what are its potential benefits?

3. What is the difference between adoption and diffusion? How does the concept of *resistance* relate to adoption?

4. Under what circumstances might a consumer follow the high-effort hierarchy of effects in adopting an innovation?

5. How can consumers be categorized in terms of their timing of adoption relative to that of other consumers?

6. What is the product life cycle, and how does it differ from product diffusion?

7. How do consumer learning requirements and social relevance affect resistance, adoption, and diffusion?

8. What characteristics of the social system affect an innovation's acceptance within a market?

Endnotes

1   Jenny Eagle, "Nestlé: 'Technology Is Fundamentally Changing the Way Consumers Buy Our Products and Engage with Our Brands,'" *Food Production Daily*, July 9, 2015, www.foodproductiondaily.com; and Deborah Ball, "After Buying Binge, Nestlé Goes on a Diet," *Wall Street Journal*, July 23, 2007, p. 1.

2   Hubert Gatignon and Thomas S. Robertson, "Innovative Decision Processes," in eds. Thomas S. Robertson and Harold H. Kassarjian, *Handbook of Consumer Behavior* (New York: Prentice-Hall, 1991), pp. 316–317; see also Everett M. Rogers, *The Diffusion of Innovations*, 5th ed. (New York: Free Press, 2003).

3   Characteristics of employees involved in new product development can also affect innovativeness; see, for example, Rajesh Sethi, Daniel C. Smith, and C. Whan Park, "Cross-Functional Product Development Teams, Creativity, and the Innovativeness of New Consumer Products," *Journal of Marketing Research* 38, February 2001, pp. 73–85.

4   Mike Isaac, "In a Shift, Rite Aid to Accept Apple and Google Mobile Payments," *New York Times*, August 11, 2015, www.nytimes.com; and "Africa: The New Pot of Gold for Telecoms," *Economic Times* (India), December 7, 2011, http://articles.economictimes.indiatimes.com.

5   Thomas S. Robertson, "The Process of Innovation and the Diffusion of Innovation," *Journal of Marketing* 31, January 1967, pp. 14–19; and Thomas S. Robertson, *Innovative Behavior and Communication* (New York: Holt, Reinhart, & Winston, 1971).

6   Scott Stein, "New Samsung Gear Watches Are Coming—Here's What They Need to Succeed," *Cnet*, August 13, 2015, www.cnet.com; and Marc E. Babej, "Will Smartwatches Spell the Death of Mechanical Watches?" *Forbes*, July 30, 2015, www.forbes.com.

7   C. Page Moreau, Arthur B. Markman, and Donald R. Lehmann, "'What Is It?' Categorization Flexibility and Consumers' Responses to Really New Products," *Journal of Consumer Research* 27, March 2001, pp. 489–498.

8   Robbie Whelan, "DHL Unit Plans Google Glass Experiment in U.S. Warehouses," *Wall Street Journal*, August 14, 2015, www.wsj.com; and Menchie Mendoza, "Google Glass Is Back But You'll Only See Them In Offices," *Tech Times*, August 2, 2015, www.techtimes.com.

9   Alfred R. Petrosky, "Extending Innovation Characteristic Perception to Diffusion Channel Intermediaries and Aesthetic Products," in eds. Rebecca Holman and Michael Solomon, *Advances in Consumer Research*, vol. 17 (Provo, Utah: Association for Consumer Research, 1991), pp. 627–634.

10 Beth Snyder Bulik, "Edible 3-D Food Printing Becomes a Reality at Hershey," *Advertising Age*, January 28, 2015, www.adage.com.

11 JoAndrea Hoegg, Joseph W. Alba, and Darren W. Dahl, "The Good, the Bad, and the Ugly: Influence of Aesthetics on Product Feature Judgments," *Journal of Consumer Psychology* 20, no. 4, 2010, pp. 419–430.

12 Customer relationship management often plays a key role in this process. See Holger Ernst, Wayne D. Hoyer, Manfred Krafft, and Katrin Krieger, "Customer Relationship Management and Company Performance," *Journal of the Academy of Marketing Science* 39, April 2011, pp. 290–306.

13 See Birud Sindhav, "Co-creation of Value: Creating New Products Through Social Media," *International Journal of Management Research*, June 2011, p. 6; and Martin Scherier, Christoph Fuchs, and Darren W. Dahl, "The Innovation Effect of User Design: Exploring Consumers' Innovation Perceptions of Firms Selling Products Designed by Users," *Journal of Marketing* 76, no. 5, 2012, pp. 18–32.

14 Donna L. Hoffman, Praveen K. Kopalle, and Thomas p. Novak, "The 'Right' Consumers for Better Concepts," *Journal of Marketing Research* 47, October 2010, pp. 854–865.

15 Wayne D. Hoyer, Rajesh Chandy, Matilda Dorotic, Manfred Krafft, and Siddharth S. Singh, "Consumer Cocreation in New Product Development," *Journal of Service Research* 13, no. 3, 2010, pp. 283–296.

16 Christoph Fuchs, Emanuela Prandelli, and Martin Schreier, "The Psychological Effects of Empowerment Strategies on Consumers' Product Demand," *Journal of Marketing* 74, January 2010, pp. 65–79.

17 Andrew MacDougall, "Beiersdorf R&D Head Says It's OK to Appreciate External Innovations," *Cosmetics Design Europe*, March 21, 2014, www.cosmeticsdesign-europe.com; and Volker Bilgram, Michael Bartl, and Stefan Biel, "Getting Closer to the Customer—How Nivea Co-creates New Products," *Marketing Review St. Gallen*, January 2011, p. 34.

18 Stefan Stern, Peter Pal Zubcsek, and Jacob Goldenberg, "People Offer Better Ideas When They Can't See What Others Suggest," *Harvard Business Review*, July 24, 2015, https://hbr.org.

19 "A Co-creation Primer," *Harvard Business Review*, February 28, 2011, http://blogs.hbr.org.

20 Lauriston Sharp, "Steel Axes for Stone Age Australians," in ed. Edward H. Spicer, *Human Problems in Technological Change* (New York: Russell Sage Foundation, 1952).

21 H. David Banta, "The Diffusion of the Computer Tomography (CT) Scanner in the United States," *International Journal of Health Services* 10, 1980, pp. 251–269, as reported in Rogers, *The Diffusion of Innovations*, pp. 231–237.

22 Shaul Oreg and Jacob Goldenberg, *Resistance to Innovation: Its Sources and Manifestations* (Chicago: University of Chicago Press, 2015).

23 Alex Wood, "The Internet of Things Is Revolutionising Our Lives, But Standards Are a Must," *The Guardian (UK)*, March 31, 2015, www.theguardian.com; and Amitav Chakravarti and Jinhong Xie, "The Impact of Standards Competition on Consumers: Effectiveness of Product Information and Advertising Formats," *Journal of Marketing Research* 43, May 2006, pp. 224–236.

24 David Glen Mick and Susan Fournier, "Paradoxes of Technology: Consumer Cognizance, Emotions, and Coping Strategies," *Journal of Consumer Research* 25, September 1998, pp. 123–143.

25 Stacy L. Wood and Joffre Swait, "Psychological Indicators of Innovation Adoption: Cross-Classification Based on Need for Cognition and Need for Change," *Journal of Consumer Psychology* 12, no. 1, 2002, pp. 1–13.

26 See Son K. Lam, Michael Ahearne, Ye Hu, and Niels Schillewaert, "Resistance to Brand Switching When a Radically New Brand Is Introduced: A Social Identity Theory Perspective," *Journal of Marketing* 74, November 2010, pp. 128–146.

27 Alexander Chernev, "Goal Orientation and Consumer Preference for the Status Quo," *Journal of Consumer Research* 31, no. 3, 2004, pp. 557–565.

28 Michal Herzenstein, Steven S. Posavac, and J. Joško Brakus, "Adoption of New and Really New Products: The Effects of Self-Regulation Systems and Risk Salience," *Journal of Marketing Research* 44, May 2007, pp. 251–260.

29 Max Willens, "Home Entertainment 2014: US DVD Sales and Rentals Crater, Digital Subscriptions Soar," *International Business Times*, January 7, 2015, www.ibtimes.com.

30 C. Page Moreau, Donald R. Lehmann, and Arthur B. Markman, "Entrenched Knowledge Structures and Consumer Response to New Products," *Journal of Marketing Research* 38, February 2001, pp. 14–29.

31 Glen Urban and Gilbert A. Churchill, "Five Dimensions of the Industrial Adoption Process," *Journal of Marketing Research* 8, August 1971, pp. 322–327; Charles R. O'Neal, Hans B. Thorelli, and James M. Utterback, "Adoption of Innovation by Industrial Organizations," *Industrial Marketing Management* 2, June 1973, pp. 235–250; and Gerald Zaltman, Robert Duncan, and Jonny Holbek, *Innovations and Organizations* (New York: Wiley, 1973).

32 Michael Arrington, "Wave Good bye to Google Wave," *TechCrunch*, August 4, 2010, www.techcrunch.com; and "Google Kills Off Seven More Products, Including Wave," *BBC News*, November 23, 2011, www.bbc.co.uk.

33 Curt Woodward, "Segway Acquired by Chinese Competitor, Months After Alleging Patent Infringement," *Boston Globe*, April 15, 2015, www.betaboston.com; and "Segway Tours: Two Wheels Good, Two Legs Bad," *Economist*, November 7, 2011, www.economist.com.

34 Rogers, *The Diffusion of Innovations*.

35 Geoffrey A. Moore, *Crossing the Chasm* (New York: Harper Business, 1991).

36 J. C. Torres, "3 Years Later, Where Are the Smartwatches?" *Slash Gear*, July 23, 2015, www.slashgear.com.

37 Marguerite Reardon, "Why Cisco Killed the Flip Mini Camcorder," *Cnet*, April 13, 2011, www.cnet.com; and Bill Machrone, "The Most Memorable Tech Flops," *PC Magazine*, January 2008, pp. 88–89.

38 Robert A. Peterson, "A Note on Optimal Adopter Category Determination," *Journal of Marketing Research* 10, August 1973, pp. 325–329; see also William R. Darden and Fred D. Reynolds, "Backward Profiling of Ma le Innovators," *Journal of Marketing Research* 11, February 1974, pp. 79–85; and Steven A. Baumgarten, "The Innovative Communicator in the Diffusion Process," *Journal of Marketing Research* 12, February 1975, pp. 12–17a. Schemes based on consumers' involvement in the new-product development process, for example, might be utilized by managers (see Jerry Wind and Vijay Mahajan, "Issues and Opportunities in New Product Development: An Introduction to the Special Issue," *Journal of Marketing Research* 34, February 1997, pp. 1–12).

39 Chuan-Fong Shih and Alladi Venkatesh, "Beyond Adoption: Development and Application of a Use-Diffusion Model," *Journal of Marketing* 68, January 2004, pp. 59–72.

40 See review in Thomas S. Robertson, Joan Zielinski, and Scott Ward, *Consumer Behavior* (Glenview, Ill.: Scott, Foresman, 1984); see also Dickerson M. D. and J. W. Gentry, "Characteristics of Adopters and Non Adopters of Home Computers," *Journal of Consumer Research* 10, no. 2, 1983, pp. 225–235.

41 Venessa Wong, "Margarine: Unilever Can't Believe It's Not Selling," *Bloomberg Businessweek*, July 29, 2013, www.businessweek.com.

42 June Cotte and Stacy L. Wood, "Families and Innovative Consumer Behavior: A Triadic Analysis of Sibling and Parental Influence," *Journal of Consumer Research* 31, no.1, 2004, pp. 78–86.

43 Richard Mader, "Year of the Mobile Payment," *Stores*, August 2011, www.stores.org.

44 Rogers, *The Diffusion of Innovations*; see also Mark S. Granovetter, "The Strength of Weak Ties," *American Journal of Sociology* 78, May 1973, pp. 1360–1380; John A. Czepiel, "Word-of-Mouth Processes in the Diffusion of a Major Technological Innovation," *Journal of Marketing Research* 11, May 1974, pp. 172–181; and Elizabeth B. Goldsmith, "Social Influence History and Theories," *Social Influence and Sustainable Consumption* (Springer International Publishing, 2015), pp. 23–39.

45 Scott A. Thompson and Rajiv K. Sinha, "Brand Communities and New Product Adoption: The Influence and Limits of Oppositional Loyalty," *Journal of Marketing* 72, November 2008, pp. 65–80.

46 Manning, Bearden, and Madden, "Consumer Innovativeness and the Adoption Process"; Jan-Benedict E. M. Steenkamp and Hans Baumgartner, "The Role of Optimum Stimulation Level in Exploratory Consumer Behavior," *Journal of Consumer Research* 19, December 1992, pp. 434–448; p. S. Raju, "Optimum Stimulation Level: Its Relationship to Personality, Demographics, and Exploratory Behavior," *Journal of Consumer Research* 7, December 1980, pp. 272–282; and Jun San Kim, Minhi Hahn, and Yeosun Yoon, "The Moderating Role of Personal Need for Structure on the Evaluation of Incrementally New Products versus Really New Products," *Psychology & Marketing* 32, no. 2, 2015, pp. 144–161.

47 Gordon R. Foxall and Christopher G. Haskins, "Cognitive Style and Consumer Innovativeness," *Marketing Intelligence and Planning*, January 1986, pp. 26–46; and Gordon R. Foxall, "Consumer Innovativeness: Novelty Seeking, Creativity and Cognitive Style," in eds. Elizabeth C. Hirschman and Jagdish N. Sheth, *Research in Consumer Behavior*, vol. 3 (Greenwich, Conn.: JAI Press, 1988), pp. 79–114.

48 Ronald E. Goldsmith and Charles F. Hofacker, "Measuring Consumer Innovativeness," *Journal of the Academy of Marketing Science* 19, Summer 1991, pp. 209–221.

49 Jan-Benedict E. M. Steenkamp, Frenkel ter Hofstede, and Michael Wedel, "A Cross-National Investigation into the Individual and National Cultural Antecedents of Consumer Innovativeness," *Journal of Marketing* 63, April 1999, pp. 55–69.

50 Hubert Gatignon and Thomas S. Robertson, "A Propositional Inventory for New Diffusion Research," *Journal of Consumer Research*, March 1985, pp. 849–867; see also John O. Summers, "Media Exposure Patterns of Consumer Innovators," *Journal of Marketing* 36, January 1972, pp. 43–49.

51 James J. Engel, Robert J. Kegerreis, and Roger D. Blackwell, "Word-of-Mouth Communication by the Innovator," *Journal of Marketing* 33, July 1969, pp. 15–19.

52 Papatla, Purushottam, "Consumer Habits and Adoption of Multiple-Functions of Mobile Phones," *Journal of Business Theory and Practice* 3, no. 1, 2015, pp. 1–17; see also Gatignon and Robertson, "A Propositional Inventory for New Diffusion Research."

53 "Cell Phones in Africa: Communication Lifeline," *Pew Research Center*, April 15, 2015, www.pewglobal.org; and Aaron Smith, "Smartphone Adoption and Usage," *Pew Internet*, July 11, 2011, www.pewinternet.org.

54 Naresh Kumar, "Review of Innovation Diffusion Models," Working Paper no. 1, *Research Gate*, 2015, www.researchgate.net/publication/279099570_Review_of_Innovation_Diffusion_Models; Frank M. Bass, "New Product Growth

Models for Consumer Durables," *Management Science* 16, September 1969, pp. 215–227; and Douglas Tigart and Behrooz Farivar, "The Bass New Product Growth Model: A Sensitivity Analysis for a High Technology Product," *Journal of Marketing* 45, Fall 1981, pp. 81–90.

55 Micah Mertes, "At Local Libraries, e-Book Collections Are Growing, But Print Is Still King," *Omaha World-Herald*, August 2, 2015, www.omaha.com; Harry Wallop, "The Kindle Is Dead, the Book Is Back. Or Is It?" *The Telegraph (UK)*, January 9, 2015, www.telegraph.co.uk; and "Amazon Sells More ebooks than Print Books," *International Business Times*, May 19, 2011, www.ibtimes.com.

56 Naresh Kumar, "A Review of Innovation Diffusion Models;" D. R. Rink and J. E. Swan, "Product Life Cycle Research: A Literature Review," *Journal of Business Research* 7, September 1979, pp. 219–242; and Robertson, *Innovative Behavior and Communication*.

57 Rayna McInturf, "Crash Course: Fitness Goals Lagging a Bit?" *Los Angeles Times*, February 17, 2005, p. E23.

58 Raghuram Iyengar, Christophe Van den Bulte, and Jae Young Lee, "Social Contagion in New Product Trial and Repeat," *Marketing Science* 34, no. 3, May–June 2015, pp. 408–429; Rex Yuxing Du and Wagner A. Kamakura, "Measuring Contagion in the Diffusion of Consumer Packaged Goods," *Journal of Marketing Research* 48, no. 1, 2011, pp. 28–47; and "What Drives Social Contagion in New Product Adoption?" *Marketing Science Institute*, November 8, 2013, www.msi.org.

59 Marianne Cusanto, "5 New Home Trends for 2015," *Fortune*, May 13, 2015, http://fortune.com.

60 David H. Henard and David M. Szymanski, "Why Some New Products Are More Successful Than Others," *Journal of Marketing Research* 38, August 2001, pp. 362–375.

61 David L. Alexander, John G. Lynch Jr., and Qing Wang, "As Time Goes by: Do Cold Feet Follow Warm Intentions for Really New Versus Incrementally New Products?" *Journal of Marketing Research* 45, June 2008, pp. 307–319.

62 Min Zhao, Steve Hoeffler, and Darren W. Dahl, "The Role of Imagination-Focused Visualization on New Product Evaluation," *Journal of Marketing Research* 46, February 2009, pp. 46–55.

63 James E. Burroughs and David Glen Mick, "Exploring Antecedents and Consequences of Consumer Creativity in a Problem Solving Context," *Journal of Consumer Research* 31, no. 2, 2004, pp. 402–411.

64 Ashley Rodriguez, "American Express Launches Apple Pay Spot Featuring Classic Ads," *Advertising Age*, February 8, 2015, www.adage.com; and Susan Pandy, "Current Perspectives on the Mobile Wallet Evolution," *Mobile Payments Industry Workgroup, April 9–10, 2015 Meeting Report – Federal Reserve Bank of Boston*, July 8, 2015, www.bostonfed.org.

65 Geoffrey A. Fowler, "Ditch Your Old Hi-Fi: Wireless Speakers Make Home Audio Easier," *Wall Street Journal*, July 14, 2015, www.wsj.com.

66 Stephen Lawson, "Why Internet of Things 'Standards' Got More Confusing in 2014," *PC World*, December 24, 2014, www.pcworld.com.

67 Jan-Benedict E. M. Steenkamp and Katrijn Gielens, "Consumer and Market Drivers of the Trial Probability of New Consumer Packaged Goods," *Journal of Consumer Research* 30, December 2003, pp. 368–384.

68 Steve Hoeffler, "Measuring Preferences for Really New Products," *Journal of Marketing Research* 40, November 2003, pp. 406–420.

69 Paschalina Ziamou and S. Ratneshwar, "Promoting Consumer Adoption of High-Technology Products: Is More Information Always Better?" *Journal of Consumer Psychology* 12, no. 4, 2002, pp. 341–351.

70 Raquel Castano, Mita Sujan, Manish Kacker, and Harish Sujan, "Managing Consumer Uncertainty in the Adoption of New Products," *Journal of Marketing Research* 45, June 2008, pp. 320–336.

71 Brian Barrett, "You Should Take Kindle's Last Rival Seriously," *Wired*, April 10, 2015, www.wired.com.

72 Gatignon and Robertson, "A Propositional Inventory for New Diffusion Research"; and Vijay Mahajan, Eitan Muller, and Frank M. Bass, "New Product Diffusion Models in Marketing: A Review and Directions for Research," *Journal of Marketing* 54, April 1990, pp. 1–27.

73 Hilar y Greenbaum and Dana Rubinstein, "Who Made That? Fleece," *New York Times Magazine*, November 27, 2011, p. 28.

74 Julia Glotz, "Marco's Range Dropped as Bernard Changes Tack," *Grocer*, August 20, 2011, p. 31; and "Marco Pierre White's Bernard Matthews Turkey Meals Are Chopped After Just Six Months," *Daily Mail (UK)*, August 21, 2011, www.dailymail.co.uk.

75 Rogers, *The Diffusion of Innovations*.

76 Ibid.

77 Debora Viana Thompson, Rebecca W. Hamilton, and Roland T. Rust, "Feature Fatigue: When Product Capabilities Become Too Much of a Good Thing," *Journal of Marketing Research* 42, November 2005, pp. 431–442.

78 Ashesh Mukherjee and Wayne D. Hoyer, "The Effect of Novel Attributes on Product Evaluation," *Journal of Consumer Research* 28, December 2001, pp. 462–472.

79 Katherine A. Burson, "Consumer– Product Skill Matching: The Effects of Difficulty on Relative Self-Assessment and Choice," *Journal of Consumer Research* 34, no. 1, 2007, pp. 104–110.

80 Al Doyle, "Getting the Perfect Picture," *Technology & Learning*, January 2002, pp. 9–11.

81 Sarah Halzack, "Campbell Soup Looks to Hummus and Cold-Pressed Juices To Stay Relevant," *Washington Post*, July 23, 2015, www.washingtonpost.com; and "Campbell Planning $100 Million Repositioning Effort," *Radio Business Report*, July 13, 2010, www.rbr.com.

82 Bill Rigby, "Exclusive: Microsoft's Digital Assistant to Head to Android, Apple Devices," *Reuters*, March 13, 2015, www.reuters.com.

83 Amanda Kooser, "Pepsi Vending Machine Takes Facebook Love, Not Money," *Cnet*, June 4, 2013, www.cnet.com; and Tim Hornyak, "Pepsi Vending Machines Like Your Social Network," *Cnet*, April 29, 2011, http://news.cnet.com.

84 "Silvercar Contributes to Oscars VIP Gift Bag," *Auto Rental News*, February 18, 2015, www.autorentalnews.com.

85 Carolyn Heneghan, "Single-Servings' Role in the Future of Food and the Environment," *Food Dive*, March 27, 2015, www.fooddive.com; and Mark Reilly, "Behold, the K-O Cup: General Mills Will Debut Keurig-Ready Oatmeal," *Minneapolis-St. Paul Business Journal*, April 16, 2014, www.bizjournals.com.

86 Maria Gallucci, "Which States Have the Most Electric Vehicles? Map Shows Cleaner Cars Are Rolling Out in a Patchwork of States," *International Business Times*, December 10, 2014, www.ibtimes.com.

87 Eric Mack, "Yes, Someone Put an Apple Watch in a Blender," *Cnet*, April 28, 2015, www.cnet.com; and Sujan Patel, "6 Companies Killing It on YouTube—What You Can Learn," *Small Business Trends*, February 23, 2015, www.smallbiztrends.com.

88 Liz Stinson, "So Smart: New Ikea App Places Virtual Furniture in Your Home," *Wired*, August 20, 2013, www.wired.com.

89 Robert J. Fisher and Linda L. Price, "An Investigation into the Social Context of Early Adoption Behavior," *Journal of Consumer Research* 19, December 1992, pp. 477–486.

90 Sandra D. Atchison, "Lifting the Golf Bag Burden," *BusinessWeek*, July 25, 1994, p. 84.

91 June Fletcher, "New Machines Measure That Holiday Flab at Home," *Wall Street Journal*, December 26, 1997, p. B8.

92 Rogers, *The Diffusion of Innovations*, p. 99.

93 C. Whan Park, Bernard J. Jaworski, and Deborah J. MacInnis, "Strategic Brand Concept–Image Management," *Journal of Marketing* 50, October 1986, pp. 135–145.

94 Fisher and Price, "An Investigation into the Social Context of Early Adoption Behavior."

95 Bill Wilson, "Bright Start for Fifa's Chinese World Cup Sponsor," *BBC News*, November 23, 2011, www.bbc.co.uk.

96 Petrosky, "Extending Innovation Characteristic Perception to Diffusion Channel Intermediaries and Aesthetic Products."

97 Kia Kokalitcheva, "Blue Bottle Raises $70 Million For an Artisanal Coffee Empire," *Fortune*, June 4, 2015, www.fortune.com.

98 Alfred Petrosky labels this factor *genrefication* and discusses it in the context of aesthetic innovations in "Extending Innovation Characteristic Perception to Diffusion Channel Intermediaries and Aesthetic Products."

99 Diane Brady, "A Thousand and One Noshes," *BusinessWeek*, June 14, 2004, pp. 54–56.

100 Jagdish N. Sheth and S. Ram, *Bringing Innovation to Market* (New York: Wiley, 1987).

101 Everett M. Rogers and F. Floyd Shoemaker, *Communication of Innovations* (New York: Free Press, 1971); and Elizabeth C. Hirschman, "Consumer Modernity, Cognitive Complexity, Creativity and Innovativeness," in ed. Richard p. Bagozzi, *Marketing in the 80s: Changes and Challenges* (Chicago: American Marketing Association, 1980), pp. 152–161.

102 Seth Stevenson, "I'd Like to Buy the World a Shelf-Stable Children's Lactic Drink," *New York Times Magazine*, March 10, 2002, p. 38; John C. Jay, "The Valley of the New," *American Demographics*, March 2000, pp. 58–59; and Norihiko Shirouzu, "Japan's High-School Girls Excel in Art of Setting Trends," *Wall Street Journal*, April 24, 1998, pp. B1, B7.

103 Gatignon and Robertson, "A Propositional Inventory for New Diffusion Research"; and Tolga Bilgicer, Kamel Jedidi, Donald R. Lehmann, and Scott A. Neslin, "Social Contagion and Customer Adoption of New Sales Channels," *Journal of Retailing* 91, no. 2, 2015, pp. 254–271.

104 Jaishankar Ganesh, V. Kumar, and Velavan Subramaniam, "Learning Effect in Multinational Diffusion of Consumer Durables," *Journal of the Academy of Marketing Science* 25, Summer 1997, pp. 214–228; and Gatignon and Robertson, "A Propositional Inventory for New Diffusion Research."

105 Dorothy Leonard-Barton, "Experts as Negative Opinion Leaders in the Diffusion of a Technological Innovation," *Journal of Consumer Research* 11, March 1985, pp. 914–926.

106 Seung Hwan (Mark) Lee, June Cotte, and Theodore J. Noseworthy, "The Role of Network Centrality in the Flow of Consumer Influence," *Journal of Consumer Psychology* 20, no. 1, 2010, pp. 66–77.

107 Zhenfeng Ma, Zhiyong Yang, and Mehdi Mourali, "Consumer Adoption of New Products: Independent versus Interdependent Self Perspectives," *Journal of Marketing* 78, no. 2, 2012, pp. 101–117.

108 Everett M. Rogers and D. Lawrence Kincaid, *Communication Networks: Toward a New Paradigm for Research* (New York: Free Press, 1981).

109 Frank M. Bass, "The Relationship Between Diffusion Curves, Experience Curves, and Demand Elasticities for Consumer Durable Technological Innovations," *Journal of Business*, July 1980, pp. s51–s57; Dan Horskey and Leonard S. Simon, "Advertising and the Diffusion of New Products," *Marketing Science* 2, Winter 1983, pp. 1–17; Vijay Mahajan and Eitan Muller, "Innovation Diffusion and New Product Growth Models in Marketing," *Journal of Marketing* 43, Fall 1979, pp. 55–68; and Mahajan, Muller, and Bass, "New Product Diffusion Models in Marketing: A Review and Directions for Research."

CHAPTER 16

Symbolic Consumer Behavior

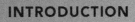

LEARNING OBJECTIVES

After studying this chapter, you will be able to:

▶ Discuss how products, special possessions, and consumption activities gain symbolic meaning and how this meaning is conveyed from one consumer to another.

▶ Identify how marketers can influence or make use of the symbolic meaning that consumption may have for consumers.

▶ Distinguish between sacred and profane entities, and show why this distinction is important for marketing strategy.

▶ Understand the process of gift giving and describe how marketers can use knowledge of this process to market more effectively.

iStockphoto.com/Ostill

Frances Roberts/Alamy Stock Photo

INTRODUCTION

Many different products, including (again) newly popular vinyl LP records, can have symbolic meaning, the focus of this chapter. The first section examines how symbolic meaning develops in products such as LPs or consumption experiences such as buying and collecting records. It also looks at the functions symbolic consumption serves and how symbolic consumption can affect our self-concept. The next section explains why some products (such as colored-vinyl LPs) are more meaningful than others. Some products are special—even sacred—and require consumption practices to keep them so, the way many LP buyers download music instead of actually playing their records.[1] The final section discusses how meaning is transferred from person to person through gift giving (see Exhibit 16.1). Knowing how symbolic meaning affects consumer behavior can help marketers develop and identify target markets, create needs-satisfying offerings, and plan appropriate communications.

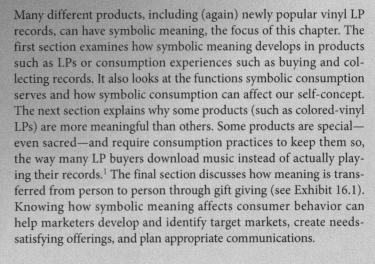

Exhibit 16.1 ▶ Chapter Overview: Symbolic Consumer Behavior

Products and consumption activities can symbolize something about ourselves and our relationships with others. In this chapter, we consider how products and consumption activities take on and communicate meaning. We also show how some possessions and consumption activities take on special or even sacred meaning. Finally, we discuss how gift giving can symbolize how we feel toward a gift recipient.

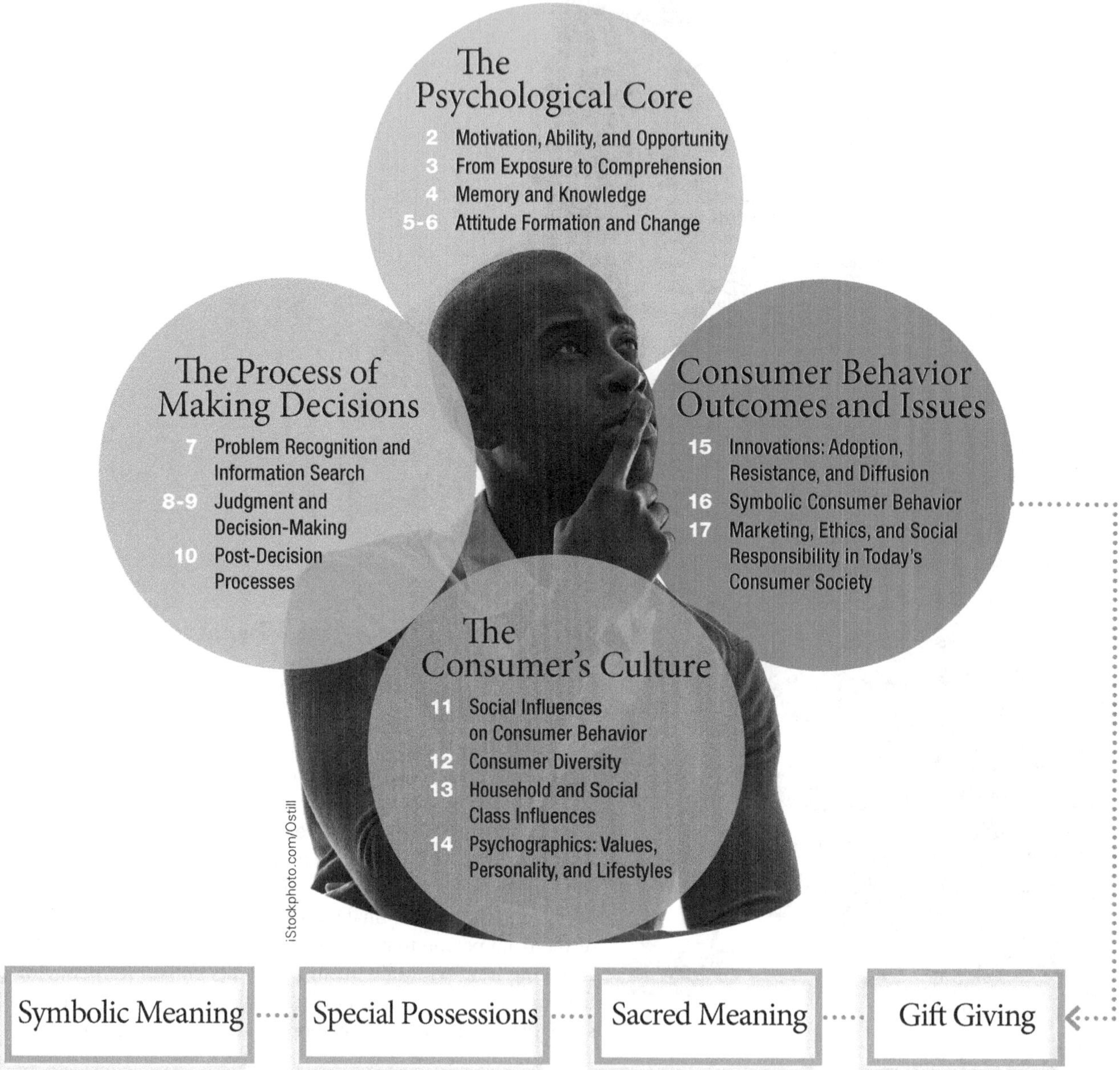

The
Psychological Core

2   Motivation, Ability, and Opportunity
3   From Exposure to Comprehension
4   Memory and Knowledge
5-6 Attitude Formation and Change

The Process of
Making Decisions

7   Problem Recognition and
    Information Search
8-9 Judgment and
    Decision-Making
10 Post-Decision
    Processes

Consumer Behavior
Outcomes and Issues

15 Innovations: Adoption,
    Resistance, and Diffusion
16 Symbolic Consumer Behavior
17 Marketing, Ethics, and Social
    Responsibility in Today's
    Consumer Society

The
Consumer's Culture

11 Social Influences
    on Consumer Behavior
12 Consumer Diversity
13 Household and Social
    Class Influences
14 Psychographics: Values,
    Personality, and Lifestyles

iStockphoto.com/Ostill

| Symbolic Meaning | ····· | Special Possessions | ····· | Sacred Meaning | ····· | Gift Giving |

16-1 Sources and Functions of Symbolic Meaning

To understand why some consumers believe vinyl LPs are special, consider where the meaning associated with these products comes from and what functions these offerings and practices fulfill. As shown in Exhibit 16.2, this meaning can stem from either our culture or ourselves as individuals.

16-1a MEANING DERIVED FROM CULTURE

Part of the meaning associated with products comes from our culture (see Exhibit 16.3).[2] Anthropologists show that we have **cultural categories** for such things as time (as in work time and leisure time), space (such as home, office, and safe or unsafe places), and occasions (such as festive vs. somber events). We also have cultural categories that reflect characteristics of people, such as categories of gender, age, social class, and ethnicity.

Implicit in cultural categories are **cultural principles**—ideas or values that specify how aspects of our culture are thought about and evaluated. For example, the cultural principles associated with "work time" dictate time that is structured, organized, and precise, and that we should feel tired afterward. The principles associated with "leisure time" are quite different. Cultural principles give meaning to products. This explains why the clothing we associate with work time is also more structured and organized than the clothing we associate with leisure time. In addition, we have categories for occasions, including festive (vibrant, active, and energetic) and somber (dark, quiet, and inactive) occasions. The clothing that we consider appropriate for those occasions mirrors these qualities.

We also have cultural principles linked with social status, gender, age, and ethnicity. For example, the category "women"

> **Cultural categories** The natural grouping of objects that reflect our culture.
>
> **Cultural principles** Ideas or values that specify how aspects of our culture are organized and/or how they should be perceived or evaluated.

has historically been associated with concepts like delicate, whimsical, expressive, and changeable. In contrast, the category "men" has historically been associated with concepts like disciplined, stable, and serious. Marketers make products and consumers use them in ways that are consistent with these principles. Thus, women's clothing in many cultures has traditionally been more delicate, whimsical, expressive, and changeable than men's clothing. Exhibit 16.3 indicates that by matching product characteristics with cultural principles and categories, we transfer the meaning associated with the cultural principles to the product. For example, we might classify certain clothing as "feminine" or as "suitable for work" because we associate it with the corresponding cultural principles and categories.

Exhibit 16.3 also shows that many agents can play a role in this association and matching process. First, product designers and manufacturers introduce new products with characteristics that reflect cultural principles. For example, the Harley-Davidson motorcycle has characteristics that make it "macho." This fit between cultural principles and offerings explains why U.S. consumers perceive a rodeo as more authentic if it reflects freedom, independence, and competition, qualities closely associated with the American West.[3] Marketers may also confer meaning by associating their offerings with certain cultural categories or myths. Therefore, Harley-Davidson develops clothing, accessories, and information that communicate what it means to be a "biker"—younger and older bikers, men and women bikers, and bikers who care about the planet.[4]

Meaning comes from nonmarketing sources, as well. Specific people may serve as opinion leaders who shape, refine, or reshape cultural principles and the products and attributes they are linked to (see Chapter 11). Celebrities are often important opinion leaders who influence the meanings associated with brands.[5] Sometimes groups on the margins of society can be agents of change, as when

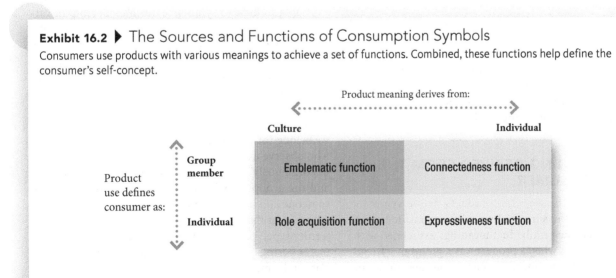

Exhibit 16.2 ▶ The Sources and Functions of Consumption Symbols

Consumers use products with various meanings to achieve a set of functions. Combined, these functions help define the consumer's self-concept.

Product meaning derives from:

Culture ⟵ · ⟶ Individual

Product use defines consumer as:

Group member	Emblematic function	Connectedness function
Individual	Role acquisition function	Expressiveness function

Exhibit 16.3 ▶ Transfer of Meaning from the Culture to the Product and to the Consumer

Meaning that exists at the level of the culture (e.g., youthfulness) can become associated with a product (e.g., Burton snowboards). Both marketers and nonmarketers (e.g., opinion leaders, the media) can play a powerful role in this association process. The meaning associated with the product can in turn be transferred to the consumer who uses it.

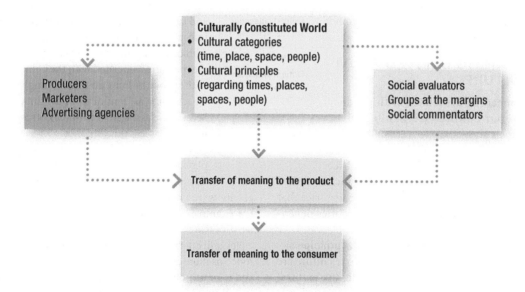

Source: Adapted from Grant McCracken, "Culture and Consumption: A Theoretical Account of the Structure and Movement of the Cultural Meaning of Consumer Goods," *Journal of Consumer Research*, 1986, pp. 71–84. Reprinted with permission of The University of Chicago Press.

brash, distinctive street-smart clothing worn by inner-city teens influences what mainstream designers produce.[6]

Journalists also shape cultural principles and the products associated with them. For example, restaurant reviewers may determine whether a restaurant is associated with principles like status, and style editors may determine whether clothes are associated with young and hip categories. Magazines like *Runner's World* communicate meanings associated with the runner category, such as what runners wear and eat, and what they like to do. Websites like www.bicycling.com communicate the meanings of extreme biking trips and the shoes, gloves, helmets, and energy bars that go with such activities. Celebrities like Taylor Swift and Jay Z can also create meaning in products by how they use them. Through all of these sources, the meaning inherent in the product is transferred to the consumer.

16-1b MEANING DERIVED FROM THE CONSUMER

In addition to the way that products derive symbolic meaning from the surrounding culture, consumers can develop their own individual meanings associated with products, such as when a product was a gift from a friend or relative. Whether meaning stems from the culture or the consumer, however, consumption symbols can be used to say something about the consumer as a member of a group or as a unique individual. Combining these two dimensions produces the emblematic, role acquisition, connectedness, and expressiveness functions of symbols described in the next section.

16-1c THE EMBLEMATIC FUNCTION

Meaning derived from culture allows us to use products to symbolize our membership in various social groups—what we call an **emblematic function**. Dresses are associated with women, and robes are associated with judges and school graduation. The music we listen to may symbolize our age, and the car we drive may symbolize our social status. Consciously or unconsciously, we use brands and products to symbolize the groups to which we belong (or want to belong[7]). At the same time, people who observe us using these products may consciously or unconsciously categorize and make inferences about us and the groups to which we belong. Just by looking at someone and his or her possessions, we might be able to tell whether that person is a member of the "surfer," "fraternity type," or "rich kid" social categories.[8] In particular, offerings can serve as geographic, ethnic, or social class emblems.

> **Emblematic function** The use of products to symbolize membership in social groups.

Geographic Emblems

Products can symbolize geographic identification. For example, brightly colored, loose-fitting clothing symbolizes identification with sunnier regions of the United States, such as California, Arizona, and Hawaii. Products may also symbolize geographic identification with a region even if they are used by people who live elsewhere.

Ethnic Emblems

Products and consumption activities can symbolize identification with a specific culture or subculture. African Americans sometimes wear African garb to symbolize identification with that culture. In India, Sikh men wear five K's as symbols of their ethnic and religious affiliation: *kesh* (hair), *kada* (bangle), *kangha* (comb), *kacha* (underpants), and *kirpan* (dagger). Some consumers use ethnic emblems of other cultures or subcultures to differentiate themselves.

Consumers also use food to express ethnic identity. For example, grilled chicken, chicken mole, and steamed yellowfish reflect U.S., Mexican, and Chinese identities, respectively. U.S. consumers put ketchup on their fries, but Dutch consumers use mayonnaise. Cornmeal serves as an ethnic emblem for Haitians immigrating to the United States.[9] In addition, we can express ethnic identification by how and when we eat. Cultures differ in whether all elements of the meal are served at once or one item at a time.[10] U.S. families typically eat dinner before 7:00 PM, but dinnertime is much later in Spain and Italy.

Social Class Emblems

Products can also symbolize social class. For example, in China, emblems of status include large luxury yachts (for the very wealthy), high-end imported cars, imported whisky, and fine imported wine (for younger consumers).[11] Rolls-Royce is a particularly prized status symbol among car buyers worldwide (see Exhibit 16.4). The century-old brand's sales have soared in recent years, despite difficult economic conditions in some nations. Its top five markets are the United States, China, the United Arab Emirates, Great Britain, and Saudi Arabia.[12] Interestingly, men and women may use products symbolizing luxury as emblems, but for different reasons. Men use them to signal their attractiveness to women, whereas women use them to signal to other women that their partners are devoted to them.[13]

Different social classes use different symbols in consumption rituals. For example, higher and lower social classes in the United States differ greatly in the types of clothing they wear at holiday time, the importance they place on etiquette, the types of serving dishes they use at formal family dinners, and even the way that they serve certain foods. Upper-class consumers may express their values, status, and group membership via subtle clues that set them apart from the mainstream while identifying them to others of their class.[14] Countering this type of social-class emblematic function, nearly 20 percent of U.S. public schools require students to wear uniforms, as is common in many other countries. The purpose is to remove social class emblems, reduce students' anxiety about keeping up with peers, and encourage identification with the school community.[15]

Gender Emblems

Food, clothing, jewelry, and alcoholic beverages are only some of the product categories associated with membership in the male and female gender categories. One study of consumers in France revealed that meat and certain other foods are viewed as "man" foods, whereas celery and other foods are viewed as "woman" foods. The way that a food is eaten also reflects its gender appropriateness: Steak and meats that may be cut roughly and chewed intensively are viewed in some cultures as more consistent with male characteristics.[16] Other researchers have found gender differences in food preferences, with boys preferring chunky peanut butter, for instance, and girls preferring the smooth variety. These preferences may be related to culturally derived associations with boys (rough) and girls (not rough).[17]

Large, rugged, powerful vehicles such as pickup trucks are often associated with male characteristics and, not surprisingly, are marketed primarily to men. For example, most commercials and Facebook promotions for Ford's F-150 and F-250 trucks feature images of guys driving heavily laden pickups across rough terrain. Ford's tagline, "Built Tough," sums up the masculine feeling of the trucks and the ads. Yet Ford also sees an opportunity to target women who want to drive a pickup. Without changing the exterior of its pickups, Ford now adds small touches that appeal to women buyers, such as pedals for shorter drivers.[18]

Reference Group Emblems

Harley-Davidson merchandise is a good example of how products can serve as emblems of membership in a reference group. One reason why Harley-Davidson consumers adopt "outlaw" symbols is that they like being members of a reference group with a counterculture ideology and independence. In general, consumers like a reference group emblem (like a T-shirt with the Harley-Davidson logo) more when an identity-consistent aspect of their self-concept (such as their image of themselves as fiercely independent) has been activated.[19] Varsity jackets, special hats, particular colors, or gang-designated jewelry may also symbolize reference group membership. Conversely, consumers may shun certain products to avoid being seen as members of a reference group— which, in turn, symbolizes membership in another reference group. Yet what constitutes an appropriate emblem can shift over time, particularly in the area of fashion. For example, in Turkey, the practice of veiling was once highly unusual among secular and urban women. However, now veiling is fashionable among middle class urban dwellers.[20]

Exhibit 16.4 ▶ Social Class Emblems
Products can indicate consumer's social class, for example, Rolls-Royce is considered a highly prized status symbol worldwide.

In addition to products, rituals are sometimes important indicators and affirmations of group membership. For example, rituals like attending graduation may reinforce our membership in the "college graduate" group. Other rituals serve as public confirmation that we have become members of a group or that we have made a life transition via a rite of passage. Wedding rituals confirm that a man or woman has transitioned from single to married status, for example.[21] Among families of Hispanic heritage, the *Quinceañera* is a ritual that marks the transition of 15-year-old girls from childhood into adulthood.

Marketing Implications

Marketers can play three roles in establishing the emblematic function of products.

Symbol Development

Marketing can link a product and its attributes to a specific cultural category and its principles. For example, when Toyota wanted to develop the symbolic associations of its redesigned Tundra pickup truck, it targeted opinion leaders it calls "true truckers," men who work in rugged situations like construction or ranching, because "they're the taste makers, the influentials," a Toyota executive explained. Later, Toyota redesigned the Tundra for a luxury-oriented target market by restyling the body to look even more muscular and refining the interior for passenger comfort.[22] Sometimes marketers need to ensure that product attributes are appropriately linked with cultural principles. Miller, for example, positioned the lite in Miller Lite as meaning "less filling and has fewer carbohydrates"—an appropriate attribute for men—rather than diet, which would have made the beer seem more feminine.[23]

Symbol development can be a challenge, as India's Tata Motors learned with its Nano car. It was designed as the world's cheapest car, with stripped-down features and high fuel efficiency. However, the actual price wound up higher than expected, which put it out of reach of the upwardly mobile, first-time car buyers who were the original target market. Consumers with a little more income could afford the Nano but did not want to be associated with its low-price symbolism. The no-frills Nano didn't sell well, so Tata phased it out and introduced the GenX Nano featuring new styling, an upgraded transmission, a trunk, and other amenities lacking in the original version.[24]

Symbol Communication

A company can use advertising to imbue a product with meaning through the setting for the ad (whether fantasy or naturalistic, interior or exterior, or rural or urban) and through other details such as the time of day and the types of people in the ad—their gender, age, ethnicity, occupation, clothing, body postures, and so on. Each ad element, including the headline and words, reinforces the meaning associated with the product. For example, Disney—known for its Disney Princess products—advertises DisneyWorld as a destination for quinceañera celebrations, with dinner-dance packages fit for a 15-year-old princess, such as La Bella del Baile (Belle of the Ball). The company also markets a line of princess-inspired ball gowns for quinceañeras.[25] In addition, symbolic meaning can be communicated by aspects of the retail channel, including how salespeople are dressed and how they treat people. For example, consumers may infer that a salesperson who is wearing an expensive watch is very successful and competent.[26] And if the salesperson represents an aspirational brand (say Prada), consumers who view the brand as part of their self-concept may be more willing to buy the brand if the salesperson somehow threatens their identity. Buying the aspirational brand may be a way of restoring their threatened identity.[27]

> **Role acquisition function** The use of products as symbols to help us feel more comfortable in a new role.

Symbol Reinforcement

Firms can design other elements of the marketing mix to reinforce the symbolic image. For instance, a company can use various pricing, distribution, and product strategies to maintain a product's status image. It may give the product a premium price, distribute it through outlets with an upscale image, and incorporate certain features that are appropriate only for the targeted segment. For example, Diageo reinforces Johnnie Walker whisky's status symbol image in Africa by emphasizing the significance of the label color (e.g., Red Label is lower priced than Black Label or Blue Label), promoting the unique taste and drinking experience, associating the brand with opinion leaders, and offering apps to educate consumers about whisky's finer points. This strategy is working: Johnnie Walker's sales in Africa are growing quickly.[28] However, a product's symbolic image may be damaged if the elements of the marketing mix clash with each other.

Symbol Removal

Some marketers have made a business of helping consumers erase symbols associated with groups with which they no longer identify. For example, the tattoo removal market is growing. Consumers may want to have tattoos removed because they are emblematic of an earlier time of life or an abandoned reference group and therefore impede the development of new personal identities. There may even be a market in erasing symbols left behind on social media sites and Web pages.

16-1d THE ROLE ACQUISITION FUNCTION

In addition to serving as emblems of group membership, offerings can help us feel more comfortable in new roles. This function is called the **role acquisition function** (look back at Exhibit 16.2).

Role Acquisition Phases

Consumers fill many roles in their lives, and these roles constantly change. You may currently occupy the role of student, son or daughter, brother or sister, and worker. At some point in your life (perhaps even now), you may occupy the role of husband or wife, uncle or aunt, parent, divorcee, grandparent, retiree, widow or widower, and so on. People typically move from one role to another in three phases.[29] The first phase is *separation* from the old role. This often means disposing of products associated with the role we are leaving, the way that children give up security blankets in their transition from baby to child. Consumers who are breaking up a relationship may symbolize the relationship's end by giving away, throwing away, or destroying products that remind them of their former partners. The second phase is the *transition* from one role to another, which may be accompanied by experimentation with new identities. During this transition, consumers may be willing to accept new possessions or styles that they otherwise would have rejected. Consumers may also construct a new identity through plastic surgery, dieting, new hairstyles, branding, body piercing, and tattooing. The final phase is *incorporation*, in which the consumer takes on the new role and the identity associated with it.

Use of Symbols and Rituals in Role Transitions

Exhibit 16.5 illustrates how and why we use symbols and rituals when we acquire a new role. We often feel uncomfortable with a new role because we are inexperienced in occupying it and have little knowledge about how to fulfill it. A common reaction is to use products stereotypically associated with that role. For example, MBAs who are insecure about their job prospects are more likely than other MBAs to use symbols generally associated with the role of a businessperson. We often use a group of products to symbolize adoption of a new role. Having the right

Exhibit 16.5 ▶ Model of Role Acquisition

When we first enter a new role (e.g., parenthood), we may lack some role confidence. As a result, we engage in activities (e.g., have baby showers) and buy groups of products (e.g., strollers) typically associated with that role. These activities and products, along with the way that others react to our behaviors, enhance our role confidence.

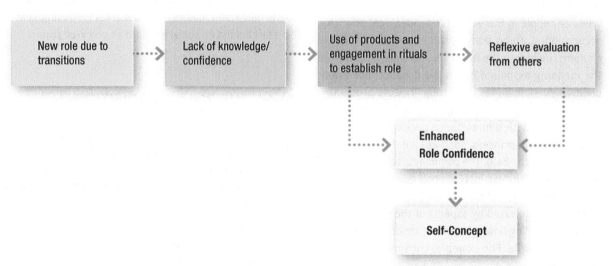

Source: Adapted from Michael Solomon, "The Role of Products as Social Stimuli: A Symbolic Interactionism Perspective," *Journal of Consumer Research*, December 1983, pp. 319–329. Reprinted with permission of The University of Chicago Press.

combination of products is important because without it we may not elicit the appropriate response from others. Imagine the reaction you would get at work if you wore white socks or sneakers with a dark business suit.

Rituals (sometimes called *rites of passage*) are an important part of role transitions. In the United States, a number of rituals mark the transition from single to married status—engagement party, wedding shower, bachelor party, rehearsal dinner, wedding, reception, and honeymoon—each with relevant enabling products. In the social media era, one ritual is changing your Facebook relationship status as part of a role transition.[30] Funeral rituals in different cultures involve symbolic consumption activities such as presenting or consuming special foods, buying flowers and cards, and displaying pictures or valuables that reflect on the deceased and the bereaved.[31]

Rituals often involve others whose participation helps validate the role transition. As shown in Exhibit 16.5, we use symbols and engage in rituals to get feedback from participants about whether we are fulfilling the role correctly. This feedback, called **reflexive evaluation**, helps us feel more confident in our role and thus validates our new status. Newly minted MBAs, for example, feel more confident in their role when experienced businesspeople acknowledge them as fellow businesspeople. The next section focuses on marital role transitions and products as symbols of this transition process.

Reflexive evalua-tion Feedback from others that tells us whether we are fulfilling the role correctly.

Marital Transitions

Products are often an important component in the transition from single to married status. As part of separating from the old phase, the couple must decide which of their possessions to dispose of and which to move to their new household. Often presents from old boyfriends or girlfriends are discarded, as are products symbolizing one's former single status. As part of the incorporation phase, the couple acquires new products that are culturally appropriate for the married role and that help them create a mutual history. Clearly, different cultures have different marital rituals.[32] For example, the mother-in-law often gives the keys to the house to a Hindu bride following the wedding, symbolically handing over the charge of running the house.

A similar process operates in the transition from married to divorced status. Here, each person takes back what was his or hers, and they divide their joint possessions. People may deliberately dispose of possessions that remind them of the other person. As one set of researchers note, "Jettisoning symbols of the ex-spouse . . . may be psychologically necessary in the process of ending the relationship."[33] Some people destroy possessions, an action that perhaps serves several functions—symbolically representing the destruction of the marriage, punishing the ex-spouse, and eliminating possessions that symbolize the marriage.

People may have difficulty fulfilling other symbolic functions as a result of ending a marriage. For example, one spouse may no longer have the conspicuous consumption items that once communicated social status. Thus, someone who loses a house (an important symbol of social prestige) may feel a loss of identity. On the other hand, people may acquire products symbolic of their new single status during this role transition, as some people do by purchasing a sports car or road bike at this time.

Cultural Transitions

Consumers may also change roles when they move to a new culture, often abandoning or disposing of old customs and symbols and adopting new ones in the process. Expatriates often face frustrating and formidable barriers to inclusion in a new culture. To reduce these barriers, they may participate in local events and rituals, adapt consumption to local customs, and become brand conscious, even though they may hold on to certain aspects of their home culture, like food, language, videos, photos, and jewelry.[34] Whether someone abandons or retains possessions that symbolize the old role may depend on how long the role is expected to last. The study of expatriates from India showed that consumers held onto possessions reminiscent of their culture of origin because they still considered the possibility of someday returning to India.

Social Status Transitions

Newly wealthy individuals, the "nouveaux riches," use possessions—usually ostentatious ones—to demonstrate their acquired status and validate their role. This behavior is consistent with the model of symbols and role transitions in Exhibit 16.5, which shows the importance of reflexive evaluation from others to indicate successful role performance. As one author notes, "Consumer satisfaction is derived from audience reactions to the wealth displayed by the purchaser in securing the product or service rather than to the positive attributes of the item in question."[35] In other words, "new money" consumers wear brand labels on the outside of their clothes to communicate, whereas "old money" consumers leave labels on the inside.

 ### Marketing Implications

Marketers can apply their knowledge of consumers' role transitions in several ways.

Role Transitions and Target Consumers

Consumers in transition represent an important target market for many firms. As Procter & Gamble's global marketing officer once observed, "Newlyweds are in some ways the ultimate consumer."[36] Many companies target engaged couples who will soon buy offerings related to the wedding, honeymoon, and new housing. For example, De Beers, a diamond trading company, targets engaged and married couples with messages reinforcing how a diamond ring can symbolize a long-lasting relationship. Its ad slogan, "A Diamond Is Forever," has been in use since 1947.[37]

Role Transitions as a Means for Developing Inventory

Because product disposition can be an important aspect of role separation, marketers of secondhand products can acquire inventory by marketing to people engaged in role transitions. For example, secondhand stores might target college students before graduation, knowing that in their role transitions many may wish to dispose of student-related paraphernalia such as furniture and clothing. Similarly, online auction sites such as www.eBay.com profit when consumers decide to dispose of items made obsolete or irrelevant by role transitions.

Role Transitions and Product Promotions

Marketers may find it useful to promote their products as instrumental in incorporating a new role. For example, marketers tout everything from shower fixtures to stock shares as acceptable wedding gifts. Wedding registries are showing up in places as diverse as Best Buy, Ace Hardware, and the Jewish Museum of New York. Interestingly, research shows that for weddings, gift-givers tend to select products that are more traditional (such as appliances and dishes) rather than unconventional (such as hardware or tools).[38] The Container Store not only has wedding and baby registries, it has registries for college students who are furnishing dorm rooms and for first-time home buyers.[39]

Selling Product Constellations

Marketers can stress the importance of groups of products to consumers in the process of role acquisition.[40] Businesses featuring product constellations include websites such as www.theknot.com, which offer access to one-stop shopping for wedding apparel, photographers, florists, limousines, catering companies, and related offerings. Company advertising can suggest that consumers will earn positive reflexive evaluation from others if they use an appropriate constellation of products associated with a given role.

Managing Rituals

Marketers can also be instrumental in developing services that help in planning and implementing rituals surrounding transitions, as funeral homes do by performing services in the death ritual. Rituals such as sending a greeting card on the occasion of a life transition have helped Hallmark build annual revenue to nearly $4 billion. The company offers paper and electronic cards for consumers to send for such diverse occasions as being newly single and losing a job. Despite the rise of e-mail and social media, greeting cards remain an important part of the rituals that mark new roles during these transitions. "Electronic communication is great for sharing information," says a Hallmark spokesperson. "Cards are better for sharing emotions."[41]

16-1e THE CONNECTEDNESS FUNCTION

Although the meaning of offerings that serve emblematic or role acquisition functions comes from the culture, product meaning can also come from the groups consumers belong to (review Exhibit 16.2).[42] Products and consumption activities that serve the **connectedness function** express our membership in a group and symbolize our personal connections to significant people, events, or experiences in our lives. For example, you may particularly like a painting or a hat because it was a gift from a close friend. Heirlooms and genealogy studies connect people with their ancestors; family photos connect them to their descendants. People may also value concert programs, ticket stubs, and other souvenirs as reminders of special people, events, and places.

> **Connectedness function** The use of products as symbols of our personal connections to significant people, events, or experiences.
>
> **Expressiveness function** The use of products as symbols to demonstrate our uniqueness—how we stand out as different from others.

Other products and acts can also symbolize connectedness. For instance, Chinese consumers use large round tables in restaurants to symbolize wholeness and the group's connectedness; Chinese New Year celebrations emphasize family ties. Knowing this, PepsiCo's Chinese New Year advertising and social media messages focus on festive family get-togethers.[43] During Muslim feasts, everyone shares food from a community plate; those who ask for a separate plate are considered rude. Rituals such as the U.S. celebration of Thanksgiving may also symbolize connectedness. Often family members show their commitment by attending the Thanksgiving gathering—even if they have to travel long distances. Moreover, cultures like those of the United States and England emphasize family connectedness during the Christmas ritual.

Each family maintains its own traditions that foster connectedness. Members often strongly resist deviating from these traditions (such as trying a new stuffing recipe for the Thanksgiving turkey). Many families foster connectedness by looking at old family photographs or videos and telling family stories. Other families pass certain cherished objects from one generation to the next as symbols

of the family's connectedness, with each owner acting as guardian of the special possessions.[44] This sense of connectedness may not only reaffirm social ties but may also make us nostalgic about past times.

16-1f THE EXPRESSIVENESS FUNCTION

As a symbol, a product has the potential to say something about our uniqueness.[45] This **expressiveness function** reflects how unique we are, not how we relate to other people. According to research, Eastern European youths like Western products because these offerings are used to create a distinct appearance that sets them apart from others.[46] We express our unique personalities through offerings like clothing, home decoration, art, leisure activities, and food consumption. We might find certain product categories, such as hairstyles, tattoos, or music, particularly appropriate for indicating who we are as individuals.[47]

Marketing Implications

The connectedness and expressive functions lead to several marketing implications. For example, marketers may wish to invoke feelings of nostalgia by connecting their product with people, places, or events. Marketers of toys and games, movies, and music have successfully encouraged consumers to connect these products with special times in their lives. Colorforms, owned by University Games, celebrated its 60th anniversary with ads promoting the rerelease of its colorful geometric set and its Michael Jackson Dress-Up Set. The target: Parents who remember playing with a Colorforms set when they were young. "Everything you loved about it as a child will be appealing to your children," says the head of University Games.[48]

In addition, marketers can suggest that their products enhance uniqueness.[49] The British fashion house Burberry invites consumers to express themselves by custom-designing a trench coat to suit their own taste. "Luxury consumers are very interested in self-expression," says a Forrester Research analyst. "If they can put a little twist on a product that makes it individualized, it suddenly sounds like a very good value proposition."[50]

16-1g MULTIPLE FUNCTIONS

A given product may serve several of the functions we just described. Crystal wine goblets received as a wedding present from the bride's grandparents could serve an emblematic function because their high price tag communicates social status. They may also serve a role acquisition function, helping the newlyweds to internalize their new marital roles. In addition, as a present from grandparents, the goblets may serve a connectedness function, symbolizing the newlyweds' special relationship with their family. Finally, if the goblets are personally appealing to the couple, they may symbolize the newlyweds' individual aesthetic tastes, thus also serving an expressiveness function. We are not always aware of a product's symbolic function. We may expect certain types of gifts when we go through role transitions like graduation and marriage, but we are probably not conscious of the fact that these products are helping us adjust to our new roles. Finally, we may really like an item that we received as a gift without realizing that we are reacting in this way because it serves as a reminder of the gift giver.

16-1h SYMBOLS AND SELF-CONCEPT

The symbolic functions of products and consumption rituals are important because together they help to define and maintain our self-concept, our mental conception of who we are.[51] Social identity theory proposes that we evaluate brands in terms of their consistency with our individual identities.[52] According to the theory, our self-concept can be decomposed into many separate identities called **actual identity schemas**, including student, worker, daughter, and so on. These identities may be driven, at least in part, by the roles that we fulfill. Some identities may be especially salient or central to our self-concept. Our actual identity may be shaped by an **ideal identity schema**—a set of ideas about how the identity that we seek would be realized in its ideal form.

> **Actual identity schema** A set of multiple, salient identities that reflect our self-concept.
>
> **Ideal identity schema** A set of ideas about how the identity would be indicated in its ideal form.

Our actual and ideal identity schemas influence which products we use and which consumption practices we engage in, even among consumers who object to the over-commercialization of contemporary culture.[53] Our actual identity might affect what we regard as aesthetically beautiful[54] or which symbols of ourselves (such as family photos or personal mugs) we bring to our workplace or put up in dorm rooms to reflect who we are.[55] Identity can also influence the amount donated to nonprofit groups. In one study, consumers contributed more when informed that another contributor who shares their identity has donated a significant amount of money.[56]

The fact that possessions help to shape our identity may explain why people who lose their possessions in natural disasters or war and people who are in institutions like the military, nursing homes, or prisons sometimes feel a loss of identity.[57] Indeed, loss of cherished possessions can induce a state of grief that resembles the death of a loved one. Some institutions, such as the military and prisons, deliberately strip individuals of their possessions to erase old identities. School and work uniforms also do this, on a more subtle level. On the other hand, millions of consumers have personal websites, blogs, and other Internet places where they use words, images, audio, links, and other elements to construct and project identities digitally, shaping and sharing their self-concept online with friends.[58]

Marketing Implications

Marketers need to consider several implications stemming from the preceding concepts.

Marketing and the Development of Consumer Self-Concepts

Marketers can play a role in both producing and maintaining an individual's self-concept. Although products may help define who we are, we also maintain our self-concept by selecting products with images that are consistent with it. For example, Converse, the athletic shoe company, allows consumers shopping in its stores or on its website to personalize their sneakers in many different ways, in line with their own self-concept. Its stores, in major cities worldwide, are equipped with special fabric printers so buyers can design and then wear their newly designed shoes on the same day. These sneakers are a good fit with self-concept because, explains a Converse executive, "the Converse customer is very creative."[59]

Product and Brand Fit with Self-Concepts

Marketers seek to create a close fit between the image of their brand and the actual or ideal identity of the consumer. The more similar a product's image is to a consumer's self-image, the more the consumer likes the product.[60] For example, in Japan, the wildly successful 60-member AKB48 all-girl singing group appeals to teen girls who see the members as kawaii (Japanese for "cute") and very much like themselves (see Exhibit 16.6). AKB48 has released one chart-topping song after another, and its branded merchandise is sold in the group's official stores in Japan, Hong Kong, and Taiwan. The group is so popular that it now has regional offshoots in five areas of Japan.[61] A close fit between the brand and the consumer's self-concept can enhance brand loyalty and reduce the possibility of brand-switching.[62]

Product Fit with Multiple Self-Concepts

Because self-images are multifaceted, marketers must also determine whether products consistent with one

YOSHIKAZU TSUNO/AFP/Getty Images

Exhibit 16.6 ▶ Fit with Self-Concepts

Products are most successful when brand images fit with consumers' self-concepts, such as the Japanese girl singing group, AKB48.

aspect of the target customers' identity may be inconsistent with another aspect. For example, a new father may react negatively to disposable diapers because even though the product is consistent with his new parent identity, it is inconsistent with his environmentally conscious identity.

Advertising Fit with Self-Concepts

Finally, ads should appeal to the identity concept appropriate for the targeted segment's gender and culture.[63] Thus, some ads that target women might emphasize mutual reliance, whereas some ads that target men might emphasize autonomy. Similarly, ads geared toward consumers in China might stress culturally appropriate themes of group goals and achievement, whereas ads for U.S. consumers might stress culturally appropriate themes of personal goals and achievement.

Increasingly, consumers are involved in two cultures and fluent in two languages due to immigration or because they leave their home country to work. When these consumers are exposed to an ad in one of the languages they know, they experience **frame switching**, activating the aspects of their self-concepts that relate to that language's cultural background. In other words, they adopt the cultural frame

> **Frame switching**
> Stimulated by language cues, a consumer who identifies with more than one culture will activate the aspects of his or her self-concept that relates to that language's cultural background.

of the language contained in the ad—but only if they are both bicultural and bilingual.[64] A U.S.-born consumer who lives and works in Japan will switch to an American cultural frame when exposed to an English-language billboard, for instance. As a result, marketers must consider how frame switching will affect consumers' emotional and cognitive processing of the arguments and images in their communications.

16-2 Special Possessions and Brands

We may feel emotionally attached to certain possessions and certain brands because we see them as part of ourselves.[65] However, some products come to hold a special, valued position in our minds, whether or not they are relevant to our self-concepts.[66] For example, one consumer may regard his lawn mower as a special possession because it is very functional, whereas another may view her skis as special because they provide such enjoyment, yet neither consumer may view these items as relevant to their self-concept.[67] This section looks at what makes a brand or product special to a consumer.

16-2a SPECIAL BRANDS

Have you ever been really, really crazy about a brand? Maybe it's your iPhone, or Zipcar, or maybe it's Top Shop, the LA Lakers, or the company you want to work for; but for whatever reason, you are a real fan of this brand. You feel connected to it,[68] and you love it.[69] It stands for what you stand for. And you think about it and talk about it a lot.[70] In fact, the brand is almost an extension of who you are.[71] You may even belong to an online group and participate in conversations about this brand. If someone criticized the brand, you might take personal offense, and defend the brand.[72] And if the brand went off the market, you'd be devastated.[73] But if the brand did something unethical, you might feel as though your own reputation was on the line and feel a sense of identity threat.[74] If this description fits you, you are described as being attached to a particular brand.[75]

Marketers are very interested in creating consumers who are highly attached to their brand, not just because of their extreme loyalty, but also by the fact that they can serve as brand ambassadors. By virtue of their brand passion, and their interests in talking about the brand, they act almost as the marketer's (unpaid) salesforce. They also buy the latest model of a given brand,[76] and can help diffusion by acting as innovators. Some research shows that attached consumers are also more likely to forgive a brand for minor mishaps that might otherwise result in consumer dissatisfaction.[77] Consumers who are highly attached to a brand may also do other things to help it. For example, people who are highly attached to the college they attended may one day become philanthropists who give the school large sums of money. But attachment can have some downsides. Researchers show that consumers who exhibit a fearful attachment style (meaning they tend to be anxious about relationships in general and tend not to trust others), want to take revenge against a brand that lets them down.[78] So in certain cases, the people who love the brand the most may, in some circumstances, feel most hurt by certain brand actions.

16-2b TYPES OF SPECIAL POSSESSIONS

Although almost any possession can be special, researchers have found that special possessions typically fall into one of several categories: pets, memory-laden objects, achievement symbols, and collections.[79]

Pets

U.S. consumers tend to regard their pets as very special and spend an estimated $55 billion every year on pet products.[80] More than 60 percent of U.S. households have a pet. Whether the economy is booming or struggling, retailers such as Petco see higher demand for gourmet pet food and other premium products because, says Petco's CEO, "we are in a pretty emotional category."[81] Not every culture treats pets as special possessions. For example, cats and dogs are not treasured as pets in the Middle East, and dog owners in Korea typically feed their pets leftovers rather than dog food.

Memory-Laden Objects

Some products acquire special meaning because they evoke memories or emotions of special people, places, or experiences. Examples include heirlooms, antiques, souvenirs, and gifts from special people. You may value a ticket stub—otherwise just a piece of paper—because it evokes memories of going to see your favorite band in concert. Such possessions can be therapeutic for elderly people because they evoke links to other people and happy times. Several researchers report the case of an individual who had to sell a favorite automobile because of a divorce but saved the license plates as a memento of this special possession. Many consumers consider photographs special because they are reminders of special people, and they create "shrines" by displaying photos on bureaus, mantles, and pianos.[82] Particular memory-laden objects can become *fetish objects*, viewed as extraordinarily magical objects. Even replicas or copies of a particularly valued item may become fetish objects. For example, a guitar reputed to have been played by George Harrison of the Beatles can be a fetish object for some consumers, even without evidence that it was actually Harrison's guitar.[83]

Achievement Symbols

People also regard possessions that symbolize achievement as special. One researcher who studied the Mormon migration to Utah in the 1800s found that people often moved possessions that demonstrated competence. For example, men brought tools, and women brought sewing machines and other objects that had a practical function but also symbolized domestic achievement.[84] Modern day symbols of achievement might include college diplomas, sports trophies, recognition plaques, or even conspicuously consumed items like Rolex watches or Porsches.

Collections

Collections are special possessions for many people. Common collectible items include model cars, sports memorabilia, seashells, minerals, coins, and childhood objects like baseball cards and dolls (see Exhibit 16.7).[85] Firms like the Bradford Exchange, the Franklin Mint, GovMint.com, and the Danbury Mint produce collectible items for consumers, but rarity makes some items particularly special. For instance, a collector paid nearly $700,000 for a Richard Mille wristwatch worn by tennis superstar Rafael Nadal during his highly successful 2010 season.[86]

Collectors often view their collections as extensions of themselves—sometimes symbolizing an aspect of their occupation, family heritage, or appearance. Collectors have the urge to "complete" the collection, such as finding the last Babe Ruth baseball card or all Beatles bootleg records, as a form of "symbolic self-completion."

Exhibit 16.7 ▶ Collections

Products can be collectible items for consumers, viewing the products as an extension of themselves.

Researchers have studied a grocery store owner who collected antique product packages, an engineer who collected pocket watches, a woman named Bunny who collected rabbit replicas, and wealthy women who collected monogrammed silver spoons.[87] For some, collections represent a fantasy image of the self. For example, men who collect baseball cards may be keeping alive the fantasy of themselves as ball players. As is often the case with people who have special possessions, collectors tend to believe that they take better care of their collections than anyone else would.[88]

16-2c THE CHARACTERISTICS THAT DESCRIBE SPECIAL POSSESSIONS

Special possessions have several distinct characteristics.[89] First, special possessions (like our family dog or the cherished silver pencil sharpener) have *few or no substitutes* according to their owners. Insurance may pay to replace furniture that was damaged in a fire, but new furniture cannot compensate for heirloom pieces that were passed down through generations. In fact, consumers see special possessions as irreplaceable because of their associations with certain events and people in their lives.[90]

Second, because of this sentimentality, consumers will not sell special possessions at market value, if at all, and often buy special possessions with little regard for their price. Economists say that special possessions have unusually low *price elasticity*, because increasing their price

has very little effect on reducing demand for them. We could never, for example, sell at any price our family pet or an afghan made by our grandmother. Collectors may pay exorbitant prices to acquire particularly sought-after objects like rare coins and one-of-a-kind wristwatches.

Third, people experience a *reluctance to discard* special possessions, even when they lose their functional value. Children often have a hard time parting with security blankets and stuffed animals and will keep these favorite objects until they are mere threads of fabric. Others have a hard time tossing out their favorite jeans. Do your parents still keep your old report cards and pictures that you drew for them? Do you still have the special gifts you got?

Some special possessions, however, are not always used for their original purpose. Some people who buy Altoids "Curiously Strong" mints retain the tin container to keep small special possessions safe.[91] Some consumers believe that a prized possession will lose valued properties if it is used to fulfill its original function, which is why some consumers preserve their new vinyl LPs and download the songs instead.

Finally, consumers frequently personify special possessions. Some name individual items in a collection, name their houses, or use a feminine or masculine pronoun when referring to their cars or boats. Perhaps even more significant, we may treat these possessions as though they were our partners, feeling such commitment and attachment that we would be devastated by their loss.[92]

16-2d WHY SOME PRODUCTS ARE SPECIAL

Possessions take on special meaning for several reasons, including their symbolic value, mood altering properties, and instrumental importance. Exhibit 16.8 shows more specific reasons that underlie these three general categories.

- *Symbolic value.* Possessions may be special, in part, because they fulfill the emblematic, role adoption, connectedness, and expressiveness functions noted earlier in the chapter. For example, we may value art, heirlooms, and jewelry because they express our style or because they were gifts and tie us to special people.[93] Thus, consumers are very reluctant to part with a possession (such as a Christmas ornament or a piece of jewelry) that has symbolic meaning because it was acquired from a much-loved family member or close friend.[94]

- *Mood-altering properties.* Possessions may be special because they have mood-altering properties. For example, trophies, plaques, collections, and diplomas can evoke feelings of pride, happiness, and joy.[95] Pets can evoke feelings of comfort. A consumer in one study described her refrigerator as a special possession because making snacks always cheered her up. Others cited music players and music as favorite possessions because these put consumers in a good mood.[96] Some research suggests that people who are most in love with their possessions are lonely and that possessions serve to reduce this sense of loneliness.[97]

- *Instrumental importance.* Possessions may also be special because they are extremely useful. A consumer who describes her cell phone or computer as special because she uses it constantly to get things done throughout the day is referring to this possession's instrumental value.

16-2e CONSUMER CHARACTERISTICS AFFECT WHAT IS SPECIAL

Social class, mobility, gender, and age are among the background characteristics that affect the types of things that become special to each of us.

- *Social class.* One study examined the meanings that people of different social classes in England gave to their possessions. People in the business class were concerned about possessions that symbolized their personal history and self-development. Unemployed people were concerned about possessions that had utilitarian value.[98] In addition, consumers who aspire to a higher social class may use

> **Possession ritual**
> Ritual we engage in when we first acquire a product that helps to make it "ours."

particular possessions to associate themselves with that social class, even misrepresenting those products to support the self-image of belonging to the higher class.[99]

- *Mobility.* Consumers' tendencies to acquire special possessions may also depend on how frequently they move. Global nomads—people who move frequently from one country to another—tend to regard their possessions more as temporary and having use value (vs. specialness) in their particular living situation at a particular time.[100]

- *Gender.* For men, products are special when they symbolize activity and physical achievement and when they have instrumental and functional features. On the other hand, women often value symbols of identity and products that symbolize their attachment to other people.[101] A study of consumers in Niger and the United States found that women's special possessions were those that symbolized their children's accomplishments or connected consumers to others. For the U.S. women, these possessions included heirlooms and pictures; for the Niger women, they included tapestries, jewelry, and other items passed on through generations. Men chose objects that showed material comfort and possessions that indicated mastery over the environment.[102] Men are more likely to collect cars, books, and sports-related objects, and women are more likely to collect jewelry, dishes, and silverware.[103]

- *Age.* Although individuals have special possessions at all ages, what they regard as special changes with age. For example, stuffed animals are very important for children, music and motor vehicles are highly prized among teenagers, and photographs take on increasing importance as consumers enter adulthood and old age.

16-2f RITUALS USED WITH SPECIAL POSSESSIONS

We often engage in rituals designed to create, energize, or enhance the meaning of special possessions. These rituals can occur at the acquisition, usage, or disposition stage of consumption.

At the acquisition stage, **possession rituals** enable the consumer to claim personal possession of new goods.[104] When you buy new jeans, for example, you may change the length, cut them at the knees, or add embellishments. You may adorn a new car with personal markers like seat covers. When you move to a new house or apartment, you hang pictures, buy curtains, and position the furniture.

Possession rituals for previously owned goods include wiping away traces of the former owner.[105] For example,

Exhibit 16.8 ▶ Reasons Why Possessions Are Special

Take a possession that you regard as special (most likely it is special to you because it has symbolic value, mood altering properties, and/or utilitarian value) and answer the following questions using a 7-point scale (1 = not true of me; 7 = very true of me).

This possession is important to me because it . . .

Symbolic Value	Symbolizes personal history	Reminds me of particular events or places
		Is a record of my personal history
		Required a lot of effort to acquire or maintain
	Represents achievement	Required a lot of effort to acquire or maintain
		Reminds me of my skills, achievements, or goals
		Reminds me of my relationship with a particular person
		Reminds me of my family or a group of people that I belong to
		Represents my family heritage or history
	Facilitates interpersonal ties	Allows me to spend time or share activities with other people
	Demonstrates status	Has social prestige value
		Gives me social status
		Makes others think well of me
	Is self-expressive	Allows me to express myself
		Expresses what is unique about me, different from others
Mood-Altering Properties	Provides enjoyment	Provides enjoyment, entertainment, or relaxation
		Improves my mood
		Provides comfort or emotional security
	Is spiritual	Provides a spiritual link to divine or higher forces
	Is appearance related	Is beautiful or attractive in appearance
		Improves my appearance or the way I look
Utilitarian Value	Is utilitarian	Allows me to be efficient in my daily life or work
		Has a lot of practical usefulness
		Provides me freedom or independence
	Has financial aspects	Is valuable in terms of money

Source: Adapted from Marsha Richens, "Valuing Things: The Public and Private Meanings of Possessions," *Journal of Consumer Research* 21, December 1994, pp. 504–521.

when you buy a new home, you thoroughly clean it, tear down old wallpaper, and take down personal markers like the name on the mailbox. However, it is not always possible to wipe away meaning. In China, for example, consumers often build new houses because of a sense that older structures are "contaminated" by the former occupants. This is the reverse of the "magic" that consumers feel when acquiring possessions that were once owned or touched by a famous person (or that person's relative), such as shoes worn by Lady Gaga or a baseball autographed by a Major League team. Some studies show that the feeling of disgust that consumers feel for certain products (such as raw meat) can carry over to products that are in physical contact with those "disgusting" products. With this in mind, grocery stores often provide plastic bags so shoppers can keep meat packages from touching other products in their shopping carts.[106]

At the consumption stage, consumers may engage in **grooming rituals** to bring out or maintain the best in special products.[107] Some consumers spend hours washing and waxing their cars or cleaning house before visitors arrive. Sometimes the grooming ritual extends to you personally, as when you spend a lot of time making yourself look good for a special event.

> **Grooming ritual**
> Ritual we engage in to bring out or maintain the best in special products.

Finally, when the offering loses its symbolic meaning, consumers engage in **divestment rituals**—wiping away all traces of personal meaning.[108] For example, many people remove the address labels before giving away magazines that they subscribe to or delete personal files before selling or donating a computer or smartphone. We might even get rid of a possession in stages, moving it from the living room to the attic before finally selling it or throwing it away.

16-2g DISPOSING OF SPECIAL POSSESSIONS

People dispose of special possessions for different reasons and in different ways. Consumers dispose of special possessions during life transitions, such as when moving to a university, to one's first home, getting married, and so on. Older consumers make disposition decisions when experiencing periods of crisis, when moving to an institution, when approaching death, and when marking rites of passage and progression—although some transfer special possessions only after death through a will. Sometimes the consumer hopes that giving the object to a relative will invoke memories, express love, or lead to a symbolic immortality; at other times the consumer seeks to control disposition decisions and timing. An older consumer generally considers which recipient will best appreciate the special object's meaning, continue to use or care for it, or uphold family traditions, or he or she may simply give it to the person who asks for it first.[109]

16-3 Sacred Meaning

Although many possessions are considered special, some are so special that they are viewed as sacred. **Sacred entities** are people, things, and places that are set apart, revered, worshiped, and treated with great respect. We may find such entities deeply moving, and we may feel anger and revulsion when they are not respected. In contrast, **profane things** are ordinary, without special power. Profane objects are often distinguished from sacred ones by the fact that they are used for more mundane purposes.[110]

Movie stars, popular singers, historic figures like John F. Kennedy and Martin Luther King Jr., and religious leaders such as the pope and the Buddha are regarded by many people as sacred. The sacred status of famous people is exemplified by the crowds visiting the graves of celebrities like Princess Diana and the homes of living or dead celebrities, such as Elvis's Graceland.

One reason why heirlooms and photographs of ancestors take on sacred status is that we may view our ancestors as heroes. A similar phenomenon explains why we treat items associated with famous statesmen such as George

Divestment ritual Ritual enacted at the disposition stage that is designed to wipe away all traces of our personal meaning in a product.

Sacred entities People, things, and places that are set apart, revered, worshiped, and treated with great respect.

Profane things Things that are ordinary, and hence have no special power.

Washington and Winston Churchill as sacred. Although not part of our personal past, these heroes were instrumental in formulating national identities. Consumers demonstrate their reverence by visiting the places that honor these historic figures.[111]

Many consumers also regard as sacred such objects as national flags, patriotic songs, art, collections, family recipes, and the Bible and such places as museums, the Alamo, the Taj Mahal, and the Great Wall of China. These sacred objects and places evoke powerful feelings, sometimes causing people to weep or feel emotional when viewing them. In addition to sacred people, objects, and places, we may identify certain times and events, religious holidays, weddings, births, deaths, and grace before meals as sacred. Sacred entities involve some mystery or myth that raises them above the ordinary.[112] The pope, for example, is viewed as being almost godlike. And legendary figures such as Elvis Presley, Marilyn Monroe, and John F. Kennedy are associated with mystery (see Exhibit 16.9). Sacred entities have qualities

Exhibit 16.9 ▶ Sacred Entities
Some famous objects, places, or people—like Elvis—are so special that they attain a sacred status and elicit emotions in consumers. That is why some ads, like this watch ad, may be successful if they combine products with an emotional response.

Image Courtesy of The Advertising Archives

that transcend time, place, or space. When you enter the Alamo, for instance, you may feel as if you are back in the period when the historic fighting took place.

Sacred objects also possess strong approach/avoidance characteristics and create an overwhelming feeling of power and fascination. For example, you may simultaneously desire to be close to but also watch from a distance people you view as heroes and heroines. Encountering sacred entities may evoke certain feelings, such as ecstasy or the sense of being smaller and humbler than the sacred entity. For instance, some people may feel that they have accomplished little in life in comparison with the achievements of heroes like Martin Luther King Jr. Some people feel humbled by the mass of humanity represented by the Vietnam Memorial. Moreover, sacred objects can create strong feelings of attachment, such as the need to take care of and nurture the sacred entity. Often sacred objects involve rituals that dictate how we should behave in the object's presence, such as the right and wrong way to treat the American flag.

Sacredness may be maintained by scarcity and exclusivity.[113] For example, the sacred status of special works of art derives from their uniqueness and the fact that their high price maintains their exclusivity. Entities that were once sacred can be made profane if they are not treated with due respect or if their sacred status is eliminated through commercialization. We can feel anger and disgust at the profaning of a sacred person or sacred object. In one study, some *Star Trek* fans said they were "barely" able to "stand watching the show" because of the way that the series was being commercially exploited.[114]

Marketing Implications

Marketers need to be aware of the sacred meanings that people, objects, places, and events can have to consumers.

Creating and Maintaining Sacredness

Sometimes marketers create sacredness in objects or people. For example, the promoters of a famous movie star might heighten his sacred status by creating or enhancing his mystery and myth, making him exclusive, and promoting the powerful emotional effect he has on people. Marketers may also help maintain sacredness— for example, by keeping the price of sacred objects like collections, fine art, and rare jewelry very high. Five decades after the Beatles shot to fame, a collector paid nearly $500,000 for a guitar played by George Harrison in 1963.[115] Before Charles Leski Auctions accepts autographed Beatles memorabilia for auction in Australia, its

experts authenticate the signatures so buyers will know they are getting what they pay for. Because some items were signed by the group's road manager rather than one of the Fab Four, "we end up breaking a lot of hearts," says an auction official.[116]

Avoiding the Profaning of Sacred Objects and Entities

Marketers sometimes unintentionally profane sacred objects through commercialization. Some consumers believe that Elvis Presley has been profaned by commercial Elvis paraphernalia. Selling religious trinkets outside the sacred properties of certain religious sites may profane these places as well. Benetton, the Italian apparel firm, touched off a worldwide controversy when its ad agency digitally manipulated photos of religious and political leaders to show them kissing each other. The company said this "Unhate" campaign was intended to "combat the culture of hatred in all its forms." One ad depicted a digitally created kiss between Pope Benedict XVI, the head of the Roman Catholic Church, and Ahmed Mohamed el-Tayeb, the leader of Cairo's al-Azhar mosque. Public outrage and official protests from the Vatican prompted Benetton to end the campaign within hours of its introduction—although it won an industry award for promoting debate.[117]

Product Involvement in Sacred Activities and Rituals

In some cases, marketers sell products regarded as instrumental to the continuation or conduct of sacred occasions and rituals. Marketers like Hallmark, Papyrus, and American Greetings profitably capitalize on sacred rituals such as Christmas celebrations by selling products (tree ornaments, ribbons, wrapping paper, cards) regarded as important parts of these events.

16-4 The Transfer of Symbolic Meaning Through Gift Giving

This chapter has shown how consumers imbue products, times, activities, places, and people with symbolic meaning. Some meanings enhance the special and /or sacred status of the product, and some are instrumental in developing or maintaining the consumer's self-concept. Another important aspect of symbolic consumption involves transferring meaning from one individual to another through gifts of physical goods (such as clothing) or experiences (such as a gift card for a restaurant).[118]

16-4a THE TIMING OF GIFTS

Some gift-giving occasions are culturally determined and timed. In the United States, these include Valentine's Day, Mother's Day, and Father's Day. Koreans celebrate the 100th day of a baby's life, and families in China celebrate when a baby is one month old. Koreans also give gifts to elders and family members on New Year's Day. Consumers in cultures around the world also celebrate various gift-giving holidays such as Valentine's Day, Hanukkah, and Kwanzaa.[119]

Some gift-giving occasions are culturally prescribed but occur at a time that is specific to each individual.[120] These are often the transitions discussed earlier: anniversaries, graduations, birthdays, weddings, bridal and baby showers, retirement parties, and religious transitions such as baptism, first communion, or bar mitzvah. Still other gift-giving occasions are ad hoc, as when we give gifts as part of a reconciliation attempt, to celebrate the birth of a child, to cheer up someone who is ill, or to thank someone for helping us.

16-4b THREE STAGES OF GIFT GIVING

Gift giving consists of three stages, as shown in Exhibit 16.10. In the **gestation stage**, we consider what to give the recipient. The **presentation stage** occurs with the actual giving of the gift. Finally, in the **reformulation stage**, we reevaluate the relationship based on the gift-giving experience.[121]

The Gestation Stage

The gestation stage before a gift is given involves the motives for and emotions surrounding giving, the nature and meaning of the gift, the value of the gift, and the amount of time spent searching for the gift.

Motives for and Emotions Surrounding Giving

During the gestation stage we develop motives for gift giving.[122] On the one hand, people may give for altruistic reasons—to help or show love for the recipient. In such cases, the gift they choose is largely based on its desirability (rather than how easy it is to obtain).[123] For example, a relative may give a large cash gift to help a young couple start their married life. We may also give for agnostic reasons because we derive positive emotional pleasure from the act of giving. Or we may give a gift for instrumental reasons, expecting the recipient to give something in return, as when a student gives a teacher a small gift in hopes of a higher grade. Consumers may also give for purely obligatory reasons because they feel the situation or the relationship demands it. Indeed, sometimes we do not

Exhibit 16.10 ▶
A Model of the Gift-Giving Process

The process of gift giving consists of three stages: (1) the *gestation stage*, at which we think about and buy the gift; (2) the *presentation stage*, at which we actually give the gift; and (3) the *reformulation stage*, at which we reevaluate our relationship based on the nature of the gift-giving experience. At each stage we can identify several issues that affect the gift-giving process.

Gestation Stage
- Motives
- Nature of the gift
- Value of the gift
- Search time

Presentation Stage
- Ceremony
- Timing and surprise elements
- Attention to the recipient
- Recipient's reaction

Reformulation Stage
- Relationship bonding
- Reciprocation

Gestation stage The first stage of gift giving, when we consider what to give someone.

Presentation stage The second stage of gift giving, when we actually give the gift.

Reformulation stage The final stage of gift giving, when we reevaluate the relationship based on the gift-giving experience.

react positively to gifts given by others because we now feel the obligation to reciprocate.

Sometimes we give gifts because we want to reduce guilt or alleviate hard feelings. In divorce, for example, the spouse who feels responsible for the breakup tends to give the partner more than a fair share in what is called *compensatory giving*.[124] Sometimes people have antagonistic motives for gift giving. For example, if you are invited to the wedding of someone you do not like, you might give the couple something you think is not very beautiful. Sometimes givers feel anxiety about giving a gift.[125] They may feel that the gift has to be absolutely perfect or worry if they lack the time or money to find a suitable gift. Interestingly, though if we have to choose a gift for multiple people (e.g., our coworkers), we don't want to give the same gift to multiple people. Instead we buy each a distinctly different gift.[126]

The Appropriateness and Meaning of the Gift

The appropriateness of the gift depends on the situation and the relationship between the gift giver and the recipient. For example, a worker would not give a boss a gift of lingerie because such items are too personal.[127] Likewise, you would not give good friends a token wedding gift because the relationship dictates something more substantial. Although token gifts may not be appropriate on a clearly defined gift-giving occasion, they can be highly significant when no gift is expected. Spontaneously giving a gift, even something small, can signify love and caring.[128]

Thus, you may feel quite touched when your significant other buys you "a little something." Token gifts are quite important for recipients with whom we do not have strong ties. It is appropriate and desirable to send holiday and birthday cards to people we see infrequently.[129]

The gift may also symbolize a particular meaning to the receiver.[130] For example, gifts can represent values we regard as appropriate for the recipient, such as domesticity for new brides and grooms or a new set of expectations. An engagement ring symbolizes expectations regarding commitment and future fidelity, just as giving golf clubs at retirement symbolizes expectations regarding future leisure. Gifts can also be symbolic of the self, as when giving a piece of art or something that the giver has created.

The Value of the Gift

The value of the gift is an important element of the gift-selection process. You might splurge on a Mother's Day gift to show your mother how much you love her. The consumer's culture can influence decisions about the value of a gift. In Japan, for example, people lose face if the gift they receive exceeds the value of the gift they have given.[131] Interestingly, consumers perceive that gifts they buy for others are more valuable, in economic terms, than gifts received from others. When giver and receiver had close connections, however, the receiver perceived higher economic value in the gift.[132] A giver may also use the value of a gift to repay a favor done by the receiver. Here, the giver's motive is to avoid feeling indebted to the receiver for the favor. The value of the purchased gift helps change what was a social exchange into an economic exchange.[133]

The Amount of Time Spent Searching

The amount of time spent searching for a gift symbolizes the nature and intensity of the giver's relationship with the recipient. Men and women differ in how much time and effort they invest in the search for a gift. Women are reportedly more involved in holiday gift shopping than are men.[134] Women also appear to spend more time searching for the perfect gift, whereas men are more likely to settle for something that "will do."[135]

The Presentation Stage

The presentation stage describes the actual exchange of the gift. Here, the ritual or ceremonial aspects of the giving process become very important.

Ceremony

During the presentation stage, the giver decides whether to wrap the gift and, if so, how. Wrapping the present nicely in appropriate paper helps to decommodify, or make more personal, a mass-produced product. However, the importance of the gift packaging depends on the formality and spontaneity of the occasion. For example, unanticipated gifts, such as a boss's surprise gift to an assistant or a wife's surprise gift to her husband, may be less formally wrapped and may even be appropriate if left unwrapped.

Timing and Surprise

Both the timing and the possibility of surprise may be important in gift giving. For example, although we know that gift giving is part of the Christmas ritual and that the wrapped gifts are even prominently displayed under the tree—sometimes for days before the actual exchange— being surprised by what they contain is often a key element. The excitement of unwrapping an item is heightened by having the recipient guess what the package contains. Although surprise is a valued part of the ritual, it is not always achieved. One study found that right before Christmas, some husbands purchase items that have been chosen in advance by their wives. Here, the gift giving is an orchestrated event with the husband playing the role of "purchasing agent."[136]

Attention to the Recipient

Paying attention to the recipient can be a critical dimension in the presentation stage. For example, attendees at wedding showers are expected to watch closely as the bride-to-be opens her gifts. Another factor to be considered is the congruence between the gift, the recipient's self-concept, and the giver's self-concept. Specifically, giving a gift that conflicts with the giver's self-concept can have a negative effect on the giver. As an example, if you give your best friend a T-shirt with an image he likes, but you find it offensive because it conflicts with your self-concept, you will not feel good about your choice.[137]

Recipient's Reaction

Another aspect is the reaction that the giver hopes to elicit from the recipient, the recipient's actual reaction, and the giver's response to the recipient's reaction. If you spent a lot of time and effort looking for the perfect gift and then the recipient opens the package quickly and goes on to the next gift without a word, you will probably feel hurt. As noted earlier, you may also feel anxious at the presentation stage if you are not sure about whether the recipient will like your gift.[138]

The Reformulation Stage

The reformulation stage marks the third and final stage of the gift-giving process. At this stage, the giver and the recipient reevaluate their relationship based on the gift-giving process.

Relationship Bonding

A gift may affect the relationship between giver and recipient in different ways, as shown in Exhibit 16.11. A gift can either maintain, strengthen, or weaken the relationship between the giver and receiver. One study found that

Exhibit 16.11 ▶ Possible Effect of Gift Giving on the Relationship

Gifts can have many different effects on a relationship— effects that range from strengthening to severing the relationship.

Relational Effect	Description	Experiential Themes
Strengthening	Gift receipt improves the quality of the relationship between giver and recipient. Feelings of connection, bonding commitment, and/or shared meaning are intensified.	Epiphany
Affirmation	Gift receipt validates the positive quality of the relationship between giver and recipient. Existing feelings of connection and/or shared meaning are validated.	Empathy Adherence Affirming farewell Recognition
Negligible effect	The gift-receipt experience has a minimal effect on perceptions of relationship quality.	Superfluity "Error" Charity Overkill
Negative confirmation	Gift receipt validates an existing negative quality of the relationship between giver and recipient. A lack of feelings of connection, bonding, and/or shared meaning is validated.	Absentee Control
Weakening	Gift receipt harms the quality of the relationship between giver and recipient. There is a newly evident or intensified perception that the relationship lacks connection, bonding, and/or shared meaning, but the relationship remains.	Burden Insult
Severing	Gift receipt so harms the quality of the relationship between giver and recipient that the relationship is dissolved.	Threat Nonaffirming farewell

Source: Julie A. Ruth, Cele C. Otnes, and Frédéric F. Brunel, "Gift Receipt and the Reformulation of Interpersonal Relationships," *Journal of Consumer Research* 25, March 1999, p. 389. Reprinted by permission of The University of Chicago Press.

gifts could strengthen a relationship by communicating feelings of connection, bonding, and commitment. Gifts can also affirm the relationship, validating existing feelings of commitment. Research suggests that a romantic relationship is likely to last longer when one member gives the other a gift to publicly announce their relationship. On the negative side, inappropriate gifts or those showing limited search effort or interest in the recipient's desires can weaken a relationship, creating the perception that the relationship lacks bonding and connection.[139] In many cultures, it is inappropriate to give money as a gift, in particular between friends and loved ones. Rituals such as wrapping the money or converting it into a gift card aim to transform money into a personal symbol.[140]

Reciprocation

The reformulation stage also has implications for how and whether the recipient will reciprocate on the next gift-giving occasion. If you gave someone a nice gift on one occasion, you would generally expect the recipient to reciprocate on the next occasion. If, on the other hand, you gave a gift that weakened the tie between you and the recipient, the latter may not give you a very nice gift or may give no gift at all on the next gift-giving occasion.

Some kinds of gift-giving situations or recipients are exempt from reciprocation.[141] For example, if you give someone a gift because she is ill or has experienced some tragedy (say, her house burned down), you will not expect her to reciprocate. However, if someone unexpectedly gives you a Christmas gift, you will usually feel guilty and want to rush out and buy him a gift, too. People of limited financial means (children, students) or lower status (a clerk, as opposed to a boss) may be regarded as exempt from giving to higher status people. Thus, it is appropriate for parents to give their children gifts and expect nothing in return. Women have also been reported to feel less obligated to reciprocate in date-related gift giving, perhaps because of culturally prescribed notions regarding men's generally higher economic power.[142]

Expectations of reciprocation depend on the culture and the relationship between the giver and the recipient. In China and Hong Kong, for instance, where gifts are commonly exchanged during certain festivals and other important occasions, reciprocity is discouraged among family members and close friends because there is no need to build ties through gift giving.[143]

Marketing Implications

Firms can build on several aspects of gift giving to market more effectively to consumers.

Promoting Products and Services as Gifts

Many marketers promote their products for gift-giving occasions, and often gift-giving occasions are the primary focus of their business. Consider the greeting card industry, which gets its biggest U.S. sales boost from the Christmas/Hanukkah/Kwanzaa season, when roughly 1.6 billion commercially produced greeting cards are bought and mailed. This figure doesn't even include homemade cards created by scrapbooking enthusiasts or the hundreds of millions of electronic cards that consumers send.[144] In some cases, uncommon gifts are promoted as appropriate for various gift-giving occasions. For example, engaged couples can now register for gift-givers to contribute toward a honeymoon trip, a home down payment, or a charitable donation in honor of the bride and groom.[145]

Technology and Gift Shopping

Technology has created major changes in the gift-giving process. Online shopping is faster and more convenient than ever, and many retail sites invite consumers to post "wish lists" showing the gifts that they would like to receive for holidays, weddings, and other occasions. Another major change affecting consumers and retailers is the growing use of plastic and digital gift cards, which have become a $125 billion business annually. Starbucks alone sells two million gift cards on Christmas Eve.[146] Knowing that consumers who receive gift cards for Christmas often go shopping right after the holiday, retailers are boosting profit margins by displaying new, full-priced products as well as discounting seasonal merchandise for postholiday shoppers. In fact, the day after Christmas is now the third-busiest shopping day for stores because of the widespread use of gift cards—and because recipients tend to spend more freely when they have a gift card.[147]

Alternatives to Traditional Gifts

Knowing that consumers are tiring of the commercialism, hassle, and materialism surrounding gift-giving occasions like Christmas, some charities ask consumers to instead give gifts to people in need. For example, the nonprofit organization Heifer International publishes a holiday catalog inviting consumers to purchase "gift" animals such as geese or bees to help families around the world become self-sufficient. As another example, giving to the United Nations refugee agency helps provide shelter and food to families displaced by famine in East Africa. Why give a donation instead of a traditional gift? "These gifts are more fun, more inspiring, and more meaningful than most gifts," according to Melissa Winkler of International Rescue Committee, a nonprofit organization.[148] Similarly, some engaged couples choose to register for gift-givers to contribute toward a charitable cause rather than buying a tangible gift.[149]

Summary:

Some offerings have symbolic meaning. Consumers use some products as conscious or unconscious badges that designate the various social categories to which they belong. Products and rituals hold symbolic significance when people undergo role transitions; serve as symbols of connection to meaningful people, places, and times; and are symbols of individuality and uniqueness. The symbolic uses of products and rituals affect the consumer's self-concept.

Consumers regard some possessions and brands as very special, nonsubstitutable, and irreplaceable. These items may be purchased with little regard for price and are rarely discarded, even if their functional value is gone; they may not even be used for their original purpose. In part, possessions are special because they serve as emblems, facilitate role transitions, connect us to others, or express our unique styles. They are special because they indicate personal mastery and achievements or are mood enhancing. Background characteristics such as social class, mobility, gender, and age all influence the type of object someone regards as special.

Some entities (possessions, people, places, objects, times, and events) are so special that they are regarded as sacred. Consumers care for and nurture these possessions and often devise special rituals to handle them. However, sacred objects can be profaned or made ordinary by commercialization, inappropriate usage, or divestment patterns. Gift giving is a process of transferring meaning in products from one person to another in three phases: gestation, presentation, and reformulation. Such occasions are often culturally prescribed but may vary in the timing. The manner in which the first two phases of gift giving are enacted can affect the long-term viability of the relationship between giver and recipient.

Questions for Review and Discussion

1. Contrast the emblematic function of a product with the role acquisition function; also contrast the connectedness function of a product with the expressive function.

2. What is reflexive evaluation, and how does it affect role acquisition?

3. How does the ideal identity schema relate to a person's actual identity schema?

4. What is frame switching, and why do marketers have to consider it when targeting bilingual, bicultural consumers?

5. What are the three main reasons why possessions take on special meaning?

6. Why do consumers engage in possession, grooming, and divestment rituals?

7. What are sacred entities, and how are they profaned?

8. Identify the three stages of gift giving, and explain how gift giving can affect relations between the giver and the recipient.

Endnotes

1   Keiron Monks, "The Future of Vinyl? Selling Music as a Lifestyle," *CNN*, August 7, 2015, www.cnn.com.

2   Grant McCracken, "Culture and Consumption," *Journal of Consumer Research* 13, June 1986, pp. 71–84; and Grant McCracken, *Culture and Consumption* (Indianapolis, Ind.: Indiana University Press, 1990).

3   Lisa Peñaloza, "Consuming the American West: Animating Cultural Meaning and Memory at a Stock Show and Rodeo," *Journal of Consumer Research* 28, December 2001, pp. 369–398.

4   See James R. Hagerty, "Harley-Davidson's Hurdle: Attracting Young Motorcycle Riders," *Wall Street Journal*, June 19, 2015, www.wsj.com; Craig J. Thompson, "Marketplace Mythology and Discourses of Power," *Journal of Consumer Research*, June 2004, pp. 162–175; Elizabeth C. Hirschman, Linda Scott, and William B. Wells, "A Model of Product Discourse," *Journal of Advertising* 27, Spring 1998, pp. 33–50; Barbara A. Phillips, "Thinking into It: Consumer Interpretation of Complex Advertising Images," *Journal of Advertising* 26, Summer 1997, pp. 77–86; Cele Otnes and Linda Scott, "Something Old, Something New: Exploring the Interaction Between Ritual and Advertising," *Journal of Advertising* 25, Spring 1996, pp. 33–50; and Jonna Holland and James W. Gentry, "The Impact of Cultural Symbols on Advertising Effectiveness: A Theory of Intercultural Accommodation," in eds. Merrie Brucks and Debbie MacInnis, *Advances in Consumer Research*, vol. 24 (Provo, Utah: Association for Consumer Research, 1997), pp. 483–489.

5   Felicia M. Miller and Chris T. Allen, "How Does Celebrity Meaning Transfer: Investigating the Process of Meaning Transfer with Celebrity Affiliates and Mature Brands," *Journal of Consumer Psychology* 22, no. 3, 2012, pp. 443–452.

6   Ruth La Ferla, "Young Shoppers Chase Up-from-the-Asphalt Niche Designers," *New York Times*, December 21, 2007, pp. G1, G10.

7   Jennifer Edson Escalas and James R. Bettman, "You Are What They Eat: The Influence of Reference Groups on Consumers' Connections to Brands," *Journal of Consumer Psychology* 13, no. 3, 2003, pp. 339–348.

8   For a discussion of how consumers use fashion to characterize their identity and infer aspects of others' identities, see Craig J. Thompson and Diana L. Haytko, "Speaking of Fashion," *Journal of Consumer Research* 19, June 1997, pp. 15–42.

9   Laura R. Oswald, "Culture Swapping: Consumption and the Ethnogenesis of Middle-Class Haitian Immigrants," *Journal of Consumer Research* 25, March 1999, pp. 303–318.

10   Elisabeth Furst, "The Cultural Significance of Food," in ed. Per Otnes, *The Sociology of Consumption: An Anthology* (Oslo, Norway: Solum Forlag, 1988), pp. 89–100.

11   Frederick Balfour, "China's Next Port of Call: Luxury Yachts," *BusinessWeek*, May 9–15, 2011, pp. 20–21; and "Breaching the Grape Wall of China," *BusinessWeek*, February 10, 2005, www. businessweek.com.

12   "Rolls-Royce Sells More Than 4,000 Cars a Year for First Time," *The Guardian (UK)*, January 5, 2015, www.theguardian. com.

13   Yajin Wang and Vladas Griskevicius, "Conspicuous Consumption, Relationships and Rivals: Women's Luxury Products as Signals to Other Women," *Journal of Consumer Research* 40, no. 5, 2014, pp. 834–854.

14   Jonah Berger and Morgan Ward, "Subtle Signs of Inconspicuous Consumption," *Journal of Consumer Research* 37, December 2010, pp. 555–569.

15   Greg Toppo, "What to Wear? Schools Increasingly Making That Decision," *USA Today*, August 18, 2013, www.usatoday .com.

16   Pierre Bourdieu, *Distinction: A Social Critique of the Judgment of Taste* (Cambridge, Mass.: Harvard University Press, 1984); for other research on gender associations with food, see Deborah Heisley, "Gender Symbolism in Food," doctoral dissertation, Northwestern University, 1991.

17   Sidney Levy, "Interpreting Consumer Mythology," *Journal of Marketing* 45, no. 3, 1982, pp. 49–62.

18   See Drew Harwell, "A Tension for America's Auto World: Winning Women Behind the Wheel," *Washington Post*, January 13, 2015, www.washingtonpost.com; and Dean Reynolds, "Ford Marketing Trucks to Women," *ABC News*, January 7, 2011, http://abcnews.go.com.

19   Americus Reed II, "Activating the Self Importance of Consumer Selves," *Journal of Consumer Research* 31, no. 2, 2004, pp. 286–295.

20   Sandiikci Ozlem and Guliz Ger, "Veiling in Style: How Does a Stigmatized Practice Become Fashionable," *Journal of Consumer Research* 40, 2014, pp. S207–S228.

21   Michelle R. Nelson and Sameer Deshpande, "Love without Borders: An Examination of Cross-Cultural Wedding Rituals," in eds. Cele C. Otnes and Tina M. Lowrey, *Contemporary Consumption Rituals* (Mahwah, NJ: Lawrence Erlbaum Associates, 2004), pp. 125–148.

22   Chris Woodyard and James R. Healey, "Toyota's New Tundra Aims for Luxury Buyers," *USA Today*, February 8, 2013, www .usatoday.com; and Jon Gertner, "From 0 to 60 to World Domination," *New York Times Magazine*, February 18, 2007, pp. 34+.

23   James B. Arndorfer, "Miller Lite: Bob Mikulay," *Advertising Age*, November 1, 2004, p. S12; and "Miller Lite," *Beverage Dynamics*, January–February 2002, p. 40.

24   Swaraj Baggonkar, "Tata Motors Bets on GenX Nano for Revival," *Business Standard (India)*, May 6, 2015, www .business-standard.com; Jyoti Thottam, "The Little Car That Couldn't," *Time*, October 24, 2011, pp. B1–B4; and "Tata's Nano: Stuck in Low Gear," *Economist*, August 20, 2011, pp. 60–61.

25   Susan Denley, "Disney Introduces Quinceañera Gowns Fit for a Princess," *Los Angeles Times*, May 23, 2013, www.latimes .com.

26   Maura L. Scott, Martin Mende, and Lisa E. Bolton, "Judging the Book by Its Cover? How Consumers Decode Conspicuous Consumption Cues in Buyer-Seller Relationships," *Journal of Marketing Research* 50, no. 3, 2013, pp. 334–347.

27   Morgan K. Ward and Darren W. Dahl, "Should the Devil Sell Prada? Retail Rejection Increases Aspiring Consumers' Desire for the Brand," *Journal of Consumer Research* 41, no. 3, 2014, 590–609.

28   Peter Evans, "Thirsty for Growth, Liquor Giant Taps Africa," *Business Day (Nigeria)*, August 7, 2015, www.businessday-online.com; and "Persuading Africans to Switch from Beer to Scotch," *Economist*, October 1, 2011, www.economist .com.

29   John W. Schouten, "Personal Rites of Passage and the Reconstruction of Self," in eds. Rebecca H. Holman and Michael R. Solomon, *Advances in Consumer Research*, vol. 18 (Provo, Utah: Association for Consumer Research, 1991), pp. 49–51.

30   Angela Woodall, "When Is It Time to Change Your Facebook Relationship Status?" *Oakland Tribune*, December 2, 2011, www.mercurynews.com.

31   See, for example, Samuel K. Bonsu and Russell W. Belk, "Do Not Go Cheaply into That Good Night: Death-Ritual Consumption in Asante, Ghana," *Journal of Consumer Research* 30, June 2003, pp. 41–55.

32   See for example, Thuc-Doan T. Nguyen and Russell W. Belk, "Harmonization Processes and Relational Meanings in Constructing Asian Weddings, *Journal of Consumer Research* 40, no. 3, 2013, pp. 518–538.

33   James H. McAlexander, John W. Schouten, and Scott D. Roberts, "Consumer Behavior and Divorce," in eds. Janeen Arnold Costa and Russell W. Belk, *Research in Consumer Behavior*, vol. 6 (Greenwich, Conn.: JAI Press, 1993), p. 162; see also Rita Fullerman and Kathleen Debevec, "Till Death Do We Part: Family Dissolution, Transition, and Consumer Behavior," in eds. John F. Sherry and Brian Sternthal, *Advances in Consumer Research*, vol. 19 (Provo, Utah: Association for Consumer Research, 1992), pp. 514–521.

34   Craig J. Thompson and Siok Kuan Tambyah, "Trying to Be Cosmopolitan," *Journal of Consumer Research* 26, December 1999, pp. 214–241.

35   Priscilla A. LaBarbera, "The Nouveaux Riches," in eds. Elizabeth C. Hirschman and Jagdish N. Sheth, *Research in Consumer Behavior* (Greenwich, Conn.: JAI Press, 1988), pp. 181–182.

36   Sarah Ellison and Carlos Tejada, "Mr., Mrs., Meet Mr. Clean," *Wall Street Journal*, January 30, 2003, pp. B1, B3.

37   Felicia Greiff, "De Beers Set to Reboot 'A Diamond is Forever' for Forevermark Brand," *Advertising Age*, June 4, 2015, www .adage.com; for more about life transitions and related products, see Paula Mergenhagen, *Targeting Transitions* (Ithaca, N.Y.: American Demographics Books, 1995).

38   Yun Kyung Oh, Ye Hu, Xin Wang, and William T. Robinson, "How Do External Reference Prices Influence Online Gift

Giving?," *International Journal of Electronic Marketing and Retailing* 5, no. 4, 2013, pp. 359–371; and Leah Burrows, "Couples, Choose Your Wedding Registry Wisely," *Brandeis Now*, May 27, 2014, www.brandeis.edu/now.

39 Catherine Curan, "Atypical Registries a Gift to Retailers," *New York Post*, August 24, 2014, www.nypost.com.

40 Otnes and Scott, "Something Old, Something New: Exploring the Interaction Between Ritual and Advertising."

41 Angela Hill, "Has Facebook Killed the Holiday Card?" *Oakland Tribune*, November 26, 2011, www.mercurynews.com.

42 In line with our notion that the meaning of the symbol may derive from the culture instead of from the individual and that symbols may have public or private meaning, see Marsha L. Richins, "Valuing Things: The Public and Private Meaning of Possessions," *Journal of Consumer Research* 21, December 1994, pp. 504–521.

43 Angela Doland, "Watch Ads from PepsiCo, Oreo, and McDonald's for Chinese New Year," *Advertising Age*, February 27, 2015, www.adage.com.

44 Carolyn Folkman Curasi, Linda L. Price, and Eric J. Arnould, "How Individuals' Cherished Possessions Become Families' Inalienable Wealth," *Journal of Consumer Research* 31, December 2004, pp. 609–622.

45 Kelly Tepper Tian, William O. Bearden, and Gar y L. Hunter, "Consumers' Need for Uniqueness," *Journal of Consumer Research* 28, June 2001, pp. 50–66; and Alexander Chernev, Ryan Hamilton, and David Gal, "Competing for Consumer Identity: Limits to Self-Expression and the Perils of Lifestyle Branding," *Journal of Marketing* 75, no. 3, 2011, pp. 66–82.

46 Gabriel Bar-Haim, "The Meaning of Western Commercial Artifacts for Eastern European Youth," *Journal of Contemporary Ethnography*, July 1987, pp. 205–226.

47 Jonah Berger and Chip Heath, "Where Consumers Diverge from Others: Identity Signaling and Product Domains," *Journal of Consumer Research* 34, August 2007, pp. 121–134.

48 Gregory Schmidt, "Toy Companies Turn to Nostalgia to Celebrate Anniversaries," *New York Times*, July 11, 2011, www.nytimes.com.

49 Stuart Elliott, "A Two-Wheeled Ride Down Memory Lane," *New York Times*, May 4, 2004, www.nytimes.com.

50 Roya Wolverson, "Styling for the Subcontinent," *Time*, December 11, 2011, p. B4; and William Lee Adams, "In the Trenches: Will Burberry Customers Pay Big for a DIY Coat?" *Time*, December 5, 2011, p. 82.

51 Vanitha Swaminathan, Karen L. Page, and Zeynep Gürhan-Canli, "'My' Brand or 'Our' Brand: The Effects of Brand Relationship Dimensions and Self-Construal on Brand Evaluations," *Journal of Consumer Research* 34, August 2007, pp. 248–259; Matthew Thomson, Deborah J. MacInnis, and C. Whan Park, "The Ties That Bind: Measuring the Strength of Consumers' Emotional Attachments to Brands," *Journal of Consumer Psychology* 15, no. 1, 2005, pp. 77–91; Jennifer Edson Escalas, "Narrative Processing," *Journal of Consumer Psychology* 14, no. 1/2, 2004, pp. 168–180; Jennifer Edson Escalas and James R. Bettman, "Self-Construal, Reference Groups, and Brand Meaning," *Journal of Consumer Research* 32, no. 3, 2005, pp. 378–389; Russell W. Belk, "Possessions and the Extended Self," *Journal of Consumer Research* 15, September 1988, pp. 139–168; A. Dwayne Ball and Lori H. Tasaki, "The Role and Measurement of Attachment in Consumer Behavior," *Journal of*

Consumer Psychology 1, no. 2, 1992, pp. 155–172; and Robert E. Kleine, Susan Schultz Kleine, and Jerome B. Kernan, "Mundane Consumption and the Self," *Journal of Consumer Psychology* 2, no. 3, 1993, pp. 209–235.

52 Kleine, Kleine, and Kernan, "Mundane Consumption and the Self "; see also M. Joseph Sirgy, "Self-Concept and Consumer Behavior," *Journal of Consumer Research* 9, December 1982, pp. 287ff; and George M. Zinkhan and J. W. Hong, "Self-Concept and Advertising Effectiveness," in eds. Rebecca Holman and Michael Solomon, *Advances in Consumer Research*, vol. 18 (Provo, Utah: Association for Consumer Research, 1991), pp. 348–354.

53 For example, see Robert V. Kozinets, "Utopian Enterprise: Articulating the Meanings of *Star Trek*'s Culture of Consumption," *Journal of Consumer Research* 28, June 2001, pp. 67–88; and Douglas B. Holt, "Why Do Brands Cause Trouble? A Dialectical Theory of Consumer Culture and Branding," *Journal of Consumer Research* 29, June 2002, pp. 70–90.

54 Claudia Townsend and Sanjay Sood, "Self Affirmation through the Choice of Highly Aesthetic Products," *Journal of Consumer Research* 39 no. 2, 2012, pp. 415–428.

55 Kelly Tian and Russell W. Belk, "Extended Self and Possessions in the Workplace," *Journal of Consumer Research* 32, no. 2, 2005, pp. 297–310.

56 Jen Shang, Americus Reed II, and Rachel Croson, "Identity Congruency Effects on Donations," *Journal of Marketing Research* 35, June 2008, pp. 351–361.

57 Baker, Stacey Menzel, and Ronald Paul Hill, "A Community Psychology of Object Meanings: Identity Negotiation During Disaster Recovery, *Journal of Consumer Psychology* 23, no. 3, 2013, pp. 275–287.

58 Hope Jensen Schau and Mary C. Gilly, "We Are What We Post? Self-Presentation in Personal Web Space," *Journal of Consumer Research* 30, December 2003, pp. 385–404.

59 Jessica Geller, "Move Over, Millennials. Gen Z Is New Target Audience," *Boston Globe*, September 1, 2015, www.bostonglobe.com; Amanda Gaines, "Breaking the Retail Code," *Retail Merchandiser*, July–August 2011, p. 1; and Emilia Terzon, "Australian First for Converse," *Inside Retail*, December 13, 2011, www.insideretailing.com.au.

60 Sirgy, "Self-Concept and Consumer Behavior."

61 Motohiro Onishi, "Through Smiles, Tears, 22 Young Girls Beat Massive Competition to Join NGT48," *Asahi Shimbun (Japan)*, August 31, 2015, http://ajw.asahi.com; and "AKB48 Takes Equal Parts Choir, Slumber Party and Beauty Pageant, Mixes Well," *Advertising Age*, December 4, 2011, www.adage.com.

62 Ashutosh Dixit, William Lundstron, and Glenna Pendleton, "Social Meanings and Brands in Marketing," *Journal of the Academy of Business and Economics* 10, no. 4, 2010, pp. 108–117.

63 Cheng Lu Wang, Terry Bristol, John C. Mowen, and Goutam Chakraborty, "Alternative Modes of Self-Construal," *Journal of Consumer Psychology* 9, no. 2, 2000, pp. 107–115.

64 David Luna, Torsten Ringberg, and Laura A. Peracchio, "One Individual, Two Identities: Frame Switching Among Biculturals," *Journal of Consumer Research* 35, August 2008, pp. 279–293.

65 Thomson, MacInnis, and Park, "The Ties That Bind: Measuring the Strength of Consumers' Emotional Attachments to Brands"; Jennifer Edson Escalas, "Narrative Processing," *Journal of Consumer Psychology* 14, no. 1/2, 2004, pp. 168–180; and Jennifer Edson Escalas and James R. Bettman, "Self-Construal, Reference Groups, and Brand Meaning," *Journal of Consumer Research* 32, no. 3, 2005, pp. 378–389.

66 67   Richins, "Valuing Things: The Public and Private Meaning of Possessions."

68 Jennifer Edson Escalas and James R. Bettman, "Self-Construal,
Reference Groups, and Brand Meaning," *Journal of Consumer
Research* 32, no. 3, 2005, pp. 378–389; Park, C. Whan, Debo-
rah J. MacInnis, Joseph Priester, Andreas Eisingerich, and
Dawn Iacobucci, "Brand Attachment and Strong Positive
Brand Attitudes: Conceptual and Empirical Differentiation
of Two Critical Brand Equity Drivers," *Journal of Marketing* 74,
November 2010, pp. 1–17; and Lucia Malar, Harley Krohmer,
Wayne D. Hoyer, and Bettina Nyffenegger, "Emotional Brand
Attachment and Brand Personality: The Relative Importance
of the Ideal and Actual Self," *Journal of Marketing* 75, no. 4,
2011, pp. 35–52.

69 Rajeev Batra, Aaron Ahuvia, and Richard p. Bagozzi, "Brand
Love," *Journal of Marketing* 76, no. 2, 2012, pp. 1–16.

70 C. Whan Park, Deborah J. MacInnis, Joseph Priester, Andreas
Eisingerich, and Dawn Iacobucci, "Brand Attachment and
Strong Positive Brand Attitudes: Conceptual and Empirical
Differentiation of Two Critical Brand Equity Drivers," *Journal
of Marketing* 74, November 2010, pp. 1–17.

71 Russell W. Belk, "Possessions and the Extended Self," *Journal
of Consumer Research* 15, September 1988, pp. 139–168; and
Russell W. Belk, "Extended Self in a Digital World, *Journal of
Consumer Research* 40, no. 3, 2013, pp. 477–500.

72 Park, MacInnis, Priester, Eisingerich, and Iacobucci, "Brand
Attachment and Strong Positive Brand Attitudes."

73 Rosellina Ferraro, Jennifer Edson Escalas, and James R.
Bettman, "Our Possessions Our Selves: Domains of Self-
Worth and the Possession–Self Link," *Journal of Consumer
Psychology* 21, no. 2, 2011, pp. 169–177; and Suzanne B. Shu
and Joann Peck, "Psychological Ownership and Affective
Reaction: Emotional Attachment Process Variables and the
Endowment Effect," *Journal of Consumer Psychology* 21, no. 4,
Special Issue, 2011, pp. 439–452.

74 Shirley Y. Cheng, Tiffany Barnette White, and Lan Chaplin Nguyen, "The Effects of Self-Brand Connections on
Responses to Brand Failure: A New Look at the Consumer-Brand Relationship," *Journal of Consumer Psychology* 22,
no. 2, 2012, pp. 280–288.

75 Matthew Thomson, Deborah J. MacInnis, and C. Whan
Park, "The Ties that Bind: Measuring the Strength of Consumers' Emotional Attachments to Brands," *Journal of Consumer Psychology* 15, no. 1, 2005, pp. 77–91; C. Whan Park,
Andreas B. Eisingerich, and Jason Whan Park, "Attachment–Aversion (AA) Model of Customer–Brand Relationships," *Journal of Consumer Psychology* 23, no. 2, 2013,
pp. 229–248.

76 Park, MacInnis, Priester, Eisingerich, and Iacobucci, "Brand
Attachment and Strong Positive Brand Attitudes."

77 Leigh Anne Novak Donovan, Joseph R. Priester, Deborah J.
MacInnis, and C. Whan Park, "Brand Forgiveness: How Close
Brand Relationships Influence Forgiveness," in eds. Susan
Fournier, Michael Breazeale, and Marc Fetscherin, *Consum-
er-Brand Relationships: Theory and Practice* (New York: Rout-
ledge, 2012), pp. 184–203.

78 Matthew Thomson, Jodie Whelan, and Allison R. Johnson,
"Why Brands Should Fear Fearful Consumers: How Attachment Style Predicts Retaliation," *Journal of Consumer Psychology* 22, no. 2, 2012, pp. 289–298.

79 Richins, "Valuing Things: The Public and Private Meaning of
Possessions."

80 Andrew Martin, "'For the Dogs' Has a Whole New Meaning,"
New York Times, June 5, 2011, pp. BU–1, BU–7.

81 Neha Dimri, "Pet Supplies Retailer Petco Files for Third IPO,"
Reuters, August 17, 2015, www.reuters.com; Diane Brady
and Christopher Palmeri, "The Pet Economy," *BusinessWeek*,
August 6, 2007, pp. 44–54; Richard C. Morais, "Dog Days,"
Forbes Global, June 21, 2004, p. 30; and Martin, " 'For the
Dogs' Has a Whole New Meaning."

82 Belk, "Possessions and the Sense of Past."

83 Karen V. Fernandez and John L. Lastovicka, "Making Magic:
Fetishes in Contemporary Consumption," *Journal of Consumer Research* 38, August 2011, pp. 278–299.

84 Russell W. Belk, "Moving Possessions: An Analysis Based
on Personal Documents from the 1847–1869 Mormon
Migration," *Journal of Consumer Research*, December 1992,
pp. 339–361.

85 Russell W. Belk, Melanie Wallendorf, John F. Sherr y Jr., and
Morris B. Holbrook, "Collecting in a Consumer Culture,"
in ed. Russell W. Belk, *Highways and Buyways* (Provo, Utah:
Association for Consumer Research, 1991), pp. 178–215.

86 Michael Clerizo, "Weird, Wild Watches," *Wall Street Journal*,
August 13, 2011, www.wsj.com.

87 Russell W. Belk, Melanie Wallendorf, John F. Sherry Jr., Morris
Holbrook, and Scott Roberts, "Collectors and Collecting," in
ed. Michael J. Houston, *Advances in Consumer Research*, vol. 15
(Provo, Utah: Association for Consumer Research, 1988),
pp. 548–553.

88 Belk, Wallendorf, Sherry, Holbrook, and Roberts, "Collectors
and Collecting."

89 Russell W. Belk, "The Ineluctable Mysteries of Possessions,"
in ed. Floyd W. Rudmin, "To Have Possessions: A Handbook
on Ownership and Property," *Journal of Social Behavior and
Personality* 6, no. 6, Special Issue, 1991, pp. 17–55.

90 Kent Grayson and David Shulman, "Indexicality and the Verification Function of Irreplaceable Possessions: A Semiotic Analysis," *Journal of Consumer Research* 27, June 2000, pp. 17–30.

91 Daniel Terdiman, "Curiously High-Tech Hacks for a Classic
Tin," *New York Times*, February 3, 2005, www.nytimes.com.

92 Susan Fournier, "The Development of Intense Consumer–
Product Relationships," *Winter AMA Educator's Conference*,
St. Petersburg, FL (February 1994).

93 Mihalyi Csikszentmihalyi and Eugene Rochberg-Halton, *The
Meaning of Things*; M. Wallendorf and E. J. Arnould, "My Favorite Things: A Cross-Cultural Inquiry into Object Attachment,
Possessiveness, and Social Linkage," *Journal of Consumer
Research* 14, March 1988, pp. 531–547; and Belk, "Moving Possessions: An Analysis Based on Personal Documents from the
1847–1869 Mormon Migration."

94 A. Peter McGraw, Philip E. Tetlock, and Orie V. Kristel, "The
Limits of Fungibility," *Journal of Consumer Research* 30, September
2003, pp. 219–228.

95 Csikszentmihalyi and Rochberg-Halton, *The Meaning of
Things*.

96 Ibid.

97 Nancy J. Sirianni and John L. Lastovicka, "Truly, Madly, Deeply:
Consumers in the Throes of Material Possession Love," *Journal of Consumer Research* 38, no. 2, 2011, pp. 323–342.

98 Helga Dittmar, "Meaning of Material Possessions as Reflections of Identity," in ed. Rudmin, *To Have Possessions*, pp. 165–
186; see also Helga Dittmar, *The Social Psychology of Material
Possessions* (New York: St. Martin's, 1992).

99 Jaideep Sengupta, Darren W. Dahl, and Gerald J. Gorn, "Misrepresentation in the Consumer Context," *Journal of Consumer Psychology* 12, no. 2, 2002, pp. 69–79.

100 Fleura Bardhi, Giana M. Eckhardt, and Eric J. Arnould, "Liquid Relationship to Possessions," *Journal of Consumer Research* 39, no. 3, 2012, pp. 510–529.

101 Dittmar, "Meaning of Material Possessions as Reflections of Identity"; and Kamptner, "Personal Possessions and Their Meanings."

102 Wallendorf and Arnould, "My Favorite Things: A Cross-Cultural Inquiry into Object Attachment, Possessiveness, and Social Linkage."

103 Russell W. Belk and Melanie Wallendorf, "Of Mice and Men: Gender Identity in Collecting," in eds. K. Ames and K. Martinez, *The Gender of Material Culture* (Ann Arbor, Mich.: University of Michigan Press), reprinted in ed. Susan M. Pearce, *Objects and Collections* (London: Routledge, 1994), pp. 240–253; and Belk Wallendorf, Sherr y, Holbrook, and Roberts, "Collectors and Collecting."

104 McCracken, "Culture and Consumption;" and McCracken, *Culture and Consumption*.

105 Ibid.

106 Andrea C. Morales and Gavan J. Fitzsimons, "Product Contagion: Changing Consumer Evaluations through Physical Contact with 'Disgusting' Products," *Journal of Marketing Research* 44, May 2007, pp. 272–283.

107 McCracken, "Culture and Consumption;" and McCracken, *Culture and Consumption*.

108 John L. Lastovicka and Karen V. Fernandez, "Three Paths to Disposition: The Movement of Meaningful Possessions to Strangers," *Journal of Consumer Research* 31, no. 4, 2005, pp. 813–823.

109 Linda L. Price, Eric J. Arnold, and Carolyn Folkman Curasi, "Older Consumers' Disposition of Special Possessions," *Journal of Consumer Research* 27, September 2000, pp. 179–201.

110 Russell W. Belk, Melanie Wallendorf, and John F. Sherry Jr., "The Sacred and the Profane in Consumer Behavior," *Journal of Consumer Research* 16, June 1989, pp. 1–38.

111 Belk, "Possessions and the Sense of Past."

112 Belk, Wallendorf, and Sherry, "The Sacred and the Profane in Consumer Behavior."

113 Amitai Etzioni, "The Socio-Economics of Property," in ed. Rudmin, *To Have Possessions: A Handbook on Ownership and Property*, Special Issue, *Journal of Social Behavior and Personality* 6, no. 6, 1991, pp. 465–468.

114 Robert V. Kozinets, "Utopian Enterprise: Articulating the Meanings of *Star Trek*'s Culture of Consumption," *Journal of Consumer Research* 28, June 2001, pp. 67–88.

115 Adam Justice, "Beatles Memorabilia Auction Sees 150 Items Under the Hammer Including Fab Four's First Record Deal," *International Business Times*, August 19, 2015, www.ibtimes.co.uk.

116 James Cockington, "Beatles Fans Can't Let It Be," *Sydney Morning Herald*, December 7, 2011, www.smh.com.au.

117 Kunur Patel, "Controversial Benetton Ad Nabs Press Grand Prix," *Advertising Age*, June 20, 2012, www.adage.com; and Rupal Parekh, "Netanyahu, Abbas Smooch in Benetton Ad," *Advertising Age*, November 16, 2011, www.adage.com.

118 Jackie Clarke, "Different to 'Dust Collectors'? The Giving and Receiving of Experience Gifts," *Journal of Consumer Behavior* 5, no. 6, 2006, pp. 533–549.

119 For historical and sociological accounts of Christmas, see Daniel Miller, "A Theory of Christmas," in ed. Daniel Miller, *Unwrapping Christmas*, pp. 3–37; Claude Levi-Strauss, "Father Christmas Executed," in ed. Miller, *Unwrapping Christmas*, pp. 38–54; Belk, "Materialism and the Making of the Modern American Christmas"; Barbara Bodenhorn, "Christmas Present: Christmas Public," in ed. Miller, *Unwrapping Christmas* (Oxford, UK: Oxford University Press), pp. 193–216; William B. Waits, *The Modern Christmas in America* (New York: New York University Press, 1993); and Stephen Nissenbaum, *The Battle for Christmas* (New York: Vantage Books, 1997). See also Elizabeth H. Pleck, "Kwanzaa: The Making of a Black Nationalist Tradition, 1966-1990," in eds. Cele C. Otnes and Tina M. Lowrey, *Contemporary Consumption Rituals* (Mahwah, NJ: Lawrence Erlbaum Associates, 2004), pp. 59–82.

120 John F. Sherry Jr., "Gift Giving in Anthropological Perspective," *Journal of Consumer Research* 10, September 1983, pp. 157–168.

121 See Sherry, "Gift Giving in Anthropological Perspective." See also, David B. Wooten and Stacy L. Wood, "In the Spotlight: The Drama of Gift Reception," in eds. Cele Otnes and Tina M. Lowrey, *Contemporary Consumption Rituals: A Research Anthology* (Mahwah, NJ: Lawrence Erlbaum, 2004), pp. 213–236.

122 For a discussion of these motives, see Sherry, "Gift Giving in Anthropological Perspective"; for research on gender differences in motives, see Mary Ann McGrath, "Gender Differences in Gift Exchanges: New Directions from Projections," *Psychology & Marketing* 12, August 1995, pp. 229–234; and Russell W. Belk, "The Perfect Gift," in eds. Cele Otnes and Richard Beltrami, *Gift Giving Behavior: An Interdisciplinary Anthology* (Bowling Green, OH: Bowling Green University Popular Press, 1996); for a discussion of the roles played by gift, see Cele Otnes, Tina M. Lowrey, and Young Chan Kim, "Gift Selection for Easy and Difficult Recipients," *Journal of Consumer Research* 20, September 1993, pp. 229–244; and Kleine, Kleine, and Allen, "How Is a Possession 'Me' or 'Not Me'?"

123 Ernest Baskin, Cheryl J. Wakslak, Yaacov Trope, and Nathan Novemsky, "Why Feasibility Matters More to Gift Receivers Than to Givers: A Construal-Level Approach to Gift Giving," *Journal of Consumer Research* 41, no. 1, 2014, pp. 169–182.

124 McAlexander, Schouten, and Roberts, "Consumer Behavior and Divorce."

125 David B. Wooten, "Qualitative Steps Toward an Expanded Model of Anxiety in Gift-Giving," *Journal of Consumer Research* 27, June 2000, pp. 84–95.

126 Mary Steffel and Robin A. LeBoeuf, "Overindividuation in Gift Giving: Shopping for Multiple Recipients Leads Givers to Choose Unique but Less Preferred Gifts," *Journal of Consumer Research* 40, no. 6, 2014, pp. 1167–1180.

127 For more on gifts in the workplace, see Julie A. Ruth, "Gift Exchange Rituals in the Workplace: A Social Roles Interpretation," in eds. Cele Otnes and Tina M. Lowrey, *Contemporary Consumption Rituals: A Research Anthology* (Mahwah, NJ: Lawrence Erlbaum, 2004), pp. 181–221.

128 Russell W. Belk and Gregory S. Coon, "Gift Giving as Agapic Love," *Journal of Consumer Research* 20, December 1993, pp. 393–417.

129 Sherry, "Gift Giving in Anthropological Perspective;" and Mary Searle-Chatterjee, "Christmas Cards and the Construction of Social Relations in Britain Today," in ed. Miller, *Unwrapping Christmas* (New York: Oxford University Press, 1993), pp. 176–192.

130 Belk and Coon, "Gift Giving as Agapic Love;" see also Sherry, "Gift Giving in Anthropological Perspective."

131 Sak Onkvisit and John J. Shaw, *International Marketing: Analysis and Strategy* (Columbus, Ohio: Merrill, 1989), pp. 241–242.

132 "The Efficiency of Gift Giving: Is It Really Better to Give Than to Receive?" *Marketing: Knowledge at Wharton*, December 15, 2004, http://knowledge.wharton.upenn.edu.

133 Jean-Sebastian Marcoux, "Escaping the Gift Economy," *Journal of Consumer Research*, December 2009, pp. 671–685.

134 Sandra Yin, "Give and Take," *American Demographics*, November 2003, pp. 12–13; and Eileen Fischer and Stephen J. Arnold, "More Than a Labor of Love: Gender Roles and Christmas Shopping," *Journal of Consumer Research* 17, December 1990, pp. 333–345.

135 John F. Sherry Jr. and Mary Ann McGrath, "Unpacking the Holiday Presence: A Comparative Ethnography of Two Gift Stores," in ed. Elizabeth C. Hirschman, *Interpretive Consumer Research* (Provo, Utah: Association for Consumer Research, 1989), pp. 148–167.

136 Mary Ann McGrath, "An Ethnography of a Gift Store: Trappings, Wrappings, and Rapture," *Journal of Retailing* 65, Winter 1989, p. 434.

137 Morgan K. Ward and Susan M. Broniarczyk, "It's Not Me, It's You: How Gift Giving Creates Gift Identity Threat as a Function of Social Closeness," *Journal of Consumer Research* 38, June 2011, pp. 164–181.

138 Wooten, "Qualitative Steps Toward an Expanded Model of Anxiety in Gift-Giving."

139 Julie A. Ruth, Cele C. Otnes, and Frederic F. Brunel, "Gift Receipt and the Reformulation of Interpersonal Relationships," *Journal of Consumer Research* 25, March 1999,

pp. 385–402; and Ming-Hui Huang and Shihti Yu, "Gifts in a Romantic Relationship: A Survival Analysis," *Journal of Consumer Psychology* 9, no. 3, 2000, pp. 179–188.

140 See p. Webley, S. E. G. Lea, and R. Portalska, "The Unacceptability of Money as a Gift," *Journal of Economic Psychology* 4, 1983, pp. 223–238.

141 Belk, "Gift Giving Behavior"; see also Sherry, "Gift Giving in Anthropological Perspective."

142 Belk and Coon, "Gift Giving as Agapic Love."

143 Annamma Joy, "Gift Giving in Hong Kong and the Continuum of Social Ties," *Journal of Consumer Research* 28, September 2001, pp. 239–256.

144 Quentin Fottrell, "5 Sentiments Still Best Expressed on Paper," *MarketWatch*, December 23, 2014, www.marketwatch.com.

145 Meena Hartenstein, "Getting Registered: Unusual Wedding Registry Options," *New York Daily News*, March 27, 2011, www.nydailynews.com.

146 Corilyn Shropshire, "Starbucks Sees Big Christmas Eve Sales in the Cards," *Chicago Tribune*, December 18, 2014, www.chicagotribune.com; and Jack Newsham, "Not Sure What to Do with That Gift Card? Now, You Can Sell It," *Boston Globe*, February 5, 2015, www.bostonglobe.com.

147 Tim Feran, "Day After Christmas Will Be Busy for Stores," *Columbus Dispatch*, November 23, 2011, www.dispatch.com.

148 Betsy Anderson, "Why Goats and Chickens Make Great Holiday Gifts," *CNN*, December 14, 2011, www.cnn.com.

149 Larisa Epatko, "Charity Database Offers Wedding Bliss of a Different Kind," *PBS News Hour*, May 14, 2014, www.pbs.org.

Marketing, Ethics, and Social Responsibility in Today's Consumer Society

iStockphoto.com/Ostill

LEARNING OBJECTIVES

After studying this chapter, you will be able to:

▶ Distinguish between social and temporal dilemmas, and explain the search for balance in decisions that involve such dilemmas.

▶ Define marketing ethics and consumer ethics, and identify some of the issues that arise from unethical or deviant acquisition, consumption, and disposition behaviors.

▶ Discuss some of the ways in which consumers and organizations use marketing for socially responsible purposes.

▶ Describe what consumers can do to resist unwanted marketing practices.

Hand-out/PEPSICO CANADA/Newscom

INTRODUCTION

In today's consumer society, marketers and consumers have the power to achieve constructive outcomes—the "bright side" of marketing. In particular, the rise of social media has empowered individuals and consumer groups to make a real difference to the planet and to the lives of others. On the other hand, ethical issues such as whether advertising contributes to obesity and whether marketing invades consumer privacy are part of the discussion about the "dark side" of marketing. Consumer behavior can have a "dark side," as well, including illegal acts (such as theft) and the compulsion to buy unneeded goods and services. Despite these extremes, marketers and consumers both seek balance when making decisions that involve dilemmas, such as between self-interest and the interests of others, and between immediate interests and long-term interests. Also, consumers can, individually and in groups, resist marketing efforts or pressure marketers to take certain steps, as this chapter explains. Exhibit 17.1 summarizes key points in marketing ethics and social responsibility.

Exhibit 17.1 ▶ Chapter Overview: Marketing, Ethics, and Social Responsibility in a Consumer Society

When making decisions, marketers and consumers must balance their self-interests with the interests of others and immediate interests with long-term interests. Certain decisions about acquisition, consumption, and disposition raise "dark side" issues of marketing ethics and consumer ethics. The "bright side" of marketing and consumer behavior is reflected in social responsibility activities geared toward constructive outcomes.

The Psychological Core

2 Motivation, Ability, and Opportunity
3 From Exposure to Comprehension
4 Memory and Knowledge
5-6 Attitude Formation and Change

The Process of Making Decisions

7 Problem Recognition and Information Search
8-9 Judgment and Decision-Making
10 Post-Decision Processes

Consumer Behavior Outcomes and Issues

15 Innovations: Adoption, Resistance, and Diffusion
16 Symbolic Consumer Behavior
17 Marketing, Ethics, and Social Responsibility in Today's Consumer Society

The Consumer's Culture

11 Social Influences on Consumer Behavior
12 Consumer Diversity
13 Household and Social Class Influences
14 Psychographics: Values, Personality, and Lifestyles

iStockphoto.com/Ostill

In Search of Balance	Marketing Ethics, Consumer Ethics, and Deviant Behavior	Social Responsibility
Potential conflicts arise in decisions that balance: • Self-interest and the interests of others • Short- and long-term interests	*Controversies related to:* • Acquisition • Consumption • Disposition	• Marketing for constructive outcomes • Initiated by consumers, marketers, or jointly

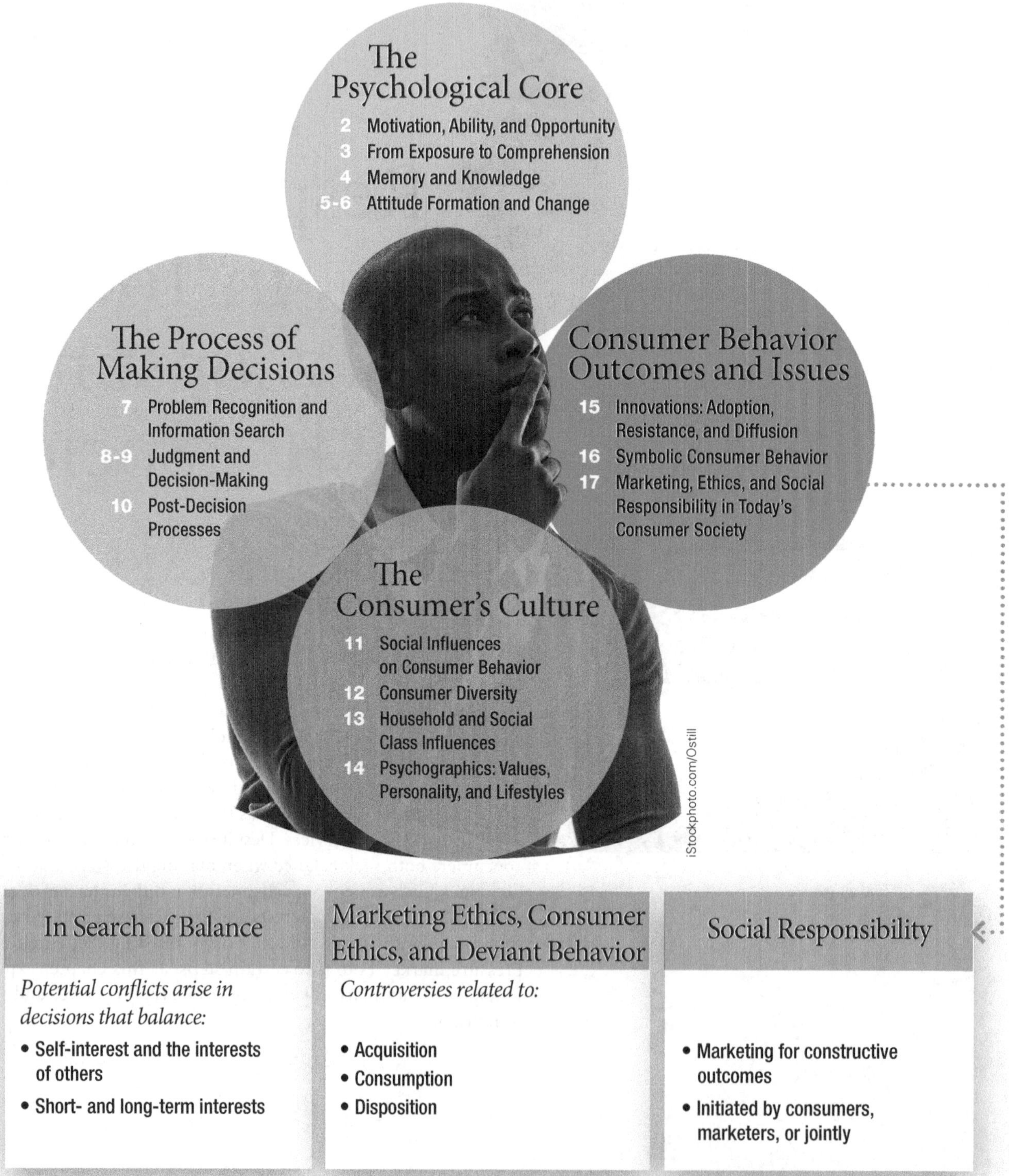

Exhibit 17.2 ▶ Social and Temporal Dilemmas

Social dilemmas focus on "who," whereas temporal dilemmas focus on "when."

Social Dilemma	Temporal Dilemma
Whose interests take priority?	*What timing takes priority?*
• Me (as an individual) **OR**	• Short-term interests **OR**
• We (my family, friends, colleagues, my employer, human beings) **OR**	• Long-term interests
• Them (others, such as competitors, people in other nations, or society at large)	

17-1 In Search of Balance

When marketers and consumers make decisions, they often face potentially conflicting priorities and outcomes. Attempts to resolve these conflicts can raise ethical issues. For example, the question of who takes priority represents a **social dilemma**: Whose interests are the priority, our own or those of others? As another example, when time is the issue, consumers face a **temporal dilemma**: Which is the priority, immediate interests or long-term interests? Exhibit 17.2 shows the dimensions of these two dilemmas.

As you learned in previous chapters, focusing on our own immediate self-interest may actually increase our happiness. At the same time, focusing on the future interests of others may increase our sense of satisfaction or be congruent with our self-concept as someone who is altruistic or charitable. But what about the extreme case of focusing on ourselves at the expense of others who might be harmed (such as exposing someone else to secondhand smoke when we light up a cigarette)? Or making an impatient choice (eating an unhealthy snack now) that may result in a negative long-term outcome (becoming overweight)?

Social dilemma
Deciding whether to put self-interest or the interests of others first.

Temporal dilemma
Deciding whether to put immediate interests or long-term interests first.

17-1a SELF-INTEREST VERSUS THE INTERESTS OF OTHERS

If we focus concretely on people close to us (such as family members or friends), our decision may be framed as concerning *me versus we*. If our focus is more abstract, such as on strangers or society at large, the decision may be framed as *me versus them*. When marketers make decisions, they may focus on *me*, meaning their own professional or personal goals. Focusing on the interests of others may frame the decision as *me or we* (the brand, product, company, or coworkers) or *me or them* (competitors or others outside the organization).

Choosing to focus on *me, we,* or *them* is not intrinsically bad. One example of *helpful other-focus* is the sharing of ideas, such as answering the questions of friends or strangers posted on social media such as Twitter or Facebook, or posting product reviews that will help others make good purchase decisions.[1]

An example of *harmful self-focus* is shoplifting. The shoplifter may perceive no or little harm to others or society because "it is only a DVD, hat, or candy bar." In reality, however, this illegal and unethical behavior costs the store money, which in turn causes it to raise prices—in effect, penalizing other shoppers while the shoplifter benefits. Every year, U.S. retailers lose merchandise worth an estimated $32 billion to shoplifters, employee theft, and supplier theft, which means the financial impact on shoppers, in the form of higher prices, is quite significant.[2] Here again is the balancing act: If retailers install antitheft devices that make honest shoppers feel spied upon, or if they raise prices too high to make up for losses, shoppers may avoid their stores, which will hurt sales and profits.

17-1b IMMEDIATE VERSUS LONG-TERM INTERESTS

In the case of a temporal dilemma, the central issue is: How will the decision affect my interests, our interests, or their interests *immediately*, compared with the *future*? In the Pepsi Refresh example, the company was focusing on long-term brand results. It did not require any purchases to qualify for funding, nor did it expect an immediate financial gain. Instead, its marketers relied on the positive word of mouth from the campaign to encourage future purchases and reinforce long-term brand loyalty. The same kind of reasoning can be applied to consumers who focus on the future. When parents save money for a child's college education, or when adults put money into a retirement fund, they are making an "investment" with the expectation of a positive future outcome.

Decisions that emphasize short-term interests may have positive or negative implications for the future. If you have an opportunity to buy a used car at a bargain price, you might decide to make the purchase right away, because you will come out ahead. If you overspend on a car, however, you may feel good about your purchase initially but discover later that you have jeopardized your financial situation. Of course, decisions that emphasize future interests may also have positive or negative implications. For instance, by focusing on the future, you might neglect or downplay pleasurable experiences in the present (forgetting to "stop and smell the roses"). This is why it's so important to balance the interests of today with the interests of tomorrow when making decisions.

17-1c "DARK SIDE" VERSUS "BRIGHT SIDE" OUTCOMES

Conflicts that arise from dilemmas in marketing sometimes lead to "dark side" outcomes, which can potentially harm consumers or marketers. For example, as discussed in the next section, should marketers advertise to children, with the goal of making sales today and encouraging loyalty tomorrow? Should consumers be able to download or share digital entertainment that they have not officially purchased or registered to receive (benefiting "me" or "we"), even if that deprives the marketers and creators ("them") of revenue?

On a larger scale, when managers in public corporations get ready to report financial results, their decisions entail both a social and a temporal dilemma. In rare and extreme cases, individuals who feel pressure to improve profits may focus too narrowly on "me" or "we" (themselves, their colleagues, company stockholders) and "now" (making today's financial performance look better). They may take unethical actions, such as inflating financial results, and when their actions are exposed, the "dark side" outcome is bankruptcy (e.g., Enron), which can hurt stockholders and put thousands of people out of work.

Of course, such extreme and far-reaching decisions are not commonplace. Most companies seek a better balance, aiming for long-term profitability *and* broadening their focus on "we" to achieve constructive, sustainable outcomes for people and the planet—the "bright side" outcome. Initially, such programs are usually funded from the firm's profits, which would seem to go against the drive for profitability. Over time, however, these programs

can shape positive brand attitudes, reinforce brand loyalty, reduce costs, and ultimately lead to higher sales and profits from new products, new markets, and new customers. Moreover, such programs toward sustainable business fit the morality of the firms and its owners.

These are some "bright side" outcomes not only for the marketer but for the consumer as well. Consumers can benefit directly from new products that meet their needs and indirectly from programs that help their communities or society at large. Even legitimate marketing techniques such as rebranding and value pricing may spark consumer distress when applied by pharmaceutical firms and religious organizations—unless their use is explained and justified in terms of the common good.[3]

17-2 Marketing Ethics, Consumer Ethics, and Deviant Consumer Behavior

Marketing ethics are rules or standards of acceptable conduct that guide individuals and organizations in making honest, fair, and respectful decisions about marketing activities, internal and external. Marketing ethics apply not just only to relationships with customers but also to relationships with employees, managers, suppliers, and other stakeholders. These standards, often formalized in ethical codes of conduct adopted by companies, professional associations, and industry groups, cover everything from targeting and communications to promotions and pricing (see Exhibit 17.3).

It is important to remember that unethical marketing behavior may not be illegal; it is unethical if it violates generally accepted rules of conduct or a formal ethical code observed by the marketer. Further, not all ethical standards are static. For instance, the growing movements toward the ethical sourcing of coffee, cocoa, lumber, and other materials as well as concerns about the ethical treatment of employees who work for overseas suppliers are relatively recent developments.

Consumer ethics are rules of acceptable conduct (such as honesty, fairness, and respect) that apply to the range of consumer behaviors. When consumers act unethically, they may not be breaking the law, but their behavior is in some way dishonest, unfair, or disrespectful to individuals or to organizations. In contrast, *deviant consumer behavior* is behavior regarded as deviant if it is either unexpected or not sanctioned by members of the society (whether or not the behavior is illegal or unethical). Unethical behavior—perceived or actual, intentional or not—on the part of marketers and consumers, as well as deviant consumer behavior, can create controversies in the context of acquisition, consumption, and disposition situations.

> **Marketing ethics**
> Rules of acceptable conduct that guide individuals and organizations in making honest, fair, and respectful decisions about marketing activities.

> **Consumer ethics**
> Rules of acceptable conduct (such as honesty, fairness, and respect) that apply to the range of consumer behaviors.

Exhibit 17.3 ▶ Marketing and Consumer Ethics

Brands like the Body Shop actively promote their marketing ethics in their ads.

17-2a ACQUISITION CONTROVERSIES

Five key controversies related to questions of ethics in marketing and consumer behavior in terms of acquisition are: (1) materialistic behavior, (2) addictive and compulsive behavior, (3) consumer theft, (4) black markets, and (5) targeting vulnerable segments.

Materialistic Behavior

Materialism is a value in many cultures (as noted in Chapter 14), not just in the West but increasingly in Asia, as well. In part, the rise in materialism among consumers in China can be attributed to wider exposure to media and marketing and to increases in income.[4] Purchases of luxury brands are increasing in Singapore, Hong Kong, and China, even during economic downturns—another sign of materialistic behavior.[5] Although materialism is a neutral value and neither unethical nor deviant, some are critical of this focus on acquiring possessions, such as consumers buying items they do not always need, sometimes do not even want, and at times, cannot afford. Moreover, whereas some research suggests that consumers with low self-esteem or lonely feelings are materialistic, there is no evidence that materialism makes people happier.[6]

Family influences can be quite strong: The children of materialistic parents tend to be more materialistic than other children.[7] At the same time, materialistic tendencies are lower when parents encourage their children's positive self-esteem.[8] Materialistic adolescents shop more, save less, and are more responsive to marketing efforts.[9] And with more marketing and media emphasis on brands, it is not surprising that children are aware of more than 200 brands by the time they reach first grade.[10] By one estimate, children between the ages of 2 and 11 are exposed to 25,600 ads per year, mainly through watching television.[11] Social comparison theory would predict that if advertising and the media show individuals with many material possessions, consumers might use advertising as a means of judging their own personal accomplishments.

Consumers who perceive that they are less well off than the comparison population may be less satisfied with their lives. Some evidence supports this idea. Consumers exposed to a lot of advertising tend to overestimate how well off the average consumer is.[12] This misperception sets up a potentially false frame of reference regarding how much the average consumer owns. Furthermore, materialistic consumers may pay undue attention to the possessions of others and make inferences about these people based on the possessions that they own.[13]

Addictive and Compulsive Behavior

Addiction reflects continued, excessive behaviors despite adverse consequences, which is typically brought on by a chemical dependency. Addicted consumers feel a great attachment to and dependence on a product or activity and believe that they must use it to function.[14] Individuals can become addicted to many goods and services, including cigarettes, drugs, alcohol, Internet use, and video games. In many cases, an addiction involves repeated acquisition and /or use of a product, even if consumption is dangerous.

> **Addiction** Excessive behavior typically brought on by a chemical dependency.

Although addicted individuals may want to stop, they believe doing so is beyond their control ("I can't help myself"). Often individuals feel shame and guilt about their addiction and try to hide it. Some addicted consumers find strength in programs like Alcoholics Anonymous and Smokenders.

Addictive behaviors can be harmful to people involved and to those around them. For example, cigarette smoking is a preventable cause of death, and a leading cause of cancer, cardiovascular disease, and chronic obstructive lung disease. According to the World Health Organization, tobacco use contributes to six million deaths worldwide each year, killing smokers and those around them who are exposed to secondhand smoke.[15]

Compulsive behavior is an irresistible urge to perform an irrational act. Unlike addictive behavior, which involves a physiological

> **Compulsive behavior**
> An irresistible urge to perform an irrational act.

dependency, compulsive behavior occurs because the consumer cannot stop doing something. For example, some individuals buy compulsively, purchasing many items that they do not need and sometimes cannot afford; they gain satisfaction from *buying*, not from *owning* (see Exhibit 17.4).

Compulsive buying has a strong emotional component, and the emotions run the gamut from the most negative to the most positive.[16] Compulsive buyers feel anxious on days when they do not buy; thus, compulsive buying may be a response to tension or anxiety. While in the store, compulsive buyers may feel great emotional arousal at the stimulation evoked by the store's atmosphere. Buying brings an immediate emotional high and a feeling of loss of control. This reaction is followed by feelings of remorse, guilt, shame, and depression.

Exhibit 17.4 ▶ Quotes from Compulsive Buyers

Compulsive buying can be an emotionally involving experience. Consumers may engage in compulsive buying to feel a thrill, gain attention, or feel that they are pleasing someone else. But this emotional high may be followed by serious financial and negative emotional consequences.

Emotional Aspects of Compulsive Buying

a. "I couldn't tell you what I bought or where I bought it. It was like I was on automatic." "I really think it's the spending. It's not that I want it, because sometimes I'll just buy it and I'll think, Ugh, another sweatshirt."

b. "But it was like, it was almost like my heart was palpitating. I couldn't wait to get in to see what was there. It was such a sensation. In the store, the lights, the people; they were playing Christmas music. I was hyperventilating and my hands were starting to sweat, and all of a sudden I was touching sweaters and the whole feel of it was just beckoning to me. And if they had a SALE sign up, forget it; I was gone. You never know when you're going to need it. I bought 10 shirts one time for $10.00 each."

 "It's almost like you're drunk. You're so intoxicated; . . . I got this great high. It was like you couldn't have given me more of a rush."

Factors Influencing Compulsive Buying

c. "The attention I got there was incredible. She waited on me very nicely, making sure it would fit and if it didn't, they would do this and that. And I guess I enjoyed being on the other end of that. I had no idea how I was going to pay for it. I never do."

 "I never bought one of anything. I always buy at least two. I still do. I can never even go into the Jewel and buy one quart of milk. I've always got to buy two . . . It's an act of pleasing.

 I had been brought up to please everybody and everyone around me because that was the way you got anything was to please. So I thought I was pleasing the store."

Financial and Emotional Consequences of Compulsive Buying

d. "I would always have to borrow between paychecks. I could not make it between paychecks. Payday comes and I'd pay all my bills, but then I'd piss the rest away, and I'd need to borrow money to eat, and I would cry and cry and cry, and everyone would say, 'Well just make a budget.' Get serious. That's like telling an alcoholic not to go to the liquor store. It's not that simple."

e. "My husband said he couldn't deal with this, and he said, 'I'm leaving you. We'll get a divorce. That's it. It's your problem. You did it. You fix it up.'"

 "I didn't have one person in the world I could talk to. I don't drink. I don't smoke. I don't do dope. But I can't stop. I can't control it. I said I can't go on like this . . . . My husband hates me. My kids hate me. I've destroyed everything. I was ashamed and just wanted to die."

Source: Thomas O'Guinn and Ronald Faber, "Compulsive Buying: A Phenomenological Perspective," *Journal of Consumer Research*, September 1989, pp. 147–157. © 1989 University of Chicago. All rights reserved.

Why do people buy compulsively? For one thing, compulsive buyers tend to have low self-esteem. In fact, the emotional high consumers experience from compulsive buying comes in part from the attention and social approval they get when they buy. The salesperson can provide considerable satisfaction—being a doting helper, telling consumers how attractive they look in a particular outfit. Consumers can also feel that they are pleasing the salesperson and the company by making purchases. This attention and the feeling of pleasing others may temporarily raise compulsive buyers' self-esteem and reinforce buying behavior (see part c of Exhibit 17.4).

The financial, emotional, and interpersonal consequences of compulsive buying can be devastating. These consumers rely extensively on credit cards, have high credit card debt, and tend to pay only the minimum monthly balance. They are also more likely to write checks for purchases, even though they know they cannot afford them. And compulsive buyers are more likely to borrow money from others to make it from paycheck to paycheck.[17] Finally, children, spouses, and friends can all be hurt by the spending habits of compulsive buyers.

Consumer Theft

Whereas compulsive buying reflects an uncontrollable desire to *purchase* things, consumer theft reflects a desire to *steal* things, which is both unethical and illegal. For U.S. retailers, shoplifting is pervasive and significant, with yearly merchandise losses topping $37 billion; worldwide, yearly shoplifting losses are estimated at $107 billion.[18] Consumer theft is a problem for nonretailers as well as for retailers. Automobile insurance fraud; credit card fraud; theft of cable TV services; piracy of music, movies, and software; fraudulent returns; and switching or altering price tags are just some of the forms of consumer theft with which companies must contend.[19] During the recent recession, consumers seeking multiple copies of store coupons began stealing newspapers from stores and driveways.[20]

As shown in Exhibit 17.5, two psychological factors seem to explain theft: (1) the temptation to steal and (2) the ability to rationalize theft behavior. These factors are, in turn, affected by aspects of the product, the purchase environment, and the consumer.

Black market An illegal market in which consumers pay often exorbitant amounts for items not readily available.

Temptation to Steal

The *temptation* to steal arises when consumers want products that they cannot legitimately buy, either to satisfy real needs or due to greed. Some researchers suggest that marketers are involved by perpetuating materialistic tendencies and creating insatiable desires for new goods and services.[21] Consumers may also be tempted to steal items that they are too embarrassed to buy through conventional channels (e.g., condoms) or that they cannot legally buy (e.g., an underage consumer stealing alcohol).[22]

Temptation is greater when consumers think that they can get away with stealing and that it is worth doing. Thus, consumers may assess the perceived risks associated with stealing and getting caught and may consider the benefits of having a product or using a service that they did not pay for.[23] Many factors in the environment affect the perceived risks of shoplifting.[24] Stores may be noisy or crowded, have little or no security, have lax return policies, have few salespeople, contain hidden nooks and crannies, or use price tags that are easily switched—leading consumers to believe their theft will be unnoticed. Also, a tendency toward thrill-seeking has been associated with many forms of consumer theft, including price tag switching and shoplifting.[25]

Rationalizations for Stealing

Consumers also steal because they can somehow *rationalize* their behavior as being either justified or driven by forces outside themselves. For example, consumers may justify stealing a low-ticket item such as a grape from a bunch at the grocery store because the item's cost seems so negligible that the word *stealing* hardly seems to apply. Some consumers may reason that a marketer "asked for it" by keeping merchandise displays open, having no security guards, or using price tags that can be readily switched.

"Everybody does it" is another rationalization, in which people feel they are "licensed to steal." After they act in a virtuous way, consumers may feel "licensed" to act less virtuously later on.[26] In one study, 11 percent of the respondents agreed that it was wrong to download online music without paying and to copy software without paying—but if they believe that "everybody else does it," they may still follow suit.[27] Interestingly, consumers who behave a little dishonestly want the expected benefits, yet try to remain honest enough to preserve their positive self-concept.[28]

Black Markets

Whereas theft represents acquisition situations in which consumers refuse to pay for available items, **black markets** represent situations in which consumers *pay* (often exorbitant amounts) for items *not* readily available. These are called "black" markets because the sellers are unauthorized, which means that the buying-selling process is usually illegal. Black markets for goods like sugar, salt, blankets, matches, and batteries fulfill functional needs; black markets for drugs, entertainment, and sexual services fulfill experiential needs; and black markets for watches and jewelry may fulfill symbolic needs.

Some items sold on the black market are legal but in short supply. For example, some consumers buy blocks of tickets to popular sporting events and concerts and resell them at much higher prices. Columbia University and other universities are cracking down on black-market sales of graduation tickets.[29] Some goods and services that

Exhibit 17.5 ▶ Motivations for Consumer Theft

Consumers may engage in theft because they (1) feel the temptation to steal and (2) can somehow rationalize their behavior. Various factors associated with the product, the environment, and the consumer can influence temptation and the ability to rationalize.

Product Factors
- Enticing product and unfulfilled aspirations
- Contraband item
- Embarrassing item

Environmental Factors
- Low perceived risk and high perceived opportunism
  - accessible product
  - limited security
  - crowded store

Consumer Factors
- Thrill-seeking tendencies

→ **Temptation**

Product Factors
- Low-ticket item

Environmental Factors
- Accessible product
- Limited security
- Crowded store

Consumer Factors
- Attitudes toward the store
- Attitudes toward big business
- Moral development
- Differential association

→ **Ability to Rationalize**

Theft

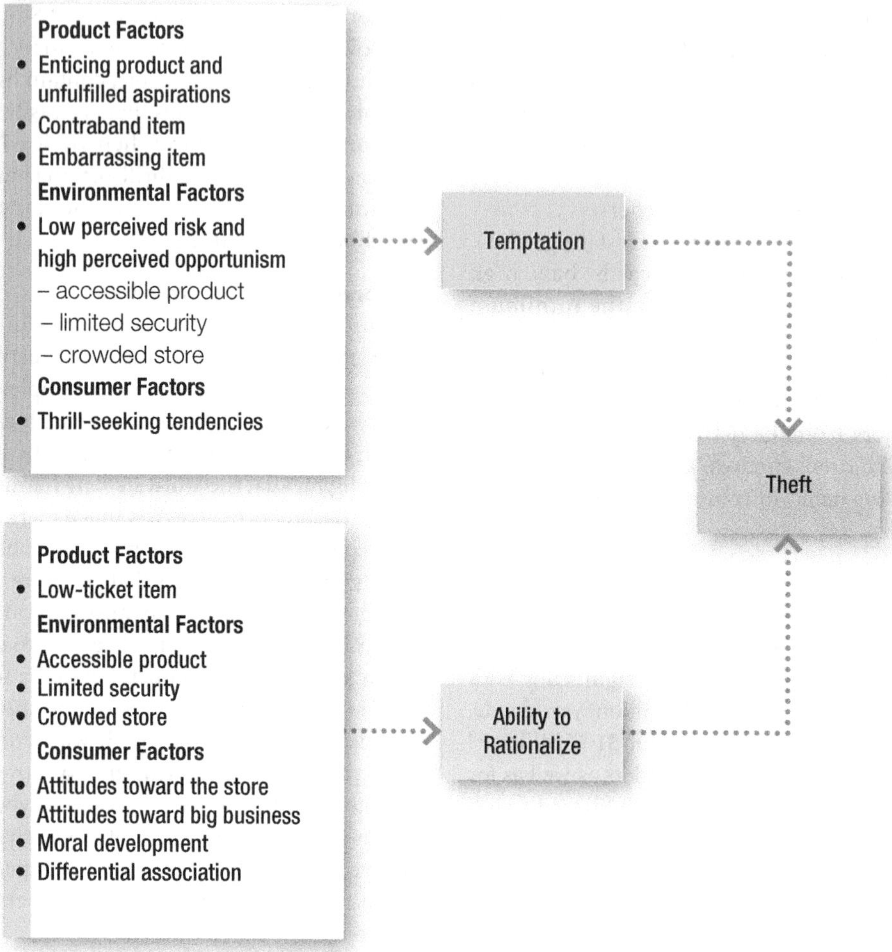

cannot legally be sold to consumers, such as components to build bombs, are sold on black markets. For example, during the years when the U.S. government banned commerce with Iran, a black market developed for American "muscle" cars such as the Camaro and Challenger.[30]

Another problem is that some goods offered on black markets are fake (see Exhibit 17.6). Counterfeits of luxury products have long been a black-market problem, fueled in part by purchases by consumers who knowingly acquire counterfeit branded items to gain the approval of others.[31] Online sales are now a problem for marketers of products in all price ranges, costing marketers up to $135 billion in lost revenue worldwide.[32] In such cases, consumers do not always know that the products they buy are fake—they only know that the prices are lower than usual.

Targeting Vulnerable Segments

Certain consumer segments are vulnerable to questionable marketing practices because of their age or because they are unprepared or unable to rationally evaluate marketing stimuli. Seniors, for instance, tend to have more difficulty processing and interpreting marketing information as they age. As another example, consumers in developing nations who have not been exposed to marketing in the past are more likely to believe a marketer's false claims or fall prey to other unethical marketing actions.

Advertising to children, in particular, has been the subject of considerable controversy focusing on the effects these ads may have on young, impressionable consumers. Research shows that by the age of two, 90 percent of U.S. children are watching videos or TV on a regular basis.[33]

AP Images/Lionel Cironneau

Exhibit 17.6 ▶ Black Markets

Some products sold on the black market are fake, such as designer handbags, and it is difficult to tell the difference between the knock-offs and the real ones.

Youngsters, particularly those under seven years, are not able to distinguish between the ad and the TV program.[34] Even at an age at which children can recognize this difference, they may not understand that the purpose of the ad is to sell them something.[35] Thus, young children do not possess the same critical reflection as adults do and are more likely to believe what they see in ads. Nonetheless, children are better at understanding the informational intent ("ads tell you about things") than the persuasive intent.[36]

Also, ad messages may prey on children's strong needs for sensual satisfaction, play, and affiliation, influencing them to choose material objects over socially oriented options.[37] Critics argue that ads teach children to become materialistic and expect immediate gratification. Unfortunately, many parents do not watch television with their children and do not educate them about advertising. As a result, children may be subject to having their attitudes and behaviors influenced by ads. Exposure to ads often prompts children to step up requests to parents about buying products, leading to family conflict and disappointed children. Children are also exposed to ads for products that shape, often negatively, their impressions of what it means to be an adult.[38] Another controversy

centers on the types of products advertised, whether toys or unhealthy foods or another product.

Concerns have also been raised about the fact that many websites targeting children feature some form of advertising.[39] Although parents can use software to block access to some sites, children may not understand the need to avoid giving out personal data and e-mail addresses. Internet access therefore raises concerns about family privacy as well as about children's ability to differentiate between advertising and nonadvertising material on the Web.

Marketing Implications

Acquisition controversies raise a number of important questions that affect marketers and their relationships with consumers and other stakeholders.

Does Marketing Perpetuate Materialism?

Clearly, many marketing activities are designed to influence consumers by making acquisition both attractive and convenient, with a wide variety of options. Despite this marketing influence, consumers in many cultures did slow their spending during the recent recession. Some entirely changed their buying habits, shopping in discount stores rather than the mid- or higher-priced stores they once preferred. Even as the economy improved, a number of these consumers continued their new, more frugal buying patterns (see Chapter 14 for more on frugality). The Poundland retail chain in England, for example, has retained so many bargain-loving customers that it acquired rival chain 99 Pence Stores to accelerate its growth strategy.[40] To reduce the influence of materialism on their lives, some consumers are choosing voluntary simplicity, as you saw in Chapter 13, often with an eye toward sustainability.

Does Marketing Encourage Addictive and Compulsive Acquisition Behaviors?

Some might argue that marketing activities encourage such behaviors. For example, cigarettes are heavily promoted in the United States—despite regulations that outlaw ads in broadcast media—and the nicotine in cigarettes is addictive (which is why it is now regulated by the Food and Drug Administration).[41] Public policy makers clearly view marketers as perpetuating this form of addictive consumption. Some countries have banned cigarette ads, and more than three dozen countries require graphic warning labels on cigarette packages because the images are presumably more effective in conveying smoking dangers than words alone.[42]

In another example, in Australia, where tobacco advertising has been forbidden since 1992, fewer than 3 percent of teenagers smoke, far fewer than in nations where ads are permitted.[43] In Canada, where graphic, full-color warnings on cigarette packs have been required for more than a decade, smoking rates have fallen; studies indicate that the warnings increase smokers' motivation to quit.[44] Many government and nonprofit marketers go further, running multimedia antismoking campaigns to change perceptions of and attitudes toward smoking, with the ultimate goal of discouraging consumers from buying tobacco products in the first place. Research continues on advertising appeals that can effectively discourage young consumers from smoking.[45]

However, in response to these bans on mass media advertising and strict regulations on tobacco packaging warnings, the tobacco industry has increased its emphasis on sponsorship marketing. Philip Morris has long been a sponsor of the Ferrari Formula One car racing team, even though its red-and-white Marlboro brand can't be displayed on the bright red car.[46] Tobacco companies are now also leveraging the power of social media to communicate with their target segments.

How Can Marketers Deal with Consumer Theft?

Businesses spend billions of dollars every year trying to prevent or reduce theft through the use of antitheft devices and improved security systems. Some companies combine closed-circuit TVs with sophisticated computer software to track suspicious behavior. With the rise of social media and some incidents of "flash mobs" in which consumers converge on a store and shoplift in a group, retailers are now monitoring social media and Internet sites for early warning signs so they can be prepared.[47]

Although security systems and procedures may reduce theft, they also may interfere with retailers' abilities to service customers. For example, retailers may have to keep merchandise in glass display cases, locked cabinets, and so on. This added security increases consumers' search costs, making it more difficult and more time-consuming for consumers to examine products and for salespeople to service customers. The added security systems may also feel intimidating to consumers.

How Can Marketers Deal with Black Markets?

Marketers are taking a variety of actions to thwart black markets, especially buying and selling online. In many

cases, products sold though black market channels are fake. U.K.-based Mulberry Group, which makes luxury leather goods, fights back against counterfeiters using software to scour the Internet for unauthorized sites that sell branded fakes. Over a two-year period, its efforts led to the shutdown of 3,321 websites that had been selling counterfeit Mulberry handbags.[48] Fake merchandise may be hazardous, such as some counterfeit food or medicines.

Should Marketers Target Children?

In light of concerns about marketers targeting children, both the Federal Trade Commission (FTC) and the Federal Communications Commission (FCC) have recommended that television stations use a separator between the program and the ad whenever the program is directed toward younger children. They recommend including a message prior to and directly after the ads—such as "We will return after these messages" before the commercial break, followed by "We now return to [name of the program]" at the end of the break—to help children to distinguish between ads and programming.[49]

The advertising industry has developed guidelines for children's advertising that are enforced by the Children's Advertising Review Unit (CARU), a wing of the Council of Better Business Bureaus. The guidelines encourage truthful and accurate advertising that recognizes children's cognitive limitations and avoids promoting unrealistic expectations about what products can do. Other countries also have agencies that regulate children's advertising and take action when necessary. For example, the U.K. Advertising Standards Authority investigates complaints about ads that target children inappropriately. It ruled that a commercial for Morrisons, a supermarket chain, promoting collectible trading cards and the chance to win a trip to Disneyland Paris, could no longer air because it encouraged children to pester parents into making purchases.[50]

17-2b CONSUMPTION CONTROVERSIES

Consumption situations can also give rise to ethical controversies. Here we discuss concerns about (1) underage drinking and smoking, (2) idealized self-images, (3) compulsive gambling, (4) overeating and obesity, and (5) privacy.

Underage Drinking and Smoking

As mentioned earlier, addictions to alcohol and tobacco represent one form of deviant consumer behavior. *Illegal*

Exhibit 17.7 ▶ Idealized Self-Images
Most models in ads are trim and attractive, representing an idealized version of the consumer.

use of these products by minors is another deviant consumer behavior. As many as 44 percent of college students have engaged in "binge drinking" (drinking more than five drinks in one sitting).[51] Nearly 90 percent of cigarette smokers tried their first cigarette by the age of 18.[52] These figures are even higher in countries where there are few bans on cigarette advertising. Underage drinking and smoking have consequences for the individual and for society. Overuse of alcohol has been implicated in campus violence, campus property damage, academic failures, teen highway fatalities, youth suicides, and campus hazing deaths.

Idealized Self-Images

Some critics say that advertising contributes to an idealized self-image (see Exhibit 17.7). Most male models shown in advertisements are trim with well-developed muscles and handsome features. The female models are mostly young, very thin, and beautiful. Because these ads represent society's conception of the ideal man or woman, they exemplify traits that many men and women will never actually achieve. A particularly salient issue for both men and women is how their bodies compare with those of thin models. Indeed, one study found that 11 percent of men said that they would trade more than five years of their lives to achieve personal weight goals—statistics that closely track women's responses.[53] In fact, many clothing manufacturers use "vanity sizing," putting a smaller size on a larger sized item, perhaps because this helps consumers feel better about themselves.[54]

Social comparison theory A theory that proposes that individuals have a drive to compare themselves with other people.

Particularly in Westernized countries, thinness is viewed as a characteristic of attractive men and women. Unfortunately, this value can be carried to extremes and can lead to eating disorders such as anorexia and bulimia, disorders that affect approximately 10 million U.S. women and 1 million U.S. men. These disorders are also increasing dramatically among young women in Japan.[55] On the other hand, binge eating is a problem for an estimated 25 million Americans.[56] With increased media and educational attention on healthy eating, a small number of consumers are taking nutrition to an extreme with orthorexia, meaning they severely limit their intake of certain foods.[57]

But do ads with thin models serve as an impetus to consumers with predispositions to eating disorders? Does identification with very thin models create dissatisfaction with one's own body and appearance?[58] Some evidence suggests the answer to these questions is yes. In fact, several countries—including France, Italy, Israel, and Spain—have laws forbidding fashion marketers from featuring super-thin models in ads and on runways. The French health minister explains: "This is an important message to young women who see these models as an aesthetic example."[59]

Social comparison theory proposes that individuals have a drive to compare themselves with other people.[60] Consistent with this theory, research shows that young women do compare themselves with models in ads and that such self-comparisons can affect self-esteem.[61] As a result, consumers feel inadequate if they do not measure up to the person with whom they are comparing themselves. Consumers who feel threatened by such comparisons will lie about their behavior to protect their self-esteem.[62] Also, consumers who have low body esteem will be less likely to want a clothing product if they try it on and notice an attractive person wearing the same product.[63]

Interestingly, some research has also found that consumers who view ads with beautiful models reduce their attractiveness ratings of average-looking women. A potential conclusion, based on the research, is that advertising can have an unintended but negative impact on how satisfied men and women are with their appearance.[64] Note that consumers do not feel bad about the comparison if the models in ads are extremely thin.[65] Other research indicates that when consumers who are interested in a product observe lower-status people being interested in the same product, this threatens their self-evaluation and causes them to have a keener interest in that product.[66]

Compulsive Gambling

Compulsive gambling, a problematic consumption behavior, affects an estimated six to nine million Americans. In one study, 85 percent of the participants aged 18 to 24 said that they had gambled, and 5 percent admitted having gambling problems.[67] Scientists have established systematic links between compulsive gambling and consumption of alcohol, tobacco, and illicit drugs.[68] Typically, compulsive gambling behavior evolves over a series of stages. Sometimes, but not always, the consumer first experiences the pleasure of a "big win."[69] Next, gambling becomes more reckless, losses pile up, and gambling becomes a central force in the individual's life. The compulsive gambler promises to stop gambling, but cannot. The final stage occurs when the gambler realizes that he or she has hit rock bottom.

Industry and marketing practices may also perpetuate behaviors like compulsive gambling.[70] Gambling is a profitable industry; although attendance at horse races is decreasing, casino gambling is on the rise, with nearly 1,000 casinos now located in 41 states in the United States—many with high-tech video slot machines.[71] Seeing the potential for higher revenue, some states spend millions of dollars advertising their lottery programs. New York, for example, takes in more than $6.5 billion in lottery revenue and spends $43 million annually to advertise its lottery and scratch-off tickets.[72] Online gambling has grown into a $12 billion industry, even though U.S. citizens cannot legally bet in online casinos.[73] In Canada, where provincial governments are considering whether to legalize online gambling, up to half of all high school and college students say they have tried Internet-based gambling.[74]

Overeating and Obesity

As noted in Chapter 1, scientists say that the rapid rise of obesity worldwide constitutes an "epidemic."[75] Overeating remains a serious problem in the United States, where one-third of all adults and 17 percent of children and teens are obese.[76] Researchers are investigating a variety of issues that may contribute to overeating and, over time, to obesity. For example, do consumers feel less guilty about eating "low fat" snack foods and therefore overeat? Research shows that consumers with high self-control consistently feel satisfied more quickly when eating unhealthy foods than when eating healthy foods, because they pay closer attention to their consumption of the unhealthy foods.[77] At the same time, marketers can help combat the tendency to overindulge by making serving size information more salient.[78] Yet when marketers calculate nutritional value using a small serving size, the food labels will report fewer calories, fat, sugar, and carbohydrates per serving, which in turn can influence consumers' anticipated consequences of consumption (i.e., guilt and purchase intentions).[79] Another factor is that consumers tend to underestimate the calorie content of foods they consume, a situation that explains the regulatory move to have restaurants post nutrition information about menu items.[80]

Moreover, consumers tend to perceive unhealthy foods as being tastier and more enjoyable than healthy foods. To address this perception, food marketers can reformulate foods to make foods healthier as well as better tasting, and revamp marketing to promote healthy foods.[81] When consumers are watching their weight, they tend to perceive food products (such as *pasta salad*) that carry names associated with less healthy eating (such as *pasta*) as less tasty and less healthful. However, when the same food product carries a healthy-sounding name (such as *salad*), product evaluations aren't affected by whether consumers are on a diet.[82] In fact, merely having a healthy option (such as *salad*) on the menu increases the possibility that consumers will order the least healthy option on the menu.[83]

Food consumption and evaluation of food products are also influenced by images of other people eating and by the presence of other people.[84] Even fork and plate sizes can make a difference: Consumers tend to eat more when they use smaller forks, and serve themselves more food when they use larger plates.[85] How large a food portion consumers choose may depend, in part, on whether they are eating in public or in private, and on whether they have a need for status.[86] When consumers feel powerless, eating in public leads to larger portions, unless eating smaller portions is associated with status.

In addition, food purchases are influenced by pricing strategies, with the result that larger-sized products offered at a value price will appeal to consumers who want to save money and will overshadow their health goals.[87] Consumers exhibit more price sensitivity when prices rise on healthy foods, and less sensitivity when prices rise on unhealthy foods. Thus, a smaller increase in price for healthy food will lead to a larger drop in demand, just as a smaller decrease in price for unhealthy food will lead to a larger increase in demand.[88]

Privacy Controversies

Privacy controversies have received more attention in recent years because a great deal of detailed information is being collected about consumers as they click around the Internet and use social media.[89] When consumers post a photo on Facebook or a message on Twitter, click on an advertising link, or watch an online video, their activities are being tracked—often by more than one company. The marketing purpose is to show relevant ads to consumers, based on their online behavior and browsing history.[90] This is useful because consumers can thus learn about products and brands that they are or might be interested in, rather than being bombarded by irrelevant ads. However, the amount and type of data collected, and what marketers might do with the data, has some consumers and privacy advocates worried.[91]

Many consumers believe that businesses collect too much personal information online, and they are concerned about threats to their personal privacy.[92] In another study, 61 percent of the participants decided not to use a financial website because of concerns about how their personal data would be handled.[93] They also worry about identity theft, especially in the wake of incidents involving theft of personal data such as credit card numbers.[94]

The extent of consumer concern and the willingness to give personal information varies according to the type of information that marketers want to collect.[95] However, although consumers often complain about privacy concerns, many still willingly provide information that could compromise their privacy.[96] Most websites post privacy policies to explain what consumer data they gather, what they do with it, how consumers can review it, and how it is protected—although often these statements do not offer complete explanations.[97] Companies can help consumers make informed decisions by describing what data they collect and how they use data to improve the consumers' online experience (such as customized offers that better fit the consumers' interests).[98]

 Marketing Implications

The consumption issues just discussed are both complex and challenging. Yet marketers must understand the questions raised by such controversies as they plan their strategy and activities. They concern balancing the interests of consumers and their own interests, in both the short and long run.

Does Marketing Encourage Underage or Excessive Drinking and Smoking?

Youngsters are exposed to a large amount of alcohol advertising as well as to non–TV-based tobacco advertising,[99] a situation that has led to calls for companies to limit kids' exposure to such advertising.[100] Although the tobacco industry avoids deliberately marketing to children, some brands continue to be advertised in adult publications that teens also read. Evidence suggests that the more young consumers view alcohol ads, the more they know about these products, and the more likely they are to use them.[101]

Similarly, most youthful smokers choose the most heavily advertised brands—which shows that advertising works and also implicates it as a cause of smoking behavior. Adolescents who have the greatest exposure to cigarette advertising in general tend to be the heaviest smokers, and the brands that do the most advertising tend to attract a greater proportion of teenagers than of adults. In particular, tobacco and alcohol ads featuring human actors or models have been found to directly produce more positive attitudes toward the ad, the brand, and the product category.[102] Children are also exposed to images of cigarette consumption in nonadvertising contexts. If scenes depicting smoking were drastically reduced in PG-13 movies, the rate of adolescent tobacco use would drop by 18 percent.[103]

However, others argue that advertising for these products has little effect on children; more critical determinants are said to include peer influence, parental smoking, and self-esteem. The alcohol industry stresses that it does not target young consumers and notes that it has invested heavily to promote responsible drinking among adult consumers (see Exhibit 17.8). Heineken, which markets beer brands worldwide, introduced a global campaign a few years ago to encourage responsible alcohol consumption. "You can't build a long term sustainable business on excessive consumption," explains the senior director of the Heineken brand.[104] Even when alcohol marketers present messages such as "Don't drink and drive," consumers may not react positively because the source is a corporate sponsor.[105]

Does Advertising Affect Self-Image?

Some companies are becoming more sensitive to the potentially negative effects of promotional messages on self-image. In the fashion industry, demand for plus-size models is up—perhaps in response to consumers' demands for different types of women in fashion products and ads.[106] Also, online retailers give consumers the option of buying and trying on clothing at home.[107]

Although some women may be unhappy about how they compare with models in ads, others are comfortable with themselves and are hostile toward advertisers that perpetuate unrealistic images of women.[108] However, because some women will still be willing to use products that entail some risk to achieve an idealized body image, marketers must disclose risks (e.g., of pharmaceutical products or dietary supplements) so that consumers can evaluate any potential negative outcomes.

Some marketers are using marketing to foster positive self-image among consumers in their target markets. Not long ago, Procter & Gamble's Always brand of personal-care products initiated a highly successful multimedia campaign to counter the misperception that girls aren't good at sports. The award-winning Always campaign, which carried the hashtag #LikeA-Girl, contrasted the reality of girls running confidently and throwing hard with adults' stereotypes of girls who could barely run or pitch a baseball. Just as important, the brand's research found that the campaign reversed teen girls' perceptions of the phrase "like a girl," turning what was formerly a negative into a positive description.[109]

Does Marketing Affect Compulsive Gambling Behavior?

The expansion of legalized gambling operations—and the marketing of such facilities—may be a problem for consumers with a tendency toward or a history of compulsive gambling. Most government-run lotteries and many casino companies set aside some funding for consumer education and treatment of compulsive gambling. Australian Leisure and Hospitality Group, for example, runs an award-winning program to combat problem gambling at hundreds of its facilities where consumers can play electronic poker.[110] Online gambling is generally illegal in the United States but legal in many countries. However, because multiple jurisdictions regulate online gambling that occurs across national borders, no one approach has been put in place to help consumers who compulsively gamble online. Finally, some research suggests that a slot machine's physical appearance—specifically, whether consumers see a hint of human resemblance—can affect consumers' perceptions of risk, a finding that may help in developing effective antigambling messages.[111]

Does Marketing Contribute to Overeating and Obesity?

The World Health Organization believes that evidence connecting junk food advertising and childhood obesity

Exhibit 17.8 ▶ Publicizing Health Concerns
To combat the advertising of tobacco and alcohol to children, federal and state agencies, interest groups, and companies publicize the adverse effects of these substances on children's health.

is convincing enough that governments should discourage marketing activities that promote unhealthy eating among youngsters.[112] In some countries, advocacy groups are campaigning for stronger restrictions on marketing of high-sugar or high-fat foods to children, whether through traditional promotions, online, or in social media. The Children's Food Campaign, for example, has complained to U.K. authorities that marketers' use of brand characters, animation, and other tools make junk foods more appealing to children who surf the Web.[113] In the United States, the USDA's "Smart Snacks in School" rule requires snack foods sold in school vending machines to meet minimum nutritional levels, as one way to encourage healthy eating and combat childhood obesity.[114]

On the other hand, more companies and media are using marketing to encourage healthier behaviors. Food manufacturers are also emphasizing the good taste of healthy foods and providing nutrition information. PepsiCo, known for its cola drinks and salty snacks, has introduced dozens of healthy snacks, from yogurt drinks to oatmeal bars, to broaden its appeal.[115] As another example, Bolthouse Farms, one of the largest U.S. growers of baby carrots, promotes consumption of its products with catchy ads carrying the slogan: "Eat 'em like junk food." The company also appeals to social media users and bargain-hunting consumers by offering digital coupons to consumers who post Instagram photos of its vegetable products or any of its ads, accompanied by the hashtags #carrotfarmers and #gotcoupon.[116] Fast-food restaurants not only post nutrition data, but also are making healthy foods a default menu choice for children. McDonald's Happy Meals now come with apples, yogurt, or clementines rather than fries. Further, since sodas were taken off the Happy Meals menu board, nearly half of all Happy Meals in America are ordered with milk or juice rather than with carbonated beverages. [117]

Do Marketers Invade Consumers' Privacy?

Online privacy is a headline issue, even though other aspects of privacy do affect consumers (such as names on mailing lists and credit card numbers retained in company databases). Giants such as Google and Facebook have become embroiled in controversy after controversy as they seek to use the volume of data they collect to better target consumers with personalized ads. Targeted online ads are already a huge business accounting for $50 billion every year.[118] Concerns about privacy are only intensifying as billions of consumers worldwide go online for information, entertainment, communication, shopping, and more. Although privacy policies are almost universally available, privacy advocates say consumers rarely read them or understand the sophisticated tracking and data collection procedures used by marketers.

Some regulators are taking action. For example, the European Union has some of the strictest online privacy rules on the planet, covering disclosure of what data are being gathered and requiring consumers to consent to being tracked by cookies.[119] Even tighter rules are on the way, giving European consumers more say over how their information may be used and clarifying when and where individuals have the "right to be forgotten" online (by having data deleted at their request).[120] Another concern is under what circumstances governmental agencies are able to request and review consumers' online, social media, and mobile messages and activities. California and a few other states now require court orders before any personal data can be released by Twitter and other companies.[121]

Meanwhile, many marketers are doing more to explain their privacy policies and reassure consumers that personal data are being safeguarded. Major Internet browsing programs have features that enable users to reject or delete cookies and avoid being tracked as individuals. Advertisers who are members of the Digital Advertising Alliance—including American Express and Walmart—voluntarily invite consumers to opt out of seeing online and mobile ads by clicking on a special icon.[122] At the same time, concerns about privacy open up the potential for marketers to develop new offerings designed to protect consumer privacy, such as apps and specialized software that allows anonymous browsing.[123]

17-2c DISPOSITION CONTROVERSIES

As discussed in Chapter 10, consumers have many options for voluntarily disposing of possessions. Some of these disposition outcomes can be controversial, especially now that more consumers and marketers are embracing sustainability and trying to protect the environment, now and into the future. This section will discuss two specific concerns: (1) disposing of products that still function and (2) disposing of products that are no longer functional.

Disposing of Products That Still Function

When products can be used, consumers who want to dispose of them can give them away to another consumer, trade for useful items, sell or auction them, donate them, or recycle them. Research about recycling demonstrates that specific beliefs about its importance and attitudes toward recycling in general can directly affect whether consumers engage in recycling behaviors and whether they perceive that recycling is inconvenient.[124]

On occasion, useful products are thrown away, a disposition behavior that can be controversial, not just because it may be perceived as wasteful. When consumers upgrade their electronics products, for example, they don't always have or take advantage of proper recycling or disposal services for their old products (in workable condition), through stores or recycling centers. As a result, many old but functional cell phones, televisions, computer monitors, and other electronics wind up in landfills, posing an environmental hazard because of materials contained in the products. In fact, this is why the European Union and individual countries have enacted strict laws regarding the safe disposal of electronic and electrical goods, whether in working order or not.[125]

Disposing of Products That Do Not Function

When consumers seek to dispose of products that no longer function, they can throw them away in a socially acceptable way (in the proper trash bin or recycle center) or abandon them in a socially unacceptable way (e.g., littering), which is controversial. Some nonfunctioning products retain a value and can be sold to consumers or businesses that want the parts or the materials. In some countries, controversy surrounds the practice of dismantling and selling old, uninhabitable buildings and other artifacts that are nonfunctional in the traditional sense, but have important historic value.

Marketing Implications

What role can or should marketers play in the disposition of functioning and nonfunctioning products, especially in controversial situations? Businesses and nonprofit organizations such as eBay, Freecycle Network, Goodwill Industries International, Oxfam, and others facilitate the disposition of functional products, as do marketing policies that encourage trade-ins toward the purchase of new goods. IKEA and others invite customers to recycle used batteries for free through bins in their stores, a responsible way to deal with products that otherwise would pile up in landfills. Marketers working for businesses, nonprofit groups, and government agencies are doing more to encourage consumers to recycle products. And nonprofit groups like the National Trust for Historic Preservation are raising money (often in partnership with businesses) to help buy and restore deteriorating historic sites, so they will not be lost forever.

In addition, many companies are being pushed by both consumers and retailers to use less product packaging or more environmentally friendly product packaging.[126] Product designers are now building in features and components that allow products to be easily disassembled for recycling or disposal. Even when products are thrown away, they can serve as raw material for companies like TerraCycle, which transforms trash into new products, marketed to green-minded consumers.[127] Such efforts may become part of the lifestyle for larger segments of consumers or perhaps entire nations or regions. Germany, for example, strictly limits the amount of waste sent to landfills, and therefore consumers have developed the habit of recycling everything that can be recycled.[128]

17-3 Social Responsibility Issues in Marketing

Economist Milton Friedman famously stated that "the social responsibility of business is to increase its profits."[129] Now, decades after his statement, most businesses do not take an "either-or" approach. Rather than framing the decision as "higher profits *or* social responsibility," they are pursuing both higher profits *and* social responsibility through marketing.

Businesses are, for the most part, thinking long-term and seeing their stakeholders as "we," making social responsibility an integral part of their overall strategy. And marketers—not just giants like Walmart, but smaller firms as well—are starting to use their influence over suppliers to encourage more socially responsible, sustainable behavior throughout the supply chain, even across national borders.[130] Brands must also be aware of how promoting their involvement in social responsibility can affect consumer perceptions. For example, luxury brands that are known for their pursuit of perfection may not gain by emphasizing their social responsibility activities, because the association tends to devalue the brand in the eyes of consumers.[131] Although marketers sometimes take the lead in addressing an issue, consumers now have the power and the voice to take the initiative; at other times, marketers and consumers collaborate to address important issues.

The following sections offer a brief overview of three social responsibility issues receiving particular marketing attention: (1) environmentally conscious behavior and ethical sourcing, (2) charitable behavior, and (3) community involvement.

17-3a ENVIRONMENTALLY CONSCIOUS BEHAVIOR AND ETHICAL SOURCING

Marketers are directly and indirectly involved in efforts to foster environmentally conscious behavior and to address concerns about global warming. Car companies, their suppliers, and gasoline companies all must comply with government requirements such as the use of unleaded gasoline and adherence to stricter emission controls to reduce environmental damage. These efforts sometimes increase marketing costs but may also open new profit opportunities. The trend toward the use of environmentally friendly products is growing, paving the way for companies like Seventh Generation, which markets eco-friendly household cleaning products.

An important aspect of behavior related to the environment is **conservation behavior**, actions taken to limit the use of scarce natural resources. Consumers are most likely to conserve when they accept personal responsibility for the pollution problem.[132] For example, consumers who perceive that there is an energy shortage because of consumption

Conservation behavior Limiting the use of scarce natural resources for the purposes of environmental preservation.

Justin Sullivan/Getty Images

Exhibit 17.9 ▶ Publicizing Health Concerns
The Environmental Protection Agency's Energy Star program labels energy-efficient appliances and computers, promoting consumer energy conservation.

by all consumers (including themselves) are more likely to do something about it. However, consumers often do not feel accountable for many environmental problems and are not motivated to act. Thus, for conservation programs to succeed, messages must make the problem personally relevant, such as educating consumers about how much energy and money they will save by cutting electrical usage. Environmentally conscious behaviors are, in fact, most likely to occur when consumers perceive that their actions will make a difference—called *perceived consumer effectiveness*.[133] When consumers perceive an issue such as sustainability to be important, they are affected more by assertive marketing messages than by nonassertive marketing messages, and they are more willing to comply with the message.[134]

A study in the Netherlands points out the importance of using social norms to influence consumers' environmental behaviors. This study found that consumers generally perceive that they are more motivated to engage in proenvironmental behavior than other households are but that they have less ability to do so.[135] Furthermore, they believe that ability is the greatest determinant and that their own behavior is influenced by others. In another study of social norms, researchers examining the behavior of hotel guests concluded that normative appeals (such as "the majority of guests in this room reuse their towels") are more effective than environmental-protection appeals in encouraging conservation behavior.[136]

Many organizations and agencies are trying to motivate consumers to be environmentally friendly. Ads sometimes encourage consumers to use products or packages that conserve resources or to engage in conservation behaviors. Providing consumers with detailed information about how to be environmentally friendly can be helpful, as well. For example, the U.S. Environmental Protection Agency and the U.S. Department of Energy's joint program ENERGY STAR, promoted through on-package labeling, manufacturers' advertising, and publicity helps consumers choose energy-efficient appliances and computers (see Exhibit 17.9). Moreover, marketers can encourage consumers to include eco-friendly products in their consideration set by proposing a list of prescreened alternatives (such as products that have earned green certification).[137] Note that credible endorsements can help combat the perception that "green" products are less effective than regular products and also to discourage consumers from using too much of a green product because they want to make up for its perceived inferiority.[138]

Another promising approach is to provide consumers with incentives to conserve. Providing consumers with a free shower-water flow device, for instance, significantly increased participation in an energy conservation program. Consumers prefer incentives such as tax credits to coercive tactics such as higher taxes. In addition, setting goals and providing feedback can help consumers curtail their energy use.

Public interest in and support for environmentally conscious behavior has resulted in a backlash against

greenwashing, the misleading use of environmental claims for marketing purposes. When marketers promote nonexistent or minimally beneficial eco-friendly claims, they risk being perceived negatively because they seem to be exploiting consumers' interest in green goods or services. For example, Volkswagen's acknowledgement that its diesel-powered cars used software to appear more eco-friendly than they really were was a blow to the German automaker's reputation.[139] To avoid confusion and deception, government regulators in many nations have established specific guidelines for how marketers can use phrases like "environmentally friendly."

> **Greenwashing** The misleading use of environmental claims for marketing purposes.

Companies and consumers are increasingly paying attention to **ethical sourcing**, which means supplies are obtained and products are produced in accordance with social responsibility and sustainability values. Starbucks, for example, is committed to ethical sourcing for its coffee sold through 21,000 locations worldwide. The company now verifies, through outside certification by outside groups, that its coffee comes from sources that meet specific economic, environmental, and social standards for the farms and farmers that grow and process the coffee.[140] How does ethical sourcing affect consumer behavior? In one study, consumers were more than twice as likely to purchase products promoted as ethically sourced when the purchase decision was made because consumers were holding themselves accountable to their own personal ethical standards. Consumers were more likely to buy products that prominently featured ethical sourcing when they were making the decision in public, such as in a store, because they wanted to appear moral in front of others and adhere to their own standards of right and wrong. Alone, consumers were more likely to buy products with less-prominent ethical cues.[141]

> **Ethical sourcing** Obtaining supplies and making products in accordance with social responsibility and sustainability values.

17-3b CHARITABLE BEHAVIOR

The influence of marketing on charitable behavior has been the focus of considerable research. For example, consumers' cognitive resources can become depleted after being exposed to a charity's foot-in-the-door techniques. In turn, it reduces their self-control and increases their tendency to respond positively to donation requests, a finding that can help charities plan more effective appeals.[142] Other research shows that asking consumers about their intentions to volunteer *time* for a charity cause activates an emotional reaction that makes more salient the idea of "giving leads to happiness." This positive mindset, in turn, increases *money* contribution. Yet, as Exhibit 17.10 shows, asking about intentions to donate money prompts consideration of monetary value, and ultimately results in a lower charitable contribution.[143] Further, consumers who perceive that a charity's beneficiaries have a lot of responsibility for their plight will tend to donate less money, out of a sense of justice. However, when they perceive that beneficiaries have little responsibility for their plight, consumers have more empathy and donate more money.[144]

Another element is whether the charity's beneficiaries are perceived to be members of a group, which leads consumers to stronger judgments. When consumers perceive the beneficiaries as belonging to a cohesive group with positive traits, they have higher feelings of concern and donate more money; the opposite is true for beneficiaries perceived to share negative traits.[145] Also, consumers with an interdependent self-construal (i.e., they think more about themselves as a member of a group) are more open to making charitable donations than consumers with independent self construals (i.e., those who are more likely to think about themselves as individuals).[146]

It is important to recognize that charitable behavior can vary by culture. According to one global survey, U.S. consumers are the most generous in volunteering their time, donating money, and helping strangers. In terms of financial contributions, Thailand ranks first, with 85 percent of consumers saying they donate to charity monthly, followed by the United Kingdom, and a tie between Ireland and the Netherlands.[147]

Thanks to social and online media, marketing to encourage charitable behavior can extend its reach and increase its impact. Consider Comic Relief, a U.K.-based charity that holds two star-studded events—Red Nose Day and Sport Relief—to raise money for fighting poverty and helping at-risk youth. Among the marketing tools it uses are the Web, Twitter, Facebook, iPhone apps, YouTube, public relations, celebrity spokespeople, and sales promotion. Comic Relief also encourages consumers to hold local fundraisers, which helps the charity raise tens of millions of dollars and help thousands of people every year. When Red Nose Day launched in the United States, the charity increased awareness by partnering with Walgreens to sell merchandise and working with NBC to present a celebrity-hosted evening telethon.[148]

Research shows, however, that consumers are less likely to donate to a charity that has corporate sponsorship, because they believe their individual donations will matter less.[149] On the other hand, nostalgia promotes charitable intentions and behavior because it fosters social connections, even more so when consumers empathize with the beneficiaries.[150]

17-3c COMMUNITY INVOLVEMENT

As the opening example shows, companies can use marketing as a catalyst for community-based social responsibility. By inviting groups to compete for grants—and giving consumers a say in which groups should receive money—Pepsi encouraged active involvement in the groups and among community members.

Marketers, large companies in particular, often have policies that encourage employees to get involved in the

Exhibit 17.10 ▶

How Requests for Time and Money Affect Charitable Contributions

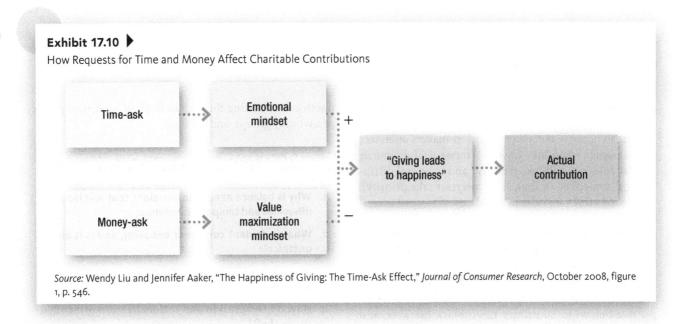

Source: Wendy Liu and Jennifer Aaker, "The Happiness of Giving: The Time-Ask Effect," *Journal of Consumer Research*, October 2008, figure 1, p. 546.

communities where they do business.[151] While this involvement usually generates goodwill and positive word of mouth, it can also benefit the company in other ways (e.g., by increasing employee satisfaction).[152] Many employees of Target, for example, volunteer as "reading buddies," reading to patients in local hospitals and to youngsters in local schools. General Electric has a Volunteers Foundation that coordinates employee volunteer efforts in 41 nations.

Sometimes, however, consumers can be confronted with high levels of injustice. When this occurs and the ways to restore justice are uncertain or not available, consumers are less likely to support fair-trade practices. However, when companies highlight how purchases can address this injustice, fair-trade support increases, especially when there are just–world beliefs and it is an indulgence product.[153]

17-4 How Can Consumers Resist Marketing Practices?

Any marketing, even "bright side" marketing in support of socially responsible outcomes, may irritate some consumers. Whether these consumers believe that they are being barraged with messages or for any other reason, consumers who are upset about certain marketing practices can resist them and try to bring about change individually, through advocacy groups, and through boycotts.[154] Consumers who are dissatisfied or unhappy with marketing practices can choose *not* to patronize the offending marketer in the future, complain to the marketer, and spread negative word of mouth. These individual consumer resistance strategies can be very effective, especially when social media are leveraged to repeat the message.

Boycott An organized activity in which consumers avoid purchasing products or services from a company whose policies or practices are seen as unfair or unjust.

Group strategies are potentially even more powerful than unorganized consumer efforts. Some formally organized advocacy groups engage in resistance by informing the public about business practices that they regard as socially inappropriate.[155] Public Citizen is a nonprofit consumer advocacy group that educates the public about issues such as online privacy and misleading marketing. *Adbusters* is an ad-free, subscription-supported magazine that informs consumers about commercial excess and encourages change by publicizing events such as Buy Nothing Day.[156]

A **boycott** is an organized activity in which consumers avoid purchasing products or services from a company whose policies or practices are seen as unfair or unjust. Boycotting is a way for consumers to hold companies accountable for perceived objectionable actions. Thus, many consumers are motivated by the opportunity and likelihood of making a difference. Also, consumers who are particularly susceptible to the normative influences of the reference group conducting the boycott will be more likely to participate than those who are less susceptible. Finally, consumers may seek to feel less guilty and hope to boost or sustain their self-esteem by joining a particular boycott.[157]

Organized boycotts are able to gain publicity and are likely to have more impact than the same number of consumers acting on their own.[158] Sometimes boycotts are directed against a company's activities rather than against a product. The primary indicators that a boycott has been successful are not that it has caused financial effects but rather that it (1) has changed the offending policies, (2) has made businesses more responsible in their plans for future activities, and (3) has forced changes in the behavior of nontargeted businesses that engage in similar practices.

Summary:

Marketing and consumer behavior can have a "bright side," leading to constructive outcomes, and a "dark side," leading to negative outcomes. Decision-makers often face ethical issues when they try to balance social dilemmas (whose interests will take priority) and temporal dilemmas (if immediate or long-term interests take priority). Marketing ethics are rules or standards of acceptable conduct that guide marketing decisions. Consumer ethics are rules of acceptable conduct that apply to the full range of consumer behaviors. Deviant consumer behavior is either unexpected or not sanctioned by society.

Five areas of controversy related to acquisition situations are materialistic behavior, addictive and compulsive behavior, consumer theft, black markets, and targeting vulnerable segments. In the context of consumption situations, controversies include underage drinking and smoking, idealized self-images, compulsive gambling, overeating and obesity, and privacy.

Disposition controversies include disposing of functional and nonfunctional products. Social responsibility issues receiving special marketing attention are environmentally conscious behavior and ethical sourcing, charitable behavior, and community involvement. Consumers can resist unwanted, disreputable, objectionable, and/or unethical marketing through individual actions, support of advocacy groups, and boycotts.

Questions for Review and Discussion

1. Why is balance needed in decisions that involve social dilemmas and temporal dilemmas?

2. What is deviant consumer behavior, and is it always unethical?

3. How does addictive behavior differ from compulsive behavior?

4. How do temptation and rationalization affect consumer theft?

5. What is social comparison theory, and how does it apply to advertising?

6. What influences conservation behavior and charitable behavior?

7. What are greenwashing and ethical sourcing, and what do they mean for consumers and marketers?

8. What can consumers do to resist unwanted marketing practices?

Endnotes

1   For more about sharing, see Yu-Jen Chen and Amna Kirmani, "Posting Strategically: The Consumer as an Online Media Planner," *Journal of Consumer Psychology* 25, no. 4, October 2015, pp. 609–621; and Russell Belk, "Sharing," *Journal of Consumer Research*, February 2010, pp. 715–734.

2   Phil Wahba, "Shoplifting, Worker Theft Cost Retailers $32 Billion Last Year," *Fortune*, June 24, 2015, www.fortune.com.

3   A. Peter McGraw, Janet A. Schwartz, and Philip E. Tetlock, "From the Commercial to the Communal: Reframing Taboo Trade-offs in Religious and Pharmaceutical Marketing," *Journal of Consumer Research* 39, no. 1, June 2012, pp. 157–173.

4   Flora F. Gu and Kineta Hung, "Materialism Among Adolescents in China: A Historical Generation Perspective," *Journal of Asia Business Studies* 3, no. 2, 2009, pp. 56–64. For another perspective, see Harold Ogden and Shen Cheng, "Cultural Dimensions and Materialism: Comparing Canada and China," *Asia Pacific Journal of Marketing and Logistics* 23, no. 4, 2011, pp. 431–447.

5   "Over 60% of Chinese Purchase Luxury Items Abroad," *China Daily*, June 12, 2015, www.chinadaily.com; and Karl Wilson,

"In Love with Luxury amid Global Gloom," *China Daily*, January 16, 2012, www.chinadaily.com.cn.

6   Ji Kyung Park and Deborah Roedder John, "More Than Meets the Eye: The Influence of Implicit and Explicit Self-Esteem On Materialism," *Journal of Consumer Psychology* 21, no. 1, Special Issue, January 2011, pp. 73–87.

7   Aaron C. Ahuvia and Nancy Y. Wong, "Personality and Values Based Materialism: Their Relationship and Origins," *Journal of Consumer Psychology* 12, no. 4, 2002, pp. 389–402; and Marvin E. Goldberg, Gerald J. Gorn, Laura A. Peracchio, and Gary Bamossy, "Understanding Materialism Among Youth," *Journal of Consumer Psychology* 13, no. 3, 2003, pp. 278–288.

8   Lan Nguyen Chaplin and Deborah Roedder John, "Interpersonal Influences on Adolescent Materialism: A New Look at the Role of Parents and Peers," *Journal of Consumer Psychology* 20, no. 2, April 2010, pp. 176–184.

9   Goldberg, Gorn, Peracchio, and Bamossy, "Understanding Materialism Among Youth."

10 Noel C. Paul, "Branded for Life?" *Christian Science Monitor*, April 1, 2002, www.csmonitor.com.

11 Lucia Moses, "Children See a Lot of Marketing Messages, Regardless of Platform," *Adweek*, March 11, 2014, www.adweek.com.

12 Marsha L. Richins, "Media, Materialism, and Human Happiness," *Advances in Consumer Research* 14, 1987, pp. 352–356.

13 See, for example, James M. Hunt, Jerome B. Kernan, and Deborah J. Mitchell, "Materialism as Social Cognition: People, Possessions, and Perception," *Journal of Consumer Psychology* 5, no. 1, 1996, pp. 65–83.

14 Elizabeth C. Hirschman, "The Consciousness of Addiction," *Journal of Consumer Research*, September 1992, pp. 155–179.

15 "Tobacco Fact Sheet," World Health Organization, July 2015, www.who.int.

16 Ronald Faber, Gary Christenson, Martina DeZwaan, and James Mitchell, "Two Forms of Compulsive Consumption: Comorbidity of Compulsive Buying and Binge Eating," *Journal of Consumer Research*, December 1995, pp. 296–304; Thomas C. O'Guinn and Ronald J. Faber, "Compulsive Buying," *Journal of Consumer Research*, September 1989, pp. 147–157; Rajan Nataraajan and Brent G. Goff, "Compulsive Buying," in ed. Floyd W. Rudman, *To Have Possessions: A Handbook on Ownership and Property* (Corte Madera, Calif.: Select Press, 1991), pp. 307–328; and Wayne S. DeSarbo and Elizabeth A. Edwards, "Typologies of Compulsive Buying Behavior," *Journal of Consumer Psychology* 5, no. 3, 1996, pp. 231–262.

17 Faber and O'Guinn, "Compulsive Consumption and Credit Abuse"; Ronald J. Faber and Thomas C. O'Guinn, "A Clinical Screener for Compulsive Buying," *Journal of Consumer Research*, December 1992, pp. 459–469; O'Guinn and Faber, "Compulsive Buying"; and James A. Roberts, "Compulsive Buying Among College Students," *Journal of Consumer Affairs*, Winter 1998, pp. 295–319.

18 "Shrinkage on the Rise," *National Retail Federation news release*, June 14, 2011, www.nrf.com; and "Shoplifting: Five-Fingered Discounts," *Economist*, October 23, 2010, p. 81.

19 Joseph C. Nunes, Christopher K. Hsee, and Elke U. Weber, "Why Are People So Prone to Steal Software?" *Journal of Public Policy and Marketing* 23, Spring 2004, pp. 43–53.

20 Rick Jervis, "Discount-Seeking Consumers Swipe Newspapers to Pad Savings," *USA Today*, August 17, 2011, www.usatoday.com.

21 Ronald A. Fullerton and Girish Punj, "The Unintended Consequences of the Culture of Consumption," *Consumption, Markets, and Culture* 1, no. 4, 1998, pp. 393–423.

22 Dena Cox, Anthony p. Cox, and George p. Moschis, "When Consumer Behavior Goes Bad," *Journal of Consumer Marketing*, September 1990, pp. 149–159.

23 Paul Bernstein, "Cheating—The New National Pastime?" *Business*, October–December 1985, pp. 24–33; and Ronald A. Fullerton and Girish Punj, "The Unintended Consequences of the Culture of Consumption: A Historical-Theoretical Analysis of Consumer Misbehavior," *Consumption, Markets and Culture* 1, no. 4, 1998, pp. 393–423.

24 Ronald A. Fullerton and Girish Punj, "Choosing to Misbehave," in eds. Leigh McAlister and Michael Rothschild, *Advances in Consumer Research*, vol. 20 (Provo, Utah: Association for Consumer Research, 1993), pp. 570–574; and Donald R. Katz, *The Big Store* (New York: Penguin, 1988).

25 Cox, Cox, and Moschis, "When Consumer Behavior Goes Bad"; and Fullerton and Punj, "The Unintended Consequences of the Culture of Consumption."

26 Uzma Khan and Ravi Dhar, "Licensing Effect in Consumer Choice," *Journal of Marketing Research*, May 2006, pp. 259–266.

27 John Fetto, "Penny for Your Thoughts," *American Demographics*, September 2000, pp. 8–9.

28 Nina Mazar, On Amir, and Dan Ariely, " The Dishonesty of Honest People: A Theory of Self-Concept Maintenance," *Journal of Marketing Research*, December 2008, pp. 633–644.

29 "Commencement Celebrations Are Not for Profit," *Columbia Spectator (Columbia University)*, April 27, 2014, www.columbiaspectator.com.

30 Marcus George, "Local Dealers Whet Iran's Appetite for U.S. Muscle Cars," *Reuters*, December 20, 2013, www.reuters.com.

31 Keith Wilcox, Hyeong Min Kim, and Sankar Sen, "Why Do Consumers Buy Counterfeit Luxury Brands?" *Journal of Marketing Research*, April 2009, pp. 247–259.

32 Shan Li, "Counterfeiters Go Downscale," *Sacramento Bee*, February 8, 2012, www.sacbee.com; and Mary Lou Costa, "The New Copycats," *Marketing Week*, September 27, 2011, www.marketingweek.co.uk.

33 F. J. Zimmerman, D. A Christakis, and A. N. Meltzoff, "Television and DVD/Video Viewing in Children Younger Than 2 Years," *Archives of Pediatric and Adolescent Medicine* 161, no. 5, 2007, pp. 473–479.

34 Andreas I. Andronikidis and Maria Lambrianidou, "Children's Understanding of Television Advertising: A Grounded Theory Approach," *Psychology & Marketing*, April 2010, pp. 299–322; and Laurene Krasney Meringoff and Gerald S. Lesser, "Children's Ability to Distinguish Television Commercials from Program Material," in ed. R. p. Adler, *The Effect of Television Advertising on Children* (Lexington, Mass.: Lexington Books, 1980), pp. 29–42.

35 M. Carole Macklin, "Preschoolers' Understanding of the Informational Function of Advertising," *Journal of Consumer Research*, September 1987, pp. 229–239; and Merrie Brucks, Gary M. Armstrong, and Marvin E. Goldberg, "Children's Use of Cognitive Defenses Against Television Advertising," *Journal of Consumer Research*, March 1988, pp. 471–482.

36 Mary C. Martin, "Children's Understanding of the Intent of Advertising: A Meta-Analysis," *Journal of Public Policy and Marketing*, Fall 1997, pp. 205–216.

37 Jon Berry, "The New Generation of Kids and Ads," *Adweek's Marketing Week*, April 15, 1991, pp. 25–28; Marvin E. Goldberg and Gerald J. Gorn, "Some Unintended Consequences of TV Advertising to Children," *Journal of Consumer Research*, June 1978, pp. 22–29; and Gary M. Armstrong and Merrie Brucks, "Dealing with Children's Advertising," *Journal of Public Policy and Marketing* 7, 1988, pp. 98–113.

38 Gerald J. Gorn and Renee Florsheim, " The Effects of Commercials for Adult Products on Children," *Journal of Consumer Research*, March 1985, pp. 962–967.

39 "For Kids on the Web, It's an Ad, Ad, Ad, Ad World," *Business-Week*, August 13, 2001, p. 108.

40 Sean Farrell, "Poundland Gets Final Clearance for 99p Stores Takeover," *The Guardian*, September 18, 2015, www.theguardian.com.

41 Michael Felberbaum, "Q&A: Former FDA Commissioner Talks about Tobacco," *Associated Press*, August 5, 2011, http://abcnews.go.com.

42 Gary Strauss, "Graphic Cigarette Labels: Will They Work?" *USA Today*, June 22, 2011, www.usatoday.com.

43 Denis Campbell, "'Plain Packs Will Make Smoking History,'" *Guardian (UK)*, January 24, 2012, www.guardian.co.uk.

44 Jacob Wittich, "Graphic Cigarette Warning Labels Reduce Smoking Rates," *Columbia Chronicle*, November 24, 2014, www.columbiachronicle.com; and Scott Hensley, "Be

Warned: FDA Unveils Graphic Cigarette Labels," *NPR*, June 21, 2011, www.npr.org.

45 See, for example, Kathleen Kelly, Maria Leonora G. Comello, Linda R. Stanley, and Gabriel R. Gonzalez, "The Power of Theme and Language in Multi-Cultural Communities," *Journal of Advertising Research*, September 2010, pp. 265–278.

46 Alex Duff, "Philip Morris Can't Kick 20-Year Ferrari Formula One Habit," *Bloomberg*, May 13, 2015, www.bloomberg.com.

47 Whit Richardson, "NRF Issues Guidelines, But Finds Flash Mobs Less Serious than Assumed," *Security Director News*, August 9, 2011, www.securitydirectornews.com.

48 Andrew Roberts, "Luxury Firms Fight Online Fraudsters Over Expensive Fakes," *Bloomberg*, July 27, 2015, www.bloomberg.com.

49 Meringoff and Lesser, "Children's Ability to Distinguish Television Commercials from Program Material."

50 Mark Sweney, "Morrisons Ad Banned for Targeting Kids," *Guardian (UK)*, October 26, 2011, www.guardian.co.uk.

51 Tyler Pager, "Underage Drinking, Binge Boozing by Minors Is on the Decline," *USA Today*, June 11, 2015, www.usatoday.com.

52 "Youth and Tobacco Use," Centers for Disease Control and Prevention, 2015, www.cdc.gov.

53 Catherine Fitzpatrick, "How Buff Is Enough? Reality Check Is in the Male," *Milwaukee Journal Sentinel*, June 24, 2001, p. 1–L.

54 Nilufer Z. Aydinoglu, and Aradhna Krishna, "Imagining Thin: Why Vanity Sizing Works," *Journal of Consumer Psychology* 22, no. 4, October 2012, pp. 565–572.

55 Isabel Reynolds, "Japan: Feature—Eating Disorders Plague Young Japanese," *Reuters*, June 20, 2001, www.reuters.com.

56 Laura Landro, "The Informed Patient: Amid Focus on Obesity and Diet, Anorexia, Bulimia Are on the Rise," *Wall Street Journal*, March 30, 2004, p. D1.

57 See Anna Brytek-Matera, Lorenzo Maria Donini, Magdalena Krupa, Eleonora Poggiogalle, and Phillipa Hay, "Orthorexia Nervosa and Self-Attitudinal Aspects of Body Image in Female and Male University Students," *Journal of Eating Disorders* 3, no. 2, 2015.

58 See also Debra Lynn Stephens, Ronald p. Hill, and Cynthia Hans on, " The Beauty Myth and Female Consumers: The Controversial Role of Advertising," *Journal of Consumer Affairs*, Summer 1994, pp. 137–154.

59 Laura Stampler, "France Just Banned Ultra-Thin Models," *Time*, April 3, 2015, www.time.com.

60 Leon Festinger, "A Theory of Social Comparison Processes," *Human Relations*, May 1954, pp. 117–140.

61 Michael Häfner, "How Dissimilar Others May Still Resemble the Self," *Journal of Consumer Psychology* 14, no. 2, 2004, pp. 187–196; Mary C. Martin and James W. Gentry, "Stuck in the Model Trap: The Effects of Beautiful Models in Ads on Female Pre-Adolescents and Adolescents," *Journal of Advertising*, Summer 1997, pp. 19–33; and Marsha L. Richins, "Social Comparison and the Idealized Images of Advertising," *Journal of Consumer Research*, June 1991, pp. 71–83.

62 Jennifer J. Argo, Katherine White, and Darren W. Dahl, "Social Comparison Theory and Deception in the Interpersonal Exchange of Consumption Information," *Journal of Consumer Research* 33, no. 1, 2006, pp. 99–108.

63 Darren W. Dahl, Jennifer J. Argo, and Andrea C. Morales, "Social Information in the Retail Environment: The Importance of Consumption Alignment, Referent Identity, and Self-Esteem," *Journal of Consumer Research* 38, no. 5, February 2012, pp. 860–871.

64 Charles S . Gulas and Kim Mc Keage, "Extending Social Comparison: An Examination of the Unintended Consequences of Idealized Advertising Imagery," *Journal of Advertising* 29, no. 2, Summer 2000, pp. 17–28.

65 Dirk Smeesters and Naomi Mandel, "Positive and Negative Media Image Effects on the Self," *Journal of Consumer Research* 32, no. 4, 2006, pp. 576–582.

66 Edith Shalev and Vicki G. Morwitz, "Influence via Comparison-Driven Self-Evaluation and Restoration: The Case of the Low-Status Influencer," *Journal of Consumer Research* 38, no. 5, February 2012, pp. 964–980.

67 Hannah Karp, "The Senior Trip to the Strip," *Wall Street Journal*, April 8, 2005, p. W4.

68 Laurence Arnold, "Link to Other Addictions Raises New Questions About Gambling," *Associated Press*, June 12, 2001.

69 Jeffrey N. Weatherly, John M. Sauter, and Brent M. King, "The 'Big Win' and Resistance to Extinction When Gambling," *Journal of Psychology*, November 2004, pp. 495–504.

70 Kevin Heubusch, " Taking Chances on Casinos," *American Demographics*, May 1997, pp. 35–40; and Rebecca Quick, "For Sports Fans, The Internet Is a Whole New Ball Game," *Wall Street Journal*, September 3, 1998, p. B9.

71 Paul Davies, "New York's Bad Bet," *New York Times*, January 22, 2012, www.nytimes.com; "Report Outlines Grim Future for Racing Industry," *Associated Press*, August 14, 2011, www.wsj.com; and "Slot Machines: The Big Gamble," *CBS News*, June 23, 2011, www.cbsnews.com.

72 Stuart Elliott, "It Only Takes an Instant, Lottery Ads Declare," *New York Times*, May 9, 2011, www.nytimes.com.

73 Matthew Garrahan, "Call for Change to US Gambling Laws," *Financial Times*, August 14, 2011, www.ft.com; and Matt Viser, "Internet Gambling Is a Target of Patrick Bill: Casino Initiative Makes It Illegal," *Boston Globe*, November 10, 2007, p. A1.

74 Tracy Johnson, "Online Gambling: The Morality Problem for Governments," *CBC News*, March 26, 2015, www.cbc.ca/news.

75 Marie Ng et al., "Global, Regional, and National Prevalence of Overweight and Obesity in Children and Adults During 1980–2013: A Systematic Analysis for the Global Burden of Disease Study 2013," *The Lancet* 384, no. 9945, August 30, 2014, pp. 766–781.

76 Shari Roan, "Obesity Rates in U.S. Appear to Be Finally Leveling Off," *Los Angeles Times*, January 17, 2012, www.latimes.com.

77 Joseph p. Redden and Kelly L. Haws, "Healthy Satiation: The Role of Decreasing Desire in Effective Self-Control," *Journal of Consumer Research* 39, no. 5, March 2013, pp. 1100–1114.

78 Brian Wansink and Pierre Chandon, "Can 'Low-Fat' Nutrition Labels Lead to Obesity?" *Journal of Marketing Research*, November 2006, pp. 605–617.

79 Gina S. Mohr, Donald R. Lichtenstein, and Chris Janiszewski, "The Effect of Marketer-Suggested Serving Size on Consumer Responses: The Unintended Consequences of Consumer Attention to Calorie Information," *Journal of Marketing* 76, no. 1, January 2012, pp. 59–75.

80 Sabrina Tavernise, "F.D.A. Extends Deadline for Calorie Counts on Menus," *New York Times*, July 9, 2015, www.nytimes.com; and Pierre Chandon and Brian Wansink, "Is Obesity Caused by Calorie Underestimation? " *Journal of Marketing Research*, February 2007, pp. 84–99.

81 Rajagopal Raghunathan, Rebecca Walker Naylor, and Wayne D. Hoyer, "The Unhealthy = Tasty Intuition and Its Effects on Taste Inferences, Enjoyment, and Choice of Food Products," *Journal of Marketing*, October 2006, pp. 170–184.

82 Caglar Irmak, Beth Vallen, and Stefanie Rosen Robinson, "The Impact of Product Name on Dieters' and Nondieters' Food Evaluations and Consumption," *Journal of Consumer Research* 38, no. 2, August 2011, pp. 390–405.

83 Alex Hutchinson, "How Salad Can Make Us Fat," *New York Times*, October 25, 2015, SR-10.

84 See Morgan Poor, Adam Duhachek, and H. Shanker Krishnan, "How Images of Other Consumers Influence Subsequent Taste Perceptions," *Journal of Marketing* 77, no. 6, November 2013, pp. 124–139; and M. L. Lowe and K. L. Haws, "(Im)moral Support: The Social Outcomes of Parallel Self-Control Decisions," *Journal of Consumer Research* 41, no. 2, August 2014, pp. 489–505.

85 Arul Mishra, Himanshu Mishra, and Tamara M. Masters, "The Influence of Bite Size on Quantity of Food Consumed: A Field Study," *Journal of Consumer Research* 38, no. 5, February 2012, pp. 791–795; and Koert Van Ittersum and Brian Wansink, "Plate Size and Color Suggestibility: The Delboeuf Illusion's Bias on Serving and Eating Behavior," *Journal of Consumer Research* 39, no. 2, August 2012, pp. 215–228.

86 David DuBois, Derek D. Rucker, and Adam D. Galinsky, "Super Size Me: Product Size as a Signal of Status," *Journal of Consumer Research* 38, no. 6, April 2012, pp. 1047–1062.

87 Kelly L. Haws and Karen Page Winterich, "When Value Trumps Health in a Supersized World," *Journal of Marketing* 77, no. 3, May 2013, pp. 48–64.

88 Debabrata Talukdar and Charles Lindsey, "To Buy or Not to Buy: Consumers' Demand Response Patterns for Healthy Versus Unhealthy Food," *Journal of Marketing* 77, no. 2, March 2013, pp. 124–138.

89 Eve M. Caudill and Patrick E. Murphy, "Consumer Online Privacy: Legal and Ethical Issues," *Journal of Public Policy and Marketing* 19, no. 1, Spring 2000, pp. 7–19.

90 Julia Angwin, "Latest in Web Tracking: Stealthy 'Supercookies,'" *Wall Street Journal*, August 18, 2011, www.wsj.com.

91 Ellen Foxman and Paula Kilcoyne, "Information Technology, Marketing Practice, and Consumer Privacy," *Journal of Public Policy and Marketing*, Spring 1993, p. 106; and Kim Bartel Sheehan and Mariea Grubbs Hoy, "Dimensions of Privacy Concern Among Online Consumers," *Journal of Public Policy and Marketing* 19, no. 1, Spring 2000, pp. 62–73.

92 Carole John, "We Say We Want Privacy Online, But Our Actions Say Otherwise," *Harvard Business Review*, October 16, 2015, http://hbr.org.

93 Michael Moss, "A Web CEO's Elusive Goal: Privacy," *Wall Street Journal*, February 7, 2000, pp. B1, B6.

94 Bob Tedeschi, "Poll Says Identity Theft Concerns Rose After High-Profile Breaches," *New York Times*, March 10, 2005, p. G5.

95 Pamela Paul, "Mixed Signals," *American Demographics*, July 2001, pp. 45–49; and Joseph Phelps, Glen Nowak, and Elizabeth Ferrell, "Privacy Concerns and Consumer Willingness to Provide Personal Information," *Journal of Public Policy and Marketing* 19, no. 1, Spring 2000, pp. 27–41.

96 Leslie K. John, Alessandro Acquisti, and George Loewenstein, "Strangers on a Plane: Context-Dependent Willingness to Divulge Sensitive Information," *Journal of Consumer Research* 37, no. 5, February 2011, pp. 858–873; Patricia A. Norberg and Daniel R. Horne, "Privacy Attitudes and Privacy-Related Behavior, *Psychology and Marketing* 24, no. 10, 2007, pp. 829–847; and John, "We Say We Want Privacy Online, But Our Actions Say Otherwise."

97 Mary J. Culnan, "Protecting Privacy Online: Is Self-Regulation Working?" *Journal of Public Policy and Marketing* 19, no.

1, Spring 2000, pp. 20–26; and Anthony D. Miyazaki and Ana Fernandez, "Internet Privacy and Security," *Journal of Public Policy and Marketing* 19, no. 1, Spring 2000, pp. 54–61.

98 George R. Milne, "Privacy and Ethical Issues in Database /Interactive Marketing and Public Policy," *Journal of Public Policy and Marketing* 19, no. 1, Spring 2000, pp. 1–6.

99 Joan Ryan, "Steroids? Alcohol Is the Real Problem," *San Francisco Chronicle*, March 17, 2005, www.sfgate.com; Vanessa O'Connell and Christopher Lawton, "Alcohol TV Ads Ignite Bid to Curb," *Wall Street Journal*, December 18, 2002, p. B2; "Study: Kids Remember Beer Ads," *ClariNet Electronic News Service*, February 11, 1994; Fara Warner, "Cheers! It's Happy Hour in Cyberspace," *Wall Street Journal*, March 15, 1995, pp. B1, B4; and Kirk Davidson, "Looking for Abundance of Opposition to TV Liquor Ads," *Marketing News*, January 6, 1997, pp. 4, 30.

100 Nicholas Bakalar, "Ad Limits Seen as Way to Curb Youth Smoking and Drinking," *New York Times*, May 22, 2007, p. F5.

101 See Jerry L. Grenard, Clyde W. Dent, and Alan W. Stacy, "Exposure to Alcohol Advertisements and Teenage Alcohol-Related Problems," *Pediatrics (American Academy of Pediatrics)* 131, no. 2, February 2013, pp. e369–e379; and Alyssa Bindman, "Children Exposed to Alcohol Ads More Likely to Drink," *The Nation's Health* 37, no. 6, 2007, p. 24.

102 Kathleen J. Kelly, Michael D. Slater, and David Karan, "Image Advertisements' Influence on Adolescents' Perceptions of the Desirability of Beer and Cigarettes," *Journal of Public Policy and Marketing*, Fall 2002, pp. 295–304.

103 James D. Sargent, Susanne Tanski, and Mike Stoolmiller, "Influence of Motion Picture Rating on Adolescent Response to Movie Smoking," *Pediatrics (American Academy of Pediatrics)* 130, no. 2, August 2012.

104 Russell Parsons, "Heineken Bids to Make Responsible Drinking 'Aspirational,'" *Marketing Week*, December 12, 2011, www.marketingweek.co.uk.

105 Lisa R. Szykman, Paul N. Bloom, and Jennifer Blazing, "Does Corporate Sponsorship of a Socially Oriented Message Make a Difference?" *Journal of Consumer Psychology* 14, no. 1/2, 2004, pp. 13–20.

106 Joanne Richard, "Curves Ahead: How Plus-Size Shopping Is Changing," *Toronto Sun*, October 2, 2015, www.torontosun.com; and Calmetta Y. Coleman, "Can't Be Too Thin, but Plus-Size Models Get More Work Now," *Wall Street Journal*, May 3, 1999, pp. A1, A10.

107 José Antonio Rosa, Ellen C. Garbarino, and Alan J. Malter, "Keeping the Body in Mind: The Influence of Body Esteem and Body Boundary Aberration on Consumer Beliefs and Purchase Intentions," *Journal of Consumer Psychology* 16, no. 1, 2006, pp. 79–91.

108 Sally Goll Beatty, "Women's Views of Their Lives Aren't Reflected by Advertisers," *Wall Street Journal*, December 19, 1995, p. B2.

109 Kristina Monllos, "How Always' Brand Director Turned an Ad Into a Movement That Shattered Stereotypes," *Adweek*, October 18, 2015, www.adweek.com.

110 Michelle Ainsworth, "David Schwarz's Responsible Gambling Program Named Best in the World," *Herald Sun (Australia)*, January 25, 2012, www.heraldsun.com.au.

111 Sara Kim and Ann L. McGill, "Gaming with Mr. Slot or Gaming the Slot Machine? Power, Anthropomorphism, and Risk Perception," *Journal of Consumer Research*, June 2011, pp. 94–107.

112 Betsy McKay, "The Children's Menu: Do Ads Make Kids Fat?" *Wall Street Journal*, January 27, 2005, pp. B1, B7.

113 Gemma Charles, "Junk Food 'Super Complaint,'" *Marketing*, February 9, 2012, www.marketingmagazine.co.uk.

114 "Healthier School Day: Tools for Schools—Focusing on Smart Snacks," U.S. Department of Agriculture Food and Nutrition Service, August 27, 2015, http://www.fns.usda.gov /healthierschoolday/tools-schools-focusing-smart-snacks.

115 Duane Stanford, "Indra Nooyi Rediscovers the Joy of Pepsi," *Businessweek*, February 2, 2012, www.businessweek.com.

116 Karlene Lukovitz, "Bolthouse Farms Leverages Innovative Instagram Tech," *Media Post*, December 12, 2013, www.medi-apost.com; and David Wright, "Baby Carrots: The Next Snack Food?" *ABC News*, February 7, 2012, http://abcnews.go.com.

117 Julie Jargon, "Less Soda Being Chosen With McDonald's Happy Meals," *Wall Street Journal*, June 25, 2015, www.wsj .com.

118 Kim Komando, "Stop Facebook Targeted Ads and Tracking," *USA Today*, October 9, 2015, www.usatoday.com.

119 John Naughton, "EU Cookie Laws Could Cause Unwary Firms to Get Their Fingers Burnt," *Guardian (UK)*, December 17, 2011, www.guardian.co.uk.

120 Mark Scott, "Privacy: A Question Over the Reach of Europe's 'Right to Be Forgotten,'" *New York Times*, February 1, 2015, www.nytimes.com; and Teri Schultz, "EU Outlines Online Privacy Recommendations," *National Public Radio*, January 27, 2012, www.npr.org.

121 Bree Fowler, "New California Law Extends Privacy Rights to Electronic Data," *ABC News*, October 9, 2015, http://abcnews. go.com.

122 Wendy Davis, "Ad Industry to Start Enforcing Mobile Privacy Rules in September," *Media Post*, May 7, 2015, www.media-post.com; and Tim Peterson, "DAA Debuts Consumer Education Campaign for Online Behavioral Advertising," *Direct Marketing News*, January 20, 2012, www.dmnews.com.

123 Eric Griffith, "How to Stay Anonymous Online," *PC Magazine*, February 10, 2014, www.pcmag.com; and Roland T. Rust, p. K. Kannan, and Peng Na, " The Customer Economics of Internet Privacy," *Journal of the Academy of Marketing Science* 30, Fall 2002, pp. 455–464.

124 John A. McCarty and L. J. Shrum, "The Influence of Individualism, Collectivism, and Locus of Control on Environmental Beliefs and Behavior," *Journal of Public Policy and Marketing* 20, no. 1, Spring 2001, pp. 93–104.

125 "Europe Expands Electronic Waste Collection, Recycling Law," *Environment News Service*, January 20, 2012, www .ens-newswire.com.

126 Jack Neff, "Eco-Wal-Mart Costs Marketers Green," *Advertising Age*, October 1, 2007, pp. 3, 42

127 Amy Patterson, "Turning Trash into Cash for the Farmington Pet Adoption Center," *Daily Journal Online (Park Hills, MO)*, September 26, 2015, www.dailyjournalonline.com.

128 See "Leaders Say Europe's Waste-Recovery Goal Is Achievable," *European Plastics News*, February 7, 2012, www.plastics-news.com.

129 See Steve Lohr, "First, Make Money. Also, Do Good," *New York Times*, August 13, 2011, www.nytimes.com.

130 Wong Lai Cheng and Jamilah Ahmad, "Incorporating Stakeholder Approach in Corporate Social Responsibility," *Social Responsibility Journal* 6, no. 4, 2005, pp. 593–610.

131 Carlos J. Torelli, Alokparna Basu Monga, and Andrew M. Kaikati, "Doing Poorly by Doing Good: Corporate Social Responsibility and Brand Concepts," *Journal of Consumer Research* 38, no. 5, February 2012, pp. 948–963.

132 Russell Belk , John Painter, and Richard Semenik, "Preferred Solutions to the Energy Crisis as a Function of Causal Attributions," *Journal of Consumer Research*, December 1981, pp. 306–312.

133 Pam Scholder Ellen, Joshua Lyle Wiener, and Cathy Cobb-Walgren, "The Role of Perceived Consumer Effectiveness in Motivating Environmentally Conscious Behaviors," *Journal of Public Policy and Marketing*, Fall 1991, pp. 102–117; and Thomas C. Kinnear, James R. Taylor, and Sadrudin A. Ahmed, "Ecologically Concerned Consumers: Who Are They?" *Journal of Marketing*, April 1972, pp. 46–57.

134 Ann Kronrod, Amir Grinstein, and Luc Wathieu, "Go Green! Should Environmental Messages Be So Assertive?" *Journal of Marketing* 76, no. 1, January 2012, pp. 95–102.

135 Rik Pieters, Tammo Bijmo, H. Fred van Raaij, and Mark de Kruijk, "Consumers' Attributions of Proenvironmental Behavior, Motivation, and Ability to Self and Others," *Journal of Public Policy and Marketing*, Fall 1998, pp. 215–225.

136 Noah J. Goldstein, Robert B. Cialdini, and Vladas Griskevicius, "A Room with a Viewpoint: Using Social Norms to Motivate Environmental Conservation in Hotels," *Journal of Consumer Research*, October 2008, pp. 472–482.

137 Julie R. Irwin and Rebecca Walker Naylor, "Ethical Decisions and Response Mode Compatibility: Weighting of Ethical Attributes in Consideration Sets Formed by Excluding versus Including Product Alternatives," *Journal of Marketing Research*, April 2009, pp. 234–246.

138 Ying-Ching Lin and Chiu-Chi Angela Chang, "Double Standard: The Role of Environmental Consciousness in Green Product Usage," *Journal of Marketing* 76, no. 5, September 2012, pp. 125–134.

139 Jeff Plungis, "Volkswagen Emissions Scandal: Forty Years of Greenwashing: The Well-Travelled Road Taken by VW," *The Independent*, September 25, 2015, www.independent. co.uk; and Jeff Plungis, "Volkswagen Admits to Cheating on U.S. Emissions Tests," *Bloomberg*, September 18, 2015, www .bloomberg.com.

140 Bruce Horovitz, "Starbucks: 99% Ethically Sourced Java," *USA Today*, April 10, 2015, www.usatoday.com.

141 John Peloza, Katherine White, and Jingzhi Shang, "Good and Guilt-Free: The Role of Self-Accountability in Influencing Preferences for Products with Ethical Attributes," *Journal of Marketing* 77, no. 1, January 2013, pp. 104–119.

142 Bob M. Fennis, Loes Janssen, and Kathleen D. Vohs, "Acts of Benevolence: A Limited-Resource Account of Compliance with Charitable Requests," *Journal of Consumer Research*, April 2009, pp. 906–924.

143 Wendy Liu and Jennifer Aaker, "The Happiness of Giving: The Time-Ask Effect," *Journal of Consumer Research*, October 2008, pp. 543–557.

144 Karen Page Winterich, Saerom Lee, and William T. Ross Jr., "I'm Moral but I Won't Help You: The Distinct Roles of Empathy and Justice in Donations," *Journal of Consumer Research* 41, no. 3, October 2014, pp. 678–696.

145 Robert W. Smith, David Faro, and Katherine A. Burson, "More for the Many: The Influence of Entitativity on Charitable Giving," *Journal of Consumer Research* 39, no. 5, March 2013, pp. 961–976.

146 Karen Page Winterich and Michael J. Barone, "Warm Glow or Cold, Hard Cash? Social Identify Effects on Consumer Choice for Donation Versus Discount Promotions," *Journal of Marketing Research* 48, no. 5, October 2011, pp. 855–868.

147 David Mills, "World Giving Index 2011," *Guardian (UK)*, December 20, 2011, www.guardian.co.uk.

148 Liza Ramrayka, "Doing the Funny Business: Why Red Nose Day USA Paid Off," *The Guardian*, May 28, 2015, www.theguardian.com.

149 Christine M. Bennett, Hakkyun Kim, and Barbara Loken, "Corporate Sponsorships May Hurt Nonprofits: Understanding Their Effects on Charitable Giving," *Journal of Consumer Psychology* 23, no. 3, July 2013, pp. 288–300.

150 Xinyue Zhou, Tim Wildschut, Constantine Kan Shi Sedikides, and Cong Feng, "Nostalgia: The Gift That Keeps on Giving," *Journal of Consumer Research* 39, no. 1, June 2012, pp. 39–50.

151 Debra Basil, Mary Runte, Michael Basil, and John Usher, "Company Support for Employee Volunteerism," *Journal of Business Research*, January 2011, pp. 61–66.

152 David A. Jones, "Does Serving the Community Also Serve the Company?" *Journal of Occupational and Organizational Psychology*, December 2010, pp. 857–878.

153 Katherine White, Rhiannon MacDonnell, and John H. Ellard, "Belief in a Just World: Consumer Intentions and Behaviors Toward Ethical Products," *Journal of Marketing* 76, no. 1, January 2012, pp. 103–118.

154 N. Craig Smith and Elizabeth Cooper-Martin, "Ethics and Target Marketing," *Journal of Marketing*, July 1997, pp. 1–20; Robert O. Hermann, " The Tactics of Consumer Resistance:

Group Action and Marketplace Exit," in eds. Leigh McAlister and Michael Rothschild, *Advances in Consumer Research*, vol. 20 (Provo, Utah: Association for Consumer Research, 1993), pp. 130–134; and Lisa Penaloza and Linda L. Price, "Consumer Resistance: A Conceptual Overview," in eds. Leigh McAlister and Michael L. Rothschild, *Advances in Consumer Research*, vol. 20 (Provo, Utah: Association for Consumer Research, 1993), pp. 123–128.

155 Robert V. Kozinets and Jay M. Handelman, "Adversaries of Consumption: Consumer Movements, Activism, and Ideology," *Journal of Consumer Research* 31, no. 3, 2004, pp. 691–704.

156 Mike Hager, "Adbusters Co-Founder Kalle Lasn Sees Power with the People," *Globe and Mail (Toronto)*, March 26, 2015, www.theglobeandmail.com.

157 Jill Gabrielle Klein, N. Craig Smith, and Andrew John, "Why We Boycott: Consumer Motivations for Boycott Participation," *Journal of Marketing Research*, July 2004, pp. 92–109; and Sakar Sen, Zeynep Gürhan-Canli, and Vicki Morwitz, "Withholding Consumption: A Social Dilemma Perspective on Consumer Boycotts," *Journal of Consumer Research*, December 2001, pp. 399–417.

158 Jonathan Baron, "Consumer Attitudes About Personal and Political Action," *Journal of Consumer Psychology* 8, no. 3, 1999, pp. 261–275.

Glossary

A

Ability The extent to which consumers have the resources needed to make an outcome happen.

Absolute threshold The minimal level of stimulus intensity needed to detect a stimulus.

Accommodation theory The more effort one puts forth in trying to communicate with an ethnic group, the more positive the reaction.

Acculturation Learning how to adapt to a new culture.

Acquisition The process by which a consumer comes to own an offering.

Activities, interests, and opinions (AIOs) The three components of lifestyles.

Actual identity schema A set of multiple, salient identities that reflects our self-concept.

Actual state Current state; the way things actually are.

Adaptability The extent to which the innovation can foster new styles.

Addiction Excessive behavior typically brought on by a chemical dependency.

Additive difference model Compensatory model in which brands are compared by attribute, two brands at a time.

Adoption A purchase of an innovation by an individual consumer or household.

Affect Low-level feelings.

Affect referral A simple type of affective tactic whereby we simply remember our feelings for the product or service.

Affect-related tactics Tactics based on feelings.

Affective decision-making model The process by which consumers base their decision on feelings and emotions.

Affective forecasting A prediction of how you will feel in the future.

Affective function Katz' notion that our feelings influence our attitudes.

Affective involvement Interest in expending emotional energy and evoking deep feelings about an offering, activity, or decision.

Affective response When consumers generate feelings and images in response to a message.

Agentic goal Goal that stresses mastery, self-assertiveness, self-efficacy, strength, and no emotion.

Alternative-based strategy Making a noncomparable choice based on an overall evaluation.

Ambiguity of information When there is not enough information to confirm or disprove one's hypotheses.

Ambivalence When our evaluations regarding a brand are mixed (both positive and negative).

Anchoring and adjustment process Starting with an initial evaluation and adjusting it with additional information.

Appraisal theory A theory of emotion that proposes that emotions are based on an individual's assessment of a situation or an outcome and its relevance to his or her goals.

Approach-approach conflict An inner struggle about which offering to acquire when each can satisfy an important but different need.

Approach-avoidance conflict An inner struggle about acquiring or consuming an offering that fulfills one need but fails to fulfill another.

Aspirational reference group A group that we admire and desire to be like.

Associative reference group A group to which we currently belong.

Attention How much mental activity a consumer devotes to a stimulus.

Attitude A relatively global and enduring evaluation of an object, issue, person, or action.

Attitude accessibility How easily an attitude can be remembered.

Attitude confidence How strongly we hold an attitude.

Attitude persistence How long our attitude lasts.

Attitude resistance How difficult it is to change an attitude.

Attitude toward the act (Aact) How we feel about doing something.

Attitude toward the ad (Aad) Whether the consumer likes or dislikes an ad.

Attraction effect When the addition of an inferior brand to a consideration set increases the attractiveness of the dominant brand.

Attractiveness A source characteristic that evokes favorable attitudes if a source is physically attractive, likable, familiar, or similar to ourselves.

Attribute balancing Picking a brand because it scores equally well on certain attributes rather than faring unequally on these attributes.

Attribute-based strategy Making a noncomparable choice by making abstract representations of comparable attributes.

Attribute determinance Attribute that is both salient and diagnostic.

Attribute processing Comparing brands, one attribute at a time.

Attribution theory A theory of how individuals find explanations for events.

Autonomic decision Decision equally likely to be made by the husband or wife, but not by both.

Availability heuristic Basing judgments on events that are easier to recall.

Avoidance-avoidance conflict An inner struggle about which offering to acquire when neither can satisfy an important but different need.

B

Baby boomers Individuals born between 1946 and 1964.

Base-rate information How often an event really occurs on average.

Behavioral intention (BI) What we intend to do.

Behavior (B) What we do.

Belief discrepancy When a message is different from what consumers believe.

Black market An illegal market in which consumers pay often exorbitant amounts for items not readily available.

Boycott An organized activity in which consumers avoid purchasing products or services from a company whose policies or practices are seen as unfair or unjust.

Brand-choice congruence The purchase of the same brand as members of a group.

Brand community A specialized group of consumers with a structured set of relationships involving a particular brand, fellow customers of that brand, and the product in use.

Brand extension Using the brand name of a product with a well-developed image on a product in a different category.

Brand familiarity Easy recognition of a well-known brand.

Brand image Specific type of schema that captures what a brand stands for and how favorably it is viewed.

Brand loyalty Buying the same brand repeatedly because of a strong preference for it.

Brand personality The set of associations included in a schema that reflect a brand's personification.

Brand processing Evaluating one brand at a time.

C

Central-route processing The attitude formation and change process when effort is high.

Choice tactics Simple rules of thumb used to make low-effort decisions.

Class average Families with an average income in a particular class.

Classic A successful innovation that has a lengthy product life cycle.

Classical conditioning Producing a response to a stimulus by repeatedly pairing it with another stimulus that automatically produces this response.

Closure The principle that individuals have a need to organize perceptions so that they form a meaningful whole.

Clustering The grouping of consumers according to common characteristics, such as demographics and consumption life-styles, using statistical techniques.

Co-branding An arrangement by which two brands form a partnership to benefit from the power of both.

Cocreation Actively involving consumers in creating value through participation in new product development, among other marketing activities.

Coercive power The extent to which the group has the capacity to deliver rewards and sanctions.

Cognitive decision-making model The process by which consumers combine items of information about attributes to reach a decision.

Cognitive function How attitudes influence our thoughts.

Cognitive involvement Interest in thinking about and learning information pertinent to an offering, an activity, or a decision.

Cognitive response Thought we have in response to a communication.

Communal goal Goal that stresses affiliation and fostering harmonious relations with others, submissiveness, emotionality, and home orientation.

Comparative message A message that makes direct comparisons with competitors.

Compatibility The extent to which an innovation is consistent with one's needs, values, norms, or behaviors.

Compensatory consumption The consumer behavior of buying products or services to offset frustrations or difficulties in life.

Compensatory model A mental cost-benefit analysis model in which negative features can be compensated for by positive ones.

Complexity The extent to which an innovation is complicated and difficult to understand or use.

Compliance Doing what the group or social influencer asks.

Comprehension The process of extracting higher-order meaning from what we have perceived in the context of what we already know.

Compromise effect When a brand gains share because it is an intermediate rather than an extreme option.

Compulsive behavior An irresistible urge to perform an irrational act.

Concreteness The extent to which a stimulus is capable of being imagined.

Confirmation bias Tendency to recall information that reinforces or confirms our overall beliefs rather than contradicting them, thereby making our judgment or decision more positive than it should be.

Conformity The tendency to behave in an expected way.

Conjoint analysis A research technique to determine the relative importance and appeal of different levels of an offering's attributes.

Conjunctive model A noncompensatory model that sets minimum cutoffs to reject "bad" options.

Connative function How attitudes influence our behavior.

Connectedness function The use of products as symbols of our personal connections to significant people, events, or experiences.

Conservation behavior Limiting the use of scarce natural resources for the purposes of environmental preservation.

Consideration (or evoked set) The subset of top-of-mind brands evaluated when making a choice.

Conspicuous consumption The acquisition and display of goods and services to show off one's status.

Conspicuous waste Visibly buying products and services that one never uses.

Construal level theory Theory describing the different levels of abstractness in the associations that a consumer has about concepts (people, products, brands, and activities) and how the consumer's psychological distance influences the abstractness of the associations (far = abstract, close = concrete) and his or her behavior.

Consumer behavior The totality of consumers' decisions with respect to the acquisition, consumption, and disposition of goods, services, time, and ideas by human decision-making units (over time).

Consumer ethics Rules of acceptable conduct (such as honesty, fairness, and respect) that apply to the range of consumer behaviors.

Consumer memory The persistence of learning over time, via the storage and retrieval of information, either consciously or unconsciously.

Consumer socialization The process by which we learn to become consumers.

Contagion The degree to which consumers influence each other in the diffusion of a new product.

Continuous innovation An innovation that has a limited effect on existing consumption patterns.

Counterargument (CA) Thought that disagrees with the message.

Credibility Extent to which the source is trustworthy, expert, or has status.

Cultural categories The natural grouping of objects that reflect our culture.

Cultural principles Ideas or values that specify how aspects of our culture are organized and/or how they should be perceived or evaluated.

Culture The typical or expected behaviors, norms, and ideas that characterize a group of people.

Customer retention The practice of retaining customers by building long-term relationships.

Cutoff level For each attribute, the point at which a brand is rejected with a noncompensatory model.

D

Data mining Searching for patterns in a company database that offer clues to customer needs, preferences, and behaviors.

Deal-prone consumer A consumer who is more likely to be influenced by price.

Decay The weakening of memory strength over time.

Decision-framing The initial reference point or anchor in the decision process.

Decision-making Making a selection among options or courses of action.

Diagnostic information That which helps us discriminate among objects.

Differential threshold/just noticeable difference (jnd) The intensity difference needed between two stimuli before they are perceived to be different.

Diffusion The percentage of the population that has adopted an innovation at a specific point in time.

Disconfirmation When expectations do not match the actual brand, product or service performance, because performance is either better or worse than expected.

Discontinuous innovation An offering that is so new that we have never known anything like it before.

Disjunctive model A noncompensatory model that sets acceptable cutoffs to find options that are "good."

Disposition The process by which a consumer discards an offering.

Dissatisfaction The feeling that a purchase decision, consumption experience, or disposition decision falls short of one's expectations.

Dissociative reference group A group we do not want to emulate.

Divestment ritual Ritual enacted at the disposition stage that is designed to wipe away all traces of our personal meaning in a product.

Dogmatism A tendency to be resistant to change or new ideas.

Domain-specific values Values that may only apply to a particular area of activities.

Door-in-the-face technique A technique designed to induce compliance by first asking an individual to comply with a very large and possibly outrageous request, followed by a smaller and more reasonable request.

Downward mobility Losing one's social standing.

Dramas Ads with characters, a plot, and a story.

Dual-mediation hypothesis Explains how attitudes toward the ad influence brand attitudes.

Dynamically continuous innovation An innovation that has a pronounced effect on consumption practices and often involves a new technology.

E

Earned status Status acquired later in life through achievements.

Ego depletion Outcome of decision-making effort that results in mental resources being exhausted.

Elaboration Transferring information into long-term memory by processing it at deeper levels.

Elimination-by-aspects model Similar to the lexicographic model but adds the notion of acceptable cutoffs.

Embedded market Market in which the social relationships among buyers and sellers change the way the market operates.

Emblematic function The use of products to symbolize membership in social groups.

Embodiment Connection between mind and body that influences and expresses consumer self-control and behavior.

Emotional accounting The intensity of positive or negative feelings associated with each mental "account" for saving or spending.

Emotional appeal A message designed to elicit an emotional response.

Emotional contagion A message designed to induce consumers to vicariously experience a depicted emotion.

Emotional detachment Emotionally disposing of a possession.

Encoding of evidence Processing the information that one experiences.

Endowment effect When ownership increases the value of an item.

Enduring involvement Long-term interest in an offering, activity, or decision.

Episodic (autobiographical) memory Knowledge we have about ourselves and our personal, past experiences.

Equity theory A theory about the fairness of exchanges between individuals, which helps in understanding consumer satisfaction and dissatisfaction.

Estimation of likelihood Judging how likely it is that something will occur.

Ethical sourcing Obtaining supplies and making products in accordance with social responsibility and sustainability values.

Ethnic group Subculture with a similar heritage and values.

Ethnographic research In-depth qualitative research using observations and interviews (often over repeated occasions) of consumers in real-world surroundings. Often used to study the meaning that consumers ascribe to a product or consumption phenomenon.

Evaluative conditioning A special case of classical conditioning, producing an affective response by repeatedly pairing a neutral conditioned stimulus with an emotionally charged unconditioned stimulus.

Even-a-penny-will-help technique A technique designed to induce compliance by asking individuals to do a very small favor—one that is so small that it almost does not qualify as a favor.

Expectancy-value model A widely used model that explains how attitudes form and change.

Expectation Belief (hypothesis) about the performance of a brand, product, or service.

Explicit memory When consumers are consciously aware that they remember something.

Exponential diffusion curve A diffusion curve characterized by rapid initial growth.

Exposure The process by which the consumer comes in physical contact with a stimulus.

Exposure to evidence Actually experiencing the brand, product, or service.

Expressiveness function The use of products as symbols to demonstrate our uniqueness—how we stand out as different from others.

Expressive roles Roles that involve an indication of family norms.

Extended family The nuclear family plus relatives such as grandparents, aunts, uncles, and cousins.

External search The process of collecting information from outside sources, for example, magazines, dealers, and ads.

Extremeness aversion Options that are extreme on some attributes are less attractive than those with a moderate level of those attributes.

F

Fad A successful innovation that has a very short product life cycle.

Fairness in the exchange The perception that the inputs and outputs of people involved in an exchange are equal.

Family life cycle Different stages of family life, depending on the age of the parents and how many children are living at home.

Fashion A successful innovation that has a moderately long and potentially cyclical product life cycle.

Favorability The degree to which we like or dislike something.

Fear appeal A message that stresses negative consequences.

Felt involvement The consumer's experience of being motivated with respect to a product or service, or decisions and actions about these.

Figure and ground The principle that people interpret stimuli in the context of a background.

Financial risk The extent to which buying, using, or disposing of an offering is perceived to have the potential to create financial harm.

Focus group A form of interview involving 8 to 12 people; a moderator leads the group and asks participants to discuss a product, concept, or other marketing stimulus.

Foot-in-the-door technique A technique designed to induce compliance by getting an individual to agree first to a small favor, then to a larger one, and then to an even larger one.

Frame switching Stimulated by language cues, a consumer who identifies with more than one culture will activate the aspects of his or her self-concept that relate to that language's cultural background.

Fraudulent symbol Symbol that becomes so widely adopted that it loses its status.

Frequency heuristic Belief based simply on the number of supporting arguments or amount of repetition.

Functional innovation A new product, service, attribute, or idea that has utilitarian benefits that are different from or better than those of alternatives.

Functional need Need that motivates the search for offerings that solve consumption-related problems.

G

Gatekeeper A source that controls the flow of information.

Gender Biological state of being male or female.

Generation X Individuals born between 1965 and 1979.

Gestation stage The first stage of gift giving, when we consider what to give someone.

Global values A person's most enduring, strongly held, and abstract values that hold in many situations.

Goal Outcome that we would like to achieve.

Goal-derived category Things viewed as belonging in the same category because they serve the same goals.

Gray market Individuals over 65 years old.

Greenwashing The misleading use of environmental claims for marketing purposes.

Grooming ritual Ritual we engage in to bring out or maintain the best in special products.

Grouping The tendency to group stimuli to form a unified picture or impression.

H

Habit A learned behavior that involves regular performance of the same act repeatedly over time. Behaviors are often performed unconsciously and may be difficult to discontinue.

Habituation The process by which a stimulus loses its attention-getting abilities by virtue of its familiarity.

Hedonic dimension When an ad creates positive or negative feelings.

Hedonic need Need that relates to sensory pleasure.

Hedonic or aesthetic innovation An innovation that appeals to our aesthetic, pleasure-seeking, and/or sensory needs.

Hedonism The principle of pleasure seeking.

Heuristics Simple rules of thumb that are used to make judgments.

High-effort hierarchy of effects A purchase of an innovation based on considerable decision-making effort.

Homophily The overall similarity among members in the social system.

Household A single person living alone or a group of individuals who live together in a common dwelling, regardless of whether they are related.

Household decision roles Roles that different members play in a household decision.

Husband-dominant decision Decision made primarily by the male head-of-household.

Hypothesis generation Forming expectations about the product or service.

Hypothesis testing Comparing prior belief or expectations with new information, such as evidence from experience.

I

Ideal identity schema A set of ideas about how the identity would be indicated in its ideal form.

Ideal state The way we want things to be.

Imagery Multi-sensory mental representation (image) of a stimulus or event.

Implicit memory Memory without any conscious attempt at remembering something.

Impulse purchase An unexpected purchase based on a strong feeling.

Incidental learning Learning that occurs from repetition rather than from conscious processing.

Independent variable The "treatment" or the entity that researchers vary in a research project.

Inept set Options that are unacceptable when making a decision.

Inert set Options toward which consumers are indifferent.

Informational influence The extent to which sources influence consumers simply by providing information.

Inherited status Status that derives from parents at birth.

Inhibition The recall of one attribute inhibiting the recall of another.

Innovation An offering that is perceived as new by consumers within a market segment and that has an effect on existing consumption patterns.

Instrumental roles Roles that relate to tasks affecting the buying decision.

Instrumental values The values needed to achieve the desired end states such as ambition and cheerfulness.

Integration of evidence Combining new information with stored knowledge.

Intensity of ethnic identification How strongly people identify with their ethnic group.

Interference When the strength of a memory deteriorates over time because of competing memories.

Internal search The process of recalling stored information from memory.

J

Judgment Evaluation of an object or estimate of the likelihood of an outcome or event.

Judgment of goodness/badness Evaluating the desirability of something.

Just noticeable difference (jnd) The intensity difference needed between two stimuli before they are perceived to be different; also known as the differential threshold.

L

Law of small numbers The expectation that information obtained from a small number of people represents the larger population.

Legitimacy The extent to which the innovation follows established guidelines for what seems appropriate in the category.

Lexicographic model A noncompensatory model that compares brands by attributes, one at a time in order of importance.

Lifestyles People's patterns of behavior.

List of Values (LOV) A survey that efficiently measures nine principal values driving consumer behavior.

Locus of control People's tendency to attribute the cause of events to the self (internal) or not the self (external, such as others, the situation, or luck).

Long-term memory (LTM) The part of memory where information is permanently stored for later use.

Low-effort hierarchy of effects Sequence of thinking-behaving-feeling.

M

Market maven A consumer on whom others rely for information about the marketplace in general.

Market test A study in which the effectiveness of one or more elements of the marketing mix is examined by evaluating sales of the product in an actual market, e.g., a specific city.

Marketing The activity, set of institutions, and processes for creating, communicating, delivering, and exchanging offerings with value for individuals, groups, and society.

Marketing ethics Rules of acceptable conduct that guide individuals and organizations in making honest, fair, and respectful decisions about marketing activities.

Marketing source Influence delivered from a marketing agent, for example, advertising, personal selling.

Marketing stimuli Information about commercial offerings communicated either by the marketer (such as ads) or by nonmarketing sources (such as word of mouth).

Match-up hypothesis Idea that the source must be appropriate for the product/service.

Materialism Placing a high importance on money and material goods.

Means-end chain analysis A technique that can help to explain how values link to attributes in products and services.

Mental accounting Categorizing spending and saving decisions into "accounts" mentally designated for specific consumption transactions, goals, or situations.

Mere exposure effect When familiarity leads to a consumer's liking an object.

Metacognitive experiences How the information is processed beyond the content of the decision.

Millennial Individuals born between 1980 and 1994; also known as Generation Y.

Modernity The extent to which consumers in the social system have positive attitudes toward change.

Motivated reasoning Processing information in a way that allows consumers to reach the conclusion that they want to reach.

Motivation An inner state of activation that provides energy needed to achieve a goal.

Multiattribute expectancy-value model A type of brand-based compensatory model.

Multibrand loyalty Buying two or more brands repeatedly because of a strong preference for them.

Multicultural marketing Strategies used to appeal to a variety of cultures at the same time.

Mystery ad An ad in which the brand is not identified until the end of the message.

N

National character The personality of a country.

Need An internal state of tension experienced when there is a discrepancy between the current and an ideal or desired physical or psychological state.

Need for cognition (NFC) A trait that describes how much people like to think.

Need for uniqueness (NFU) The desire for a unique position and experiences through the purchase, use, and disposition of products and services.

Negative word-of-mouth communication The act of consumers sharing negative information about a brand, product, or service with other consumers.

Netnography Observing and analyzing the online behavior and comments of consumers.

Noncomparable decision The process of making a decision about products or services from different categories.

Noncompensatory model A simple decision model in which negative information leads to rejection of the option.

Nonmarketing source Influence delivered from an entity outside a marketing organization, for example, friends, family, and the media.

Norm Collective decision about what constitutes appropriate behavior.

Normative choice tactics Low-elaboration decision-making that is based on others' opinions.

Normative influence How other people influence our behavior through social pressure.

Nuclear family Father, mother, and children.

O

Objective comprehension The extent to which consumers accurately understand the message a sender intended to communicate.

Offering A product, service, activity, experience, or idea offered by a marketing organization to consumers.

One-sided message A marketing message that presents only positive information.

Ongoing search A search that occurs regularly, regardless of whether the consumer is making a choice.

Online processing When a consumer is actively evaluating a brand as he/she views an ad for it.

Operant conditioning A process of learning driven by the use of rewards to reinforce desired behavior and punishment to discourage objectionable behavior.

Opinion leader An individual who acts as an information broker between the mass media and the opinions and behaviors of an individual or group.

Optimal stimulation level (OSL) The level of arousal that is most comfortable for an individual.

Overprivileged Families with an income higher than the average in their social class.

P

Parody display Status symbols that start in the lower-social classes and move upward.

Perceived risk The extent to which the consumer anticipates negative consequences of an action, for example, buying, using, or disposing of an offering, to emerge and positive consequences to not emerge.

Perception The process of determining the properties of stimuli using vision, hearing, taste, smell, and touch.

Perceptual fluency The ease with which information is processed.

Perceptual organization The process by which stimuli are organized into meaningful units.

Performance The extent to which the product/service does what it is supposed to do and fulfills consumers' needs.

Performance-related tactics Tactics based on benefits, features, or evaluations of the brand.

Performance risk The possibility that the offering will not perform as well as hoped or expected.

Peripheral cues Easily processed aspects of a message, such as music, an attractive source, a picture, or humor.

Peripheral-route processing The attitude formation and change process when effort is low.

Peripheral route to persuasion Aspects other than key message arguments that are used to influence attitudes.

Personal relevance Something that has a direct bearing on the self and has potentially significant consequences or implications for our lives.

Personality General, enduring differences between people in terms of behavior patterns, feeling, and thinking.

Physical detachment Physically disposing of an item.

Physical (or safety) risk The extent to which buying, using, or disposing of an offering is perceived to have the potential to create physical harm or harm one's safety.

Possession ritual Ritual we engage in when we first acquire a product that helps to make it "ours."

Post-decision dissonance A feeling of discomfort about whether or not the correct decision was made.

Post-decision emotions Positive or negative emotions experienced while using or disposing of the acquired brand, products, or services.

Post-decision regret The negative feeling that one should have made another purchase, consumption, or disposition decision than one actually did.

Preattentive processing The nonconscious processing of stimuli, such as in peripheral vision.

Preference for the whole The tendency to perceive more value in a whole than in the combined parts that make up a whole, even if the parts have the same objective value as the whole.

Prepurchase search A search for information that aids a specific acquisition decision.

Presentation stage The second stage of gift giving, when we actually give the gift.

Price-related tactics Simplifying decision heuristics that are based on price.

Primacy and recency effect The tendency to show greater memory for information that comes first or last in a sequence.

Primary data Data originating from a researcher and collected to provide information relevant to a specific research project.

Primary reference group Group with whom we have physical face-to-face interaction.

Priming The increased sensitivity to certain concepts and associations due to prior experience based on implicit memory.

Problem recognition The perceived difference between an actual and an ideal state.

Product life cycle A concept that suggests that products go through an initial introductory period followed by periods of sales growth, maturity, and decline.

Profane things Things that are ordinary and hence have no special power.

Prominence The intensity of stimuli that causes them to stand out relative to the environment.

Prototype The best example of a cognitive (mental) category.

Protoypicality The extent to which an object is representative of its category.

Psychographics A description of consumers based on their psychological and behavioral characteristics.

Psychological risk The extent to which buying, using, or disposing of an offering is perceived to have the potential to harm one's sense of self and thus create negative emotions.

R

Reactance Doing the opposite of what the individual or group wants us to do.

Recall The ability to retrieve information about a stimulus from memory without being reexposed to the stimulus again.

Recognition The process of identifying whether we have previously encountered a stimulus when reexposed to it.

Reference group A group of people consumers compare themselves with for information regarding behavior, attitudes, or values.

Reflexive evaluation Feedback from others that tells us whether we are fulfilling the role correctly.

Reformulation stage The final stage of gift giving, when we reevaluate the relationship based on the gift-giving experience.

Relative advantage Benefits in an innovation superior to those found in existing products.

Representativeness heuristic Making a judgment by simply comparing a stimulus with the category prototype or exemplar.

Research foundation A nonprofit organization that sponsors research on topics relevant to the foundation's goals.

Resistance A desire not to buy the innovation, even in the face of pressure to do so.

Response involvement Interest in certain decisions and behaviors.

Retrieval The process of remembering or accessing what was previously stored in memory.

Retrieval cue A stimulus that facilitates the activation of memory.

Rokeach Value Survey (RVS) A survey that measures instrumental and terminal values.

Role acquisition function The use of products as symbols to help us feel more comfortable in a new role.

S

Sacred entities People, things, and places that are set apart, revered, worshiped, and treated with great respect.

Salient attribute Attribute that is "top of mind" or more important.

Satisfaction The feeling that a purchase decision, consumption experience, or disposition decision meets or exceeds one's expectations.

Satisfice Finding a brand that satisfies a need even though the brand may not be the best brand.

Schema The set of associations linked to a concept in memory.

Script A special type of schema that represents knowledge of a sequence of actions involved in performing an activity.

Secondary data Data collected for some other purpose that is subsequently used in a research project.

Secondary reference group Group with whom we do not have direct contact.

Self-concept Our mental view of who we are.

Self-control Process consumers use to regulate feelings, thoughts, and behavior in line with long-term goals, rather than to pursue short-term goals.

Self-referencing Relating a message to one's own experience or self-image.

Semantic memory General knowledge about an entity, detached from specific episodes.

Sensation seeker A consumer who actively looks for variety.

Sensory memory Input from the five senses stored temporarily in memory.

Sexual orientation A person's preference toward sexual partners of the same and/or opposite sex.

Shaping Leading consumers through a series of steps to create a desired response.

Simple inferences Beliefs based on peripheral cues.

Situational (temporary) involvement Temporary interest in an offering, activity, or decision, often caused by situational circumstances.

Sleeper effect Consumers forget the source of a message more quickly than they forget the message.

Social class fragmentation The disappearance of class distinctions.

Social class hierarchy The grouping of members of society according to status, high to low.

Social comparison theory A theory that proposes that individuals have a drive to compare themselves with other people.

Social dilemma Deciding whether to put self-interest or the interests of others first.

Social influence Implicit or explicit pressures from individuals, groups, and the mass media that affects how a person behaves.

Social relevance The extent to which an innovation can be observed or the extent to which having others observe it has social cachet.

Social risk The extent to which buying, using, or disposing of an offering is perceived to have the potential to do harm to one's social standing.

Source derogation (SD) Thought that discounts or attacks the source of the message.

Source identification The process of determining what the perceived stimulus actually is, that is, what category it belongs to.

Spreading of activation The process by which retrieving a concept or association spreads to the retrieval of a related concept or association.

S-shaped diffusion curve A diffusion curve characterized by slow initial growth followed by a rapid increase in diffusion.

Status crystallization When consumers are consistent across indicators of social class income, education, occupation, etc.

Status float Trends that start in the lower and middle classes and move upward.

Status symbol Product or service that tells others about someone's social class standing.

Storytelling A research method by which consumers are asked to tell stories about product acquisition, usage, or disposition experiences. These stories help marketers gain insights into consumer needs and identify the product attributes that meet these needs.

Strong argument A presentation that features the best or central merits of an offering in a convincing manner.

Subjective comprehension What the consumer understands from the message, regardless of whether this understanding is accurate.

Subjective norm (SN) How others feel about our doing something.

Subliminal perception The activation of sensory receptors by stimuli presented below the perceptual threshold.

Support argument (SA) Thought that agrees with the message.

Survey A method of collecting information from a sample of consumers, predominantly by asking questions.

Symbolic innovation A product, a service, an attribute, or an idea that has new social meaning.

Symbolic need Need that relates to the meaning of our consumption behaviors to ourselves and to others. That is, how we perceive ourselves, how we are perceived by others, how we relate to others, and the esteem in which we are held by others.

Symbols External signs that consumers use to express their identity.

Syncratic decision Decision made jointly by the husband and wife.

T

Taxonomic category How consumers classify a group of objects in memory in an orderly, often hierarchical way, based on their similarity to one another.

Temporal dilemma Deciding whether to put immediate interests or long-term interests first.

Terminal values Highly desired end states such as social recognition and pleasure.

Terror management theory (TMT) A theory which deals with how we cope with the threat of death by defending our world view of values and beliefs.

Theory of planned behavior An extension of the TORA model that predicts behaviors over which consumers perceive they have control.

Theory of reasoned action (TORA) A model that provides an explanation of how, when, and why attitudes predict behavior.

Thin-slice judgments Evaluations made after very brief observations.

Tie-strength The extent to which a close, intimate relationship connects people.

Time risk The extent to which buying, using, or disposing of the offering is perceived to have the potential to lead to loss of time.

Top dog A market leader or brand with a large or the largest market share.

Trade group A professional organization made up of marketers in the same industry.

Traditional hierarchy of effects Sequential steps used in decision making involving thinking, then feeling, then behavior.

Transformational advertising Ads that try to increase emotional involvement with the product or service.

Trialability The extent to which an innovation can be tried on a limited basis before it is adopted.

Trickle-down effect Trends that start in the upper classes and then are copied by lower classes.

Truth effect When consumers believe a statement simply because it has been repeated a number of times.

Two-sided message A marketing message that presents both positive and negative information.

U

Underdog A lower-share brand that is perceived to be doing well in spite of the odds against it.

Underprivileged Families below the average income in their class.

Unity When all the visual parts of a design fit together.

Upward mobility Raising one's status level.

Usage The process by which a consumer uses an offering.

Use innovativeness Finding use for a product that differs from the product's original intended usage.

Utilitarian (or functional) dimension When an ad provides information.

V

Valence Whether information about something is good (positive valence) or bad (negative valence).

Value segmentation The grouping of consumers by common values.

Value system Our total set of values and their relative importance.

Values Enduring beliefs about abstract outcomes and behaviors that are good or bad, such as health, independence, family life, and peace.

Variety seeking Trying something different.

Vicarious exploration Seeking information simply for stimulation.

Viral marketing Rapid spread of brand/product information among a population of people, stimulated by brands.

Voluntary simplicity Limiting acquisition and consumption to live a less material life.

W

Wearout Becoming bored with a stimulus.

Weber's law The stronger the initial stimulus, the greater the additional intensity needed for the second stimulus to be perceived as different.

Wife-dominant decision Decision made primarily by the female head-of-household.

Word of mouth Influence delivered verbally from one person to another person or group of people.

Working memory (WM) The portion of memory where incoming information is encoded or interpreted in the context of existing knowledge, and kept available for more processing.

Z

Zapping Use of a remote control to switch channels during commercial breaks.

Zipping Fast-forwarding through commercials on a program recorded earlier.

Zone of acceptance The acceptable range of prices for any purchase decision.

Name/Author Index

H

Product Index

Subject Index

Note: 'e' indicates an exhibit

A

Ability, 11, 44, 60–61. *See also* Consumer ability, MAO (motivation, ability and opportunity)
  defined, 60–61
  influences, 46e
  to process information, 194–195
  recycling, 280
Absolute threshold, 84, 85
Abstract goal, 54
Abstractness, and concreteness, 79e
Academics
  consumer behavior and, 16
  consumer behavior research, 37
  high school reference group, 306e
Acceptable cutoff, 218
Accessibility/availability, brand name recall, 185–186
Accommodation theory, 336
Acculturation, 334, 375
Achievement symbols, 441
Acquisition
  consumer behavior, 6
  controversies, 461–466
  and gender, 329–330
  methods, 8e
  model of role, 436e
Active coping, 271e
Activists, complainer, 273
Activities, interests, and opinions (AIOs), 391, 392e
Actual identity schemas, 439
Actual state, 182–183
Adaptability, innovation, 422
Addiction, 461–462
  and marketing, 466–467
Additive difference model, 217
Adopter groups, 411–413
  application, 411–413
  characteristics of, 411
  profile of, 412
Adoption
  decision process, 410e
  innovation, 405e, 409
  innovation influences, 416–424
  resistance versus, 409
Advertising
  advertorial, 87
  based on feelings of regret, 260e
  boomers, 326–327
  children and, 464–465
  and consumer behavior, 19
  direct comparative, 138
  fit and self-concepts, 440
  generation X, 326
  Hispanic Americans, 335–336
  humor in, 168e

media and, 328
  messages, 324–325, 326
  position and exposure, 73
  and self-image, 469–470
  stimulating imagery through, 221e
  teens, 324–325
  transformational, 170
  values influence, 383
Advertising agencies, 36
Advertorial, 87
Aesthetic innovations, 406–407
Affect, definition, 248
Affect referral, 248
Affect-related tactics, 248
Affective decision-making models, 214
Affective (emotional) function
  attitudes, 128, 139–141
  decision-making, 218, 222–227
  high effort, 140–142
  high effort influences, 142–145
  low-effort attitudes, 160–161
  low-effort attitude influences, 165–170
Affective forecasting, 220–221, 280
Affective involvement, 47, 140
Affective responses (ARs), 140
African American consumers, 337–338
Age
  and consumer ability, 61
  and consumer behavior, 324–331, 346
  and special possessions, 448
  United States consumer spending, 5e
  and values, 382
Agentic goals, 329
Aggressive personality, 388
Alcohol, minor's illegal use, 467
Allocentric consumers, 378
Alternative-based strategy, 222
Ambiguity of information, 263
Ambivalence, definition, 128
American Consumer Satisfaction Index (ACSI), 265e
Amount of information, and consumer opportunity, 63
Analogy, attitude reasoning, 131
Analysis of reason, attitude/behavior prediction, 145
Anchoring and adjustment process, judgment, 208
Appraisal theory, 55, 56e, 220
Approach-approach conflict, 51
Approach-avoidance conflict, 51
Appropriateness, gift, 447–448
Argument quality, message, 137
Asian American consumers, 338
Aspirational reference group, 298, 299
Associative networks, 106–108, 106e, 107e
Associative reference group, 299

Attention
  characteristics, 76–77, 77e
  and consumer behavior, 11
Attitude, definition, 128
Attitude accessibility, 128
  and behavior prediction, 145
Attitude ambivalence, 128
Attitude-behavior relationship
  factors affecting, 144–146
  over time, 145
Attitude confidence, 128, 145
Attitude persistence, 128
Attitude resistance, 128
Attitude toward the act (A_{act}), TORA, 133, 133e
Attitude toward the ad (A_{ad}), high-effort, 144
Attitude toward the ad (A_{ad}), low-effort, 163
Attitudes
  affective (emotional) foundations, 139–144
  analytical processes, 131–135
  behavior prediction, 144–146
  change strategies, 134–135
  characteristics, 128–129
  cognitive foundations, 129–135
  in consumer behavior, 12
  external search, 189
  forming and changing, 12, 128–129
  foundations, 128, 129–135, 130e
  importance of, 128
  inconsistency with, 60
  low-effort situations, 157–158
  and motivation, 60
  research, 145
  specificity and behavior prediction, 145
  unconscious influences, 155–157
  values-driven, 131
Attraction effect, 211
Attractive sources, 141, 165
Attractiveness, 141
  importance of, 142e
  group, 300
  reference groups, 300
Attribute balancing, high-effort decisions, 224
Attribute determination, 187
Attribute information, external search, 197, 198
Attribute processing, 217–218
Attribution theory, 268, 269
Attributes
  and decision-making, 217–218
  recall of, 185–187
Authenticity, 380–381
Autobiographical (episodic) memory, 103
Autonomic decision, 353
Availability heuristic, 236, 237
Avoidance, consumption coping, 271e
Avoidance-avoidance conflict, 51